**CONTENTS**

Green Bay Packe

MW01280181

CLUB INFORMATION

The Green Bay Packers, Inc., is a publicly-owned, non-profit corporation. A total of 4,746,896 shares is owned by 109,723 stockholders — none of whom receives any dividend on the initial investment. The Corporation is governed by 45 directors and a seven-member executive committee.

PACKER CORPORATION MISSION STATEMENT:

The Green Bay Packers' Mission is to be a dominating force in professional football's competitive arena.

On the field, the Packers will continually strive to present their fans with the highest level of performance quality available.

In their operating activities and relations with the NFL, the Packers will also continually strive for excellence in the quality of work performed.

On-field and operating personnel will, at all times, maintain the highest ethical and moral standards in their actions, recognizing that they are all representatives of the Packers' franchise and traditions.

Overall, the Packers will commit themselves to doing their part in representing the State of Wisconsin with competitiveness, respect and dignity.

NFL Champions 1929, 1930, 1931, 1936, 1939, 1944, 1961, 1962, 1965, 1966, 1967, 1996

STREET ADDRESS
Green Bay Packers
1265 Lombardi Avenue
Green Bay, WI 54304

MAILING ADDRESS
P.O. Box 10628
Green Bay, WI 54307-0628

INTERNET ADDRESSES
www.packers.com
www.packerproshop.com

TELEPHONE NUMBERS
Main Switchboard 920/496-5700
Ticket Office 920/496-5719
Packer Pro Shop 800/992-5750

Administration FAX 920/496-5738
Public Relations FAX 920/496-5712
Ticket Office FAX 920/496-5708
Packer Pro Shop FAX 920/496-7755
Football Operations FAX 920/496-7753

Fan Information Hotline.............920/496-7722

FINGERTIP INFORMATION

TEAM COLORS: Dark Green (Pantone 553), Gold (Pantone 116) and White
CONFERENCE: National Football Conference, Central Division
STADIUM: Lambeau Field (capacity 60,790)
RADIO: Flagship WTMJ (620 AM) and state-wide Packer Radio Network
PRESEASON TV: WBAY-TV (Ch. 2) in Green Bay originates for four-station state network
TRAINING CAMP: St. Norbert College; De Pere, Wis. (since 1958)
Rookies report July 16, Veterans report July 17, Camp breaks Aug. 25

MEDIA GUIDE CREDITS
Editor: Jeff Blumb
Writers: Lee Remmel, Jeff Blumb, Mark Schiefelbein, Aaron Popkey, Paula Martin and Chris Hollenback. Additional editorial assistance provided by Elias Sports Bureau and the Pro Football Hall of Fame
Cover Photo: James Biever
Other Photos: Vernon Biever, James Biever and Harmann Studios
Prepress-formatting and design: Marathon Communications; Green Bay, Wis.
Printing: Marathon Communications; Green Bay, Wis.

GREEN BAY PACKERS FOUNDATION

The Green Bay Packers have always had a special bond with their fans and with the community – a bond which dates back to 1919, when Curly Lambeau and George Calhoun brought together athletes and organized a football team. The community supported the team in times of need, by "passing the hat" at games and by buying stock in 1923, 1935, 1950 and 1997, among other ways. To give back to the community, the Packers organization extended its hand to the needy in the state of Wisconsin with the development of the Green Bay Packers Foundation on Dec. 30, 1986.

"Our unique ownership structure gives us a strong link with fans and the community, who have supported us for so many years," said Green Bay Packers President and CEO Bob Harlan. "We have fans not just in Green Bay, but throughout the state, and the Foundation is a great way to give something back."

The Foundation assists in a wide variety of activities and programs which benefit education, civic affairs, health services, human services and youth-related programs. It is a non-profit organization created to assist charitable and worthwhile causes throughout the state of Wisconsin. All grant recipients must be public charities exempt from taxation under Section 501(c)(3) of the Internal Revenue Code.

Not all funding requests can be filled, and there are areas that do not fit the Foundation's established guidelines. Among the types of requests which cannot be filled are those for building construction, endowments, political campaigns and activities, individuals (including loans and scholarships), advertising, multi-year grant requests and projects/programs from outside Wisconsin.

The brainchild of The Honorable Robert J. Parins, the team's president from 1982-89, the Foundation has awarded nearly $500,000 in grants, including a record amount of $110,000 to 53 organizations in 1997. Contributions to individual organization made by the Foundation range from between $1,000 to $5,000. The money donated comes from the interest accrued from a trust fund established in 1988 and donations made to the Foundation from outside sources. The trust fund is the same fund which now would receive whatever monies remained after the payment of all expenses in the event that the Packers franchise would ever be sold.

The recipients of the grants are decided on by a five-person committee, made up from the club's board of directors, including a member of the seven-person executive committee. The Foundation committee, which is appointed by the president of the Green Bay Packers, meets twice a year to review hundreds of requests. Applications must be received each year by November 1, and the final decision on which organizations will receive money is made in December.

Organizations in Wisconsin interested in applying for a Foundation grant should request a guideline application letter in writing on their organization's letterhead. All requests should be sent to : Phillip A. Pionek, Secretary; Green Bay Packers Foundation; P.O. Box 10628; Green Bay, WI 54307-0628. Completed guideline application letters must be received by November 1.

The Green Bay Packers as an organization also make smaller financial contributions to various projects, in addition to donating items for charity raffles and auctions at schools, churches, hospitals and other philanthropic groups. Such requests should be directed to Sherry Schuldes, Director of Family Programs, at the above address.

Below is a complete listing of the 53 organizations which received grants from the Green Bay Packers Foundation in 1997:

1) American Legion/Sullivan-Wallen Post #11
2) Bay Lakes Council-Boy Scouts of America
3) Brian LaViolette Scholarship Foundation
4) Brown County Library
5) Brown County Task Force for the Homeless
6) Citizens Against Drug Impaired Drivers
7) Center Against Sexual & Domestic Abuse
8) Center for Blind & Visually Impaired Children, Inc.
9) Center for Childhood Safety, Inc.
10) Centro Primo Prime Center
11) Community Action, Inc., of Rock & Walworth Counties
12) Community Clothes Closet
13) De Pere Area Diamond Sports
14) Disabled American Veterans
15) Down's Syndrome Association of Wisconsin
16) Encompass Child Care, Inc.
17) Families, Abuse, Circle of Violence, Encounter of Shawano County
18) Forward Service Corporation
19) Free S.P.I.R.I.T. Riders, Inc.
20) Great Lakes Hemophilia Foundation
21) Green Bay Botanical Garden (5 of 5)
22) Green Bay Jaycees, Inc.
23) Green Bay Urban Partnership (1 of 5)
24) Harbor House Domestic Abuse Programs
25) Harambee Community School
26) Hunger Task Force of Milwaukee, Inc.

27) Jackie Nitschke Center, Inc.
28) Kewaunee County Development Center
29) Leadership Green Bay
30) Leisure Independence Network of Kenosha County
31) Make-A-Wish Foundation of Wisconsin
32) Mental Health Association (Sheboygan)
33) Milwaukee Children's Theater Company, Inc.
34) MDA-Great Lakes-Northeast Wisconsin
35) New Hope Center, Inc.
36) NHS
37) Notre Dame de la Baie Academy
38) Portal Industries, Inc.
39) Safe House of Southeast Wisconsin, Inc.
40) Safehouse International-Teen Plus
41) SCHCC Benefit Club Foundation, Inc.
42) Scholarships, Inc.
43) Sexual Abuse Survivors Support Year Round
44) Special Olympics Wisconsin-Northeastern Area
45) St. Mary's Hospital Foundation
46) Suring Community Childcare Center
47) Trees For Tomorrow, Inc.
48) United Sports Association for Youth
49) Unity Hospice
50) Veritas Society
51) Welcome, House of Modification Examples, Inc.
52) Wisconsin Committee to Prevent Child Abuse
53) Wisconsin Epilepsy Association

ADMINISTRATION

BOB HARLAN, President and CEO
MICHAEL R. REINFELDT, Vice President of Administration/Chief Financial Officer
LANCE LOPES, Assistant Vice President/General Counsel
DUKE COPP, Accountant
MIKE JELENIC, Computer Systems Analyst
JEANNE McKENNA, Assistant Director of Family Programs
TRACI NYGAARD, Accounting Assistant
JERRY PARINS, Corporate Security Officer
PHIL PIONEK, Exec. Asst. to President
SHERRY SCHULDES, Director of Family Programs
VICKI VANNIEUWENHOVEN, Accountant
WAYNE WICHLACZ, Director of Computer Services
MARGARET MEYERS, Administrative Assistant/ Business Affairs

PUBLIC RELATIONS

LEE REMMEL, Executive Director
JEFF BLUMB, Assistant Director
MARK SCHIEFELBEIN, Assistant Director/ Travel Coordinator
AARON POPKEY, Public Relations Assistant
PAULA MARTIN, Administrative Assistant
LINDA McCROSSIN, Secretary/Receptionist
CHRIS HOLLENBACK, Intern

MARKETING

JEFF CIEPLY, Director
CRAIG BENZEL, Marketing Assistant
KANDI GOLTZ, Administrative Assistant
CHARLA HARRIE, Intern
KATE HOGAN, Packer Pro Shop Manager
BRANDON ARNDT, Packer Pro Shop
LISA BERG, Packer Pro Shop Asst./Retail Sales
JULIE POCQUETTE, Packer Pro Shop
JULIE SCHURK, Packer Pro Shop Assistant/ Catalog Sales
TREVOR VANNIEUWENHOVEN, Packer Pro Shop Assistant/Warehouse

TICKETS

MARK WAGNER, Director
CAROL EDWIN, Assistant Director
ANN MARIE LAES, Ticket Office Assistant
CHRIS WAHLEN, Ticket Office Assistant

FRONT OFFICE STAFF

ANN DABECK, Receptionist
LaFAWN JOSLIN, Receptionist
JUDY MEHLBERG, Mail Clerk

FOOTBALL OPERATIONS

RON WOLF, Executive V.P./General Manager
TED THOMPSON, Director of Player Personnel
JEANNE BRUETTE, Administrative Assistant/ General Manager

COACHES

MIKE HOLMGREN, Head Coach
SHERMAN LEWIS, Offensive Coordinator
FRITZ SHURMUR, Defensive Coordinator
LARRY BROOKS, Defensive Line
NOLAN CROMWELL, Wide Receivers
KEN FLAJOLE, Defensive Asst./Quality Control
JOHNNY HOLLAND, Special Teams
KENT JOHNSTON, Strength and Conditioning
JIM LIND, Linebackers
TOM LOVAT, Offensive Line
ANDY REID, Quarterbacks
GARY REYNOLDS, Offensive Asst./Quality Control
MIKE SHERMAN, Tight Ends/Asst. Offensive Line
HARRY SYDNEY, Running Backs
BOB VALESENTE, Defensive Backs
SUSAN KLUCK, Administrative Assistant (Holmgren)
BILL NAYES, Administrative Assistant/Football
BARRY RUBIN, Strength and Conditioning Assistant
DIANE CORON, Secretary

PRO PERSONNEL

REGGIE McKENZIE, Director
WILL LEWIS, Pro Personnel Assistant
AUTUMN THOMAS-BEENENGA, Administrative Asst.

COLLEGE SCOUTING

JOHN DORSEY, Director (Southeast)
DANNY MOCK, Scouting Coordinator
MATT BOOCKMEIER, Scout (East)
SHAUN HEROCK, Scout (Midwest)
SCOT McCLOUGHAN, Scout (Rocky Mountains)
JOHNNY MEADS, Scout (Southwest)
SAM SEALE, Scout (West)
LEE GISSENDANER, Scout (National Football Scouting)
JOHN 'RED' COCHRAN, Scout (North)

VIDEO

AL TREML, Director
BOB ECKBERG, Assistant Director
CHRIS KIRBY, Video Assistant

EQUIPMENT

GORDON 'RED' BATTY, Manager
TOM BAKKEN, Assistant Manager
BRYAN NEHRING, Assistant Manager
TIM O'NEILL, Equipment Assistant

MEDICAL

PEPPER BURRUSS, Head Trainer
DR. PATRICK McKENZIE, Team Physician
DR. JOHN GRAY, Associate Team Physician
KURT FIELDING, Assistant Trainer
SAM RAMSDEN, Assistant Trainer
BRYAN ENGEL, Intern

BUILDINGS AND GROUNDS

TED EISENREICH, Buildings Supervisor
TODD EDLEBECK, Fields Supervisor
PATRICK 'OLLIE' HELF, Maintenance Assistant
ALLEN JOHNSON, Grounds Assistant
BILL RASMUSSEN, Maintenance Assistant
DAVE TILOT, Maintenance Assistant

GAME DAY STAFF

VERNON J. BIEVER, Sideline Photographer
JAMES V. BIEVER, Sideline Photographer
HARMANN STUDIOS, Portrait Photographers
LOVELL IVES, Halftime Director
JIM LAWLER, JR., Program Sales

BOB HARLAN

President and Chief Executive Officer

A visionary and aggressive leader, as well as a man of his word, Bob Harlan has kept his promise.

When he was elected president and chief executive officer of the Green Bay Packers, Inc., in June of 1989, he promptly established an ambitious agenda for himself and the organization, announcing, "I want to move this franchise ahead in every area.

"We've got to be successful from top to bottom to succeed. And," he promised, "we're going to succeed."

Succeed, assuredly, he and the Packers have – beyond all reasonable expectations, both corporately and competitively. The organization he heads up today – currently being cited as a model for franchises across the entire spectrum of professional sports – reigns as the elite, the standard of professional football.

Thus, in less than a decade, Harlan has taken his place among the most productive and accomplished chief executives in the Green Bay Packers' long and storied history. Now in his tenth year as the operating head of pro football's unique organization, he is respected throughout the National Football League for triggering the return of the Lombardi Trophy to Green Bay – which became a long-awaited reality in January of 1997 when the Packers triumphed over New England in Super Bowl XXXI – as well as for the extensive and innovative agenda he has implemented since taking over the office of president and chief executive officer.

A member of the club's front office since 1971, the veteran Packer official made two major and historic decisions late in the 1991 season, moves that have had a profoundly positive effect upon the Green Bay franchise and its future. Convinced the organization was merely treading water competitively, he first relieved then-executive vice president Tom Braatz of his responsibilities November 20, 1991, and, one week later, named former Raiders personnel chief Ron Wolf as executive vice president and general manager, with total authority over football operations.

In the light of subsequent events, the latter decision already ranks among the most significant in the 79-year history of the Packers, the NFL's only publicly-owned franchise. Wolf was chosen 'NFL Executive of the Year' following his first full season with the Packers, which saw him hire ex-49ers offensive coordinator Mike Holmgren to replace Lindy Infante as head coach and also acquire Pro Bowl quarterback Brett Favre for a first-round draft choice in pro football's most acclaimed trade of 1992.

During the productive interim, the Packers have advanced to the playoffs each of the last five years – the first such accomplishment in franchise history – climaxed their 1996 achievements by reaching and winning the Super Bowl for the first time in 29 years and followed that singular achievement by returning to the Super Bowl in January of this year.

Holmgren had responded to his original challenge by directing the Packers to a 9-7 record – a five-victory improvement over '91 – in his first season, one in which Favre established himself as the Packers' field general, and to two more 9-and-7 marks in both 1993 and 1994, thus bringing Green Bay three consecutive winning seasons for the first time since 1965-66-67 and the 'Lombardi Era.' He subsequently led the Green and Gold to an 11-5 record in 1995 and their first NFC Central Division title since 1972, surpassed that considerable achievement by escorting them to a record-tying, 13-3 regular-season record in 1996 and the team's first Super Bowl title since 1967, then led his defending champions to another 13-3 season in 1997 and a return trip to the Super Bowl.

The hiring of Wolf was the centerpiece in a series of key moves Harlan has effected since succeeding Judge Robert J. Parins as president of the corporation at the annual stockholders meeting June 5, 1989, including the 1994 decision to leave Milwaukee and play all home games in Green Bay's Lambeau Field and the 1997 decision to launch the fourth stock sale in team annals – a highly successful venture which brought in more than 100,000 new shareholders and produced in excess of $24 million, assuring the Packers' fiscal future well into the 21st century.

Once elected – on June 2, 1989 – the Packers' then-new chief executive officer lost little time initiating his first major project. Ten weeks later, in late August of 1989, he announced plans to construct 1,920 club seats – a historic first in Lambeau Field – and 36 new private boxes, an $8,263,000 expansion. It was completed in time for the start of 1990 preseason play.

A firm believer in the importance of ongoing, person-to-person dialogue with the team's fans, Harlan also scheduled and staged the first 'Breakfast with the Packers' functions in club history, gatherings for fans selected at random by computer, at which he invited questions and feedback from them about the Packers organization.

Committed to making the fans' day at the stadium as enjoyable as possible, he in 1990 also directed the formation of a comprehensive program designed to encourage responsible drinking by fans in Lambeau Field, and in 1993 implemented a no-smoking policy in the stadium seating areas at all home games. Results in the first eight years of the responsible drinking program's existence indicate it has been a success, with arrests for misconduct down appreciably from previous years.

A year earlier, while still executive vice president of administration, Harlan was the catalyst in the implementation and development of a long-term marketing program, launched with the hiring of a director of marketing and the opening of an official outlet store in the Packers' administration building, a project which has become a solid success in the intervening nine years and has produced even greater dividends following a major expansion of the team pro shop and on the heels of the team's recent success.

In 1992, he initiated plans for a comprehensive upgrade and expansion of the team's administration building and training quarters – a 20,000-square foot addition, encompassing a 74-by-80 foot gymnasium with a suspended running track as well as new public relations and marketing offices. The project, completed in time for the opening of 1993 training camp, also permitted enlargement of the team pro shop to 2,000 square feet – six times its original size.

Two years later, in 1994, Harlan authorized and directed the construction of a new, $4.7-million "state-of-the-art" indoor practice facility, The Don Hutson Center – the finest such structure in professional football – which was completed in time for use during the '94 season.

In 1994, he also presided over a historic move – the decision to leave Milwaukee and play all home games in Green Bay, a sensitive issue since the Packers had had a 62-year presence in the state's largest city. But as a condition of the transfer, necessitated by addressing an annual $2.5 million disparity in income which resulted from playing games in County Stadium, Harlan made sure Milwaukee's fans were not forgotten, offering them a three-game ticket package in Lambeau Field.

The latter expressed their appreciation in highly positive terms, 96 percent of Milwaukee's 48,000 season ticket holders subsequently availing themselves of the opportunity.

Three years ago, he facilitated two other major additions to the Packer complex – 90 new private boxes spanning the north end zone of Lambeau Field and the construction of a 60-seat auxiliary press box to enhance the stadium's accommodations for the media.

In 1997, convinced that the organization was in need of additional capital reserves to be competitive well into the 21st century – via improvements to Lambeau Field and the team's training facilities – he launched the team's first stock sale since 1950. More than 100,000 shares, at $200 per share, were sold during the offering, initiated in mid-November and concluded on March 16, 1998, adding more than $24 million to the corporation's capital reserves.

That success, in turn, produced what may have been the largest shareholders' meeting in the history of the nation's corporate business – one held in Green Bay's Lambeau Field July 8 of this year and attended by 18,707 stockholders.

At the time of his election in 1989, Harlan had addressed what he termed the two key "bottom lines...Obviously, one is winning football games, and the other is keeping the organization financially solvent and strong so it can always remain in Green Bay and compete with the other 27 clubs in this league."

Becoming president of the Green Bay Packers, he also revealed on that historic day, had exceeded his fondest dreams.

"In 1960, when I had just graduated from Marquette University and was working as sports information director at Marquette, just getting started in public relations, I attended a Packer game at Milwaukee County Stadium," he told members of the media following his election. "I made a comment to my wife then that I hope I can grow in the public relations field and become competent enough that some day I can become the public relations director for the Green Bay Packers. When the opportunity came along 11 years later to join this fine organization, I jumped at it...To be associated with the NFL and the Packers, I have been highly honored...That honor has reached a new and incredible level."

The ninth president in the team's 79-year existence, Harlan is the team's first CEO to come up through the ranks. All previous presidents of the NFL's only publicly-owned franchise had come from the business and professional areas of the community as members of the board of directors.

The genial Iowan, who has been involved in every area of the club's operations over the course of his 27-year Green Bay career, joined the organization as assistant general manager on June 1, 1971, after serving as director of public relations for the St. Louis baseball Cardinals. He later was named corporate general manager in 1975, corporate assistant to the president in 1981 and executive vice president of administration on February 16, 1988.

In the latter role, he had been responsible for team travel, negotiating radio and preseason television contracts, front office personnel, ticket office operations, purchasing, the leasing of Lambeau Field's private boxes, insurance, game-day entertainment and the scheduling of preseason games.

Prior to 1985, he also had negotiated all player contracts for 14 years.

Harlan, in his tenth year as club president, is the third-longest tenured chief executive officer in Packers history. Only Dominic Olejniczak, who served 24 years (1958-82), and Lee H. Joannes, 17 years (1930-47), have headed the corporation longer.

Harlan, who earned a B.S. degree in journalism from Marquette in 1958, had a brief tour of duty in the U.S. Army before spending six months as a general reporter for *United Press International* in Milwaukee. He subsequently became sports information director at Marquette in 1959, serving six years in that capacity, after which he joined the St. Louis baseball Cardinals in 1965, serving as director of community relations and the speakers' bureau for two years and as director of public relations for three-and-a-half years before coming to the Packers.

Born Robert Ernest Harlan in Des Moines, Iowa, on September 9, 1936, he is active in the greater Green Bay community as a member of the board of trustees of St. Norbert College and the advisory board of Firstar Bank of Green Bay. He also is a member of the executive board of the 65 Roses Sports Club, which was created to generate awareness of cystic fibrosis and to raise money for research to find a cure for the dreaded disease.

In 1993, he was honored by the Green Bay Rotary Club with its 'Free Enterprise Award' for his numerous contributions to the community, both individually and on behalf of the Packer Corporation. In 1996, he was presented with the Green Bay Visitor and Convention Bureau's annual 'Tourism Recognition Award' for "outstanding contributions to the Green Bay area tourism industry," as well as being saluted as Northeastern Wisconsin's 'Executive of the Year' by *Marketplace* magazine.

In 1997, he was thrice honored by his alma mater, Marquette University. He was presented with the 1997 Marquette University 'Alumni Community Service Award' during the alumni association's National Awards Week (April 25-27), presented with an honorary doctor of laws degree at the institution's commencement exercises May 18 and, on June 3, saluted as "Master of the Game" by Marquette's National Sports Law Institute at its annual awards dinner in Milwaukee in recognition of his "humanitarian efforts, commitment to public service, great sense of ethics and integrity as a professional within the sports field."

On April 4 of this year, he also was presented with the 'Distinguished Service Award' at the first Lee Remmel Sports Awards Banquet for leading the Packers' franchise out of mediocrity to professional football's heights.

Bob and his wife, Madeline, have three sons – Kevin, 38, who is a play-by-play broadcaster on telecasts of NFL games for CBS Sports and also will be 'voicing' college basketball games for the network next season, as well as NBA games for TNT; Bryan, 36, who is director of public relations for the Chicago Bears; and Michael, 29, a sales executive who is manager of the Milwaukee Brewers' Gold Club.

An ardent golfer, Harlan also is an "involved" fan, closely monitoring the athletic fortunes of the Milwaukee Brewers and Milwaukee Bucks as well as those of the University of Wisconsin-Green Bay, the University of Wisconsin-Madison and his alma mater, Marquette.

RON WOLF

Exec. Vice President and General Manager

Tireless, aggressive and uncommonly resourceful, Ron Wolf has presided over one of the swiftest and most stunning turnabouts in National Football League history, converting the Green Bay Packers from perennial also-rans into Super Bowl champions and the standard of the pro football world in the short span of six years.

A remarkably prosperous period by any measure, his tenure as the organization's executive vice president and general manager has been punctuated by six consecutive winning seasons – the Packers' first such parlay since the 1960s. It also has included:

- **Green Bay's first Super Bowl championship in 29 years;**

- **Back-to-back Super Bowl appearances (1996 and 1997);**

- **Five consecutive playoff berths, for the first time in team annals;**

- **Back-to-back NFC Championships (1996 and 1997);**

- **Three consecutive NFC Central Division titles (1995-1996-1997);**

- **The first "trifecta" of double-digit winning regular seasons for a Green Bay team since 1961-62-63 (11-5 in 1995 and 13-3 in both 1996 and 1997);**

- **Pro football's best regular-season, won-lost record over the past three years (1995-96-97), 37-11-0;**

- **The first 16-victory campaign in the Packers' 79-year history (1996); and**

- **An amazing 37 wins in the last 38 games – including playoffs – in the team's Lambeau Field home.**

In the history-making process, Wolf thus has emphatically fulfilled the commitment he made in taking over the Packers' football operations as executive vice president and general manager in late November of 1991, launching the renaissance of a franchise that had had only four winning seasons during a 24-year span.

And, in so doing, he has made a more profound impact upon the Packers organization and its artistic fortunes than anyone since the arrival of the legendary Vince Lombardi upon the Green Bay scene nearly 40 years ago.

During a 1992 speaking appearance, early in his Packer tenure, Wolf had succinctly delineated the challenge he accepted in taking over his current responsibilities by declaring with characteristic brevity, "I was brought here to win."

As the recent record eloquently suggests, seldom has anyone responded to a challenge with greater celerity than the man who earlier had played a major role in developing the Oakland/Los Angeles Raiders into one of professional football's most successful franchises.

The inexhaustible Wolf, who spends countless hours grinding video of college players and NFL free agents – an ongoing process which he supplements by frequently venturing into the field each fall to personally scout players at colleges and universities throughout the nation – has delivered a consistent contender and, now, a Super Bowl champion, with the aid of the head coach he selected to direct the on-field operations, former 49ers offensive coordinator Mike Holmgren.

In appreciation for his considerable achievements, Wolf twice has been rewarded with three-year extensions of his original five-year contract – the first in 1994 and the most recent on April 7, 1997. The latest document will have him presiding over the Packers' competitive fortunes into the next century – through the year 2002.

Packers President Bob Harlan paid tribute to Wolf's accomplishments in announcing the most recent extension, asserting, "I think Ron is the best general manager in the National Football League, and he obviously has done a remarkable job in the past five years to put us back on top in the league.

"I also think continuity and stability in that position are vitally important. And this is a way for us to show our appreciation for his accomplishments."

Wolf, in turn, calls his "the ultimate job" in his profession, "particularly (for) a person at my level. Green Bay is it, as far as I'm concerned, for that very reason. There isn't an owner whose ego needs to be stroked. You're given everything you need to do the job. To me, that's so important. Nobody has denied us anything."

A man with a deep appreciation for the game and its history – and the Packers' history and tradition, in particular – he said at the announcement of his second contract extension, "To me, it's a distinct honor to be able to continue my association with professional football's most historic and traditional franchise, the Green Bay Packers. It's an honor and a privilege."

Wolf's highly successful rebuilding program began with the signing of Holmgren, his first major hire after taking over the Packers' football operation, one which proved to be a master stroke.

In the months that followed, Wolf supplemented that contribution by executing two significant trades, later with a series of shrewd acquisitions via the waiver wire and free agent market.

The key transaction saw him acquire Brett Favre, a highly-talented young quarterback, from the Atlanta Falcons with a first-round draft choice, a move that has paid spectacular dividends, Favre having presided over the offense in each of those six consecutive winning seasons and closed out a record-breaking 1995 campaign by universally being acclaimed as the NFL's 'Most Valuable Player,' an honor he again was incredibly accorded following the 1996 and 1997 seasons.

Wolf subsequently added center/guard Frank Winters, signed from the Kansas City Chiefs in Plan B, who has been a key performer in the offensive line, moving from center to shore up the left guard position each season from 1992-94 when injuries felled successive starters Rich Moran and Guy McIntyre.

These, and several other timely and profitable moves, helped the Packers to forge their second-best record since 1972, a 9-7 mark that saw them remain in the NFC Central Division race until the final game of the '92 season.

In the wake of that remarkable turnaround – the Packers had been 4-and-12 in 1991 after going 6-and-10 in 1990 – Wolf was saluted as 'NFL Executive of the Year' by *The Sporting News*, thus becoming the first Packer executive ever to be so honored.

Wolf, who came to the Packers from the New York Jets, typically deflected credit from himself, preferring to generalize in labeling the *Sporting News* award "a great honor for the Packer organization."

But Harlan, the Packers' chief executive officer – and the man who hired him – offers a more specific analysis.

"I think I can tell you, Ron Wolf spends every minute of every waking hour thinking about what he can do to make this football team better," Harlan said. "He's dedicated and working at it so constantly. With that work ethic, you think, 'We're going to make it.' "

In 1993, Wolf further bolstered the team's talent level by venturing aggressively into the free agent market, following the advent of unrestricted free agency, bringing in Reggie White, considered by many the greatest defensive end in pro football history, and starting guard Harry Galbreath, among others.

Again, the moves paid immediate dividends. The Packers repeated 1992's 9-7 record against a much more demanding schedule – it included six playoff teams – and not only qualified for the playoffs for the first time since 1982 but advanced to the second round, defeating the Detroit Lions (28-24) in their first postseason assignment before falling to the Super Bowl Champion Dallas Cowboys (27-17) in a divisional playoff.

In 1994, Wolf moved quickly to offset the free agency loss of linebacker Tony Bennett by signing defensive end Sean Jones of the Houston Oilers, who proceeded to lead the Green Bay defense in quarterback sacks. He also added ex-Viking Fred Strickland to step in for the retired Johnny Holland at inside linebacker, former Bear Steve McMichael to upgrade the defensive line and converted the departure of left guard Doug Widell – who moved to the Detroit Lions as a free agent – into a plus by signing five-time Pro Bowler McIntyre, who shook off an early blood clot problem to spearhead a much-improved Packer run-

ning game over the last 10 weeks of the season.

Holmgren, skillfully melding these new elements into the overall mix, then led the Packers to a third consecutive 9-7 record, capping the regular season with three straight victories to qualify for the playoffs for the second year in a row. They followed with a fourth straight triumph in their opening postseason test, turning back the Lions, 16-12, before bowing to the Cowboys at Dallas in another divisional playoff.

In 1995, Wolf upgraded the secondary, drafting cornerback Craig Newsome from Arizona State in the first round. Newsome, a tough, physical corner, went on to earn NFL all-rookie honors and trigger the Packers' divisional playoff victory over the defending Super Bowl champion 49ers, scooping up an Adam Walker fumble and returning it 31 yards for a touchdown which shot Green Bay into an early and permanent lead.

That 27-17 victory propelled the Packers into the NFC Championship Game, for the first time since 1967, before the Green and Gold's Super Bowl quest ended in Dallas – one step removed from Super Bowl XXX.

Already recognized throughout the National Football League for triggering the Packers' return to prominence during his tenure in the organization, Wolf also was saluted in 1996 for his skill and cooperation in another, related area, when he was honored by the Pro Football Writers of America for his contributions to their professional efforts. The PFWA announced that Wolf had been selected to receive the organization's prestigious 'Horrigan Award,' presented annually "to the league official or player for his or her professional style in helping football writers do their job." The award is named in honor of the late Jack Horrigan, former publicity director of the American Football League and vice president of public relations for the Buffalo Bills.

Then, in 1996, came the coupe de grace – the culmination of Wolf's quest for pro football's ultimate prize. Aware his team was close to the coveted goal, he added three key performers to the personnel mix – free safety Eugene Robinson by way of an offseason trade and defensive tackle Santana Dotson and punt returner Desmond Howard as unrestricted free agents. Under Holmgren's shrewd and demanding tutelage, all three played major roles as Favre, the NFL's 'Most Valuable Player' for the second year in a row, and the charismatic White led the Packers to their first Super Bowl title since 1967, despite playing the league's most demanding schedule.

With the formula firmly in place, the pattern of success continued in 1997, Favre leading the Packers to another 13-3 record, a second consecutive NFC Championship and a second straight Super Bowl appearance. Two important moves made by Wolf that offseason helped guarantee the team's continued success. Wolf first drafted Iowa's Ross Verba in the first round to solidify the uncertain left tackle position, then plucked unknown Ryan Longwell, who would stabilize the Packers' placekicking fortunes, off the waiver wire right before the start of training camp.

In the interim, Wolf has been honored by the National Quarterback Club for his multiple contributions to the Packers' artistic renaissance. He was presented with the organization's 'Lifetime Achievement Award' at its annual recognition dinner (June 4, 1998).

The Packers' dramatic turnaround since Wolf's arrival, accompanied by increasingly high expectations from the team's excited loyalists, has documented Harlan's decision to bring him in late in 1991 with total authority over the organization's football operation.

"When we started the search to fill the position," Harlan said at the time of the announcement, "we put together a list of eight names. Ron's name was at the top of the list."

Wolf, who previously had spent 25 years in the front office of the Raiders, took over a position new to the Packers' organizational structure in terms of authority and responsibility, said authority including hiring and supervising the head coach and the scouting staff, conducting the draft and making all football decisions for the organization.

With the sweeping mandate, Wolf moved swiftly. He made his first major decision in a span of 24 days after his appointment, dismissing Lindy Infante as head coach on December 22, 1991, his second in hiring Mike Holmgren as Infante's successor just 20 days later – January 11, 1992.

The 59-year-old executive, who agreed to a five-year contract in leaving the New York Jets to join the Packers, credits his long experience in the Raiders' front office with preparing him for his current responsibilities.

"I had an opportunity to learn from – to me – the greatest figure in the game today, Al Davis," he said. "He knows every aspect of the game of professional football – not just the X's and O's but from the business standpoint and the talent standpoint. He is totally involved, and he taught me. I was very, very fortunate to work for him."

Wolf launched his professional football career under Davis in 1963 when he joined the then-fledgling

Raiders as a talent scout.

Subsequently, when Davis was named American Football League commissioner in 1966, Wolf accompanied him to the league office as the AFL's coordinator of talent. He returned to the Raiders with Davis prior to the opening of the 1966 season and played a major role in the club's personnel operation until the spring of 1975.

At that time, the then 37-year-old Wolf was named to oversee the formation of the newly-franchised Tampa Bay Buccaneers of the NFL as vice president of operations. He remained in that capacity until 1978, when he re-joined the Raiders, for whom he headed up player personnel operations until he signed on with the Jets organization in June of 1990.

His efforts in behalf of the Tampa Bay franchise bore fruit in 1979 when the players Wolf assembled carried the Buccaneers to the NFC Central title and, in the playoffs, as far as the National Football Conference Championship Game before they bowed to the then-Los Angeles Rams in a defensive struggle, 9-0.

Born in New Freedom, Pa., on December 30, 1938, Wolf attended the University of Oklahoma, where he majored in history. He earlier had served with Army Intelligence in Europe for three years.

Wolf has said he decided he wanted to make professional football his life's work "when I was in the service in '58 or '59, and I was stationed in Berlin, Germany. I think that appealed to me as something I would really like to do if I could do it. I never thought I'd be able to get my foot in the door."

His first job in the field was with *Pro Football Illustrated*, a publication based in Chicago, in 1961. He subsequently returned to the University of Oklahoma in 1962, he said, "and then Al Davis called me in 1963, after I'd taken my last final examination at Oklahoma...The very day, he called me."

On those rare occasions when he is not immersed in football operations today, Wolf can be found reading. "I like to read novels – and when I really get serious – I like to delve into the Civil War or World War II," he says of himself. "That's when I get into a serious mode, which runs for about two weeks...Then I get off it."

Wolf, who has a corollary and highly developed interest in the lives of legendary military leaders, such as George S. Patton, George Custer and Douglas MacArthur, et al, said, "What fascinates me – and I can't pin the answer down – is where do all these people come from...the great people that emerge in time of crisis? Where have they been? Why do they suddenly appear on the scene at the precise moment of history?"

Ron's family includes his wife, Edie, and five children – daughters Saralyn, Celli and Joan, and two sons, Jonathan and Eliot, both of the latter students at Green Bay's Notre Dame Academy. Mrs. Wolf is a psychologist who has established a practice in Green Bay.

MICHAEL R. REINFELDT

Vice Pres. of Admin./Chief Financial Officer

The possessor of an extensive background in finance as an athletics administrator in both the college and professional ranks, as well as nearly a decade of playing experience at football's highest level, Michael R. 'Mike' Reinfeldt brings the best of two professional worlds to his dual role as the Packer Corporation's vice president of administration and chief financial officer.

As a former All-Pro defensive back, he thus has brought an important and complementary dimension to his responsibilities as chief financial officer, which include negotiating player contracts as well as supervising the Packers' financial operations and accounting staff and directing the preparation of all corporate and departmental budgets.

As vice president of administration, an additional position to which he was named by President Bob Harlan January 1, 1994, he also is responsible for overseeing all of the organization's other extensive non-football operations.

A native of Baraboo, Wis., Reinfeldt was named chief financial officer on November 8, 1990, coming to the Packers from the University of Southern California, where he had served as the school's associate athletic director. He previously had been chief financial officer for the then-Los Angeles Raiders from 1985 through 1987.

Reinfeldt, who earned an MBA degree in management and finance from Houston Baptist University, earlier had obtained a bachelor of science degree from the University of Wisconsin-Milwaukee, where he starred as a four-year starter on the varsity football team and holds the school record for most interceptions in a career (24). It is a mark that is not likely to be broken because his alma mater dropped football following his senior year.

He holds another distinction in UWM's annals – he is the only alumnus in the institution's history ever to play in the National Football League.

Following graduation, Reinfeldt went on to a distinguished career in the professional ranks, launched when he signed with the then-Oakland Raiders as a free agent in 1975. After spending that season with the Raiders, he went on to play eight years (1976-83) with the Houston Oilers, starting 102 consecutive games, calling defensive signals for the secondary and leading the team in interceptions in 1977, 1979 and 1981. In the process, he played in two AFC Championship Games for Houston (against Pittsburgh in both 1978 and 1979) and also acquired his MBA degree while attending Houston Baptist in the offseason.

Reinfeldt enjoyed his best season in 1979, when he led the NFL in interceptions with 12, earned consensus All-Pro honors, started in the Pro Bowl and was named 'Player of the Year' in the American Football Conference.

Subsequently, upon retiring as an active player, he returned to the Raiders as chief financial officer, overseeing the organization's financial and accounting operations and negotiating the majority of player contracts. He also dealt with local television and radio contracts, and was responsible for staff personnel.

Reinfeldt left professional football in 1988 to join the athletic department at the University of Southern California, where he served as the school's assistant athletic director for one year, then was promoted to associate athletic director, a position he held until formally joining the Packers organization on January 7, 1991.

At USC, he was responsible for the formation and control of the athletic department's $17 million budget, and handled negotiations on major contracts with radio and television networks, sponsors and outside suppliers.

In 1997, the 45-year-old Reinfeldt was honored by his alma mater. He was presented with the University of Wisconsin-Milwaukee Alumni Association's 'Distinguished Alumnus Award' during a pre-commencement ceremony (May 10). The award recognizes UWM graduates who have distinguished themselves with outstanding achievements in their careers, civic involvement, or both. Reinfeldt graduated from UWM in 1975 with a bachelor's degree in marketing.

Born May 6, 1953, in Baraboo, Reinfeldt was a high school sports star there, earning six letters in football and basketball. Still an athlete, he regularly is involved in a variety of sports, including tennis, golf, bicycling, basketball and racquetball. Also an omnivorous reader, he is committed to reading "as many different books as I can...I try to read three or four books a week – some fiction, some historical fiction and some factual...some biography...a little bit of everything."

Reinfeldt and his wife, Susan, are the parents of two children – a son, Jared Michael, born January 29, 1994, and a daughter, Elise Marie, born March 9, 1995.

LANCE LOPES

Assistant Vice President/General Counsel

Lance Lopes, the Packer Corporation's general counsel since 1993, this year has taken on new and additional responsibilities as assistant vice president of the organization.

An attorney since 1989, Lopes received the promotion from Bob Harlan, the Packers' president and chief executive officer, in February.

In his expanded role, the 34-year-old Nevada native handles all legal matters for the organization, assists in player contract negotiations and front office administration and also represents the corporation at league meetings.

Most recently, Lopes played a major role in connection with the Packers' latest stock sale, launched last November. He was instrumental in obtaining approval from securities officials and the National Football League, and also designed and administered the distribution plan and helped coordinate the marketing activities, which concluded in March following the sale of more than $24 million in stock.

Prior to joining the Packer Corporation, Lopes was in the private civil practice of law from 1989 until 1993 – for two years in Honolulu and three years in Seattle.

An honors graduate of Linfield College (McMinville, Ore.) with a B.A. degree, he subsequently earned his law degree at the University of Oregon in 1988.

Earlier an accomplished athlete at Lowry High School in Winnemucca, Nev., he claimed 10 letters playing varsity football, basketball, baseball and golf. A tight end, he then went on to play for two NAIA Division II national championship football teams at Linfield College.

Born in Winnemucca September 20, 1963, Lopes is married – his wife, Mari, currently practices law part-time – and they have three children: Katie (born 6/21/93), Sydney (born 5/6/96) and Peter (born 4/30/98).

Lance lists golf, skiing and travel as his favorite hobbies.

TED THOMPSON

Director of Player Personnel

Possessor of an extensive resume that has included a 10-year playing career in the National Football League, Ted Thompson is in his seventh year in the Packers' player personnel operation, the focal point of the organization.

Director of pro personnel from 1993 until 1997, Thompson was promoted to director of player personnel by Executive Vice President/General Manager Ron Wolf May 30, 1997, to "oversee all of our college and pro scouting operations."

In his latest role, Thompson is responsible for supervising the college scouting staff, headed by director John Dorsey, and pro scouting activities, coordinated by Reggie McKenzie, director of pro personnel.

A native of Atlanta, Texas, the 45-year-old Thompson joined the Packers organization January 15, 1992, following 10 seasons with the Houston Oilers as a 'nickel' linebacker. A graduate of Southern Methodist University, where he was a three-year starting linebacker, he closed out his pro career at the end of the 1984 NFL season.

One of the most durable players in Oilers history, he played in 146 regular-season games, missing only one contest during his 10 seasons. He also played in seven playoff games following the 1978-80 seasons. A reserve kicker in addition to his linebacker duties, he made 4 of 4 PATs against the New York Jets in an emergency situation during the 1981 season.

Thompson, born in Atlanta, Texas, January 17, 1953, earned a bachelor's degree in business administration at SMU, where he gained Academic All-Southwest Conference honors. He operated his own investment business in Houston prior to signing on with the Packers as assistant director of pro personnel in 1992.

JOHN DORSEY
Director of College Scouting

John Dorsey, an effective player for the Packers during the '80s, is in his second year as Green Bay's director of college scouting. He was named to his current position by Executive Vice President/General Manager Ron Wolf on February 27, 1997, to succeed the retiring John Math.

The 38-year-old Dorsey began his career in player personnel in May of 1991, when he was hired by the Packers to scout linebackers. Retained by Wolf the following year, his scouting assignments subsequently have included the midlands, southwest and southeast regions, current responsibilities are east of the Mississippi River with a watchful eye on the all-important southeast.

Selected by Green Bay in the fourth round of the 1984 draft, Dorsey played five seasons for the Packers (1984-88) at linebacker and on special teams before spending a final year on injured reserve in 1989. He totaled 130 tackles as a pro, in addition to 2 fumble recoveries and 1 pass defensed. Dorsey led Green Bay's special teams in solo tackles in three of his first four seasons, a level of play which helped earn him selection as the Packers' special teams captain. Possessor of a streak of 76 consecutive non-strike games played, Dorsey saw that string end when he suffered a freak knee injury in pre-game warmups of the '89 season opener.

A four-year starter at Connecticut, Dorsey was named 'Defensive Player of the Year' in the Yankee Conference during each of his final two collegiate seasons, also earning Division I-AA All-America recognition as a senior.

Heavily involved in the community throughout his playing career, especially with the Wisconsin Cystic Fibrosis Foundation, he was voted as the Packers' 'Man of the Year' in 1987 for his civic contributions.

Born August 31, 1960, in Leonardtown, Md., Dorsey is the father of two sons, Bryant, 11, and Austin, 7.

Dorsey enjoys playing golf, water skiing and reading when not traversing the country looking for players.

REGGIE McKENZIE
Director of Pro Personnel

Reggie McKenzie, possessor of four years experience in Green Bay's pro personnel department and a seven-year National Football League playing career at linebacker, begins his second year as director of pro personnel for the Packers in 1998.

McKenzie, a pro personnel assistant since joining the Packers in 1994, was promoted to director of pro personnel by Executive Vice President/General Manager Ron Wolf in May of 1997.

A 10th-round draft choice out of the University of Tennessee in 1985 by the then-Los Angeles Raiders, McKenzie went on to win all-rookie honors and was the team's second-leading tackler during each of his first two seasons. After four years with the Raiders (1985-88), McKenzie spent two seasons (1989-90) with the Arizona Cardinals and one year (1992) with the San Francisco 49ers before a knee injury forced him to retire. Prior to signing with the 49ers, he played with the World League's Montreal Machine in the spring of 1992.

While out of football in 1991, McKenzie spent a season as a defensive coach for Dorsey High School in South Central Los Angeles. Led by Sharman Shah, who would later change his name to Karim Abdul-Jabbar and become a Miami Dolphins running back, the school captured the league championship.

McKenzie returned to Tennessee and served as an assistant under head coach Phil Fulmer in 1993. While back in Knoxville, he also pursued a master's degree in education administration.

Born in Knoxville, Tenn., February 8, 1963, McKenzie earned a bachelor's degree in business administration with an emphasis in personnel management at Tennessee. A two-way football star at Austin East High School in Knoxville, McKenzie was valedictorian of his 1981 graduating class. A twin brother, Raleigh, also attended Tennessee and is now enjoying his 14th season of professional football, currently as a center with the San Diego Chargers.

McKenzie is the president of the 'McKenzie Foundation,' a non-profit youth foundation in Knoxville. The organization awards academic scholarships to graduating seniors at Austin East High School. During the NFL's offseason, he also operates an annual three-day football clinic in Knoxville.

McKenzie and his wife, June, a Green Bay attorney, have two daughters, Jasmin (born 1/28/92) and Mahkayla (born 8/7/93), and a son, Reginald Kahlil (born 1/3/97).

In his spare time, McKenzie enjoys spending time with his family.

LEE REMMEL

Executive Director of Public Relations

Lee Remmel enters his 25th year as a member of the Packers' front office in 1998, having served previously as director of public relations in 1974 and from 1980 through 1988, and as director of publicity from 1975 through 1979.

He was named executive director of public relations in March of 1989 by Bob Harlan, then executive vice president of administration, with responsibility for overseeing the public relations, marketing and community relations areas. Prior to joining the Packer organization on March 24, 1974, Remmel was a sports writer and columnist for the *Green Bay Press-Gazette* for 29½ years.

In the course of his two "careers," he has been involved in staffing all 32 Super Bowls played to date, the first eight representing the *Press-Gazette,* the next 22 as a member of the National Football League's auxiliary media relations staff and the last two years with the Packers' front office.

Remmel also has been a member of the NFL public relations directors' Professional Football Writers of America liaison, statistics and NFL Films committees.

While at the *Press-Gazette*, he was the only sports writer in Wisconsin to have been directly involved in coverage of the Packers throughout all of the team's coaching regimes to that point, beginning with Packers' founder E.L. 'Curly' Lambeau and continuing until the naming of Bart Starr in 1975. His personal longevity may be best illustrated by the fact that he witnessed his 100th Packer-Bear game on November 12, 1995, in the 150th regular-season meeting of the arch enemies.

Remmel's half-century of close association with the Packers was duly recognized on March 30, 1996, when he was inducted into the Green Bay Packer Hall of Fame.

In 1967, he was voted Wisconsin 'Sports Writer of the Year.' He also is a past president of the former Wisconsin Pro Football Writers' Association.

Remmel, a native of Shawano, Wis., where he was born June 30, 1924, began his career as the sports editor of a weekly newspaper while a Shawano High School freshman. He and his wife, Noreen, celebrate their 50th wedding anniversary on August 21 of this year.

Active in the community, the first annual Lee Remmel Sports Awards Banquet, honoring Wisconsin professional, collegiate, amateur and prep althetes, was held last April, raising $20,000 for scholarship funds at the University of Wiconsin-Green Bay, St. Norbert College and area high schools. More than 725 people attended the inaugural event, which will be staged on April 8 next year.

He also is a member of the executive committee of the Brown County Civic Music Association, along with his wife, as well as of the executive board of the 65 Roses Sports Club (cystic fibrosis). He additionally is a member of the St. Norbert College Fine Arts Committee, the Green Bay School/Business/Industry Partnership Council and the board of directors of the Green Bay Packer Hall of Fame.

The seven-member Executive Committee of the Green Bay Packers presently is composed of (from left to right) Peter M. Platten, III, Secretary; John J. Fabry, Vice President; Dr. Donald F. Harden, Member; Robert E. Harlan, President; Donald J. Schneider, Member; James A. Temp, Member; and John R. Underwood, Treasurer.

Now in their 80th season of professional football, the Green Bay Packers are a team and an organization unique in both structure and accomplishment. They represent — from an organizational standpoint — the only publicly-owned franchise in the 30-club National Football League. On the field, they have won more championships — twelve — than any other team in the NFL's 78-year history.

Green Bay Packers, Inc., was founded as a non-profit corporation in 1922 under the leadership of A.B. Turnbull, then publisher of the *Green Bay Press-Gazette,* who became the organization's first president. There are 4,746,896 shares of stock owned by 109,723 stockholders. The corporation is governed by a seven-member Executive Committee, elected from a 45-person board of directors.

BOARD OF DIRECTORS

Thomas D. Arndt	Robert E. Harlan	Peter M. Platten, III
Daniel C. Beisel	Philip J. Hendrickson	Herman J. Reckelberg
John F. Bergstrom	Rosemary Hinkfuss	Michael R. Reese
Terry J. Bogart	Dr. Oliver M. Hitch	Pat Richter
John E. Broeren	John C. Koeppler	Ronald Sadoff
Robert C. Buchanan	James F. Kress	Leo J. Scherer
The Hon. George A. Burns, Jr.	Bernard C. Kubale	Paul J. Schierl
Tony Canadeo	Theodore M. Leicht	Donald J. Schneider
James M. Christensen	Donald J. Long, Sr.	Allan H. "Bud" Selig
Willie D. Davis	Thomas J. Lutsey, Jr.	K.C. Stock
John H. Dickens	John N. MacDonough	James A. Temp
Richard Dougherty	Dr. Thomas A. Manion	Fred N. Trowbridge, Jr.
John J. Fabry	John C. Meng	William J. Tyrrell
Robert C. Gallagher	Stewart C. Mills, Jr.	John R. Underwood
Dr. Donald F. Harden	Thomas M. Olejniczak	Michael A. Wier

DIRECTORS EMERITUS

Robert G. Bush	Paul F. Kelly	Lee G. Roemer
Arthur T. Chermak	Howard L. Levitas	George J. Stathas
Frank M. Cowles	Fred H. Lindner	Bernard C. Ziegler
Warren H. Dunn	Arthur H. Mongin, Jr.	
Woodrow R. Jepsen	The Hon. Robert J. Parins	

MIKE HOLMGREN

Head Coach

Prepossessing Michael George Holmgren, a masterful motivator with a rare capacity for extracting optimum performance from his players, has added major dimensions to the Packers' lustrous history in six eminently successful seasons as the eleventh head coach in the team's 79-year annals.

Until the towering Californian's arrival upon the Green Bay scene, only two figures were preeminent in the Packers' long coaching history – team founder E.L. 'Curly' Lambeau and the fabled Vince Lombardi.

But those storied icons, who had the "stage" to themselves for decades, are mutually exclusive no longer, historically speaking. Holmgren formally joined them in the team's pantheon of elite following a hallmark 1996 season, one majestically crowned by a Super Bowl title – the Packers' first in 29 years – and further established himself in their company by leading the Green and Gold to a second consecutive Super Bowl appearance last January.

Surpassing the legendary Lombardi's success in Lambeau Field en route, he thus has forged a substantial niche in Packers archives for all time, becoming the third head coach in team annals to bring a world championship to what had come to be known as Titletown in an earlier era.

Prior to that signal accomplishment, he already occupied a lofty plateau in the team's rich and proud history, having become just the third field leader in the club's lengthy existence to own a winning record – a distinction he also shares with Lambeau and Lombardi.

A Californian born and bred, Holmgren had left the picturesque hills and haute cuisine of his native San Francisco in 1992 to take on a classic challenge in Green Bay, the smallest city in the National Football League.

Fresh from two Super Bowl victories in his role as offensive coordinator for his hometown 49ers, he immediately set his primary priority upon assuming on-field direction of the Packers. It was typically succinct: "Establishing a winning attitude," which he identified as an essential about-face for a team burdened by two decades of mediocrity.

As recent history well illustrates, he clearly has succeeded beyond even the most optimistic expectations.

Although the Super Bowl success – a 35-21 triumph over the New England Patriots in SB XXXI at New Orleans in January of 1997 – is his crowning achievement to date, the list of his coaching credits, compiled within the short span of six years, is both long and lustrous.

Putting an end to a protracted drought in the process – the Packers had enjoyed only two winning seasons in the previous 19 – the former high school history teacher has:

- **Strung together six consecutive winning seasons,** a feat last forged by the storied Lombardi in the '60s;

- **Directed the Packers to five consecutive** National Football League playoff berths – for the first time in team history;

- **Led them to three straight NFC Central Division championships (1995-96-97)** for the first time in team annals;

- **Produced Green Bay's first conference titles (back-to-back championships in 1996 and 1997)** since 1967;

- **Maneuvered his team to 13-3 records in both 1996 and 1997** (the Packers' best since 1966, when they were 12-2 in a 14-game season);

- **Orchestrated the first 16-victory season** (including three playoff wins) in team history, in 1996;

- **Led the Packers to 23 consecutive, regular-season victories at home,** the longest winning streak in the team's 79-year history, and the second longest home-field streak in league annals; and

- **Escorted the Green and Gold to three consecutive, double-digit winning seasons,** the first such "trifecta" since 1961-62-63 (11 wins in 1995, 13 in both 1996 and 1997).

Additionally, in this productive process, he has quickly amassed the third-most coaching victories in team history, parlaying his overall record to 73-36-0, including a 64-32-0 mark in regular-season play and a 9-4 record in playoff competition.

Near the end of the '96 season, Holmgren became only the eighth coach in NFL history to win 50 regular-season games within his first five years in the league (Lombardi, Don Shula, Chuck Knox, Joe Gibbs, Mike Ditka, George Seifert and Bill Cowher were the others before him).

And these figures encompass a Holmgren home record that is little short of remarkable. Not even the legendary Lombardi put up the "home" numbers he has – 40 victories in 44 games overall in Lambeau Field, including five victorious playoff appearances, for an imposing .909 winning percentage. Lombardi, for purposes of comparison, was 32-7-1 in his 40 career games in "Lambeau," including playoffs, an .813 percentage. Holmgren now has not lost a game at home since the opening contest of the 1995 season.

Wolf, taking note of these imposing accomplishments, paid high tribute to Holmgren.

"Mike Holmgren is interested in one thing – and one thing only – and that's winning ball games," the Packers' general manager asserted. "He's very special at teaching players how to play and communicating with players. He also has tremendous dignity and character. I think all those qualities come through to our football team. I think that's the reason why the Packers are as successful as they have been under his tenure."

Initially, however, it was not that easy. Taking over a club which had finished with a dismal 4-and-12 record in 1991, Holmgren saw his first team lose five of its first seven games in his baptismal, '92 season. Rebounding from that early adversity, he led his first three Packers teams to as many consecutive 9-and-7 records, a span of success Green Bay had not known since the now-distant "Lombardi Era."

The 50-year-old San Franciscan embellished these accomplishments by escorting the Green and Gold to an 11-5 mark in 1995 – the 11 victories representing the third-highest such total in team annals – and to its first NFC Central Division championship in 23 years, then guiding his squad to back-to-back wild-card and divisional playoff victories in the postseason and a berth in the National Football Conference title game for the first time since 1967.

When the Packers saw the Cowboys come from behind to prevail in the latter contest at Dallas, Holmgren made a promise to his players in the somber visitors' dressing room at Texas Stadium.

"Next year," he told the team, "those last ten minutes will be ours."

And, proving himself something of a prophet, it came to pass. Employing "the next logical step on paper is the Super Bowl" as his theme, Holmgren called upon his considerable leadership ability to meld diverse talents and personalities into the overall mix – exemplified by the late-season addition of controversial wide receiver Andre Rison following injuries to starting receivers Robert Brooks and Antonio Freeman – and plug them in when and where needed without diminishing the team's focus or togetherness.

Preseason additions of free safety Eugene Robinson – acquired in a trade with Seattle – and defensive tackle Santana Dotson, along with that of Rison, became other shining examples of Holmgren's ability to pull all such elements together and produce the desired results. In this case, a Super Bowl championship, climaxing a season which saw Robinson emerge as the team's interception leader, Dotson provide a needed inside pass rush and Rison contribute the first touchdown in the Packers' SB XXXI victory over New England.

En route to professional football's summit, Holmgren's Packers certified their right to primacy with a rare competitive coupling, leading the NFL in scoring (a club-record 456 points) and fewest points allowed (210), thus becoming the first team to forge such a parlay since 1972. In so doing, the defense also set a league record for a 16-game schedule by permitting only 19 opponent touchdowns, breaking the mark set by the 1985 Chicago Bears.

In the wake of the Super Bowl triumph, Holmgren was honored as 'NFL Coach of the Year' for a second time, having been presented with the 1997 "Victor Award" by vote of the Sportswriters and Broadcasters of America. He also was named VISA's 'NFL Coach of the Year' in a vote by fans.

Not one to dwell upon successes achieved, Holmgren then prepared himself – and his team – for the next challenge. Feeling the need "to re-direct my time and energies toward a Super Bowl repeat," he announced in early March that he had canceled his television and radio shows for the 1997 season, also mentioning a desire to spend more time at home with his family.

Although a surprising decision to some, it typified the depth of Holmgren's commitment, one which complements an impressive faculty for overcoming adversity, as evidenced throughout his six-year tenure.

And his dedication to the task at hand, transmitted to the players with the aid of his coaching staff, paid handsome dividends in 1997, leading all the way to a repeat appearance in the "Big Dance."

"One of the highlights for me…was how this football team – the players, coaches, trainers, everybody – approached the season after winning the Super Bowl last year," he said in a season-end review, three days after the 31-24 loss to the Broncos in SB XXXII at San Diego. "We were able to accomplish things that a lot of world champions had not been able to do following their Super Bowl win."

Although he made no mention of it, the latter included a historic 15-4 overall record, marking only the second time in Packers annals the Green and Gold have won as many as 15 games in a season – following upon their record, 16-victory campaign en route to capturing Super Bowl honors in 1996.

Those 15 victories, in turn, produced a third consecutive NFC Central Division championship, a second straight NFC Championship and, as indicated, the aforementioned second consecutive Super Bowl appearance.

Last season, on a personal level he became only the second head coach in NFL history to win at least one playoff game in five straight seasons, joining Oakland's John Madden (1973-77).

Earlier in his Green Bay tenure, Holmgren demonstrated a rare talent for dealing with adversity, forging a 9-and-7 record for the third time in 1994 despite the premature retirement of leading tackler Johnny Holland and the injury loss of starters Guy McIntyre (six games), LeRoy Butler (three games) and Roland Mitchell (15 games) – plus key contributors Lenny McGill (nine games) and Gilbert Brown (three games) during the course of the season.

The former USC field general again proved himself a highly resourceful leader in 1995, following a career-ending injury to Sterling Sharpe, the most prolific pass receiver in Packers history. Calling upon his players to "crank it up a notch" to offset the loss of a primary weapon, he developed an exceptional team unity which played a major role in producing the Packers' first division title in nearly a quarter-century – a togetherness which later prompted elder statesman Reggie White to observe, "The chemistry on this team is as good as any I've ever been around."

Appropriately, Holmgren's efforts have been duly recognized and rewarded. Even prior to his third straight winning season in 1994, the Packer organization expressed its appreciation for his accomplishments – and unqualified confidence in his future leadership – when President Bob Harlan extended his contract for three years, one which is slated to have him presiding over the team's on-field operations until the next century. The extension takes him through the year 1999.

Earlier honored as National Football Conference 'Coach of the Year' in 1992, he had maneuvered the Packers to within one game of the playoffs in his first season, leading them to a six-game winning streak – their longest since 1965 – en route.

The following year, he managed to take his team to the next level – the playoffs – despite the loss of four starters to injuries, three of them members of the offensive line (center James Campen, left guard Rich Moran and right tackle Tootie Robbins), plus linebacker Brian Noble, a consistently productive performer and a team leader.

In plotting and executing his offensive strategy, Holmgren also had to deal with the fact that his principal weapon, Sharpe, was not able to practice the last eight weeks of the '93 season – and throughout the play-offs – because of a nagging turf toe injury, and thus was not at his physical best in the drive for a postseason berth.

Holmgren's resourceful handling of these challenges loomed large in the late stages of the '93 season as the Packers rebounded from a season-ending loss to Detroit to score a last-minute, come-from-behind victory over the Lions in their wild-card playoff encounter a week later, thus recording their first postseason victory in more than a decade.

A year later, Holmgren again exhibited impressive ability to rally his team, re-grouping the Green and Gold in the wake of a late, three-game losing streak – two of the losses coming against 1993 Super Bowl principals Buffalo and Dallas – to sweep its final three games and qualify for the playoffs for the second year in a row.

A reasoned and compassionate perfectionist, he has exercised admirable patience along the way in continuing to develop his highly-talented young quarterback, Brett Favre, patience which has been amply rewarded. Favre has responded with record-breaking seasons each of the past three years, efforts that have brought him three consecutive NFL 'Most Valuable Player' honors.

In complete command of his football team throughout his six-year tenure, Holmgren has evinced a quiet confidence from the beginning, perhaps traceable to the league-wide reputation as one of professional football's premier offensive coaches that he had brought with him from the San Francisco 49ers – together with a long-time identification with success.

Gil Haskell, one of his assistant coaches during Holmgren's first six seasons in Green Bay, cites another explanation. "My impression is that he has prepared himself to be a head coach," Haskell said of Holmgren. "Many people get head coaching jobs that never expected to get them. He didn't...He's been planning this for some time."

Holmgren's initial success in 1992 stemmed in large part from his ability to achieve what he listed as his number one priority. At the outset, he pinpointed the need "to establish a winning attitude," asserting, "We have to establish the fact that good things are going to happen in the second half of games, not bad things. And that's a mindset."

The Packers' 9-7 record in that baptismal season is eloquent evidence that Holmgren's words were taken to heart. Over the course of the campaign, the Packers compiled an imposing 8-0 record in games in which they led at halftime, a shining example of the positive approach. And, poetically, they came from behind in the final minute of play to post their first regular-season victory of the 'Holmgren Era,' scoring with 13 seconds remaining to shade the Cincinnati Bengals, 24-23, in Week 3.

Holmgren, who at 6-feet-5 inevitably cuts an imposing figure (he is the tallest head coach in Packers history), became the eleventh head coach in team annals when he was signed to a five-year contract January 11, 1992, by Ron Wolf, the Packers' executive vice president and general manager.

It was in the nature of a coup for Wolf since Holmgren had been sought after by no fewer than six NFL clubs following the 1991 season in recognition of his accomplishments as offensive coordinator for the 49ers.

Earlier quarterbacks coach under the celebrated Bill Walsh for three seasons, he became San Francisco's offensive coordinator in 1989 and proceeded to put his personal stamp on the club's attack. Under him, the 49er offense ranked no lower than third in the league during his three years as coordinator.

Over this span, the 49ers compiled the NFL's best overall record, posting 71 wins compared to only 23 losses, with one tie, a .753 percentage.

Individually, Holmgren did perhaps the finest job of his San Francisco tenure in 1991. Despite losing quarterbacks Joe Montana and Steve Young to injuries, the 49ers' offense finished third in the league under his leadership. With third-string quarterback Steve Bono taking over for the injured Young, who had replaced an injured Montana at the start of the season, the 49ers won five of their last six games.

The ability to win with three different quarterbacks, a singular achievement, helped to make Holmgren the NFL's most sought-after assistant as head coaching opportunities began to develop following the '91 season.

Under his direction, the 49ers' offense had been the NFL's top-ranked unit in 1989, his first season as the team's offensive coordinator. Earlier, in 1987, Holmgren's guidance was credited with helping Montana capture his first league passing championship. He also was cited for the manner in which he prepared Young to step in for Montana when injuries forced the latter to the sideline, and the adjustments he implemented to help Bono succeed in his interim role.

A native of San Francisco, Holmgren had returned home in 1986 to take on his first coaching assignment in the professional ranks. He came to the 49ers from Brigham Young University, where he had been a member of LaVell Edwards' staff for four years (1982-85). There, he tutored Young in his role as quarterbacks coach, helping the Cougars to maintain one of college football's most potent passing offenses. During Holmgren's tenure, BYU won the school's first national championship in 1984.

Holmgren also has known personal success on the football field as a performer, having been named 1965's 'Prep Athlete of the Year' while playing for San Francisco's Lincoln High School. A quarterback, he went on to play four years of college football at the University of Southern California (1966-69) and was selected by the St. Louis Cardinals in the eighth round of the 1970 draft. He subsequently was in training camp with both the Cardinals and the New York Jets that year, prior to returning to his high school alma mater, Lincoln High, to begin his coaching career in 1971 – and teach history.

A year later, Holmgren moved to San Francisco's Sacred Heart High as a teacher and assistant coach, struggling through 4-and-24 adversity from 1972-1974 at a school which had no practice facilities, before transferring to nearby Oak Grove High from 1975-80, a period during which the school won a Central Coast Sectional football championship.

The Packers' future head coach next entered the college ranks, serving as quarterbacks coach and offensive coordinator at San Francisco State in 1981, preceding his move to Brigham Young in 1982.

Of Swedish-Norwegian descent, Holmgren was born June 15, 1948, in San Francisco. Following graduation from Lincoln High School, he earned his bachelor of science degree at USC in 1970.

Mike and his wife, Kathy, have four daughters — married twins Calla and Jenny (born 9/27/73), who graduated from North Park College (their mother's alma mater) in 1995; Emily (born 1/21/77), now in her fourth year at Gordon College; and Gretchen (born 7/14/81), a senior at Ashwaubenon High School.

In 1997, the Packers' head coach was honored by North Park College when the institution conferred a doctor of laws degree upon him during annual commencement ceremonies.

He also received a more visible honor on August 17, 1997, when Gross Street in Green Bay's Village of Ashwaubenon was formally dedicated as 'Holmgren Way' in recognition of the Packers' Super Bowl triumph. Ironically, the newly-christened 'Holmgren Way' intersects Lombardi Avenue only two blocks east of Lambeau Field, running parallel to the stadium.

Professionally, aside from his responsibilities in the Packers organization, Holmgren co-chairs the NFL Competition Committee along with Buccaneers General Manager Rich McKay, having succeeded the retired Shula in that role in 1996. Holmgren previously had served as chairman of the Competition Committee Coaches Subcommittee since 1994.

Although a relatively new resident, Holmgren has long-standing Wisconsin ties. His maternal grandfather, Jens Bugge, was born on a farm in the Badger state. Known as 'Colonel' in the family because of his service as an officer in the United States Army, Bugge was the author of a book on military strategy, a copy of which reposes in the West Point library.

Away from football, the Packers' coach spends most of his leisure time with his family. Golf is his favorite pastime and he also is fond of reading, particularly historical books.

Already substantially involved in the Green Bay community and his adopted state, he has seen his Mike Holmgren Celebrity Invitational Golf Tournament raise approximately $25,000 annually for the 65 Roses Sports Club (cystic fibrosis) each of the past seven years.

Holmgren, who enjoys riding his motorcycle in rare moments of leisure, additionally served as honorary co-chairman of the 'Harley 100-Mile Run for Muscular Dystrophy' from 1995-97. In another civic role, Holmgren was honorary chairman for the Wisconsin Arthritis Foundation telethon in 1992 and '93.

He also annually heads up 'Mike Holmgren's Golf for Kids,' an event held at Lake Geneva, Wis., with the proceeds going for summer camp scholarships for inner city Chicago youths and funding for the Urban Outreach Program at North Park College.

COACHING BACKGROUND: 1981 (San Francisco State, offensive coordinator/quarterbacks coach); 1982-85 (Brigham Young University, quarterbacks coach); 1986-1991 (San Francisco 49ers, quarterbacks coach 1986-88, offensive coordinator 1989-91); 1992-98 (Green Bay Packers, head coach).

HEAD COACHING RECORD

Year	Team	W	L	T	Pct.	Finish
1992	Green Bay	9	7	0	.563	2nd, NFC Central
1993	Green Bay	9	7	0	.563	3rd, NFC Central
1994	Green Bay	9	7	0	.563	2nd, NFC Central
1995	Green Bay	11	5	0	.688	1st, NFC Central
1996	Green Bay	13	3	0	.813	1st, NFC Central
1997	Green Bay	13	3	0	.813	1st, NFC Central
Regular-Season Totals		**64**	**32**	**0**	**.677**	
Postseason		**9**	**4**	**0**	**.692**	
Career Record		**73**	**36**	**0**	**.670**	

SHERMAN LEWIS

Offensive Coordinator

In the six-year tenure of scholarly Sherman Lewis as Green Bay's offensive coordinator (1992-97), the Packers' offense has escalated from one plateau – making steady, sure and appreciable progress over the first four seasons – to quite another…record-breaking, league-high production over the past two.

The evolutionary process reached an explosive peak in the 1996 season, one in which the offense amassed 456 points to establish a new club standard en route to winning Super Bowl XXXI and the National Football League championship.

Green Bay's 56 touchdowns and 456 points in '96 also were NFL highs, marking the first time that the Packers had led the league in points since 1962 (and only the fifth time overall).

The offense followed that record season with another league-leading performance in 1997, pacing the NFC in scoring with 422 points – an average of 26.4 points per game – and also topping the conference in touchdowns with 50.

Significantly, the 456-point eruption in '96 marked the fourth consecutive year the offense had made substantial improvement in the ultimate bottom line, the production of points – improving from 276 in 1992, to 340 in 1993, to 382 in 1994 and to 404 in 1995.

The 422-point total in 1997 also continued a major trend, marking the third consecutive season that the Packers had scaled the 400-point plateau in scoring.

In breaking the club scoring record in '96, the Packers routinely demonstrated a quick-strike capability with 12 regular-season touchdowns coming from 50 yards or more, the most in a season by any team since 1970, a statistic punctuated during the playoffs by four additional scores of 50-plus yards, including three in the Super Bowl.

Green Bay's offense had invaded the record book a year earlier under Sherman's direction, rolling up 5,750 yards, the third-highest such total in the team's long National Football League history. A key element in mounting that impressive figure was a league-leading third down efficiency percentage, 49.1.

Lewis' expertise paid immediate and practical dividends in 1992, his first season as overseer of the offense, when the Packers' attack he coordinated proceeded to produce 4,786 yards, the most by a Green Bay offensive unit since 1989. Moving the chains consistently, the Packers registered 291 first downs along the way, compared to 259 a year earlier.

In 1993, his second season at the offensive controls, the improvement was more dramatic, the Packers rolling up 340 points, 66 more than in the previous campaign.

In 1994, they manifested even greater firepower, amassing 382 points, the most a Green Bay team had scored in a decade – since the '84 Green and Gold posted 390. In the process, the Packers also stacked up 5,361 yards – the most they had gained in a season since 1989.

Such accomplishments were not unexpected. When Mike Holmgren became head coach of the Packers in January of 1992, the identity of his offensive coordinator was a foregone conclusion. Without question, it was going to be Sherman Lewis.

"I wanted Sherm to be my offensive coordinator when I became head coach here in Green Bay because I knew he was an outstanding football coach," Holmgren later said. "We had worked together in San Francisco...and he was a key member of the staff. He's one of the brightest and most innovative coaches I've ever been around."

Holmgren since has reinforced that testimonial. In his year-end review following the '95 season, he described Lewis as "the best kept secret in this league." He added, "I don't want to lose him (to a potential head-coaching opportunity), but he certainly deserves his chance, and he would be very good."

Lewis brought an impressive coaching pedigree with him to Green Bay, having helped the 49ers develop one of the most productive attacks in the National Football League under Bill Walsh en route to three Super Bowl victories during the '80s.

Named to the Packers staff on January 18, 1992 – one week after Holmgren became Green Bay's head coach – Lewis was a member of the 49ers staff for nine seasons, the first six as running backs coach, tutoring such outstanding performers as perennial Pro Bowl running back Roger Craig and fullback Tom Rathman. Lewis subsequently coached the wide receivers during his final three seasons in San Francisco and helped hone the skills of Jerry Rice and John Taylor, who have been selected to a combined 13 Pro Bowls.

Sherman's responsibilities during his first season on the Green Bay staff also included coaching the receivers, duties he turned over to Jon Gruden prior to the 1993 season.

The 56-year-old Kentucky native had been an assistant coach at his alma mater, Michigan State, for 14 seasons prior to joining the 49ers, serving as assistant head coach and defensive coordinator for his final three years at MSU. Originally hired by the late Hugh 'Duffy' Dougherty, he later served on the staffs of Denny Stolz, Darryl Rodgers and Frank 'Muddy' Waters.

Lewis earlier had been a two-way All-America halfback at Michigan State, where he was second runnerup for the 1963 Heisman Trophy (behind Roger Staubach of Navy and Billy Lothridge of Georgia Tech) and named college football's 'Player of the Year' by *Football News*.

Sherman, who earned his master's degree in education administration from MSU in 1974, also was a standout track and field performer for the Spartans.

Born in Louisville, Ky., June 29, 1942, Lewis and his wife, Toni, have two sons, Kip (born 2/6/67), a former University of Arizona football player who now is a sports anchor/reporter for Green Bay's WLUK-TV, and Eric (born 1/2/76), who closed out a distinguished prep football career at St. Francis High School in Mountain View, Calif., in 1993 and, after receiving a football scholarship to San Diego State University, became a starting cornerback for the Aztecs.

COACHING BACKGROUND: 1969-82 (Michigan State); 1983-91 (San Francisco 49ers); 1992-98 (Green Bay Packers).

FRITZ SHURMUR

Defensive Coordinator

Innovator, author and consummate tactician, Leonard "Fritz" Shurmur has had considerably more than his share of coaching successes during a 23-year career in the National Football League – one which finds him pro football's elder statesman in terms of service as a defensive coordinator – and he continues to add to his collection of accomplishments each year.

In 1997, for most recent example, his defense set a modern-era club record for fewest touchdown passes permitted in a season with 10 – sharing league honors with the New York Giants – as Green Bay marched to a second straight appearance in the Super Bowl on the heels of a 13-3 regular-season record for the second consecutive year. Ranked 23rd in the league after 11 games, Shurmur's defensive unit was top-ranked over the final five regular-season games, allowing an average of only 224.8 yards per contest, and had skyrocketed to seventh place by year's end.

Particularly tough was the Packers' pass defense, which did not permit an opponent touchdown pass in the final 35 quarters (nearly nine full games) of the year, including playoffs, and just one opposition score through the air in the last 46 quarters. The final touchdown pass by a Green Bay foe in 1997 came, remarkably, on November 16 in the first quarter of a game at Indianapolis.

The Green Bay defense provided 32 take-aways in 1997, producing 110 points, 36 of which were immediate as three interceptions and three fumbles were returned for touchdowns.

Upon defeating the San Francisco 49ers in the most recent NFC Championship Game, the Packers became the first NFL team to limit an opponent to less than 100 rushing yards and 300 total yards in five consecutive playoff games (over the last two seasons). Each was a victory.

All of this was accomplished in 1997 despite numerous obstacles along the way. Starting cornerback Craig Newsome was lost to a season-ending knee injury on the very first play of the year, thrusting unproven Tyrone Williams into the lineup for the balance of the season. Injuries nagged three of Green Bay's four starting defensive linemen – Gilbert Brown (knee/ankle), Reggie White (back) and Gabe Wilkins (knee) – throughout the season, at times reducing their effectiveness.

A year earlier, the genial Michigan native was truly at the top of his game, presiding over a dominating defense which swept 1996, regular-season league honors and played a major role in the Packers' postseason surge to their first Super Bowl title in 29 years.

In that heady process, the Packers limited their opponents to 210 points, 248 first downs and an average of 259.8 yards per game, all three league lows, in emerging as the NFL's regular-season leader in defense (on a yardage basis) for the first time since 1967 and the fourth time overall since 1933.

In so doing, Shurmur's defenders punctuated their efforts by permitting the opposition only 19 touchdowns, a league record for a 16-game schedule, implemented in 1978, and in six games held opponents to a touchdown or less.

Along the way, the defense restricted the opposition to only 82 second-half points over the 16-game regular season, demonstrating an ability to shut down offenses and take over a game after intermission. This point was further magnified over the final six regular-season games and three postseason contests as Green Bay allowed but 33 points in the second half, including just seven in the fourth quarter. The Packers' three playoff opponents failed to score in the all-important final period.

The Green Bay defense also did its part to help the team's offense in 1996, producing an NFC-best 39 take-aways, which in turn resulted in 132 Packer points. Included among those 39 take-aways was a conference-high 26 interceptions.

Another important factor in the success of Green Bay's '96 defense was its ability to shut down the opposition at other critical junctures, Packer opponents converted at just 32.7% on third down – second-best in the NFL.

Under Shurmur, the Packers also have proven to be strong in the area of preparation and game-planning. In the team's last 37 games (including playoffs), Green Bay has allowed only two touchdowns on its opponent's opening drive – a strong testament to the players' strategic readiness for the battle at hand.

Such exploits should have come as no surprise to those familiar with Shurmur's career and coaching acumen. The resourceful veteran long since had gained wide recognition over a distinguished career for his creative defensive schemes and masterful game plans.

Now in his 19th year as a coordinator, Shurmur once again had demonstrated his ability to develop both long- and short-term solutions to problems during the '95 season.

In the former, he saw his defense force 56 three-and-out series over the '95 seasons, the most in the NFL.

In the latter, he devised an aggressive game plan which short-circuited San Francisco's vaunted passing game in the divisional playoffs, one which saw Green Bay defenders trigger and convert a running back's fumble into a touchdown on the game's opening series and then constantly harry quarterback Steve Young, sacking him three times and forcing two interceptions en route to a highly convincing, 27-17 victory in the 49ers' own 3Com Park.

Shurmur, now in his fifth season with the Packers and his 24th in the NFL overall, lost no time in putting his personal stamp upon the defensive platoon when named coordinator by Head Coach Mike Holmgren on January 31, 1994.

Despite the injury-enforced retirements of linebacker Johnny Holland and right cornerback Roland Mitchell – and voluntarily confining himself to the scheme of predecessor Ray Rhodes in the interests of a smooth and effective transition – he presided over a defense that finished the '94 season fifth in the National Football Conference and a highly respectable sixth in the league as a whole.

His defenders then climaxed those efforts in the postseason by setting an all-time playoff record in their wild-card game against Detroit (December 31), holding the redoubtable Barry Sanders and the Lions to negative rushing yardage en route to a 16-12 victory in Green Bay's Lambeau Field. In that performance, the Packers held the Lions to minus-4 yards in 15 attempts, breaking a 31-year-old playoff record while restricting league rushing champion Sanders to a career-low minus-1 yard in 13 attempts.

Shurmur earlier demonstrated a classic example of his flair for innovation in 1989 when, as defensive coordinator for the Los Angeles Rams, he was confronted with the challenge of revamping an injury-depleted defensive unit. Utilizing linebackers as down linemen and compensating for the absence of two regular inside linebackers until the season's 10th game, he developed a 2-5 'Eagle' defense which allowed only three running backs to gain 100 yards, finished fifth in the NFC with 42 quarterback sacks and led the Rams to two postseason victories.

On the Phoenix staff for three years prior to joining the Packers, he produced comparable results in becoming the Cardinals' defensive coordinator in 1991. Developing a unit featuring seven new starters, he turned out a defense which held opponents to 52 fewer points than the previous season and limited the opposition to two touchdowns or less on nine occasions, scored three touchdowns on turnovers and shared the league low for touchdown passes allowed with 12.

Shurmur's '11 men to the football' concept also triggered 37 fumbles, the third-highest single-season total in franchise history, while the Cardinals' 21 fumble recoveries ranked second in the NFC and third in the league.

A year later, his schematic originality paid dividends for Phoenix with a 'Big Nickel' alignment that featured four down linemen, two linebackers and five defensive backs. It fueled a defensive surge that limited foes to 67.5 yards rushing per game over the final six weeks of the season and enabled the Big Red to finish with the fifth-rated defense in the conference. The unit also held opponents to 101 first downs, the best effort in club history over a 16-game schedule.

The following season, 1993, Shurmur's 4-2-5 Cardinal defense again proved highly effective, closing out the season seventh in the NFL in points allowed with 269 – an average of 16.9 per game – the team's lowest total since the 16-game schedule was implemented.

Shurmur had joined the Cardinals following nine seasons with the Los Angeles Rams' successful defense, eight of them as its coordinator. He signed on as the Rams' defensive line coach for the strike-shortened 1982 season and became their defensive coordinator the following year, in which the Rams improved from 27th to 15th in total defense. In 1985 and '86, his efforts continued to bear fruit as the Rams led the NFL with 56 quarterback sacks in '85 and finished fifth in total defense both seasons. Overall, the Rams qualified for postseason play six times during Shurmur's nine-year tenure.

The 66-year-old Wyandotte, Mich., native made his NFL coaching debut with the Detroit Lions in 1975 as defensive line coach. He later was named Detroit's defensive coordinator in 1977. Four seasons in New England, the last two as defensive coordinator, followed. During this span, his 1979 Patriots defense led the NFL with 57 sacks.

Shurmur launched his coaching career in 1954 as a graduate student at his alma mater, Albion (Mich.) College, where he served as assistant football coach and swimming coach through 1961 before moving to the University of Wyoming as an assistant football coach. He was the Cowboys' defensive line coach from 1962-70 prior to being named head coach in 1971. As Wyoming's defensive coach, Shurmur's teams led the nation in rushing defense twice and in total defense once. During his stay in Laramie, the Cowboys paced the Western Athletic Conference in defense in 1963 and from 1965-69.

Blessed with writing skills to complement his football knowledge, Shurmur has authored four books – *Coaching Team Defense*, which covers all phases of defensive football and has elicited acclaim from his peers and fans alike; *The Five Linebacker Eagle Defense; Coaching Team Defense, Second Edition;* and most recently, *Coaching the Defensive Line*, published in 1996.

Shurmur also has taken his teaching skills to screen, having produced a 50-minute video, *Coaching the Defensive Line.*

Born July 15, 1932, Shurmur attended Roosevelt High School in his native Wyandotte. He later earned All-Michigan Athletic Association honors as a center at Albion College and was named the conference's most valuable player. Fritz, who graduated with a master's degree in education administration in 1956, also was named to the all-conference baseball team and is a charter member of Albion's Athletic Hall of Fame.

On May 10, 1997, he was honored by his alma mater when he was presented with an honorary degree – doctor of pedagogy – during Albion's annual commencement exercises.

Shurmur and his wife, Peggy, have three children – Sally Ann Michalov, 41; Scott, 39; and Susie Plumb, 35. Sally Ann, an award-winning sports reporter for the *Casper Star-Tribune*, was named the 1990 Wyoming 'Sportswriter of the Year.'

COACHING BACKGROUND: 1954-55 (Albion, graduate assistant); 1956-61 (Albion); 1962-74 (Wyoming, head coach 1971-74); 1975-77 (Detroit Lions); 1978-81 (New England Patriots); 1982-90 (Los Angeles Rams); 1991-93 (Phoenix Cardinals); 1994-98 (Green Bay Packers).

LARRY BROOKS

Defensive Line

Now in his 24th season in professional football, Larry Brooks brings a distinguished pedigree to his role on the Packers' coaching staff, one highlighted by the defensive line's significant contribution to the National Football League's premier defense in 1996 en route to a Super Bowl championship and further accentuated by another strong performance in making a repeat visit to the "Big Dance" in 1997.

His front line troops – chief among them left end Reggie White and tackles Santana Dotson and Gilbert Brown – played a major and collective role on a '97 unit which held the opposition to an average of 17.6 points per game, a scoring defense which ranked a highly respectable fifth in the NFL as a whole.

That achievement came on the heels of a hallmark effort in 1996 when the defense limited opponents to a league-low average of 259.8 yards per game and a modest 3.5-yard average per rush, lowest in the National Football Conference, in sweeping to Super Bowl success.

It was the kind of execution Brooks had come to expect of himself as a player, having earlier been a perennial Pro Bowl performer during an 11-year playing career in the NFL with the then-Los Angeles Rams. Named to the Pro Bowl for five consecutive seasons (1976-80), he also was an All-Pro selection in 1977, '78 and '79. Along the way, he was the starting left defensive tackle in the Rams' only Super Bowl appearance (against the Pittsburgh Steelers) in January of 1980. He also started three National Football Conference Championship Games.

The 48-year-old Virginian, now in his fifth year as the Packers' defensive line coach, was named to the Green Bay coaching staff by Head Coach Mike Holmgren February 15, 1994. His arrival in Titletown reunited him with Packers defensive coordinator Fritz Shurmur, under whom he previously had served as an assistant defensive line coach with the Rams for eight seasons.

A Virginia State alumnus, he had been a late-round selection (14th) of the Rams in the 1972 draft. Becoming a defensive starter midway through his rookie year, Brooks went on to play an important role alongside Jack Youngblood, Cody Jones and Fred Dryer as the Rams won seven consecutive NFC Western Division championships during his 11-year playing career (1972-82).

Following his retirement as a player, Larry joined the Rams' coaching staff as assistant defensive line coach in 1983, a position he held through the 1990 season. Out of football in 1991, he returned to his collegiate alma mater as assistant athletic director and assistant football coach in 1992. He subsequently was named interim athletic director in 1993.

As a collegian, Brooks was named to the *Associated Press* Little All-America team. He also earned all-conference accolades and was honored as 'Virginia Small College Lineman of the Year' in 1971.

Born June 10, 1950, at Prince George, Va., he is an ardent outdoorsman who enjoys hunting and fishing. Larry is married (Colleen) and the father of a son, Larry, Jr., 28, who lives in Orange County, Calif.

COACHING BACKGROUND: 1983-90 (Los Angeles Rams); 1992-93 (Virginia State University); 1994-98 (Green Bay Packers).

ASSISTANT COACHES

NOLAN CROMWELL

Wide Receivers

An All-America quarterback as a collegian, later a perennial Pro Bowler as a safety and most recently the Packers' special teams coach, versatile Nolan Cromwell takes on a new role in 1998 as Green Bay's wide receivers coach.

Now in his eighth year as an NFL coach, Cromwell was named to the position by Head Coach Mike Holmgren in February, succeeding Gil Haskell, who had left to become offensive coordinator for Carolina.

Although the responsibilities are new to him, the 43-year-old Cromwell is no stranger to receivers, having spent 11 playing seasons (1977-87) studying their every move while performing at safety for the then-Los Angeles Rams – and enjoyed considerable success in the process.

In that role, he had one of the more distinguished playing careers in recent pro football history, becoming a four-time Pro Bowl selection along the way and ending his on-field career as the Rams' all-time leader in interception return yardage with 671 yards on 37 interceptions.

Also a premier special teams performer in his playing days with the Rams, the native Kansan has gone on to enjoy comparable success in his most recent role as coach of the Packers' kamikaze units over the past six seasons.

The former University of Kansas All-American's greatest success in the latter assignment came as the Packers swept to a third Super Bowl championship in 1996. Presented with a new weapon in former Redskin and Jaguar Desmond Howard just prior to the opening of training camp, he proceeded to maximize the newcomer's talents with an effective blocking scheme and opportune return "calls." The combination was so successful that the Packers closed out the 1996 regular season as the National Football League's leader in punt return yardage, 875, with an average of 15.1 yards for 58 returns, as Howard set a new league single-season, individual record for punt return yards.

Besides its first-place ranking in the NFL in punt return average (15.1), the Green Bay special teams excelled in other ways in 1996. The Packers also were first in opponent net punting average, holding foes to an NFL-low 32.45 yards. Green Bay additionally scored more points on special teams (24) than any other club in '96, adding two additional touchdowns (12 points) in the postseason, and for the second straight season did not allow any points to be scored against the Packers on special teams. Cromwell's troops also limited the opposition to the fourth-worst kickoff starting point (24.5-yard line) in the NFL.

Five different times during the 1996 season, Cromwell had one of his players earn NFC 'Special Teams Player of the Week' honors. His players also set two NFL records and established nine new Packer records (tying two other team marks). Cromwell's coverage teams took their performance to an even higher level during the '96 playoffs, holding opponents to an impressive 17.4-yard average on kickoff returns and a 7.1-yard punt return average.

Under his guidance, punter Craig Hentrich also made record-breaking progress. He weighed in with a new club record in 1996, depositing 28 punts inside the opposition's 20-yard line, breaking his own mark for the second year in a row, and then set a new club mark for punting average in 1997, averaging 45.0 yards for 75 punts.

Cromwell also was able to successfully work through an initially-unstable placekicking situation last season, overcoming widespread concern through the emergence of Ryan Longwell, who went on to score the second-most points by a rookie in team history (120).

Earlier, in 1995, Cromwell's Green Bay coverage teams had peaked, appropriately, during the playoffs. The punt coverage team held the Falcons, 49ers and Cowboys to an average of 4.3 yards per return and the kickoff coverage unit limited them to an average of 20.0 yards per runback over three postseason games.

Cromwell's punt return team also made Packers history during the '95 playoffs, rookie Antonio Freeman returning a second-quarter punt 76 yards for a touchdown in the wild-card playoff victory over Atlanta December 31, establishing a club postseason record with the first TD runback of a punt or kickoff in team annals.

In 1994, his return units made headlines, Robert Brooks becoming the first Packer since 1969 to return both a punt and a kickoff for a touchdown in the same season – posting an 85-yard scoring runback of a punt against the Los Angeles Rams October 9 and a 96-yard kickoff return TD against the Detroit Lions December 4.

Cromwell's troops earlier had a highly productive year in 1993, his second season on the Green Bay staff. Based on a statistical analysis of 17 special teams categories by the *Dallas Morning News*, the Packers tied for fourth in the league, a dramatic rise from 1992's 24th place.

A native of Smith Center, Kan., Cromwell was a second-round draft choice of the Rams in 1977. In addition to earning Pro Bowl recognition at safety, he also was a standout special teams player, serving as holder for extra points and field goals, scoring three rushing touchdowns on fake field goal attempts in the latter assignment.

In addition to his Pro Bowl honors, Nolan was named NFC 'Defensive Player of the Year' by the Kansas City Committee of 101 in 1980 and was chosen NFL 'Defensive Back of the Year' in 1984 by *Football Digest.*

As a collegian, he was accorded All-America laurels as a junior quarterback in the Kansas wishbone offense and, as a senior, set an NCAA record for rushing yardage by a quarterback by posting 294 yards from scrimmage. Also a gifted decathlete in track, he had moved to offense after spending first two seasons on defense at safety.

Cromwell launched his coaching career in 1991 as a defensive and special teams assistant on Coach John Robinson's Rams staff. Following retirement as a player and prior to re-joining the Rams as a coach, he owned and operated three tire stores in the Los Angeles area.

Nolan, who was born January 30, 1955, and his wife, Mary, have two children – Lance (born 6/15/86) and Jennifer (born 4/13/88).

COACHING BACKGROUND: 1991 (Los Angeles Rams); 1992-98 (Green Bay Packers).

KEN FLAJOLE
Defensive Assistant/Quality Control

Ken Flajole, who has spent the last 21 years in the collegiate coaching ranks, is in his first season as defensive assistant/quality control coach on Green Bay's staff.

Flajole, named to his current position by Head Coach Mike Holmgren on February 25, 1998, most recently had served as the co-defensive coordinator/secondary coach at Nevada for the past two seasons. In 1996, his first year on the job, the Wolf Pack finished first in its conference in total defense, scoring defense and passing defense, up from fourth place in all three categories the previous season.

In addition to his quality control responsibilities on defense, Flajole will assist Johnny Holland with the Packers' special teams, working with punt and kickoff receivers, and also assist defensive backs coach Bob Valesente with his charges.

Previous to joining the Nevada staff, Flajole (pronounced FLAY-jull), had coached in the college ranks at six other institutions of higher learning, beginning with a stint at his alma mater, Pacific Lutheran (1977-78), followed by stops at Washington (1979), Montana (1980-85), Texas-El Paso (1986-88), Missouri (1989-93), Richmond (1993-94) and Hawaii (1995).

All of Flajole's coaching positions have been on the defensive side of the ball, including responsibilities as defensive coordinator at Richmond as well as during his final two seasons at Montana.

Earlier, as an athlete, he was an all-conference outside linebacker, first at Wenatchee (Wash.) Valley Community College, then at Pacific Lutheran in Tacoma, Wash. He received a B.S. degree in education from Pacific Lutheran in 1976.

Flajole was born October 4, 1954, in Seattle. He and his wife, Teri, have two daughters – Kelly (born

ASSISTANT COACHES

2/11/82) and Kori (born 1/16/84).

COACHING BACKGROUND: 1977-78 (Pacific Lutheran); 1979 (University of Washington); 1980-85 (Montana); 1986-88 (Texas-El Paso); 1989-93 (Missouri); 1993-94 (Richmond); 1995 (Hawaii); 1996-97 (Nevada); 1998 (Green Bay Packers).

JOHNNY HOLLAND

Special Teams

Johnny Holland, one of the premier linebackers in Packers history as a player, moves into new and substantially expanded responsibilities as special teams coach in 1998 – in his fourth season as a member of the team's coaching staff.

The 33-year-old Holland, defensive assistant/quality control the past three years, succeeds Nolan Cromwell, named wide receivers coach in February. He takes over with a substantial amount of familiarity with special teams, having participated with the units as a player and later assisting Cromwell with the special teams in his role as defensive assistant/quality control. In addition to working with Cromwell, Holland focused his attention on aiding Jim Lind with the Green Bay linebackers.

Holland, who originally joined the Packers as a second-round draft selection out of Texas A&M, proceeded to become a key and highly productive performer in the Green Bay defense, posting more than 100 tackles for six consecutive seasons (1988-1993) and leading his platoon in tackles each of his last two seasons.

In 1992, he suffered the first of two neck injuries that were to cut short his playing career. Sidelined with two games remaining in the regular season by a herniated cervical disk, he underwent a corrective vertebrae fusion. He returned to action in 1993, starting all 16 games, and led the defense with a career-high 145 tackles while helping the Packers gain the National Football League playoffs for the first time in 11 years.

Following the season, however, it was discovered he had developed a second herniated disk in his neck and, after consultation with the Packers' medical staff, he decided to forego a second surgical procedure and announced his retirement from football May 20, 1994, ending a seven-year NFL career.

He subsequently entered business in Sugar Land, Texas, and remained in the workaday world until February 21, 1995, when Head Coach Mike Holmgren persuaded Johnny to join the Packers' coaching staff.

As a collegian, the genial Texan was a three-year starter and four-time letterman at Texas A&M, leading the Aggies in total tackles in each of his last three seasons and earning consensus All-America honors as a junior despite missing one game. In the process, he earned the nickname 'Mr. Anywhere' for his ability to consistently be where the ball was.

Earlier, he won 12 letters at Hempstead (Texas) High School – four each in football and basketball, three in track and one in baseball.

Born March 11, 1965, in Belleville, Texas, Johnny and his wife, Faith, have two children – a son, Jordan (born 3/15/94), and a daughter, Joli (born 8/26/96).

COACHING BACKGROUND: 1995-98 (Green Bay Packers).

KENT JOHNSTON
Strength and Conditioning

Amiable and soft-spoken Kent Johnston, who directs and coordinates the Packers' strength and conditioning program on a year-round basis, has been credited with making a major contribution to the Green and Gold's on-field success over the past six seasons, which have been punctuated by back-to-back trips to the Super Bowl following the last two.

Implementing a comprehensive program upon his arrival in Green Bay – one which has included weight control and nutrition as well as conditioning – Johnston has contributed to the cause in areas beyond his customary domain, the weight room. Primarily, he has been credited with rendering valuable assistance in the rehabbing of injured players while also helping with advice and guidance on nutrition.

Since joining the Packers, the genial Texan has structured specific training programs for each player – as he previously had done at Tampa Bay, where he implemented karate as a segment of the Bucs' conditioning regimen. In the process, he also has conducted karate classes as an element of the Packers' conditioning program.

In addition, he has traveled around the country in the offseason to monitor the conditioning progress of those players who do not live in the Green Bay area on a year-round basis.

The 42-year-old native of Mexia, Texas, was honored in February of 1997 for his professional excellence over a decade-long career in the National Football League when he was saluted as "Strength and Conditioning Coach of the Year" by the Professional Football Strength and Conditioning Coaches' Society during the organization's annual meeting.

Kent earlier earned high marks as a strength and conditioning coach at the University of Alabama under then-head coach Ray Perkins in 1985 and 1986 when the Crimson Tide's weight program was regarded as one of the nation's finest. The athletes he helped develop during that span include premier linebackers Cornelius Bennett (Atlanta Falcons) and Derrick Thomas (Kansas City Chiefs), as well as Derrick McKey of the NBA's Indiana Pacers.

Johnston launched his coaching career in 1978 at Teague (Texas) High School as an assistant coach before signing on at Northwestern (La.) State in 1979. He next moved to Northeast Louisiana as strength coach in 1980 before returning to the prep ranks at Willis (Texas) High School in 1982. A year later, he joined Perkins' University of Alabama staff as a graduate assistant for two seasons (1983-84) before being named strength and conditioning coach in 1985. When Perkins became head coach at Tampa Bay in 1987, Johnston joined the Buccaneers' staff.

A graduate of Stephen F. Austin University, he played defensive back in football en route to earning his bachelor's degree in physical education and history. He secured his master's degree in physical education from Alabama in 1984.

Born February 21, 1956, in Mexia, Texas, a hometown he shares with Philadelphia Eagles head coach Ray Rhodes, Allen Kent Johnston graduated from Mexia High School, where he participated in football, tennis and track. Kent and his wife, Pam, have four sons – Kody (born 5/30/90), Kole (born 5/7/92), Clay (born 8/8/96) and Cade (born 6/24/98).

COACHING BACKGROUND: 1979 (Northwestern La. State); 1980-81 (Northeast Louisiana); 1983-84 (Alabama, graduate assistant); 1985-86 (Alabama); 1987-91 (Tampa Bay Buccaneers); 1992-98 (Green Bay Packers).

JIM LIND
Linebackers

A 24-year coaching veteran, Jim Lind is in his fourth season as the Packers' linebackers coach, his seventh as a member of the Green Bay coaching staff.

Lind, defensive assistant/quality control in his first three Green Bay seasons, was named to his current position by Head Coach Mike Holmgren on February 18, 1995. He replaced Bob Valesente, who took over the defensive backs.

A 50-year-old native of Isle, Minn., Lind spent nine years as a head coach in the college ranks before joining the Packers organization in 1992, a move which teamed him with Holmgren for a second time. They previously had coached together in 1982 when the Green Bay head coach was a member of LaVell Edwards' staff at Brigham Young University and Lind was a graduate assistant.

Head coach at the University of Minnesota-Morris from 1983 through 1986, Lind directed the UM-M Cougars to two championships in the Northern Intercollegiate Conference. In the process, he was named NIC 'Coach of the Year' in 1984 and NAIA District 13 'Coach of the Year' in 1986.

Lind subsequently served as head coach at the University of Wisconsin-Eau Claire from 1987 through 1991 prior to joining the Green Bay staff.

He began his college coaching career at St. Cloud (Minn.) State, where he was a graduate assistant in 1977 and offensive coordinator in 1978. He then moved to neighboring St. John's University in 1979, serving as defensive coordinator under John Gagliardi.

Earlier, Jim entered his profession in 1974 as head football coach at Underwood (Minn.) High School, a position he held until moving to St. Cloud State.

Born November 11, 1947, Lind played football and participated in track at Isle (Minn.) High School before enrolling at Bethel College, where he played linebacker for one year. Moving to Bemidji (Minn.) State, from which he received his undergraduate degree, he played defensive back for two years. Jim later earned his master's degree at St. Cloud State and earned his doctorate in Professional Leadership in Physical Education and Athletics at BYU in 1987.

Lind and his wife, Cindy, have two sons – Erik (born 1/6/87) and Bryan (born 1/31/90).

COACHING BACKGROUND: 1977 (St. Cloud State, graduate assistant); 1978 (St. Cloud State); 1979-80 (St. John's University); 1981-82 (Brigham Young, graduate assistant); 1983-86 (Minnesota-Morris, head coach); 1987-91 (Wisconsin-Eau Claire, head coach); 1992-98 (Green Bay Packers).

TOM LOVAT
Offensive Line

A superior teacher of offensive line technique, patient and paternal Tom Lovat saw his efforts bear impressive, record-setting fruits during the 1997 season, when his offensive line established a club standard for fewest sacks allowed (26) since the NFL adopted the 16-game schedule in 1978. The feat is made even more impressive by the fact that Lovat was playing with a rookie left tackle, Ross Verba, for much of the season.

In addition, Lovat's productive unit cleared the way for 1,909 rushing yards – the Packers' highest production since 1985 – and helped Dorsey Levens come within 39 yards of Jim Taylor's all-time Green Bay single-season rushing record as Levens became just the second 1,000-yard rusher for the team over the past two decades.

The first assistant to be hired by then-new Head Coach Mike Holmgren (January 14, 1992), Lovat has presided over a front five that has delivered the most effective pass protection Green Bay quarterbacks have had since the NFL implemented the current 16-game schedule format. In addition to last season's record-breaking performance, Lovat's forward walls have required opponents to be content with 30 sacks in 1993 and 33 in both 1994 and 1995, the lowest such totals permitted by a Packers offensive line in the 20-year span that the 16-game format has been in place.

Despite the loss of the line's veteran anchor, left tackle Ken Ruettgers, who was able to start only one game in 1996 because of what became a career-ending knee problem, Lovat also was still able to extract efficient performances from his front line during the Packers' drive to Super Bowl XXXI in 1996, particularly down the stretch. Over the last eight games including playoffs, it gave up only 16 sacks – an average of just two per game – en route to capturing a second straight NFC Central Division title and setting a new team scoring record by amassing 456 points. Lovat also saw his center, Frank Winters, become the first Packers offensive lineman to play in the Pro Bowl since Larry McCarren in 1983.

Now in his seventh season on the Green Bay staff and his 19th year in the NFL, Lovat has been able to consistently draw quality efforts from his charges despite major injury problems, such as those which beset his athletes in both 1993 and '94. The 59-year-old Bingham Canyon, Utah, native did perhaps the finest coaching job of his professional career in '93. Despite the injury loss of three of five starters during the course of the season (center James Campen, guard Rich Moran and right tackle Tootie Robbins), he was able to maintain a consistent, productive and well-coordinated unit over the 16-game regular-season schedule and throughout the playoffs.

So effective was the Packers' O-Line under his direction that repeating Super Bowl champion Dallas was the only National Football Conference team to yield fewer sacks (29) during the '93 season than Green Bay's front five, which gave up an average of only 1.9 per game.

In 1994, Lovat had to overcome the early loss of starting left guard Guy McIntyre, his premier run blocker, shelved by a blood clot for six games during the first half of the season, thus requiring him to move center Winters to left guard and bring Jamie Dukes off the bench to step in for Winters.

In 1995, Lovat's contributions to the Packers' offensive success were reflected in a league-leading third down efficiency ratio, 49.1 percent, and the club's first 1,000-yard rusher since 1978 in Edgar Bennett.

Earlier he enjoyed good success in 1992, the first year of his second tour of duty with the Packers. Although handicapped by injury problems which caused Moran to miss half of the season and Campen to sit out three games, the Green and Gold's offense ranked among the leaders in both third- and fourth-down efficiency, a development traceable in no small measure to the performance of Lovat's line.

The genial westerner, a 30-plus-year coaching veteran and a member of the Phoenix Cardinals' staff prior to re-joining the Packers, previously served as a Green Bay offensive line assistant (to Ernie McMillan) in 1980 under Bart Starr.

Well respected for his teaching skills, Lovat launched his coaching career at the University of Utah in 1967 while completing his master's degree, received in 1968.

He moved to Idaho State and then to Saskatchewan of the Canadian Football League, taking on his first professional assignment as defensive coach for the Roughriders in 1971.

Lovat returned to Utah as an assistant in 1972 and later was named the school's head coach in 1974, a position he held through the 1976 season. He then moved to Stanford, where he was a member of the Bill Walsh staff from 1977 through 1979, before signing on with the Packers for the first time in 1980.

Tom next joined the Cardinals for the first time in 1981, serving as offensive line coach through the 1984 season. He then became assistant head coach-offense of the Indianapolis Colts, holding that position from 1985 through 1988 under Ron Meyer, the Colts leading the American Football Conference in rushing in '85 under his direction.

Lovat subsequently spent the 1989 season as offensive line coach at the University of Wyoming before re-joining the then-Phoenix Cardinals in 1990. That '90 season his offensive line allowed only 43 quarterback sacks, the lowest total by the Cardinals in 11 seasons and one that the Phoenix forward wall matched in 1991. In the '90 process, Lovat's line paved the way for rookie Johnny Johnson to rush for 924 yards and earn Pro Bowl honors.

Born in Bingham Canyon, Utah, on December 28, 1938, Lovat is a 1961 graduate of the University of Utah, where he was a three-year football and baseball letterman for the Utes, earning All-Skyline honors in baseball.

Tom and his wife, Lyn, have three children – a daughter, Johna Rae Griese, and two sons, Matthew and Mark.

COACHING BACKGROUND: 1967 (Utah); 1968-70 (Idaho State); 1971 (Saskatchewan Roughriders, CFL); 1972-76 (Utah, head coach 1974-76); 1977-79 (Stanford); 1980 (Green Bay Packers); 1981-84 (St. Louis Cardinals); 1985-88 (Indianapolis Colts); 1989 (Wyoming); 1990-91 (Phoenix Cardinals); 1992-1998 (Green Bay Packers).

ANDY REID

Quarterbacks

Andy Reid, who had enjoyed success in coaching both tight ends and offensive linemen over a 15-year career, added another major accomplishment to his coaching dossier in 1997.

Responsible for presiding over the quarterbacks for the first time in his professional life, he saw his primary charge, Brett Favre, continue to prosper without missing a beat – capturing the National Football League's 'Most Valuable Player' honor for the third consecutive year – a laurel Favre shared with the Detroit Lions' Barry Sanders.

The 40-year-old Brigham Young alumnus was assigned to his current responsibilities by Head Coach Mike Holmgren February 10, 1997, replacing the departed Marty Mornhinweg, after serving as tight ends and assistant offensive line coach in his first five years on the Packers' coaching staff.

Reid had enjoyed substantial success in his previous role. Under his patient and resourceful tutelage, tight end has been a consistently productive position during his tenure, a span punctuated by Mark Chmura being named to the Pro Bowl following the 1995 season – the first such honor for a Packers tight end since 1983 – and Keith Jackson to an identical honor following the 1996 campaign.

Andy, who built a reputation for developing outstanding offensive lines while in the college ranks, saw Chmura and predecessor Jackie Harris put up near-record numbers under his direction upon his arrival in Green Bay. Harris registered 55 receptions in 1993, a total only one shy of the Packers' single-season record, prior to signing on as a free agent with Tampa Bay in 1994, and Chmura posted 54 catches in 1995, the third-highest collection in team annals.

And, in 1996, Reid elicited a hallmark season from Jackson, whose 10 touchdown receptions fell only one short of the Packers' record for TD catches by a tight end and who played a major role in the Green and Gold's drive to a Super Bowl XXXI triumph.

Reid may well have done the best coaching job of his Packer tenure two years earlier when he was called upon to juggle and utilize the talents of four different tight ends over the course of the 1994 season, among them 11-year veteran Ed West, handicapped by a pair of refractory knees; incoming Reggie Johnson, periodically hampered by a hamstring problem; then third-year pro Chmura, thrust into a late-season starting role by the injury factor; and rookie Jeff Wilner, inserted on a spot basis. He was able to garner a total of 57 receptions from this quartet, including a career-high 31 by the gimpy West.

Earlier, Harris matured into one of the NFL's premier tight ends under Reid's demanding, yet reinforcing, direction in 1992 and '93 prior to signing with the Bucs. Harris caught 97 passes over that two-year span.

Reid, who had been offensive line coach at the University of Missouri since 1988, was named to the Packers' staff by Holmgren on January 21, 1992, to assist Tom Lovat with the offensive line in addition to coaching the tight ends.

Quality pass-blocking offensive lines, in both the Division I and II ranks, had been Reid's hallmark since launching his coaching career at San Francisco State in 1983. The school led the nation in passing offense and total offense for three consecutive years (1983-84-85) while he served as offensive coordinator, offensive line coach and strength coach.

Reid moved to Northern Arizona as offensive line coach in 1986, then to Texas-El Paso in 1987. When Bob Stull took over as head coach at Missouri in 1989, he joined Stull's Tiger staff, where he spent three years prior to being "recruited" by the Packers in 1992.

Andy received his coaching start at his alma mater, BYU, as a graduate assistant under LaVell Edwards in 1982. An offensive tackle/guard on three Holiday Bowl teams as a collegian, Reid earned three varsity football letters, graduating with a bachelor's degree in physical education. He also received a master's degree in Professional Leadership in Physical Education and Athletics.

Born in Los Angeles on March 19, 1958, Reid and his wife, Tammy, have five children – Garrett (born 4/13/83), Britt (born 4/28/85), Crosby (born 3/17/88), Drew Ann (born 3/9/90) and Spencer (born 6/9/92).

COACHING BACKGROUND: 1982 (Brigham Young, graduate assistant); 1983-85 (San Francisco State); 1986 (Northern Arizona); 1987-88 (Texas-El Paso); 1989-91 (Missouri); 1992-98 (Green Bay Packers).

GARY REYNOLDS

Offensive Assistant/Quality Control

On staff since 1993, Gary Reynolds is in his third year as offensive assistant/quality control, having fully shed his original responsibilities this year as administrative assistant/football operations, a position he had held since joining the club.

A 31-year-old Texan, he was assigned the added duties on the offensive staff by Head Coach Mike Holmgren in February of 1996, replacing Marty Mornhinweg, who had been named quarterbacks coach.

In his role, Reynolds is in charge of all computer input and analysis for the offensive coaching staff, in addition to film breakdown.

A Texas A&M alumnus with a bachelor of science degree in engineering (1988) and a master's degree in education (1992), Reynolds joined the Packers organization in July of 1993 after serving as assistant recruiting coordinator at the University of Tennessee. He previously had been graduate assistant/assistant recruiting coordinator at Texas A&M from January 1991 until August 1992, when he joined the University of Tennessee staff.

Born October 15, 1966, in Boston, Reynolds graduated from Dulles High School in Sugar Land, Texas, in 1984. He is married to the former Beth Epperly of Knoxville, Tenn.

COACHING BACKGROUND: 1991 (Texas A&M); 1992 (Tennessee); 1993-98 (Green Bay Packers).

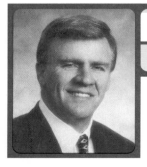

MIKE SHERMAN

Tight Ends/Assistant Offensive Line

Mike Sherman, in his second year as a member of the Packers' staff, marks a major coaching milestone with the advent of the 1998 season. He now is in his 20th year in his chosen profession, including 16 seasons at the college level, where he was associated in coaching no fewer than eight bowl teams.

Named tight ends coach by Head Coach Mike Holmgren February 19, 1997, he replaced Andy Reid, who took over a new assignment as quarterbacks coach. In his first season on the job, tight end Mark Chmura was voted to the Pro Bowl.

Immediately prior to joining the Packers' board of strategy, Sherman had been a member of the Texas A&M staff for seven of the past eight years and was serving as the Aggies' offensive coordinator at the time he was invited to join the Green Bay staff.

He launched his coaching career at Stamford (Conn.) High School in 1979 and entered the college ranks at the University of Pittsburgh in 1981. Following two years at Pitt, he joined the Tulane football staff in 1983 and subsequently moved to Holy Cross as offensive coordinator for the 1985 season.

ASSISTANT COACHES

The 43-year-old Sherman later spent five years as offensive line coach at Texas A&M (1989-93) before moving to UCLA in the same role for one year, he then returned to A&M as offensive line coach in 1995. He was named offensive coordinator for the Aggies following the 1996 season.

Over his collegiate career, Sherman has had substantial "big game" experience, serving on staffs that took four teams to the Cotton Bowl and one to the Sugar Bowl among eight postseason appearances.

He also has coached a number of offensive linemen who have gone on to play and star in the National Football League, among them Richmond Webb of the Miami Dolphins, a seven-time Pro Bowl selection, and Jonathan Ogden of UCLA, who was the Baltimore Ravens' first-round draft selection in 1996, the fourth player chosen overall, and who went to his initial Pro Bowl last season.

During his own playing career, Sherman was an offensive guard/tackle and linebacker for three seasons at Central Connecticut State University (1974, 1976-77).

Born December 19, 1954, in Norwood, Mass., Sherman and his wife, Karen, have four children – Sarah, 15; Emily, 11; Matthew, 9; and Benjamin, 5.

COACHING BACKGROUND: 1981-82 (University of Pittsburgh); 1983-84 (Tulane); 1985-88 (Holy Cross); 1989-93 (Texas A&M); 1994 (UCLA); 1995-96 (Texas A&M); 1997-1998 (Green Bay Packers).

HARRY SYDNEY

Running Backs

His resume already enhanced by having helped two teams win Super Bowls, Harry Sydney added another major credit to his professional dossier in 1997, presiding over Dorsey Levens' emergence as the most productive running back in the Packers' 77-year National Football League history.

Under Sydney's tutelage, Levens made the most of becoming the team's featured back in the absence of the injured Edgar Bennett, amassing 1,805 yards (1,435 rushing and 370 receiving) to establish a new, Packers single-season record for most yards gained from scrimmage.

Levens also shattered the Packers' single-game rushing record along the way, churning out 190 yards in 33 attempts to break Jim Taylor's 36-year-old record while spearheading a 45-17 triumph over the Dallas Cowboys November 23, then continued his assault on the club's record book in the playoffs, swelling his career production to 840 yards (524 rushing and 316 receiving), thereby setting a Green Bay record for yards from scrimmage in the postseason.

Two years earlier, in 1995, Sydney officiated at Bennett's development into the Packers' first 1,000-yard rusher (1,067) since 1978, when Terdell Middleton turned the trick.

In 1996, improving upon that achievement, he tutored an offensive backfield trio – Bennett, Levens and blocker extraordinaire William Henderson – that amassed the imposing total of 2,817 rushing and receiving yards and 18 touchdowns as the Packers swept to a 13-3 regular-season record and through the playoffs to capture Super Bowl honors.

Sydney, who took over as running backs coach in '95, thus has put to productive use the expertise he gleaned in 10 pro playing seasons, helping maximize his charges' contributions to Head Coach Mike Holmgren's offense.

A veteran of two Super Bowl victories as a player for the 49ers, the voluble North Carolinian is in his fifth year on the Green Bay staff. He had been a general assistant in 1994, his first season as an NFL coach.

Harry, a fullback during his on-field career, played on Super Bowl championship teams in 1988 and '89 during a five-year tenure with San Francisco in which he served as the Niners' special teams captain.

In one subsequent season with the Packers, 1992, he was a substantial contributor to the cause, catching 49 passes for 384 yards and rushing for 163 yards in 51 carries while helping the Green and Gold post a 9-7 record, their second-best mark in a 20-year span.

Sydney earlier played in the United States Football League for three years and in the Canadian Football League for one season prior to joining the 49ers in 1987. A wishbone quarterback at the University of

Kansas as a collegian, he moved to running back prior to his junior season and earned All-Big Eight honors at the position.

Born Harry Flanroy Sydney III in Petersburg, Va., on June 26, 1959, he was an all-state performer in both football and basketball at Seventy-First High School in Fayetteville, N.C.

Sydney, who owns a degree in criminal justice from the University of Kansas, is the possessor of a highly eclectic resume. In addition to having taught a high school psychology course on a "sabbatical" from pro football in 1986, he also reports having had a variety of odd jobs in earlier years – cook, factory worker, basketball referee and driver of a soft drink truck, among others.

Harry and his wife, Madonna, have eight children – Harry IV, Zachary, Nathan, Taylor, Krystal, Jacquie, Alyse and Eric.

COACHING BACKGROUND: 1994-1998 (Green Bay Packers).

BOB VALESENTE
Defensive Backs

The epitome of versatility, Bob Valesente has coached in every area of the game during a distinguished, 36-year career, one which has seen him literally touch all of the professional bases – as a head coach, offensive coordinator, defensive coordinator and special teams coach, among other assignments.

Valesente, who made his tutorial debut in 1962, also has coached at all three levels – high school, college and professional – and has had extensive experience on both sides of the football, including time at seven colleges and universities.

He joined Head Coach Mike Holmgren's staff as linebackers coach in 1992, then was asked to take over the defensive backs in 1995, replacing Dick Jauron, who had resigned to become defensive coordinator for the expansion Jacksonville Jaguars. It was a smooth transition for Valesente since – earlier in his career – he had coached the defensive secondary for a total of 12 seasons while in the college ranks and later in the NFL with the Baltimore Colts.

Under his positive direction and painstaking tutelage the past three seasons, the Packers' secondary has made substantial improvement each year, punctuating its upsurge with 26 interceptions in 1996. The Packers' 26 interceptions overall shared National Football Conference honors with the St. Louis Rams, who also had 26 thefts.

In the process, Green Bay's "outfield" emerged as the league's No. 1 pass defense in 1996, forcing opposing quarterbacks to settle for a 55.4 passer rating during the regular season and a 45.8 mark for the three playoff games, during which Packer defensive backs intercepted eight passes. One of Valesente's charges, strong safety LeRoy Butler, also earned Pro Bowl and All-Pro honors.

The secondary again emerged as one of the NFL's most miserly in 1997, holding the opposition to a 51.2 passing percentage (second-lowest in the league) over the regular-season route and highlighting that performance by not yielding a touchdown pass over the last 23 quarters of the regular season. It allowed only 10 passing touchdowns overall to tie the New York Giants for league honors and also set a Packers record for a 16-game season. And Butler once more received Pro Bowl and All-Pro recognition.

The 58-year-old Valesente earlier had presided over Bryce Paup's rise to Pro Bowl status at linebacker in 1994, a season which Paup climaxed by amassing 19 tackles, 2 sacks and 1 interception in two playoff games to emerge as the defensive unit's postseason leader.

Bob, who joined the Packers' staff in 1992 after two seasons with the Pittsburgh Steelers, is on his third NFL coaching assignment. In addition to his tour of duty with the Steelers, he previously had been secondary/special teams coach for the then-Baltimore Colts in 1982-83.

Valesente began his coaching career at Ithaca (N.Y.) High School in 1962, then left the profession temporarily after one year to play professional baseball for the Chicago Cubs organization in 1963 and '64. Bob then launched his college coaching career at Cornell University as freshman defensive coordinator in the fall of 1964. After 10 seasons at Cornell, the last five as varsity secondary coach, he moved to the

ASSISTANT COACHES

University of Cincinnati as secondary coach in 1975-76, then to Arizona (1977-79) and to Mississippi State (1980-81) as defensive coordinator/linebackers coach.

Bob then received his first NFL coaching opportunity at Baltimore in 1982, later returning to the college ranks as assistant head coach/quarterbacks coach at the University of Kansas in 1984. He subsequently was named head coach at Kansas in 1986, then spent one year as offensive coordinator/quarterbacks coach at Maryland in 1988 before joining the University of Pittsburgh staff.

Valesente later was named linebackers coach for the Steelers by then-head coach Chuck Noll on March 9, 1990, after serving as assistant head coach/defensive coordinator at Pitt in 1989. Under his tutelage, both David Little and Greg Lloyd blossomed into All-Pro performers, helping the Steelers earn the league's No. 1 ranking on defense in 1990.

A graduate of Ithaca College, Valesente played halfback on the varsity football team and was a catcher-outfielder for the baseball team that reached the 1962 College World Series. Drafted by the Chicago Cubs, he played at the Class A level in 1963-64.

Valesente, who is a member of the Ithaca College Hall of Fame, graduated in 1962 with a bachelor's degree in physical education, later earning his master's degree from the same institution in 1965.

Born in Seneca Falls, N.Y., on July 19, 1940, Bob and his wife, Joan, have three children – a son, Rob, 30, and two daughters, Ginger Valesente Weekly, 32, and Michelle, 18.

COACHING BACKGROUND: 1964-74 (Cornell); 1975-76 (University of Cincinnati); 1977-79 (Arizona); 1980-81 (Mississippi State); 1982-83 (Baltimore Colts); 1984-87 (Kansas, head coach 1986-87); 1988 (Maryland); 1989 (University of Pittsburgh); 1990-91 (Pittsburgh Steelers); 1992-98 (Green Bay Packers).

PRONUNCIATION GUIDE

PLAYERS

Joe Andruzzi	ann-DROOZ-ee
LeRoy Butler	luh-ROY
Mark Chmura	cha-MER-ah
Keaton Cromartie	crow-MAR-tee
Jeff Dellenbach	DELL-en-bahk
Lee DeRamus	da-RAY-mis
Brett Favre	FARVE
Paul Frase	FRAYS
George Koonce	KOONTZ
Bob Kuberski	ka-BER-ski
Blaine McElmurry	MACK-el-murry
Scott McGarrahan	ma-GAIR-a-han
Glyn Milburn	GLIN
Doug Pederson	PEE-der-son
Roell Preston	row-EL
Bill Schroeder	SHRAY-der
Pat Terrell	TARE-el
Kyle Wachholtz	WAH-holtz
Mike Wahle	WALL
Doug Widell	why-DELL

COACHES

Fritz Shurmur	SHER-mer
Ken Flajole	FLAY-jull
Tom Lovat	luh-VAHT
Bob Valesente	val-a-SEN-tay

GORDON 'RED' BATTY
Equipment Manager

Gordon 'Red' Batty enters his fifth season as equipment manager for the Green Bay Packers, a position which sees him responsible for properly outfitting players with the safest and most advanced equipment, as well as ordering and maintaining all of the team's equipment and sideline apparel. Immediately prior to joining the Packers, he had spent 13 seasons (1981-93) in the same position with the then-Houston Oilers.

A 39-year-old native of Montreal, Batty remarkably is in his 26th season in the equipment field in 1998. He began his career in 1973 at the age of 14, working as a ball boy for the Montreal Alouettes of the Canadian Football League. Six years later, he was elevated to the position of equipment manager for the Alouettes. During Batty's tenure in Montreal, the Alouettes won two Grey Cups (1974 and '77).

Batty subsequently joined the Oilers in June of 1981, in the process becoming the NFL's youngest equipment manager at age 22. He now has been a participant in the NFL playoffs each of the last 11 seasons – the past four with Green Bay after seven straight postseason appearances with Houston. Batty also purports to be the first native-born Canadian to garner both a Grey Cup and Super Bowl ring, the latter distinction earned when the Packers culminated the 1996 campaign by capturing Super Bowl XXXI.

Holder of a league-wide reputation as one of the best in the business, Batty is part of the seven-member NFL equipment managers advisory council. He also previously has assisted NFL Properties with two of its events: *The NFL Experience*, a popular fan attraction staged at Super Bowl sites; and *The NFL Quarterback Challenge*, an annual competition held among the league's top passers.

Upon being named to the Packers' staff on January 24, 1994, Batty became only the fifth person in club history to hold the title of equipment manager.

Born November 18, 1958, in Montreal, Batty (pronounced BAT-ee) and his wife, Joanne, have one daughter, Chelsei (born 8/30/91), and one son, Cameron (born 7/28/96).

A devout fan of the National Hockey League, Batty has had the privilege of working several NHL All-Star Games and roughly 30 other league games. Additionally, he attended the final Canadiens game ever played at his famed home town Montreal Forum. He also continues to play the game of hockey himself and assists the local Green Bay Gamblers USHL hockey club whenever possible.

PEPPER BURRUSS
Head Trainer

One of the more visible people in the Packers organization, Pepper Burruss begins his sixth season as the team's head trainer, his 22nd in the NFL overall. Overseer of the club's medical care on a daily basis, Burruss, a certified athletic trainer and physical therapist, joined Green Bay in 1993 following 16 seasons with the New York Jets as an assistant athletic trainer.

The 44-year-old Burruss was hired by the Jets in 1977 after receiving his B.S. degree in physical therapy from Northwestern University Medical School. One year earlier, he had graduated with honors from Purdue University, where he earned a B.A. degree in health and safety education. At Purdue, Burruss was fortunate to be a student trainer working under a legend in the field, the late William 'Pinky' Newell.

The Jets' training staff was twice honored during his stint with the team. In 1985, they were the first-

FOOTBALL STAFF

ever recipients of 'NFL Athletic Training Staff of the Year' recognition, an award given by their peers. The staff was honored again at the National Athletic Trainers Association (NATA) clinical symposium in 1994 by former Jets defensive lineman Dennis Byrd, who credited the team's emergency care as a contributing factor in his miraculous recovery from quadriplegia. Byrd had suffered a fractured neck by virtue of an on-field collision in a 1992 game with Kansas City at the Meadowlands.

Professionally, Burruss has served two terms on the executive committee of the Professional Football Athletic Trainers Society (PFATS), first as an AFC assistant trainer representative, then as the NFC head trainer representative.

He is a native of Wappingers Falls, N.Y., where he attended Ketcham High School.

Born Thomas Pepper Burruss April 15, 1954, in Beacon, N.Y., he and his wife, Nancy, have one son, Shane (born 10/22/88), and one daughter, Christina (born 9/18/93). Also a medical practitioner, Nancy is a clinical nurse specialist for cardiothoracic surgery, along with serving as an assistant professor at Bellin College of Nursing in Green Bay.

Burruss currently serves on the resources development committee of the Green Bay YMCA and on the corporate board of Curative Rehabilitation Center in Green Bay.

A gifted public speaker, Burruss routinely gives lectures throughout the state of Wisconsin, armed with an extensive array of photo slides to supplement his presentation. His hobbies include collecting and studying firearms cartridges, in addition to home maintenance projects.

BARRY RUBIN
Strength and Conditioning Assistant

Possessor of a 17-year background in his field, genial Barry Rubin is in his fourth year as strength and conditioning assistant for the Packers.

The 41-year-old Louisianan joined the Packers organization May 19, 1995, following a third tenure as head strength coach at Northeast Louisiana University, thus becoming the first full-time strength and conditioning assistant in club history.

In assisting Kent Johnston, Green Bay's strength and conditioning coach, his responsibilities include monitoring the team's cardiovascular conditioning (running) program, as well as player workouts in the weight room and assisting in setup of player nutritional profiles.

A native of Monroe, La., where he was born June 25, 1957, Rubin began his career in the strength and conditioning field in 1981 as a graduate assistant at Northeast Louisiana following his graduation from Northwestern (La.) State University. In addition to seven years of service at Northeast, in three separate tenures, he also spent two years as head strength coach at Louisiana State, one year as a personal trainer to then-Pittsburgh Steelers quarterback Bubby Brister and four years at a health club in Monroe, La.

Rubin, who is single, was a tight end and punter as a collegian at Northwestern (La.) State from 1978-80, where his teammates included future NFL performers Bobby Hebert, Mark Duper, Joe Delaney and Gary Reasons. He was named to the Jewish All-America football team as a senior in 1979, a year in which he set a school record with a 75-yard punt.

A devout baseball fan, he pledges his personal allegiance to the Milwaukee Brewers. He also is an avid collector of baseball cards, his collection including the rookie cards of Hank Aaron and Sandy Koufax.

AL TREML
Video Director

Al Treml, the only video director the Packers franchise has ever known, enters his 35th season of work for the club, the 32nd in a full-time capacity. In his position, he oversees the production and editing of all game and practice tapes for the organization's football operations, as well as the regular exchange of video with other teams. In addition, he is in charge of the purchase and maintenance of the team's vast array of video equipment.

Hired full-time by then-Packers head coach Vince Lombardi in March of 1967, Treml first began filming games for the team on a part-time basis in 1964 while still working for a Green Bay television station, his responsibilities then also included all film processing, printing and editing. He currently enjoys the longest continuous employment of anyone in the Packers organization.

A Green Bay native, Treml had been employed by local stations WFRV-TV (1960-63) and WBAY-TV (1964-67) as a news and sports photographer prior to joining the Packers. He was named 'TV Photographer of the Year' by the Wisconsin Press Photographers in 1960 and '62.

Elected by his peers in 1986 as the first chairman of the NFL Video Directors Committee, he subsequently served as co-chairman of the committee from 1992-98. More recently, he was appointed to the NFL's Digital Media Group, a committee formed by Commissioner Paul Tagliabue to study future digital media use in the league.

Under Treml's direction, the Packers were the first club in the NFL to utilize non-linear digital editing, a system now used by 17 league teams.

Treml entered the Army in October of 1955, right out of high school, serving until 1958. He attended the Army Photo School in Ft. Monmouth, N.J., in '55, then spent two-and-a-half years as an Army photographer and lab technician in Orleans, France.

Once discharged from the Army, Treml worked for a small daily newspaper, the *Twin City News Record* in Neenah, Wis., as a photographer, engraver and lab worker before moving over into the television field.

Born December 3, 1936, in Green Bay, Treml graduated from the city's Central Catholic High School in 1955. He and his wife of 41 years, Judy, have six grown children – Terri Sanborn, Tom, Tracy Atkinson, Karen Oettinger, Gary and Tricia.

Treml, an avid collector of antique cameras, also enjoys watching college basketball, playing golf and traveling in his leisure time.

PACKERS COACHING HISTORY
(562-449-36)

Years	Coach	Record	Pct.
1921-49	Earl (Curly) Lambeau	212-106-21	(.656)
1950-53	Gene Ronzani*	14-31-1	(.315)
1953	Hugh Devore - Ray (Scooter) McLean**	0-2-0	(.000)
1954-57	Lisle Blackbourn	17-31-0	(.354)
1958	Ray (Scooter) McLean	1-10-1	(.125)
1959-67	Vince Lombardi	98-30-4	(.758)
1968-70	Phil Bengtson	20-21-1	(.488)
1971-74	Dan Devine	25-28-4	(.474)
1975-83	Bart Starr	53-77-3	(.410)
1984-87	Forrest Gregg	25-37-1	(.405)
1988-91	Lindy Infante	24-40-0	(.375)
1992-97	Mike Holmgren	73-36-0	(.670)

* Resigned after 10 games in 1953   ** Co-coaches

Brandon Arndt
Packer Pro Shop

Tom Bakken
*Assistant Equipment
Manager*

Craig Benzel
Marketing Assistant

Lisa Berg
*Packer Pro Shop
Assistant/Retail Sales*

Jeff Blumb
*Assistant Public Relations
Director*

Matt Boockmeier
College Scout (East)

Jeanne Bruette
*Administrative Asst./
General Manager*

Jeff Cieply
Director of Marketing

'Red' Cochran
College Scout (North)

Duke Copp
Accountant

Diane Coron
Coaches' Secretary

Ann Dabeck
Receptionist

Bob Eckberg
Assistant Video Director

Todd Edlebeck
Fields Supervisor

Carol Edwin
Assistant Ticket Director

Ted Eisenreich
Buildings Supervisor

STAFF PHOTOS

Kurt Fielding
Assistant Trainer

Lee Gissendaner
College Scout (National Football Scouting)

Kandi Goltz
Administrative Assistant/ Marketing

Dr. John Gray
Associate Team Physician

'Ollie' Helf
Maintenance Assistant

Shaun Herock
College Scout (Midwest)

Kate Hogan
Packer Pro Shop Manager

Chris Hollenback
Public Relations Intern

Mike Jelenic
Computer Systems Analyst

Allen Johnson
Grounds Assistant

LaFawn Joslin
Receptionist

Chris Kirby
Video Assistant

Susan Kluck
Administrative Asst./ Coach Holmgren

Ann Marie Laes
Ticket Office Assistant

Will Lewis
Pro Personnel Assistant

Paula Martin
Administrative Asst./ Public Relations

STAFF PHOTOS

Scot McCloughan
College Scout (Rocky Mountains)

Linda McCrossin
Public Relations Secretary

Jeanne McKenna
Assistant Director of Family Programs

Dr. Patrick McKenzie
Team Physician

Johnny Meads
College Scout (Southwest)

Judy Mehlberg
Mail Clerk

Margaret Meyers
Administrative Asst./ Business Affairs

Danny Mock
College Scouting Coordinator

Bill Nayes
Administrative Assistant/ Football

Bryan Nehring
Assistant Equipment Manager

Traci Nygaard
Accounting Assistant

Tim O'Neill
Equipment Assistant

Jerry Parins
Corporate Security Officer

Phil Pionek
Executive Assistant to President

Julie Pocquette
Packer Pro Shop

Aaron Popkey
Public Relations Assistant

Sam Ramsden
Assistant Trainer

Bill Rasmussen
Maintenance Assistant

Mark Schiefelbein
*Assistant Public Relations
Director/Travel Coordinator*

Sherry Schuldes
*Director of Family
Programs*

Julie Schurk
*Packer Pro Shop
Assistant/Catalog Sales*

Sam Seale
College Scout (West)

Autumn Thomas-Beenenga
*Administrative Asst./
Pro Personnel*

Dave Tilot
Maintenance Assistant

Trevor Vannieuwenhoven
*Packer Pro Shop
Assistant/Warehouse*

Vicki Vannieuwenhoven
Accountant

Mark Wagner
Ticket Director

Chris Wahlen
Ticket Office Assistant

Wayne Wichlacz
*Director of Computer
Services*

Antonio Freeman, a showman-like performer who established career highs in catches (81), receiving yards (1,243) and receiving TDs (12) in 1997 while emerging as the Packers' go-to receiver in each of the past two seasons, is second in the NFL to the Vikings' Cris Carter in touchdown receptions over that two-year period with 21. Freeman, who has 100-or-more yards receiving in both of the last two Super Bowls, already holds or shares 13 all-time club playoff records.

RONNIE ANDERSON 82

Wide Receiver
College: Allegheny College
NFL Exp.: 1st Season   **Packers Exp.:** 1st Season
Ht.: 6-1   **Wt.:** 189   **Born:** 2/27/74   **Acq:** FA-97

PRO: Having served his first year apprenticeship by spending much of the 1997 season on the Packers' practice squad, running pass routes with vigor daily in the hope that opportunity might eventuate along the way, Ronnie Anderson finds himself in a position to contend for a berth on the active roster the second time around...Green Bay offensive coordinator Sherm Lewis is convinced the wiry Ohioan has the physical and mental assets to take the next step..."Ronnie has good size and speed to go along with excellent hands," Lewis says of the 24-year-old Cleveland native. "He also has shown a good work ethic and dedication to learning the offense as quickly as possible. He's had a year in the system as a practice squad member and will challenge for a spot on the 53-man roster this year."...**1997:** Signed to Green Bay's 53-man roster on the eve of Super Bowl XXXII (Jan. 23) to replace Don Beebe, who was placed on injured reserve with a hamstring injury, after spending a good deal of the season on the Packers' practice squad...Was inactive for the Super Bowl...Originally had signed with the Packers as an undrafted free agent April 25...Played in three preseason games — vs. New England (Aug. 31), at Oakland (Aug. 8) and vs. Buffalo (Aug. 16)...Posted 1 solo tackle on special teams, on kick coverage in the Buffalo contest...Placed on waivers Aug. 18, he was later re-signed to the practice squad (Oct. 7).

COLLEGE: Three-year starter and letter winner (1994-96) at Allegheny (Pa.) College...Finished his career as the school's all-time leader in receptions (125), receiving yards (1,783) and touchdowns (18)...Named first-team All-North Coast Athletic Conference in 1995 and '96...Helped Allegheny post a three-year record of 29-2, including two conference titles and two NCAA Division II playoff bids...Led conference with 10 touchdown receptions as a senior, among 40 catches for 570 yards...Also averaged 20.7 yards on 19 career kickoff returns...Won four letters in track, competing in the 100-, 200- and 400-meter dashes, in addition to the relays and the long jump...Named as track team's MVP in both 1995 and '96...Earned two degrees, one in English and another in history.

PERSONAL: Given the name Ronnie Derrell Anderson...Born in Cleveland...Is engaged to Annette Bailey of San Diego, the couple plans to marry right after the 1998 season...Earned all-state honors in both football and basketball at University School in Hunting Valley, Ohio...Caught 48 passes for 858 yards as a senior, helping team forge a 9-1 record...Named as school's 'Athlete of the Year' in both his junior and senior year...Earned four letters each in football (as a wide receiver and free safety), basketball and track...Hobbies include writing poetry, reading and playing Sega...Has volunteered his time with Big Brothers in Meadville, Pa., and by playing in charity basketball games with the Packers' team this past offseason...Residence: Green Bay.

PRO STATISTICS:

Games/Starts—Green Bay 1997 (practice squad).

THE PLAYERS

JOE ANDRUZZI **70**

Offensive Guard
College: Southern Connecticut State
NFL Exp.: 2nd Season   **Packers Exp.:** 2nd Season
Ht.: 6-3 **Wt.:** 310   **Born:** 8/23/75   **Acq:** FA-97

PRO: An unheralded, undrafted free agent a year ago, Joe Andruzzi prepped for advancement in '98 with a year as a reserve on the Packers' roster and an impressive season with the Scottish Claymores in NFL Europe during the spring of this year, thereby developing into a contender for the starting assignment at left guard, a position left open when incumbent Aaron Taylor signed with the San Diego Chargers as an unrestricted free agent…"I think he's a promising football player," Green Bay offensive line coach Tom Lovat says of the brawny Brooklyn native. "I hope he can compete with Marco (Rivera) for that left guard job. His is another situation a lot similar to that of (Adam) Timmerman, with respect to the (college) program he's come from. That's why we sent Joe to Europe to get that experience, that next level up. I think he's a promising football player. If he doesn't do it this year, he's certainly going to be around. He's strong, he has good athleticism. And he can run – he does all the things you can measure as well. The thing that's going to be interesting is how much he picked up last year and how far it will carry him in the preseason. They like him in Europe – (the Claymores) thought he was their best lineman – that's what they told us. And he might have been one of the top linemen in the whole league."…**NFL EUROPE:** Started all 10 games for the Scottish Claymores, earning a spot on the All-NFL Europe team in the process…Helped Claymores to finish with the third-best team rushing total in the league (averaging 100.0 yards per game), as team runners notched three 100-yard rushing days during the season…**1997:** Battled way onto team's opening day roster by dint of an impressive early performance in the preseason when he was described by General Manager Ron Wolf as "one of the surprises of training camp"…Was inactive for all 16 regular-season games and the Packers' three playoff contests, including Super Bowl XXXII…Missed the last month of the preseason after spraining the medial collateral ligament in his left knee in game against New England (July 31)…Returned to the practice field the second week of the regular season…Had signed with the Packers as an undrafted free agent on April 25, 1997.

COLLEGE: Four-year starter (1993-96) at Southern Connecticut State in New Haven, Conn. …A NCAA Division III first-team All-America selection by the National Football Coaches Association in 1995 and '96…Played center, tackle and guard during his collegiate career…Was a first-team all-conference selection as a senior, when he helped the Owls set season records for total yards (4,783), touchdowns (52), passing yards (2,153) and completions (142)…Served as team captain his senior year and helped team win 15 games over his final two seasons…Majored in liberal studies.

PERSONAL: Given name Joseph Dominick Andruzzi…Born in Brooklyn, N.Y. …Single…All-city selection in football at Tottenville High School in Staten Island, N.Y., where he was an offensive and defensive tackle…Hobbies include playing racquetball and weightlifting…Did volunteer work with special education students while in college…Residence: Staten Island, N.Y.

PRO STATISTICS:

Games/Starts—Green Bay 1997 (0/0); 1997 Playoffs (0/0); Scottish Claymores (NFL Europe) 1998 (10/10).

VAUGHN BOOKER — 96

Defensive End

College: Cincinnati
NFL Exp.: 5th Season **Packers Exp.:** 1st Season
Ht.: 6-5 **Wt.:** 295 **Born:** 2/24/68 **Acq:** T-98 (KC)

PRO: An established and productive starter acquired in an offseason trade with the Kansas City Chiefs, Vaughn Booker adds veteran and quality depth to the defensive line...Capable of playing both end and tackle with equal facility, the 30-year-old University of Cincinnati alumnus also provides flexibility – and a strong work ethic...Defensive coordinator Fritz Shurmur, addressing the latter asset, says of him, "He's just a guy who plays with extreme effort all the time. And he's got some skills. The best part about him is that his motor runs all the time."...Acquired from Kansas City May 13, 1998, in exchange for defensive lineman Darius Holland, Booker had been a three-year starter for the Chiefs, playing in 56 games over four seasons – with 33 starts...Closed out his Kansas City tenure with 164 tackles, including 7 sacks, plus 132 quarterback pressures, 5 forced fumbles, 5 fumble recoveries and 5 passes defensed...Had joined the Chiefs as a free agent in 1994 following two seasons as a Canadian import with Winnipeg of the CFL...A starter at defensive end for the Blue Bombers in both seasons, he recorded 103 total tackles and 6 sacks before signing with the Chiefs prior to the '94 NFL season...**1997:** Started at left defensive tackle in 13 games, sitting out three contests (Sept. 28 vs. Seattle, Dec. 14 at San Diego and Dec. 21 vs. New Orleans) due to a knee injury...Ranked third on the defensive unit in quarterback pressures with 31 and posted a career-high 4 sacks...Also contributed 46 tackles (26 solo)...Sacked Seahawks' Warren Moon twice at Seattle (Nov. 23)...Made a season-high 7 tackles, including a sack, vs. San Diego (Oct. 16)...Posted 6 stops, plus a season-best 7 quarterback pressures, vs. Carolina (Sept. 14)...Had three other games of 5-or-more tackles...Sacked the Raiders' Jeff George, in addition to recording a forced fumble and a fumble recovery, vs. Oakland (Dec. 7)...Also started Chiefs' divisional playoff game against the Denver Broncos (Jan. 4), making 1 solo tackle...**1996:** Was hindered at the end of the season by an ankle injury, but still managed to see action in 14 games, making 10 starts...Continued to make progress in his third season with the Chiefs, registering a career-high 51 tackles (37 solo), as well as 1 sack, 1 fumble recovery and 2 forced fumbles...Also was fifth on the team in quarterback pressures with 43...Was credited with a career-best 10 tackles (8 solo), 2 QB pressures and a forced fumble at San Diego (Sept. 29)...Recorded 6 tackles, 4 QB pressures, a forced fumble and a fumble recovery at Denver (Oct. 27)...Had a season-best 9 QB hurries in win over Green Bay (Nov. 10)...Did not start at Houston (Sept. 1), at Minnesota (Nov. 3) and at Detroit (Nov. 28) as the Chiefs began the game in their 'nickel' package...Was held out of the starting lineup vs. Chicago (Nov. 17) with a back injury...Suffered a sprained ankle at Oakland (Dec. 9), he was inactive the final two weeks of the season, missing games against Indianapolis and Buffalo...**1995:** Worked his way into the starting lineup after entering the season as a backup to Neil Smith at left end and Darren Mickell at right end...Became a full-time starter at right end vs. New England (Oct. 15) and started the final nine games there...Had made first NFL start at Arizona (Oct. 1) when Mickell was injured...Played in all 16 games for the only time in his pro career, starting 10 (nine at right end, one at left end)...Finished the year with 43 tackles, 1.5 sacks, 49 QB pressures (fifth-most on the team), 1 fumble recovery (returned for his lone NFL touchdown) and 2 passes defensed...Made the biggest play of his career with 1:52 left vs. Denver (Dec. 17) and Kansas City clinging to a four-point lead when he scooped up a John Elway fumble, forced by Mickell, and returned it 14 yards for a score...Earlier had a season-high 7 tackles, including one-half sack, at Denver (Oct. 22)...Posted first full sack of his career at San Diego (Nov. 12)...In a wild-card playoff game against Indianapolis (Jan. 7), recorded 7 tackles, his first postseason sack, a forced fumble and 5 QB pressures...**1994:** Made an impact in his first NFL season as a backup defensive end to Smith and Mickell...Registered 24 tackles, one-half sack, 2 forced fumbles, 2 fumble recoveries and 9 QB pressures...Recovered an Elway fumble to seal a hectic, 31-28 comeback victory at Denver (Oct. 17)...Made his other fumble recovery at San Diego (Oct. 9)...Had a season-high 5 tackles, including a half-sack, in rematch with Broncos (Dec. 4)...**CANADIAN FOOTBALL LEAGUE:** Played two seasons (1992-

93) for the Winnipeg Blue Bombers, starting at defensive end...Totaled 103 tackles (56 solo), including 6 sacks, plus 4 fumble recoveries...Had 77 stops (41 unassisted), 2 sacks and recovered 4 fumbles in his initial season north of the border...Undrafted by NFL teams, signed with Winnipeg as a free agent in 1992.

COLLEGE: Played two seasons (1987, 1991) for the University of Cincinnati with a three-year stint in the United States Army sandwiched in between...Was redshirted in 1986...Led Bearcats in tackles as a 216-pound freshman linebacker, amassing 118 stops, including 2 quarterback sacks...Set a school single-game record with 24 tackles in '87 contest against East Carolina...Returned from the Army in 1991, a season which saw him post 32 tackles and 5½ sacks...Majored in criminology.

PERSONAL: Given name Vaughn Jamel Booker...Nicknamed 'V99' and 'Book'...Born in Cincinnati...Married to Sheila, couple has three children – Breana (born 12/31/90), DeVaughn (born 6/9/93) and Devon (born 12/2/96)...Was a two-time all-city performer in football, tight end and placekicker...Caught 23 passes for 676 yards and 6 touchdowns as a senior...Earned three letters in football and basketball, plus one in track...Boxed while in the U.S. Army from 1988-90...Brother, Anthony, played defensive tackle at Indiana State (1988-91)...Worked with two charities while playing for the Chiefs: 'Dream Factory,' which grants the wishes of terminally ill children; and 'Two Loaves, Three Fish,' which assists the homeless...Also had his own in-season radio show in Kansas City...Hobbies include fishing, movies, travel and spending time with his family...Residence: Overland Park, Kan.

PRO STATISTICS:

Year	G/S	UT	AT	Sacks	Int.	FR	FF	PD
1994 Kansas City 13/0		18	6	½	0	2	2	1
1995 Kansas City 16/10		28	15	1½	0	1	0	2
1996 Kansas City 14/10		37	14	1	0	1	2	1
1997 Kansas City 13/13		26	20	4	0	1	1	1
Totals 56/33		109	55	7	0	5	5	5
Playoffs 3/2		8	3	1	0	0	1	0

Touchdowns: 1, 14-yard fumble return vs. Denver (12/17/95)
Kickoff Returns: 2 for 10 yards, 5.0 avg., LG 10 in 1994

ROBERT BROOKS — 87

Wide Receiver
College: South Carolina
NFL Exp.: 7th Season   **Packers Exp.:** 7th Season
Ht.: 6-0   **Wt.:** 180   **Born:** 6/23/70   **Acq:** D3-92

PRO: A legitimate medical marvel and a man with a single-minded mission, Robert Brooks rebounded from a devastating, career-threatening knee injury to capture National Football League 'Comeback Player of the Year' honors in 1997 with one of the most remarkable recoveries in pro football history...Punctuating his return to action by once again becoming a 1,000-yard receiver, he earned high praise and open admiration from veteran Head Trainer Pepper Burruss, who says in wonder, "Robert Brooks could set the standard for how someone should approach conditioning and rehabilitation. He has made the greatest recovery I've ever seen in my 20 years as a trainer. And now that he has had an offseason without having to rehabilitate that knee – and suffer the pain and discomfort associated with that process – he will be even better this year. Last year he was playing catch-up. This year he has a chance to get ahead."...The wiry South Carolinian's spectacular comeback came as no surprise to Burruss or Number 87's coaches and teammates...A classic example of grit, tenacity and commitment, he has proved throughout his pro career to be one of the most resilient and remarkable athletes in Packers annals – a performer who openly thrives on challenges...When called upon to succeed the departed Sterling Sharpe as the "go-to-guy" in Green Bay's offense three years ago, he promptly proceeded to eclipse two of Sharpe's all-time club records with a season-long performance of rare brilliance, amassing 1,497 yards receiving to surpass Sharpe's previous mark of 1,461, and registering nine 100-yard receiving days, two more than Sharpe's 1992 record of seven...Then, in 1996, Brooks was presented with an even more formidable challenge when he suffered one of the most devastating knee injuries in team history in a game against San Francisco Oct. 14, tearing the anterior cruciate ligament, the patellar tendon and the medial collateral ligament in his right knee, along with incurring a significant bone chip...Aided by his strong Christian faith, he since has become something of a medical miracle, easily exceeding projections on the length of time his arduous rehab program would require and eliciting profound admiration from the team's training staff for his recuperative powers in the process..."We've seen anterior cruciates come back before and we've seen the patellar tendon come back before," says Burruss, "but never the two together. His recovery is about 99 percent attributable to Robert's dedication and work ethic. He also has been blessed with an extremely strong faith."...One of those patently delighted with Brooks' incredible rehab success – and his '97 comeback – is Packers offensive coordinator Sherm Lewis, who observes, "Robert appears to be 100 percent recovered from his 1996 knee injury. And he looked extremely quick and elusive in our minicamps this offseason. He also will provide leadership and inspiration to our younger receivers. He's such a great example – his work ethic is as good as anybody's I've ever been around. He's dedicated, he works hard. He's a great, great competitor – probably one of the toughest guys I've ever coached."...The former South Carolina Gamecock continued to invade the Packers' record book in 1997, pairing with Antonio Freeman to become the first wide receiver tandem in team annals to post companion 1,000-yard seasons, jointly amassing a team-record 2,253 yards (the old record was 2,130 by James Lofton/John Jefferson in 1983)...Brooks, with 60 receptions last season, now is tied with Carroll Dale for eighth place in Packers history with 275 career catches (for 3,805 yards and 29 touchdowns)...He also has made considerable inroads in the club's postseason record book despite missing the playoffs in 1996, holding two marks: *Most Passes Caught (career)* – 43; and *Most Yards Catching Passes (career)* – 620...He also shares three other club playoff records: *Most Consecutive Games, One or More Pass Receptions* – 10, an active string which he splits with teammate Dorsey Levens; *Most Games, 100 or More Yards Pass Receiving (career)* – 3 (with Freeman); and *Most Consecutive Games, 100 or More Yards Pass Receiving* – 2 in 1995 (with Sharpe and Freeman)...Additionally, his 15.3-yard career punt return average (14 for 214 yards) in the postseason is the NFL's all-time best, and he needs only 52 more yards to pass Dave Meggett (265) for the most career punt return yardage in league playoff history, currently standing fourth...Had held the record for longest pass reception in Green Bay postseason history – 73 yards at Dallas in the 1995 playoffs – until Freeman's 81-yard catch-and-run in Super Bowl XXXI at New Orleans in the 1996 postseason...Tied with John Brockington for 23rd place in Packers career scoring with 192 points...Forever will remain a part NFL record books as the eighth player in league history to catch a 99-yard touchdown pass, accomplished in Week 2 of 1995 at Chicago – also a team record...Holds two other club marks: *Most Yards Catching Passes (season)* – 1,497 in 1995; and *Most Games, 100 or More Yards Pass Receiving (season)* – 9 in 1995...Is the owner of 13 career 100-yard receiving games and two 1,000-yard seasons...Brooks' absence from the lineup for much of 1996 season was a major blow to the fans as well as the team...He had quickly become a folk hero as a first-year starter in 1995, endearing himself to the faithful by leaping into the stands to share his elation with them following his touchdown receptions...Lewis also applauds Brooks' penchant for jumping into the stands to share with the fans..."The fans love it," he says, "and I think it's something that just happened and became kind of contagious, and went through the team. The next thing we know it was all over the country – people were showing it. That's what football used to be like – that's the way it should be."...A productive player in whatever area he is called upon, led the NFL in kickoff returns in 1993 with a 26.6-yard average...Possesses a 24.3-yard career average on 51 kickoff returns, as well as an 8.8-yard average for 67 punt runbacks as a pro...**1997:** Finished second on the team with 60 receptions (tied for 13th in the NFC) for 1,010 yards (10th in the NFC) and 7 touchdowns, thus becoming only the seventh player in team history to record three-or-more 50-catch seasons...Had a career-best 16.8-yard average per catch, first among the NFC's leading receivers...Selected as NFL 'Comeback Player of the Year' by the Pro Football Writers of America/*Pro Football Weekly*...Took on added responsibility of club's punt return duties for the playoffs, a role he had filled during his first three NFL seasons (1992-94)...After reaching the required 10 returns, he became the league's all-time postseason leader in career punt return average (15.3 yards)...Started 15 of the team's 16 regular-season games, plus all three playoff contests, including Super

Bowl XXXII...Had started the first 10 games of the season at flanker until missing the Indianapolis contest (Nov. 16) after suffering a rib injury the previous week vs. St. Louis (Nov. 9)...Enjoyed six regular-season games where he averaged better than 20 yards per reception, including each of the last five contests...Started season opener vs. Chicago (Sept. 1) and led team with 71 receiving yards on 3 catches to "officially" launch his comeback campaign, his production including a diving, 18-yard touchdown reception from Brett Favre just before halftime, giving the Packers an 18-11 lead in the eventual 38-24 win; he also had made a 44-yard catch across the middle on the previous play to help set up his score...Led club in receiving at Philadelphia (Sept. 7) with 6 receptions for 90 yards...Made 4 catches for a team-high 72 yards in win over Miami (Sept. 14)...Had 92 yards receiving on 5 receptions vs. Minnesota (Sept. 21), including a 19-yard touchdown catch he snared between two Viking defenders late in the first quarter of 38-32 victory...Turned in an outstanding performance at Detroit (Sept. 28), when he caught a team-leading 9 passes for a career-high 164 yards – his lone 100-yard receiving day of the season and the 13th of his career...Led the team with 67 receiving yards (on 6 catches) at New England (Oct. 27), including a 20-yard touchdown reception late in the third quarter, giving the Packers a 21-10 lead in eventual 28-10 win...Scored the Packers' only offensive touchdown in 20-10 victory over Detroit (Nov. 2), when he caught a 26-yard scoring pass late in the second quarter; had a team-leading 77 yards receiving on 5 catches in the Lions rematch...Caught a 36-yard pass in the initial quarter to set up Green Bay's first touchdown in 45-17 triumph over Dallas (Nov. 23), but did not return to the game after that play when he suffered dizziness from an earlier hit...Scored the Packers' first touchdown of the game in 27-11 win at Minnesota (Dec. 1), pulling in a 18-yard strike from Favre while sandwiched among three defenders...Posted a touchdown reception for the second straight contest, snagging a 43-yard scoring pass late in the first quarter at Tampa Bay (Dec. 7) to give the Packers a 7-3 lead in the eventual 17-6, division-clinching win...Had 3 catches for 71 yards overall (23.7 avg.) in Bucs game...Caught a TD pass for the third consecutive game Dec. 14 at Carolina, when he snared a 20-yard pass between two defenders and barged into the end zone, giving the Packers a 14-0 lead in the first quarter of a 31-10 victory...Caught 4 passes for a team-leading 83 yards, playing just the first half, in the Packers' 31-21 win over Buffalo (Dec. 20), in the process scaling the 1,000-yard plateau for the second time as a pro...Was fourth among Green Bay receivers during the postseason with 7 catches for 73 yards...Was named 'Special Teams Player of the Week' by the NFL for the divisional playoff round after he returned 3 punts for 47 yards (a 15.7-yard average) in 21-7 win over Tampa Bay (Jan. 4); he also caught 1 pass for 21 yards...Made 3 receptions for 36 yards in 23-10, NFC Championship Game triumph at San Francisco (Jan. 11), including catches of 18 and eight yards on the Packers' opening drive; he also drew a 24-yard pass interference penalty on the team's initial possession, one which culminated in a field goal...Caught 3 passes for 16 yards in Super Bowl XXXII vs. Denver...**1996:** Made 23 receptions for 344 yards and 4 touchdowns in seven starts at flanker prior to his injury to rank eighth on the team...Posted two 100-yard receiving games – 5 catches for 130 yards and 2 TDs vs. Philadelphia (Sept. 9) and 8 receptions for 108 yards against San Diego (Sept. 15) – to pad his career total to 12...Caught an 18-yard pass for the game's first score in 37-6 thumping of Chicago (Oct. 6)...Suffered a concussion on the Packers' first offensive play at Seattle (Sept. 29), forcing him out for the remainder of the game and, in the process, ending his streak of consecutive games with at least one reception at 37...Had a 13-yard TD catch for game's opening score at Minnesota (Sept. 22)...Suffered season-ending injury on first offensive play vs. San Francisco (Oct. 14), tearing the anterior cruciate ligament and patellar tendon in his right knee while blocking the 49ers' Tyronne Drakeford on a running play to the opposite side of the field...Underwent surgery on Oct. 18 and was placed on injured reserve eight days later...**1995:** Started all 16 games for the second straight year, finishing with a team-record 1,497 yards on 102 receptions, including 13 TDs...En route, he became only the second player in club history to catch 100-or-more passes in a season, his total representing the third-highest in Green Bay annals, behind only Sharpe's 112 in 1993 and 108 in '92...Became only the fifth receiver in team history to post a 1,000-yard season, joining Don Hutson, Billy Howton, Lofton and Sharpe...Also became just the ninth receiver in Packer annals to post as many as two 50-catch seasons...First-team All-Pro choice of *USA Today*...Also named to 'All-Madden Team' by Fox Sports analyst John Madden...Was one of nine National Football League players to have at least 100 catches, he finished eighth in the NFC in receptions and fifth in receiving yards...In addition, his 13 receiving touchdowns tied him for fourth in the conference and equaled the third-best one-season total in club annals (behind Sharpe's 18 in '94 and the 17 of Hutson in 1942)...Also ranked seventh in conference scoring among non-kickers with 78 points...Had three consecutive 100-yard games during a mid-season stretch (at Detroit Oct. 29, at Minnesota Nov. 5 and vs. Chicago Nov. 12), one shy of the team record and the first such trifecta by a Packers receiver since Lofton turned the trick in 1984...Four times he caught 2 touchdown passes in a game and had six contests with at least 8 receptions...Made a minimum of 4 catches in 16 of the Packers' 17 games, including playoffs, the exception being a 2-reception effort vs. Minnesota (Oct. 22)...His 29 third-down receptions ranked sixth in the NFC...Had a team-leading 8 receptions for 70 yards in opener with St. Louis (Sept. 3)...Named NFC 'Offensive Player of the Week' for his outstanding performance at Chicago (Sept. 11), when he caught 8 passes for a season-high 161 yards and 2 touchdowns...One of the latter was an NFL record-tying, 99-yard scoring reception from Favre early in the second quarter, which also was a new team record (previously held by Billy Grimes, who collaborated with Tobin Rote on a 96-yard hookup at San Francisco Dec. 10, 1950), and only the eighth time in league history that this feat had been accomplished...Made 5 catches for 47 yards, including a 19-yard TD reception midway through the second quarter (after which he executed his first 'Lambeau Leap') in win over N.Y. Giants (Sept. 17)...Caught a six-yard TD pass at Jacksonville (Sept. 24) among 4 receptions for 30 yards vs. Jaguars...Had 10 receptions for 124 yards at Dallas (Oct. 8)...Caught his fifth touchdown pass of the season – a 12-yarder midway through the third quarter – and had 4 catches for 66 yards overall in win over Detroit (Oct. 15)...Had his third 100-yard receiving day of the season in rematch at Detroit (Oct. 29) when he totaled 127 yards on 6 receptions, including a weaving 77-yard TD late in the second quarter, the second-longest of his career...Posted his second consecutive 100-yard receiving game Nov. 5 at Minnesota, snaring 9 passes for 120 yards...Turned in another outstanding performance, this time vs. Chicago (Nov. 12), when he caught 6 passes for 138 yards and 2 TDs (covering 29 and 44 yards) in key divisional triumph over Bears for third straight 100-yard day...Registered sixth 100-yard game of the season in win over Tampa Bay (Nov. 26), catching 6 passes for 114 yards and 2 TDs – a 54-yard reception late in the second quarter and a three-yard scoring catch midway through the fourth quarter...Had a team record-tying seventh 100-yard receiving game of the season in Buccaneers rematch at Tampa (Dec. 10)...Established a new club record with his eighth 100-yard effort of the season at New Orleans (Dec. 16), when he caught 5 passes for 118 yards and 2 touchdowns – on first-half scoring strikes of 17 and 40 yards...Extended his own team record with his ninth 100-yard receiving game of the season Dec. 24 vs. Pittsburgh, when he caught a career-high 11 passes for 137 yards and a touchdown, including 8 receptions (for 116 yards) in the first half plus another 3 after halftime to surpass the century mark...Continued to excel in the playoffs, starting all three games and leading the team in receptions (17), yards (281) and TDs (3)...Helped fuel Packers' 37-20, wild-card victory over the Falcons (Dec. 31), snaring 1 TD among 7 receptions for 73 yards...Posted 103 yards on 4 catches in 27-17 upset win over defending Super Bowl champion San Francisco 49ers (Jan. 6) at 3Com Park...Notched second consecutive 100-yard receiving day in NFC Championship Game at Dallas (Jan. 14) with 105 yards on 6 receptions – including a then-Packer postseason record 73-yard scoring pass from Favre and a second TD late in the third quarter which gave Green Bay a 27-24 lead heading into the final period...**1994:** Starting all 16 games for the first time, he entrenched himself as a quality, starting NFL receiver, pulling in 58 passes for 648 yards and 4 touchdowns...Teamed with Sharpe to give the Packers their first pair of wide receivers with 50-plus catches in a season since 1983, when Lofton and Jefferson engineered a similar parlay...Also became the first Packer to return both a punt and a kickoff for touchdowns in the same season since the late Travis Williams accomplished the feat in 1969, and set a then-club season record for punt returns with 40 runbacks...Was third on the team and tied for 18th in the National Football Conference in receptions, averaging 4.25 catches per game over the final eight games of the season (34 total)...Also a highly productive performer in the postseason, he turned in consecutive 100-yard offensive performances in the '94 playoffs, posting 101 yards in a 16-12 wild-card victory over Detroit (Dec. 31), with 7 receptions for 88 yards and 13 additional yards on 1 rushing attempt – the longest run from scrimmage by either team in the contest...Subsequently had 161 total yards in divisional playoff loss at Dallas (Jan. 8), equaling his season best with 8 catches for 138 yards, including a long of 59 yards, and 2 rushes for 23 yards...Averaged 8.8 yards (seventh in the NFC) on punt returns and an imposing 28.9 yards for 9 kickoff returns...Caught at least one pass in every game, including a season-high 8 for 74 yards against Atlanta in the Packers' last game at Milwaukee County Stadium (Dec. 18), three of his receptions coming on the final, game-winning drive (two for first downs)...Had posted the first 100-yard receiving game of his pro career a week earlier against the Chicago Bears, making 6 receptions for 105 yards and 1 touchdown in 40-3 victory...Registered a 96-yard kickoff return for a score and caught 4 passes for 79 yards at Detroit (Dec. 4)...Made 3 catches for 32 yards, including an 11-yard touchdown reception on the Packers' opening drive of the game, in a 17-10 win over the N.Y. Jets (Nov. 13)...Had one of his better days as a pro vs. Detroit (Nov. 6), when he caught 2 TD passes from Favre (of 12 and 28 yards) in Packers' 38-30 win over

Lions – the first multiple-touchdown game of his NFL career...Earned NFC 'Special Teams Player of the Week' honors after posting momentum-swinging, 85-yard scoring punt return vs. L.A. Rams (Oct. 9) midway through the third quarter, tying the game at 17-17 in eventual 24-17 victory...Started first game since his '92 rookie season in opener vs. Minnesota (Sept. 4) and responded with 4 catches for 35 yards...**1993:** Played in 14 games and supplemented his contributions as a receiver by emerging as a premier kickoff returner, averaging 26.6 yards per runback to lead the NFL, thus becoming the first Packer to lead the league in this specialty since Steve Odom captured NFL honors in 1978...Served as primary backup at both wide receiver positions...Closed out season as team's sixth-ranking receiver with 20 catches for 180 yards...Also averaged 8.4 yards on 16 punt returns after assuming those duties from Terrell Buckley beginning with the Kansas City game (Nov. 8) and continuing until incurring a shoulder separation late in the Chicago contest (Dec. 5), which caused him to be inactive for the next two games...Returned to action vs. L.A. Raiders (Dec. 26), although he had no receptions...Turned in outstanding performance at Dallas (Oct. 3), returning a third-quarter kickoff 95 yards for a touchdown, the Packers' first scoring return of a kickoff since 1991...Averaged 44.5 yards on 2 KOR, including a 68-yarder on the opening kickoff, in 30-27 win over Denver (Oct. 10)...Caught his first pass of season at Minnesota (Sept. 26)...Had outstanding day on returns at New Orleans (Nov. 14), averaging 30.5 yards on 2 KOR and 24 yards on 2 punt returns, including a 35-yarder...Snared 4 passes for 56 yards at Chicago before suffering shoulder separation...Made significant contributions during playoffs, particularly on special teams, returning 2 punts for 43 yards in 28-24 wild-card victory at Detroit (Jan. 8) and amassing 134 all-purpose yards in 27-17 loss to Dallas (Jan. 16), including an acrobatic 13-yard touchdown catch in the third quarter...**1992:** Played in all 16 games, making one start...Caught 12 passes overall for 126 yards and 1 touchdown to rank ninth on the team...Finished second among both Green Bay punt and kickoff returners, averaging 9.3 yards for 11 punt returns and 18.8 yards for 18 kickoff runbacks...Caught first career TD pass vs. Pittsburgh (Sept. 27), an eight-yard slant and fade, beating the Steelers' Rod Woodson in the fourth quarter...Earlier had seen action at wide receiver vs. Minnesota (Sept. 6) in three- and four-receiver sets, starting as Packers opened game with three WRs...Third-round draft choice (62nd overall, and seventh wide receiver) of Green Bay in 1992.

COLLEGE: Set South Carolina career receiving record with 19 touchdown catches, surpassing Sharpe's previous mark of 17...Also established all-time SC record with 76 career kickoff returns...Ranked second (to Sharpe) in school history in career receptions (156) and receiving yards (2,211)...A four-year starter for the Gamecocks (1988-91), he also lettered three years in track...Led team in receiving all four years, including a career-high 55 catches (for 684 yards, 5 TDs) as a senior...Earned B.S. degree in retailing.

PERSONAL: Given name Robert Darren Brooks...Nicknamed 'Shoo-in'...Born in Greenwood, S.C. ...Married to Diana, couple is expecting a child in early August...Lettered three years in football, starting his last two seasons at tailback, and three years in track at Greenwood (S.C.) High School...An all-area, all-region and all-state choice as a senior, he rushed for 780 yards and 14 touchdowns in nine games, missing three contests due to injury...Named as team's 'Most Valuable Player'...Also was a two-time state champion in track (300 intermediate hurdles and 110 high hurdles)...Scored 5 touchdowns and made an interception on defense in the first organized football game in which he ever played – at the age of 6...President of his own record company, 'Shoo-in 4 Life Records, Inc.,' located in Columbia, S.C. ...Musically-oriented, also is a self-taught keyboard player...Released a CD single, *Jump*, in August of 1996, which he wrote, arranged, performed, produced and mixed...Has plans to release more songs off the 'Shoo-in' label...Also actively maintains his own website on the internet (www.robert brooks.com)...Equally talented as a barber, has been known to cut the hair of his teammates at the Packers' facilities...Hobbies include music, hunting and fishing...Popularized the consumption of all-natural juices in 1996 (fruit and vegetable), a trend which now extends nearly team-wide; he first began blending and drinking the concoctions himself during the 1995 season, and credits his personal use as a contributing factor in the rehabilitation of his major knee injury...Has held the 'Robert Brooks Football Camp,' designed for kids ages 8-18, in the Green Bay area each of the past two summers...Along with Packers teammate LeRoy Butler, threw out the first pitch at the Milwaukee Brewers' 1996 Opening Day...Locally has worked on behalf of Special Olympics, including 'Packer Roast '96' in Green Bay which saw him roasted by a collection of friends and teammates; the Salvation Army; the United Way; and the Leukemia Society...Will serve as the Packers' 1998 United Way spokesman...Has been involved in the 'Outreach' program and with the Red Cross in Columbia, S.C. ...Also enjoys any charity work "pertaining to God"...Residence: Scottsdale, Ariz.

PRO STATISTICS:

			RECEIVING				RUSHING				
Year	G/S	No.	Yds.	Avg.	LG	TD	No.	Yds.	Avg.	LG	TD
1992 Green Bay 16/1		12	126	10.5	18	1	2	14	7.0	8	0
1993 Green Bay 14/0		20	180	9.0	25	0	3	17	5.7	21	0
1994 Green Bay 16/16		58	648	11.2	35	4	1	0	0.0	0	0
1995 Green Bay 16/16		102	1,497	14.7	*99t	13	4	21	5.3	21	0
1996 Green Bay 7/7		23	344	15.0	38	4	4	2	0.5	6	0
1997 Green Bay 15/15		60	1,010	16.8	48	7	2	19	9.5	15	0
Totals 84/55		275	3,805	13.8	99t	29	16	73	4.6	21	0
Playoffs 10/8		43	620	14.4	73t	4	5	56	11.2	20	0

			PUNT RETURNS				KICKOFF RETURNS				
Year	No.	FC	Yds.	Avg.	LG	TD	No.	Yds.	Avg.	LG	TD
1992 Green Bay 11		1	102	9.3	22	0	18	338	18.8	30	0
1993 Green Bay 16		4	135	8.4	35	0	23	611	*26.6	95t	1
1994 Green Bay 40		13	352	8.8	85t	1	9	260	28.9	96t	1
1995 Green Bay 0		0	0	0.0	0	0	1	28	28.0	28	0
1996 Green Bay 0		0	0	0.0	0	0	0	0	0.0	0	0
1997 Green Bay 0		0	0	0.0	0	0	0	0	0.0	0	0
Totals.....................67		18	589	8.8	85t	1	51	1,237	24.3	96t	2
Playoffs 14		4	214	15.3	43	0	2	36	18.0	19	0

*Led NFL

Forced Fumbles: 1 in 1996
Special Teams Tackles: 2 (2-0) in 1993
Miscellaneous Tackles: 2 in 1992; 1 in 1994; 2 in 1995; 2 in 1996; 3 in 1997; 2 in 1997 Playoffs for total of 10
100-Yard Receiving Games: 1 in 1994; 1 in 1994 Playoffs; 9 in 1995; 2 in 1995 Playoffs; 2 in 1996; 1 in 1997 for total of 13

CAREER SINGLE-GAME HIGHS

Most Receptions: 11, vs. Pittsburgh (12/24/95); **Most Receiving Yards:** 164, at Detroit (9/28/97); **Longest Reception:** 99t, at Chicago (9/11/95); **Most TD Receptions:** 2, six times (last: vs. Philadelphia, 9/9/96)

GILBERT BROWN   93

Defensive Tackle
College: Kansas
NFL Exp.: 6th Season   **Packers Exp.:** 6th Season
Ht.: 6-2   **Wt.:** 350   **Born:** 2/22/71   **Acq:** W-93 (Minn)

PRO: A fan favorite and something of a folk hero, massive Gilbert Brown long since has entrenched himself in the heart of the Packers' front four, where he is consistently preeminent among elite nose tackles across the National Football League...Defensive coordinator Fritz Shurmur, addressing Brown's awesome impact, says of the super-strong Detroit native, "Without question, Gilbert has the potential to be the most dominant inside player in the league."...Over Brown's five-year career, the only impediment to

optimum performance for the 27-year-old wide-body has been injury, a factor which caused him to sit out three games in both the 1994 and 1995 seasons and four games in 1997...When in good health, he has effectively controlled the line of scrimmage, as demonstrated in 1996 when – as a first time starter – he started all 16 games and played a major role in the Packers' miserly defense, which yielded only 19 touchdowns over the regular season to set a league record...Shurmur, taking note of Brown's impressive contributions to that considerable accomplishment, observed, "We are expecting the same type of year that he had in 1996. In 1997, when he played, he dominated. But his problem was that he had a series of injuries throughout the year that prevented him from playing – and we need him to be a full-time player. He has the ability to be able to control the center of the defense, often draws double-team blocks, and is a force. He has the ability to be able to draw enough attention so that the linebackers can move without being impeded by too many blockers. Gilbert and Santana Dotson also complement each other extremely well. Gilbert is the big guy who pushes the pile and Santana is the quick guy who makes the move on 'em. And so, by moving those two guys around, we get that little bit of a change-of-pace in the middle of our defense. And the fact that those two guys are in there – especially Gilbert and his size – it allows us to play with smaller, quicker linebackers. Gilbert, probably in terms of football strength, is the strongest player on our team. He can knock 'em back – he can knock offensive linemen off the ball. And, I think, probably without question, has the potential to be the most dominant inside player in the league."...Somewhat facetiously described by Head Coach Mike Holmgren as "a guy-and-a-half wide," Brown originally was drafted by Minnesota in 1993...He subsequently was waived by the Vikings on the final cutdown and claimed by the Packers...A much-coveted unrestricted free agent following the 1996 season, he chose to re-sign with Green Bay (Feb. 18, 1997)..."Everybody knew how I felt," Brown said of his decision to remain with the Packers. "Nobody really gave me a chance once Minnesota let me go. Green Bay gave me a chance and my loyalty is to Green Bay. My heart was here."...**1997:** Started 12 regular-season games, plus all three playoff contests, including Super Bowl XXXII...Was inactive for four games – and missed parts of others – due to separate knee and ankle injuries...Started the first five games, then was inactive for two contests because of a knee problem, returned to start the next seven games before missing the final two games with an ankle injury...Came back to start the three playoff games...Finished regular season with 26 tackles, including 3 sacks (a total which equaled his career high), and 1 pass defensed...Enjoyed a productive postseason, registering 12 tackles (11 solo) to rank sixth on the team (second among defensive linemen), forcing 1 fumble and being credited with 1 pass defensed...Helped limit the Prospectors to only 33 yards rushing in 23-10 NFC Championship Game victory over the 49ers at San Francisco (Jan. 11)...Had 5 tackles vs. Tampa Bay in the divisional playoff a week earlier (Jan. 4), including 4 stops and a forced fumble among the Buccaneers' first nine running plays...Matched his season high with 6 stops in Super Bowl defeat at the hands of Denver (Jan. 25)...Posted 4 tackles, including a sack, in 38-24, opening day win over Chicago (Sept. 1)...Recorded a sack among 2 tackles at Philadelphia (Sept. 7)...Saw limited duty in three early-season games due to a strained knee suffered in the first quarter against Miami (Sept. 14)...Subsequently was inactive for games 6 and 7 (vs. Tampa Bay and at Chicago) and was aided in his rehabilitation by Green Bay's ensuing bye week...Returned to start at New England (Oct. 27) following the bye and made his presence felt with 4 tackles and one-half sack...Enjoyed second impressive outing in a row following his return, this time vs. Detroit (Nov. 2), when he had 5 tackles, including one-half sack, and batted down a Scott Mitchell pass...Made a season-best 6 tackles in Packers' 17-7 win over St. Louis (Nov. 9)...Subsequently suffered a high sprain of his right ankle a week later on the Colts' seventh play from scrimmage at Indianapolis (Nov. 16) and did not return in the 41-38 loss...Started the following game vs. Dallas (Nov. 23) and his presence helped stifle the Cowboys' vaunted running game, though he played only on a spot basis after not practicing throughout the week...Had 1 stop at Tampa Bay (Dec. 7), helping the Green Bay defense hold the Buccaneers to just 67 yards rushing...Was inactive for the team's final two regular-season games – at Carolina (Dec. 14) and vs. Buffalo (Dec. 20) – while attempting to heal nagging ankle injury...**1996:** Started all 16 games for the first time as a pro and led all Green Bay defensive linemen with a career-high 56 total tackles, 26 better than his previous career best of 30 in 1994...Also registered 1 sack, 1 forced fumble and 1 pass defensed...Additionally started all three playoff games at nose tackle, including Super Bowl XXXI...Named to the 'All-Madden Team' by Fox Sports analyst John Madden...Had his most productive day of the season, statistically, at Seattle (Sept. 29) with a career-high 7-tackle effort...Also had a standout performance in the Packers' second win over Chicago (Dec. 1), forging 6 tackles and batting down a Dave Krieg pass...Had 5-stop performances against San Francisco (Oct. 14), Tampa Bay (Oct. 27), at Kansas City (Nov. 10) and vs. Minnesota (Dec. 22)...Posted his lone sack of the season against the Lions in his hometown of Detroit (Dec. 15)...Forced a fumble by the Bucs' Jerry Ellison in the first quarter of the opener at Tampa Bay (Sept. 1)...Continued to exert a dominant presence in the postseason, posting 8 tackles in the playoffs...Was a key reason why the featured ball carriers of the 49ers (Terry Kirby), Panthers (Anthony Johnson) and Patriots (Curtis Martin) gained only 14, 31 and 42 yards rushing, respectively, in the Packers' three playoff games...Forced a fumble by Johnson (recovered by LeRoy Butler) in the NFC title game which deflated Carolina's hopes on its drive immediately following Green Bay's assumption of a 27-13 lead in an eventual, 30-13 victory (Jan. 12)...Registered 2 solo tackles in Super Bowl triumph over New England (Jan. 26)...**1995:** Assumed starting role at defensive tackle beginning with Cleveland game (Nov. 19), giving Packers' run defense a major lift...Saw action in 13 games, starting seven, over the course of the season...Finished regular season with 27 tackles (18 solo)...Had returned nicely from torn anterior cruciate ligament injury suffered late in the 1994 season, coming back in time for the opener against St. Louis (Sept. 3)...Suffered additional setback, however, when he sprained a ligament in his left elbow in Rams contest...Was inactive for three successive games before returning against Dallas (Oct. 8)...Started his first game of the season at Detroit (Oct. 29) as Packers opened in their 'nickel' package and equaled his season high with 4 tackles...Also made 4 stops vs. the Browns and Buccaneers (Nov. 26)...In his first game back as a full-time starter, provided a strong inside surge at Cleveland, which played a big role in stopping a Browns fourth-and-one play at the Green Bay 10-yard line in the waning minutes of the game, giving the Packers the ball back to run out the clock in 31-20 victory...Practiced for the first time coming off knee injury prior to the final preseason game vs. Washington (Aug. 25)...Starter in team's three postseason games, posting all 3 of his tackles in wild-card playoff win over Atlanta (Dec. 31)...Left upset win at San Francisco (Jan. 6) late in the first quarter with a left knee contusion, but returned to start the following week in NFC Championship Game at Dallas...**1994:** Played in 13 games with one start (vs. Miami Sept. 11, his first NFL start) before suffering a season-ending tear of the anterior cruciate ligament in his left knee at Detroit (Dec. 4)...Was placed on injured reserve Dec. 6 and underwent corrective surgery Dec. 12...Frequently replaced Steve McMichael on second and third down, his playing time increased as the season progressed up until he was hurt...Finished fourth among team's defensive linemen with 30 tackles, 18 of them solos, including 3 quarterback sacks...Twice equaled his season best with 4-tackle efforts – at Chicago Oct. 31, including a sack of the Bears' Erik Kramer, and at Buffalo Nov. 20, among them a sack of the Bills' Jim Kelly...Also played a major role in helping Packer defense limit the Vikings to only 1.2 yards per rush at Minnesota (Oct. 20)...Earlier was a key factor in restricting former high school teammate Jerome Bettis to 65 yards rushing in victory over L.A. Rams (Oct. 9) as Packers permitted only 2.7 yards per rush...Registered his first career sack at Philadelphia (Sept. 18), felling the Eagles' Randall Cunningham...Saw extensive action from scrimmage in opener vs. Minnesota (Sept. 4) as Packers held the Vikings to an average of 2.8 yards per rush...**1993:** Although he played in only two games after being claimed on waivers from the Minnesota Vikings Aug. 31, he exhibited sufficient skills to convince Green Bay coaches he had a chance to play at the NFL level...Did not play in three games and was officially inactive for the other 11...Got initial playing time as a Packer against Denver (Oct. 10) after being inactive for first four games...Later played at Tampa Bay (Oct. 24) and quickly made his presence felt, registering a solo tackle on his first play from scrimmage...Also was on active roster for four other games – at Kansas City (Nov. 8), vs. Detroit (Nov. 21), vs. Tampa Bay (Nov. 28) and at Chicago (Dec. 5) – but did not play...Saw reserve duty in Detroit playoff game (Jan. 8), then again was on active roster, though he did not play, in Dallas postseason contest the following week (Jan. 16)...Second of two third-round draft choices (79th overall) by Minnesota in 1993.

COLLEGE: Started 35 games in four seasons for Kansas (1989-92)...Tied for sixth in school history in tackles by a defensive lineman with 168 and fifth in career tackles for loss with 30...Also had 7½ career sacks...Finished second on the team in sacks, tackles for loss and fumbles recovered in 1991 while helping the Jayhawks hold opponents to an average of 150.9 yards per game on the ground, then the best run defense at Kansas since 1968...A year earlier, as a sophomore, was named as Jayhawks' 'Co-Defensive Most Valuable Player' and earned second-team All-Big Eight recognition...Started nine games at nose guard as a freshman...An All-Academic Big Eight selection in 1991...Majored in human development.

PERSONAL: Given name Gilbert Jesse Brown...Nicknamed 'The Gravedigger'...Born in Detroit...Single...Has a son, Jamal (born 3/5/93)...Recorded 89 tackles and 10 sacks at Detroit's MacKenzie High School his senior year to earn all-state honors...Played both nose guard and offensive tackle...Also lettered in track, competing in the shot put and 100- and 200-meter dashes...Gained a measure of notoriety late in the 1996 season through his regular consumption of the 'Gilbertburger' – a Double

Whopper with extra everything, cut in half with extra cheese, no pickles – at the Oneida St. Burger King in Green Bay...Favorite pastimes: spending time with his son and reading...Splits residence between Detroit and Green Bay.

PRO STATISTICS:

Year	G/S	UT	AT	Sacks	Int.	FR	FF	PD
1993 Green Bay 2/0		1	0	0	0	0	0	1
1994 Green Bay 13/1		18	12	3	0	0	0	0
1995 Green Bay 13/7		18	9	0	0	0	0	0
1996 Green Bay 16/16		36	20	1	0	0	1	1
1997 Green Bay 12/12		19	7	3	0	0	0	1
Totals 56/36		92	48	7	0	0	1	3
Playoffs 10/9		18	5	0	0	0	2	3

LeROY BUTLER   36

Safety
College: *Florida State*
NFL Exp.: *9th Season*   **Packers Exp.:** *9th Season*
Ht.: *6-0*   **Wt.:** *198*   **Born:** *7/19/68*   **Acq:** *D2-90*

PRO: Fearless and flamboyant, with a "shoot-from-the-hip" approach to both life and football, LeRoy Butler has firmly entrenched himself as the premier strong safety in the National Football League with back-to-back Pro Bowl seasons in 1996 and 1997...His primacy at the position was underscored when his second consecutive hallmark season also earned him selection to the *Associated Press* All-Pro team for the second year in a row and the third time overall (he was named for the first time in 1993), as well as several other All-Pro squads...Butler also made major inroads in Green Bay archives in '97, his team-leading 5 interceptions lifting him above the legendary Don Hutson and into a tie with Mark Lee for fifth place on the team's lifetime list with 31 "picks"...He thus enters the 1998 season only two thefts behind fourth-ranking Irv Comp, who posted 33 over a seven-year career (1943-49)...Packers defensive coordinator Fritz Shurmur paid the ebullient and voluble Floridian the ultimate compliment following the '97 campaign, asserting, "LeRoy Butler is the most versatile safety playing in the National Football League. He not only has coverage skills that are mostly identified in cornerbacks, but also has the ability to play up on the line of scrimmage – much like a linebacker – or blitz like a linebacker. And he is effective in all those areas. He is probably as instinctive a football player as I've ever been around – he has a great feel for where the ball is and is going to be. Just a playmaker – I think he's the ultimate playmaker at the safety position in the National Football League from the strong safety point of view. I think that his ability to make big plays from that position sets him apart from the rest of the strong safeties in the league."...This season, Shurmur is counting upon the ninth-year pro – a bona fide team leader as well as a "big play" performer of the first magnitude – to take a more prominent leadership role following the departure of veteran free safety Eugene Robinson in free agency..."LeRoy is a leader on our team and I think he appreciated very much the ability of Eugene Robinson to be the manager back there," Shurmur noted. "I think, however, that LeRoy has a lot of those skills and that, with a younger secondary, he will be the guy who will step it up in terms of being a bigger contributor as a manager with our defense."...A cornerback in his first two NFL seasons, Butler also has other talents, having entertained Packer loyalists by executing impromptu dance "routines" after making big plays, some of which have found their way into the team's highlight videos...His fancy footwork has provided a graphic illustration of how far Butler has come from an impoverished childhood in the Blodgett Homes project of Jacksonville, which once found him wheelchair-bound...There was a time when dancing would have been impossible for him – because the bones in his feet were extremely weak, creating a misalignment which permitted him to walk only short distances and prevented him from running...For much of his childhood, his feet were in braces or casts, and there were periods when he was bound to a wheelchair...By the time he reached seventh grade, however, his feet had healed and he was on his way to Florida State and the NFL...Although teammate Robert Brooks has taken it to a new level, LeRoy was the originator of what has come to be known as the "Lambeau Leap," in which Packers players have made it a habit to soar into the stands after scoring a touchdown on home turf, a "flight" Butler first attempted late in 1993 against the then-Los Angeles Raiders following the scoring return of a fumble recovery...On the heels of his 1997 pace-setting performance, now has led or tied for the team lead in interceptions in five different seasons (also 1990-91, 1993 and 1995), a feat surpassed in Green Bay history only by Bobby Dillon's seven times (1952-58) and equaled by Willie Wood's five times (1961-63, 1965, 1970)...Is tied with six teammates for the Packers' postseason record for most career games played (13), each having passed the previous record-holder, Ray Nitschke (11) during the '97 playoffs...Now possesses the longest tenure on the Green Bay roster (1990-97), not to mention the fact that he is the lone remaining player from the "Lindy Infante era"...**1997:** Started all 16 regular-season games for the third straight year and the fifth time in his career, he also opened at strong safety in all three of the Packers' postseason games, including Super Bowl XXXII...Finished with 101 tackles to tie Brian Williams for third place on the Packers' defense...It was the third 100-tackle season of his career (he also surpassed the century mark in 1993 and '95)...Ranked fourth on the team in total tackles in the postseason with 17, including 10 solo and 1 quarterback sack...Led Green Bay in interceptions for the fifth time with 5, tying him for sixth place in the National Football Conference and just one pick shy of the career-high 6 he recorded in 1993...Finished third on the team with 10 passes defensed, swelling his career total to 101, and tied for fourth with 3 sacks...Also forced 1 fumble...Voted as the starter at strong safety for the NFC's Pro Bowl squad, his second consecutive trip to Hawaii and third honor overall (he played in reserve role in 1993)...Named All-Pro by AP, Sports Illustrated, Pro Football Weekly/Pro Football Writers of America, Sporting News, USA Today and College & Pro Football Newsweekly...Garnered second team All-NFL honors from Football Digest...Also an All-NFC selection of Football News and PFW...Turned in a standout performance in 20-10 Sunday night win over Detroit (Nov. 2), when he contributed 8 tackles, 2 interceptions and a forced fumble...Paced the team with 9 stops in 17-7 victory over St. Louis (Nov. 9), including his second sack of the year...Also had 9 stops at Indianapolis (Nov. 16)...Led Packers with a season-high 10 stops in 27-11 win at Minnesota (Dec. 1)...Had another of his patented big-play performances, this time in win at New England (Oct. 27), when he recorded 6 tackles, a sack of Patriots quarterback Drew Bledsoe and an interception in the end zone on a 'Hail Mary' pass attempt as the first half ended...Also limited New England's All-Pro tight end Ben Coates to just 3 catches for 14 yards...Earlier in the year, had turned in a courageous effort vs. Minnesota (Sept. 21), when he had two second-quarter interceptions (which led to 10 Green Bay points) and 5 total tackles, despite having his arm heavily taped due to a strained biceps injury suffered a week earlier vs. Miami...Also ran down the Vikings' Robert Smith from behind to make a touchdown-saving tackle, pushing him out of bounds at the six-yard line; Minnesota eventually missed a short field goal attempt...Had made 8 stops in win over Miami (Sept. 14), suffering the arm injury and a "stinger" in his right arm when he tackled the Dolphins' Karim Abdul-Jabbar for a four-yard loss in the third quarter...Had 4 tackles, including his third sack of the season when he felled Panthers quarterback Kerry Collins on a perfectly-timed blitz, in the Packers' 31-10 win over Carolina (Dec. 14)...Sacked the Bucs' Trent Dilfer among 4 tackles as Green Bay defeated Tampa Bay 21-7 in a divisional playoff contest (Jan. 4)...Posted 4 tackles in 23-10, NFC Championship Game victory over the 49ers (Jan. 11)...Amassed 9 stops in Super Bowl XXXII vs. Denver (Jan. 25), while also holding Broncos All-Pro TE Shannon Sharpe to a mere 38 yards on 5 receptions...Had missed the opening week of training camp practices after straining his right hamstring during workouts in his hometown of Jacksonville in the days leading up to camp...**1996:** Started all 16 games at strong safety for the second consecutive year...Finished third on the club in tackles with 92, including 70 unassisted stops, and third in passes defensed with 13...Made big plays game after game throughout the season, he finished the year with 5 interceptions, tying him for sixth in the NFC and one off his career high...Also emerged as the runner-up to team leader Reggie White in quarterback sacks with a career-best 6½ a total which left him only one-half sack shy of the NFL single-season record for defensive backs, 7, set by Chicago Bears safety Dave Duerson in 1986...An All-Pro selection of AP, PFW/PFWA, USA Today, SI, TSN and Football Digest...Also was chosen All-NFC by United Press International and Football News...Voted as the NFC's starting strong safety in the Pro Bowl, marking his second trip to the NFL's all-star contest...Also named to the 14th annual 'All-Madden Team' by Fox Sports analyst John Madden...Turned in a dominating performance vs. Tampa Bay (Oct. 27), forging a season-high 11 tackles and 1½ sacks...Helped seal win over Buccaneers when he teamed with Williams to sack Dilfer on fourth down with 1:14 left in the game and the Packers clinging to a 13-7 lead...Had a club-high 10 tackles at Minnesota (Sept. 22), including his first sack and lone forced fumble of the season on the same play when he felled the Vikings' Warren Moon in the fourth quarter (the fumble was recovered by White)...Also made 10 stops in initial meeting with Chicago (Oct. 6)...Earned NFC 'Defensive Player of the Week' honors after making 2 interceptions vs. San Diego (Sept. 15), returning the second pick 90 yards for a touchdown...Also had 2 interceptions in season opener at Tampa Bay (Sept. 1), including an acrobatic theft of a Dilfer pass...Intercepted an Elvis Grbac pass on the game's first offensive series vs. San Francisco (Oct. 14)...Turned in another exceptional performance – this time at St. Louis (Nov. 24) – when he had 5 tackles, including a career-high 2 sacks, plus a fumble recovery...Put together a fine all-around game vs. Denver (Dec. 8), when he notched a sack of quarterback Bill Musgrave among his 5 stops and recorded a pass defensed...Contributed 5 stops, including a sack, in initial win over Detroit (Nov. 3)...Maintained his high performance level in the postseason, which saw him represent the defense – along with White – as one of six playoff captains named by the team...Started all three postseason games, including Super Bowl XXXI...Amassed 15 tackles overall in the playoffs to tie Williams for the club lead...Had 7 stops in the Packers' 35-21 triumph over New England in the Super Bowl (Jan. 26), including a memorable sack of the Patriots' Bledsoe which saw him run over halfback Dave Meggett before pulling Bledsoe down with one arm...Knocked down 2 passes in divisional playoff win over San Francisco (Jan. 4)...Made a key fumble recovery vs. Carolina in the NFC Championship Game (Jan. 12), halting what might have been the Panthers' final serious effort to get back into the contest...**1995:** Started all 16 games en route to becoming the first Green Bay defensive back to lead the team in tackles (with 117) since Mark Murphy achieved that distinction in 1990...His 5 accompanying interceptions tied him for 10th in the NFC...Turned in excellent game at Chicago (Sept. 11), making 7 tackles and intercepting an Erik Kramer flea-flicker pass between two potential Bears wide receivers at the Packers' 1-yard line, wrestling the ball away from Curtis Conway and blunting a potential scoring drive (Green Bay scored on the subsequent possession – Brett Favre to Brooks for a 99-yard TD)...Had 6 stops in front of friends and family Sept. 24 at Jacksonville...Recorded a season-high 13 tackles (also equaling his career high), including 12 solo stops, at Dallas (Oct. 8)...Intercepted a Kramer pass in the end zone with 1:53 left in 35-28 victory over Chicago (Nov. 12), halting a potential game-tying drive by the Bears, who had reached the Green Bay 22-yard line...Also weighed in with 8 tackles and his lone sack of the season in rematch with Midway Monsters...Made his second interception in as many weeks midway through the fourth quarter at Cleveland (Nov. 19), when he waylaid a Vinny Testaverde pass intended for Andre Rison at the Packers' 15-yard line; he then got up and raced 76 yards to the Browns' 9, setting up a Favre TD run two plays later which gave the Packers a 31-13 lead en route to a 31-20 win...Intercepted his fourth pass of the year on Dec. 3 vs. Cincinnati, when he picked off a Jeff Blake aerial in the end zone on a fourth-down play midway through the fourth quarter...Had one of his finest performances of the season at Tampa Bay (Dec. 10), when he registered a team-leading 9 solo stops and 3 passes defensed, as well as his fifth interception of the year...Made 8 tackles in division-clinching victory over Pittsburgh (Dec. 24), including stop of Kordell Stewart for a one-yard loss on a third-and-goal play at the Packers' 5-yard line with 16 seconds left in the game – setting up a fourth-down pass play which fell incomplete...Started all three playoff games, making 26 tackles to rank second on the team (behind Wayne Simmons) in the postseason...Had 9 stops each in playoff games against San Francisco and Dallas...**1994:** Overcame serious September episode with viral pneumonia to lead the team's defensive backs and finish fourth overall with 63 total tackles (47 solo)...Also tied for second on club with 3 interceptions among his 5 passes defensed...Inactive for three games (vs. Philadelphia Sept. 18, Tampa Bay Sept. 25 and New England Oct. 2) due to pneumonia, then missed most of another with a shin injury...Started 13 games, including the last 11 in succession...Also started both playoff contests, leading Green Bay defenders in tackles during the postseason with 11...Recorded 8 stops vs. Atlanta (Dec. 18), his second-highest tackle output of the season...Made key play vs. Chicago (Dec. 11) when he intercepted a Steve Walsh pass and returned it 51 yards to the Bear 4-yard line, setting up an Edgar Bennett touchdown which gave the Packers a 17-3 lead in an eventual 40-3 victory...Earlier had a career-high 13 tackles at Buffalo (Nov. 20) to lead Green Bay's defense...Recorded his second interception in as many games Nov. 6 vs. Lions, when he picked off a Scott Mitchell pass at the Packers' three-yard line to halt a second-quarter Detroit drive...Led a strong defensive effort at Chicago (Oct. 31) with 7 tackles, he also intercepted his first pass of the season when he waylaid a Walsh throw in the end zone early in the fourth quarter, ending a Bears penetration which had reached the Green Bay 13-yard line...Suffered a bruised shin on first defensive play from scrimmage at Minnesota (Oct. 20) and subsequently was unable to return to the game...Returned to starting lineup against Rams (Oct. 9) after recovering from pneumonia and registered 6 tackles...Stepped up to make a big play on first play from scrimmage vs. Dolphins (Sept. 11), sacking quarterback Dan Marino and forcing a fumble, on the same play...**1993:** Tied for second in the National Football Conference while leading the team with 6 interceptions – equaling the most thefts in one season by a Green Bay defender since 1989 – and starting all games at strong safety...His 25 passes defensed also were an unofficial team record (since broken by Doug Evans), that total being the most in one season by a Packers defender since the club began keeping the statistic in 1981...Surpassed 100 tackles for the first time in his career, his 111 stops (including 89 solos) ranking third on the defense behind linebackers Johnny Holland and George Koonce...Named first team All-Pro by *AP, PFW/PFWA, SI, TSN* and *Football Digest*...Also chosen to All-NFC squads of *UPI* and *Football News*, he was named to the Pro Bowl as an alternate, eventually replacing the Dallas Cowboys' Thomas Everett, who was sidelined by injury...Selected as the Packers' 'Most Valuable Defensive Player'...Had 4 tackles, 1 interception and 4 passes defensed in season-opening victory over L.A. Rams (Sept. 5)...Turned in standout performance vs. Denver (Oct. 10), coupling 9 tackles with 4 passes defensed...Posted an interception and 2 passes defensed, plus 3 solo tackles, in a 37-14 victory at Tampa Bay (Oct. 24), then forged another fine effort vs. Chicago (Oct. 31)...With the Bears driving for the game-tying TD at the Packers' 12-yard line early in the fourth quarter, he sacked QB Jim Harbaugh, causing a fumble which he then recovered, thwarting Chicago's comeback bid...Finished the Bears contest with 9 tackles, 1 sack, 1 interception (off a Peter Tom Willis pass on the Bears' final series, sealing the win) plus a forced fumble and recovery...With Packers nurturing a 19-17 lead and 3:49 left in game, made key interception of a Rodney Peete pass vs. Detroit (Nov. 21) and returned it 22 yards to the Lions' 14-yard line, setting up Bennett's victory-clinching TD in an eventual 26-17 win...Also had 4 tackles and 2 passes defensed vs. Detroit...Authored another clutch performance in Packers' 20-13 win at San Diego (Dec. 12), posting 3 tackles, an interception and 2 passes defensed...Made a key INT early in the second quarter of Chargers contest when, after San Diego had just intercepted a Favre pass one play earlier, Stan Humphries threw deep for Nate Lewis but Butler came out of nowhere to leap high and snare the ball from Lewis at the Green Bay 13 and returned it 39 yards to the S.D. 48...Scored his first NFL touchdown vs. the Raiders the following week (Dec. 26), when he forced a fumble by Randy Jordan on the L.A. 40-yard line; the ball was scooped up by teammate White, who lumbered 10 yards before lateraling back to Butler, who ran into the end zone from 25 yards out, giving the Packers a 21-0 lead early in the fourth quarter of an eventual 28-0 shutout...Also was defensive standout in playoffs, tying for third on the team with 16 stops...Forged 8 tackles in 28-24, come-from-behind victory over Lions in wild-card contest at Pontiac (Mich.) Silverdome (Jan. 8)...Registered 8 solo tackles, recovered a fumble to halt one Cowboy drive at the Dallas 43-yard line in the first quarter and intercepted a Troy Aikman pass at the Packers' 30 early in the second quarter to blunt another threat in divisional playoff contest (Jan. 16)...Also sacked Aikman for a five-yard loss in fourth quarter...**1992:** Replacing departed Murphy, he started 15 games – at strong safety in 14 games and at right inside cornerback in one (vs. Falcons)...Finished fourth on the defensive unit with 73 total tackles (56 solo) and ranked second on the team in passes defensed with 14...Registered season-high 9 tackles at N.Y. Giants (Nov. 8)...Had lone interception in 17-3 victory over Bears at Chicago (Nov. 22)...Also forced 1 fumble and recovered 1...**1991:** Installed as the starter at right cornerback, he started all 16 games...Posted 3 interceptions to share team lead with Murphy and Chuck Cecil...Also was credited with 63 total tackles, including 53 solos, 10 passes defensed, 1 forced fumble and 1 fumble recovery...All three of his interceptions proved highly opportune...The first of the year, made in the season opener against the Philadelphia Eagles (Sept. 1), saved a touchdown when he waylaid a Jim McMahon pass in the Green Bay end zone...His second, at the L.A. Rams on Sept. 29, came at Green Bay's 18-yard line, sparing the Packers potential embarrassment, and his third against Indianapolis (Nov. 24) snuffed a budding Colts threat at the Indy 46...Also forced a Thomas Sanders fumble deep in Green Bay territory vs. Philadelphia, which was recovered by the Packers at their 9-yard line...Had best statistical day of the season Oct. 6 against Cowboys, posting 7 total tackles...**1990:** Made an immediate impact in his rookie season, playing in all 16 games as a reserve and sharing team interception honors with Murphy and Jerry Holmes, each posting 3 thefts...Made 2 of his 3 interceptions in one game – vs. Minnesota at Milwaukee (Oct. 28), forging his first interception as a professional on the fourth play of the final quarter in 24-10 victory...Also intercepted a Peete pass in the Packers' end zone vs. Detroit (Dec. 22)...Credited with breaking up 11 passes over the season and forcing 1 fumble...Involved in 19 tackles overall, 18 of them unassisted...Augmented these efforts with substantial contributions on special teams, emerging as the Packers' fourth-ranked kamikaze under the team's point system then in effect...Registered 10 tackles on coverage units, 8 of them solo...Second-round draft choice

(48th overall) of Green Bay in 1990.

COLLEGE: Three-year starter (1987-89) at Florida State...Totaled 194 tackles (117 solo), 9 interceptions, 2 fumble recoveries, 3 forced fumbles, 1 sack and 14 passes defensed for Seminoles...First-team All-America selection of *AP, UPI* and Walter Camp in 1989...Starting at right cornerback, he finished third on the team in tackles as a senior with 94 (53 solo)...Also ranked 11th in nation with 7 interceptions for a then-school season record of 139 yards in returns, surpassing previous mark of Deion Sanders, and deflected 9 total passes...Part of one of the more memorable plays in college football history in 1988, when he stunned 82,500 Clemson fans by rushing 78 yards on a fake punt from the Seminoles' 21-yard line, setting up a 19-yard game-winning field goal with 1:33 left for a 24-21 FSU victory...Majored in social science.

PERSONAL: Given name LeRoy Butler III...Nicknamed 'The Butler'...Born in Jacksonville...Married long-time girlfriend Rhodesia Lee, a former Florida State majorette, this past June 20, the couple has two daughters, L'Oreal (born 10/8/93) and Gabrielle (born 11/29/94)...He also has a third daughter, Sharon (born 12/30/85)...Prep All-American at Robert E. Lee High School in Jacksonville...'Super 24' Senior selection and played in the annual Florida-Georgia all-star game...Made 139 tackles and 5 interceptions from his safety position as a senior, he also averaged 15.3 yards on 31 rushing attempts at running back...Won seven letters – three in football and two each in basketball and track...Was a high school and college teammate of one-time Packers teammate Bennett...Leader in the Fellowship of Christian Athletes while at Florida State...Has set up the 'LeRoy Butler Foundation' in Jacksonville, which is in the preliminary stages of attempting to build a 15,000-square foot youth center (the LeRoy Butler Youth Center) for underprivileged kids right in the inner city, within a mile of where he grew up…Held a golf tournament this past July 13 in Green Bay in an effort to raise funds for the project…Previously has worked with 'Underprivileged Kids' organization, PAL (Police Athletic League), Boy's Hope and Big Brothers/Big Sisters in Jacksonville...Former owner of two Jacksonville-based businesses, a beauty salon – 'LB Hair Design' – and a management company – 'Oyy-lee Productions,' which handles musical groups...Along with Packers teammate Brooks, threw out the first pitch at the Milwaukee Brewers' 1996 Opening Day...Serves on a periodic basis as the co-host of a television show aired in Green Bay and Milwaukee...Hobbies include spending time with his kids, deep sea fishing, golf and shopping...Residence: Jacksonville.

PRO STATISTICS:

Year	G/S	UT	AT	Sacks	Int.	Yds.	LG	TD	FR	FF	PD
1990 Green Bay 16/0		18	1	0	3	42	28	0	0	1	11
1991 Green Bay 16/16		53	10	0	3	6	6	0	1	1	10
1992 Green Bay 15/15		56	18	0	1	0	0	0	1	1	14
1993 Green Bay 16/16		89	22	1	6	131	39	0	1	3	25
1994 Green Bay 13/13		47	16	1	3	68	51	0	0	1	5
1995 Green Bay 16/16		97	20	1	5	105	76	0	0	1	13
1996 Green Bay 16/16		70	22	6½	5	149	90t	1	1	1	13
1997 Green Bay 16/16		70	31	3	5	4	2	0	0	1	10
Totals 124/108		**500**	**140**	**12½**	**31**	**505**	**90t**	**1**	**4**	**10**	**101**
Playoffs 13/13		**62**	**23**	**3**	**1**	**14**	**14**	**0**	**2**	**0**	**8**

Other Touchdowns: 1, 25-yard fumble return vs. L.A. Raiders (12/26/93)
Special Teams Tackles: 10 (8-2) in 1990

MOST INTERCEPTIONS — PACKERS — CAREER

52	Bobby Dillon, 1952-59 (8 seasons)
48	Willie Wood, 1960-71 (12 seasons)
39	Herb Adderley, 1961-69 (9 seasons)
33	Irv Comp, 1943-49 (7 seasons)
31	Mark Lee, 1980-90 (11 seasons)
31	LeROY BUTLER, 1990-97 (8 seasons)
30	Don Hutson, 1935-45 (11 seasons)

MARK CHMURA **89**

Tight End
College: Boston College
NFL Exp.: 7th Season   **Packers Exp.:** 7th Season
Ht.: 6-5   **Wt.:** 255   **Born:** 2/22/69   **Acq:** D6-92

PRO: A Pro Bowl selection in 1997 for the second time in his career, Mark Chmura has quietly taken his place among the NFL's premier tight ends…He also continues to make significant inroads in the Packers' archives, having forged into fifth place on the team's all-time list among tight ends with 136 career receptions…The sure-handed, six-year veteran closed out the '97 season with 38 catches, the second-highest total of his NFL career, while returning to center stage at his position after sharing "go-to" responsibilities with the now-retired Keith Jackson in 1996…Led all NFL tight ends in touchdown receptions with 7 in 1995, when he also was named to the Pro Bowl as a backup following a career-best 54 catches, only two receptions shy of the club single-season record for a tight end…Green Bay offensive coordinator Sherm Lewis is expecting another productive campaign from Number 89, observing, "Mark has really worked hard in the offseason to improve his strength and flexibility. Coming off his second Pro Bowl year, I know he is looking forward to his best season ever. Brett Favre likes to throw the ball to the tight end, work the middle of the field and go to the tight end in 'Red Zone' situations – so I also expect Mark to have another Pro Bowl-type year."…At 6-5 and 255 pounds, the imposing Boston College alumnus presents an inviting target for Favre, with whom he has combined for 16 touchdowns to date, including 4 postseason scores (he also has caught one touchdown pass from Ty Detmer)…Now stands fourth among tight ends on Green Bay's all-time scoring list with 80 career points, right behind Ron Kramer (90)…Is tied with six teammates for the Packers' postseason record for most career games played (13), each having passed record-holder Ray Nitschke (11) in the '97 playoffs…**1997:** Started 14 games during the regular season, playing in 15 of 16 games overall, he also started all three contests in the playoffs, including Super Bowl XXXII…Named as a reserve on the NFC's Pro Bowl squad, the second time in his career he was so honored…Finished the regular season fifth on the team in receptions with 38 (for 417 yards and 6 touchdowns)…Suffered a sprained posterior cruciate ligament in his left knee as he was being tackled after making a 30-yard reception in the season opener vs. Chicago (Sept. 1)…Subsequently missed only the Philadelphia contest the following week (Sept. 7)…Returned against Miami on Sept. 14, after an initial prognosis that he would miss 4 to 6 weeks…Played with a protective brace on his knee vs. the Dolphins, but still caught a season-high 5 passes for 57 yards, including a 23-yard reception…Pulled in a two-yard touchdown pass from Favre late in the third quarter against Minnesota (Sept. 21), giving the Packers a 38-22 lead in an eventual 38-32 win…It marked his first touchdown reception since late in the 1995 season (Dec. 24 vs. Pittsburgh)…Caught 2 passes for 18 yards at Detroit (Sept. 28), but suffered a concussion on a first-quarter reception near the Packers' goal line when he banged his head on the turf after making the catch…Established a career best with 2 touchdown catches at Chicago (Oct. 12), of two and 12 yards…Enjoyed an exceptional performance in win at New England (Oct. 27), when he made 4 receptions for a season-high 60 yards, including a 32-yard touchdown reception (his longest scoring catch as a pro) on a strike from Favre with 22 seconds left in the second quarter, giving the Packers a 14-10 lead at the half of an eventual 28-10 win…Caught touchdown passes of four and two yards (matching his career high) in the third quarter, giving Green Bay a 24-10 lead in a 45-17 triumph over Dallas (Nov. 23)…Tied for the team lead with 5 receptions (for 52 yards) vs. the Cowboys…Equaled his season best with 5 catches (for 37 yards) in division-clinching win at Tampa Bay (Dec. 7)…Was the club's third-ranking receiver during the postseason with 8 catches for 81 yards, including 2 touchdowns…Had 2 receptions for 20 yards, including a three-yard TD catch to open the scoring, in the Packers' 21-7 divisional playoff win over Tampa Bay (Jan. 4), then caught 2 balls for 18 yards in 23-10 victory at San Francisco in NFC Championship Game (Jan. 11)…Closed out the postseason with 4 receptions for 43 yards and 1 touchdown in Super Bowl XXXII vs. Denver; his score, a six-yard strike from Favre in the back right corner of the end zone with 12 seconds left in the first half, trimmed the Broncos' lead to 17-14 at the intermission...**1996:** Overcame mid-season arch injury to finish the year in strong fashion, catching 10 passes in the Packers' final three regular-season contests...Started 13 games at tight end over the course of the season and finished sixth on the team with 28 receptions for 370 yards...Had started in team's first 10 games, splitting action routinely with fellow Pro Bowler Jackson, until suffering a severe sprain of his left arch at Kansas City (Nov. 10), which caused him to miss the next three games (at Dallas and St. Louis and vs. Chicago)...Came back from the arch injury to start against the Broncos (Dec. 8) and responded with 4 catches (equaling his season high) for a season-best 70 yards, including a season-long 29-yard catch...Also had 4 receptions in regular-season finale vs. Minnesota (Dec. 22)...Played one of his best games of the year in Tampa Bay rematch (Oct. 27) when he caught 3 passes for 59 yards, including a 26-yard reception...Also had 3 catches in win at Seattle (Sept. 29)...Earlier had made a season-best 4 receptions (for 35 yards) in victory over San Diego (Sept. 15)...Started all three playoff games, including Super Bowl XXXI...Caught 2 passes for 13 yards against home state Patriots in the Super Bowl (Jan. 26), punctuating his postseason efforts by making a 2-point conversion reception (from Favre) after the Packers' final touchdown in 35-21 triumph...Versatile, served as the team's long-snapper on punts when healthy...**1995:** Started 15 of 16 regular-season games and two of three playoff contests...Finished as the team's third-leading receiver, his 54 catches surpassing his previous career best, 14 in 1994, by 40...It also was only two shy of the club record for a tight end (56 by Paul Coffman in 1979)...Led all NFL tight ends in touchdown receptions with 7, one more than Ben Coates of New England and Keith Jennings of Chicago, and was named to the Pro Bowl as a backup...Accounted for 679 receiving yards, a 12.6-yard average, and his 7 TD catches were the most by a Green Bay tight end since Coffman had 11 in 1983...First-team All-Pro selection of *College & Pro Football Newsweekly* and *Football Digest*...Also named to All-NFC squads of *Football News* and *United Press International* (second team)...Was utilized as the team's long-snapper on punts in addition to receiving duties, posting 2 special teams tackles in the regular season plus 3 in the playoffs...Turned in auspicious performance in season opener vs. St. Louis Rams (Sept. 3), establishing a personal career high with 7 catches for 97 yards and his first NFL touchdown, a seven-yarder from Favre midway through the third quarter...Made 3 catches for 35 yards at Chicago (Sept. 11), but severely sprained his left ankle late in the game...Started vs. the Giants six days later despite ankle problem, catching 2 passes for 22 yards...Caught 2 passes for 24 yards at Jacksonville (Sept. 24) and also had a touchdown catch nullified by a penalty...Additionally recovered an onside kick attempt by the Jaguars late in the game...Made 2 catches for 32 yards, including a leaping, 11-yard TD reception from Favre early in the fourth quarter, at Dallas (Oct. 8)...Also had a special teams tackle and forced a fumble on punt coverage vs. Cowboys...Had a team-leading 5 catches for 61 yards, including a career-long 33-yard reception in win vs. Detroit (Oct. 15)...Enjoyed outstanding performance in the Packers' victory over Minnesota (Oct. 22), when he caught 5 passes for 101 yards and a 12-yard touchdown – the initial 100-yard effort of his pro career and the first by a Green Bay tight end since 1993...Included in Chmura's 5 receptions were two acrobatic catches – one on a third-down play in which he out-jumped two Minnesota defenders for a 21-yard gain early in the second quarter; the other a 22-yard diving reception (in which he was parallel to the ground) that gave the Packers a first-and-goal at the Vikings' 5-yard line and led to a Green Bay touchdown...Caught a two-yard touchdown pass from Detmer early in the fourth quarter of rematch at Minnesota (Nov. 5), then subsequently scored the two-point conversion on a diving catch off a tipped Detmer pass...Had a three-yard TD catch early in second quarter of Packers' win at Cleveland (Nov. 19)...Made 7 receptions, tying his career high, for a career-best 109 yards vs. Cincinnati (Dec. 3) – including an eight-yard scoring reception early in the third quarter for the team's final points in 24-10 victory...Pulled in his seventh scoring pass of the season in finale vs. Pittsburgh (Dec. 24), when he caught a one-yard throw from Favre midway through the third quarter for eventual winning points in a 24-19 triumph...Continued his season-long productivity in the playoffs by snaring 6 passes for 50 yards and 2 scores...Caught a two-yard touchdown pass from Favre, one of 2 receptions, in 37-20 wild-card victory over Atlanta (Dec. 31)...Registered another TD reception, a 13-yarder from Favre, in the second quarter of 27-17 win over the defending Super Bowl champion 49ers in San Francisco (Jan. 6), providing what proved to be the eventual winning points...Ended day with 3 catches for 19 yards...Started Pro Bowl at tight end, replacing an injured Jay Novacek (knee) for NFC squad coached by the Packers' Mike Holmgren, and caught 1 pass for 15 yards in 20-13 victory...**1994:** Started final four regular-season games plus both playoff contests in place of an injured Ed West (ankle)...Finished seventh on the team with 14 receptions for 165 yards...Saw action in 14 total regular-season games, was inactive for the other two...Played a prominent role in Packers' 16-12 victory over Detroit in wild-card playoff (Dec. 31), equaling his then-career high with 5 receptions for 75 yards, including a career-long catch of 33 yards...Was Green Bay's fourth-leading receiver in the postseason with 7 receptions for 88 yards...Earlier caught 2 passes for 46 yards in regular-season finale at Tampa Bay (Dec. 24), an effort which followed perhaps his best performance of the season, registered against Atlanta Dec. 18, when he caught a season-high 5 passes for 63 yards, including two clutch receptions of 25 and eight yards on the Packers' game-winning drive in a last-minute, 21-17 victory...Started first game as a professional Dec. 4 at Detroit and responded with 3 catches for 26 yards...Caught 3 passes for 28 yards at Dallas (Nov. 24), his first receptions of the season...Was sixth on the squad in special teams tackles with 6, including 2 vs. the N.Y. Jets (Nov. 13)...Later was forced out of the Jets game with a concussion...Earlier had missed Philadelphia (Sept. 18) and Tampa Bay (Sept. 25) games after aggravating a training camp hamstring injury vs. Miami (Sept. 11)...Returned to play in front of family and friends Oct. 2 at New England...Had missed part of camp after he suffered a right hamstring injury in practice (July 24)...Returned to practice Aug. 16 and played in final two preseason games...**1993:** Saw extensive action on special teams, in addition to his appearances as a backup tight end, playing in 14 games overall...Played in two-tight end sets vs. Detroit (Nov. 21), Tampa Bay (Nov. 28), L.A. Raiders (Dec. 26) and at Detroit (Jan. 2), as well as in both playoff games (at Detroit Jan. 8 and at Dallas Jan. 16), when usual starter Jackie Harris was sidelined by knee injuries...Caught his first NFL pass, a six-yarder from Favre, vs. the Raiders...Also caught a seven-yarder in regular-season finale vs. Lions...Suffered a bruised right shoulder recovering an onside kick Oct. 24 at Tampa Bay, causing him to be inactive for the ensuing two games...Returned to action Nov. 14 at New Orleans, making 1 special teams tackle...**1992:** Suffered a lower back injury early in training camp and subsequently was placed on injured reserve Aug. 24...Sixth-round draft choice (157th selection overall and ninth tight end) of Green Bay in 1992.

COLLEGE: Set Boston College's all-time career record for receptions with 164...Also ranked third on school's all-time receiving yards list with 2,046...Caught 11 touchdown passes as a collegian...Four-year starter (1988-91) for the Eagles...Redshirted in 1987...All-America first-team selection by the Football Writers Association of America as a senior, also garnering second-team honors from *Associated Press*...Also was an All-Big East first-team choice...Became the sixth BC player to receive the Harry Agganis Award, given annually to the outstanding senior football player in New England...Majored in sociology.

PERSONAL: Given name Mark William Chmura...Born in Deerfield, Mass. ...Married to Lynda, couple has two sons, Dylan (born 11/25/94) and Dyson (born 2/25/97)...Two-time All-Western Massachusetts and team 'Most Valuable Player' at Frontier Regional High School in South Deerfield, Mass. ...Played both linebacker and tight end...Three-time All-Western Massachusetts pick in basketball, scoring over 1,000 points and snaring more than 1,000 rebounds during his career...Also excelled in track, setting a school record in the 50-meter dash...Won four letters in football and basketball and three in baseball...Brother, Matt, was a tight end at New Hampshire...Works on behalf of the 'Neurofibromatosis Foundation' in South Windsor, Conn., donating $100 for every reception he makes to help combat the childhood nerve disease...Has been involved locally with Children's Hospital of Wisconsin and Big Brothers/Big Sisters...Was Packers' 1996 NFL 'Man of the Year'...While in college participated in the 'Big East Care' program, working with inner-city children in Boston...Hobbies include water sports, golf and target shooting...Residence: Hobart, Wis.

PRO STATISTICS:

			RECEIVING			
Year	G/S	No.	Yds.	Avg.	LG	TD
1992 Green Bay ....injured reserve						
1993 Green Bay.................14/0		2	13	6.5	7	0
1994 Green Bay.................14/4		14	165	11.8	27	0
1995 Green Bay..............16/15		54	679	12.6	33	7
1996 Green Bay...............13/13		28	370	13.2	29	0
1997 Green Bay...............15/14		38	417	11.0	32t	6
Totals 72/46		136	1,644	12.1	33	13
Playoffs 13/10		24	247	10.3	33	4

Two-Pt. Conversions: 2, at Minnesota (11/5/95) and vs. New England (1/26/97-Super Bowl XXXI)
Kickoff Returns: 1 for 0 yards in 1993
Special Teams Tackles: 1 (1-0) in 1993; 6 (6-0) in 1994; 2 (1-1) in 1995; 3 (3-0) in 1995 Playoffs; 2 (2-0) in 1996 ; 1 (1-0) in 1996 Playoffs for total of 11 (10-1)
Special Teams Forced Fumbles: 1 in 1995
Miscellaneous Tackles: 2 in 1994; 1 in 1997; 1 in 1997 Playoffs for total of 3
100-Yard Receiving Games: 2 in 1995

CAREER SINGLE-GAME HIGHS

Most Receptions: 7, vs. St. Louis (9/3/95) and vs. Cincinnati (12/3/95); **Most Receiving Yards:** 109, vs. Cincinnati (12/3/95); **Longest Reception:** 33, vs. Detroit (12/31/94-postseason) and vs. Detroit (10/15/95); **Most TD Receptions:** 2, at Chicago (10/12/97) and vs. Dallas (11/23/97)

BRETT CONWAY 10

Kicker

College: Penn State
NFL Exp.: 2nd Season   **Packers Exp.:** 2nd Season
Ht.: 6-2   **Wt.:** 191   **Born:** 3/8/75   **Acq:** D3-97

PRO: The top-rated placekicker in the 1997 draft, and one of the most heralded specialists to come out of the collegiate ranks in recent years, Brett Conway returns to bid for the Packers' kicking assignment after seeing a highly promising debut season in the National Football League come to an early and unhappy end when he suffered a leg injury midway through the preseason...A third-round selection in the draft, a high selection for a placekicker, he had entered training camp as the heir apparent to departed veteran Chris Jacke...But it was not to be...What initially appeared to be a right thigh strain, a problem which surfaced as he warmed up for the Packers' preseason game against the Raiders at Oakland Aug. 8, prompted Head Coach Mike Holmgren to hold him out of the game upon advice of the medical staff...The injury failed to respond to treatment and Conway was not to get back on the field in 1997, he subsequently was placed on injured reserve shortly after the regular season began...Fellow rookie Ryan Longwell stepped into the assignment, went on to lead the team in scoring with 120 points and, as might be expected, represents Conway's primary competition in his efforts to capture the assignment in 1998...Johnny Holland, the Packers' new special teams coach, assures he will have equal opportunity to do so, observing, "Ryan Longwell finished up last season as our kicker, but we always want to make it competitive – and want to give Brett a chance to win the job also. Both of them are super-competitive guys and willing to accept the challenge of competition. As far as Brett is concerned, he's been having a good offseason and he's been back kicking, which is good. He's a hard-working guy and wants to prove he can kick in this league. And I believe that he can overcome the injury and that he can kick in this league. He was a third-round draft pick, and that says a lot about a kicker. Unfortunately, the injury came along."...**1997:** Appeared in two preseason games – vs. Miami July 26 and vs. New England July 31...Made two of three field goal attempts against the Dolphins, converting on 20- and 24-yard kicks, before missing wide right on a 39-yard kick...Missed all three attempts vs. New England (32, 44 and 40 yards)...Averaged 63.9 yards for 7 kickoffs, with 3 touchbacks in the first two contests, with a long of 79 yards on his first effort in the preseason opener vs. Miami...Suffered right thigh strain in pregame warmups at Oakland (Aug. 8), he was held out of the game...Injury did not respond to treatment and forced him to miss remainder of preseason...Subsequently was inactive for regular-season opener vs. Chicago (Sept. 1) and was placed on injured reserve Sept. 3, ending his season...The first kicker selected, he was Green Bay's third-round draft choice (90th overall) in 1997.

COLLEGE: Four-year letter winner at Penn State (1993-96), he was a first-team All-Big Ten selection as a senior and a two-time semifinalist for the Lou Groza Award, given annually to the nation's premier placekicker...Left Penn State second on the school's all-time scoring list with 276 points, having hit on 45 of 61 field goal attempts and 141 of 142 PAT tries...His 45 field goals were the second-most in school history and he set a Big Ten record by making 129 consecutive conversions (including bowl games), also a school mark...As a senior, led Nittany Lions with 93 points and had two game-winning field goals: a 25-yarder with 1:23 to play vs. Wisconsin and a 30-yarder with 12 seconds left in a 32-29 win over Michigan State...Made career-long 52-yarder vs. Temple in 1996...Additionally, boomed 49 of his 69 kickoffs into or out of the end zone as a senior...As a junior, led team in scoring with 85 points and was a second-team All-Big Ten pick...Was second on the team in scoring as a sophomore with 92 points...Primarily handled kickoff duties as a freshman...Majored in hotel management.

PERSONAL: Given name Brett Alan Conway...Born in Atlanta...Single...An all-state and All-America choice in both soccer and football at Parkview High School in Lilburn, Ga. ...Converted 4 kicks of more than 50 yards his junior and senior seasons, including a 58-yarder...Was a *Parade* All-America and second-team *USA Today* choice his senior year...His soccer team won the state title and was ranked No. 3 in the nation by *USA Today*...Earned three letters in football and four in soccer...Hobbies include soccer and golf...Has worked with 'The Second Mile,' a charitable organization in State College, Pa., that assists underprivileged children...Residence: Atlanta.

PRO STATISTICS:

Games/Starts—Green Bay 1997 (injured reserve).

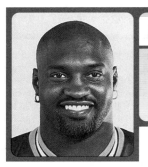

ERIC CURRY   75

Defensive End
College: Alabama
NFL Exp.: 6th Season   **Packers Exp.:** 1st Season
Ht.: 6-6   **Wt.:** 275   **Born:** 2/3/70   **Acq:** UFA-98 (TB)

PRO: One of the most heralded athletes to enter the 1993 National Football League draft when coming out of the college ranks, Eric Curry joins the Packers as a sixth-year veteran with impressive pass-rushing potential...Consistent on-field success has eluded the former University of Alabama standout, signed as an unrestricted free agent April 1, 1998, but Green Bay defensive coordinator Fritz Shurmur is optimistic over Curry's chances of becoming a contributor to the Packers' cause..."Eric Curry is a guy who has never achieved at the level that everybody expected him to," Shurmur says. "He came out of Alabama as a great potential player and then, for one reason or another, has not had the playing time that it would take for a guy to reach the upper levels of play in the National Football League. We expect him to compete for a position."...Tampa Bay's first-round selection in the '93 draft – the sixth player chosen – he was a starter at right end during his first three seasons with the Buccaneers, but has been primarily a backup the past two years...Over his five seasons with Tampa Bay, he recorded 84 tackles – including 12 sacks – while starting 44 of 59 games...He also was credited with 7 forced fumbles...**1997:** Played in six games, starting the season finale against the Chicago Bears (Dec. 21) at left end when Chidi Ahanotu was slowed by the flu...Was inactive for the Bucs' other 10 regular-season games plus both of the club's playoff contests...Closed out the year with 1 solo tackle, recorded at Indianapolis (Nov. 2)...**1996:** Played in 12 games with three starts...Served as the Bucs' primary substitute at both end positions, he also saw action on special teams...Began the season as the starter at left defensive end while Ahanotu was sidelined by a broken hand, playing the first three games at that position...Had 2 sacks and 3 tackles for loss among his 9 total stops over the course of the season...Turned in his best game of the year at Detroit (Sept. 8), contributing 4 tackles, 1 forced fumble and his initial sack of the season...Made another strong showing the following week at Denver (Sept. 15) before suffering a third-quarter knee injury which kept him out of action for three weeks...Returned from the injury at Arizona (Oct. 20) as a sub for defensive end Regan Upshaw...Recorded his second sack of the year Dec. 8 vs. the Redskins, dropping QB Gus Frerotte for a six-yard loss that forced an errant Washington field goal attempt...**1995:** Started all 16 games (at right end) for the only time as a pro, in the process becoming one of only three Tampa Bay defensive players to start every contest...Totaled a career-best 29 tackles (25 solo), 2 sacks, 1 fumble recovery, 1 forced fumble and 2 passes defensed...Was forced to leave game in the second quarter of overtime victory over Vikings (Oct. 15) with a strained hip...Equaled his career high with 5 tackles in a loss to Atlanta (Oct. 22), he also pressured Falcons QB Jeff George into a shovel pass which was intercepted and returned for a touchdown by teammate Warren Sapp...Enjoyed perhaps his most effective game of the season in finale against Detroit (Dec. 23), posting a pair of sacks to match his career best and earn 'Player of the Game' honors...**1994:** Was Buccaneers' starter at right end, playing in 15 games with 14 starts (inactive at Green Bay Sept. 25, did not start vs. Chicago Nov. 6)...Ended season with 24 tackles (18 solo), 2 forced fumbles and 3 sacks...Had a sack of Warren Moon among 4 stops in overtime victory at Minnesota (Nov. 27)...Sacked Redskins QB Heath Shuler, forcing a fumble which was recovered by teammate Barney Bussey to set up a key field goal, in 26-21 victory over Washington (Dec. 4)...Made a career-high 5 tackles vs. Indianapolis (Sept. 11)...**1993:** Played in and started 10 games as a rookie, finishing with 21 tackles (16 solo), 5 sacks (tied for second on the team), 3 forced fumbles and 1 fumble recovery...Despite signing late, was impressive in training camp and earned starting job at right defensive end...Missed final six games of the season after suffering ankle sprain in first series of Vikings contest (Nov. 21)...Had streak of at least one sack in four straight games (one short of team record), including a career-high 2 at Minnesota (Oct. 10)...Drafted in the first round (sixth overall) by Tampa Bay in 1993...Chosen one pick behind Alabama teammate and fellow defensive end John Copeland, marking the third time in NFL history that two players who played the same position at the same college were selected consecutively in the first round.

COLLEGE: Enjoyed an outstanding three-year career (1990-92) at Alabama as a defensive end, amassing 114 career tackles (77 solo) and 22.5 sacks...Finished second (behind Derrick Thomas) on the school's all-time sacks list, posting six multi-sack games...Finished with 40 tackles (30 solo) and a career-high 10½ sacks his senior season as Crimson Tide went 13-0 and captured the national championship...Selected 'Defensive Player of the Year,' by Chevrolet...Named 'Lineman of the Year' by *United Press International* and Washington Pigskin Club...First-team All-America selection of *Associated Press, UPI,* Walter Camp, Kodak, *The Sporting News* and *College & Pro Football Newsweekly*...Also was a finalist for the Lombardi Award and finished ninth in balloting for the Heisman Trophy...Was first-team All-Southeastern Conference choice...As a junior, made 46 tackles, including 4 sacks, while earning second-team all-conference honors...Had 8 sacks among 28 tackles as a sophomore...Suffered a foot injury in the summer prior to his freshman year, causing him to miss the season...Despite his original admission under the NCAA's Proposition 48, he went on to win Alabama's 'Commitment to Academic Excellence Award' and made the Dean's List...Holds B.S. degree in criminal justice with a minor in sociology.

PERSONAL: Given name Eric Felece Curry...Nicknamed 'Big E' and 'Skillet'...Born in Thomasville, Ga. ...Single...Attended Thomasville (Ga.) High School, lettering in football and basketball...Played defensive end, cornerback, free safety, wide receiver and tight end as a prep...Has three cousins who have played in the NFL – William Andrews (Falcons 1979-83, 1986), Lomas Brown (Lions 1985-95, Cardinals 1996-97) and Guy McIntyre (49ers 1984-93, Packers 1994 and Eagles 1995-96)...Funds and administers two college scholarship programs through his All-Sports Foundation, which strives to help Tampa underprivileged kids...Also has donated considerable time to YMCA programs in Tampa...Hobbies include billiards, playing ping-pong and basketball, traveling and reading...Residence: Tampa.

PRO STATISTICS:

Year	G/S	UT	AT	Sacks	Int.	FR	FF	PD
1993 Tampa Bay.................10/10	16	5	5	0	1	3	0
1994 Tampa Bay.................15/14	18	6	3	0	0	2	0
1995 Tampa Bay.................16/16	25	4	2	0	1	1	2
1996 Tampa Bay.................12/3	9	0	2	0	0	1	1
1997 Tampa Bay...................6/1	1	0	0	0	0	0	0
Totals 59/44	69	15	12	0	2	7	3
Playoffs 0/0	0	0	0	0	0	0	0

CHRIS DARKINS 44

Cornerback
College: *Minnesota*
NFL Exp.: *3rd Season*   **Packers Exp.:** *3rd Season*
Ht.: *6-0*   **Wt.:** *205*   **Born:** *4/30/74*   **Acq:** *D4-96*

PRO: Previously a running back with intriguing potential, Chris Darkins this season makes what is considered to be football's most challenging transition – to the "other side" of the ball at defensive back..."He's a project," Green Bay defensive coordinator Fritz Shurmur acknowledged in addressing the switch. "(But) a couple things we do know – he's an excellent athlete with great speed, and he's a competitor. Whether or not those defensive instincts and things are there, only time will tell. But we like the fact that he's such a willing competitor, that he's a bright guy and that he's blessed with really great athletic skills. All those things at least make him a candidate to be a cornerback in this league."...Packers head coach Mike Holmgren also is impressed with the credentials Number 44 brings to the task, observing, "Chris is a very fast, physical football player. He's never been a defensive player, but he shows good ability in his hips to make turns."...The inherent challenge for Darkins, Green Bay pro personnel director Reggie McKenzie noted, stems from the fact that, in his previous role "he was always running forward, with the ball in his hand – always running forward. Now he will be doing just the opposite – running backwards (in coverage)."...Darkins, in a separate appraisal, agreed, conceding, "The footwork is a tough part. And so is reading quarterbacks and reading routes."...The 24-year-old University of Minnesota alumnus, who made his practice field debut at the position during the Packers' passing camp in mid-May, also noted, "It makes me feel comfortable knowing that they are saying this is a project and let's see how it works out."...Holmgren has had good fortune with similar experiments in the past, receivers Corey Harris and Keith Crawford both having made the switch to defensive back with reasonable success...**1997:** Played a prominent role on special teams, excelling on kick coverage while playing in 14 of 16 games...Finished third on special teams units with 13 tackles, 8 of them solo...Posted a career-high 3 special teams tackles against Miami (Sept. 14), he later made 2 stops vs. Minnesota (Sept. 21), at New England (Oct. 27) and at Indianapolis (Nov. 16)...Also served as a deep man on kickoffs in the second half of initial Vikings contest (replacing Bill Schroeder), returning 4 for 68 yards (17.0 avg.)...Was inactive at Detroit (Sept. 28) and vs. Buffalo (Dec. 20), the latter contest because of an abdominal strain suffered six days earlier at Carolina...Played on special teams in all three postseason games, including Super Bowl XXXII against Denver, and registered 1 solo tackle in kick coverage (vs. the Broncos)...Enjoyed an impressive training camp, enabling him to make the Packers' opening day roster, leading the team in rushing during the preseason with 197 yards and 2 touchdowns on 32 attempts for a robust 6.2-yard average...**1996:** Played in the team's first preseason game, Aug. 2 vs. New England...Gained 4 yards in 3 rushing attempts and caught 2 passes for 12 yards before suffering a dislocated left shoulder...Underwent corrective surgery on Aug. 13, he was placed on injured reserve six days later...Drafted in the fourth round (123rd overall) by Green Bay in 1996.

COLLEGE: Four-year letterwinner (1992-95) as a running back at the University of Minnesota, starting the last two-and-a-half seasons...Closed out his collegiate career with 3,235 rushing yards (on 643 attempts) – the second-highest total school history – including a single-season record of 1,443 yards as a junior...Also ranked fourth in Golden Gophers' history with 21 career rushing touchdowns...Caught 66 passes for 737 yards (11.2 avg.) and 5 touchdowns over his four seasons...Had nine games of 100-or-more yards rushing, including three of 200-plus yards...Served as a team captain during his junior and senior seasons...Set a school single-game rushing record by amassing 294 yards on a career-high 38 carries in a 1995 win over Purdue...Carried 164 times for 825 yards and 6 TDs as he struggled through an injury-filled (high left ankle sprain) senior season...Won the 'Paul Giel Award,' given to the player who exemplifies unselfishness and the most concern about the school, as a senior...Also garnered 'Bronko Nagurski Award' as team MVP...Averaged career-best 5.2 yards per carry his junior season, when he was a first-team All-Big Ten pick, received All-America honorable mention and was a finalist for the 'Doak Walker Award'...Also starred in track, was the 1996 Indoor Big Ten Champion in the 55 meters with a time of 6.27; qualified for the NCAA indoor meet, but did not advance to the finals...Majored in political science.

PERSONAL: Given name Christopher Oji Darkins...Middle name (African) means "Brave Warrior"...Nicknamed 'Darkside'...Born in San Francisco...Married to Paula...Has a son, Andre (born 3/25/94)...Earned all-state and all-conference honors in football at Strake Jesuit College Prep in Houston...Rushed for over 1,300 yards and scored 18 touchdowns as a senior...Also was an all-state and all-conference selection in both soccer and track...Won a total of seven state 4A private school titles in track...Captured state crowns in the 100, 200, long jump and 400-meter relay as a senior...Won the high jump and long jump as a junior and was on the winning 400-meter relay team as a sophomore...Helped lead his school to the state team title each season...Won two letters in football and four each in track and soccer...Elected student body president as a senior...Spent the offseason operating his four Minneapolis-based companies: UCS Computer Corp., UCS Solutions Group (network services), UCS Cabling (communications cabling) and Gerard Industries (trucking)...Is an active participant in Twin Cities (Minneapolis-St. Paul) elementary school reading programs...Gave time to the Jacob Wetterling Foundation while in college...Hobbies include reading (especially computer books) and bowling...Residence: Minneapolis.

PRO STATISTICS:

Year	G/S	No.	RUSHING Yds.	Avg.	LG	TD	No.	KICKOFF RETURNS Yds.	Avg.	LG	TD
1996 Green Bay ....injured reserve											
1997 Green Bay 14/0		0	0	0.0	0	0	4	68	17.0	20	0
Totals **14/0**		**0**	**0**	**0.0**	**0**	**0**	**4**	**68**	**17.0**	**20**	**0**
Playoffs **3/0**		**0**	**0**	**0.0**	**0**	**0**	**0**	**0**	**0.0**	**0**	**0**

Special Teams Tackles: 13 (8-5) in 1997; 1 (1-0) in 1997 Playoffs

ROB DAVIS   60

Long Snapper
College: *Shippensburg*
NFL Exp.: *3rd Season*   **Packers Exp.:** *2nd Season*
Ht.: *6-3*   **Wt.:** *290*   **Born:** *12/10/68*   **Acq:** *FA-97*

PRO: A consistent, top-level long snapper who aspires to ply his valued skill for the Packers again in 1998 after joining the team last year at midseason...Previously played in 1996 for Green Bay's long-time nemesis, the Chicago Bears...Had labored three years for an opportunity to play in the NFL, spending two training camps with the N.Y. Jets (1993-94), a year in the Canadian Football League with the Baltimore

THE PLAYERS

Stallions (1995) and a preseason with Kansas City (1996), before reaching his goal..."He's one of the best long snappers I have seen in 8-10 years," says Green Bay special teams coach Johnny Holland. "Having a long snapper is very valuable to the punt team and field goal team. Rob has done a great job at being consistent in getting the ball to the punter and kicker accurately. He has good control and wrist action and a good snap. This offseason Rob has worked hard every day. He takes pride in working to be the best in the NFL."...Is the first player ever from Shippensburg (Pa.) University to play in the NFL...**1997:** Signed with Green Bay as a free agent on Nov. 4 after usual punt snapper Paul Frase was sidelined by a back injury...Handled all of the Packers' long-snapping duties for the last seven regular-season games, beginning with win over St. Louis (Nov. 9), as well as all three playoff contests, including Super Bowl XXXII...Had been waived by Chicago right before the start of the regular season (Aug. 27) and was out of football until joining Green Bay...**1996:** Played in all 16 games for Chicago, serving as the Bears' long snapper for both punts and placements...Made 10 tackles on special teams, including a career-high 3 in a season-opening win over Dallas (Sept. 2)...Had been signed by Chicago on Aug. 28 after being waived by Kansas City in the roster cutdown to 60 players (Aug. 20)...Originally had signed with the Chiefs on April 22...**1995:** Served as the long snapper and a backup nose tackle for the Baltimore Stallions of the Canadian Football League after joining the team in April...**1994:** Failed to make the Jets' roster in his second attempt, he was waived on Aug. 22...Returned to coach at Shippensburg following his release...Had re-signed with New York on May 2...**1993:** Waived by the Jets on Aug. 24, he spent the year out of football...Signed by the New York Jets as an undrafted free agent on May 10.

COLLEGE: Four-year starter (1988-89, 1991-92) at defensive tackle for Shippensburg (Pa.) University, where he started all 43 games of his career...Redshirted in 1987 and took the 1990 season off...Finished as the school's all-time leading tackler among defensive linemen with 353 total stops...Tied the Red Raiders' career record with 34 tackles for loss...Set the school's single-season sacks record with 13 his junior season...Was a first-team All-Eastern College Athletic Conference selection as a junior and senior...Helped Shippensburg to the NCAA Division II playoffs in 1991...Earned a degree in criminal justice/law enforcement.

PERSONAL: Given name Robert Emmett Davis...Born in Washington, D.C. ...Single...Lettered in football, wrestling and lacrosse at Eleanor Roosevelt High School in Greenbelt, Md. ...Played tight end and center as a prep...Has worked part-time as a bodyguard for the Chicago Bulls' Dennis Rodman...Speaks frequently in Green Bay area schools, he previously was a regular speaker at Boys & Girls Clubs and schools in Chicago...Also worked with Big Brothers/Big Sisters and volunteered for the Chris Zorich Foundation while with the Bears...Counseled juvenile delinquents during the 1993-95 offseasons in Pennsylvania...Played for the Packers' basketball team, Titans of the Tundra, the past offseason...Hobbies include playing golf and movies...Would like to further his education and eventually become a dean at a school after football...Residence: De Pere, Wis.

PRO STATISTICS:

> **Games/Starts**—Baltimore (CFL) 1995 (18/0); Chicago 1996 (16/0); Green Bay 1997 (7/0); 1997 Playoffs (3/0). NFL totals: 23/0. Playoff totals: 3/0. CFL totals: 18/0.

> **Special Teams Tackles:** 10 (3-7) in 1996; 1 (1-0) in 1997 for total of 11 (4-7)

THE PLAYERS

TYRONE DAVIS   81

Tight End
College: Virginia
NFL Exp.: 3rd Season   **Packers Exp.:** 2nd Season
Ht.: 6-4   **Wt.:** 252   **Born:** 6/30/72   **Acq:** FA-97

PRO: A one-time wide receiver who gives the Packers an explosive downfield threat from the tight end spot...Has the size, speed and receiving skills to thrive in the Green Bay offense...Spent his first two NFL seasons with the N.Y. Jets (1995-96) before initially joining the Packers in a trade just prior to the start of the '97 season..."Tyrone is an excellent target with outstanding speed for a tight end," says Sherm Lewis, the Packers' offensive coordinator. "He has the speed to play outside as a receiver and the size to play as an effective blocking tight end. We plan on utilizing him in various offensive formations and personnel groupings this year."...Emerged as one of the Packers' top special teams players and got more involved with the offense as the 1997 season progressed...Is still learning his position, having moved to tight end as he headed into his second season in the pros...Played wide receiver throughout college and as an NFL rookie...**1997:** Got into 13 games on special teams in his maiden Green Bay season, seeing increased duty at tight end in the latter half of the year and throughout the playoffs...Also played in all three postseason contests, including Super Bowl XXXII...Tied for fifth on the club in special teams tackles with 11...Caught 2 passes for 28 yards and 1 touchdown during the regular season, adding another reception of 17 yards during the playoffs...Served as the team's No. 2 tight end for three of the final four regular-season games – at Minnesota (Dec. 1), at Carolina (Dec. 14) and vs. Buffalo (Dec. 20) – as usual backup Jeff Thomason was inactive due to an ankle sprain...Scored the first two touchdowns of his NFL career in finale vs. Bills...The first score came when he recovered a fumbled punt in the end zone less than two minutes into the game, giving Green Bay a quick 7-0 lead, while the second came on a two-yard pass from Brett Favre to the right edge of the end zone midway through the second quarter, swelling the Packers' lead to 21-0 in the eventual 31-21 win...Had seen his first extended action of the year on offense at Indianapolis (Nov. 16) after Thomason left the game with ankle sprain, he also recorded 2 special teams stops against the Colts...Made a career-high 3 special teams tackles vs. Dallas (Nov. 23), equaling that total eight days later in a Monday night game at Minnesota (Dec. 1)...Caught his first pass with Green Bay, a career-long 26-yarder, in win over Detroit (Nov. 2)...Later made a 17-yard reception at San Francisco in the NFC Championship Game (Jan. 11)...Acquired from the N.Y. Jets on Aug. 25 in a trade for past considerations, he played in each of Green Bay's first two games, including a role as a second tight end at Philadelphia (Sept.7) with Mark Chmura sidelined by a knee injury...Was inactive for the ensuing two contests after suffering a slight left hamstring injury against the Eagles...Subsequently waived on Sept. 24, he was re-signed just five days later...**1996:** Was enjoying an impressive training camp at tight end before suffering a sprained left foot in the Jets' annual preseason game with the New York Giants (Aug. 17), an injury which would nag him throughout the regular season...Played in only two games...Was inactive for 11 contests and did not play in the other three though dressed...Caught his only pass of the year (a six-yarder from Frank Reich) vs. Buffalo (Oct. 20)...Later saw action in season finale against Miami (Dec. 22)...**1995:** Played in the Jets' first two and last two games, primarily on special teams but also as a wide receiver...Spent the intervening 12 weeks on the club's practice squad...Made his initial NFL reception (a nine-yarder from Bubby Brister) in his first pro game, Sept. 3 at Miami...Waived by the Jets on Sept. 13, was inked to New York's practice squad two days later, where he remained until re-joining the active roster on Dec. 11...Was the second of two fourth-round draft choices (107th overall) by the New York Jets in 1995.

COLLEGE: Three-year starter and four-time letterman (1991-94) at the University of Virginia as a wide receiver...Was a second-team All-Atlantic Coast Conference selection his senior season after winning honorable mention as a junior...Set a school record with 28 career touchdown receptions (No. 2 all-time in ACC history, behind only the 38 of Duke's Clarkston Hines), breaking the previous mark of 27 held by Herman Moore (Lions)...Totaled 2,153 receiving yards (on 103 catches) to rank third in school history, while averaging 20.9 yards per reception...Three times led the Cavaliers in receiving yards – 465 in '91, 548 in '92 and 691 in '94...Was the team's leading receiver as a senior with 38 catches (for 691 yards and 10 touchdowns)...Enjoyed four career 100-yard games, including three during his senior season...Made a career-high 9 receptions (for 119 yards and 3 touchdowns) in Cavs' 1994 game against Navy...Was one of only three true freshmen to play in 1991...Scored a touchdown on each of the first two receptions of his collegiate career, including a 72-yarder vs. Georgia Tech on his initial catch...Majored in history.

PERSONAL: Given name Tyrone Davis...Born in Halifax, Va. ...Married to Melissa, couple has two sons, Jarrett (born 8/26/89) and Damien (born 12/22/97), and one daughter, Mariah (born 6/5/92)...Played one year of football at Fork Union (Va.) Military Academy after graduating from Halifax (Va.) High School, where he was a three-sport star...Was an all-district selection as a wide receiver, while leading his team in both scoring and receptions, in his lone season of football at Halifax...Captained the basketball and track and field squads, earning two letters in each sport...Was an all-state jumper (high jump, triple jump, long jump) as a junior...Averaged 22.3 points per game as a member of the basketball team to merit all-district honors...Hobbies include watching television and video games...Residence: Green Bay.

PRO STATISTICS:

			RECEIVING			
Year	G/S	No.	Yds.	Avg.	LG	TD
1995 N.Y. Jets	4/0	1	9	9.0	9	0
1996 N.Y. Jets	2/0	1	6	6.0	6	0
1997 Green Bay	13/0	2	28	14.0	26	1
Totals	**19/0**	**4**	**43**	**10.8**	**26**	**1**
Playoffs	**3/0**	**1**	**17**	**17.0**	**17**	**0**

Special Teams Touchdowns: 1, fumble recovery in end zone vs. Buffalo (12/20/97)
Special Teams Tackles: 1 in 1995; 11 (7-4) in 1997 for total of 12

CAREER SINGLE-GAME HIGHS

Most Receptions: 1, four times; **Most Receiving Yards:** 26, vs. Detroit (11/2/97); **Longest Reception:** 26, vs. Detroit (11/2/97); **Most TD Receptions:** 1, vs. Buffalo (12/20/97)

JEFF DELLENBACH　　67

Center/Guard
College: Wisconsin
NFL Exp.: 14th Season　　　**Packers Exp.:** 3rd Season
Ht.: 6-6　**Wt.:** 300　**Born:** 2/14/63　**Acq:** FA-96

PRO: One of the team's most versatile athletes, Jeff Dellenbach has been a valuable addition to the Packers' offensive line since his arrival late in the '96 season...Now entering his second full season with Green Bay, he has provided some valued depth and experience during the team's last two trips to the Super Bowl...A versatile, solid veteran, he was signed as a free agent late in the '96 regular season to upgrade the club's depth at center, but can play any of the five positions on the offensive line...Also has served as the Packers' long-snapper for placements...Is a veteran of 179 NFL games, including 97 starts...Also possesses 11 games of experience in the postseason (three starts)...Played 10 seasons for the Miami Dolphins (1985-94), the team which originally drafted him, before moving to New England as an unrestricted free agent...Was with the Patriots for a little over one season (1995-96)...Started at four of the five offensive line positions during his career with the Dolphins (47 starts at center, 25 at left tackle, eight at right tackle and seven at right guard), adding five starts at center while in New England...Also has five starts for the Packers (three at center, two at left guard)...Green Bay offensive line coach Tom Lovat looks for Dellenbach to assume the same role he did last year, saying, "Jeff is an experienced veteran who has good football savvy. He filled in at left guard and center for us last year and did a good job. He makes few mental errors because of his experience. We like his versatility because he can play all five positions on the line."...A native of Wisconsin, he grew up in Wausau, which is approximately 85 miles west of Green Bay...**1997:** Played in 14 of the team's 16 regular-season games...Started five games (three at center, two at left guard)...Made his first NFL start at left guard for the injured Aaron Taylor (knee) as the Packers gained 144 yards rushing in win at New England (Oct. 27)...Also started at left guard in 20-10 win over Detroit (Nov. 2)...Earlier had started three consecutive games at center (vs. Miami Sept. 14, vs. Minnesota Sept. 21 and at Detroit Sept. 28) while Frank Winters was out with a foot sprain...Started his first game as a Packer against the Dolphins and helped Green Bay gain 142 yards rushing in 23-18 win...Filled in for the injured Taylor (knee) at left guard at Chicago (Oct. 12), entering the game in the second quarter, and performed well despite practicing at that position for just that week...Saw action on special teams over the first nine games, serving as the club's regular long-snapper for field goals and extra points...Did not play at Indianapolis (Nov. 16) and vs. Dallas (Nov. 23)...Also did not get into any of the three postseason games, including Super Bowl XXXII...**1996:** Joined the Packers as a free agent on Dec. 3...Saw action on special teams in each of Green Bay's final three regular-season games plus all three playoff contests, including Super Bowl XXXI...Assumed role as the team's snapper for field goals and extra points in regular-season finale vs. Minnesota (Dec. 22) after snapping for Green Bay's final extra point in 31-3 win at Detroit one week earlier...Had appeared in two games with the Patriots before being waived Sept. 10...**1995:** Played in 15 games with the Patriots, starting the first five at center, before a lower back injury vs. Denver (Oct. 8) forced him to miss the next week's contest at Kansas City...His replacement in the lineup, Dave Wohlabaugh, played well enough to retain the job for the remainder of the season...Got into the team's final 10 games in a reserve capacity...Had signed with the Patriots on March 6 as an unrestricted free agent...**1994:** Started all 16 games at center for the Dolphins, anchoring a line which allowed just 17 sacks all season...Also started two playoff games as Miami advanced to the second round as champions of the AFC East...**1993:** Started all 16 games for Miami, 11 at center and five at right guard...Took part in one of the more unusual plays of the season during the Dolphins' 16-14 victory over the Dallas Cowboys on Thanksgiving (Nov. 25), when, with Miami trailing 14-13, the Cowboys' Jimmie Jones blocked a 41-yard field goal attempt...When Leon Lett of Dallas attempted to recover the ball at the 7-yard line and pushed it to the 1, it became live and Dellenbach recovered with three seconds left in the game...Miami subsequently converted the second-chance field goal attempt and won the game as time expired...**1992:** Saw action in 16 games with the Dolphins, including eight starts...Alternated at right tackle by quarter with Mark Dennis...Also played in two postseason contests, starting the AFC Championship Game vs. Buffalo (Jan. 17)...**1991:** Opened the season as Miami's starting left tackle in place of Richmond Webb, who was recovering from a knee injury...Played in 15 games over the course of the season with two starts...Was inactive at Kansas City (Oct. 13) due to a calf strain suffered in practice...**1990:** Played in 15 regular-season games and two playoff contests...Had missed the entire preseason due to contract negotiations...Signed Aug. 30 and was granted a two-week roster exemption...Activated Sept. 8, but did not play in the opener against New England, snapping a 35-game starting streak...**1989:** Started all 16 games and was voted as 'Offensive Lineman of the Year' by South Florida media...Started all 19 games of Dolphins' record-setting sack-less streak (1988-89), with 13 coming at center and six at left tackle...**1988:** Replaced All-Pro center Dwight Stephenson, who had suffered a career-ending leg injury late in the '87 season, in the lineup and started in all 16 games, contributing to line that allowed only 7 sacks all season...**1987:** Played in 11 non-strike games, starting six...Filled in at left tackle for Jon Giesler early in the year, he later took over Stephenson's spot at center for the final three contests...Helped offensive line end the Washington Redskins' streak of 63 games with at least one sack (Dec. 20)...**1986:** Played in 13 games, making six starts (at left tackle and right guard), after a severe ankle sprain suffered in training camp limited his early-season action...**1985:** Played in 11 regular-season games and each of the Dolphins' two playoff games...Made the first (and only) start of his rookie season Nov. 24 at Buffalo...Was the second of two fourth-round picks (111th overall) by Miami in the 1985 draft.

COLLEGE: A four-year letter winner at the University of Wisconsin (1981-84)...Named to the *Associated Press* All-America third team as a senior, also receiving honorable mention from *United Press International*...Selected as Big Ten 'Offensive Lineman of the Year' by conference broadcasters...Was a first-team All-Big Ten selection by *AP* and *UPI*...Started 35 consecutive games to finish collegiate career...Garnered second-team all-conference honors as a 1983 junior...Switched to offensive line as a sophomore after playing in 10 games on the defensive line during his freshman season...Majored in recreation and resource management.

PERSONAL: Given name Jeffrey Alan Dellenbach...Nicknamed 'Delly'...Born in Wausau, Wis. ...Married to Mary, couple has three sons, Dane (born 4/21/89), Dax (born 4/13/90) and Dilon (born 4/30/93)...Was a multiple sport standout at Wausau (Wis.) East High School, lettering twice in football and three times each in hockey and baseball...Was an All-America and all-state selection as an offensive and defensive lineman...Also served as the team's placekicker and averaged 42 yards per kick as a punter...Earned all-conference recognition as a hockey goalie...Later played junior varsity hockey at Wisconsin (1981 and '82)...While in Miami, worked with a variety of community organizations, including the 'Say No to Drugs' campaign, cerebral palsy, cystic fibrosis, Miami Children's Hospital and the Children's Miracle Network...Also sponsored charity golf tournaments to benefit the Boys & Girls Club of Palm Beach County and The Starting Place...Was selected as the Dolphins' NFL 'Man of the Year' nominee in 1991...Appeared with Miami teammate Dan Marino in movie *Ace Ventura, Pet Detective*...Hobbies include hunting and fishing...Residence: Ft. Lauderdale, Fla.

PRO STATISTICS:

Games/Starts—Miami 1985 (11/1); 1985 Playoffs (2/0); 1986 (13/6); 1987 (11/6); 1988 (16/16); 1989 (16/16); 1990 (15/0); 1990 Playoffs (2/0); 1991 (15/2); 1992 (16/8); 1992 Playoffs (2/1); 1993 (16/16); 1994 (16/16); 1994 Playoffs (2/2); New England 1995 (15/5); 1996 (2/0); Green Bay 1996 (3/0); 1996 Playoffs (3/0); 1997 (14/5); 1997 Playoffs (0/0). Career totals: 179/97. Playoff totals: 11/3.

EARL DOTSON · 72

Offensive Tackle
College: Texas A&I
NFL Exp.: 6th Season   **Packers Exp.:** 6th Season
Ht.: 6-4   **Wt.:** 315   **Born:** 12/17/70   **Acq:** D3-93

PRO: Having matured into one of the National Football League's superior offensive tackles, huge Texan is poised to deliver a Pro Bowl season in his fourth year as a starter...Offensive line coach Tom Lovat, Earl Dotson's position coach since he arrived upon the Green Bay scene as a third-round draft selection in 1993, is convinced that lofty possibility is at hand for the 27-year-old Texas A&I alumnus in his sixth NFL campaign..."He's in the best shape he's been in, since he's been here, physically," said Lovat in making his case. "He's at a good weight and he looks good. He is probably on the verge of being a Pro Bowler. He just needs a break. I think he got some votes last year – I'm sure – not that that's the criterion for good linemen, but I think he's one of the top tackles in the league. I don't know how they rate 'em or where he would fit on the scale, but he's made the strides since we got him that would indicate to me that he's on the verge of being a very fine football player. He's always been a superb drive blocker – he's got great explosion. He's got very good feet for re-positioning and all the things that athletes have to do. And now he's been with us five years – he knows the system – and he gives us good stability."...Made his first major advances in 1995, his third NFL season, when faced with what he termed a do-or-die situation as training camp opened, he proceeded to establish himself as the starter at offensive right tackle...Dotson, who had played only four games as a second-year pro in part because of an elbow injury, said in explanation of his salutary renaissance, "I just started taking the game more seriously. It was do-or-die for me. I pretty much had to come in and prove myself. I finally realized that to make it, I had to make it in the weight room, then bring it on the field. The offseason is one of the most important times of a player's career."...**1997:** Started 13 of the Packers' 16 regular-season games at right tackle, as well as all three postseason games, including Super Bowl XXXII...Missed three games because of injury...Inactive for the Tampa Bay (Oct. 5) and Chicago (Oct. 12) contests after suffering a back injury (bulging disk) on the last offensive play of practice on Oct. 1...Returned to the starting lineup at New England (Oct. 27) and helped the club post a then season-high 144 yards rushing...Earlier had dressed, and was ready go in an emergency situation, but did not play vs. Miami (Sept. 14) after suffering a left ankle/turf toe sprain the previous week at Philadelphia (Sept. 7)...Returned to start ensuing Minnesota game (Sept. 21)...Suffered a concussion in the second half of St. Louis contest (Nov. 9) from which he did not return to the game...Helped Green and Gold amass a season-high 220 yards rushing in 45-17 win over Dallas (Nov. 23), including a club-record 190 yards on the ground by Dorsey Levens...Incurred a shoulder sprain in the Packers' 31-10 victory over Carolina (Dec. 14), causing him to miss the second half...Recovered a Levens fumble against the Eagles, enabling drive to continue, one which culminated with a Ryan Longwell 22-yard field goal...Developed swelling in his right knee during training camp as the result of offseason arthroscopic surgery (Jan. 30), causing him to miss the team's first three preseason games...Returned to the practice field on Aug. 10... **1996:** Started 15 of 16 regular-season games at right tackle, sitting out the eighth contest of the year – the rematch vs. Tampa Bay (Oct. 27) – with a sprained left ankle...Originally had suffered the injury in the second half of the Packers' overtime win over San Francisco (Oct. 14)...Returned to start vs. Detroit (Nov. 3) before leaving in the second quarter because of back spasms, he later returned to Lions contest in the second half...Was one of those primarily responsible for the marked improvement in the Packers' running game, which raised its rushing average to 114.9 yards per contest during the '96 season – up substantially from an 89.3-yard average in '95...Also started all three postseason games at right tackle, including Super Bowl XXXI...Played a key blocking role as the Packers churned out 201 rushing yards in their 30-13, NFC Championship Game triumph over Carolina (Jan. 12), many of those yards coming over his side of the line...**1995:** Started all 16 regular-season games plus the team's three playoff contests at right tackle after shedding 15 pounds during an offseason weight-reduction program to enhance his quickness and endurance...Prevented a possible touchdown at Cleveland (Nov. 19) when he chased down the Browns' Tim Goad – following a Brett Favre fumble – and tackled him at the Packers' 28-yard line; Cleveland eventually had to settle for a field goal on the drive...Also made a crunching, key block on the Lions' Robert Porcher on a reverse that enabled Robert Brooks to gain 21 yards in a win over Detroit (Oct. 15)...Later left Lions contest in the fourth quarter after straining his left calf...Though not at full strength, he started and played the entire game in the Packers' win over Minnesota the following week (Oct. 22)...Earlier posted a fine performance at Chicago (Sept. 11) when he was lined up against the Bears' Alonzo Spellman, even as he was playing through a painful elbow injury in the second half (the same elbow he had dislocated one year earlier)...Started his first NFL game vs. the St. Louis Rams (Sept. 3) in Green Bay's regular-season inaugural when he opened at right tackle...**1994:** Had his season abbreviated by an early injury, suffering a dislocated right elbow vs. Tampa Bay (Sept. 25) when he lined up as an eligible receiver on a short-yardage play...Subsequently was inactive for the Packers' final 12 regular-season games after seeing action in each of the first four contests, playing primarily on special teams...Saw most extensive action of the year with offense at Philadelphia (Sept. 18) when starting right tackle Paul Hutchins left the game with a knee injury...Returned to practice, after recovering from the elbow problem, in latter portion of year...Was the backup to Joe Sims at right tackle when Sims suffered a left foot sprain vs. New England in preseason finale...Had been scheduled to start regular-season opener vs. Vikings the following week (Sept. 4), but sprained his ankle in practice the week prior to the game and gave way to Hutchins...Inactive for both playoff games...**1993:** Played in 13 games as a rookie, almost exclusively on special teams...Inactive for other three games with a foot sprain, incurred at Dallas (Oct. 3)...Returned to action at Kansas City (Nov. 8) and played in every game thereafter...Was primary backup to Sims over the final four regular-season games after starting right tackle Tootie Robbins suffered a season-ending triceps injury at Chicago on Dec. 5...Also saw reserve action in both playoff games...Third-round draft choice (81st overall) of Green Bay in 1993.

COLLEGE: Two-year starter (1991-92) at Texas A&I after transferring from Tyler (Texas) Junior College...First-team All-America selection by *NFL Draft Report, Associated Press, Football Gazette* and Kodak in 1992...Also was a unanimous All-Lone Star Conference first-team pick, winning 'Lineman of the Year' recognition...Did not give up a sack the entire '92 season, he also did not allow any tackles by his opponent in six games...Was not penalized for holding or offside in any contest his senior season while registering 78 knockdown blocks as the Javelinas' ground game ranked 11th in the nation, averaging 262.5 yards per game...Also won all-conference selection in 1991...Majored in sociology.

PERSONAL: Given name Earl Christopher Dotson...Nicknamed 'Big E'...Born in Beaumont, Texas...Married to Janell...Has a daughter, Ashley (born 6/11/91), and a son, Jared (born 8/26/93)...An All-America, all-state and all-conference selection as an offensive and defensive tackle at Beaumont (Texas) Westbrook High School, the same school which produced long-time NFL defensive lineman Jerry

Ball...Lettered twice in football and once in track...Hobbies include reading and cars...Splits residence between Green Bay and Longview, Texas

PRO STATISTICS:

Games/Starts—Green Bay 1993 (13/0); 1993 Playoffs (2/0); 1994 (4/0); 1994 Playoffs (0/0); 1995 (16/16); 1995 Playoffs (3/3); 1996 (15/15); 1996 Playoffs (3/3); 1997 (13/13); 1997 Playoffs (3/3). Career totals: 61/44. Playoff totals: 11/9.

Miscellaneous Tackles: 3 in 1995; 1 in 1995 Playoffs; 1 in 1996 for total of 4

SANTANA DOTSON   71

Defensive Tackle
College: Baylor
NFL Exp.: 7th Season   **Packers Exp.:** 3rd Season
Ht.: 6-5   **Wt.:** 286   **Born:** 12/19/69   **Acq:** UFA-96 (TB)

PRO: The Packers' most consistent defensive lineman the past two seasons, has proven to be a valuable signee since his arrival two years ago as an unrestricted free agent...Consistently provides all-important inside pass rush, while playing the run effectively...Enters the '98 campaign as a legitimate candidate for All-Pro and Pro Bowl recognition...Has played a major role in the club's defense as Green Bay has advanced to the last two Super Bowls...Extremely durable, he has yet to miss a game in his six NFL seasons (96 consecutive regular-season games played, 102 including playoffs)...Joined the Packers prior to the 1996 season after four productive years with the Tampa Bay Buccaneers...Green Bay defensive coordinator Fritz Shurmur believes that Dotson has played exceptionally well during his stint with the Packers and is one of the NFL's best at his position, saying, "Santana is one of the premier defensive tackles in the league. He has been with us for two years and it is no accident that our defense has achieved at such a high level since he's been here. He has been a steady force. He has started and played every down he has been scheduled to play, never missed any playing time and he has performed at a high level. Last year when we had a number of injuries in the defensive line, he was the rock, the guy who was there every week. He is a force rushing the passer as an inside player, and in this day and age of three- and five-step drops where the quarterback is closer to the line of scrimmage, you need someone who can get in his face quickly – and Santana does that. He does it all."...Had 23 career sacks for Bucs, fourth on that club's all-time sacks list when he left...Led Tampa Bay in sacks in two of his four seasons...Recorded 195 tackles (140 solo), 5 forced fumbles, 4 fumble recoveries and 8 passes defensed over his four seasons with the Buccaneers...**1997:** Started (at defensive tackle) in all 16 regular-season games for the second time as a pro...Also was the club's starter for all three playoff contests, including Super Bowl XXXII...Had the most tackles by a Green Bay defensive lineman with 67 (48 solo) to rank seventh on the team overall...Also tied (with Gabe Wilkins) for second on the Packers with 5½ sacks, matching his 1996 total...Also forced 2 fumbles and broke up 2 passes...Was tops among Green Bay linemen during the postseason with 15 tackles (8 solo), in addition to 1 pass defensed...Enjoyed perhaps his best game of the season at Indianapolis (Nov. 16), when he recorded a season-high 2 sacks among his 7 tackles and forced a fumble right before halftime which led to a Green Bay touchdown...Had registered 8 stops (his regular-season best), including a sack, one week earlier in win over St. Louis (Nov. 9)...Turned in a solid performance in 21-16 win against Tampa Bay (Oct. 5) as he made 7 tackles and threw a key block on the Bucs' Mike Alstott on Wilkins' pivotal 77-yard interception return for a touchdown...Posted 6 tackles, including a sack of the Vikings' Brad Johnson late in the third quarter, in victory over Minnesota (Sept. 21)...Sacked Bears QB Erik Kramer and forced a fumble on the same play (recovered by Wilkins for a touchdown) late in the Packers' 38-24 win over Chicago (Sept. 1)...Had a key third-down stop of the Cowboys' Emmitt Smith for -2 yards midway through the fourth quarter of 45-17 win over Dallas (Nov. 23), at a time when the game's outcome still was in doubt...Made 5 tackles, including a shared sack with Reggie White, in Green Bay's

27-11 win at Minnesota (Dec. 1)...Recorded 4 tackles and knocked down a Trent Dilfer pass in divisional playoff win over Tampa Bay (Jan. 4)...Equalled his career best with 10 tackles against Denver in Super Bowl XXXII (Jan. 25)...**1996:** Started 15 of Green Bay's 16 regular-season games at defensive tackle for the league's No. 1-ranked defense, his only non-start of the season came at Dallas (Nov. 18) when the Packers opened in a 3-4 defense...Also started all three playoff games, including Super Bowl XXXI, in the first postseason action of his pro career...Recorded 45 tackles to rank second among club defensive linemen and ninth on the team overall...Was third on the club in sacks with 5½, the second-highest output of his career (10 in 1992)...Also had a forced fumble, a fumble recovery and 6 passes defensed...Continued his effectiveness in the postseason as he recorded 8 tackles, including a sack, and a pass breakup...Had one of his best games in a Green Bay uniform in team's 28-18 win over Detroit (Nov. 3), when he had a season-high 2 sacks among 5 tackles, 2 additional quarterback pressures, a forced fumble and batted down a season-best 2 passes at the line of scrimmage...Posted a team-leading 1½ sacks in Monday night game against Philadelphia (Sept. 9), including a shared sack with White for a safety in 39-13 win...Made a season-high 6 tackles in overtime win vs. San Francisco (Oct. 14)...Registered 5 stops, including a sack, in curbed action at Kansas City (Nov. 10)...Played mostly in passing situations against the Chiefs due to limited practice time the previous week after swelling in his knee surfaced following the Detroit contest...Had a sack among 4 tackles, plus 2 other quarterback pressures, at Minnesota (Sept. 22)...Recovered a Rick Mirer fumble in 31-10 win at Seattle (Sept. 29), returning it eight yards to the Seahawks' 28-yard line, leading to a Packer touchdown...Had a fourth-quarter sack among 3 total tackles, plus a pass defensed, in Super Bowl triumph over New England (Jan. 26)...Had signed with Green Bay on March 7 as an unrestricted free agent after playing his first four NFL seasons with Tampa Bay...**1995:** Appeared in all 16 games for the Buccaneers in his final season with the team, starting eight as he alternated with '95 first-round draft choice Warren Sapp...Made eight consecutive starts at right defensive tackle beginning with Bucs' sixth game, Oct. 8 vs. Cincinnati...Led Tampa Bay with 5 sacks, the second time in four years he had led the team in that category...Also made 38 tackles, recovered 2 fumbles and broke up 2 passes...Was named Bucs' 'Player of the Game' for excellent performance in front of hometown Houston fans Oct. 29, when he tallied a season-high 9 tackles plus a sack and fumble recovery vs. the Oilers...Recorded a sack, knocked down a pass and made 2 solo tackles in Bucs' opening day win at Philadelphia (Sept. 3)...Contributed 3 solo tackles, a sack and a fumble recovery vs. Washington (Sept. 24)...Responded with 2 tackles and 4 QB pressures in Bengals start...Had 5 tackles vs. Atlanta (Oct. 22), including 1 sack and 3 others for loss...Also recorded a sack at Green Bay (Nov. 26)...**1994:** Saw action in all 16 contests, including starts in nine of the team's first 10 games (seven at right defensive tackle and two at left end)...Finished season with 23 tackles (18 solo) and 2 passes defended, he also tied for second on the club with 3 sacks...Suffered broken left hand in first quarter of win over Detroit (Oct. 2), but remained in game and continued to play in subsequent weeks with protective cast...Recorded sacks at San Francisco (Oct. 23), at Seattle (Nov. 20) and vs. L.A. Rams (Dec. 11)...Made a season-best 4 tackles in consecutive games, against 49ers and Minnesota (Oct. 30)...**1993:** Played in all 16 games with 13 starts (11 at right defensive tackle, two at left end)...Ranked fifth on the squad with 63 tackles (41 solo), 5 sacks (tied for second on team), a club-leading 3 forced fumbles and a pass defensed...Led Tampa Bay defensive linemen in tackles for the second straight season...Made a season-best 8 tackles and forced a fumble vs. the 49ers (Nov. 14), he had three other 8-tackle efforts...Deflected a pass against Washington (Dec. 5) which was intercepted in the end zone by teammate Ray Seals for a Bucs touchdown...**1992:** Enjoyed sensational rookie campaign which saw him win multiple league rookie accolades...Named NFL 'Rookie of the Year' by *The Sporting News*...Also chosen NFL 'Defensive Rookie of the Year' by both *Football Digest* and *College & Pro Football Newsweekly*...Honored as NFC 'Defensive Rookie of the Year' by NFLPA/*USA Today*...Was a consensus all-rookie pick...Had a career-best 71 tackles (57 solo), including a career-high 10 sacks, plus 2 forced fumbles, 2 fumble recoveries and 3 passes defensed...Broke the Tampa Bay rookie sack record, doubling the previous mark of 5 shared by Hall of Famer Lee Roy Selmon (1976) and Chris Washington (1984)...Became just the third player in team history to record a double-digit sack total (Selmon 1977-79, '83 and Broderick Thomas 1991)...Started all 16 games (14 at right defensive tackle and the final two at left end)...Had 9 tackles, including 2 sacks and a forced fumble, in his first NFL regular-season game, Sept. 6 against Phoenix...Made a career-best 10 tackles and had 2 sacks in 31-3 victory over Green Bay (Sept. 13)...Scored his only career touchdown when he scooped up a fourth-quarter Barry Sanders fumble and returned it 42 yards for a score Sept. 27 at Detroit...Also had a sack in 27-23 triumph over Lions, earning NFC 'Defensive Player of the Week' honors in the process...Recorded 2 sacks vs. Minnesota (Nov. 8) for third multiple sack game of season...Started at left end at San Francisco (Dec. 19),

contributing 7 tackles and a sack...Was the second of two fifth-round selections (132nd overall) by Tampa Bay in the 1992 draft, a pick which had been obtained from Kansas City for linebacker Ervin Randle.

COLLEGE: A three-year starter and four-time letterwinner (1988-91) at Baylor...Redshirted in 1987...Finished collegiate career with 193 total tackles, including 18 sacks, plus 4 forced fumbles and 1 fumble recovery...Was a three-time first-team All-Southwest Conference pick...Consensus first-team All-America selection as a senior, when he registered 60 tackles, 4 sacks and 2 blocked kicks...Also was a finalist for both the Outland and Lombardi trophies and named as SWC 'Defensive Player of the Year'...Earned conference 'Newcomer of the Year' recognition from *Dallas Morning News* as a freshman despite his reserve role...Holds B.A. degree in telecommunications.

PERSONAL: Given name Santana N. Dotson...Nicknamed 'S.D.'...Is named after Native American Chief Santana whose philosophy was "with unity comes strength"...Born in New Orleans...Married to Monique, couple has a son, Khari (born 1/12/96), and a daughter, Amani (born 3/24/97)...Was a prep All-America selection in football at Jack Yates High School in Houston...Lettering three times, helped lead team to three-year record of 36-4, including 1985 state title...Also earned one letter in track as a discus thrower and shot putter...Father, Alphonse, was a second-round draft choice of Green Bay in 1965, who instead chose to sign with the rival AFL's Kansas City Chiefs, playing five years professionally as a defensive lineman with the Chiefs (1965), Miami (1966) and Oakland (1968-70)...Hobbies include jet skiing, video games and reading...Has been involved with Big Brothers/Big Sisters in Northeast Wisconsin and Houston...Set up a scholarship fund through his high school for kids in extracurricular activities who attain a certain GPA...Also has established the Santana Dotson Foundation in Houston, which gives scholarships to inner-city kids who otherwise could not afford to go to college...Served during the 1997 season as co-host of *Monday Night Kickoff*, a weekly television show which aired on WBAY-TV in Green Bay...Residence: Houston.

PRO STATISTICS:

Year	G/S	UT	AT	Sacks	Int.	FR	FF	PD
1992 Tampa Bay 16/16		57	14	10	0	2	2	3
1993 Tampa Bay 16/13		41	22	5	0	0	3	1
1994 Tampa Bay 16/9		18	5	3	0	0	0	2
1995 Tampa Bay 16/8		24	14	5	0	2	0	2
1996 Green Bay................16/15		27	18	5½	0	1	1	6
1997 Green Bay................16/16		48	19	5½	0	0	2	2
Totals 96/77		**215**	**92**	**34**	**0**	**5**	**8**	**16**
Playoffs 6/6		**14**	**9**	**1**	**0**	**0**	**0**	**2**

PACKERS WHO HAVE WON THE HEISMAN TROPHY

(1941)	Bruce Smith, B, Minnesota, 1945-48
(1961)	Paul Hornung, B, Notre Dame, 1957-62, 1964-66
(1990)	Ty Detmer, QB, Brigham Young, 1992-95
(1991)	Desmond Howard, WR, Michigan, 1996

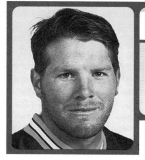

BRETT FAVRE

4

Quarterback
College: Southern Mississippi
NFL Exp.: 8th Season   **Packers Exp.:** 7th Season
Ht.: 6-2   **Wt.:** 230   **Born:** 10/10/69   **Acq:** T-92 (Atl)

PRO: Ron Wolf, the Packers' astute general manager and veteran of 35 years in professional football, calls Brett Favre "the greatest player in the game"...And, after only six seasons as a starting quarterback – and at the remarkably youthful age of 28 – freewheeling Brett Lorenzo Favre clearly is in a class apart...He has, beyond question, already forged a permanent niche for himself among pro football's all-time elite at his position...And his undisputed primacy at quarterback in today's NFL – in which he has led the Packers to a Super Bowl championship in 1996 and a repeat trip to the league's ultimate game last season – has been emphatically underscored by his selection as the NFL's 'Most Valuable Player' by the *Associated Press* for a record, third consecutive year...Named in "co"-status with the Detroit Lions' Barry Sanders in 1997, he thus became the first player in NFL history to win the *AP* honor three times, let alone in three consecutive years, setting him apart from all of his predecessors...Favre's acknowledged dominance at his position is based in large part on his remarkable productivity, best exemplified by the fact that the swashbuckling Mississippian has thrown the imposing total of 145 touchdown passes in the past four years, leaving his fellow quarterbacks distantly behind...Next up, for best available comparison, is Denver's John Elway with 95 TD throws during the same span...Favre owns a comparably substantial margin over the past two seasons, having posted 74 scoring passes to the 55 by New England's Drew Bledsoe in the same period...His 145 TD passes also represent the second-best four-year stretch in NFL history (behind only Dan Marino's 148 from 1984-87)...Standing 32nd all-time in career touchdown passes entering the 1998 season with 182, Favre likely will crack the league's Top Twenty this year, needing 19 to tie #20 Roman Gabriel (201), and, should he maintain the 30.3 per season average he has thrown touchdown passes at over his six years in Green Bay, he could ascend all the way to third on the all-time list within only four more seasons...Already the possessor of the third-highest quarterback rating in NFL annals, 89.3 – based on 1,971 completions on 3,206 career attempts for 22,591 yards and 182 touchdowns with 95 interceptions – he further entrenched himself in league history last season by becoming the first passer in its 78-year existence to throw 30-or-more touchdown passes in four consecutive seasons (1994-97); Marino also did it four times, but not consecutively...Now has three of the eight highest one-season touchdown pass totals in league annals (39 in 1996, 38 in 1995 and 35 in 1997)...In firing 35 scoring passes, he also became only the fourth player in NFL history to lead the league in TD passes in as many as three consecutive seasons (1995-97), in the process joining Hall of Famer Arnie Herber as the only Green Bay quarterbacks to lead the NFL in touchdown passes in three different seasons (Herber did it in 1932, '34 and '36)...In 1998, Favre will be attempting to join Johnny Unitas (1957-60) as the only quarterbacks in the NFL's long history to lead the league in touchdown passes four straight seasons...Became just the fourth quarterback in league annals to post six consecutive 3,000-yard seasons, his 3,867-yard production enabling him to join Marino (9 straight, 1984-92); Elway (7, 1985-91) and Boomer Esiason (6, 1985-90) in a highly exclusive fraternity...Has more yards passing (16,061) over the last four seasons than any other NFL quarterback...Holds the fourth-best career passing percentage, 61.48%, in league history...Also an indomitable competitor and acknowledged team leader, he has led Green Bay to six straight winning seasons, five consecutive berths in the NFL playoffs (a feat unprecedented in the team's rich postseason history), three straight NFC Central Division titles, three consecutive NFC Championship Games and to back-to-back Super Bowl appearances, including a 35-21 victory over New England in SB XXXI, the Packers' first Super Bowl triumph in 29 years...Favre last year became only the seventh player in NFL history to pass for more than 3,000 yards in the postseason, swelling his career total to 3,098 yards for 13 playoff appearances...In so doing, he joined Joe Montana (5,772 yards in 23 games), Elway (4,273 in 19 games), Jim Kelly (3,863 in 17 games), Terry Bradshaw (3,833 in 19 games), Marino (3,741 in 14 games) and Troy Aikman (3,372 in 14 games)...Favre, who with 23 has the sixth-most career TD passes in league playoff history, now has thrown for a touchdown in 9 consecutive playoff games and thus is tied with Elway (1984-89) for the fourth-longest such string in NFL postseason annals, ranking behind only Marino (13 games, 1983-95), Ken Stabler (10 games, 1973-77) and Montana (10 games, 1988-93)…The NFL's fifth-ranked all-time postseason passer (92.0), he is the possessor of virtually every significant passing

ON A TOUCHDOWN PASS PACE FOR ALL-TIME?

Packers quarterback Brett Favre, with 182 career touchdown passes, after only seven seasons already is tied for 32nd in NFL history and poised to crack the league's All-Time Top 20 in 1998. Should he continue to throw touchdown passes at his current rate – he has averaged 30.3 per season over his six years in Green Bay – he will make major inroads into NFL history (illustrated below) and could even rise to as high as third all-time within a span of only four more seasons. If he were to maintain his present pace through the life of his current contract (which runs through the year 2003), he would stand to be second all-time in NFL history, behind only Dan Marino.

MOST TOUCHDOWN PASSES – NFL – CAREER

1)	385	Dan Marino, Miami, 1983-97
	364	*(PROJECTED) Brett Favre, Atlanta-Green Bay, 1991-2003*
2)	342	Fran Tarkenton, Minnesota-N.Y. Giants 1961-78
	334	*(PROJECTED) Brett Favre, Atlanta-Green Bay, 1991-2002*
	303	*(PROJECTED) Brett Favre, Atlanta-Green Bay, 1991-2001*
3)	290	Johnny Unitas, Baltimore-San Diego, 1956-73
4)	279	Warren Moon, Houston-Minnesota-Seattle, 1984-97
5)	278	John Elway, Denver, 1983-97
6)	273	Joe Montana, San Francisco-Kansas City, 1979-94
	273	*(PROJECTED) Brett Favre, Atlanta-Green Bay, 1991-2000*
7)	261	Dave Krieg, Seattle-Kansas City-Detroit-Arizona-Chicago-Tennessee, 1980-97
8)	255	Sonny Jurgensen, Philadelphia-Washington, 1957-74
9)	254	Dan Fouts, San Diego, 1973-87
10)	247	Boomer Esiason, Cincinnati-N.Y. Jets-Arizona, 1984-97
11)	244	John Hadl, San Diego-L.A. Rams-Green Bay-Houston, 1962-77
	243	*(PROJECTED) Brett Favre, Atlanta-Green Bay, 1991-99*
12)	242	Y.A. Tittle, Baltimore-San Franciso-N.Y. Giants, 1950-64
13)	239	Len Dawson, Pittsburgh-Cleveland-Dallas Texans-Kansas City, 1957-75
14)	237	Jim Kelly, Buffalo, 1986-96
15)	236	George Blanda, Chicago Bears-Baltimore-Houston-Oakland, 1949-75
16)	214	John Brodie, San Francisco, 1957-73
17)	212	Terry Bradshaw, Pittsburgh, 1970-83
	212	*(PROJECTED) Brett Favre, Atlanta-Green Bay, 1991-98*
18)	209	Jim Hart, St. Louis-Washington, 1966-84
19)	203	Jim Everett, L.A. Rams-New Orleans-San Diego, 1986-97
20)	201	Roman Gabriel, L.A. Rams-Philadelphia, 1962-77
21)	199	Phil Simms, N.Y. Giants, 1979-83
22)	197	Ken Anderson, Cincinnati, 1971-86
23)	196	Bobby Layne, Chicago Bears-N.Y. Bulldogs-Detroit-Pittsburgh, 1948-62
	196	Joe Ferguson, Buffalo-Detroit-Tampa Bay-Indianapolis, 1973-90
	196	Norm Snead, Washington-Philadelphia-Minnesota-N.Y. Giants-San Francisco, 1961-76
26)	194	Ken Stabler, Oakland-Houston-New Orleans, 1970-84
27)	193	Steve DeBerg, San Francisco-Denver-Tampa Bay-Kansas City-Miami, 1978-93
	193	Steve Young, Tampa Bay-San Francisco, 1985-97
29)	192	Bob Griese, Miami, 1967-80
30)	186	Sammy Baugh, Washington, 1937-52
31)	183	Craig Morton, Dallas-N.Y. Giants-Denver, 1965-82
32)	182	Steve Grogan, New England, 1975-90
	182	BRETT FAVRE, Atlanta-Green Bay, 1991-97

 **THE PLAYERS**

record in the Packers' postseason annals, having extended five team, career playoff records in '97: *Most Passes Completed (career)* – 250; *Most Passes Attempted (career)* – 414; *Most Yards Gained on Passes (career)* – 3,098; *Most Touchdown Passes (career)* – 23; and *Most Consecutive Games, Throwing Touchdown Pass* – 9…Is now tied with six teammates for the Green Bay postseason record for most career games played (13), each having passed the previous record-holder, Ray Nitschke (11) during the '97 playoffs…Blessed, additionally, with remarkable durability, he has started 93 consecutive regular-season games – the longest active streak among current NFL quarterbacks by nearly three full seasons (Tampa Bay's Trent Dilfer is second with 48), as well as the longest current string by a Green Bay player…Has the opportunity entering the 1998 season to become just the third quarterback since the 1970 AFL-NFL merger to make 100-or-more consecutive regular-season starts, a milestone he would reach in the Packers' seventh game, Oct. 25 vs. Baltimore; should he remain healthy enough to do so, he would join two quarterbacks from the 1970s and '80s in this durability club – Philadelphia's Ron Jaworski (116) and Buffalo's Joe Ferguson (107)…His starting streak, currently the fourth-longest since 1970, extends to 106 consecutive games with the inclusion of 13 straight postseason appearances over the past five seasons…In the process, he has compiled a glittering 63-30 regular-season record as a starter, a .677 percentage that is second only to the .700 mark of Steve Bono (28-12) among the NFL's active quarterbacks with 20-or-more starts entering the 1998 season…Possessor of one of the most potent and accurate passing arms in pro football history, Favre has attempted and completed more passes (1,971 of 3,206) for more touchdowns (182) than any other passer in Packers history…He also is the holder of the club lifetime mark for passing percentage (61.57)…Overall, he owns 17 Packers passing records, five of which were added in 1997: *Most Passes Completed (career)* – 1,971; *Most Passes Attempted (career)* – 3,206; *Most Games, 300 Yards Passing (career)* – 16; *Most Touchdown Passes (career)* – 182; and *Most Consecutive Seasons Leading League, Touchdown Passes* – 3…Figures to surpass, this season, the only significant Packers career standard he does not own – for passing yards (24,718), now held by Bart Starr…Favre enters the 1998 season within ready range (2,127 yards) of the record with 22,591 yards…Has an exceptional ratio (better than 3-to-1) of touchdown passes to interceptions over his past 39 regular-season games (95 TD passes compared to 31 INTs)…Also has thrown at least one touchdown pass in 82 of his 93 career regular-season starts with the Packers, failing to do so in only three games since the start of the 1995 season…With two such efforts in '97, he now has 12 career games with four-or-more touchdown passes, fourth-highest in NFL history, behind only Marino (20), Unitas (17) and George Blanda (13)…Since the start of the '95 season, he has thrown three-or-more touchdown passes in 21 regular-season games (in 30 games overall during his career)…Remarkably effective in cold weather, particularly for one born and reared in the south, he has forged a perfect 23-0 record (including five postseason victories) as a starter at home (19 in Green Bay, four in Milwaukee) when the game-time temperature is 35 degrees or below…In those 23 games, he has completed 453 of 701 passes (64.6%) for 5,338 yards and 50 touchdowns with only 13 interceptions for an overall passer rating of 103.7…In another testament to his exceptional leadership qualities, Favre has authored 11 come-from-behind victories in his pro career...**1997 HONORS:** Chosen as the starting quarterback for the NFC in the Pro Bowl for the third consecutive year, though due to a lingering knee injury he did not play in the game for the first time...His selection marked the fifth time in his six Green Bay seasons (in 1992 and '93 as a reserve) that Favre has been named to NFL's all-star game...In addition to being named NFL 'Most Valuable Player' by *AP* for a third consecutive year, an honor he shared with Sanders, Favre also was a unanimous choice at quarterback across the board, being named at the position on every major All-Pro team, including *AP*, *Sports Illustrated, Pro Football Weekly, The Sporting News, College & Pro Football Newsweekly, Football Digest* and *USA Today*...Named All-NFC by *Pro Football Weekly* and *Football News*...His preeminence at his position was further underscored when he was honored as 'Professional Quarterback of the Year' for the third consecutive year by the National Quarterback Club (June 4)...**1997:** Started all 16 games for the fifth straight season and finished third in the NFC with a 92.6 passer rating, based on 304 completions in 513 attempts for 3,867 yards and 35 touchdowns, with 16 interceptions...Was especially effective in the 'Red Zone' (inside the opponents' 20-yard line)...During the regular season, he threw 24 touchdown passes – without an interception – while completing 46 of 79 passes for 341 yards and a passer rating of 108.2...Including the '97 postseason, he completed 52 of 94 attempts for 392 yards and 27 touchdowns – without an interception – in the 'Red Zone,' a passer rating of 105.1...Also led the NFC in completions (304) and passing yards (3,867), finishing second in the league as a whole to Oakland's Jeff George (3,917) in the latter...Closed out the regular season with a team-record 182 career TD passes, having eclipsed the previous mark of 152 – set by Starr over a 16-year career – in the fourth game of just his sixth season (vs. Minnesota Sept. 21)...Also became the second-fastest player in NFL history to get to 150 career TD passes, reaching that milestone in his 84th career game, a rate bettered only by Marino (62 games), and second-fastest to throw for 20,000 career yards when he accomplished the feat in 86 games (behind only Marino's 74 games)...In the Packers' 16 regular-season games, he threw at least 2 touchdown passes in 11 games and 3-or-more in six contests...Finished as Green Bay's second-leading rusher with 187 yards and 1 TD on 58 carries...Was the only player in the league to have thrown every one of his team's passes until the regular-season finale vs. Buffalo (Dec. 20), when he gave way to Bono after leading the Packers to a 21-0 halftime advantage...Escorted the Packers to a 45-17 triumph over long-time nemesis, the Dallas Cowboys (Nov. 23), as he threw 4 touchdown passes, completing 22 of 35 passes for

SPEEDING TO A SPECIAL PLACE IN NFL HISTORY

FASTEST QUARTERBACKS TO 200 CAREER TOUCHDOWN PASSES – NFL HISTORY

89 games	Dan Marino, Miami 1983-89
*97 games	BRETT FAVRE, Atlanta 1991; Green Bay 1992-97
121 games	Johnny Unitas, Baltimore 1956-65
132 games	Jim Kelly, Buffalo 1986-94
135 games	Dave Krieg, Seattle 1980-91; Kansas City 1992
137 games	Fran Tarkenton, Minnesota 1961-66; N.Y. Giants 1967-70
143 games	Joe Montana, San Francisco 1979-89
	Dan Fouts, San Diego 1973-84

enters 1998 season 18 touchdown passes shy of 200 career touchdown passes

FASTEST QUARTERBACKS TO 150 CAREER TOUCHDOWN PASSES – NFL HISTORY

62 games	Dan Marino, Miami 1983-87
84 games	BRETT FAVRE, Atlanta 1991; Green Bay 1992-97
87 games	Johnny Unitas, Baltimore 1956-63
90 games	Dave Krieg, Seattle 1980-89

FASTEST QUARTERBACKS TO 100 CAREER TOUCHDOWN PASSES – NFL HISTORY

44 games	Dan Marino, Miami 1983-86
53 games	Johnny Unitas, Baltimore 1956-60
62 games	BRETT FAVRE, Atlanta 1991; Green Bay 1992-95
65 games	Dave Krieg, Seattle 1980-86
	Jim Everett, L.A. Rams 1986-90

 **THE PLAYERS**

203 yards, with only 1 INT...Earlier turned in his best statistical effort of the season in a losing venture at Indianapolis (Nov. 16), throwing for a season-high 363 yards (fourth-highest total of his career) and 3 touchdowns, completing 18 of 25 passes with 2 INTs for a passer rating of 120.4...His 14.52-yard average

DOMINATING HIS ERA IN THE TOUCHDOWN PASS CATEGORY

MOST 30-PLUS TOUCHDOWN PASS SEASONS – NFL HISTORY
4	Dan Marino, Miami 1984-86, 1994
	BRETT FAVRE, Green Bay 1994-97
2	Sonny Jurgensen, Philadelphia 1961, Washington 1967
	Y.A. Tittle, N.Y. Giants 1962-63
	Daryle Lamonica, Oakland 1967, 1969
	Dan Fouts, San Diego 1980-81
	Steve Bartkowski, Atlanta 1980-81
	Warren Moon, Houston 1990, Minnesota 1995

MOST CONSECUTIVE SEASONS LEADING NFL IN TOUCHDOWN PASSES – NFL HISTORY
4	Johnny Unitas, Baltimore 1957-60
3	Dan Marino, Miami 1984-86
	Steve Young, San Francisco 1992-94
	BRETT FAVRE, Green Bay 1995-97
2	Cecil Isbell, Green Bay 1941-42
	Sid Luckman, Chicago Bears 1945-46
	Tobin Rote, Green Bay 1955-56
	Y.A. Tittle, N.Y. Giants 1962-63
	Dan Fouts, San Diego 1981-82
	Jim Everett, L.A. Rams 1988-89

BEST FOUR-SEASON SPAN OF TOUCHDOWN PASSES IN A CAREER – NFL HISTORY
148	Dan Marino, Miami 1984-87
145	BRETT FAVRE, Green Bay 1994-97
111	George Blanda, Houston 1960-63
111	Daryle Lamonica, Oakland 1967-70
111	Dan Fouts, San Diego 1978-81

MOST TOUCHDOWN PASSES – NFL – SEASON
48	Dan Marino, Miami, 1984
44	Dan Marino, Miami, 1986
39	BRETT FAVRE, Green Bay, 1996
38	BRETT FAVRE, Green Bay, 1995
36	George Blanda, Houston, 1961
	Y.A. Tittle, N.Y. Giants, 1963
35	Steve Young, San Francisco, 1994
	BRETT FAVRE, Green Bay, 1997

MOST GAMES, FOUR-OR-MORE TOUCHDOWN PASSES – NFL – CAREER
20	Dan Marino, Miami 1983-97
17	Johnny Unitas, Baltimore 1958-72; San Diego 1973
13	George Blanda, Chicago Bears 1949, 1950-58; Baltimore 1950; Houston 1960-66; Oakland 1967-75
12	Sonny Jurgensen, Philadelphia 1957-63; Washington 1964-74
	Fran Tarkenton, Minnesota 1961-66, 1972-78; N.Y. Giants 1967-71
	Dan Fouts, San Diego 1973-87
	BRETT FAVRE, Atlanta 1991; Green Bay 1992-97

per pass play vs. the Colts, helped by a season-long 74-yard connection with Derrick Mayes, was the third-highest single-game average in team history, as well as the best by a Packers quarterback since 1958...A quick-strike artist against Indy, he led the Packers on six scoring drives – averaging 63.0 yards – of 4, 2, 5, 3, 11 and 3 plays...Helped Green Bay post a 17-7 win over St. Louis (Nov. 9) by throwing for 1 touchdown and rushing for another, while amassing 306 yards passing (his first 300-yard performance of the season)...Directed Packers to an impressive 27-11 win at Minnesota (Dec. 1), completing 15 of 29 passes for 196 yards and an 18-yard TD pass to Robert Brooks...Subsequently led the Packers to their third straight NFC Central Division title by orchestrating 17-6 win at Tampa Bay (Dec. 7), a day which saw him complete a season-high 25 passes in 33 attempts for 280 yards and 2 touchdowns...Closed out game with a passer rating of 108.1 against the Bucs as he completed a season-best 75.8 percent of his passes...Directed Packers to their third straight road victory a week later, presiding at a 31-10 conquest of Carolina (Dec. 14), completing 18 of 34 throws for 256 yards and 3 touchdowns with 1 interception...Led Green and Gold to 31-21 victory over Buffalo in finale, completing 12 of 18 attempts for 156 yards and 2 TDs for a season-high 130.8 passer rating...Threw 3 scoring passes to lead the Packers to a 24-23 win at Chicago (Oct. 12) while completing 19 of 35 passes...Had 3 TD passes for second straight game, this time at New England (Oct. 27), when he earned NFC 'Offensive Player of the Week' honors by completing 23 of 34 passes for 239 yards and an interception in leading the Packers to a 28-10 victory in a rematch of Super Bowl XXXI...Directed Green Bay to a 20-10 win over Detroit (Nov. 2), when he hit on 15 of 28 attempts for 181 yards and 1 touchdown, with 1 INT...Maneuvered Green Bay to pivotal win over previously unbeaten Tampa Bay (Oct. 5) when he completed 21 of 31 passes for 191 yards and 2 touchdowns – without an interception...Tied the team record and his career high when he threw 5 touchdown passes in leading the Packers to 38-32 win over Minnesota (Sept. 21), earning Miller Lite 'Player of the Week' honors in the process...Broke Starr's club mark for career touchdown passes when he found Antonio Freeman from 28 yards out with 10:51 remaining in the second quarter of Vikings contest...His 5 scoring throws represented the single-game high by an NFC quarterback during the 1997 season...Overall, completed 18 of 31 passes for 266 yards with 2 INTs against the Vikings...Led Packers to 38-24 victory over Chicago (Sept. 1) in season opener as he threw for 226 yards and 2 TDs, completing 15 of 22 passes with 1 interception...Orchestrated 23-18 win over Miami (Sept. 14) as he completed 24 of 37 attempts for 253 yards and 2 TDs, throwing to seven different receivers in the process...Threw for 279 yards at Philadelphia (Sept. 7), completing 19 of 41 attempts, with 1 interception...Did not throw a touchdown pass against the Eagles, marking the first time in 13 regular-season games he did not post a scoring pass, dating back to Oct. 27 of the 1996 season vs. Tampa Bay...Rebounded to throw for at least one score in each of the final 14 games...Passed for 295 yards at Detroit (Sept. 28), completing 22 of a season-high 43 passes, with 1 TD and 3 INTs (his first 3-interception game since Oct. 29, 1995, at Detroit)...**1997 PLAYOFFS:** Completing 56 of 97 passes for 668 yards and 5 touchdowns, with just 3 interceptions, Favre directed Green Bay through the playoffs to its second successive appearance in the NFL's ultimate game, the Super Bowl...Completed 15 of 28 passes for 190 yards and 1 touchdown, with 2 interceptions, in leading Green Bay past Tampa Bay, 21-7, in the Packers' first postseason test – a divisional playoff game in Lambeau Field (Jan. 4)...The TD strike – a three-yarder to tight end Mark Chmura, staked the Packers to a 7-0 advantage in the first quarter, a lead they never relinquished; he later added his first career two-point conversion against the Bucs...A masterful mudder, the resourceful field general hit on 16 of 27 attempts for 222 yards and 1 TD – without an interception – in escorting the Green and Gold to a decisive, 23-10 victory over the 49ers in the NFC Championship Game at San Francisco (Jan. 11), triggering the Packers' return to the Super Bowl...Threw 3 TD passes against Denver in SB XXXII at San Diego's Qualcomm Stadium (Jan. 25), tying his own postseason best, but it wasn't enough to carry the day against the Broncos, who prevailed 31-24...Completed 25 of 42 passes for 256 yards, with 1 INT, vs. Denver...Two of his touchdowns (22 and 13 yards) went to his split end, Freeman, and another (a six-yarder) to Chmura for the Packers' other touchdown...Represented Packers throughout the postseason as one of team's six playoff captains...**1996 HONORS:** Named as the starting quarterback for the NFC in the Pro Bowl for the second straight year...In addition to being voted as the NFL's 'Most Valuable Player' by AP for the second year in a row, he earned the same award from the Professional Football Writers of America and PFW...Earned 'Player of the Year' honors from TSN, Football Digest, Miller Lite, the Maxwell Club, the Touchdown Club of Columbus and the Victor Awards...Selected as Pro Football 'Performer of the Year' by ESPN's ESPY Awards...Named league 'Offensive Player of the Year' by PFW, College & Pro Football Newsweekly and the Newspaper Enterprise Association...Selected NFC 'Player of the Year' by Football News...Also chosen NFC 'Offensive Player of the Year' by United Press International and the

FAVRE ALREADY IS AMONG THE NFL'S ALL-TIME BEST

HIGHEST PASSER RATING – NFL – CAREER (MINIMUM 1,500 ATTEMPTS)

97.0	Steve Young, Tampa Bay 1985-86; San Francisco 1987-97
92.3	Joe Montana, San Francisco 1979-90, 1992; Kansas City 1993-94
89.3	BRETT FAVRE, Atlanta 1991; Green Bay 1992-97
87.8	Dan Marino, Miami 1983-97
84.4	Jim Kelly, Buffalo 1986-96

BEST PASSING EFFICIENCY – NFL – CAREER (MINIMUM 1,500 ATTEMPTS)

64.83%	Steve Young, Tampa Bay 1985-86; San Francisco 1987-96 (2,300-3,548)
63.24%	Joe Montana, San Francisco 1979-90, 1992; Kansas City 1993-94 (3,409-5,391)
62.01%	Troy Aikman, Dallas 1989-97 (2,292-3,696)
61.48%	BRETT FAVRE, Atlanta 1991; Green Bay 1992-97 (1,971-3,206)
60.14%	Jim Kelly, Buffalo 1986-96 (2,874-4,779)

MOST CONSECUTIVE 3,000-YARD PASSING SEASONS – NFL HISTORY

9	Dan Marino, Miami, 1984-92
7	John Elway, Denver, 1985-91
6	Boomer Esiason, Cincinnati, 1985-90
	BRETT FAVRE, Green Bay 1992-97

Kansas City Committee of 101...Tabbed as NFL 'Quarterback of the Year' by the National Quarterback Club and Footaction...Garnered first-team All-Pro honors from *AP, College & Pro Football Newsweekly, Football Digest, PFW/PFWA, TSN, SI* and *USA Today*...Earned 'All-NFC' honors from *Football News* and *UPI*...Named 'Newsmaker of the Year' by the Wisconsin Newspaper Association, an inaugural award given out to honor someone whose "spirit of service is demonstrated through acts which reflect positively on Wisconsin"...**1996:** In throwing for 39 touchdowns, one more than he had in 1995, set NFC and Green Bay records for most touchdown passes in a season for the second straight year...It ranks as the third-highest single-season total in NFL history (behind Marino's 48 in 1984 and 44 in '86)...Starting all 16 games for the fourth straight season, he also led the NFL in touchdown passes for the second year in a row, thus becoming only the third Packer (Cecil Isbell in 1941-42 and Tobin Rote in 1955-56) and 10th player in NFL annals to lead the league in TD passes in consecutive seasons...Threw for an NFC-best 3,899 yards, becoming only the sixth passer in NFL history to throw for 3,000 yards in five consecutive seasons...In the process tied Joe Namath for the honor of being the third-fastest player in league annals to reach 15,000 yards passing, scaling that plateau in his 66th game (Marino was the fastest, turning the trick in 56 games, followed by Jim Everett, who did it in 64 games)...At his best in key situations, Favre ranked second in the NFC in both fourth-quarter passing (96.2 rating) and third-down passing (93.6), including a conference-high 12 touchdown passes on third down...Authored five 4-touchdown games in 1996, the second-highest single-season total in NFL history, behind only the 6 of Marino in 1984 (Marino also had 5 in 1986)...Also was Green Bay's third-leading rusher with 136 yards and 2 touchdowns on 49 carries and the only NFL player (among qualifiers) to register a perfect 100 percent success rate on third-and-one rushing, converting all 8 of his attempts...Left each of the Packers' first three games – all blowout victories – early...Was named NFC 'Offensive Player of the Week' for his 4-touchdown performance in season opener at Tampa Bay (Sept. 1) as he completed 20 of 27 passes (74.1%) for 247 yards, with no interceptions, for single-game season bests in passer rating (141.5) and completion percentage...Passed for 3 touchdowns in 39-13 win over Philadelphia (Sept. 9) and for 231 yards and 3 TDs in 42-10 win over San Diego (Sept. 15)...Threw for 2 touchdowns at Minnesota (Sept. 22) and for 4 TDs at Seattle (Sept. 29), completing 20 of 34 passes for 209 yards vs. Seahawks...Named NFC 'Offensive Player of the Month' for September, passing for 16 TDs in leading the Packers to a 4-1 record during the month...Tied his season best for a second time by firing 4 TD passes at Chicago on Oct. 6, including a 50-yard 'Hail Mary' throw to Freeman for a score on the last play of the first half, leading Green Bay to a 37-6 win while completing 18 of 27 passes for 246 yards...Amassed 395 passing yards, the second-highest total of his career and the fourth-highest in Packers history, against the 49ers the following week (Oct. 14) in escorting Green Bay to a 23-20 victory in overtime...Led Packers on three scoring drives in second half of Niners contest which ended with field goals in the fourth quarter and overtime, resulting in the 11th game-winning comeback of his career...Completed 28 of a team-record 61 passes, including a 59-yard TD throw to Don Beebe, with 2 interceptions...Posted 178 passing yards in win over Tampa Bay (Oct. 27), but failed to throw a touchdown pass for the first time in 15 regular-season games (his last previous game without a TD pass had come nearly one year earlier – on Nov. 5, 1995 at Minnesota)...Equaled his season high with 4 TD passes in leading Packers to 28-18 victory over Detroit (Nov. 3) – three to his new pair of starting wide receivers, Beebe and Terry Mickens...Threw for 314 yards and 2 touchdowns at Kansas City (Nov. 10), completing 27 of 49 passes as he moved past Dickey (132) and into sole possession of second place on the team's career touchdown pass list...Directed Green Bay to key win at St. Louis (Nov. 24), ending two-game losing streak, throwing 2 touchdown passes while completing 25 of 38 passes for 192 yards...Ran for 1 TD and passed for another in triggering a 28-17 repeat victory over Chicago (Dec. 1)...Threw for 4 touchdowns, including 3 to Freeman, against the NFL's then-No. 1 ranked defense in the Packers' 41-6 triumph over Denver (Dec. 8), completing 20 of 38 attempts for 280 yards...Completed 16 of 25 passes for 240 yards and 1 touchdown, with 1 interception, in 31-3 win at Detroit (Dec. 15)...Rounded out the regular season by capturing NFC 'Offensive Player of the Week' honors for the second time in '96 as he threw for 3 TDs against Minnesota in finale (Dec. 22), completing 15 of 23 passes for 202 yards before leaving the game early in the fourth quarter of 38-10 triumph...**1996 PLAYOFFS:** Along with center Frank Winters, he represented the offense as one of the playoff captains named by the team...Under control and on target throughout the playoffs, Favre set or tied no fewer than four club records during the postseason while completing 44 of 71 passes, a 62.0 percentage, for 617 yards and 5 touchdowns – with

AT THE TOP OF HIS GAME IN THE PLAYOFFS

HIGHEST PASSER RATING – NFL POSTSEASON – CAREER (MINIMUM 150 ATTEMPTS)

104.8	Bart Starr, Green Bay, 10 games
96.0	Troy Aikman, Dallas, 14 games
95.6	Joe Montana, San Francisco-Kansas City, 23 games
93.5	Ken Anderson, Cincinnati, 6 games
92.0	BRETT FAVRE, Green Bay, 13 games

MOST YARDS PASSING – NFL POSTSEASON – CAREER

5,772	Joe Montana, San Francisco-Kansas City, 23 games
4,273	John Elway, Denver, 19 games
3,863	Jim Kelly, Buffalo, 17 games
3,833	Terry Bradshaw, Pittsburgh, 19 games
3,741	Dan Marino, Miami, 14 games
3,372	Troy Aikman, Dallas, 14 games
3,098	BRETT FAVRE, Green Bay, 13 games

MOST TOUCHDOWN PASSES – NFL POSTSEASON – CAREER

45	Joe Montana, San Francisco-Kansas City, 23 games
30	Terry Bradshaw, Pittsburgh, 19 games
29	Dan Marino, Miami, 14 games
24	Roger Staubach, Dallas, 20 games
	John Elway, Denver, 19 games
23	BRETT FAVRE, Green Bay, 13 games

MOST CONSECUTIVE GAMES WITH A TOUCHDOWN PASS – NFL POSTSEASON

13	Dan Marino, Miami, 1983-95
10	Ken Stabler, Oakland, 1973-77
	Joe Montana, San Francisco-Kansas City, 1988-93
9	John Elway, Denver, 1984-89
	BRETT FAVRE, Green Bay, 1995-97 (current)

only 1 interception – for a passer rating of 107.5...Playing within himself in horrific weather conditions vs. San Francisco in the Packers' 35-14 divisional playoff win (Jan. 4), he completed 11 of 15 passes for 79 yards and 1 TD...Under frigid but more playable conditions, he threw for 292 yards on 19-of-29 passing in the NFC Championship Game at Lambeau Field a week later (Jan. 12), including state-of-the-art touchdown tosses to Dorsey Levens (29 yards) and Freeman (six yards)...Two weeks later (Jan. 26) in the NFL's championship contest, he launched the day's scoring on a 54-yard touchdown pass to wideout Andre Rison on his first throw of the game, coming on a called audible, and later found Freeman with a Super Bowl-record, 81-yard scoring strike where he perfectly lofted the ball over a Pats defender...In total, Favre frisked New England's vaunted defense for 246 yards, completing 14 of 27 attempts without an interception, to trigger a 35-21 triumph in Super Bowl XXXI at the Louisiana Superdome in New Orleans, returning the Lombardi Trophy to Green Bay for the first time in 29 years...It had to have been an especially magic moment for Favre, who had disclosed off-the-field problems in May, then stated upon returning from a 45-day stay in the Menninger Clinic at Topeka, Kan., "You know, I'm going to beat thing. I'm going to win a Super Bowl. And all I can tell people if they don't believe me is, 'Just bet against me.'"...**1995 HONORS:** Selected to start in the Pro Bowl for the initial time after two appearances as a reserve...Earned NFL 'Most Valuable Player' awards from *AP*, PFWA, *PFW* and *SI*...Named 'Player of the Year' by *TSN*, *Football Digest*, Miller Lite, the Maxwell Club and the Touchdown Club of Columbus...Selected as Pro Football 'Performer of the Year' by ESPN's ESPY Awards...Named league 'Offensive Player of the Year' by *AP*, *PFW*, *College & Pro Football Newsweekly* and NEA...Selected NFC 'Player of the Year' by *Football News* and the Touchdown Club of Columbus...Also named NFC 'Offensive Player of the Year' by *UPI* and the Kansas City Committee of 101...Received first-team All-Pro honors from *AP*, *College & Pro Football Newsweekly*, *Football Digest*, PFW/PFWA, *TSN*, *SI* and *USA Today*...Garnered 'All-NFC' honors from *Football News* and *UPI*...Presented NFL 'Quarterback of the Year' honors by the National Quarterback Club...Lauded as 'Wisconsin Sports Person of the Year' by Wisconsin Sports Authority/Milwaukee Pen & Mike Club...**1995:** Became only the third 4,000-yard passer in team history after a 308-yard performance at New Orleans (Dec. 16)...Finished the season with NFL-best 4,413 passing yards, second-highest total in team history and only 45 yards shy of Dickey's team record 4,458 (1983)...Earlier, became the first player in team history to post four 3,000-yard passing seasons, achieved in four consecutive seasons...Established a new team record with seven 300-yard passing games, breaking Don Majkowski's previous record of six in 1989...Led the NFC (and was second in the NFL) with a 99.5 passer rating – only the Colts' Jim Harbaugh with a 100.7 rating had better...Paced the NFC in third-down passing with a 103.8 passer rating...Threw 3-or-more TD passes in seven games and for at least 4 TD passes in three games...Had thrown at least 1 touchdown pass in 17 straight games dating back to Week 8 of '94 – the second-longest string in club annals, behind only the 22 of Isbell (1941-42) – until streak was snapped at Minnesota (Nov. 5)...Also had thrown at least 2 touchdown passes in 12 consecutive games, equaling the NFL record also held by Unitas (1959), Don Meredith (1965-66) and Marino (1986-87), until the string ended at Dallas (Oct. 8)...Led the league in completions of 20-or-more yards with 59, he also had the NFL's highest completion percentage inside the 'Red Zone' (66.2%)...Started all 16 games for third straight season, plus all three of the team's playoff contests...Rebounded from an ankle injury at Minnesota (Nov. 5) to complete 70.3 percent of his passes (166-236) in the ensuing seven games for 2,046 yards and 21 touchdowns, with only 2 interceptions – an imposing passer rating of 123.0...Tied for team lead with his career-best 3 rushing scores...Turned in gutty performance in leading Packers to their division-clinching, 24-19 victory over Pittsburgh (Dec. 24) when, despite having to stop twice during the game after getting the wind knocked out of him, he threw for 301 yards and 2 touchdowns...On one sequence, he was hit hard by three Steeler defenders while scrambling on a play; the Packers called a timeout and Favre, who coughed up blood on the sidelines during a break in the action, returned to throw a one-yard scoring pass to Chmura on the following play...Threw 4 TD passes – all in the first half – in the Packers' 34-23 win at New Orleans (Dec. 16)...Completed 21 of 38 passes for 308 yards against the Saints...Had 287 yards passing and 1 touchdown with 1 interception – completing 27 of 46 passes – in rematch at Tampa Bay (Dec. 10)...Threw his first interception in 126 attempts when the Bengals' Corey Sawyer picked off a pass late in the fourth quarter vs. Cincinnati (Dec. 3), but still led Packers to 24-10 win over the Bengals, throwing for 339 yards and 3 touchdowns while completing a season-high 31 passes (in 43 attempts)...Named NFC 'Offensive Player of the Month' for December, passing for 1,233 yards on 102 completions in 151 attempts with 10 TDs and only 2 INTs (109.0 passer rating) in leading Green Bay to three victories during the month...Had a stellar outing vs. Tampa Bay (Nov. 26), completing 16 of 24 passes for 267 yards and 3 TDs...Led the Packers to a tough road win at Cleveland (Nov. 19) when,

GREEN BAY PACKERS NAMED AS NFL 'MOST VALUABLE PLAYER'

Don Hutson, End	1941-42
Paul Hornung, Halfback	1961
Jim Taylor, Fullback	1962
Bart Starr, Quarterback	1966
BRETT FAVRE, Quarterback	1995-97

despite still being limited with an ankle injury, he passed for 3 touchdowns and ran for another...Completed 23 of 28 passes for 210 yards against Browns for a career-best 82.1 completion percentage...Had arguably his best performance as a professional in a rematch with Chicago (Nov. 12) when, not knowing until late in the week if he was even going to play due to a severely sprained ankle the week before, he threw for a career-high and team-record tying 5 touchdown passes to lead the Packers to a key 35-28 victory over the Bears...Subsequently was named NFC 'Offensive Player of the Week' (for the second time in four weeks) after completing 25 of 33 passes for 336 yards with no interceptions against Chicago, giving him a career-high single-game passer rating of 147.2...Had suffered a severely sprained left ankle late in second quarter of rematch at Minnesota one week earlier (Nov. 5) – an injury which later would require offseason surgery (Feb. 27, 1996) to remove several bone chips and one large spur...Left Vikings game for the remainder of the first half, then played three series in the second half before the injury hindered his play and he gave way to Ty Detmer...Completed 17 of 30 passes for 177 yards with 2 interceptions against Minnesota...Had a bittersweet outing in the Silverdome, throwing for 304 yards and 1 TD (a 77-yarder to Brooks) but was intercepted 3 times...Saluted as NFL's recipient of the 'Extra Effort Award' for the month of October...Earned his first-ever NFC 'Offensive Player of the Week' honor with an outstanding performance in initial game with Minnesota (Oct. 22), tying a then-career high with 4 touchdown passes in leading the Packers to a 38-21 win...Completed 22 of 43 passes for 295 yards without an interception against the Vikings...Led Packers to a win over Detroit (Oct. 15), when he threw for a season-best 342 yards and 2 TDs on 23-of-34 passing...Triggered a valiant comeback attempt at Dallas (Oct. 8), when he rushed for a career-high 2 TDs and threw for another score to rally the Packers from a 21-point, second-half deficit to within seven at 31-24 with 8:13 remaining in the game...Completed 21 of 41 passes for 295 yards vs. the Cowboys...Led the Packers to a win at Jacksonville (Sept. 24), passing for 202 yards and 2 TDs, completing 20 of 30 passes while rushing for 39 net yards, including a career-best 40-yard run...Had a solid game in win over the N.Y. Giants (Sept. 17) as he threw 2 TD passes and completed 14 of 25 attempts for 141 yards...Turned in outstanding performance at Chicago (Sept. 11), completing 21 of 37 passes for 312 yards and 3 TDs, including a team-record 99-yard TD pass to Brooks early in the second quarter – only the eighth time in NFL history that feat had been accomplished...Completed 29 of a season-high 51 passes for 299 yards and 2 TDs with 3 INTs in season opener vs. St. Louis Rams (Sept. 3)...**1995 PLAYOFFS:** Utilizing no fewer than nine receivers, Favre completed 24 of 35 passes for 199 yards and 3 touchdowns in leading the Packers to a 37-20 wild-card victory over Atlanta in Lambeau Field (Dec. 31), presiding over scoring drives of 85, 78 and 70 yards and throwing for 3 touchdowns in the process...He was even more precise in a divisional playoff at San Francisco the following week (Jan. 6), hitting on 21 of 28 passes (for a team postseason record completion percentage of 75.0) for 299 yards and 2 touchdowns – with no interceptions – in leading the Packers to a 27-17 triumph over the favored 49ers, defending Super Bowl champions...Named NFL 'Offensive Player of the Week' for performance vs. Niners...Completed 21 of 39 attempts for 307 yards and 3 touchdowns in the NFC Championship Game at Dallas (Jan. 14), the Packers' first such appearance since 1967, but it wasn't sufficient to carry the day, the Cowboys eventually prevailing, 38-27...Favre, who had not thrown an interception in two earlier '95 playoff appearances, was picked off twice...**1994:** Finished

MULTIPLE WINNERS OF *ASSOCIATED PRESS* NFL 'MOST VALUABLE PLAYER' AWARD

3	BRETT FAVRE, Green Bay	1995-97
2	Jim Brown, Cleveland	1957, 1965
2	Johnny Unitas, Baltimore	1964, 1967
2	Joe Montana, San Francisco	1989-90
2	Steve Young, San Francisco	1992, 1994

second in the NFL only to Steve Young of San Francisco's Super Bowl champion 49ers with a passer rating of 90.7...Ranked third in the NFC in passing yards with 3,882...In the process, he became only the second player in team history to throw for 3,000 yards in three different seasons...Also posted third-lowest interception percentage (2.4) in the NFC among qualifying passers...Ended season second in the NFL with 33 TD passes, which also represented a Green Bay record at the time, surpassing the 32 of Dickey in 1983...Set two other club records, his 363 completions eclipsing the previous mark of 353 by Majkowski in 1989, and closing out the season with a 3.24 career interception percentage, bettering Majkowski's 3.48 career mark...Ranked second in the NFC in passing attempts with 582 (17 shy of Majkowski's Packers single-season record of 599 in '89)...Was particularly effective over the last half of the season, throwing for 23 touchdowns over the last eight games and only 7 interceptions over the final nine games (his 14 interceptions overall were 10 fewer than he threw in 1993)...Started all 16 games plus both playoff contests...Named second-team All-Pro by *Football Digest*...Produced probably the Packers' biggest play of the year in the second-to-last game of the regular season...With Green Bay needing a victory to keep their playoff hopes alive, he engineered a come-from-behind, 67-yard drive in the final 1:58 against Atlanta (Dec. 18), capping the march with his diving, nine-yard TD run into the right corner of the end zone with only 14 seconds remaining in the game to give the Packers a 21-17 win...Completed 6 of 9 passes for 58 yards in that eleventh-hour drive...Completed 29 of 44 passes for 321 yards and 2 TDs overall against Falcons...Led Packers to a 34-19, playoff-clinching victory at Tampa Bay a week later (Dec. 24), completing 24 of 36 passes for 291 yards and 3 TDs (all to Sterling Sharpe)...Hit on 19 of 31 passes for 250 yards and 3 TDs in a 40-3 win over Chicago (Dec. 11)...Also had a 26-yard run on a scramble against the Bears...Had a big statistical day in a losing cause at Detroit (Dec. 4), completing 29 of 43 passes for season-high 366 yards and 3 touchdowns...Turned in excellent performance at Dallas (Nov. 24), throwing 4 touchdown passes while completing 27 of 40 passes – without an interception – for 257 yards against the NFL's then-No. 1 rated defense...Had 3 TD passes at Buffalo Nov. 20, completing 22 of 40 for 214 yards, with only 1 INT...Completed 20 of 28 passes for 183 yards and 2 TDs – without an interception – in leading Packers to 17-10 win over the Jets a week earlier...Escorted Packers to their second consecutive win vs. Detroit (Nov. 6), throwing 3 TD passes in a 38-30 victory at Milwaukee...Mounted one of his finest

FAVRE HAS ONLY ONE PACKERS CAREER PASSING RECORD LEFT TO ATTAIN

MOST YARDS PASSING – PACKERS – CAREER

24,718	Bart Starr, 1956-71 (16 seasons)
22,591	BRETT FAVRE, 1992-97 (6 seasons)
21,369	Lynn Dickey, 1976-77, 1979-85 (9 seasons)

MOST TOUCHDOWN PASSES – PACKERS – CAREER

182	BRETT FAVRE, 1992-97 (6 seasons)
152	Bart Starr, 1956-71 (16 seasons)
133	Lynn Dickey, 1976-77, 1979-85 (9 seasons)

MOST 300-YARD PASSING GAMES – PACKERS – CAREER

16	BRETT FAVRE, 1992-97 (6 seasons)
15	Lynn Dickey, 1976-77, 1979-85 (9 seasons)
9	Don Majkowski, 1987-92 (6 seasons)
5	Bart Starr, 1956-71 (16 seasons)

MOST PASSES COMPLETED – PACKERS – CAREER

1,971	BRETT FAVRE, 1992-97 (6 seasons)
1,808	Bart Starr, 1956-71 (16 seasons)
1,592	Lynn Dickey, 1976-77, 1979-85 (9 seasons)

MOST PASSES ATTEMPTED – PACKERS – CAREER

3,206	BRETT FAVRE, 1992-97 (6 seasons)
3,149	Bart Starr, 1956-71 (16 seasons)
2,831	Lynn Dickey, 1976-77, 1979-85 (9 seasons)

performances at Chicago on Oct. 31, running for 1 touchdown and throwing for another in a cold, cyclonic rainstorm...The former came late in the second quarter, when he rolled out to his right and raced 36 yards (diving over a Bear defender into the end zone) to give the Packers a 14-0 lead...Later, in the fourth quarter, he connected with Edgar Bennett for a 13-yard touchdown, raising the Packers' lead to 27-0...His 58 yards rushing against the Bears represented a career high...Had thrown a touchdown pass in nine straight games – the final three regular-season contests of '93 plus the first six games of '94 – until the streak was broken at Minnesota (Oct. 20) when he left the game after the first quarter with a severely bruised left hip...It was the first time since he became the starting quarterback early in 1992 that he had been forced to leave a game due to injury...Put together a similar nine-game string over the final nine games of the season, throwing for at least one score in each...Rallied Packers from a 14-point halftime deficit to a 24-17 win over the L.A. Rams (Oct. 9), completing 25 of 41 passes for 222 yards and 1 TD (an eight-yarder to Sharpe in the third quarter, cutting Rams' lead to 17-10)...Led offense on a go-ahead TD drive at New England (Oct. 2) when Green Bay drove 64 yards to score...Hit Sharpe for 17 yards on a fourth-and-10, found Ron Lewis for 38 yards two plays later, then scrambled for 11 yards on a third-and-10 to the N.E. 1, before a Reggie Cobb score...Completed 25 of 47 passes for 294 yards and 1 TD, with 2 interceptions, against the Patriots...Played one of the finest games of his career in 30-3 win over Tampa Bay (Sept. 25), earning Miller Lite 'NFL Player of the Week' honors as he completed 30 of 39 passes for 306 yards and 3 touchdowns, with no interceptions...Had a 37-yard scoring pass to Cobb at Philadelphia (Sept. 18) as he hit on 24 of 45 passes for 280 yards...Came together against Miami after a slow start (Sept. 11), completing 31 of 51 passes for 362 yards and 2 TDs...Completed 22 of 36 passes for 185 yards and 1 touchdown (a 14-yarder to Sharpe) in season-opening win over the Vikings (Sept. 4)...**1994 PLAYOFFS:** Played a key role in Packers' 16-12 wild-card playoff victory over Detroit in Green Bay's Lambeau Field (Dec. 31)...Moving the chains effectively during a tight defensive duel, he completed 23 of 38 passes for 262 yards – without an interception – mustering 18 first downs in a masterful "ball control" performance...Hit on 18 of 35 attempts for 211 yards, with 1 INT, in divisional playoff at Dallas a week later (Jan. 8)...**1993:** Started all 16 games – one of only seven NFL quarterbacks to do so...Became the most accurate career passer in Packers history, supplanting the legendary Starr...Finished the year eighth in the NFC with a 72.2 passer rating, completing 318 of 522 passes (60.9%) for 3,303 yards and 19 touchdowns, with 24 interceptions...Was first among all NFC passers (second in NFL) with 318 completions and his 19 TDs ranked third in the conference (fifth in the NFL)...His 3,303 passing yards were second in the NFC to Young (sixth in the NFL)...Played in the Pro Bowl as a reserve when the Giants' Phil Simms could not take part due to a shoulder problem...Completed 19 of 24 passes for 264 yards and 2 TDs, with 1 INT, to lead Packers 36-6 win over L.A. Rams in season opener (Sept. 5)...Scored game's only TD vs. Vikings (Sept. 26) as Packers took opening kickoff and marched 85 yards in 14 plays (8:55 elapsed), capped by his diving two-yard plunge to give Green Bay the early lead...Turned in strong performance vs. Denver (Oct. 10), completing 20 of 32 passes for 235 yards and 1 TD (a 66-yarder to TE Jackie Harris)...Had highly productive outing at Tampa Bay (Oct. 24) when he completed 20 of 35 passes for 268 yards and a season-high 4 touchdowns (all of the latter to Sharpe), escorting Packers to 37-14 win...Led Packers to 17-3 victory over Chicago Bears (Oct. 31), connecting on 15 of 24 passes for 136 yards and 1 TD (a 21-yarder to Sharpe)...Staged gritty performance in leading Packers to 19-17, come-from-behind victory over Saints in New Orleans (Nov. 14)...Came up with the biggest play of the season to that point when, on a second-and-20 play from the Packers' 27-yard line with 52 seconds left and the Packers down 17-16, he rolled out of the pocket to his left and hit Sharpe with a 54-yard strike that led to a game-winning field goal...Closed out day with 18 completions in 32 attempts for 150 yards and 1 TD...Directed Packers to 26-17 win over Detroit (Nov. 21), throwing for 259 yards (24 of 33 – for a season-best 72.7%)...Led Packers to a come-from-behind, 13-10 win over Tampa Bay (Nov. 28) when he engineered a 15-play, 75-yard scoring drive late in the fourth quarter, capping it with a two-yard TD pass to Sharpe with 1:16 left to produce the victory...On the play previous to his scoring strike to Sharpe he had suffered a deep thigh bruise on a one-yard rollout to the right sideline, but, even though he was limping noticeably, threw the game-winner on the next play...Finished the Bucs contest with 23 completions in 36 attempts for 159 yards and 1 TD, with no INTs...Set a Green Bay single-game record with 36 completions at Chicago (Dec. 5), breaking the previous record of 35 set by Dickey in 1980...Also threw for a career-high 402 yards vs. Bears – the third-most in team history (behind Dickey's 418 vs. Tampa Bay in 1980 and Don Horn's 410 vs. the Cardinals in 1969)...It also represented the first 300- and 400-yard passing games of Favre's career...Also threw for 2 TDs vs. Bears (an 18-yarder to Sharpe and a 22-yarder to Mark Clayton)...Led Packers to 20-13 win at San Diego (Dec. 12), completing 13 of 23 passes for 146 yards...Turned in solid outing vs. Raiders (Dec. 26) in -22 degree wind chill, passing for 190 yards and 1 TD (a 23-yarder to Sharpe in the third quarter) on 14 completions in 28 attempts, with no INTs...Completed 23 of 37 passes for 190 yards and 1 TD (a 39-yarder to Bennett) in season-ending loss to Detroit (Jan. 2), but also threw a career-high 4 interceptions...**1993 PLAYOFFS:** Pulled off one of the

BRETT FAVRE'S PERFECT RECORD AT HOME IN COLD WEATHER

Packers quarterback Brett Favre, a Mississippi native, holds a perfect 23-0 record at home (18-0 regular season, 5-0 playoffs) when the game-time temperature is 35° or below – a complete listing of those games can be found below. He lost his only road contest with sub-35° temperatures, a 1996 game at Kansas City. Including slightly balmier weather, he is 34-5 in all games (29-5 regular season, 5-0 playoffs) when temperatures are 45° or less.

AT HOME

1992

Date	Opponent		W/L	A-C-Yds.-Pct.-TD-Int.-Rating
Nov. 15	Philadelphia (Milw.)	28°, partly sunny	W	33-23-275-69.7-2-2-89.8
Nov. 29	Tampa Bay (Milw.)	32°, partly sunny	W	41-26-223-63.4-1-0-85.7
Dec. 6	Detroit (Milw.)	26°, light snow	W	19-15-214-78.9-3-0-153.2
Dec. 20	L.A. Rams	8°, sunny	W	23-14-188-60.9-2-1-97.7
1993				
Nov. 28	Tampa Bay	29°, partly cloudy	W	36-23-159-63.9-1-0-83.0
Dec. 26	L.A. Raiders	0°, sunny	W	28-14-190-50.0-1-0-83.9
1994				
Dec. 11	Chicago	15°, sunny	W	31-19-250-61.3-3-1-105.6
Dec. 18	Atlanta (Milw.)	33°, sunny	W	44-29-321-65.9-2-1-93.1
*Dec. 31	Detroit	33°, partly cloudy	W	38-23-262-60.5-0-0-81.3
1995				
Nov. 12	Chicago	22°, cloudy	W	33-25-336-75.8-5-0-147.2
Nov. 26	Tampa Bay	34°, cloudy	W	24-16-267-66.7-3-0-143.6
Dec. 3	Cincinnati	32°, partly cloudy	W	43-31-339-72.1-3-1-108.6
Dec. 24	Pittsburgh	24°, cloudy	W	32-23-301-71.9-2-0-122.0
*Dec. 31	Atlanta	30°, light fog	W	35-24-199-68.6-3-0-111.5
1996				
Dec. 1	Chicago	29°, flurries	W	27-19-231-70.4-1-0-108.7
Dec. 8	Denver	31°, mostly cloudy	W	38-20-280-52.6-4-2-89.8
Dec. 22	Minnesota	31°, overcast	W	23-15-202-65.2-3-0-132.6
*Jan. 4	San Francisco	34°, rain	W	15-11-79-73.3-1-0-107.4
*Jan. 12	Carolina	3°, sunny	W	29-19-292-65.5-2-1-107.3
1997				
Nov. 2	Detroit	35°, cloudy	W	28-15-181-53.6-1-1-70.7
Nov. 23	Dallas	22°, partly cloudy	W	35-22-203-62.9-4-1-104.8
Dec. 20	Buffalo	31°, cloudy	W	18-12-156-66.7-2-0-130.8
*Jan. 4	Tampa Bay	28°, cloudy	W	28-15-190-53.6-1-2-57.1
Totals				**701-453-5,338-64.6-50-13-103.7**

ON THE ROAD

1996

Date	Opponent		W/L	A-C-Yds.-Pct.-TD-Int.-Rating
Nov. 10	at Kansas City	30°, overcast	L	49-27-314-55.1-2-1-79.8

*playoff game

BRETT FAVRE'S 11 GAME-WINNING COMEBACKS
(occasions where he has brought team back from a fourth-quarter deficit or tie to win the game)

1992

Game		Deficit	Final	
Sept. 20	Cincinnati	3-17	24-23	
Nov. 15	Philadelphia	21-24	27-24	
Nov. 29	Tampa Bay	12-14	19-14	

1993

Nov. 14	at New Orleans	16-17	19-17	
Nov. 21	Detroit	16-17	26-17	
Nov. 28	Tampa Bay	6-10	13-10	
Jan. 8	at Detroit	21-24	28-24	(postseason)

1994

Oct. 9	L.A. Rams	17-17	24-17	
Dec. 18	Atlanta	14-17	21-17	

1995

Nov. 12	Chicago	28-28	35-28	

1996

Oct. 14	San Francisco	14-17	23-20	(overtime)

most spectacular plays in team history in wild-card playoff at Detroit the following week (Jan. 8)...With the Packers trailing 24-21 in the final minute of play, he scrambled out of the pocket to his left, found an "unguarded" Sharpe in the open and unleashed an across-the-body throw from extreme left to extreme right; Sharpe ran under the football in the end zone with 55 seconds left and the Packers shortly became 28-24 winners...Had thrown 2 earlier TD passes to Sharpe (a 12-yarder in the second quarter and a 28-yarder in the third period) while completing 15 of 26 passes for 204 yards overall...Threw 2 more TD passes in losing effort (27-17) in divisional playoff at Dallas the following week (Jan. 16) – a two-yarder to Brooks and a 29-yarder to Sharpe...Closed out day with 28 completions in 45 attempts for 331 yards (one yard short of Packers' single-game playoff record) and 2 TDs...**1992:** Acquired from Atlanta by Wolf for a first-round draft selection in an offseason trade (Feb. 10)...Was so impressive in escorting Green Bay to its second-best record in 20 years (9-7) – soaring from designated backup to Pro Bowler in just three months' time – that Head Coach Mike Holmgren was prompted to observe, "If Brett can stay healthy, he will be the cornerstone of our football team for many years to come."...Beginning the 1992 season as the understudy to incumbent Majkowski, he was hastily summoned from the bench to replace an injured Majkowski in the first quarter of Game 3 vs. Cincinnati (Sept. 20) and proceeded to take a stranglehold on the QB position, staking an immediate claim by leading the Packers to an electrifying, come-from-behind, 24-23 victory over the Bengals, forged by way of a 35-yard scoring pass to wideout Kitrick Taylor with only 13 seconds remaining in the game...Performing in storybook fashion, he went on to compile an 8-5 record as a starter and establish two new Green Bay passing records in the process – single-season marks for passing percentage (64.12%) and most consecutive 200-yard passing games (11)...Named as third QB for NFC Pro Bowl squad after finishing fifth among conference passers with an 85.3 overall rating, based on 302 completions in 471 attempts for 3,227 yards and 18 touchdowns with only 13 interceptions...At the time, was youngest quarterback ever to play in AFC-NFC Pro Bowl (since 1971) at 23 years, 3 months, 28 days of age...His 302 completions tied him with Aikman of Super Bowl champion Dallas Cowboys for first-place honors in NFC...Also ranked second in conference to Young with his 64.12 passing percentage, which broke Starr's Green Bay single-season record of 63.74, set in 1968...Had third-lowest interception percentage among all NFL quarterbacks (2.76)...Also became only the fourth Packers QB to pass for over 3,000 yards in a season...Had a string of 111 passes without an interception broken at Oilers on Dec. 13...Did not play vs. Minnesota in regular-season opener on Sept. 6, but saw action in relief role the next week at Tampa Bay (Sept. 13), completing 8 of 14 passes for 73 yards in second-half play...Engineered two TD drives in last eight minutes of the game to pull out 24-23 victory over Cincinnati (Sept. 20) after relieving injured Majkowski in opening quarter...Threw for season-high 289 yards against Bengals on 22 of 39 passing...Made first NFL start on Sept. 27 vs. Pittsburgh and responded by completing 14 of 19 passes for 210 yards and 2 TDs, including a 76-yarder to Sharpe, with no interceptions...Played well at Atlanta (Oct. 4) despite heavy pressure from Falcons defense, completing 33 of 43 passes for 276 yards and 1 TD...Led Packers to 27-13 victory over Detroit (Nov. 1) at Silverdome, completing 22 of 37 passes for 212 yards and 2 TDs...Completed 27 of a season-high 44 attempts for 279 yards at N.Y. Giants (Nov. 8) but had 3 interceptions, his first multiple-interception contest of the season...Also forced a fumble vs. Giants – recovered by teammate Sanjay Beach – in an impromptu role as a tackler, hitting New York's Pepper Johnson after Johnson had intercepted a pass...Staged an inspiring performance vs. Philadelphia (Nov. 15), leading Packers to a 27-24, come-from-behind victory despite suffering a first-degree separation of his left (non-throwing) shoulder early in the game...Completed 23 of 33 for 275 yards and 2 scores with 2 interceptions in upset of Eagles...Had a five-yard TD run (his first NFL touchdown) at the Bears a week later (Nov. 22) during a fine overall performance, which saw him complete 16 of 24 passes for 209 yards and 1 TD (a 49-yard strike to Sharpe) in 17-3 triumph...Had productive afternoon in return meeting with Tampa Bay (Nov. 29), completing 26 of 41 passes for 223 yards and 1 TD (a nine-yard throw to Harris in fourth quarter) in leading the Packers to a 19-14 win...Posted high percentage performance in rematch with Lions (Dec. 6), hitting on 15 of 19 passes for 214 yards and 3 TDs (the first 3-touchdown game of his career) in escorting Packers to a 38-10 victory...Also effective at Houston (Nov. 13), completing 19 of 30 passes for 155 yards in 16-14 win over Oilers...Closed out regular-season home schedule with a 14 for 23 effort vs. L.A. Rams (Dec. 20), good for 188 yards and 2 TDs (both to Sharpe) in a 28-13 victory...**1991:** Was second-round draft selection by Falcons (33rd overall and third quarterback, after Dan McGwire and Todd Marinovich)...Completed 14 of 32 passes for 160 yards and 2 touchdowns, with 1 interception, in the preseason...Active for three games during the regular season, he played in two (Oct. 27 vs. L.A. Rams and Nov. 10 at Washington), attempting 5 passes without a completion in Redskins contest.

COLLEGE: Led his Southern Mississippi team to 29 victories, including two bowl triumphs, during four varsity seasons (1987-90), and climaxed his collegiate career by earning a 'Most Valuable Player' award in the East-West Shrine game featuring the nation's best seniors...Set school records for passing yards (8,193), pass attempts (1,234), completions (656), passing percentage (53.0) and touchdowns (55), with only 35 interceptions...His production included five 300-yard passing games and five 3-TD performances, while his 7,695 regular-season passing yards ranked him among the top 30 of all-time NCAA passers...His 1.57 interception ratio in 1988 was the lowest among the 50 top-ranked passers in the nation, and his 2.9 interception rate for his four-year career (based on only 34 in 1,169 attempts) also ranks as one of the best in NCAA history...Overcame injuries in a serious summer car accident prior to his senior season to lead his team to an 8-3 record and just eight points from an undefeated season...Suffered internal injuries in the accident on July 14, 1990, he subsequently had 30 inches of his intestines surgically removed 24 days later (Aug. 7)...Shocked his coaches and teammates by returning to the starting lineup a month later (Sept. 8) and escorting the Golden Eagles to an upset over Alabama...Also was MVP of All-American Bowl at conclusion of senior year...Became starter at Southern Miss in third game of his freshman season...Majored in special education.

PERSONAL: Given name Brett Lorenzo Favre...Born in Gulfport, Miss. ...Grew up in Kiln, Miss. (pronounced KILL)...Married long-time girlfriend Deanna Tynes on July 14, 1996, after a 12-year courtship, the couple has a daughter, Brittany (born 2/6/89)...Earned five letters in baseball (he led team in batting all five seasons) and three in football at Hancock North Central High School in Kiln, where his father, Irvin, was his coach...Played quarterback and strong safety, also serving as punter and placekicker...Played in Mississippi high school all-star game following senior season...Had his high school jersey (number 10) retired in April, 1993...Then had the number 4 jersey he had worn at Southern Mississippi retired in September, 1993...Subsequently was inducted into the Southern Miss Sports Hall of Fame in April, 1997...Father pitched for Southern Mississippi baseball varsity...Older brother, Scott, played quarterback for Mississippi State and younger brother, Jeff, was a free safety on Southern Mississippi football team...Sister, Brandi, is a former 'Miss Teen Mississippi'...Grew up idolizing a pair of Southern quarterbacks, Saints' Archie Manning and Cowboys' Roger Staubach...Started in 1996 the 'Brett Favre Fourward Foundation,' which this year donated $120,000 of the $230,000 raised by his annual golf tournament (held May 8-10 in Gulfport, Miss.) to four Mississippi charities – Special Olympics, Make-A-Wish, Hope Haven (a home for battered women and children) and Gaits to Success (therapeutic horsemanship for the mentally disabled) – the latter two are located in the county (Hancock) where he grew up...This year's golf tournament featured a benefit concert by Hootie and the Blowfish, which raised $15,000 for the foundation...Also has raised in excess of $255,000 for the Boys & Girls Club of Green Bay over the past three seasons by donating $150 for each touchdown pass and rushing TD he has, a monetary total augmented by matching corporate contributions; he generated $80,000 in 1997 after raising $80,000 and $95,000 in the 1995 and 1996 seasons, respectively...Received the 'Community Service Award' from the Green Bay Chamber of Commerce in August of 1997 in recognition of his work with the area Boys & Girls Club, in addition to Special Olympics and Cystic Fibrosis...Has worked at Thanksgiving with the Salvation Army in Green Bay and Gulfport, Miss., to donate food baskets to needy families...Gave time during the 1993-95 seasons as the Packers' player representative to the state Punt, Pass & Kick competition...Had his fourth grade teacher, Billy Ray Dedeaux of Hancock North Central Elementary School in his native Kiln, Miss., named as the NFL's 'Teacher of the Month' for September, 1994...Has been one of the country's most marketable athletes since leading Green Bay to a Super Bowl victory in January of 1997...Appears in a national ad for DirecTV in 1998, he also continues his endorsements of Nike and Sprint, having appeared in national commercials for both...Previously was in national television commercials for Edge Shave Gel (along with teammate Reggie White) and Choice Hotels...Also did a national 'Milk Mustache' ad, which was on billboards in 1997...Has endorsement deals with Rawlings, Pepsi, Repel Insect Block, Cellular One (regional) and Koss headphones...Also serves as a spokesman for the Wisconsin Department of Tourism, Wisconsin Milk Marketing Board, Bergstrom Automotive (Wisconsin car dealerships), Acclaim video games, Kohl's department stores and Fun Jet Vacations...Also is involved with the NFL Quarterback Club...Came out with his own line of clothing in 1996, sold at Kohl's...Will be opening a 'Brett Favre Steakhouse' in Green Bay in November of 1998 after successfully launching the first such restaurant in September of 1997 in downtown Milwaukee...Had over 2 million of his candy bars, the 'Brett Favre MVP Bar,' sold through fund-raising groups in its first year, the most ever sold by the Morley Candy Company...Sold over 100,000 copies of his authorized autobiography, entitled *Favre For The Record*..., which was published by Doubleday late in the summer of 1997, an updated version of the book which includes a chapter on the 1997 season and Super Bowl XXXII will appear in paperback in September of 1998...Makes an appearance near the end of the 1998 movie *There's Something About Mary* as the boyfriend of co-star Cameron Diaz...Previously had made a cameo as a janitor in *Reggie's Prayer*, the 1997 movie project of teammate Reggie White...Will appear this season as the periodic co-host of a television program, *Pack Attack*, which will be filmed at his Milwaukee restaurant, alternating with three teammates in those duties...Was a guest on *The Tonight Show with Jay Leno* in the days following Super Bowl XXXII earlier this year, he later played himself in one episode of the weekly HBO series *Arliss*...Had made appearances on *The Late Show with David Letterman* and *The Late, Late Show with Tom Snyder* in the days immediately following Green Bay's Super Bowl triumph over New England in January of 1997...Previously had a cameo on *The Tonight Show* the week of Super Bowl XXX from Phoenix...Won 'long throw' portion of 1995 NFL Quarterback Challenge...Hobbies include playing basketball, golf and fishing...Splits residence between Hattiesburg, Miss., and Green Bay.

PRO STATISTICS:

PASSING

Year		G/S	Att.	Comp.	Yds.	Pct.	TD	Int.	LG	Rating
1991	Atlanta 2/0		5	0	0	0.0	0	2	0	0.0
1992	Green Bay 15/13		471	302	3,227	64.1	18	13	76t	85.3
1993	Green Bay 16/16		522	318	3,303	60.9	19	24	66t	72.2
1994	Green Bay 16/16		582	363	3,882	62.4	33	14	49	90.7
1995	Green Bay 16/16		570	359	*4,413	63.0	*38	13	*99t	99.5
1996	Green Bay 16/16		543	325	3,899	59.9	*39	13	80t	95.8
1997	Green Bay 16/16		513	304	3,867	59.3	*35	16	74	92.6
Totals 97/93			3,206	1,971	22,591	61.5	182	95	99t	89.3
Playoffs................13/13			414	250	3,098	60.4	23	10	81t	92.0

*Led NFL

RUSHING

Year		No.	Yds.	Avg.	LG	TD
1991	Atlanta 0		0	0.0	0	0
1992	Green Bay 47		198	4.2	19	1
1993	Green Bay 58		216	3.7	27	1
1994	Green Bay 42		202	4.8	36t	2
1995	Green Bay 39		181	4.6	40	3
1996	Green Bay 49		136	2.8	23	2
1997	Green Bay 58		187	3.2	16	1
Totals 293			1,120	3.8	40	10
Playoffs 36			59	1.6	12	1

Two-Pt. Conversions: 1, vs. Tampa Bay (1/4/98-postseason)
Receptions: 1 for -7 yards in 1992
Forced Fumbles: 1 in 1992; 1 in 1994 for total of 2
Miscellaneous Tackles: 2 in 1992; 4 in 1993; 2 in 1994; 2 in 1995; 1 in 1996 for total of 11

FAVRE'S SINGLE-GAME CAREER-HIGHS

Attempts
61	vs. San Francisco, Oct. 14, 1996
54	at Chicago, Dec. 5, 1993
51	vs. Miami, Sept. 11, 1994
51	vs. St. Louis, Sept. 3, 1995

Completions
36	at Chicago, Dec. 5, 1993
33	at Atlanta, Oct. 4, 1992
31	vs. Miami, Sept. 11, 1994
31	vs. Cincinnati, Dec. 3, 1995

Passing Yards
402	at Chicago, Dec. 5, 1993
395	vs. San Francisco, Oct. 14, 1996
366	at Detroit, Dec. 4, 1994
363	at Indianapolis, Nov. 16, 1997
362	vs. Miami, Sept. 11, 1994

Completion Percentage (min. 20 att.)
82.1	at Cleveland, Nov. 19, 1995
78.9	vs. Detroit, Dec. 6, 1992
76.9	vs. Tampa Bay, Sept. 25, 1994
76.7	at Atlanta, Oct. 4, 1992
75.8	vs. Chicago, Nov. 12, 1995
75.8	at Tampa Bay, Dec. 7, 1997

Touchdown Passes
5	vs. Chicago, Nov. 12, 1995
5	vs. Minnesota, Sept. 21, 1997
4	at Tampa Bay, Oct. 24, 1993
4	at Dallas, Nov. 24, 1994
4	vs. Minnesota, Oct. 22, 1995
4	at New Orleans, Dec. 16, 1995
4	at Tampa Bay, Sept. 1, 1996
4	at Seattle, Sept. 29, 1996
4	at Chicago, Oct. 6, 1996

4	vs. Detroit, Nov. 3, 1996
4	vs. Denver, Dec. 8, 1996
4	vs. Dallas, Nov. 23, 1997

Interceptions
4	at Detroit, Jan. 2, 1994
3	8 times (last: at Detroit, Sept. 28, 1997)

Longest Passes
99t	at Chicago, Sept. 11, 1995 (to Brooks)
+81t	vs. New England, Jan. 26, 1997 (to Freeman)
80t	at Minnesota, Sept. 22, 1996 (to Beebe)
77t	at Detroit, Oct. 29, 1995 (to Brooks)
76t	vs. Pittsburgh, Sept. 27, 1992 (to Sharpe)
74	at Indianapolis, Nov. 16, 1997 (to Mayes)

Passer Rating (min. 20 att.)
147.2	vs. Chicago, Nov. 12, 1995
143.6	vs. Tampa Bay, Nov. 26, 1995
142.8	at New Orleans, Dec. 16, 1995
141.5	at Tampa Bay, Sept. 1, 1996
133.6	at Cleveland, Nov. 19, 1995
*132.9	at San Francisco, Jan. 6, 1996

Longest Runs
40	at Jacksonville, Sept. 24, 1995
36t	at Chicago, Oct. 31, 1994
27	vs. Tampa Bay, Nov. 28, 1993

*playoff game
+Super Bowl XXXI

FAVRE'S 1992 GAME-BY-GAME PASSING

Date	Opponent	Att.	Comp.	Yds.	Pct.	TD	Int.	LG	Sack	W/L
Sept. 6	Minnesota				-did not play-					
Sept. 13	at Tampa Bay	14	8	73	57.1	0	1	20	4	-
Sept. 20	Cincinnati	39	22	289	56.4	2	0	42	5	-
Sept. 27	Pittsburgh	19	14	210	73.7	2	0	76t	2	W
Oct. 4	at Atlanta	43	33	276	76.7	1	1	24	2	L
Oct. 18	at Cleveland	33	20	223	60.6	0	0	21	2	L
Oct. 25	Chicago	37	20	214	54.1	1	1	45	4	L
Nov. 1	at Detroit	37	22	212	59.5	2	0	30t	2	W
Nov. 8	at N.Y. Giants	44	27	279	61.4	0	3	43	1	L
Nov. 15	Philadelphia	33	23	275	69.7	2	2	34	2	W
Nov. 22	at Chicago	24	16	209	66.7	1	0	49t	1	W
Nov. 29	Tampa Bay	41	26	223	63.4	1	0	27	1	W
Dec. 6	Detroit	19	15	214	78.9	3	0	65t	1	W
Dec. 13	at Houston	30	19	155	63.3	1	1	21	3	W
Dec. 20	L.A. Rams	23	14	188	60.9	2	1	43	3	W
Dec. 27	at Minnesota	35	23	187	65.7	0	3	29	1	L

FAVRE'S 1993 GAME-BY-GAME PASSING

Date	Opponent	Att.	Comp.	Yds.	Pct.	TD	Int.	LG	Sack	W/L
Sept. 5	L.A. Rams	29	19	264	65.5	2	1	50t	3	W
Sept. 12	Philadelphia	24	12	111	50.0	2	2	28	1	L
Sept. 26	at Minnesota	31	20	150	64.5	0	2	16	0	L
Oct. 3	at Dallas	37	21	174	56.8	0	0	20	1	L
Oct. 10	Denver	32	20	235	62.5	1	3	66t	0	W
Oct. 24	at Tampa Bay	35	20	268	57.1	4	1	51	2	W
Oct. 31	Chicago	24	15	136	62.5	1	1	21t	2	W
Nov. 8	at Kansas City	34	20	213	58.8	1	3	35t	4	L
Nov. 14	at New Orleans	32	18	150	56.3	1	0	54	6	W
Nov. 21	Detroit	33	24	259	72.7	0	2	36	1	W
Nov. 28	Tampa Bay	36	23	159	63.9	1	0	28	2	W
Dec. 5	at Chicago	54	36	402	66.7	2	3	34	1	L
Dec. 12	at San Diego	23	13	146	56.5	0	1	25	2	W
Dec. 19	Minnesota	33	20	256	60.6	2	1	42	1	L
Dec. 26	L.A. Raiders	28	14	190	50.0	1	0	26	2	W
Jan. 2	at Detroit	37	23	190	62.2	1	4	39t	2	L
*Jan. 8	at Detroit	26	15	204	57.7	3	1	40t	0	W
*Jan. 16	at Dallas	45	28	331	62.2	2	2	48	2	L

FAVRE'S 1994 GAME-BY-GAME PASSING

Date	Opponent	Att.	Comp.	Yds.	Pct.	TD	Int.	LG	Sack	W/L
Sept. 4	Minnesota	36	22	185	61.1	1	0	24	3	W
Sept. 11	Miami	51	31	362	60.8	2	1	35	4	L
Sept. 18	at Philadelphia	45	24	280	53.3	1	2	48	6	L
Sept. 25	Tampa Bay	39	30	306	76.9	3	0	36	0	W
Oct. 2	at New England	47	25	294	53.2	1	2	38	4	L
Oct. 9	L.A. Rams	41	25	222	61.0	1	1	26	2	W
Oct. 20	at Minnesota	10	6	32	60.0	0	1	7	1	L
Oct. 31	at Chicago	15	6	82	40.0	1	0	22	0	W
Nov. 6	Detroit	36	24	237	66.7	3	1	28t	1	W
Nov. 13	N.Y. Jets	28	20	183	71.4	2	0	17t	1	W
Nov. 20	at Buffalo	40	22	214	55.0	3	1	29t	1	L
Nov. 24	at Dallas	40	27	257	67.5	4	0	36t	2	L
Dec. 4	at Detroit	43	29	366	67.4	3	2	47t	1	L
Dec. 11	Chicago	31	19	250	61.3	3	1	35	2	W
Dec. 18	Atlanta	44	29	321	65.9	2	1	40	2	W
Dec. 24	at Tampa Bay	36	24	291	66.7	3	1	49	1	W
*Dec. 31	Detroit	38	23	262	60.5	0	0	33	1	W
*Jan. 8	at Dallas	35	18	211	51.4	0	1	59	1	L

FAVRE'S 1995 GAME-BY-GAME PASSING

Date	Opponent	Att.	Comp.	Yds.	Pct.	TD	Int.	LG	Sack	W/L
Sept. 3	St. Louis	51	29	299	56.9	2	3	29	4	L
Sept. 11	at Chicago	37	21	312	56.8	3	1	99t	2	W
Sept. 17	N.Y. Giants	25	14	141	56.0	2	0	19t	4	W
Sept. 24	at Jacksonville	30	20	202	66.7	2	1	29t	2	W

Date	Opponent	Att.	Comp.	Yds.	Pct.	TD	Int.	LG	Sack	W/L
Oct. 8	at Dallas	41	21	295	51.2	1	1	30	0	L
Oct. 15	Detroit	34	23	342	67.7	2	0	35	2	W
Oct. 22	Minnesota	43	22	295	51.2	4	0	32	3	W
Oct. 29	at Detroit	43	26	304	60.5	1	3	77t	1	L
Nov. 5	at Minnesota	30	17	177	56.7	0	2	21	4	L
Nov. 12	Chicago	33	25	336	75.8	5	0	44t	3	W
Nov. 19	at Cleveland	28	23	210	82.1	3	0	27	2	W
Nov. 26	Tampa Bay	24	16	267	66.7	3	0	54t	1	W
Dec. 3	Cincinnati	43	31	339	72.1	3	1	29	1	W
Dec. 10	at Tampa Bay	46	27	285	58.7	1	1	35	0	L
Dec. 16	at New Orleans	30	21	308	70.0	4	0	40t	2	W
Dec. 24	Pittsburgh	32	23	301	71.9	2	0	28	2	W
*Dec. 31	Atlanta	35	24	199	68.6	3	0	20	1	W
*Jan. 6	at San Francisco	28	21	299	75.0	2	0	53	1	W
*Jan. 14	at Dallas	39	21	307	53.9	3	2	73t	4	L

FAVRE'S 1996 GAME-BY-GAME PASSING

Date	Opponent	Att.	Comp.	Yds.	Pct.	TD	Int.	LG	Sack	W/L
Sept. 1	at Tampa Bay	27	20	247	74.1	4	0	51t	1	W
Sept. 9	Philadelphia	31	17	261	54.8	3	0	38	1	W
Sept. 15	San Diego	33	22	231	66.7	3	1	32	2	W
Sept. 22	at Minnesota	27	14	198	51.9	2	1	80t	7	L
Sept. 29	at Seattle	34	20	209	58.8	4	0	28	2	W
Oct. 6	at Chicago	27	18	246	66.7	4	1	50t	1	W
Oct. 14	San Francisco	61	28	395	45.9	1	2	59t	2	W
Oct. 27	Tampa Bay	31	19	178	61.3	0	1	26	2	W
Nov. 3	Detroit	35	24	281	68.6	4	1	65t	4	W
Nov. 10	at Kansas City	49	27	314	55.1	2	1	49	4	L
Nov. 18	at Dallas	37	21	194	56.8	1	0	25	4	L
Nov. 24	at St. Louis	38	25	192	65.8	2	2	14	1	W
Dec. 1	Chicago	27	19	231	70.4	1	0	41	2	W
Dec. 8	Denver	38	20	280	52.6	4	2	51t	1	W
Dec. 15	at Detroit	25	16	240	64.0	1	1	40	3	W
Dec. 22	Minnesota	23	15	202	65.2	3	0	37	2	W
*Jan. 4	San Francisco	15	11	79	73.3	1	0	18	1	W
*Jan. 12	Carolina	29	19	292	65.5	2	1	66	1	W
+Jan. 26	New England	27	14	246	51.9	2	0	81t	5	W

FAVRE'S 1997 GAME-BY-GAME PASSING

Date	Opponent	Att.	Comp.	Yds.	Pct.	TD	Int.	LG	Sack	W/L
Sept. 1	Chicago	22	15	226	68.2	2	1	44	2	W
Sept. 7	at Philadelphia	41	19	279	46.3	0	1	30	1	L
Sept. 14	Miami	37	24	253	64.9	2	0	48	1	W
Sept. 21	Minnesota	31	18	266	58.1	5	2	28t	2	W
Sept. 28	at Detroit	43	22	295	51.2	1	3	45	2	L
Oct. 5	Tampa Bay	31	21	191	67.7	2	0	31t	3	W
Oct. 12	at Chicago	35	19	177	54.3	3	1	18	0	W
Oct. 27	at New England	34	23	239	67.6	3	0	32t	1	W
Nov. 2	Detroit	28	15	181	53.6	1	1	28	2	W
Nov. 9	St. Louis	37	18	306	48.6	1	2	45	2	W
Nov. 16	at Indianapolis	25	18	363	72.0	3	2	74	3	L
Nov. 23	Dallas	35	22	203	62.9	4	1	36	2	W
Dec. 1	at Minnesota	29	15	196	51.7	1	0	31	1	W
Dec. 7	at Tampa Bay	33	25	280	75.8	2	1	43t	0	W
Dec. 14	at Carolina	34	18	256	52.9	3	1	58t	3	W
Dec. 20	Buffalo	18	12	156	66.7	2	0	38	0	W
*Jan. 4	Tampa Bay	28	15	190	53.6	1	2	26	4	W
*Jan. 11	at San Francisco	27	16	222	59.3	1	0	40	1	W
#Jan. 25	Denver	42	25	256	59.5	3	1	27	1	L

*playoff game   +Super Bowl XXXI   #Super Bowl XXXII

THE PLAYERS

MIKE FLANAGAN — 58

Center
College: UCLA
NFL Exp.: 3rd Season **Packers Exp.:** 3rd Season
Ht.: 6-5 **Wt.:** 290 **Born:** 11/10/73 **Acq:** D3a-96

PRO: Third-year center who entered the league with tremendous promise as a third-round draft choice of the Packers...Has yet to take the field for any measurable period of time due to the dark cloud of injury which has overshadowed his pro career almost from the beginning...Broke two bones in his leg midway through the preseason of his 1996, rookie campaign...Has since been stymied by complications which have dictated several additional surgeries related to his original injury...Despite a vigorous work ethic, to this point has been unable to withstand the physical rigors of daily participation...Will continue to rehabilitate and strengthen his leg with hopes of returning to unrestrained action for the 1998 season..."When we drafted him and had him on the field, he showed a lot of promise," says Tom Lovat, Green Bay's offensive line coach. "He's a good athlete. He's got very good feet and movement. And he's smart. We had him on the field for a limited time last year and it appeared that he was sharp and did the things that would give him a chance. Now he's back in the process of rehabbing. If it mends like it should, he'll compete and very easily could become our backup center. But all that's supposition heading into training camp."...Standing 6-feet, 5-inches, is taller than the prototype center...Has ample room to add bulk to his angular frame...**1997:** Was sidelined for a second consecutive season when the muscle and nerve damage associated with his 1996 leg injury were slow to respond...Initially went on reserve/physically unable to perform during training camp (Aug. 19), forcing him to miss at least the league-mandated first six games...Recovered sufficiently to practice with the team, beginning Oct. 22, for the allowable three-week period at midseason...Subsequently was placed on season-ending PUP Nov. 11 following a determination by the club's coaching and medical staffs that he needed continued rehabilitation...**1996:** Spent his entire rookie season on injured reserve after suffering a fracture to both bones in his lower right leg while blocking on the opening kickoff of the team's second preseason game, Aug. 11 vs. Pittsburgh...Underwent surgery the next day to place a stabilizing rod in the larger bone of his lower leg...Later was placed on IR Aug. 19...Was the first of two third-round draft choices (90th overall and second center) by Green Bay in 1996.

COLLEGE: Three-year starter and letterman (1993-95) for UCLA...Started his final 32 consecutive games, longest streak on the Bruins...Was a first-team All-Pacific 10 Conference selection as a junior and senior...Also earned third-team All-America recognition from *Football News* in 1995...Was co-offensive winner of school's 'Kenneth S. Washington Award' for outstanding senior, when he registered 79 knockdown blocks...Began the '93 season as a backup, but started the final nine games of the season after injuries to two players, including Jonathan Ogden (Ravens), created an opportunity...Went on that year to be chosen as one of three offensive winners of the 'Captain Don Brown Memorial Trophy' for most improved player...Played in one game in 1992, but did not letter...Was redshirted in 1991...Earned a spot on the Director's (academic) Honor Roll three times...Majored in history.

PERSONAL: Given name Michael Christopher Flanagan...Born in Washington, D.C. ...Single...Was an all-state, all-league and all-city selection in football at Rio Americano High School in Sacramento, Calif. ...Played offensive and defensive tackle, lettering twice...Helped lead team to an 11-1 record and the CIF Sacramento section finals as a senior, when he recorded 91 tackles and 13½ sacks...Served as a team captain...Also earned two letters in basketball...Hobbies include hunting...Residence: Green Bay.

PRO STATISTICS:

Games/Starts—Green Bay 1996 (injured reserve); 1997 (reserve/physically unable to perform).

PAUL FRASE   97

Defensive End
College: Syracuse
NFL Exp.: 10th Season   **Packers Exp.:** 2nd Season
Ht.: 6-5   **Wt.:** 275   **Born:** 5/6/65   **Acq:** T-97 (Jax)

PRO: Veteran defensive end/long snapper who became a valuable member of the team after joining Green Bay just prior to the start of the 1997 season...Acquired in a trade with the Jacksonville Jaguars on the day of the NFL's final '97 roster cutdown (Aug. 24)...Immediately helped to solidify the Packers' special teams with his long-snapping ability, in addition to his role as a backup defensive end...Green Bay defensive coordinator Fritz Shurmur believes that Frase came through in 1997 when the team needed him most, saying, "Paul really bailed us out in some situations last year. He was a savior for us in some situations when we had difficulty with injuries at the defensive end position. Initially he came in here as a backup defensive end and long snapper, but worked himself into a role where he played a lot of snaps during the year – and played well for us. He is a steady football player who works hard at his job and competes hard on every down."...Has seen action at every position on the defensive line as a pro, a career which has seen him play in 128 games with 49 starts...Spent his first seven years (1988-94) with the New York Jets, sitting out the 1990 campaign due to hyperthyroidism...Chosen by Jacksonville in the 1995 expansion draft, was with the Jaguars for two seasons (1995-96) before coming over to Green Bay in a trade...Has 269 career tackles, 11 sacks, 6 forced fumbles, 3 fumble recoveries, 7 passes defensed and 2 blocked field goals...Handled long-snapping duties for the Jets from 1992-94...Also did some snapping for the Jaguars in 1996, then for the Packers in '97...Re-signed with Green Bay this past April 24...**1997:** Played in nine regular-season games in his first year with the Packers, he was inactive for the team's other seven contests...Got into each of Green Bay's first two playoff games, but was inactive for Super Bowl XXXII when injury concerns in the secondary dictated keeping an extra defensive back active...Finished the regular season with 3 total tackles...Served as a backup defensive end and as the team's long-snapper for punts for the third through eighth games...Injured his back in practice the week prior to New England contest (Oct. 27); played against the Patriots but the injury lingered, causing him to be inactive vs. Detroit (Nov. 2)...Subsequently had a microdiskectomy, a surgical procedure to repair a herniated disk, on Nov. 4, putting him out for five more games...Returned to action at Carolina (Dec. 14) and saw extensive action at left defensive end, mostly in the second half, he had 1 tackle against the Panthers...Saw reserve action at left end Oct. 12 at Chicago, he helped the Packers' defense make one of its biggest plays of the season when, with Green Bay clinging to a 24-23 lead with 1:59 left in the game and the Bears attempting a game-deciding two-point conversion, he pressured QB Erik Kramer, whose swing pass to Raymont Harris fell incomplete...Saw extensive action at right end vs. Tampa Bay (Oct. 5), recording 1 tackle...Also was inactive for opener vs. Chicago (Sept. 1)...Played much of the second half of divisional playoff win over Tampa Bay (Jan. 4) at right end after Gabe Wilkins went out with a knee injury in the second quarter, making 1 tackle...Recovered a Steve Young fumble late in NFC Championship Game win at San Francisco (Jan. 11)...Acquired from Jacksonville Aug. 24 in exchange for a 1998 sixth-round draft choice...**1996:** Played in 14 games in a reserve capacity, seeing action at defensive end and defensive tackle...Had 7 tackles (6 solo), 2 hurries and 1 pass defensed...Received the majority of his playing time on special teams, recording a career-high 7 tackles on kick coverage...Handled snapping responsibilities for first time as a Jaguar Oct. 6 at New Orleans...Played in all three of Jacksonville's postseason contests...Started at defensive tackle in Jaguars' goal-line defense in AFC Championship Game loss at New England (Jan. 12)...Handled snapping for last four punts against the Patriots after an injury to usual snapper Rich Griffith...Recorded 2 defensive stops and 2 special teams tackles during the playoffs...Was inactive at Pittsburgh (Nov. 17) and at Baltimore (Nov. 24)...**1995:** In his first year with Jacksonville, started the final five games after a season-ending foot injury to Jeff Lageman, who was a teammate with both the Jets and Jaguars...Played in nine games overall, posting 29 tackles and a sack...Was inactive for the club's other seven contests...Sacked Chris Chandler at Houston (Oct. 1)...Made 7 tackles at Tampa Bay (Nov.

19)...Made first Jaguars start a week later against Cincinnati (Nov. 26)...Forced a fumble which set up an early field goal at Denver (Dec. 3)...Selected by his teammates as the 'Ed Block Courage Award' recipient for the second time in his career...Selected by Jacksonville in the ninth round (17th overall) of the 1995 expansion draft (Feb. 15)...**1994:** Started the first five games of the season in his final year with the Jets – four at right defensive tackle, one at left defensive end – while playing in all 16 contests...Had 35 tackles, 1 sack, 1 forced fumble, 1 fumble recovery and 2 passes defensed...Recorded 5 tackles and forced a fumble at Houston (Dec. 24)...Had 1 sack plus 2 tackles for loss the previous week against San Diego (Dec. 18)...**1993:** Played in all 16 games, starting the final four at defensive tackle when Leonard Marshall was sidelined by an arm injury…Had 40 tackles, 1 sack, 1 forced fumble, a career-high 2 fumble recoveries and 1 pass defensed...Posted 14 tackles in his four starting assignments...Had his lone sack of the year at Miami (Sept. 12)...**1992:** Started 12 straight games while playing in all 16 contests…Recorded 47 tackles, including a career-high 5 sacks (tied for second on the team), and a career-best 2 forced fumbles...Had 1 sack and blocked a field goal try at Indianapolis (Oct. 11)...Posted 3 tackles, 2 sacks and a forced fumble in his first start of the season, Oct. 4 vs. New England...Awarded a game ball after contributing 4 tackles and 1 quarterback hurry vs. Miami (Nov. 1)…Handled the team's punt-snapping duties throughout the season…**1991:** Played in all 16 games after having missed the previous season with Graves disease, earning the 'Ed Block Courage Award' in a vote of his teammates...Had 18 tackles, including a season-high 5 against the Packers (Nov. 3)...Also handled the team's long-snapping duties against Green Bay...Saw reserve action in the Jets' wild-card loss at Houston (Dec. 29)…Played the final three games with a broken thumb...**1990:** Recovering from an offseason bout with hyperthyroidism (Graves disease), was placed on the reserve/non-football injury list Aug. 27, where he spent the entire year…Practiced with the Jets' scout team in the latter half of the season…**1989:** Started the final 14 games, the last 13 at left defensive end, while playing in all 16 contests...Led Jets' defensive linemen with a career-high 59 total tackles...Had a sack in consecutive games, vs. the L.A. Raiders (Oct. 9) and at New Orleans (Oct. 15)…Blocked a field goal at Miami (Sept. 24), which George Radachowsky returned 78 yards for a touchdown...**1988:** Played in all 16 games as a rookie, including seven starts at left defensive end...Had 31 tackles, including his first pro sack Dec. 10 vs. Indianapolis, 1 forced fumble and 2 passes defensed...Saw most of his action on special teams the first seven games before replacing Mark Gastineau in the lineup...Drafted in the sixth round (146th overall) by the New York Jets in 1988.

COLLEGE: A two-year starter and four-time letter winner (1984-87) at Syracuse...Redshirted in 1983…Earned honorable mention All-America and second-team All-Big East honors as a senior, when he recorded 51 tackles and 6 sacks...Helped lead the Orangemen to an 11-0 regular season and a berth in the Sugar Bowl his senior year...Had 2 sacks vs. Gerald Perry in the Senior Bowl and 1 sack against Randall McDaniel in the Japan Bowl at the conclusion of his collegiate career…Had 76 tackles, 2½ sacks and 1 interception as a junior...Holds a B.A. degree in psychology.

PERSONAL: Given name Paul Miles Frase...Nicknamed 'Frasee'...Born in Elmira, N.Y. ...Married to Alison, couple has one son, Joshua (born 2/2/95)...Won four letters in basketball and three in football at Spaulding High School in Barrington, N.H. …Earned all-state honors in football as a junior and senior…Also was named all-state in basketball his senior year...Started the Joshua Frase Foundation, named after his son, who has congenital myopathy, to help in the research and prevention of the rare muscle disease...Has played host to a variety of fundraisers to support research for myotubular and other congenital myopathies, he co-hosted a 1996 holiday event for the Muscular Dystrophy Association...Active with the Fellowship of Christian Athletes...Father, James, is a minister...Hobbies include riding his Harley Davidson motorcycle and reading...Residence: Jacksonville.

PRO STATISTICS:

Year		G/S	UT	AT	Sacks	Int.	FR	FF	PD
1988	N.Y. Jets	16/7	23	8	1	0	0	1	2
1989	N.Y. Jets	16/14	46	13	2	0	0	0	0
1990	N.Y. Jets	reserve/non-football illness							
1991	N.Y. Jets	16/2	15	3	0	0	0	0	0
1992	N.Y. Jets	16/12	34	13	5	0	0	2	1
1993	N.Y. Jets	16/4	27	13	1	0	2	1	1
1994	N.Y. Jets	16/5	24	11	1	0	1	1	2
1995	Jacksonville	9/5	16	13	1	0	0	1	0
1996	Jacksonville	14/0	1	6	0	0	0	0	1
1997	Green Bay	9/0	2	1	0	0	0	0	0
Totals		**128/49**	**188**	**81**	**11**	**0**	**3**	**6**	**7**
Playoffs		**6/1**	**2**	**1**	**0**	**0**	**1**	**0**	**0**

Special Teams Tackles: 1 in 1991; 1 in 1992; 1 in 1993; 7 in 1996; 2 in 1996 Playoffs; 1 in 1997 for total of 11

Blocked Field Goals: 2, at Miami (9/24/89) and at Indianapolis (10/11/92)

ANTONIO FREEMAN ⟩ 86

Wide Receiver
College: Virginia Tech
NFL Exp.: 4th Season **Packers Exp.:** 4th Season
Ht.: 6-1 **Wt.:** 198 **Born:** 5/27/72 **Acq:** D3d-95

PRO: One of the National Football League's emerging young superstars at the wide receiver position, fourth-year pro has taken his play to a new, higher level each year…A tremendous runner after the catch who sees the field well, he brings an element of style and showmanship to his performance…Consistently has taken his 'A' game to the playoffs, helping the Packers to reach the Super Bowl each of the past two seasons…"The bigger the game, the better Antonio plays," says Green Bay offensive coordinator Sherm Lewis. "With Robert Brooks coming off a knee injury last season, he developed into our go-to receiver, making many clutch and acrobatic catches. Antonio is finally starting to get the recognition that he deserves and, in my mind, should be ready to break into that level of Pro Bowl receivers in 1998."…Gifted athlete who is especially effective in the 'Red Zone' (inside the opponents' 20-yard line)…Has 21 touchdown receptions over the past two seasons, a total second in the NFL over that span and surpassed by only the 23 of Minnesota's Cris Carter…From his split end spot has led Green Bay in receptions and receiving yards each of the last two years, including one of the top six seasons in club history in 1997…Enters the '98 season in 20th place on Green Bay's all-time receiving list with 145 career receptions (for 2,282 yards and 22 touchdowns)…Has totaled 10 career 100-yard receiving games (seven in the regular season, three in the playoffs)…"His speed is a little deceiving," Lewis adds. "You know, there are guys playing that are a lot faster than he is, no question about that – but you never see him get run down. He's fast enough that if he catches it, he's going to take it. He's a big-play guy. I think he's really excellent in the 'Red Zone;' when we get around that end zone, he's going to make some plays for you. I think another thing he does, he gives you that guy who has the ability to run after the catch."…Already has carved out a significant place in the Packers' postseason history, holding or sharing no less than 13 all-time club playoff records…Also possesses the third-best playoff punt return average in NFL history, his 14.3-yard career average (10-143) is bettered only by the 15.3-yard average of current teammate Robert Brooks (14-214) and the 15.2-yard average set by Anthony Carter of the Vikings and Lions (17-259)…Has a current string of at least one reception in nine consecutive playoff games, one off the team record of 10…In club playoff history, is tied (with Boyd Dowler) for fourth in career receptions (30) and stands third in career receiving yards (525)…Also is third in team postseason history with 42 career points…"I've always said about him that he seems to do the right thing," continues Lewis. "In the gray area, when things aren't quite like you put on the board – they're not quite black, not quite white – he does the right thing. That is why he is a great player. And he's probably picked this offense up quicker than anybody that I've ever been around."…Holds seven team playoff records: *Longest Reception* – 81 yards vs. New England in Super Bowl XXXI; *Most Touchdowns (career)* – 7; *Most Consecutive Games, Scoring Touchdown* – 3; *Most Kickoff Returns (career)* – 20; *Most Yards Gained on Kickoff Returns (career)* – 413; *Highest Punt Return Average (game-3 returns)* – 24.0 yards vs. Atlanta in 1995; and *Longest Punt Return* – 76 yards vs. Atlanta in 1995…Is tied for six other club postseason marks: *Most Passes Caught (game)* – 9 vs. Denver in Super Bowl XXXII; *Most Games, 100 or More Yards Pass Receiving (career)* – 3; *Most Consecutive Games, 100 or More Yards Pass Receiving* – 2 (which remains current); *Most Touchdown Passes Received (career)* – 5; *Most Consecutive Games, Touchdown Pass Received* – 2 (twice, one of which remains current); *Most Kickoff Returns (game)* – 7 in 1995 NFC Championship Game at Dallas…Had stepped his game up during the 1996 season in the injury-forced absence of other receivers and first emerged as the team's go-to guy…Initially had made his mark on special teams as a 1995 rookie, returning both punts and kickoffs…Enhanced his contributions that year in the playoffs, making several important catches to go along with numerous big plays on returns…**1997:** Taking his play to new levels, led Green Bay in receiving during the regular season for the second straight year, posting career-high numbers in receptions (81), receiving yards (1,243) and touchdown receptions (12)…Joined Sterling Sharpe and Brooks as the only players in team history to catch 80-or-more passes in one season as he registered the sixth-highest, one-season reception total in club record books…Was fifth in the NFC in receptions (eighth in the NFL) and fourth in the conference in receiving yards (seventh in the league)…Became just the sixth 1,000-yard receiver in team history in recording his first career 1,000-yard season…Teamed with Brooks to form the first-ever pair of Green Bay pass-catchers to each have over 1,000 yards receiving, the duo posting a team-record 2,253 yards (old record: 2,130 by James Lofton and John Jefferson in 1983)…Finished second in the NFC, behind the Vikings' Carter, with 12 TD catches…Tied three other players for second in the NFL in third-down receptions (29), trailing only the 31 of the Cardinals' Frank Sanders…Additionally was fourth in conference scoring among non-kickers with 72 points and 11th in the NFC in total yards from scrimmage (1,257)…Tied for sixth in average yards per catch (15.3) among the NFC's top 20 receivers…Started all 16 regular-season games for the first time as a pro, opening 15 at split end and one at flanker (Nov. 16 at Indianapolis when Brooks was inactive due to a rib injury)…Also started all three playoff contests, including Super Bowl XXXII, in elevating his personal game during the postseason…Led the team in receptions (17), receiving yards (308) and touchdown receptions (3) during the playoffs…Put himself in line for game MVP honors (with a different final score) with a magnificent performance in 31-24 Super Bowl loss to Denver (Jan. 25), catching 9 passes (for 126 yards and 2 touchdowns) to equal the Packers' all-time playoff record…Made a tremendous, 22-yard, over-the-shoulder grab at the very back of the end zone for the game's first score less than five minutes into the Super Bowl, he later added a 13-yard touchdown on a crossing route to tie the contest at 24 early in the fourth quarter…Had turned in a similar showing in the NFC Championship Game two weeks earlier at San Francisco (Jan. 11)…Made 4 receptions for 107 yards (a season-high 26.8-yard average) and 1 touchdown in Green Bay's 23-10 triumph over the 49ers…Two plays after a long Eugene Robinson interception return had given the Packers the ball at the San Francisco 28-yard line, he caught a short slant pass from Brett Favre, cut back across the grain, breaking several tackles in the process, for a memorable 27-yard touchdown and a 10-0 Green Bay lead…Later hauled in a 40-yard reception from Favre seconds before halftime to set up a Ryan Longwell field goal which made the score 13-3…Took on the added responsibility of returning kickoffs during the postseason, running back 9 for 158 yards…Had four regular-season games where he caught 2 touchdown passes and three contests of 100-plus yards…After not catching a pass in the season opener, made at least 3 receptions in every game thereafter…Equaled his career high with 10 receptions (for a season-best 166 yards and touchdowns of 58 and 6 yards) in a 31-10 win at Carolina (Dec. 14) to earn NFC 'Offensive Player of the Week' honors…Earlier had received conference 'Offensive Player of the Week' recognition after making a team-leading 7 catches for 160 yards vs. St. Louis (Nov. 9), including a 25-yard TD reception, in the 17-7 victory…Had enjoyed one of his better games of the season early in the year vs. Minnesota (Sept. 21), catching 7 passes for 122 yards and 2 TDs; his first scoring catch allowed him to become part of Packers history as he was on the receiving end

THE PLAYERS

FREEMAN SCORES TOUCHDOWNS WITH THE BEST OF THEM

MOST TOUCHDOWN RECEPTIONS – NFL – 1996-97 SEASONS COMBINED

23	Cris Carter, Minnesota (10 in 1996, 13 in 1997)
21	ANTONIO FREEMAN, Green Bay (9 in 1996, 12 in 1997)
20	Tony Martin, San Diego (14 in 1996, 6 in 1997)
19	Joey Galloway, Seattle (7 in 1996, 12 in 1997)
18	Derrick Alexander, Baltimore (9 in 1996, 9 in 1997)
	Michael Jackson, Baltimore (14 in 1996, 4 in 1997)

of Favre's 153rd career touchdown pass to break Bart Starr's long-standing team record of 152...Hauled in touchdown receptions of 31 and 6 yards to lead Green Bay to a 21-16 win over previously-unbeaten Tampa Bay (Oct. 5)...Led Packers with 7 catches for 86 yards at Chicago (Oct. 12) the following week...Had 2 touchdowns (of 16 and 26 yards) at Indianapolis (Nov. 16) among a team-high 5 receptions for 93 yards, he also provided excellent downfield blocking on Dorsey Levens' 52-yard scoring run along the right sideline...Caught 3 passes for 56 yards vs. Dallas (Nov. 23), including a 23-yard touchdown reception midway through the fourth quarter; the Cowboys had closed to within 24-17 until Freeman's TD catch made it 31-17 in the Packers' eventual 45-17 triumph...Also had drawn a 34-yard pass interference penalty on the Cowboys' Deion Sanders on Green Bay's opening drive of the second half, setting up a touchdown two plays later which put the Packers out front 17-10...Made a team-leading 6 receptions for a game-high 85 yards in the Packers' 27-11 win at Minnesota (Dec. 1), including key third-down catches on each of the club's first two scoring drives; he also had his first NFL carry against the Vikings on a 14-yard reverse...Posted a club-high 6 receptions (for 63 yards), a four-yard touchdown catch among them, in 31-21, season-closing win over Buffalo (Dec. 20)...Had caught his first TD pass of the season on Sept. 14 vs. Miami, when he hauled in a two-yard throw from Favre early in the second quarter of 23-18 victory...**1996:** Emerged in training camp to win the Packers' starting split end job...Despite missing four weeks due to injury, he still led the team in both receptions (56) and receiving yards (933) for the first time...Also finished second on the club (to Keith Jackson) with 9 touchdown catches...Had his personal season interrupted for a month when he suffered a fractured left forearm (ulna) early in the second Tampa Bay game (Oct. 27), an injury which necessitated surgery two days later to stabilize the fracture and to attach a plate...Was inactive for the ensuing four games before he returned to the field with his arm in a cast, a protective measure he was forced to endure for the balance of the season...Went on a blistering pace after coming back from his injury-forced hiatus, catching 25 passes for 452 yards and 4 touchdowns during the team's perfect, 4-0 December to earn NFC 'Offensive Player of the Month' honors...Made a career-high 10 receptions (for 156 yards) vs. Chicago (Dec. 1) in his memorable return to the lineup...Had a second straight outstanding game the ensuing week against Denver, when he caught 9 passes for a career-high 175 yards and a career-best 3 touchdowns in a 41-6 shellacking of the Broncos (Dec. 8)...His production vs. Denver included a 14-yard TD grab to give Green Bay a 13-3 lead just before halftime and a 51-yard touchdown catch, where he broke the tackle of the Broncos' Tory James, midway through the third quarter to crack the game wide open at 20-6...His 331 receiving yards in successive weeks against Chicago and Denver represented the fifth-highest two-game total in club annals and the most in consecutive games since Lofton had a team-record 368 yards two straight weekends in 1984...Made at least one big play in each of the Packers' three playoff games en route to Green Bay's 12th world championship...Caught a pivotal touchdown pass in Super Bowl XXXI vs. New England (Jan. 26) to give the Packers a 17-14 lead and swing the momentum back to Green Bay after the Patriots had scored 14 unanswered points for a 14-10 advantage...It stands as the longest reception in Super Bowl history, an 81-yard catch-and-run along the right sideline where he beat the bump-and-run coverage of Pats strong safety Lawyer Milloy at the line, then outran free safety Willie Clay, who was giving chase from across the field...Totaled 3 receptions for 105 yards against New England...Made an impressive over-the-shoulder touchdown reception of 6 yards on a fade pattern late in the first half of NFC Championship Game vs. Carolina (Jan. 12), giving Green Bay a 14-10 lead in the eventual 30-13 triumph over the Panthers...Recovered an Edgar Bennett fumble in the end zone for the Packers' fourth touchdown in 35-14, divisional playoff victory over San Francisco (Jan. 4), a score which capped a 72-yard drive by Green Bay immediately following a quick 49ers TD early in the third quarter which had pulled them to within 21-14...Set a new club postseason record for most consecutive games scoring a touchdown with his score in each of the Packers' three '96 contests...Was second on the team (behind Levens) in receptions during the playoffs with 9 for 174 yards and 2 touchdowns...Finished the regular season 12th in the NFC in receiving yards and 20th in the conference in catches...Enjoyed the first five (four regular season, one postseason) 100-yard receiving games of his pro career in his inaugural year as a starter...Had the third-highest percentage of first downs to receptions in the NFL (30 catch minimum), his 82.1% (46 first downs among 56 receptions) left him behind only the Redskins' Henry Ellard (94.2%) and the Bears' Bobby Engram (84.8%)...Named to the 'All-Madden Team' by Fox Sports analyst John Madden...Though 14 of his 15 total starts (12 regular season, three postseason) were at split end, he frequently was called upon early in the year to fill in for Brooks at flanker...Initially did so in win at Seattle (Sept. 29) after Brooks went out with a concussion on the Packers' first play from scrimmage, responding with 7 catches (2 for touchdowns) and his first career 100-yard game (108) as a pro...Followed that performance with an exceptional outing on Oct. 6 at Chicago, making 7 receptions for 146 yards, including two amazing touchdown catches – the first coming on a 50-yard "Hail Mary" pass on the last play of the first half, the second an acrobatic, 35-yard grab over a Bear defender late in the third quarter to give Green Bay a 34-6 lead in the eventual 37-6 victory...His only start of the year at flanker came in the same Buccaneers contest in which he was injured as Brooks had gone out for the season one game earlier vs. San Francisco...Made a team-leading 6 receptions for 82 yards in season-opening victory at Tampa Bay (Sept. 1)...**1995:** Got opportunity early in his rookie season to contribute as a return man after incumbent Charles Jordan was hampered by shoulder and knee injuries, he never really relinquished the role...Subsequently became more involved in the offense as the year went on, seeing regular duty in four-receiver formations by the time the playoffs rolled around...Twice was named NFL 'Special Teams Player of the Week' during the playoffs as a result of his performances against Atlanta (Dec. 31) and at Dallas in the NFC Championship Game (Jan. 14)...Broke open close playoff game with Falcons by returning a Dan Stryzinski punt 76 yards for a touchdown midway through the second quarter – the first-ever scoring return of either a punt or kickoff in Green Bay's storied postseason history...Also had 2 kickoff returns for 54 yards vs. Atlanta, including a 42-yarder right after the Falcons had scored a quick touchdown for an early 7-0 lead...Totaled 202 return yards in Cowboys contest – 7 for 148 yards on kickoffs and 4 for 54 yards on punts...His 39-yard punt return late in the first quarter of NFC title game triggered a Green Bay touchdown three plays later which gave the Packers a 17-14 advantage...One week earlier had made a favorable impression as a receiver at San Francisco (Jan. 6), catching 2 passes for first downs on the opening drive of 27-17 triumph over 49ers...Led team and finished fifth in the NFC in kickoff returns with a 23.2-yard average (24 returns for 556 yards)...Set club rookie record with 37 punt returns (for 292 yards)...Also caught 8 passes for 106 yards and 1 touchdown...Made 2 receptions vs. the N.Y. Giants (Sept. 17) in his initial league game...Scored his first touchdown in the NFL at New Orleans (Dec. 16) when he caught an 11-yard pass from Favre late in the second quarter among his season-high 3 receptions...Provided Packers with great field position in key, 35-28 win over Chicago (Nov. 12) with a 26-yard punt return in the first quarter and a 45-yard kickoff return in the third period – both runbacks set up a Green Bay touchdown on the very next play...Averaged an impressive 35.3 yards on 3 kickoff returns in same Bears contest...Saw action in 11 regular-season games as a reserve, was inactive for four contests and did not play in another...Played in all three postseason games, making his first career start in NFC Championship Game at Dallas (Jan. 14) when Packers opened in a four-wide receiver formation...Caught 4 passes for 43 yards in the playoffs, he also averaged 14.3 yards returning punts (10-143) and 23.2 yards returning kickoffs (11-255)...Had enjoyed a tremendous preseason, leading club with 10 receptions and averaging 12.4 yards per punt return...Was the last of four third-round draft choices (90th overall pick and ninth wide receiver) by Green Bay in 1995.

COLLEGE: Three-year starter and four-time letterman (1991-94) at Virginia Tech...Was redshirted in 1990...Departed as the Hokies' all-time leader in receptions with 121 (for 2,207 yards)...Also set school record with 22 career receiving touchdowns – 11 of which went for 45 yards or more...Established himself as one of the country's top punt returners in his final collegiate season...Was team leader in catches each of his last three years...Earned All-Big East second-team honors as both a wide receiver and punt returner in 1994, when he caught a career-best 38 passes for 586 yards and 5 TDs...Led conference and finished sixth nationally in punt returns as a senior, setting a school single-season record for yardage with 467 on 39 returns (12.0 avg.)...Returned a punt 80 yards for a touchdown in '94 game against Pittsburgh...Made 32 receptions for 644 yards as a junior, including a Tech single-season record 9 touchdown catches...Set Big East one-game record with 194 receiving yards vs. Temple, he also equaled school mark with 3 TD receptions in same contest...Was a third-team pick on 'Sophomore All-America' squad of *Football News* in

1992...Averaged a school-record 22.0 yards per catch (32 receptions for 703 yards and 6 touchdowns)...Became just second player in Tech history to catch 3 touchdown passes of 60-plus yards in one season; included in that group was an 83-yard score against West Virginia...Finished third on team in receptions in 1991 with 19 for 274 yards and 2 TDs...Holds B.S. degree in human resources.

PERSONAL: Given name Antonio Michael Freeman...Nicknamed 'Free' and 'Buttons'...Born in Baltimore...Single...Named prep 'Offensive Player of the Year' by the *Baltimore Sun* and received honorable mention on *USA Today* All-America team as a 1989 senior at Polytechnic High School in Baltimore, his team went 10-0 that year, won the Maryland Group A title and was ranked 23rd in the nation...Averaged 23 yards per reception during his senior season, when he caught 47 passes for 1,079 yards and 9 touchdowns...Lettered twice in football as a wide receiver and cornerback, he also won two letters in basketball...Was the first player in the history of Polytechnic High School to have his football jersey number retired, when his number 80 was put into mothballs in October of 1996...Sponsored a basketball team in Baltimore's Oliver Recreation League (which he played in as a youth) from 1996-97, his team advanced to the national AAU tournament in '97...Is a devout fan of his hometown Baltimore Orioles...Hobbies include music and basketball...Residence: Baltimore.

PRO STATISTICS:

			RECEIVING					RUSHING			
Year	G/S	No.	Yds.	Avg.	LG	TD	No.	Yds.	Avg.	LG	TD
1995 Green Bay..........11/0		8	106	13.3	28	1	0	0	0.0	0	0
1996 Green Bay........12/12		56	933	16.7	51t	9	0	0	0.0	0	0
1997 Green Bay........16/16		81	1,243	15.3	58t	12	1	14	14.0	14	0
Totals.................39/28		145	2,282	15.7	58t	22	1	14	14.0	14	0
Playoffs 9/7		30	525	17.5	81t	5	0	0	0.0	0	0

			PUNT RETURNS					KICKOFF RETURNS			
Year	No.	FC	Yds.	Avg.	LG	TD	No.	Yds.	Avg.	LG	TD
1995 Green Bay 37		3	292	7.9	26	0	24	556	23.2	45	0
1996 Green Bay 0		0	0	0.0	0	0	1	16	16.0	16	0
1997 Green Bay 0		0	0	0.0	0	0	0	0	0.0	0	0
Totals.....................37		3	292	7.9	26	0	25	572	22.9	45	0
Playoffs 10		2	143	14.3	76t	1	20	413	20.7	42	0

Other Touchdowns: 1, fumble recovery in end zone vs. San Francisco (1/4/97-postseason)
Miscellaneous Tackles: 1 in 1995; 1 in 1996; 1 in 1997 for total of 3
100-Yard Receiving Games: 4 in 1996; 1 in 1996 Playoffs; 3 in 1997; 2 in 1997 Playoffs for total of 7

CAREER SINGLE-GAME HIGHS

Most Receptions: 10, vs. Chicago (12/1/96) and at Carolina (12/14/97); **Most Receiving Yards:** 175, vs. Denver (12/8/96); **Longest Receptions:** 81t, vs. New England at N.O. (1/26/96-postseason) / 58t, at Carolina (12/14/97); **Most TD Receptions:** 3, vs. Denver (12/8/96)

BERNARDO HARRIS   55

Linebacker
College: North Carolina
NFL Exp.: 4th Season   **Packers Exp.:** 4th Season
Ht.: 6-2   **Wt.:** 248   **Born:** 10/15/71   **Acq:** FA-95

PRO: Emerging young player who earned his stripes on special teams for two years before becoming a full-time performer last season...Won the starting spot at middle linebacker during the '97 training camp in the absence of incumbent starter George Koonce (who was rehabilitating a knee injury), then lived up to his preseason performance by leading the team in tackles...Quiet and unassuming, should further grow into his leadership role with another year of experience..."We are very comfortable with him as a starter," says Green Bay defensive coordinator Fritz Shurmur. "Last year he went in there and really had an outstanding year as the middle linebacker and the signal-caller for our defense. I think the biggest thing he does well is understand the defense from a physical standpoint, then turn that into playing the defense well. He understands pass coverage and does as good of a job as we've had done in there at the middle linebacker position. The thing you always have to do is become more adept at running a defense, and that is make the adjustments, make the calls and do all those kinds of things. And as he gets more and more familiar with it, he gets more and more comfortable with it, he has more and more experience in it, he'll be more effective at it. He's a bright guy, and we feel confident that we'll see him take the next step."...Led or tied for the team lead in tackles in seven different 1997 games, including four double-digit performances...Had been an excellent special teams player for Green Bay during the 1995-96 seasons...Took a tremendous amount of pride in leading the Packers' highly-regarded coverage units in tackles during the club's Super Bowl-winning campaign of '96...Overcame his naturally mild-mannered personality last season to become the defensive leader that his middle linebacker position demands..."I think he fought his way through that," Shurmur adds. "He became more forceful and became louder. He's a quiet guy, and it's not natural for him to be a loud guy, but I think he understands more and more that he's got to exert himself a little more, to be more forceful with the calls and the things he does, because it's just a matter of hearing and, when 80,000 people are screaming, you've got to be able to go above and beyond that and communicate what he needs to communicate to them."...Has played all three linebacker positions for the Packers, having concentrated on outside linebacker during each of his initial two seasons with the team...Battled through a broken arm in training camp his first year in Green Bay to make the team's 53-man roster in 1995 as a virtually unknown free agent...Had spent the '94 season out of football, working at an auto parts dealership in his hometown, after a short-lived attempt for a roster spot with the Chiefs...**1997:** Mounted an impressive training camp performance to earn the starting job at middle linebacker...Started all 16 regular-season games for the first time, he also started all three of the club's playoff contests, including Super Bowl XXXII...Led the team with a career-high 119 stops (86 solo) – his first-ever 100-tackle season...Also had 1 sack, 1 interception and 5 passes defensed...Finished second (to Eugene Robinson) in tackles during the postseason with 24 (15 solo), including 1 sack, plus 1 pass defensed...Sacked Steve Young in the fourth quarter of 23-10, NFC Championship Game victory at San Francisco (Jan. 11) among 6 total tackles...Made 11 stops in Super Bowl loss to Denver, a total bettered only by Robinson (14)...Earlier had posted four double-digit tackle games during the regular season to lead the club...Made a career-high 14 stops (8 solo) at Chicago (Oct. 12) in a game which also saw him set up the eventual winning points in 24-23 victory...Recorded a key, diving interception – the first of his NFL career – in the fourth quarter at the Bears' 19-yard line after running back Raymont Harris was hit by teammate Brian Williams and the ball popped into the air; Green Bay subsequently kicked a field goal for its final points of the afternoon...One week earlier vs. Tampa Bay (Oct. 5), had contributed 13 stops, including a season-best 10 solo tackles...Had started a personal, three-game span of 10-or-more tackles with 11 stops at Detroit (Sept. 28)...Began season with an 11-tackle effort in the opener vs. the Bears (Sept. 1)...Led or tied for the team lead in tackles seven times, including six of the first seven games...Made 9 stops at Philadelphia (Sept. 7) and vs. Minnesota (Sept. 21) to also pace club...Gave

Packers a big lift going into halftime of eventual 17-7 win over St. Louis (Nov. 9), blocking a Rams field goal attempt as time expired to protect a 3-0 Green Bay lead as the teams headed to the locker rooms...Recorded his first-ever NFL sack in 45-17 triumph over Dallas (Nov. 23), blitzing the Cowboys' Troy Aikman on the second play of the game...**1996:** Primarily a backup at the 'Buck' (left outside) linebacker position, in addition to his extensive special teams responsibilities, played in all 16 regular-season games for the initial time as a pro...Also got into the club's three playoff contests, including Super Bowl XXXI...Led the Packers with 21 tackles (14 solo) on special teams during the regular season, the most by a Green Bay player since Jackie Harris had posted 22 in 1990...Subsequently tied (with Travis Jervey) for the club lead in special teams stops during the postseason with 6...Enjoyed one of the best coverage games by a Packer in recent memory when he equaled his career high with 4 special teams tackles in NFC Championship Game triumph over home state Carolina Panthers (Jan. 12)...Earlier had recorded 4 stops with the special teams in 41-6 shellacking of Denver (Dec. 8)...Posted 2 tackles on kick coverage in five other regular-season games as well as in the Super Bowl...Forced a fumble by Andre Coleman on kickoff coverage late in the first half of win over San Diego (Sept. 15), which teammate Tyrone Williams recovered...Totaled 5 tackles (4 solo) as a member of the defense...Received playing time at linebacker in games at Tampa Bay (Sept. 1), at Seattle (Sept. 29), at Chicago (Oct. 6), vs. Broncos and at Detroit (Dec. 15)...Made a season-best 3 stops in Bears contest...**1995:** Saw action in 11 regular-season games plus all three postseason contests, mostly in a special teams capacity...Received his most extensive defensive action of the season at Cleveland (Nov. 19) when starting middle linebacker Fred Strickland left the game in the first quarter due to a knee injury...Responded to the challenge by posting a season-high 4 tackles vs. the Browns...Also got prolonged duty at middle linebacker three weeks later at Tampa Bay (Dec. 10), playing in Joe Kelly's stead in the first half after Kelly shifted outside to replace an injured Koonce (wrist)...Ranked seventh on the team in special teams tackles with 11, including a season-best 2 vs. Detroit (Oct. 15), Chicago (Nov. 12) and New Orleans (Dec. 16)...Blocked a John Jett punt on the opening series at Dallas in NFC Championship Game (Jan. 14), leading to a Green Bay field goal...Had played in Packers' first three preseason games, performing well, until fracturing his left arm in the third, Aug. 19 vs. Indianapolis...Subsequently was inactive for each of Green Bay's first four regular-season contests...Got first playing time in the NFL on Oct. 8 vs. the Cowboys at Texas Stadium, he made 1 special teams tackle that day...Later was inactive in finale against Pittsburgh (Dec. 24) due to a lingering ankle sprain originally suffered three weeks earlier vs. Cincinnati...Had joined the Packers on Jan. 13, 1995, as a free agent...**1994:** Originally signed by the Kansas City Chiefs on June 2, 1994, as an undrafted free agent, he suffered a minor knee injury in practice within the first week of training camp...Subsequently was waived on Aug. 4 after the completion of his rehabilitation...Spent the remainder of the season out of football, working in the auto parts department of a BMW dealership in Chapel Hill, N.C.

COLLEGE: Two-year starter and four-time letterman (1990-93) at University of North Carolina...Finished his collegiate career with 224 tackles (117 solo), including 15 for loss and 7 sacks, as an outside linebacker...Also recorded 2 forced fumbles, 2 fumble recoveries and 1 interception...Was a second-team All-Atlantic Coast Conference selection as a senior when he had 85 tackles and 4½ sacks...Made a career-high 90 stops his junior season, the most by a Tar Heel outside linebacker since Lawrence Taylor had posted 95 in 1979...Had a career-best 18 stops in 1992 game with Army...Majored in physical education.

PERSONAL: Given name Bernardo Jamaine Harris...Born in Chapel Hill, N.C. ...Married to Kellie, couple has two sons, Bradley (born 5/4/94) and Blake (born 12/18/97)...Was an all-area and all-conference tight end and linebacker at Chapel Hill (N.C.) High School...As a senior, had 115 tackles and 4 interceptions at linebacker and caught 10 passes for 300 yards and 5 touchdowns at tight end...Earned three letters in football and one in basketball...Having grown up in Chapel Hill, then attended UNC, is an ardent fan of the North Carolina basketball team...Was involved with the 'Hometown Heroes' program in Durham, N.C., in 1996, he assisted with a football camp for area youth...Hobbies include playing basketball and golf, billiards and spending time with his family...Residence: Green Bay.

PRO STATISTICS:

Year	G/S	UT	AT	Sacks	Int.	Yds.	FR	FF	PD
1995 Green Bay 11/0		7	0	0	0	0	0	0	0
1996 Green Bay 16/0		4	1	0	0	0	0	0	0
1997 Green Bay 16/16		86	33	1	1	0	0	0	5
Totals 43/16		97	34	1	1	0	0	0	5
Playoffs 9/3		15	9	1	0	0	0	0	1

Special Teams Tackles: 11 (8-3) in 1995; 2 (1-1) in 1995 Playoffs; 21 (14-7) in 1996; 6 (5-1) in 1996 Playoffs; 1 (1-0) in 1997; 1 (1-0) in 1997 Playoffs for total of 33 (23-10)
Special Teams Forced Fumbles: 1 in 1996
Blocked Field Goals: 1, vs. St. Louis (11/9/97)
Blocked Punts: 1, at Dallas (1/14/96-postseason)

RAYMONT HARRIS · 29

Running Back
College: Ohio State
NFL Exp.: 5th Season   **Packers Exp.:** 1st Season
Ht.: 6-0 **Wt.:** 230 **Born:** 12/23/70 **Acq:** UFA-98 (Chi)

PRO: Versatile backfield performer and a 1,000-yard rusher in 1997, fifth-year running back joins Packers in 1998 after spending the past four seasons with the Chicago Bears...A solid all-around performer, equally adept at rushing and receiving, joins starters Dorsey Levens and William Henderson to add another weapon to the already potent Green Bay running backs corps...Packers offensive coordinator Sherm Lewis is pleased to work Harris into Green Bay's offensive plans for the '98 season, saying, "He's a quality back, a proven NFL back. He's a tough, hard-nosed, good inside runner and yet he's also got the speed to go all the way. So he's got a good combination of speed, size and toughness. He'll be a good addition. You can never get too many quality backs because you never know when they're going to go down. I've been in games when we've lost our first two backs in the first quarter, so he's definitely a great addition."...A veteran of 42 games with 35 starts, had rushed for 2,245 yards and 15 touchdowns on 592 carries (3.8 avg.) with the Bears...Leaves Bears in 12th place on the club's all-time rushing list...Lining up as a fullback, halfback and in single back sets, he also caught 100 passes for 651 yards and 1 touchdown during his four years in Chicago...Originally designated as the Bears' transition player (Feb. 13), the tag was removed April 20 and he subsequently signed with the Packers as an unrestricted free agent on July 19, turning down several other teams' offers and ending weeks of speculation around the league...**1997:** Started 13 games for Chicago and finished with career highs in carries (275), rushing yards (1,033) and touchdowns (10), becoming just the seventh running back in the Bears' history to post a 1,000-yard season...Led Bears in all three categories, his rushing touchdown total was second-best in the NFC, while his rushing yardage was sixth-highest in the conference...Also caught 28 passes for 115 yards to rank sixth on the team...Posted five 100-yard rushing games...Started first three contests at fullback before moving to running back in Week 4 at New England (Sept. 21), he proceeded to start at the position in 10 of the next 11 contests...Personal season came to an end vs. Buffalo (Dec. 7), when he suffered a fractured left leg upon being tackled at the end of a 20-yard run in the third quarter...Subsequently was placed on injured reserve Dec. 9 and underwent corrective surgery three days later...Had enjoyed a productive performance in season opener at Green Bay (Sept. 1), tying a career high with 122 rushing yards on 13 carries, with 2 touchdowns (also a career best)...His effort against the Packers included a career-long 68-yard TD run...Rushed for 120 yards on 29 carries at Dallas (Sept. 28)...Carried 27 times for 101 yards and 1 TD in second contest vs. Green Bay (Oct. 12)...Topped century mark again at Miami (Oct. 27), finishing with 106 yards and 1 TD on 25 rushing attempts...Left in third quarter of contest at Minnesota (Nov. 9) with a bruised side...Inactive for following week's contest vs. N.Y.

Jets (Nov. 16) with the side injury...Posted 116 yards and 1 TD on a career-high 33 carries vs. Tampa Bay (Nov. 23)...**1996:** Played in 12 games with 10 starts...Led Bears with 748 rushing yards on 194 carries with 4 touchdowns...Registered three 100-yard rushing games...Also posted a career-high 296 receiving yards on 32 receptions, with 1 touchdown...Became first Bear since Neal Anderson in 1987 to register both a 100-yard rushing and receiving game in the same season...Opened season with a career-high 103 receiving yards on 3 receptions vs. Dallas (Sept. 2), including a career-long 47 reception from punter Todd Sauerbrun on a fake punt...Also among his production vs. the Cowboys was a 33-yard touchdown catch, thrown by wide receiver Curtis Conway, which remains Harris' lone receiving TD in the NFL...Suffered knee injury vs. Minnesota (Sept. 15) and subsequently sat out the next four contests (Sept. 22 at Detroit, Sept. 29 vs. Oakland, Oct. 6 vs. Green Bay and Oct. 13 at New Orleans)...Returned to action at Minnesota (Oct. 28) and posted 61 yards on 15 carries...Was back in starting lineup vs. Tampa Bay (Nov. 3) and registered his first career 100-yard rushing day with 118 yards and 1 TD on 19 attempts...Carried 23 times for 112 yards at Denver (Nov. 10)...Notched another 100-yard game with 122 yards on 27 attempts vs. Detroit (Nov. 24)...Bettered 100 yards in total offense at Green Bay (Dec. 1) with 79 rushing (24 carries) and 28 receiving (5 catches)...Nabbed a season-high 6 receptions (22 yards) in finale at Tampa Bay (Dec. 22), when he also chipped in 26 rushing yards and 1 TD...**1995:** Started season opener vs. Minnesota (Sept. 3), but broke right collarbone upon falling out of bounds after a four-yard reception on the Bears' second play from scrimmage...Was inactive for the following 11 games before being placed on season-ending injured reserve (Nov. 29)...**1994:** Played in all 16 games as a rookie, making 11 starts at fullback...Rushed for 464 yards (second on team) on 123 carries, with 1 touchdown...Also caught a career-high 39 passes (for 236 yards), also good for second on club...Had just 4 rushing attempts fail to reach the line of scrimmage, best of all NFL backs with at least 100 carries...Also started both playoff contests, leading the team in rushing in winning effort at Minnesota (Jan. 1) with 67 yards on 13 carries, his production including a 29-yard TD...Again led team in rushing a week later at San Francisco (Jan. 7) with 26 yards on 8 carries in divisional playoff matchup...Also had 5 receptions for 24 yards vs. 49ers...Established a career high with 7 receptions (for 51 yards) at Miami (Nov. 13), tying it a week later (7 for 53) vs. Detroit (Nov. 20)...Registered a season-high 92 yards and his first professional touchdown among 23 carries vs. L.A. Rams (Dec. 18)...Recovered a fumbled punt at N.Y. Jets (Sept. 25)...Drafted in the fourth round (114th overall, and 16th running back) by Chicago in 1994.

COLLEGE: A four-year letter winner at Ohio State (1990-93), starting the final two years...Finished as the Buckeyes' fifth-ranking rusher of all-time with 2,649 yards on 574 carries (4.6 avg.), with 27 touchdowns...Also had 17 receptions for 122 yards and 1 TD as a collegian...As a senior, notched five 100-yard rushing efforts and posted 1,344 yards and 12 touchdowns overall on 273 carries...Had career day in senior year performance in the Holiday Bowl, rushing for 235 yards and 3 TDs on 39 carries, helping Buckeyes to 28-21 victory over Brigham Young...Performance ranked as Ohio State's fourth-best single-game total and the school's best-ever bowl game total...Gained starting halfback position as a junior and finished year with 463 yards and 5 TDs on 106 carries...Redshirted in 1989...Majored in communications.

PERSONAL: Given name Raymont LaShawn Harris...Nicknamed 'Quiet Storm' and 'UltraBack'...Born in Lorain, Ohio...Married to Leslie, couple has a son, Elijah (born 1/7/98)...Also has a daughter, Shakia (born 9/1/90)...Earned two letters in football, three in baseball and one in track at Admiral King High School in Lorain, Ohio...Played in just four games as a senior due to a broken collarbone...Has given time to United Negro College Fund...Hobbies include playing golf and writing poetry...Residence: Libertyville, Ill.

PRO STATISTICS:

Year		G/S	No.	Yds.	Avg.	LG	TD	No.	Yds.	Avg.	LG	TD
			RUSHING					**RECEIVING**				
1994	Chicago	16/11	123	464	3.8	13	1	39	236	6.1	18	0
1995	Chicago	1/1	0	0	0.0	0	0	1	4	4.0	4	0
1996	Chicago	12/10	194	748	3.9	23	4	32	296	9.3	47	1
1997	Chicago	13/13	275	1,033	3.8	68t	10	28	115	4.1	16	0
Totals		42/35	592	2,245	3.8	68t	15	100	651	6.5	47	1
Playoffs		2/2	21	93	4.4	29	1	8	44	5.5	10	0

Kickoff Returns: 1 for 18 yards in 1994
100-Yard Rushing Games: 3 in 1996; 5 in 1997 for total of 8
100-Yard Receiving Games: 1 in 1996

WILLIAM HENDERSON 33

Fullback

College: North Carolina
NFL Exp.: 4th Season   **Packers Exp.:** 4th Season
Ht.: 6-1   **Wt.:** 245   **Born:** 2/19/71   **Acq:** D3b-95

PRO: Perhaps the best blocking fullback in the National Football League, Green Bay's running fortunes have taken a decided upturn over the past two seasons with him in the starting lineup...Dominating, he takes tremendous pride in pummeling opponents – with secondary desire to carry the football...Is a bona fide Pro Bowl candidate, though one who in the past has been overlooked due to his conference counterparts who play more of a headliner role in their teams' offenses...Was credited by teammate Dorsey Levens as a key component in Levens' 1,435-yard season on the ground (second-best in team history) in 1997...That success followed just one year after the Packers' rushing average jumped better than 25 yards per game from the year before in his initial season as the starter...Has proven to be a surprisingly effective pass-catcher out of the backfield, averaging 34 receptions per season as the club's starter...Also has done the job consistently as a short-yardage rusher, picking up a first down on 80% (8-of-10) of his 1997 carries where two-or-fewer yards was needed to move the chains, including a perfect 3-of-3 on third down..."William may be the best blocking fullback in the NFL," says Green Bay offensive coordinator Sherm Lewis, "and is one of the key reasons for the success Dorsey Levens enjoyed in '97. Our coaches feel that he is a much better runner than he is given credit for, and we would like to see him get more carries this season. He also has demonstrated a rare ability to make first defenders miss after catching short passes out of the backfield. William is a very unselfish player who only cares about winning and enjoys the role he plays."...Ironically, the destruction he routinely causes when matching up head-to-head with opposition linebackers and defensive backs belie the quiet, focused Christian man he is on the inside...Highly dependable, missed only nine snaps with the base offense last season...Had won the starting fullback job late in '96 training camp over incumbent Levens, in large part due to his extraordinary blocking skills...Also adds another, less noticeable element to the Green Bay attack, according to Lewis, who says, "He brings a degree of toughness to the field. I like to refer to him as a tempo setter for us. He kind of sets the tempo for the offense by being physical."...In this day of increased emphasis on individual accolades, Henderson takes a uniquely simplistic approach to his duties, saying, "My job is to block. I consider myself a glorified guard here. I feel like I'm a lineman. I won't have the perfect game until every linebacker is lying flat on their backs."...Despite the fact that he wasn't invited to any postseason all-star games or the NFL scouting combine after a collegiate career lacking in stats, was targeted by the Packers as the player they wanted to draft in 1995 to help jump-start the Green Bay running game...Subsequently had his rookie season push for the starting lineup short-circuited by a knee injury early in training camp, but since has lived up to the club's lofty expectations over the past two seasons...**1997:** Played in all 16 regular-season games for the second straight year, starting all but two (each time when the Packers opened with an extra wide receiver)...Served a vital role in Levens' 1,435-yard rushing season (No. 2 in club record books) and helped the Packers to improve their team rushing average by another five yards over the year before, up to 119.3...Also started all three playoff contests, Super Bowl XXXII among them, in the process helping Levens to average 105.3 yards per game on the ground during the postseason, including two 100-yard rushing performances (112 vs. Tampa Bay and 114 at San Francisco – which also

111

stand as the top two individual performances in Green Bay playoff history)…Finished fourth on the team in receptions during the regular season with a career-best 41 (for a career-high 367 yards)…Also was the club's fourth-ranking rusher with 113 yards on 31 carries…Gained a season-high 32 yards rushing, including a season-long 15-yard run, in a 31-10 win at Carolina (Dec. 14) – with his lead blocking spurring the balance of a 218-yard effort on the ground vs. the Panthers…Made a team-leading and career-high 7 receptions (for 60 yards), including a 10-yard touchdown catch late in the fourth quarter, in 23-18 victory over Miami (Sept. 14)…Also helped the Packers to gain 142 yards rushing against the Dolphins…Caught 4 passes for 45 yards and enjoyed one of the better blocking games of his career at Indianapolis (Nov. 16), helping to spring Levens on numerous long plays, including a 56-yard screen pass and a 52-yard touchdown run down the right sideline…Continued his blocking dominance in the following two games, vs. Dallas (Nov. 23) and at Minnesota (Dec. 1)…Helped Green Bay to rush for a season-best 220 yards against the Cowboys, including a team-record 190 yards by Levens, he also caught 5 passes himself in the 45-17 triumph…Then was a catalyst for 139 yards on the ground vs. the Vikings, 108 by Levens…Made a season-long 25-yard reception in win over St. Louis (Nov. 9)…Carried a season-high 6 times (for 16 yards) and had 4 catches at Philadelphia (Sept. 7)…**1996:** In his initial season as the Packers' full-time starter at fullback, played in all 16 games for the first time in his pro career, starting all but five (when Green Bay opened in double-tight end or four-wide receiver formations)…Served as a primary catalyst for the better than 25-yard improvement in the Packers' running game over the year before (114.9 yards per game in 1996 vs. 89.3 in '95)…Finished fourth on the team in rushing in his limited opportunity to carry the ball, gaining 130 yards on 39 carries…Also made 27 receptions (for 203 yards and 1 touchdown) to rank seventh on the club…Started all three postseason games, including Super Bowl XXXI, and assisted Green Bay to an even better rushing average than during the regular season (151.7 yards per game)…Made a season-high 5 receptions for 62 yards, including a career-long 27-yarder, at Kansas City (Nov. 10)…Scored the first touchdown of his NFL career on Sept. 15 vs. San Diego, when he caught an eight-yard pass from Brett Favre late in the second quarter to give the Packers a 21-3 halftime lead in an eventual 42-10 victory…Had 4 catches total against the Chargers…Had rushed for a career-best 40 yards on only 6 carries in Monday night thrashing of Philadelphia just six days earlier (Sept. 9)…Was given starting fullback job over Levens late in training camp after demonstrating superior blocking throughout the preseason…**1995:** Played in final 15 regular-season games, including first NFL start in finale vs. Pittsburgh (Dec. 24)…Had been inactive for opener vs. St. Louis (Sept. 3) while rehabbing from arthroscopic knee surgery…Rebounded from early setback of knee injury to become one of Packers' most effective blockers by the end of his rookie season, frequently rotating into the offense as a powerful blocker in running situations…Finished campaign fourth on the team in rushing with 35 yards on 7 carries, he also caught 3 passes for 21 yards…Missed all four preseason games after suffering torn cartilage in his left knee Aug. 1 in a training camp practice…Subsequently had knee scoped on Aug. 9…Turned in career-long 17-yard run on his first professional carry, Sept. 24 at Jacksonville…Got extensive playing time Oct. 8 at Dallas as usual starter Levens was inactive due to a knee injury…Turned in banner blocking effort Nov. 19 at Cleveland, often going head-to-head with Browns LB Pepper Johnson…Saw reserve duty in all three playoff games…Regularly played at fullback in short-yardage and goal-line situations with Levens moving to halfback…Was the second of four third-round draft choices (66th overall) by Green Bay in 1995.

COLLEGE: A four-time letter winner at North Carolina (1991-94)…Redshirted in 1990 as he continued rehabilitation on a high school knee injury…Averaged better than five yards per carry (5.2) as a collegian…Carried 145 times for 750 yards and 8 touchdowns during his career, he also caught 14 passes for 97 yards…Split playing time with Malcolm Marshall each of his final two seasons…Rushed for 251 yards (on 47 carries) and served as co-captain his senior year…Helped pave the way for two different Tar Heel tailbacks to rush for over 1,000 yards as a junior, when he personally gained 242 yards on 51 attempts…Missed only one game in 1992, but injuries limited his availability for much of the season, he carried only twice for five yards…Was co-recipient of the 'Jeffrey Cowell Memorial Award' in '91 as the Tar Heels' 'Most Outstanding First-Year Player' after rushing for a career-high 252 yards on 45 attempts…Had a career-best 101-yard rushing day vs. Maryland in 1991…Holds a B.S. degree in physical education with a concentration in sports science, he also minored in African-American studies.

PERSONAL: Given name William Terrelle Henderson…Nicknamed 'Boogie'…Born in Richmond, Va. …Single…Sat out his senior season at Thomas Dale High School in Chester, Va., after suffering a severe knee injury (torn anterior cruciate ligament) in the team's first scrimmage of the year…Still was selected as one of the state's top five prospects by the *Roanoke Times*…Played fullback, linebacker and placekicker, earning two letters…Chosen second-team all-state as a junior, when he gained 707 yards and scored 11

touchdowns...Also earned all-region and all-district honors on offense and defense...Rushed for 606 yards and 7 TDs as a sophomore...Had a career long field goal of 52 yards...Lettered four times in track as well, finishing second in the discus at the state meet...Spent this past offseason studying for his athletic training certification exam, he plans to eventually work toward a master's degree in physical therapy...Hobbies include drawing, arts and crafts, watching cartoons (*South Park* is his favorite) and relaxing...The Redskins' John Riggins was his hero as a kid...Did landscaping work while in college...Enjoys charity work involving children...Has worked with Special Olympics in Milwaukee and North Carolina, as well as with Big Brothers/Big Sisters, the Leukemia Society, the Crippled Children's Fund and the Rainbow Games...Splits residence between Green Bay and Chapel Hill, N.C.

PRO STATISTICS:

Year	G/S	RUSHING					RECEIVING				
		No.	Yds.	Avg.	LG	TD	No.	Yds.	Avg.	LG	TD
1995 Green Bay..........15/1		7	35	5.0	17	0	3	21	7.0	9	0
1996 Green Bay........16/11		39	130	3.3	14	0	27	203	7.5	27	1
1997 Green Bay........16/14		31	113	3.6	15	0	41	367	9.0	25	1
Totals.................47/26		77	278	3.6	17	0	71	591	8.3	27	2
Playoffs 9/6		10	14	1.4	4	0	9	46	5.1	8	0

Kickoff Returns: 2 for 38 yards, 19.0 avg., LG 23 in 1996
Special Teams Tackles: 1 (1-0) in 1995
Miscellaneous Tackles: 1 in 1996; 3 in 1997 for total of 4

CAREER SINGLE-GAME HIGHS

Most Rushing Attempts: 6, vs. Philadelphia (9/9/96) and at Philadelphia (9/7/97); **Most Rushing Yards:** 40, vs. Philadelphia (9/9/96); **Longest Run:** 17, at Jacksonville (9/24/95); **Most Receptions:** 7, vs. Miami (9/14/97); **Most Receiving Yards:** 62, at Kansas City (11/10/96); **Longest Reception:** 27, at Kansas City (11/10/96); **Most TD Receptions:** 1, vs. San Diego (9/15/96) and vs. Miami (9/14/97)

ANTHONY HICKS 　 **50**

Linebacker
College: *Arkansas*
NFL Exp.: *2nd Season*　　**Packers Exp.:** *2nd Season*
Ht.: *6-1*　**Wt.:** *243*　**Born:** *3/31/74*　**Acq:** *D5-97*

PRO: A well-equipped athlete with good size, speed and quickness who should compete for a roster spot as a backup linebacker...Spent his entire 1997, rookie year on injured reserve after suffering a preseason leg injury..."In spurts, he has shown that he has the talent to compete for a position as a backup and special teams player," says Packers defensive coordinator Fritz Shurmur. "After having moved him around several times, it appears as though the middle linebacker position is the one in which he'll challenge for a spot on the roster. We expect him to display skills as a front-line special teams performer and, if this happens, he has an excellent chance to make the roster."...**1997:** Strained his right quadriceps in the team's third preseason game, at Oakland (Aug. 8)...Subsequently was placed on season-ending injured reserve on Aug. 19...Had totaled 3 tackles during the preseason...Drafted in the fifth round (160th overall) by Green Bay in 1997.

COLLEGE: A one-year starter and four-time letter winner (1993-96) at Arkansas...Redshirted in 1992...Played in 33 games for the Razorbacks, he overcame injuries early in his collegiate career to start

13 contests his last two seasons, including 10 starts as a senior...Totaled 129 career tackles, including 2 sacks and 3 for loss, 1 interception, 1 fumble recovery and 6 passes defensed...Had a career-high 61 stops as a senior, including a single-game career-best 9 vs. Auburn...Suffered a knee injury during the preseason that caused him to miss the majority of his 1994, sophomore year...Received a B.A. degree in retail management (1996) and administrative management (1997).

PERSONAL: Given name Anthony O'neil Hicks...Nicknamed 'Wildman' and 'Triple H'...Born in Strong, Ark. ...Single...Has a son, Zachary (born 6/29/96)...Was an all-district and all-state selection in football as a senior at Arkadelphia (Ark.)/Strong High School...Earned two letters as a fullback, tailback and cornerback...Produced over 1,000 all-purpose yards as a senior, including 759 yards rushing...Was an all-district pick and lettered three times each in basketball and track...Also captained the football, basketball and track teams...Hobbies include reading, listening to music, meeting new people and sports...Has worked with Arkansas Athletes Outreach...Father, Randy, played college basketball at Henderson State...Splits residence between Green Bay and Arkadelphia, Ark.

PRO STATISTICS:

Games/Starts—Green Bay 1997 (injured reserve).

LAMONT HOLLINQUEST ⟩ 56

Linebacker
College: Southern California
NFL Exp.: 5th Season   **Packers Exp.:** 3rd Season
Ht.: 6-3   **Wt.:** 250   **Born:** 10/24/70   **Acq:** FA-96

PRO: A very athletic and intelligent player with excellent size, speed and command of the game...Has made a great contribution to the Green Bay defense and special teams since joining the team in 1996...A valuable backup player who can play all three linebacker positions and also in the 'dime' defense..."When he has been asked to play, he has played and contributed in all positions," says Packers defensive coordinator Fritz Shurmur. "He is one of the leaders on our special teams. We are very comfortable when he is asked or called upon to play in a backup role."...Originally drafted by Washington in 1993, he played for the Redskins in '93 and for most of the 1994 campaign before being waived near the end of his second season...Immediately claimed by Cincinnati, he was waived during the ensuing, 1995 preseason and spent the remainder of the year out of football...Subsequently signed with Green Bay as a free agent...**1997:** Was the primary backup at both outside linebacker spots...A top special teams performer, especially on kick coverage, where he led the Packers during the regular season with 16 total tackles (12 solo)...Played in all 16 regular-season games for the second consecutive year and the third time in his career...Saw action in all three playoff games, including Super Bowl XXXII...Tied for the club postseason lead in special teams stops with 3, including 2 in win over Tampa Bay (Jan. 4)...Recorded a season-high 3 stops on kick coverage vs. Buffalo (Dec. 20)....Earlier had made 2 tackles with the specialty units at New England (Oct. 27)...Saw limited time on defense, registering 4 tackles – 1 each at Philadelphia (Sept. 7), vs. Dallas (Nov. 23), at Carolina (Dec. 14) and vs. the Bills...Had led the team in tackles during the preseason with 21...**1996:** Played in all 16 regular-season games after making the Packers' roster largely on the strength of his special teams play...Went on to finish second on the club (to Bernardo Harris) in special teams tackles with 15 (13 solo)...Also got into all three playoff contests, including Super Bowl XXXI, in a special teams capacity, making 1 solo tackle vs. New England in the title game...Had registered a season-high 3 special teams tackles vs. San Francisco (Oct. 14)...Contributed 6 tackles, 1 interception and 2 pass breakups defensively over the course of the year, including a season-best 4 stops Sept. 9 against Philadelphia...Recorded the second interception of his career Sept. 1 at Tampa Bay, when he picked off a Trent Dilfer pass late in the fourth quarter...Saw late-season action at linebacker vs. Denver and Detroit, making 1 stop in each contest...Had signed with Green Bay as a free agent on Jan. 18...**1995:** Released by Cincinnati during training camp (Aug. 21), he spent the balance of the year out of football...**1994:** Played in first 15 games for Washington and led the club in special teams tackles with 25...Had 19 total tackles (12 solo), including one-half sack, on defense, plus his first career interception, which he returned for 39 yards vs. Indianapolis (Oct. 23)...Waived on Dec. 20, he was claimed on waivers by Cincinnati the following day and was inactive for the Bengals' final regular-season game...**1993:** Played in all 16 games as a rookie, primarily on special teams...Contributed 13 coverage stops and blocked a field goal attempt (Oct. 7 vs. N.Y. Giants)...Led all Washington special teamers in "total hits" with 90...Began to see action in Redskins' 'nickel' package midway through the season, making 9 stops on defense in addition to 3 quarterback hurries...Drafted in the eighth round (212th overall) by Washington in 1993.

COLLEGE: A two-year starter and four-time letter winner at Southern California (1988-89, 1991-92)...Sat out the 1990 season...Totaled 94 tackles over collegiate career...Began as a safety for the Trojans before finishing at linebacker, where he played his entire senior season when he made 31 tackles, including 2 sacks and 6 for loss...Had a career-best 48 stops as a junior (playing both safety and linebacker), recording a single-game career-high 9 tackles (plus a fumble recovery to set up a touchdown) at California...Backed up Mark Carrier (Lions) at safety during his first two seasons...Majored in public administration.

PERSONAL: Given name Lamont Bertrell Hollinquest...Born in Los Angeles...Married to Lynne, couple has two sons, Chaz (born 11/30/90) and Miles (born 3/7/98), and a daughter, Courtney (born 6/22/93)...Was regarded as one of the top prep defensive backs in the nation despite missing his entire senior season at Pius X High School in Downey, Calif., due to a broken ankle...Broke the ankle on the first play in the first game of his senior year...Still was named to numerous all-state and All-America squads, including a first-team spot on the *Los Angeles Herald-Examiner's* 'Super 11,' on the basis of an outstanding junior campaign...Had 121 tackles and 8 interceptions, returning two for touchdowns, on defense, and caught 4 touchdown passes as a tight end during junior year...Earned three letters in both football and basketball, he also garnered first-team all-state honors in hoops, averaging more than 23 points per game as a senior...Cousin, Charles Smith, was a wide receiver with the Philadelphia Eagles from 1974-81...Is the owner of a music and talent production company – 'One Big Family Productions' — in Los Angeles and Washington, D.C. ...Has worked with the United Way in Northern Virginia...Hobbies include music, playing basketball and riding motorcycles...Residence: Kansas City, Mo.

PRO STATISTICS:

Year		G/S	UT	AT	Sacks	Int.	Yds.	FR	FF	PD
1993	Washington	16/0	6	3	0	0	0	0	0	0
1994	Washington	15/0	12	7	½	1	39	0	0	3
	Cincinnati	0/0	0	0	0	0	0	0	0	0
1995		out of football								
1996	Green Bay	16/0	4	2	0	1	2	0	0	2
1997	Green Bay	16/0	3	1	0	0	0	0	0	0
Totals		63/0	25	13	½	2	41	0	0	5
Playoffs		6/0	1	0	0	0	0	0	0	0

Special Teams Tackles: 13 in 1993; 25 (21-4) in 1994; 15 (13-2) in 1996; 1 (1-0) in 1996 Playoffs; 16 (12-4) in 1997; 3 (3-0) in 1997 Playoffs for total of 69

Blocked Field Goals: 1, vs. N.Y. Giants (10/7/93)

TRAVIS JERVEY — 32

Running Back
College: The Citadel
NFL Exp.: 4th Season   **Packers Exp.:** 4th Season
Ht.: 6-0   **Wt.:** 222   **Born:** 5/5/72   **Acq:** D5b-95

PRO: Already one of the top special teams players in the NFL – a fact validated by his selection to the Pro Bowl last year – is hopeful of parlaying his success on kick coverage into an increased role in the offensive backfield...Moved to fullback late in the '97 training camp, is expected to return to his prior halfback role this season...Has seen the majority of his personal playing time on special teams during his initial three NFL seasons...Arguably the fastest player on the team, he twice has competed in the NFL's Fastest Man Competition (1996-97)...Has been one of the Packers' top special teams performers during his first three NFL seasons, registering 32 kick coverage tackles, he routinely disrupts opposition blocking schemes by his quick ascent up the field...Durable and the owner of great physical skills, has yet to miss a game as a pro..."Travis is one of the most versatile players on the team," says Green Bay offensive coordinator Sherm Lewis. "He can play both halfback and fullback. He has great physical tools – outstanding speed and strength. He is the fastest of all the backs. His goal is to become a starting running back."...**1997:** Named to the NFC Pro Bowl squad as its special teams player, the first time a Green Bay player ever had been so honored...Also was tabbed to the All-Pro team of *Pro Football Weekly* as its special teamer...Played in all 16 regular-season games for the third consecutive year, primarily in a special teams capacity...Also got into each of the club's three playoff contests, including Super Bowl XXXII...Was shifted to fullback (his collegiate position) late in training camp, where he served throughout the season as the backup to William Henderson...Finished the regular season with 10 special teams tackles (seventh on the club), adding 1 additional coverage stop during the postseason...Equaled his career high with 3 special teams tackles vs. Buffalo (Dec. 20)...Made 2 tackles on kick coverage at New England (Oct. 27)...Showed flashes of promise rushing the ball in the preseason, when he gained 118 yards on 19 carries (6.2 avg.)...**1996:** Saw reserve action in all 16 regular-season games for the second straight year...Also got into each of club's three playoff contests, including Super Bowl XXXI...A regular contributor in all areas of special teams, he also served as a backup at halfback...Tied Bernardo Harris for the team lead in special teams tackles during the postseason with 6, including 3 (equaling his career best) vs. Carolina in the NFC Championship Game (Jan. 12) and 2 against New England in the Super Bowl (Jan. 26)...Ranked sixth on the club with 9 special teams stops during the regular season...Also served as a deep man on kickoffs at varying times throughout the season...Was fifth on the team with 106 yards rushing on 26 carries...Carried 5 times for a career-best 35 yards in 38-10 win over Minnesota (Dec. 22)...Gained 25 yards on a career-high 6 carries at Chicago (Oct. 6)...Saw extended playing time at running back late in blowout wins over Tampa Bay (Sept. 1), Philadelphia (Sept. 9), San Diego (Sept. 15) and Denver (Dec. 8)...**1995:** Got into all 16 games on special teams...Tied for fifth on the club with 13 special teams tackles...Also served as deep man on kickoff return group and averaged 20.6 yards on 8 returns...Had a career-best 28-yard kickoff return vs. Detroit (Oct. 15)...Recorded a career-high 3 special teams stops in season opener vs. St. Louis (Sept. 3)...Made 2 special teams tackles in four other games...Forced a fumble by the Bears' Michael Timpson on kickoff coverage at Chicago (Sept. 11)...Returned the first kickoff of his NFL career for 27 yards at Jacksonville (Sept. 24)...Also saw action in all three playoff contests, recording 2 special teams stops...Had finished the preseason as the Packers' second-leading rusher with 119 yards on 35 carries...Was the second of two fifth-round draft choices (170th overall) by Green Bay in 1995.

COLLEGE: A three-year letter winner for The Citadel (1992-94)...Finished his collegiate career with 1,490 yards and 15 rushing touchdowns on 211 carries...Career rushing average of 7.1 yards per carry was a school record...Made 1 career reception as a collegian...Had only 319 rushing yards going into his senior season, a year which saw him have a breakthrough campaign by rushing for 1,171 yards and 12 TDs on 152 carries, an impressive 7.7 yards per carry...Averaged 106.5 yards rushing per game as a senior, third-best in the Southland Conference...Was a second-team all-conference pick...Rushed for a career-high 224

yards on only 10 carries (22.4 avg.) vs. Virginia Military Institute, including a school-record 96-yard run from scrimmage...Played in two games as a 1991 freshman, but did not letter...Also ran track (55-meter dash) for the Cadets...Majored in business administration.

PERSONAL: Given name Travis Richard Jervey...Nicknamed 'Beef'...Born in Columbia, S.C. ...Single...An all-state and all-conference selection in football at Wando High School in Mt. Pleasant, S.C. ...Played in the 1990 Shrine Bowl (South Carolina vs. North Carolina)...Named as team's 'Most Valuable Player'...Won three letters in football...Finished his prep career with 2,221 yards and 22 touchdowns on 281 carries...Helped lead team to two state playoff appearances...Competed in the NFL's Fastest Man Competition for two straight years (1996-97), he advanced to the finals in 1997 by defeating Herschel Walker in his first race and subsequently finished fourth...Hobbies include surfing and water sports...Father, Ned, also is a graduate of The Citadel...Has done work for Children's Hospital and visited local schools in Charleston, S.C. ...Also has volunteered his time for Children's Miracle Network by visiting hospitals and giving talks to kids...Has been one of five winners of the *Muscle & Fitness* 'Best Physique' award each of the last two years...Spent most of this past offseason surfing in Costa Rica...Residence: Isle of Palms, S.C.

PRO STATISTICS:

Year	G/S	RUSHING					KICKOFF RETURNS				
		No.	Yds.	Avg.	LG	TD	No.	Yds.	Avg.	LG	TD
1995 Green Bay	16/0	0	0	0.0	0	0	8	165	20.6	28	0
1996 Green Bay	16/0	26	106	4.1	12	0	1	17	17.0	17	0
1997 Green Bay	16/0	0	0	0.0	0	0	0	0	0.0	0	0
Totals	48/0	26	106	4.1	12	0	9	182	20.2	28	0
Playoffs	9/0	0	0	0.0	0	0	3	35	11.7	19	0

Special Teams Tackles: 13 (9-4) in 1995; 2 (1-1) in 1995 Playoffs; 9 (6-3) in 1996; 6 (6-0) in 1996 Playoffs; 10 (10-0) in 1997; 1 (1-0) in 1997 Playoffs for total of 32 (25-7)
Special Teams Forced Fumbles: 1 in 1995

CAREER SINGLE-GAME HIGHS
Most Rushing Attempts: 6, at Chicago (10/6/96); **Most Rushing Yards:** 35, vs. Minnesota (12/22/96); **Longest Run:** 12, vs. Minnesota (12/22/96); **Most Special Teams Tackles:** 3, vs. St. Louis (9/3/95), vs. Carolina (1/12/97-postseason) and vs. Buffalo (12/20/97)

SETH JOYNER
59

Linebacker
College: Texas-El Paso
NFL Exp.: 13th Season   **Packers Exp.:** 2nd Season
Ht.: 6-2   **Wt.:** 245   **Born:** 11/18/64   **Acq:** FA-97

PRO: One of the game's most versatile linebackers over the past dozen years, the savvy play-maker now enters his second season with the Packers...Continues to be one of the top students of the game even after 12 years in the NFL, spending countless hours poring over videotape of upcoming opponents...Will benefit from a full training camp at his more familiar outside linebacker position this summer after spending the 1997 camp learning the Packers' middle linebacker position; he later moved back outside and became a starter after the mid-season trade of incumbent Wayne Simmons...Is expected to compete with George Koonce in 1998 for a starting spot at outside linebacker...Packers defensive coordinator Fritz Shurmur appreciated Joyner's efforts last season and expects more of the same in 1998, saying, "Seth has had a great career. He's played in a lot of places, but last year he came in and we played him as an inside linebacker to start the year. In the middle of the season, he was asked to switch to the outside linebacker position when Wayne Simmons was traded. He did a great job of learning on the run, called on all of his

experience and instinctiveness as a football player and did a great job for us as an outside linebacker in our base defense as a starter. He also was a very effective pass rusher for us in our 'dime' defense – came up with several big plays. As a result, he became a leader of our defense. We're looking for the same kind of output from him this year. He will compete for the outside linebacker position and also for a spot in our 'dime' defense as end."…A veteran of 179 games with 171 starts, he has posted 1,201 career tackles (795 solo), 52½ sacks, 24 interceptions, 11 fumble recoveries, 27 forced fumbles and 59 passes defensed…Has started all 16 games eight times as a pro, including the seven seasons immediately prior to last year…Additionally has made eight career postseason starts, accumulating 33 tackles (28 solo), 3 INTs, 8 passes defensed and 1 forced fumble…Upon joining the Packers in 1997, was reunited with friend and former teammate Reggie White, with whom he had played for seven years in Philadelphia…"Seth is the type of guy that, put in the right spot, he can take a game over," says White…A consummate professional, his mere presence is a benefit to club…"He contributes in the locker room and in meetings," Shurmur adds. "He has impeccable work habits. He devotes large amounts of time to extra study and preparation and, as a result, he's a great role model for our younger players."…A three-time Pro Bowl selection (1991, 1993-94), he was named NFL 'Player of the Year' by *Sports Illustrated* and garnered runner-up honors for *Associated Press* 'Defensive Player of the Year' in 1991…Posted career-highs in tackles (136) and interceptions (4) in 1988…Has seven 100-plus tackle seasons in his career, including six consecutive campaigns (1988-93) with Philadelphia…As a testament to his play-making abilities, has contributed five defensive touchdowns (two interception returns and three fumble returns) during his 12-year career…A highly-sought after free agent after his release from the Arizona Cardinals in June of 1997, he signed with the Packers on July 18, ending weeks of speculation around the league…Originally an eighth-round selection by the Philadelphia Eagles in 1986, he spent his first 11 years in the NFC East, with eight seasons in Philadelphia (1986-93) and three with Arizona (1994-96)…**1997:** Played in 11 games, starting the final 10 contests at 'Buck' (left outside) linebacker in his initial season with the Packers…Finished with 34 total tackles, including 3 sacks, plus 1 pass defensed and 1 blocked punt…Totaled 9 additional tackles, plus 1 pass defensed, in the playoffs, starting all three postseason contests, including Super Bowl XXXII…Made 6 stops and knocked down 1 pass in NFC Championship Game win at San Francisco (Jan. 11)…Notched 2 tackles vs. Broncos in Super Bowl XXXII (Jan. 25)…Earlier, had made 2½ sacks in Green Bay's last four regular-season contests, finishing the year strong as the Packers used him at a variety of attacking positions…As a pass-rusher on obvious throwing downs, harassed quarterbacks from the inside and outside with equally impressive results…Registered a season-high 8 tackles in Monday night win at Minnesota (Dec. 1), his stops including a five-yard sack of Vikings QB Brad Johnson…A week later, notched 1½ sacks among 3 tackles in division-clinching win at Tampa Bay (Dec. 7)…Registered first career blocked punt in Packers' 31-21 win vs. Buffalo (Dec. 20)…Set defensive tone in 45-17 win over Dallas (Nov. 23), stuffing Emmitt Smith for a three-yard loss on the Cowboys' first play from scrimmage…Posted a half-sack among 3 tackles in victory vs. St. Louis (Nov. 9)…Made 5 total tackles in first start of season, Oct. 12, at Chicago…Start came on heels of trade that sent Simmons to Kansas City (Oct. 7), allowing Joyner to move to the strong side linebacker position after initial work at middle linebacker…Made first appearance as a Packer vs. Tampa Bay (Oct. 5), seeing reserve duty…Initial contributions to team were delayed by ongoing swelling in his left knee during training camp which eventually required arthroscopic surgery (Aug. 30), he subsequently missed the final preseason contest and was inactive for club's first four games…Signed with Green Bay as a free agent on July 18…**1996:** Started all 16 games – for the seventh straight year – at left outside linebacker in his final season with Arizona…Finished third on the team in tackles with 124 (71 solo), surpassing the century mark for the seventh time as a pro…Tied for second on the squad with 5 quarterback sacks…Also had 10 tackles for loss, 3 forced fumbles, 1 INT and 1 fumble recovery…Was a second-team All-Pro selection by *United Press International*…Registered a season-high 13 tackles in a 17-3 loss at Dallas (Oct. 13)…Recorded 12 tackles, 1 sack and forced 2 fumbles in a 36-30 win over Philadelphia (Nov. 24)…Also posted 12 tackles the following week at Minnesota (Dec. 1)…Recovered a fumble at Philadelphia in the final game of the season (Dec. 22)…Picked off his only pass of the season in the opener at Indianapolis (Sept. 1)…**1995:** Started all 16 games for the Cardinals, 12 at linebacker and four at strong safety, helping out in an injury-depleted secondary…Had 82 tackles (47 solo) to finish third on the club…Posted a season-high 8 tackles – including 1 sack – and 1 interception at the N.Y. Giants (Oct. 8), his drop of quarterback Dave Brown on the final play of the game sent the contest into overtime…Had 5 tackles, recovered a fumble and blocked a field goal at Carolina (Nov. 19), which teammate Aeneas Williams returned for a score…Started final four contests at strong safety – vs. Giants (Nov. 30), at San Diego (Dec. 9), at Philadelphia (Dec. 17) and vs. Dallas (Dec. 25) – when injuries shorted the defensive backfield…**1994:** Made an immediate impact in his first season with Arizona, helping the Cardinals to a third-place defensive ranking – their best defensive effort in a quarter-century...Started all 16 games and finished sixth on the team with 86 tackles (68 solo)...Further contributed 6 sacks, 3 interceptions, 2 forced fumbles and 11 tackles for loss...Voted to his third career Pro Bowl and was a second-team All-NFC pick by *UPI*...Named NFC 'Defensive Player of the Week' after his performance in a 12-6 win over Philadelphia (Nov. 20), his effort against his former teammates included 5 tackles, 2 sacks (tying a career high), 2 passes defensed and 3 tackles for loss...Forced 2 fumbles in 17-7 win over Minnesota (Oct. 2)...Notched a season-high 10 tackles at Dallas (Oct. 9)...Blocked a Chip Lohmiller field goal attempt in overtime contest at Washington (Oct. 16), subsequently enabling Arizona to pull out a 19-16 win over the Redskins later in the sudden-death period...Had signed with the Cardinals as an unrestricted free agent on April 19...**1993:** Earned second Pro Bowl selection, pacing the Eagles with 113 tackles (80 solo)...Also contributed 2 sacks and 1 forced fumble as he started all 16 games in his final season in Philadelphia...Named All-Pro by the Pro Football Writers of America and *Pro Football Weekly*...Also was an All-NFC pick by *PFW*...Recorded 11 tackles and his lone interception of the season vs. Chicago (Oct. 10)...Registered a season-high 13 tackles at Miami (Nov. 14)...**1992:** Started all 16 games and helped lead the Eagles to the playoffs, finishing third on the team with 121 tackles, including 7 sacks...Added 3 forced fumbles, 1 fumble recovery and 4 interceptions – 2 of which were returned for touchdowns...Named to second-team All-NFL squad by *AP, College & Pro Football Newsweekly* and Newspaper Enterprise Association...Garnered NFC 'Defensive Player of the Week' honors following 7-3 win over Phoenix (Oct. 25), setting up Eagles' decisive TD with a fumble recovery and also snaring 1 interception...Returned an interception for a career-high 43 yards and a touchdown in a 47-34 victory at the Giants (Nov. 22)...Picked off a pass and raced 24 yards for a touchdown in a 28-17 win vs. Minnesota (Dec. 6)...Made 9 tackles in two postseason contests, also registering a 14-yard interception return in 36-20 wild-card playoff win at New Orleans (Jan. 3)...**1991:** Fashioned perhaps his best season as a professional...Started all 16 games and was selected to his first Pro Bowl...Named NFL 'Player of the Year' by *SI*...Runner-up to New Orleans linebacker Pat Swilling for *AP* 'Defensive Player of the Year'...Also earned All-Pro honors from *PFWA* and *NEA*, second-team All-Pro recognition from *AP* and All-NFC accolades from *PFW*...Registered 110 tackles (68 solo), finishing sixth among Philadelphia defenders, including 6½ sacks...Added 3 interceptions, 6 passes defensed, a career-best 6 forced fumbles and 4 fumble recoveries – 2 of them for touchdowns, tying an NFL single-season record...Returned a fumble 34 yards for a score and forced a fumble in end zone that resulted in another touchdown in a 34-14 win at Phoenix (Nov. 24)...Had 8 tackles, 2 sacks (tying a career high), 2 forced fumbles and 2 fumble recoveries en route to NFC 'Defensive Player of the Week' honors Dec. 2 at Houston...Also recovered a Vinny Testaverde fumble in the end zone for a touchdown at Tampa Bay (Oct. 6)...**1990:** Started all 16 games and led Philadelphia with 132 tackles (including a career-high 91 solo stops)...Also posted a career-best 7½ sacks, 1 interception, 7 passes defensed and 3 forced fumbles...Registered 11 tackles and picked off a pass at Buffalo (Dec. 2)...Made 7 tackles and tipped a pass that was returned for a touchdown in a 30-7 win over the Giants (Nov. 4)...**1989:** Started 14 games and tied for sixth on the club with 123 tackles...Also registered 5 sacks, 1 interception, 5 passes defensed and 3 forced fumbles...Left game vs. Minnesota (Nov. 19) after suffering knee injury early in second half, subsequently sat out next two contests – at Dallas (Nov. 23) and at N.Y. Giants (Dec. 3)...Established single-game career high of 2 sacks among 14 tackles in 10-7 win over the then-Los Angeles Raiders (Oct. 22)...Tied his career high with 16 tackles against Washington (Nov. 12)...Had an interception in 21-7 wild-card loss to the then-Los Angeles Rams (Dec. 31)...**1988:** Posted 136 tackles (third on the club) and 4 interceptions – both career highs – as he started all 16 contests...Also recorded 3½ sacks, 11 passes defensed and 2 forced fumbles...All 4 of his interception returns rewarded the Eagles with possession inside the opponent's 20-yard line...Had 10-or-more solo tackles five times, including a career-high 16-tackle effort in a 23-17 win at Phoenix (Dec. 10)...Registered an interception in divisional playoff loss at Chicago (Dec. 31)...**1987:** In strike-shortened season, made switch from right to left linebacker and started all 12 union games for the Eagles...Registered 96 tackles (65 solo) to rank third on the club...Also posted 4 sacks, 2 INTs, 5 passes defensed, 2 fumble recoveries and 2 forced fumbles...Scored his first NFL touchdown on an 18-yard fumble return in a 27-17 win over New Orleans (Sept. 20)...Made 10-plus tackles four times, including a season-high 15-tackle effort in a 28-23 win at St. Louis (Nov. 1)...Made a key interception in overtime of 34-31 win at New England (Nov. 29)...Had 10 tackles and blocked a field goal attempt in overtime at the Giants (Dec. 6)...**1986:** Played in 14 games with seven starts at right linebacker as a rookie...Finished with 44 tackles, 2 sacks, 1 INT and 1 fumble recovery...Recorded 25 stops (20 solo) on special teams...Notched 10 tackles in his first NFL start, vs. the New York Giants (Nov. 9)...Snared his first NFL interception, while also registering a sack, the following

week vs. Detroit (Nov. 16)…Released on the final training camp cutdown (Sept. 1), he re-signed two weeks later (Sept. 17)…Drafted in the eighth round (208th overall) by Philadelphia in 1986.

COLLEGE: A four-year letterman (1982-85) at Texas-El Paso…Suited up at outside linebacker his first three years before switching to the middle as a senior…Led the Miners in tackles his final two seasons…Had 98 tackles as a junior and 89 stops his senior year…Majored in mass communications.

PERSONAL: Given name Seth Joyner…Born in Spring Valley, N.Y. …Married to Wanda…Has a daughter, Jasmine (born 9/7/88)…Garnered all-state honors at fullback and all-league honors at linebacker as a senior at Spring Valley (N.Y.) High School…Lettered three years in football, he also was a two-time letterman in basketball, playing forward…Founded 'Wizzo Wear' with a business partner in October of 1997; the company markets golf wear, sportswear, hats and sunglasses, among other sporting items…Active in many charities, he worked with the Jerome Brown Foundation and 'People for People' while playing in Philadelphia and has given time to Children's Hospital in both Philadelphia and Phoenix…Also has worked on behalf of D.A.R.E. in his home state of New York…Received honor from his high school this past May when it retired his jersey number (30)…Event was part of "D.A.R.E. to Dream" weekend, which included a celebrity golf tournament, with proceeds going to his and other high schools in the conference…Considering the pursuit of a broadcasting career when his playing days are over…Hobbies include "golf, golf and more golf…and bowling"…Residence: Paradise Valley, Ariz.

PRO STATISTICS:

Year		G/S	UT	AT	Sacks	Int.	Yds.	LG	TD	FR	FF	PD
1986	Philadelphia	14/7	34	10	2	1	4	4	0	0	1	2
1987	Philadelphia	12/12	65	31	4	2	42	29	0	2	2	5
1988	Philadelphia	16/16	86	50	3½	4	96	30	0	0	2	11
1989	Philadelphia	14/14	76	47	5	1	0	0	0	0	3	5
1990	Philadelphia	16/16	91	41	7½	1	9	9	0	0	3	7
1991	Philadelphia	16/16	68	42	6½	3	41	41	0	4	6	6
1992	Philadelphia	16/16	85	36	7	4	88	43t	2	1	3	7
1993	Philadelphia	16/16	80	33	2	1	6	6	0	0	1	4
1994	Arizona	16/16	68	18	6	3	2	2	0	0	2	4
1995	Arizona	16/16	47	35	1	3	9	11	0	3	1	6
1996	Arizona	16/16	71	53	5	1	10	10	0	1	3	4
1997	Green Bay	11/10	24	10	3	0	0	0	0	0	0	1
Totals		**179/171**	**795**	**406**	**52½**	**24**	**307**	**43t**	**2**	**11**	**27**	**63**
Playoffs		**8/8**	**28**	**5**	**0**	**3**	**23**	**14**	**0**	**0**	**1**	**8**

Other Touchdowns: 3, 18-yard fumble return vs. New Orleans (9/20/87); fumble recovery in end zone at Tampa Bay (10/6/91); and 34-yard fumble return at Phoenix (11/24/91)
Special Teams Tackles: 25 (20-5) in 1986
Blocked Field Goals: 3, at N.Y. Giants (12/6/87); at Washington (10/16/94); and at Carolina (11/19/95)
Blocked Punts: 1, vs. Buffalo (12/20/97)

GEORGE KOONCE) 53

Linebacker
College: East Carolina
NFL Exp.: 7th Season   **Packers Exp.:** 7th Season
Ht.: 6-1   **Wt.:** 245   **Born:** 10/15/68   **Acq:** FA-92

PRO: A proven NFL starting linebacker who never fully regained his past form last season as he returned to the field after the 10-month rehabilitation of a serious knee injury suffered during the 1996 playoffs…Played every linebacker position for Green Bay over his four-and-a-half years as a starter (1992-

96)…Scheduled to compete in '98 with incumbent Seth Joyner for the starting job at 'Buck' (left outside) linebacker, a spot he played during parts of the 1992 and '93 seasons…"I think the knee affected him dramatically," says Fritz Shurmur, the Packers' defensive coordinator. "I don't think he ever was near 100 percent last year. I do believe that he's very close to being 100 percent now and I fully expect that he's going to challenge for a starting role as an outside linebacker on our team. He definitely is a starting linebacker and has demonstrated his ability to be able to play well as an outside linebacker. And if something were to happen to (starting middle linebacker) Bernardo Harris, he would go in and play the middle and play it exceptionally well."…Registered 100-or-more tackles in three of the four seasons prior to last year (1993-94, 1996)…Remains a true fan favorite, who, at home games, is the frequent recipient of hearty chants of 'Kooooonce'...Of humble NFL beginnings, he was cut by the Atlanta Falcons as an undrafted player in 1991, then played for the worst team in the World League before joining the Packers as an obscure free agent in '92 — remaining, to this day, as one of Green Bay's top free agent finds over the past decade…Versatile, he also has demonstrated his unselfishness on several occasions by switching positions at the drop of a hat…"He can play all three linebacker positions extremely well," Shurmur adds. "That makes him very valuable. And he works very hard at his job. I don't think we have anyone on our team that understands the defense any better than he does. And so as a result he's very valuable from the standpoint of everybody around him having a feeling of security."…Had enjoyed a highly-productive year in 1996 on the heels of an offseason which had seen him work extremely hard after a '95 campaign where his level of play had dipped by his own admission…But since then has suffered through the personal disappointment of a season-ending knee injury in '96, which caused him to watch both the NFC Championship Game and Super Bowl XXXI from the sidelines, and his limited return to the field in 1997…Remains the second-longest tenured player on the Green Bay defense behind only LeRoy Butler…**1997:** Returned to the field late in the season after a 10-month rehabilitation of the knee injury he had suffered in the '96 playoffs…Saw reserve action at linebacker and special teams duty in the club's final four regular-season games plus all three playoff contests…Played in Super Bowl XXXII vs. Denver after having missed the Super Bowl a year earlier due to his knee injury…Totaled 5 tackles during the regular season, including a season-best 2 in each of his first two games back, at Minnesota (Dec. 1) and at Tampa Bay (Dec. 7), he also recorded a special teams stop vs. the Vikings…Contributed a solo tackle in each of the three postseason contests…Had been placed on reserve/physically unable to perform during training camp (Aug. 19), a move which mandated that he miss at least the first six weeks of the regular season…While still on PUP, began practicing with the team on Oct. 29…Was activated on Nov. 18, but was inactive for Dallas contest five days later…**1996:** Made the switch from 'Plugger' (right outside) linebacker to 'Mike' (middle) linebacker with only a week left in the preseason to create room in the lineup for the emerging Brian Williams…Started all 16 regular-season games for the third consecutive season, though all were at his new position…Also started divisional playoff contest with San Francisco (Jan. 4), contributing 3 tackles and 1 pass breakup, but tore the anterior cruciate ligament in his right knee in the second half of win over the 49ers…Subsequently underwent reconstructive surgery on Jan. 9 and was placed on injured reserve the following day…Led the team in tackles for the second time in his career, making 117 stops (76 solo)…Also turned in a career-high 3 interceptions after he had picked off just one pass in his first four league seasons…Enjoyed one of the shining moments of his NFL career when he intercepted a Warren Moon pass at Minnesota (Sept. 22) and returned it 75 yards up the sideline for his first pro touchdown, giving the Packers a 21-17 lead late in the third quarter…Made a season-high 14 tackles at Kansas City (Nov. 10), 10 unassisted…Had 11 stops in each game against the Bears, also intercepting a Dave Krieg pass in the initial meeting, Oct. 6 at Chicago…Intercepted a Rodney Peete pass, which had been tipped into the air by teammate Santana Dotson, in Monday night triumph over Philadelphia (Sept. 9)…**1995:** Started all 16 games for the second straight year, including 14 at 'Plugger' linebacker, plus all three playoff contests…Finished fifth on the team in tackles with 84, including 46 solo stops and 1 sack…Also contributed his first NFL interception and 3 passes defensed…Registered a season-best 13 tackles in NFC Championship Game at Dallas (Jan. 14) among his 20 total stops in the postseason…Had 6 tackles and picked off a Moon pass deep in Minnesota territory (Oct. 22), his 12-yard return of the interception to the Vikings' seven-yard line set up a Green Bay touchdown two plays later which staked the Packers to a 14-7 lead in an eventual 38-21 victory…Missed a portion of game at Tampa Bay (Dec. 10) after spraining his left wrist…Registered his lone sack of the year Oct. 29 at Detroit…Had been forced to play some at middle linebacker late in training camp after injuries decimated the team's linebacking corps…**1994:** Moved into 'Plugger' linebacker position in Green Bay's new 4-3 alignment, a spot vacated when Johnny Holland was forced into retirement by a neck injury, and started all 16 games for first time in his career...Went on to lead Packers in total (119) and solo (78) stops for the initial time, posting his second consecutive 100-tackle season in the process...Made a season-high 12 tackles on two occasions — Sept. 18 at Philadelphia and Nov. 20 at Buffalo...Registered 10 stops and recovered an early Errict Rhett fumble in season finale at Tampa Bay (Dec. 24)...Had forced a Craig Heyward fumble and led club with 9 tackles only one week earlier vs. Atlanta...Set up Packers' first offensive touchdown in eventual 38-30 triumph over Detroit (Nov. 6), when he recovered a Krieg fumble at the Lions' 20-yard line in second quarter...After missing '93 playoffs due to injury, started first two postseason games of his career...Recorded 15 total tackles, including 11 in NFC divisional playoff contest at Dallas (Jan. 8)...**1993:** Started 15 of 16 regular-season games, he did not play in Dec. 26 Raiders contest after suffering a sprained foot one week earlier vs. Minnesota...Returned to start in finale at Detroit (Jan. 2), but incurred a dislocated shoulder in second quarter of Lions tilt, necessitating his placement on injured reserve the next day and causing him to miss both playoff games...Finished second (to Holland) on the team in total tackles with a career-high 125 (70 solo), marking his first 100-tackle season as a pro...Named Miller Lite 'Player of the Game' for his 12-tackle effort at Minnesota (Sept. 26)...Made a career-high 18 tackles (9 solo), including a sack, on Halloween vs. Chicago...Also contributed sacks at Dallas (Oct. 3) and New Orleans (Nov. 14)...Prior to the season had been scheduled to move inside to vacate the 'Buck' linebacker position — the spot he had played in '92 — for 1993 first-round draft choice Wayne Simmons...Remained at 'Buck,' however, when Simmons tore knee cartilage early in training camp, starting first two regular-season games there...Subsequently volunteered to move inside to 'Mike' linebacker position (LILB) beginning with third game when Brian Noble suffered a career-ending knee injury vs. Philadelphia and with Simmons once again available for duty...Remained at 'Mike' for balance of season until going down with shoulder problem himself...**1992:** One of the most pleasant surprises of training camp, joined Green Bay as a free agent after taking the World League by storm...Made himself virtually impossible to cut by leading Packers in tackles during the preseason with 23...Went on to play in all 16 games with 10 starts, primarily at 'Buck' linebacker...Began season in a backup role and as one of Packers' more prominent special teams players, he first was inserted into the starting lineup Oct. 25 vs. Chicago...Finished year seventh on team in tackles with 55 (34 solo), also contributing 1½ sacks and 2 passes defensed...Made 3 special teams tackles and also recovered Rod Woodson's muffed punt, which immediately led to Green Bay's final touchdown, in 17-3 victory over Pittsburgh (Sept. 27)...Had a season-high 14 tackles, including 9 solo, at Minnesota (Dec. 27)...Picked up first full sack in NFL vs. Detroit on Dec. 6...Signed with Packers as a free agent on June 1, 1992...**WORLD LEAGUE:** Signed with Ohio Glory of World League of American Football on Dec. 17, 1991...Established himself as one of the top defensive players in the WLAF during the '92 season...Led the World League with 91 total tackles, setting a league single-season record in the process...Also had 2½ sacks as he started all 10 games...Nominated multiple times for World League Player of the Week honors, but did not receive the recognition he deserved due to Glory's 1-9 record...Made a season-high 12 stops vs. the Birmingham Fire on May 24...**1991:** Signed with the Atlanta Falcons as an undrafted free agent on April 30, 1991, he subsequently was waived on the final cutdown of training camp (Aug. 26).

COLLEGE: Played two seasons (1989-90) at East Carolina, starting and lettering in '90 for the Pirates...Began collegiate career at Chowan Junior College in Murfreesboro, N.C. (1987-88)...Recorded 107 total tackles (59 solo) at ECU, including 18 for loss...Also had 8 sacks, 1 fumble recovery and 5 passes defensed...Started every game at outside linebacker as a senior, making 84 tackles (50 solo), including a team-leading 7 sacks and 16 TFL...Earned second-team All-South Independent honors from the *Associated Press* in '90...Saw action at defensive end and linebacker for Pirates in 1989...As he was limited to six games (two starts) due to knee, wrist and groin injuries, he did not letter...At Chowan, racked up 183 total tackles (104 solo), 1 sack, 1 interception, 4 fumble recoveries and 3 passes defensed...Was a second-team All-America selection by *NJCAA* and *Gridwire* as a sophomore, also earning first-team all-conference honors...Named 'Coastal Carolina Defensive Player of the Year' in 1988, when he started every game and made 131 total tackles (74 solo)...Majored in industrial technology.

PERSONAL: Given name George Earl Koonce, Jr. ...Born in New Bern, N.C. ...Was married to the former Judi Zellner on Nov. 4, 1996, by teammate Reggie White, the couple has a son, Trey (born 7/27/96), and a daughter, Arienna (born 1/2/98)...Also has another son, Bryan (born 3/4/89)...Attended West Craven High School in Vanceboro, N.C., earning three letters as a linebacker and tight end...Owner of a kennel – 'Koonce's Kennel' – in New Bern, N.C., where he breeds beagles...Also is the owner of 100 apartment units in New Bern under the 'Koonce Properties' moniker...Hobbies include playing basketball, hunting and fishing...Is an avid rabbit hunter...Made a $50,000 "Shared Visions Campaign" gift to East Carolina in November of 1995 for the expansion of Dowdy-Ficklen Stadium...Has attended classes at East Carolina in past offseasons, working toward the completion of his degree in industrial technology and communications...Previously was enrolled in classes in the business school at St. Norbert College (in De Pere, Wis.) in '94...Worked part-time in management at a catfish farm (Carolina Classic) in Greenville, N.C., during the 1995 offseason...Played shooting guard for Packers' basketball team in the offseason from 1993-95...Served as a spokesman for Children's Hospital of Eastern North Carolina for five years (1993-97)...Also has worked on behalf of Ronald McDonald House in Greenville, Children's Hospital of Wisconsin and Milwaukee-based Athletes for Youth...Splits residence between Green Bay and Greenville, N.C.

PRO STATISTICS

Year	G/S	UT	AT	Sacks	Int.	Yds.	LG	TD	FR	FF	PD
1992 Green Bay 16/10		34	21	1½	0	0	0	0	0	0	2
1993 Green Bay 15/15		70	55	3	0	0	0	0	0	0	2
1994 Green Bay 16/16		78	41	1	0	0	0	0	2	1	3
1995 Green Bay 16/16		46	38	1	1	12	12	0	0	0	3
1996 Green Bay 16/16		76	41	0	3	84	75t	1	1	0	5
1997 Green Bay 4/0		4	1	0	0	0	0	0	0	0	0
Totals 83/73		308	197	6½	4	96	75t	1	3	1	15
Playoffs.......................9/6		29	12	0	0	0	0	0	0	0	2

Special Teams Tackles: 8 (8-0) in 1992; 1 (1-0) in 1997 for total of 9 (9-0)
Special Teams Fumble Recoveries: 1 in 1992

WLAF STATISTICS

Year	G/S	UT	AT	Sacks	Int.	FR	FF	PD
1992 Ohio Glory..............10/10		65	26	2½	0	3	1	5

Special Teams Tackles: 1 in 1992

BOB KUBERSKI   94

Defensive Tackle
College: Navy
NFL Exp.: 4th Season   **Packers Exp.:** 4th Season
Ht.: 6-4 **Wt.:** 298   **Born:** 4/5/71   **Acq:** D7-93

PRO: Coming off his most productive season as a professional, Bob Kuberski has become a valued contributor as a reserve defensive tackle...Bounced back strongly from a preseason knee injury in 1996 to have his best year in 1997...Filled in nicely last season when regular starter Gilbert Brown went down with knee and ankle injuries...Green Bay defensive coordinator Fritz Shurmur believes one of Kuberski's best attributes is his desire to be the best he can be, saying, "Bob was a great contributor on our team last year. He is the ultimate effort guy. He does not play a down that's anything less than all-out effort, whether it's practice or a game. Bob is effective when he plays because he brings a special kind of competitiveness to his position and a realization that every play has to be an all-out effort. He, like most of our other guys, is a person of impeccable character, a bright guy and a real team player."...A seventh-round draft pick in 1993, has played only three seasons for the Packers due to an initial two-year military hiatus...Did not play the entire '93 and '94 seasons while fulfilling his service commitment to the Navy...**1997:** Served as the backup to Brown at nose tackle...Saw action in 11 regular-season games, starting three in Brown's absence...Also saw action in all three playoff games, including Super Bowl XXXII...Had been inactive for each of the team's first five games...Finished the regular season with a career-high 24 tackles (14 solo), tops among Green Bay's reserves...Saw extensive duty at Indianapolis (Nov. 16) after Brown injured his ankle on the Colts' seventh play from scrimmage, he responded with a career-high 9 tackles...Had made his first NFL start at Chicago (Oct. 12) with Brown out due to a knee injury, recording 6 tackles...Also played a major role in the Packers' fourth-quarter goal-line stand against the Bears as he teamed with Gabe Wilkins to stop QB Erik Kramer on a fourth-down sneak at the one-yard line midway through the fourth quarter and the Packers clinging to a 21-17 lead in eventual 24-23 win...Later started each of the club's final two regular-season games (at Carolina Dec. 14 and vs. Buffalo Dec. 20)...Made 3 tackles in the Packers' 27-11 win at Minnesota (Dec. 1), including a two-yard tackle-for-loss on the Vikings' LeRoy Hoard in the first quarter...Blocked an early field goal attempt by the Bucs' Michael Husted in 21-7 divisional playoff win over Tampa Bay (Jan. 4)...Had led all defensive linemen in tackles during the preseason with 10...**1996:** Had the start of his season delayed when he experienced swelling in his right knee after a week of training camp...Subsequently underwent arthroscopic surgery on Aug. 5 to address cartilage damage and did not return to full practice until Sept. 25...Was inactive for 14 regular-season games and all three postseason contests, including Super Bowl XXXI...Saw his only action of the season at St. Louis (Nov. 24)...Had dressed for the first time, though he did not play, six days earlier at Dallas...**1995:** Had a strong training camp to secure a roster spot...Saw action in nine games on special teams and in certain short-yardage and goal-line situations...Inactive for club's seven other contests...Finished the regular season with 6 tackles, including 2 sacks, and 1 pass defensed...Had 1 tackle at Cleveland (Nov. 19) as he saw his most extensive action of the season...Recorded the first sack of his NFL career at Jacksonville (Sept. 24), when he brought down the Jaguars' Mark Brunell early in the fourth quarter...Had his second sack of the season in regular-season finale vs. Pittsburgh (Dec. 24), dropping Neil O'Donnell in the second quarter...Batted down a Jeff Blake pass vs. Cincinnati (Dec. 3)...Inactive for first two playoff contests before recording 2 tackles against Dallas in the NFC Championship Game (Jan. 14)...Had been reinstated to the Packers' active roster on April 18...**1994:** Spent season fulfilling his Naval commitments...**1993:** Drafted in the seventh round (183rd overall) by Green Bay in 1993...Signed by Packers on June 7, he took all of his personal leave time from the Navy to spend roughly a month at Green Bay's training camp...Placed on the Reserve/Military list Aug. 23 after his return to the service.

COLLEGE: A three-year starter and letter winner at Navy (1990-92)...Was a two-time All-East first-team selection (1991-92)...Totaled 240 tackles (152 solo), including 4 sacks and 20 for loss, plus 2 fumble recoveries, 2 forced fumbles and 5 passes defensed as a collegian...Led Middies' defensive linemen with 80 tackles (fourth on team) as a senior...Also had a team-high 11 tackles for loss and broke up 3 passes...Paced Navy defensive linemen in stops as a junior with 86 (third on team), including 52 solo tackles...Also had a team-leading 5 tackles for loss, 1 fumble recovery and 1 forced fumble...Started final seven games at defensive tackle in 1990 after playing with the Plebe/JV team as a freshman...Holds a B.S. degree in political science.

PERSONAL: Given name Robert Kenneth Kuberski, Jr. ...Born in Chester, Pa. ...Married to Janet, couple has a daughter, Brooke (born 4/6/97)...An all-league, all-county and All-Southeastern Pennsylvania selection in football at Ridley High School in Folsom, Pa. ...Earned three letters in football as a fullback and defensive end...Also lettered twice in lacrosse and once in wrestling, where, as a fill-in heavyweight, he pinned his opponent to clinch the county championship as a senior...Played high school football with NFL quarterback Matt Blundin...Spent the past offseason as a financial advisor with Morgan Stanley Dean Witter...Has passed the Series 7 test for his brokerage license and now is a registered stock broker...Hobbies include fishing and hunting...Is an active speaker in the offseason, mostly to schools and civic groups...Residence: De Pere, Wis.

PRO STATISTICS:

Year	G/S	UT	AT	Sacks	Int.	FR	FF	PD
1993 Green Bay ....reserve/military								
1994 Green Bay ....reserve/military								
1995 Green Bay 9/0	4	2	2	0	0	0	1
1996 Green Bay 1/0	0	0	0	0	0	0	0
1997 Green Bay 11/3	14	10	0	0	0	0	0
Totals 21/3	18	12	2	0	0	0	1
Playoffs......................4/0	1	1	0	0	0	0	0

Blocked Field Goals: 1, vs. Tampa Bay (1/4/98-postseason)

SEAN LANDETA 7

Punter
College: Towson State
NFL Exp.: 14th Season   **Packers Exp.:** 1st Season
Ht.: 6-0   **Wt.:** 200   **Born:** 1/6/62   **Acq:** UFA-98 (TB)

PRO: Reliable veteran punter, now in his 14th NFL season, brings sure-footed confidence to the Green Bay special teams…Is expected to take over team punting duties after the free agency departure of Craig Hentrich, the Packers' punting specialist the last four seasons…A two-time Pro Bowl selection (1986, 1990), he also has earned two Super Bowl rings as a member of the New York Giants (1986, 1990)…Green Bay special teams coach Johnny Holland is excited to have a punter of Landeta's caliber in the Packers' fold, saying, "We'll definitely look to Sean for his veteran leadership. It's going to valuable to have a guy that has a lot of experience as a punter in a lot of games. There's nothing that he hasn't seen. His experience will be valuable. His knowledge of the punting game and what we're looking for from a punt in every situation – hang time, distance, whatever it takes – will be an asset."…With a 43.6-yard career average, he currently ranks eighth on the NFL's all-time punting list…Has led the NFC in punting four times during his career and finished third-or-better in eight seasons…Possesses a better than 2-to-1 ratio on punts 'inside the 20' (231) vs. touchbacks (112)…Earned singular recognition when he was named to the NFL's All-1980s team in 1989 by the Pro Football Hall of Fame selection committee…Has faced the entire gamut of game conditions and scenarios in his career, valuable experience not lost on Holland…"Sean has proven he can get the job done," Holland explains. "He's punted in bad weather before – in New York – he's punted for different teams. He's punted in big games before – been to the playoffs, two Super Bowls. We know we can count on him."…An experienced postseason performer, owns a 40.8-yard average on 54 punts – with an impressive 36.3-yard net – in 11 career playoff games…Possesses a greater than 3-to-1 ratio (14-4) of punts landed 'inside the 20' vs. touchbacks in the playoffs…Signed with the Packers as an unrestricted free agent on Feb. 26, 1998, leaving the Tampa Bay Buccaneers…A one-time United States Football League punter who was a member of two league championship teams with the Philadelphia/Baltimore Stars, he originally had signed with the New York Giants as a free agent prior to the start of training camp in 1985…Spent eight-and-a-half years (1985-93) punting for the Giants before being waived at the midpoint of the 1993 season; he subsequently signed with the then-Los Angeles Rams, finishing the season…Remained with the Rams for three-and-a-half seasons (1993-96)…Out of football to start the 1997 season, he signed on with Tampa Bay in Week 7 and remained with the Buccaneers for the balance of the year…**1997:** Punted in 10 games for the Buccaneers, finishing with a 42.1-yard average (10th in the NFC)…Had signed with Tampa Bay on Oct. 9 to replace Tommy Barnhardt, who was placed on injured reserve after sustaining a broken collarbone at Green Bay (Oct. 5)…Played well at Indianapolis, punting 6 times for a 43.3-yard average and booming the Bucs out of late trouble twice with punts of 56 and 54 yards, respectively…Had string of 355 punts without a block broken on final punt of day at New York Jets (Dec. 14)…Boomed career-long 74-yarder earlier in game against the Jets, his fourth career punt of at least 70 yards…Landed a season-high 3 punts 'inside the 20' vs. Green Bay (Dec. 7)…In Bucs' two postseason contests, averaged 41.2 yards on 9 punts, with a 35.4-yard net average, and registered 3 'inside the 20' efforts…**1996:** Matched career high with 44.8-yard punting average, as he played in all 16 games in his last season with the Rams…Tied for second place in gross punting average in the NFC and for sixth place in the NFL overall…Turned in fine performance vs. Jacksonville (Oct. 20), including a season-long 70-yard effort among 5 punts for a 48.6-yard average…Closed out season in fine fashion vs. New Orleans (Dec. 21), punting for a season-high 49.2-yard net average, having three punts travel more than 50 yards and surpassing the 35,000-yard career mark…Ran his consecutive punts without a block string to 307 by season's end…Finished his tenure with the Rams as the club's all-time leading punter with a 44.4-yard career gross average…**1995:** Played in all 16 games and finished with a 44.3-yard average on career highs in both punts (83) and yards (3,679)…Effort was tops in NFC and good for third place in the NFL overall…Averaged over 40 yards per punt in all 16 games and boasted a net average of at least 40 yards in three games...Landed 23 punts 'inside the 20'...Named as first alternate to Pro Bowl and earned All-Pro honors from *USA Today* and second-team All-NFC recognition from *United Press International*...Named NFC 'Special Teams Player of the Month' for November after posting a 44.2-yard gross and 40.0-yard net average on 17 punts during the month...Experienced bout with pneumonia Saturday before game at Carolina (Sept. 17), but recovered in time to average 42.4 yards on 7 punts in contest vs. Panthers...Became the 24th punter in NFL annals to top the 30,000-yard mark with a 63-yard blast at Philadelphia (Oct. 29)...Notched single-game career highs for both punts (10) and yards (484) at New York Jets on Dec. 3...**1994:** Tied his career high with an NFL-leading 44.8-yard average on 78 punts in his first full season with the Rams...Punted in all 16 games, finishing with a net average of 34.3...Landed 23 punts 'inside the 20'...Was a second-team All-NFC pick by *UPI*...Tied franchise record with a single-game, career-high 52.5-yard average on 4 punts in contest at Kansas City (Sept. 25), earning NFC 'Special Teams Player of the Week' and, later, 'Special Teams Player of the Month' (September) in the process...Stuck a career-high 5 punts 'inside the 20' vs. Atlanta (Oct. 2)...**1993:** Played in eight games for the Giants, averaging 42.1 yards on 33 punts (with 1 block), before being released (Nov. 9)...Signed three days later with the then-L.A. Rams and punted in that team's final eight games, collecting a 43.5-yard average on 42 punts...Overall, finished the season with a 42.9-yard average, good for a seventh-place tie among NFC punters...**1992:** Averaged 43.7 yards on 53 punts, pacing all NFL non-dome punters...His average was good for fourth place overall among all NFC punters...Had 2 blocked punts...Suffered a season-ending knee injury vs. Philadelphia (Nov. 22), he subsequently had surgery and was placed on injured reserve two days later, causing him to miss the Giants' five remaining contests...**1991:** Notched another fine season, finishing with a 43.3-yard average (fourth in the NFC) on 64 punts, while playing in 15 games for the Giants...Enjoyed consistency throughout the season, averaging over 40 yards per punt in all but one game...**1990:** A unanimous All-Pro selection at punter for the second consecutive year, averaged an NFC-high 44.0 yards on 75 efforts...Named to the Pro Bowl for the second time in his career...Equaled his career high by landing 24 punts 'inside the 20'...Performed well in the playoffs, averaging 42.1 yards on 10 punts, as Giants won Super Bowl XXV over Buffalo...**1989:** A unanimous All-Pro selection at punter, led the NFL with a career-high 37.8-yard net punting average on 70 efforts, appearing in all 16 games for the Giants...Tied for second place in the NFC with a 43.1-yard gross average...Named as punter on the NFL's All-1980s team, chosen by the Hall of Fame selection committee...In playoff loss vs. L.A. Rams (Jan. 7), averaged 37.2 yards, but with 3 returns for a minus-1 yard, resulted in an excellent 37.4-yard net average...**1988:** Suffered lower back injury in season opener vs. Washington (Sept. 5), he was placed on injured reserve two days later...**1987:** In a strike-shortened season, finished fourth in the NFL and third in the NFC with a 42.7-yard average on 65 punts, playing in all 12 union games...Suffered his first blocked punt in the NFL at New Orleans (Nov. 22)...**1986:** Earned near-consensus All-Pro honors in his second season, establishing a career high with an NFC-leading 44.8-yard punting average...Net average of 37.1 yards also was tops in the conference...Selected to represent NFC in the Pro Bowl as he punted in all 16 games for the Giants, dropping a career-high 24 punts 'inside the 20'...Notched a 43.7-yard average on 16 postseason punts (38.8-yard net) as the Giants captured Super Bowl XXI with a win over Denver...**1985:** Punted in all 16 games for the Giants in his rookie NFL season after signing as a free agent at the conclusion of the USFL campaign...Finished with a 42.9-yard average on 81 punts, good for third place in the NFC...Was a second-team All-NFC selection by *UPI* and an All-Rookie pick by *Football Digest*...Averaged 37.6 yards on 14 punts in the playoffs...Signed with New York Giants as a free agent on July 14...While with the newly-relocated Baltimore Stars, finished with a 41.8-yard average and had 18 punts 'inside the 20,' as team won second consecutive USFL championship...**1984:** Was a first-team All-USFL selection for the second straight year as the Philadelphia Stars won their first league championship...Led USFL with 38.1-yard net average while averaging 41.1 yards per punt...**1983:** Punted to 41.9-yard gross and 36.5-yard net averages, earning first-team All-USFL honors as a member of the Stars...Led league with 31 punts 'inside the 20'...Was a 14th-round selection by Philadelphia in the 1983 USFL draft.

COLLEGE: A three-year letterman (1980-82) at Towson State...Was a three-time All-Eastern College Athletic Conference selection for the Tigers (1980-82)...Was nation's leading punter among Division II schools in 1980 with a 43.4-yard average, also chipping in with 14 field goals...Ranked among the top five punters in Division II in 1981 and 1982, with 41.1- and 44.7-yard averages, respectively...Named a Kodak Division II All-American and *Associated Press* Little All-American following his 1982 efforts...Played, but did not letter, in 1979...Majored in communications.

PERSONAL: Given name Sean Edward Landeta...Born in Baltimore, Md. ...Married to Pam, couple has a son, Joseph (born 3/6/97)...An all-county and all-metro punter as a senior at Loch Raven High School in Towson, Md. ...Lettered one year in football and three years in baseball...Has been and continues to be involved in many charities, including the American Cancer Society, the Juvenile Diabetes Foundation, Leukemia Society of America and Special Olympics...Also heavily involved in children's charities...Hobbies include watching sporting events, reading and spending time with his family – particularly his fast-growing son, Joseph...Residence: Manhasset, N.Y.

PRO STATISTICS:

Year		G	No.	Yds.	Gross Avg.	Net Avg.	TB	In 20	LG	Blk.
1985	N.Y. Giants	16	81	3,472	42.9	36.4	14	19	68	0
1986	N.Y. Giants	16	79	3,539	44.8	37.1	11	24	61	0
1987	N.Y. Giants	12	65	2,773	42.7	31.0	6	13	64	1
1988	N.Y. Giants	1	6	222	37.0	35.8	0	1	53	0
1989	N.Y. Giants	16	70	3,019	43.1	37.8	7	19	71	0
1990	N.Y. Giants	16	75	3,306	44.0	37.3	11	24	67	0
1991	N.Y. Giants	15	64	2,768	43.3	35.3	8	16	61	0
1992	N.Y. Giants	11	53	2,317	43.7	31.5	9	13	71	2
1993	N.Y. Giants	8	33	1,390	42.1	35.0	3	11	57	1
	L.A. Rams	8	42	1,825	43.5	32.9	7	7	66	0
1994	L.A. Rams	16	78	3,494	44.8	34.3	9	23	62	0
1995	St. Louis Rams	16	83	3,679	44.3	36.7	12	23	63	0
1996	St. Louis Rams	16	78	3,491	44.8	36.1	9	23	70	0
1997	Tampa Bay	10	54	2,274	42.1	34.1	6	15	74	1
Totals		**177**	**861**	**37,569**	**43.6**	**35.5**	**112**	**231**	**74**	**5**
Playoffs		**11**	**54**	**2,203**	**40.8**	**36.3**	**4**	**14**	**63**	**0**

Passing: 0 of 1 in 1985
Rushing: 2 for 0 yards, 0.0 avg., LG 0 in 1996

CAREER SINGLE-GAME HIGHS

Most Punts: 10, at N.Y. Jets (12/3/95); **Most Yards Punting:** 484, at N.Y. Jets (12/3/95); **Highest Punting Average (min. 4 att.):** 52.5, at Kansas City (9/25/94); **Longest Punt:** 74, at N.Y. Jets (12/14/97); **Most Punts Inside the 20:** 5, vs. Atlanta (10/2/94)

DORSEY LEVENS > 25

Running Back
College: *Georgia Tech*
NFL Exp.: *5th Season*   **Packers Exp.:** *5th Season*
Ht.: *6-1*   **Wt.:** *228*   **Born:** *5/21/70*   **Acq.:** *D5b-94*

PRO: A big back, one whom opponents struggle to bring down, enjoyed a breakthrough 1997 season in his first year as Green Bay's featured ball carrier...Emerged as one of the NFL's best halfbacks last season on the heels of a strong finish in 1996...Posted the second-best season running the football in the Packers' storied history, while becoming the club's sixth 1,000-yard rusher ever, after the team's incumbent halfback, Edgar Bennett, was lost early in the year due to a torn Achilles' tendon...Was the first Green Bay running back voted to the Pro Bowl in nearly two decades, when he was named as a starter on the NFC squad alongside 2,000-yard rusher Barry Sanders…"After getting his chance to start," says Packers offensive coordinator Sherm Lewis, "Dorsey took advantage of the opportunity and never looked back. He started every game and became a Pro Bowl player for us. He is a very versatile performer who was just as effective on inside runs as he was outside. And he is a definite threat as a pass receiver, with the ability to go all the way every time he touches the ball."…Particularly strong at the beginning and end of games, he averaged 5.0 yards per carry (74-372) in the first quarter and 4.7 yards per carry (98-457) in the fourth quarter during the '97 regular season…Demonstrated that he could be the desired workhorse by setting a team record for most rushing attempts in one season…Able to wear other teams down, a fact born out by his 10-or-more carries in the final period six times last year – Sept. 1 vs. Chicago, Oct. 27 at New England, Nov. 23 vs. Dallas and Dec. 1 at Minnesota in the regular season, plus Jan. 4 vs. Tampa Bay and Jan. 11 at San Francisco in the playoffs – and all were victories…Toted the rock 13 times for 91 yards – an impressive 7.0-yard average – in the fourth quarter of 45-17 triumph over Cowboys en route to an all-time Green Bay single-game rushing record of 190 yards…Has had four separate and very distinct seasons with the Packers since first joining the club in 1994 as a fifth-round draft choice…Saw minimal playing time as a rookie, primarily on special teams, he then started at fullback in 1995, excelling as a pass-catcher and leading the way for Bennett's 1,067-yard season…Ceding the fullback job to bruising William Henderson in 1996, he backed up Bennett at halfback and received most of his playing time in single-back sets…Emerged late in the '96 campaign with outstanding performances in several big games, particularly the Packers' victory over Carolina in the NFC Championship Game, as Green Bay went on to capture Super Bowl XXXI…Then faced his greatest challenge athletically early last season when Bennett went down and, in an instant, he became the primary runner for the defending Super Bowl champions…Responded beautifully, running for 100-plus yards six times during the regular season – double the previous best for a Mike Holmgren-coached Green Bay team – before adding two more century efforts during the playoffs…"Dorsey has got a rare combination of size and speed," Lewis adds. "He's really fast for a guy his size. He's more elusive than some of our other backs – he can make people miss. He's got quickness and he can change direction. Plus, he's got enough speed that he can out-run angles; when a defender is coming he can out-run him to the sideline. And he's got enough confidence in himself that he knows he can take it outside and out-run linebackers."…Named as Green Bay's franchise player this past February, he has begun to make his mark in club history…Already holds three team records: *Most Rushing Attempts (season)* – 329 in 1997; *Most Rushing Yards Gained (game)* – 190 vs. Dallas in 1997; and *Most Total Yards From Scrimmage (season)* – 1,805 in 1997…Also is tied for one club mark: *Most Consecutive Games, 100 or More Yards Rushing* – 3 in 1997…Enters the 1998 season 12th on Green Bay's all-time rushing list with 2,136 yards (on 491 carries), with the chance to quickly crack the Top Ten by surpassing #11 Ted Fritsch (2,200) and #10 Tobin Rote (2,205)…Raised his personal level of play during the '97 postseason as he averaged 105.3 yards per game rushing – more than 15 yards better than his superb average during the regular season (89.7) – and set new all-time club single-game rushing marks in consecutive weeks…Had greater than one-third of his playoff carries (25 of 71) last year come in the fourth quarter…Ran for a higher-than-normal average (4.6 yards) during the second half of the team's three '97 postseason games, when he gained 187 yards on 41 carries…Is the Packers' second-leading rusher of all-time in the postseason with 524 career yards, only 37 yards behind the leader, Bennett (561)…Also is the second-leading receiver in Green Bay's playoff history with 32 catches, he trails just Robert Brooks (43)…Does hold three team playoff records: *Most Yards Gained Rushing (game)* – 114 yards at San Francisco in the 1997 NFC Championship Game; *Most Games, 100 or More Yards Rushing (career)* – 2; *Most Consecutive Games, 100 or More Yards Rushing* – 2 in 1997…Is tied for two other club postseason marks: *Most Consecutive Games, Rushing Touchdowns* – 2 in 1997; *Most Consecutive Games, One or More Pass Receptions* – 10 (tied with Brooks)…A proven pass-catcher of measurable quality in addition to his running skills, is on the brink of also cracking the Packers' all-time Top Twenty receivers, he enters the '98 season with 133 career receptions (for 1,039 yards)…Has more total touchdowns – 29 (15 rushing, 14 receiving) – over the past three seasons than any other player on the Green Bay roster…**1997:** Became the team's featured ball carrier early in the season when '96 starter Bennett was lost for the year (torn Achilles' tendon) in the first preseason game…Went on to enjoy one of the best seasons ever by a Green Bay runner…Led the Packers and finished second in the NFC (fourth in NFL) with 1,435 rushing yards and 7 touchdowns on 329 attempts (4.4 avg.)…His 1,435 yards represented the second-highest, single-season rushing total in team history, only 39 yards behind Jim Taylor's club-record 1,474 yards in 1962…Became just the sixth 1,000-yard rusher in the Packers' history and only the second in nearly two decades…Set a team record with 1,805 total yards from scrimmage – second in the NFC – topping Bennett's previous single-season mark of 1,715 yards, posted in 1995…Named to the NFC Pro Bowl team as a starter at running back, he became the first Green Bay runner voted to the NFL's annual all-star contest since Terdell Middleton in 1978 (Brent Fullwood played as an injury replacement in 1989)...Also was selected for the All-NFC teams of *Pro Football Weekly* and *Football News*...Was a second-team All-NFL pick by *Football Digest* and *College & Pro Football Newsweekly*...Broke Bennett's club single-season record for carries (316 in 1995) with 329 rushing attempts...Also made a career-best 53 receptions (for 370 yards and 5 touchdowns) to rank third on the team...Finished third in NFC scoring among non-kickers with 74 points (12 touchdowns, 1 two-point conversion)...Started all 16 regular-season games (at halfback) for the first time as a pro, he also started all three of the club's playoff games, including Super Bowl XXXII...Led the team in rushing during the postseason with 316 yards and 2 touchdowns on 71 carries (4.5 avg.), he also was the club's second-leading receiver in the playoffs with 14 catches for 112 yards...Finished the regular season with six 100-yard rushing games, twice the previous high total since the Mike Holmgren era began in 1992 – and just one short of Taylor's club single-season record of 7, accomplished in 1962 – he subsequently had two more 100-yard efforts in the playoffs...Enjoyed undoubtedly his most memorable day as a pro in 45-17 triumph over Dallas (Nov. 23), when he set a Green Bay single-game rushing record with 190 yards on the ground, breaking the previous mark of 186 set by Taylor vs. the N.Y. Giants in Milwaukee Dec. 3, 1961, to earn national Miller Lite NFL 'Player of the Week' honors...Gained 145 of his rushing yards against the Cowboys in the second half (on 24 attempts) – the first time a Green Bay running back had 100-or-more yards on the ground in one half since 1987, when Kenneth Davis rushed for 107 yards in the first half of a game at Detroit Oct. 25 – including an average of 7.0 yards per carry (13 for 91 yards) in the fourth quarter...Had a career-high 33 carries in Cowboys contest, the second-highest number ever by a Packers running back, and scored 2 touchdowns – a seven-yard reception for the first score of the game and a five-yard run in the closing minutes which broke Taylor's 36-year-old record...One week earlier, played an outstanding game at Indianapolis (Nov. 16), when he had the lone 3-touchdown game of his pro career (2 rushing, 1 receiving) while rushing for 103 yards on only 14 attempts – a season-high 7.4 yards per carry average...Also caught 4 passes for 92 yards against the Colts, including a season-long 56-yarder on a screen, giving him 195 total yards from scrimmage...His career-long 52-yard scoring run in the second quarter at Indianapolis was Green Bay's longest rush from scrimmage in nearly four years...On the heels of his efforts vs. the Colts and Cowboys, tied John Brockington's 1971 club record of three consecutive 100-yard rushing games when he gained 108 yards (on 31 carries) in 27-11, Monday night victory at Minnesota (Dec. 1), scoring twice on runs of three and five yards...Also set a new team mark with 533 total yards from scrimmage during the same three-game stretch...His 33 rushing attempts against the Cowboys and 31 vs. the Vikings in consecutive weeks represented two of the five highest one-game carry totals in club history...Was on pace for a career performance at Chicago (Oct. 12) when he gained 74 yards rushing in the first half on just 12 carries (6.2 avg.), but had to leave the game late in the second quarter after injuring his clavicle on a running play...Initially stayed in Bears contest after injury, he caught a one-yard touchdown pass two plays later with 1:40 left in the first half, giving Green Bay a 14-10 halftime lead...Turned in an outstanding and gutsy performance in important win two weeks later at New England (Oct. 27) as he led the team in both rushing and receiving despite pain from the clavicle, gaining 100 yards on the ground while catching 7 passes (for 40 yards)...Also scored 2 touchdowns vs. the Patriots – one on a six-yard pass late in the first quarter, the other on a three-yard run with 2:46 left in the game to give the Packers their final, 28-10 advantage...Had the first 100-yard rushing day of his pro career vs. Miami (Sept. 14), when he churned out 121 yards (on 21 carries), including 93 in the second half of the 23-18 win...Averaged 6.7 yards per carry two weeks later at Detroit (Sept. 28) as he rushed 16 times for 107 yards...Gained 73 yards rushing despite sitting out the majority of the second half in the Packers' 31-10 victory at Carolina (Dec. 14)...Rushed for 71 yards during regular-season finale vs. Buffalo (Dec. 20) in three quarters of action, but fell 39 yards shy of Taylor's single-season record for yards rushing...Registered the first two-point conversion of his pro career in season opener vs. Chicago (Sept. 1)...Had a career-high 8 receptions in each victory over the Buccaneers during the regular season, including an important eight-yard touchdown catch in the rematch, a 17-6, division-clinching win at Tampa (Dec. 7)...Saved his best for last, though, when it came to the Bucs, setting a Green Bay single-game postseason rushing record – 112 yards on 25 carries, breaking the previous mark of 108 by Bennett in 1995 – in 21-7 divisional playoff victory over Tampa Bay (Jan. 4)...Followed that up by establishing a new club record for the second week in a row, when he rushed for 114 yards on 27 carries in the Packers' 23-10, NFC Championship Game triumph at San Francisco (Jan. 11)...His 100-plus yard rushing effort against the 49ers was the first allowed by that team during the 1997 season and included a five-yard touchdown run late in the game to virtually cement the issue at 23-3...Gained 90 yards on 19 rushing attempts in 31-24, Super Bowl XXXII loss to Denver, he also caught 6 passes (for 56 yards), including receptions on four consecutive plays during the Packers' final, unsuccessful bid to tie the game in the last two minutes...**1996:** Saw the bulk of his personal playing time come in the team's single-back sets for much of the season...Received additional snaps late in the year and throughout the postseason when he began to emerge as a true offensive threat who struck fear into opponents...Played in all 16 regular-season games for the initial time, starting once (Dec. 1 vs. Chicago) when the Packers opened in a four-receiver formation...Also got into all three playoff contests, including Super Bowl XXXI...Finished second (to Bennett) on the team in rushing with 566 yards (14th in the NFC) on 121 carries...His impressive 4.7 yards-per-carry average was second only to Detroit's Sanders (5.1) among the top 20 rushers in the conference...It also was the the best by a Green Bay runner with 100-or-more carries since 1988...Tied for fourth on the club with 31 receptions for 226 yards...Scored 10 touchdowns (5 rushing, 5 receiving), tying him for seventh in NFC scoring among non-kickers as well as for second on the Packers...Finished the year strong, averaging 66.8 rushing yards per contest over Green Bay's final four regular-season games, then generating an average of 65.0 yards per contest on the ground in the playoffs...Gained 195 yards on 39 carries in the postseason, behind only Bennett's 219 yards on the team...Led the Packers in receptions during the playoffs with 10 for 156 yards and 1 touchdown...Merited selection to the 'All-Madden Team' by Fox Sports analyst John Madden based on his strong year-end performance...Enjoyed at the time the professional game of his life in NFC Championship Game victory over Carolina (Jan. 12), earning NFL 'Offensive Player of the Week' honors in the process...Had 205 total yards from scrimmage vs. the Panthers, including 88 yards rushing (then a career high) on only 10 carries for an 8.8-yard average and 117 yards through the air (his lone 100-yard receiving day as a pro) among a team-leading 5 receptions...Broke a big 35-yard run off tackle on third-and-one on the last play of the first quarter against Carolina, then made a fabulous 29-yard touchdown catch just inside the right edge of the end zone on the initial snap of the second period for Green Bay's first TD...Later vs. the Panthers, ran 66 yards up the right sideline on a screen pass to set up a four-yard touchdown by Bennett on the next play, putting the Packers ahead 27-13 in the eventual 30-13 triumph...His 117 receiving yards in the NFC title contest was the most by a Green Bay running back in a four-quarter game since 1951, when Jug Girard gained 130 yards on 4 catches at the N.Y. Yanks (Oct. 28)...Had better than half of the Packers' rushing total in their Super Bowl win over New England (Jan. 26), leading the team with 61 yards on 14 carries...Rushed for '96 regular-season high of 86 yards on 14 carries in 41-6 thrashing of Denver (Dec. 8)...Had enjoyed a stirring performance one week earlier at Chicago, when he rushed for 69 yards on only 5 attempts – a 13.8-yard average – and scored on a 10-yard run early in the fourth quarter, giving Green Bay a 21-10 lead in the eventual 28-17 win...Closed out the regular season with 73 yards and 1 touchdown on the ground vs. Minnesota (Dec. 22), a game which also saw him catch a 13-yard screen pass for another score...Made a season-best 5 receptions (for a team-leading 83 yards) at Kansas City (Nov. 10)...**1995:** Beat out Henderson in training camp to win the starting fullback job following the offseason move of '94 starter Bennett to halfback...Played in 15 regular-season games, making 12 starts at fullback...Finished third on the team in rushing with 120 yards and 3 touchdowns on 36 carries...Also was club's fourth-ranking receiver with 48 receptions for 434 yards and 4 TDs...Was consistently productive as a receiver, catching at least one pass in every game he played (including playoffs)...Made a season-high 6 receptions (for 50 yards) at Detroit (Oct. 29)...Had a one-yard touchdown catch among his 5 receptions in the Packers' 35-28 win over Chicago (Nov. 12), he also rushed for a season-high 26 yards that day...First had a career-best 2 rushing scores vs. Tampa Bay (Nov. 26)...Was inactive at Dallas (Oct. 8) due to a sprained left knee suffered in practice three days earlier...Played in all three playoff games, starting the first two...Was team's third-leading receiver in the postseason with 7 receptions for 47 yards...Made looping, 18-yard touchdown catch along the right sideline midway through the fourth quarter, sealing 37-20 first-round playoff victory over Atlanta (Dec. 31)...Usually moved to halfback (with Henderson coming in at fullback) in goal-line and short-yardage situations...**1994:** Won preseason duel with veteran Dexter McNabb for backup fullback position behind Bennett...Played in the Packers' final 14 regular-season games, plus both playoff contests, after he was inactive for the first two games of the year...Saw the majority of his action on special teams, but also was utilized periodically as a blocking back for Bennett in short-yardage situations...Carried 5 times for 15 yards during the regular season...Had Green Bay's lone touchdown – a three-yard run off left tackle on fourth-and-one to cap Packers' opening drive – in 16-12 wild-card playoff victory over Detroit at Lambeau Field (Dec. 31)...Caught 1 pass for 9 yards in his most extensive action of the season, Nov. 13 vs. the N.Y. Jets, when he played the entire second half in place of Bennett, who had left in the second quarter with a bruised knee...One week earlier vs. the Lions had forced a fumble by Detroit's Derrick Moore on kickoff coverage which the Packers recovered, leading to an early field goal in eventual 38-30 victory...Contributed 5 solo tackles on special teams, adding 1 stop with the coverage group in the postseason...Second of two fifth-round draft choices (149th overall and

18th running back) by Green Bay in 1994.

COLLEGE: Played two years (1992-93) at Georgia Tech after transferring from Notre Dame, where he spent his first two collegiate seasons (1989-90)...Forced to sit out redshirt year in 1991...Totaled 1,221 yards and 13 touchdowns on 207 rushing attempts as a collegian, including 1,036 yards and 10 TDs at Tech...Also caught 25 total passes for 323 yards and 2 scores (21-276-2 for GT)...Was a first-team All-Atlantic Coast Conference choice as a senior, when he led the Yellowjackets in rushing with 823 yards and 8 touchdowns on 114 attempts...Set a school record with his 7.2 yards-per-carry average...Scored 3 touchdowns and rushed for a career-high 141 yards on 20 attempts vs. Wake Forest...Was expected to be No. 1 tailback for the Irish entering the 1990 season, but suffered a knee injury which hampered his play and limited him to eight games...Had lettered as a freshman, carrying 25 times for 132 yards and 1 score...Holds B.A. degree in business management.

PERSONAL: Given name Herbert Dorsey Levens...Nicknamed 'Horse'...Born in Syracuse, N.Y. ...Single...Lettered four times as a running back, safety and linebacker at Nottingham High School in Syracuse, N.Y. ...All-America selection of *Parade* and *SuperPrep* magazines, he also was named 'Offensive Player of the Year' in the Northeast by the latter...Chosen Gatorade Circle of Champions 'Player of the Year' in New York and was rated as the top player in the state by *Scholastic Coach*...Earned all-state and all-league honors and was 'Co-Player of the Year' for Central New York as a senior, when he rushed for 1,307 yards...Scored 7 touchdowns and kicked 8 PATs for 50 total points in one game his senior year...Also earned three letters in basketball, serving as team captain his senior season...Hobbies include bowling and fishing...Is a big movie buff as well...Held a charity basketball game – the 'Dorsey Levens All-Star Basketball Challenge' – in Syracuse during the 1995 offseason to benefit the Sherman Park Football Association (a children's league he had played in as a youngster)...Also signed autographs in Syracuse to benefit the NAACP in 1996 and '97...Previously worked in the 'Mentor' program while at Georgia Tech, tutoring kids...Residence: Atlanta.

PRO STATISTICS:

Year	G/S	RUSHING					RECEIVING				
		No.	Yds.	Avg.	LG	TD	No.	Yds.	Avg.	LG	TD
1994 Green Bay 14/0		5	15	3.0	5	0	1	9	9.0	9	0
1995 Green Bay 15/12		36	120	3.3	22	3	48	434	9.0	27	4
1996 Green Bay 16/1		121	566	4.7	24	5	31	226	7.3	49	5
1997 Green Bay 16/16		329	1,435	4.4	52t	7	53	370	7.0	56	5
Totals 61/29		491	2,136	4.4	52t	15	133	1,039	7.8	56	14
Playoffs.................11/5		115	524	4.6	35	3	32	316	9.9	66	2

Two-Pt. Conversions: 1, vs. Chicago (9/1/97)

Kickoff Returns: 2 for 31 yards, 15.5 avg., LG 16 in 1994; 1 for 13 yards in 1994 Playoffs; 5 for 84 yards, 16.8 avg., LG 29 in 1996 for total of 7 for 115 yards, 16.4 avg., LG 29

Special Teams Tackles: 5 (5-0) in 1994; 1 (1-0) in 1994 Playoffs; 2 (0-2) in 1995 for total of 7 (5-2)

Miscellaneous Tackles: 2 in 1995; 1 in 1997 for total of 3

100-Yard Rushing Games: 6 in 1997; 2 in 1997 Playoffs

100-Yard Receiving Games: 1 in 1996 Playoffs

CAREER SINGLE-GAME HIGHS

Most Rushing Attempts: 33, vs. Dallas (11/23/97); **Most Rushing Yards:** 190, vs. Dallas (11/23/97); **Longest Run:** 52t, at Indianapolis (11/16/97); **Most TD Runs:** 2, three times (last: at Minnesota, 12/1/97); **Most Receptions:** 8, vs. Tampa Bay (10/5/97) and at Tampa Bay (12/7/97); **Most Receiving Yards:** 117, vs. Carolina (1/12/96-postseason) / 92, at Indianapolis (11/16/97); **Longest Reception:** 66, vs. Carolina (1/12/96-postseason) / 56, at Indianapolis (11/16/97); **Most TD Receptions:** 1, 14 times

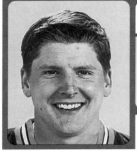

RYAN LONGWELL) 8

Kicker
College: California
NFL Exp.: 2nd Season   **Packers Exp.:** 2nd Season
Ht.: 6-0   **Wt.:** 192   **Born:** 8/16/74   **Acq:** W-97 (SF)

PRO: Second-year placekicker, looks to build upon last season's success as unlikely Packers specialist...Rose from ranks of being a "camp leg" to become Green Bay's leading scorer as he seized a preseason Cinderella opportunity...Originally joined Packers as a waiver wire acquisition just prior to start of training camp, simply hoping for the chance to get enough work to gain notice from another NFL club; a little over seven weeks later, he was making his NFL debut on *Monday Night Football* as the kicker for the defending Super Bowl champions...Made most of opportunity when expected Green Bay kicker, third-round draft choice Brett Conway, suffered what would become a season-ending quadriceps injury...Capitalized on an excellent preseason performance to gain a roster spot and went on to have one of the most productive rookie seasons for a kicker in Packers history...Green Bay special teams coach Johnny Holland expects Longwell to pick up right where he left off in 1997, saying, "We would hope he continues to improve. He proved that he could kick in this league. He did a good job for us last year, but this year I think he can improve and even do better. We're looking for big things from him this year. He's got the rookie 'shakes' off of him now – some of the nervousness will go away. I think that he should even be better this year."...Will compete with Conway during this year's training camp for placekicking duties, a situation Holland believes will benefit everyone..."It's a great situation for the team," Holland continues. "I think they'll both be great kickers in this league and whichever one doesn't make the team, I'm sure someone will want him on their team as the kicker. We just want to make it a fair competition. No one has the job yet, so it's still wide open. The competition is good for the team and will only make Ryan and Brett better."...**1997:** Enjoyed an immensely successful rookie season, connecting on 24/30 field goal tries and was a perfect 48/48 on PAT attempts while appearing in all 16 games...Led team and ranked third in NFC scoring with 120 points, the second-highest rookie total in team annals – trailing only Chester Marcol's 128-point production in 1972...Joined Marcol, Chris Jacke and Jan Stenerud as only the fourth kicker (and ninth player overall) in team annals to score 100-or-more points in a season...His 80.0 percent conversion rate was the fifth-best single-season field goal percentage in team history...Of his six misses, two were blocked and two hit uprights...Total of 24 field goals ranked as the fourth-best single-season mark in club annals and his 48 extra points were the team's third-best total...Had 29 of his 89 regular-season kickoffs reach the end zone, including 11 touchbacks (12.4%), as the Packers finished third in NFL kickoff coverage...Kicked at least one field goal in each of Green Bay's final eight games...Turned in a stellar performance in the playoffs, hitting on 6/7 field goal attempts (85.7%) and on 6/6 PAT tries, to lead the NFL's kickers in postseason scoring with 24 points...Already stands in third place in Green Bay's postseason annals for most field goals made (career) with 6, trailing only Jacke (15) and Don Chandler (9)...Was 3/3 on PATs and converted a 27-yard field goal attempt in Super Bowl XXXII vs. Denver (Jan. 25)...Connected on 3/4 field goal tries in NFC Championship Game victory at San Francisco (Jan. 11), falling one short of team postseason single-game, field goal record...Effort against the 49ers – the team which had released him in the preseason – included a 43-yard field goal into a tough wind as the half ended, giving the Packers a 13-3 intermission lead...One week earlier (Jan. 4), had connected on two second-quarter field goals (from 21 and 32 yards), staking the Packers to a 13-0 halftime lead in eventual 21-7 divisional playoff victory over Tampa Bay...Nailed a clutch, 44-yard field goal with 6:44 remaining in contest vs. Detroit (Nov. 2), giving Packers 10-point cushion in a 20-10 victory; the kick was his second three-pointer of the evening...Converted on 2/3 field goal attempts and all 3 PAT tries to help Green Bay to a 27-11 victory at Minnesota (Dec. 1) as Packers broke a five-game losing streak at the Metrodome...Made good on both PAT efforts and booted a key 27-yard field goal with 6:24 remaining in game at Tampa Bay (Dec. 7), staking Green Bay to eventual, 17-6 margin of victory and its third consecutive division title...Provided Packers with winning margin at Chicago (Oct. 12), as he hit a 37-yard field goal into swirling winds, giving Green Bay a 24-17 lead with 2:38 remaining in eventual 24-23 victory...Nailed a career-long 50-yard field goal among three successful kicks at Detroit (Sept. 28)...Also chalked up three field goals in each of Green Bay's first three games – vs. Chicago (Sept. 1), at Philadelphia (Sept. 7) and vs. Miami (Sept. 14) – with the Bears' contest producing his first NFL three-pointer and establishing his single-game career high for points (12)...Had enjoyed a perfect preseason, hitting on 6/6 field goal tries and 10/10 extra point attempts to earn a roster spot after Conway suffered a quadriceps injury in pregame warmups at Oakland (Aug. 8), making it necessary for the Packers to keep a second kicker into the regular season...Connected on all three attempts vs. Raiders as he stepped in for Conway on a last-minute basis, hitting from 21, 44 and 34 yards...Two weeks later, he solidified his hold on the placekicking duties in the final preseason contest, against the Giants in Madison (Aug. 22), as he converted field goals of 50, 28 and 49 yards to keep the Packers within striking distance; Green Bay later scored 2 touchdowns in the final 5:20 for a 22-17 win...When Conway's injury did not respond to treatment, and he eventually was placed on injured reserve (Sept. 3), Longwell was provided with his season-long opportunity...Originally was signed by the San Francisco 49ers as an undrafted free agent on April 28, 1997...Subsequently was waived by the Niners on July 9 and claimed the next day by Green Bay.

COLLEGE: A four-year letter winner (1993-96) at the University of California, acting as both the punter and placekicker during his final three seasons in Berkeley...Also served as Cal's punter as a freshman...Finished career as the school's eighth-leading scorer with 177 total points...Was successful on 32/56 field goal attempts and 81/85 PAT tries (including Aloha Bowl)...Had a 41.9-yard career punting average at Cal (including bowl games), good for third place (tie) in Golden Bears' annals...As a senior, earned first-team All-Pacific 10 Conference honors as a punter and was voted second-team All-Pac 10 as a placekicker...Led team with 76 points as he converted 12/17 field goal efforts and 40/41 PAT attempts (including Aloha Bowl)...Had a long field goal of 53 yards against San Diego State...Ranked ninth in the NCAA in 1996 with a 45.2-yard average on punts, the second-best mark in Cal history...Booted a season-long, 72-yard punt against Navy in the Aloha Bowl...Saw the opposition return just 30 of his 66 kickoffs in 1996...Twice was named Pac 10 'Special Teams Player of the Week' (Sept. 14 and Sept. 28)...Was one of three team captains during the '96 campaign...As a junior, hit on 12/17 field goal attempts...Earned B.A. degree in English.

PERSONAL: Given name Ryan Walker Longwell...Born in Seattle...Single...Was one of the top kicking prospects on the West Coast coming out of Bend (Ore.) High School...A three-year letterman in football, he was an all-conference selection as a junior and senior...Averaged 44.3 yards per punt as a senior and put 82 percent of his kickoffs into the end zone...Additionally served as the backup quarterback his senior year...Also was a three-time letterman in baseball as a third baseman, earning all-conference honors as a junior and senior...This past April he received the first annual Lee Remmel Sports Award for Professional Achievement in honor of his outstanding 1997 rookie season...Enjoys speaking to school groups and other organizations about the benefits of having a positive outlook and attitude...Was involved with Big Brothers/Big Sisters while at Cal...Has given time to Special Olympics in Bend, Ore., volunteering at ski races and speaking at other events...Hobbies include playing golf...Has a cousin, Michael Orr, who was a member of the 1992 and 1996 U.S. Olympic cycling team...Residence: Bend, Ore.

PRO STATISTICS:

Year	G	PATs Made/Att.	Pct.	Blk.	FIELD GOALS Made/Att.	Pct.	LG.	Blk.	Total Pts.
1997 Green Bay	16	48/48	100.0	0	24/30	80.0	50	2	120
Playoffs	3	6/6	100.0	0	6/7	85.7	43	0	24

ACCURACY BY DISTANCE

Year	1-19 Yards	20-29 Yards	30-39 Yards	40-49 Yards	50+ Yards
1997 Green Bay	4/4	7/8	10/13	2/4	1/1
Playoffs	1/1	3/3	1/1	1/2	0/0

KICK BY KICK

1997: (38G,36G,29G) (22G,18G,27G,28N) (26G,24G,39G) (34G) (36G,19G,50G) (47B) (37G) ( ) (23G,44G) (44G) (18G) (34N,32G) (30G,35N,19G) (31B,27G) (31G) (45N,35G) **PS:** (21G,32G) (19G,47N,43G, 25G) (27G)

KICKOFFS

Year	No.	No. in EZ	TB	Pct. of TB
1997 Green Bay	89	29	11	12.4
Playoffs	15	2	1	6.7

CAREER SINGLE-GAME HIGHS

Most Field Goals Made: 3, four times (last: at Detroit, 9/28/97); **Most Field Goals Attempted:** 4, at Philadelphia (9/7/97); **Longest Field Goal Made:** 50, at Detroit (9/28/97); **Longest Field Goal Attempted:** 50, at Detroit (9/28/97); **Most PATs Made:** 6, vs. Dallas (11/23/97); **Most PATs Attempted:** 6, vs. Dallas (11/23/97); **Most Points Scored:** 12, vs. Chicago (9/1/97); **Most Kickoffs:** 8, vs. Chicago (9/1/97) and vs. Dallas (11/23/97); **Most Kickoffs in End Zone:** 4, vs. Chicago (9/1/97); **Most Touchbacks:** 2, vs. Minnesota (9/21/97)

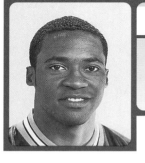

DERRICK MAYES 80

Wide Receiver
College: Notre Dame
NFL Exp.: 3rd Season   **Packers Exp.:** 3rd Season
Ht.: 6-0   **Wt.:** 205   **Born:** 1/28/74   **Acq:** D2-96

PRO: One of the most talented receivers on the Packers' roster, Derrick Mayes is looking for a breakthrough year in 1998...Has showed flashes of brilliance his first two seasons, but has been somewhat limited due to injuries...Slowed initially by a shoulder injury as a rookie, ankle injuries forced him to miss time last season...Has the ability to make circus-type catches and can get the ball in traffic...Green Bay offensive coordinator Sherm Lewis and the entire coaching staff have high expectations for Mayes this season..."We expect Derrick to make his biggest contribution to date this year," Lewis says. "Derrick has been hampered with injuries his first two years, but appears to be kicking off the '98 season healthier than ever before. He possesses great hands and can make the acrobatic catches. He will start the season as the number three receiver with hopes of pushing (Robert) Brooks and (Antonio) Freeman for a starting spot."...Also saw his first NFL action as a punt returner in the latter part of the 1997 season...After wearing the number 1 in college, chose number 80 for the pros as a salute to personal friend Lake Dawson (formerly of the Chiefs), who was his immediate predecessor as Notre Dame's go-to receiver and who also wore that number for Kansas City...**1997:** Played in 12 regular-season games with three starts...Saw most of his action as the Packers' No. 3 wide receiver...Started once when Brooks was sidelined with a rib injury, the other occasions when Green Bay opened in a multiple receiver formation...Was inactive for three other games and did not play in one contest due to separate injuries to both of his ankles...Played in all three postseason contests, including Super Bowl XXXII...Finished sixth on the team during the regular season with a career-high 18 receptions for 290 yards (16.1 avg.)...Replaced the injured Brooks in the starting lineup at Indianapolis (Nov. 16) and caught 3 passes for a career-high 119 yards (his first 100-yard game as a pro) in his hometown, including a career-long 74-yard reception – the longest catch by a Packer in 1997 – which saw him fall one yard shy of the end zone...Saw extensive action the following week vs. Dallas (Nov. 23) when Brooks (concussion) left the game in the first quarter...Had 4 receptions for 30 yards against the Cowboys to equal his career best...Made one of the bigger plays of his pro career at Philadelphia (Sept. 7), when, with the Packers down 10-9 and facing a fourth-and-16 from their own 41 with 1:38 left in the game, he caught a 28-yard pass from Brett Favre to give Green Bay a first down at the Eagles' 31-yard line...Started season opener vs. Chicago (Sept. 1) as Packers opened in four wide receiver set, and made a career-high 4 receptions (for 54 yards)...Caught 3 passes for 22 yards in the Packers' 17-6, division-clinching win at Tampa Bay (Dec. 7)...Also served as the club's punt returner, primarily during a three-week, late-season stretch, he returned 14 punts for a 10.1-yard average over the course of the season...Had 6 punt returns for 78 yards (13.0 avg.), including a 26-yard runback, in the Packers' 27-11 win at Minnesota (Dec. 1)...Did not play in regular-season finale vs. Buffalo (Dec. 20), one week after he was inactive at Carolina (Dec. 14) due to a sprained left ankle suffered on Dec. 11 in practice...Earlier had suffered a right ankle sprain on the Packers' first possession at Detroit (Sept. 28), from which he did not return, causing him to be inactive vs. Tampa Bay (Oct. 5) and at Chicago (Oct. 12)...Caught 3 passes for 47 yards during the postseason...Caught a 14-yard pass on third-and-9 to set up Mark Chmura's touchdown reception on the next play, putting the Packers ahead 7-0, in divisional playoff win over Tampa Bay (Jan. 4)...Later in same contest made a 23-yard, circus-type catch, where he ended up snaring the ball between his legs, to the Bucs' 22-yard line on a crucial third-and-18 play late in the third quarter...More importantly, the catch kept the drive alive, a possession which resulted in Green Bay's final touchdown in a 21-7 victory...Also had a key reception, where he bulled over the 49ers' Tyronne Drakeford to pick up a first down, early in the third quarter of NFC Championship Game win at San Francisco (Jan. 11)...**1996:** Limited by a shoulder injury early in his rookie season, returned to play in seven games as a backup receiver, catching 6 passes for 46 yards and 2 touchdowns...Was inactive for the team's other nine regular-season contests plus all three playoff games, including Super Bowl XXXI...Scored his first NFL touchdown at Kansas City (Nov. 10), making a tough, one-handed grab off of a fade route late in the game, cutting the Packers' deficit to 27-20 with 1:02 left in the game...Also tied his season high with 2 receptions against the Chiefs...Caught his second touchdown pass in as many weeks at Dallas (Nov. 18), when he pulled in a three-yarder from Favre...Saw his first action of the year late in Green Bay's 37-6 win at Chicago (Oct. 6)...Caught his first NFL pass in Monday night win over San Francisco (Oct. 14), a five-yard reception immediately prior to Green Bay's game-winning field goal in overtime...Saw his most extensive action of the season Oct. 27 against Tampa Bay, when he caught a season-best 2 passes for 20 yards after Freeman went out with a broken arm early in the game...Had dislocated his left shoulder in the final seconds of the team's third preseason contest, at Baltimore (Aug. 17), when he made a reception on a crossing pattern during the Packers' game-winning drive...Subsequently missed the balance of training camp before returning to full practice on Sept. 18, he was inactive for the team's first five regular-season games...Drafted in the second round (56th overall and 11th wide receiver) by Green Bay in 1996.

COLLEGE: A two-year starter and four-time letterman (1992-95) at Notre Dame...Finished his collegiate career as Notre Dame's all-time leader in receiving yards (2,512) and touchdown catches (22), while he stood fifth in receptions (129)...Had nine career 100-yard receiving games for the Irish...Was a second-team All-America selection as a senior by *Football News* as well as a third-team pick of the *Associated Press*, when he led the Fighting Irish with 48 receptions for 881 yards and 6 TDs... Also was chosen as one of five senior captains...Tabbed as one of 10 semi-finalists for the 'Fred Biletnikoff Award,' presented annually to the top receiver in the nation, each of his final two years...Named as Notre Dame's MVP in a vote of his teammates in both 1994 and '95...Was an honorable mention All-America choice of *United Press International* as a junior...Broke school's single-season record for TD receptions in 1994 with 11, while leading the team with 47 catches (for 847 yards)...Made 24 receptions for 512 yards and 2 scores as a sophomore...Caught 10 passes (for 272 yards) as a freshman, including touchdowns on each of the first three receptions...Earned a B.A. degree in communications.

PERSONAL: Given name Derrick Binet Mayes...Nicknamed 'A-mayes-ing'...Born in Indianapolis...Single...Was an honorable mention All-America selection by *USA Today* at North Central High School in Indianapolis...Also named Gatorade Circle of Champions Indiana 'Player of the Year' by *Scholastic Coach* as a senior...Was an all-state pick and was selected to play in Indiana North-South all-star game...Caught 45 passes for 738 yards and 4 TDs as a senior on the heels of 45 receptions for 720 yards and 9 TDs his junior year...Also lettered twice each in basketball and track...Hobbies include playing golf...Is in the trophy engraving business with his father, David...Mother, Ann, is a junior high school principal who taught former Miami Dolphins standout Mark Clayton in the seventh grade...Residence: Phoenix.

PRO STATISTICS:

Year	G/S	No.	RECEIVING Yds.	Avg.	LG	TD	No.	FC	PUNT RETURNS Yds.	Avg.	LG	TD
1996 Green Bay	7/0	6	46	7.7	12	2	0	0	0	0.0	0	0
1997 Green Bay	12/3	18	290	16.1	74	0	14	3	141	10.1	26	0
Totals	19/3	24	336	14.0	74	2	14	3	141	10.1	26	0
Playoffs	3/0	3	47	15.7	23	0	0	0	0	0.0	0	0

Miscellaneous Tackles: 1 in 1996
100-Yard Receiving Games: 1 in 1997

CAREER SINGLE-GAME HIGHS

Most Receptions: 4, vs. Chicago (9/1/97) and vs. Dallas (11/23/97); **Most Receiving Yards:** 119, at Indianapolis (11/16/97); **Longest Reception:** 74 at Indianapolis (11/16/97); **Most TD Receptions:** 1, two times

BLAINE McELMURRY > **38**

Safety
College: *Montana*
NFL Exp.: *1st Season*   **Packers Exp.:** *1st Season*
Ht.: *6-0*   **Wt.:** *187*   **Born:** *10/23/73*   **Acq:** *FA-97*

PRO: Intelligent, hard-hitting safety prospect who looks to have an increased impact in his second year with Green Bay...Solid in all of the fundamentals...Spent the bulk of his rookie campaign on the Packers' practice squad, then saw limited playing time late in the season as a member of the active roster..."He's an excellent athlete," says Packers defensive coordinator Fritz Shurmur. "He's a guy who's got great skills in terms of ability to be able to cover, change directions and do all of those kinds of things. We're looking for him to compete for a safety position, either as a strong safety or free safety. He's a good tackler, should be a good special teams player and will make a legitimate run at a roster spot."...Earlier had earned Division I-AA All-America honors both on the field and in the classroom at the University of Montana...**1997:** First joined Green Bay in Week 2, when he was signed to the Packers' practice squad (Sept. 3)...Was elevated to the active roster on Nov. 25 after 11 weeks on the practice squad...Saw action on special teams in Monday night, 27-11 victory at Minnesota (Dec. 1)...Was inactive for the ensuing final three regular-season games, plus all three postseason contests, including Super Bowl XXXII...Had begun training camp with the newly-relocated Tennessee Oilers, but was waived on the final cutdown (Aug. 24)...Claimed by Philadelphia, he remained with the Eagles for less than one week before his release on Aug. 29...Signed with the Tennessee Oilers as an undrafted free agent on May 2.

COLLEGE: Three-year starter and four-time letterman (1993-96) at University of Montana...Redshirted in 1992...Started 44 consecutive games over his final three seasons, including the Grizzlies' 11 playoff

contests…Had 253 career tackles (141 solo) and 13 interceptions, two of which he returned for touchdowns…Was a Division I-AA All-America selection as a senior…Twice chosen first-team All-Big Sky Conference (1995-96)…Also was named as UM's 'Golden Helmet Award' winner in both '95 and '96, an honor given to the school's hardest hitter…Led or tied for the team lead in interceptions each of his final three seasons, including a career-high 5 in 1996…Helped the Grizzlies to win the I-AA national championship in 1995, then reach the title game again the next season before losing to Marshall…Was voted to the GTE Academic All-America team his senior year, when he posted a 3.6 grade point average, he also was an honors student and a four-time academic all-conference selection…Earned a B.S. degree as a microbiology pre-med major.

PERSONAL: Given name Blaine Richard McElmurry…Born in Helena, Mont. …Married to Kristine…Earned 12 letters at Troy (Mont.) High School – four each in football, basketball and track…A quarterback and safety for the football team, he won all-state, all-conference and team MVP honors as both a junior and senior…Also participated in Montana's annual East-West Shrine Game…Was a member of the 1991 Troy squad which captured the state 'B' football championship and was coached by his father, Richard, who himself had played football at Carroll College (Helena, Mont.)…Also won state titles in the long and triple jumps as a senior, while posting personal bests of 22' 2" and 44' 8", respectively…Was a two-time all-state pick in basketball as well…Had a perfect 4.0 GPA to merit prep academic All-American status…With aspirations for an eventual post-football career in orthopedics (and a medical school acceptance already in hand), he spent a portion of this past offseason observing the surgeries of Dr. Patrick McKenzie, the Packers' orthopedist…Sister, Katie, played guard for the women's basketball team at the University of Montana the last four years…Hobbies include hunting, fishing and water skiing…Residence: Green Bay.

PRO STATISTICS:

Year	G/S	UT	AT	Sacks	Int.	FR	FF	PD
1997 Green Bay 1/0		0	0	0	0	0	0	0
Playoffs **0/0**		**0**	**0**	**0**	**0**	**0**	**0**	**0**

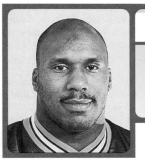

KEITH McKENZIE) **95**

Defensive End
College: Ball State
NFL Exp.: 3rd Season **Packers Exp.:** 3rd Season
Ht.: 6-3 **Wt.:** 264 **Born:** 10/17/73 **Acq:** D7b-96

PRO: Talented young pass-rusher who possesses the necessary skills to make a legitimate run at a starting position as a defensive end…Will contribute at minimum as an accomplished special teams player and as a situational rusher…Has finished the last two years strong when given increased opportunity, flashing tremendous potential during the playoffs while making a valued defensive contribution in runs to the Super Bowl…"Keith McKenzie is a very instinctive football player," says Packers defensive coordinator Fritz Shurmur, "who has exceptional ability to be able to rush the passer, to tackle and to do all those kinds of things. He is an outside player on the line of scrimmage with his hand on the ground. His size limits his ability to be able to play inside. But he also has enough linebacker skill to be able to use him as a pass-dropper in some situations, and he's also effective as a special teams player. He has the kind of ability where you look for ways to get him on the field."…Has led Green Bay in sacks each of the past two preseasons, and even led the entire NFL in 1996…Has added roughly 10 pounds over this past offseason, increasing his weight to 264 in an effort to better withstand the physical element of NFL defensive line play…With 4 career postseason sacks, now is tied with Sean Jones for the second-most in Green Bay playoff history, trailing only the 8 of Reggie White…"In the stretch run the last two years when our defense has played really well over the last seven or eight games of each of those seasons, he has been a significant contributor from the standpoint of rushing the passer and coming up with sacks," Shurmur adds. "He's got a great feel for working off the corners of the blocker, which is what pass rush is all about. And he's relentless in his effort. His feet are always moving up the field. And, as a result, he just wins some pass-rush battles with sheer determination."...Has primarily been utilized as a situational rush end and on special teams during his initial two seasons...Played linebacker in college for three seasons before moving to defensive end for his senior year...His outside pass-rush skills, along with his small-college background and jersey number (95), have invited comparisons to former Packer and current Jacksonville Jaguar Bryce Paup...**1997:** Stepped up his personal production on defense dramatically during the playoffs after seeing primarily special teams duty throughout the regular season...Played in all 16 games for the first time as a pro, he also got into each of the club's three playoff contests, including Super Bowl XXXII...Registered 3 sacks during the postseason to tie the Broncos' Neil Smith and the Bucs' Warren Sapp for the NFL lead...Sacked Steve Young twice in the fourth quarter of NFC Championship Game win at San Francisco (Jan. 11), the first of which, on a fourth down deep in 49ers territory, resulted in a Dorsey Levens touchdown for Green Bay's final points in 23-10 triumph, while the second snuffed out the Niners' last gasp scoring effort when he knocked the ball loose from Young for teammate Paul Frase to recover...One week earlier in the divisional playoffs, had sacked the Buccaneers' Trent Dilfer for a 15-yard loss in the final period of 21-7 win over Tampa Bay (Jan. 4)...Finished fourth on the club in special teams tackles during the regular season with 12, equaling his career high with 2 at Indianapolis (Nov. 16)...Posted 1½ sacks among his 3 total tackles in limited regular-season play on defense...Had a season-best 2 stops, including one-half sack, in win over St. Louis (Nov. 9)...Had recorded his lone "full" sack one week earlier vs. his hometown Lions (Nov. 2), dropping Detroit QB Scott Mitchell late in the game...Led the team in sacks during the preseason (with 2½) for the second straight year...**1996:** Made an immediate impression on the Green Bay coaching staff as a rookie when he led the NFL in sacks during the preseason with 5½...Played in 10 regular-season games and in all three postseason contests, including Super Bowl XXXI...Was inactive for club's other six games...Along with 1 sack and a forced fumble, posted 5 tackles during the regular season, including a season-high 2 in Monday night walloping of Philadelphia (Sept. 9)...Enjoyed a strong finish to his personal year...Picked up his first "full" sack as a pro in NFC Championship Game win over Carolina (Jan. 12), felling the Panthers' Kerry Collins late in the contest...Followed that performance up by registering 2 special teams tackles in the first half of Green Bay's Super Bowl triumph over New England (Jan. 26)...Earlier had established his career high of 2 special teams stops in regular-season finale vs. Minnesota (Dec. 22)...Totaled 5 total tackles on kickoff and punt coverage over the course of the regular season...Forced a fumble by Rams quarterback Tony Banks late in the Packers' 24-9 victory at St. Louis (Nov. 24), sharing a sack with teammate Wayne Simmons on the same play...Had split a sack with Shannon Clavelle early in the season, when the pair got together to drop San Diego's Sean Salisbury (Sept. 15)...Was the second of two seventh-round draft choices (252nd overall) by Green Bay in 1996.

COLLEGE: Two-year starter and three-time letterman (1993-95) at Ball State...Played linebacker his first three years before switching to defensive end as a senior...Left as school's all-time sacks leader with 25 after pacing Cardinals in this category each of his last two seasons...Recorded 195 career tackles (121 solo), including 33 for loss, as well as 3 fumble recoveries, 1 forced fumble, 1 interception, 3 passes defensed and 2 blocked punts...Was an All-Mid American Conference first-team pick by league coaches and *Football News* as a senior...Also received team's MVP award and served as a tri-captain in 1995, when he led the squad with 11 sacks (15th in the nation) and the MAC with 18 tackles for loss...Paced team in sacks with 9 among a career-best 82 tackles as a junior...Posted a career-high 18 tackles at Toledo...Named MAC 'Defensive Player of the Week' vs. Western Michigan, when he registered 7 tackles and 4 sacks...Played in every game, including the Las Vegas Bowl, his sophomore campaign...Saw action in six 1992 games, though he did not letter...Was redshirted in 1991...Played in four games for Ball State's basketball team as a senior and also competed in the shot put for the school at one track meet, placing third...Earned a B.S. degree in history.

PERSONAL: Given name Keith Derrick McKenzie...Born in Detroit...Single...Was an all-conference and all-metro selection in football at Highland Park (Mich.) High School...Played offensive guard and linebacker, earning three letters...Had 65 tackles, 4 sacks and 2 interceptions as a senior...Also served as team's punter, averaging 40 yards per kick...Lettered three times in track, he competed in the 200-meter dash (best time was 23.9) and was a state qualifier in the shot put (best mark was 55' 0")...Also lettered twice in wrestling and once in tennis...Uncle, Reggie McKenzie, played for the Buffalo Bills (1972-82) and Seattle Seahawks (1983-84)...Served as a training camp ballboy for the Seahawks for three summers while in high school...Has worked with his uncle's charity, the 'Reggie McKenzie Foundation,' in Detroit...Hobbies include basketball, watching television (especially nature shows), fishing, hunting (bow hunting in particular) and playing video

games…Residence: Detroit.

PRO STATISTICS:

Year		G/S	UT	AT	Sacks	Int.	FR	FF	PD
1996	Green Bay	10/0	2	3	1	0	0	1	0
1997	Green Bay	16/0	1	2	1½	0	0	0	0
Totals		26/0	3	5	2½	0	0	1	0
Playoffs		6/0	4	0	4	0	0	1	0

Special Teams Tackles: 5 (2-3) in 1996; 2 (2-0) in 1996 Playoffs; 12 (9-3) in 1997; 1 (1-0) in 1997 Playoffs for total of 17 (11-6)

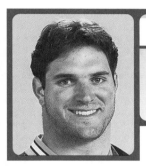

JOHN MICHELS   77

Offensive Tackle
College: Southern California
NFL Exp.: 3rd Season   **Packers Exp.:** 3rd Season
Ht.: 6-7   **Wt.:** 300   **Born:** 3/19/73   **Acq:** D1-96

PRO: Impressively hewn Californian, the Packers' first-round selection in the 1996 NFL draft, returns for his third NFL season in a new role…The monolithic ex-Trojan, possessor of 14 games' experience as a starter over his first two seasons, takes on the significant, "swing tackle" assignment in the offensive line, one which will find him backing up both Ross Verba and Earl Dotson, the starters at left and right tackle, respectively…Opened the 1997 season as the designated successor to the retired Ken Ruettgers as the starter at left tackle, but was hampered by injury in both training camp and the early weeks of the regular season, subsequently giving way to Verba, the Packers' top pick in the 1997 draft…Green Bay offensive line coach Tom Lovat, for one, remains confident that Michels can be a valuable contributor to the cause…"John has started, what, 12 or 15 ball games? So he's got experience that you look for," Lovat observed. "You know, of course, he's had his opportunities to be the starter. He just can't seem to hang on to it when he's in there. Maybe in this offseason he will have improved himself so that he will be a little more at ease and maybe do the things that we've been trying to get him to do for the last two to three years. I know this – if you look around the league, with 30 teams, there are a lot of people that would like to have a guy like John. He just happens to be in a spot where we've got two pretty good football players. And I think this – there are a lot of teams playing with a lot less-talented guys than John at the tackle position."…**1997:** Started the first five games of the regular season before yielding to Verba on the heels of knee and thumb injuries…Suffered a sprain of the medial collateral ligament in his right knee on the Packers' first offensive series vs. Minnesota (Sept. 21)…Although unable to return to the game, he started the following week at Detroit (Sept. 28), but aggravated the sprain early in the third quarter, forcing him out of Lions contest…Saw action solely on special teams beginning with Tampa Bay contest (Oct. 5), and also in the next three games, before being inactive for the team's final seven regular-season contests…Also was inactive throughout the playoffs…Originally had been slowed in training camp after sustaining a dislocated left thumb in practice July 15…Did not miss a practice, but subsequently played with a protective cast…**1996:** Played in 15 games, making nine starts at left tackle, and was inactive for one contest…Also saw action in all three playoff games, including Super Bowl XXXI, primarily in a special teams capacity…Named to all-rookie teams of *Pro Football Weekly*/PFWA and *College & Pro Football Newsweekly* upon completion of his rookie campaign…Following a strong initial showing in training camp, and with Ruettgers sidelined due to a knee problem, it had appeared in mid-August that he would be the Packers' opening day starter at left tackle…Then suffered a sprained right ankle just before halftime of the team's third preseason game, Aug. 17 at Baltimore…Though he returned to play in the Packers' first four regular-season games almost exclusively in a special teams role, he did not fully recover from the injury until making his first NFL start on Sept. 29 at Seattle, replacing Gary Brown in the lineup...Also started the following week at Chicago (Oct. 6) before spraining the medial collateral ligament in his right knee early in Bears contest...Inactive for the ensuing Monday night game with San Francisco (Oct. 14), he returned to start each of the next three games, vs. Tampa Bay (Oct. 27), Detroit (Nov. 3) and at Kansas City (Nov. 10)...With the Bucs contest, however, he began sharing time with Ruettgers, who had returned from his own knee difficulties...Backed up Ruettgers in Monday night loss at Dallas, then became the starter again for following four games when Ruettgers retired on Nov. 20...Held the Rams' highly-regarded Leslie O'Neal to only 1 tackle in key win at St. Louis the next week (Nov. 24)...Subsequently yielded the left tackle position to veteran Bruce Wilkerson for regular-season finale vs. Minnesota and the playoffs...Drafted in the first round (27th overall) by Green Bay in 1996.

COLLEGE: One-year starter and three-time letterman (1993-95) for Southern California...Had started his collegiate career as a defensive lineman before moving to offensive tackle midway through the '93 season...Redshirted in 1991...Started every game at left tackle for the Rose Bowl champion Trojans in 1995...Reached personal preseason goal when he earned All-Pacific 10 Conference first-team honors...Made 8 knockdown blocks in his first start, a 45-7 rout of San Diego State...Had a season-high 9 knockdown blocks as USC offense amassed 405 yards in a 31-0 win over Arizona...Backed up All-American Tony Boselli (Jaguars) at left tackle in 1994...Played behind Willie McGinest (Patriots) at defensive end and tackle in '93...Did not see any action as a defensive tackle/outside linebacker in 1992 as a redshirt freshman...Holds B.A. degree in religion.

PERSONAL: Given name John Spiegel Michels...Born in La Jolla, Calif. ...Married to Melissa, the couple has one daughter, Lauren (born 7/14/98)...Was an All-America selection as a defensive tackle at La Jolla (Calif.) High School, lettering three times...Had 90 tackles and 13 sacks in 13 games as a senior, along with 8 pass deflections, 3 forced fumbles and 3 fumble recoveries...Also lettered three years each in basketball and track (discus, hurdles, high jump)...Was league champion in the discus...Along with then-teammate Aaron Taylor, threw out the first pitch at the Milwaukee Brewers' 1997 Opening Day...Hobbies include youth ministry, playing the guitar, singing, playing golf and jet skiing...Speaks to youth groups during the offseason, both in Northeast Wisconsin and in California...Has worked with the local Leap of Faith ministry for the past two years, he previously was involved with 'The Gathering,' a youth ministry in San Diego...Also has served Athletes in Action and the Fellowship of Christian Athletes...Residence: Green Bay.

PRO STATISTICS:

Games/Starts—Green Bay 1996 (15/9); 1996 Playoffs (3/0); 1997 (9/5); 1997 Playoffs (0/0). Career totals: 24/14. Playoff totals: 3/0.

GLYN MILBURN   30

Running Back/Kick Returner
College: Stanford
NFL Exp.: 6th Season   **Packers Exp.:** 1st Season
Ht.: 5-8   **Wt.:** 174   **Born:** 2/19/71   **Acq:** T-98 (Det)

PRO: One of the top return men in the NFL, Glyn Milburn brings his wide range of talents to the Packers after spending the last two years with divisional rival Detroit...Is expected to contend for a role as a third-down back along with vying to become the team's kick return specialist, a capacity in which he has shined over his five pro seasons to date, earning Pro Bowl recognition in 1995...Acquired by Green Bay in an offseason trade with the Lions this past April 23 in exchange for a conditional 1999 draft choice...Had begun his NFL career in 1993 with Denver, playing three seasons for the Broncos, before being traded to Detroit..."Glyn has really impressed the offensive coaches with his quickness and receiving ability," says Packers offensive coordinator Sherm Lewis. "He is respected around the league as an outstanding kickoff and punt returner. We're hoping to utilize his receiving skills coming out of the backfield."...A very versatile player, he has played running back, wide receiver and returned punts and kickoffs during his five-year NFL career with the Broncos (1993-95) and Lions (1995-96)...Though slight in stature, has yet to miss a game as a pro, playing in 80 consecutive regular-season contests plus two playoff games...Was a Pro Bowl selection as a kick return specialist in 1995 while with Denver, a year which saw him lead the NFL with a 27.0-yard average on kickoffs...Has averaged 24.1 yards on 215 career kickoff returns and 9.7 yards on 193 career punt returns...Now has accumulated 8,882 total yards in the NFL...Set a league record with 404 all-purpose yards in a 1995 game with Seattle...**1997:** Played in all 16 regular-season games with one start, also seeing action in the Lions' playoff loss at Tampa Bay...Began the year as the club's third receiver, but became solely a return man later in the season...Named as an alternate to the NFC Pro Bowl squad as a kick returner...Finished the season with 5 receptions for 77 yards (15.4 avg.)...Was sixth in the NFC in kickoff returns, averaging 23.9 yards on 55 runbacks, while finishing 10th in the conference in punt returns (47 for 433 yards)...Caught a season-long 43-yard pass in opener vs. Atlanta (Aug. 31)...Had a season-high 2 receptions (for 19 yards) vs. Tampa Bay (Sept. 7)...Lone start of the season came at New Orleans (Sept. 21) as Lions opened the game with three receivers...Posted a career-high 189 kickoff return yards (on 5 attempts) in 55-20, Thanksgiving Day victory over Chicago (Nov. 27)...Had a season-long 40-yard punt return at Tampa Bay (Oct. 12)...Turned in a fine return performance at Washington (Nov. 9), when he averaged 17.3 yards on 4 punt returns and 26.2 yards on 5 kickoff returns...Returned 5 kickoffs for 140 yards (28.0 avg.) in wild-card playoff loss to Buccaneers (Dec. 28)...**1996:** Served primarily as a kick returner while playing in all 16 games in his first season with Detroit after being acquired in an offseason trade...Set a club single-season record for most kickoff return yards – 1,627 – breaking Mel Gray's previous mark of 1,276 yards...Also established a new team record for most kickoff returns in a season with 64, surpassing the previous high of 48, set by Herman Hunter in 1986...Finished fourth in the NFC (fifth in the NFL) with a 25.4-yard kickoff return average...Helped set up a fourth-quarter touchdown with a 49-yard kickoff return at Philadelphia (Sept. 15)...Had his longest punt return of the season (33 yards) vs. Atlanta (Oct. 6), setting up Detroit's first touchdown...Had a season-long 65-yard kickoff return vs. the N.Y. Giants (Oct. 27) to position the Lions for their only touchdown, he also averaged a season-high 35.8 yards per kickoff return in the game...Compiled a season-high 148 kickoff return yards on 5 runbacks (29.6 avg.) at San Diego (Nov. 11)...Had a 48-yard kickoff return to set up a go-ahead field goal vs. Kansas City (Nov. 28) on Thanksgiving Day...Returned a season-high 6 kickoffs (for 140 yards) vs. Green Bay (Dec. 15)...Had joined the Lions in an April 12 trade with Denver...**1995:** Named to the AFC Pro Bowl squad as a kick return specialist in his final season with the Broncos...Saw action in all 16 games as a return man, wide receiver and tailback...Led the NFL with a 27.0-yard kickoff return average, returning 47 for 1,269 yards...Also averaged 11.4 yards on (31) punt returns, third in the AFC and fifth in the NFL...Along with the Redskins' Brian Mitchell, was one of only two players to rank among the top five in the NFL in both kickoff and punt return average...Named first-team All-Pro as a kick returner by *The Sporting News*...Garnered second-team All-Pro honors from the *Associated Press* and *College & Pro Football Newsweekly*...Was an All-AFC pick of *Pro Football Weekly* and *Football News*...Earned AFC 'Special Teams Player of the Week' honors for his performance against San Diego (Nov. 19), when he totaled 177 yards on 4 kickoff returns (44.3 avg.) and added 20 yards on 2 punt returns...Opened the game against the Chargers with a career-long 86-yard kickoff return...Had 178 kickoff return yards – on 7 runbacks, an average of 25.4 yards – at Houston (Nov. 26)...Set an NFL record with 404 total yards vs. Seattle (Dec. 10) as he rushed a career-high 18 times for a career-best 131 yards (7.3 avg.) – his lone 100-yard rushing performance as a pro – caught 5 passes for 45 yards, returned 5 punts for a career-high 95 yards (19.0 avg.) and brought back 5 kickoffs for 133 yards (26.6 avg.)...Accounted for 193 total yards at Philadelphia (Nov. 12), when he had 5 kickoff returns for 140 yards (28.0 avg.), caught 4 passes for 23 yards and rushed twice for 30 yards...Gained all of his yards from scrimmage against the Eagles on Denver's final drive as he was the Broncos' featured back...Averaged 26.8 yards on 5 kickoff runbacks at Dallas (Sept. 10)...Made his only start of the season at tailback Dec. 17 at Kansas City, replacing an injured Terrell Davis, and totaled 114 all-purpose yards...**1994:** Got into all 16 games with three starts...Compiled 1,818 all-purpose yards, including 201 rushing on 58 attempts, 549 receiving on a career-high 77 receptions, 793 on 37 kickoff returns and 379 on 41 punt returns...His 77 catches were the most by an NFL running back in '94 and the most ever in one season by a Broncos running back...Finished sixth in the AFC with a 9.2-yard punt return average...Posted 202 total yards and scored on a 20-yard reception at the L.A. Rams (Nov. 6)...Earlier had career highs for receptions (9) and receiving yards (85) vs. the L.A. Raiders (Sept. 18)...Scored the lone rushing touchdown of his pro career Dec. 17 at San Francisco on an 11-yard run...Had a season-long 44-yard punt return at San Diego (Oct. 23)...**1993:** Played in all 16 regular-season games, starting two, he also saw action in the club's playoff loss at the L.A. Raiders...Put together a solid rookie season as he gained 1,125 total yards...Rushed for 231 yards on 52 attempts, caught 38 passes for 300 yards and 3 touchdowns, averaged 10.6 yards on 40 punt returns (fifth in the AFC and eighth in the NFL) and returned 12 kickoffs for 188 yards...Accounted for 148 all-purpose yards in his first NFL game, Sept. 5 at the N.Y. Jets, including a career-long 50-yard reception, a 36-yard punt return and a 25-yard touchdown catch...Caught a season-high 8 passes at Kansas City (Sept. 20)...Had a career-long 54-yard punt return vs. Tampa Bay (Dec. 26)...Gained a season-high 173 total yards vs. Minnesota (Nov. 14) and 129 all-purpose yards in the postseason vs. the Raiders (Jan. 9)...Drafted in the second round (43rd overall) by Denver in 1993.

COLLEGE: Was a three-year starter and letterman (1990-92) for Stanford after beginning his collegiate career at the University of Oklahoma (1988)...Totaled 25 touchdowns and 6,363 yards − 2,387 rushing, 1,512 receiving, 1,161 on punt returns and 1,303 on kickoff returns − between the two schools, including 6,049 at Stanford...Sat out redshirt season in 1989 following his transfer...As a senior, ran for a career-high 851 yards and 8 touchdowns while averaging 4.8 yards per carry, caught 37 passes for 405 yards and 2 TDs, returned 15 kickoffs for 316 yards and had an astounding 17.3-yard punt return average (34 for 589 yards)...Garnered first-team All-America recognition from the *Associated Press*...Was the first player in Stanford history to return 3 punts for TDs in one season when he did so in 1992, a feat which was just one shy of the NCAA record, and left with the school's career record for punt return touchdowns (4)...Among his numerous senior year highlights was a 199-yard rushing performance vs. Notre Dame and punt return touchdowns of 75 yards against UCLA, 79 yards vs. Oregon State and 76 yards against arch rival California...Was a second-team all-conference choice in 1991, when he averaged 137.6 all-purpose yards per game...Set a school mark with 2,222 all-purpose yards in 1990, including 196 yards rushing vs. Cal...Received honorable mention on the All-America teams of *AP, United Press International* and *Football News*...Also was a member of the Cardinal track team his first two years at Stanford...Earned a B.A. degree in public policy.

PERSONAL: Given name Glyn Curt Milburn...Born in Los Angeles...Single...Attended Santa Monica (Calif.) High School, where he was a prep All-America selection in football by *SuperPrep* and *USA Today* (second team)...Earned California 'Offensive Player of the Year' honors from the *Los Angeles Times* and 'Best of the West' recognition from the *Long Beach Press Telegram*...Set state prep records for rushing yards (2,718) and rushing touchdowns (38) as a 1987 senior...Ran for over 200 yards in 10 of his games, including one 383-yard, 5-TD effort...His first high school carry went for a 65-yard touchdown...Earned three letters in football (as a running back and cornerback) and track, plus one in basketball...Cousin, Rod Milburn, won a gold medal at the 1972 Olympics in Munich, Germany, in the 110-meter high hurdles...Hobbies include computers, reading (mostly Christian books) and public speaking...Worked as an investment analyst this past offseason at Bodri Capital, an investment firm in Palo Alto, Calif. ...Previously had worked in the operations department of Direct Gas Supply, a Houston petroleum company, during the 1995-96 offseasons...Participated in the Presidential Inauguration Committee in 1996, his efforts included on-site work the day that President Clinton was sworn in for a second term...Ran for student body president while attending Stanford...Very community oriented, among the groups he has been involved with are Special Olympics, the American Diabetes Foundation, Kiwanis Club, Optimists Club, Athletes in Action and Champions for Christ...Residence: Green Bay.

PRO STATISTICS:

Year	G/S	RUSHING No.	Yds.	Avg.	LG	TD	RECEIVING No.	Yds.	Avg.	LG	TD
1993 Denver	16/2	52	231	4.4	26	0	38	300	7.9	50	3
1994 Denver	16/3	58	201	3.5	20	1	77	549	7.1	33	3
1995 Denver	16/1	49	266	5.4	29	0	22	191	8.7	23	0
1996 Detroit	16/0	0	0	0.0	0	0	0	0	0.0	0	0
1997 Detroit	16/1	0	0	0.0	0	0	5	77	15.4	43	0
Totals	80/7	159	698	4.4	29	1	142	1,117	7.9	50	6
Playoffs	2/0	2	-2	-1.0	1	0	5	8	1.6	6	0

Year	PUNT RETURNS No.	FC	Yds.	Avg.	LG	TD	KICKOFF RETURNS No.	Yds.	Avg.	LG	TD
1993 Denver	40	11	425	10.6	54	0	12	188	15.7	26	0
1994 Denver	41	4	379	9.2	44	0	37	793	21.4	40	0
1995 Denver	31	17	354	11.4	44	0	47	1,269	27.0	86	0
1996 Detroit	34	19	284	8.4	33	0	64	1,627	25.4	65	0
1997 Detroit	47	26	433	9.2	40	0	55	1,315	23.9	69	0
Totals	193	77	1,875	9.7	54	0	215	5,192	24.1	86	0
Playoffs	5	1	43	8.6	18	0	11	225	20.5	50	0

100-Yard Rushing Games: 1 in 1995

CAREER SINGLE-GAME HIGHS

Most Rushing Attempts: 18, vs. Seattle (12/10/95); **Most Rushing Yards:** 131, vs. Seattle (12/10/95); **Longest Run:** 29, vs. Seattle (12/10/95); **Most TD Runs:** 1, at San Francisco (12/17/94); **Most Receptions:** 9, vs. L.A. Raiders (9/18/94); **Most Receiving Yards:** 85, vs. L.A. Raiders (9/18/94); **Longest Reception:** 50, at N.Y. Jets (9/5/93); **Most TD Receptions:** 1, six times; **Most Punt Returns:** 5, four times (last: vs. Indianapolis, 11/23/97); **Most Punt Return Yards:** 95, vs. Seattle (12/10/95); **Longest Punt Return:** 54, vs. Tampa Bay (12/26/93); **Most Kickoff Returns:** 7, at L.A. Raiders (12/11/94); **Most Kickoff Return Yards:** 189, vs. Chicago (11/27/97); **Longest Kickoff Return:** 86, vs. San Diego (11/19/95)

RODERICK MULLEN) 28

Cornerback/Safety

College: Grambling State

NFL Exp.: 4th Season   **Packers Exp.:** 4th Season

Ht.: 6-1   **Wt.:** 202   **Born:** 12/5/72   **Acq:** FA-95

PRO: Multi-skilled player who doubles as both a cornerback and safety...Also is one of Green Bay's better special teams players...Smart, has a strong knowledge of the assignments of all positions in the secondary, allowing him to effectively serve as a backup everywhere...Has ideal size to play a physical style, while still possessing enough athleticism for good range..."I would describe Roderick Mullen as a versatile guy – there's no guy on our team who can play all four secondary positions, plus the inside spot in the 'dime', but he can," says Fritz Shurmur, the Packers' defensive coordinator. "He's a very cerebral guy. He understands our defense – understands the free safety, strong safety and both corner positions as well as, I said, the fifth defensive back or the inside cover corner in our 'nickel' and 'dime' defenses – so he's a very valuable guy for us. We're very comfortable with him in any of those roles should he be a starter."...Proved those words prophetic in 1997 in an early-season game at Detroit when he was called to action..."He was thrust into the starting role last year as a cornerback when Doug Evans couldn't play in the Detroit game – and against Herman Moore," Shurmur recalls. "He did an exceptional job that game."...Concentrated more on the cornerback position during his collegiate career at Grambling State before moving into the dual role he now carries out...Originally drafted by the New York Giants in 1995, spent training camp and the early part of that season on their practice squad before directly joining the Packers' 53-man roster as a free agent...**1997:** Received increased playing time on defense in his third season...Spent the first eight games as an extra defensive back in the club's 'dime' package before yielding to Darren Sharper...Finished with a career-high 17 tackles (15 solo), as well as 1 interception, 1 fumble recovery and 4 passes defensed...Also contributed a career-best 9 stops as a member of the special teams (7 unassisted)...Played in all 16 regular-season games for the first time as a pro, starting once...Also saw action in all three of the team's playoff contests, including Super Bowl XXXII...Recorded 2 special teams tackles against Denver in the Super Bowl among 3 coverage stops during the postseason...Made his first-ever NFL start when he opened at right cornerback in place of the injured Evans (hamstring) at Detroit (Sept. 28)...Rose up and did an excellent job of guarding Moore, the Lions' Pro Bowl receiver, while making 2 tackles and breaking up 1 pass...One week earlier vs. Minnesota (Sept. 21), had posted the most productive game of his pro career with a career-best 6 tackles (5 solo)...Saw extensive playing time late in Vikings contest as he subbed in for the injured Evans with the Packers clinging to a 38-32 lead and Minnesota driving for the potential winning touchdown...Made his first NFL interception in Green Bay's season opener vs. Chicago (Sept. 1), when he ran down an Erik Kramer pass at the Packers' 20-yard line late in the second quarter...Had season-high 2 stops on special teams at Carolina (Dec. 14), he also made his initial fumble recovery as a pro late in the 31-10 thrashing of the Panthers when he got in at cornerback...Enjoyed an excellent preseason, leading the team in passes defensed with 6 and finishing second among Green Bay tacklers with 20 stops...**1996:** Played in each of the Packers' first 14 regular-season games, primarily in a special teams capacity, before spraining the medial collateral ligament in his right knee vs. Denver (Dec. 8)...Was inactive for final two contests, he subsequently returned to see action in all three of Green Bay's playoff games, including Super Bowl XXXI...Totaled 3 tackles on defense in his occasional role in the club's 'dime' package...Made a season-high 2 stops (both solo) in win over Detroit (Nov. 3), adding an assisted tackle one week later at Kansas City...Contributed 3 unassisted tackles on special teams during the regular season, he augmented those efforts with a solo stop in club's divisional playoff win over San Francisco (Jan. 4)...**1995:** Saw reserve action in final eight regular-season games plus two of Packers' three playoff contests after hitching on with the team Oct. 18 as a free agent directly off the practice squad of the Giants...Contributed 3 unassisted tackles on defense and 3 additional stops (1 solo) on special teams over the last half of the year...Was inactive for his initial two games after signing with Green Bay before he worked his way into special teams role...Made season-high 2 tackles at Tampa Bay (Dec. 10), when he received added playing time as a sixth defensive back in a secondary which had been depleted by injuries to George Teague and Craig Newsome...Also had seen duty in team's 'dime' package in fourth quarter of win at Cleveland (Nov. 19), chipping in 1 solo stop that day...Contributed 1 assisted stop on special teams during playoffs, at Dallas in NFC Championship Game (Jan. 14)...Was inactive for Atlanta postseason contest...Had spent entire training camp with Giants before his release on final cutdown (Aug. 27), signed to that team's practice squad two days later...Fifth-round draft choice (153rd overall) of the New York Giants in 1995.

COLLEGE: Two-year starter (1993-94) at cornerback for Grambling State after spending his first two college seasons on the sideline...Totaled 58 tackles (45 solo), 6 interceptions, 26 passes defensed, 1 tackle for loss and 1 fumble recovery for the Tigers...Was a second-team All-Southwestern Athletic Conference selection as a senior, when he recorded 39 tackles (30 unassisted), 4 interceptions and 17 pass breakups...Honored as school's MVP of 1994 Bayou Classic battle with Southern after he intercepted 2 passes...Granted a medical redshirt season in 1992 due to a seriously broken leg suffered during spring drills...Volunteered in Grambling's sports information department while injured...Had sat out his freshman season under the NCAA's Proposition 48...Holds a B.S. degree in criminal justice.

PERSONAL: Given name Roderick Louis Mullen...Born in St. Francisville, La. ...Nicknamed 'Money'...Married to Deneca, couple has one daughter, Meagan (born 5/10/94), and one son, Roderick II (born 11/26/96)...Won all-state and All-District 10-AA honors at West Feliciana High School in St. Francisville, La. ...Lettered three times in football as a running back and defensive back, he also earned two letters in basketball and one in track...Hobbies include hunting and fishing...Splits residence between Green Bay and St. Francisville, La.

PRO STATISTICS:

Year	G/S	UT	AT	Sacks	Int.	FR	FF	PD
1995 N.Y. Giants ....practice squad								
Green Bay 8/0	3	0	0	0	0	0	0
1996 Green Bay..............14/0	2	1	0	0	0	0	0
1997 Green Bay..............16/1	15	2	0	1	1	0	4
Totals **38/1**	**20**	**3**	**0**	**1**	**1**	**0**	**4**
Playoffs **8/0**	**0**	**0**	**0**	**0**	**0**	**0**	**0**

Special Teams Tackles: 3 (1-2) in 1995; 1 (0-1) in 1995 Playoffs; 3 (3-0) in 1996; 1 (1-0) in 1996 Playoffs; 9 (7-2) in 1997; 3 (3-0) in 1997 Playoffs for total of 15 (11-4)

CRAIG NEWSOME ⟩ 21

Cornerback
College: *Arizona State*
NFL Exp.: *4th Season* **Packers Exp.:** *4th Season*
Ht.: *6-0* **Wt.:** *190* **Born:** *8/10/71* **Acq:** *D1-95*

PRO: One of the NFL's more physical cornerbacks, returns in 1998 from a major knee injury which limited his '97 season to a mere one play...Took part fully in all of the team's offseason minicamps...Highly skilled at bump-and-run coverage, is a focused and intense player who refuses to back off of anybody...Also provides top-notch run support...Was Green Bay's first-round draft choice in 1995, and when healthy has since met all of the expectations ingrained with that perch..."He's a tough guy who can go up and challenge guys. He gets in their face and stays with them," says Packers defensive coordinator Fritz Shurmur. "If you're going to beat Craig Newsome, it's a full-time job. He brings a special kind of temperament to our defense. He is the epitome of the hard-nosed, tough, competitive guy who plays hard and plays physical on every down. He is the kind of guy who leads by his example. He is the kind of guy who doesn't say much or talk about how to do it – he just does it, then everyone else does it because they see him do it."...Had the most passes defensed (42) by a Green Bay defensive back in his first two seasons since the advent of this statistic in 1981...Also made the most total tackles (156) of any Packers DB in his initial two NFL campaigns since safety Tom Flynn recorded 174 stops over the 1984-85 seasons...From all appearances, looks to be fully recovered from the serious knee injury which derailed his third pro season almost immediately..."I think what we have witnessed is absolutely no residual limitation as a result of his knee surgery," Shurmur adds. "He has done everything in the camps, has had a minimum of discomfort or flare-up in terms of the knee itself, so I fully expect that he will not be limited at all by anything."...A quiet and mature person, he became the Packers' starting left corner the day he arrived in Green Bay three summers ago, surrendering that post only through injury...Consistently displays excellent work habits on the field, a trait perhaps attributable to the two post-high school years he spent laboring in the hot California sun as a block mason..."Craig Newsome is a guy who never misses an opportunity to get better," Shurmur says. "Every play in practice, whether it's in pads, without pads or whatever, he is a 100-miles-an-hour guy. He's going full speed, he's trying to make plays, he is in a sense trying to get better every time he does something out there. And as a result he makes continual improvement."...Is a proven big-game performer, a quality he demonstrated during the playoffs of his first two seasons...Intercepted a pass in each of the Packers' three victories en route to their 1996 world championship, tying the NFL record and establishing a new club postseason mark for most consecutive games with one interception (3), a streak which remains current entering the '98 campaign...One year earlier as a rookie, had recovered and returned a San Francisco fumble for a touchdown to start Green Bay's scoring in its upset postseason triumph over the 49ers...Adding his pickoff in the '95 San Francisco playoff game, after only three seasons he already is tied with Pro Football Hall of Famer Herb Adderley and Eugene Robinson for the Packers' all-time postseason record with 4 career interceptions...Tested throughout his 1995, rookie season, he refused to back down and by year's end had merited selection to several all-rookie teams and established a club rookie record for passes defensed...**1997:** Tore the anterior cruciate ligament in his left knee on the first play from scrimmage of the regular season while reacting to an out-and-up move by Chicago's Ricky Proehl (Sept. 1)...Placed on season-ending injured reserve two days later...Underwent corrective surgery on Sept. 9...**1996:** Started every game (19 including playoffs) at left cornerback for the second successive season...Was a primary component in Green Bay's top-rated pass defense...As a testament to the consistency of his play, did not incur a pass interference or illegal contact penalty through the first 18 games (16 regular season, two playoffs) before he was flagged for interference in the first quarter of Super Bowl XXXI...Posted 71 tackles (61 solo) to rank sixth on the club...Also contributed 1 forced fumble and 2 interceptions, as well as a career-best and team-leading 23 passes defensed...Recorded season-high totals in tackles (8) and passes defensed (3) at Minnesota (Sept. 22)...Later made 8 stops in first meeting with Detroit (Nov. 3)...Also broke up 3 passes at Tampa Bay (Sept. 1), in rematch with the Vikings (Dec. 22) and in divisional playoff contest with San Francisco (Jan. 4)...Intercepted the Seahawks' Rick Mirer (Sept. 29) and Minnesota's Brad Johnson (Dec. 22) during the regular season...Forced a fumble by the Bucs' Alvin Harper which led to Green Bay's fourth touchdown in 34-3, opening day victory over Buccaneers...Continuing his fine play in the playoffs he totaled a team-high 7 passes defensed, among them interceptions of the 49ers' Elvis Grbac, the Panthers' Kerry Collins and the Patriots' Drew Bledsoe in consecutive games...Also drilled New England receiver Vincent Brisby in the final minutes of the Super Bowl, jarring the ball loose for teammate Brian Williams to intercept and giving Green Bay the ball back to down twice to run out the game clock...Made 13 postseason tackles to tie for fourth on the club...**1995:** Started all 19 games (16 regular season, three in the playoffs) at left cornerback as a rookie...Finished fourth on the team in tackles with a career-high 85 (72 solo)...Also had a club rookie record 19 passes defensed, including his first NFL interception Dec. 16 at New Orleans, when he picked off a Jim Everett throw in the end zone...Earned selection to all-rookie teams of *Football News* and *College & Pro Football Newsweekly*...Also was named to the All-Madden Team by Fox analyst John Madden...Chosen as Packers' 'Rookie of the Year'...Played especially well late in the season and into the playoffs...Made his first pro touchdown particularly memorable and meaningful, when he scooped up an Adam Walker fumble on the 49ers' first play from scrimmage of NFC divisional playoff contest and raced 31 yards into the end zone to give the Packers a 7-0 lead in eventual 27-17 upset win at San Francisco (Jan. 6)...Also had 4 solo tackles and 2 passes defensed, including a late interception of the Niners' Steve Young...One week earlier had posted 7 stops and broken up 2 Jeff George throws in first-round postseason victory over Atlanta (Dec. 31)...Ended playoffs with 14 total tackles (13 solo), 1 fumble recovery, 1 interception and 4 passes defensed...Recorded single-game career highs in tackles (13) and passes defensed (5) in 24-19 triumph over Pittsburgh in regular-season finale (Dec. 24)...Had 11 stops plus 2 pass breakups in win over Tampa Bay (Nov. 26)...Limited Herman Moore, the Lions' Pro Bowl wide receiver, to only 3 receptions — this despite 13 throws in his direction — in 30-21 victory over Detroit (Oct. 15)...Drafted in the first round (32nd overall and third cornerback) by Green Bay in 1995.

COLLEGE: Two-year starter (1993-94) at Arizona State after beginning his collegiate career at San Bernardino (Calif.) Valley Junior College...Recorded 99 tackles (71 solo), 4 interceptions, 14 passes defensed, 2 fumble recoveries and 1 forced fumble for ASU...Was a first-team All-Pacific 10 Conference selection in 1993, when he picked off 4 passes and broke up 12 to go along with 57 tackles (38 solo)...Also was a candidate for the Jim Thorpe Award, given annually to the nation's top defensive back...Missed first four games of his senior season while meeting academic requirements, returned to start Sun Devils' last seven contests at left cornerback...Posted a career-best 12 stops against Washington State...Earlier had been a two-year starter (1991-92) for San Bernardino Valley Junior College...Was a first-team All-Foothill Conference choice and was named as league's 'Most Valuable Defensive Back' in each of his two seasons...Also merited second-team All-America selection in 1992 from *JC Gridwire*...Set a national junior college record with a 103-yard interception return for a touchdown vs. Riverside City College in '92...Majored in criminal justice.

PERSONAL: Given name Craig Newsome...Nicknamed 'C-New'...Born in San Bernardino, Calif. ...Has a son, Garrett (born 11/22/90), and two daughters, Alexis (born 12/21/94) and Alena (born 10/24/97)...Was an all-conference selection in football at Eisenhower High School in Rialto, Calif. ...Lettered two seasons as a wide receiver and cornerback, he caught 45 passes for 758 yards and 12 touchdowns as a senior...Right out of high school worked for two years in construction in the Los Angeles

area as a block mason, building brick walls, before deciding to attend junior college...Has given time to 'Make A Wish' in Milwaukee...Hobbies include playing golf, fishing, playing video games and spending time with his family...Residence: Scottsdale, Ariz.

PRO STATISTICS:

Year	G/S	UT	AT	Sacks	Int.	Yds.	LG	FR	FF	PD
1995 Green Bay...............16/16		72	13	0	1	3	3	0	0	19
1996 Green Bay...............16/16		61	10	0	2	22	20	0	1	23
1997 Green Bay...................1/1		0	0	0	0	0	0	0	0	0
Totals.......................33/33		133	23	0	3	25	20	0	1	42
Playoffs 6/6		24	3	0	4	40	35	1	0	11

Touchdowns: 1, 31-yard fumble return at San Francisco (1/6/96-postseason)

DOUG PEDERSON) 18

Quarterback
College: Northeast Louisiana
NFL Exp.: 6th Season   **Packers Exp.:** 4th Season
Ht.: 6-3   **Wt.:** 216   **Born:** 1/31/68   **Acq:** FA-95

PRO: After serving as Green Bay's third quarterback for almost two-and-a-half seasons, is expected to be the Packers' No. 2 signal-caller in 1998...Has elevated his play and gained the confidence of the coaching staff with his solid performances in preseason and in practice...Originally signed by the Miami Dolphins in 1991 as an undrafted free agent...Spent one year (1992) on Miami's practice squad, then was a reserve for that club for parts of three seasons (1993-95)...Has received the majority of his personal playing time in the World League, he was with the N.Y./N.J. Knights in 1992 and the Rhein Fire in 1995...Highlight of pro career came in 1993 contest at Philadelphia, when he entered the game after starter Scott Mitchell went out with a shoulder injury and directed the Dolphins to a 19-14, come-from-behind victory – giving Don Shula his 325th career victory to make him the winningest coach in NFL history...Joined Green Bay as a free agent late in the 1995 season after injuries hit the quarterback position...Also previously had two separate stints in the World League...Green Bay offensive coordinator Sherm Lewis states that Pederson is ready to be the immediate backup to Brett Favre, saying, "Doug will be our No. 2 quarterback this year. His knowledge of the offense is outstanding. He demonstrated his ability to effectively get the team in the end zone during the 1997 preseason. Doug has a strong arm and outstanding mobility in the pocket. The coaching staff has great confidence in Doug's ability to effectively run the team."...**1997:** Served as the team's inactive 'Third Quarterback' for all 16 regular-season games as well as for all three playoff contests, including Super Bowl XXXII...Did see action late in fourth quarter of regular-season finale vs. Buffalo (Dec. 20), when he knelt down three straight times to end the game...Enjoyed an excellent preseason, completing 31 of 57 passes for 423 yards and 4 touchdowns with just 1 interception for a 94.4 passer rating...**1996:** Served as the Packers' inactive 'Third Quarterback' for 14 regular-season games as well as for all three playoff contests, including Super Bowl XXXI...Was the No. 2 QB on Dec. 1 vs. Chicago, though he did not play, and vs. Denver (Dec. 8) as usual backup Jim McMahon was sidelined by a rib injury...Saw late fourth-quarter action in blowout win over the Broncos, handing off three times...Had a strong training camp to turn away challenge from rookie Kyle Wachholtz...Completed 32 of 56 passes for 390 yards and 2 touchdowns with just 1 interception during preseason games, seeing added playing time with McMahon out due to arthroscopic knee surgery...**1995:** Had been selected by the Carolina Panthers on Feb. 15 in the Expansion Draft but the Panthers withdrew their qualifying offer on May 22, terminating their rights to him...Subsequently signed by the Dolphins as a free agent for the fifth straight season (July 11)...Waived by Miami in training camp (Aug. 21), later re-signed with the Dolphins on Oct. 10...Was inactive for two games before he was released on Oct. 24...Signed with Green

Bay as a free agent roughly a month later (Nov. 21)...Served as team's inactive 'Third Quarterback' for three of Green Bay's last five regular-season games plus all three playoff contests...Simply was inactive for two other regular-season games as Packers carried four quarterbacks on their roster...**WORLD LEAGUE:** Played in two games for the Rhein Fire in 1995, completing 11 of 26 passes for 186 yards and 1 touchdown with 2 interceptions...Got into the team's final two contests (vs. Barcelona and Amsterdam) in relief of Andy Kelly...**1994:** Was a member of the Dolphins throughout the season after re-signing with team on April 14...Inactive for all 16 regular-season games and both playoff contests...**1993:** Re-signed by the Dolphins as a free agent on March 1...Played in seven games as a reserve...Saw action at quarterback three times, including two occasions in an emergency role following injuries...Completed 4 of 8 passes for 41 yards over the course of the season...Initially waived on final cutdown (Aug. 30) and began year on Miami's practice squad...Moved up to 53-man roster on Oct. 23 and made NFL debut the following day against Indianapolis as holder for field goal and extra point attempts...Saw first pro action at quarterback Oct. 31 vs. Kansas City in relief of Mitchell late in the game, though he did not attempt a pass and lost one yard on his only carry...Also replaced Mitchell, who suffered a left (throwing) shoulder separation, in third quarter at Philadelphia (Nov. 14) and hit on 3 of 6 passes for 34 yards, leading drives for two field goals to bring the Dolphins back from a 14-13 deficit to a 19-14 win — providing Shula with his 325th career victory to make him the winningest coach in league annals...Replaced the injured Steve DeBerg (jaw/lip) briefly in third quarter against the N.Y. Giants (Dec. 5) and completed 1 of 2 passes for 7 yards...Waived by the Dolphins on Dec. 14...**1992:** Released by Miami on the final cutdown (Aug. 31), signed to the Dolphins' practice squad two days later...Spent five weeks on practice squad until his termination on Oct. 5...Earlier had re-signed with Dolphins as a free agent June 3...**WORLD LEAGUE:** Played with New York/New Jersey Knights in 1992 and finished season with 70 completions in 128 attempts for 1,077 yards and 8 touchdowns with 3 interceptions...Saw action mostly as a reserve...Led Knights to their first win of the season in his first start, when he completed 18 of 39 passes for 257 yards and 2 touchdowns against Frankfurt Galaxy...Enjoyed his best performance of the year in season finale at Montreal Machine as he threw for 309 yards and 2 touchdowns, completing 17 of 27 passes...**1991:** Signed by Miami as an undrafted free agent on April 30, but was waived in training camp (Aug. 16).

COLLEGE: Three-year starter and four-time letterman (1987-90) at Northeast Louisiana...Redshirted in 1986...Finished collegiate career with 571 completions on 1,032 attempts for 6,445 yards and 33 touchdowns with 41 interceptions...Led Southland Conference in passing as a senior, when he hit on 205 of 367 passes for 2,282 yards and 10 touchdowns with 14 interceptions...Threw for 2,603 yards and 16 TDs as a junior...Holds B.A. degree in business management.

PERSONAL: Given name Douglas Irvin Pederson...Born in Bellingham, Wash. ...Married to Jeannie, couple has two sons, Drew (born 2/2/95) and Josh (born 9/22/97)...An all-league selection as a quarterback, safety and kicker at Ferndale (Wash.) High School...Finished high school career with 106 completions in 250 attempts for 1,880 yards and 19 touchdowns...Earned three letters each in football, basketball and baseball...Hobbies include water sports and golf...Has worked with the Cerebral Palsy Telethon in Louisiana...Volunteered his time by speaking to elementary schools in Monroe, La., during this past offseason...Residence: Monroe, La.

PRO STATISTICS:

Year		G/S	Att.	Comp.	Yds.	Pct.	TD	Int.	LG	Rating
1992	Miami	practice squad								
1993	Miami	7/0	8	4	41	50.0	0	0	12	65.1
1994	Miami	0/0	0	0	0	0.0	0	0	0	0.0
1995	Miami	0/0	0	0	0	0.0	0	0	0	0.0
	Green Bay	0/0	0	0	0	0.0	0	0	0	0.0
1996	Green Bay	1/0	0	0	0	0.0	0	0	0	0.0
1997	Green Bay	1/0	0	0	0	0.0	0	0	0	0.0
Totals		9/0	8	4	41	50.0	0	0	12	65.1
Playoffs		0/0	0	0	0	0.0	0	0	0	0.0

Rushing: 2 for -1 yard, -0.5 avg., LG 0 in 1993; 3 for -4 yards, -1.3 avg., LG -1 in 1997 for total of 5 for -5 yards, -1.0 avg., LG 0

WORLD LEAGUE PASSING STATISTICS									
Year	G/S	Att.	Comp.	Yds.	Pct.	TD	Int.	LG	Rating
1992 N.Y./N.J. Knights 7/1		128	70	1,077	54.7	8	3	67t	93.8
1995 Rhein Fire 2/0		26	11	186	42.3	1	2	44	47.9
Totals 9/1		154	81	1,263	52.6	9	5	67t	86.0

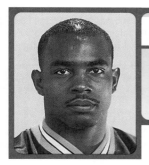

ROELL PRESTON   **49**

Wide Receiver/Kick Returner
College: Mississippi
NFL Exp.: 3rd Season   **Packers Exp.:** 1st Season
Ht.: 5-10 Wt.: 195   **Born: 6/23/72   Acq: FA-98**

PRO: Quick receiver who excels running after the catch...Provides extra value as a top-level return man...Returns in 1998 for a second stay with the Packers...Had made an immediate impression in a one-game stint with Green Bay in 1997, setting an all-time club record for kickoff return yards...Spent his initial two NFL seasons playing in the run-and-shoot offense with Atlanta (1995-96)..."Roell was very effective as a return man for us last year in the Indianapolis game," says Sherm Lewis, the Packers' offensive coordinator. "He will be given a good look as a wide receiver this year. He's been impressive in all of our preseason mini-camps."...Was re-signed by Green Bay on Feb. 27, 1998...Perfected a touchdown celebration in college where he dives into the end zone, an art he has continued (with more limited opportunity) in the pros; originally took the idea from his older brother, Tyrone, who, like him, played collegiately at Ole Miss...**1997:** Had a brief, though somewhat memorable, season as he played in just one game...After his preseason release by Atlanta, was signed by the Packers as a free agent on Nov. 12, only four days prior to their contest at Indianapolis, in an effort to spark the club's return game...Subsequently had 211 kickoff return yards (on 7 runbacks) vs. the Colts to set an all-time Green Bay single-game record, breaking the previous mark of 208, established by Harlan Huckleby in 1983...Also returned 1 punt for 0 yards...Released by the Packers Nov. 18, he signed with Washington as a free agent on Dec. 4...Inactive for one game with the Redskins before he was let go five days later...Earlier had been waived by the Falcons on the final cutdown (Aug. 24)...**1996:** Saw increased playing time at wide receiver in his second season with Atlanta...Caught 21 passes for 208 yards and 1 touchdown...Made two starts among 15 games played...Caught a team-high 6 passes (for 74 yards) at Detroit (Oct. 6) in his first-ever NFL start...Had a career-best 9 receptions (for 69 yards) vs. Houston (Oct. 13) the following week in second straight start...Earlier had made 6 receptions (for 65 yards), including a 17-yard TD grab, at San Francisco (Sept. 29)...Did not handle the Falcons' kickoff return duties extensively until the latter portion of the season, but still managed 32 returns for 681 yards...Had a season-high 176 kickoff return yards, including a career-best 50-yarder, at Cincinnati (Nov. 24)...**1995:** Amassed 756 all-purpose yards as a rookie after making the Falcons' roster largely on the strength of his return skills...Returned 30 kickoffs for 627 yards during his maiden season while playing in 14 games...Also caught 7 passes for 129 yards and 1 TD...Made dazzling, 61-yard catch-and-run for a touchdown at Arizona (Nov. 26), which saw him manage to stay on his feet despite being hit by three defenders at the Cardinals' 38-yard line...Had caught his first two passes in the NFL at Tampa Bay (Oct. 22)...Began his season with a bang by returning 4 kickoffs for 98 yards in opener vs. Carolina (Sept. 3), including a 44-yarder...Was inactive for the Falcons' playoff game at Green Bay (Dec. 31)...Drafted in the fifth round (145th overall) by Atlanta in 1995.

COLLEGE: Was a two-year starter (1993-94) for the University of Mississippi following two seasons at Northwest Mississippi Community College (1991-92)...Made 73 career receptions for 1,143 yards and 11 touchdowns for the Rebels, including 38 for 688 yards and 8 TDs as a senior...Saved the best game of his Ole Miss career for the last, when he totaled 150 yards on 7 catches, a 30-yard TD among them, in 1994 vs. Mississippi State...Named as the most outstanding player on the Gray squad in the annual Blue-Gray Game

after catching 4 passes for 122 yards, including a 40-yard score...Earlier had been a two-time all-state J.C. pick at Northwest Mississippi, helping the Rangers capture the national championship in 1992...Had 84 catches for 1,655 yards and 19 touchdowns as a junior college player, including 58 for 1,026 yards and 9 TDs in '92...Totaled 157 receptions for 2,798 yards and 30 touchdowns over his four seasons at the two schools...Majored in criminal justice.

PERSONAL: Given name Roell Preston...Nicknamed 'Goat'...Born in Miami...Single...Has a son, Cameron (born 7/25/96)...Was a first-team All-Dade County selection his senior year at Hialeah High School in Miami...Earned two letters in football as a quarterback, running back, wide receiver and free safety, he also lettered twice in track...Has three brothers who played college football: Rock, 1994-96 at Florida State, who is with the CFL's Calgary Stampeders; Tyrone Ashley, 1989-91 at Mississippi (who was in the Chicago Bears' 1992 training camp); and Clarence Ashley, at Fayetteville State...Hobbies include playing video games...Spent a portion of this past offseason playing on the Packers' basketball team...Residence: Miami.

PRO STATISTICS:

Year		G/S	No.	RECEIVING Yds.	Avg.	LG	TD	No.	KICKOFF RETURNS Yds.	Avg.	LG	TD
1995	Atlanta	14/0	7	129	18.4	61t	1	30	627	20.9	44	0
1996	Atlanta	15/2	21	208	9.9	17t	1	32	681	21.3	50	0
1997	Green Bay	1/0	0	0	0.0	0	0	7	211	30.1	43	0
	Washington	0/0	0	0	0.0	0	0	0	0	0.0	0	0
Totals		**30/2**	**28**	**337**	**12.0**	**61t**	**2**	**69**	**1,519**	**22.0**	**50**	**0**
Playoffs		**0/0**	**0**	**0**	**0.0**	**0**	**0**	**0**	**0**	**0.0**	**0**	**0**

Punt Returns: 1 for 0 yards in 1997

CAREER SINGLE-GAME HIGHS

Most Receptions: 9, vs. Houston (10/13/96); **Most Receiving Yards:** 79, at Arizona (11/26/95); **Longest Reception:** 61t, at Arizona (11/26/95); **Most TD Receptions:** 1, at Arizona (11/26/95) and at San Francisco (9/29/96); **Most Kickoff Returns:** 7, at Cincinnati (11/24/96) and at Indianapolis (11/16/97); **Most Kickoff Return Yards:** 211, at Indianapolis (11/16/97); **Longest Kickoff Return:** 50, at Cincinnati (11/24/96)

MIKE PRIOR · 39

Safety
College: *Illinois State*
NFL Exp.: *13th Season*　　**Packers Exp.:** *6th Season*
Ht.: *6-0*　**Wt.:** *208*　**Born:** *11/14/63*　**Acq:** *FA-98*

PRO: A consummate professional on and off the field, brings both experience and consistency to his role as a backup in the Packers' young defensive backfield...Represents the ideal makeup of a backup player...Has been a dependable and versatile player during his five years with the Packers following six seasons as a starter for the Indianapolis Colts...A big contributor in Green Bay's 'nickel' and 'dime' packages, he also excels on special teams coverage units and as an occasional punt returner...Able to play either safety position in the defensive backfield...Is one of the surest tacklers on the club...Has played in all 93 of the Packers' games (80 regular season, 13 in playoffs) since he joined Green Bay in 1993...Has now played in 16 regular-season games 10 times in his career, including each of the last six years...Is tied with six teammates for the Packers' postseason record for most career games played (13)...With 3 career playoff interceptions as a Packer, now is just one shy of the club's all-time postseason mark, shared by three players...According to Green Bay defensive coordinator Fritz Shurmur, Prior is a player all young athletes should emulate, saying, "Mike is a pro's pro. He is the guy that when you think of the way a professional athlete should conduct himself, how he should approach his job – his relationship with the rest of the team, with the coaching staff, with the media – and how he should conduct himself off the field, he is the prototype. He is the epitome of a professional. Mike is always ready to play. He has been a starter in our 'dime' defense as a safety, but has also been asked to play linebacker positions in the 'dime.' Mike also can play either strong or free safety in situations where someone has been injured, and has always played at a high level. He understands as much about our defense as any player we have and he can communicate that. He is very valuable to young players in that he helps direct them into the right way to not only play but also conduct themselves. I always look at Mike as a very stabilizing factor for our defense and our secondary."…Waived by the Packers this past Feb. 27, was re-signed by the club on April 24…Originally had been acquired by Green Bay as an unrestricted free agent in 1993 after six years with Indianapolis…Began his pro career as a seventh-round selection of the Tampa Bay Buccaneers in the 1985 draft…Spent his rookie season with the Bucs before signing on with the Colts as a free agent in 1987…Had 27 career interceptions for the Colts (tied for sixth in club history) and has had three seasons of 6 thefts…Also known for his top-notch tackling ability, he has 688 career tackles along with 34 INTs, 93 passes defended, 9 fumble recoveries, 7 forced fumbles and 3½ sacks…Is tied for 14th among active NFL players with his 34 career interceptions…Appeared in 86 games with the Colts from 1987-92, starting 78…**1997:** Played in all 16 regular-season games for the sixth straight year (the last five with the Packers) and the 10th time in his career…Also saw action in all three postseason games, including Super Bowl XXXII…Served as the backup to LeRoy Butler at strong safety, in addition to being a regular contributor in the 'nickel' and 'dime' packages as well as on special teams…Finished the regular season with 22 tackles, tops among reserves in the secondary…Also was second on the team with 4 interceptions – the most he has had since 1992, when he had 6 with Indianapolis – and third with 11 passes defended…Finished second on the club with 14 special teams tackles…Intercepted the Bucs' Trent Dilfer late in divisional playoff victory over Tampa Bay (Jan. 4), he also totaled 2 tackles during the postseason…One of the club's six playoff captains, he added 2 special teams stops during the postseason…Had an interception in two of the Packers' final three regular-season games…Picked off an Alex Van Pelt pass in finale vs. Buffalo (Dec. 20) and returned it 49 yards in the Packers' 31-21 win…Two weeks earlier, had made a key interception in the Packers' 17-6, division-clinching win at Tampa Bay (Dec. 7) when he picked off a Steve Walsh pass at the GB 15-yard line with 3:49 left in the game…Had a season-high 3 special teams tackles in the Packers' 45-17 win over Dallas (Nov. 23)…Intercepted a Mark Rypien pass with 3:00 left in the game vs. St. Louis (Nov. 9); Green Bay subsequently ran out the clock for a 17-7 win…Picked off a Dan Marino pass just before halftime in the Packers' 23-18 win over Miami (Sept. 14)…Made a season-high 4 tackles on defense at Detroit (Sept. 28)…Had 2 stops on kick coverage vs. Chicago (Sept. 1), in Lions rematch (Nov. 2) and at Minnesota (Dec. 1)…Also served as one of the Packers' punt returners in "pooch" punt situations…**1996:** Played in all 16 regular-season games…Also got into each of the club's three playoff games, including Super Bowl XXXI…Regularly saw action in the team's 'nickel' and 'dime' substitution packages…Had 34 total tackles to rank first among backup players, in addition to 1 interception, 1 forced fumble and 6 passes defended…Tied for sixth on the club with 9 special teams tackles, including a season-high 3 at St. Louis (Nov. 24)…Also came up with another big play in the Rams contest when, after St. Louis had recorded a safety, he recovered Craig Hentrich's ensuing free kick, giving Green Bay the ball at the Rams' 37-yard line – a possession which subsequently led to a field goal as the first half expired…Named as one of club's six captains for the playoffs (representing special teams)…Added 8 tackles defensively and 5 special teams stops (third on the club) during the postseason…Also intercepted a Drew Bledsoe pass in the Super Bowl, a turnover which led to Green Bay's third touchdown, giving the Packers a 27-14 halftime lead in the eventual 35-21 triumph…Made 3 tackles on coverage, including a forced fumble, and had 6 stops on defense in divisional playoff victory over San Francisco (Jan. 4)…Made a season-best 7 tackles in 39-13 win over Philadelphia (Sept. 9)…Intercepted a pass and had a season-best 2 passes defended in 34-3, opening day win over Tampa Bay (Sept. 1)…Filled in for the injured Eugene Robinson (ankle) at free safety during the second half of 28-18 win over Detroit (Nov. 3) and contributed 2 tackles plus a pass defensed…Forced a fumble among 2 tackles vs. Chicago (Dec. 1)…**1995:** Played in all 16 games as a key backup at both free and strong safety, in addition to duty as team's regular 'dime' and sometime 'nickel' back, though he did make two starts…Finished the regular season with 62 tackles – eighth on the team, tops among the club's reserves and his personal high in three seasons with Green Bay – plus 1½ sacks, 1 interception, 1 forced fumble and 4 passes defended…Also was a valuable special teams performer, tying for fifth place with 13 tackles…Started at free safety in place of the injured George Teague (toe) at Tampa Bay (Dec. 10), he responded with a team-leading and season-high 9 tackles…Sacked quarterback Jeff Blake (his first full sack of the season), causing a fumble in the process, Dec. 3 vs. Cincinnati, which helped to stop a fourth-quarter Bengals drive in the eventual 24-10 victory…Combined with teammate Sean Jones to sack Dilfer in win over Tampa Bay (Nov. 26) while also recording 5 tackles...Started his first game of the season Oct. 15 vs. Detroit as Green Bay opened in its 'nickel' package and tied his season high with 9 tackles...Sealed win over the N.Y. Giants (Sept. 17), when he intercepted a Dave Brown pass at the Green Bay 22-yard line with 15 seconds left in the game and the Packers clinging to a 14-6 lead...Made a season-high 4 special teams tackles, had 2 tackles on defense and returned a punt 10 yards in win vs. Minnesota (Oct. 22)...Played in all three playoff games, starting against multiple-receiver offense of Atlanta (Dec. 31)...Led reserves with 11 total tackles in the postseason...Stopped a potential scoring drive when he intercepted a Steve Young pass near the goal-line in the Packers' playoff win at San Francisco (Jan. 6)...**1994:** Played in all 16 games, also seeing action in both of the Packers' playoff games...Led club in special teams tackles with 17, the most he had contributed since making 21 in 1987 with the Colts...Backed up Teague at free safety, also filling role as backup strong safety for three straight games while Tim Hauck was out with a knee injury...Enhanced his value to the special teams by at times serving as a second punt return man...Contributed 17 total stops plus a pass breakup with the defense...Had perhaps his best game of the season Dec. 11 vs. Chicago, making a season-best 4 tackles, knocking down 1 pass and recording a stop on special teams...Also registered 4 tackles Nov. 24 at Dallas in extensive playing time in the defensive backfield...Made a crucial downfield block on Robert Brooks' momentum-turning, 85-yard punt return for a touchdown in 24-17 victory over L.A. Rams (Oct. 9)...Had five games where he recorded 2 special teams tackles...**1993:** Saw action in all 16 games in his first Green Bay season, starting four at free safety before giving way to one of the team's first-round draft choices, Teague...Finished the year with 36 total tackles (32 solo), tying for 12th on the club...Had 5 tackles and helped teammate Bryce Paup nail L.A. Rams RB Cleveland Gary in the end zone for a safety in the Packers' 36-6 win (Sept. 5)...Made a season-high 10 solo tackles at Minnesota (Sept. 26)...Played a prominent role on special teams as he led Green Bay in punt returns, averaging 11.4 yards on 17 returns...Also finished fourth on the club with 12 special teams tackles...Played a major part in the Packers' win at San Diego (Dec. 12) as he stepped in for the injured Brooks at punt returner and had 4 returns for 39 yards, also intercepting a Stan Humphries pass with four seconds left in the game to seal Green Bay's 20-13 win over the Chargers...Had perhaps his best game of the season vs. the Vikings (Dec. 19), returning 4 punts for 50 yards, including a 21-yarder, and making 3 special teams tackles...Returned 5 punts for 56 yards and had 2 special teams tackles against the L.A. Raiders (Dec. 26)...Got into both playoff games in backup role...Signed with the Packers as an unrestricted free agent on April 16...**1992:** Started all 16 games for the Colts...Finished second on the team with 91 tackles (74 solo), 1 forced fumble and 1 fumble recovery...Led the squad with 6 interceptions, while his 12 passes defensed was third-best...Best game of season came vs. Phoenix (Dec. 20) with 7 tackles, 3 passes defensed and a club single-game record-tying 3 interceptions...Had a season-high 12 tackles (11 solo) vs. Houston on Sept. 13...Also hit double figures in tackles at Buffalo (Sept. 20), when he recorded 10 (9 solo)...Made an interception and recovered a fumble at Miami (Oct. 25)...Had an interception and forced fumble at N.Y. Jets (Dec. 13)...Caught a 17-yard pass from punter Rohn Stark vs. Dolphins (Nov. 8)...**1991:** Saw action in nine games, starting seven at free safety...Finished the season with 45 tackles (36 solo), 3 interceptions, 4 passes defensed and 1 fumble recovery...Had started 52 consecutive games before an abdominal injury forced him into backup duty vs. New England (Sept. 1)...Started games 2-6 before being placed on injured reserve (Oct. 11) with the abdominal problem...Was activated on Dec. 6 and started the final two games...Made 10 tackles vs. Buffalo (Dec. 15)...Had interceptions at Miami (Sept. 8), at Seattle (Sept. 29) and at Tampa Bay (Dec. 22)...**1990:** Started all 16 games for the third consecutive season...Had a career-high 113 tackles (81 solo), 3 interceptions, 15 passes defensed, 2 fumble recoveries and 1 forced fumble...Had five double-digit tackle games and at least 8 tackles in eight contests...Also had 6 special teams tackles...Caught a 40-yard pass from Stark at N.Y. Jets (Dec. 16)...**1989:** Posted fine numbers with 98 tackles (74 solo), 6 interceptions, 9 passes defensed, 1 quarterback pressure, 1 forced fumble and 1 fumble recovery...Won AFC 'Defensive Player of the Week' honors vs. Cleveland (Dec. 10) with 9 tackles, 1 forced fumble, 1 fumble recovery and a 58-yard interception return for a touchdown in overtime, giving Colts 23-17 triumph...Picked off 2 passes vs. New England (Oct. 29)...**1988:** Started all 16 games (15 at FS, one at SS)...Made 98 tackles (69 solo), 1 sack, 3 quarterback pressures, 3 interceptions, 18 passes defensed, 1 forced fumble and 1 fumble recovery...Had double-digit tackles in four contests...**1987:** Signed with the Colts as a free agent on Feb. 27, but was waived Aug. 31...Subsequently re-signed with Indianapolis on Sept. 24...Played in 13 games with seven starts, including divisional playoff game at Cleveland (Jan. 9)...Tied for AFC lead with 6 interceptions and tied for NFL lead with 9 takeaways...Totaled 68 tackles (44 solo), 1 sack, 9 passes defensed and 3 fumble recoveries...Had three double-digit tackle games...Also led Colts with 21 special teams tackles...**1986:** Waived by Tampa Bay in training camp (Aug. 25), he spent the remainder of the year out of football...**1985:** Saw limited duty defensively for the Buccaneers as a rookie...Had 4 stops in the defensive backfield...Did excel on special teams with 22 tackles...Also returned 13 punts for an 8.1-yard average and 10 kickoffs for a 13.1-yard average...Drafted in the seventh round (176th overall) by Tampa Bay in 1985.

COLLEGE: A four-year starter (1981-84) at Illinois State...Was a three-time Division I-AA All-American at safety...Earned All-America second-team and All-Missouri Valley Conference first-team honors in 1982 and '83...Ranked as all-time MVC interception leader with 24...Made 344 career tackles, including a school-record 133 his sophomore year...Had 8 interceptions and 67 tackles as a senior...Led MVC in punt returns as a junior and senior (had 3 career returns for TDs)...Had his college jersey number (15) retired in October of 1995...Also was a three-time letter winner (1983-85) in baseball for the Redbirds...Ended baseball career as school's all-time batting average leader (.388)...Had 32 career home runs, 137 RBI and 55 stolen bases...Set a school record with 19 HR as a senior...A 17th-round pick by the Baltimore Orioles in the 1984 baseball draft...Also was drafted by the Los Angeles Dodgers (fourth round) in 1985 and by the Houston Astros in 1986...Played centerfield and was an emergency relief pitcher...Earned a B.S. degree in business administration.

PERSONAL: Given name Michael Robert Prior...Born in Chicago Heights, Ill. ...Married to Diane, couple has three daughters – Nicole (born 5/30/86), Briana (born 1/12/89) and Paige (born 12/1/90)...Won four letters each in football, wrestling and baseball at Marian High School in Chicago Heights, Ill. ...Played wide receiver and defensive back...Hobbies include softball, tennis and golf...Has worked with cystic fibrosis in Indianapolis...Received an 'Outstanding Young Alumni' award from Illinois State in 1997...Residence: Indianapolis.

PRO STATISTICS:

Year		G/S	UT	AT	Sacks	Int.	Yds.	LG	TD	FR	FF	PD
1985	Tampa Bay	16/0	4	0	0	0	0	0	0	0	0	0
1986		out of football										
1987	Indianapolis	13/7	44	24	1	6	57	38	0	3	1	9
1988	Indianapolis	16/16	69	29	1	3	46	23	0	1	1	18
1989	Indianapolis	16/16	74	24	0	6	88	58t	1	1	1	9
1990	Indianapolis	16/16	81	32	0	3	66	36	0	2	1	15
1991	Indianapolis	9/7	36	9	0	3	50	37	0	1	0	4
1992	Indianapolis	16/16	74	17	0	6	44	19	0	1	1	12
1993	Green Bay	16/4	32	4	0	1	1	1	0	0	0	4
1994	Green Bay	16/0	14	3	0	0	0	0	0	0	0	1
1995	Green Bay	16/2	49	13	1½	1	9	9	0	0	1	4
1996	Green Bay	16/0	22	12	0	1	7	7	0	0	1	6
1997	Green Bay	16/0	17	5	0	4	72	49	0	0	0	11
Totals		**182/84**	**516**	**172**	**3½**	**34**	**440**	**58t**	**1**	**9**	**7**	**93**
Playoffs		**14/2**	**21**	**11**	**0**	**3**	**25**	**13**	**0**	**0**	**0**	**4**

Year				PUNT RETURNS					KICKOFF RETURNS			
		No.	FC	Yds.	Avg.	LG	TD	No.	Yds.	Avg.	LG	TD
1985	Tampa Bay	13	6	105	8.1	19	0	10	131	13.1	29	0
1986		out of football										
1987	Indianapolis	0	0	0	0.0	0	0	3	47	15.7	22	0
1988	Indianapolis	1	5	0	0.0	0	0	0	0	0.0	0	0
1989	Indianapolis	0	3	0	0.0	0	0	0	0	0.0	0	0
1990	Indianapolis	2	6	0	0.0	0	0	0	0	0.0	0	0
1991	Indianapolis	0	2	0	0.0	0	0	0	0	0.0	0	0
1992	Indianapolis	1	12	7	7.0	7	0	0	0	0.0	0	0
1993	Green Bay	17	3	194	11.4	24	0	0	0	0.0	0	0
1994	Green Bay	8	4	62	7.8	16	0	0	0	0.0	0	0
1995	Green Bay	1	2	10	10.0	10	0	0	0	0.0	0	0
1996	Green Bay	0	1	0	0.0	0	0	0	0	0.0	0	0
1997	Green Bay	1	3	0	0.0	0	0	0	0	0.0	0	0
Totals		**44**	**47**	**378**	**8.6**	**24**	**0**	**13**	**178**	**13.7**	**29**	**0**
Playoffs		**0**	**3**	**0**	**0.0**	**0**	**0**	**0**	**0**	**0.0**	**0**	**0**

statistics continued on next page

Receptions: 1 for 40 yards in 1990; 1 for 17 yards in 1992 for total of 2 for 57 yards, 28.5 avg., LG 40
Special Teams Tackles: 22 in 1985; 21 (12-9) in 1987; 2 (2-0) in 1988; 6 (3-3) in 1990; 2 (1-1) in 1991; 2 (2-0) in 1992; 12 (8-4) in 1993; 17 (14-3) in 1994; 1 (1-0) in 1994 Playoffs; 13 (10-3) in 1995; 9 (7-2) in 1996; 5 (4-1) in 1996 Playoffs; 14 (9-5) in 1997; 2 (1-1) in 1997 Playoffs for total of 120
Special Teams Forced Fumbles: 1 in 1996 Playoffs

MARCO RIVERA   62

Offensive Guard
College: Penn State
NFL Exp.: 3rd Season   *Packers Exp.:* 3rd Season
Ht.: 6-4   *Wt.:* 305   *Born:* 4/26/72   *Acq:* D6-96

PRO: Strong, aggressive, up-and-coming third-year player with the opportunity to become the Packers' starting left guard in 1998...With the free agency departure of three-year starter Aaron Taylor, has the inside track on securing the only open slot in the Green Bay offensive line...Will compete with second-year player Joe Andruzzi for the starting spot...Packers offensive line coach Tom Lovat fully expects Rivera to make a solid run at the position, saying, "If Marco goes out and just performs like he should, he'll probably have the job. We've seen what he's done and the improvement he's made since he's been here. He did play in the World League (in 1997), and played well, then came back last year and showed improvement. So we know what he's capable of doing."...A former sixth-round pick who made the team as a long-shot rookie in 1996, he has used his two-year backup experience as well as a season with the World League's Scottish Claymores to put himself in position to reach the next level in the pros – that of a starter...Spent much of this past offseason in Green Bay, working out diligently in preparation for his chance to win a spot in the lineup..."I think he can play in this league," Lovat continues. "It's just a matter of him getting reps. He's probably one of the stronger guys we have. Plus he's got a great work habit – he's done really well this offseason and he's getting better. He's smart and knows the offense – no problem there. He just has to play."...**1997:** Played in 14 regular-season games, primarily on special teams...Participated on the field goal and extra point units as well as the kickoff return group...Was inactive for the Packers' first two games before seeing action in the club's final 14 games as well as all three playoff contests, including Super Bowl XXXII...Saw first action with the offensive line as he stepped in at left guard in the fourth quarter of a 31-10 win at Carolina (Dec. 14)...Served as the primary backup at center behind Jeff Dellenbach for three early-season games (Sept. 14 vs. Miami, Sept. 21 vs. Minnesota and Sept. 28 at Detroit) while regular starter Frank Winters was sidelined with a foot injury...**WORLD LEAGUE:** Played for the Scottish Claymores of the World League (now NFL Europe) during the 1996 offseason, starting all 10 games and helping his team finish third (out of six clubs) in the league in total offense...Named honorable mention All-World League by *Pro Football Weekly*...**1996:** Was one of the preseason's surprise success stories, playing well in camp and earning a spot on team's final roster...Inactive for all 16 regular-season games and three playoff contests...Drafted in the sixth round (208th overall) by Green Bay in 1996.

COLLEGE: A three-year starter and four-time letter winner (1992-95) for Penn State...Played in 41 career games for the Nittany Lions, making 31 starts...Experience also included appearances in three bowl games – the Outback, Rose and Blockbuster...Initially played guard, but moved to tackle as a sophomore before switching back to guard in 1994...Earned second-team All-Big Ten honors as a junior and senior...Starter on 1994 squad which led the nation in scoring (47.8 points per game) and total offense (520.2 yards per game), in addition to breaking 19 individual and 14 team records, on the way to Big Ten and Rose Bowl championships...Started first nine games in 1993 before a shoulder injury ended his season...Redshirted in 1991...Earned a B.S. degree in administration of justice.

PERSONAL: Given name Marco Anthony Rivera...Born in Brooklyn, N.Y. ...Single...An All-New York and all-county selection in football at Elmont Memorial High School in Long Island, N.Y. ...Also garnered All-America honorable mention from *USA Today* and *SuperPrep*...A four-year letterman, he played guard, defensive end and linebacker...Had 16 sacks among nearly 300 career tackles and also registered 6 interceptions...Member of football team that captured three conference titles...Also earned all-conference honors in basketball (three letters) and lacrosse (four letters)...Experienced some of his heritage this past June when he traveled to Puerto Rico (his mother is a native Puerto Rican and his grandmother still lives there) and visited cancer patients at St. Holland's Hospital in San Juan...Also ran a youth football clinic for approximately 200 participants (10 to 16-year olds) while in Puerto Rico...Has given time to Big Brothers/Big Sisters in the Green Bay area...Served as a television commercial spokesman for a Chevy truck importer in Glasgow, Scotland, during his time as a player in the World League...While at Penn State, worked with 'Second Mile,' an organization which helps needy kids...Father, Bill, has been a butcher for 35 years in Brooklyn, N.Y., operating two family-owned meat markets, 'Two Brothers Meat Market' (which he himself owns) and 'Sunrise Meat Market'...With a family history in cuisine, Marco specializes in preparing 'Spaghetti Rivera,' his own pasta creation based on a long-time family recipe...Hobbies include playing golf, hunting and fishing...Residence: Green Bay.

PRO STATISTICS:

Games/Starts—Green Bay 1996 (0/0); 1996 Playoffs (0/0); 1997 (14/0); 1997 Playoffs (3/0). Career totals: 14/0. Playoff totals: 3/0.

BILL SCHROEDER   84

Wide Receiver
College: *Wisconsin-La Crosse*
NFL Exp.: *3rd Season*   **Packers Exp.:** *2nd Season*
Ht.: *6-3* **Wt.:** *200* **Born:** *1/9/71* **Acq:** *FA-97 (D6c-94)*

PRO: A highly-regarded physical talent and successful special teams player, looks to further develop his every-down skills and become a regular offensive contributor in 1998...Made impact in his first full NFL season last year on Packers' special teams, ranking in the NFC's top ten in both punt and kickoff returns...A small college success story, had achieved last year's breakthrough after persevering through his first three NFL seasons, spending years one and three on Green Bay's practice squad and year two on New England's injured reserve list...Enjoyed a standout, 1997 season in the World League leading into the '97 NFL campaign...Packers offensive coordinator Sherm Lewis is impressed with what Schroeder brings to the table, saying, "He's one of the fastest players on the team with excellent hands. Bill's a great down-the-field threat and uses his speed well after making short or intermediate catches."...With three years of experience overall in Green Bay's system, knowledge should bode well as he enters training camp in 1998..."We expect Bill to challenge for the number three or four receiver spot," Lewis adds. "And he's done well on special teams, so he'll continue to perform on most of those squads."...Re-signed with the Packers this past April 22 as an exclusive rights free agent...Originally a sixth-round selection of Green Bay in 1994, he spent his rookie season on the Packers' practice squad before making a two-week playoff appearance on the active roster...Was traded to New England during the ensuing, 1995 training camp; he suffered a broken bone in his foot in a preseason game and spent the year on injured reserve...Waived during the following, 1996 preseason, he subsequently was signed to the Packers' practice squad where he spent the remainder of the year...**1997:** In his first regular-season NFL action, played in 15 games for the Packers, making one start when Green Bay opened a game with four wide receivers...Was inactive for one regular-season contest and for all three playoff games, including Super Bowl XXXII...Served as Packers' main punt returner for first 10 contests of season and also saw time as a deep man on kickoffs...Finished eighth among NFC punt returners with a 10.4-yard average on 33 runbacks...Ranked ninth in the conference on kickoff returns with a 23.4-yard average on 24 returns...Served as team's fourth receiver several times during the season, finishing with 2 receptions for 15 yards and 1 touchdown...Also contributed with 5 tackles (4 solo) on special teams…Earned NFC 'Special Teams Player of the Week' honors for excellent return performance in season opener vs. Chicago (Sept. 1), which included a career-high 107 yards on 5 punt returns (a 21.4-yard average) and another 53 yards on 2 kickoff returns…Bears contests also marked his first NFL start, as he was on the field when the Packers opened in a four receiver set…First punt return vs. Chicago (and first of NFL career) went for a career-long 46 yards…Established a career long with a 40-yard kickoff return a week later at Philadelphia (Sept. 7), later equaling it in regular-season finale vs. Buffalo (Dec. 20)…Posted another fine day on punt returns in initial win over Minnesota (Sept. 21), gaining 65 yards on 3 returns for a career-high 21.7-yard average…Entered contest at Detroit (Sept. 28) as the backup punt and kickoff return specialist, but was forced into primary duty at both spots when injuries felled both Derrick Mayes (ankle) and Don Beebe (concussion)…Later in same contest, scored first NFL touchdown on a diving end zone reception of a pass that deflected off of teammate Antonio Freeman's helmet…Had a career-high 6 punt returns vs. St. Louis (Nov. 9)…Established single-game career highs in both kickoff returns (4) and kickoff return yards (84) vs. Dallas on Nov. 23…Inactive at Tampa Bay (Dec. 7)…Had re-signed with the Packers on Feb. 7, 1997…**WORLD LEAGUE:** Allocated to the Rhein Fire of the World League in 1997…Finished second in the league in receiving yards (702) and tied for second in receptions (43)…Also caught 6 touchdown passes (tied for second in scoring among receivers and tied for fourth overall)…Finished fourth in the World League with 720 total yards from scrimmage (702 receiving, 18 rushing)…Named to All-World League team at wide receiver, as selected by members of the league's media…Made 2 receptions for 36 yards in World Bowl '97 loss to Barcelona…Had three 100-yard receiving days – 131 yards on 6 receptions at Frankfurt (May 17), 131 yards on 5 receptions at Barcelona (May 31) and 102 yards on 4 receptions at Amsterdam (May 3)…**1996:** Waived by New England on Aug. 14, subsequently was signed to the Packers' practice squad on Aug. 28, where he spent the entire Super Bowl season…**1995:** Traded to New England, along with tight end Jeff Wilner in exchange for center Mike Arthur, during training camp (Aug. 12), he suffered a broken bone in his foot in the Patriots' preseason finale at Oakland (Aug. 25) and spent the entire season on injured reserve…**1994:** Spent most of the season on the Packers' practice squad before being activated on Dec. 29, following season-ending injury to Sterling Sharpe…Played on special teams in both playoff contests – vs. Detroit (Dec. 31) and at Dallas (Jan. 8)…Earlier had been released on the final cutdown of training camp (Aug. 28), subsequently was signed to the practice squad two days later…Was the third of four sixth-round draft choices (181st overall) by Green Bay in 1994.

COLLEGE: Played one season (1993) of college football for Wisconsin-La Crosse, snaring 30 passes for 752 yards (25.1 avg.) and 8 touchdowns as Eagles won the Wisconsin State University Conference Championship…Also a return man, he averaged 12.1 yards on 27 punt returns and 24.8 yards on 22 kickoff returns…Enjoyed an excellent track career at UW-La Crosse as he garnered NCAA Division III All-America honors 17 times…Captured Division III titles in the triple jump in 1992 and the long jump in 1993…Was a conference champion 16 times at La Crosse, he left campus holding eight school track records…Holds B.S. degree in physical education/teaching.

PERSONAL: Given name William Fredrich Schroeder…Nicknamed 'Schrades'…Born in Eau Claire, Wis. …Married the former Shelly Rud this past April 18…Won four letters in track, two in football and two in basketball at Sheboygan (Wis.) South High School…Played quarterback, defensive back and returned punts and kickoffs…Father, brother and uncle all played college football…Culminated college education in April of 1996 when he received his B.S. degree in physical education/teaching…During offseason, plays for 'Titans of the Tundra,' the Packers' charity basketball team…Also enjoys many other offseason charitable outings, including playing in celebrity golf tournaments and speaking to groups at childrens' hospitals and elementary schools…Took part in a youth football camp with 200 kids this past June in Palmer, Alaska…Is a part-time wildlife art dealer…Hobbies include playing golf, hunting, fishing and "all other sports"…Residence: De Pere, Wis.

PRO STATISTICS:

			RECEIVING					RUSHING			
Year	G/S	No.	Yds.	Avg.	LG	TD	No.	Yds.	Avg.	LG	TD
1994 Green Bay ....practice squad											
1995 New England ......injured reserve											
1996 Green Bay ....practice squad											
1997 Green Bay..........15/1	2	15	7.5	8	1		0	0	0.0	0	0
Totals 15/1	**2**	**15**	**7.5**	**8**	**1**		**0**	**0**	**0.0**	**0**	**0**
Playoffs.................2/0	**0**	**0**	**0.0**	**0**	**0**		**0**	**0**	**0.0**	**0**	**0**

Year		No.	FC	PUNT RETURNS Yds.	Avg.	LG	TD	No.	KICKOFF RETURNS Yds.	Avg.	LG	TD
1994	Green Bay ....practice squad											
1995	New England ....injured reserve											
1996	Green Bay ....practice squad											
1997	Green Bay 33	33	8	342	10.4	46	0	24	562	23.4	40	0
Totals	33	33	8	342	10.4	46	0	24	562	23.4	40	0
Playoffs	0	0	0	0	0.0	0	0	0	0	0.0	0	0

Special Teams Tackles: 5 (4-1) in 1997

			WORLD LEAGUE STATISTICS RECEIVING						RUSHING			
Year		G/S	No.	Yds.	Avg.	LG	TD	No.	Yds.	Avg.	LG	TD
1997	Rhein Fire 10/10	10/10	43	702	16.3	73t	6	2	18	9.0	21	0
World Bowl	..............1/1	1/1	2	36	18.0	30	0	0	0	0.0	0	0

Kickoff Returns: 1 for 20 yards in 1997; 1 for 12 yards in World Bowl '97
Miscellaneous Tackles: 1 in 1997

CAREER SINGLE-GAME HIGHS

Most Receptions: 1, vs. Miami (9/14/97) and at Detroit (9/28/97); **Most Receiving Yards:** 8, vs. Miami (9/14/97); **Longest Reception:** 8, vs. Miami (9/14/97); **Most TD Receptions:** 1, at Detroit (9/28/97); **Most Punt Returns:** 6, vs. St. Louis (11/9/97); **Most Fair Catches:** 3, vs. Detroit (11/2/97); **Most Punt Return Yards:** 107, vs. Chicago (9/1/97); **Longest Punt Return:** 46, vs. Chicago (9/1/97); **Most Kickoff Returns:** 4, vs. Dallas (11/23/97); **Most Kickoff Return Yards:** 84, vs. Dallas (11/23/97); **Longest Kickoff Return:** 40, at Philadelphia (9/7/97) and vs. Buffalo (12/20/97)

DARREN SHARPER   42

Safety
College: *William & Mary*
NFL Exp.: *2nd Season*   **Packers Exp.:** *2nd Season*
Ht.: *6-2* **Wt.:** *210*   **Born:** *11/3/75*   **Acq:** *D2-97*

PRO: A superb athlete with great range, looks to add to his "big-play" resume as he vies for the starting free safety spot in 1998...Moves back to his collegiate position of free safety after spending the majority of his rookie year as the team's fourth corner in its 'dime' package...An outstanding play-maker in college, he continued his knack for the exceptional with three defensive touchdowns in 1997, breaking a club rookie record and tying a team record in the process...Will be relied upon to take his high level of play to an every-down basis this year, a step Packers defensive coordinator Fritz Shurmur is confident he can make..."As a rookie, Darren made a really significant impact on our defense," Shurmur says. "He became a starter as a corner in our 'dime' defense at the mid-year point and had three huge plays – three touchdowns. This year we are counting on him to take over as the starting free safety. He needs a lot of work and development in the area of making calls and adjustments and those kinds of things, but they come with experience. He's a very bright, gifted athlete and we expect him to do well."...Has immersed himself in offseason studies along with extra work at mini-camps in preparation for

157

his new role with the team…"I think there's no question that there has been a realization over the offseason," Shurmur continued, "of just what it takes and what kind of effort it will take on his part – what kind of input he'll have to have – to be able to play at a high level in our secondary as a starter."…**1997:** A regular, year-long contributor on special teams, saw increased playing time in the Packers' 'dime' package as the season progressed…Played in 14 regular-season games, he was inactive for the club's other two contests…Also appeared in all three postseason games, including Super Bowl XXXII…Finished with 13 tackles (10 solo), 2 interceptions, 1 fumble recovery, 2 forced fumbles and 2 passes defensed…Also had 7 tackles on special teams…Scored three touchdowns – two interception returns and one fumble return – to tie Hall of Famer Herb Adderley's three interception return effort in 1965 for the team record for most defensive touchdowns in a season…Three touchdown success also broke the club's rookie record of 2, previously held by Charles 'Buckets' Goldenberg in 1933…His 18 points also were good for sixth place on the club scoring list…Assumed punt return duties in the final two regular-season games, finishing with a 4.6-yard average on 7 runbacks, his production included a 23-yard return vs. Buffalo (Dec. 20)…Became a regular in Green Bay's 'dime' package Nov. 2 vs. Detroit and marked the occasion by intercepting a Scott Mitchell pass – while covering Lions Pro Bowl receiver Herman Moore – and returning it 50 yards down the sideline for a touchdown, giving Green Bay a 14-7, second-quarter lead in the eventual 20-10 victory…Theft was both his first NFL interception and first pro touchdown…Notched his second score of the season in contest against Dallas (Nov. 23), when he forced a fumble by Cowboys running back Sherman Williams, then returned it 34 yards for Green Bay's final touchdown in a 45-17 triumph…His third and final TD of the season came vs. Buffalo (Dec. 20), as he stepped in front of an Alex Van Pelt pass and returned it 20 yards for a touchdown and 31-14 lead in ensuing 31-21 win…Also recovered an onside kick attempt by the Bills, in addition to registering a forced fumble on a spectacular hit of Bills tight end Lonnie Johnson, who had just hauled in a pass reception on a fake punt play…Made a season-high 3 tackles vs. St. Louis (Nov. 9)…Had seen his first extended play in the 'dime' package on Sept. 28 at Detroit when Doug Evans was inactive due to a hamstring injury…Played late in game vs. Minnesota (Sept. 21) and helped Packers thwart a late Vikings drive in 38-32 win…Inactive vs. Tampa Bay (Oct. 5) and at Chicago (Oct. 12)…In postseason duty, notched 2 total tackles and 4 passes defensed (second among Green Bay defenders in the playoffs), and added 1 special teams stop…Had 2 solo tackles and a pass defensed in divisional playoff victory over Tampa Bay (Jan. 4)…Notched 2 passes defensed in NFC Championship triumph at San Francisco (Jan. 11)…In preseason action, made 10 tackles and had 2 passes defensed; he also enjoyed a 13.5-yard average on 12 punt returns…Drafted in the second round (60th overall) by Green Bay in 1997.

COLLEGE: A three-year starter and four-time letterman (1993-96) at William & Mary…Was a two-time Division I-AA All-America selection as well as three-time first-team All-Yankee Conference pick…Played in 40 career games with 37 starts…Intercepted 24 passes during his collegiate career, tops in school history…His 486 career interception return yards made him the all-time leader in I-AA as well as Yankee Conference history…His 3 career interception returns for touchdowns also was a conference record…Recorded 296 total tackles and had 44 passes defensed…An effective punt returner for the Tribe, he averaged 10.2 yards per return over a three-year period, including an 80-yard punt return for a touchdown as a senior…Left school as the Tribe's career punt return yardage leader (1,037 yards)…A first-team I-AA All-America selection as a senior…Also earned Yankee Conference 'Defensive Player of the Year' honors and was a first-team East Coast Athletic Conference and All-Virginia pick…Led the conference and tied for top honors nationally among I-AA players with 10 interceptions…His 228 interception return yards was the highest in I-AA…Made a career-best 116 total tackles…Garnered national Division I-AA 'Defensive Player of the Week' honors for his performance vs. James Madison, when he had 16 tackles and 2 interceptions, one of which he returned 88 yards for a touchdown…Had an 80-yard punt return for a touchdown vs. Jackson State in the first round of the NCAA playoffs…Set a school record with 500 punt return yards…Earned first-team All-America and All-Yankee Conference honors as a junior…Led the conference and was tied for eighth nationally with 7 interceptions…Won the Penn contest when he returned an interception 40 yards for a deciding, fourth-quarter score…Received honorable mention All-America honors and was a first-team All-Yankee Conference choice as a sophomore…Tied for the conference lead and ranked 12th nationally with 7 interceptions…Had a 36-yard interception return for a touchdown vs. Villanova…Returned a blocked punt 34 yards for a touchdown vs. Rhode Island…Played in the last five games of his freshman season, starting two…Earned a B.A. degree in sociology.

PERSONAL: Given name Darren Mallory Sharper…Born in Richmond, Va. …Single…Was an all-district choice in football at Hermitage High School in Richmond, Va., where he earned four letters…Played

uarterback and led team to a 20-9 record as the starting signal-caller...Also was an all-district selection in asketball (four letters) and in track (three letters) as a hurdler...Enjoys public speaking and regularly peaks to school and charity groups, including a visit to Richmond elementary schools on 'National eading Day' this past offseason...Also runs a 'Mentorship Program' in Williamsburg, Va., that helps keep ids on the right path academically and socially...Spoke at an annual fund-raiser for a Richmond-area doption agency this past March...Since joining the Packers, also has given time to the Green Bay-area nited Way...Brother, Jamie, who also was chosen in the second round of the 1997 draft, was a 15-game tarter for the Baltimore Ravens last season; the brothers will face one another on Oct. 25 of this year vhen the Ravens visit Lambeau Field, giving Darren opportunity to exact revenge for the two collegiate lefeats his William & Mary team suffered at the hands of Jamie's University of Virginia squad...Father, larry, went to training camp with the Kansas City Chiefs in 1971 after a standout career at Virginia state...Hobbies include working out, playing the piano and water sports – both jet and water kiing...Residence: Glen Allen, Va.

PRO STATISTICS:

Year	G/S	UT	AT	Sacks	Int.	Yds.	LG	TD	FR	FF	PD
1997 Green Bay	14/0	10	3	0	2	70	50t	2	1	2	2
Playoffs	3/0	2	0	0	0	0	0	0	0	0	4

Other Touchdowns: 1, 34-yard fumble return vs. Dallas (11/23/97)
Punt Returns: 7 for 32 yards, 4.6 avg., 3 FC, LG 23 in 1997
Kickoff Returns: 1 for 3 yards in 1997
Special Teams Tackles: 7 (4-3) in 1997; 1 (1-0) in 1997 Playoffs

JERMAINE SMITH — 99

Defensive Tackle
College: Georgia
NFL Exp.: 2nd Season   **Packers Exp.:** 2nd Season
Ht.: 6-3   **Wt.:** 298   **Born:** 2/3/72   **Acq.:** D4-97

PRO: A second-year pro who saw more playing time as the regular season progressed in 1997...Extremely quick and agile for his size...Saw spot duty in the defensive line last season...Suffered a compound fracture of his right elbow, along with muscle and ligament damage, in a June 28 motorcycle accident in Green Bay, an injury which may sideline him for the entire 1998 season...Green Bay defensive coordinator Fritz Shurmur looks for Smith to mature and develop as an NFL player eventually, saying, "Last year Jermaine showed us some signs that he was going to be a good defensive lineman in this league. He has to play faster and get more done when he's playing. He needs to make plays – getting the runner with the ball or being effective as a pass rusher and playing fast. He needs to get all those things done at another level. Jermaine has to mature as a contributing football player. He has to take the next step."...**1997:** Served as the backup to Santana Dotson at defensive tackle...Saw action in nine regular-season games, including the last eight...Was inactive for six other games and did not play in one contest...Also was inactive for all three playoff games, including Super Bowl XXXII...Finished the regular season with 3 solo tackles, including 1 sack, plus 2 passes defensed...Also recorded a tackle on special teams...Played perhaps his best game of the season in the Packers' 20-10 win vs. Detroit (Nov. 2), when he registered his first NFL sack (of Scott Mitchell) on fourth down at the Lions' 45-yard line with 3:03 left in the game...Also saw extensive action during a four week stretch late in the season – vs. St. Louis (Nov. 9), at Indianapolis (Nov. 16), vs. Dallas (Nov. 23) and at Minnesota (Dec. 1) – making a solo tackle against both the Rams and Colts...Had received the first action of his rookie year Oct. 12 at Chicago, he batted down an Erik Kramer pass...Later had a pass defensed in regular-season finale against Buffalo (Dec. 20)...Did not play in opener vs. Bears (Sept. 1), then was inactive for the next five games...Also was inactive at New England (Oct. 27)...Drafted in the fourth round (126th overall) by Green Bay in 1997.

COLLEGE: A two-year starter and letter winner (1995-96) at Georgia...Played in 22 career games for the Bulldogs with 15 starts...Totaled 111 tackles, 3½ sacks, 14 tackles for loss, 4 fumble recoveries, 1 forced fumble and 3 passes defensed in his two-year stint at Georgia...Was an All-Southeastern Conference first-team selection in 1996, when he led the team in tackles for loss (11) and fumble recoveries (3)...Also recorded 68 tackles and 2½ sacks...Had 43 stops, including 3 tackles for loss and a sack, as a 1995 junior...Had transferred to Georgia from Georgia Military College, where he started at a defensive end in 1993 and '94...Named team's 'Defensive Player of the Year' in 1994, when he had 53 tackles, including 12 sacks and 9 others for loss, plus 8 forced fumbles as school finished 10-1 and was ranked 12th in the nation...Majored in child and family development.

PERSONAL: Given name Matt Jermaine Smith...Nicknamed 'Big Cat'...Born in Augusta, Ga. ...Single...Was an all-area honorable mention choice in football at Laney High School in Augusta, Ga., earning two letters...Named as team's 'Best Defensive Lineman' by the coaching staff...Had 93 tackles and 13 sacks as a senior...Also started at fullback, gaining 584 yards and scoring 4 touchdowns as a senior, when he had runs of 85 and 79 yards...Hobbies include playing video games...Residence: Memphis, Tenn.

PRO STATISTICS:

Year	G/S	UT	AT	Sacks	Int.	FR	FF	PD
1997　Green Bay..................9/0		3	0	1	0	0	0	2
Playoffs.......................0/0		0	0	0	0	0	0	0

Special Teams Tackles: 1 (0-1) in 1997

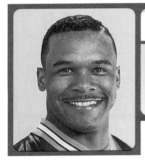

PAT TERRELL　　40

Safety
College: *Notre Dame*
NFL Exp.: *9th Season*　　**Packers Exp.:** *1st Season*
Ht.: *6-1*　**Wt.:** *208*　**Born:** *3/18/68*　**Acq:** *UFA-98 (Car)*

PRO: Veteran safety added to the Packers' roster in the offseason after time with three other NFL teams...Is expected to bring leadership and experience to the Green Bay secondary...Packers defensive coordinator Fritz Shurmur indicates that Terrell's experience is what appealed most to him, saying, "Pat brings experience at this point in his career. He's been on some good teams. I had him when he was a rookie with the Rams. Now it's a matter of him being able to fit into our scheme and then competing for a job. I expect that he will do that. Pat is an intelligent, classy guy who conducts himself like a pro. He is a good addition to a secondary where there are jobs open."...Has played in 123 career games with 67 starts...Has 417 career tackles, 10 interceptions and 30 passes defensed in his eight-year NFL career...Signed with Green Bay as an unrestricted free agent this past April 1...Spent the previous three seasons with the Carolina Panthers (1995-97) after playing with the New York Jets in 1994...Originally drafted by the Los Angeles Rams in 1990, he played four seasons with the Rams (1990-93) before moving to New York as an unrestricted free agent...**1997:** Played in all 16 games, making five starts, in his final season with Carolina...Saw action mainly in 'dime' situations...Served as the backup at both strong and free safety...Finished third among defensive backs (10th overall) with 58 tackles and 4 passes defensed...Also recorded 5 special teams tackles...Started first three games at free safety...Equaled his career high with 12 tackles in opener vs. Washington (Aug. 31)...Had 6 stops and a pass defensed a week later at Atlanta (Sept. 7)...Broke up a pass and registered 3 tackles at San Diego (Sept. 14)...Made 7 stops against San Francisco (Sept. 29) and vs. Oakland (Nov. 2)...**1996:** Started all 16 games (at free safety) for the second time as a pro...Led Carolina defensive backs with a career-high 90 tackles (tied for third on the team)...Also had 3 interceptions to equal his career best among 6 passes defensed...Earned NFC 'Defensive Player of the Week' honors for his performance vs. the N.Y. Giants (Nov. 10), when had the first 2-interception game of his NFL career, 5 tackles and 2 passes defensed...Led the team and equaled his season high with 10 stops at New Orleans (Sept. 8)...Also made 10 tackles vs. Baltimore (Dec. 15)...Had picked off his first pass of the season Sept. 29 at Jacksonville, in addition to registering 5 tackles...Had 8 tackles vs. St. Louis (Oct. 13), at Philadelphia (Oct. 27) and in rematch at Rams (Nov. 17)...Started both playoff contests, contributing 13 tackles, 1 interception and a pass defensed...Intercepted a Troy Aikman pass in the closing minutes of divisional playoff game vs. Dallas (Jan. 5) and returned it 49 yards (a career long) to set up a field goal that clinched the 26-17 win...Made 8 tackles in NFC Championship Game at Green Bay (Jan. 12)...**1995:** Started 13 games at free safety...Had 73 tackles (61 solo), second-best among Panthers' defensive backs...Had career highs in interceptions (3) and passes defensed (8)...Also had a forced fumble, a fumble recovery and 6 stops on special teams...Spent the first three games of the season playing on special teams and with the defense in its 'dime' package before taking over as the starting free safety...Made a career-high 12 tackles in his first start with Carolina, Oct. 1 vs. Tampa Bay...Recorded a key, fourth-quarter interception and made 6 tackles in the Panthers' 13-7 win at San Francisco (Nov. 5)...Also had an interception vs. Indianapolis (Dec. 3)...Made one of the season's most memorable plays in the fourth quarter of Atlanta contest (Dec. 17), when he deflected a fourth-down pass intended for Bert Manuel to highlight a goal-line stand and seal a Carolina win in the team's final game at Clemson...Also had his third interception of the season, 7 tackles and 2 passes defensed against the Falcons...Had signed with Carolina as a free agent on Aug. 23 following his termination by the Jets two days earlier...**1994:** Saw action in all 16 games with two starts in his lone season with the N.Y. Jets...Registered 26 tackles (20 solo) and 1 pass defensed...Also had 7 special teams tackles...Started his first game for New York in place of an injured Ronnie Lott Nov. 13 at Green Bay, contributing 8 tackles and a pass defensed...Recorded 7 stops in subsequent start vs. San Diego (Dec. 18)...Signed with Jets as an unrestricted free agent on May 19...**1993:** Played in 13 games in his final season with the Rams, making three starts...Tied for the team lead with 2 interceptions and finished third on the club with 6 passes defensed...Recorded 29 total stops...Had his best game of the season at Houston (Sept. 26), when he intercepted a pass in addition to 5 tackles and 3 passes defensed as a starter in Rams' 'nickel' package...Had a season-high 6 tackles in start at strong safety vs. Atlanta (Nov. 14)...Suffered a neck injury the following week against Washington (Nov. 21), causing him to be inactive for the next three games...In season finale vs. Chicago (Jan. 2), helped secure a 20-6 victory with a fourth-quarter interception...**1992:** Started 11 games while playing in 15 overall...Finished the season with 55 tackles (seventh on the team) and 1 forced fumble...Suffered a neck injury in season opener at Buffalo (Sept. 6), causing him to miss ensuing New England contest (Sept. 13)...Returned to action at Miami (Sept. 20)...Later started the Rams' final nine games...Had a season-high 9 tackles vs. San Francisco (Nov. 22)...**1991:** Started all 16 games for the first time as a pro...Registered 74 tackles (third on the team), 1 interception and 4 passes defensed...Intercepted a John Friesz pass to preserve 30-24 win over San Diego (Oct. 13)...Recorded a season-high 9 tackles vs. New Orleans (Sept. 15)...Had a team-leading 7 stops at the N.Y. Giants (Sept. 8) and vs. Green Bay (Sept. 29)...**1990:** Saw action in 15 games with one start as a rookie...Named to the all-rookie team of *Football News*...Finished the season with 12 tackles, 1 interception, 1 forced fumble, 1 fumble recovery and 1 pass defensed...Excelled on special teams, where he ranked second on the club with a career-best 16 coverage tackles...Made his first NFL start a memorable one at San Francisco (Nov. 25), when he picked off a Joe Montana pass for his first career interception...Drafted in the second round (49th overall) by the Los Angeles Rams in 1990.

COLLEGE: A two-year starter and four-time letter winner (1986-89) at Notre Dame...Finished collegiate career with 100 tackles (61 solo) and 9 interceptions...Named first-team All-America by *Gannett News Service* as a senior, when he had 53 tackles and 6 interceptions...Was the starting free safety in 1988 when the Fighting Irish captured the national championship...Played cornerback as a freshman, moved to wide receiver as a sophomore (catching 2 passes for 63 yards), then settled in at free safety as a junior...Earned a B.A. degree in business marketing and a minor in international marketing.

PERSONAL: Given name Patrick Christopher Terrell...Nicknamed 'P.T.'...Born in Memphis, Tenn. ...Married to Elizabeth, couple has a son...Received all-state and honorable mention All-America recognition as a wide receiver at Lakewood High School in St. Petersburg, Fla. ...Also played quarterback and safety...Won four letters in football and four in baseball as a centerfielder...Attended same high school as William Floyd (Panthers), Tom Carter (Bears) and former Houston Oiler Ernest Givins...One of his hobbies is aviation – he is licensed as a private, multi-engine and instrument rating pilot...Last year

THE PLAYERS

was involved with American Diabetes in Charlotte, helping to raise $30,000…Also has been involved with the United Way in Gastonia, N.C. …Residence: Charlotte, N.C.

PRO STATISTICS:

Year	G/S	UT	AT	Sacks	Int.	Yds.	LG	FR	FF	PD
1990 L.A. Rams 15/1		8	4	0	1	6	6	1	1	1
1991 L.A. Rams 16/16		64	10	0	1	4	4	0	0	4
1992 L.A. Rams 15/11		45	10	0	0	0	0	0	1	0
1993 L.A. Rams 13/3		24	5	0	2	1	1	0	0	6
1994 N.Y. Jets.................16/2		20	6	0	0	0	0	0	0	1
1995 Carolina 16/13		61	12	0	3	33	21	1	1	8
1996 Carolina 16/16		60	30	0	3	6	6	0	0	6
1997 Carolina 16/5		38	20	0	0	0	0	0	0	4
Totals 123/67		**320**	**97**	**0**	**10**	**50**	**21**	**2**	**3**	**30**
Playoffs.........................2/2		**9**	**4**	**0**	**1**	**49**	**49**	**0**	**0**	**1**

Special Teams Tackles: 16 (15-1) in 1990; 1 (1-0) in 1991; 7 in 1994; 6 (1-5) in 1995; 5 (1-4) in 1997 for total of 35

JEFF THOMASON   83

Tight End
College: Oregon
NFL Exp.: 6th Season   **Packers Exp.:** 4th Season
Ht.: 6-5   **Wt.:** 255   **Born:** 12/30/69   **Acq:** FA-95

PRO: Coming off his best season as a pro, looks for even more playing time in 1998 at a position that is one of the deepest on the squad…Became the Packers' No. 2 tight end last year following the retirement of Keith Jackson, he served as the backup to starter Mark Chmura after two seasons with the club as a third tight end…Responded well to the challenge, making a career-high 9 receptions in '97 after catching 10 total passes in his previous four seasons combined…Excels on special teams, he has been one of Green Bay's top special teams players the last three seasons, especially on kick coverage…Looks to have an injury-free campaign in '98 after an ankle injury caused him to be inactive for three games last season, snapping a streak of 44 consecutive games played (all with the Packers)…Had seen most of his action on special teams and as a third tight end during his first two seasons with the Packers after beginning his NFL career with Cincinnati and spending one year (1994) out of football…Possesses good size and soft hands, he also is a much-improved blocker…Already an accomplished special teams player, he has added long-snapping to his repertoire…"Jeff has worked hard to improve his receiving and blocking skills," says Green Bay offensive coordinator Sherman Lewis. "He is a good blocker who has excellent running skills after the catch. He is a big target that can get down the field as a deep threat when called upon."…Started his pro career with the Cincinnati Bengals in 1992 as an undrafted free agent…Spent two seasons with the Bengals (1992-93) prior to making the Green Bay roster in 1995…**1997:** Played in 13 regular-season games, he was inactive for the other three due to an ankle injury…Also played in all three playoff contests, including Super Bowl XXXII…Finished seventh on the team with a career-high 9 receptions for 115 yards (12.8 avg.) and 1 touchdown…Also finished tied for fifth on the club during the regular season with 11 tackles on kick coverage…Had the best game of his pro career in season opener vs. Chicago (Sept. 1) when he caught a team-leading and career-high 5 passes for 58 yards, including his first career touchdown – a one-yard scoring reception from Brett Favre in the second quarter…Suffered an ankle injury vs. the Bears, but still started the following week at Philadelphia (Sept. 7) as regular starter Chmura missed Eagles contest with a knee injury…Turned in a courageous effort against the Eagles as he had 2 receptions for 32 yards despite being hindered by his sore ankle...Had a strong performance in rematch at Chicago (Oct. 12), when he caught an 11-yard pass to the Bears' two-yard line, setting up a touchdown three plays later which gave Green Bay a 14-10 halftime lead...Also made 2 special teams tackles in second Bears game...Later had 2 tackles on kick coverage in wins over the Lions (Nov. 2) and St. Louis (Nov. 9)...Caught 1 pass for 14 yards and made 4 tackles – 2 on kick coverage and 2 miscellaneous tackles after interceptions – at Detroit (Sept. 28)...Sprained his right ankle in first half of game at Indianapolis (Nov. 16) and did not return...Saw action vs. Dallas (Nov. 23) but ankle problems continued to linger, causing him to be inactive at Minnesota (Dec. 1)...Also was inactive at Carolina (Dec. 14) and vs. Buffalo (Dec. 20) with same ankle injury after coming back and trying to play at Tampa Bay (Dec. 7)...**1996:** Saw action in all 16 regular-season games for the second consecutive year, primarily in a special teams role...Also got into each of the club's three postseason games, including Super Bowl XXXI...Served as the Packers' second tight end for the three games immediately following starter Chmura's arch injury at Kansas City (Nov. 10)...Made 3 receptions for 45 yards over the course of the season...Finished fifth on the club with 11 special teams tackles, including a season-best 2 at Tampa Bay (Sept. 1) and vs. Philadelphia (Sept. 9)...Additionally made 2 special teams tackles vs. Carolina in the NFC Championship Game (Jan. 12), he at times in that contest also was an effective run blocker vs. Panthers linebacker Kevin Greene...Made vigorous tackle of Patriots' Dave Meggett on the kickoff following Desmond Howard's momentum-turning kickoff return for a touchdown in Green Bay's Super Bowl triumph...Saw limited duty at tight end in club's first nine games before getting additional playing time vs. the Chiefs after Chmura went out early...Made second-ever NFL start at St. Louis (Nov. 24) as the Packers opened in two-tight end formation...Caught a 16-yard pass and returned a kickoff 20 yards at Dallas (Nov. 18)...Also had a reception at Tampa Bay (Sept. 1) and at Chicago (Oct. 6)...Recovered an onside kickoff late in Bears rematch (Dec. 1) to help preserve a 28-17 win...**1995:** Was Packers' backup tight end through first part of season, but saw role on offense diminish somewhat following arrival of Jackson in October...Got most of his playing time on special teams...Finished the year strong on special teams, making 13 of his 15 tackles over the final six games...His 15 stops with Green Bay's coverage units tied him for third on the club...Made a career-high 4 tackles (3 solo) on special teams at New Orleans (Dec. 16)...Earlier had 3 special teams stops at Cleveland (Nov. 19) and vs. Tampa Bay (Nov. 26)...Played in all 16 games for the first time as a pro, starting once (Oct. 15 vs. Detroit) when the Packers opened in a two-tight end formation...Ended season with 3 catches for 32 yards...Caught seven-yard pass Sept. 3 vs. St. Louis for first reception as a Packer...Later made catches in victories at Chicago (Sept. 11) and Jacksonville (Sept. 24)...Saw action in all three of the club's postseason games, contributing 2 solo tackles on special teams...Left Minnesota contest (Oct. 22) early after suffering a concussion on a kickoff return...Sprained medial collateral ligament in his left knee in a training camp practice Aug. 16, causing him to miss the final two preseason games...Had signed with Green Bay as a free agent on Jan. 12...**1994:** Released by Cincinnati July 29, he was claimed on waivers by the Packers on Aug. 1...Subsequently let go by Green Bay Aug. 22, he spent the remainder of the season out of football...**1993:** Played in three games for the Bengals over course of the season...Was inactive for the team's other 13 contests...Made 2 receptions for 8 yards...Caught passes at Pittsburgh (Sept. 19) and vs. Houston (Nov. 14)...Also saw action against Seattle (Sept. 26)...**1992:** Originally signed with Cincinnati as an undrafted free agent on April 29...Spent majority of the season on injured reserve with a knee injury...Placed on IR Sept. 1, where he stayed until activated on Dec. 5...Played in the last four games of the season for the Bengals, catching 2 passes for 14 yards...Also contributed 1 solo tackle on special teams.

COLLEGE: A four-time letter winner (1988-91) at Oregon, where he started his last two seasons...Served as team captain his senior year...Finished his collegiate career with 63 receptions for 818 yards and 10 touchdowns...Caught a career-high 30 passes for 396 yards and 6 TDs in 1990...Made 21 receptions as a senior and 12 as a sophomore...Holds B.S. degree in psychology.

PERSONAL: Given name Jeffrey David Thomason...Born in San Diego...Single...Lettered two years in football at Corona Del Mar High School in Newport Beach, Calif. ...Played linebacker and tight end...Also lettered four years in swimming...Spoke to various schools in Green Bay and Newport Beach, Calif., during the offseason...Is taking courses towards an MBA degree over the internet from the University of Phoenix, he is scheduled to graduate in the year 2000...Hobbies include reading, surfing and golf...Residence: Newport Beach, Calif.

PRO STATISTICS:

Year		G/S	No.	RECEIVING Yds.	Avg.	LG	TD
1992	Cincinnati 4/0		2	14	7.0	10	0
1993	Cincinnati 3/0		2	8	4.0	5	0
1994	...........................out of football						
1995	Green Bay 16/1		3	32	10.7	15	0
1996	Green Bay 16/1		3	45	15.0	24	0
1997	Green Bay 13/1		9	115	12.8	27	1
Totals	....................52/3		**19**	**214**	**11.3**	**27**	**1**
Playoffs	....................9/0		**0**	**0**	**0.0**	**0**	**0**

Kickoff Returns: 1 for 16 yards in 1995; 1 for 20 yards in 1996 for total of 2 for 36 yards, 18.0 avg., LG 20
Special Teams Tackles: 1 (1-0) in 1992; 15 (12-3) in 1995; 2 (2-0) in 1995 Playoffs; 11 (10-1) in 1996; 3 (1-2) in 1996 Playoffs; 11 (9-2) in 1997; 1 (1-0) in 1997 Playoffs for total of 38 (32-6)
Miscellaneous Tackles: 1 in 1993; 2 in 1997 for total of 3

CAREER SINGLE-GAME HIGHS
Most Receptions: 5, vs. Chicago (9/1/97); **Most Receiving Yards:** 58, vs. Chicago (9/1/97); **Longest Reception:** 27, at Philadelphia (9/7/97); **Most TD Receptions:** 1, vs. Chicago (9/1/97)

ADAM TIMMERMAN) 63)
Offensive Guard
College: South Dakota State
NFL Exp.: 4th Season   **Packers Exp.:** 4th Season
Ht.: 6-4   **Wt.:** 300   **Born:** 8/14/71   **Acq:** D7-95

PRO: Coming off his best season as a professional in 1997, Adam Timmerman has quietly emerged as one of the team's leaders in the trenches...Now entering his fourth NFL season, his third as a starter, he has made significant progress in his short tenure with the Packers...Just three years after he went to training camp with hopes of simply making the club, he now has started 32 consecutive games (40 including playoffs) for the Green and Gold...A fierce and intense competitor on the field who is able to play both guard spots...Green Bay offensive line coach Tom Lovat points out that Timmerman has benefited from experience..."Last season was a good one for Adam," Lovat states. "He is now an experienced player. He now has the instincts and confidence that he did not have in prior years. Adam has gotten better every year. He is a strong, smart player and a better athlete than you think. But he still has to improve."...Had received his professional football baptism during the 1995 playoffs when a knee injury put starter Aaron Taylor out and thrust him into the lineup at left guard...Hails from a farming background, still returns to his native Cherokee, Iowa, every spring to assist his family in planting the crops on its 800-acre bean and corn farm...Well-liked due to his genuine demeanor off the field, serves as a highly-visible television ad pitchman for regional Chevy Super Dealers...**1997:** Started at right guard in all 16 games, the club's only offensive lineman to start every contest...Also started all three playoff games, including Super Bowl XXXII...Did not miss a play the entire regular season and postseason...Helped the Packers' running attack to average 119.3 yards on the ground during the regular season, including a season-high 220 yards rushing in Green Bay's 45-17 win over Dallas (Nov. 23) as Dorsey Levens set a team record with 190 yards...Part of an offensive line that enabled the Packers to gain 218 yards rushing in a 31-10 victory at

Carolina (Dec. 14)...Teamed with Frank Winters and Taylor to hold the 49ers' heralded inside duo of Dana Stubblefield and Bryant Young without a sack and to a collective 8 tackles in 23-10, NFC Championship Game victory at San Francisco (Jan. 11)...**1996:** Started all 16 regular-season games (at right guard) for the first time as a professional...Also started each of the team's three postseason contests, including Super Bowl XXXI...Helped Packers' ground game average 114.9 yards rushing per contest, up from 89.3 in 1995...Won the starting job at the vacant right guard position with a strong training camp performance...Also saw some action on special teams...**1995:** Served as a backup at both guard positions...Saw action on special teams in 13 regular-season games...Was inactive for three games early in the year (Giants, Jaguars, Cowboys)...Pressed into service during the playoffs when Taylor went down with a season-ending knee injury late in the second quarter of Atlanta postseason contest (Dec. 31)...Played remainder of win over Falcons, then had successive starts at left guard at San Francisco (Jan. 6) and at Dallas (Jan. 14) in NFC Championship Game...Drafted in the seventh round (230th overall) by Green Bay in 1995.

COLLEGE: Was a four-time letterman (1990, 1992-94) at South Dakota State, including the last three years as a starter...Earned Division II All-America recognition as a junior and senior...Also was a three-time All-North Central Conference performer for the Jackrabbits...Twice won first-team academic all-conference honors...Received the 'Jim Langer Award,' presented to the nation's top Division II lineman, as a 1994 senior...Granted a medical redshirt year in 1991 after suffering a season-ending ankle injury in the first game...Also was redshirted in 1989 as a true freshman...Graduated from SDSU following the fall semester in late 1993, he returned home for six months to help tend the family farm...Still had one year of football eligibility left, so he decided to return to play his final season...Holds a B.S. degree in agriculture business.

PERSONAL: Given name Adam Larry Timmerman...Born in Cherokee, Iowa...Married to Jana...An all-conference and honorable mention all-state performer in football at Washington High School in Cherokee, Iowa...Also was team captain, he played guard, tackle and defensive tackle...Won two letters in football, two in basketball and three in track...Finished eighth in the state track meet in the 110 high hurdles...Was a National Honor Society member...He and wife, Jana, have given their time to many area charities, among them Children's Hospital, United Way and have served as the honorary chairpersons for the March of Dimes in 1997 and '98...Has spoken at various schools in his free time...Also is involved with Athletes in Action...Served as co-host of a regular Friday radio show, 'Breakfast with the Boys,' on Green Bay's WIXX Radio each of the past two seasons...Hobbies include fixing up old cars – he has a 1965 Mustang – farming and golf...Splits residence between Green Bay and Cherokee, Iowa.

PRO STATISTICS:

Games/Starts—Green Bay 1995 (13/0); 1995 Playoffs (3/2); 1996 (16/16); 1996 Playoffs (3/3); 1997 (16/16); 1997 Playoffs (3/3). Career totals: 45/32. Playoff totals: 9/8.

ROSS VERBA · 78

Offensive Tackle
College: Iowa
NFL Exp.: 2nd Season   Packers Exp.: 2nd Season
Ht.: 6-4   Wt.: 302   Born: 10/31/73   Acq: D1-97

PRO: Now entrenched at left tackle, tenacious and imposing Iowan looks to continue his impressive development as blind-side protector of three-time NFL MVP Brett Favre...The Packers' first-round draft choice in 1997, added stabilizing dimension – and a mean streak – to offensive line when he assumed permanent duties at left tackle in Week 6 last year...Recipient of all-rookie accolades in '97, has emerged as a viable Pro Bowl candidate in 1998...After missing initial two weeks of training camp last summer due to contractual stalemate, is looking forward to a full camp in 1998 to further cultivate his very promising skills, a scenario Green Bay offensive line coach Tom Lovat feels will certainly help him..."When he missed some time last year, he had to make up for a lot of lost ground on the job," says Lovat. "And he did that. Being in camp this year will give him a chance to look at what he needs to do – he'll have more time. He'll improve technically this year, and he has to. Last year he played on brute determination and brute desire and did a good job. We don't want to take that away from him, but he's been around the block now. People have seen him and they know what his shortcomings are, too. It may be a little tougher for him in that respect."...Calm, off-the-field demeanor is stark contrast to aggressive, take-no-prisoners attitude on the gridiron – a temperament readily accepted and appreciated by his teammates and coaches..."He comes to play the game," agrees Lovat. "He'll battle you. If he's what we think he is, he'll be around for a long time. He's got the tools and the potential to be one of the good ones."...**1997:** Played in all 16 games, starting the final 11 contests at left tackle...Also started all three playoff games, including Super Bowl XXXII – becoming the first rookie ever to start at left tackle in the Super Bowl...Garnered all-rookie honors from Pro Football Writers of America/*Pro Football Weekly, College & Pro Football Newsweekly* and *Football News*...Took advantage of opportunity when injuries sidelined incumbent left tackle John Michels in two early-season contests...Primarily playing on special teams in Packers' first five contests, saw initial action at left tackle vs. Minnesota (Sept. 21), when he stepped in for an injured Michels (leg) after the first offensive series and played the remainder of the game...A week later at Detroit (Sept. 28), replaced an injured Michels (knee) in the third quarter and played the duration...Subsequently made his first NFL start the ensuing week vs. Tampa Bay (Oct. 5), he played well enough to cement the starting spot...Helped pave way as Packers set a season-high rushing total of 220 yards in 45-17 win over the Cowboys (Nov. 23), including Dorsey Levens' club-record 190 yards on the ground...Also assisted in Green Bay's 218-yard rushing effort at Carolina (Dec. 14)...Turned in outstanding performance in NFC Championship victory at San Francisco (Jan.11), holding the 49ers' Chris Doleman without a sack and helping to open up running lanes for Levens...A tight end in high school, earlier in the season had seen playing time on the offensive line as an eligible receiver vs. Chicago (Sept.1), when regular tight ends Mark Chmura and Jeff Thomason suffered knee and ankle injuries, respectively...In initial game with Detroit, was on the unsuccessful receiving end of a Favre pass in the end zone as he ran a pattern as an eligible receiver...Was a late arrival to training camp (Aug. 1), missing time due to contractual holdout...Drafted in the first round (30th overall) by Green Bay in 1997.

COLLEGE: A four-year starter (1993-96) for the University of Iowa...Started 35 career games for the Hawkeyes after moving from tight end to offensive tackle prior to the start of the 1993 season...An intense and tireless worker on the field, he earned the team's offensive hustle award six times during his college career and received the 'Coaches Hustle Award' for offense in 1996...Was a first-team All-Big Ten selection as a senior, when he started all 12 games at left tackle...Honored as school's 'co-Most Valuable Player', he also served as one of four co-captains for the entire '96 season...Earned offensive MVP honors three times – vs. Penn State, Illinois and Wisconsin – plus offensive hustle award vs. Indiana and Northwestern...Was the leader of an offensive line that paved the way for running back Sedrick Shaw to gain over 1,000 yards rushing for the third straight season...Selected to play in the Senior Bowl...In an injury-plagued junior year, started seven contests...Had started the first five games of the season before a sprained ankle vs. Indiana forced him to miss next two contests...Was injured a second time at Northwestern...Saw action, but did not start, in final two regular-season contests...Played in all 11 games as a sophomore, making 10 starts...Member of 1994 offensive line that helped Iowa to 2,431 yards rushing, the third-best total in school history, and allowed just 10 sacks in 11 games...As a redshirt freshman, saw action in nine games, starting the final six contests...Was redshirted in 1992...Majored in sports management.

PERSONAL: Given name Ross Robert Verba...Born in Des Moines, Iowa...Single...Was a *Parade* All-America selection as a senior tight end at Dowling High School in West Des Moines, Iowa...Also was picked as Iowa's 'Player of the Year' by *Parade*...Earned all-state and all-conference honors as well...Served as a captain and was named team MVP...Caught 35 passes for 434 yards and 7 touchdowns his senior year as team went 9-2...Had moved to tight end as a junior after starting high school career as an offensive lineman...Also played defensive end, making 75 tackles and recovering 2 fumbles...Recorded 60 tackles defensively, plus 300 receiving yards and 4 touchdowns on offense, as a junior...Earned three letters in football, he also played basketball for two years...Attended same high school as Packers President Bob Harlan...With an eye already fixed on his post-football career, started his own sports marketing agency, 'Boss Ross 78,' this past January; the agency represents himself and other pro football players in their marketing endeavors...Has given time to the 'Joshua Frase Foundation,' the organization named after the son of Packers teammate Paul Frase who suffers from congenital myopathy, a rare muscle disease...Also enjoys public speaking, regularly making appearances in front of school and business groups...Served as the 1998 honorary chairperson for the Muscular Dystrophy Association's annual

THE PLAYERS

'Harley Run,' a 100-mile ride with more than 1,000 motorcycles which raised over $50,000 from this year's event, held June 6...Hobbies include jet skiing and riding his Harley-Davidson motorcycle...Residence: Green Bay.

PRO STATISTICS:

Games/Starts—Green Bay 1997 (16/11); 1997 Playoffs (3/3). Career totals: 16/11. Playoff totals: 3/3.

Miscellaneous Tackles: 1 in 1997

REGGIE WHITE > 92

Defensive End
College: Tennessee
NFL Exp.: 14th Season   **Packers Exp.:** 6th Season
Ht.: 6-5   **Wt.:** 300 **Born:** 12/19/61 **Acq:** UFA-93 (Phil)

PRO: The most-honored athlete ever to play defensive end in the National Football League's long history, Reggie White returns for the 14th and what he has termed the final season of a singular and distinguished career...Hampered by a persistent back problem in 1997, he earlier had announced his retirement from the game – on the second day of the 1998 NFL draft (April 19) – but subsequently decided to play one more year to fulfill a promise he had made to Packers management when he signed a new, five-year contract late in the 1996 season – a commitment to play at least two seasons...Remembering that promise, he announced on April 21, had triggered his decision to return...Long a legitimate icon in his game, in which he last season was a Pro Bowl selection at his position for a record 12th consecutive year, White has seen his talents, performance and persona elicit the ultimate in superlatives for more than a decade...The prepossessing Tennessean, a certain Hall of Famer as soon as he becomes eligible, is larger than life, literally and figuratively – a man apart, both at his position and off the field...Green Bay defensive coordinator Fritz Shurmur, openly admiring, has paid him the ultimate compliment, calling White "the cornerstone and foundation of this football team"...Confident Number 92 will make substantial contributions to the cause in '98, Shurmur observed, "As we have seen with him over the years, whenever he has had some kind of a physical difficulty, in most cases those types of things put the average guy on the shelf. But he has played through dislocated elbows, holes in his hamstring muscle, and last year with a bad back. So I would not be a bit surprised to see him come back and achieve at a high level. I know he has recommitted, rededicated himself to working as much as humanly possible to rehabilitate his injured back. And, again, if it's humanly possible for anyone to do it, Reggie will do it. As a result, I fully expect that he'll be there and be a contributor to our defense again. Obviously, the leadership skills are unparalleled in this league. His impact on our team, on our fans, on our city and on our state is immeasurable. And when it comes to great football players, there's no question that he's probably the greatest to ever play the position. But, more significantly, I've never been around a guy who has more legitimate concerns for his fellow man and for bettering the place in society of his fellow man or for those who do not have the same kind of advantages we have. So he's a great human being and a great football player."...Addressing what White's presence and performance have meant to the Packers over the past five seasons, Shurmur asserted, "Actually, when we look around at our team and what's happened with our team, the most important – the pivotal move – was to bring Reggie White here. When he came here, he came here with the idea that he was going to help this team get to a Super Bowl, and did and everything he could as an individual to try to get there – including personal sacrifices and all those kinds of things. He was the ultimate team player – a team leader to the point where he has a very positive influence on the rest of our people. I think if I were to take three words that kind of characterize our team, they are commitment, character and chemistry – and all of those words describe Reggie and his commitment to this team. He is a rare football player, a rare individual. He is rare in his capacity to play the game consistently. He has tremendous strength and explosiveness, to go with speed. He's probably the most unselfish team player I've ever been around and it rubs off. If you were to look at one guy whose demeanor and whose mode of living is an example for all of us to follow, it's Reggie White. He leads by example better than any player I've been around – he never misses a turn in practice."...These accolades having been delivered, there remains no way to adequately measure White's electrifying impact upon the defense in his five seasons as a Packer...But his unit's performance in 1996, for prime example, offers an eloquent testimonial to his contributions...The Packers' defense – under White's leadership – reached the summit in '96, finishing as the NFL's top-ranked unit in for the first time since 1967...White and his colleagues led the league in fewest points allowed (210) and set an NFL record for fewest touchdowns allowed in a 16-game season (19)...His unit's rankings have consistently held top spots in many defensive categories since his arrival upon the Green Bay scene...The Green Bay defense soared to second place in 1993 (from a distant 23rd the previous year), when the former Philadelphia Eagles superstar joined the Green and Gold as the most sought-after performer to become available with the advent of unrestricted free agency in the National Football League...It subsequently finished a highly-respectable sixth in 1994 despite the loss of starters Johnny Holland, Tony Bennett and Roland Mitchell from the '93 unit...The defense continued to be a positive constant in 1995...Although it finished 14th overall statistically, it closed out the season ranking fourth in fewest points allowed (314)...Head Coach Mike Holmgren, for one, was able to put the 1993 performance in practical perspective...White "made us a better football team – no question about it," Holmgren said, documenting this assertion by noting, "We went from 23 on defense (in the league as a whole) to two – with no noticeable dramatic personnel changes, except for one man."...Still at the very top of his game after 13 years, White again saw his on-field superiority documented in 1997 by his selection to the Pro Bowl for an NFL-record 12th straight year, breaking a tie with the San Francisco 49ers' Jerry Rice (1986-96) and the Cincinnati Bengals' Anthony Munoz (1981-91) for the most consecutive times chosen since the 1970 league merger...It also represented his fifth trip to the Pro Bowl in a Green Bay uniform, tying Willie Davis (1963-67) for the Packers' record for a defensive lineman...He had received even more singular recognition for professional football's all-time sacks leader – his election to the National Football League's 75th Anniversary All-Time Team in August of 1994...In 1997, he continued his reign as the league's official all-time leader in quarterback sacks, notching 11 to increase his career total to 176½ over his 13-year NFL tenure...In the process, became only the second player in league history to post at least 10 sacks in each of 11 seasons (Buffalo's Bruce Smith had become the first earlier in '97)...Is tied with Smith for the most career sacks in NFL postseason history, each having posted 12 in the playoffs...Also ranks as the Packers' career sacks leader in the playoffs, having recorded 8 in a Green Bay uniform...Has 52½ sacks

MOST SACKS – NFL HISTORY (COMPILED SINCE 1982)

176.5	REGGIE WHITE, Philadelphia 1985-92; Green Bay 1993-97
154.0	Bruce Smith, Buffalo 1985-97
137.5	Richard Dent, Chicago 1983-93, 1995; San Francisco 1994; Indianapolis 1996; Philadelphia 1997
133.0	Kevin Greene, L.A. Rams 1985-92; Pittsburgh 1993-95; Carolina 1996; San Francisco 1997
132.5	Lawrence Taylor, N.Y. Giants 1982-93
128.0	Rickey Jackson, New Orleans 1982-93; San Francisco 1994-95

with the Packers during the regular season, placing him second on the club's all-time list (since sacks became an official NFL stat in 1982), behind only Tim Harris (55)...Now has sacked 64 different quarterbacks over his NFL career, having added the Eagles' Ty Detmer and the Bills' Alex Van Pelt to his collection in 1997...Earlier in his career, he had become the fastest player in league history to record 100 career sacks, reaching the century mark in only 93 games, 21 games faster than No. 2 Lawrence Taylor (114)...One of the game's most durable performers, he missed a non-strike game for the first time in his career late in the 1995 season (Dec. 10 at Tampa Bay due to a hamstring problem), but was back at his customary stand the following week...Had played in 166 consecutive 'union' contests to that point, one of the longest such streaks in NFL history...The 36-year-old White is the only player in NFL history to register double-digit sack totals in nine consecutive seasons (1985 through 1993)...He in 1993 also became the first Packers defensive end chosen for the Pro Bowl since Ezra Johnson in 1978...Impressively productive since his selection by the Eagles as a first-round pick in the NFL's supplemental draft of USFL players in 1984, White has amassed 1,079 tackles (772 solo), including his 176½ sacks...He also has posted 3

MOST SACKS – PACKERS HISTORY (COMPILED SINCE 1982)

55.0	Tim Harris, 1986-90
52.5	REGGIE WHITE, 1993-97
41.5	Ezra Johnson, 1977-87
36.0	Tony Bennett, 1990-93
32.5	Bryce Paup, 1990-94

interceptions, 51 passes defensed, forced 28 fumbles and recovered 20, two of the latter for touchdowns...In addition, he has supplemented these contributions by registering 2 safeties and blocking 4 kicks (2 FGs, 1 PAT and 1 punt)...The only player to be selected by *Pro Football Weekly* on its 1980s All-Decade team and also to be projected to its All-1990s team, he has customarily lined up at defensive end, but also has used his strength and speed to wreak havoc on blocking schemes from various positions along the line during his career...Launched his pro career with the USFL's Memphis Showboats (1984-85), posting 193 tackles (120 solo), 23½ sacks and forcing 7 fumbles in 34 starts...**1997 HONORS:** Elected to the Pro Bowl for the 12th straight year, breaking a tie with the Rice and Munoz for the most consecutive times chosen since the 1970 merger of the National and American Football Leagues...In addition, was named to the All-NFC team of *Football News*...Also was selected as a second-team All-Pro by *College & Pro Football Newsweekly*...**1997:** Was team's starter at left end for all 16 regular-season games for the third time in five years with Green Bay (and for the ninth time in his 13 NFL seasons)...Led the Packers in sacks for the third straight season and for the fourth time in his five years with 11, a total which earned him seventh place in the National Football Conference...Finished second among the team's defensive linemen with 46 tackles (36 solo), plus 2 fumble recoveries and 6 passes defensed...Played in the 200th regular-season game of his career in the Packers' finale vs. Buffalo (Dec. 20)...Posted 3½ sacks over an important two-game stretch late in the season – both wins on the road, against Minnesota and Tampa Bay...Enjoyed maybe his best game of the year at the Vikings (Dec. 1), when he recorded a season-high 2½ sacks among his 3 tackles in the Packers' 27-11 victory (his second multiple-sack game of '97) despite not playing on every down due to his lingering back problem...Registered a key, third-down sack of Bucs QB Trent Dilfer late in the first half, in the Packers' 17-6, division-clinching win at Tampa Bay (Dec. 7)...Then had a sack among 2 tackles in the Packers' 31-21 victory over the Bills (Dec. 20)...Posted 6 tackles (5 solo), including a half-sack, and batted down 2 Erik Kramer passes in season-opening win over Chicago (Sept. 1)...Had 2 sacks of Dilfer and made 5 stops in initial, 21-16 victory over Tampa Bay (Oct. 5)...Turned in an outstanding performance in his return to Philadelphia (Sept. 7), the city in which he played his first eight NFL seasons, registering 1 sack, batting down 2 Detmer passes and recovering a Detmer fumble at the Green Bay two-yard line to stop an almost certain Eagles scoring drive...Came up with a clutch effort in win over Minnesota two weeks later (Sept. 21) when, with the Packers clinging to a 38-32 lead and Minnesota driving (at its own 46-yard line) for the potential game-winning score in the waning moments of the game (1:45 left), he hit Brad Johnson's arm as the Vikings quarterback attempted a fourth-down pass that fell incomplete; Green Bay subsequently ran out the clock to preserve the win...White also had a sack of Johnson earlier in the game and tipped a Johnson pass that was intercepted by teammate LeRoy Butler at the Minnesota 12-yard line with 54 seconds left in the first half, leading to a Ryan Longwell field goal as the Packers forged a 31-7 halftime lead...Had 2 tackles and a sack at Detroit (Sept. 28)...Two weeks later, against Chicago (Oct. 12), he tipped a Kramer pass which then was intercepted by teammate Brian Williams at the Green Bay 47; the subsequent Packers drive led to a touchdown, giving Green Bay a 14-10 lead...Also had a season-high 7 tackles (6 solo) in rematch with the Bears...Recovered a Curtis Martin fumble (forced by teammate Eugene Robinson) to halt an early long drive by the Patriots at New England (Oct. 27); the Packers' following possession resulted in a touchdown in the eventual 28-10 win...Sacked Lions quarterback Scott Mitchell on a big third-down play at the Green Bay 40-yard line late in the fourth quarter (Nov. 2) and the Packers went on to stop Detroit on fourth down, helping to preserve a 20-10 victory...Went out late in the game at Indianapolis (Nov. 16) due to a flare-up of a chronic back problem, but still started the ensuing Sunday's match with Dallas (Nov. 23) despite limited practice time during the week...**1997 PLAYOFFS:** Started all three postseason games, including Super Bowl XXXII, and thus is now tied with six teammates for the Green Bay postseason record for most career games played (13), each having passed the previous record-holder, Ray Nitschke (11) in '97...Collected 6 tackles, including 1 sack and 1 forced fumble, in the playoffs...Notched the 12th postseason sack of his career, a five-yard trap of the 49ers' Steve Young in the fourth quarter of the

Packers' 23-10 victory in the NFC Championship Game at San Francisco (Jan. 11), the take-down tying him with Buffalo's Smith for NFL postseason career sack honors...The sack, among 4 tackles overall vs. the 49ers, precipitated a Young fumble that was recovered by San Francisco...Earlier had 1 solo stop in the Packers' 21-7 divisional playoff triumph over Tampa Bay (Jan. 4)...Closed out the postseason with 1 solo tackle in Super Bowl XXXII (Jan. 25)...Again represented defense, along with LeRoy Butler, as one of the team's six playoff captains throughout the postseason...**1996 HONORS:** Elected to the Pro Bowl for the 11th consecutive year...Was a first-team All-Pro selection by *College & Pro Football Newsweekly* and a first-team All-NFC selection by *Football News* and *United Press International*...Chosen second-team All-Pro by *Associated Press* and *Football Digest*...Also named to the 'All-Madden Team' by Fox Sports analyst John Madden...Recipient of the NFL's 'Extra Effort Award' for the month of October for his work with Wisconsin schoolchildren...**1996:** Started all 16 regular-season games (at left defensive end) for the second time with Green Bay and for the eighth time in his 12-year NFL career...Even though double-teamed week in and week out, he led the Packers in sacks (8½) for the third time in his four seasons with the team...Also registered 36 total tackles, plus 1 interception, a team-leading 3 fumble recoveries (tie), a club-best 3 forced fumbles, 6 passes defensed and a blocked punt...His 3 fumble recoveries equaled his career high, originally set with Philadelphia in 1991...Played perhaps his best game of the regular season Dec. 15 at Detroit – three days after re-signing with Green Bay – when he registered 2 sacks among his 3 tackles, plus a forced fumble, while applying unremitting pressure on Lions' Mitchell...Also enjoyed a particularly strong performance vs. San Diego (Sept. 15), when he had 2 sacks, 1 forced fumble and 1 pass defensed...Made a season-high 5 tackles at Kansas City (Nov. 10)...Had 3 stops, including a sack and a forced fumble, in rematch with Minnesota (Dec. 22)...Recorded a sack of the 49ers' Elvis Grbac among 3 stops in overtime victory over San Francisco (Oct. 14)...Had made 4 stops at Chicago (Oct. 6)...Turned in an exceptional effort vs. Tampa Bay (Oct. 27), when he blocked the first punt of his career in the first quarter – setting up a Green Bay field goal – and also pressured Bucs' Dilfer repeatedly, including a sack in the third period...Intercepted the third pass of his NFL career, when he picked off a Rick Mirer throw in the first quarter at Seattle (Sept. 29) and returned it 46 yards to the Seahawks' 21-yard line, triggering a field goal on the Packers' ensuing series...He also had a season-high 4 passes defensed against Seattle...Recovered a fourth-quarter fumble by Broncos quarterback Bill Musgrave on Dec. 8 vs. Denver, Green Bay converting the turnover into points on its following possession...Had 5 pressures of Dilfer plus a fumble recovery in season opener at Tampa Bay (Sept. 1)...Later posted 3 pressures and a recovered fumble at Minnesota (Sept. 22)...**1996 PLAYOFFS:** Started all three of the Packers' postseason games and forged 5 tackles, all unassisted, including a Super Bowl-record 3 sacks of New England quarterback Drew Bledsoe in the Packers' 35-21 triumph over the Patriots in SB XXXI (Jan. 26)...Registered the first two sacks of Bledsoe on consecutive plays (second and third down) late in the third quarter, halting the New England possession immediately following Desmond Howard's momentum-turning, 99-yard kickoff return for a touchdown, later adding his third sack on the Pats' final stab at a comeback...Represented defense, along with Butler, as one of the team's six playoff captains throughout the postseason...**1995 HONORS:** Elected to the Pro Bowl for the 10th straight year...First-team All-Pro selection by *AP, Pro Football Weekly*/Pro Football Writers of America, *USA Today, Sports Illustrated, The Sporting News, College & Pro Football Newsweekly* and *Football Digest*...All-NFC choice of *UPI* and *Football News*...Selected as NFC 'Defensive Player of the Year' by the Kansas City Committee of 101...Honored as NFC 'Defensive Player of the Year' at the annual Mackey Awards...Also was named to the 'All-Madden Team'...**1995:** Finished third in the NFC with 12 sacks – the 10th time he had enjoyed a double-digit sack year in his first 11 NFL seasons...Played in 15 games, making 13 starts...Was the team's second-leading tackler among defensive linemen with 46 total stops...Also forced 2 fumbles and was credited with 4 passes defensed...Made a miraculous recovery in final weeks of the season when an initial prognosis of surgery to repair a torn left hamstring suffered in Dec. 3 victory over Cincinnati (which would have ended his personal year) proved premature when he returned to practice on Dec. 14 (a Thursday), the day after the presumed need for surgery was announced (Wednesday, Dec. 13)...First felt renewed strength in the hamstring at his home the evening of the 13th, then confirmed those thoughts during a late-night workout at the Packers' indoor practice facility, The Don Hutson Center, under the supervision of Kent Johnston, the team's strength and conditioning coach...Saw action in pass-rushing situations two days later at New Orleans (Dec. 16), recording 1 solo tackle...Subsequently returned to the starting lineup for regular-season finale vs. Pittsburgh the following week (Dec. 24)...Had missed the first non-strike game of his NFL career when he was inactive for Bucs rematch at Tampa (Dec. 10) with the hamstring injury suffered a week earlier...Had his third sack in as many weeks against Bengals, but also suffered hamstring tear in his left leg in the

REGGIE WHITE HIT PARADE – 1985-97

Reggie White's 176.5 regular season sacks have come against the following 64 quarterbacks

Player	Sacks	Player	Sacks
Phil Simms, Giants	15.5	Erik Kramer, Bears	2.0
Neil Lomax, Cardinals	13.0	Dan Marino, Dolphins	2.0
Jeff Hostetler, Giants/Raiders	7.5	Ken O'Brien, Jets	2.0
Tommy Kramer, Vikings	6.5	Tom Ramsey, Patriots	2.0
Chris Miller, Falcons/Rams	6.5	Mark Rypien, Redskins	2.0
Troy Aikman, Cowboys	6.0	Wade Wilson, Saints	2.0
John Elway, Broncos	5.5	Vince Evans, Raiders	1.5
Trent Dilfer, Buccaneers	5.0	Jim McMahon, Chargers/Vikings	1.5
Warren Moon, Vikings	5.0	Rodney Peete, Lions/Eagles	1.5
Steve Pelluer, Cowboys	5.0	Vinny Testaverde, Buccaneers	1.5
Brad Johnson, Vikings	4.5	Steve Beuerlein, Cowboys	1.0
Scott Mitchell, Lions	4.0	Jeff Blake, Bengals	1.0
Jim Plunkett, Raiders	4.0	Drew Bledsoe, Patriots	1.0
Jeff Rutledge, Redskins	4.0	Bubby Brister, Steelers	1.0
Don Majkowski, Packers/Lions	3.5	Mark Brunell, Jaguars	1.0
Jim Everett, Rams	3.0	Randall Cunningham, Eagles	1.0
Stan Gelbaugh, Cardinals/Seahawks	3.0	Ty Detmer, Eagles	1.0
Timm Rosenbach, Cardinals	3.0	Craig Erickson, Buccaneers	1.0
Cliff Stoudt, Cardinals	3.0	Joe Ferguson, Bills	1.0
Jack Trudeau, Colts	3.0	Vince Ferragamo, Bills	1.0
Bobby Hebert, Saints	2.5	Rich Gannon, Vikings	1.0
Dave Krieg, Chiefs/Lions/Bears	2.5	Jason Garrett, Cowboys	1.0
Joe Montana, 49ers	2.5	Elvis Grbac, 49ers	1.0
Jay Schroeder, Redskins/Raiders	2.5	Steve Grogan, Patriots	1.0
Danny White, Cowboys	2.5	Blair Kiel, Packers	1.0
David Archer, Falcons	2.0	Bernie Kosar, Browns	1.0
Boomer Esiason, Bengals	2.0	Sean Salisbury, Vikings	1.0
Jim Harbaugh, Bears	2.0	Mike Tomczak, Bears	1.0
Mark Hermann, Chargers	2.0	Alex Van Pelt, Bills	1.0
Gary Hogeboom, Cowboys	2.0	Doug Williams, Redskins	1.0
Stan Humphries, Chargers	2.0	Eric Zeier, Browns	1.0
Jim Kelly, Bills	2.0	Anthony Dilweg, Packers	0.5

Quarterbacks Never Sacked by White But Whom He May Face in 1998: Kerry Collins (Panthers), Steve Young (49ers), Kordell Stewart (Steelers), Danny Kanell (Giants), Bobby Hoying (Eagles), Steve McNair (Oilers)

fourth quarter...Felled the Bucs' Dilfer for a 10-yard loss late in the third quarter vs. Tampa Bay (Nov. 26)...Sacked Browns quarterback Eric Zeier for an 11-yard loss among his 3 tackles in the Packers' win at Cleveland (Nov. 19)...Turned in gutty performance in Green Bay's key, 35-28 victory over Bears (Nov. 12), when he had a season-high 6 tackles, a half-sack and batted down a Kramer pass – despite not knowing until pre-game warmups if he was even going to play, due to the knee injury he had suffered a week earlier...Notched a sack in rematch at Minnesota (Nov. 5), but left the game in the fourth quarter after suffering a sprained medial collateral ligament in his right knee following a collision with teammate Sean Jones on an attempted quarterback sack...Had another in a long line of outstanding performances, this time in first '95 meeting with Minnesota (Oct. 22), when he recorded 2 quarterback sacks and forced a Warren Moon fumble which was recovered in the end zone by Jones for a Green Bay touchdown, giving the Packers a 35-14 lead en route to eventual, 38-21 triumph...Dominated each of the three players the Vikings lined up at right tackle across from him...Made 4 tackles and recorded 1 sack at Dallas (Oct. 8) despite constant double-team blocking by the Cowboys...Made 3 tackles and registered 1 sack (another sack was nullified due to a penalty) in the Packers' win at Jacksonville (Sept. 24)...Made another in a long line of big plays when, Sept. 11 at Chicago, with Green Bay clinging to a 27-24 lead, he sacked Kramer, forcing him to fumble, the ball being recovered by teammate Wayne Simmons at the Bears' 22-yard line with only 1:59 remaining in the game...Launched '95 season with a dominating performance against St. Louis Rams (Sept. 3), recording 2½ sacks despite being double- and triple-teamed...**1995 PLAYOFFS:** Registered 2 solo tackles and 1 sack during three postseason appearances, the latter a five-yard trap of Dallas quarterback Troy Aikman on the Cowboys' first offensive series in NFC Championship Game (Jan. 14)...Though he had no stats to show for his efforts, continually harassed 49ers quarterback Young in 27-17 upset win at San Francisco (Jan. 6) as Green Bay defense shut down Niners' vaunted offensive attack...Did not start wild-card playoff with Atlanta (Dec. 31), but saw considerable duty as a reserve...**1994:** Durable as well as devastating, he had started 117 consecutive games – tying him with five other players for the longest active streak in the NFL – until the string was snapped Nov. 24 at Dallas when he did not start the game because of an elbow injury, suffered in the previous weekend's Buffalo contest (Nov. 20)...He did, however, come in with the first 'nickel' unit in the first quarter and played much of the rest of the game...Played in all 16 regular-season games, missing only the start against Dallas...Finished second among team's defensive linemen with 59 total tackles and was second on the club with 8 sacks...Also forced 2 fumbles, recovered 1 and knocked down 7 passes...Started both playoff games at defensive tackle, his domination of the middle of the line vs. Detroit (Dec. 31) was a primary reason that

MOST SACKS – POSTSEASON – NFL HISTORY (COMPILED SINCE 1982)

12.0	REGGIE WHITE, Philadelphia 1985-92; Green Bay 1993-97
12.0	Bruce Smith, Buffalo 1985-97
11.0	Charles Haley, San Francisco 1986-91; Dallas 1992-96

the Packers were able to hold the Lions to an NFL postseason record -4 yards rushing on 15 attempts and league rushing champion Barry Sanders to a career-low -1 yard on 13 carries...Made his presence felt Dec. 11 vs. Chicago while moving to the interior of the defensive line at times to make up for the injury loss of Gilbert Brown, the Bears rushed for only 27 yards on 14 carries...Sacked Detroit's Dave Krieg among 2 tackles at the Lions (Dec. 4)...Although hampered by an elbow injury, turned in the type of dominating performance which has become his trademark at Dallas on Thanksgiving Day, posting 6 tackles and 1 sack, an 11-yard drop of Cowboys QB Jason Garrett; he also applied heavy pressure and forced Garrett into an intentional grounding infraction during the contest...Also, on a number of occasions, he lifted 325-pound Dallas offensive tackle Larry Allen off the ground, literally with one arm because his left elbow was in a brace, as he strove to move upfield...Played against Cowboys when, only two days earlier, he had been declared out of the contest medically due to the elbow injury suffered vs. the Bills...Had 2 tackles at Buffalo, but suffered sprained medial ligament in his left elbow midway through the third quarter, an injury which forced him to leave the game...Equaled his season high with 6 tackles in the Packers' 38-30 win over Detroit (Nov. 6), he also batted down a Krieg pass...Had one of the most dominating performances of his career Oct. 20 at Minnesota...After flushing Moon out of the pocket, he promptly took WR Cris Carter (who was between White and Moon) and flung him at Moon's feet before sacking the Viking QB for a 15-yard loss...On another play, he grabbed 331-pound Minnesota lineman Bernard Dafney and threw him off his feet with his right arm as he made a move upfield...Earlier had sacked Moon among 6 tackles in season-opening, 16-10 win (Sept. 4) over Minnesota, also knocking down a pass in the same contest – all while lining up against All-Pro Chris Hinton...Registered a season-high 2 sacks vs. L.A. Rams (Oct. 9), including one of QB Chris Miller that ended the Rams' final drive as Miller also fumbled the football in the process...Sacked Bledsoe at New England (Oct. 2) among 5 total tackles, while also batting down a pass...Had a sack and forced a fumble (both on the same play) on the Bucs' Craig Erickson, and recovered a Vince Workman fumble on an attempted reverse – all in the second quarter – in the Packers' 30-3 win over Tampa Bay (Sept. 25)...Applied heavy pressure to Philadelphia QB Randall Cunningham in his initial return to the city where he played his first eight NFL seasons (Sept. 18), posting 3 solo tackles and drawing 2 holding penalties...Named to *SI* All-Pro team, he also was chosen second-team All-Pro by *AP, College & Pro Football Newsweekly* and *Football Digest*...Additionally voted to *UPI* and *Football News* All-NFC teams, in addition to selection as Pro Bowl starter...Along with the Bills' Smith, was honored in June of 1995 at the annual Mackey Awards banquet as the NFL's outstanding defensive linemen for the '94 season, selection coming in a vote of the league's players...As testimony to his characteristic candor, also was named to the 'All-Interview Team' of the Pro Football Writers of America...**1993:** Started all 16 games at left defensive end in his first Packers season and became an immediate team leader, both by example and contribution...Became NFL's all-time sacks leader in season's first Bears contest (Oct. 31), surpassing

THE PLAYERS

Taylor, and went on to close out year as NFC's 1993 co-leader (with Renaldo Turnbull of New Orleans) with 13...Led Green Bay's defensive line in total tackles with 98 (67 solo)...Also tied for team lead in forced fumbles (3) and fumble recoveries (2)...Elected to the Pro Bowl for the eighth consecutive year (as a starter in '93), he also was named a first-team All-Pro by *TSN* and was a second-team All-Pro choice of *AP, Football Digest* and *College & Pro Football Newsweekly*...Also tabbed for *UPI* and *Football News* All-NFC teams...Turned in exceptional performance in "reunion" meeting with Philadelphia (Sept. 12), posting 8 tackles, 1 sack and forcing 2 fumbles...Later named Pro Football Writers of America-Classic Games 'Player of the Week' for an outstanding, clutch effort vs. Denver (Oct. 10), when he had 5 tackles and 3 sacks, including sacks on consecutive plays (third and fourth down) late in the fourth quarter to seal a 30-27 victory for the Packers after the Broncos had advanced to the Green Bay 43-yard line...Contributed another sterling performance vs. Bears (Oct. 31), posting a season-high 10 tackles, 2 sacks and 1 forced fumble...Registered 7 tackles and 1 sack in a *Monday Night Football* appearance at Kansas City (Nov. 8)...Had 2 more sacks among his 8 tackles in the Packers' 19-17, come-from-behind win at New Orleans (Nov. 14) to earn NFC 'Defensive Player of the Week' honors...Recorded 6 tackles and 1 sack in Packers' 26-17 victory over Detroit at Milwaukee (Nov. 21)...Forged another dominating performance Dec. 26 vs. the L.A. Raiders, posting 8 tackles, 2½ sacks, 1 pass defensed and 1 fumble recovery – the latter forced by Butler off the Raiders' Randy Jordan, which White scooped up and ran 10 yards with before lateraling back to Butler, who ran 25 yards for a TD, giving Packers a 21-0 lead in an eventual 28-0 victory...Equaled '93 best with 10 total tackles, including a season-high 8 solo stops, in regular-season finale at Detroit (Jan. 2)...Started both postseason contests, played a significant defensive role in Packers' 28-24 playoff victory over the Lions (Jan. 8), collecting 4 tackles and sacking Detroit QB Kramer twice...**1992:** Led Eagles' defense in the first round of the NFC playoffs at New Orleans, making the two biggest plays of the game...The first came on a third-and-one for the Saints, which saw White stop RB Craig Heyward for no gain, forcing New Orleans to settle for a field goal...He then sacked QB Bobby Hebert to cause a subsequent safety, sealing a 36-20 win...A week later, in a 34-10 loss to eventual Super Bowl XXVII Champion Dallas, White weighed in with 7 tackles and a sack...Earlier finished regular season with 14 sacks...Had perhaps his best performance of season Nov. 22 at the N.Y. Giants, registering 3½ sacks, 7 QB hurries and 8 tackles...Posted season-high tackle total of 11 vs. the L.A. Raiders (Nov. 8), his output including 1½ sacks...Returned a fumble (by Phoenix QB Chris Chandler) 37 yards for the game's final touchdown against Cardinals...Played in his 120th consecutive non-strike game for Eagles in regular-season finale vs. Giants...Chosen to NFC's Pro Bowl squad for seventh consecutive season, an Eagles record...Named All-Pro by *PFW/PFWA*, Newspaper Enterprise Association, *College & Pro Football Newsweekly* and *Football Digest*...Also earned All-NFC recognition from *UPI* and was a second-team All-Pro selection by *AP*...**1991:** Was undisputed leader of the Eagles' defense, a unit that achieved a rare triple honor by ranking No. 1 in the NFL against the run, the pass and overall, in terms of fewest yards allowed...A near-unanimous first-team All-Pro pick, he subsequently was selected a starter in the Pro Bowl for the sixth straight year...Also was named NFL 'Defensive Player of the Year' by *PFW*...Closed out season as Eagles' leader in both QB sacks (15) and hurries (55)...Tied for second in the NFL in sacks with William Fuller (Oilers), trailing only Saints' Pat Swilling (17)...When he joined teammates Jerome Brown and Clyde Simmons as NFC starters in the Pro Bowl, it marked the first time since 1981 – and only the sixth time ever – that three defensive linemen from the same team were selected to the Pro Bowl...Made the 100th consecutive regular-season start of his career at Phoenix on Nov. 24...Had one of his finer days as an Eagle at Green Bay in the season opener – 3 sacks, 2 forced fumbles (one of which he recovered) and batted a Don Majkowski pass which then was intercepted by linemate Mike Golic...Forged other multiple sack performances vs. the Giants (Nov. 4), Cincinnati (Nov. 17) and Washington (Dec. 22), registering an interception vs. Bengals as Golic returned the favor, tipping a Boomer Esiason pass into the air for White...In a CBS Sports poll, conducted during the season and asking NFL club general managers which player they would build their defense around, White was named most often...**1990:** Selected as an NFC Pro Bowl starter for the fifth consecutive season...Earned near unanimous All-NFL acclaim and was named 'Defensive Lineman of the Year' by the NFL Players' Association...Led Eagles defense with 14 QB sacks, ranking second in the NFC to the 49ers' Charles Haley and fourth in NFL...Had season-high 3 sacks vs. Indianapolis (Sept. 30)...Made his first career interception on a deflected pass thrown by Washington QB Jeff Rutledge in a *Monday Night Football* matchup, returning it 33 yards...Sacked QB Jim Everett on Sept. 23 at the L.A. Rams, forcing a fumble which set up Eagles' first points of the game...**1989:** Was a Pro Bowl starter and a near-consensus first-team All-NFL and All-NFC pick...Recorded 11 sacks while helping Philadelphia set a team record of 62...Posted three multiple-sack games, including a season-high 2½-sack effort vs. the 49ers (Sept. 24)...Forced a fumble by Giants' Phil Simms that Eagles returned for a touchdown on opening series of a key matchup between NFC East leaders at Giants Stadium (Dec. 3)...**1988:** Led the NFL in sacks (18) for second straight year...Named NFL 'Player of the Year' by the Washington Touchdown Club and was a unanimous selection as a Pro Bowl starter...Finished second to Chicago's Mike Singletary in *AP* balloting for NFL defensive MVP, while gaining near-unanimous first-team All-NFL recognition...Had six multiple-sack games, including the third 4-sack game of his career (at Minnesota on Sept. 25)...Led Eagles' linemen with 133 total tackles...Earned NFC 'Defensive Player of the

MOST SACKS – POSTSEASON – PACKERS HISTORY (COMPILED SINCE 1982)	
8.0	REGGIE WHITE, 1993-97
4.0	Sean Jones, 1994-96
4.0	Keith McKenzie, 1996-97
3.0	Tony Bennett, 1990-93
3.0	LeRoy Butler, 1990-97
3.0	Bryce Paup, 1990-94

Month' honors in December, punctuating his performance with a 14-tackle, 2-sack effort at Dallas (Dec. 18)...**1987:** Paced the NFL with an NFC-record 21 sacks (one short of league standard of 22 set by Jets' Mark Gastineau in 1984) – in only 12 games as the season was abbreviated by a player strike...Named NFL 'Defensive Player of the Year' by *NEA*, NFL Films and *Touchdown* magazine...Also voted NFC 'Defensive Player of the Year' by *UPI, PFW* and the Kansas City Committee of 101, as well as garnering 'Defensive Lineman of the Year' recognition from NFL Alumni...Unanimous All-NFL selection and a Pro Bowl starter...Had a sack in 11 of the Eagles' 12 non-strike games, including nine multiple-sack contests...Stole the ball from Washington QB Doug Williams and ran 70 yards for his first NFL touchdown (Sept. 13)...**1986:** Selected as a Pro Bowl starter and subsequently became game's MVP when he tied a Pro Bowl record with 4 sacks...Earned first-team All-NFL and All-NFC honors after ranking third in both the league and conference in sacks (18, then an Eagles record) behind Taylor (20½) and the Redskins' Dexter Manley (18½)...Made 15 of his 18 sacks over the final eight games, including 3 at Dallas on Dec. 14 which earned him NFC 'Defensive Player of the Week' honors...**1985:** Officially became an Eagle on Sept. 20 when Philadelphia purchased his rights from the USFL's Memphis Showboats...Joined Eagles in Week 4 and went on to be named NFC 'Defensive Rookie of the Year' by the NFLPA, first-team NFL all-rookie and honorable mention All-Pro...Made memorable debut on Sept. 29 vs. N.Y. Giants, recording 2½ sacks and deflecting a pass which teammate Herman Edwards intercepted and returned for a touchdown...Became starting left defensive end the following week in 3-4 defense Eagles then were playing...Ended season tied for team lead in sacks with 13 (fifth in NFC)...Had played in 20 regular and postseason games for the Showboats prior to joining Philadelphia, earning first-team All-USFL honors after ranking third in the league with 12½ sacks...**1984:** Began pro career with Memphis Showboats in January and made USFL all-rookie team with 11-sack performance...Selected by Eagles as their first-round choice (the fourth player chosen overall) in the NFL's 1984 supplemental draft of USFL players.

COLLEGE: Nicknamed 'Minister of Defense,' he was a consensus All-American and Southeastern Conference 'Player of the Year' as a senior...Also was one of four finalists for the Lombardi Award, given annually to the nation's outstanding college lineman, his final season...Holds a B.A. degree in human services.

PERSONAL: Given name Reginald Howard White...Born in Chattanooga, Tenn. ...Married to Sara, couple has a son, Jeremy (born 5/12/86), and a daughter, Jecolia (born 5/24/88)...Attended Howard High School in Chattanooga, where he lettered three times in football (as a nose tackle and tight end) and basketball and once in track...Was an All-America choice in football and earned all-state selection in basketball...Known nearly as well for his work in the community as for his football accomplishments, he was saluted by the National Football League Players' Association in 1992, when it conferred the prestigious 'Byron "Whizzer" White Humanitarian Award' upon him for his "service to team, community and country in the spirit of Supreme Court Justice Byron White"...Was presented with the Simon Wiesenthal Center's 'Tolerance Award' in New York City in May of 1996, given to him "for his commitment to fostering tolerance and pursuing his vision for a better America"...Also was named as the winner of the 1996 'Jackie Robinson Humanitarian Award'...Working with community leaders, in April of 1997 launched Urban Hope Partnership, an effort to increase jobs, home ownership, entrepreneurship and education in

Green Bay's central-city neighborhoods; program graduated its first two classes (25 and 30 members, respectively), during this past offseason...Previously in 1995, he helped pioneer the Inner City Community Investment Corporation in Knoxville, Tenn. with a personal $1 million grant...In its first year of operation, the corporation's Knoxville Community Development Bank distributed micro loans to 89 people who either were small business owners or individuals wanting to start a small business – borrowers generally regarded by other banks as "at risk"...Had another busy offseason in 1998, as he appeared on several national television and radio programs, among them ABC-TV's *20/20* and CNN's *Crossfire*, and initiated several new projects...In June, announced the launch of 'Reggie White Studios, Inc.,' a joint venture with several investors, including Richard Monfort, co-owner of baseball's Colorado Rockies, and Rodney Linafelter, CEO of the Dakota Corporation...Studios will produce major motion pictures, made-for-TV movies and original television programming with a "family-safe" focus...Along with his family, embarked on a "Wisconsin Pilgrimage Tour" this past March, a 10-day tour of the Holy Land...White's family and 315 people traveled to the Middle East and visited such Holy sites as Jerusalem, the Sea of Galilee, Jericho and the Jordan River, where travelers had the opportunity to be baptized...The Whites plan to cruise the Greek Islands in May of 1999 to follow the footsteps of St. Paul...This past May, Reggie and his wife, Sara, became senior partners in the Alexis de Tocqueville Institution, a Virginia-based establishment that is involved with school choice, urban economic hope, revitalization of communities and the securing of people's basic rights...In 1998, will serve as the spokesperson for 'Lifeline,' a Merivision long-distance telephone company that donates 10 percent of its proceeds to charities across the United States, with White's own proceeds being given to Urban Hope...Has two new books coming out this fall, *God's Playbook*, a devotional bible written along with Steve Hubbard, and *Complete Image of God*, co-authored by Andrew Payton Thomas...Also is scheduled to introduce a career memoir video, *Why I Play the Game*, a motivational documentary, with a soundtrack which will be available on CD...A bean bag baby bearing his likeness also is set to be sold this fall...An avid wrestling fan, he lost to former Chicago Bear and Green Bay Packer Steve McMichael in a WCW pay-per-view match in May of 1997...Appeared as a gymnastics coach, coaching U.S. Olympian Kerry Strug, in a 1997 episode of CBS-TV's *Touched By An Angel*...Earlier, had been a celebrity contestant on the television game show *Jeopardy*...Along with teammate Brett Favre, appeared on a television commercial for Edge Shave Gel in 1997...Opened his second retail store, 'One On Sport,' in Atlanta in July of 1997, after opening an initial football merchandise store, 'Reggie White's Pro Shop,' in Green Bay during the 1996 playoffs...Also is an investor in two 18-hole golf courses, starting the second – 'Royal Oaks Golf Course' in Maryville, Tenn. – in the '97 offseason with a consortium of other NFL players past and present...Had produced his autobiography, starred in a movie and filmed an instructional video during the 1996 offseason...Penned his autobiography, entitled *In the Trenches*, in collaboration with Jim Denney, which was published in the fall of 1996, with a second edition that came out in September of 1997...Beginning in May of 1996, filmed the movie *Reggie's Prayer* in Portland, Ore., a story about a professional football player who retires so he can work with at-risk teens...The film, which was released to theaters early in 1997 and later, to home video, included actors Pat Morita, Cylk Cozart and Melba Joyce, in addition to NFL personalities Mike Holmgren, Favre, Keith Jackson, Bryce Paup, Gale Sayers, Rosey Grier, Jerome Bettis, William Roaf and Eddie George...In another '96 offseason project, Reggie filmed an instructional video for defensive linemen...During the 1989-92 seasons, Reggie spent his post-practice Friday afternoons on Philadelphia street corners, trying to educate area youngsters about the perils of drugs and alcohol as well as on the importance of staying in school...An ordained minister, he has preached regularly in churches of various denominations and on the streets...Is a member of The Inner City Church in Knoxville, Tenn., which was destroyed by fire during the early morning hours of Jan. 8, 1996, in an apparent case of arson...Since that time, more than $230,000 of the approximately $1 million needed to rebuild has been raised from Wisconsin residents in a strong outpouring of support, with another $5,000 having been raised by Knoxville community leaders; the church re-opened this past spring...Appeared on NBC-TV's *Unsolved Mysteries* program early in 1996 as the burning of his church was profiled...A large portion of the proceeds from his 1991 book, *The Reggie White Touch Football Playbook: Winning Plays, Rules and Safety Tips*, was earmarked for the maternity home which he and Sara formerly maintained on their property...His multiple off-the-field interests include a three-piece line of home fitness equipment, 'Reggie White's All-Pro Workout System'...An impressionist of some note, he can "present" a highly credible Muhammad Ali, Rodney Dangerfield, Clint Eastwood, Elvis Presley and Bill Cosby...He also can perform a realistic imitation of a growling guard dog...Hobby: "spending time with my family"...Residence: Green Bay.

PRO STATISTICS:

NFL STATISTICS

Year		G/S	UT	AT	Sacks	Int.	Yds.	FR	FF	PD
1985	Philadelphia	13/12	62	38	13	0	0	2	0	0
1986	Philadelphia	16/16	83	15	18	0	0	0	1	5
1987	Philadelphia	12/12	62	14	21	0	0	1	4	0
1988	Philadelphia	16/16	96	37	18	0	0	2	1	0
1989	Philadelphia	16/16	82	41	11	0	0	2	3	2
1990	Philadelphia	16/16	59	24	14	1	33	1	4	4
1991	Philadelphia	16/16	72	28	15	1	0	3	2	13
1992	Philadelphia	16/16	54	27	14	0	0	1	3	2
1993	Green Bay	16/16	67	31	13	0	0	2	3	2
1994	Green Bay	16/15	41	18	8	0	0	1	2	7
1995	Green Bay	15/13	37	9	12	0	0	0	2	4
1996	Green Bay	16/16	21	15	8½	1	46	3	3	6
1997	Green Bay	16/16	36	10	11	0	0	2	0	6
Totals		200/196	772	307	176½	3	79	20	28	51
Playoffs		18/17	46	4	12	0	0	0	1	1

Touchdowns: 2, 70-yard fumble return at Washington (9/13/87) and 37-yard fumble return at Phoenix (9/13/92)
Safeties: 2, vs. Washington (12/8/85) and at New Orleans (1/3/93-postseason)
Blocked Field Goals: 2, at N.Y. Giants (10/12/86) and vs. St. Louis Cardinals (12/7/86)
Blocked PATs: 1, vs. Atlanta (10/30/88)
Blocked Punts: 1, vs. Tampa Bay (10/27/96)

USFL STATISTICS

Year		G/S	UT	AT	Sacks	Int.	FR	FF
1984	Memphis	16/16	52	43	11	0	1	2
1985	Memphis	18/18	68	30	12½	0	1	5
Totals		34/34	120	73	23½	0	2	7
Playoffs		2/2	NA	NA	NA	NA	NA	NA

Touchdowns: 1, 30-yard fumble return vs. Birmingham (5/3/85)

DOUG WIDELL | 74

Offensive Guard
College: Boston College
NFL Exp.: 10th Season   **Packers Exp.:** 2nd Season
Ht.: 6-4   **Wt.:** 285   **Born:** 9/23/66   **Acq:** FA-98

PRO: Long-time NFL guard with nine years of starting experience...Returns for his second stint with the Packers after spending the 1993 season as the team's left guard...Likely will compete for a roster spot as a backup at both guard spots...Also offers veteran insurance at the vacant left guard position where younger players are slated to compete for the starting job...Gritty player who will battle his opponent to the dying end...Has played for Denver (1989-92), Green Bay (1993), Detroit (1994-95) and Indianapolis (1996-97)...Did not miss a game until the 1995 season and has sat out only five contests (all in '95) over his entire nine-year pro career...Possessor of 139 career games played, including

126 starts...Also has started nine playoff contests, including two AFC Championship Games (1989, 1991) and one Super Bowl (XXIV)..."He did a pretty good job for us when he was here before," says Tom Lovat, Green Bay's offensive line coach. "Then he went over to Detroit and we watched him – he played about the same there. And about the same in Indianapolis. Right now Doug is insurance for us, and he knows that. He's a veteran, and if you get into a situation where he had to play you know you're going to get a professional job from him. Those old pros, they're nice to have around in those roles – they've been there."...Was primarily a right guard early in his pro career (1989-92, also 1994), but has played more left guard in recent years (1993, 1995-97)...Signed with Green Bay as a free agent on April 22, 1998, after being terminated by the Colts on Feb. 20...**1997:** Served as the starting left guard for Indianapolis for the second straight season...Started all 16 games...Part of an offensive line which helped the Colts rush for 100-or-more yards in seven of their last eight games...**1996:** Was one of only four Colts players to start all 16 regular-season games (all at left guard) in his initial year with Indianapolis...Also started playoff loss at Pittsburgh (Dec. 29)...Had signed with the Colts as an unrestricted free agent on March 18...**1995:** Moved to left guard in his second season with the Lions, starting 11 times...Was inactive for two early-season games with an ankle injury, including Sept. 17 contest with Arizona which snapped a streak of 98 consecutive games played (106 including playoffs)...It also marked the first game he had missed during his first seven NFL seasons...Later was inactive for Detroit's final two regular-season games plus playoff contest at Philadelphia (Dec. 30) due to an ankle injury...Also dressed, but did not play, in mid-season game vs. Cleveland...Played a part in Barry Sanders' No. 2 league ranking in both rushing yards (1,500) and total yards from scrimmage (1,898)...**1994:** Stepped into the starting lineup at right guard for Detroit after jumping to the Lions in free agency...Missed only one play all year (Dec. 10 at N.Y. Jets) while starting all 16 regular-season games...Also started club's playoff loss at Green Bay (Dec. 31)...Played a part in a Detroit offense which led the NFC in rushing (and was third overall in the NFL) with 2,080 yards...Helped open holes for league rushing champion Sanders (1,883 yards), who had 10 100-yard games...Had signed with Detroit as an unrestricted free agent on June 2...**1993:** Joined Green Bay late in training camp, coming over in a trade with the Broncos...Played in all 16 regular-season games for the Packers, making nine starts...Backed up both guard spots over the first half of the season, starting at left guard vs. Denver (Oct. 10) when Frank Winters slid over to center in place of an injured James Campen...Later became the full-time starter at left guard for the final eight games of the season, beginning with contest at New Orleans (Nov. 14), when regular starter Rich Moran irritated a previous knee injury in practice prior to Saints game and subsequently went on injured reserve...Also started both playoff games, at Detroit and at Dallas...Had been acquired in an Aug. 24 trade with Denver in exchange for the Packers' seventh-round pick in 1994...**1992:** Starting all 16 games at right guard, boosted his total of consecutive regular-season starts to 58 in his final year with Denver...Along with right tackle Ken Lanier, was one of only two Bronco offensive players to start every game from 1990-92...**1991:** Was in the starting lineup at right guard for all 16 games for the second straight season...Also started both of the club's playoff contests...**1990:** Started all 16 games (all at right guard) for the first time in his pro career...Was one of only four Denver offensive players to start every game...**1989:** Moved into the starting lineup at right guard prior to the Broncos' seventh game, Oct. 22 at Seattle...While playing in all 16 regular-season games, he started the final 10...Also started all three playoff contests, including the team's Super Bowl XXIV loss to San Francisco...Earned selection to the all-rookie team of *College & Pro Football Newsweekly*...Was the first of two second-round draft choices (41st overall) by Denver in 1989.

COLLEGE: Two-year starter and three-time letterman (1986-88) at Boston College...Played right tackle as a senior, taking over the position of his brother, Dave, who had graduated...Had played alongside Dave at right guard as a junior...Saw the majority of his action on special teams in 1986...Was second on the depth chart at left guard in 1985, but did not letter...Redshirted in 1984...Holds a B.S. degree in marketing.

PERSONAL: Given name Douglas Joseph Widell...Born in Hartford, Conn. ...Married to Colleen, couple has one daughter, Morgan (born 1/20/95), and one son, Matthew (born 7/16/97)...Attended South Catholic High School in Hartford, Conn., lettering twice as a two-way tackle...Earned all-state and all-conference honors...Played with his brother, Dave (Atlanta Falcons), from 1990-92 with Denver to become only the sixth brother combination in NFL history to play together at the same time, for the same team, at the same position (offensive line)...Was a spokesperson for Indiana Family and Social Services Fatherhood Campaign while with the Colts...Hobbies include woodwork, golf and spending time with his family...Residence: Parker, Colo.

PRO STATISTICS:

Games/Starts—Denver 1989 (16/10); 1989 Playoffs (3/3); 1990 (16/16); 1991 (16/16); 1991 Playoffs (2/2); 1992 (16/16); Green Bay 1993 (16/9); 1993 Playoffs (2/2); Detroit 1994 (16/16); 1994 Playoffs (1/1); 1995 (11/11); 1995 Playoffs (0/0); Indianapolis 1996 (16/16); 1996 Playoffs (1/1); 1997 (16/16). Career totals: 139/126. Playoff totals: 9/9.

BRUCE WILKERSON) 64

Offensive Tackle
College: *Tennessee*
NFL Exp.: *12th Season*   **Packers Exp.:** *3rd Season*
Ht.: *6-5*   **Wt.:** *315*   **Born:** *7/28/64*   **Acq:** *FA-96*

PRO: A versatile, veteran offensive lineman who can step in at either tackle spot and also has seen action at the guard position...Adds quality depth and experience across the line...Begins his 12th year as a pro, a career in which he has played in 147 regular-season games, including 94 starts...Has 11 additional games of playoff experience (six starts)...Last season marked the fourth occasion in his NFL career that he had played in every game for his team, though the first time since 1991 with the then-Los Angeles Raiders..."Bruce brings the experience factor to our line," says Green Bay offensive line coach Tom Lovat. "When he's in there, you don't worry. He's a cagey, smart, but not real physical guy at this point of his career. He's been through the war and gets the job done."...Originally drafted by the Raiders, he was with the Silver and Black for eight seasons (1987-94), playing in 107 regular-season games with 89 starts...Subsequently spent the 1995 campaign with the first-year Jacksonville Jaguars before signing with Green Bay on the eve of the 1996 draft (April 19)...**1997:** Played in all 16 regular-season games for the first time in his two-year career with the Packers, primarily on special teams, but did start three games at right tackle...Got into all three playoff games, including Super Bowl XXXII, in a special teams role...Started for injured Earl Dotson (back) at right tackle in wins over Tampa Bay (Oct. 5) and at Chicago (Oct. 12)...Also got the start for Dotson (ankle/turf toe) against Miami (Sept. 14) as the Packers gained 142 yards rushing...Filled in for Dotson (shoulder) at Carolina (Dec. 14), playing the entire second half at right tackle...Came in for Dotson (concussion) late in the third quarter vs. St. Louis (Nov. 9) and played the remainder of the game...Saw action on special teams the other 11 games...Battled through back spasms during training camp to return to practice on a limited basis for the first time on Aug. 10, he subsequently played in the club's fourth preseason game, vs. Buffalo at Toronto (Aug. 16)...**1996:** Moved into the Packers' starting left tackle position the last week of the regular season after serving as the primary reserve at both tackle spots throughout most of the year...Remained at left tackle through the playoffs, providing steady play and peace of mind as the Packers captured Super Bowl XXXI...Saw action in 14 regular-season games, including two starts, he was inactive for the club's two other contests...Assumed the starting left tackle position from rookie John Michels in the regular-season finale vs. Minnesota (Dec. 22) and held the spot from that point forward...Did not allow a sack through the first two postseason games, he also helped to pave the way for a 479-yard offensive performance – a season high and a Green Bay postseason record – in NFC Championship Game victory over Carolina (Jan. 12)...Earlier had started at right tackle in win over Tampa Bay (Oct. 27) as usual starter Dotson was inactive due to an ankle injury...Stepped in for Dotson against San Francisco (Oct. 14), playing the majority of the second half and overtime in 23-20 triumph over the 49ers...Also saw some action vs. Detroit (Nov. 3) after Dotson left the game briefly with back spasms...Received the bulk of his early-season playing time on special teams...Was inactive at Seattle (Sept. 29) and at Chicago (Oct. 6)...**1995:** Signed with the expansion Jacksonville Jaguars as an unrestricted free agent on June 15...Played in 10 games for Jacksonville in a reserve capacity, seeing action primarily on special teams, before his offseason release on April 17, 1996...**1994:** Got into 11 games, making six starts, for the Raiders in his final season in Los Angeles...Was inactive for

the last five contests of the year...**1993:** Started 14 regular-season games, missing two contests (Sept. 12 at Seattle and Sept. 19 vs. Cleveland) due to a knee injury...Also started both of the club's playoff contests...**1992:** Started Raiders' first 15 games at left tackle...Placed on injured reserve Dec. 22 with a broken right foot...**1991:** Started all 16 games plus wild-card playoff contest against Kansas City at left tackle...Was granted free agency Feb. 1 through 'Plan B,' but re-signed with the Raiders on July 24...**1990:** Saw action in eight games, making one start, as well as reserve duty in both playoff contests after missing the first half of the season on injured reserve (Sept. 4-Nov. 3) with a knee injury...In his first game back, he started at left tackle at Kansas City (Nov. 4)...**1989:** Was a starter at tackle in all 16 games...**1988:** Started all 16 games during the season, 15 at right guard and one at right tackle...**1987:** Developed quickly as a pro pass protector and a powerful run blocker in his rookie season...Played in 11 games, starting five...Drafted in the second round (52nd overall) by the Los Angeles Raiders in 1987.

COLLEGE: A three-year starter and four-time letterman at Tennessee (1983-86)...Redshirted in 1982...Was one of the nation's top offensive linemen as a senior, when he earned honorable mention All-America recognition from the *Associated Press* and *United Press International*...Also was a consensus first-team All-Southeast Conference selection...Chosen second-team All-America by *The Sporting News* his junior year, in addition to winning All-SEC laurels...Majored in sociology.

PERSONAL: Given name Bruce Alan Wilkerson...Born in Loudon, Tenn. ...Married to Antionette...He has two children, a daughter, Starkicia Nicole (born 11/2/86), and a son, Jeremy (born 2/25/92)...Was an all-state and all-county choice in football at Loudon (Tenn.) High School...Lettered three years as an offensive and defensive tackle...Also earned two letters in basketball as a center...Named all-county and was elected team captain of hoops squad as a senior...Hobbies include hunting, fishing and tinkering with cars and motorcycles...Made a donation to the Loudon (Tenn.) Quarterback Club in recent years to help pay for lights to be installed at the pee-wee football field...Residence: Knoxville, Tenn.

PRO STATISTICS:

Games/Starts—L.A. Raiders 1987 (11/5); 1988 (16/16); 1989 (16/16); 1990 (8/1); 1990 Playoffs (2/0); 1991 (16/16); 1991 Playoffs (1/1); 1992 (15/15); 1993 (14/14); 1993 Playoffs (2/2); 1994 (11/6); Jacksonville 1995 (10/0); Green Bay 1996 (14/2); 1996 Playoffs (3/3); 1997 (16/3); 1997 Playoffs (3/0). Career totals: 147/94. Playoff totals: 11/6.

BRIAN WILLIAMS   51

Linebacker
College: Southern California
NFL Exp.: 4th Season   **Packers Exp.:** 4th Season
Ht.: 6-1   **Wt.:** 245   **Born:** 12/17/72   **Acq:** D3c-95

PRO: On the verge of Pro Bowl status entering the 1998 campaign, has developed into one of the outstanding young linebackers in the NFL as he heads into his fourth season...Has put together two top-notch seasons at his weakside (right outside) linebacker spot for the Packers while starting 32 consecutive regular-season games for the Green and Gold (38 including playoffs)...Emerging after a non-descript rookie season in 1995 which saw him slowed by injury, he has become a major player on one of the NFL's best defenses the last two years...Has averaged just under 100 tackles per season (98) during his two seasons as a starter...Only beginning to receive the recognition he assuredly deserves, was named to the All-Pro team of *USA Today* last season...An every-down player, he possesses great speed and is one of the Packers' best tacklers...Green Bay defensive coordinator Fritz Shurmur is one who has seen first-hand how Williams has elevated his play, saying, "Brian has had two exceptional years as a starter at outside linebacker for us in our base defense and also as the starting linebacker in our 'nickel' and 'dime' defenses. He has exceptional ability and instincts – speed and toughness – and all the things that it takes to be an outstanding linebacker in this league. Brian is a very bright, instinctive player who achieves at a high level.

I look for him to take another step. I think the Pro Bowl has eluded him, but I think he has the potential to have that kind of year – and we're looking forward to having it happen this year."...Made such an immediate impact at 'Plugger' (right outside) linebacker in the '96 preseason that incumbent George Koonce was moved inside to the middle linebacker position in the final weeks of training camp...Went on to finish second on the team in tackles that year, then tied for the club lead in stops during the Packers' postseason run to capture Super Bowl XXXI...**1997:** Opened all 16 regular-season games for the second straight year at weakside linebacker...Also started all three playoff contests, including Super Bowl XXXII...Tied (with LeRoy Butler) for third on the team in tackles with 101 (74 solo) – his first 100-tackle season as a pro...Also registered 1 sack, 2 interceptions, 1 fumble recovery and a career-high 6 passes defensed...Tabbed for the All-Pro team of *USA Today*...Earned Miller Lite 'Player of the Week' honors at Chicago (Oct. 12) as he played one of the finest games of his pro career...Intercepted an Erik Kramer pass at the Packers' 47-yard line late in the second quarter and returned it 25 yards to the Bears' 28, setting up a Green Bay touchdown six plays later...Also posted 10 tackles against the Bears, while breaking up a season-high 2 passes...Turned in another strong performance the following week at New England (Oct. 27), when he made 9 tackles, intercepted a Drew Bledsoe pass – the second straight game he made an INT – and tipped another aerial...Pressured Lions QB Scott Mitchell into a second-quarter interception, which teammate Darren Sharper returned 50 yards for a touchdown, in the Packers' 20-10 victory over Detroit (Nov. 2)...Had a team-leading and season-high 11 tackles in win over Miami (Sept. 14)...Turned in a fine all-around performance vs. Tampa Bay (Oct. 5), when he made 4 tackles, recovered a Warrick Dunn fumble (which led to Green Bay touchdown) and batted down a Trent Dilfer pass late in the second quarter of 21-16 win over the Bucs...Recorded the first full sack of his career in the Packers' 31-10 victory at Carolina (Dec. 14)...Finished third on the team in tackles during the postseason with 20 (12 solo), including 8 in the Packers' 23-10 NFC Championship Game win at San Francisco (Jan. 11)...**1996:** Started all 16 regular-season games at the 'Plugger' linebacker spot...Finished second on the club with 95 tackles, including 60 solo stops...Also tied with Reggie White for the team lead with 3 fumble recoveries, to go along with 4 passes defensed...Started each of the club's three postseason games, including Super Bowl XXXI, and tied Butler for the team lead in tackles with 15...Also had an interception, a fumble recovery and a forced fumble in the playoffs...Had such a strong training camp at 'Plugger' linebacker that '95 starter Koonce was moved inside in the final weeks of the preseason...Made a career-high 16 tackles vs. Tampa Bay (Oct. 27) and helped to seal a Green Bay win when he combined with Butler to sack the Bucs' Dilfer on a fourth-down play with 1:14 left in the game and the Packers clinging to a 13-7 lead...Had 15 tackles in the Packers' overtime win over San Francisco (Oct. 14)...Forced and recovered a William Floyd fumble early in the fourth quarter of divisional playoff win over San Francisco (Jan. 4) among his 6 solo tackles...Also had 6 stops vs. Carolina in the NFC Championship Game (Jan. 12)...Contributed 3 tackles and intercepted a bobbled Bledsoe pass, taking the ball away from New England for the final time, in the Packers' Super Bowl triumph (Jan. 26)...Made 6 tackles and recovered a fumble in the Packers' win at St. Louis (Nov. 24) despite fighting the flu...Turned in another fine performance, this time vs. Denver (Dec. 8), when he had 3 tackles, a pass defensed near the goal line and a fumble recovery in the Packers' 41-6 win...Showed his tremendous speed against Philadelphia (Sept. 9), when he chased down the Eagles' Irving Fryar from behind at the Green Bay 1-yard line after Fryar had the ball lateraled to him from teammate Chris T. Jones at the Packers' 34...Had emerged as a player who had to be on the field by leading the team in tackles during the preseason with 23...**1995:** Bothered by a chronic groin injury which limited his development, served as a backup to Koonce at 'Plugger' linebacker as a rookie...Played in 13 regular-season games, primarily on special teams...Recorded 6 tackles as a member of the kick coverage units...Made a career-high 2 special teams stops vs. Cincinnati (Dec. 3)...Made key recovery of an onside kick late in 14-6 win over N.Y. Giants (Sept. 17)...Was inactive for the last three games of October (Detroit, Minnesota and at Detroit)...Got into all three playoff contests on special teams...Originally suffered groin injury on June 1 in a rookie mini-camp...Subsequently missed first several weeks of training camp until he returned to practice on Aug. 7...Was the third of the Packers' four selections in the third round (73rd overall) in 1995.

COLLEGE: A three-year starter and four-time letterman (1991-94) at Southern California...Totaled 264 tackles (185 solo), including 7 sacks and 32 for loss, for Trojans...Also had 2 interceptions, 5 forced fumbles, 3 fumble recoveries and 7 pass breakups...Earned second-team All-Pacific 10 Conference honors as a senior, when he made 79 tackles, including a team-best 10 stops for loss and 3 sacks...Also served as USC's co-captain...Chosen 'Defensive MVP' of the East-West Shrine Game following his senior season...Was second on the team with 69 tackles as a junior...Led the Trojans in tackles as a sophomore with 91, including 13 for loss and 3 sacks...Holds degree in public administration.

PERSONAL: Given name Brian Marcee Williams...Nicknamed 'B-Dub'...Born in Dallas...Single...An All-America selection in football as a senior at Bishop Dunne High School in Dallas...Named as state's 'Athlete of the Year' in 3-A...Led team to a 12-0 record and Texas 3-A championship in 1990...Lettered three times as a linebacker, running back and punter...Collected 143 tackles, 6 sacks, 17 forced fumbles, 6 fumble recoveries (4 for TDs) and had 4 interceptions...Also was an all-district choice and conference 'Defensive Player of the Year'...Gained 144 yards and scored 2 touchdowns on just 7 carries in 1990 state semifinal game, he subsequently rushed for 126 yards and 2 TDs in title contest...Named all-state, all-district and was league 'Defensive Player of the Year' as a junior, when he had 117 tackles, 5 interceptions and 4 fumble recoveries...High school team finished second in the state his junior year and was state champion his sophomore season...Also was an all-district choice in basketball (three letters), baseball (four letters) and track (three letters)...Fulfilled promise to his family and completed college courses in May of 1996, graduating with a degree in public administration...Has sponsored kids at his prep alma mater, Bishop Dunne, paying for a portion of their tuition...As a youngster performed in a saxophone quartet that played gospel music in Dallas churches...Hobbies include playing video games (John Madden football is a favorite)...Residence: Dallas.

PRO STATISTICS:

Year		G/S	UT	AT	Sacks	Int.	Yds.	LG	FR	FF	PD
1995	Green Bay	13/0	0	0	0	0	0	0	0	0	0
1996	Green Bay	16/16	60	35	½	0	0	0	3	0	4
1997	Green Bay	16/16	74	27	1	2	30	25	1	0	6
Totals		**45/32**	**134**	**62**	**1½**	**2**	**30**	**25**	**4**	**0**	**10**
Playoffs		**9/6**	**24**	**11**	**0**	**1**	**16**	**16**	**1**	**1**	**1**

Special Teams Tackles: 6 (2-4) in 1995

TYRONE WILLIAMS   37

Cornerback
College: Nebraska
NFL Exp.: 3rd Season   **Packers Exp.:** 3rd Season
Ht.: 5-11   **Wt.:** 192   **Born:** 5/31/73   **Acq:** D3b-96

PRO: Third-year pro who in 1997 unwittingly became a starter when Craig Newsome went down on the first play of the season...A fierce competitor who is not afraid to come up and play bump-and-run coverage, traits which belie his soft-spoken demeanor off the field...Is a proven winner who has been on a championship team at every level of competition (high school, college, pro) and, amazingly, has played in a title game each year since 1993..."I think Tyrone Williams exhibited as a rookie two years ago that he had the ability to be able to play in this league," says Green Bay defensive coordinator Fritz Shurmur. "People attacked him and challenged him, and he responded magnificently. He has the perfect temperament for playing – he's a tough, competitive guy who is unaffected by the last play. And as a result, he has the capacity to be able to challenge on every down. Last season he was thrust into the role of being a full-time starter for us and immediately became a big contributor to our team."...After filling Newsome's spot at left cornerback last season, in 1998 moves back to his more natural position of right corner following the departure of Doug Evans in free agency...Had regularly contributed as a 1996 rookie, subbing in when the Packers put extra defensive backs onto the field in passing situations..."Tyrone has a great background from the standpoint of competitive football," Shurmur adds. "He comes from Nebraska, has played in a lot of big games and showed that from the very beginning. Plus, he's a mature guy. And he's a good tackler who always plays hard."...Now has played in a championship game in five consecutive seasons – 1993-95 at the University of Nebraska and 1996-97 with the Packers – he ended up on the winning side of the ledger in the middle three contests, narrowly losing the first and the last...Is the first player ever to play on back-to-back collegiate national championship teams (Nebraska 1994-95), then play for a Super Bowl winner in his rookie year (Green Bay 1996)...Earlier, as a 1989 sophomore, his Manatee High School (Bradenton, Fla.) team had won a Florida state prep title...**1997:** Playing in all 16 regular-season games for the second straight year, started the final 15 at left cornerback after usual starter Newsome suffered a season-ending knee injury on the year's first play from scrimmage...Also started all three playoff contests, including Super Bowl XXXII...Led the team in passes defensed for the first time with 13...Also had a career-high 74 tackles (fifth on team), 1 interception and forced 2 fumbles during the regular season...Made a career-best 10 stops (8 solo) in initial meeting with the Lions, Sept. 28 at Detroit...Forced a Warrick Dunn fumble among 9 total stops the following week in 21-16 win over Tampa Bay (Oct. 5), the turnover at the Bucs' 24-yard line three plays later led to a Green Bay touchdown and a 7-3 advantage...Enjoyed a breakthrough game in 28-10, Monday night triumph at New England (Oct. 27) as he made two big defensive efforts in the Packers' third-quarter goal-line stand...Broke up passes on consecutive plays (third and fourth down) while covering the Patriots' Ben Coates and Keith Byars, respectively, with Green Bay clinging to a slim 14-10 margin right after halftime...Made his lone interception of the year in regular-season finale vs. Buffalo (Dec. 20), picking off Alex Van Pelt...Had forced a fumble late in 31-10 victory at Carolina six days earlier...Limited the Cowboys' Anthony Miller and Vikings' Jake Reed to just 4 receptions combined in successive wins over Dallas (Nov. 23) and at Minnesota (Dec. 1)...Made his first-ever NFL start in Week 2 at Philadelphia (Sept. 7), responding with 6 tackles...Had played virtually the entire season opener vs. Chicago (Sept. 1) as Newsome was sidelined right away...Additionally led the Packers in passes defensed during the postseason with 6, including a season-high (and career-best tying) 3 in the NFC Championship Game win at San Francisco (Jan. 11)...Also forced a fumble among 6 total tackles against the Niners...Caused the Broncos' Terrell Davis to fumble on the first play from scrimmage of the second half in Super Bowl XXXII (Jan. 25), recovering it himself to set up a Ryan Longwell field goal which evened the score at 17...Earlier had intercepted the Bucs' Trent Dilfer late in the first half of 21-7, divisional playoff victory over Tampa Bay (Jan. 4), leading to a Longwell field goal which made the score 13-7 heading into the locker room...Finished the postseason with 11 solo tackles to tie for seventh on the team...**1996:** Contributed throughout his rookie year in the 'dime' package of Green Bay's top-rated pass defense...Played in all 16 regular-season games plus the team's three playoff contests, including Super Bowl XXXI...Was second in total tackles (to Mike Prior) among the Packers' non-starters during the regular season with 22 (19 solo), he also broke up 6 passes...Additionally made 12 special teams tackles to tie for third on the club, adding 1 fumble recovery with the coverage units...Really stepped the level of his play up at the end of the regular season and throughout the playoffs...Rose to the occasion when challenged by Carolina in the NFC Championship Game (Jan. 12), equaling his career best of 3 passes defensed...Among those breakups was his first interception as a pro, a sensational, diving grab of an errant Kerry Collins throw in the final minute of the first half, which subsequently led to a field goal that put Green Bay ahead 17-10 at halftime of the eventual 30-13 triumph...Had been partner to a series of never-ending blocks on the 49ers' Curtis Buckley during Desmond Howard's 71-yard punt return for a touchdown to open the scoring a week earlier vs. San Francisco in the divisional playoffs (Jan. 4)...Made 1 stop against New England in the Super Bowl...Posted a season-best 5 tackles and established his career high for passes defensed (3) in second meeting with the Lions, at Detroit (Dec. 15)... Recorded a career-high 2 special teams tackles in four different games: at Seattle (Sept. 29), vs. Detroit (Nov. 3), at Detroit (Dec. 15) and vs. San Francisco in the playoffs (Jan. 4)...Recovered a fumble on kickoff coverage vs. San Diego (Sept. 15)...Saw his most extensive action of the season on Nov. 10 at Kansas City when he replaced starting right cornerback Evans, who was ejected after the first play of the second quarter...Made 1 tackle and broke up 1 pass against the Chiefs...Was the second of two third-round draft choices (93rd overall) by Green Bay in 1996.

COLLEGE: Was a three-year starter (1993-95) at right cornerback for Nebraska after sitting out his 1992 freshman season...Finished with 95 career tackles (64 solo), including 3 for loss, plus 5 interceptions, 11 passes defensed, 4 fumble recoveries and 1 forced fumble...Earned first-team All-Big Eight Conference honors as a junior and senior...Had the opportunity to play in three straight national championship games (two Orange Bowls, one Fiesta Bowl), with the Cornhuskers emerging victorious each of the last two years...Started all 12 games as a senior, including title matchup with Florida in the Fiesta Bowl...Missed only the West Virginia game, starting every other contest, in 1994, when he posted career highs in tackles (38), interceptions (3) and passes defensed (5)...Contributed 4 stops in Orange Bowl triumph over Miami

(Fla.) as a junior...Moved into the starting lineup in the fourth game of 1993, eventually earning conference 'Co-Defensive Newcomer of the Year' honors from Big Eight coaches...Tied for the conference lead with 3 fumble recoveries...Had career-high numbers in tackles (9) and passes defensed (3) in 18-16, Orange Bowl loss to Florida State in '93 national title bout...Majored in family science.

PERSONAL: Given name Upton Tyrone Williams...Born in Bradenton, Fla. ...Married to Shantel, couple has two sons, Cameron (born 8/7/88) and Michael (born 9/20/89), and one daughter, Tyra (born 1/13/98)...Was an all-state selection in football and basketball at Manatee High School in Bradenton, Fla. ...Earned three letters in football, four in basketball and two in track...Was a teammate of quarterback Tommie Frazier in both high school and college...Along with Frazier and another college teammate, Barron Miles, helped to save a neighbor's house from burning down in the summer of 1993...Took time prior to the 1995 Orange Bowl game with Miami to speak to kids in the Dade County housing projects about staying in school and identifying good role models...Enjoys working with underprivileged children...Held the first-ever 'Tyrone Williams Charity Weekend' this past May in his hometown of Bradenton, the event consisted of a celebrity basketball camp as well as a football clinic for kids age 8 up through college...Hobbies include fishing and watching movies with his family...Splits residence between Green Bay and Bradenton, Fla.

PRO STATISTICS:

Year		G/S	UT	AT	Sacks	Int.	Yds.	LG	FR	FF	PD
1996	Green Bay...............16/0		19	3	0	0	0	0	0	0	6
1997	Green Bay..............16/15		58	16	0	1	0	0	0	2	13
Totals	.....................32/15		77	19	0	1	0	0	0	2	19
Playoffs	........................6/3		13	0	0	2	14	14	1	2	9

Special Teams Tackles: 12 (9-3) in 1996; 3 (1-2) in 1996 Playoffs; 1 (1-0) in 1997 for total of 13 (10-3)

Special Teams Fumble Recoveries: 1 in 1996

MATT WILLIG · 76

Offensive Tackle
College: *Southern California*
NFL Exp.: *6th Season*   **Packers Exp.:** *1st Season*
Ht.: *6-7* **Wt.:** *315* **Born:** *1/21/69* **Acq:** *UFA-98 (Atl)*

PRO: A towering, versatile offensive lineman who possesses ample NFL starting experience...Will compete for a roster spot in Green Bay as a backup, swing tackle after joining the team in the offseason as an unrestricted free agent...Has played in 62 games since entering the league as an undrafted player in 1992 with the New York Jets, starting 28 contests, including 13 career starts at the all-important left tackle position...Also has played guard and once lined up as a tight end...A defensive end in college at USC, successfully made the transition to offensive tackle in the early part of his NFL career..."He brings experience to the position and he has started in the league," says Packers offensive line coach Tom Lovat. "We'll get him some action in the preseason and let him compete with the rest of the guys. If he's going to make the team, his role would be to swing between both tackles."...Spent parts of four seasons with the N.Y. Jets (1992-95), followed by two years with the Atlanta Falcons (1996-97) before moving to the Packers this past May 5...**1997:** Played in all 16 contests for the third time in his career, starting the last 13 at right tackle for Atlanta...Contributed to the team's strong 7-4 finish following an 0-5 start...Had seen duty as a reserve tackle in the club's initial three games...**1996:** Saw action in 12 games, mainly on special teams, in his first year with Atlanta...Competed on the offensive line over a five-week stretch late in the season...Received his most extensive playing time when he replaced an injured Bob Whitfield at left tackle in the first half at Cincinnati (Nov. 24)...Acquired by the Falcons May 2, 1996, in a trade with the Jets for a conditional seventh-round draft choice in 1998...**1995:** Played in all 16 games, starting 12 at left tackle...Returned to the starting lineup for the final seven contests after seeing strictly special teams duty in games 6-9...Also started at left tackle the first five weeks of the season, the offensive line did not allow a sack in games 2 and 3...Held Bills' All-Pro defensive end Bruce Smith without a sack in start at left tackle (Nov. 19)...**1994:** Saw action in all 16 games, starting three (two at left guard, one at left tackle)...Replaced the injured Roger Duffy (ankle) in the lineup at left guard for the final two games...Had made his first NFL start Nov. 20 at Minnesota, filling in at left tackle for the injured Jeff Criswell (back), and helped the line earn the offensive game ball in a 31-21 win...Stood in Criswell in four other games, including contest at Green Bay Nov. 13...Saw action as a tight end in goal-line situations vs. Indianapolis (Oct. 9), when injuries sidelined James Thornton and Fred Baxter...Participated on special teams in every game...**1993:** Made a full-time transition to offensive tackle...Played in two games, some at tackle, though mostly on special teams...Dressed for, but did not play in, one contest and was inactive for the other 13...**1992:** Spent the majority of the season on the Jets' practice squad, playing both defensive and offensive tackle...Added to the team's roster (as a tackle) Dec. 24 for the season finale against New Orleans two days later, but did not play...Released in training camp (Aug. 24) by the Jets, joined the club's practice squad Sept. 2...Originally had signed with the New York Jets as an undrafted rookie free agent May 6.

COLLEGE: A four-year letter winner (1988-91) for Southern California...Redshirted in 1987...Played on the defensive line, he recorded 22 tackles as a senior and 23 stops, including 5 sacks, his junior year...Saw the majority of his action on special teams during his initial two seasons...Was a member of three bowl teams, playing in the Rose Bowl (twice) and the John Hancock Bowl...Was a college teammate of future NFL players Junior Seau, Mark Carrier and Dan Owens...Part of a Trojans squad which went undefeated in the Pacific 10 Conference his first two years...Nearing a degree in public administration, he needs to take only one more class to receive his diploma.

PERSONAL: Given name Matthew Joseph Willig...Nicknamed 'Gig'...Born in La Mirada, Calif. ...Single...Attended St. Paul High School in Santa Fe Springs, Calif., where he earned three letters each in football (as an offensive and defensive tackle) and basketball...Following college he had a role in the movie *Full Contact*, where he played a martial arts fighter; although he didnt have any speaking lines, he did a lot of "growling and grunting"...Four of his five brothers played college football — Chuck, Northern Arizona 1978-80; Chris, Cerritos College 1981-82; Bob, University of Washington 1985-88; and Greg, Rice University 1989-92...Brother, Greg, also went to training camp with the Jets in 1993 as a free agent quarterback...Hobbies include playing golf, working out and "hanging out at the ocean"...Residence: Mission Viejo, Calif.

PRO STATISTICS:

> **Games/Starts**—N.Y. Jets 1992 (0/0); 1993 (2/0); 1994 (16/3); 1995 (16/12); Atlanta 1996 (12/0); 1997 (16/13). Career totals: 62/28.

FRANK WINTERS · 52

Center
College: *Western Illinois*
NFL Exp.: *12th Season*   **Packers Exp.:** *7th Season*
Ht.: *6-3*   **Wt.:** *300*   **Born:** *1/23/64*   **Acq:** *PB-92 (KC)*

PRO: The unquestionable leader of the Packers' offensive line, Frank Winters has combined smarts and toughness to emerge as one of the league's best centers...Has consistently been one of Green Bay's most durable and dependable performers...Had rarely missed a snap in his first five seasons with the team until he sat out three games last season after suffering a mid-foot sprain in Week 2, snapping a string of 82 consecutive games played (longest on the team), including 74 straight starts...Had started all 16 regular-season games for Green Bay for four straight seasons (1993-96) until his injury last season...Finally received long-overdue recognition after the 1996 season when he got the opportunity to play in the Pro Bowl for the first time in his career...Though he has played mostly center in recent seasons, he also has proven to be an effective guard and long-snapper...Is tied with six teammates for the Green Bay postseason record for most career games played (13), each having passed the previous record-holder, Ray Nitschke (11) last year...Green Bay offensive line coach Tom Lovat knows how important Winters is to the team..."We couldn't play without Frank," Lovat says emphatically. "He knows the offense so well he could coach it. He has to identify the front. Any changes in schemes start with him and he has to know what the change is. He is such a tough competitor; he's probably our meanest guy along the front. And he has better athleticism than he gets credit for. Frank is a smart blocker who uses finesse and power. He's also one of the team leaders. He leads by his actions, but when he talks his teammates listen."...Originally came to the Packers in 1992 as a 'Plan B' free agent, signed away from Kansas City...Now has played in 168 regular-season games, plus 20 playoff contests, in an 11-year career which has seen him suit up for four different NFL clubs...A 'Plan B' veteran, he previously had joined both the Chiefs and N.Y. Giants through the league's former free agency system...Began his pro career with Cleveland, where he played in 28 games from 1987-88, then played in 15 games for the Giants in 1989, and subsequently saw action in 32 league contests with K.C. ...**1997:** Started in 13 regular-season games at center, plus all three playoff contests, including Super Bowl XXXII...Inactive for three early-season games (Miami Sept. 14, Minnesota Sept. 21, Detroit Sept. 28) after suffering a left mid-foot sprain at Philadelphia (Sept. 7), snapping a string of 82 consecutive games played (longest on the team), including 74 straight starts...Helped hold the Vikings' John Randle without a sack in 27-11 win at Minnesota (Dec. 1)...Was part of Green Bay's season-best 220-yard rushing effort in the Packers' 45-17 win over Dallas (Nov. 23), including Dorsey Levens' club-record 190 yards on the ground...Teamed with guards Aaron Taylor and Adam Timmerman to hold the 49ers' vaunted inside duo of Dana Stubblefield and Bryant Young without a sack and to a collective 8 tackles in NFC Championship Game victory at San Francisco (Jan. 11)...Was one of the club's two offensive captains during the playoffs for the second straight year...Also served as the Packers' long-snapper on punts vs. Detroit (Nov. 2), replacing the injured Paul Frase (back)...**1996:** Started all 16 regular-season games for the fourth straight year, exclusively at center...Threw a key downfield block on the Vikings' Orlando Thomas to help spring Levens' 13-yard touchdown reception off a screen pass, a score which put the Packers ahead of Minnesota 17-10 early in the fourth quarter en route to a 38-10 win (Dec. 22)...Also served for much of the season as the Packers' long-snapper for placements...Anchored an offensive line which paved the way for a Green Bay running attack that averaged 114.9 yards per game, up from 89.3 in 1995...Also started all three postseason games, including Super Bowl XXXI...Represented the offense, along with Brett Favre, as one of the team's six playoff captains...Played in the Pro Bowl for the initial time in his career, going as the first alternate when the Cowboys' Ray Donaldson withdrew due to an elbow injury...**1995:** Enjoyed one of the better seasons of his career...Started all 16 games (all at center) for the third season in a row...Also was the starting center for each of the team's three playoff contests...Served as the regular long-snapper for field goals and extra points and was the backup snapper for punts...Did come in as the Packers' long-snapper on punts at Jacksonville (Sept. 24) after regular snapper Mike Bartrum left the game with a broken arm...Had 1 stop on special teams...**1994:** Showed his versatility and dependability as he started all 16 regular-season games – 10 at center and six at left guard...Also started at center for both playoff games...Was the Packers' starter at center throughout training camp, even starting at the position in the regular-season opener vs. Minnesota (Sept. 4)...Shifted to left guard and started there in games 2-7 as usual starter Guy McIntyre was out with a blood clot in his calf...Made the move back to center beginning with Monday night contest at Chicago (Oct. 31) as McIntyre returned to left guard spot...Made big play vs. Atlanta (Dec. 18) when he recovered a Favre fumble at the Packers' 14...Served as team's long-snapper on kicks and backed up Mark Chmura in that role on punts, recording 1 solo special teams tackle...**1993:** Quietly had an outstanding season, missing only one snap the entire year (including preseason)...Started at left guard in the first four games after incumbent starter Rich Moran went down with a knee injury in training camp...Shifted to center to start the final 12 regular-season games plus both playoff contests after usual starter, James Campen, suffered a season-ending hamstring injury at Dallas (Oct. 3)...Handled all of the team's long-snapping duties, contributing 5 special teams tackles (3 solo) as part of that role...**1992:** Appeared in all 16 games with 11 starts in his first season with Green Bay...Started three games at center after Campen (knee) went on injured reserve...Also started last eight games at left guard after Moran (knee) was placed on IR...Saw brief action at center in season opener vs. Minnesota (Sept. 6) and vs. Pittsburgh (Sept. 27) after Campen left both games due to injury...Also subbed in at left guard at Detroit (Nov. 1) when Moran first suffered his knee injury...Served as team's long-snapper...Signed with Packers as a 'Plan B' free agent on March 17...**1991:** Played in all 16 games and two playoff contests for the Kansas City Chiefs...**1990:** Acquired by the Chiefs on March 27 as a 'Plan B' free agent from the New York Giants...Saw action in all 16 regular-season games plus playoff contest at Miami...Started six of first seven games at left guard...Handled all of the Chiefs' deep-snapping chores...**1989:** Signed with the Giants as a 'Plan B' free agent from the Cleveland Browns on March 20...Appeared in 15 games as a deep-snapper and reserve offensive lineman...**1988:** Played in all 16 games for the Browns plus playoff contest vs. Denver...For second straight year took care of all of the Browns' deep-snapping duties and was a backup offensive lineman...**1987:** Named to all-rookie team of Pro Football Writers of America following the season...Handled all long-snapping chores for Browns and saw reserve action in the offensive line...Made squad after being selected in the 10th round (276th overall) by Cleveland in 1987.

COLLEGE: A four-year letterman (1983-86) at Western Illinois...Won the starting job at center midway through his freshman season...Showed durability by starting 42 successive games thereafter...Was a NCAA Division I-AA All-America selection by Kodak and *The Sporting News* as a senior...Also was an All-Gateway Conference pick and the team's MVP...Graduated with a degree in political science.

PERSONAL: Given name Frank Mitchell Winters...Born in Hoboken, N.J. ...Married to Alita, couple has two daughters, Aubre (born 9/2/88) and Alexa (born 1/15/90)...Named 'Offensive Lineman of the Year' and won all-league honors at Emerson High School in Union City, N.J. ...Enjoys listening to music and reading...Owns two restaurants in Cleveland called 'Paninis,' specializing in pizza and sandwiches...Residence: Overland Park, Kan.

PRO STATISTICS:

Games/Starts—Cleveland 1987 (12/0); 1987 Playoffs (2/0); 1988 (16/0); 1988 Playoffs (1/0); N.Y. Giants 1989 (15/0); 1989 Playoffs (1/0); Kansas City 1990 (16/6); 1990 Playoffs (1/0); 1991 (16/0); 1991 Playoffs (2/0); Green Bay 1992 (16/11); 1993 (16/16); 1993 Playoffs (2/2); 1994 (16/16); 1994 Playoffs (2/2); 1995 (16/16); 1995 Playoffs (3/3); 1996 (16/16); 1996 Playoffs (3/3); 1997 (13/13); 1997 Playoffs (3/3). Career totals: 168/94. Playoff totals: 20/13.

The final selection in the first round of the 1997 NFL draft, Iowa's Ross Verba fully lived up to his advance billing. Demonstrating equal amounts of grace and contentiousness, Verba was able to win the Packers' starting left tackle post by the sixth game, becoming the all-important protector of league MVP Brett Favre's blind side, and went on to earn all-rookie honors. He climaxed his inaugural season by becoming the first rookie left tackle ever to start in a Super Bowl.

VONNIE HOLLIDAY　　90

Defensive End/Defensive Tackle
College: *North Carolina*
Ht.: *6-5*　　**Wt.:** *296*　　**Born:** *12/11/75*　　**Acq:** *D1*

COLLEGE: The Packers' first-round selection (19th overall) in 1998...A four-year letter winner (1994-97) at North Carolina, starting the last two-and-a-half years...Played in 46 games with 28 starts for the Tar Heels...Totaled 162 tackles (83 solo), including 11 sacks and 28 for loss, plus 6 forced fumbles and 11 passes defensed...A first-team All-Atlantic Coast Conference player last season at defensive tackle, will have the opportunity to play both defensive end and tackle with the Packers according to Green Bay defensive coordinator Fritz Shurmur, who says, "I think he will challenge for a starting position at defensive end. And, obviously, he would be in a position to play as a backup and in an alternating role as an inside player in our base defense and with a chance to be a starter as an inside pass rusher in our 'dime' and 'nickel' defense."...Shurmur likes the ability Holliday possesses, adding, "He brings athleticism and an intensity level with a motor that's always running. He has the ability to do athletically, everything that you need to have done on the defensive line at both the inside and outside positions. We expect him to be a big contributor this year."...Appeared in four bowl games, including two starts, during his four years in Chapel Hill...**1997:** A first-team All-ACC selection...Started all 11 games for the Tar Heels and finished the season with a career-high 64 total tackles...His production included 5 sacks (tied for second on the team) and 13 tackles for loss...Also added 2 forced fumbles and 5 passes defensed...Served as a co-captain...Received 'Charlie Justice Award' for outstanding contribution on defense...Notched at least one tackle for loss in nine of 11 games...Contributed with 10-tackle outings against both Virginia and TCU...Recovered a third-quarter Wake Forest fumble that led to the go-ahead touchdown in an eventual 30-12 victory...Had 8 tackles, including 3 for loss, vs. Virginia Tech in the Gator Bowl...**1996:** Emerged as a solid player for North Carolina in his first season as a full-time starter...Played in all 11 games with 10 starts...Took over for the departed Tar Heel All-American Marcus Jones, finishing the season with 47 total tackles, including 5 sacks (tied for second on the team) and 11 tackles for loss...Started off N.C. State contest with a bang, sacking quarterback Jamie Barnette on the first play of the game, causing a fumble which was recovered in the end zone for a Tar Heel touchdown by linebacker Kivuusama Mays...Later added a second sack against the Wolfpack in 52-20 victory...Had dominating game in shutout of Georgia Tech with 7 tackles that included 2 sacks and 4 tackles for loss...Turned in a strong showing in the Gator Bowl vs. West Virginia with 7 tackles, including both a sack and tackle for loss...**1995:** Played extensively for the Tar Heels, making appearances in 10 games, including five starts...Finished the season with 39 tackles, including 17 solo stops...Also had 1 sack and 4 tackles for loss...Had a season-high 6 tackles in a 22-17 victory over Virginia...Forced 2 fumbles and made 5 stops vs. Georgia Tech...Enjoyed a strong Carquest Bowl performance with 4 tackles (2 TFL), 1 fumble recovery and a pass defensed in victory over Arkansas...Recovery of Razorback quarterback Brian Lunney's fumble deep in UNC territory thwarted a fourth-quarter Arkansas drive and helped to preserve the Tar Heels' 20-10 win...**1994:** Was one of only three true freshmen to see playing time, he appeared in 10 of the Tar Heels' 11 games...Finished with 12 total tackles...Also appeared in Sun Bowl, making 2 tackles vs. Texas.

HIGH SCHOOL: A first-team all-state selection and 3-A 'Lineman of the Year' as a senior at Camden (S.C.) High School...Also garnered city 'Player of the Year' honors and was team's 'Most Valuable Player' as a senior...Was a three-year all-area and all-conference selection as a defensive player, lining up as a linebacker, defensive end and tackle during his career...Offensively, played tight end as a freshman – garnering all conference honors – before moving to center as a sophomore...Handled team's long-snapping duties...A four-year letter winner in basketball, he was a three-time all-conference player as a forward and center...Earned conference 'Defensive Player of the Year' honors as a senior, leading his team to a 28-3 record and the state semifinals...A three-year letterman in baseball, he pitched, caught and played first and third bases, earning all-conference honors as a junior.

PERSONAL: Majored in communications...Single...Nicknamed 'Chocolate Thunder,' a name he acquired during a strong showing in his initial practices with the Tar Heels...Hobbies include fishing, basketball, golf and spending time with family and friends...Worked the summers of 1996 and '97 as a customer service representative at 'Crown Honda and Volvo' in Chapel Hill, N.C. ...Worked high school summers at a law office in Camden, S.C., which in turn fueled his desire to someday start a juvenile foundation, "Vonnie's Kids," to work with disadvantaged youth...Was member of 15-player leadership committee at North Carolina...Cousin, Corey Holliday, also attended North Carolina and is a wide receiver for the Pittsburgh

Steelers...Former New York Giants linebacker Harry Carson serves as his mentor...Born Dimetry Giovonni Holliday in Camden, S.C. ...Residence: Carrboro, N.C.

COLLEGE STATISTICS:

Year	UT	AT	Sacks	Int.	FR	FF	PD	TFL
1994 North Carolina	5	7	0	0	0	0	2	0
1995 North Carolina	17	22	1	0	0	2	3	4
1996 North Carolina	32	15	5	0	0	2	1	11
1997 North Carolina	29	35	5	0	0	2	5	13
Totals	**83**	**79**	**11**	**0**	**0**	**6**	**11**	**28**

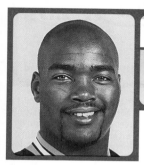

JONATHAN BROWN — 91

Defensive End
College: *Tennessee*
Ht.: 6-4   **Wt.:** 265   **Born:** 11/28/75   **Acq:** D3

COLLEGE: The Packers' third-round selection (90th overall) in 1998...A two-year starter and four-time letterman (1994-97) at Tennessee...Was an All-Southeastern Conference selection as a senior...Played in 45 career games with the Volunteers with 26 starts...Lined up at both defensive end positions at Tennessee and finished with 25 career sacks, good for third place in school annals behind the Packers' Reggie White (32) and former teammate Leonard Little (28)...Also totaled 115 tackles (74 solo), 4 fumble recoveries, 6 forced fumbles, 2 passes defensed and 8 tackles for loss...An exceptional pass-rusher, he is expected to immediately contribute to the Packers' defense..."He has unique abilities and skills as a pass rusher at the outside position as a defensive end," says Fritz Shurmur, Green Bay's defensive coordinator. "He also, however, has demonstrated the ability to be able to play against the run in a base defense. We are certainly not looking at him as purely a situational player. We are looking at him as a candidate for a defensive end position. We expect him to challenge that way. He will have the opportunity to not only to make this team, but also be a guy who figures in the mix when it comes to playing time."...**1997:** A first-team All-SEC selection, started all 12 games at left defensive end for Tennessee...A second-team All-SEC pick by conference coaches...Finished with 37 total tackles, including a team-high and an SEC-leading 13½ sacks...Added 3 forced fumbles and 2 fumble recoveries...Had five multiple-sack games...Had 2½ of a team record-tying 8 sacks against South Carolina...Had 2 sacks among 8 tackles in victory over Georgia...Recovered a fumble and registered 3 tackles in Orange Bowl vs. Nebraska...**1996:** Started all 11 games for the Volunteers, recording 39 total tackles...Tackle total included 6½ sacks (second on the team) and 5 stops for loss...Played the first nine games at right defensive end before moving to left defensive end for the remainder of the season...Authored a five-game sack streak during the season...Enjoyed productive outing in victory over Alabama, contributing 7 tackles, with 1 sack and 1 TFL, and 1 fumble recovery...**1995:** Played in all 11 games with one start...As mainly a backup at right defensive end, notched 26 total tackles, including 3 sacks...In his only start of the season, at left defensive end vs. Arkansas, registered a sack among 4 tackles and added a forced fumble...**1994:** Saw action in all 11 games as a true freshman, making two starts...Finished season with 13 total tackles, including 2 sacks...Had memorable collegiate debut vs. UCLA, notching 4 tackles, including a sack and a tackle for loss.

HIGH SCHOOL: An All-America selection by *SuperPrep* and *Blue Chip Illustrated* as a senior at Booker T. Washington High School in Tulsa, Okla. ...Also was named district 'Player of the Year' as a senior...Had 14 sacks among 118 tackles as a senior...A four-year starter and three-year all-conference player at defensive tackle, he started the final three years on the offensive line at tackle and guard as well...A three-year letter winner in basketball (power forward) and track (shot)...Member of the National Honor Society.

PERSONAL: Majored in psychology...Single...Nicknamed 'J.B.'...While at Tennessee, was involved in 'Say No to Drugs' and 'Stay in School' campaigns...Hopes to establish a community involvement program in his hometown of Tulsa with R.W. McQuarters, the San Francisco 49ers' 1998 first-round draft choice out of Oklahoma State and a close friend from their elementary and high school days...Was the best man in the wedding of Marcus Nash, a former teammate at Tennessee who was a 1998 first-round draft choice of the Denver Broncos...Hobbies include listening to music...Born Jonathan Bernard Brown in Chickasha, Okla. ...Residence: Knoxville, Tenn.

THE DRAFT CHOICES

COLLEGE STATISTICS:

Year	UT	AT	Sacks	Int.	FR	FF	PD	TFL
1994 Tennessee.......................9	4	2	0	1	2	0	1
1995 Tennessee.......................13	13	3	0	0	1	0	1
1996 Tennessee.......................22	17	6½	0	1	0	0	5
1997 Tennessee.......................30	7	13½	0	2	3	2	1
Totals **74**	**41**	**25**	**0**	**4**	**6**	**2**	**8**

ROOSEVELT BLACKMON · 23

Cornerback
College: Morris Brown
Ht.: 6-1 **Wt.: 185** **Born: 9/10/74** **Acq: D4**

COLLEGE: The Packers' fourth-round selection (121st overall) in 1998...A four-year starter (1994-97) at Morris Brown...Played in 34 career games with 31 starts...Had 12 career interceptions, returning 2 for touchdowns...Recorded 140 total tackles (81 solo), 4 fumble recoveries, 4 forced fumbles, 62 passes defensed and 2 tackles for loss as a collegian...Also an accomplished punt returner, was a Division II All-American as a return specialist in 1996...Had a 14.0-yard average (38 returns for 531 yards and 2 touchdowns) over his collegiate career...Unrecruited because of only one year playing experience in high school, was a walk-on at Morris Brown before earning a scholarship...Somewhat raw in technique, has shown plenty of the enthusiasm and potential needed to succeed in the NFL..."He demonstrates coverage skill that will allow him to be able to challenge for the third corner position," says Packers defensive coordinator Fritz Shurmur. "We look to him to be a backup corner this year in our base defense and to challenge for a starting role as the third corner in our 'nickel' and 'dime' defenses."...His 1994, walk-on season at Morris Brown was the culmination of dedicated effort to reach a personal goal...After playing only one season of high school football due to size concerns of his coaches (he was only 160 pounds as a high school senior), he was not recruited by any colleges...Enrolled at Bethune-Cookman College in Daytona Beach, Fla., but stayed only one semester...After leaving, he held down jobs as a used car salesman and a gravedigger at the local (Belle Glade, Fla.) cemetery, before leaving for Morris Brown in late summer...Due to procedural problems, he was not able to enroll for the fall semester...Worked as assistant equipment manager for the Morris Brown football team during the 1993 season, before finally enrolling for the spring semester and walking on to the football team the following fall...Also was a collegiate sprinter at Morris Brown, he competed in the 55- (indoors), 100- and 200-meter dashes...Earned Division II All-America status in the 100 meters during the 1997 season, placing fourth at the national championships...**1997:** In a season interrupted with injury, played in just five games...Finished with 25 total tackles, 1 interception and 7 passes defensed...Suffered a fractured bone in his lower back in season opener vs. Clark-Atlanta, subsequently sat out five games while recovering from the injury...In second game back from injury, had back-to-back passes defensed on the final two plays of the game to preserve a 24-23 victory over Savannah State...In contest vs. Benedict College, had 58-yard punt return to the two-yard line, setting up winning touchdown in 7-6 victory...**1996:** Started all 11 games and finished with 25 total tackles, 2 interceptions and 17 passes defensed...Was an All-Southern Intercollegiate Athletic Conference first-team selection...Also returned 19 punts for 305 yards and 2 touchdowns to garner Division II All-Amercia honors as a returner...His 16.1-yard average on punt returns ranked second in the nation among Division II athletes...Had 95-yard interception return for a touchdown against Tuskegee...Essayed a memorable performance against Alabama A&M, returning back-to-back punts for touchdowns...The two 87-yard returns, within a minute of each other, provided the Wolverines with their only scores in a 16-8 victory...Had a 33-yard interception return for a touchdown against Kentucky State...**1995:** Started all 10 games and totaled 39 tackles...Also added 4 interceptions and 21 passes defensed...Had 76 yards on 7 punt returns during the season...Saw emergency duty as a quarterback and completed 2 of 4 passes for 99 yards and 1 touchdown...Also had 1 carry for 7 yards...**1994:** Played in 10 games with eight starts...Notched 51 total tackles, 5 interceptions, 17 passes defensed, 3 fumble recoveries and 3 forced fumbles...Had an impressive performance vs. Alabama A&M with 7 tackles, 5 passes defensed and 88-yard interception return for a touchdown...Made mark in collegiate debut vs. Clark-Atlanta with 2 interceptions and 2 fumble recoveries.

HIGH SCHOOL: Played wide receiver for one season at Glades Central High School in Belle Glade, Fla. ...Also served as the team's third-string quarterback.

PERSONAL: Majored in health and physical education...Single...Nicknamed 'Tadpole,' a moniker that developed from his own father's nickname of 'Frog'...Hobbies include golf and spending time with his family...Close friend of Tampa Bay wide receiver Reidel Anthony with whom he attended high school...Has trained during the past five summers with Cincinnati cornerback Jimmy Spencer, who also attended the same high school...Has organized a football camp in Belle Glade, Fla., primarily for high school players each of the last five summers...Born Roosevelt Blackmon, III, in Pahokee Fla. ...Residence: Belle Glade, Fla.

COLLEGE STATISTICS:

Year	UT	AT	Sacks	Int.	FR	FF	PD	TFL
1994 Morris Brown	32	19	0	5	3	3	17	0
1995 Morris Brown	14	25	0	4	1	0	21	0
1996 Morris Brown	15	10	0	2	0	0	17	2
1997 Morris Brown	20	5	0	1	0	1	7	0
Totals	**81**	**59**	**0**	**12**	**4**	**4**	**62**	**2**

Rushing: 1 for 7 yards in 1995
Passing: 2 of 4 for 99 yards, 1 TD in 1995
Punt Returns: 7 for 76 yards, 10.6 avg. in 1995; 19 for 305 yards, 16.1 avg., LG 87, 2 TDs in 1996; 12 for 150 yards, 12.5 avg., LG 58 in 1997 for total of 38 for 531 yards, 14.0 avg., LG 87, 2 TDs

COREY BRADFORD 85

Wide Receiver
College: Jackson State
Ht.: 6-1   **Wt.:** 197   **Born:** 12/8/75   **Acq:** D5

COLLEGE: The Packers' fifth-round selection (150th overall) in 1998...Played but one season of college football, making 11 starts for Jackson State last year...Began his football career after transferring from junior college, where he was on a track scholarship...A great athlete, he has been compared to former Green Bay wide receiver Sterling Sharpe in terms of size and strength by Packers offensive coordinator Sherm Lewis..."He's got a great work ethic," Lewis says. "He's going to be a tough kid. He's got great size and good speed."...Although he joins the Packers with only one year of college football experience, Lewis feels he should have a presence this season, saying, "I think he'll contribute on special teams at first and then contribute a little at receiver. But I think he is going to make us a better football team."...**1997:** Started all 11 games in his only college football season and made 48 receptions for 937 yards (19.5 avg.) and a team-high 9 touchdowns...A first-team All-Southeastern Athletic Conference selection, he also was named SWAC 'Newcomer of the Year'...Also contributed 282 yards and 1 touchdown on 10 kickoff returns (28.2 avg.)...Averaged 117.2 all-purpose yards per game...Receiving yardage total (937) was third-best in school history...His 48 receptions and 9 TD catches each were the fifth-best one-season performances in team annals...A long-distance threat, 4 of his 9 touchdown receptions covered 50-or-more yards...Enjoyed a particularly productive day vs. Mississippi Valley State with 4 receptions for 111 yards and 1 TD, also gaining 116 yards on 3 kickoff returns with one going 83 yards for a touchdown...A week later, turned in a memorable performance vs. Texas Southern, snaring 10 receptions for 200 yards and 3 TDs...Scampered 72 yards for a rushing touchdown vs. Arkansas-Pine Bluff...Hauled in an 81-yard touchdown pass in his first collegiate game, against Alabama State...**1996:** Sat out the season for academic reasons...**Junior College:** A two-year letterwinner (1994-95) in track at Hinds (Miss.) Community College, he finished eighth in the triple jump and sixth in the long jump nationally in 1995.

HIGH SCHOOL: A four-year letter winner and all-state defensive back as a senior at Clinton (La.) High School...Also played quarterback as a junior and senior...A four-time letterman in basketball and track, as a senior he was all-district in basketball and also captured the state long jump championship.

PERSONAL: Majored in recreation administration...Single...Nicknamed 'Louisiana Lightning'...Hobbies include fishing and basketball...A cousin, Tim Sensly, is a defensive back who has been in training camp with the New York Giants and Carolina Panthers the past two years...Born Corey Lamon Bradford in Baton Rouge, La. ...Residence: Clinton, La.

COLLEGE STATISTICS:

Year	No.	Yds.	RECEIVING Avg.	LG	TD
1997 Jackson State.............48		937	19.5	81	9
Totals 48		937	19.5	81	9

Rushing: 2 for 70 yards, 35.0 avg., LG 72, 1 TD in 1997
Kickoff Returns: 10 for 282 yards, 28.2 avg., LG 83, 1 TD in 1997

SCOTT McGARRAHAN　34

Safety
College: New Mexico
Ht.: 6-1　**Wt.:** 197　**Born:** 2/12/74　**Acq:** D6a

COLLEGE: The Packers' first of two sixth-round selections (156th overall) in 1998...A three-year starter and four-time letterman (1994-97) at New Mexico...Started in 34 straight games for the Lobos, playing in 46 contests overall...A first-team All Western Athletic Conference selection and the school's defensive 'Most Valuable Player' as a senior, finished his career with 316 total tackles (tied for 13th place on Lobos' all-time list), 3 interceptions, 5 sacks, 6 forced fumbles, 19 passes defensed and 5 tackles for loss...According to Green Bay defensive backs coach Bob Valesente, is a player who developed a great understanding of the game as the quarterback for New Mexico's defensive secondary..."He is a real hard-nosed, vocal leader who controlled a very good defense last year," says Valesente. "He is very instinctive and will take the proper angles on his run support and in pass defense. He carries with him a sense of confidence."...An excellent special teams player, should be a contributor immediately on the Packers' coverage teams...**1997:** A first-team All-WAC selection, team's defensive 'MVP' and outstanding special teams player...Started all 12 games for the Lobos and finished as defense's third-leading tackler with 97 total stops...Also contributed 4 sacks, 2 interceptions, 2 tackles for loss, 2 forced fumbles and 6 passes defensed...Served as team co-captain...Had double-digit tackle totals in five games, including a career-high 17 stops (16 solo) against Rice...Returned an interception 66 yards to the one-yard line in game against Tulsa...In contest at San Diego State, made 11 tackles and forced 2 fumbles, one of which stalled an Aztec drive at the Lobos' 20-yard line...Made 12 stops in Insight.com Bowl vs. Arizona...**1996:** Started all 11 games and finished fourth on the squad with 73 total tackles...Also had 2 forced fumbles and 5 passes defensed, tying for the team lead in both categories...Made a season-high 14 stops against Northern Arizona...**1995:** Earned honorable mention All-WAC honors while starting all 11 games...Finished with a career-best 101 total tackles, good for third place among Lobo defenders...His 9.4 tackles per game was tied for the sixth-best average in the WAC...Also had 7 passes defensed, 1 interception and 2 forced fumbles...Turned in 15-tackle performances in consecutive weeks vs. Air Force and Fresno State...**1994:** Saw action in all 12 games as a reserve free safety...Finished with 45 total tackles...**1993:** Redshirted.

HIGH SCHOOL: An all-area, all-district and all-city selection as a cornerback and safety his senior season at Lamar High School in Arlington, Texas...A two-year starter and three-year letter winner, he also played slotback on offense...Notched 65 tackles and 5 interceptions as a senior, returning one INT for a touchdown...Lamar posted a 35-4 record during his three years as a starter, winning 33 straight district games and finishing as the state runner-up in 1990...Also lettered one year in wrestling.

PERSONAL: Majored in business...Single...Nicknamed 'Mac'...Hobbies include playing the guitar...Grandfather, Leon Pickett, was a tackle on TCU's 1938 national championship team...Older brother, Chris, played football for Southwest Texas State...While at New Mexico, was involved with Campus Crusade for Christ and Champions for Christ...Born John Scott McGarrahan in Arlington, Texas...Residence: Albuquerque, N.M.

COLLEGE STATISTICS:

Year	UT	AT	Sacks	Int.	FR	FF	PD	TFL
1993 New Mexico ....Redshirted								
1994 New Mexico 25	20	0	0	0	0	1	0
1995 New Mexico 68	33	0	1	1	2	7	1
1996 New Mexico 59	14	1	0	0	2	5	2
1997 New Mexico 78	19	4	2	0	2	6	2
Totals 230	**86**	**5**	**3**	**1**	**6**	**19**	**5**

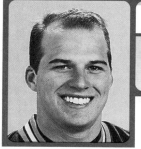

MATT HASSELBECK   11

Quarterback
College: *Boston College*
Ht.: *6-4*   **Wt.:** *217*   **Born:** *9/25/75*   **Acq:** *D6b*

COLLEGE: The Packers' second of two sixth-round selections (187th overall) in 1998...A two-year starter and four-year letter winner (1994-97) at Boston College...Finished fifth on the Eagles' career passing list with 4,548 yards, completing 390 of 701 passes with 22 touchdowns and 26 interceptions...Ranks fourth in school annals in both completions and attempts...Started 21 games and played in 37 overall...Green Bay quarterbacks coach Andy Reid feels Hasselbeck's skills make him a good fit for the team's offense, saying, "I see a good football player who will fit in tremendously with the things that we are doing here in the passing game."...Reid also feels Hasselbeck's play-making ability is a plus, adding, "If he were in a bad situation, he could get you out of that situation with a positive play. He has a tremendous feel in the pocket, and that constitutes having good feet. He possesses a better-than-average arm and good accuracy. He's the complete package."...**1997:** Started 10 games for the Eagles, missing one contest due to injury...Completed 188 of 305 passes for 2,239 yards and 11 touchdowns with 10 interceptions...Completion percentage performance (61.6%) tied the fourth-best single-season mark in school history...Co-winner of the 'Thomas F. Scanlon Award' as the outstanding senior scholar-athlete...Averaged 226.3 yards per game of total offense...Connected on 25 of 41 passes for 277 yards and 2 touchdowns in season-opener at Temple...Was named Big East Conference 'Player of the Week' for his performance against Rutgers, converting on 21 of 27 passes for 314 yards and a touchdown; he also rushed for a score...Suffered hip, knee and right thumb injuries in fourth quarter of Cincinnati contest, he subsequently sat out game vs. Georgia Tech...Threw for 277 yards in a 22-of-33 performance that included a Boston College-record 14 consecutive completions in contest vs. Notre Dame...Completed 24 of 38 passes for 268 yards in victory over Pittsburgh, his effort including a 41-yard strike to set up the game-winning field goal...Authored a great finish to his Eagles career, completing 31 of 46 attempts for a career-high 393 yards and 3 touchdowns, including the game-winner, in a 24-20 victory over Army...**1996:** Played in 11 games with 10 starts...Hit on 171 of 330 passes for 1,990 yards and 9 touchdowns with 9 interceptions...Averaged 161.5 yards of total offense per game, ranking fifth in the Big East...Came off the bench in the fourth quarter to rally Boston College to a dramatic 24-21 win over Hawaii in the season opener...Threw a three-yard touchdown pass, successfully completed the two point conversion, and, after the Eagles regained possession from the Rainbows, he connected on two passes to set up a 42-yard game-winning field goal as time expired...Threw for 292 yards and 3 touchdowns in victory over Navy...Completed 24 of 46 passes for 304 yards and 2 TDs vs. West Virginia...Threw for over 200 yards vs. Cincinnati, Virginia Tech, Rutgers and Pittsburgh...Suffered a separated right shoulder vs. Temple which caused him to miss season-ending contest vs. Miami (Fla.)...**1995:** In role as the Eagles' main backup quarterback, he played in 11 games with one start...Completed 27 of 60 passes for 280 yards and 2 touchdowns, with 7 interceptions...Notched his first collegiate touchdown pass – a five-yard toss to tight end Todd Pollack – in a 5-of-8 performance for 62 yards against Michigan...Again saw significant playing time in game vs. West Virginia, completing 10 of 19 attempts for 102 yards and 1 TD...Made first career start vs. Army, connecting on 12 of 27 passes for 116 yards with 4 interceptions in miserable weather conditions...**1994:** Saw action in five games...Had notable performance in 30-11 victory over Notre Dame as he entered the game as the holder on a fake field goal attempt, taking the snap and running for a first down...Connected on 4 of 6 passes for 39 yards in limited action vs. Army...**1993:** Redshirted.

HIGH SCHOOL: An honorable mention All-America selection by USA Today as a senior at Xaverian Brothers High School in Westwood, Mass. ...Also garnered All-East honors from *Blue Chip Illustrated* and All-New England honors from *SuperPrep*...Was named all-state by the *Boston Herald* and all-scholastic by the *Boston Globe*...Completed 90 of 120 passes for 1,490 yards and 7 touchdowns as a senior...Also ran for 400 yards and 3 TDs...Team captured conference title and was the runner-up in Massachusetts' Division 1-A Super Bowl...Was a three-year starter at quarterback...Also lettered in basketball (3 years) and baseball (2 years).

PERSONAL: Received a B.S. degree in marketing and finance (1997) and is currently in Boston College's Carroll School of Management MBA program with a concentration in international management...Single...Interned during the summers of 1996 and '97 at Fidelity Capital Market in Boston's World Trade Center...Was the 1996 recipient of Boston College's 'St. Ignatius Award for Student Involvement,' an honor presented by the university's Dean for Student Development to an outstanding student leader...As a junior, participated in Boston College Chaplain's Office Ignatio Volunteer Program in Jamaica during spring break, working with victims of leprosy and teaching children at a Kingston school...Also was a member of the Student Athlete Advisory Board for four years...Helped raise money for the Boston College Campus School, a program for assisting physically and mentally challenged children...Also involved with the Fellowship of Christian Athletes...Father, Don, played tight end in the NFL for nine seasons with the Patriots (1977-83), Raiders (1983), Vikings (1984) and Giants (1985) after enjoying a fine college career at the University of Colorado...A younger brother, Tim, is a Boston College quarterback who should challenge for the starting job this fall as a redshirt sophomore...Another family quarterback, his youngest brother Nathanael, will be a junior this fall at Xaverian Brothers High School in Westwood, Mass. ...Has an uncle, Steve Hasselbeck, who was a wide receiver at Penn...Born Matthew Michael Hasselbeck in Boulder, Colo. ...Residence: Chestnut Hill, Mass.

COLLEGE STATISTICS:

		PASSING						
Year	Att.	Comp.	Yds.	Pct.	TD	Int.	LG
1993 Boston College	Redshirted						
1994 Boston College	6	4	39	66.7	0	0	13
1995 Boston College	60	27	280	45.0	2	7	27
1996 Boston College	330	171	1,990	51.8	9	9	46
1997 Boston College	305	188	2,239	61.6	11	10	60
Totals	701	390	4,548	55.6	22	26	60

Rushing: 5 for 8 yards, 1.6 avg., LG 8 in 1994; 10 for -6 yards, -0.6 avg., LG 8, 1TD in 1995; 87 for -214 yards, -2.5 avg., LG 16, 2 TDs in 1996; 71 for 24 yards, 0.3 avg., LG 17, 1 TD in 1997 for total of 173 for -188 yards, -1.1 avg., LG 17, 4 TDs

EDWIN WATSON   35

Fullback
College: Purdue
Ht.: 6-0   **Wt.:** 225   **Born:** 9/29/76   **Acq:** D7

COLLEGE: The Packers' seventh-round selection (218th overall) in 1998...A four-year letter winner (1994-97) at Purdue, he started for three-and-a-half seasons...Started 32 of 40 career games for the Boilermakers...Finished as the school's fourth all-time leading rusher with 2,520 yards on 530 carries...Scored 25 rushing touchdowns, good for fifth place in school annals...Notched five career 100-yard rushing games...An accomplished receiver, he totaled 676 yards on 63 career receptions, with 2 touchdowns...Ranks eighth on Purdue's all-time scoring list with 164 points...Played both running back and fullback during his career at Purdue, is expected to contend for backup fullback job behind William Henderson...Has skills necessary of a running back to perform in the Packers' version of the 'West Coast' offense..."He caught the eyes of our coaching staff with his unusual ability to catch the ball coming out of the backfield in college," says Green Bay offensive coordinator Sherm Lewis. "He has good size and speed, which also should make him very valuable as a special teams player."...**1997:** An honorable mention All-Big Ten selection, played in 12 games with 11 starts...Finished with a team-leading 927 yards and 11 touchdowns on 175 carries...Seventh-leading rusher in the Big Ten...Also had 31 receptions for 411 yards and 2 touchdowns...Topped the century mark three times to end the season in games against Michigan State (115), Penn State (133) and Indiana (163)...Michigan State effort included a three-yard game-winning plunge with 40 seconds left in a 22-21 victory...Had 65- and 21-yard touchdowns among 4 receptions for 115 yards in win over Minnesota, also adding a rushing score...Again notched 3 touchdowns, all by way of the ground, in game vs. Wisconsin...A 75-yard score against the Badgers was the longest by a Boilermaker since 1982...Enjoyed a strong Alamo Bowl performance with 5 receptions for 102 yards and 41 rushing yards on 13 rushes...**1996:** Started all 11 games and finished with a team-high 768 yards and 6 touchdowns on 194 carries...Was the third-leading receiver for the Boilermakers with 220 yards on 25 catches...Named Big Ten 'Offensive Player of the Week' after rushing for a career-high 229 yards on 29 carries, with 3 TDs, vs. North Carolina State...**1995:** Made seven starts and played in all 11 games, finishing as the team's second-leading rusher with 553 yards on 102 carries, with 5 touchdowns...Also caught 6 passes for 41 yards...Romped for 194 yards and 2 TDs on 21 carries against Wisconsin...Matched with Mike Alstott's 204 yards against the Badgers, the combined total of 398 yards was the school record for most rushing yards by two Purdue backs in one game...Received Purdue's 'Leonard Wilson Award' for unselfishness and dedication...**1994:** Played in seven games, starting the final three...Finished as Purdue's third-leading rusher with 272 yards on 59 carries, with 3 touchdowns...Opened his college career with 13 rushes for 89 yards and a touchdown in a victory over Ball State.

HIGH SCHOOL: A first-team all-state selection as a senior at Pontiac (Mich.) Northern High School...Also was a second-team all-metro and all-county selection by the *Detroit Free Press*...A four-year letter winner, he rushed for 1,053 yards and 22 touchdowns on 123 carries as a senior...Returned 9 kickoffs for 186 yards...Also was a four-year letter winner in both track (100-, 200-, and 400-meters) and wrestling.

PERSONAL: Majored in recreational management...Single...Nicknamed 'E-Watts'...Hobbies include bowling and fishing...Has spent the last seven years serving as a mentor and tutor at Herrington Elementary School in Pontiac, Mich. ...Born Edwin David Watson, II, in New Orleans...Residence: West Lafayette, Ind.

COLLEGE STATISTICS:

		RUSHING				RECEIVING				
Year	No.	Yds.	Avg.	LG	TD	No.	Yds.	Avg.	LG	TD
1994 Purdue 59		272	4.6	18	3	1	4	4.0	4	0
1995 Purdue 102		553	5.4	63	5	6	41	6.8	12	0
1996 Purdue 194		768	4.0	49	6	25	220	8.8	28	0
1997 Purdue 175		927	5.3	75	11	31	411	13.3	65	2
Totals.................530		**2,520**	**4.8**	**75**	**25**	**63**	**676**	**10.7**	**65**	**2**

INSIDE 1265

Inside 1265 is the official television program of the Green Bay Packers. The show, which debuted near the end of the 1997 season, provides viewers with a behind-the-scenes look at what is happening with their favorite team from within the Packers' offices at 1265 Lombardi Avenue in Green Bay.

The show is co-hosted by Jessie Garcia, sportscaster at WTMJ-TV in Milwaukee, and Packer Hall of Famer Larry McCarren, sports director at Green Bay's WFRV-TV.

The program regularly boasts exclusive, one-on-one interviews with the Packers' hierarchy, including President and CEO Bob Harlan, Executive Vice President/General Manager Ron Wolf, Head Coach Mike Holmgren and Vice President of Administration/Chief Financial Officer Mike Reinfeldt.

Other recent stories on *Inside 1265* have included an in-depth profile of the Packers' 1998 first-round draft choice, Vonnie Holliday; extended interviews with assistant coaches Nolan Cromwell (wide receivers) and Johnny Holland (special teams), who both took on new assignments in 1998; a look at what some of the players did during this past offseason; and a behind-the-scenes peek at the football camp of tight end Mark Chmura.

The show also includes a special "strategy" session, where McCarren provides viewers with an in-depth look at a specific player and an aspect of his game. Recent strategy topics have consisted of strong safety LeRoy Butler demonstrating how he blitzes the quarterback and of defensive tackle Santana Dotson on how he takes on an opposing offensive lineman.

Inside 1265 airs on a state-wide basis approximately once every two months, appearing on WTMJ-TV (Ch. 4) in Milwaukee, WFRV-TV (Ch. 5) in Green Bay, WISC-TV (Ch. 3) in Madison, WSAW-TV (Ch. 7) in Wausau and WLAX-TV (Ch. 25) in La Crosse. Air dates and times vary by market.

MIKE WAHLE

68

Offensive Tackle
College: Navy
Ht.: 6-6   **Wt.:** 306   **Born:** 3/29/77   **Acq:** SD2

COLLEGE: The Packers' first and only selection in the 1998 supplemental draft, chosen in the 24th position of the second round (and the second of two picks overall in the draft)...A two-year letter winner at Navy (1996-97), including last season as a starter...A late bloomer physically, he entered the Naval Academy in 1995 as a 210-pound wide receiver and continued to grow, reaching his present, 6-6, 306-pound stature this spring...Packers offensive line coach Tom Lovat is impressed with Wahle's potential, saying, "He's got good size and, with his history as a receiver and quarterback, it would indicate that he's a good athlete. He's definitely not a project in the sense that he'd be starting from scratch."...Had established himself as a top-flight player and leader at Annapolis, evidenced by his selection as a team co-captain for the upcoming 1998 season in a vote by his coaches and teammates, but due to an NCAA ruling, he had to forfeit his senior year eligibility...After resigning from the academy, he has no further military obligations...Made a strong impression both on and off the field during his stay at Navy with head coach Charlie Weatherbie saying, "He's got great feet, he's very strong and quick, a great athlete who's very capable of playing in the NFL. More people have asked about his character and I've told them he's a great person, the kind of man you'd want your son to grow up to be like."...As a result of Wahle's selection, the Packers surrendered their second-round choice in the 1999 NFL draft...**1997:** Started all 11 games at left tackle for Navy, helping to pave the way for the nation's third-best rushing offense...**1996:** Made transition to offensive line and played in six games as a reserve tackle and on special teams...**1995:** Played on the junior varsity squad as a wide receiver...Did not see any varsity action.

HIGH SCHOOL: Was an all-conference selection and league MVP as a tight end at Rim of the World High School in Lake Arrowhead, Calif. ...A three-year letter winner, he also played quarterback and strong safety...Also was a three-time letterman in basketball, he garnered league MVP and all-region honors as a senior point guard...Additionally played baseball, winning four letters as a pitcher.

PERSONAL: Majored in economics...Single...Nicknamed 'Beagle'...Hobbies include wakeboarding, cooking, weightlifting and reading suspense novels...Worked with Rim Education Foundation while in high school...Father, Chris, played defensive line at Oregon State...Has two friends from grade school currently playing college football – John Merandi, a center at Notre Dame; and Scott Allmon, a center at Wyoming...Born Michael James Wahle in Portland, Ore. ...Residence: Blue Jay, Calif.

G **OTHER FREE AGENTS**

MAGIC BENTON (WR, 6-0, 185, 1/10/76, Rookie, Miami of Fla.): Signed with the Packers as an undrafted free agent on April 24, 1998...A three-year letter winner at the University of Miami (1995-97)...Played in 30 career games with the Hurricanes, making seven starts...Finished with 50 receptions for 760 yards (15.2 avg.) and 6 touchdowns...Also had 24 punt returns for 210 yards (8.8 avg.) and 1 TD, and 18 kickoff returns for 391 yards (21.7 avg.) in his career...Enjoyed outstanding junior season in 1996, posting career highs in receptions (38), receiving yards (547) and touchdown receptions (4), as he became the first player in Miami history to open a season with three consecutive 100-yard receiving games...Majored in communications...A *Parade* All-American and two-time all-state selection as a wide receiver at Northwestern High School in Miami...A three-year letterman in football, he also played cornerback and free safety on defense...A four-time letter winner in track, he captured the state championship in the 400-meter dash as a senior and set school records in the 100-, 200- and 400-meters...Nicknamed 'Magic Man'...Hobbies include playing basketball and watching TV...Through college course work, volunteered for a semester at a local juvenile detention center...Aspires to one day be a television broadcaster...Single, resides in Miami...Given name Magic Dawel Benton, born in Miami.

MICHAEL BLAIR (FB, 5-11, 245, 11/26/74, 1st Year, Ball State): Signed with the Packers as a free agent on April 22, 1998...Originally had signed as an undrafted free agent with the Kansas City Chiefs on April 28, 1997, he later was waived during training camp (Aug. 15) and spent the remainder of the year out of football...A four-year starter and letter winner (1993-96) at Ball State...Finished as the school's second-ranking career rusher with 3,051 yards on 668 carries (4.6 avg.), with a school-record 31 touchdowns...Also had 92 receptions for 889 yards and 6 touchdowns as he started 41 of 44 career games for the Cardinals...His 37 total touchdowns is also a school record...Posted 12 career 100-yard games with Ball State, second in team annals...Earned second-team All-Mid-America Conference honors as a senior in 1996, rushing for 680 yards and 8 touchdowns on 147 carries...Was an All-MAC second-team selection as a junior, finishing with 819 yards rushing on 218 carries, with 4 touchdowns...As a freshman, garnered first-team All-MAC honors and was named 'Freshman of the Year,' as he rushed for 738 yards and 8 touchdowns...Also contributed 41 receptions for 351 yards and 2 TDs as the Cardinals captured the MAC title; he added a two-yard touchdown pass in Ball State's Las Vegas Bowl appearance...Redshirted in 1992...Also participated in track, lettering once...Earned B.S. degree in journalism, emphasizing in graphic design...Rushed for 1,200 yards and racked up 1,800 all-purpose yards as a senior at Thornwood (South Holland, Ill.) High School...A tailback and cornerback, he lettered four years in football...Also lettered four times in track...Interests include studying dinosaurs, science fiction and geology...Single, resides in Dolton, Ill. ...Given name Michaelangelo Christopher Blair, born in Chicago.

MIKE BOWMAN (WR, 6-1, 198, 9/16/74, Rookie, Valdosta State): Signed with Green Bay as an undrafted free agent on April 28, 1998...A two-year letter winner at NCAA Division II Valdosta State (1996-97), including last year as a starter...Started all 11 games as a senior, hauling in 43 receptions for 728 yards (16.9 avg.) and 11 touchdowns...Played in eight games in 1996, totaling 138 yards and 1 TD on 11 receptions...Majored in environmental geography...Attended University of Florida and lettered two years in track (1993-94), before transferring to Valdosta State...A four-time letterman at Interlachen (Fla.) High School...Played quarterback and safety...Also earned four letters in basketball, three letters in track and two letters in baseball...Nicknamed 'Bo Do'...Hobbies include playing the bass guitar...Has done construction work the past two summers and also has worked as a personal trainer...Has given time to the March of Dimes in Florida...Single, resides in Valdosta, Ga. ...Given name Michael David Bowman, born in Gainesville, Fla.

KEATON CROMARTIE (LB, 6-2, 238, 4/19/76, Rookie, Tulane): Signed with the Packers as an undrafted free agent on April 24, 1998...A four-year letter winner at Tulane (1994-97), including last year as a starter...Played in 42 career games with 10 starts, finishing with 103 tackles (62 solo), 9 sacks, 15 tackles for loss, 1 interception and 2 blocked kicks...A linebacker his first three seasons, made move to defensive end and started 10 games as a senior, registering 41 tackles, including 9 sacks and 12 tackles for

OTHER FREE AGENTS

loss...Majored in social science...An all-district selection at linebacker as a senior at Southeast High School in Bradenton, Fla. ...Senior year's squad went 15-0 to capture the Class 4A state championship and was rated sixth nationally by *USA Today*...Earned three letters in football and two in track (shot put)...Nicknamed 'Keatieboy'...Hobbies include running track, playing basketball and training for football...Friend of the family, Robert Goff, was a nine-year NFL defensive lineman, playing with Tampa Bay (1988-89), New Orleans (1990-95) and Minnesota (1996)...Has worked on behalf of 'Jack and Jill,' an African-American teen organization...Single, resides in Bradenton, Fla. ...Given name Keaton Alfred Cromartie, born in Bradenton, Fla.

JASON DAVIS (P, 6-0, 219, 1/24/75, Rookie, Oklahoma State): Signed with the Packers as an undrafted free agent on April 24, 1998...A three-year letter winner at Oklahoma State (1995-97)...Left school as the second-leading punter in Cowboys' annals with a 43.9-yard career average...As a senior, averaged 43.9 yards on 50 punts, ranking second in the Big 12 Conference and 13th in the NCAA...Was a third-team All-Big 12 selection...In 1996, averaged 44.0 yards on 59 punts, good for 18th in the NCAA and fifth in the conference...Effort included a school-record 82-yard boot at Colorado...Earned B.A. degree in business management with a marketing minor...In 1995 at Blinn Junior College, averaged 43 yards per punt and did not have a block...An all-conference punter at Troy High School in Kerrville, Texas...Won two letters in football and also played wide receiver, running back, kicker and kick returner...Also lettered two years in track...Hobbies include fishing, hunting and outdoor sports...Has done carpentry work during the previous 10 summers for his father's company...Married to Tracy, couple resides in Stillwater, Okla. ...Given name Jason Lee Davis, born in Austin Texas.

LEE DeRAMUS (WR, 6-1, 210, 8/24/72, 3rd Year, Wisconsin): Signed with the Packers on March 17, 1998...Originally a sixth-round selection of New Orleans in 1995, played two years with the Saints (1995-96) before being waived in training camp last year (Aug. 18)...Spent 1997 out of football...In two seasons with Saints, caught 21 passes for 182 yards and 1 touchdown...Played in 15 games in 1996 with four starts, catching 15 passes for 182 yards and 1 touchdown...Made first career start at Cincinnati (Sept. 15) and made 2 receptions for 25 yards...Notched first career touchdown on a 28-yard reception vs. Chicago (Oct. 13), his only catch of the day...Made three other starts – vs. Houston (Nov. 10), vs. Atlanta (Dec. 8), and at New York Giants (Dec. 15)...Played in final eight games of 1995 after spending the first half of the season on the reserve/non-football injury list while rehabilitating broken leg suffered prior to his senior year at Wisconsin...Activated to the 53-man roster on Oct. 30, he went on to catch 6 passes for 76 yards, and added 1 special teams tackle...Posted career, single-game highs in receptions (4) and yards (56) vs. Green Bay (Dec. 16)...A three-time letter winner at Wisconsin (1991-93), starting two-and-a-half years...Missed entire 1994, senior season after suffering a broken left leg in practice a week before the season opener...In three years with the Badgers, started 27 of 33 games and totaled 1,974 yards and 15 touchdowns on 119 receptions, leading the team each year...An All-Big Ten selection in 1993, hauled in 54 receptions for 920 yards and 6 TDs, eclipsing Al Toon's school record in the process...Also participated in track at Wisconsin, running the 100- and 200-meter dashes and the 4 x 100-meter relay...Majored in sociology...A *Blue Chip Illustrated* and *SuperPrep* All-America selection as a wide receiver at Edgewood Regional High School in Tansboro, N.J. ...Also played defensive back...Was a four-year letter winner in football, basketball and track...Nicknamed 'Famous' and 'Babe'...Hobbies include playing and recording music, playing basketball and video games, and going to movies...Winner of Saints' 1995 'Ed Block Courage Award,' in honor of his diligent rehabilitation of his broken leg – he was just the second NFL rookie to receive the award since its inception in 1984...Is a part-owner – with his father, Lee Sr. – of 'Lee's Precision Cut Barber Shop' in Tansboro, N.J. ...Has given time to Boys & Girls Club in Tansboro and also has run a basketball camp there the past three summers for 8 to 12-year olds...Additionally, has helped his father, a pastor at Mount Zion Baptist in Tansboro, with church youth groups...Has an uncle, Jim Smith, who played wide receiver for the Pittsburgh Steelers from 1977-82...Single, resides in Sicklerville, N.J. ...Given name Lee Collins DeRamus, born in Stratford, N.J.

TERRELL FARLEY (CB/S, 6-0, 195, 8/16/75, Rookie, Nebraska): Signed with the Packers for the '98 season on Jan. 12, 1998...Undrafted in 1997, he spent the season out of football...A two-time letter winner at Nebraska (1995-96), starting the last year-and-a-half...Played in 19 career games as a linebacker, with 12 starts, and finished tenure with 105 tackles (42 solo), 8 sacks, 19 tackles for loss, 3 interceptions, 7 passes defensed, 3 blocked kicks and 1 fumble recovery...Returned 2 interceptions for touchdowns...Played in eight games, with seven starts, as a 1996 senior, garnering third-team All-Big 12 honors from the *Associated Press*...Finished with 43 tackles, 3 sacks and 10 tackles for loss...As a junior, earned second-team All-America honors from *AP* and was named Big Eight Defensive 'Newcomer of the Year'...Totaled 62 tackles, 5 sacks, 9 tackles for loss and 3 interceptions, with 2 being returned for touchdowns...Was teammate of current Packers cornerback Tyrone Williams...Majored in criminal justice...Played at Independence Junior College in 1993-94...An all-state selection and defensive 'Player of the Year' as a linebacker at Kendrick High School in Columbus, Ga. ...Lettered three years each in football and track...Hobbies include playing Sony PlayStation...Has worked with the Nate Odomes Foundation charity basketball game in Columbus, Ga. ...Single, resides in Atlanta...Given name Terrell Dwayne Farley, born in Columbus, Ga.

ANTHONY FOGLE (CB, 6-0, 193, 2/23/75, 1st Year, Oklahoma): Re-signed with the Packers on Jan. 28, 1998...Originally had signed as an undrafted free agent with the New York Jets on April 28, 1997, he later was waived during training camp (Aug. 25)...Was signed to the Packers' practice squad on Nov. 26 of last year, where he spent the remainder of the season...Allocated to the Barcelona Dragons of NFL Europe this past spring, he played in all 10 games with five starts and finished third on the team with 43 tackles (32 solo), plus 1 interception and 8 passes defensed...Also returned 18 punts for 128 yards (7.1 avg.) and 1 touchdown...Earned NFL Europe's special teams 'Player of the Week' honors for Week 7 when he returned a punt 50 yards for a touchdown to seal a 31-24 victory over the previously-undefeated Rhein Fire...Added 5 kickoff returns for 81 yards...A three-year starter and letter winner at Oklahoma (1994-96)...As a senior with the Sooners, recorded career highs in tackles (46), tackles for loss (19), forced fumbles (3), fumble recoveries (2) and passes defensed (7)...Posted two interceptions as a junior...Majored in film and video studies...Earned three letters in football as a prep, he was an all-state and all-region selection as an option quarterback at Westbury High School in Houston, rushing for 1,010 yards and 13 touchdowns as a senior...Also lettered three times in track, competing in the 100- and 200-meter dashes and the 4 x 100-meter relay...Also was an All-Houston academic selection...Hobbies include fishing...Has been involved with Fellowship of Christian Athletes...Has a brother, Julius, a sergeant in the Army, who is a highly-ranked amateur boxer and two-time Golden Glove winner at the middleweight level...Has a daughter, Cydney (born 4/26/95)...Resides in Norman, Okla. ...Given name Anthony Lee Fogle, born in New York, N.Y.

DAVID HOELSCHER (DE, 6-6, 281, 11/27/75, Rookie, Eastern Kentucky): Signed with the Packers as an undrafted free agent on April 24, 1998...A four-year starter and letter winner at Eastern Kentucky, collected 201 tackles (121 solo), 17 sacks and 44 stops for loss...As a senior, made 61 tackles (34 solo), 3½ sacks, 1 interception and a team-leading 14 tackles for loss...Also had 2 blocked kicks...Majored in speech communications...A three-year letterman as a tight end and defensive end at Versailles (Ohio) High School...Also earned three letters in track...Hobbies include all sports...Worked at a plastics recycling company in the summer of 1997...Single, resides in Yorkshire, Ohio...Given name David Henry Hoelscher, born in Coldwater, Ohio.

OTHER FREE AGENTS

ANTONIO LONDON (LB, 6-2, 238, 4/14/71, 6th Year, Alabama): Signed with Green Bay on Feb. 24, 1998...Originally a third-round selection by Detroit in 1993, has played in 75 career games with 19 starts for the Lions (1993-97)...Also has played in four postseason games with one start...During his career he has registered 13 sacks among 141 total tackles (83 solo)...Played in all 16 games with six starts for Detroit in 1997, finishing with 46 tackles and 2 sacks...Also started postseason game at Tampa Bay (Dec. 28) in place of injured Reggie Brown and had 1 sack among 6 tackles...Started 13 games and played in 14 overall in 1996, finishing with a career-high 70 tackles (40 solo) and 3 sacks...Registered a career-high 7 sacks among 14 tackles in 1995 as he saw action in 15 games...Posted a career, single-game high with 3 sacks vs. Minnesota (Nov. 23)...A three-year starter and four-time letterman (1989-92) at Alabama...Totaled 9 sacks during his tenure at Alabama...Was one of only two true freshmen to letter...Telecommunications and film major...Was a *Parade* All-America selection, a member of the *Sporting News'* 'Top 100 squad' and an all-state pick as a senior linebacker at Tullahoma (Tenn.) High School...Started for four years at linebacker and wide receiver...Also participated in track (four years) and basketball (three years)...Nicknamed 'Stick'...Hobbies include fishing, sleeping and spending time with his family...Served as a substitute teacher (grades K-12) in Tullahoma during the 1995 and '96 offseasons...Conducted football camps in Tullahoma from 1992-95, helping out 8 to 16-year olds...While in Detroit, remained involved with the 'Boys and Men' program in Tullahoma and invited 10 youths each year to a Lions game at the Pontiac (Mich.) Silverdome...Married to Gloria, couple has three children – a daughter, Tiffany (born 3/28/84), and two sons, Antonio II (born 1/17/95), and Auston (born 7/8/97) – and resides in Belvidere, Tenn. ...Given name Antonio Monte London, born in Tullahoma, Tenn.

BILLY LYON (DT, 6-5, 295, 12/10/73, 1st Year, Marshall): Re-signed with Green Bay on Jan. 28, 1998...Originally had signed as an undrafted free agent with the Kansas City Chiefs on April 28, 1997, he later was waived during training camp (Aug. 15)...Was out of football until being signed to the Packers' practice squad on Nov. 20, 1997, where he spent the remainder of the regular season and playoffs...A four-year starter and letter winner at Marshall (1993-96)...Played in three NCAA Division I-AA championship games with the Thundering Herd, capturing a national championship in the 1996 contest...Played in 59 games overall with 54 starts, finishing career with 304 tackles (164 solo), 30 sacks, 148 quarterback pressures, 13 passes defended, 12 forced fumbles and 3 fumble recoveries...Was a NCAA Division I-AA consensus All-America and first-team All-Southern Conference selection as a senior, when he finished with 91 tackles (51 solo), 9 sacks, 3 forced fumbles and 3 passes defended...Garnered first-team All-America honors from the *Associated Press* and first-team all-conference recognition as a junior...As a sophomore, received first-team All-Southern Conference honors and was an honorable mention All-American...Moved from tight end to tackle as a redshirt freshman...Redshirted in 1992...Earned B.S. degree in occupational safety...Earned first-team all-conference selection in football as a senior at Lloyd High School in Erlanger, Ky. ...Earned three letters in football as a linebacker and tight end...Nicknamed 'Billy'...Hobbies include building model cars and watching sports...Engaged to marry Tasha Gadd in February of 1999, has a son, Tyler (born 6/15/96)...Resides in Morningview, Ky. ...Given name William Morton Lyon, born in Ashland, Ky.

CHRIS McCOY (RB, 5-10, 195, 7/13/75, Rookie, Navy): Signed by the Packers as an undrafted free agent on June 3, 1998...Was a three-year starter and letter winner as a quarterback at Navy (1995-97)...Finished career as second-ranking rusher on Navy's all-time list with 3,401 yards on 682 carries (5.0 avg.), a total behind only the 4,179 yards posted by Napoleon McCallum (1981-85)...Rushing total is second only to the 3,612 yards gained by Air Force's Dee Dowis (1986-89) for a NCAA quarterback...Also registered 43 rushing touchdowns, breaking McCallum's school record of 31...Additionally posted 2,486 career passing yards on 152 completions in 323 attempts, with 21 touchdowns and 17 interceptions...As a senior, registered 1,370 rushing yards and 20 touchdowns on 246 carries (5.6 avg.), and passed for 1,203 yards and 11 TDs on 69 completions in 135 attempts...Earned degree in economics...An All-West Georgia selection as a defensive back at Randolph/Clay High School in Morris, Ga. ...Served as a captain his final two years and earned team MVP honors as a senior...Also lettered in baseball, earning team MVP honors...Single, resides in Morris, Ga. ...Given name Christopher Cornelius McCoy, born in Eutanla, Ala.

OTHER FREE AGENTS

ANTHONY McKINNEY (TE, 6-2, 253, 12/8/74, 1st Year, Connecticut): Signed with the Packers for the '98 season on Dec. 30, 1997...Originally had signed with the Minnesota Vikings as an undrafted free agent on May 1, 1997, he later was waived during training camp (July 29) and spent the remainder of the year out of football...A three-year starter and letter winner at the University of Connecticut (1994-96), starting in 31 of his last 33 games...A second-team All-Yankee Conference selection as a senior, finishing second on the team with 23 receptions for 226 yards and 2 touchdowns...Also rushed 11 times for 53 yards as a senior...Overall, finished his Huskies career with 52 receptions for 701 yards and 4 touchdowns...Was a third-team all-conference pick as a 1995 junior...Redshirted in 1992...Earned a B.A. degree in sociology...Was an all-conference selection as a senior offensive tackle for Fairfield (Conn.) Prep...Also a defensive tackle, he earned three letters in football...Won two letters in track...Hobbies include reading and taking long walks...Single, has a son Kyran (born 3/5/96)...Resides in Charlotte...Given name Anthony Louis McKinney, born in Queens, N.Y.

DEXTER NOTTAGE (DT, 6-4, 284, 11/14/70, 4th Year, Florida A&M): Signed as a free agent by the Packers on March 19, 1998...Originally a sixth-round draft choice of the Washington Redskins in 1994...Spent three seasons with the Redskins (1994-96), playing in 47 games with five starts...Played in 16 games, starting four, for Washington in 1996, finishing with career highs in tackles (50) and sacks (5)...Played in all 16 games in 1995, posting 32 tackles, 3 fumble recoveries and 1 forced fumble...Saw action in 15 contests in his 1994 rookie season, starting once, and recorded 34 tackles and 1 sack...Waived by Washington late in its '97 training camp (Aug. 25), he was out of football until signing with Kansas City on Sept. 24...Spent five weeks with the Chiefs, appearing in one game (vs. Seattle, Sept. 28) and registering 1 tackle...Inactive for the next four games, he was waived on Nov. 7 and spent the rest of the season out of football...A two-year starter and letter winner at Florida A&M (1990-91), he left school after his sophomore year to help support his family after some members had experienced health problems...In two years at Florida A&M, he played in 13 career games, posting 65 tackles and 6½ sacks...Majored in physical therapy...An all-state selection at defensive tackle and fullback at Hollywood (Fla.) Hills High School...Also played tight end...Earned three letters each in football, basketball and track...Hobbies include playing basketball, swimming and spending time with his family...Speaks to elementary and junior high school students in the Washington D.C.-Northern Virginia area on the importance of staying in school and furthering their education...Married to Roxanne, couple has two sons, Dexter II (born 5/20/93) and Mythyus (born 9/18/96), and resides in Green Bay...Given name Dexter Alexander Nottage, born in Nassau, Bahamas.

EMORY SMITH (FB, 6-0, 245, 5/21/74, 1st Year, Clemson): Re-signed with the Packers on Jan. 28, 1998...Originally had signed with Green Bay as an undrafted free agent on April 25, 1997, he later was waived in training camp (Aug. 19)...Was signed to the Dallas practice squad on Oct. 22, he spent the remainder of the Cowboys' season with that team...Subsequently was signed to the Packers' practice squad (Dec. 30) for the balance of Green Bay's postseason after his regular-season practice squad contract with the Cowboys had expired...A four-time letterman (1993-96) and two-year starter at Clemson...Redshirted in 1992...Rushed for 1,568 career yards and scored 25 touchdowns, including bowl games, for the Tigers...Played in 47 games, starting 31...Had his best season as a 1995 junior, when he rushed for 712 yards (third-best in school history by a fullback) and scored 15 TDs (14 rushing, 1 receiving)...Named as the offensive MVP of the Peach Bowl in 1993...Earned a B.A. degree in marketing...Was a first-team all-state selection as a linebacker at Escambia High School in Pensacola, Fla. ...Averaged 10 tackles per game...Named Pensacola area's 'Defensive Player of the Year'...Also rushed for 1,001 yards and 13 touchdowns as a senior...Selected to play in the Florida-Georgia all-star game...Brother, Emmitt, is a star running back for the Dallas Cowboys...Nicknamed 'Em'...Hobbies include fishing, hunting, golf, water skiing and all outdoor sports...Enjoys speaking to elementary and middle school students in Pensacola, Fla., on the importance of education...Single, resides in Pensacola, Fla. ...Given name Emory Gerald Smith, born in Pensacola, Fla.

KYLE WACHHOLTZ (TE, 6-4, 248, 5/17/72, 1st Year, Southern California): Re-signed with the Packers on Feb. 24, 1998...Originally a seventh-round draft pick by Green Bay in 1996, he was waived in training camp (Aug. 25) and spent the remainder of the year on the Packers' practice squad before being signed to the active roster (Jan. 10, 1997) when George Koonce was placed on injured reserve...Inactive for both the NFC Championship Game and Super Bowl XXXI...Drafted as a quarterback, he impressed coaches as a scout team tight end during his '96 season on the Green Bay practice squad, prompting the position switch to begin the '97 camp...Waived during the 1997 preseason (Aug. 18), he was signed a week later (Aug. 26) to the Packers' practice squad, where he spent the balance of the year...A two-year letter winner as a quarterback (1993, 1995) at Southern California...A backup in 1992 and '93, split time as a senior...Finished career with 128 completions in 206 attempts for 1,469 yards and 13 touchdowns, with only 4 interceptions...Selected to play in Senior Bowl...As a senior, threw for 1,231 yards and 11 touchdowns with 3 interceptions on 105 completions in 171 attempts (61.4%)...Redshirted in 1991...Majored in history...A *Blue Chip* All-America second-team selection at quarterback for Norco (Calif.) High School...As a senior, led team to league championship and was named league's MVP, as he completed 116 of 198 passes for 1,868 yards and 20 touchdowns...Also played baseball and basketball, earning all-league honors in baseball and league MVP honors in basketball as a senior...Uncle, Larry Wachholtz, was an All-America defensive back at Nebraska in 1966...Nicknamed 'Wacky'...Hobbies include basketball, paint ball and golf...Single, he splits residence between Corona, Calif., and Green Bay...Given name Kyle John Wachholtz, born in Fullerton, Calif.

JUDE WADDY (LB, 6-2, 220, 9/12/75, Rookie, William & Mary): Signed with Green Bay as an undrafted free agent on April 24, 1998...A four-year starter and letter winner at William & Mary (1994-97)...Played in 45 career games with 41 starts, finishing career with 422 tackles (254 solo), 19 sacks and 15 stops for loss...Was an All-Eastern College Athletic Conference selection as a senior, when he led the team with 112 tackles (59 solo) while starting all 11 games...Redshirted in 1993...Earned B.S. degree in kinesiology...An all-state and all-county selection at linebacker his senior year at Suitland (Md.) High School...Lettered three years in football, also lining up as an offensive guard, tight end and halfback...Earned three letters in wrestling, taking county and regional titles and a third-place state finish as a senior...Hobbies include motorcycle racing, a pastime he experienced in high school...Worked with the African-American Male Coalition while at William & Mary...College teammate of current Packers safety Darren Sharper...Single, resides in Yorktown, Va. ...Given name Jude Michael Waddy, born in Washington, D.C.

OFFENSE

WR:	86	Antonio Freeman	80	Derrick Mayes	49	Roell Preston	
			85	Corey Bradford	19	Mike Bowman	
LT:	78	Ross Verba	77	John Michels	68	Mike Wahle	
LG:	62	Marco Rivera	70	Joe Andruzzi			
C:	52	Frank Winters	58	Mike Flanagan	67	Jeff Dellenbach	
RG:	63	Adam Timmerman	74	Doug Widell	67	Jeff Dellenbach	
RT:	72	Earl Dotson	64	Bruce Wilkerson	76	Matt Willig	
TE:	89	Mark Chmura	83	Jeff Thomason	81	Tyrone Davis	
			47	Kyle Wachholtz	48	Anthony McKinney	
WR:	87	Robert Brooks	82	Ronnie Anderson	84	Bill Schroeder	
			46	Lee DeRamus	16	Magic Benton	
QB:	4	Brett Favre	18	Doug Pederson	11	Matt Hasselback	
					9	David Klingler	
RB:	25	Dorsey Levens	32	Travis Jervey	29	Raymont Harris	
			30	Glyn Milburn	41	Chris McCoy	
FB:	33	William Henderson	22	Emory Smith	35	Edwin Watson	
					27	Michael Blair	

DEFENSE

LE:	92	Reggie White	96	Vaughn Booker	75	Eric Curry	
			95	Keith McKenzie	79	David Hoelscher	
T:	71	Santana Dotson	73	Dexter Nottage			
NT:	93	Gilbert Brown	94	Bob Kuberski	98	Billy Lyon	
RE:	90	Vonnie Holliday	97	Paul Frase	91	Jonathon Brown	
LOLB:	53	George Koonce	59	Seth Joyner	45	Keaton Cromartie	
MLB:	55	Bernardo Harris	56	Lamont Hollinquest	50	Anthony Hicks	
ROLB:	51	Brian Williams	57	Antonio London	54	Jude Waddy	
LCB:	21	Craig Newsome	28	Roderick Mullen	44	Chris Darkins	
					24	Anthony Fogle	
RCB:	37	Tyrone Williams	26	Terry McDaniel	23	Roosevelt Blackmon	
					43	Terrell Farley	
SS:	36	LeRoy Butler	39	Mike Prior	38	Blaine McElmurry	
FS:	42	Darren Sharper	40	Pat Terrell	34	Scott McGarrahan	

SPECIAL TEAMS

K:	8	Ryan Longwell	10	Brett Conway			
P:	7	Sean Landeta	2	Jason Davis			
H:	18	Doug Pederson	11	Matt Hasselbeck			
PR:	30	Glyn Milburn	49	Roell Preston	23	Roosevelt Blackmon	
			84	Bill Schroeder	80	Derrick Mayes	
KR:	30	Glyn Milburn	49	Roell Preston	85	Corey Bradford	
					84	Bill Schroeder	
PC:	60	Rob Davis	97	Paul Frase	94	Bob Kuberski	
KC:	60	Rob Davis	67	Jeff Dellenbach	52	Frank Winters	

Rookies and first-year players are underlined

No.	Name	Pos.	Ht.	Wt.	Birth-date	NFL Exp.	College	High School Hometown
82	Anderson, Ronnie	WR	6-1	189	2/27/74	1	Allegheny College	Hunting Valley, Ohio
70	Andruzzi, Joe	G	6-3	310	8/23/75	2	Southern Conn. State	Staten Island, N.Y.
16	Benton, Magic	WR	6-0	185	1/10/76	R	Miami (Fla.)	Miami, Fla.
23	Blackmon, Roosevelt	CB	6-1	185	9/10/74	R	Morris Brown	Belle Glade, Fla.
27	Blair, Michael	RB	5-11	245	11/26/74	1	Ball State	South Holland, Ill.
96	Booker, Vaughn	DE	6-5	300	2/24/68	5	Cincinnati	Cincinnati, Ohio
19	Bowman, Mike	WR	6-1	198	9/16/74	R	Valdosta State	Interlachen, Fla.
85	Bradford, Corey	WR	6-1	197	12/8/75	R	Jackson State	Clinton, La.
87	Brooks, Robert	WR	6-0	180	6/23/70	7	South Carolina	Greenwood, S.C.
93	Brown, Gilbert	DT	6-2	350	2/22/71	6	Kansas	Detroit, Mich.
91	Brown, Jonathan	DE	6-4	265	11/28/75	R	Tennessee	Tulsa, Okla.
36	Butler, LeRoy	S	6-0	198	7/19/68	9	Florida State	Jacksonville, Fla.
89	Chmura, Mark	TE	6-5	255	2/22/69	7	Boston College	South Deerfield, Mass.
10	Conway, Brett	K	6-2	191	3/8/75	2	Penn State	Lilburn, Ga.
45	Cromartie, Keaton	LB	6-2	238	4/19/76	R	Tulane	Bradenton, Fla.
75	Curry, Eric	DE	6-6	275	2/3/70	6	Alabama	Thomasville, Ga.
44	Darkins, Chris	CB	6-0	205	4/30/74	3	Minnesota	Houston, Texas
2	Davis, Jason	P	6-0	219	1/24/75	R	Oklahoma State	Kerrville, Texas
60	Davis, Rob	LS	6-3	290	12/10/68	3	Shippensburg	Greenbelt, Md.
81	Davis, Tyrone	TE	6-4	252	6/30/72	3	Virginia	Halifax, Va.
67	Dellenbach, Jeff	C/G	6-6	300	2/14/63	14	Wisconsin	Wausau, Wis.
46	DeRamus, Lee	WR	6-1	210	8/24/72	3	Wisconsin	Tansboro, N.J.
72	Dotson, Earl	T	6-4	315	12/17/70	6	Texas A&I	Beaumont, Texas
71	Dotson, Santana	DT	6-5	286	12/19/69	7	Baylor	Houston, Texas
43	Farley, Terrell	CB/S	6-0	195	8/16/75	R	Nebraska	Columbus, Ga.
4	Favre, Brett	QB	6-2	230	10/10/69	8	Southern Mississippi	Kiln, Miss.
58	Flanagan, Mike	C	6-5	290	11/10/73	3	UCLA	Sacramento, Calif.
24	Fogle, Anthony	CB	6-0	193	2/23/75	1	Oklahoma	Houston, Texas
97	Frase, Paul	DE	6-5	275	5/6/65	10	Syracuse	Rochester, N.H.
86	Freeman, Antonio	WR	6-1	198	5/27/72	4	Virginia Tech	Baltimore, Md.
55	Harris, Bernardo	LB	6-2	248	10/15/71	4	North Carolina	Chapel Hill, N.C.
29	Harris, Raymont	RB	6-0	230	12/23/70	5	Ohio State	Lorain, Ohio
11	Hasselbeck, Matt	QB	6-4	217	9/25/75	5	Boston College	Norfolk, Mass.
33	Henderson, William	FB	6-1	245	2/19/71	4	North Carolina	Chester, Va.
50	Hicks, Anthony	LB	6-1	243	3/31/74	2	Arkansas	Arkadelphia, Ark.
79	Hoelscher, David	DE	6-6	281	11/27/75	R	Eastern Kentucky	Versailles, Ohio
90	Holliday, Vonnie	DE	6-5	296	12/11/75	R	North Carolina	Camden, S.C.
56	Hollinquest, Lamont	LB	6-3	250	10/24/70	5	Southern California	Downey, Calif.
32	Jervey, Travis	RB	6-0	222	5/5/72	4	The Citadel	Mt. Pleasant, S.C.
59	Joyner, Seth	LB	6-2	245	11/18/64	13	Texas-El Paso	Spring Valley, N.Y.
9	Klingler, David	QB	6-3	215	2/17/69	7	Houston	Stratford, Texas
53	Koonce, George	LB	6-1	245	10/15/68	7	East Carolina	Vanceboro, N.C.
94	Kuberski, Bob	DT	6-4	298	4/5/71	4	Navy	Folsom, Pa.
7	Landeta, Sean	P	6-0	200	1/6/62	14	Towson State	Towson, Md.
25	Levens, Dorsey	RB	6-1	228	5/21/70	5	Georgia Tech	Syracuse, N.Y.
57	London, Antonio	LB	6-2	238	4/14/71	6	Alabama	Tullahoma, Tenn.
8	Longwell, Ryan	K	6-0	192	8/16/74	2	California	Bend, Ore.
98	Lyon, Billy	DT	6-5	295	12/10/73	1	Marshall	Erlanger, Ky.
80	Mayes, Derrick	WR	6-0	205	1/28/74	3	Notre Dame	Indianapolis, Ind.

1998 PACKERS ROSTER

No.	Name	Pos.	Ht.	Wt.	Birth-date	NFL Exp.	College	High School Hometown
41	McCoy, Chris	RB	5-10	195	7/13/75	R	Navy	Morris, Ga.
26	McDaniel, Terry	CB	5-10	180	2/8/65	11	Tennessee	Saginaw, Mich.
38	McElmurry, Blaine	S	6-0	187	10/23/73	1	Montana	Troy, Mont.
34	McGarrahan, Scott	S	6-1	197	2/12/74	R	New Mexico	Arlington, Texas
95	McKenzie, Keith	DE	6-3	264	10/17/73	3	Ball State	Highland Park, Mich.
48	McKinney, Anthony	TE	6-2	253	12/8/74	1	Connecticut	Fairfield, Conn.
77	Michels, John	T	6-7	300	3/19/73	3	Southern California	La Jolla, Calif.
30	Milburn, Glyn	RB/KR	5-8	174	2/19/71	6	Stanford	Santa Monica, Calif.
28	Mullen, Roderick	CB/S	6-1	202	12/5/72	4	Grambling State	St. Francisville, La.
21	Newsome, Craig	CB	6-0	190	8/10/71	4	Arizona State	Rialto, Calif.
73	Nottage, Dexter	DT	6-4	284	11/14/70	4	Florida A&M	Hollywood, Fla.
18	Pederson, Doug	QB	6-3	216	1/31/68	6	Northeast Louisiana	Ferndale, Wash.
49	Preston, Roell	WR/KR	5-10	195	6/23/72	3	Mississippi	Hialeah, Fla.
39	Prior, Mike	S	6-0	208	11/14/63	13	Illinois State	Chicago Heights, Ill.
62	Rivera, Marco	G	6-4	305	4/26/72	3	Penn State	Elmont, N.Y.
84	Schroeder, Bill	WR	6-3	200	1/9/71	3	Wisconsin-La Crosse	Sheboygan, Wis.
42	Sharper, Darren	S	6-2	210	11/3/75	2	William & Mary	Richmond, Va.
22	Smith, Emory	FB	6-0	245	5/21/74	1	Clemson	Pensacola, Fla.
99	Smith, Jermaine	DT	6-3	298	2/3/72	2	Georgia	Augusta, Ga.
40	Terrell, Pat	S	6-1	208	3/18/68	9	Notre Dame	St. Petersburg, Fla.
83	Thomason, Jeff	TE	6-5	255	12/30/69	6	Oregon	Newport Beach, Calif.
63	Timmerman, Adam	G	6-4	300	8/14/71	4	South Dakota State	Cherokee, Iowa
78	Verba, Ross	T	6-4	302	10/31/73	2	Iowa	West Des Moines, Iowa
47	Wachholtz, Kyle	TE	6-4	248	5/17/72	1	Southern California	Norco, Calif.
54	Waddy, Jude	LB	6-2	220	9/12/75	R	William & Mary	Suitland, Md.
68	Wahle, Mike	T	6-6	306	3/29/77	R	Navy	Lake Arrowhead, Calif.
35	Watson, Edwin	FB	6-0	225	9/29/76	R	Purdue	Pontiac, Mich.
92	White, Reggie	DE	6-5	300	12/19/61	14	Tennessee	Chattanooga, Tenn.
74	Widell, Doug	G	6-4	285	9/23/66	10	Boston College	Hartford, Conn.
64	Wilkerson, Bruce	T	6-5	315	7/28/64	12	Tennessee	Loudon, Tenn.
51	Williams, Brian	LB	6-1	245	12/17/72	4	Southern California	Dallas, Texas
37	Williams, Tyrone	CB	5-11	192	5/31/73	3	Nebraska	Bradenton, Fla.
76	Willig, Matt	T	6-7	315	1/21/69	6	Southern California	Santa Fe Springs, Calif.
52	Winters, Frank	C	6-3	300	1/23/64	12	Western Illinois	Union City, N.J.

A player will be credited with a year of NFL experience for each season in which he accumulates six games on the Active List, Inactive List, Reserve/Injured List, or Reserve/Physically Unable to Perform List — six games on a combination of any of these lists. Rookies are players in their first year of professional football who have not been on the roster of another professional football team for any regular-season or postseason games. Players who have played in other professional sports leagues (Canadian Football League, etc.), have participated in previous NFL training camps, or have been on the above lists for fewer than six games are listed as first-year NFL players ("1").

Year	Record	Draft (32)	Trades (4)	Free Agents (45)
1990	6-10-0	S LeRoy Butler D2		
1992	9-7-0	WR Robert Brooks D3	QB Brett Favre (Atl)	LB George Koonce
		TE Mark Chmura D6		C Frank Winters
1993	9-7-0	T Earl Dotson D3		DE Reggie White (UFA)
		DT Bob Kuberski D7		
1994	9-7-0	RB Dorsey Levens D5b		
1995	11-5-0	CB Craig Newsome D1		LB Bernardo Harris
		FB William Henderson D3b		CB/S Roderick Mullen
		LB Brian Williams D3c		QB Doug Pederson
		WR Antonio Freeman D3d		TE Jeff Thomason
		RB Travis Jervey D5b		
		G Adam Timmerman D7		
1996	13-3-0	T John Michels D1		C/G Jeff Dellenbach
		WR Derrick Mayes D2		DT Santana Dotson (UFA)
		C Mike Flanagan D3a		LB Lamont Hollinquest
		CB Tyrone Williams D3b		T Bruce Wilkerson
		CB Chris Darkins D4		
		G Marco Rivera D6		
		DE Keith McKenzie D7b		
1997	13-3-0	T Ross Verba D1	DE Paul Frase (Jax)	WR Ronnie Anderson
		S Darren Sharper D2		G Joe Andruzzi
		K Brett Conway D3		LS Rob Davis
		DT Jermaine Smith D4		TE Tyrone Davis
		LB Anthony Hicks D5		LB Seth Joyner
				S Blaine McElmurry
				WR Bill Schroeder (D6c-94)
1998		DE Vonnie Holliday D1	DE Vaughn Booker (KC)	WR Magic Benton
		DE Jonathan Brown D3	RB/KR Glyn Milburn (Det)	FB Michael Blair
		CB Roosevelt Blackmon D4		WR Mike Bowman
		WR Corey Bradford D5		LB Keaton Cromartie
		S Scott McGarrahan D6a		DE Eric Curry (UFA)
		QB Matt Hasselbeck D6b		P Jason Davis
		FB Edwin Watson D7		WR Lee DeRamus
		T Mike Wahle SD2		CB/S Terrell Farley
				CB Anthony Fogle
				RB Raymont Harris (UFA)
				DE David Hoelscher
				QB David Klingler
				P Sean Landeta (UFA)
				LB Antonio London
				DT Billy Lyon
				RB Chris McCoy
				CB Terry McDaniel
				TE Anthony McKinney
				DT Dexter Nottage
				WR/KR Roell Preston
				S Mike Prior
				FB Emory Smith
				S Pat Terrell (UFA)
				TE Kyle Wachholtz (D7a-96)
				LB Jude Waddy
				G Doug Widell
				T Matt Willig (UFA)

Waivers (2): DT Gilbert Brown (from Minnesota), 1993; K Ryan Longwell (from San Francisco), 1997

15-4 Record (13-3 Regular Season)
NFC Champions • NFC Central Division Champions

PRESEASON GAMES

Date	Opponent	GB	Opp.	Attendance	Weather
Sat., July 26	Miami Dolphins	20	0	59,089	Partly cloudy & 82
Thurs., July 31	New England Patriots	7	3	60,778	Clear & 76
Fri., Aug. 8	at Oakland Raiders	37	24	42,956	Clear & 72
Sat., Aug. 16	Buffalo Bills ^	35	3	53,896	Indoors
Fri., Aug. 22	New York Giants +	22	17	76,704	Clear & 70
	TOTAL POINTS:	121	47		

REGULAR-SEASON GAMES

Date	Opponent	GB	Opp.	Attendance	Weather
Mon., Sept. 1	Chicago Bears	38	24	60,766	Hot, humid & 73
Sun., Sept. 7	at Philadelphia Eagles	9	10	66,803	Sunny &78
Sun., Sept. 14	Miami Dolphins	23	18	60,075	Cloudy & 70
Sun., Sept. 21	Minnesota Vikings	38	32	60,115	Mostly sunny & 59
Sun., Sept. 28	at Detroit Lions	15	26	78,110	Indoors
Sun., Oct. 5	Tampa Bay Buccaneers	21	16	60,100	Sunny, windy & 75
Sun., Oct. 12	Chicago Bears	24	23	62,212	Sunny, windy & 73
Mon., Oct. 27	at New England Patriots	28	10	59,972	Cloudy, cool & 52
Sun., Nov. 2	Detroit Lions	20	10	60,126	Cloudy & 35
Sun., Nov. 9	St. Louis Rams	17	7	60,093	Cloudy & 42
Sun., Nov. 16	at Indianapolis Colts	38	41	60,928	Indoors
Sun., Nov. 23	Dallas Cowboys	45	17	60,111	Partly cloudy & 22
Mon., Dec. 1	at Minnesota Vikings	27	11	64,001	Indoors
Sun., Dec. 7	at Tampa Bay Buccaneers	17	6	73,523	Clear & 56
Sun., Dec. 14	at Carolina Panthers	31	10	70,887	Cloudy & 40
Sat., Dec. 20	Buffalo Bills	31	21	60,108	Cloudy & 31
	TOTAL POINTS:	422	282		

POSTSEASON GAMES

Date	Opponent	GB	Opp.	Attendance	Weather
Sun., Jan. 4	Tampa Bay Buccaneers	21	7	60,327	Cloudy & 28
Sun., Jan. 11	San Francisco 49ers	23	10	68,987	Rain & 56
Sun., Jan. 25	Denver Broncos *	24	31	68,912	Sunny & 67
	TOTAL POINTS:	68	48		

* Super Bowl XXXII at San Diego
^ game played at Toronto, Canada
+ game played at Madison, Wis.

ATTENDANCE SUMMARY
Total Preseason Attendance: 293,423 (3 Home: 196,571; 1 Away: 42,956; 1 Neutral: 53,896)
Total Regular-Season Attendance: 1,017,930 (63,621 avg.)
8 Home: 481,494 (60,187 avg.)
8 Away: 536,436 (67,055 avg.)
Total Postseason Attendance: 198,226 (1 Home: 60,327; 1 Away: 68,987; 1 Neutral: 68,912)

1997 PACKERS STATISTICS

TEAM STATISTICS

	PACKERS	OPPONENTS
TOTAL FIRST DOWNS	325	288
Rushing	103	105
Passing	191	156
Penalty	31	27
3rd Down: Made/Att.	80/202	77/232
3rd Down Pct.	39.6	33.2
4th Down: Made/Att.	5/5	12/24
4th Down Pct.	100.0	50.0
POSSESSION AVG.	30:05	29.55
TOTAL NET YARDS	5614	4827
Avg. Per Game	350.9	301.7
Total Plays	1008	1047
Avg. Per Play	5.6	4.6
NET YARDS RUSHING	1909	1876
Avg. Per Game	119.3	117.3
Total Rushes	459	443
NET YARDS PASSING	3705	2951
Avg. Per Game	231.6	184.4
Sacked/Yards Lost	26/191	41/274
Gross Yards	3896	3225
Attempts/Completions	523/309	563/288
Completion Pct.	59.1	51.2
Had Intercepted	16	21
PUNTS/AVERAGE	75/45.0	90/42.5
NET PUNTING AVERAGE	75/36.0	90/36.6
PENALTIES/YARDS	93/718	114/945
FUMBLES/BALL LOST	24/16	25/11
TOUCHDOWNS	50	30
Rushing	9	16
Passing	35	10
Returns	6	4

SCORE BY PERIODS

	1	2	3	4	OT	Total
Packers	82	151	87	102	0	422
Opponents	48	78	56	100	0	282

SCORING

	TD	Ru	Pa	Rt	K-PAT	FG	S	Pts.
Longwell	0	0	0	0	48/48	24/30	0	120
Levens	12	7	5	0	0/0	0/0	0	74
Freeman	12	0	12	0	0/0	0/0	0	72
R.Brooks	7	0	7	0	0/0	0/0	0	42
Chmura	6	0	6	0	0/0	0/0	0	36
Sharper	3	0	0	3	0/0	0/0	0	18
T.Davis	2	0	1	1	0/0	0/0	0	12
Wilkins	2	0	0	2	0/0	0/0	0	12
Favre	1	1	0	0	0/0	0/0	0	6
Hayden	1	1	0	0	0/0	0/0	0	6
Henderson	1	0	1	0	0/0	0/0	0	6
Mickens	1	0	1	0	0/0	0/0	0	6
Schroeder	1	0	0	1	0/0	0/0	0	6
Thomason	1	0	1	0	0/0	0/0	0	6
Packers Total	50	9	35	6	48/48	24/30	0	422
Opp. Total	30	16	10	4	18/18	24/30	0	282

2-Pt. Conversions: Levens 1, Packers 1-2, Opponents 6-12

FIELD GOALS

	1-19	20-29	30-39	40-49	50+
Longwell	4/4	7/8	10/13	2/4	1/1
Packers Total	4/4	7/8	10/13	2/4	1/1
Opp. Total	0/0	7/8	8/10	8/11	1/1

Longwell: (38G,36G,29G) (22G,18G,27G,28N) (26G,24G,39G) (34G) (36G,19G,50G) (47B) (37G) () (23G,44G) (44G) (18G) (34N,32G) (30G,35N,19G) (31B,27G) (31G) (45N,35G)

Opponents: (42G) (48N,32G) (24G,31G,22G,34G) (22N,31G) (53G,44G,22G,39G) (23G) (41G) (38G) (34G) (37B,36N) (42G,42N,41G,35G,20G) (29G) (42G,44N) (24G,48G) (43G) ()

RUSHING

	No.	Yds.	Avg.	LG	TD
Levens	329	1435	4.4	52t	7
Favre	58	187	3.2	16	1
Hayden	32	148	4.6	21	1
Henderson	31	113	3.6	15	0
R.Brooks	2	19	9.5	15	0
Freeman	1	14	14.0	14	0
Bono	3	-3	-1.0	-1	0
Pederson	3	-4	-1.3	-1	0
Packers Total	459	1909	4.2	52t	9
Opp. Total	443	1876	4.2	68t	16

RECEIVING

	No.	Yds.	Avg.	LG	TD
Freeman	81	1243	15.3	58t	12
R.Brooks	60	1010	16.8	48	7
Levens	53	370	7.0	56	5
Henderson	41	367	9.0	25	1
Chmura	38	417	11.0	32t	6
Mayes	18	290	16.1	74	1
Thomason	9	115	12.8	27	1
Beebe	2	28	14.0	23	0
T.Davis	2	28	14.0	26	1
Schroeder	2	15	7.5	8	1
Hayden	2	11	5.5	7	0
Mickens	1	2	2.0	2t	1
Packers Total	309	3896	12.6	74	35
Opp. Total	288	3225	11.2	62	10

INTERCEPTIONS

	No.	Yds.	Avg.	LG	TD
Butler	5	4	0.8	2	0
Prior	4	72	18.0	49	0
Evans	3	33	11.0	27	0
Sharper	2	70	35.0	50t	2
B.Williams	2	30	15.0	25	0
Wilkins	1	77	77.0	77t	1
Robinson	1	26	26.0	26	0
Mullen	1	17	17.0	17	0
Harris	1	0	0.0	0	0
T.Williams	1	0	0.0	0	0
Packers Total	21	329	15.7	77t	3
Opp. Total	16	305	19.1	52t	3

PUNTING

	No.	Yds.	Avg.	Net	TB	In20	LG	Blk.
Hentrich	75	3378	45.0	36.0	21	26	65	0
Packers Total	75	3378	45.0	36.0	21	26	65	0
Opp. Total	90	3828	42.5	36.6	1	29	59	1

PUNT RETURNS

	Ret.	FC	Yds.	Avg.	LG	TD
Schroeder	33	8	342	10.4	46	0
Mayes	14	3	141	10.1	26	0
Sharper	7	3	32	4.6	23	0
Preston	1	0	0	0.0	0	0
Prior	1	3	0	0.0	0	0
Packers Total	56	17	515	9.2	46	0
Opp. Total	32	15	255	8.0	38	0

KICKOFF RETURNS

	No.	Yds.	Avg.	LG	TD
Schroeder	24	562	23.4	40	0
Preston	7	211	30.1	43	0
Beebe	6	134	22.3	39	0
Hayden	6	141	23.5	35	0
Darkins	4	68	17.0	20	0
Mickens	1	0	0.0	0	0
Sharper	1	3	3.0	3	0
Packers Total	49	1119	22.8	43	0
Opp. Total	78	1599	20.5	49	0

PASSING

	Att.	Comp.	Yards	Pct.	Yds./Att.	TD	Int.	LG	Sack/Lost	Rating
Favre	513	304	3867	59.3	7.54	35	16	74	25/176	92.6
Bono	10	5	29	50.0	2.90	0	0	14	1/15	56.3
Packers Total	523	309	3896	59.1	7.45	35	16	74	26/191	91.9
Opp. Total	563	288	3225	51.2	5.73	10	21	62	41/274	59.0

1997 DEFENSIVE STATISTICS

Player	Total Tackles	Solo	Asst.	Sacks/ Yards	Int./ Yards	Fum. Rec.	For. Fum.	Pass Def.
Harris	119	86	33	1.0/10.0	1/0	0	0	5
Robinson	113	78	35	2.5/19.0	1/26	2	1	7
B.Williams	101	74	27	1.0/11.0	2/30	1	0	6
Butler	101	70	31	3.0/20.0	5/4	0	1	10
T.Williams	74	58	16	0.0/0.0	1/0	0	2	13
Evans	71	55	16	1.0/6.0	3/33	0	2	12
S.Dotson	67	48	19	5.5/42.5	0/0	0	2	2
White	46	36	10	11.0/73.5	0/0	2	0	6
Wilkins	40	25	15	5.5/26.5	1/77	3	1	1
Joyner	34	24	10	3.0/16.0	0/0	0	0	1
Simmons	29	18	11	0.0/0.0	0/0	0	0	3
Brown	26	19	7	3.0/19.5	0/0	0	0	1
Kuberski	24	14	10	0.0/0.0	0/0	0	0	0
Prior	22	17	5	0.0/0.0	4/72	0	0	11
Mullen	17	15	2	0.0/0.0	1/17	1	0	4
Sharper	13	10	3	0.0/0.0	2/70	1	2	2
Holland	11	7	4	0.0/0.0	0/0	0	0	0
Koonce	5	4	1	0.0/0.0	0/0	0	0	0
Hollinquest	4	3	1	0.0/0.0	0/0	0	0	0
J.Smith	3	3	0	1.0/7.0	0/0	0	0	2
Frase	3	2	1	0.0/0.0	0/0	0	0	0
McKenzie	3	1	2	1.5/10.0	0/0	0	0	0
Collins	1	1	0	0.0/0.0	0/0	0	0	3
Johnson	1	1	0	0.0/0.0	0/0	0	0	0
G.Williams	1	1	0	0.0/0.0	0/0	0	0	0
Clavelle	1	0	1	0.0/0.0	0/0	0	0	0

TOUCHDOWNS: Sharper 3, 50-yard interception return vs. Detroit (11/2), 34-yard fumble return vs. Dallas (11/23) and 20-yard interception return vs. Buffalo (12/20); Wilkins 2, 1-yard fumble return vs. Chicago (9/1) and 77-yard interception return vs. Tampa Bay (10/5)

1997 OFFICIAL SPECIAL TEAMS STATISTICS

Player	TT	UT	AT	FR	FF
Hollinquest	16	12	4	0	0
Prior	14	9	5	0	0
Darkins	13	8	5	0	0
McKenzie	12	9	3	0	0
Thomason	11	9	2	0	0
T.Davis	11	7	4	0	0
Jervey	10	10	0	0	0
Mickens	9	7	2	0	0
Mullen	9	7	2	0	0
Sharper	7	4	3	0	0
Schroeder	5	4	1	0	0
Hayden	4	2	2	0	0
Kinder	4	2	2	0	0
B.Brooks	3	3	0	0	0
R.Davis	1	1	0	0	0
Frase	1	1	0	0	0
Harris	1	1	0	0	0
Koonce	1	1	0	0	0
T.Williams	1	1	0	0	0
J.Smith	1	0	1	0	0
Winters	1	0	1	0	0

TOUCHDOWNS: T.Davis 1, fumble recovery in end zone vs. Buffalo (12/20)
BLOCKED PUNTS: Joyner 1, vs. Buffalo (12/20)
BLOCKED FIELD GOALS: Harris 1, vs. St. Louis (11/9)

Miscellaneous Tackles: R.Brooks 3, Henderson 3, Taylor 3, Thomason 2, Chmura 1, E.Dotson 1, Freeman 1, Levens 1, Timmerman 1, Verba 1

TT = Total Tackles; UT = Unassisted Tackles; AT = Assisted Tackles; FR = Fumble Recoveries; FF = Forced Fumbles

1997 GAME-BY-GAME STATISTICS

PACKERS:

Date	Opponent	Total	Rush	Pass	Pen.	Made	Att.	Made	Att.	Plays	Yds.	Avg.	No.	Yds.	TD	Att.	Comp.	Yds.	TD	Int.	Sack	No.	Yds.	No.	Lost	Made	Att.	TIME
		FIRST DOWNS				**3RD DOWNS**		**4TH DOWNS**		**TOTAL OFFENSE**			**NET RUSHING**			**NET PASSING**						**PENALTIES**		**FUMBLES**		**2-PT. CONV.**		**POSS.**
9/1	Chicago	18	7	10	1	5	9	1	1	55	315	5.7	31	107	1	22	15	208	2	0	2	6	28	1	1	1	1	27:13
9/7	at Philadelphia	21	5	13	3	3	13	1	1	70	380	5.4	28	107	0	41	19	273	1	2	1	7	15	2	2	0	0	28:29
9/14	Miami	22	8	13	1	7	14	1	1	67	392	5.9	29	142	0	29	24	250	2	1	1	7	69	2	2	0	0	31:23
9/21	Minnesota	24	4	15	5	7	8	0	0	55	350	6.4	22	93	0	31	18	257	5	1	2	5	40	2	1	0	0	26:55
9/28	at Detroit	23	5	13	5	5	12	0	0	63	396	6.3	18	107	1	43	22	289	2	0	3	5	65	2	0	0	0	29:19
10/5	Tampa Bay	13	4	9	0	5	11	0	0	52	234	4.5	18	64	0	31	21	170	2	0	0	5	38	2	1	0	0	25:39
10/12	at Chicago	22	5	14	3	5	12	0	0	60	277	4.6	25	100	1	35	19	177	3	1	1	5	55	2	0	0	0	27:40
10/27	at New England	27	12	15	0	11	16	0	0	74	371	5.0	39	144	1	34	23	227	3	1	2	7	25	2	1	0	0	34:20
11/2	Detroit	11	4	7	0	5	14	0	0	55	244	4.4	11	81	0	28	15	163	1	2	2	4	54	1	1	0	0	27:19
11/9	St. Louis	18	4	12	2	5	14	0	0	64	387	6.0	20	96	0	37	18	291	1	1	3	7	66	1	1	0	0	27:40
11/16	at Indianapolis	20	6	13	1	2	6	0	0	44	441	10.0	16	107	2	25	22	334	3	1	1	8	53	0	0	0	0	23:06
11/23	Dallas	29	6	12	6	13	17	0	0	78	409	5.2	36	220	2	35	22	187	4	1	2	3	23	2	0	0	0	37:19
12/1	at Minnesota	17	8	8	1	4	16	2	2	64	326	4.9	36	139	2	29	15	280	2	1	3	6	41	2	0	0	0	30:30
12/7	at Tampa Bay	20	8	15	0	5	11	0	0	78	458	5.9	41	82	0	34	18	240	3	0	0	3	21	3	0	0	0	34:41
12/14	at Carolina	26	14	12	2	8	16	0	1	78	272	4.3	41	218	1	28	17	170	0	3	3	3	10	2	3	0	0	37:44
12/20	Buffalo	14	3	10	1	3	13	0	0	63	272	4.3	41	102	0	17	17	170	3	0	1	13	115	3	3	1	1	32:08
TOTALS		**325**	**103**	**191**	**31**	**80**	**202**	**5**	**5**	**1008**	**5614**	**5.6**	**459**	**1909**	**9**	**523**	**309**	**3705**	**35**	**16**	**26**	**93**	**718**	**24**	**16**	**1**	**2**	**avg. 30:05**
*1/4	Tampa Bay	16	9	10	0	5	14	1	1	64	289	4.5	32	118	1	28	15	171	0	2	4	7	90	3	1	1	1	32:03
*1/11	at San Francisco	19	8	10	1	4	12	0	0	60	325	5.4	32	106	1	27	16	219	2	1	1	9	62	1	0	0	0	31:40
*1/25	Denver (at S.D.)	21	4	14	3	5	10	0	1	63	350	5.6	20	95	0	42	25	255	3	1	1	9	59	2	2	0	0	27:35

OPPONENT:

Date	Opponent	Total	Rush	Pass	Pen.	Made	Att.	Made	Att.	Plays	Yds.	Avg.	No.	Yds.	TD	Att.	Comp.	Yds.	TD	Int.	Sack	No.	Yds.	No.	Lost	Made	Att.	TIME
		FIRST DOWNS				**3RD DOWNS**		**4TH DOWNS**		**TOTAL OFFENSE**			**NET RUSHING**			**NET PASSING**						**PENALTIES**		**FUMBLES**		**2-PT. CONV.**		**POSS.**
9/1	Chicago	19	6	11	2	5	16	1	1	74	336	4.5	30	164	0	41	17	172	1	0	3	13	91	1	0	1	1	32:47
9/7	at Philadelphia	16	6	10	0	6	17	1	3	65	258	4.0	30	100	0	32	19	158	1	1	3	5	23	2	0	0	0	31:31
9/14	Miami	20	9	11	0	3	16	2	2	69	299	4.3	30	59	0	47	21	240	3	2	1	7	67	0	0	0	0	28:37
9/21	Minnesota	22	9	12	1	8	17	1	2	74	393	5.3	37	185	1	34	19	208	3	0	2	9	115	1	1	0	0	33:05
9/28	at Detroit	18	9	12	0	4	14	1	2	65	376	5.8	36	173	2	27	17	203	1	1	3	9	107	0	0	0	0	30:41
10/5	Tampa Bay	23	10	14	1	6	14	1	2	68	372	5.5	36	217	2	29	16	155	0	2	2	3	30	2	1	0	0	34:21
10/12	at Chicago	18	3	13	2	6	12	0	1	69	353	5.1	34	121	1	35	22	232	1	4	2	3	53	2	0	0	0	32:20
10/27	at New England	18	10	6	2	7	12	0	2	58	324	5.6	28	69	0	47	21	255	0	4	2	6	15	1	2	0	0	25:40
11/2	Detroit	16	4	8	4	4	17	2	4	79	256	3.2	41	125	1	41	18	203	2	0	0	4	20	3	1	0	0	32:41
11/9	St. Louis	26	8	17	1	4	16	4	4	70	269	3.8	25	66	0	25	12	120	2	0	4	15	110	2	1	0	0	33:20
11/16	at Indianapolis	11	6	5	0	7	9	0	1	46	213	4.6	24	93	0	42	21	154	1	0	6	11	45	3	1	0	0	36:54
11/23	Dallas	17	8	9	2	6	18	0	0	72	253	3.5	20	99	1	26	10	154	1	0	3	6	103	3	2	3	3	22:41
12/1	at Minnesota	8	6	5	0	6	16	0	1	52	161	3.1	24	67	0	26	7	94	1	3	1	6	40	2	0	0	0	29:30
12/7	at Tampa Bay	9	6	3	0	3	15	1	4	53	172	3.2	24	140	0	36	7	32	0	3	1	6	33	3	0	0	0	25:19
12/14	at Carolina	18	5	12	0	5	12	0	0	67	325	4.9	24	51	0	24	24	274	0	0	0	10	93	1	1	0	0	22:16
12/20	Buffalo																											27:52
TOTALS		**288**	**105**	**156**	**27**	**77**	**232**	**12**	**24**	**1047**	**4827**	**4.6**	**443**	**1876**	**16**	**563**	**288**	**2951**	**10**	**21**	**41**	**114**	**945**	**25**	**11**	**6**	**12**	**avg. 29:55**
*1/4	Tampa Bay	15	1	11	0	5	13	4	4	66	263	4.0	27	90	1	37	23	173	2	2	3	11	38	2	0	0	0	27:57
*1/11	at San Francisco	15	14	11	3	3	14	2	2	60	257	4.3	18	33	0	38	23	224	2	1	1	9	64	4	1	0	0	28:20
*1/25	Denver (at S.D.)	21	14	5	2	5	10	3	0	61	302	5.0	39	179	4	22	12	123	0	1	1	6	65	1	1	0	0	32:35

*playoff game

TEAM STATISTICS

	PACKERS	OPPONENTS
TOTAL FIRST DOWNS	56	51
Rushing	18	19
Passing	34	25
Penalty	4	7
3rd Down: Made/Att.	14/41	13/39
3rd Down Pct.	34.1	33.3
4th Down: Made/Att.	1/2	2/7
4th Down Pct.	50.0	28.6
POSSESSION AVG.	30:29	29:31
TOTAL NET YARDS	964	822
Avg. Per Game	321.3	274.0
Total Plays	187	187
Avg. Per Play	5.2	4.4
NET YARDS RUSHING	319	302
Avg. Per Game	106.3	100.7
Total Rushes	84	84
NET YARDS PASSING	645	520
Avg. Per Game	215.0	173.3
Sacked/Yards Lost	6/23	6/53
Gross Yards	668	573
Attempts/Completions	97/56	97/47
Completion Pct.	57.7	48.5
Had Intercepted	3	4
PUNTS/AVERAGE	14/38.4	14/37.0
NET PUNTING AVERAGE	14/36.8	14/31.7
PENALTIES/YARDS	25/211	16/167
FUMBLES/BALL LOST	6/3	7/2
TOUCHDOWNS	7	6
Rushing	2	5
Passing	5	0
Returns	0	1

SCORE BY PERIODS

	1	2	3	4	OT	Total
Packers	17	23	3	25	0	68
Opponents	7	13	14	14	0	48

SCORING

	TD	Ru	Pa	Rt	K-PAT	FG	S	Pts.
Longwell	0	0	0	0	6/6	6/7	0	24
Freeman	3	0	3	0	0/0	0/0	0	18
Chmura	2	0	2	0	0/0	0/0	0	12
Levens	2	2	0	0	0/0	0/0	0	12
Favre	0	0	0	0	0/0	0/0	0	2
Packers Total	7	2	5	0	6/6	6/7	0	68
Opp. Total	6	5	0	1	6/6	2/3	0	48

2-Pt. Conversions: Favre 1, Packers 1-1, Opponents 0-0

FIELD GOALS

	1-19	20-29	30-39	40-49	50+
Longwell	1/1	3/3	1/1	1/2	0/0
Packers Total	1/1	3/3	1/1	1/2	0/0
Opp. Total	0/0	1/1	0/0	0/1	1/1

Longwell: (21G,32G) (19G,47N,43G,25G) (27G)
Opponents: (43B) (28G) (51G)

RUSHING

	No.	Yds.	Avg.	LG	TD
Levens	71	316	4.5	21	2
Henderson	5	6	1.2	3	0
R.Brooks	1	5	5.0	5	0
Favre	7	-8	-1.1	6	0
Packers Total	84	319	3.8	21	2
Opp. Total	84	302	3.6	27	5

RECEIVING

	No.	Yds.	Avg.	LG	TD
Freeman	17	308	18.1	40	3
Levens	14	112	8.0	22	0
Chmura	8	81	10.1	21	2
R.Brooks	7	73	10.4	21	0
Henderson	5	24	4.8	7	0
Mayes	3	47	15.7	23	0
T.Davis	1	17	17.0	17	0
Mickens	1	6	6.0	6	0
Packers Total	56	668	11.9	40	5
Opp. Total	47	573	12.2	52	0

INTERCEPTIONS

	No.	Yds.	Avg.	LG	TD
Robinson	2	75	37.5	58	0
T.Williams	1	14	14.0	14	0
Prior	1	13	13.0	13	0
Packers Total	4	102	25.5	58	0
Opp. Total	3	0	0.0	0	0

PUNTING

	No.	Yds.	Avg.	Net	TB	In20	LG	Blk.
Hentrich	14	538	38.4	36.8	0	10	52	0
Packers Total	14	538	38.4	36.8	0	10	52	0
Opp. Total	14	518	37.0	31.7	0	3	48	0

PUNT RETURNS

	Ret.	FC	Yds.	Avg.	LG	TD
R.Brooks	5	2	74	14.8	28	0
Packers Total	5	2	74	14.8	28	0
Opp. Total	3	7	23	7.7	21	0

KICKOFF RETURNS

	No.	Yds.	Avg.	LG	TD
Freeman	9	158	17.6	25	0
Hayden	1	19	19.0	19	0
Packers Total	10	177	17.7	25	0
Opp. Total	14	307	21.9	95t	1

PASSING

	Att.	Comp.	Yards	Pct.	Yds./Att.	TD	Int.	LG	Sack/Lost	Rating
Favre	97	56	668	57.7	6.89	5	3	40	6/23	83.2
Packers Total	97	56	668	57.7	6.89	5	3	40	6/23	83.2
Opp. Total	97	47	573	48.5	5.91	0	4	52	6/53	49.9

Player	Total Tackles	Solo	Asst.	Sacks/ Yards	Int./ Yards	Fum. Rec.	For. Fum.	Pass Def.
Robinson	28	16	12	0.0/0.0	2/75	0	0	2
Harris	24	15	9	1.0/8.0	0/0	0	0	1
B.Williams	20	12	8	0.0/0.0	0/0	0	0	0
Butler	17	10	7	1.0/12.0	0/0	0	0	1
S.Dotson	15	8	7	0.0/0.0	0/0	0	0	1
Brown	12	11	1	0.0/0.0	0/0	0	1	1
T.Williams	11	11	0	0.0/0.0	1/14	1	2	6
Evans	11	9	2	0.0/0.0	0/0	0	0	3
Joyner	9	8	1	0.0/0.0	0/0	0	0	1
White	6	6	0	1.0/5.0	0/0	0	1	0
Koonce	3	3	0	0.0/0.0	0/0	0	0	0
McKenzie	3	3	0	3.0/28.0	0/0	0	1	0
Sharper	2	2	0	0.0/0.0	0/0	0	0	4
Prior	2	0	2	0.0/0.0	1/13	0	0	1
Frase	1	1	0	0.0/0.0	0/0	1	0	0
Hollinquest	1	1	0	0.0/0.0	0/0	0	0	0
Wilkins	1	1	0	0.0/0.0	0/0	0	0	1
Holland	1	0	1	0.0/0.0	0/0	0	0	0

1997 OFFICIAL PLAYOFF SPECIAL TEAMS STATISTICS

Player	TT	UT	AT	FR	FF
Hollinquest	3	3	0	0	0
Mickens	3	3	0	0	0
Mullen	3	3	0	0	0
Prior	2	1	1	0	0
Darkins	1	1	0	0	0
Harris	1	1	0	0	0
Jervey	1	1	0	0	0
McKenzie	1	1	0	0	0
Sharper	1	1	0	0	0
Thomason	1	1	0	0	0

BLOCKED FIELD GOALS: Kuberski 1, vs. Tampa Bay (1/4)

Miscellaneous Tackles: R.Brooks 2, Chmura 1

TT = Total Tackles; UT = Unassisted Tackles; AT = Assisted Tackles; FR = Fumble Recoveries; FF = Forced Fumbles

POSITION ABBREVIATION INDICATES START; WR3-Started as 3rd Wide Receiver; WR4-Started as 4th Wide Receiver; SUB-Played; DNP-Did Not Play; IAF-Inactive Friday; IAS-Inactive Sunday; 3QB-Inactive Third Quarterback (*-DNP); PS-Practice Squad; IR-Injured Reserve; PUP-Reserve/Physically Unable to Perform

Week → Player	1 Chi	2 @Phi	3 Mia	4 Min	5 @Det	6 TB	7 @Chi	9 @NE	10 Det	11 StL	12 @Ind	13 Dal	14 @Min	15 @TB	16 @Car	17 Buf	GP/GS/DNP/IA
Anderson	—	—	—	—	—	—	PS	PS	PS	PS	PS	PS	PS	PS	PS	PS	0/0/0/0
Andruzzi	IAF	IAF	IAF	IAF	IAF	IAS	IAS	IAF	IAF	IAF	IAF	IAF	IAF	IAF	IAF	IAF	0/0/0/16
Beebe	IAF	IAS	IAS	IAS	SUB	IAF	SUB	SUB	SUB	SUB	SUB	SUB	SUB	SUB	SUB	IAS	10/0/0/6
Bennett	IR	IR	IR	IR	IR	IR	IR	IR	IR	IR	IR	IR	IR	IR	IR	IR	0/0/0/0
Bono	DNP	DNP	DNP	DNP	DNP	DNP	DNP	DNP	DNP	DNP	DNP	DNP	DNP	DNP	SUB	SUB	2/0/14/0
Brooks, B.	—	—	—	—	SUB	SUB	SUB	IAS	IAS	IAS	IAS	IAS	—	—	—	—	3/0/0/5
Brooks, R.	WR	WR	WR	WR	WR	WR	WR	WR	WR	WR	IAF	WR	WR	WR	WR	WR	15/15/0/1
Brown	NT	NT	NT	NT	NT	IAF	IAF	NT	NT	NT	NT	NT	NT	NT	IAF	IAF	12/12/0/4
Butler	SS	SS	SS	SS	SS	SS	SS	SS	SS	SS	SS	SS	SS	SS	SS	SS	16/16/0/0
Chmura	SUB	IAF	TE	TE	TE	TE	TE	TE	TE	TE	TE	TE	TE	TE	TE	TE	15/14/0/1
Clavelle	SUB	SUB	SUB	SUB	SUB	SUB	IAF	—	—	—	—	—	—	—	—	—	6/0/0/1
Collins	—	—	—	—	—	—	—	—	—	—	—	—	IAF	IAS	IAS	SUB	1/0/0/3
Conway	IAF	IR	IR	IR	IR	IR	IR	IR	IR	IR	IR	IR	IR	IR	IR	IR	0/0/0/1
Darkins	SUB	SUB	SUB	SUB	IAF	SUB	SUB	SUB	SUB	SUB	SUB	SUB	SUB	SUB	SUB	IAF	14/0/0/2
Davis, R.	—	—	—	—	—	—	—	—	—	SUB	SUB	SUB	SUB	SUB	SUB	SUB	7/0/0/0
Davis, T.	SUB	SUB	IAF	IAF	—	SUB	SUB	SUB	SUB	SUB	SUB	SUB	SUB	SUB	SUB	SUB	13/0/0/2
Dellenbach	SUB	SUB	C	C	C	SUB	SUB	LG	LG	SUB	DNP	DNP	SUB	SUB	SUB	SUB	14/5/2/0
Dotson, E.	RT	RT	DNP	RT	RT	IAF	IAF	RT	RT	RT	RT	RT	RT	RT	RT	RT	13/13/1/2
Dotson, S.	DT	DT	DT	DT	DT	DT	DT	DT	DT	DT	DT	DT	DT	DT	DT	DT	16/16/0/0
Evans	RCB	RCB	RCB	RCB	IAS	RCB	RCB	RCB	RCB	RCB	RCB	RCB	RCB	RCB	RCB	RCB	15/15/0/1
Favre	QB	QB	QB	QB	QB	QB	QB	QB	QB	QB	QB	QB	QB	QB	QB	QB	16/16/0/0
Flanagan	PUP	PUP	PUP	PUP	PUP	PUP	PUP	PUP	PUP	PUP	PUP	PUP	PUP	PUP	PUP	PUP	0/0/0/0
Fogle	—	—	—	—	—	—	—	—	—	—	—	—	PS	PS	PS	PS	0/0/0/0
Frase	IAS	SUB	SUB	SUB	SUB	SUB	SUB	SUB	IAF	IAF	IAF	IAF	IAF	IAF	SUB	SUB	9/0/0/7
Freeman	WR	WR	WR	WR	WR	WR	WR	WR	WR	WR	WR	WR	WR	WR	WR	WR	16/16/0/0
Harris	MLB	MLB	MLB	MLB	MLB	MLB	MLB	MLB	MLB	MLB	MLB	MLB	MLB	MLB	MLB	MLB	16/16/0/0
Hayden	SUB	SUB	SUB	SUB	SUB	SUB	SUB	SUB	SUB	SUB	SUB	IAS	IAS	SUB	SUB	SUB	14/0/0/2
Henderson	SUB	FB	FB	FB	FB	FB	FB	FB	FB	FB	FB	FB	SUB	FB	FB	FB	16/14/0/0
Hentrich	SUB	SUB	SUB	SUB	SUB	SUB	SUB	SUB	SUB	SUB	SUB	SUB	SUB	SUB	SUB	SUB	16/0/0/0
Heese	PS	PS	PS	PS	PS	PS	PS	PS	PS	PS	PS	PS	PS	PS	PS	—	0/0/0/0
Hicks	IR	IR	IR	IR	IR	IR	IR	IR	IR	IR	IR	IR	IR	IR	IR	IR	0/0/0/0
Holland	SUB	SUB	SUB	SUB	SUB	NT	SUB	IAF	IAF	IAF	IAS	SUB	SUB	SUB	SUB	SUB	12/1/0/4
Hollinquest	SUB	SUB	SUB	SUB	SUB	SUB	SUB	SUB	SUB	SUB	SUB	SUB	SUB	SUB	SUB	SUB	16/0/0/0
Jervey	SUB	SUB	SUB	SUB	SUB	SUB	SUB	SUB	SUB	SUB	SUB	SUB	SUB	SUB	SUB	SUB	16/0/0/0
Johnson	—	SUB	SUB	SUB	SUB	—	—	—	—	—	—	—	—	—	—	—	4/0/0/0
Joyner	IAF	IAF	IAF	IAF	IAF	SUB	LOLB	LOLB	LOLB	LOLB	LOLB	LOLB	LOLB	LOLB	LOLB	LOLB	11/10/0/5
Kinder	PS	SUB	SUB	SUB	SUB	SUB	SUB	IAS	IAS	IAS	—	—	—	—	—	—	6/0/0/3
Kitts	—	—	—	—	PS	—	—	—	—	—	—	—	—	—	—	—	0/0/0/0
Koonce	PUP	PUP	PUP	PUP	PUP	PUP	PUP	PUP	PUP	PUP	PUP	IAF	SUB	SUB	SUB	SUB	4/0/0/1
Kuberski	IAS	IAS	IAF	IAS	IAF	SUB	NT	SUB	SUB	SUB	SUB	SUB	SUB	SUB	NT	NT	11/3/0/5
Lee	PS	PS	PS	PS	—	—	—	—	—	—	—	—	—	—	—	—	0/0/0/0
Levens	RB	RB	RB	RB	RB	RB	RB	RB	RB	RB	RB	RB	RB	RB	RB	RB	16/16/0/0
Longwell	SUB	SUB	SUB	SUB	SUB	SUB	SUB	SUB	SUB	SUB	SUB	SUB	SUB	SUB	SUB	SUB	16/0/0/0
Lyon	—	—	—	—	—	—	—	—	—	—	—	PS	PS	PS	PS	PS	0/0/0/0
Mayes	WR3	SUB	SUB	SUB	SUB	IAF	IAS	SUB	SUB	SUB	WR	SUB	WR3	SUB	IAF	DNP	12/3/1/3
McElmurry	—	PS	PS	PS	PS	PS	PS	PS	PS	PS	PS	PS	PS	IAF	IAS	IAS	1/0/0/3
McKenzie	SUB	SUB	SUB	SUB	SUB	SUB	SUB	SUB	SUB	SUB	SUB	SUB	SUB	SUB	SUB	SUB	16/0/0/0
Michels	LT	LT	LT	LT	LT	SUB	SUB	SUB	SUB	IAS	IAS	IAS	IAS	IAS	IAS	IAS	9/5/0/7
Mickens	SUB	SUB	SUB	SUB	SUB	SUB	SUB	SUB	SUB	SUB	IAF	IAF	IAS	IAS	SUB	SUB	11/0/0/5
Mullen	SUB	SUB	SUB	SUB	RCB	SUB	SUB	SUB	SUB	SUB	SUB	SUB	SUB	SUB	SUB	SUB	16/1/0/0
Newsome	LCB	IR	IR	IR	IR	IR	IR	IR	IR	IR	IR	IR	IR	IR	IR	IR	1/1/0/0
Pederson	*3QB	*3QB	*3QB	*3QB	*3QB	*3QB	*3QB	*3QB	*3QB	*3QB	*3QB	*3QB	*3QB	*3QB	*3QB	3QB	1/0/0/15
Preston	—	—	—	—	—	—	—	—	—	—	SUB	—	—	—	—	—	1/0/0/0
Prior	SUB	SUB	SUB	SUB	SUB	SUB	SUB	SUB	SUB	SUB	SUB	SUB	SUB	SUB	SUB	SUB	16/0/0/0

1997 PARTICIPATION CHART

Week	1	2	3	4	5	6	7	9	10	11	12	13	14	15	16	17	GP/GS/
Player	Chi	@Phi	Mia	Min	@Det	TB	@Chi	@NE	Det	StL	@Ind	Dal	@Min	@TB	@Car	Buf	DNP/IA
Rivera	IAS	IAS	SUB	SUB	SUB	SUB	SUB	SUB	SUB	SUB	SUB	SUB	SUB	SUB	SUB	SUB	14/0/0/2
Robinson	FS	FS	FS	FS	FS	FS	FS	FS	FS	FS	FS	FS	FS	FS	FS	FS	16/16/0/0
Rowe	PS	PS	PS	PS	PS	PS	PS	PS	PS	PS	PS	—	—	—	—	—	0/0/0/0
Schroeder	WR4	SUB	SUB	SUB	SUB	SUB	SUB	SUB	SUB	SUB	SUB	SUB	SUB	IAF	SUB	SUB	15/1/0/1
Sharper	SUB	SUB	SUB	SUB	SUB	IAS	IAS	SUB	SUB	SUB	SUB	SUB	SUB	SUB	SUB	SUB	14/0/0/2
Simmons	LOLB	LOLB	LOLB	LOLB	LOLB	LOLB	—	—	—	—	—	—	—	—	—	—	6/6/0/0
Smith, J.	DNP	IAF	IAS	IAS	IAS	IAS	SUB	IAS	SUB	SUB	SUB	SUB	SUB	SUB	SUB	SUB	9/0/1/6
Taylor	LG	LG	LG	LG	LG	LG	LG	IAF	IAF	LG	LG	LG	LG	LG	LG	LG	14/14/0/2
Thomason	SUB	TE	SUB	SUB	SUB	SUB	SUB	SUB	SUB	SUB	SUB	SUB	SUB	IAF	SUB	IAF	13/1/0/3
Timmerman	RG	RG	RG	RG	RG	RG	RG	RG	RG	RG	RG	RG	RG	RG	RG	RG	16/16/0/0
Verba	SUB	SUB	SUB	SUB	SUB	LT	LT	LT	LT	LT	LT	LT	LT	LT	LT	LT	16/11/0/0
Wachholtz	PS	PS	PS	PS	PS	PS	PS	PS	PS	PS	PS	PS	PS	PS	PS	PS	0/0/0/0
White	LDE	LDE	LDE	LDE	LDE	LDE	LDE	LDE	LDE	LDE	LDE	LDE	LDE	LDE	LDE	LDE	16/16/0/0
Wilkerson	SUB	SUB	RT	SUB	SUB	RT	RT	SUB	SUB	SUB	SUB	SUB	SUB	SUB	SUB	SUB	16/3/0/0
Wilkins	RDE	RDE	RDE	RDE	RDE	RDE	RDE	RDE	RDE	RDE	RDE	RDE	RDE	RDE	RDE	RDE	16/16/0/0
Williams, B.	ROLB	ROLB	ROLB	ROLB	ROLB	ROLB	ROLB	ROLB	ROLB	ROLB	ROLB	ROLB	ROLB	ROLB	ROLB	ROLB	16/16/0/0
Williams, G.	—	—	—	—	—	—	—	DNP	SUB	SUB	SUB	SUB	—	—	—	—	4/0/1/0
Williams, T.	SUB	LCB	LCB	LCB	LCB	LCB	LCB	LCB	LCB	LCB	LCB	LCB	LCB	LCB	LCB	LCB	16/15/0/0
Winters	C	C	IAS	IAF	IAS	C	C	C	C	C	C	C	C	C	C	C	13/13/0/3

1997 PLAYOFF PARTICIPATION

POSITION ABBREVIATION INDICATES START; SUB-Played; DNP-Did Not Play; IAF-Inactive Friday; IAS-Inactive Sunday; 3QB-Inactive Third Quarterback (-DNP); PS-Practice Squad; IR-Injured Reserve; PUP-Reserve/Physically Unable to Perform*

Playoff Game	1	2	SB	GP/GS/
Player	TB	@SF	Den	DNP/IA
Anderson	PS	PS	IAF	0/0/0/1
Andruzzi	IAF	IAF	IAF	0/0/0/3
Beebe	IAF	IAF	IR	0/0/0/2
Bennett	IR	IR	IR	0/0/0/0
Bono	DNP	DNP	DNP	0/0/3/0
Brooks, R.	WR	WR	WR	3/3/0/0
Brown	NT	NT	NT	3/3/0/0
Butler	SS	SS	SS	3/3/0/0
Chmura	TE	TE	TE	3/3/0/0
Collins	IAS	IAS	SUB	1/0/0/2
Conway	IR	IR	IR	0/0/0/0
Darkins	SUB	SUB	SUB	3/0/0/0
Davis, R.	SUB	SUB	SUB	3/0/0/0
Davis, T.	SUB	SUB	SUB	3/0/0/0
Dellenbach	DNP	DNP	DNP	0/0/3/0
Dotson, E.	RT	RT	RT	3/3/0/0
Dotson, S.	DT	DT	DT	3/3/0/0
Evans	RCB	RCB	RCB	3/3/0/0
Favre	QB	QB	QB	3/3/0/0
Flanagan	PUP	PUP	PUP	0/0/0/0
Fogle	PS	PS	PS	0/0/0/0
Frase	SUB	SUB	IAS	2/0/0/1
Freeman	WR	WR	WR	3/3/0/0
Harris	MLB	MLB	MLB	3/3/0/0
Hayden	SUB	SUB	SUB	3/0/0/0
Henderson	FB	FB	FB	3/3/0/0
Hentrich	SUB	SUB	SUB	3/0/0/0
Hicks	IR	IR	IR	0/0/0/0
Holland	SUB	SUB	SUB	3/0/0/0
Hollinquest	SUB	SUB	SUB	3/0/0/0
Jervey	SUB	SUB	SUB	3/0/0/0
Joyner	LOLB	LOLB	LOLB	3/3/0/0

Playoff Game	1	2	SB	GP/GS/
Player	TB	@SF	Den	DNP/IA
Koonce	SUB	SUB	SUB	3/0/0/0
Kuberski	SUB	SUB	SUB	3/0/0/0
Levens	RB	RB	RB	3/3/0/0
Longwell	SUB	SUB	SUB	3/0/0/0
Lyon	PS	PS	PS	0/0/0/0
Mayes	SUB	SUB	SUB	3/0/0/0
McElmurry	IAF	IAF	IAF	0/0/0/3
McKenzie	SUB	SUB	SUB	3/0/0/0
Michels	IAS	IAS	IAS	0/0/0/3
Mickens	SUB	SUB	SUB	3/0/0/0
Mullen	SUB	SUB	SUB	3/0/0/0
Newsome	IR	IR	IR	0/0/0/0
Pederson	*3QB	*3QB	*3QB	0/0/0/0
Prior	SUB	SUB	SUB	3/0/0/0
Rivera	SUB	SUB	SUB	3/0/0/0
Robinson	FS	FS	FS	3/3/0/0
Schroeder	IAS	IAS	IAS	0/0/0/3
Sharper	SUB	SUB	SUB	3/0/0/0
Smith, E.	PS	PS	PS	0/0/0/0
Smith, J.	IAF	IAF	IAF	0/0/0/3
Taylor	LG	LG	LG	3/3/0/0
Thomason	SUB	SUB	SUB	3/0/0/0
Timmerman	RG	RG	RG	3/3/0/0
Verba	LT	LT	LT	3/3/0/0
Wachholtz	PS	PS	PS	0/0/0/0
White	LDE	LDE	LDE	3/3/0/0
Wilkerson	SUB	SUB	SUB	3/0/0/0
Wilkins	RDE	RDE	RDE	3/3/0/0
Williams, B.	ROLB	ROLB	ROLB	3/3/0/0
Williams, T.	LCB	LCB	LCB	3/3/0/0
Winters	C	C	C	3/3/0/0

SEPT. 1: Coming off their first undefeated-untied preseason in three decades, the Super Bowl XXXI champions launched their bid for a repeat season at home on ABC-TV's *Monday Night Football* with a 38-24 win over the Chicago Bears.

After Green Bay took a 3-0 lead to the end of the first quarter, Chicago jumped to an 8-3 lead early in the second. The Packers then re-took the lead when Doug Evans intercepted an Erik Kramer pass and returned it 27 yards to the Chicago 1-yard line. Brett Favre connected with Jeff Thomason on the next play for the score, and, with a two-point conversion, the Packers were on top, 11-8. Chicago tied the game, 11-11, with 1:56 left in the half, on a Jeff Jaeger field goal. Green Bay retaliated with a five-play, 80-yard drive, capped by an 18-yard pass by Favre to Robert Brooks in the left corner of the end zone with only 48 seconds on the clock. The score gave the Green and Gold an 18-11 lead, one which they never relinquished.

Rookie free agent Ryan Longwell connected on field goals of 36 and 29 yards in the third quarter and a one-yard Levens run to open the fourth quarter increased the Packers' lead to 31-11. Chicago pulled within 14 points with 2:08 left on a 68-yard run by Raymont Harris, but time ran out for the Bears.

Favre connected on 15 of 22 passes for 226 yards and a pair of touchdowns, with one interception. The Packers' return game featured Bill Schroeder, who alone amassed 160 yards (107 on five punt returns and 53 on two kickoff returns). The win did not come without a price. Craig Newsome suffered a torn anterior cruciate ligament in his left knee on the game's first play from scrimmage and was lost for the season.

SEPT. 21: The Packers got back on the winning track with back-to-back victories over Miami, 23-18, and Minnesota, 38-32, after the team's nine-game win streak came to an end in a 10-9 loss in Philadelphia on Sept. 7.

In the victory over Minnesota, Favre connected twice to Antonio Freeman and fired one touchdown each to Brooks and Terry Mickens to give Green Bay a 31-7 halftime lead. The game had the makings of a blowout, but Minnesota turned things around in opening the second half. The Vikings converted two Packer turnovers into touchdowns to close the gap to 31-22 with less then five minutes expired in the third quarter.

The Packers retaliated with a nine-play, 81-yard drive, which was capped by a two-yard strike from Favre to Mark Chmura in the right corner of the end zone, increasing Green Bay's lead to 38-22 with 4:41 remaining in the third quarter. The Vikings opened the fourth period with a 10-play, 48-yard drive, culminating in a 31-yard field goal. Later, Brad Johnson hit Jake Reed with a 27-yard touchdown pass and it was 38-32 with 6:44 left in the game. But the Packers' defense prevailed, forcing three straight incompletions to stop the Vikings on downs, and Green Bay proceeded to then run out the clock.

Favre had a history-making performance, throwing for five touchdowns, thus tying the team's single-game record and surpassing the club's career mark for touchdown passes. Favre broke the old mark of 152, set by Bart Starr, in the second quarter when he threw his 153rd career touchdown. The long-time rivals produced over 700 yards of offense between them. Freeman, who posted a fourth two-touchdown (or better) performance of his three-year career, finished the day with 7 catches for 122 yards, the fifth 100-yard game of his career.

OCT. 5: The Green and Gold returned home to face the undefeated, NFC Central-leading Tampa Bay Buccaneers (5-0) after suffering their second road loss of the season, having fallen to the Detroit Lions 26-15 a week earlier.

The Buccaneers led 3-0 at the end of the first quarter, but a 21-point second quarter, headed by Favre, who was responsible for 14 of those points, gave Green Bay a 21-3 halftime lead. The Packers' first score came less than a minute into the quarter after Tyrone Williams forced a Buccaneers fumble and Brian Williams made the recovery at the Tampa Bay 35. On third-and-six, Favre fired a strike to Freeman, who ran 31 yards for the touchdown to give Green Bay its first lead, 7-3.

In the Packers' next series, Favre fumbled a quarterback sneak on third-and-one and the Buccaneers recovered on the Green Bay 18. Gabe Wilkins intercepted a Trent Dilfer screen pass on the next play, though, then hurdled would-be tackler Dilfer and, with a key block on Mike Alstott from Santana Dotson, ran 77 yards for a touchdown. With 44 seconds remaining in the quarter, Favre connected with Freeman again, this time on a six-yard pass to cap a seven-play, 50-yard drive, to provide the winning margin. The Buccaneers scored in the third and fourth quarters on one- and two-yard runs, respectively, keeping the game close, but they ultimately fell short, 21-16.

The Packers managed a victory despite the Buccaneers' advantage in total yards (372-234), offensive plays (68-52) and time of possession (34:21-25:39). Levens led the Green Bay attack with 105 total yards of offense.

OCT. 12: Green Bay headed into the bye week and completed a four-game swing around the division with a 24-23 victory over winless Chicago at Soldier Field. The triumph was the eighth straight over the Bears and gave the Packers, 5-2, a share of the division lead with Tampa Bay and Minnesota.

Chicago jumped to a 10-0 first-quarter lead, but Green Bay struck back in the second when Favre connected with Chmura for a two-yard touchdown with 6:38 left in the half to close out an 11-play, 80-yard drive. On the next series, linebacker Brian Williams intercepted a Kramer pass and returned it 25 yards to Chicago's 28-yard line. Five plays later Favre hit Levens, who crossed the goal line untouched. Longwell's second conversion of the game gave the Packers a 14-10 halftime lead.

The Bears took the second half kickoff and marched 73 yards in 12 plays to take a 17-14 lead. As the quarter came to a close, Favre threw his third touchdown of the day – his second to Chmura – to climax an eight-play, 55-yard drive. Chmura pulled in the ball at the four-yard line and barged into the end zone with less than a minute remaining as the Packers took the lead for good.

Early in the fourth quarter, Chicago found itself knocking on the door with the aid of a 35-yard pass interference penalty on Tyrone Williams that gave the Bears possession on Green Bay's 5-yard line. But four plays later, on fourth-and-goal from the 1, the Packers' Wilkins and Bob Kuberski rose up to stop Kramer a half-yard short of the goal line. After an exchange of possessions, Green Bay then stretched its lead on a 37-yard field goal by Longwell.

The victory wasn't secure until 1:54 remained in the game when Chicago failed on what would have been a go-ahead two-point conversion. Kramer had driven the Bears 67 yards for a touchdown, but his subsequent pass to Harris on the conversion try was incomplete and the Packers held on to win.

OCT. 27: The Packers returned to the gridiron after a bye and uncustomary entire week off from practice for a rematch of Super Bowl XXXI in New England on *Monday Night Football*. The time off proved to be beneficial for Green Bay as they came out and handled the Patriots with ease en route to a 28-10 win.

Leading just 14-10 at halftime, the Packers put together two long, clock-consuming scoring drives, while holding New England scoreless. The Patriots took the second half kickoff and moved the ball in seven plays to the Green Bay 1-yard line. On first down, Santana Dotson and LeRoy Butler combined to stop Curtis Martin for no gain. That was followed by three consecutive incomplete passes, the latter two broken up by Tyrone Williams. Favre then led the offense on a 17-play, 99-yard scoring drive, the NFL's longest of the season, eating up nine minutes and 31 seconds and capping it off with a 20-yard TD pass to Brooks.

In addition to the 99-yard effort, the Packers put together three other long scoring drives. The first, an 81-yard, 13-play march, took 4:43 and was finished by a six-yard Favre-to-Levens connection. The second, a nine-play, 75-yard production, was completed by a 32-yard Favre bullseye to Chmura and ate up 1:50 on the clock. The final drive, a 15-play, 85-yard project for the last touchdown, was finished off by Levens' three-yard run and took 7:24 to complete.

Favre, spreading the ball out to six receivers, closed out the evening with 23 completions in 34 pass attempts for 239 yards and 3 touchdowns, also rushing nine times for 32 yards. In the process, he eclipsed another club career passing record – passes completed – by notching his 1,809th completion, breaking the old standard of 1,808 set by Starr. Levens finished the game with 140 yards of total offense – 100 yards rushing in 26 attempts and 7 catches for 40 yards.

NOV. 23: It was the game for which Packers fans were waiting years – the Dallas Cowboys in Lambeau Field. Following two home wins, 20-10 over Detroit Nov. 2 and 17-7 over St. Louis Nov. 9, Green Bay was looking to rebound from a disappointing 41-38 loss at Indianapolis a week earlier. The Packers subsequently manhandled the Cowboys 45-17 to end the Texans' eight-game winning streak and position themselves alone atop the NFC Central.

The first half ended in a 10-10 standoff, each team having possessed the ball for exactly 15 minutes, and there was no hint of the Green Bay domination to come. The Packers came out in the second half and took control, putting together drives of 69, 73, 61 and 88 yards and scoring on all four possessions. They had mounted a 38-17 lead with just under two minutes remaining in the game. Rookie Darren Sharper completed the scoring for the day by recovering a fumble – one he had forced himself – and returning it 34 yards for a touchdown with 1:33 showing on the clock.

For the second time of the season, Favre finished the day with four touchdowns, connecting for three in the second half – four- and two-yard throws to Chmura and a 23-yard toss to Freeman. Levens finished the day with a club-record 190 rushing yards on 33 carries, including 145 yards in 24 attempts in the second half. Compared to the even share of minutes in the first half, Green Bay held the ball for 22:19 to the Cowboys' 7:41 in the second half. After holding a modest 34-28 edge in offensive plays at halftime, the Packers ran off 44 to the Cowboys' 18 in the final half. And after settling for a 9-6 first down margin in the first half, the Green and Gold totaled 20 to Dallas' 5 in the second. The Packers' defense limited Troy Aikman and the Cowboys to 213 net yards (93 rushing, 120 passing).

DEC. 1: The Packers assured themselves of a fifth consecutive playoff berth by defeating the Minnesota Vikings 27-11 on *Monday Night Football*. The win also broke a five-year losing streak in the Metrodome.

Midway through the first quarter, Favre found Freeman with a 31-yard strike to the Minnesota 29 and, six plays later, including seven- and 10-yard runs by Levens, the Packers settled for a 30-yard field goal by Longwell. The Vikings evened the score in the second quarter on a 42-yard field goal. Two possessions later, Favre led an 11-play, 86-yard drive, topped off by an 18-yard bullet to Brooks in the end zone to give the Packers a 10-3 halftime lead.

Green Bay converted two second-half turnovers, an Evans interception and a Wilkins fumble recovery, into 10 points to mount a 20-3 lead midway through the fourth quarter. Evans' third-quarter interception positioned the Packers at the Vikings' 37-yard line on the second play of the quarter. After being thrown for a one-yard loss on first down, Levens took charge two plays later, bolting up the middle for 10 yards. He again shot up the middle, this time for nine yards, and then pulled in a pass for 16 yards to the Minnesota 3-yard line. Levens finished the drive on the next play, surging up the middle and into the end zone for the score. Wilkins recovered a Johnson fumble at the Vikings' 10-yard line early in the fourth quarter, leading to Green Bay's second field goal and the final score, a 19-yarder by Longwell.

Levens rolled up 133 yards of offense, including 108 rushing, his sixth 100-yard effort of the season. Reggie White paced the defense, posting 2½ sacks, as the Green Bay defenders registered six sacks in all.

DEC. 7: A 17-6 win over the Tamp Bay Buccaneers secured Green Bay its third consecutive NFC Central Division title – the first time since 1965-66-67 – and a first-round bye in the playoffs.

Trailing 3-0 in the first quarter, Favre scrambled right to avoid Buccaneer pressure, faked a run, then pulled up and unfurled a perfect strike to Brooks, who fell backward in the end zone for the score with 4:46 left in the period. In the third quarter, nursing a 7-6 lead, Favre put together a 10-play, 73-yard drive, which culminated in another vintage play from his arsenal of moves. From the Bucs' 8-yard line, Favre moved toward the line of scrimmage, about to take off running, then flipped the ball to Levens who subsequently spun and bolted into the end zone, getting hit as he crossed the goal line.

On the Packers' next series, Favre orchestrated a 16-play, 88-yard drive which began in the 14th minute of the third quarter and consumed nearly two-thirds of the fourth period – a total of 10 minutes and 31 seconds. The drive, to which Levens and William Henderson contributed 71 of the 88 yards, was finished off by a 27-yard Longwell field goal to give the Green and Gold a 17-6 margin in the eventual victory.

Favre closed out the day with 25 completions in 33 attempts for 280 yards and two touchdowns. Levens weighed in with 118 yards of total offense. The Packers' defense sacked Dilfer four times.

DEC. 20: Wrapping up a three-game road sweep with a 31-10 over the Carolina Panthers – the first such three-game road success for the Green and Gold since 1963 – the Packers returned home to close out the regular season with a 31-21 win over the Buffalo Bills. Assured of a playoff berth, first-round bye and home-field advantage for its first postseason game, Green Bay extended its regular-season winning streak at home to 23 games – the longest in team history and the second-longest in NFL annals.

The Packers converted three Buffalo turnovers for its first and final touchdowns, plus a field goal. The recovery of a Buffalo fumble in the end zone by Tyrone Davis in the game's second minute was the first Packers score and Sharper's 20-yard interception return with under five minutes left in the game closed out Green Bay's scoring for the day. It was Sharper's second interception return for a touchdown of the year; his first had come with a 50-yard return Nov. 2 against Detroit.

Freeman produced Green Bay's second touchdown on a four-yard strike from Favre late in the first quarter. Tyrone Davis, who had scored his first NFL touchdown on the first-quarter fumble recovery, caught a two-yard pass in the right corner of the end zone for the Packers' third touchdown. Mike Prior's third-quarter interception and 49-yard return led to a 35-yard Longwell field goal, staking the Packers to a 24-0 lead before Buffalo was permitted to score. Antowain Smith posted the Bills' first score one play after Buffalo recovered a Steve Bono fumble. In the fourth quarter, Smith again scored from one yard out. With the Packers substituting liberally during the late stages, the Bills made it a 10-point margin, scoring the day's final touchdown with 2:05 left to play.

THE PLAYOFFS

JAN. 4: Green Bay advanced to the NFC Championship Game for the third consecutive year by way of a 21-7 win over the Tampa Bay Buccaneers in Lambeau Field and earned the right to face the San Francisco 49ers in 3Com Park with the winner advancing to Super Bowl XXXII.

The Green and Gold held a 13-0 halftime lead on a Favre three-yard touchdown pass to Chmura and two Longwell field goals of 21 and 32 yards, respectively. It appeared Green Bay was in a position to put the game away when Freeman returned the second half kickoff 90 yards for what would have been a touchdown, but a holding penalty put the Packers on their own 10-yard line to start the second half. Favre quickly moved the Green Bay offense to the Tamp Bay 25, but the drive ended when Tampa Bay intercepted a Favre pass on the 6-yard line. The Bucs then drove 94 yards in eight plays with Mike Alstott scoring from six yards out to make it a six-point game.

The Packers got even two exchanges later as Favre drove 54 yards in nine plays, capped by Levens crossing the goal line from two yards out and Favre running in the two-point conversion.

Levens was a key factor in the winning process, setting a new Packers postseason single-game rushing record, 112 yards on 25 carries; he also caught 4 passes for 29 yards. Bob Kuberski authored one of the day's bigger plays, knocking snapper Dave Moore back from the line of scrimmage and blocking Michael Husted's 43-yard field goal attempt, which would have provided the first points of the game. The win extended the Packers' all-time home winning streak in the playoffs to a perfect 12 victories.

JAN. 11: The Packers earned a second consecutive trip to the "Big Dance" by defeating the San Francisco 49ers 23-10 on the rain-drenched, soggy soil of 3Com Park. Green Bay, which had won back-to-back titles in Super Bowls I and II, would travel to San Diego for Super Bowl XXXII to face the AFC champion Denver Broncos.

With the Packers leading 3-0, the game took a turn on Eugene Robinson's interception less than three minutes into the second quarter. San Francisco faced a third-and-eight situation at the Green Bay 28 when Robinson swept in front of Brent Jones, pulled in the ball and headed up the field. Cutting back to his right, he ran 58 yards to the 49ers' 28-yard line. On second-and-nine, Favre connected with Freeman, who raced 27 yards into the end zone. Longwell's conversion padded the Packers' lead to 10-0. A 28-yard field goal put the 49ers on the board, but Longwell retaliated with a 43-yarder on the final play of the first half, giving the Green and Gold a 13-3 lead.

After a scoreless third quarter, Longwell kicked his third field goal of the day, a 25-yarder, with 5:12 left on the clock, and Levens added a five-yard run up the middle two minutes later to wrap up the Packers' offensive attack. San Francisco returned the ensuing kickoff 95 yards for a touchdown, but it was all the 49ers could put together as Green Bay captured the win.

Levens' 114 rushing yards – 71 in the second half – surpassed his 112-yard effort the week before and set a new club single-game, postseason record. The Packers' defense, which had shut down the Tampa Bay offense the week prior, held the 49ers to a lone field goal and without an offensive touchdown.

JAN. 26: History did not repeat itself for the Packers, who were seeking to win their second straight Super Bowl title for the second time (Green Bay previously had won Super Bowls I and II). Standing in their way were the Denver Broncos and their eventual Super Bowl MVP, Terrell Davis. The Broncos defeated the Packers 31-24 in what many have called the greatest Super Bowl of all-time.

Green Bay struck first, scoring on the game's opening drive when Favre hit Freeman with a 22-yard pass to close an eight-play, 76-yard march. The Packers' 7-0 lead would be their only one of the day, however. Denver answered back with a drive of its own on its first series, capped by Davis' first one-yard touchdown run of the day. Two Green Bay turnovers – a Favre interception and fumble – resulted in 10 Bronco points, giving them a 17-7 lead in the second quarter. Green Bay closed the gap to 17-14 with 12 seconds left in the half, when Favre connected with Chmura on a six-yard throw on a drive that went 95 yards in 17 plays – the longest such production in Green Bay's playoff history.

The second half opened with Tyrone Williams recovering a Broncos fumble on the first play from scrimmage of the half at the Denver 26, and seven plays later Longwell had tied the contest, 17-17, on a 27-yard field goal. A series later, Craig Hentrich blasted a 51-yard punt to put the Broncos' 8-yard line, but John Elway orchestrated a 92-yard, 13-play drive for the go-ahead touchdown, a one-yard run by Davis – his second of the day.

An exchange of turnovers closed out the third quarter as Freeman fumbled the ensuing kickoff and Denver recovered at the Packers' 22-yard line; Robinson intercepted Elway on the next play, returning the theft to the Packers' 15-yard line from two yards deep in the end zone. Favre took advantage of the opportunity, escorting the Packers into the end zone in just four plays, hitting Freeman from 13 yards out for what would be Green Bay's final score of the day, tying the score 24-24. With 3:27 remaining in the game, Denver took over on the Green Bay 49-yard line and in five plays the Broncos were in the end zone, Davis' third one-yard run of the day capping the drive. The Packers, giving one last effort, started on their own 30 and swept to the Denver 35-yard line in three plays. On first down, Levens picked up four yards on a pass, but Favre's next pass bounced off the hands of a closely guarded Freeman and his third-down pass intended for Brooks fell incomplete. Favre's throw on fourth down with 32 seconds remaining in the game was intended for Chmura – but was knocked away. So, with 28 ticks left on the clock, Green Bay's reign as world champions came to an end.

The Packers out-gained the Broncos, 350 yards to 302, and emerged with a 255 to 123 advantage in net passing, but one statistic made the difference: the rushing numbers. Denver mounted a 179-yard assault against Green Bay, Davis accounting for 157 yards in 30 carries, with three touchdowns. Favre, who finished the day with 256 yards and three touchdowns on 25-of-42 passing, became only the seventh player in NFL history to amass more than 3,000 passing yards in the playoffs.

PACKERS' RETIRED NUMBERS

No.	Pos.	Player	Year Retired
3	B	Tony Canadeo	1952
14	E/DB	Don Hutson	1951
15	QB	Bart Starr	1973
66	LB	Ray Nitschke	1983

Dorsey Levens, a one-time fifth-round draft choice, was thrust into a starting role early in the 1997 preseason when incumbent halfback Edgar Bennett suffered a season-ending tear of his Achilles' tendon. A big, physical runner, Levens impressively answered the gauntlet thrown his way, rushing for 1,435 yards, the second-highest one-season total in team history and became the first Green Bay running back voted to the Pro Bowl in nearly two decades, starting alongside 2,000-yard rusher Barry Sanders. Wearing opponents down in the fourth quarter on a consistent basis, Levens averaged 4.7 yards per carry in the final period last year.

PACKERS 38, CHICAGO 24
Monday, September 1, at Green Bay

CHICAGO	0	11	0	13	—	24
GREEN BAY	3	15	6	14	—	38

Scoring
GB FG Longwell 38
CB R.Harris 1 run (Flanigan-Sauerbrun pass)
GB Thomason 1 pass from Favre (Levens-Favre pass)
CB FG Jaeger 42
GB R.Brooks 18 pass from Favre (Longwell kick)
GB FG Longwell 36
GB FG Longwell 29
GB Levens 1 run (Longwell kick)
CB Proehl 22 pass from Kramer (two-pt. attempt failed)
GB Wilkins 1 fumble return (Longwell kick)
CB R.Harris 68 run (Jaeger kick)

TEAM STATISTICS
	Packers	Bears
First Downs	18	19
Total Net Yards	315	336
Total Plays	55	74
Net Yards Rushing	107	164
Net Yards Passing	208	172
Passes (A-C-I)	22-15-1	41-17-2
Penalties-Yards	6-28	13-91
Fumbles (No.-Lost)	1-1	1-1

Rushing
Packers — Levens 22-80; Favre 7-18; Henderson 2-9.
Bears — R.Harris 13-122; Salaam 16-41; Kramer 1-1.

Receiving
Packers — Thomason 5-58; Mayes 4-54; R.Brooks 3-71; Henderson 2-13; Chmura 1-30.
Bears — R.Harris 4-36; Wetnight 3-32; Engram 3-24; Proehl 2-30; Penn 2-28; Salaam 2-20; Jennings 1-22.

Passing
Packers — Favre 22-15-1 (226 yards).
Bears — Kramer 41-17-2 (192 yards).

PHILADELPHIA EAGLES 10, PACKERS 9
Sunday, September 7, at Philadelphia

GREEN BAY	0	6	3	0	—	9
PHILADELPHIA	0	0	3	7	—	10

Scoring
GB FG Longwell 22
GB FG Longwell 18
PE FG Boniol 32
GB FG Longwell 27
PE Solomon 2 pass from Detmer (Boniol kick)

TEAM STATISTICS
	Packers	Eagles
First Downs	21	16
Total Net Yards	380	258
Total Plays	70	65
Net Yards Rushing	107	100
Net Yards Passing	273	158
Passes (A-C-I)	41-19-1	32-19-0
Penalties-Yards	2-15	5-23
Fumbles (No.-Lost)	2-1	2-1

Rushing
Packers — Levens 22-91; Henderson 6-16.
Eagles — Watters 23-81; Garner 3-18; Turner 1-1; Detmer 3-0.

Receiving
Packers — R.Brooks 6-90; Freeman 4-63; Henderson 4-41; Mayes 2-40; Thomason 2-32; Levens 1-13.
Eagles — Fryar 8-125; Watters 3-0; Timpson 2-18; Solomon 2-9; Seay 1-8; Garner 1-5; Lewis 1-5; Turner 1-3.

Passing
Packers — Favre 41-19-1 (279 yards).
Eagles — Detmer 32-19-0 (173 yards).

PACKERS 23, MIAMI DOLPHINS 18
Sunday, September 14, at Green Bay

MIAMI	6	3	3	6	—	18
GREEN BAY	0	10	3	10	—	23

Scoring
MD FG Mare 24
MD FG Mare 31
GB Freeman 2 pass from Favre (Longwell kick)
MD FG Mare 22
GB FG Longwell 26
MD FG Mare 34
GB FG Longwell 24
GB FG Longwell 39
GB Henderson 10 pass from Favre (Longwell kick)
MD Jordan pass from Marino (two-pt. attempt failed)

TEAM STATISTICS
	Packers	Dolphins
First Downs	22	20
Total Net Yards	392	299
Total Plays	67	69
Net Yards Rushing	142	59
Net Yards Passing	250	240
Passes (A-C-I)	37-24-0	47-21-1
Penalties-Yards	7-69	7-67
Fumbles (No.-Lost)	2-2	0-0

Rushing
Packers — Levens 21-121; Favre 5-11; Henderson 3-10.
Dolphins — Abdul-Jabbar 15-45; Spikes 3-4; Kidd 1-4; Jordan 1-2; McPhail 1-2; Parmalee 1-2.

Receiving
Packers — Henderson 7-60; Chmura 5-57; Freeman 5-52; R.Brooks 4-72; Levens 2-4; Schroeder 1-8.
Dolphins — Jordan 4-100; McDuffie 4-36; McPhail 4-24; Barnett 3-22; Drayton 2-31; Abdul-Jabbar 2-2; Manning 1-14; Parmalee 1-11.

Passing
Packers — Favre 37-24-0 (253 yards).
Dolphins — Marino 47-21-1 (240 yards).

PACKERS 38, MINNESOTA VIKINGS 32
Sunday, September 21, at Green Bay

MINNESOTA	7	0	15	10	—	32
GREEN BAY	7	24	7	0	—	38

Scoring

MV R.Smith 1 run (Davis kick)
GB R.Brooks 19 pass from Favre (Longwell kick)
GB Freeman 28 pass from Favre (Longwell kick)
GB Freeman 15 pass from Favre (Longwell kick)
GB Mickens 2 pass from Favre (Longwell kick)
GB FG Longwell 34
MV Carter 3 pass from Johnson (Davis kick)
MV Reed 7 pass from Johnson (Evans run)
GB Chmura 2 pass from Favre (Longwell kick)
MV FG Davis 31
MV Reed 27 pass from Johnson (Davis kick)

TEAM STATISTICS

	Packers	Vikings
First Downs	24	22
Total Net Yards	350	393
Total Plays	55	74
Net Yards Rushing	93	185
Net Yards Passing	257	208
Passes (A-C-I)	31-18-2	34-19-2
Penalties-Yards	5-40	9-115
Fumbles (No.-Lost)	2-1	0-0

Rushing

Packers — Levens 17-79; Favre 4-10; Henderson 1-4.
Vikings — R.Smith 28-132; Johnson 3-33; Evans 5-17; Green 1-3.

Receiving

Packers — Freeman 7-122; R.Brooks 5-92; Levens 2-22; Henderson 1-21; Mayes 1-5; Chmura 1-2; Mickens 1-2.
Vikings — Reed 9-119; Carter 5-32; R.Smith 4-38; Glover 1-28.

Passing

Packers — Favre 31-18-2 (266 yards).
Vikings — Johnson 34-19-2 (217 yards).

DETROIT LIONS 26, PACKERS 15
Sunday, September 28, at Pontiac, Mich.

GREEN BAY	6	3	6	0	—	15
DETROIT	0	17	3	6	—	26

Scoring

GB FG Longwell 36
GB FG Longwell 19
DL Brown 45 interception return (Hanson kick)
DL Chryplewicz 4 pass from Mitchell (Hanson kick)
GB FG Longwell 50
DL FG Hanson 53
GB Schroeder 7 pass from Favre (two-pt. attempt failed)
DL FG Hanson 44
DL FG Hanson 22
DL FG Hanson 39

TEAM STATISTICS

	Packers	Lions
First Downs	23	18
Total Net Yards	396	376
Total Plays	63	65
Net Yards Rushing	107	173
Net Yards Passing	289	203
Passes (A-C-I)	43-22-3	27-17-0
Penalties-Yards	9-65	9-107
Fumbles (No.-Lost)	2-1	1-0

Rushing

Packers — Levens 16-107; Favre 1-1; Hayden 1-(-1).
Lions — Sanders 28-139; Morton 1-20; Rivers 1-13; Vardell 3-3; Mitchell 3-(-2).

Receiving

Packers — R.Brooks 9-164; Freeman 5-91; Levens 3-(-1); Chmura 2-18; Thomason 1-14; Schroeder 1-7; Henderson 1-2.
Lions — Moore 6-105; Morton 6-61; Sanders 1-20; Milburn 1-11; Vardell 1-8; Metzelaars 1-6; Chryplewicz 1-4.

Passing

Packers — Favre 43-22-3 (295 yards).
Lions — Mitchell 27-17-0 (215 yards).

PACKERS 21, TAMPA BAY BUCCANEERS 16
Sunday, October 5, at Green Bay

TAMPA BAY	3	0	7	6	—	16
GREEN BAY	0	21	0	0	—	21

Scoring

TB FG Husted 23
GB Freeman 31 pass from Favre (Longwell kick)
GB Wilkins 77 interception return (Longwell kick)
GB Freeman 6 pass from Favre (Longwell kick)
TB Alstott 1 run (Husted kick)
TB Dunn 2 run (two-pt. attempt failed)

TEAM STATISTICS

	Packers	Bucs
First Downs	13	23
Total Net Yards	234	372
Total Plays	52	68
Net Yards Rushing	64	217
Net Yards Passing	170	155
Passes (A-C-I)	31-21-0	29-16-1
Penalties-Yards	5-38	3-30
Fumbles (No.-Lost)	2-1	2-1

Rushing

Packers — Levens 13-44; Favre 4-17; Hayden 1-3.
Buccaneers — Dunn 16-125; Alstott 17-56; Anthony 1-18; Dilfer 1-13; Ellison 1-5.

Receiving

Packers — Levens 8-61; R.Brooks 4-29; Freeman 3-57; Chmura 3-23; Henderson 3-21.
Buccaneers — Copeland 5-53; Alstott 4-34; Anthony 3-44; Harris 1-19; Hape 1-13; Moore 1-12; Dunn 1-4.

Passing

Packers — Favre 31-21-0 (191 yards).
Buccaneers — Dilfer 29-16-1 (179 yards).

PACKERS 24, CHICAGO BEARS 23
Sunday, October 12, at Chicago

GREEN BAY	0	14	7	3	—	24
CHICAGO	10	0	7	6	—	23

Scoring

CB R.Harris 1 run (Jaeger kick)
CB FG Jaeger 41
GB Chmura 2 pass from Favre (Longwell kick)
GB Levens 1 pass from Favre (Longwell kick)
CB Kramer 3 run (Jaeger kick)
GB Chmura 12 pass from Favre (Longwell kick)
GB FG Longwell 37
CB Penn 22 pass from Kramer (two-pt. attempt failed)

TEAM STATISTICS

	Packers	Bears
First Downs	22	26
Total Net Yards	277	353
Total Plays	60	69
Net Yards Rushing	100	121
Net Yards Passing	177	232
Passes (A-C-I)	35-19-1	35-22-2
Penalties-Yards	5-55	6-53
Fumbles (No.-Lost)	0-0	0-0

Rushing

Packers — Levens 12-74; Hayden 7-21; Favre 4-5; Henderson 2-0.
Bears — R.Harris 27-101; Autry 2-7; Conway 1-6; Kramer 3-5; Tn.Carter 1-2.

Receiving

Packers — Freeman 7-86; Henderson 3-20; R.Brooks 2-24; Chmura 2-14; Hayden 2-11; Levens 2-11; Thomason 1-11.
Bears — Penn 7-77; Conway 5-77; Engram 3-17; Jennings 2-34; R.Harris 2-8; Tn.Carter 2-4; Wetnight 1-15.

Passing

Packers — Favre 35-19-1 (177 yards).
Bears — Kramer 35-22-2 (232 yards).

PACKERS 28, NEW ENGLAND PATRIOTS 10
Monday, October 27, at Foxboro, Mass.

GREEN BAY	7	7	7	7	—	28
NEW ENGLAND	0	10	0	0	—	10

Scoring

GB Levens 6 pass from Favre (Longwell kick)
NE Coates 11 pass from Bledsoe (Vinatieri kick)
NE FG Vinatieri 38
GB Chmura 32 pass from Favre (Longwell kick)
GB R.Brooks 20 pass from Favre (Longwell kick)
GB Levens 3 run (Longwell kick)

TEAM STATISTICS

	Packers	Patriots
First Downs	27	18
Total Net Yards	371	324
Total Plays	74	58
Net Yards Rushing	144	69
Net Yards Passing	227	255
Passes (A-C-I)	34-23-0	36-20-3
Penalties-Yards	4-25	3-15
Fumbles (No.-Lost)	2-1	2-1

Rushing

Packers — Levens 26-100; Favre 9-32; Hayden 2-6; Henderson 2-6.

Patriots — Martin 18-65; Meggett 1-4; Bledsoe 1-0.

Receiving

Packers — Levens 7-40; R.Brooks 6-67; Chmura 4-60; Freeman 3-32; Henderson 2-20; Mayes 1-20.
Patriots — Glenn 7-163; Martin 4-52; Jefferson 3-18; Coates 3-14; Meggett 1-15; Byars 1-3; Gash 1-3.

Passing

Packers — Favre 34-23-0 (239 yards).
Patriots — Bledsoe 36-20-3 (268 yards).

PACKERS 20, DETROIT LIONS 10
Sunday, November 2, at Green Bay

DETROIT	7	3	0	0	—	10
GREEN BAY	0	14	3	3	—	20

Scoring

DL Vardell 1 run (Hanson kick)
GB R.Brooks 26 pass from Favre (Longwell kick)
GB Sharper 50 interception return (Longwell kick)
DL FG Hanson 34
GB FG Longwell 23
GB FG Longwell 44

TEAM STATISTICS

	Packers	Lions
First Downs	11	18
Total Net Yards	244	256
Total Plays	55	79
Net Yards Rushing	81	125
Net Yards Passing	163	131
Passes (A-C-I)	28-15-1	47-21-4
Penalties-Yards	7-54	4-20
Fumbles (No.-Lost)	2-1	2-0

Rushing

Packers — Levens 20-59; Favre 4-13; Henderson 1-9.
Lions — Sanders 23-105; Mitchell 3-18; Vardell 2-2.

Receiving

Packers — R.Brooks 5-77; Freeman 5-44; Levens 3-6; Chmura 1-28; T.Davis 1-26.
Lions — Moore 9-50; Sloan 5-29; Morton 4-35; Schlesinger 1-33; Metzelaars 1-7; Vardell 1-4.

Passing

Packers — Favre 28-15-1 (181 yards).
Lions — Mitchell 47-21-4 (158 yards).

PACKERS 17, ST. LOUIS RAMS 7
Sunday, November 9, at Green Bay

ST. LOUIS	0	0	7	0	—	7
GREEN BAY	0	3	7	7	—	17

Scoring

GB FG Longwell 44
GB Freeman 25 pass from Favre (Longwell kick)
SL Phillips 8 run (Wilkins kick)
GB Favre 7 run (Longwell kick)

TEAM STATISTICS

	Packers	Rams
First Downs	18	16

Total Net Yards	387	269
Total Plays	64	70
Net Yards Rushing	96	66
Net Yards Passing	291	203
Passes (A-C-I)	37-18-2	41-18-1
Penalties-Yards	9-66	15-110
Fumbles (No.-Lost)	1-1	1-0

Rushing
Packers — Levens 21-81; Favre 4-15.
Rams — Phillips 15-41; Moore 2-9; Lee 4-8; Banks 2-6; Heyward 1-1; Rypien 1-1.

Receiving
Packers — Freeman 7-160; R.Brooks 4-48; Chmura 3-45; Henderson 2-39; Levens 2-14.
Rams — Lee 5-104; Moore 4-38; Small 4-38; Bruce 3-34; Kennison 1-17; Heyward 1-4.

Passing
Packers — Favre 37-18-2 (306 yards).
Rams — Banks 23-9-0 (103 yards); Rypien 18-9-1 (132 yards).

INDIANAPOLIS COLTS 41, PACKERS 38
Sunday, November 16, at Indianapolis

GREEN BAY	14	14	0	10	—	38
INDIANAPOLIS	9	18	3	11	—	41

Scoring
GB Levens 3 pass from Favre (Longwell kick)
IC FG Blanchard 42
GB Levens 52 run (Longwell kick)
IC Harrison 17 pass from Justin (two-pt. attempt failed)
IC Fontenot 33 fumble return (Stablein-Justin pass)
IC Belser 50 interception return (Blanchard kick)
GB Levens 1 run (Longwell kick)
GB Freeman 16 pass from Favre (Longwell kick)
IC FG Blanchard 41
IC FG Blanchard 35
GB FG Longwell 18
IC Warren 3 run (Harrison-Justin pass)
GB Freeman 26 pass from Favre (Longwell kick)
IC FG Blanchard 20

TEAM STATISTICS
	Packers	Colts
First Downs	20	26
Total Net Yards	441	467
Total Plays	44	66
Net Yards Rushing	107	147
Net Yards Passing	334	320
Passes (A-C-I)	25-18-2	30-24-0
Penalties-Yards	8-53	6-45
Fumbles (No.-Lost)	1-1	3-1

Rushing
Packers — Levens 14-103; Henderson 1-4; Favre 1-0.
Colts — Faulk 17-116; Crockett 10-27; Warren 3-3; Justin 4-1.

Receiving
Packers — Freeman 5-93; Levens 4-92; Henderson 4-45; Mayes 3-119; Chmura 2-14.

Colts — Harrison 8-98; Dilger 6-96; Dawkins 5-83; Bailey 2-33; Crockett 1-19; Warren 1-6; Faulk 1-5.

Passing
Packers — Favre 25-18-2 (363 yards).
Colts — Justin 30-24-0 (340 yards).

PACKERS 45, DALLAS COWBOYS 17
Sunday, November 23, at Green Bay

DALLAS	3	7	0	7	—	17
GREEN BAY	7	3	14	21	—	45

Scoring
GB Levens 7 pass from Favre (Longwell kick)
DC FG Cunningham 29
DC Sanders 50 interception return (Cunningham kick)
GB FG Longwell 32
GB Chmura 4 pass from Favre (Longwell kick)
GB Chmura 2 pass from Favre (Longwell kick)
DC E.Smith 21 run (Cunningham kick)
GB Freeman 23 pass from Favre (Longwell kick)
GB Levens 5 run (Longwell kick)
GB Sharper 34 fumble return (Longwell kick)

TEAM STATISTICS
	Packers	Cowboys
First Downs	29	11
Total Net Yards	409	213
Total Plays	78	46
Net Yards Rushing	220	93
Net Yards Passing	189	120
Passes (A-C-I)	35-22-1	25-12-0
Penalties-Yards	3-23	11-103
Fumbles (No.-Lost)	0-0	3-2

Rushing
Packers — Levens 33-190; Favre 3-21; Henderson 5-9.
Cowboys — E.Smith 11-59; Walker 3-16; Sh.Williams 3-15; Aikman 3-3.

Receiving
Packers — Chmura 5-52; Henderson 5-12; Mayes 4-30; Levens 4-17; Freeman 3-56; R.Brooks 1-36.
Cowboys — Irvin 4-57; Bjornson 4-38; E.Smith 2-2; Miller 1-26; St.Williams 1-7.

Passing
Packers — Favre 35-22-1 (203 yards).
Cowboys — Aikman 24-12-0 (130 yards); Wilson 1-0-0 (0 yards).

PACKERS 27, MINNESOTA VIKINGS 11
Monday, December 1, at Minneapolis

GREEN BAY	3	7	7	10	—	27
MINNESOTA	0	3	0	8	—	11

Scoring
GB FG Longwell 30
MV FG Murray 42
GB R.Brooks 18 pass from Favre (Longwell kick)
GB Levens 3 run (Longwell kick)
GB FG Longwell 19
MV Hoard 4 run (Carter-Cunningham pass)

GB   Levens 5 run (Longwell kick)

TEAM STATISTICS

	Packers	Vikings
First Downs	17	17
Total Net Yards	326	253
Total Plays	66	72
Net Yards Rushing	139	99
Net Yards Passing	187	154
Passes (A-C-I)	29-15-0	42-21-1
Penalties-Yards	6-41	7-40
Fumbles (No.-Lost)	0-0	2-1

Rushing
Packers — Levens 31-108; Favre 4-17; Freeman 1-14.
Vikings — R.Smith 16-54; Cunningham 3-39; Evans 2-4; Hoard 3-2.

Receiving
Packers — Freeman 6-85; Levens 4-25; R.Brooks 2-43; Henderson 2-34; Chmura 1-9.
Vikings — Carter 6-52; Palmer 5-35; Reed 3-50; Glover 2-32; Walsh 2-13; R.Smith 2-6; Hoard 1-1.

Passing
Packers — Favre 29-15-0 (196 yards).
Vikings — Johnson 30-15-1 (117 yards); Cunningham 12-6-0 (72 yards).

PACKERS 17, TAMPA BAY BUCCANEERS 6
Sunday, December 7, at Tampa

GREEN BAY	7	0	7	3	—	17
TAMPA BAY	3	3	0	0	—	6

Scoring
TB   FG Husted 24
GB   R.Brooks 43 pass from Favre (Longwell kick)
TB   FG Husted 48
GB   Levens 8 pass from Favre (Longwell kick)
GB   FG Longwell 27

TEAM STATISTICS

	Packers	Bucs
First Downs	20	8
Total Net Yards	362	161
Total Plays	64	52
Net Yards Rushing	82	67
Net Yards Passing	280	94
Passes (A-C-I)	33-25-1	26-10-1
Penalties-Yards	3-21	6-33
Fumbles (No.-Lost)	2-2	1-1

Rushing
Packers — Levens 22-54; Favre 6-13; Henderson 2-11; R.Brooks 1-4.
Buccaneers — Alstott 10-34; Dunn 12-33.

Receiving
Packers — Levens 8-64; Freeman 5-73; Chmura 5-37; R.Brooks 3-71; Mayes 3-22; Henderson 1-13.
Buccaneers — Williams 5-87; Thomas 2-19; Dunn 2-9; Harris 1-2.

Passing
Packers — Favre 33-25-1 (280 yards).

Buccaneers — Dilfer 17-6-0 (67 yards); Walsh 9-4-1 (50 yards).

PACKERS 31, CAROLINA PANTHERS 10
Sunday, December 14, at Charlotte

GREEN BAY	14	3	7	7	—	31
CAROLINA	0	3	0	7	—	10

Scoring
GB   Freeman 58 pass from Favre (Longwell kick)
GB   R.Brooks 20 pass from Favre (Longwell kick)
CP   FG Kasay 43
GB   FG Longwell 31
GB   Freeman 6 pass from Favre (Longwell kick)
CP   Lane 35 run (Kasay kick)
GB   Hayden 6 run (Longwell kick)

TEAM STATISTICS

	Packers	Panthers
First Downs	26	9
Total Net Yards	458	172
Total Plays	78	53
Net Yards Rushing	218	140
Net Yards Passing	240	32
Passes (A-C-I)	34-18-1	26-7-0
Penalties-Yards	1-10	0-0
Fumbles (No.-Lost)	2-0	2-1

Rushing
Packers — Hayden 14-86; Levens 17-73; Henderson 5-32; R.Brooks 1-15; Favre 1-15; Bono 3-(-3).
Panthers — Lane 19-119; Collins 2-10; Carruth 1-6; Johnson 1-4; Greene 1-1.

Receiving
Packers — Freeman 10-166; R.Brooks 2-43; Beebe 2-28; Levens 2-0; Chmura 1-11; Henderson 1-8.
Panthers — Carruth 4-28; Mills 1-22; Muhammad 1-6; Walls 1-0.

Passing
Packers — Favre 34-18-1 (256 yards).
Panthers — Collins 26-7-0 (56 yards).

PACKERS 31, BUFFALO BILLS 21
Saturday, December 20, at Green Bay

BUFFALO	0	0	8	13	—	21
GREEN BAY	14	7	3	7	—	31

Scoring
GB   T.Davis fumble recovery in end zone (Longwell kick)
GB   Freeman 4 pass from Favre (Longwell kick)
GB   T.Davis 2 pass from Favre (Longwell kick)
GB   FG Longwell 35
BB   A.Smith 5 run (Riemersma-Van Pelt pass)
BB   A.Smith 1 run (two-pt. failed)
GB   Sharper 20 interception return (Longwell kick)
BB   Van Pelt 1 run (Christie kick)

TEAM STATISTICS

	Packers	Bills
First Downs	14	21
Total Net Yards	272	325
Total Plays	63	67

Net Yards Rushing	102	51
Net Yards Passing	170	274
Passes (A-C-I)	28-17-0	45-24-3
Penalties-Yards	13-115	10-93
Fumbles (No.-Lost)	3-3	3-1

Rushing
Packers — Levens 22-71; Hayden 7-33; Henderson 1-3; Pederson 3-(-4); Favre 1-(-1).
Bills — Thomas 7-28; A.Smith 10-20; Van Pelt 2-4; Holmes 2-(-1).

Receiving
Packers — Freeman 6-63; R.Brooks 4-83; Henderson 3-18; Chmura 2-17; T.Davis 1-2; Levens 1-2.
Bills — Early 7-120; Johnson 4-44; Riemersma 4-42; A.Smith 4-32; Moulds 3-31; Reese 1-13; Holmes 1-2.

Passing
Packers — Favre 18-12-0 (156 yards); Bono 10-5-0 (29 yards).
Bills — Van Pelt 44-23-3 (255 yards); Mohr 1-1-0 (29 yards).

PACKERS 21, TAMPA BAY BUCCANEERS 7
Sunday, January 4, 1998, at Green Bay

TAMPA BAY	0	0	7	0 —	7
GREEN BAY	7	6	0	8 —	21

Scoring
GB Chmura 3 pass from Favre (Longwell kick)
GB FG Longwell 21
GB FG Longwell 32
TB Alstott 6 run (Husted kick)
GB Levens 2 run (Favre run)

TEAM STATISTICS
	Packers	Bucs
First Downs	16	15
Total Net Yards	289	263
Total Plays	64	66
Net Yards Rushing	118	90
Net Yards Passing	171	173
Passes (A-C-I)	28-15-2	37-12-2
Penalties-Yards	7-90	3-38
Fumbles (No.-Lost)	3-1	2-0

Rushing
Packers — Levens 25-112; Henderson 2-4; Favre 5-2.
Buccaneers — Dunn 18-64; Alstott 7-21; Anthony 1-5; Walsh 1-0.

Receiving
Packers — Freeman 4-75; Levens 4-29; Mayes 2-37; Chmura 2-20; Henderson 2-8; R.Brooks 1-21.
Buccaneers — Copeland 4-44; Moore 3-54; Dunn 2-34; Anthony 1-52; Thomas 1-16; Davis 1-0.

Passing
Packers — Favre 28-15-2 (190 yards).
Buccaneers — Dilfer 36-11-2 (200 yards); Walsh 1-1-0 (0 yards).

PACKERS 23, SAN FRANCISCO 49ERS 10
Sunday, January 11, 1998, at San Francisco

GREEN BAY	3	10	0	10 —	23
SAN FRANCISCO	0	3	0	7 —	10

Scoring
GB FG Longwell 19
GB Freeman 27 pass from Favre (Longwell kick)
SF FG Anderson 28
GB FG Longwell 43
GB FG Longwell 25
GB Levens 5 run (Longwell kick)
SF Levy 95 kickoff return (Anderson kick)

TEAM STATISTICS
	Packers	49ers
First Downs	19	15
Total Net Yards	325	257
Total Plays	60	60
Net Yards Rushing	106	33
Net Yards Passing	219	224
Passes (A-C-I)	27-16-0	38-23-1
Penalties-Yards	9-62	6-64
Fumbles (No.-Lost)	1-0	4-1

Rushing
Packers — Levens 27-114; Henderson 3-2; Favre 2-(-10).
49ers — Kirby 6-21; Hearst 8-12; Young 2-1; Floyd 2-(-1).

Receiving
Packers — Freeman 4-107; Levens 4-27; R.Brooks 3-36; Chmura 2-18; T.Davis 1-17; Mayes 1-10; Henderson 1-7.
49ers — Owens 6-100; Stokes 6-87; Kirby 4-7; Hearst 3-14; Uwaezuoke 2-14; Clark 1-16; Jones 1-12.

Passing
Packers — Favre 27-16-0 (222 yards).
49ers — Young 38-23-1 (250 yards).

DENVER BRONCOS 31, PACKERS 24
Sunday, January 25, 1998, at San Diego

GREEN BAY	7	7	3	7 —	24
DENVER	7	10	7	7 —	31

Scoring
GB Freeman 22 pass from Favre (Longwell kick)
DB Davis 1 run (Elam kick)
DB Elway 1 run (Elam kick)
DB FG Elam 51
GB Chmura 6 pass from Favre (Longwell kick)
GB FG Longwell 27
DB Davis 1 run (Elam kick)
GB Freeman 13 pass from Favre (Longwell kick)
DB Davis 1 run (Elam kick)

TEAM STATISTICS
	Packers	Broncos
First Downs	21	21
Total Net Yards	350	302
Total Plays	63	61
Net Yards Rushing	95	179
Net Yards Passing	255	123
Passes (A-C-I)	42-25-1	22-12-1

1997 GAME-BY-GAME REVIEW

Penalties-Yards 9-59   7-65
Fumbles (No.-Lost) 2-2   1-1

Rushing
Packers — Levens 19-90; R.Brooks 1-5.
Broncos — Davis 30-157; Elway 5-17; Hebron 3-3; Griffith 1-2.

Receiving
Packers — Freeman 9-126; Levens 6-56; Chmura 4-43; R.Brooks 3-16; Henderson 2-9; Mickens 1-6.
Broncos — Sharpe 5-38; McCaffrey 2-45; Davis 2-8; Griffith 1-23; Hebron 1-5; Carswell 1-4.

Passing
Packers — Favre 42-25-1 (256 yards).
Broncos — Elway 22-12-1 (123 yards).

FAX ON DEMAND

The Green Bay Packers provide a fax on demand service for the benefit of media covering the team. The system, which efficiently provides updated information, is accessible 24 hours a day, seven days a week, and is updated each Monday during the season after 6 p.m. (central).

Instructions for using the fax on demand system, which can deliver press releases, rosters, statistics and selected biographies, follow:

Step 1 (to access information)
• Dial 920/496-7779 from the handset of your fax machine.
• You will hear the following prompt: "If you know the number of the document you wish to receive, press 1. To select from a menu, press 2. If you wish to receive a complete list of all available documents, press 3."

Step 2 (to select documents)
• If you select 1:
   Enter the three-digit number of the document(s) you wish to receive, if you know it.
   You may select up to three documents.
   After each document selection, press the star (*) key. After your last selection press the pound (#) key.

• If you select 2:
   Follow the prompts.
   Press 1 for schedules and rosters, press 2 for statistics, press 3 for biographies, etc.

Step 3 (to receive documents)
• To receive the document(s) you have requested, press the "start" or "receive" key on your fax machine when instructed and hang up the receiver. Your documents will be sent immediately.

Following is the fax on demand menu:
110   Packers schedule
120   NFL schedule
130   Packers numerical roster
140   Packers alphabetical roster
150   Packers depth chart
210   Packers offensive and defensive statistics
220   NFL statistics
230   Packers supplemental statistics
240   Most recent Packers play-by-play
310   Bio of Packers Head Coach Mike Holmgren
320   Bio of Packers quarterback Brett Favre
330   Bio of Packers defensive end Reggie White
340   Bio of Packers President Bob Harlan
350   Bio of Packers Executive Vice President/General Manager Ron Wolf
710   Packers week-of-game press release with stats and rosters
720   Tentative training camp practice times
730   Weekly injury report for Packers and their opponent
740   Packers' weekly updated biographies
750   List of Packers' transactions

Please call the Packers' public relations department at 920/496-5705 with any questions or problems.

1997 NFL FINAL STANDINGS

NATIONAL FOOTBALL CONFERENCE
Eastern Division

	W	L	T	PF	PA	H	A	AFC	NFC	DIV
*N.Y. Giants	10	5	1	307	265	6-2	4-3-1	1-3	9-2-1	7-0-1
Washington	8	7	1	327	289	5-2-1	3-5	1-3	7-4-1	4-3-1
Philadelphia	6	9	1	317	372	6-2	0-7-1	2-1-1	4-8	3-5
Dallas	6	10	0	304	314	5-3	1-7	2-2	4-8	3-5
Arizona	4	12	0	286	379	3-5	1-7	1-3	3-9	2-6

Central Division

	W	L	T	PF	PA	H	A	AFC	NFC	DIV
*Green Bay	13	3	0	422	282	8-0	5-3	3-1	10-2	7-1
# Tampa Bay	10	6	0	299	263	5-3	5-3	3-1	7-5	3-5
# Detroit	9	7	0	379	306	6-2	3-5	2-2	7-5	6-2
# Minnesota	9	7	0	354	359	5-3	4-4	3-1	6-6	3-5
Chicago	4	12	0	263	421	2-6	2-6	2-2	2-10	1-7

Western Division

	W	L	T	PF	PA	H	A	AFC	NFC	DIV
*San Francisco	13	3	0	375	265	8-0	5-3	2-2	11-1	8-0
Carolina	7	9	0	265	314	2-6	5-3	2-2	5-7	4-4
Atlanta	7	9	0	320	361	3-5	4-4	2-2	5-7	4-4
New Orleans	6	10	0	237	327	3-5	3-5	2-2	4-8	1-7
St. Louis	5	11	0	299	359	2-6	3-5	0-4	5-7	3-5

AMERICAN FOOTBALL CONFERENCE
Eastern Division

	W	L	T	PF	PA	H	A	AFC	NFC	DIV
*New England	10	6	0	369	289	6-2	4-4	9-3	1-3	7-1
# Miami	9	7	0	339	327	6-2	3-5	8-4	1-3	4-4
N.Y. Jets	9	7	0	348	287	5-3	4-4	6-6	3-1	2-6
Buffalo	6	10	0	255	367	4-4	2-6	5-7	1-3	5-3
Indianapolis	3	13	0	313	401	2-6	1-7	2-10	1-3	2-6

Central Division

	W	L	T	PF	PA	H	A	AFC	NFC	DIV
*Pittsburgh	11	5	0	372	307	7-1	4-4	9-3	2-2	6-2
#Jacksonville	11	5	0	394	318	7-1	4-4	9-3	2-2	6-2
Tennessee	8	8	0	333	310	6-2	2-6	4-8	4-0	2-6
Cincinnati	7	9	0	355	405	6-2	1-7	5-7	2-2	3-5
Baltimore	6	9	1	326	345	3-4-1	3-5	4-8	2-1-1	3-5

Western Division

	W	L	T	PF	PA	H	A	AFC	NFC	DIV
* Kansas City	13	3	0	375	232	8-0	5-3	9-3	4-0	7-1
# Denver	12	4	0	472	287	8-0	4-4	9-3	3-1	6-2
Seattle	8	8	0	365	362	4-4	4-4	6-6	2-2	4-4
Oakland	4	12	0	324	419	2-6	2-6	2-10	2-2	2-6
San Diego	4	12	0	266	425	2-6	2-6	3-9	1-3	1-7

AFC

Wild Card Playoffs
DENVER 42, Jacksonville 17
NEW ENGLAND 17, Miami 3

Divisional Playoffs
PITTSBURGH 7, New England 6
Denver 14, KANSAS CITY 10

AFC Championship
Denver 24, PITTSBURGH 21

NFC

Wild Card Playoffs
Minnesota 23, N.Y. GIANTS 22
TAMPA BAY 20, Detroit 10

Divisional Playoffs
SAN FRANCISCO 38, Minnesota 22
GREEN BAY 21, Tampa Bay 7

NFC Championship
Green Bay 23, SAN FRANCISCO 10

Super Bowl XXXII
at San Diego, California
Denver 31, Green Bay 24

*Division Champion; #Wild Card team   Home teams in playoff games are indicated by CAPITAL LETTERS

Long coveted, shares of stock in the Green Bay Packers were sold to fans all across America late last year and early in 1998 during a limited time offering, the first such sale held in 47 years. A total of 109,723 persons (representing 4,746,896 shares) now can lay claim to an ownership interest in the franchise.

While shares of stock do include voting rights, the redemption price is minimal, no dividends are ever paid, the stock cannot appreciate in value and there are no season ticket privileges associated with stock ownership. No shareholder is allowed to own more than 200,000 shares, a safeguard to ensure that no one individual is able to assume control of the club.

There now have been four stock sales in the 79-year history of the team. The first, in 1923, saw local merchants raise $5,000 by selling 1,000 shares for $5 apiece, with a stipulation at that time that the purchaser also had to buy at least six season tickets.

The second, in 1935, raised $15,000 in new capital after the corporation had gone into receivership. At that point, the non-profit corporation was reorganized as the Green Bay Packers, Inc., the present company, with 300 shares of stock outstanding.

The third, in 1950, came on the heels of founder Curly Lambeau's 30-year dominion, when the club's officers arranged to amend the corporation's bylaws to permit the sale of up to 10,000 total shares of stock (opening up more than 9,500 shares for purchase), to limit the number of shares that any individual could own and to increase the number of directors from 15 to 25.

The response to the '50 drive was inspiring, with people from all across Wisconsin, as well as former Green Bay residents living in other states, coming forward to buy the $25 shares of stock. Roughly $50,000 was raised in one 11-day period alone. Reportedly, one woman from a farm near Wrightstown, Wis., showed up at the team's offices with $25 worth of quarters in a match box. A total of about $118,000 was generated through this major stock sale, helping to put the Packers on a sound financial basis once again.

The most recent stock sale, launched late in 1997, added 105,989 new shareholders and raised more than $24 million, monies which are earmarked for upcoming physical enhancements to Lambeau Field and to the team's training facilities. Priced at $200 per share, 120,010 shares were purchased during the 17-week sale, which ended March 16, 1998.

With National Football League support of the plan already in hand, the existing 1,940 shareholders overwhelmingly voted to amend the articles of the corporation on November 13 of last year, authorizing the Packers to sell up to one million shares to raise funds for capital improvements, and received a 1,000 to 1 split on their original shares. Fans immediately were able to call a special toll free phone number or tap into the team's internet site for information on how to buy the 400,000 shares made available to the public.

The initial response to the stock offering was staggering. In the first 11 days of the sale, roughly one-third – or $7.8 million – of the total amount transacted was sold. Paid orders poured in at a rate of 3,500 per day during this early period, generating about $700,000 each day. The sale hit its high point during the first week of December as fans purchased shares as holiday gifts.

Shares of stock were purchased by citizens from all 50 states, in addition to fans in Guam and the U.S. Virgin Islands. Over half (or roughly 64,300) of the shares sold during the most recent offering were bought by Wisconsin residents, followed by inhabitants of Illinois (9,600), Minnesota (4,300), California (3,700), Florida (2,900), Michigan (2,800), Texas (2,500) and Ohio (2,000).

Today, an annual meeting of stockholders is held in July – the 1998 meeting was conducted July 8 inside Lambeau Field. As a means of running the corporation, a 45-person board of directors is elected by the stockholders. Each year, 15 positions come up for election, each individual being voted in for a three-year term. The board of directors in turn elect a seven-member Executive Committee (officers) of the corporation, consisting of a president, vice president, treasurer, secretary and three members-at-large. The president is the only officer who receives compensation, the balance sitting gratis.

Shares of stock cannot be re-sold, except back to the team for a fraction of the original price. Limited transfer of shares (ie., to heirs and relatives) is permissible.

Based on the original 'Articles of Incorporation for the (then) Green Bay Football Corporation' put into place in 1923, if the Packers franchise ever were to be sold, after the payment of all expenses any remaining monies would go to the Sullivan-Wallen Post of the American Legion in order to build "a proper soldier's memorial." This stipulation was enacted to ensure that the club remained in Green Bay and that there could never by any financial enhancement for the shareholder. The beneficiary was changed from the Sullivan-Wallen Post to the Green Bay Packers Foundation on the basis of a shareholder vote at the November, 1997, meeting.

Jim Taylor (31), who rushed for 1,474 yards in 1962 to set the Packers' all-time record, watched Dorsey Levens mount a serious challenge to that mark last year. While Levens fell 39 yards shy of Taylor's single-season record – which remains the longest-standing record of its type among all NFL teams by over a decade – he did in 1997 break Taylor's single-game mark for rushing yards with a 190-yard effort against Dallas. Still the leading career rusher in team history with 8,207 yards, Taylor had held the single-game record even longer, having rushed for 186 yards in a 1961 victory over the New York Giants in Milwaukee.

RUSHING
Attempts
Most Attempts (career)
1,811, Jim Taylor, 1958-1966 (9 seasons)
1,293, John Brockington, 1971-77 (7 seasons)
1,171, Clarke Hinkle, 1932-41 (10 seasons)
1,025, Tony Canadeo, 1941-44, 1946-52 (11 seasons)
936, Edgar Bennett, 1992-96 (5 seasons)

Most Attempts (season)
329, Dorsey Levens, 1997 (16 games)
316, Edgar Bennett, 1995 (16 games)
284, Terdell Middleton, 1978 (16 games)
274, John Brockington, 1972 (14 games)
272, Jim Taylor, 1962 (14 games)

Most Attempts (game)
39, Terdell Middleton, vs. Minnesota, Nov. 26, 1978 (110 yards)
33, Dorsey Levens, vs. Dallas, Nov. 23, 1997 (190 yards)
32, Jim Grabowski, vs. Chicago, Sept. 24, 1967 (111 yards)
32, John Brockington, at Minnesota, Nov. 17, 1974 (137 yards)
31, Dorsey Levens, at Minnesota, Dec. 1, 1997 (108 yards)
30, Jim Taylor, vs. Pittsburgh, Nov. 3, 1963 (141 yards)
30, John Brockington, at Chicago, Nov. 7, 1971 (142 yards)
30, Harlan Huckleby, at New York Giants, Oct. 4, 1981 (88 yards)
30, Edgar Bennett, at Chicago, Sept. 11, 1995 (96 yards)

Most Seasons Leading Team
8, Clarke Hinkle, 1932-34, 1937-41
7, Jim Taylor, 1960-66
5, John Brockington, 1971-75
4, Tony Canadeo, 1943, 1948-50
3, Ted Fritsch, 1944-46
3, Gerry Ellis, 1981, 1983-84
3, Edgar Bennett, 1994-96

Most Consecutive Seasons Leading Team
7, Jim Taylor, 1960-66
5, Clarke Hinkle, 1937-41
5, John Brockington, 1971-75
3, Clarke Hinkle, 1932-34
3, Ted Fritsch, 1944-46
3, Tony Canadeo, 1948-50
3, Edgar Bennett, 1994-96

Most Attempts, Rookie (season)
216, John Brockington, 1971
126, Gerry Ellis, 1980
121, Willard Harrell, 1975
114, Kenneth Davis, 1986
108, Bob Monnett, 1933

Yardage
Most Yards Gained (career)
8,207, Jim Taylor, 1958-66 (9 seasons)
5,024, John Brockington, 1971-77 (7 seasons)
4,197, Tony Canadeo, 1941-44, 1946-52 (11 seasons)
3,860, Clarke Hinkle, 1932-41 (10 seasons)
3,826, Gerry Ellis, 1980-86 (7 seasons)

Most Yards Gained (season)
1,474, Jim Taylor, 1962 (272 attempts)
1,435, Dorsey Levens, 1997 (329 attempts)
1,307, Jim Taylor, 1961 (243 attempts)
1,169, Jim Taylor, 1964 (235 attempts)
1,144, John Brockington, 1973 (265 attempts)
1,116, Terdell Middleton, 1978 (284 attempts)
1,105, John Brockington, 1971 (216 attempts)
1,101, Jim Taylor, 1960 (230 attempts)
1,067, Edgar Bennett, 1995 (316 attempts)
1,052, Tony Canadeo, 1949 (208 attempts)
1,027, John Brockington, 1972 (274 attempts)
1,018, Jim Taylor, 1963 (248 attempts)

Most Yards Gained (game)
190, Dorsey Levens, vs. Dallas, Nov. 23, 1997 (33 attempts)
186, Jim Taylor, vs. New York Giants, Dec. 3, 1961 (27 attempts)
167, Billy Grimes, vs. New York Yanks, Oct. 8, 1950 (10 attempts)
165, Jim Taylor, at Los Angeles Rams, Dec. 13, 1964 (17 attempts)
164, Jim Taylor, at Minnesota, Oct. 14, 1962 (17 attempts)

Most Seasons Leading Team
7, Jim Taylor, 1960-66
6, Clarke Hinkle, 1932, 1934, 1936-37, 1940-41
5, Tony Canadeo 1943, 1946-49
5, John Brockington, 1971-75
3, Ted Fritsch, 1942, 1944-45
3, Tobin Rote, 1951-52, 1956
3, Gerry Ellis, 1981, 1983-84
3, Eddie Lee Ivery, 1980, 1982, 1985
3, Edgar Bennett, 1994-96

Most Consecutive Seasons Leading Team
7, Jim Taylor, 1960-66
5, John Brockington, 1971-75
4, Tony Canadeo, 1946-49
3, Edgar Bennett, 1994-96
2, By many players

Longest Runs From Scrimmage
97 yards, Andy Uram, vs. Chicago Cardinals, Oct. 8, 1939 (touchdown)
84 yards, Jim Taylor, vs. Detroit, Nov. 8, 1964 (touchdown)
83 yards, James Lofton, at New York Giants, Sept. 20, 1982 (touchdown)
80 yards, Jessie Clark, at St. Louis, Sept. 29, 1985 (no touchdown)
77 yards, Tom Moore, vs. Detroit, Sept. 22, 1963 (touchdown)
76 yards, Terdell Middleton, vs. Detroit, Oct. 1, 1978 (touchdown)
73 yards, Billy Grimes, at Chicago Bears, Oct. 15, 1950 (touchdown)

Most Seasons, 1,000 or More Yards Rushing
5, Jim Taylor, 1960-64
3, John Brockington, 1971-73
1, Tony Canadeo, 1949
1, Terdell Middleton, 1978
1, Edgar Bennett, 1995
1, Dorsey Levens, 1997

Most Games, 100 or More Yards Rushing (career)
26, Jim Taylor
13, John Brockington
9, Tony Canadeo
6, Edgar Bennett, Dorsey Levens
5, Terdell Middleton, Eddie Lee Ivery, Gerry Ellis

Most Games, 100 or More Yards Rushing (season)
7, Jim Taylor, 1962
6, Dorsey Levens, 1997
5, Tony Canadeo, 1949
5, Jim Taylor, 1960
4, Jim Taylor (3 times), 1961, 1963, 1964
4, John Brockington (2 times), 1971, 1973
4, Terdell Middleton, 1978

Most Consecutive Games, 100 or More Yards Rushing
3, John Brockington, 1971
3, Dorsey Levens, 1997
2, Tony Canadeo (2 times), 1949
2, Tobin Rote, 1951
2, Jim Taylor (8 times)
2, John Brockington, 1973

Highest Average Gain (game – 10 attempts)
16.70, Billy Grimes, vs. N.Y. Yanks, Oct. 8, 1950 (10-167)

Most Yards Gained, Rookie (season)
1,105, John Brockington, 1971
545, Gerry Ellis, 1980
519, Kenneth Davis, 1986
445, Cecil Isbell, 1938
412, Bob Monnett, 1933

Touchdowns
Most Seasons Leading Team
6, Verne Lewellen, 1926-31
6, Clarke Hinkle, 1932, 1936-1939, 1941
5, Ted Fritsch, 1943-47
5, Tobin Rote, 1951-52, 1954-56
5, Paul Hornung, 1957-60, 1965
4, Jim Taylor, 1961-64

4, Donny Anderson, 1967-68, 1970-71
4, John Brockington, 1972-75
4, Brent Fullwood, 1987-90
4, Tony Canadeo, 1948-49, 1952
3, Gerry Ellis, 1980, 1983, 1985
3, Edgar Bennett, 1993-95

Most Consecutive Seasons Leading Team
6, Verne Lewellen, 1926-31
5, Ted Fritsch, 1943-47
4, Clarke Hinkle, 1936-39
4, Paul Hornung, 1957-60
4, Jim Taylor, 1961-64
4, John Brockington, 1972-75
4, Brent Fullwood, 1987-90
3, Tobin Rote, 1954-56
3, Edgar Bennett, 1993-95

Most Touchdowns (season)
19, Jim Taylor, 1962
15, Jim Taylor, 1961

Most Touchdowns, Rookie (season)
5, Buckets Goldenberg, 1933
5, Gerry Ellis, 1980
5, Brent Fullwood, 1987
4, Bob Monnett, 1933
4, Charlie Sample, 1942
4, Tom Moore, 1960
4, Dave Hampton, 1969
4, John Brockington, 1971
4, Scott Hunter, 1971
3, Clarke Hinkle, 1932
3, George Sauer, 1935
3, Tony Canadeo, 1941
3, Irv Comp, 1943
3, Jack Cloud, 1950
3, Paul Hornung, 1957

Most Consecutive Games, Rushing for Touchdown
7, Paul Hornung, 1960
6, Terdell Middleton, 1978
5, Tobin Rote, 1956
5, Jim Taylor (2 times), 1961, 1964
4, Verne Lewellen (3 times), 1929, 1929-30, 1931
4, Charlie Sample, 1942
4, Jim Taylor (3 times), 1961, 1962 (twice)
4, Donny Anderson, 1971

FORWARD PASSING

Most Seasons Leading League
3, Arnie Herber, 1932, 1934, 1936
3, Bart Starr, 1962, 1964, 1966

Most Consecutive Seasons Leading League
2, Cecil Isbell, 1941-42

Most Passes Completed (career)
1,971, Brett Favre, 1992-97 (6 seasons)
1,808, Bart Starr, 1956-71 (16 seasons)
1,592, Lynn Dickey, 1976-77, 1979-85 (9 seasons)
889, Don Majkowski, 1987-92 (6 seasons)
826, Tobin Rote, 1950-56 (7 seasons)

Most Passes Completed (season)
363, Brett Favre, 1994 (attempted 582)
359, Brett Favre, 1995 (attempted 570)
353, Don Majkowski, 1989 (attempted 599)
325, Brett Favre, 1996 (attempted 543)
318, Brett Favre, 1993 (attempted 522)

Most Passes Completed (game)
36, Brett Favre, at Chicago, Dec. 5, 1993 (54 attempts)
35, Lynn Dickey, at Tampa Bay, Oct. 12, 1980 (51 attempts)
34, Don Majkowski, at Detroit, Nov. 12, 1989 (59 attempts)
33, Brett Favre, at Atlanta, Oct. 4, 1992 (43 attempts)
31, Brett Favre, vs. Miami, Sept. 11, 1994 (51 attempts)
31, Brett Favre, vs. Cincinnati, Dec. 3, 1995 (43 attempts)

Most Passes Attempted (career)
3,206, Brett Favre, 1992-97 (6 seasons)
3,149, Bart Starr, 1956-71 (16 seasons)
2,831, Lynn Dickey, 1976-77, 1979-85 (9 seasons)
1,854, Tobin Rote, 1950-56 (7 seasons)
1,607, Don Majkowski, 1987-92 (6 seasons)

Most Passes Attempted (season)
599, Don Majkowski, 1989
582, Brett Favre, 1994
570, Brett Favre, 1995
543, Brett Favre, 1996
522, Brett Favre, 1993

Most Passes Attempted (game)
61, Brett Favre, vs. San Francisco, Oct. 14, 1996 (completed 28)
59, Don Majkowski, at Detroit, Nov. 12, 1989 (completed 34)
54, Randy Wright, vs. San Francisco, Oct. 26, 1986 (completed 30)
54, Brett Favre, at Chicago, Dec. 5, 1993 (completed 36)
53, Don Majkowski, at Tampa Bay, Dec. 3, 1989 (completed 25)
52, Randy Wright, at Detroit, Dec. 4, 1988 (completed 29)

Fewest Passes Intercepted (season)
3, Bart Starr, 1966 (251 attempts)

Most Passes Intercepted (season)
29, Lynn Dickey, 1983 (484 attempts)
25, Lynn Dickey, 1980 (478 attempts)
24, Tobin Rote, 1950 (224 attempts)
24, Brett Favre, 1993 (522 attempts)
23, Randy Wright, 1986 (492 attempts)
21, Irv Comp, 1944 (177 attempts)
21, Jack Jacobs, 1948 (184 attempts)
21, John Hadl, 1975 (353 attempts)

Most Passes Intercepted (game)
6, Tom O'Malley, vs. Detroit, Sept. 17, 1950 (15 attempts)
5, Cecil Isbell, at New York Giants, Nov. 20, 1938 (19 attempts)
5, Jack Jacobs, at New York Giants, Nov. 23, 1947 (24 attempts)
5, Tobin Rote, vs. Los Angeles Rams, Oct. 16, 1955 (40 attempts)
5, Bart Starr, vs. Chicago, Sept. 24, 1967 (19 attempts)
5, Randy Wright, at New Orleans, Sept. 14, 1986 (44 attempts)
5, Don Majkowski, at Tampa Bay, Oct. 14, 1990 (42 attempts)

Most Consecutive Passes Thrown Without Interception
294, Bart Starr, 1964-65

Most Yards Gained on Passes (career)
24,718, Bart Starr, 1956-71 (16 seasons)
22,591, Brett Favre, 1992-97 (6 seasons)
21,369, Lynn Dickey, 1976-77, 1979-85 (9 seasons)
11,535, Tobin Rote, 1950-56 (7 seasons)
10,870, Don Majkowski, 1987-92 (6 seasons)

Most Yards Gained on Passes (season)
4,458, Lynn Dickey, 1983 (484 attempts)
4,413, Brett Favre, 1995 (570 attempts)
4,318, Don Majkowski, 1989 (599 attempts)
3,899, Brett Favre, 1996 (543 attempts)
3,882, Brett Favre, 1994 (582 attempts)
3,867, Brett Favre, 1997 (513 attempts)
3,529, Lynn Dickey, 1980 (478 attempts)
3,303, Brett Favre, 1993 (522 attempts)
3,247, Randy Wright, 1986 (492 attempts)
3,227, Brett Favre, 1992 (471 attempts)
3,195, Lynn Dickey, 1984 (401 attempts)

Most Yards Gained on Passes (game)
418, Lynn Dickey, at Tampa Bay, Oct. 12, 1980 (35 completions)
410, Don Horn, vs. St. Louis, Dec. 21, 1969 (22 completions)
402, Brett Favre, at Chicago, Dec. 5, 1993 (36 completions)
395, Brett Favre, vs. San Francisco, Oct. 14, 1996 (28 completions)
387, Lynn Dickey, vs. Washington, Oct. 17, 1983 (22 completions)
384, Lynn Dickey, vs. San Diego, Oct. 7, 1984 (25 completions)
383, Lynn Dickey, vs. Minnesota, Oct. 23, 1983 (23 completions)
371, Lynn Dickey, at Denver, Oct. 15, 1984 (27 completions)
367, Don Majkowski, vs. Detroit, Oct. 29, 1989 (29 completions)
366, Lynn Dickey, at Atlanta, Nov. 27, 1983 (25 completions)
366, Brett Favre, at Detroit, Dec. 4, 1994 (29 completions)

Longest Completed Passes (all TDs)
*99 yards, Brett Favre to Robert Brooks, at Chicago, Sept. 11, 1995
96 yards, Tobin Rote to Billy Grimes, at San Francisco, Dec. 10, 1950
95 yards, Lynn Dickey to Steve Odom, at Minnesota, Oct. 2, 1977
92 yards, Arnie Herber to Don Hutson, vs. Chicago Cardinals, Oct. 8, 1939
91 yards, Bart Starr to Boyd Dowler, at Los Angeles Rams, Dec. 17, 1960
90 yards, Babe Parilli to Bill Howton, vs. Washington, Oct. 5, 1952
90 yards, Babe Parilli to Bill Howton, at San Francisco, Dec. 14, 1952

Shortest Completed Pass (for touchdown)
4 inches, Cecil Isbell to Don Hutson, vs. Cleveland Rams, Oct. 18, 1942

Most Seasons Leading League, Yards Gained
3, Arnie Herber, 1932, 1934, 1936

INDIVIDUAL RECORDS

Most Seasons Leading Team, Yards Gained
12, Bart Starr, 1957, 1959-68, 1970
8, Lynn Dickey, 1976-77, 1980-85
7, Arnie Herber, 1932-37, 1939
6, Tobin Rote, 1950-51, 1953-56
6, Brett Favre, 1992-97

Most Consecutive Seasons Leading Team, Yards Gained
10, Bart Starr, 1959-68
6, Arnie Herber, 1932-37
6, Lynn Dickey, 1980-85
6, Brett Favre, 1992-97
4, Tobin Rote, 1953-56
3, Cecil Isbell, 1940-42
3, Irv Comp, 1944-46
3, Don Majkowski, 1988-90

Most Passes Attempted, Rookie (season)
224, Tobin Rote, 1950   127, Don Majkowski, 1987
177, Babe Parilli, 1952   106, Stan Heath, 1949
163, Scott Hunter, 1971

Most Passes Completed, Rookie (season)
83, Tobin Rote, 1950   55, Don Majkowski, 1987
77, Babe Parilli, 1952   50, David Whitehurst, 1977
75, Scott Hunter, 1971

Most Yards Gained, Rookie (season)
1,416, Babe Parilli, 1952   875, Don Majkowski, 1987
1,231, Tobin Rote, 1950   662, Irv Comp, 1943
1,210, Scott Hunter, 1971

Most Games, 300 Yards Passing (career)
16, Brett Favre, 1992-97   2, Randy Wright, 1984-88
15, Lynn Dickey, 1976-77, 1979-85   1, Cecil Isbell, 1938-42
9, Don Majkowski, 1987-92   1, Don Horn, 1967-70
5, Bart Starr, 1956-71   1, Mike Tomczak, 1991
2, Tobin Rote, 1950-56

Most Games, 300 Yards Passing (season)
7, Brett Favre, 1995   4, Lynn Dickey, 1984
6, Don Majkowski, 1989   4, Brett Favre, 1994
5, Lynn Dickey, 1983   3, Lynn Dickey, 1980

Most Consecutive Games, 300 Yards Passing
3, Lynn Dickey, 1984
2, Lynn Dickey (2 times), 1983 (twice)
2, Don Majkowski, 1989
2, Brett Favre, 1995
2, Brett Favre, 1997

Most Touchdown Passes (career)
182, Brett Favre, 1992-97 (6 seasons)
152, Bart Star, 1956-71 (16 seasons)
133, Lynn Dickey, 1976-77, 1979-85 (9 seasons)
89, Tobin Rote, 1950-56 (7 seasons)
64, Arnie Herber, 1930-40 (11 seasons)

Most Touchdown Passes (season)
39, Brett Favre, 1996
38, Brett Favre, 1995
35, Brett Favre, 1997
33, Brett Favre, 1994
32, Lynn Dickey, 1983

Most Touchdown Passes (game)
5, Cecil Isbell, vs. Chicago Cardinals, Nov. 1, 1942
5, Don Horn, vs. St. Louis, Dec. 21, 1969
5, Lynn Dickey, at New Orleans, Dec. 13, 1981
5, Lynn Dickey, at Houston, Sept. 4, 1983
5, Brett Favre, vs. Chicago, Nov. 12, 1995
5, Brett Favre, vs. Minnesota, Sept. 21, 1997
4, Roy McKay, vs. Detroit, Oct. 7, 1945
4, Babe Parilli, vs. Philadelphia, Oct. 26, 1958
4, Lamar McHan, vs. Detroit, Oct. 4, 1959
4, Bart Starr, at Minnesota, Nov. 1, 1964
4, Bart Starr, at Dallas, Oct. 28, 1968
4, David Whitehurst, vs. New Orleans, Sept. 10, 1978
4, Lynn Dickey, vs. Cleveland, Nov. 6, 1983
4, Lynn Dickey, vs. Detroit, Oct. 28, 1984
4, Lynn Dickey, vs. Minnesota, Nov. 11, 1984

4, Don Majkowski, vs. Dallas, Oct. 8, 1989
4, Brett Favre, at Tampa Bay, Oct. 24, 1993
4, Brett Favre, at Dallas, Nov. 24, 1994
4, Brett Favre, vs. Minnesota, Oct. 22, 1995
4, Brett Favre, at New Orleans, Dec. 16, 1995
4, Brett Favre, at Tampa Bay, Sept. 1, 1996
4, Brett Favre, at Seattle, Sept. 29, 1996
4, Brett Favre, at Chicago, Oct. 6, 1996
4, Brett Favre, vs. Detroit, Nov. 3, 1996
4, Brett Favre, vs. Denver, Dec. 8, 1996
4, Brett Favre, vs. Dallas, Nov. 23, 1997

Most Games, Four or More Touchdown Passes (career)
12, Brett Favre, 1992-97 (6 seasons)
5, Lynn Dickey, 1976-77, 1979-85 (9 seasons)
2, Bart Starr, 1956-71 (16 seasons)

Most Games, Four or More Touchdown Passes (season)
5, Brett Favre, 1996
3, Brett Favre, 1995
2, Lynn Dickey (2 times), 1983, 1984
2, Brett Favre, 1997

Most Consecutive Games, Four or More Touchdown Passes
2, Brett Favre (Weeks 5-6 in 1996)

Most Consecutive Games, Throwing Touchdown Pass
22, Cecil Isbell (Weeks 1-11 in 1941, Weeks 1-11 in 1942)
17, Brett Favre (Weeks 8-16 in 1994, Weeks 1-8 in 1995)
15, Don Majkowski (Weeks 15-16 in 1988, Weeks 1-13 in 1989)
14, Brett Favre (Weeks 10-16 in 1995, Weeks 1-7 in 1996)
14, Brett Favre (Weeks 3-16 in 1997) (current)
13, Tobin Rote (Weeks 7-12 in 1955, Weeks 1-7 in 1956)

Most Touchdown Passes, Rookie (season)
13, Babe Parilli, 1952
7, Cecil Isbell, 1938
7, Irv Comp, 1943
7, Tobin Rote, 1950
7, Scott Hunter, 1971

Most Consecutive Completions
18, Lynn Dickey, at Houston, Sept. 4, 1983
18, Don Majkowski, vs. New Orleans, Sept. 17, 1989

Best Passing Efficiency (career – minimum 500 attempts)
61.48%, Brett Favre, 1992-97 (1,971-3,206)
57.42%, Bart Starr, 1956-71 (1,808-3,149)
56.23%, Lynn Dickey, 1976-77, 1979-85 (1,592-2,831)
55.32%, Don Majkowski, 1987-92 (889-1,607)
53.80%, Randy Wright, 1984-88 (602-1,119)

Best Passing Efficiency (season – minimum 140 attempts)
64.12%, Brett Favre, 1992 (302-471)
63.74%, Bart Starr, 1968 (109-171)
62.98%, Brett Favre, 1995 (359-570)
62.46%, Bart Starr, 1962 (178-285)
62.37%, Brett Favre, 1994 (363-582)

Best Passing Efficiency (game – minimum 20 attempts)
90.48%, Lynn Dickey, at New Orleans, Dec. 13, 1981 (19-21)

PASS RECEIVING

Most Passes Caught (career)
595, Sterling Sharpe, 1988-94 (7 seasons)
530, James Lofton, 1978-86 (9 seasons)
488, Don Hutson, 1935-45 (11 seasons, 118 games)
448, Boyd Dowler, 1959-69 (11 seasons)
345, Max McGee, 1954, 1957-67 (12 seasons)

Most Passes Caught (season)
112, Sterling Sharpe, 1993 (16 games)
108, Sterling Sharpe, 1992 (16 games)
102, Robert Brooks, 1995 (16 games)
94, Sterling Sharpe, 1994 (16 games)
90, Sterling Sharpe, 1989 (16 games)
81, Antonio Freeman, 1997 (16 games)
78, Edgar Bennett, 1994 (16 games)
74, Don Hutson, 1942 (11 games)
71, James Lofton, 1980 (16 games)
71, James Lofton, 1981 (16 games)

69, James Lofton, 1985 (16 games)
69, Sterling Sharpe, 1991 (16 games)
67, Sterling Sharpe, 1990 (16 games)
65, Gerry Ellis, 1981 (16 games)
64, James Lofton, 1986 (15 games)
62, James Lofton, 1984 (16 games)
61, Edgar Bennett, 1995 (16 games)

Most Passes Caught (game)
14, Don Hutson, at New York Giants, Nov. 22, 1942 (134 yards)
13, Don Hutson, vs. Cleveland Rams, Oct. 18, 1942 (209 yards)
12, Ken Payne, at Denver, Sept. 29, 1975 (167 yards)
12, Vince Workman, vs. Minnesota, Sept. 6, 1992 (50 yards)
11, Don Hutson, vs. Card-Pitt, Oct. 8, 1944 (207 yards)
11, Bob Mann, at Los Angeles Rams, Dec. 16, 1951 (123 yards)
11, Billy Howton, at Baltimore, Oct. 24, 1954 (147 yards)
11, Eddie Lee Ivery, at Tampa Bay, Oct. 12, 1980 (128 yards)
11, Gerry Ellis, at Tampa Bay, Nov. 22, 1981 (76 yards)
11, James Lofton, at Denver, Oct. 15, 1984 (206 yards)
11, Sterling Sharpe, at New York Giants, Nov. 8, 1992 (160 yards)
11, Robert Brooks, vs. Pittsburgh, Dec. 24, 1995 (137 yards)
11, Don Beebe, vs. San Francisco, Oct. 14, 1996 (220 yards)
10, Don Hutson, at Chicago Bears, Nov. 15, 1942 (117 yards)
10, Max McGee, at Minnesota, Oct. 14, 1962 (159 yards)
10, James Lofton, vs. Detroit, Oct. 6, 1985 (124 yards)
10, Sterling Sharpe, vs. Minnesota, Nov. 26, 1989 (157 yards)
10, Sterling Sharpe, at Phoenix, Nov. 18, 1990 (157 yards)
10, Sterling Sharpe, vs. Denver, Oct. 10, 1993 (70 yards)
10, Sterling Sharpe, at Tampa Bay, Oct. 24, 1993 (147 yards)
10, Sterling Sharpe, at Chicago, Dec. 5, 1993 (114 yards)
10, Edgar Bennett, vs. Miami, Sept. 11, 1994 (78 yards)
10, Sterling Sharpe, at Detroit, Dec. 4, 1994 (115 yards)
10, Robert Brooks, at Dallas, Oct. 8, 1995 (124 yards)
10, Antonio Freeman, vs. Chicago, Dec. 1, 1996 (156 yards)
10, Antonio Freeman, at Carolina, Dec. 14, 1997 (166 yards)

Most Consecutive Games, One or More Pass Receptions
103, Sterling Sharpe, 10th in 1988 through 16th in 1994
60, Edgar Bennett, 1st in 1993 through 12th in 1996
58, James Lofton, 8th in 1979 through 8th in 1983
50, Don Hutson, 3rd in 1941 through 10th in 1945
50, Paul Coffman, 3rd in 1979 through 4th in 1982
49, Max McGee, 8th in 1959 through 13th in 1961 and 1st in 1962 through 1963
44, Don Hutson, 1st in 1937 through 10th in 1938 and 1st in 1939 through 1st in 1941

Most Touchdown Passes Received (career)
99, Don Hutson, 1935-45 (11 seasons)
65, Sterling Sharpe, 1988-94 (7 seasons)
50, Max McGee, 1954, 1957-67 (12 seasons)
49, James Lofton, 1978-86 (9 seasons)
43, Billy Howton, 1952-58 (7 seasons)

Most Touchdown Passes Received (season)
18, Sterling Sharpe, 1994 (16 games)
17, Don Hutson, 1942 (11 games)
13, Billy Howton, 1952 (12 games)
13, Sterling Sharpe, 1992 (16 games)
13, Robert Brooks, 1995 (16 games)
12, Billy Howton, 1956 (12 games)
12, Sterling Sharpe, 1989 (16 games)
12, Antonio Freeman, 1997 (16 games)
11, Don Hutson, 1943 (12 games)
11, Paul Coffman, 1983 (16 games)
11, Sterling Sharpe, 1993 (16 games)

Most Touchdown Passes Received (game)
4, Don Hutson, vs. Detroit, Oct. 7, 1945
4, Sterling Sharpe, at Tampa Bay, Oct. 24, 1993
4, Sterling Sharpe, at Dallas, Nov. 24, 1994
3, Johnny (Blood) McNally, at Providence, Nov. 26, 1931
3, Don Hutson, at Cleveland Rams, Oct. 17, 1937
3, Don Hutson, vs. Cleveland Rams, Sept. 11, 1938
3, Don Hutson, at Cleveland Rams, Oct. 30, 1938
3, Don Hutson, at Washington, Nov. 30, 1941
3, Don Hutson, vs. Chicago Cardinals, Nov. 1, 1942
3, Andy Uram, vs. Chicago Cardinals, Nov. 1, 1942
3, Don Hutson, at Cleveland Rams, Nov. 8, 1942

3, Bob Mann, vs. Philadelphia, Oct. 14, 1951
3, Billy Howton, at Detroit, Nov. 27, 1952
3, Max McGee, at Philadelphia, Oct. 30, 1954
3, Max McGee, at Los Angeles Rams, Dec. 7, 1963
3, James Lofton, vs. New Orleans, Sept. 10, 1978
3, James Lofton, vs. Pittsburgh, Sept. 11, 1983
3, Sterling Sharpe, at Tampa Bay, Dec. 24, 1994
3, Keith Jackson, at Tampa Bay, Sept. 1, 1996
3, Antonio Freeman, vs. Denver, Dec. 8, 1996

Most Yards Catching Passes (career)
9,656, James Lofton, 1978-86 (9 seasons)
8,134, Sterling Sharpe, 1988-94 (7 seasons)
7,991, Don Hutson, 1935-45 (11 seasons)
6,918, Boyd Dowler, 1959-69 (11 seasons)
6,346, Max McGee, 1954, 1957-67 (12 seasons)

Most Yards Catching Passes (season)
1,497, Robert Brooks, 1995
1,461, Sterling Sharpe, 1992
1,423, Sterling Sharpe, 1989
1,361, James Lofton, 1984
1,300, James Lofton, 1983
1,294, James Lofton, 1981
1,274, Sterling Sharpe, 1993
1,243, Antonio Freeman, 1997
1,231, Billy Howton, 1952
1,226, James Lofton, 1980
1,211, Don Hutson, 1942
1,188, Billy Howton, 1956
1,153, James Lofton, 1985
1,119, Sterling Sharpe, 1994
1,105, Sterling Sharpe, 1990
1,010, Robert Brooks, 1997

Most Yards Catching Passes (game)
257, Billy Howton, vs. Los Angeles Rams, Oct. 21, 1956 (7 receptions)
237, Don Hutson, at Brooklyn, Nov. 21, 1943 (8 receptions)
220, Don Beebe, vs. San Francisco, Oct. 14, 1996 (11 receptions)
209, Don Hutson, vs. Cleveland Rams, Oct. 18, 1942 (13 receptions)
207, Don Hutson, vs. Chicago Cardinals, Nov. 1, 1942 (5 receptions)
207, Don Hutson, vs. Card-Pitt, Oct. 8, 1944 (11 receptions)
206, James Lofton, at Denver, Oct. 15, 1984 (11 receptions)
205, Carroll Dale, vs. Detroit, Sept. 29, 1968 (6 receptions)
200, Billy Howton, at Los Angeles Rams, Dec. 7, 1952 (6 receptions)

Most Combined Net Yards Gained (season)
1,896, Billy Grimes, 1950 (480 Rush., 261 Rec., 555 PR, 600 KOR)
1,805, Dorsey Levens, 1997 (1,435 Rush., 370 Rec.)
1,715, Edgar Bennett, 1995 (1,067 Rush., 648 Rec.)
1,654, Dave Hampton, 1971 (303 Rush., 37 Rec., 1,314 KOR)
1,617, Walter Stanley, 1986 (19 Rush., 723 Rec., 316 PR, 559 KOR)

Longest Pass Receptions
*99, Robert Brooks (from Brett Favre, at Chicago, Sept. 11, 1995)
96, Billy Grimes (from Tobin Rote, at San Francisco, Dec. 10, 1950)
95, Steve Odom (from Lynn Dickey, at Minnesota, Oct. 2, 1977)

Most Seasons Leading League
*8, Don Hutson, 1936-37, 1939, 1941-45
3, Sterling Sharpe, 1989, 1992-93

Most Consecutive Seasons Leading League
*5, Don Hutson, 1941-45
2, Sterling Sharpe, 1992-93

Most Seasons Leading Team
10, Don Hutson, 1936-45
8, James Lofton, 1978, 1980-86
7, Boyd Dowler, 1959, 1962-65, 1967-68
7, Sterling Sharpe, 1988-94
6, Billy Howton, 1952-57
4, Max McGee, 1958, 1960-62

Most Consecutive Seasons Leading Team
10, Don Hutson, 1936-45
7, James Lofton, 1980-86
7, Sterling Sharpe, 1988-94
6, Billy Howton, 1952-57
4, Boyd Dowler, 1962-65

Most Seasons, 50 or More Pass Receptions
7, James Lofton, 1979-81, 1983-86
7, Sterling Sharpe, 1988-94
3, Don Hutson, 1941-42, 1944
3, Billy Howton, 1952, 1954, 1956
3, Paul Coffman, 1979, 1981, 1983
3, Edgar Bennett, 1993-95
3, Robert Brooks, 1994-95, 1997
2, Boyd Dowler, 1963, 1967
2, Gerry Ellis, 1981, 1983
2, Antonio Freeman, 1996-97

Most Pass Receptions, Rookie (season)
55, Sterling Sharpe, 1988
53, Billy Howton, 1952
48, Gerry Ellis, 1980
46, James Lofton, 1978
39, Keith Woodside, 1988

Most Games, 200 or More Yards Pass Receiving (career)
4, Don Hutson, 1935-45   1, James Lofton, 1978-86
2, Billy Howton, 1952-58   1, Don Beebe, 1996-97
1, Carroll Dale, 1965-72

Most Games, 200 or More Yards Pass Receiving (season)
2, Don Hutson, 1942

Most Games, 100 or More Yards Pass Receiving (career)
32, James Lofton, 1978-86
29, Sterling Sharpe, 1988-94
24, Don Hutson, 1935-45
19, Boyd Dowler, 1959-69
17, Billy Howton, 1952-58

Most Games, 100 or More Yards Pass Receiving (season)
9, Robert Brooks, 1995
7, Sterling Sharpe, 1992
6, Don Hutson, 1942
6, Billy Howton, 1952
6, James Lofton, 1984
6, Sterling Sharpe, 1989
5, James Lofton (2 times), 1980, 1983
5, Sterling Sharpe, (2 times), 1993, 1994
4, Don Hutson (2 times), 1939, 1945
4, Billy Howton, 1954
4, James Lofton, 1981
4, Antonio Freeman, 1996

Most Consecutive Games, 100 or More Yards Pass Receiving
4, Don Hutson, 1945   3, James Lofton, 1984
4, James Lofton, 1982-83   3, Robert Brooks, 1995
3, Billy Howton, 1952   3, Robert Brooks, 1995

Most Seasons Leading League, Yards Gained
*7, Don Hutson, 1936, 1938-39, 1941-44

Most Consecutive Seasons Leading League, Yards Gained
*4, Don Hutson, 1941-44

Most Seasons Leading Team, Yards Gained
11, Don Hutson, 1935-45
9, James Lofton, 1978-86
7, Sterling Sharpe, 1988-94
6, Billy Howton, 1952-57
6, Carroll Dale, 1966, 1968-72
5, Max McGee, 1958-62
4, Boyd Dowler, 1963-65, 1967

Most Consecutive Seasons Leading Team, Yards Gained
11, Don Hutson, 1935-45
9, James Lofton, 1978-86
7, Sterling Sharpe, 1988-94
6, Billy Howton, 1952-57
5, Max McGee, 1958-62
5, Carroll Dale, 1968-72
3, Boyd Dowler, 1963-65

Most Seasons, 1,000 or More Yards, Pass Receiving
5, James Lofton, 1980-81, 1983-85

5, Sterling Sharpe, 1989-90, 1992-94
2, Billy Howton, 1952, 1956
2, Robert Brooks, 1995, 1997
1, Don Hutson, 1942
1, Antonio Freeman, 1997

Most Yards Gained, Rookie (season)
1,231, Billy Howton, 1952
818, James Lofton, 1978
791, Sterling Sharpe, 1988
614, Max McGee, 1954
549, Boyd Dowler, 1959

Touchdowns
Most Seasons Leading League
*9, Don Hutson, 1935-38, 1940-44

Most Consecutive Seasons Leading League
*5, Don Hutson, 1940-44
4, Don Hutson, 1935-38

Most Touchdowns, Rookie (season)
*13, Billy Howton, 1952   5, Ray Pelfrey, 1951
9, Max McGee, 1954   5, Carl Elliott, 1951
6, Don Hutson, 1935   4, Boyd Dowler, 1959
6, James Lofton, 1978   4, Ed West, 1984

Most Consecutive Games, Touchdowns
7, Don Hutson (2 times), 1941-42, 1943-44
6, Billy Howton, 1956
6, Sterling Sharpe, 1994
5, Don Hutson, 1942
5, Billy Howton, 1952
4, Don Hutson, 1936
4, Steve Odom, 1975
4, James Lofton (2 times), 1982-83, 1984

INTERCEPTIONS BY
Most Interceptions (career)
52, Bobby Dillon, 1952-59 (8 seasons)
48, Willie Wood, 1960-71 (12 seasons)
39, Herb Adderley, 1961-69 (9 seasons)
33, Irv Comp, 1943-49 (7 seasons)
31, Mark Lee, 1980-90 (11 seasons)
31, LeRoy Butler, 1990-97 (8 seasons)

Most Interceptions (season)
10, Irv Comp, 1943 (10 games)
9, Bobby Dillon, 1953 (12 games)
9, Bobby Dillon, 1955 (12 games)
9, Bobby Dillon, 1957 (12 games)
9, John Symank, 1957 (12 games)
9, Willie Wood, 1962 (14 games)
9, Willie Buchanon, 1978 (16 games)
9, Tom Flynn, 1984 (16 games)
9, Mark Lee, 1986 (16 games)
8, Don Hutson, 1943
8, Bob Forte, 1947
8, Bob Jeter, 1967

Most Interceptions (game)
*4, Bobby Dillon, at Detroit, Nov. 26, 1953
*4, Willie Buchanon, at San Diego, Sept. 24, 1978

Most Season Leading Team
7, Bobby Dillon, 1952-58
5, Willie Wood, 1961-63, 1965, 1970
5, LeRoy Butler, 1990-91, 1993, 1995, 1997
4, Herb Adderley, 1963-65, 1969
3, Don Hutson, 1940, 1942, 1945
3, Joe Symank, 1957, 1959, 1961
3, Ken Ellis, 1971-73
3, Mark Murphy, 1988, 1990-91

Most Consecutive Seasons Leading Team
7, Bobby Dillon, 1952-58
3, Willie Wood, 1961-63
3, Herb Adderley, 1963-65
3, Ken Ellis, 1971-73

Most Interceptions, Rookie (season)
10, Irv Comp, 1943
9, John Symank, 1957
9, Tom Flynn, 1984
7, Rebel Steiner, 1950

Longest Interception Returns (all touchdowns)
99 yards, Tim Lewis, vs. Los Angeles Rams, Nov. 18, 1984
94 yards, Rebel Steiner, vs. Chicago Bears, Oct. 1, 1950
91 yards, Hal Van Every, at Pittsburgh, Nov. 23, 1941
90 yards, LeRoy Butler, vs. San Diego, Sept. 15, 1996
88 yards, Bob Summerhays, vs. Philadelphia, Oct. 14, 1951

Most Touchdowns (career)
7, Herb Adderley, 1961-69
5, Bobby Dillon, 1952-59
3, Charley Brock, 1939-47
3, Doug Hart, 1964-71
3, Ken Ellis, 1970-75

Most Touchdowns (season)
3, Herb Adderley, 1965
2, Don Perkins, 1944
2, Charley Brock, 1945
2, Bob Jeter, 1966
2, Darren Sharper, 1997

Most Touchdowns, Rookie (season)
2, Darren Sharper, 1997

SCORING
Most Points (career)
823, Don Hutson, 1935-45 (11 seasons), (105 touchdowns, 172 extra points, 7 field goals)
820, Chris Jacke, 1989-96 (8 seasons), (301 extra points, 173 field goals)
760, Paul Hornung, 1957-62, 1964-66 (9 seasons), (62 touchdowns, 190 extra points, 66 field goals)
546, Jim Taylor, 1958-66 (9 seasons), (91 touchdowns)
521, Chester Marcol, 1972-80 (9 seasons), (1 touchdown, 155 extra points, 120 field goals)

Most Points (season)
*176, Paul Hornung, 1960 (15 touchdowns, 41 extra points, 15 field goals)
146, Paul Hornung, 1961 (10 touchdowns, 41 extra points, 15 field goals)
138, Don Hutson, 1942 (17 touchdowns, 33 extra points, 1 field goal)

Most Points (game)
33, Paul Hornung, vs. Baltimore, Oct. 8, 1961 (4 touchdowns, 6 extra points, 1 field goal)
31, Don Hutson, vs. Detroit, Oct. 7, 1945 (4 touchdowns, 7 extra points)
30, Paul Hornung, at Baltimore, Dec. 12, 1965 (5 touchdowns)
28, Paul Hornung, vs. Minnesota, Sept. 16, 1962 (3 touchdowns, 4 extra points, 2 field goals)

Most Points (one quarter)
29, Don Hutson, vs. Detroit, Oct. 7, 1945 (4 touchdowns, 5 extra points)

Most Consecutive Games Scoring One or More Points
45, Jan Stenerud (4 in 1980, 16 in 1981, 9 in 1982, 16 in 1983)
42, Don Chandler, 1965-67
42, Chris Jacke, (9 in 1991, 16 in 1992, 16 in 1993, 1 in 1994)
41, Al Del Greco, 1984-86
40, Don Hutson, 1940-44
39, Paul Hornung, 1958-61

Most Seasons Leading League
*5, Don Hutson, 1940-44
3, Paul Hornung, 1959-61
2, Chester Marcol, 1972, 1974

Most Consecutive Seasons Leading League
*5, Don Hutson, 1940-44
3, Paul Hornung, 1959-61

TOUCHDOWNS
Most Touchdowns (career)
105, Don Hutson, 1935-45 (11 seasons)

91, Jim Taylor, 1958-66 (9 seasons)
66, Sterling Sharpe, 1988-94 (7 seasons)
62, Paul Hornung, 1957-62, 1964-66 (9 seasons)
51, Max McGee, 1954, 1957-67 (12 seasons)

Most Touchdowns (season)
19, Jim Taylor, 1962
18, Sterling Sharpe, 1994
17, Don Hutson, 1942
16, Jim Taylor, 1961
15, Paul Hornung, 1960
15, Jim Taylor, 1964

Most Touchdowns (game)
5, Paul Hornung, at Baltimore, Dec. 12, 1965
4, Don Hutson, vs. Detroit, Oct. 7, 1945
4, Paul Hornung, vs. Baltimore, Oct. 8, 1961
4, Jim Taylor, at Cleveland, Oct. 15, 1961
4, Jim Taylor, at Chicago, Nov. 4, 1962
4, Jim Taylor, at Philadelphia, Nov. 11, 1962
4, Donny Anderson, vs. Cleveland, Nov. 12, 1967
4, Terdell Middleton, vs. Seattle, Oct. 15, 1978
4, Sterling Sharpe, at Tampa Bay, Oct. 24, 1993
4, Sterling Sharpe, at Dallas, Nov. 24, 1994

Most Seasons Leading League
*8, Don Hutson, 1935-38, 1941-44

Most Consecutive Seasons Leading League
*4, Don Hutson, 1935-38, 1941-44

Most Seasons Leading Team
11, Don Hutson, 1935-45
5, Verne Lewellen, 1926-30
5, Jim Taylor, 1959, 1961-64
5, Sterling Sharpe, 1989-90, 1992-94
3, Billy Howton, 1952, 1956-57
3, Donny Anderson, 1967, 1970-71
3, Barty Smith, 1976-77, 1979
3, Paul Coffman, 1979, 1983-84

Most Consecutive Seasons Leading Team
11, Don Hutson, 1935-45
5, Verne Lewellen, 1926-30
4, Jim Taylor, 1961-64
3, Sterling Sharpe, 1992-94
2, Johnny (Blood) McNally, 1931-32
2, Billy Howton, 1956-57
2, Donny Anderson, 1970-71
2, Barty Smith, 1976-77
2, Paul Coffman, 1983-84
2, Sterling Sharpe, 1989-90
2, Dorsey Levens, 1996-97

Most Touchdowns, Rookie (season)
13, Billy Howton, 1952
9, Max McGee, 1954
8, Gerry Ellis, 1980
7, Don Hutson, 1935
7, Dave Hampton, 1969

Most Consecutive Games Scoring Touchdowns
7, Don Hutson (2 times), 1941-42, 1943-44
7, Paul Hornung, 1960
6, Clarke Hinkle, 1937
6, Billy Howton, 1956
6, Terdell Middleton, 1978
6, Brent Fullwood, 1988
6, Sterling Sharpe, 1994
5, Chuck Sample, 1942
5, Don Hutson, 1942
5, Billy Howton, 1952
5, Fred Cone, 1953
5, Tobin Rote, 1956
5, Jim Taylor (2 times), 1961, 1964
5, Dave Hampton, 1969
4, Verne Lewellen (5 times), 1928, 1929, 1929-30, 1930, 1931
4, Don Hutson, 1936
4, Ted Fritsch, 1945
4, Billy Grimes, 1950

4, Fred Cone, 1956-57
4, Jim Taylor (4 times), 1961, 1962 (twice), 1964
4, Donny Anderson (2 times), 1967, 1971
4, Steve Odom, 1975
4, Gerry Ellis (2 times), 1980, 1984
4, James Lofton (2 times), 1982-83, 1984
4, Sterling Sharpe, 1989
4, Dorsey Levens, 1997

POINTS
Most Consecutive Seasons Leading Team
7, Don Hutson, 1939-45
5, Verne Lewellen, 1926-30
5, Fred Cone, 1953-57
5, Chris Jacke, 1989-93
4, Ted Fritsch, 1946-49
4, Paul Hornung, 1958-61
3, Don Chandler, 1965-67
3, Chester Marcol, 1972-74
3, Jan Stenerud, 1981-83
3, Al Del Greco, 1984-86

Most Points, No Touchdowns (season)
128, Chester Marcol, 1972
128, Chris Jacke, 1993
120, Ryan Longwell, 1997
115, Jan Stenerud, 1983
114, Chris Jacke, 1996
108, Chris Jacke, 1989
101, Jan Stenerud, 1981

Most Seasons, 100 or More Points
3, Paul Hornung, 1960-61, 1964
3, Chris Jacke, 1989, 1993, 1996
2, Don Hutson, 1942-43
2, Jan Stenerud, 1981, 1983
1, Ted Fritsch, 1946
1, Jim Taylor, 1962
1, Chester Marcol, 1972
1, Sterling Sharpe, 1994
1, Ryan Longwell, 1997

Most Consecutive Seasons, 100 or More Points
2, Don Hutson, 1942-43
2, Paul Hornung, 1960-61

Most Points, Rookie (season)
128, Chester Marcol, 1972
120, Ryan Longwell, 1997
108, Chris Jacke, 1989
78, Billy Howton, 1952
61, Al Del Greco, 1984

FIELD GOALS
Most Field Goals (career)
173, Chris Jacke (1989-96)
120, Chester Marcol (1972-80)
66, Paul Hornung (1957-62, 1964-66)
59, Jan Stenerud (1980-83)
53, Fred Cone (1951-57)

Most Field Goals (season)
33, Chester Marcol, 1972 (48 attempts)
31, Chris Jacke, 1993 (37 attempts)
25, Chester Marcol, 1974 (39 attempts)
24, Ryan Longwell, 1997 (30 attempts)
23, Chris Jacke, 1990 (30 attempts)

Longest Field Goals
54 yards, Chris Jacke, at Detroit, Jan. 2, 1994
53 yards, Jan Stenerud, at Tampa Bay, Nov. 22, 1981
53 yards, Chris Jacke, vs. Los Angeles Rams, Sept. 9, 1990
53 yards, Chris Jacke, at New York Jets, Nov. 3, 1991
53 yards, Chris Jacke, at Detroit, Nov. 1, 1992
53 yards, Chris Jacke, vs. San Francisco, Oct. 14, 1996
52 yards, Ted Fritsch, at New York Yanks, Oct. 19, 1950
52 yards, Paul Hornung, vs. Chicago (free kick), Sept. 13, 1964
52 yards, Chester Marcol, at Baltimore, Sept. 22, 1974
52 yards, Chris Jacke, vs. Atlanta, Oct. 1, 1989
52 yards, Chris Jacke, vs. Detroit, Nov. 21, 1993

Most Field Goals (game)
5, Chris Jacke, at Los Angeles Raiders, Nov. 11, 1990
5, Chris Jacke, vs. San Francisco, Oct. 14, 1996
4, Paul Hornung, at Pittsburgh, Oct. 30, 1960
4, Paul Hornung, at Minnesota, Oct. 22, 1961
4, Jerry Kramer, vs. Pittsburgh, Nov. 3, 1963
4, Chester Marcol, at Cleveland, Sept. 17, 1972
4, Chester Marcol, vs. Detroit, Dec. 3, 1972
4, Chester Marcol, vs. St. Louis, Nov. 11, 1973
4, Chester Marcol, vs. Detroit, Sept. 29, 1974
4, Chester Marcol, at Minnesota, Nov. 17, 1974
4, Tom Birney, at Detroit, Dec. 15, 1979
4, Jan Stenerud, vs. New York Giants, Nov. 8, 1981
4, Jan Stenerud, vs. Buffalo, Dec. 5, 1982
4, Jan Stenerud, at Tampa Bay, Dec. 12, 1983
4, Al Del Greco, at Detroit, Dec. 15, 1985
4, Al Del Greco, vs. Chicago, Sept. 22, 1986
4, Max Zendejas, at Minnesota, Oct. 16, 1988
4, Chris Jacke, at Chicago, Dec. 17, 1989
4, Chris Jacke, vs. Tampa Bay, Nov. 29, 1992
4, Chris Jacke, at New Orleans, Nov. 14, 1993
4, Chris Jacke, vs. Detroit, Nov. 21, 1993
4, Chris Jacke, vs. Chicago, Dec. 11, 1994

Most Seasons Leading Team
8, Chris Jacke, 1989-96
6, Ted Fritsch, 1942, 1945-46, 1948-50
6, Fred Cone, 1951, 1953-57
6, Chester Marcol, 1972-74, 1976-78
5, Clarke Hinkle, 1933, 1937-38, 1940-41
5, Paul Hornung, 1958-61, 1964
4, Cub Buck, 1922-25
3, Tiny Engebretsen, 1936, 1938-39
3, Don Chandler, 1965-67
3, Jan Stenerud, 1981-83
3, Al Del Greco, 1984-86

Most Consecutive Seasons Leading Team
8, Chris Jacke, 1989-96
5, Fred Cone, 1953-57
4, Cub Buck, 1922-25
4, Paul Hornung, 1958-61
3, Ted Fritsch, 1948-50
3, Don Chandler, 1965-67
3, Chester Marcol (2 times), 1972-74, 1976-78
3, Jan Stenerud, 1981-83
3, Al Del Greco, 1984-86

Most Field Goals Attempted (career)
224, Chris Jacke (1989-96)
195, Chester Marcol (1972-80)
128, Paul Hornung (1957-62, 1964-66)
98, Ted Fritsch (1942-50)
89, Fred Cone (1951-57)

Most Field Goals Attempted (season)
48, Chester Marcol, 1972
39, Chester Marcol, 1974
38, Paul Hornung, 1964
37, Chris Jacke, 1993
35, Chester Marcol, 1973

Most Field Goals, Rookie (season)
33, Chester Marcol, 1972
24, Ryan Longwell, 1997
22, Chris Jacke, 1989
11, Joe Danelo, 1975
9, Al Del Greco, 1984

Most Consecutive Games Scoring Field Goals
12, Jan Stenerud, 1980-81
12, Chris Jacke, 1991-92
10, Fred Cone, 1955
10, Chris Jacke, 1989-90
10, Chris Jacke, 1993
9, Don Chandler, 1967
9, Chester Marcol (2 times), 1972-73, 1976-77
8, Paul Hornung, 1960
8, Ryan Longwell, 1997

Most Consecutive Field Goals
17, Chris Jacke, 1993
15, Chris Jacke, 1989-90
11, Jan Stenerud, 1981
10, Max Zendejas, 1987
9, Chris Jacke, 1990
9, Chris Jacke, 1992-93
9, Chris Jacke, 1995

Highest Field Goal Percentage (career – 50 attempts)
80.82, Jan Stenerud (59/73)
77.23, Chris Jacke (173/224)
66.67, Al Del Greco (50/75)
61.54, Chester Marcol (120/195)
60.00, Don Chandler (48/80)

Highest Field Goal Percentage (season – 1 attempt per game)
91.67, Jan Stenerud, 1981 (22/24)
84.21, Max Zendejas, 1987 (16/19)
83.78, Chris Jacke, 1993 (31/37)
80.77, Jan Stenerud, 1983 (21/26)
80.00, Ryan Longwell, 1997 (24/30)

Most Field Goals, 50 or More Yards (career)
17, Chris Jacke (1989-96)
3, Chester Marcol (1972-80)
2, Ted Fritsch (1942-50)
2, Paul Hornung (1957-62, 1964-66)
2, Jan Stenerud (1980-83)
2, Al Del Greco (1984-87)
1, Tom Birney (1979-80)
1, Eddie Garcia (1983-84)
1, Ryan Longwell (1997)

Most Field Goals, 50 or More Yards (season)
6, Chris Jacke, 1993
3, Chris Jacke, 1995
2, Chester Marcol, 1972
2, Jan Stenerud, 1981
2, Al Del Greco, 1986
2, Chris Jacke (2 times), 1990, 1992

POINTS AFTER TOUCHDOWN

Most Seasons Leading League
3, Don Hutson, 1941-42, 1945

Most Seasons Leading Team
8, Chris Jacke, 1989-96
7, Fred Cone, 1951-57
7, Chester Marcol, 1972-74, 1976-79
6, Don Hutson, 1940-45
5, Paul Hornung, 1958-61, 1964
4, Cub Buck, 1922-25
4, Red Dunn, 1927, 1929-31

Most Consecutive Seasons Leading Team
8, Chris Jacke, 1989-96
7, Fred Cone, 1951-57
6, Don Hutson, 1940-45
4, Cub Buck, 1922-25
4, Paul Hornung, 1958-61
4, Chester Marcol, 1976-79
3, Red Dunn, 1929-31
3, Ernie Smith, 1935-37
3, Don Chandler, 1965-67
3, Chester Marcol, 1972-74
3, Jan Stenerud, 1981-83
3, Al Del Greco, 1984-86

Most Points After Touchdown Attempted (career)
306, Chris Jacke, 1989-96
214, Fred Cone, 1951-57
194, Paul Hornung, 1957-62, 1964-66
184, Don Hutson, 1935-45
164, Chester Marcol, 1972-80

Most Points After Touchdown Attempted (season)
53, Chris Jacke, 1996
52, Jan Stenerud, 1983
48, Ryan Longwell, 1997
46, Jerry Kramer, 1963
43, Paul Hornung, 1964
43, Don Chandler, 1966
43, Chris Jacke, 1994
43, Chris Jacke, 1995

Most Consecutive Points After Touchdown
134, Chris Jacke, 1990-94
99, Paul Hornung, 1960-62, 1964
87, Chris Jacke, 1994-96

74, Al Del Greco, 1985-87
67, Jan Stenerud, 1982-83

Highest Point After Touchdown Percentage (career – minimum 100 PATs)
98.37, Chris Jacke (301/306)
98.25, Al Del Greco (112/114)
97.94, Paul Hornung (190/194)
97.50, Don Chandler (117/120)
97.46, Jan Stenerud (115/118)

Most Points After Touchdown (career)
301, Chris Jacke, 1989-96
200, Fred Cone, 1951-57
190, Paul Hornung, 1957-62, 1964-66
172, Don Hutson, 1935-45
155, Chester Marcol, 1972-80

Most Points After Touchdown (season)
52, Jan Stenerud, 1983 (52 attempts)
51, Chris Jacke, 1996 (53 attempts)
48, Ryan Longwell, 1997 (48 attempts)
43, Jerry Kramer, 1963 (46 attempts)
43, Chris Jacke, 1995 (43 attempts)
42, Chris Jacke, 1989 (42 attempts)

Most Points After Touchdown (game)
8, Don Chandler, vs. Atlanta, Oct. 23, 1966
7, Don Hutson, vs. Detroit, Oct. 7, 1945
7, Paul Hornung, at Cleveland, Oct. 15, 1961
7, Paul Hornung, vs. Chicago, Sept. 30, 1962
7, Jerry Kramer, at Philadelphia, Nov. 11, 1962
7, Don Chandler, vs. Cleveland, Nov. 12, 1967
7, Jan Stenerud, vs. Tampa Bay, Oct. 2, 1983

SAFETIES
Most Safeties (season)
*2, Tom Nash, 1932   *2, Tim Harris, 1988

KICKOFF RETURNS
Most Kickoff Returns (career)
179, Steve Odom, 1974-79 (4,124 yards)
153, Al Carmichael, 1953-58 (3,907 yards)
120, Herb Adderley, 1961-69 (3,080 yards)
77, Travis Williams, 1967-70 (2,058 yards)
75, Tony Canadeo, 1941-44, 1946-52 (1,736 yards)

Most Kickoff Returns (season)
46, Dave Hampton, 1971 (1,314 yards)
42, Steve Odom, 1975 (1,034 yards)
41, Harlan Huckleby, 1983 (757 yards)
39, Del Rodgers, 1984 (843 yards)
35, Charles Wilson, 1990 (798 yards)

Most Kickoff Returns (game)
8, Harlan Huckleby, vs. Washington, Oct. 17, 1983 (208 yards)
8, Gary Ellerson, at St. Louis, Sept. 29, 1985 (164 yards)
7, Steve Odom, vs. Detroit, Sept. 29, 1974 (160 yards)
7, Roell Preston, at Indianapolis, Nov. 16, 1997 (211 yards)
6, Al Carmichael, at L.A. Rams, Dec. 16, 1956 (146 yards)
6, Lew Carpenter, vs. L.A. Rams, Nov. 20, 1960 (105 yards)
6, Herb Adderley, at Baltimore, Nov. 5, 1961 (180 yards)
6, Dave Hampton, at Detroit, Oct. 10, 1971 (140 yards)
6, Steve Odom, vs. Dallas, Nov. 12, 1978 (149 yards)
6, Mark Lee, at Chicago, Dec. 7, 1980 (134 yards)
6, Del Rodgers, at Baltimore, Dec. 19, 1982 (106 yards)
6, Tim Lewis, at Houston, Sept. 4, 1983 (116 yards)
6, Phillip Epps, at Tampa Bay, Sept. 30, 1984 (122 yards)
6, Del Rodgers, vs. Seattle, Oct. 21, 1984 (88 yards)
6, Corey Harris, at New York Giants, Nov. 8, 1992 (131 yards)
6, Desmond Howard, at Dallas, Nov. 18, 1996 (120 yards)

Most Kickoff Returns, Rookie (season)
35, Charles Wilson, 1990 (798 yards)
33, Vince Workman, 1989 (547 yards)
31, Steve Odom, 1974 (713 yards)

Most Kickoff Return Yards (career)
4,124, Steve Odom, 1974-79 (179 returns)
3,907, Al Carmichael, 1953-58 (153 returns)
3,080, Herb Adderley, 1961-69 (120 returns)

2,084, Dave Hampton, 1969-71 (74 returns)
2,058, Travis Williams, 1967-70 (77 returns)

Most Kickoff Return Yards (season)
1,314, Dave Hampton, 1971 (46 returns)
1,034, Steve Odom, 1975 (42 returns)
927, Al Carmichael, 1956 (33 returns)
843, Del Rodgers, 1984 (39 returns)
798, Charles Wilson, 1990 (35 returns)

Most Kickoff Return Yards (game)
211, Roell Preston, at Indianapolis, Nov. 16, 1997 (7 returns)
208, Harlan Huckleby, vs. Washington, Oct. 17, 1983 (8 returns)
194, Dave Hampton, vs. New York Giants, Sept. 19, 1971 (5 returns)
189, Al Carmichael, vs. Chicago Bears, Oct. 7, 1956 (5 returns)
189, Dave Hampton, vs. New Orleans, Nov. 28, 1971 (5 returns)
180, Herb Adderley, at Baltimore, Nov. 5, 1961 (6 returns)

Longest Kickoff Returns (all TDs)
*106, Al Carmichael, vs. Chicago Bears, Oct. 7, 1956
104, Travis Williams, at Los Angeles Rams, Dec. 9, 1967
103, Herb Adderley, vs. Baltimore, Nov. 18, 1962
101, Dave Hampton, vs. Minnesota, Oct. 4, 1970
100, Al Carmichael, at Cleveland Browns, Oct. 23, 1955
100, Larry Krause, at Pittsburgh, Dec. 6, 1970
100, Aundra Thompson, vs. New York Jets, Nov. 4, 1979

Most Kickoff Return Yards, Rookie (season)
798, Charles Wilson, 1990 (35 returns)
739, Travis Williams, 1967 (18 returns)
713, Steve Odom, 1974 (31 returns)

Highest Kickoff Return Average (career - 50 returns)
28.2, Dave Hampton, 1969-71 (74 returns, 2,084 yards)
26.7, Travis Williams, 1967-70 (77 returns, 2,058 yards)
26.5, Tom Moore, 1960-65 (71 returns, 1,882 yards)
25.7, Herb Adderley, 1961-69 (120 returns, 2,080 yards)
25.5, Al Carmichael, 1953-58 (153 returns, 3,907 yards)

Highest Kickoff Return Average (season - 12 returns)
*41.1, Travis Williams, 1967 (18 returns, 739 yards)
33.1, Tom Moore, 1960 (12 returns, 397 yards)
29.86, Al Carmichael, 1955 (14 returns, 418 yards)
29.85, Herb Adderley, 1963 (20 returns, 597 yards)
28.6, Dave Hampton, 1971 (46 returns, 1,314 yards)

Highest Kickoff Return Average, Rookie (season -12 returns)
*41.1, Travis Williams, 1967 (18 returns, 739 yards)
33.1, Tom Moore, 1960 (12 returns, 397 yards)
28.5, Larry Krause, 1970 (18 returns, 513 yards)
26.6, Herb Adderley, 1963 (18 returns, 478 yards)
26.5, Dave Hampton, 1969 (22 returns, 582 yards)

Most Touchdowns (career)
5, Travis Williams, 1967-70
3, Dave Hampton, 1969-71
2, Al Carmichael, 1953-58
2, Herb Adderley, 1961-69
2, Steve Odom, 1974-79
2, Robert Brooks, 1992-97

Most Touchdowns (season)
*4, Travis Williams, 1967
1, by many players

Most Touchdowns (game)
*2, Travis Williams, vs. Cleveland, Nov. 12, 1967

Most Touchdowns, Rookie (season)
*4, Travis Williams, 1967
1, Dave Hampton, 1969
1, Larry Krause, 1970
1, Terdell Middleton, 1977
1, Darrell Thompson, 1990

PUNTING

Longest Punts
90 yards, Don Chandler, vs. San Francisco, Oct. 10, 1965
78 yards, Jack Jacobs, vs. Chicago Cardinals, Oct. 10, 1948
75 yards, Boyd Dowler, at Minnesota, Oct. 22, 1961
75 yards, Boyd Dowler, vs. San Francisco, Oct. 21, 1962

Highest Punting Average (career - 150 punts)
42.8 yards, Craig Hentrich, 1994-97 (289 punts)
42.6 yards, Dick Deschaine, 1955-57 (181 punts)
42.0 yards, Bucky Scribner, 1983-84 (154 punts)
41.6 yards, Max McGee, 1954, 1957-67 (256 punts)
39.7 yards, Don Bracken, 1985-90 (368 punts)

Highest Punting Average (season - 35 punts)
45.0 yards, Craig Hentrich, 1997 (75 punts)
44.7 yards, Jerry Norton, 1963 (51 punts)
44.1 yards, Boyd Dowler, 1961 (38 punts)
43.5 yards, Jack Jacobs, 1947 (57 punts)
43.2 yards, Dick Deschaine, 1955 (56 punts)

Highest Punting Average (game – 4 punts)
61.6 yards, Roy McKay, vs. Chicago Cardinals, Oct. 28, 1945
(5-308)

Most Punts (career)
495, David Beverly, 1975-80 (37.9 yd. avg.)
368, Don Bracken, 1985-90 (39.7 yd. avg.)
315, Donny Anderson, 1966-71 (39.6 yd. avg.)
289, Craig Hentrich, 1994-97 (42.8 yd. avg.)
256, Max McGee, 1954, 1957-67 (41.6 yd. avg.)

Most Punts (season)
106, David Beverly, 1978 (35.5 yd. avg.)
86, David Beverly, 1980 (38.2 yd. avg.)
86, Paul McJulien, 1991 (40.4 yd. avg.)
85, David Beverly, 1977 (39.9 yd. avg.)
85, Bucky Scribner, 1984 (42.3 yd. avg.)
85, Don Bracken, 1988 (38.7 yd. avg.)
83, David Beverly, 1976 (37.0 yd. avg.)
82, Ray Stachowicz, 1981 (40.6 yd. avg.)

Most Punts (game)
11, Clarke Hinkle, at Chicago Bears, Dec. 10, 1933 (407 yards)
11, Jug Girard, at Chicago Bears, Oct. 15, 1950 (418 yards)
11, Jug Girard, at Los Angeles Rams, Dec. 3, 1950 (402 yards)
10, Roy McKay, at Philadelphia, Oct. 13, 1946 (421 yards)
10, Jack Jacobs, at Chicago Bears, Nov. 14, 1948 (392 yards)
10, Max McGee, at New York Giants, Nov. 1, 1959 (437 yards)
10, Don Chandler, vs. Dallas, Oct. 24, 1965 (400 yards)
10, David Beverly, at Cincinnati, Sept. 26, 1976 (366 yards)
10, David Beverly, vs. Minnesota, Nov. 26, 1978 (305 yards)
10, David Beverly, at Chicago, Dec. 10, 1978 (307 yards)
10, Don Bracken, vs. L.A. Raiders, Sept. 13, 1987 (489 yards)
10, Craig Hentrich, at Minnesota, Oct. 20, 1994 (460 yards)

PUNT RETURNS

Most Punt Returns (career)
187, Willie Wood, 1960-71 (returned 1,391 yards)
100, Al Carmichael, 1953-58 (returned 753 yards)
100, Phillip Epps, 1982-88 (returned 819 yards)
87, Walter Stanley, 1985-88 (returned 720 yards)
85, Johnnie Gray, 1975-83 (returned 656 yards)

Most Punt Returns (season)
58, Desmond Howard, 1996 (returned 875 yards)
40, Robert Brooks, 1994 (returned 352 yards)
37, Johnnie Gray, 1976 (returned 307 yards)
37, Antonio Freeman, 1995 (returned 292 yards)
36, Phillip Epps, 1983 (returned 324 yards)
33, Steve Odom, 1978 (returned 298 yards)
33, Walter Stanley, 1986 (returned 316 yards)
33, Bill Schroeder, 1997 (returned 342 yards)

Most Punt Returns (game)
8, Phillip Epps, vs. Minnesota, Nov. 21, 1982 (returned 49 yards)
7, Johnnie Gray, vs. Minnesota, Nov. 21, 1976 (returned 30 yards)
7, Robert Brooks, vs. New England, Oct. 2, 1994 (returned 34 yards)
7, Desmond Howard, vs. San Diego, Sept. 15, 1996 (returned 118 yards)
6, Ken Ellis, at Cleveland, Sept. 17, 1972 (returned 45 yards)
6, Steve Odom, vs. Detroit, Oct. 1, 1978 (returned 66 yards)
6, Phillip Epps, at Dallas, Sept. 23, 1984 (returned 22 yards)
6, Robert Brooks, vs. Tampa Bay, Nov. 28, 1993 (returned 39 yards)
6, Charles Jordan, vs. St. Louis, Sept. 3, 1995 (returned 61 yards)
6, Antonio Freeman, vs. New York Giants, Sept. 17, 1995 (returned 51 yards)
6, Antonio Freeman, at Minnesota, Nov. 5, 1995 (returned 62 yards)

6, Desmond Howard, vs. San Francisco, Oct. 14, 1996 (returned 28 yards)
6, Bill Schroeder, vs. St. Louis, Nov. 9, 1997 (returned 23 yards)

Most Punt Returns, Rookie (season)
37, Antonio Freeman, 1995 (returned 292 yards)
30, Jeff Query, 1989 (returned 247 yards)
24, Veryl Switzer, 1954 (returned 306 yards)

Most Punt Return Yards (career)
1,391, Willie Wood, 1960-71 (187 returns)
875, Desmond Howard, 1996 (58 returns)
834, Billy Grimes, 1950-52 (63 returns)
819, Phillip Epps, 1982-88 (100 returns)
753, Al Carmichael, 1953-58 (100 returns)

Most Punt Return Yards (season)
*875, Desmond Howard, 1996 (58 returns)
555, Billy Grimes, 1950 (29 returns)
352, Robert Brooks, 1994 (40 returns)
342, Bill Schroeder, 1997 (33 returns)
324, Phillip Epps, 1983 (36 returns)

Most Punt Return Yards, Rookie (season)
306, Veryl Switzer, 1954 (24 returns)
292, Antonio Freeman, 1995 (37 returns)
247, Jeff Query, 1989 (30 returns)

Most Fair Catches (career)
102, Willie Wood, 1960-71
41, Elijah Pitts, 1961-69, 1971
38, Jon Staggers, 1972-74
31, Phillip Epps, 1982-88
28, Johnnie Gray, 1975-83

Most Fair Catches (season)
20, Jon Staggers, 1972
18, Willie Wood, 1970
16, Desmond Howard, 1996
13, Phillip Epps, 1983
13, Robert Brooks, 1994
12, Jon Staggers, 1973

Most Fair Catches (game)
5, Willie Wood, vs. Chicago, Nov. 15, 1970

Highest Punt Return Average (career - 50 returns)
15.1, Desmond Howard, 1996 (58 returns, 875 yards)
13.2, Billy Grimes, 1950-52 (63 returns, 834 yards)
9.4, Jeff Query, 1989-91 (76 returns, 712 yards)
9.2, Jon Staggers, 1972-74 (50 returns, 460 yards)
8.9, Steve Odom, 1974-79 (64 returns, 569 yards)

Highest Punt Return Average (season - 14 returns)
19.1, Billy Grimes, 1950 (29 returns, 555 yards)
16.1, Willie Wood, 1961 (14 returns, 225 yards)
15.4, Ken Ellis, 1972 (14 returns, 215 yards)
15.1, Desmond Howard, 1996 (58 returns, 875 yards)
13.3, Willie Wood, 1964 (19 returns, 252 yards)

Highest Punt Return Average, Rookie (season - 14 returns)
12.79, Walter Stanley, 1985 (14 returns, 179 yards)
12.75, Veryl Switzer, 1954 (24 returns, 306 yards)
12.73, Steve Odom, 1974 (15 returns, 191 yards)
11.6, Fred Provo, 1948 (18 returns, 208 yards)
10.0, Terrell Buckley, 1992 (21 returns, 210 yards)

Longest Punt Returns (all TDs)
95 yards, Steve Odom, vs. Chicago, Nov. 10, 1974
94 yards, Mark Lee, vs. New York Giants, Nov. 8, 1981
93 yards, Veryl Switzer, at Chicago Bears, Nov. 7, 1954
92 yards, Desmond Howard, at Detroit, Dec. 15, 1996
90 yards, Andy Uram, vs. Brooklyn, Oct. 12, 1941
90 yards, Phillip Epps, vs. Tampa Bay, Oct. 2, 1983

Most Touchdowns (career)
3, Desmond Howard, 1996
2, Billy Grimes, 1950-52
2, Willie Wood, 1960-71
2, Jon Staggers, 1972-74

Most Touchdowns (season)
3, Desmond Howard, 1996
2, Billy Grimes, 1950
2, Willie Wood, 1961

COMBINED KICK RETURNS
Most Touchdowns (career)
6, Travis Williams, 1967-70 (5 kickoffs, 1 punt)

MISCELLANEOUS
Most Unassisted Tackles (season)
151, Rich Wingo, 1979
146, Mike Douglass, 1981

Most Kicks Blocked (season)
*7, Ted Hendricks, 1974 (3 FGs, 3 punts, 1 PAT)

Most Consecutive Games, Kick Blocked
4, Gary Lewis, 1982

Most Opponent Fumbles Recovered (career)
21, Willie Davis (1960-69)
20, Ray Nitschke (1958-72)
20, Johnnie Gray (1975-83)

Longest Fumble Runs
76 yards, Scott Stephen, at Chicago, Dec. 17, 1989
70 yards, Mike Butler, vs. Minnesota, Nov. 11, 1979 (TD)
68 yards, George Cumby, vs. Tampa Bay, Oct. 11, 1981
60 yards, Henry Jordan, at Dallas, Nov. 29, 1964 (TD)

Most Opponent Fumbles Recovered For Touchdown (season)
*2, Mike Douglass, 1983

SERVICE
Most Years Head Coach
31, Earl L. "Curly" Lambeau, 1919-49
9, Vince Lombardi, 1959-67
9, Bart Starr, 1975-83

Most Years Active Player
16, Bart Starr, 1956-71
15, Ray Nitschke, 1958-72
14, Forrest Gregg, 1956, 1958-70

Most Consecutive Games Played
187, Forrest Gregg, 1956, 58-70
162, Willie Davis, 1960-69
162, Larry McCarren, 1973-84
150, Boyd Dowler, 1959-69

* – Shares or Holds NFL Record

WISCONSIN ATHLETIC HALL OF FAME

1951 — Don Hutson, E/DB
   Clarke Hinkle, B
1955 — Howard "Cub" Buck, T
1957 — Joseph "Red" Dunn, B
1960 — Johnny "Blood" McNally, B
1961 — Earl "Curly" Lambeau, Coach & B
1967 — Lavvie Dilweg, E
   Arnie Herber, B
   Verne Lewellen, B
1970 — Mike Michalske, G

1973 — Tony Canadeo, B
   Charles "Buckets" Goldenberg, G/B
1976 — Vince Lombardi, Coach-GM
1978 — Lisle Blackbourn, Coach
1981 — Ray Nitschke, LB
   Bart Starr, QB
1988 — Willie Davis, DE
1990 — Paul Hornung, B
1993 — Jerry Kramer, G

TEAM RECORDS

YARDS GAINED

Most Yards Gained (season)
6,172, 1983 (1,807 rushing, 4,365 passing)
5,780, 1989 (1,732 rushing, 4,048 passing)
5,750, 1995 (1,428 rushing, 4,322 passing)
5,614, 1997 (1,909 rushing, 3,705 passing)
5,535, 1996 (1,838 rushing, 3,697 passing)

Most Gross Yards Passing (season)
4,688, 1983   3,977, 1994
4,539, 1995   3,938, 1996
4,325, 1989

Most Net Yards Passing (season)
4,365, 1983   3,773, 1994
4,322, 1995   3,705, 1997
4,048, 1989

Most Net Yards Gained Passing (game)
423, vs. Chicago Cardinals, Nov. 1, 1942 (27 att., 13 comp., 6 TDs, 1 INT)
422, vs. St. Louis, Dec. 21, 1969 (34 att., 23 comp., 5 TDs, 1 INT)
415, vs. Tampa Bay, Oct. 12, 1980 (51 att., 35 comp., 1 TD, 2 INTs)
403, vs. Washington, Oct. 17, 1983 (32 att., 23 comp., 3 TDs, 1 INT)

Fewest Net Yards Gained Passing (game)
-35, vs. Cincinnati, Sept. 26, 1976
-12, vs. Chicago, Nov. 4, 1973
-10, vs. Dallas, Oct. 24, 1965
-2, vs. Detroit, Nov. 7, 1965

Most Yards Gained Rushing (season)
2,460, 1962   2,248, 1963
2,350, 1961   2,227, 1971
2,276, 1964

Most Yards Gained Rushing (game)
366, vs. Detroit, Oct. 26, 1947 (50 attempts)
312, vs. New York Yanks, Oct. 8, 1950 (40 attempts)
303, vs. Baltimore, Oct. 18, 1953 (56 attempts)
301, at Washington, Dec. 1, 1946 (64 attempts)
298, at Chicago, Dec. 16, 1973 (53 attempts)

Most Yards Gained (game)
628, at Philadelphia, Nov. 11, 1962 (294 rushing, 334 passing)

Most Rushing Attempts, Both Teams (game)
*108, GB (38) at Chicago Cardinals (70), Dec. 5, 1948
102, GB (51) vs. Pittsburgh (51), Nov. 20, 1949

Fewest Rushing Attempts (game)
7, vs. Miami, Sept. 11, 1994
10, vs. Seattle, Dec. 9, 1990
11, at Chicago, Nov. 27, 1988
12, vs. San Diego, Oct. 7, 1984
12, at Buffalo, Nov. 20, 1994
13, at Tampa Bay, Oct. 14, 1990
13, vs. Philadelphia, Sept. 1, 1991
13, at Minnesota, Dec. 27, 1992

Most Touchdowns Rushing (season)
*36, 1962 (14 games)
29, 1960 (12 games)

Most Seasons Leading League
4 (1946, 1961-62, 1964)

Fewest Yards Rushing (game)
13, vs. Seattle, Dec. 9, 1990 (10 attempts)
17, vs. Boston Redskins, Sept. 17, 1933 (37 attempts)
18, vs. Chicago Cardinals, Oct. 21, 1934 (29 attempts)
20, at Boston Redskins, Nov. 8, 1936 (30 attempts)
20, at Baltimore, Oct. 28, 1956 (18 attempts)
22, at Los Angeles Rams, Nov. 28, 1965 (16 attempts)
22, at Chicago, Nov. 27, 1988 (11 attempts)

FIRST DOWNS

Seasons Leading League
5 (1940, 1942, 1944, 1960, 1962)

Most First Downs (season)
342, 1989 (114 rushing, 207 passing, 21 penalty)
340, 1983 (99 rushing, 214 passing, 27 penalty)
339, 1995 (84 rushing, 235 passing, 20 penalty)
338, 1996 (118 rushing, 197 passing, 23 penalty)
325, 1997 (103 rushing, 191 passing, 31 penalty)

Most First Downs (game)
37, at Philadelphia, Nov. 11, 1962 (21 rushing, 15 passing, 1 penalty)
32, at Tampa Bay, Oct. 12, 1980 (11 rushing, 21 passing)
31, vs. Tampa Bay, Dec. 1, 1985 (12 rushing, 17 passing, 2 penalty)
31, at Detroit, Nov. 12, 1989 (10 rushing, 19 passing, 2 penalty)
30, vs. Detroit, Oct. 28, 1984 (10 rushing, 16 passing, 4 penalty)
30, vs. Detroit, Oct. 6, 1985 (16 rushing, 13 passing, 1 penalty)
29, at Minnesota, Oct. 14, 1962 (13 rushing, 15 passing, 3 penalty)
29, vs. San Francisco, Oct. 26, 1986 (17 rushing, 12 passing)
29, vs. New Orleans, Sept. 17, 1989 (10 rushing, 18 passing, 1 penalty)
29, at Los Angeles Rams, Sept. 24, 1989 (9 rushing, 16 passing, 4 penalty)
29, at Chicago, Dec. 5, 1993 (8 rushing, 20 passing, 1 penalty)
29, vs. Minnesota, Dec. 22, 1996 (18 rushing, 11 passing)
29, vs. Dallas, Nov. 23, 1997 (11 rushing, 12 passing, 6 penalty)

Fewest First Downs to Opponent (game)
*0, vs. New York Giants, Oct. 1, 1933

FORWARD PASSING

Most Passes Completed (season)
375, 1994 (609 attempts)   340, 1992 (527 attempts)
372, 1995 (593 attempts)   328, 1996 (548 attempts)
354, 1989 (600 attempts)

Most Passes Attempted (season)
609, 1994 (375 completed)   582, 1988 (319 completed)
600, 1989 (354 completed)   565, 1986 (305 completed)
593, 1995 (372 completed)

Most Passes Attempted (game)
61, vs. San Francisco, Oct. 14, 1996 (28 completed)
60, at Detroit, Nov. 12, 1989 (35 completed)
59, at New Orleans, Sept. 14, 1986 (28 completed)
57, vs. San Francisco, Oct. 26, 1986 (32 completed)
56, at Los Angeles Rams, Dec. 16, 1951 (27 completed)

Best Passing Efficiency (season - 250 minimum)
64.5%, 1992 (340 completions in 527 attempts)
62.7%, 1995 (372 completions in 593 attempts)
61.6%, 1994 (375 completions in 609 attempts)
61.0%, 1993 (322 completions in 528 attempts)
60.7%, 1966 (193 completions in 318 attempts)

Fewest Passes Attempted (game)
*0, vs. Portsmouth, Oct. 8, 1933

Most Passes Attempted, Both Teams (game)
100, GB (47) at New England (53), Oct. 2, 1994
100, GB (61) vs. San Francisco (39), Oct. 14, 1996

Most Seasons Leading League, Passing Yardage
5 (1934, 1935, 1936, 1937, 1942)

Fewest Yards Gained Passing, Both Teams (game)
*-11, GB (-10) vs. Dallas (-1), Oct. 24, 1965

Most Touchdown Passes (season)
39, 1995   33, 1994
39, 1996   30, 1984
35, 1997   28, 1942
33, 1983

Most Touchdown Passes (game)
6, vs. Chicago Cardinals, Nov. 1, 1942
6, vs. Detroit, Oct. 7, 1945

Most Passes Had Intercepted (game)
8, vs. New York Giants, Nov. 21, 1948
7, vs. Chicago Bears, Sept. 22, 1940
7, vs. Detroit, Oct. 20, 1940
7, vs. Detroit, Sept. 17, 1950

Most Times Sacked (game)
11, vs. Detroit, Nov. 7, 1965

Most Times Sacked, Both Teams (game)
*18, GB (10) at San Diego (8), Sept. 24, 1978

Fewest Quarterback Sacks Allowed (season)
17, 1972 (14 games)   17, 1974 (14 games)

Fewest Yards Allowed by Quarterback Sacks (season)
104, 1972   126, 1974

Seasons Leading League, Completion Percentage
7 (1936, 1941, 1961-62, 1964, 1966, 1968)

Fewest Passes Had Intercepted (season)
*5, 1966 (318 attempts)
6, 1964 (321 attempts)

Most Passes Had Intercepted, Both Teams (game)
11, GB (4) at Cleveland Rams (7), Oct. 30, 1938
11, GB (7) vs. Detroit (4), Oct. 20, 1940

Most Seasons Leading League, Net Yards Gained Rushing and Passing
3 (1937-38, 1940)

SCORING

Most Touchdowns (season)
56, 1996 (16 games)   51, 1984 (16 games)
53, 1962 (14 games)   50, 1997 (16 games)
52, 1983 (16 games)

Most Touchdowns Rushing (season)
*36, 1962 (14 games)   23, 1964 (14 games)
29, 1960 (12 games)   22, 1963 (14 games)
27, 1961 (14 games)

Most Points After Touchdown (season)
52, 1962 (53 attempts)   48, 1984 (50 attempts)
52, 1983 (52 attempts)   48, 1995 (48 attempts)
51, 1996 (53 attempts)   48, 1997 (48 attempts)
49, 1961 (49 attempts)   43, 1963 (46 attempts)

Seasons Leading League, Touchdowns
6 (1932, 1937-38, 1961-62, 1996)

Most Field Goals (season)
33, 1972 (48 attempts)   24, 1997 (30 attempts)
31, 1993 (37 attempts)   23, 1990 (30 attempts)
25, 1974 (39 attempts)

Most Points (season)
456, 1996 (16 games)   415, 1962 (14 games)
429, 1983 (16 games)   404, 1995 (16 games)
422, 1997 (16 games)

Fewest Points (season)
80, 1922 (11 games)   113, 1927 (10 games)
85, 1923 (10 games)   114, 1949 (12 games)
108, 1924 (11 games)

Most Points Scored (game)
57, vs. Detroit, Oct. 7, 1945 (57-21)
56, vs. Atlanta, Oct. 23, 1966 (56-3)
55, vs. Chicago Cardinals, Nov. 1, 1942 (55-24)
55, vs. Cleveland, Nov. 12, 1967 (55-7)
55, vs. Tampa Bay, Oct. 2, 1983 (55-14)

Most Points, Both Teams (game)
95, GB (48) vs. Washington (47), Oct. 17, 1983
88, GB (41) at Atlanta (47), Nov. 27, 1983 (ot)
87, GB (35) at Detroit (52), Nov. 22, 1951
84, GB (44) at Detroit (40), Nov. 27, 1986
83, GB (31) at Chicago Bears (52), Nov. 6, 1955

Most Points (one team, one quarter)
*41, GB vs. Detroit (second quarter), Oct. 7, 1945
35, GB vs. Cleveland (first quarter), Nov. 12, 1967
35, GB vs. Tampa Bay (second quarter), Oct. 2, 1983

Most Points (one team, one half)
*49, GB vs. Tampa Bay (first half), Oct. 2, 1983 (55-14)
45, GB vs. Cleveland (first half), Nov. 12, 1967 (55-7)

Most Touchdowns Rushing (game)
6, at Pittsburgh, Nov. 23, 1941
6, at Cleveland, Oct. 15, 1961
6, at Philadelphia, Nov. 11, 1962

Most Field Goals Attempted (season)
48, 1972 (made 33)   37, 1993 (made 31)
39, 1974 (made 25)   35, 1973 (made 21)

Most Field Goals Attempted, Both Teams (game)
11, GB (6) vs. Detroit (5), Sept. 29, 1974

Fewest Field Goals (season - since 1932)
0, 1932   0, 1944

Most Field Goals, Both Teams (game)
8, GB (4) vs. Detroit (4), Sept. 29, 1974

Most Points After Touchdown (game)
8, vs. Atlanta, Oct. 23, 1966
7, vs. Chicago Cardinals, Nov. 1, 1942
7, vs. Detroit, Oct. 7, 1945
7, at Cleveland, Oct. 15, 1961
7, vs. Chicago Bears, Sept. 30, 1962
7, at Philadelphia, Nov. 11, 1962
7, vs. Cleveland, Nov. 12, 1967
7, vs. Tampa Bay, Oct. 2, 1983

Most Touchdowns (game)
8, vs. Chicago Cardinals, Nov. 1, 1942
8, vs. Detroit, Oct. 7, 1945
8, vs. Atlanta, Oct. 23, 1966

Fewest Points, Shutout Victory (game)
2, at Chicago Bears, Oct. 16, 1932

PUNTING

Most Punts (season)
106, 1978 (16 games)   87, 1949 (12 games)
95, 1975 (14 games)   87, 1970 (14 games)
93, 1987 (16 games)   87, 1980 (16 games)

Fewest Punts (season)
42, 1982 (9 games)
48, 1944 (10 games)
48, 1960 (12 games)

Most Punts, Both Teams (game)
*31, at Chicago Bears (17) vs. GB (14), Oct. 22, 1933

PUNT RETURNS

Seasons Leading League, Punt Returns
6 (1950, 1953-54, 1961, 1972, 1996)

Most Yards, Punt Returns (season)
*875, 1996 (16 games)
729, 1950 (12 games)

Most Fair Catches (game)
6, at Chicago, Dec. 16, 1973

Most Touchdowns, Punt Returns (season)
3, 1996 (16 games)

KICKOFF RETURNS

Most Yards, Kickoff Returns (season)
1,546, 1971 (58 returns, 26.7 avg.)

Fewest Yards, Kickoff Returns (season)
381, 1940 (11 games)

Most Touchdowns, Kickoff Returns (season)
*4, 1967 (14 games)

Most Touchdowns, Kickoff Returns (game)
*2, vs. Cleveland, Nov. 12, 1967

Most Yards Allowed, Kickoff Returns (game)
304, at Chicago Bears, Nov. 9, 1952 (7 returns)

FUMBLES

Fewest Fumbles (season)
11, 1944 (10 games)
13, 1942 (11 games)

Most Fumbles (season)
44, 1988 (16 games)
42, 1992 (16 games)
41, 1991 (16 games)
40, 1952 (12 games)

Most Fumbles Lost (season)
31, 1952 (12 games)

Most Opponents' Fumbles Recovered (season)
28, 1946 (11 games)
27, 1975 (14 games)

Most Opponents' Fumbles (game)
9, at San Diego, Sept. 24, 1978

Most Touchdowns, Opponents' Fumbles Recovered (game)
*2, at Dallas, Nov. 29, 1964

Most Fumbles, Both Teams (game)
13, GB (7) vs. Detroit (6), Oct. 6, 1985

PENALTIES
Most Seasons Leading League, Fewest Penalties
5 (1955-56, 1966-67, 1974)

Most Penalties, Both Teams (game)
33, GB (11) vs. Brooklyn (22), Sept. 17, 1944

Most Yards Penalized, Both Teams (game)
309, GB (184) vs. Boston Yanks (125), Oct. 21, 1945

DEFENSIVE RECORDS
SCORING
Seasons Leading League, Fewest Points Allowed
6 (1935, 1947, 1962, 1965-66, 1996)

Fewest Touchdowns Allowed (season - since 1932)
8, 1932 (14 games)

Fewest Touchdowns Allowed (16-game season)
*19, 1996

Fewest Points Allowed (season)
24, 1929 (13 games)
34, 1923 (10 games)
38, 1924 (11 games)

Most Points Allowed (season)
439, 1983 (16 games)
418, 1986 (16 games)
406, 1950 (12 games)

YARDS GAINED
Most Yards Allowed (season)
6,403, 1983 (16 games)

Fewest Yards Allowed (season)
2,161, 1935 (12 games)

FIRST DOWNS
Most First Downs Allowed (season)
366, 1983 (16 games)

Fewest First Downs Allowed, Rushing (season)
40, 1939 (12 games)

Fewest First Downs Allowed, Penalty (season)
4, 1943 (10 games)

RUSHING
Fewest Yards Allowed, Rushing (season)
932, 1982 (9 games)
1,112, 1943 (10 games)
1,130, 1944 (10 games)

Most Yards Allowed, Rushing (season)
2,882, 1979 (16 games)
2,641, 1983 (16 games)
2,619, 1956 (12 games)

PASSING
Fewest Touchdowns Allowed, Passing (season)
3, 1932 (14 games)
3, 1934 (13 games)

Seasons Leading League, Fewest Yards Allowed
9 (1947-48, 1962, 1964-68, 1996)

Fewest Yards Allowed, Passing (season)
1,229, 1944 (10 games)
1,288, 1946 (11 games)

Most Yards Allowed, Passing (season)
3,762, 1983 (16 games)   3,383, 1980 (16 games)
3,640, 1995 (16 games)   3,383, 1990 (16 games)
3,401, 1994 (16 games)   3,339, 1989 (16 games)

Most Total Net Yards Allowed (season)
6,403, 1983 (16 games)
5,782, 1980 (16 games)

Most Opponent Passes (season)
616, 1995 (16 games)   551, 1984 (16 games)
605, 1994 (16 games)   544, 1996 (16 games)
563, 1997 (16 games)

Most Opponent Passes Completed (season)
351, 1995 (16 games)   305, 1991 (16 games)
337, 1994 (16 games)   302, 1989 (16 games)
315, 1984 (16 games)

Highest Opponent Passing Percentage (season)
63.6, 1989 (16 games)
59.6, 1986 (16 games)
59.5, 1987 (16 games)

INTERCEPTIONS BY
Seasons Leading League
8 (1940, 1942-43, 1947, 1955, 1957, 1962, 1965)

Most Passes Intercepted By (season)
42, 1943 (10 games)
40, 1940 (11 games)

Most Passes Intercepted By (game)
9, at Detroit, Oct. 24, 1943

Most Touchdowns, Returning Interceptions (season)
6, 1966

PUNT RETURNS
Fewest Opponents' Punt Returns (season)
13, 1967 (14 games)

Fewest Yards Allowed, Punt Returns (season)
*22, 1967 (14 games)

Most Yards Allowed, Punt Returns (season)
*932, 1949 (12 games)

Highest Average Allowed, Punt Returns (season)
*18.6, 1949 (50-932)

Most Touchdowns Allowed, Punt Returns (season)
3, 1949 (12 games)

MISCELLANEOUS
Most Kicks Blocked (season)
12, 1974 (4 FGs, 4 punts, 4 PATs)

Most Safeties (season)
3, 1932   3, 1975

Most League Championships
*12 (1929-30-31, 1936, 1939, 1944, 1961-62, 1965-66-67, 1996)

Most Consecutive League Championships
*3 (1929-30-31 and 1965-66-67)

Most First Place Finishes, Regular Season (since 1933)
15 (1936, 1938-39, 1944, 1960-62, 1965-67, 1972, 1982, 1995-97)

Most Games Won (season)
13, 1962   12, 1929
13, 1996   12, 1931
13, 1997

Most Consecutive Games Without Defeat
23, 1928-30 (won 21, tied 2)

Most Consecutive Games Won
11, 1928-29
11, 1961-62

Most Consecutive Games Won (season)
10, 1929
10, 1962

Most Consecutive Games Without Defeat (season)
13, 1929

Most Consecutive Games Without Defeat, Start of Season
13, 1929 (entire season)

Most Consecutive Home Games Won
23, 1995-97   20, 1929-32

Most Consecutive Home Games Without Defeat
*30, 1928-33 (won 27, tied 3)

Most Consecutive Road Games Without Defeat
12, 1928-30 (won 10, tied 2)

Most Consecutive Shutout Games Won or Tied (since 1932)
3, 1932 (won 3)

Most Shutout Games Won or Tied (season - since 1932)
7, 1932 (won 6, tied 1)

Most Games Lost (season)
12, 1986
12, 1988
12, 1991

Most Consecutive Games Lost
9, 1948-49
8, 1951-52
8, 1953-54

Most Consecutive Games Lost (season)
7, 1948   7, 1984
7, 1951   7, 1988
7, 1958

Most Penalties (game)
17, vs. Boston Yanks, Oct. 21, 1945 (184 yards)

Most Yards Penalized (game)
184, vs. Boston Yanks, Oct. 21, 1945 (17 penalties)

'Most' Happy Returns: Phillip Epps, shown in the midst of a runback, holds the Packers' record for most punt returns in a game. The former Texas Christian speedster registered 8 runbacks against the Vikings at the Minneapolis Metrodome November 21, 1982, breaking the previous record of 7, set by Johnnie Gray — also against Minnesota — November 21, 1976, and subsequently equaled by Robert Brooks (vs. New England Oct. 2, 1994) and by Desmond Howard (vs. San Diego Sept. 15, 1996). Epps had the longest punt return of his career — a 90-yarder — against Tampa Bay October 2, 1983. It remains the sixth-longest in Packers annals.

LEADERS BY SEASON

RUSHING
based on net yards gained

Year	Player	Att.	Yds.	Avg.	TD	NFC Rank	NFL Rank
1923	Curly Lambeau	133	416	3.1	1	—	NA
1924	Curly Lambeau	132	457	3.5	0	—	NA
1925	Myrt Basing	149	430	2.9	4	—	NA
1926	Verne Lewellen	83	275	3.3	3	—	NA
1927	*Verne Lewellen	91	305	3.4	5	—	NA
1928	Verne Lewellen	106	349	3.3	6	—	NA
1929	Johnny (Blood) McNally	104	406	3.9	2	—	NA
1930	*Bo Molenda	146	458	3.1	2	—	NA
1931	Bo Molenda	100	425	4.3	3	—	NA
1932	Clarke Hinkle	113	451	4.0	3	—	NA
1933	Clarke Hinkle	145	419	2.9	3	—	7
1934	Clarke Hinkle	142	384	2.7	1	—	13
1935	Bob Monnett	68	336	4.9	1	—	7
1936	Clarke Hinkle	100	476	4.8	5	—	9
1937	Clarke Hinkle	129	552	4.3	5	—	2
1938	Cecil Isbell	85	445	5.2	2	—	4
1939	Cecil Isbell	132	407	3.1	2	—	10
1940	Clarke Hinkle	109	383	3.5	2	—	6
1941	Clarke Hinkle	129	393	3.0	5	—	5
1942	Ted Fritsch	74	323	4.4	0	—	11
1943	Tony Canadeo	94	489	5.2	3	—	5
1944	Ted Fritsch	94	322	3.4	4	—	t11
1945	Ted Fritsch	88	282	3.2	7	—	10
1946	Tony Canadeo	122	476	3.9	0	—	t4
1947	Tony Canadeo	103	464	4.5	2	—	3
1948	Tony Canadeo	123	589	4.8	4	—	5
1949	Tony Canadeo	208	1,052	5.1	4	—	2
1950	Billy Grimes	84	480	5.7	5	—	12
1951	Tobin Rote	76	523	6.9	3	—	8
1952	Tobin Rote	58	313	5.4	2	—	23
1953	Floyd Reid	95	492	5.2	3	—	8
1954	Floyd Reid	99	507	5.1	5	—	9
1955	Howie Ferguson	192	859	4.5	4	—	2
1956	Tobin Rote	84	398	4.7	11	—	21
1957	Don McIlhenny	100	384	3.8	1	—	21
1958	Paul Hornung	69	310	4.5	2	—	26
1959	Paul Hornung	152	681	4.5	7	—	8
1960	Jim Taylor	230	1,101	4.8	11	—	2
1961	Jim Taylor	243	1,307	5.4	15	—	2
1962	Jim Taylor	272	1,474	5.4	19	—	1
1963	Jim Taylor	248	1,018	4.1	9	—	2
1964	Jim Taylor	235	1,169	5.0	12	—	2
1965	Jim Taylor	207	734	3.5	4	—	5
1966	Jim Taylor	204	705	3.5	4	—	10
1967	Jim Grabowski	120	466	3.9	2	—	19
1968	Donny Anderson	170	761	4.5	5	—	9
1969	Travis Williams	129	536	4.2	4	—	14
1970	Donny Anderson	222	853	3.8	5	4	7
1971	John Brockington	216	1,105	5.1	4	1	2
1972	John Brockington	274	1,027	3.7	8	4	9
1973	John Brockington	265	1,144	4.3	3	1	2
1974	John Brockington	266	883	3.3	5	2	6
1975	John Brockington	144	434	3.0	7	20	42
1976	Willard Harrell	130	435	3.3	3	23	48
1977	Barty Smith	166	554	3.3	2	16	31
1978	Terdell Middleton	284	1,116	3.9	11	4	6
1979	Terdell Middleton	131	495	3.8	2	20	39
1980	Eddie Lee Ivery	202	831	4.1	3	8	12
1981	Gerry Ellis	196	860	4.4	4	11	19
1982	Eddie Lee Ivery	127	453	3.6	9	11	21
1983	Gerry Ellis	141	696	4.9	4	14	27
1984	Gerry Ellis	123	581	4.7	4	16	30
1985	Eddie Lee Ivery	132	636	4.8	2	17	33
1986	Kenneth Davis	114	519	4.6	0	19	t35
1987	Kenneth Davis	109	413	3.8	3	19	40
1988	Brent Fullwood	101	483	4.8	7	17	37
1989	Brent Fullwood	204	821	4.0	5	9	16
1990	Michael Haddix	98	311	3.2	0	30	58

LEADERS BY SEASON

Year	Player	Att.	Yds.	Avg.	TD	NFC Rank	NFL Rank
1991	Darrell Thompson	141	471	3.3	1	15	36
1992	Vince Workman	159	631	4.0	2	11	21
1993	Darrell Thompson	169	654	3.9	3	12	24
1994	Edgar Bennett	178	623	3.5	5	12	26
1995	Edgar Bennett	316	1,067	3.4	3	10	15
1996	Edgar Bennett	222	899	4.0	2	7	14
1997	Dorsey Levens	329	1,435	4.4	7	2	4

*stats do not include one game where only incomplete statistics are available

PASSING

Year	Player	Att.	Comp.	Pct.	Yds.	LG	TD	Int.	NFC/NFL Rank
1932	Arnie Herber	101	37	45.5	637	—	9	9	—
1933	Arnie Herber	124	50	40.3	656	—	4	12	—
1934	Arnie Herber	115	42	36.5	799	—	8	12	—
1935	Arnie Herber	106	40	37.7	729	—	8	14	—
1936	Arnie Herber	173	77	44.5	1,239	—	11	13	—
1937	Arnie Herber	104	47	45.2	684	—	7	10	—
1938	Cecil Isbell	91	37	40.7	659	—	7	10	—
1939	Arnie Herber	139	57	41.0	1,107	—	8	9	—
1940	Cecil Isbell	150	68	45.3	1,037	—	9	12	3
1941	Cecil Isbell	206	117	56.8	1,479	—	15	11	—
1942	Cecil Isbell	268	146	54.5	2,021	73t	24	14	—
1943	Irv Comp	92	46	50.0	662	79t	7	4	3
1944	Irv Comp	177	80	45.2	1,159	55t	12	21	4
1945	Irv Comp	106	44	41.5	865	75t	7	11	8
1946	Irv Comp	94	27	28.7	333	35	1	8	16
1947	Jack Jacobs	242	108	44.6	1,615	69t	16	17	4
1948	Jack Jacobs	184	82	44.6	848	64t	5	21	15
1949	Jug Girard	175	62	35.4	881	50	4	12	12
1950	Tobin Rote	224	83	37.1	1,231	96t	7	24	17
1951	Tobin Rote	256	106	41.4	1,540	85	15	20	15
	Bob Thomason	221	125	56.6	1,306	75t	11	9	16
1952	Tobin Rote	157	82	52.2	1,268	81t	13	8	2
	Babe Parilli	177	77	43.5	1,416	90t	13	17	3
1953	Tobin Rote	185	72	38.9	1,005	80t	5	15	13
	Babe Parilli	166	74	44.6	830	45	4	19	16
1954	Tobin Rote	382	180	47.1	2,311	82t	14	18	16
1955	Tobin Rote	342	157	45.9	1,977	60t	17	19	12
1956	Tobin Rote	308	146	47.4	2,203	66t	18	15	8
1957	Bart Starr	215	117	54.4	1,489	77t	8	10	4
1958	Babe Parilli	157	68	43.3	1,068	80t	10	13	9
1959	Bart Starr	134	70	52.2	972	44	6	7	9
1960	Bart Starr	172	98	57.0	1,358	91t	4	8	6
1961	Bart Starr	295	172	58.3	2,418	78t	16	16	3
1962	Bart Starr	285	178	62.5	2,438	83t	12	9	1
1963	Bart Starr	244	132	54.1	1,855	53t	15	10	7
1964	Bart Starr	272	163	59.9	2,144	55	15	4	1
1965	Bart Starr	251	140	55.8	2,055	77t	16	9	4
1966	Bart Starr	251	156	62.2	2,257	83t	14	3	1
1967	Bart Starr	210	115	54.8	1,823	84	9	17	6
1968	Bart Starr	171	109	63.7	1,617	63t	15	8	4
1969	Bart Starr	148	92	62.2	1,161	51	9	6	2
1970	Bart Starr	255	140	54.9	1,645	65t	8	13	13/21
1971	Scott Hunter	163	75	46.0	1,210	77t	7	17	12/22
1972	Scott Hunter	199	86	43.2	1,252	49	6	9	11/24
1973	Jerry Tagge	106	56	52.8	720	50	2	7	18/38
1974	John Hadl	184	89	48.4	1,072	68t	3	8	—
1975	John Hadl	353	191	54.1	2,095	54	6	21	13/25
1976	Lynn Dickey	243	115	47.3	1,465	69t	7	14	13/26
1977	Lynn Dickey	220	113	51.4	1,346	95t	5	14	12/26
1978	David Whitehurst	328	168	51.2	2,093	58	10	17	10/21
1979	David Whitehurst	322	179	55.6	2,247	78t	10	18	11/23
1980	Lynn Dickey	478	278	58.2	3,529	69t	15	25	10/20
1981	Lynn Dickey	354	204	57.6	2,593	75t	17	15	4/10
1982	Lynn Dickey	218	124	56.9	1,790	80t	12	14	9/16
1983	Lynn Dickey	484	289	59.7	4,458	75t	32	29	5/8
1984	Lynn Dickey	401	237	59.1	3,195	79t	25	19	5/7
1985	Lynn Dickey	314	172	54.8	2,206	63	15	17	9/15

LEADERS BY SEASON

Year	Player	Att.	Comp.	Pct.	Yds.	LG	TD	Int.	NFC/NFL Rank
1986	Randy Wright	492	263	53.5	3,247	62	17	23	10/22
1987	Randy Wright	247	132	53.4	1,507	66	6	11	14/27
1988	Don Majkowski	336	178	53.0	2,119	56	9	11	10/19
1989	Don Majkowski	599	353	58.9	4,318	79t	27	20	5/8
1990	Don Majkowski	264	150	56.8	1,925	76t	10	12	10/21
1991	Mike Tomczak	238	128	53.8	1,490	75t	11	9	12/22
1992	Brett Favre	471	302	64.1	3,227	76t	18	13	5/6
1993	Brett Favre	522	318	60.9	3,303	66t	19	24	8/20
1994	Brett Favre	582	363	62.4	3,882	49	33	14	2/2
1995	Brett Favre	570	359	63.0	4,413	99t	38	13	1/2
1996	Brett Favre	543	325	59.9	3,899	80t	39	13	2/2
1997	Brett Favre	513	304	59.3	3,867	74	35	16	3/3

RECEIVING
based on number of receptions

Year	Player	Rec.	Yds.	Avg.	LG	TD	NFC/NFL Rank
1932	Johnny (Blood) McNally	14	168	12.0	—	3	—
1933	Roger Grove	18	215	11.9	—	0	—
1934	Clarke Hinkle	12	113	9.4	69t	1	—
1935	Johnny (Blood) McNally	25	404	16.2	70t	3	—
1936	Don Hutson	34	526	15.5	58t	8	1
1937	Don Hutson	41	552	13.5	78t	7	1
1938	Don Hutson	32	548	17.1	54	9	—
1939	Don Hutson	34	846	24.9	92t	6	1
1940	Don Hutson	45	664	14.8	36t	7	2
1941	Don Hutson	58	738	12.7	45t	10	1
1942	Don Hutson	74	1,211	16.4	73t	17	1
1943	Don Hutson	47	776	16.5	79t	11	1
1944	Don Hutson	58	866	14.9	55t	9	1
1945	Don Hutson	47	834	17.7	75t	9	1
1946	Clyde Goodnight	16	308	19.3	51t	1	t17
	Nolan Luhn	16	224	14.0	36	2	t17
1947	Nolan Luhn	42	696	16.5	44	7	t4
1948	Clyde Goodnight	28	448	16.0	57	3	t14
1949	Ted Cook	25	442	17.7	50	1	t20
1950	Al Baldwin	28	555	19.8	85t	3	23
1951	Bob Mann	50	696	13.9	52	8	4
1952	Billy Howton	53	1,231	23.2	90t	13	6
1953	Billy Howton	25	463	18.5	80t	4	t25
1954	Billy Howton	52	768	14.8	59	2	4
1955	Billy Howton	44	697	15.8	60	5	t3
1956	Billy Howton	55	1,188	21.6	66t	12	2
1957	Billy Howton	38	727	19.1	77t	5	6
1958	Max McGee	37	655	17.7	80t	7	9
1959	Boyd Dowler	32	549	17.2	35	4	t19
1960	Max McGee	38	787	20.7	57t	4	t13
1961	Max McGee	51	883	17.3	53	7	11
1962	Max McGee	49	820	16.7	64	3	t15
	Boyd Dowler	49	724	14.8	41	2	t15
1963	Boyd Dowler	53	901	17.0	53t	6	9
1964	Boyd Dowler	45	623	13.8	50t	5	t15
1965	Boyd Dowler	44	610	13.9	47t	4	t15
1966	Jim Taylor	41	331	8.1	21	2	t24
1967	Boyd Dowler	54	836	15.5	57t	4	9
1968	Boyd Dowler	45	668	14.8	72t	6	10
1969	Carroll Dale	45	879	19.5	48	6	t17
1970	Carroll Dale	49	814	16.6	89t	2	7/8
1971	Carroll Dale	31	598	19.3	77t	4	t25/t46
1972	MacArthur Lane	26	285	11.0	49	2	t38/t74
1973	MacArthur Lane	27	255	9.4	30	1	t33/t61
1974	John Brockington	43	314	7.3	29	0	t10/t12
1975	Ken Payne	58	766	13.2	54	0	2/4
1976	Ken Payne	33	467	14.2	57t	4	t24/t46
1977	Barty Smith	37	340	9.2	42	1	t14/t31
1978	James Lofton	46	818	17.8	58t	6	t16/t28
1979	Paul Coffman	56	711	12.7	78t	4	11/22
1980	James Lofton	71	1,226	17.3	47	4	3/5
1981	James Lofton	71	1,294	18.2	75t	8	5/t7
1982	James Lofton	35	696	19.9	80t	4	t8/t21

246

Year	Player	Rec.	Yds.	Avg.	LG	TD	NFC/NFL Rank
1983	James Lofton	58	1,300	22.4	74t	8	9/t20
1984	James Lofton	62	1,361	22.0	79t	7	10/t24
1985	James Lofton	69	1,153	16.7	56t	4	6/14
1986	James Lofton	64	840	13.1	36	4	8/19
1987	Walter Stanley	38	672	17.7	70t	3	t19/t49
1988	Sterling Sharpe	55	791	14.4	51	1	20/33
1989	Sterling Sharpe	90	1,423	15.8	79t	12	1/1
1990	Sterling Sharpe	67	1,105	16.5	76t	6	8/14
1991	Sterling Sharpe	69	961	13.9	58t	4	7/18
1992	Sterling Sharpe	108	1,461	13.5	76t	13	1/1
1993	Sterling Sharpe	112	1,274	11.4	54	11	1/1
1994	Sterling Sharpe	94	1,119	11.9	49	18	4/5
1995	Robert Brooks	102	1,497	14.7	99t	13	8/8
1996	Antonio Freeman	56	933	16.7	51t	9	20/t41
1997	Antonio Freeman	81	1,243	15.3	58t	12	5/8

INTERCEPTIONS
based on number made

Year	Player	Int.	Yards	TD	NFC Rank	NFL Rank
1923	Charlie Mathys	4	58	0	—	NA
	Curly Lambeau	4	10	0	—	NA
1924	Walter Voss	8	NA	NA	—	NA
1925	Fred Larson	7	NA	NA	—	NA
1926	Verne Lewellen	9	NA	NA	—	NA
1927	Red Dunn	4	NA	NA	—	NA
	Curly Lambeau	4	NA	NA	—	NA
1928	Eddie Kotal	10	NA	NA	—	NA
1929	Lavvie Dilweg	7	NA	NA	—	NA
1930	Lavvie Dilweg	6	NA	NA	—	NA
1931	Johnny (Blood) McNally	6	NA	NA	—	NA
1932	Arnie Herber	6	NA	NA	—	NA
	Johnny (Blood) McNally	6	NA	NA	—	NA
1933	Roger Grove	5	NA	NA	—	t3
1934	Hank Bruder	4	108	1	—	t2
	Joe Laws	4	35	0	—	t2
1935	Chester Johnston	4	17	0	—	NA
1936	George Svendsen	5	122	0	—	NA
1937	Clarke Hinkle	5	77	0	—	NA
1938	Clarke Hinkle	6	15	0	—	NA
1939	Charley Brock	8	133	1	—	NA
1940	Don Hutson	6	24	0	—	t1
1941	Hal Van Every	3	104	1	—	t11
1942	Don Hutson	7	71	0	—	2
1943	Irv Comp	10	149	1	—	2
1944	Ted Fritsch	6	115	1	—	t3
	Irv Comp	6	54	0	—	t3
1945	Charley Brock	4	122	2	—	t6
	Don Hutson	4	15	0	—	t6
1946	Herm Rohrig	5	134	0	—	t4
1947	Bob Forte	8	140	1	—	t3
1948	Ted Cook	6	81	0	—	t8
1949	Ted Cook	5	52	0	—	t13
1950	Rebel Steiner	7	190	1	—	t10
1951	Jug Girard	5	25	0	—	t9
1952	Ace Loomis	4	115	1	—	t21
	Bob Forte	4	50	0	—	t21
	Bobby Dillon	4	35	0	—	t21
1953	Bobby Dillon	9	112	1	—	t5
1954	Bobby Dillon	7	111	1	—	t7
1955	Bobby Dillon	9	153	0	—	t2
1956	Bobby Dillon	7	244	1	—	t5
1957	John Symank	9	198	0	—	t4
	Bobby Dillon	9	180	1	—	t4
1958	Bobby Dillon	6	134	1	—	t7
1959	Bill Forester	2	48	0	—	t34
	John Symank	2	46	0	—	t34
	Bob Freeman	2	22	0	—	t34

Year	Player	Int.	Yards	TD	NFC Rank	NFL Rank
	Emlen Tunnell	2	20	0	—	t34
1960	Jesse Whittenton	6	101	0	—	t7
1961	John Symank	5	99	0	—	t16
	Jesse Whittenton	5	98	1	—	t16
	Hank Gremminger	5	54	0	—	t16
	Willie Wood	5	52	0	—	t16
1962	Willie Wood	9	132	0	—	1
1963	Herb Adderley	5	86	0	—	t14
	Willie Wood	5	67	0	—	t14
1964	Herb Adderley	4	56	0	—	t12
1965	Herb Adderley	6	175	3	—	t3
	Willie Wood	6	65	0	—	t3
1966	Bob Jeter	5	142	2	—	t9
	Dave Robinson	5	60	0	—	t9
1967	Bob Jeter	8	78	0	—	t3
1968	Tom Brown	4	66	0	—	t19
1969	Herb Adderley	5	169	1	—	t7
1970	Willie Wood	7	110	0	t2	t5
1971	Ken Ellis	6	10	0	t4	t9
1972	Ken Ellis	4	106	1	t7	t20
	Willie Buchanon	4	62	0	t7	t20
	Jim Hill	4	37	0	t7	t20
1973	Ken Ellis	3	53	1	t24	t41
	Jim Hill	3	53	0	t24	t41
	Jim Carter	3	44	1	t24	t41
1974	Ted Hendricks	5	74	0	t6	t13
1975	Perry Smith	6	97	0	t4	t7
1976	Johnnie Gray	4	101	1	t11	t24
1977	Steve Luke	4	9	0	t15	t29
	Mike C. McCoy	4	2	0	t15	t29
1978	Willie Buchanon	9	93	1	t1	t2
1979	Johnnie Gray	5	66	0	t8	t17
1980	Johnnie Gray	5	54	0	t10	t24
1981	Maurice Harvey	6	217	0	t11	t14
	Mark Lee	6	50	0	t11	t14
1982	John Anderson	3	22	0	t8	t21
1983	Tim Lewis	5	111	0	t12	t23
	John Anderson	5	54	1	t12	t23
1984	Tom Flynn	9	106	0	1	2
1985	Tim Lewis	4	4	0	t22	t39
1986	Mark Lee	9	33	0	t2	t2
1987	Jim Bob Morris	3	135	0	t17	t31
	Dave Brown	3	16	0	t17	t31
1988	Mark Murphy	5	19	0	t7	t13
1989	Dave Brown	6	12	0	t3	t7
1990	LeRoy Butler	3	42	0	t17	t33
	Jerry Holmes	3	39	0	t17	t33
	Mark Murphy	3	6	0	t17	t33
1991	Chuck Cecil	3	76	0	t22	t42
	Mark Murphy	3	27	0	t22	t42
	LeRoy Butler	3	6	0	t22	t42
1992	Chuck Cecil	4	52	0	t9	t22
1993	LeRoy Butler	6	131	0	t2	t7
1994	Terrell Buckley	5	38	0	t5	t10
1995	LeRoy Butler	5	105	0	t10	t15
1996	Eugene Robinson	6	107	0	t2	t4
1997	LeRoy Butler	5	4	0	t6	t10

SCORING
based on total points

Year	Player	TD	FG	PAT	Pts.	NFC Rank	NFL Rank
1921	Curly Lambeau	2	3	7	28	—	t11
1922	Curly Lambeau	3	1	3	24	—	t14
1923	Cub Buck	0	6	5	23	—	18
1924	Walter Voss	5	0	0	30	—	t12
1925	Myrt Basing	6	0	0	36	—	t9
	Marty Norton	6	0	0	36	—	t9
1926	Verne Lewellen	7	0	0	42	—	9
1927	Verne Lewellen	5	0	0	30	—	t10

Year	Player	TD	FG	PAT	Pts.	NFC Rank	NFL Rank
1928	Verne Lewellen	9	0	0	54	—	2
1929	Verne Lewellen	8	0	0	48	—	6
1930	Verne Lewellen	9	0	0	54	—	2
1931	Johnny (Blood) McNally	14	0	0	84	—	1
1932	Johnny (Blood) McNally	4	0	0	24	—	t6
	Hank Bruder	4	0	0	24	—	t6
1933	Charles Goldenberg	6	0	0	42	—	6
1934	Bob Monnett	2	4	6	30	—	t12
1935	Don Hutson	7	0	1	43	—	2
1936	Don Hutson	9	0	0	54	—	3
1937	Clarke Hinkle	7	2	8	56	—	2
1938	Clarke Hinkle	7	3	7	58	—	1
1939	Don Hutson	6	0	2	38	—	t7
1940	Don Hutson	7	0	15	57	—	1
1941	Don Hutson	12	1	20	95	—	1
1942	Don Hutson	17	1	33	138	—	1
1943	Don Hutson	12	3	36	117	—	1
1944	Don Hutson	9	0	31	85	—	1
1945	Don Hutson	10	2	31	97	—	2
1946	Ted Fritsch	10	9	13	100	—	1
1947	Ted Fritsch	6	6	2	56	—	8
1948	Ted Fritsch	1	6	5	29	—	38
1949	Ted Fritsch	1	5	11	32	—	t27
1950	Billy Grimes	8	0	0	48	—	t16
1951	Fred Cone	1	5	29	50	—	t15
1952	Billy Howton	13	0	0	78	—	7
1953	Fred Cone	6	5	23	74	—	6
1954	Fred Cone	0	9	27	54	—	t11
	Max McGee	9	0	0	54	—	t11
1955	Fred Cone	0	16	30	78	—	4
1956	Fred Cone	4	5	33	72	—	t4
	Bill Howton	12	0	0	72	—	t4
1957	Fred Cone	2	12	26	74	—	3
1958	Paul Hornung	2	11	22	67	—	t7
1959	Paul Hornung	7	7	31	94	—	1
1960	Paul Hornung	15	15	41	176	—	1
1961	Paul Hornung	10	15	41	146	—	1
1962	Jim Taylor	19	0	0	114	—	1
1963	Jerry Kramer	0	16	43	91	—	4
1964	Paul Hornung	5	12	41	107	—	4
1965	Don Chandler	0	17	37	88	—	8
1966	Don Chandler	0	12	41	77	—	t16
1967	Don Chandler	0	19	39	96	—	4
1968	Carroll Dale	8	0	0	48	—	t22
1969	Travis Williams	9	0	0	54	—	t22
1970	Dale Livingston	0	15	19	64	18	31
1971	Lou Michaels	0	8	19	43	18	41
1972	Chester Marcol	0	33	29	128	1	1
1973	Chester Marcol	0	21	19	82	10	18
1974	Chester Marcol	0	25	19	94	1	1
1975	Joe Danelo	0	11	20	53	14	40
1976	Chester Marcol	0	10	24	54	t13	t32
1977	Chester Marcol	0	13	11	50	16	32
1978	Terdell Middleton	12	0	0	72	t7	t19
1979	Tom Birney	0	7	7	28	t48	t104
	Chester Marcol	0	4	16	28	t48	t104
1980	Gerry Ellis	8	0	0	48	t26	t47
1981	Jan Stenerud	0	22	35	101	t6	t12
1982	Jan Stenerud	0	13	25	64	4	9
1983	Jan Stenerud	0	21	52	115	7	9
1984	Al Del Greco	0	9	34	61	22	39
1985	Al Del Greco	0	19	38	95	11	20
1986	Al Del Greco	0	17	29	80	14	28
1987	Max Zendejas	0	16	13	61	15	t27
1988	Brent Fullwood	8	0	0	48	t23	t48
1989	Chris Jacke	0	22	42	108	t5	t8
1990	Chris Jacke	0	23	28	97	6	12
1991	Chris Jacke	0	18	31	85	t11	t21
1992	Chris Jacke	0	22	30	96	7	13
1993	Chris Jacke	0	31	35	128	2	3

Year	Player	TD	FG	PAT	Pts.	NFC Rank	NFL Rank
1994	Sterling Sharpe	18	0	0	108	5	t10
1995	Chris Jacke	0	17	43	94	13	26
1996	Chris Jacke	0	21	51	114	7	12
1997	Ryan Longwell	0	24	48	120	3	t5

FIELD GOALS MADE
based on number made

Year	Player	Att.	Made	Pct.	LG	NFC Rank	NFL Rank
1921	Curly Lambeau	12	3	25.0	NA	—	4
1922	Charlie Mathys	2	1	50.0	NA	—	t11
	Curly Lambeau	6	1	16.7	NA	—	t11
	Cub Buck	10	1	10.0	NA	—	t11
1923	Cub Buck	16	6	37.5	NA	—	t5
1924	Cub Buck	11	3	27.3	NA	—	t7
1925	George Abramson	6	2	33.3	NA	—	t13
1926	Pid Purdy	7	2	28.6	NA	—	t8
1927	Pid Purdy	3	1	33.3	NA	—	t7
1928	Harry O'Boyle	6	3	50.0	NA	—	1
1929	Red Dunn	4	2	50.0	NA	—	t2
1930			— none made —				
1931			— none made —				
1932			— none made —				
1933	Clarke Hinkle	7	2	28.6	NA	—	t5
1934	Bob Monnett	7	4	57.1	NA	—	t2
1935	Ade Schwammel	NA	4	NA	NA	—	t4
1936	Paul Engebretsen	NA	5	NA	NA	—	t3
1937	Clarke Hinkle	NA	2	NA	NA	—	t6
1938	Clarke Hinkle	9	3	33.3	NA	—	t4
1939	Paul Engebretsen	8	4	50.0	NA	—	t3
1940	Clarke Hinkle	14	9	64.3	45	—	1
1941	Clarke Hinkle	14	6	42.9	NA	—	1
1942	Ted Fritsch	5	4	80.0	NA	—	t2
1943	Don Hutson	5	3	60.0	25	—	t1
1944			— none made —				
1945	Ted Fritsch	8	3	37.5	49	—	6
1946	Ted Fritsch	17	9	52.9	46	—	1
1947	Ward Cuff	16	7	43.8	39	—	t1
1948	Ted Fritsch	16	6	37.5	47	—	t3
1949	Ted Fritsch	20	5	25.0	46	—	t5
1950	Ted Fritsch	17	3	17.6	52	—	t11
1951	Fred Cone	7	5	71.4	37	—	t11
1952	Bill Reichardt	20	5	25.0	43	—	8
1953	Fred Cone	16	5	31.3	44	—	t8
1954	Fred Cone	16	9	56.3	45	—	5
1955	Fred Cone	24	16	66.7	45	—	1
1956	Fred Cone	8	5	62.5	45	—	t9
1957	Fred Cone	17	12	70.6	39	—	4
1958	Paul Hornung	21	11	52.4	45	—	t5
1959	Paul Hornung	17	7	41.2	46	—	t8
1960	Paul Hornung	28	15	53.6	47	—	t2
1961	Paul Hornung	22	15	68.2	51	—	t3
1962	Jerry Kramer	11	9	81.8	37	—	t11
1963	Jerry Kramer	34	16	47.1	46	—	4
1964	Paul Hornung	38	12	31.6	52	—	t10
1965	Don Chandler	26	17	65.4	49	—	t3
1966	Don Chandler	28	12	42.9	47	—	13
1967	Don Chandler	29	19	65.5	49	—	4
1968	Mike Mercer	12	7	58.3	45	—	15
1969	Mike Mercer	17	5	29.4	48	—	15
1970	Dale Livingston	28	15	53.6	49	11	19
1971	Lou Michaels	14	8	57.1	44	12	t24
1972	Chester Marcol	48	33	68.8	51	1	1
1973	Chester Marcol	35	21	60.0	46	t7	t13
1974	Chester Marcol	39	25	64.1	52	1	1
1975	Joe Danelo	16	11	68.8	48	10	19
1976	Chester Marcol	19	10	52.6	45	t11	t22
1977	Chester Marcol	21	13	61.9	44	6	t13
1978	Chester Marcol	19	11	57.9	48	t11	t21
1979	Tom Birney	9	7	77.8	46	14	28

Year	Player	Att.	Made	Pct.	LG	NFC Rank	NFL Rank
1980	Tom Birney	12	6	50.0	50	14	28
1981	Jan Stenerud	24	22	91.7	53	4	t7
1982	Jan Stenerud	18	13	72.2	48	3	7
1983	Jan Stenerud	26	21	80.8	48	7	t10
1984	Al Del Greco	12	9	75.0	45	14	t26
1985	Al Del Greco	26	19	73.1	46	t9	t18
1986	Al Del Greco	27	17	63.0	50	t8	t16
1987	Max Zendejas	19	16	84.2	48	t7	t15
1988	Max Zendejas	16	9	56.3	50	15	26
1989	Chris Jacke	28	22	78.6	52	t6	t11
1990	Chris Jacke	30	23	76.7	53	t4	t6
1991	Chris Jacke	24	18	75.0	53	10	t19
1992	Chris Jacke	29	22	75.9	53	4	t8
1993	Chris Jacke	37	31	83.8	54	2	t3
1994	Chris Jacke	26	19	73.1	50	10	22
1995	Chris Jacke	23	17	73.9	51	13	t26
1996	Chris Jacke	27	21	77.8	53	t10	t20
1997	Ryan Longwell	30	24	80.0	50	8	t12

PUNT RETURNS

Year	Player	Ret.	Yds.	Avg.	LG	TD	NFC/NFL Rank
1941	Andy Uram	7	121	17.3	90t	1	—
1942	Tony Canadeo	7	76	10.9	26	0	—
1943	Joe Laws	10	84	8.4	19	0	7
1944	Joe Laws	15	118	6.1	23	0	7
1945	Joe Laws	11	71	6.4	21	0	10
1946	Bob Nussbaumer	12	98	8.2	21	0	11
1947	Jim Gillette	11	168	15.3	26	0	8
1948	Fred Provo	18	208	11.6	40	0	9
1949	Ralph Earhart	14	161	11.5	57t	1	14
1950	Billy Grimes	29	555	19.1	85t	2	2
1951	Billy Grimes	16	100	6.3	26	0	20
1952	Billy Grimes	18	179	9.9	72	0	11
1953	Al Carmichael	20	199	10.0	52	0	2
1954	Veryl Switzer	24	306	12.8	93t	1	1
1955	Veryl Switzer	24	158	6.6	38	0	8
1956	Al Carmichael	21	165	7.9	22	0	6
1957	Al Carmichael	25	190	7.6	48	0	2
1958	Jim Shanley	14	105	7.5	26	0	7
1959	Lew Carpenter	13	150	11.5	51	0	2
1960	Willie Wood	16	106	6.6	33	0	7
1961	Willie Wood	14	225	16.1	72t	2	1
1962	Willie Wood	23	273	11.9	65	0	2
1963	Willie Wood	19	169	8.9	41	0	10
1964	Willie Wood	19	252	13.3	64	0	2
1965	Willie Wood	13	38	2.9	14	0	14
1966	Willie Wood	22	82	3.7	13	0	11
1967	Donny Anderson	9	98	10.9	43	0	3
1968	Tom Brown	16	111	6.9	52t	1	10
1969	Elijah Pitts	16	60	3.8	10	0	10
1970	Willie Wood	11	58	5.3	12	0	N-Q
1971	Ken Ellis	22	107	4.9	30	0	11/24
1972	Ken Ellis	14	215	15.4	80t	1	1/1
1973	Jon Staggers	19	90	4.7	26	0	13/28
1974	Steve Odom	15	191	12.7	95t	1	t5/t11
1975	Willard Harrell	21	136	6.5	25	0	16/26
1976	Johnnie Gray	37	307	8.3	27	0	11/21
1977	Willard Harrell	28	253	9.0	75t	1	5/16
1978	Steve Odom	33	298	9.0	48	0	5/11
1979	Steve Odom	15	80	5.3	19	0	12/26
1980	Ron Cassidy	17	139	8.2	20	0	t11/t19
1981	Mark Lee	20	187	9.4	94t	1	6/11
1982	Phillip Epps	20	150	7.5	35	0	9/19
1983	Phillip Epps	36	324	9.0	90t	1	6/13
1984	Phillip Epps	29	199	6.9	39	0	11/t22
1985	Walter Stanley	14	179	12.8	27	0	N-Q
1986	Walter Stanley	33	316	9.6	83t	1	4/7
1987	Walter Stanley	28	173	6.2	48	0	12/22
1988	Ron Pitts	9	93	10.3	63t	1	N-Q
1989	Jeff Query	30	247	8.2	15	0	11/15
1990	Jeff Query	32	308	9.6	25	0	4/t6

Year	Player	Ret.	Yds.	Avg.	LG	TD	NFC/ NFL Rank
1991	Vai Sikahema	26	239	9.2	62	0	6/10
1992	Terrell Buckley	21	211	10.0	58t	1	5/t10
1993	Mike Prior	17	194	11.4	24	0	N-Q
1994	Robert Brooks	40	352	8.8	85t	1	7/14
1995	Charles Jordan	21	213	10.1	18	0	t5/t10
1996	Desmond Howard	58	875	15.1	92t	3	1/1
1997	Bill Schroeder	33	342	10.4	46	0	8/t15

N-Q: Non-Qualifier

KICKOFF RETURNS

Year	Player	Ret.	Yds.	Avg.	LG	TD	NFC/ NFL Rank
1941	Tony Canadeo	4	110	27.5	55	0	—
1942	Andy Uram	8	208	26.0	98t	1	—
1943	Tony Canadeo	10	242	24.2	43	0	6
1944	Ted Fritsch	11	288	26.1	44	0	2
1945	Ted Fritsch	8	279	34.9	79	0	5
1946	Tony Canadeo	6	163	27.1	38	0	15
1947	Ed Cody	10	269	26.9	39	0	t5
1948	Ed Smith	12	287	23.7	36	0	8
1949	Jack Kirby	14	315	22.5	34	0	10
1950	Tony Canadeo	16	411	25.7	48	0	10
1951	Dom Moselle	20	547	27.4	44	0	4
1952	Billy Grimes	18	422	23.4	34	0	15
1953	Al Carmichael	26	641	24.7	43	0	8
1954	Al Carmichael	20	531	26.6	49	0	3
1955	Al Carmichael	14	418	29.9	100t	1	1
1956	Al Carmichael	33	927	28.1	106t	1	3
1957	Don McIlhenny	14	362	25.9	53	0	6
1958	Al Carmichael	29	700	24.1	60	0	5
1959	John Symank	14	338	24.1	39	0	5
1960	Tom Moore	12	397	33.1	84	0	1
1961	Tom Moore	15	409	27.3	60	0	7
1962	Herb Adderley	15	418	27.9	103t	1	3
1963	Herb Adderley	20	597	29.9	98t	1	3
1964	Tom Moore	16	431	26.9	55	0	5
1965	Tom Moore	15	361	24.1	52	0	15
1966	Donny Anderson	23	533	23.2	61	0	15
1967	Travis Williams	18	739	41.1	104t	4	1
1968	Herb Adderley	14	331	23.6	50	0	11
1969	Dave Hampton	22	582	26.5	87t	1	5
1970	Larry Krause	18	513	28.5	100t	1	3/7
1971	Dave Hampton	46	1,314	28.6	90t	1	3/3
1972	Ike Thomas	21	572	27.2	89	0	5/7
1973	Ike Thomas	23	527	22.9	34	0	t9/t22
1974	Steve Odom	31	713	23.0	52	0	14/25
1975	Steve Odom	42	1,034	24.6	93t	1	6/11
1976	Mike C. McCoy	18	457	25.4	65	0	4/t9
1977	Steve Odom	23	468	20.3	37	0	17/30
1978	Steve Odom	25	677	27.1	95t	1	1/1
1979	Aundra Thompson	15	346	23.1	100t	1	N-Q
1980	Mark Lee	30	589	19.6	35	0	t15/t28
1981	Mark Lee	14	270	19.3	31	0	19/40
1982	Del Rodgers	20	436	21.8	76	0	11/21
1983	Harlan Huckleby	41	757	18.5	57	0	17/37
1984	Del Rodgers	39	843	21.6	97t	1	6/14
1985	Gary Ellerson	29	521	18.0	32	0	15/32
1986	Walter Stanley	28	559	20.0	55	0	9/t22
1987	Brent Fullwood	24	510	21.3	46	0	9/13
1988	Brent Fullwood	21	421	20.0	31	0	9/22
1989	Vince Workman	33	547	16.6	46	0	16/31
1990	Charles Wilson	35	798	22.8	36	0	3/5
1991	Charles Wilson	23	522	22.7	82t	1	t3/t5
1992	Corey Harris	23	485	21.1	50	0	11/t14
1993	Robert Brooks	23	611	26.6	95t	1	1/1
1994	Corey Harris	29	618	21.3	59	0	12/t23
1995	Antonio Freeman	24	556	23.2	45	0	5/14
1996	Desmond Howard	22	460	20.9	40	0	17/34
1997	Bill Schroeder	24	562	23.4	40	0	t8/t14

N-Q: Non-Qualifier

PUNTING

Year	Player	Punts	Gross Avg.	LG	Blk.	NFC/NFL Rank
1939	Clarke Hinkle	43	40.7	65	0	
1940	Clarke Hinkle	22	37.2	59	0	—
1941	Clarke Hinkle	22	44.5	63	0	18
1942	Lou Brock	32	38.3	52	2	—
1943	Lou Brock	32	36.4	72	1	—
1944	Tony Canadeo	13	36.8	46	0	9
1945	Roy McKay	44	41.2	73	0	13
1946	Roy McKay	64	42.7	64	1	1
1947	Jack Jacobs	57	43.5	74	1	1
1948	Jack Jacobs	69	40.3	78	1	1
1949	Jug Girard	69	39.0	72	1	3
1950	Jug Girard	71	38.2	63	3	5
1951	Jug Girard	52	40.4	66	2	13
1952	Babe Parilli	65	40.7	63	0	6
1953	Clive Rush	60	37.7	60	0	10
1954	Max McGee	72	41.7	63	0	13
1955	Dick Deschaine	56	43.2	73	0	5
1956	Dick Deschaine	62	42.7	57	0	2
1957	Dick Deschaine	63	42.0	71	2	2
1958	Max McGee	62	42.3	61	0	6
1959	Max McGee	64	42.4	61	1	4
1960	Max McGee	31	41.6	58	1	7
1961	Boyd Dowler	38	44.1	75	1	10
1962	Boyd Dowler	36	43.1	75	0	5
1963	Jerry Norton	51	44.7	61	0	6
1964	Jerry Norton	56	42.2	61	0	6
1965	Don Chandler	74	42.9	90	0	11
1966	Don Chandler	60	40.9	58	0	5
1967	Donny Anderson	65	36.6	63	0	10
1968	Donny Anderson	59	40.0	65	1	14
1969	Donny Anderson	58	40.2	58	0	9
1970	Donny Anderson	81	40.8	62	0	9
1971	Donny Anderson	50	40.4	58	0	6/15
1972	Ron Widby	65	41.8	64	0	8/17
1973	Ron Widby	56	43.1	60	2	5/10
1974	Randy Walker	69	38.4	58	0	3/6
1975	David Beverly	66	37.6	55	0	8/18
1976	David Beverly	83	37.0	60	0	13/24
1977	David Beverly	85	39.9	59	1	12/25
1978	David Beverly	106	35.5	57	1	t5/t7
1979	David Beverly	69	40.4	65	0	15/29
1980	David Beverly	86	38.3	55	0	4/10
1981	Ray Stachowicz	82	40.6	72	0	14/t26
1982	Ray Stachowicz	42	40.2	53	2	11/t18
1983	Bucky Scribner	69	41.6	70	0	11/17
1984	Bucky Scribner	85	42.3	61	1	3/10
1985	Joe Prokop	56	39.5	66	0	3/8
1986	Don Bracken	55	40.1	63	0	14/28
1987	Don Bracken	72	40.9	65	2	11/21
1988	Don Bracken	85	38.7	62	1	5/9
1989	Don Bracken	66	40.6	63	1	12/24
1990	Don Bracken	64	38.0	59	0	7/11
1991	Paul McJulien	86	40.4	62	1	13/25
1992	Bryan Wagner	30	40.7	52	0	10/t19
1993	Bryan Wagner	74	42.9	60	0	N-Q
1994	Craig Hentrich	81	41.4	70	0	t6/t12
1995	Craig Hentrich	65	42.2	61	0	t7/t17
1996	Craig Hentrich	68	42.4	65	2	7/t14
1997	Craig Hentrich	75	45.0	65	0	3/t5

N-Q: Non-Qualifier

SACKS
based on number made, official stat since 1982

Year	Player	Sacks	NFC Rank	NFL Rank
1972	Clarence Williams	9.0	NA	NA
1973	Mike P. McCoy	6.0	NA	NA
1974	Clarence Williams	6.0	NA	NA

Year	Player	Sacks	NFC Rank	NFL Rank
1975	Dave Pureifory	11.0	NA	NA
1976	Mike P. McCoy	8.5	NA	NA
	Alden Roche	8.5	NA	NA
1977	Dave Pureifory	8.0	NA	NA
	Dave Roller	8.0	NA	NA
1978	Ezra Johnson	20.5	2	2
1979	Bob Barber	6.0	NA	NA
	Ezra Johnson	6.0	NA	NA
1980	Mike Butler	9.0	NA	NA
	Ezra Johnson	9.0	NA	NA
1981	Mike Butler	10.5	NA	NA
1982	Ezra Johnson	5.5	t13	t21
1983	Ezra Johnson	14.5	3	7
1984	Mike Douglass	9.0	21	t37
1985	Ezra Johnson	9.5	19	30
1986	Tim Harris	8.0	t18	t34
1987	Tim Harris	7.0	t16	t25
1988	Tim Harris	13.5	5	5
1989	Tim Harris	19.5	2	2
1990	Tim Harris	7.0	t21	t40
1991	Tony Bennett	13.0	t3	t6
1992	Tony Bennett	13.5	t6	t13
1993	Reggie White	13.0	t1	t4
1994	Sean Jones	10.5	t5	t10
1995	Reggie White	12.0	3	t6
1996	Reggie White	8.5	17	26
1997	Reggie White	11.0	7	10

ALL-TIME PACKER 'TOP 20' RUSHERS AND RECEIVERS

TOP 20 RUSHERS

Name	Att.	Yds.	Avg.	LG	Yrs.
Jim Taylor	1,811	8,207	4.5	84t	9
John Brockington	1,293	5,024	3.9	53	7
Tony Canadeo	1,025	4,197	4.1	54	11
Clarke Hinkle	1,171	3,860	3.3	58	10
Gerry Ellis	836	3,826	4.6	71	7
Paul Hornung	893	3,711	4.2	72	9
Edgar Bennett	936	3,353	3.6	39t	5
Donny Anderson	787	3,165	4.0	54	6
Eddie Lee Ivery	667	2,933	4.4	49	8
Tobin Rote	419	2,205	5.3	55t	7
Ted Fritsch	619	2,200	3.6	55	9
Dorsey Levens	491	2,136	4.4	52t	4
Howie Ferguson	544	2,120	3.9	57	6
Tom Moore	503	2,069	4.1	77t	6
Terdell Middleton	559	2,044	3.7	76t	5
Floyd Reid	459	1,964	4.4	69t	6
Barty Smith	544	1,942	3.6	33	7
Joe Laws	470	1,932	4.1	—	12
MacArthur Lane	484	1,711	3.5	41	3
Brent Fullwood	433	1,702	3.9	38	4

TOP 20 RECEIVERS

Name	No.	Yds.	Avg.	LG	Yrs.
Sterling Sharpe	595	8,134	13.7	79t	7
James Lofton	530	9,656	18.2	80t	9
Don Hutson	488	7,991	16.4	92t	11
Boyd Dowler	448	6,918	15.4	91t	11
Max McGee	345	6,346	18.4	82t	12
Paul Coffman	322	4,223	13.1	78t	8
Bill Howton	303	5,581	18.4	90t	7
Carroll Dale	275	5,422	19.7	89t	8
Robert Brooks	275	3,805	13.8	99t	6
Gerry Ellis	267	2,514	9.4	69t	7
Edgar Bennett	242	1,920	7.9	40	5
Ed West	202	2,321	11.5	50	11
Phillip Epps	192	2,884	15.0	63	7
Jim Taylor	187	1,505	8.0	41	9
Perry Kemp	182	2,341	12.9	39	4
Rich McGeorge	175	2,370	13.5	51	9
Ron Kramer	170	2,594	15.3	55	7
Eddie Lee Ivery	162	1,612	10.0	62	8
John Jefferson	149	2,253	15.1	50	4
Antonio Freeman	145	2,282	15.7	58t	3

Player	Years	TD	PAT	FG	Pts.
Don Hutson	35-45	105	172	7	823
Chris Jacke	89-96	0	301	173	820
Paul Hornung	57-62, 64-66	62	190	66	760
Jim Taylor	58-66	91	0	0	546
Chester Marcol	72-80	1	155	120	521
Fred Cone	51-57	16	200	53	455
Sterling Sharpe	88-94	66	0	0	396
Ted Fritsch	42-50	35	62	36	380
Clarke Hinkle	32-41	44	31	28	379
Verne Lewellen	24-32	51	1	0	307
Max McGee	54, 57-67	51	0	0	306
James Lofton	78-86	50	0	0	300
Jan Stenerud	80-83	0	115	59	292
Al Del Greco	84-87	0	112	50	262
Don Chandler	65-67	0	117	48	261
Billy Howton	52-58	43	0	0	258
Boyd Dowler	59-69	40	0	0	240
Paul Coffman	78-85	39	0	0	234
Johnny McNally	29-33, 35-36	38	2	0	230
Carroll Dale	65-72	35	0	0	210
Gerry Ellis	80-86	35	0	0	210
Elijah Pitts	61-69, 71	35	0	0	210
John Brockington	71-77	32	0	0	192
Robert Brooks	92-97	32	0	0	192
Donny Anderson	66-71	31	0	0	186
Tony Canadeo	41-44, 46-52	31	0	0	186
Eddie Lee Ivery	79-86	30	0	0	180
Tobin Rote	50-56	30	0	0	180
Edgar Bennett	92-96	29	0	0	**178
Jerry Kramer	58-68	0	90	29	177
Dorsey Levens	94-97	29	0	0	*176
Tom Moore	60-65	27	0	0	162
Ed West	84-94	26	0	0	*158
Antonio Freeman	95-97	22	0	0	132
Gary Knafelc	54-62	21	0	0	126
Joe Laws	34-45	21	0	0	126
Barty Smith	74-80	21	0	0	126
Ryan Longwell	97	0	48	24	120
Brent Fullwood	87-90	19	0	0	114
Terdell Middleton	77-81	19	0	0	114
Curly Lambeau	21-29	12	20	6	110
Floyd Reid	50-56	18	0	0	108
Max Zendejas	87-88	0	30	25	105
Bob Mann	50-54	17	0	0	102
Travis Williams	67-70	17	0	0	102
Lou Brock	40-45	16	2	0	98
Andy Uram	38-43	16	2	0	98
Phillip Epps	82-88	16	0	0	96
Hank Bruder	31-39	15	4	0	94
Jessie Clark	83-87	15	0	0	90
Ron Kramer	57, 59-64	15	0	0	90
Bob Monnett	33-38	8	27	5	90
Steve Odom	74-79	15	0	0	90
Bart Starr	56-71	15	0	0	90
Vince Workman	89-92	15	0	0	90
Lavvie Dilweg	27-34	14	2	0	86
Paul Engebretsen	34-41	0	43	14	85
Mark Chmura	93-97	13	0	0	*80
Nolan Luhn	45-49	13	0	0	+80
Clyde Goodnight	45-49	13	0	0	78
Dave Hampton	69-71	13	0	0	78
Harlan Huckleby	80-85	13	0	0	78
Rich McGeorge	70-78	13	0	0	78
Marv Fleming	63-69	12	0	0	72
Hurdis McCrary	29-33	12	0	0	72
Carl Mulleneaux	38-41, 45-46	12	0	0	72
Mike Mercer	68-69	0	35	12	71
Ed Jankowski	37-41	10	4	1	67

Player	Years	TD	PAT	FG	Pts.
Irv Comp	43-49	11	0	0	66
Jim Grabowski	66-70	11	0	0	66
Keith Jackson	95-96	11	0	0	66
John Jefferson	81-84	11	0	0	66
MacArthur Lane	72-74	11	0	0	66
Dale Livingston	70	0	19	15	64
Bo Molenda	28-32	9	10	0	64
Cecil Isbell	38-42	10	3	0	63
Tom Birney	79-80	0	21	13	60
Red Dunn	27-31	1	48	2	60
Wuert Englemann	30-33	10	0	0	60
Brett Favre	92-97	10	0	0	60
Charles Goldenberg	33-45	10	0	0	60
Billy Grimes	50-52	10	0	0	60
Scott Hunter	71-73	10	0	0	60
Eddie Kotal	25-29	10	0	0	60
Ernie Smith	35-37, 39	0	42	6	60
Roger Grove	31-35	7	16	0	58
Herb Adderley	61-69	9	0	0	54
Myrt Basing	23-27	9	0	0	54
Cub Buck	21-25	0	24	10	54
Lynn Dickey	76-77, 79-85	9	0	0	54
Willard Harrell	75-77	9	0	0	54
Jackie Harris	90-93	9	0	0	54
Don Majkowski	87-92	9	0	0	54
Darrell Thompson	90-94	9	0	0	54
Eric Torkelson	74-79, 81	9	0	0	54
Joe Danelo	75	0	20	11	53
Ward Cuff	47	0	30	7	51
Paul Ott Carruth	86-88	8	0	0	48
Milt Gantenbein	31-40	8	0	0	48
Anthony Morgan	93-96	8	0	0	48
Walt Schlinkman	46-49	8	0	0	48
Aundra Thompson	77-81	8	0	0	48
Keith Woodside	88-91	8	0	0	48
Arnie Herber	30-40	7	2	0	44
Lou Michaels	71	0	19	8	43
Al Carmichael	53-58	7	0	0	42
Carlton Elliott	51-54	7	0	0	42
Howie Ferguson	53-58	7	0	0	42
Carl Lidberg	26, 29-30	7	0	0	42
Don McIlhenny	57-59	7	0	0	42
Babe Parilli	52-53, 57-58	7	0	0	42
George Sauer	35-37	7	0	0	42
Jon Staggers	72-74	7	0	0	42
David Whitehurst	77-83	7	0	0	42
Don Beebe	96-97	6	0	0	36
Harry Jacunski	39-44	6	0	0	36
Perry Kemp	88-91	6	0	0	36
Marty Norton	25	6	0	0	36
Walter Stanley	85-88	6	0	0	36
Charlie Mathys	22-26	5	0	1	33
Doug Hart	64-71	5	0	0	+32
Jack Cloud	50-51	5	0	0	30
Kenneth Davis	86-88	5	0	0	30
Bobby Dillon	52-59	5	0	0	30
Gary Ellerson	85-86	5	0	0	30
Ken Ellis	70-75	5	0	0	30
Rex Enright	26-27	5	0	0	30
Herman Fontenot	89-90	5	0	0	30
Harry O'Boyle	28, 32	1	15	3	30
Ken Payne	74-77	5	0	0	30
Ray Pelfrey	51-52	5	0	0	30
Pid Purdy	26-27	1	15	3	30
Jeff Query	89-91	5	0	0	30
Al Rose	32-36	5	0	0	30
Chuck Sample	42, 45	5	0	0	30
Veryl Switzer	54-55	5	0	0	30

Player	Years	TD	PAT	FG	Pts.
Walter Voss	24	5	0	0	30
Bill Reichardt	52	1	5	5	26
Ade Schwammel	34-36, 43-44	0	8	6	26
Tim Webster	71	0	8	6	26
Chuck Mercein	67-69	2	7	2	25
Willie Wood	60-71	4	1	0	25
Charley Brock	39-47	4	0	0	24
Reggie Cobb	94	4	0	0	24
Ted Cook	48-50	4	0	0	24
Paul Duhart	44	4	0	0	24
Ralph Earhart	48-49	4	0	0	24
Bob Forte	46-53	4	0	0	24
Earl Gros	62-63	4	0	0	24
John Hilton	70	4	0	0	24
Joe Johnson	54-58	4	0	0	24
Bob Long	64-67	4	0	0	24
Paul Miller	36-38	4	0	0	24
Dick O'Donnell	24-30	4	0	0	24
Steve Pritko	49-50	4	0	0	24
Del Rodgers	82, 84	4	0	0	24
Bernie Scherer	36-38	4	0	0	24
Barry Smith	73-75	4	0	0	24
Ed Cody	47-48	2	11	0	23
Eddie Garcia	83-84	0	14	3	23
Tom Nash	28-32	3	0	0	++22
Dutch Hendrian	24	3	0	1	21
Roy McKay	44-47	3	3	0	21
Paul Fitzgibbons	30-32	3	1	0	19
Steve Atkins	79-81	3	0	0	18
Al Baldwin	50	3	0	0	18
Willie Buchanon	72-78	3	0	0	18
Mark Clayton	93	3	0	0	18
Larry Coutre	50, 53	3	0	0	18
Mike Douglass	78-85	3	0	0	18
Jug Girard	48-51	3	0	0	18
Michael Haddix	89-90	3	0	0	18
Jack Harris	25-26	3	0	0	18
Desmond Howard	96	3	0	0	18
Mark Ingram	95	3	0	0	18
Mike Meade	82-83	3	0	0	18
Terry Mickens	94-97	3	0	0	18
Stan Mills	22-23	3	0	0	18
Dom Moselle	51-52	3	0	0	18
Frankie Neal	87	3	0	0	18
Don Perkins	43-45	3	0	0	18
Darren Sharper	97	3	0	0	18
Harry Sydney	92	3	0	0	18
Jerry Tagge	72-74	3	0	0	18
Hal Van Every	40-41	3	0	0	18
Randy Wright	84-88	3	0	0	18
Bob Adkins	40-41, 45	2	4	0	16
Willie Davis	60-69	2	0	0	++16
Booth Lusteg	69	0	12	1	15
Craig Hentrich	94-97	0	5	3	14
Mike Michalske	29-35, 37	2	0	0	+14
Bruce Smith	45-48	2	0	0	+14
Carl Bland	89-90	2	0	0	12
Tom Brown	64-68	2	0	0	12
Terrell Buckley	92-94	2	0	0	12
LeRoy Butler	90-97	2	0	0	12
Lee Roy Caffey	64-69	2	0	0	12
Jack Clancy	70	2	0	0	12
Tyrone Davis	97	2	0	0	12
Preston Dennard	85	2	0	0	12
Clint Didier	88-89	2	0	0	12
Bill DuMoe	21	2	0	0	12
Dick Flaherty	26	2	0	0	12
William Henderson	95-97	2	0	0	12
Cal Hubbard	29-33, 35	2	0	0	12
Jack Jacobs	47-49	2	0	0	12
Claudis James	67-68	2	0	0	12
Bob Jeter	63-70	2	0	0	12
Chester Johnston	31, 34-38	2	0	0	12
Charles Jordan	94-95	2	0	0	12
Walt Landers	78-79	2	0	0	12
Gary Lewis	81-84	2	0	0	12
Mark Lewis	85-87	2	0	0	12
Tim Lewis	83-86	2	0	0	12
Larry Marks	28	2	0	0	12
John Martinkovic	51-56	2	0	0	12
Joel Mason	42-45	2	0	0	12
Aubrey Matthews	88-89	2	0	0	12
Derrick Mayes	96-97	2	0	0	12
Blake Moore	84-85	2	0	0	12
Ray Nitschke	58-72	2	0	0	12
Art Schmaehl	21	2	0	0	12
Herm Schneidman	35-39	2	0	0	12
Ben Starret	42-45	2	0	0	12
John Thompson	79-82	2	0	0	12
Gabe Wilkins	94-97	2	0	0	12
Ben Wilson	67	2	0	0	12
Charles Wilson	90-91	2	0	0	12
Faye Wilson	30-31	2	0	0	12
Ben Agajanian	61	0	8	1	11
John Anderson	78-89	1	1	1	10
Dale Dawson	88	0	1	3	10
Tim Harris	86-90	1	0	0	++10
Whitey Woodin	22-31	1	4	0	10
George Abramson	25	0	2	2	8
Robert Brown	82-92	1	0	0	+8
Bryce Paup	90-94	1	0	0	+8
Frank Balazs	39-41	1	1	0	7
Nate Abrams	21	1	0	0	6
Lionel Aldridge	63-71	1	0	0	6
Bill Anderson	65-66	1	0	0	6
Bert Askson	75-77	1	0	0	6
Frank Baker	31	1	0	0	6
Norm Barry	21	1	0	0	6
Don Barton	53	1	0	0	6
Sanjay Beach	92	1	0	0	6
Wayland Becker	36-38	1	0	0	6
Tony Bennett	90-93	1	0	0	6
J.R. Boone	53	1	0	0	6
Zeke Bratkowski	63-68, 71	1	0	0	6
Mark Brunell	93-94	1	0	0	6
Bill Butler	59	1	0	0	6
Mike Butler	77-82, 85	1	0	0	6
Ivan Cahoon	26-29	1	0	0	6
Lew Carpenter	59-63	1	0	0	6
Fred Carr	68-77	1	0	0	6
Jim Carter	70-75, 77-78	1	0	0	6
Joe Carter	42	1	0	0	6
Paul Christman	50	1	0	0	6
Jack Concannon	74	1	0	0	6
Larry Craig	39-49	1	0	0	6
Bernie Crimmins	45	1	0	0	6
Tommy Cronin	22	1	0	0	6
Ray Crouse	84	1	0	0	6
Jim Crowley	25	1	0	0	6
Dan Currie	58-64	1	0	0	6
Dave Davis	71-72	1	0	0	6
Gib Dawson	53	1	0	0	6
Dean Dorsey	88	0	3	1	6
Wally Dreyer	50	1	0	0	6
Doug Evans	93-97	1	0	0	6
Tony Falkenstein	43	1	0	0	6

Player	Years	TD	PAT	FG	Pts.
Bobby Jack Floyd	52	1	0	0	6
Joe Francis	58-59	1	0	0	6
Milton Gardner	22-26	1	0	0	6
Jim Gillette	47	1	0	0	6
Leland Glass	72-73	1	0	0	6
Les Goodman	73-74	1	0	0	6
Johnnie Gray	75-83	1	0	0	6
Tiger Greene	86-90	1	0	0	6
Tom Greenfield	39-41	1	0	0	6
Hank Gremminger	56-65	1	0	0	6
Joey Hackett	87-88	1	0	0	6
James Hargrove	87	1	0	0	6
Maurice Harvey	81-83	1	0	0	6
Aaron Hayden	97	1	0	0	6
Les Hearden	24	1	0	0	6
Stan Heath	49	1	0	0	6
Estus Hood	78-84	1	0	0	6
Don Horn	67-70	1	0	0	6
Lynn Howard	21-22	1	0	0	6
Bob Ingalls	42	1	0	0	6
Jim Jensen	81-82	1	0	0	6
Glenn Johnson	49	1	0	0	6
Randy Johnson	76	1	0	0	6
Bruce Jones	27-28	1	0	0	6
Sean Jones	94-96	1	0	0	6
Henry Jordan	59-69	1	0	0	6
Jim Keane	52	1	0	0	6
Bill Kelley	49	1	0	0	6
Blair Kiel	88-91	1	0	0	6
George Koonce	92-97	1	0	0	6
Larry Krause	70-71, 73-74	1	0	0	6
Bill Larson	80	1	0	0	6
Mark Lee	80-90	1	0	0	6
Ace Loomis	51-53	1	0	0	6
Steve Luke	75-80	1	0	0	6
Larry Mason	88	1	0	0	6
Al Matthews	70-75	1	0	0	6
Mike P. McCoy	70-76	1	0	0	6
Lamar McHan	59-60	1	0	0	6
Steve Meilinger	58, 60	1	0	0	6
Lee Morris	87	1	0	0	6
Mark Murphy	80-85, 87-91	1	0	0	6
Ed Neal	45-51	1	0	0	6
Brian Noble	85-93	1	0	0	6
Dan Orlich	49-51	1	0	0	6
Ernie Pannell	41-42, 45	1	0	0	6
Johnny Papit	53	1	0	0	6
Keith Paskett	87	1	0	0	6
Shawn Patterson	88-91, 93	1	0	0	6
Ron Pitts	88-90	1	0	0	6
Keith Ranspot	42	1	0	0	6
Ray Riddick	40-42, 46	1	0	0	6
Alan Risher	87	1	0	0	6
Andre Rison	96	1	0	0	6
John Roach	61-63	1	0	0	6
Ken Roskie	48	1	0	0	6
Dan Ross	86	1	0	0	6
Russ Saunders	31	1	0	0	6
Francis Schammel	37	1	0	0	6
Bill Schroeder	94, 97	1	0	0	6
Patrick Scott	87-88	1	0	0	6
John Simmons	86	1	0	0	6
Nate Simpson	77-79	1	0	0	6
Ollie Smith	76-77	1	0	0	6
John Spilis	69-71	1	0	0	6
Rebel Steiner	50-51	1	0	0	6
John Stephens	93	1	0	0	6
Ken Stills	85-89	1	0	0	6

Player	Years	TD	PAT	FG	Pts.
Bob Summerhays	49-51	1	0	0	6
Don Summers	87	1	0	0	6
Earl Svendsen	37, 39	1	0	0	6
Karl Swanke	80-86	1	0	0	6
Len Szafaryn	50, 53-56	1	0	0	6
Claude Taugher	22	1	0	0	6
Cliff Taylor	76	1	0	0	6
Kitrick Taylor	92	1	0	0	6
Lavale Thomas	87-88	1	0	0	6
Jeff Thomason	95-97	1	0	0	6
Gerald Tinker	75	1	0	0	6
Mike Tomczak	91	1	0	0	6
Walter Tullis	78-79	1	0	0	6
Alex Urban	41, 44-45	1	0	0	6
Eddie Usher	22, 24	1	0	0	6
Val Joe Walker	53-56	1	0	0	6
Clarence Weathers	90-91	1	0	0	6
Lyle Wheeler	21-23	1	0	0	6
Jesse Whittenton	58-64	1	0	0	6
Clarence Williams	70-77	1	0	0	6
Perry Williams	69-73	1	0	0	6
Paul Winslow	60	1	0	0	6
Dave Conway	71	0	5	0	5
Joe Ethridge	49	0	1	1	4
Errol Mann	68, 76	0	4	0	4
Dave Pureifory	72-77	0	2	0	+4
Herman Rohrig	41, 46-47	0	1	1	4
Chet Adams	43	0	0	1	3
Greg Boyd	83	0	0	0	+2
Bob Brown	66-73	0	0	0	+2
Curtis Burrow	88	0	2	0	2
Bill Forester	53-63	0	0	0	+2
Dave Hanner	52-64	0	0	0	+2
Ted Hendricks	74	0	0	0	+2
Walter Niemann	22-24	0	0	0	+2
Urban Odson	46-49	0	0	0	+2
Tom Toner	73, 75-77	0	0	0	+2
Dick Weisgerber	38-40, 42	0	2	0	2
Dick Wildung	46-51, 53	0	0	0	+2
Cal Clemens	36	0	1	0	1
Glen Sorenson	43-45	0	1	0	1
Clayton Tonnemaker	50, 53-54	0	1	0	1
Rich Wingo	79, 81-84	0	1	0	1

+ - includes Safety
++ - includes 2 Safeties
* - includes 2-Pt. Conversion
** - includes 2 2-Pt. Conversions

THE LAST TIME...

(Regular Season Games Only)

RUSHING

200 Yards Rushing
BY PACKERS — Never
BY OPPONENT — Greg Bell, Sept. 24, 1989, at L.A. Rams (221 yards)

100 Yards Rushing
BY PACKERS — Dorsey Levens, Dec. 1, 1997, at Minnesota (108 yards)
BY OPPONENT — Fred Lane, Dec. 14, 1997, at Carolina (119 yards)

100 Yards Rushing in One Half
BY PACKERS — Dorsey Levens, Nov. 23, 1997, vs. Dallas (145 yards in second half)
BY OPPONENT — Barry Sanders, Nov. 3, 1996, vs. Detroit (105 yards in first half)

100 Yards Rushing and Receiving
BY PACKERS — Never
BY OPPONENT — Chuck Nelson, Nov. 13, 1983, at Minnesota (119 yards rushing, 137 receiving)

Two 100-Yard Rushers
BY PACKERS — Eddie Lee Ivery (109 yards) and Gerry Ellis (101), Dec. 1, 1985, vs. Tampa Bay
BY OPPONENT — Tony Dorsett (149 yards) and Robert Newhouse (101), Nov. 12, 1978, vs. Dallas at Milw.

4 Touchdowns Rushing
BY PACKERS — Terdell Middleton, Oct. 15, 1978, vs. Seattle at Milw. (5,14, 2, 9 yards)
BY OPPONENT — Bobby Douglass, Nov. 4, 1973, vs. Chicago (1, 1, 2, 1 yards)

3 Touchdowns Rushing
BY PACKERS — Brent Fullwood, Oct. 9, 1988, vs. New England at Milw. (33, 7, 31 yards)
BY OPPONENT — James Jones, Oct. 9, 1983, at Detroit (1, 13, 1 yards)

2 Touchdowns Rushing
BY PACKERS — Dorsey Levens, Dec. 1, 1997, at Minnesota (3, 5 yards)
BY OPPONENT — Antowain Smith, Dec. 20, 1997, vs. Buffalo (5, 1 yards)

PASSING

400 Yards Passing
BY PACKERS — Brett Favre, Dec. 5, 1993, at Chicago (402 yards)
BY OPPONENT — Joe Montana, Nov. 4, 1990, vs. San Francisco (411 yards)

300 Yards Passing
BY PACKERS — Brett Favre, Nov. 16, 1997, at Indianapolis (363 yards)
BY OPPONENT — Paul Justin, Nov. 16, 1997, at Indianapolis (340 yards)

5 Touchdown Passes
BY PACKERS — Brett Favre, Sept. 21, 1997, vs. Minnesota (19, 28, 15, 2, 2 yards)
BY OPPONENT — Dan Marino, Dec. 8, 1985, vs. Miami (10, 21, 16, 2, 61 yards)

4 Touchdown Passes
BY PACKERS — Brett Favre, Nov. 23, 1997, vs. Dallas (7, 4, 2, 23 yards)
BY OPPONENT — Dan Marino, Dec. 8, 1985, vs. Miami (5 TDs — 10, 21, 16, 2, 61 yards)

3 Touchdown Passes
BY PACKERS — Brett Favre, Dec. 14, 1997, at Carolina (58, 20, 6 yards)
BY OPPONENT — Brad Johnson, Sept. 21, 1997, vs. Minnesota (3, 7, 27 yards)

6 Interceptions
BY PACKERS — Tom O'Malley, Sept. 17, 1950, vs. Detroit
BY OPPONENT — Don Horn, Sept. 26, 1971, vs. Denver at Milw.

5 Interceptions
BY PACKERS — Don Majkowski, Oct. 14, 1990, at Tampa Bay
BY OPPONENT — Rich Gannon, Oct. 28, 1990, vs. Minnesota at Milw.

4 Interceptions
BY PACKERS — Brett Favre, Jan. 2, 1994, at Detroit
BY OPPONENT — Scott Mitchell, Nov. 2, 1997, vs. Detroit

RECEIVING

10 Receptions
BY PACKERS — Antonio Freeman, Dec. 14, 1997, at Carolina (10 rec.)
BY OPPONENT — Jackie Harris, Nov. 26, 1995, vs. Tampa Bay (10 rec.)

200 Yards Receiving
BY PACKERS — Don Beebe, Oct. 14, 1996, vs. San Francisco (220 yards)
BY OPPONENT — Jim Phillips, Nov. 16, 1958, vs. L.A. Rams (208 yards)

100 Yards Receiving
BY PACKERS — Antonio Freeman, Dec. 14, 1997, at Carolina (166 yards)
BY OPPONENT — Quinn Early, Dec. 20, 1997, vs. Buffalo (120 yards)

100 Yards Receiving in One Half
BY PACKERS — Robert Brooks, Sept. 28, 1997, at Detroit (139 yards in first half)
BY OPPONENT — Keenan McCardell, Nov. 19, 1995, at Cleveland (102 yards in second half)

Two 100-Yard Receivers
BY PACKERS — Sterling Sharpe (115 yards) and Anthony Morgan (103), Dec. 4, 1994, at Detroit
BY OPPONENT — Curtis Conway (126 yards) and Jeff Graham (108), Nov. 12, 1995, vs. Chicago

4 Touchdown Receptions
BY PACKERS — Sterling Sharpe, Nov. 24, 1994, at Dallas (1, 36, 30, 5 yards)
BY OPPONENT — Never

3 Touchdown Receptions
BY PACKERS — Antonio Freeman, Dec. 8, 1996, vs. Denver (14, 51, 25 yards)
BY OPPONENT — Herman Moore, Oct. 29, 1995, at Detroit (10, 69, 29 yards)

2 Touchdown Receptions
BY PACKERS — Antonio Freeman, Dec. 14, 1997, at Carolina (58, 6 yards)
BY OPPONENT — Jake Reed, Sept. 21, 1997, vs. Minnesota (7, 27 yards)

INTERCEPTIONS

4 Interceptions
BY PACKERS — Willie Buchanon, Sept. 24, 1978, at San Diego
BY OPPONENT — Never

3 Interceptions
BY PACKERS — Tom Flynn, Oct. 28, 1984, vs. Detroit
BY OPPONENT — Vencie Glenn, Dec. 27, 1992, at Minnesota

2 Interceptions
BY PACKERS — LeRoy Butler, Nov. 2, 1997, vs. Detroit
BY OPPONENT — Willie Clay, Oct. 29, 1995, at Detroit

Interception Returned for Touchdown
BY PACKERS — Darren Sharper, Dec. 20, 1997, vs. Buffalo (20 yards)
BY OPPONENT — Deion Sanders, Nov. 23, 1997, vs. Dallas (50 yards)

SCORING

5 Touchdowns
BY PACKERS — Paul Hornung, Dec. 12, 1965, at Baltimore (2, 50, 9, 3, 65 yards)
BY OPPONENT — Never

4 Touchdowns
BY PACKERS — Sterling Sharpe, Nov. 24, 1994, at Dallas (1, 36, 30, 5 yards)
BY OPPONENT — Bobby Douglass, Nov. 4, 1973, vs. Chicago (1, 1, 2, 1 yards)

3 Touchdowns
BY PACKERS — Dorsey Levens, Nov. 16, 1997, at Indianapolis (3, 52, 1 yards)
BY OPPONENT — Greg Hill, Nov. 10, 1996, at Kansas City (8, 34, 24 yards)

FIELD GOALS/PATs

5 Field Goals Made
BY PACKERS — Chris Jacke, Oct. 14, 1996, vs. San Francisco (30, 25, 35, 31, 53 yards)
BY OPPONENT — Chris Boniol, Nov. 18, 1996, at Dallas (7 FGs — 45, 37, 42, 45, 35, 39, 28 yards)

4 Field Goals Made
BY PACKERS — Chris Jacke, Oct. 14, 1996, vs. San Francisco (5 FGs — 30, 25, 35, 31, 53 yards)
BY OPPONENT — Cary Blanchard, Nov. 16, 1997, at Indianapolis (42, 41, 35, 20 yards)

50-Yard Field Goal
BY PACKERS — Ryan Longwell, Sept. 28, 1997, at Detroit
BY OPPONENT — Jason Hanson, Sept. 28, 1997, at Detroit

Blocked Field Goal
BY PACKERS — Bernardo Harris, Nov. 9, 1997, vs. St. Louis (37-yard J.Wilkins att.)
BY OPPONENT — Hardy Nickerson, Dec. 7, 1997, at Tampa Bay (31-yard R.Longwell att.)

2-Point Conversion
BY PACKERS — Dorsey Levens, Sept. 1, 1997, vs. Chicago (pass from Brett Favre)
BY OPPONENT — Jay Riemersma, Dec. 20, 1997, vs. Buffalo (pass from Alex Van Pelt)

Point After Touchdown Missed
BY PACKERS — Chris Jacke, Dec. 15, 1996, at Detroit (2nd att.)
BY OPPONENT — Kevin Butler, Dec. 8, 1991, at Chicago (4th att.)

Blocked Point After Touchdown
BY PACKERS — Matt Brock, Nov. 11, 1990, at L.A. Raiders (Jeff Jaeger's 2nd att.)
BY OPPONENT — Oliver Barnett, Nov. 20, 1994, at Buffalo (Chris Jacke's 1st att.)

PUNTING

70-Yard Punt
BY PACKERS — Craig Hentrich, Nov. 13, 1994, vs. N.Y. Jets (70 yards)
BY OPPONENT — Sean Landeta, Nov. 8, 1992, at N.Y. Giants (71 yards)

60-Yard Punt
BY PACKERS — Craig Hentrich, Nov. 16, 1997, at Indianapolis (65 yards)
BY OPPONENT — Sean Landeta, Nov. 24, 1996, at St. Louis (62 yards)

Blocked Punt
BY PACKERS — Seth Joyner, Dec. 20, 1997, vs. Buffalo (Chris Mohr punter)
BY OPPONENT — Anthony Marshall, Sept. 11, 1995, at Chicago (Craig Hentrich punter)

10 Punts
BY PACKERS — Craig Hentrich, Oct. 20, 1994, at Minnesota (460 yards)
BY OPPONENT — Mike Saxon, Oct. 20, 1994, at Minnesota (396 yards)

0 Punts
BY PACKERS — Dec. 17, 1989, at Chicago
BY OPPONENT — Nov. 22, 1981, at Tampa Bay

OTHER SPECIAL TEAMS

Kickoff Returned for Touchdown
BY PACKERS — Don Beebe, Oct. 6, 1996, at Chicago (90 yards)
BY OPPONENT — Mel Gray, Nov. 6, 1994, vs. Detroit at Milw. (91 yards)

Punt Returned for Touchdown
BY PACKERS — Desmond Howard, Dec. 15, 1996, at Detroit (92 yards)
BY OPPONENT — Carl Pickens, Sept. 20, 1992, vs. Cincinnati (95 yards)

Blocked (Opponent) Field Goal Returned for Touchdown
BY PACKERS — Willie Buchanon, Dec. 17, 1972, at New Orleans (57 yards)
BY OPPONENT — Clarence Scott, Sept. 17, 1972, at Cleveland (55 yards)

Blocked Punt Returned for Touchdown
BY PACKERS — Tiger Greene, Dec. 2, 1990, at Minnesota (36 yards — Harry Newsome punter)
BY OPPONENT — Bennie Blades, Nov. 1, 1992, at Detroit (7 yards — Paul McJulien punter)

Recovered Own Onside Kick Attempt
BY PACKERS — Bryce Paup, Dec. 9, 1990, vs. Seattle at Milw. (Chris Jacke kicker)
BY OPPONENT — Jocelyn Borgella, Nov. 3, 1996, vs. Detroit (Jason Hanson kicker)

DEFENSE

Shutout Posted
BY PACKERS — Dec. 26, 1993, vs. L.A. Raiders (28-0)
BY OPPONENT — Oct. 17, 1991, vs. Chicago (17-0)

Fumble Returned for Touchdown
BY PACKERS — Tyrone Davis, Dec. 20, 1997, vs. Buffalo (recovered in end zone)
BY OPPONENT — Al Fontenot, Nov. 16, 1997, at Indianapolis (33 yards)

Safety Scored
BY PACKERS — TEAM, Sept. 9, 1996, vs. Philadelphia (Peete sacked by S.Dotson and White)
BY OPPONENT — Kevin Carter, Nov. 24, 1996, at St. Louis (Favre sacked)

5 Sacks
BY PACKERS — Ezra Johnson, Sept. 3, 1978, at Detroit

4 Sacks
BY PACKERS — Bryce Paup, Sept. 15, 1991, vs. Tampa Bay (4½)
BY OPPONENT — Keith Millard, Oct. 15, 1989, at Minnesota

3 Sacks
BY PACKERS — Bryce Paup, Nov. 8, 1993, at Kansas City
BY OPPONENT — Michael Strahan, Sept. 17, 1995, vs. N.Y. Giants

MISCELLANEOUS

0 Penalties
BY PACKERS — Nov. 25, 1990, vs. Tampa Bay at Milw.
BY OPPONENT — Dec. 14, 1997, at Carolina

Game Without A Touchdown
BY PACKERS — Sept. 7, 1997, at Philadelphia
BY OPPONENT — Dec. 7, 1997, at Tampa Bay

50 Points Scored in a Game
BY PACKERS — 55, Oct. 2, 1983, vs. Tampa Bay
BY OPPONENT — 55, Dec. 20, 1986, at N.Y. Giants

40 Points Scored in a Game
BY PACKERS — 45, Nov. 23, 1997, vs. Dallas
BY OPPONENT — 41, Nov. 16, 1997, at Indianapolis

500 Yards Total Offense
BY PACKERS — 516, Dec. 11, 1994, vs. Chicago
BY OPPONENT — 539, Nov. 22, 1984, at Detroit

SUPER BOWL RESULTS

I -	Green Bay 35, Kansas City, 10, at Los Angeles, Jan. 15, 1967.
II -	Green Bay 33, Oakland, 14, at Miami, Jan. 14, 1968.
III -	New York Jets 16, Baltimore 7, at Miami, Jan. 12, 1969.
IV -	Kansas City 23, Minnesota 7, at New Orleans, Jan. 11, 1970.
V -	Baltimore 16, Dallas 13, at Miami, Jan. 17, 1971.
VI -	Dallas 24, Miami 3, at New Orleans, Jan. 16, 1972.
VII -	Miami 14, Washington 7, at Los Angeles, Jan. 14, 1973.
VIII -	Miami 24, Minnesota 7, at Houston, Jan. 13, 1974.
IX -	Pittsburgh 16, Minnesota 6, at New Orleans, Jan. 12, 1975.
X -	Pittsburgh 21, Dallas 17, at Miami, Jan. 18, 1976.
XI -	Oakland 32, Minnesota 14, at Pasadena, Jan. 9, 1977.
XII -	Dallas 27, Denver 10, at New Orleans, Jan. 15, 1978.
XIII -	Pittsburgh 35, Dallas 31, at Miami, Jan. 21, 1979.
XIV -	Pittsburgh 31, Los Angeles 19, at Pasadena, Jan. 20, 1980.
XV -	Oakland 27, Philadelphia 10, at New Orleans, Jan. 25, 1981.
XVI -	San Francisco 26, Cincinnati 21, at Pontiac, MI, Jan. 24, 1982.
XVII -	Washington 27, Miami 17, at Pasadena, Jan. 30, 1983.
XVIII -	L.A. Raiders 38, Washington 9, at Tampa, Jan. 22, 1984.
XIX -	San Francisco 38, Miami 16, at Palo Alto, CA, Jan. 20, 1985.
XX -	Chicago 46, New England 10, at New Orleans, Jan. 26, 1986.
XXI -	New York Giants 39, Denver 20, at Pasadena, Jan. 25, 1987.
XXII -	Washington 42, Denver 10, at San Diego, Jan. 31, 1988.
XXIII -	San Francisco 20, Cincinnati 16, at Miami, Jan. 22, 1989.
XXIV -	San Francisco 55, Denver 10, at New Orleans, Jan. 28, 1990.
XXV -	New York Giants 20, Buffalo 19, at Tampa, Jan. 28, 1991.
XXVI -	Washington 37, Buffalo 24, at Minneapolis, Jan. 26, 1992.
XXVII -	Dallas 52, Buffalo 17, at Pasadena, Jan. 31, 1993.
XXVIII -	Dallas 30, Buffalo 13, at Atlanta, Jan. 30, 1994.
XXIX -	San Francisco 49, San Diego 26, at Miami, Jan. 29, 1995.
XXX -	Dallas 27, Pittsburgh 17, at Tempe, AZ, Jan. 28, 1996.
XXXI -	Green Bay 35, New England 21, at New Orleans, Jan. 26, 1997.
XXXII -	Denver 31, Green Bay 24, at San Diego, Jan. 25, 1998.

Herb Adderley, who returned an interception 60 yards for a touchdown in Green Bay's Super Bowl II victory over Oakland, singly held the Packers' all-time record for most defensive touchdowns in one season, established with 3 scoring returns of interceptions in 1965, until rookie Darren Sharper tied the mark last year. Among the more notable team records Adderley continues to possess are those for most interception returns for touchdowns in a career (7) and most career postseason interceptions (4), a mark he shares with two players of recent time, Craig Newsome and Eugene Robinson.

TWELVE TIMES WORLD CHAMPIONS

The Green Bay Packers have won more championships — twelve — than any other team in National Football League history. They won their first three by league standing (1929, 1930 and 1931) and nine since the NFL's playoff system was established in 1933 (1936, 1939, 1944, 1961, 1962, 1965, 1966, 1967 and 1996). Green Bay also is the only NFL team to win three straight titles, having done it twice (1929-30-31 and 1965-66-67).

In addition, the Packers won the first two Super Bowls (over Kansas City in 1966, 35-10, and over Oakland in 1967, 33-14), as well as a more recent one (over New England in 1996, 35-21).

Chicago's Bears rank second with nine NFL titles, followed by the Giants with six, the Cowboys, Redskins and 49ers with five each, and the Lions and Browns with four apiece.

GREEN BAY'S CHAMPIONSHIP RECORD

1929	12 Wins	0 Defeats	1 Tie
1930	10 Wins	3 Defeats	1 Tie
1931	12 Wins	2 Defeats	0 Ties
1936	Packers 21 ....Boston Redskins 6	..........at New York	...........(29,545)
1938	N.Y. Giants 23 ....Packers 17	..........at New York	...........(48,120)
1939	Packers 27 ..............N.Y. Giants 0	..........at Milwaukee	...........(32,279)
1944	Packers 14 ..............N.Y. Giants 7	..........at New York	...........(46,016)
1960	Philadelphia 17 ....Packers 13	..........at Philadelphia	...........(67,325)
1961	Packers 37 ..............N.Y. Giants 0	..........at Green Bay	...........(39,029)
1962	Packers 16 ..............N.Y. Giants 7	..........at New York	...........(64,892)
1965	Packers 23 ....Cleveland 12	..........at Green Bay	...........(50,777)
1966	Packers 34 ....Dallas 27	..........at Dallas	...........(74,152)
1967	Packers 21 ....Dallas 17	..........at Green Bay	...........(50,861)
1995	*Dallas 38...............Packers 27	..........at Irving, Texas	...........(65,135)
1996	*Packers 30 ....Carolina 13	..........at Green Bay	...........(60,216)
1997	*Packers 23 ....San Francisco 10	..........at San Francisco	...........(68,987)

*NFC Championship Game

SUPER BOWL

1966	Packers 35 ....Kansas City 10	..........at Los Angeles	...........(61,946)
1967	Packers 33 ....Oakland 14	..........at Miami	...........(75,546)
1996	Packers 35 ....New England 21	..........at New Orleans	...........(72,301)
1997	Denver 31 ....Packers 24	..........at San Diego	...........(68,912)

PACKERS SUPER BOWL STORY

SUPER BOWL I
January 15, 1967

Memorial Coliseum; Los Angeles, Calif.

Paid Attendance: 61,946

Green Bay 35, Kansas City 10

The Packers launched the Super Bowl series by whipping Kansas City's American Football League champions 35-10 behind the passing of Bart Starr, the receiving of Max McGee and a key interception by All-Pro safety Willie Wood.

Vince Lombardi's repeating NFL champions broke open the game with three second-half touchdowns, the first of which was set up by Wood's 50-yard return of an interception to the Chiefs' 5-yard line with the Packers leading by only 14-10. The pass, authored by the Chiefs' Len Dawson, had been intended for Kansas City tight end Fred Arbanas.

McGee, filling in for ailing Boyd Dowler (injured on the Packers' first offensive series) after having caught only four passes all season, snared seven from Starr for 138 yards and two touchdowns. Elijah Pitts ran for two other scores, counting one on a five-yard run in the third quarter and the other on a one-yard bolt in the final period.

The Chiefs' 10 points came in the second quarter, the only touchdown on a seven-yard pass from Dawson to Curtis McClinton.

Starr completed 16 of 23 passes for 250 yards and two touchdowns and was chosen the game's most valuable player. His scoring strikes came on a 37-yard collaboration with McGee in the first quarter and a 13-yard pitch to the aging end in the decisive third period.

The Packers collected $15,000 per man and the Chiefs $7,500 apiece — the largest single-game shares in the history of team sports at the time.

Game I Scoring					
Kansas City (AFL).............0	10	0	0	—	10
PACKERS (NFL)................7	7	14	7	—	35

G.B. — McGee 37 pass from Starr (Chandler kick) (8:56)
K.C. — McClinton 7 pass from Dawson (Mercer kick) (4:20)
G.B. — Taylor 14 run (Chandler kick) (10:23)
K.C. — FG Mercer 31 (14:06)
G.B. — Pitts 5 run (Chandler kick) (2:27)
G.B. — McGee 13 pass from Starr (Chandler kick) (14:09)
G.B. — Pitts 1 run (Chandler kick) (8:25)

SUPER BOWL II
January 14, 1968

Orange Bowl; Miami, Fla.

Paid Attendance: 75,546

Green Bay 33, Oakland 14

Having acquired a third consecutive NFL championship just two weeks earlier, the Packers embellished that record-tying parlay by winning the Super Bowl title for the second straight year. This time, they dispatched the AFL champion Raiders 33-14 in a game that drew the first $3-million gate in football history.

Bart Starr again was chosen the game's most valuable player as he completed 13 of 24 passes for 202 yards and one touchdown and directed a Packers attack that was in control all the way after building up a 16-7 halftime lead.

Don Chandler kicked four field goals (39, 20, 43 and 31 yards), and All-Pro cornerback Herb Adderley highlighted the Green Bay scoring with a 60-yard interception return of a Daryle Lamonica pass.

After leading by only 3-0 at the quarter, the Packers padded their margin to 16-7 at halftime by way of three Chandler field goals and a 62-yard scoring pass from Starr to split end Boyd Dowler. They then left the Raiders behind with a 10-point third period, Donny Anderson scoring on a two-yard run and Chandler with his final field goal.

The game marked the last for Vince Lombardi as Packers coach, ending nine years at Green Bay in which he won six Western Conference championships, five NFL titles and two Super Bowls, a record unprecedented in pro football history.

Game II Scoring					
PACKERS (NFL)................3	13	10	7	—	33
Oakland (AFL) 0	7	0	7	—	14

G.B. — FG Chandler 39 (5:07)
G.B. — FG Chandler 20 (3:08)
G.B. — Dowler 62 pass from Starr (Chandler kick) (4:10)
Oak. — Miller 23 pass from Lamonica (Blanda kick) (8:45)
G.B. — FG Chandler 43 (14:59)
G.B. — Anderson 2 run (Chandler kick) (9:06)
G.B. — FG Chandler 31 (14:58)
G.B. — Adderley 60 interception return (Chandler kick) (3:57)
Oak. — Miller 23 pass from Lamonica (Blanda kick) (5:47)

SUPER BOWL XXXI
January 26, 1997

Louisiana Superdome; New Orleans, La.

Paid Attendance: 72,301

Green Bay 35, New England 21

Using several momentum-turning big plays, the Packers held off resilient New England to capture their first world championship in 29 years. For Green Bay, the victory also marked its league-high 12th NFL championship as well as its third Super Bowl triumph.

The Packers jumped to an early 10-0 lead. Brett Favre, sensing a Patriots blitz, audibled on Green Bay's second play from scrimmage, hitting late-season pickup Andre Rison on a wide-open post pattern for a 54-yard touchdown pass. On the ensuing New England possession, Doug Evans intercepted Drew Bledsoe at the Patriots' 28, which led to a 37-yard field goal by Chris Jacke.

New England then was able to turn the tide in its favor, however, as Bledsoe took his club on two long drives for touchdowns. The first, which covered 79 yards and culminated in a short pass to Keith Byars, was aided by two long throws to Pats running backs and a 26-yard pass interference penalty. The second, starting at the New England 43, was spurred by a leaping, 44-yard reception by rookie Terry Glenn. When tight end Ben Coates caught a four-yard TD pass from Bledsoe, the Patriots momentarily had their only lead of the game and had completed the highest-scoring first quarter in Super Bowl history.

Green Bay rebounded to re-take the lead when Favre, seeing Patriots' strong safety Lawyer Milloy at the line of scrimmage in tight coverage on Antonio Freeman, watched Freeman elude Milloy's "bump" and lofted a perfect aerial to Freeman along the right sideline. Freeman, able to out-run New England's late-arriving free safety, covered 81 yards for the longest reception in Super Bowl history. After another Jacke field goal, Favre took advantage of a Mike Prior interception and escorted his troops on a nine-play, 74-yard march just before halftime which ended when, on a bootleg left, he lunged the ball over the goal line as he was rolling out of bounds.

Taking a 27-14 edge out of the locker room at halftime, Green Bay maintained that lead until late in the third quarter, when the Patriots' Curtis Martin made a magnificent 18-yard run up the middle of the Packer defense to pull New England to within six points at 27-21.

That margin was short-lived, though, as Desmond Howard returned the ensuing kickoff 99 yards for a back-breaking touchdown (the longest in Super Bowl history), bursting through the center of the Packers' well-blocked wedge, then juking kicker Adam Vinatieri to bolt free. Howard, who had 244 total return yards in the game including key punt runbacks of 32 and 34 yards, was voted the game's most valuable player, becoming the first special teams player to be so honored. A subsequent, successful two-point conversion, where Favre found Mark Chmura along the back of the end zone, gave the Green and Gold an insurmountable two-touchdown lead.

The top-ranked Green Bay defense, which had four interceptions of Bledsoe, was led by Reggie White, who sacked the New England quarterback a Super Bowl-record three times, including twice in a row on the possession immediately following Howard's scoring return.

Favre, playing less than an hour from his hometown of Kiln, Miss., completed 14 of 27 passes for 246 yards and two touchdowns without an interception, while his counterpart, Bledsoe, threw for 253 yards and two scores on 25-of-48 passing.

Game XXXI Scoring

New England (AFC)	14	0	7	0	—	21
PACKERS (NFC)	10	17	8	0	—	35

G.B. — Rison 54 pass from Favre (Jacke kick) (3:32)
G.B. — FG Jacke 37 (6:18)
N.E. — Byars 1 pass from Bledsoe (Vinatieri kick) (8:25)
N.E. — Coates 4 pass from Bledsoe (Vinatieri kick) (12:27)
G.B. — Freeman 81 pass from Favre (Jacke kick) (0:56)
G.B. — FG Jacke 31 (6:45)
G.B. — Favre 2 run (Jacke kick) (13:49)
N.E. — Martin 18 run (Vinatieri kick) (11:33)
G.B. — Howard 99 kickoff return (Chmura-Favre pass) (11:50)

SUPER BOWL XXXII
January 25, 1998
Qualcomm Stadium; San Diego, Calif. **Paid Attendance: 68,912**
Denver 31, Green Bay 24

Behind a dominating rushing performance by San Diego native Terrell Davis, four-time Super Bowl loser Denver garnered its first-ever victory in the NFL's title game to dethrone the reigning champion Packers in what some called "the best Super Bowl ever." In the process, the Broncos also ended a 13-game Super Bowl winning streak by the National Football Conference representative and sent Green Bay to its initial Super Bowl defeat after three triumphs.

Davis, named as the game's most valuable player, averaged 5.2 yards per carry as he rushed for 157 yards and three touchdowns, including the final, decisive score with less than two minutes remaining.

After the opening possession — a 76-yard scoring sequence by Green Bay — it appeared (falsely) that the game might turn into just another rout by the NFC against an overmatched AFC opponent. The Packers easily traversed the field, capping the drive with an arching, 22-yard touchdown pass from Brett Favre to Antonio Freeman at the back of the end zone, Freeman tap-dancing to get his feet down, and Green Bay had a 7-0 lead less than five minutes into the contest.

But the Broncos stormed back, scoring the first three times that they had the ball to commandeer a 17-7 advantage. After Davis went over from a yard out for Denver's initial points, the Broncos forced a pair of turnovers in Green Bay territory. First, Favre was intercepted when he prematurely unloaded a pass for Robert Brooks while under a heavy blitz, a miscue which resulted in a one-yard touchdown run by Broncos quarterback John Elway on a bootleg to the right. Then, after Favre fumbled when hit by Denver safety Steve Atwater on another blitz, the Broncos tacked on a long field goal by Jason Elam.

Green Bay mounted an impressive, 95-yard touchdown drive to consume the latter half of the second quarter and pull to within 17-14. Favre lofted a perfect aerial to tight end Mark Chmura in the back right corner of the end zone just 12 seconds before halftime, a pass which narrowly skirted the finger tips of a leaping defender.

Davis, who had missed the entire second quarter after experiencing migraine headache symptoms, fumbled on the first play from scrimmage the second half, an error which turned into a game-tying Ryan Longwell field goal only minutes later.

The Broncos went ahead again late in the third period, when Davis scored his second touchdown of the game to culminate 92-yard, seven-plus minute drive. And when, on the ensuing kickoff, Freeman fumbled at his own 22, things looked dire for Green Bay as it stared at a potential two-touchdown deficit heading into the final quarter. But when the Broncos went for the jugular on their first play, free safety Eugene Robinson intercepted Elway in the end zone.

Favre completed three passes to Freeman on the ensuing Green Bay possession, including a 13-yard crossing route for the receiver's second touchdown which knotted the score at 24 with thirteen-and-a-half minutes remaining. Freeman made nine receptions (for 126 yards) on the day to equal the club's all-time playoff record.

After the Packers failed to take advantage of one fourth quarter-drive which neared midfield, Denver ran the ball down their throat for the game's winning touchdown, a drive which covered 49 yards in only five plays — four on the ground. Davis strolled into the end zone untouched up the middle for a 31-24 lead with just 105 ticks of the clock left.

Still facing the relentless blitzing which had characterized the play of the Denver defense throughout the game, from his own 30-yard line Favre moved the Packers 39 yards down the field on four straight passes to Dorsey Levens to reach the Broncos' 31 with 42 seconds remaining. But when his next three throws fell incomplete, including a fourth-down pass intended for Chmura which was knocked down by linebacker John Mobley, the game was Denver's, giving Elway a long-awaited Super Bowl victory after he had endured three losses. In the process, the Broncos became just the second wild-card team to capture a Super Bowl in NFL history.

Favre, while not turning in his usual MVP-like performance, completed 25 of 42 passes for 256 yards and three touchdowns with one interception. Elway, who did not complete a pass to one of his wide receivers until late in the third quarter, threw for 123 yards on 12-of-22 passing while being intercepted once.

Game XXXII Scoring						
PACKERS (NFC)	7	7	3	7	—	24
Denver (AFC)	7	10	7	7	—	31

G.B. — Freeman 22 pass from Favre (Longwell kick) (4:02)
Den. — Davis 1 run (Elam kick) (9:21)
Den. — Elway 1 run (Elam kick) (0:05)
Den. — FG Elam 51 (2:39)
G.B. — Chmura 6 pass from Favre (Longwell kick) (14:48)
G.B. — FG Longwell 27 (3:01)
Den. — Davis 1 run (Elam kick) (14:26)
G.B. — Freeman 13 pass from Favre (Longwell kick) (1:28)
Den. — Davis 1 run (Elam kick) (13:15)

265

PACKERS IN THE PLAYOFFS

Overall: 22-9 • **Home: 12-0 (10-0 in Green Bay, 2-0 in Milwaukee)** • **Away: 6-8** • **Neutral: 4-1**

Date	Round	Opponent	Result	Score	Attendance
12/13/36	NFL Championship	Boston Redskins (@ New York)	W	21-6	29,545
12/11/38	NFL Championship	at New York Giants	L	17-23	48,120
12/10/39	NFL Championship	New York Giants (@ Milwaukee)	W	27-0	32,279
12/14/41	Western Division Playoff	at Chicago Bears	L	14-33	43,425
12/17/44	NFL Championship	at New York Giants	W	14-7	46,016
12/26/60	NFL Championship	at Philadelphia Eagles	L	13-17	67,325
12/31/61	NFL Championship	New York Giants	W	37-0	39,029
12/30/62	NFL Championship	at New York Giants	W	16-7	64,892
12/26/65	Western Conf. Championship	Baltimore Colts	W	13-10 (ot)	50,484
1/2/66	NFL Championship	Cleveland Browns	W	23-12	50,777
1/1/67	NFL Championship	at Dallas Cowboys	W	34-27	74,152
1/15/67	Super Bowl I	Kansas City Chiefs (@ Los Angeles)	W	35-10	61,946
12/23/67	Western Conf. Championship	Los Angeles Rams (@ Milwaukee)	W	28-7	49,861
12/31/67	NFL Championship	Dallas Cowboys	W	21-17	50,861
1/14/68	Super Bowl II	Oakland Raiders (@ Miami)	W	33-14	75,546
12/24/72	NFC Divisional Playoff	at Washington Redskins	L	3-16	53,140
1/8/83	NFC First-Round Playoff	St. Louis Cardinals	W	41-16	54,282
1/16/83	NFC Divisional Playoff	at Dallas Cowboys	L	26-37	63,972
1/8/94	NFC Wild Card Playoff	at Detroit Lions	W	28-24	68,479
1/16/94	NFC Divisional Playoff	at Dallas Cowboys	L	17-27	64,790
12/31/94	NFC Wild Card Playoff	Detroit Lions	W	16-12	58,125
1/8/95	NFC Divisional Playoff	at Dallas Cowboys	L	9-35	64,745
12/31/95	NFC Wild Card Playoff	Atlanta Falcons	W	37-20	60,453
1/6/96	NFC Divisional Playoff	at San Francisco 49ers	W	27-17	69,311
1/14/96	NFC Championship	at Dallas Cowboys	L	27-38	65,135
1/4/97	NFC Divisional Playoff	San Francisco 49ers	W	35-14	60,787
1/12/97	NFC Championship	Carolina Panthers	W	30-13	60,216
1/26/97	Super Bowl XXXI	New England Patriots (@ New Orleans)	W	35-21	72,031
1/4/98	NFC Divisional Playoff	Tampa Bay Buccaneers	W	21-7	60,327
1/11/98	NFC Championship	at San Francisco 49ers	W	23-10	68,987
1/25/98	Super Bowl XXXII	Denver Broncos (@ San Diego)	L	24-31	68,912

'36 PACKERS 21, BOSTON REDSKINS 6
NFL Championship
Dec. 13 at Polo Grounds, New York

Although New York was not represented in the title playoff, the game was played in the Polo Grounds because the Redskins' franchise was being shifted to Washington, D.C., by George Preston Marshall. A turnout of 29,545 saw Don Hutson take a 48-yard touchdown pass from Arnie Herber in the first three minutes, and the Packers were never behind. Green Bay's two second-half scores were set up, respectively, by a 52-yard pass from Herber to Johnny (Blood) McNally and when Lon Evans blocked a punt.

PACKERS ....7 0 7 7 — 21
Boston ....0 6 0 0 — 6
G.B. — Hutson 48 pass from Herber (E.Smith kick)
Bos. — Rentner 2 run (kick failed)
G.B. — Gantenbein 8 pass from Herber (E.Smith kick)
G.B. — Monnett 2 run (Engebretsen kick)

'38 NEW YORK 23, PACKERS 17
NFL Championship
Dec. 11 at Polo Grounds, New York

The Packers overcame an early 9-0 New York lead, spawned by two blocked punts deep in their territory, but could not hold off the Giants in the second half. Green Bay began to close in early in the second period, Arnie Herber capitalizing on a Paul (Tiny) Engebretsen interception by lofting a 40-yard touchdown strike to Carl Mulleneaux, cutting the Giants' margin to 9-7.

The Giants shortly converted a midfield fumble by Packer fullback Eddie Jankowski into a 16-7 lead before Green Bay again trimmed the deficit to two points before the half was over, Clarke Hinkle crashing over from the 6-inch line following a 66-yard Cecil Isbell pass to Wayland Becker.

The Packers then forged in front in the opening minutes of the second half for the first and only time in the game, an Engebretsen field goal presenting them with a 17-16 edge. The Giants, however, stormed back with a 61-yard scoring drive, capped by a 23-yard pass from Ed Danowski to Hank Soar. Soar fought his way over the goal line from the 2, with Hinkle clinging to one leg, for what proved to be the winning touchdown. A crowd of 48,120, a playoff record, sat in on the proceedings.

PACKERS ....0 14 3 0 — 17
New York 9   7 7 0 — 23
N.Y. — FG Cuff 14
N.Y. — Leemans 6 run (kick failed)
G.B. — C.Mulleneaux 40 pass from Herber (Engebretsen kick)
N.Y. — Barnard 21 pass from Danowski (Cuff kick)
G.B. — Hinkle 1 run (Engebretsen kick)
G.B. — FG Engebretsen 15
N.Y. — Soar 23 pass from Danowski (Cuff kick)

'39 PACKERS 27, NEW YORK 0
NFL Championship
Dec. 10 at State Fair Park, Milwaukee

The Packers made playoff history by scoring the first shutout ever registered in an NFL championship game. Despite bitter 35 m.p.h. winds, both Arnie Herber and Cecil Isbell passed for touchdowns in leading Green Bay to its fifth world championship before 32,279 fans.

Green Bay mounted a 7-0 halftime lead, by dint of a Herber scoring strike to Milt Gantenbein as the Giants missed on three field goal attempts. The Packers pulled away in the third quarter on a 29-yard field goal by Paul (Tiny) Engebretsen and a long TD pass from Isbell to Joe

Laws, set up by Laws' 30-yard punt return. The Packers added 10 more points in the fourth quarter on a 42-yard field goal by Ernie Smith and a short scoring run by fullback Eddie Jankowski. Green Bay intercepted the Giants six times and held them to only 164 total yards.

New York ....0 0 0 0 — 0
PACKERS ....7 0 10 10 — 27
G.B. — Gantenbein 7 pass from Herber (Engebretsen kick)
G.B. — FG Engebretsen 29
G.B. — Laws 31 pass from Isbell (Engebretsen kick)
G.B. — FG E.Smith 42
G.B. — Jankowski 1 run (E.Smith kick)

'41 CHICAGO BEARS 33, PACKERS 14
Western Division Playoff
Dec. 14 at Wrigley Field, Chicago

In a Western Division playoff contest necessitated when the two teams finished the year with identical 10-1 records, each having given the other its lone loss, the Packers fell victim to Chicago's offensive trio of George McAfee, Norm Standlee and Hugh Gallarneau in the 16-degree cold at Wrigley Field.

After the Bears fumbled the opening kickoff, Green Bay grabbed an early 7-0 lead. Gallarneau returned a punt 81 yards for a touchdown to narrow the gap to 7-6, before Chicago exploded for 24 second-quarter points to essentially settle the issue. The Bears rushed for 277 yards this day, McAfee leading the way with a team record 119 and Standlee adding 79 plus two touchdowns.

Green Bay's prolific end, Don Hutson, was held to only one catch for 19 yards.

PACKERS ....7 0 7 0 — 14
Chicago ....6 24 0 3 — 33
G.B. — Hinkle 1 run (Hutson kick)
Chi. — Gallarneau 81 punt return (kick blocked)
Chi. — FG Snyder 24
Chi. — Standlee 3 run (Stydahar kick)
Chi. — Standlee 2 run (Stydahar kick)
Chi. — Swisher 9 run (Stydahar kick)
G.B. — Van Every 10 pass from Isbell (Hutson kick)
Chi. — FG Snyder 26

'44 PACKERS 14, NEW YORK 7
NFL Championship
Dec. 17 at Polo Grounds, New York

With peerless pass catcher Don Hutson employed primarily as a decoy against the Giant defense, fullback Ted Fritsch emerged as the offensive hero of Packers' sixth world title victory.

Fritsch scored both Green Bay touchdowns, one a one-yard run on fourth-and-goal and the other on a 28-yard pass-and-run collaboration with Irv Comp in the third. Ward Cuff scored the Giants' touchdown with a one-yard plunge on the initial play of the final period, a drive which saw New York advance past its own 35-yard line for the first time in the game. Joe Laws, the Packers' veteran, 34-year-old all-purpose halfback, had a brilliant day, setting a playoff record with three interceptions and claiming ground gaining honors with 74 yards in 13 carries.

PACKERS ....0 14 0 0 — 14
New York 0   0 0 7 — 7
G.B. — Fritsch 1 run (Hutson kick)
G.B. — Fritsch 28 pass from Comp (Hutson kick)
N.Y. — Cuff 1 run (Strong kick)

'60 PHILADELPHIA 17, PACKERS 13
NFL Championship
Dec. 26 at Franklin Field, Philadelphia

Packers erected a 6-0 lead in the second period and were out in front by 13-10 in the fourth quarter before yielding to a late surge by the Eagles, who scored the deciding points on a five-yard burst by Ted Dean.

The Packers had stopped Philadelphia at its own four late in the third period, then recaptured the lead on a seven-yard TD pass from Bart Starr to Max McGee. A 58-yard return by Dean on the ensuing kickoff ignited the Eagles, however, and led to Philadelphia's winning touchdown with 5:21 remaining. Green Bay made a final, last-ditch effort, driving to the Eagles' 22. But, after catching a Starr pass, Packers fullback Jim Taylor was stopped at the 8-yard line by Chuck Bednarik as time expired.

The contest marked the first title game appearance by the Packers in 16 years and, remarkably, became the only playoff loss ever suffered by their legendary coach, Vince Lombardi.

PACKERS.......................3   3   0   7   —   13
Philadelphia ....0 10   0   7   —   17
G.B. — FG Hornung 20
G.B. — FG Hornung 23
Phil. — McDonald 35 pass from Van Brocklin (Walston kick)
Phil. — FG Walston 15
G.B. — McGee 7 pass from Starr (Hornung kick)
Phil. — Dean 5 run (Walston kick)

'61 PACKERS 37, NEW YORK 0
NFL Championship
Dec. 31 at City Stadium, Green Bay (renamed Lambeau Field in 1965)

Paul Hornung, on leave from the Army, scored a playoff record-tying 19 points to key the Packers' decimation of the Giants in the first title game ever played in Green Bay.

A record Packer home crowd of 39,029 watched the Green and Gold erupt for 24 points in the second quarter. In all, the Packers scored seven times against the NFL's top defensive team of 1961, amassing four touchdowns and three field goals. The defense, meanwhile, was proving a devastating complement to the attack, intercepting four Giant passes and recovering one fumble, while limiting New York to only six first downs and 130 total yards.

Two interceptions, by Ray Nitschke and defensive back Hank Gremminger, set up touchdowns No. 2 and 3, while the fumble recovery (by Forrest Gregg) led to Hornung's second field goal and a Jesse Whittenton interception to Hornung's final FG.

New York 0   0   0   0   —   0
PACKERS.......................0 24 10   3   — 37
G.B. — Hornung 6 run (Hornung kick)
G.B. — Dowler 13 pass from Starr (Hornung kick)
G.B. — R.Kramer 14 pass from Starr (Hornung kick)
G.B. — FG Hornung 17
G.B. — FG Hornung 22
G.B. — R.Kramer 13 pass from Starr (Hornung kick)
G.B. — FG Hornung 19

'62 PACKERS 16, NEW YORK 7
NFL Championship
Dec. 30 at Yankee Stadium, New York

Out front all the way in a raw, cyclonic setting (13-degree temperatures and 40-mile per hour winds), Packers weather siege by vengeful Giants in primitive,

hand-to-hand struggle. Ray Nitschke proves principal frustration to New Yorkers, seeking redemption for shutout humiliation in '61 title game. His deflection triggers interception to blunt early Giant drive to Green Bay 10. On way to being named game's most valuable player, he also registers two fumble recoveries, one of which led to the Packers' only touchdown of the afternoon. The other set up a 29-yard field goal by Jerry Kramer, whose trio of three-pointers provided the eventual margin.

Giants' only TD comes on block of Max McGee punt in Green Bay end zone midway through the third quarter.

A battered Jim Taylor sets playoff record with 31 rushing attempts, good for 85 yards.

PACKERS.......................3   7   3   3   —   16
New York 0   0   7   0   —   7
G.B. — FG J.Kramer 26
G.B. — Taylor 7 run (J.Kramer kick)
N.Y. — Collier blocked punt recovery in end zone (Chandler kick)
G.B. — FG J.Kramer 29
G.B. — FG J.Kramer 30

'65 PACKERS 13, BALTIMORE 10 (ot)
Western Conference Championship
Dec. 26 at Lambeau Field, Green Bay

Don Chandler's second field goal provided the winning margin for the Packers at 13:39 of sudden death overtime as Green Bay defeated Baltimore 13-10 in front of 50,484 partisans. His 25-yard kick ended the only overtime playoff game in Packer history, a contest necessitated when the two teams ended the regular season with matching 10-3-1 records.

Chandler's first field goal, a 22-yarder with 1:58 remaining in regulation to tie the game, remains controversial to this day, Baltimore loyalists claiming it was wide right. The kick sailed high above the uprights, making it difficult for game officials to determine its accuracy. Uprights were lengthened for the next season in an effort to avoid a recurrence of this situation.

The Colts, who were playing without starting quarterback Johnny Unitas (knee) and his backup, Gary Cuozzo (dislocated shoulder), used halfback Tom Matte as a fill-in. He completed only five passes, but did gain 57 yards rushing. Baltimore took a 10-0 halftime lead, scoring first 21 seconds into the game when linebacker Don Shinnick scooped up a Bill Anderson fumble and went 25 yards for a touchdown. Packers quarterback Bart Starr injured his ribs on the play, Green Bay's first from scrimmage, when he tried to get to Shinnick.

Zeke Bratkowski replaced Starr for the balance of the afternoon, completing 22 of 39 passes for 248 yards. The Packers moved to within 10-7 in the third quarter when Paul Hornung scored on a one-yard run, setting the stage for Chandler's heroics.

Baltimore................7   3   0   0   —   10
PACKERS 0   0   7   3   3   —   13
Balt. — Shinnick 25 fumble return (Michaels kick)
Balt. — FG Michaels 15
G.B. — Hornung 1 run (Chandler kick)
G.B. — FG Chandler 22
G.B. — FG Chandler 25

'65 PACKERS 23, CLEVELAND 12
NFL Championship
Jan. 2 at Lambeau Field, Green Bay

Field softened by four-inch snow made Packer backs only run harder as Lambeau Field crowd of 50,777 celebrated team's third championship in five years. Jim Taylor (27-96) and Paul Hornung (18-105) amassed 201 yards rushing in rally that overcame Browns' early 9-7 lead.

Packer defenders, meanwhile, collared Cleveland's Jim Brown, the NFL's leading rusher during the regular season with 1,544 yards, and held him to but 50 yards. The game was a see-saw battle throughout and saw kickers Don Chandler and Lou Groza boot a total of five field goals.

Bart Starr finally settled the issue in the third quarter, escorting the Packers on a 90-yard, 11-play scoring drive climaxed by Hornung's 13-yard sweep of Browns' right perimeter.

Cleveland	9	3	0	0	—	12
PACKERS	7	6	7	3	—	23

G.B. — Dale 47 pass from Starr (Chandler kick)
Clev.— Collins 17 pass from Ryan (kick failed)
Clev.— FG Groza 24
G.B. — FG Chandler 15
G.B. — FG Chandler 23
Clev.— FG Groza 28
G.B. — Hornung 13 run (Chandler kick)
G.B. — FG Chandler 29

'66 PACKERS 34, DALLAS 27
NFL Championship
Jan. 1 at Cotton Bowl, Dallas

Bart Starr has one of his finest hours, passing for four touchdowns as the Packers win their second straight title and fourth in six years. Tom Brown thwarts last-minute Cowboy bid, and the majority of 74,152 Cotton Bowl fans, with end zone interception of Don Meredith's fourth-down pass from the Green Bay 2 with 28 seconds left.

Packers mounted quick 14-0 lead on a 17-yard Starr pass to Elijah Pitts and 18-yard scoring run with a fumble recovery by rookie Jim Grabowski, but led only 21-17 at halftime following explosive Cowboy comeback. After a 32-yard Danny Villanueva field goal had cut the Packer lead to a tenuous 21-20, Starr hit Boyd Dowler and Max McGee with 16- and 28-yard scoring passes, respectively, to provide a cushion against the Cowboys' late surge.

PACKERS	14	7	7	6	—	34
Dallas	14	3	3	7	—	27

G.B. — Pitts 17 pass from Starr (Chandler kick)
G.B. — Grabowski 18 fumble return (Chandler kick)
Dal. — Reeves 3 run (Villanueva kick)
Dal. — Perkins 23 run (Villanueva kick)
G.B. — Dale 51 pass from Starr (Chandler kick)
Dal. — FG Villanueva 11
Dal. — FG Villanueva 32
G.B. — Dowler 16 pass from Starr (Chandler kick)
G.B. — McGee 28 pass from Starr (kick blocked)
Dal. — Clarke 28 pass from Meredith (Villanueva kick)

'67 PACKERS 28, LOS ANGELES 7
Western Conference Championship
Dec. 23 at County Stadium, Milwaukee

Travis Williams scored two touchdowns, on runs of 46 and two yards, and the Packers were able to weather three early turnovers as Green Bay downed the Los Angeles Rams, 28-7, in the first regularly-scheduled conference playoff in NFL history. After L.A. got on the board first via a 29-yard scoring pass from Roman Gabriel to Bernie Casey, the Packers responded with 28 unanswered points in one of the more memorable games at Milwaukee County Stadium.

Williams rushed for 88 yards on 18 total carries, while quarterback Bart Starr set a team record by completing 73.9% of his passes (17-23) for 222 yards and one touchdown. End Carroll Dale was the recipient of Starr's

scoring toss, it covering 17 yards, and finished the afternoon with six catches for 109 yards. The Packer defense sacked Gabriel five times, including three-and-a-half by tackle Henry Jordan.

The victory was Green Bay's first on a three-game run which would see the Packers defeat Dallas in the legendary "Ice Bowl" game eight days later, then top the Oakland Raiders for a second straight Super Bowl victory.

Los Angeles	7	0	0	0	—	7
PACKERS	0	14	7	7	—	28

L.A. — Casey 29 pass from Gabriel (Gossett kick)
G.B. — Williams 46 run (Chandler kick)
G.B. — Dale 17 pass from Starr (Chandler kick)
G.B. — Mercein 6 run (Chandler kick)
G.B. — Williams 2 run (Chandler kick)

'67 PACKERS 21, DALLAS 17
NFL Championship
Dec. 31 at Lambeau Field, Green Bay

With thermometer shuddering at 13 below zero and a wind chill of minus 46, Bart Starr scores winning touchdown from 1-yard line with 13 seconds remaining, sealing record third straight championship for Packers and their fifth in seven years.

Starr's touchdown, on third down with no timeouts remaining, climaxed a 68-yard drive in 12 plays which had begun with 4:50 on the clock, in front of 50,861 partisans at now legendary "Ice Bowl" game.

As was the case in 1966, Packers grabbed early 14-0 advantage. But this time Cowboys came from behind to take the lead, forcing storybook finish by Green Bay to win contest later voted the greatest game in pro football history.

Starr's touchdown passes of eight and 43 yards to Boyd Dowler built the first-quarter bulge, trimmed in the second quarter by George Andrie's seven-yard scoring return of a Starr fumble and a 21-yard Danny Villanueva field goal which also was set up by a Green Bay fumble. Dan Reeves' 50-yard scoring strike to Lance Rentzel on the first play of the fourth quarter triggered the dramatic denouement.

Dallas	0	10	0	7	—	17
PACKERS	7	7	0	7	—	21

G.B. — Dowler 8 pass from Starr (Chandler kick)
G.B. — Dowler 43 pass from Starr (Chandler kick)
Dal. — Andrie 7 fumble return (Villanueva kick)
Dal. — FG Villanueva 21
Dal. — Rentzel 50 pass from Reeves (Villanueva kick)
G.B. — Starr 1 run (Chandler kick)

'72 WASHINGTON 16, PACKERS 3
NFC Divisional Playoff
Dec. 24 at Robert F. Kennedy Stadium; Washington, D.C.

Chester Marcol's 17-yard field goal early in the second quarter puts the Packers out front, but a Bill Kilmer-to-Roy Jefferson touchdown pass late in the same period gave the Redskins a lead they never yielded. Curt Knight kicked three field goals to provide the Redskins' other points before a crowd of 53,140 fans on Sunday afternoon, December 24.

John Brockington, the Packers' 1,000-yard rusher, had to settle for nine yards on 13 carries as the Redskins used a five-man defensive line to shut down Green Bay's running game. Brockington's Washington counterpart, Larry Brown, rushed for 101 yards on 25 carries.

PACKERS	0	3	0	0	—	3
Washington	0	10	0	6	—	16

G.B. — FG Marcol 17
Wash. — Jefferson 32 pass from Kilmer (Knight kick)
Wash. — FG Knight 42
Wash. — FG Knight 35
Wash. — FG Knight 46

'82 PACKERS 41, ST. LOUIS 16
NFC First-Round Playoff
Jan. 8 at Lambeau Field, Green Bay

Making their first postseason appearance in Lambeau Field since celebrated "Ice Bowl" game of 1967 against Dallas, Packers halt Cardinal drive at 1-yard line in the first quarter, then proceed to forge an all-time club scoring record in their opening Super Bowl Tournament contest following the strike-shortened 1982 season.

Green Bay stages two long scoring drives with touchdown passes from Lynn Dickey to his wide receivers, John Jefferson and James Lofton. The Packers subsequently capitalized on a pair of St. Louis turnovers in Cardinals territory, turning each possession into points with a touchdown by Eddie Lee Ivery.

Out front 28-9 at halftime, they pad lead to 41-9 in the fourth quarter before permitting Cards a consolation touchdown. Dickey ties Packer playoff record by passing for four touchdowns (17 of 23 for 260 yards and zero intercepts overall) and Jefferson sets club postseason mark with 148 receiving yards on six catches, including a 60-yard TD reception — another Packer playoff record. Placekicker Jan Stenerud also establishes a club playoff mark with a 46-yard field goal. St. Louis quarterback Neil Lomax throws for 385 yards on 32-of-51 passing.

St. Louis	3	6	0	7 —	16
PACKERS	7	21	10	3 —	41

St.L — FG O'Donoghue 18
G.B. — Jefferson 60 pass from Dickey (Stenerud kick)
G.B. — Lofton 20 pass from Dickey (Stenerud kick)
G.B. — Ivery 2 run (Stenerud kick)
G.B. — Ivery 4 pass from Dickey (Stenerud kick)
St.L — Tilley 5 pass from Lomax (kick blocked)
G.B. — FG Stenerud 46
G.B. — Jefferson 7 pass from Dickey (Stenerud kick)
G.B. — FG Stenerud 34
St.L — Shumann 18 pass from Lomax (O'Donoghue kick)

'82 DALLAS 37, PACKERS 26
NFC Divisional Playoff
Jan. 16 at Texas Stadium; Irving, Texas

Packers amass 466 yards, a team playoff record, but are unable to overcome slow start which finds them trailing 20-7 at halftime. They roll up 363 yards and out-score Cowboys 19-17 in the second half, pulling within four points (30-26) on a 22-yard scoring runback of an interception by Mark Lee in the fourth quarter. But Cowboys retaliate with a 74-yard scoring drive to end Green Bay hopes with 63,972 fans looking on.

Quarterback Lynn Dickey throws for 332 yards (19 of 36), a Packer playoff record, in losing cause. Split end James Lofton emerges with 109 yards on five receptions. Lofton also spices Packers' second-half comeback with 71-yard reverse for a TD, tying all-time NFL playoff record for a run from scrimmage.

The Cowboys' Dennis Thurman intercepted three passes, one for a 39-yard touchdown and a final theft which sealed the victory for Dallas in the fourth quarter.

PACKERS	0	7	6	13 —	26
Dallas	6	14	3	14 —	37

Dal. — FG Septien 50
Dal. — FG Septien 34
G.B. — Lofton 6 pass from Dickey (Stenerud kick)
Dal. — Newsome 2 run (Septien kick)

Dal. — Thurman 39 interception return (Septien kick)
G.B. — FG Stenerud 30
G.B. — FG Stenerud 33
Dal. — FG Septien 24
G.B. — Lofton 71 run (kick blocked)
Dal. — Cosbie 7 pass from D.White (Septien kick)
G.B. — Lee 22 interception return (Stenerud kick)
Dal. — Newhouse 1 run (Septien kick)

'93 PACKERS 28, DETROIT 24
NFC Wild Card Playoff
Jan. 8 at Pontiac Silverdome; Pontiac, Mich.

In one of the most electrifying victories in their rich postseason history, the Packers come from behind to shade NFC Central Division champion Detroit, 28-24, at Pontiac Silverdome on a dramatic, 40-yard touchdown pass from Brett Favre to Sterling Sharpe in the final minute. Favre's decisive strike, a scrambling, across-the-body throw from extreme left to extreme right, finds Sharpe wide open in the end zone with 55 seconds remaining, capping a see-saw battle.

Earlier, rookie free safety George Teague had written himself into the NFL postseason record book with a 101-yard interception return for a touchdown, his pickoff of Lions' Erik Kramer lifting Green Bay into a 21-17 lead. Sharpe equalled a league playoff mark himself by catching three touchdown passes in the contest, among his five receptions for 101 yards.

Lions' Barry Sanders, in his first game back from a knee injury, ignites Silverdome crowd of 68,479 with 169 yards rushing.

PACKERS	0	7	14	7 —	28
Detroit	3	7	7	7 —	24

Det. — FG Hanson 47
G.B. — Sharpe 12 pass from Favre (Jacke kick)
Det. — Perriman 1 pass from Kramer (Hanson kick)
Det. — Jenkins 15 interception return (Hanson kick)
G.B. — Sharpe 28 pass from Favre (Jacke kick)
G.B. — Teague 101 interception return (Jacke kick)
Det. — D.Moore 5 run (Hanson kick)
G.B. — Sharpe 40 pass from Favre (Jacke kick)

'93 DALLAS 27, PACKERS 17
NFC Divisional Playoff
Jan. 16 at Texas Stadium; Irving, Texas

Packers grab early 3-0 lead over eventual Super Bowl champions, the points ensuing when Bill Bates' run on a fourth-down fake punt is stopped short by the Green Bay defense. Momentum swings Cowboys' way shortly, however, as Dallas mounts 17-point surge in the second quarter, eventually prevailing 27-17.

Quarterback Brett Favre passes for 331 yards (one yard shy of Packers' postseason record) and Sterling Sharpe turns in second straight 100-yard effort (six receptions for 128 yards). But Cowboys' aerial duo matches up, quarterback Troy Aikman completing 28 of 37 passes for 302 yards and three touchdowns, while wideout Michael Irvin adds nine catches for 126 yards.

PACKERS	3	0	7	7 —	17
Dallas	0	17	7	3 —	27

G.B. — FG Jacke 30
Dal. — Harper 25 pass from Aikman (Murray kick)
Dal. — FG Murray 41
Dal. — Novacek 6 pass from Aikman (Murray kick)
Dal. — Irvin 19 pass from Aikman (Murray kick)
G.B. — Brooks 13 pass from Favre (Jacke kick)
Dal. — FG Murray 38
G.B. — Sharpe 29 pass from Favre (Jacke kick)

'94 PACKERS 16, DETROIT 12
NFC Wild Card Playoff
Dec. 31 at Lambeau Field, Green Bay

Spurred by a classic, postseason record defensive performance, the Packers outlast Detroit Lions 16-12 in team's first home playoff game since 1982 season. Coordinator Fritz Shurmur's defensive charges hold the NFL's leading rusher, Barry Sanders, to a career-low -1 yard on 13 attempts and limit Lions collectively to -4 yards on the ground — erasing a 31-year-old league playoff record.

Quarterback Brett Favre directs several long drives, helping the Packers control the ball for 37-plus minutes, including a 76-yard excursion on the game's opening series, capped by a three-yard touchdown run by Dorsey Levens. Green Bay plays turnover-free football throughout, entertaining home playoff record crowd of 58,125. Chris Jacke adds three field goals to team's cause, including a Packer postseason record 51-yarder.

But Lions pull to within 13-10 in the fourth quarter on a three-yard touchdown pass from Dave Krieg to Brett Perriman and reach the Packers' 11-yard line on final drive in game's closing moments. Green Bay defense stiffens, however, recapturing the ball on downs, before Packer punter Craig Hentrich takes intentional safety to run out final seven seconds on the clock.

Detroit	0	0	3	9	— 12
PACKERS	7	3	3	3	— 16

G.B. — Levens 3 run (Jacke kick)
G.B. — FG Jacke 51
Det. — FG Hanson 38
G.B. — FG Jacke 32
Det. — Perriman 3 pass from Krieg (Hanson kick)
G.B. — FG Jacke 28
Det. — Safety, Hentrich ran out of end zone

'94 DALLAS 35, PACKERS 9
NFC Divisional Playoff
Jan. 8 at Texas Stadium; Irving, Texas

After falling behind 21-3 in the second quarter and 28-9 at halftime, the Packers find themselves unable to mount a second-half comeback, falling to Dallas in divisional playoff contest, 35-9. Green Bay is able to amass 327 yards of total offense but few points, and team's defense is victim of the Cowboys' arsenal of offensive superstars.

Trailing only 7-3 in the first quarter, the Packers pin Dallas deep in its own territory, only to have their back broken when Cowboys connect on an NFL playoff-record 94-yard touchdown pass from Troy Aikman to Alvin Harper. Aikman throws for 337 yards overall, while three different Dallas receivers — Michael Irvin (111), Harper (108) and Jay Novacek (104) — have 100-yard days. Dallas backup Blair Thomas rushes for 70 yards and two scores after replacing Emmitt Smith, who left the game in the first quarter after aggravating a hamstring injury.

Packer flanker Robert Brooks, moving into spot usually occupied by the injured Sterling Sharpe, equals his career best with eight receptions for a game-high 138 yards.

PACKERS	3	6	0	0	— 9
Dallas	14	14	0	7	— 35

Dal. — E.Smith 5 run (Boniol kick)
G.B. — FG Jacke 50
Dal. — Harper 94 pass from Aikman (Boniol kick)
Dal. — B.Thomas 1 run (Boniol kick)
G.B. — Bennett 1 run (pass failed)
Dal. — Galbraith 1 pass from Aikman (Boniol kick)
Dal. — B.Thomas 2 run (Boniol kick)

'95 PACKERS 37, ATLANTA 20
NFC Wild Card Playoff
Dec. 31 at Lambeau Field, Green Bay

Utilizing a balanced offensive attack, including a Packer postseason record 108 yards on the ground from Edgar Bennett, Green Bay toppled the Atlanta Falcons 37-20 on a foggy, 30-degree afternoon. The Packers had earned an opening round home playoff game for the second straight season, this time by virtue of winning their first outright NFC Central crown in 23 years.

After a 65-yard touchdown pass from Jeff George to Eric Metcalf three minutes into the game gave Atlanta a 7-0 lead and stunned the home playoff record crowd of 60,453, the Packers quickly regained control, scoring two first-quarter touchdowns to seize a 14-7 lead. Following a Falcons field goal which narrowed the gap to four, Green Bay broke the game open midway through the second period when rookie Antonio Freeman returned a punt 76 yards for a touchdown — the first scoring return of a punt or kickoff in club postseason history. Mark Chmura's two-yard touchdown catch from Brett Favre with less than a minute remaining before halftime, capping a 14-play, 85-yard drive, gave the Packers a commanding 27-10 advantage as the teams headed into the locker room.

Green Bay matched the Falcons score for score in the second half, Favre's third TD toss of the day — a beautiful, lofting throw to fullback Dorsey Levens with just under eight minutes to play — cementing the issue. Favre completed passes to nine different Packer receivers in the contest, while Bennett averaged 4.5 yards and scored once on 24 rushing attempts. George threw for 366 yards and two touchdowns for Atlanta on 30-of-54 passing, while Metcalf caught eight balls for 114 yards.

Atlanta	7	3	0	10	— 20
PACKERS	14	13	0	10	— 37

Atl. — Metcalf 65 pass from J.George (Andersen kick)
G.B. — Bennett 8 run (Jacke kick)
G.B. — R.Brooks 14 pass from Favre (Jacke kick)
Atl. — FG Andersen 31
G.B. — Freeman 76 punt return (bad snap)
G.B. — Chmura 2 pass from Favre (Jacke kick)
Atl. — Birden 27 pass from J.George (Andersen kick)
G.B. — Levens 18 pass from Favre (Jacke kick)
Atl. — FG Andersen 22
G.B. — FG Jacke 25

'95 PACKERS 27, SAN FRANCISCO 17
NFC Divisional Playoff
Jan. 6 at 3Com Park, San Francisco

Physically menacing the 49er offense throughout the day, Green Bay pulled off a shocking upset of defending Super Bowl champion San Francisco in its home stadium, 27-17, and advanced to the NFC Championship Game for the first time since the 1970 league merger. The victory was especially sweet for Packers head coach Mike Holmgren, a native San Franciscan who, for the first time, was opposing the team with which he had gotten his NFL start.

After an opening drive by the Packers which had reached the 49ers' 26-yard line only to end in a blocked field goal, Green Bay's defense immediately set the tone for the rest of the game. On San Francisco's first play from scrimmage, linebacker Wayne Simmons drilled Niners fullback Adam Walker, the recipient of a screen pass in the right flat, Walker fumbling and the ball being scooped up by rookie cornerback Craig Newsome, who ran 31 yards into the end zone for a 7-0 lead. The Packers subsequently mounted 62- and 72-yard scoring drives on their next two possessions, Brett Favre throwing touchdown passes to Keith Jackson and Mark Chmura respectively, to assume an authoritative 21-0 advantage four minutes into the second quarter.

Favre, the league MVP during the regular season, played like, well, the league MVP, completing a club playoff record 75.0% of his passes (21-28) in the win. Jackson, who had two long receptions over the middle to help set up Green Bay scores, caught four passes for 101 yards, while flanker Robert Brooks also had over 100 yards receiving (103) on an identical number of catches.

The 49ers did close to within 21-10 midway through the third quarter before Packers kicker Chris Jacke booted two important field goals to stretch the Green Bay lead back to 17 points. San Francisco later added a meaningless touchdown in the game's last minute for the final margin.

The Packer defense, which forced four turnovers, battered 49ers quarterback Steve Young all afternoon, sacking him three times and knocking him down on countless other occasions as he attempted an NFL playoff record 65 passes in a futile comeback bid. Jerry Rice, San Francisco's receiver nonpareil, while making 11 receptions was limited to virtually no yards after the catch.

PACKERS........................14   7   3   3   —   27
San Francisco................0   3   7   7   —   17

G.B. — Newsome 31 fumble return (Jacke kick)
G.B. — Jackson 3 pass from Favre (Jacke kick)
G.B. — Chmura 13 pass from Favre (Jacke kick)
S.F. — FG Wilkins 21
S.F. — Young 1 run (Wilkins kick)
G.B. — FG Jacke 27
G.B. — FG Jacke 26
S.F. — Loville 2 run (Wilkins kick)

'95 DALLAS 38, PACKERS 27
NFC Championship
Jan. 14 at Texas Stadium; Irving, Texas

Packers, one victory away from their first Super Bowl appearance in 28 years, hold lead into the fourth quarter before finally succumbing to offensive firepower of eventual Super Bowl champion Dallas, 38-27. Emmitt Smith, behind Cowboys' massive offensive line, rushes for 150 yards and three touchdowns on 35 carries as Green Bay sees its season end at Texas Stadium for the third straight year.

After a blocked punt leads to a quick field goal by the Packers, Dallas comes back, quarterback Troy Aikman throwing two TD passes to Michael Irvin. Green Bay answers, however, with two quick scores of its own — a team postseason record 73-yard pass from Brett Favre to Robert Brooks as well as a Favre-to-Keith Jackson connection — to vault into the lead, 17-14. Cowboys score another 10 points before halftime, though, to go up 24-17.

Green Bay gets first 10 points of the second half, including a one-yard touchdown pass from Favre to Brooks, to hold a 27-24 advantage heading into the final 15 minutes. Smith's talents glisten in the fourth quarter, however, as he rushes for two touchdowns — sandwiched around a drive-killing interception by the Cowboys' Larry Brown in Dallas territory — to give Texans their third Super Bowl appearance in four years.

PACKERS........................10   7   10   0   —   27
Dallas 14   10   0   14   —   38

G.B. — FG Jacke 46
Dal. — Irvin 6 pass from Aikman (Boniol kick)
Dal. — Irvin 4 pass from Aikman (Boniol kick)
G.B. — R.Brooks 73 pass from Favre (Jacke kick)

G.B. — Jackson 24 pass from Favre (Jacke kick)
Dal. — FG Boniol 34
Dal. — E.Smith 1 run (Boniol kick)
G.B. — FG Jacke 37
G.B. — R.Brooks 1 pass from Favre (Jacke kick)
Dal. — E.Smith 5 run (Boniol kick)
Dal. — E.Smith 16 run (Boniol kick)

'96 PACKERS 35, SAN FRANCISCO 14
NFC Divisional Playoff
Jan. 4 at Lambeau Field, Green Bay

Jump-started by their special teams, specifically two punt returns by Desmond Howard, the Green Bay Packers took the first step toward an eventual berth in Super Bowl XXXI by knocking the San Francisco 49ers out of the playoffs for the second straight year. With rain having fallen since early morning on a cold and dreary day, the playing field offered less-than-ideal footing throughout the contest and deteriorated into a quagmire by game's end. Despite the weather, 60,787 spectators (three no-shows) still showed up.

After the 49ers went three-and-out on their opening possession, Howard caught Tommy Thompson's punt at his own 29 and weaved his way through several San Francisco defenders for a 71-yard touchdown just 2:15 into the game. Midway through the first quarter, Howard broke free on a second punt return, traveling 46 yards before he was tripped up by his heel only seven yards from the end zone. Moments later, Brett Favre hit Andre Rison with a four-yard touchdown pass to give Green Bay a 14-0 advantage.

The Packers extended their lead to 21-0 before two special teams miscues by Green Bay turned into 14 points for the Niners and brought the game back to within reach. First, a San Francisco punt bounced off the leg of the Packers' Chris Hayes to give the 49ers possession at the Green Bay 26-yard line, leading to a Terry Kirby touchdown seven plays later. Then, when the Packers failed to field a short kickoff to open the second half, San Francisco recovered at the Green Bay 4, and, on the next play, quarterback Elvis Grbac ran around left end on a naked bootleg for another score.

To their credit, the Packers stormed right back on their next possession, going 72 yards in 12 plays, a drive capped off by Antonio Freeman's fumble recovery in the end zone after Edgar Bennett fumbled just shy of the goal line.

Neither team gained many yards in the sloppy conditions. Green Bay racked up only 210 yards, including a club postseason low 71 yards passing. Bennett was the Packers' workhorse, running for 80 yards and two touchdowns on 17 carries. San Francisco, which lost usual starting quarterback Steve Young after two series when he could not function effectively due to two broken ribs suffered one week earlier, gained only 196 yards itself.

San Francisco................0   7   7   0   —   14
PACKERS........................14   7   7   7   —   35

G.B. — Howard 71 punt return (Jacke kick)
G.B. — Rison 4 pass from Favre (Jacke kick)
G.B. — Bennett 2 run (Jacke kick)
S.F. — Kirby 8 pass from Grbac (Wilkins kick)
S.F. — Grbac 4 run (Wilkins kick)
G.B. — Freeman fumble recovery in end zone (Jacke kick)
G.B. — Bennett 11 run (Jacke kick)

'96 PACKERS 30, CAROLINA 13
NFC Championship
Jan. 12 at Lambeau Field, Green Bay

After twice falling behind early due to turnovers, the Packers rebounded to defeat the upstart Carolina

Panthers and win their first trip to the Super Bowl in 29 years, largely on the strength of a 205-yard performance by Dorsey Levens. It was the first title game played in Green Bay since the legendary "Ice Bowl" in 1967.

Panthers linebacker Sam Mills intercepted a Brett Favre pass deep in Green Bay territory not quite 10 minutes into the game, which quickly led to a three-yard touchdown toss from Kerry Collins to fullback Howard Griffith. Levens out-jumped Carolina cornerback Eric Davis at the right edge of the end zone for a 29-yard touchdown catch on the first snap of the second quarter to even the score, only one play after he had rushed for 35 yards on a third-and-one situation.

Carolina took advantage of a Favre fumble near midfield to add a John Kasay field goal, but the Packers stormed back to score 10 points in the final minute of the first half. Favre connected with Antonio Freeman for a touchdown on a six-yard fade pattern with 48 seconds remaining, capping a 15-play, 71-yard drive. When the Panthers then attempted to move down field, Green Bay rookie cornerback Tyrone Williams made a diving interception of Collins at the Packers' 38-yard line, which four plays later eventuated into a 31-yard Chris Jacke field goal with 10 seconds remaining before halftime.

The teams traded field goals in the second half before the Packers' Edgar Bennett strolled through the middle of the line untouched on a four-yard touchdown run late in the third quarter to somewhat cement the issue at 27-13. Bennett's score was set up by a 66-yard catch-and-run along the right sideline by Levens on a perfectly-executed screen pass one play earlier.

Green Bay put up 479 net yards, an all-time team playoff record. Spearheading the attack was a ground game which churned out 201 yards, 99 yards on 25 carries by Bennett and 88 yards on only 10 attempts by Levens. Levens also made five receptions for 117 yards. Favre completed 19 of 29 passes for 292 yards.

While the weather certainly was cold — 3 degrees with a wind chill of -17 — the storyline heading into the game was the field itself, ravaged the previous week against San Francisco when rainy conditions turned it into a mud pit. The contest was played on an all-new grass field, put into place in the days prior to the game with sod trucked in from Maryland on better than two dozen semis.

The George S. Halas Trophy, symbolic of the National Football Conference Championship, was presented to Packers President Bob Harlan, General Manager Ron Wolf and Head Coach Mike Holmgren in an on-field ceremony immediately following the game.

Carolina	7	3	3	0	— 13
PACKERS	0	17	10	3	— 30

Car. — Griffith 3 pass from Collins (Kasay kick)
G.B. — Levens 29 pass from Favre (Jacke kick)
Car. — FG Kasay 22
G.B. — Freeman 6 pass from Favre (Jacke kick)
G.B. — FG Jacke 31
G.B. — FG Jacke 32
Car. — FG Kasay 23
G.B. — Bennett 4 run (Jacke kick)
G.B. — FG Jacke 28

'97 PACKERS 21, TAMPA BAY 7
NFC Divisional Playoff
Jan. 4 at Lambeau Field, Green Bay

In a hard-fought, defensive struggle — much like the two earlier meetings of the divisional foes — the Packers used their offensive superiority to overwhelm Tampa Bay on a gray afternoon. A record-breaking

rushing performance by Dorsey Levens helped Green Bay to maintain control of the contest.

The Buccaneers, making their first appearance in the playoffs since the 1982 season, squandered three first-half opportunities for a field goal. On the first, the Packers' Bob Kuberski surged up the middle to block Micheal Husted's 43-yard effort. Keith McKenzie stuffed Tampa Bay's attempt at a fake field goal for no gain the second time around, then the Bucs' long snapper, Dave Moore, sailed the ball over his holder's head on the third.

Green Bay moved 67 yards down the field for its first score, a short touchdown pass to Mark Chmura from Brett Favre, following the initial Buccaneers failed field goal attempt. The Packers then got two field goals from rookie kicker Ryan Longwell just before halftime, the second resulting after a Tyrone Williams interception in Tampa Bay territory.

A Favre interception on Green Bay's first possession of the second half eventuated in the Buccaneers' lone points, a six-yard run by fullback Mike Alstott to culminate a 94-yard drive by the Floridians. But the Packers were able to keep the upstart Bucs at arm's length, Levens punching in a short touchdown run early in the fourth quarter and Favre following that up with a successful two-point conversion on a quarterback draw.

Levens finished the day with a team playoff record 112 yards rushing, including 88 in the second half. Favre, meanwhile, was being harassed by the Tampa Bay defense, particularly defensive tackle Warren Sapp, who had three sacks and forced two fumbles. The two combatants openly jawed throughout the contest in an intriguing side show.

Tampa Bay	0	0	7	0	— 7
PACKERS	7	6	0	8	— 21

G.B. — Chmura 3 pass from Favre (Longwell kick)
G.B. — FG Longwell 21
G.B. — FG Longwell 32
T.B. — Alstott 6 run (Husted kick)
G.B. — Levens 2 run (Favre run)

'97 PACKERS 23, SAN FRANCISCO 10
NFC Championship
Jan. 11 at 3Com Park, San Francisco

Green Bay, making its third straight appearance in the NFC Championship Game, never allowed the 49ers' offense to get started and advanced to play in the Super Bowl for the second year in a row. In the process, the Packers dispatched San Francisco from the playoffs for the third consecutive season, the second time in the Niners' home park.

From the outset of the rain-swept afternoon, the Packers were able to pick on San Francisco's cornerbacks, moving 76 yards downfield on their opening possession, though the drive was stalled and Green Bay was forced to settle for a short Ryan Longwell field goal.

San Francisco managed a drive to the Packers' 28-yard line early in the second quarter, but it was snuffed out when free safety Eugene Robinson stepped in front of a Steve Young pass intended for Brent Jones. Robinson, weaving across the field, returned 58 yards to the 49ers' 28. Two plays later, Antonio Freeman caught a short slant from Brett Favre, cut back against the grain, breaking several tackles in the process, for a 27-yard touchdown grab and a 10-0 Green Bay lead.

The 49ers put together another long drive late in the opening half, but had to settle for a field goal when three straight passes from the Green Bay 10-yard line fell incomplete. The Packers, after showing little desire to mount a scoring drive in the final minute before halftime, connected on a 40-yard bomb from Favre to Freeman in the waning seconds to set up a successful 43-yard field goal try from Longwell against a difficult wind on the final play before the teams headed to the locker room.

Longwell, who had attended nearby Cal just one season earlier and had been released by the 49ers just before training camp, added his third field goal of the game midway through the fourth quarter, giving Green Bay a more comfortable 13-point lead.

The Packers' defense, which held San Francisco to just 33 yards rushing on 18 carries over the course of the day, went into the attack mode on Young in the fourth quarter, sacking him four times, including two by Keith McKenzie. When Young was sacked on fourth down at his own 11-yard line with just under four minutes remaining, Green Bay quickly took advantage, moving into the end zone on two Dorsey Levens runs.

Levens established a club playoff rushing mark for the second week in a row, churning out 114 yards — the first 100-yard rushing day allowed by the 49ers during the '97 season — and again did much of his work in the second half. Freeman totaled 107 yards receiving on four catches, and punter Craig Hentrich helped Green Bay to handily win the field position battle by depositing all five of his punts inside the 49ers' 20.

The Niners' Chuck Levy returned the kickoff following Levens' score 95 yards for San Francisco's lone touchdown of the day, though it proved to be of little significance as only 2:52 showed on the clock.

With only a smattering of Green Bay fans remaining in the stands, the George S. Halas Trophy, representative of the National Football Conference Championship, was handed over to the rain-soaked trio of Packers President Bob Harlan, General Manager Ron Wolf and Head Coach Mike Holmgren in a presentation on the field.

PACKERS..........................3 10   0 10 — 23
San Francisco.................0   3   0   7 — 10
G.B. — FG Longwell 19
G.B. — Freeman 27 pass from Favre (Longwell kick)
S.F. — FG Anderson 28
G.B. — FG Longwell 43
G.B. — FG Longwell 25
G.B. — Levens 5 run (Longwell kick)
S.F. — Levy 95 kickoff return (Anderson kick)

DON HUTSON'S PASS RECEIVING

Most Passes Caught
74-one season
14-one game

Most Touchdown Passes
99-eleven seasons
17-one season
4-one game

Most Yards Gained Catching Passes
7,991-eleven seasons
1,211-one season
237-one game

Longest Completed Pass
92 yards

Shortest Completed Pass
4 inches

Total Points Scored
823-eleven seasons
138-one season
31-one game

Total Touchdowns Scored
105

Most Touchdowns
17-one season
4-one game

Most Points After Touchdown
172-eleven seasons
7-one game

HUTSON'S YEAR-BY-YEAR STATISTICS

	Games	Rec.	Yards	LG	TD		Games	Rec.	Yards	LG	TD
1935	10	18	420	83	6	1941	11	58	738	45	10
1936	12	34	536	87	9	1942	11	74	1211	73	17
1937	11	41	552	78	7	1943	10	47	776	79	11
1938	10	32	548	54	9	1944	10	58	866	55	9
1939	11	34	846	92	6	1945	10	47	834	75	9
1940	11	45	664	36	7	Totals	117	488	7991	92	99

RUSHING

Most Attempts (career)
63, Edgar Bennett (10 games)
46, Jim Taylor (7 games)
15, Dorsey Levens (11 games)

Most Attempts (game)
31, Jim Taylor, at New York Giants, Dec. 30, 1962
27, Jim Taylor, vs. Cleveland, Jan. 2, 1966
27, Dorsey Levens, at San Francisco, Jan. 11, 1998
25, Edgar Bennett, vs. Carolina, Jan. 12, 1997
25, Dorsey Levens, vs. Tampa Bay, Jan. 4, 1998

Most Yards Gained (career)
561, Edgar Bennett (10 games)
524, Dorsey Levens (11 games)
508, Jim Taylor (7 games)

Most Yards Gained (game)
114, Dorsey Levens, at San Francisco, Jan. 11, 1998 (27 attempts)
112, Dorsey Levens, vs. Tampa Bay, Jan. 4, 1998 (25 attempts)
108, Edgar Bennett, vs. Atlanta, Dec. 31, 1995 (24 attempts)
105, Jim Taylor, at Philadelphia, Dec. 26, 1960 (24 attempts)
105, Paul Hornung, vs. Cleveland, Jan. 2, 1966 (18 attempts)

Longest Runs From Scrimmage
71, James Lofton, at Dallas, Dec. 16, 1983 (touchdown)
46, Travis Williams, vs. Los Angeles Rams, Dec. 23, 1967
(touchdown)
35, Max McGee, at Philadelphia, Dec. 26, 1960
35, Dorsey Levens, vs. Carolina, Jan. 12, 1997

Most Games, 100 or More Yards Rushing (career)
2, Dorsey Levens (11 games)
1, Jim Taylor (7 games)
1, Paul Hornung (5 games)
1, Edgar Bennett (7 games)

Most Consecutive Games, 100 or More Yards Rushing
2, Dorsey Levens (1997)
1, three times

Most Touchdowns (career)
5, Edgar Bennett (10 games)
3, Paul Hornung (5 games)
3, Dorsey Levens (11 games)
2, Clarke Hinkle (4 games)
2, Elijah Pitts (6 games)
2, Jim Taylor (7 games)
2, Travis Williams (3 games)

Most Touchdowns (game)
2, Elijah Pitts, vs. Kansas City, Jan. 15, 1967
2, Travis Williams, vs. Los Angeles Rams, Dec. 23, 1967
2, Edgar Bennett, vs. San Francisco, Jan. 4, 1997

Most Consecutive Games, Rushing Touchdowns
2, Paul Hornung (1965)
2, Edgar Bennett (1994-95)
2, Edgar Bennett (1996)
2, Dorsey Levens (1997)

FORWARD PASSING

Most Passes Completed (career)
250, Brett Favre (13 games)
130, Bart Starr (10 games)
36, Lynn Dickey (2 games)

Most Passes Completed (game)
28, Brett Favre, at Dallas, Jan. 16, 1994
25, Brett Favre, vs. Denver, Jan. 25, 1998
24, Brett Favre, vs. Atlanta, Dec. 31, 1995

Most Passes Attempted (career)
414, Brett Favre (13 games)
213, Bart Starr (10 games)
59, Lynn Dickey (2 games)

Most Passes Attempted (game)
45, Brett Favre, at Dallas, Jan. 16, 1994
42, Brett Favre, vs. Denver, Jan. 25, 1998
39, Brett Favre, at Dallas, Jan. 14, 1996

Most Yards Gained on Passes (career)
3,098, Brett Favre (13 games)
1,753, Bart Starr (10 games)
592, Lynn Dickey (2 games)

Most Yards Gained on Passes (game)
332, Lynn Dickey, at Dallas, Jan. 16, 1983
331, Brett Favre, at Dallas, Jan. 16, 1994
307, Brett Favre, at Dallas, Jan. 14, 1996

Most Games, 300 Yards Passing (career)
2, Brett Favre (13 games)
1, Bart Starr (10 games)
1, Lynn Dickey (2 games)

Most Consecutive Games, 300 Yards Passing
1, four times

Most Touchdown Passes (career)
23, Brett Favre (13 games)
15, Bart Starr (10 games)
5, Lynn Dickey (2 games)

Most Touchdown Passes (game)
4, Bart Starr, at Dallas, Jan. 1, 1967
4, Lynn Dickey, vs. St. Louis, Jan. 8, 1983
3, Bart Starr, vs. New York Giants, Dec. 31, 1961
3, Brett Favre, at Detroit, Jan. 8, 1994
3, Brett Favre, vs. Atlanta, Dec. 31, 1995
3, Brett Favre, at Dallas, Jan. 14, 1996
3, Brett Favre, vs. Denver, Jan. 25, 1998
2, seven times

Most Consecutive Games, Throwing Touchdown Pass
9, Brett Favre (1995-97) (current)
6, Bart Starr (1965-67)
3, Arnie Herber (1936, 1938-39)
2, Cecil Isbell (1939, 1941)
2, Bart Starr (1960-61)
2, Lynn Dickey (1983)
2, Brett Favre (1993)

Most Passes Intercepted (career)
10, Brett Favre (13 games)
4, Arnie Herber (3 games)
3, Irv Comp (1 game)
3, Bart Starr (10 games)
3, Lynn Dickey (2 games)

Most Passes Intercepted (game)
3, Arnie Herber, vs. New York Giants, Dec. 10, 1939
3, Irv Comp, at New York Giants, Dec. 17, 1944
3, Lynn Dickey, at Dallas, Jan. 8, 1983
2, Zeke Bratkowski, vs. Baltimore, Dec. 26, 1965
2, Brett Favre, at Dallas, Jan. 16, 1994
2, Brett Favre, at Dallas, Jan. 14, 1996
2, Brett Favre, vs. Tampa Bay, Jan. 4, 1998

Longest Completed Passes
#81, Brett Favre to Antonio Freeman, vs. New England, Jan. 26,
1997 (touchdown)
73, Brett Favre to Robert Brooks, at Dallas, Jan. 14, 1996
(touchdown)
66, Cecil Isbell to Wayland Becker, at New York Giants,
Dec. 11, 1938
66, Brett Favre to Dorsey Levens, vs. Carolina, Jan. 12, 1997
62, Bart Starr to Boyd Dowler, vs. Oakland, Jan. 14, 1968
(touchdown)
60, Lynn Dickey to John Jefferson, vs. St. Louis, Jan. 8, 1983
(touchdown)

Best Passing Efficiency (career - minimum 50 attempts)
61.03%, Bart Starr (130-213)
61.02%, Lynn Dickey (36-59)
60.39%, Brett Favre (250-414)

Best Passing Efficiency (game - minimum 20 attempts)
75.00%, Brett Favre, at San Francisco, Jan. 6, 1996 (21-28)
73.91%, Bart Starr, vs. Los Angeles Rams, Dec. 23, 1967
(17-23)
73.91%, Lynn Dickey, vs. St. Louis, Jan. 8, 1983 (17-23)
69.57%, Bart Starr, vs. Kansas City, Jan. 15, 1967 (16-23)

PASS RECEIVING

Most Passes Caught (career)
43, Robert Brooks (10 games)
32, Dorsey Levens (11 games)
31, Edgar Bennett (10 games)
30, Boyd Dowler (10 games)
30, Antonio Freeman (9 games)

Most Passes Caught (game)
9, Edgar Bennett, at Dallas, Jan. 16, 1994
9, Antonio Freeman, vs. Denver, Jan. 25, 1998
8, Bill Anderson, vs. Baltimore, Dec. 26, 1965
8, Robert Brooks, at Dallas, Jan. 8, 1995
7, Max McGee, vs. Kansas City, Jan. 15, 1967
7, Robert Brooks, vs. Detroit, Dec. 31, 1994
7, Robert Brooks, vs. Atlanta, Dec. 31, 1995

Most Consecutive Games, One or More Pass Receptions
10, Robert Brooks (1993-95, 1997) (current)
10, Dorsey Levens (1994-97) (current)
9, Antonio Freeman (1995-97) (current)
8, Carroll Dale (1965-72)
6, Boyd Dowler (1960-66)
6, Keith Jackson (1995-96)

Most Yards Catching Passes (career)
620, Robert Brooks (10 games)
534, Carroll Dale (8 games)
525, Antonio Freeman (9 games)

Most Yards Catching Passes (game)
148, John Jefferson, vs. St. Louis, Jan. 8, 1983
138, Max McGee, vs. Kansas City, Jan. 15, 1967
138, Robert Brooks, at Dallas, Jan. 8, 1995
128, Carroll Dale, at Dallas, Jan. 1, 1967
128, Sterling Sharpe, at Dallas, Jan. 16, 1994

Most Games, 100 or More Yards Pass Receiving (career)
3, Robert Brooks (10 games)
3, Antonio Freeman (9 games)
2, Carroll Dale (8 games)
2, Sterling Sharpe (2 games)

Most Consecutive Games, 100 or More Yards Pass Receiving
2, Sterling Sharpe (1993)
2, Robert Brooks (1995)
2, Antonio Freeman (1997) (current)

Most Touchdown Passes Received (career)
5, Boyd Dowler (10 games)
5, Antonio Freeman (9 games)
4, Max McGee (7 games)
4, Sterling Sharpe (2 games)
4, Robert Brooks (10 games)
4, Mark Chmura (13 games)
3, Carroll Dale (8 games)

Most Touchdown Passes Received (game)
**3, Sterling Sharpe, at Detroit, Jan. 8, 1994
2, Ron Kramer, at Philadelphia, Dec. 26, 1960
2, Max McGee, vs. Kansas City, Jan. 15, 1967
2, Boyd Dowler, vs. Dallas, Dec. 31, 1967
2, John Jefferson, vs. St. Louis, Jan. 8, 1983
2, Robert Brooks, at Dallas, Jan. 14, 1996
2, Antonio Freeman, vs. Denver, Jan. 25, 1998

Most Consecutive Games, Touchdown Pass Received
2, Carroll Dale (1965-66)
2, Max McGee (1966)
2, Boyd Dowler (1967)
2, James Lofton (1982)
2, Sterling Sharpe (1993)
2, Mark Chmura (1995)
2, Keith Jackson (1995)
2, Antonio Freeman (1996)
2, Antonio Freeman (1997) (current)

INTERCEPTIONS BY

Most Interceptions (career)
4, Herb Adderley (9 games)
4, Craig Newsome (6 games)
4, Eugene Robinson (6 games)
3, Joe Laws (4 games)
3, Mike Prior (13 games)
2, by seven players

Most Interceptions (game)
3, Joe Laws, at New York Giants, Dec. 17, 1944
2, Charley Brock, vs. New York Giants, Dec. 10, 1939
2, Eugene Robinson, vs. San Francisco, Jan. 4, 1997

Most Consecutive Games, One Interception
**3, Craig Newsome (1996) (current)
2, Herb Adderley (1967)
2, Terrell Buckley (1993)
2, Eugene Robinson (1997)

Longest Interception Returns
*101, George Teague, at Detroit, Jan. 8, 1994 (touchdown)
60, Herb Adderley, vs. Oakland, Jan. 14, 1968 (touchdown)
58, Eugene Robinson, at San Francisco, Jan. 11, 1998
50, Willie Wood, vs. Kansas City, Jan. 15, 1967

SCORING

Most Points (career)
73, Chris Jacke (15 field goals, 28 extra points) (10 games)
49, Don Chandler (9 field goals, 22 extra points) (7 games)
42, Antonio Freeman (7 touchdowns) (9 games)

Most Points (game)
19, Paul Hornung, vs. New York Giants, Dec. 31, 1961
(1 touchdown, 3 field goals, 4 extra points)
18, Sterling Sharpe, at Detroit, Jan. 8, 1994
(3 touchdowns)
15, Don Chandler, vs. Oakland, Jan. 14, 1968 (4 field goals,
3 extra points)

Most Consecutive Games, Scoring One or More Points
10, Chris Jacke (1993-96)
7, Don Chandler (1965-67)
3, Antonio Freeman (1996)
3, Ryan Longwell (1997) (current)

Most Touchdowns (career)
7, Antonio Freeman (9 games)
5, Boyd Dowler (10 games)
5, Edgar Bennett (10 games)
5, Dorsey Levens (11 games)
4, Max McGee (7 games)
4, Sterling Sharpe (2 games)
4, Robert Brooks (7 games)
4, Mark Chmura (13 games)

Most Touchdowns (game)
3, Sterling Sharpe, at Detroit, Jan. 8, 1994

Most Consecutive Games, Scoring Touchdown
3, Antonio Freeman (1996)
2, 13 times

Most Field Goals Attempted (career)
22, Chris Jacke (10 games)
12, Don Chandler (7 games)
7, Ryan Longwell (3 games)

Most Field Goals Attempted (game)
5, Jerry Kramer, at New York Giants, Dec. 30, 1962
4, Don Chandler, vs. Oakland, Jan. 14, 1968
4, Chris Jacke, vs. Detroit, Dec. 31,1994
4, Chris Jacke, vs. Carolina, Jan. 12, 1997
4, Ryan Longwell, at San Francisco, Jan. 11, 1998
3, six times

Most Field Goals Made (career)
15, Chris Jacke (10 games)
9, Don Chandler (7 games)
6, Ryan Longwell (3 games)

Most Field Goals Made (game)
##4, Don Chandler, vs. Oakland, Jan. 14, 1968
3, Paul Hornung, vs. New York Giants, Dec. 31, 1961
3, Jerry Kramer, at New York Giants, Dec. 30, 1962
3, Don Chandler, vs. Cleveland, Jan. 2, 1966
3, Chris Jacke, vs. Detroit, Dec. 31, 1994
3, Chris Jacke, vs. Carolina, Jan. 12, 1997
3, Ryan Longwell, at San Francisco, Jan. 11, 1998

Most Consecutive Field Goals Made
5, Don Chandler (1965)
5, Chris Jacke (1996)
4, Don Chandler (1967)
4, Jan Stenerud (1982)
4, Chris Jacke (1994)
4, Chris Jacke (1995)
3, Paul Hornung (1960)
3, Ryan Longwell (1997)
3, Ryan Longwell (1997) (current)

Longest Field Goals
51 yards, Chris Jacke, vs. Detroit, Dec. 31, 1994
50 yards, Chris Jacke, at Dallas, Jan. 8, 1995
46 yards, Jan Stenerud, vs. St. Louis, Jan. 8, 1983
46 yards, Chris Jacke, at Dallas, Jan. 14, 1996

Most (One-Point) Points After Touchdown (career)
28, Chris Jacke (10 games)
22, Don Chandler (7 games)
7, Jan Stenerud (2 games)

Most (One-Point) Points After Touchdown (game)
5, Don Chandler, vs. Kansas City, Jan. 15, 1967
5, Jan Stenerud, vs. St. Louis, Jan. 8, 1983
5, Chris Jacke, vs. San Francisco, Jan. 4, 1997
4, Paul Hornung, vs. New York Giants, Dec. 31, 1961
4, Don Chandler, at Dallas, Jan. 1, 1967
4, Don Chandler, vs. Los Angeles Rams, Dec. 23, 1967
4, Chris Jacke, at Detroit, Jan. 8, 1994
4, Chris Jacke, vs. Atlanta, Dec. 31, 1995

Safeties
none

KICKOFF RETURNS

Most Kickoff Returns (career)
20, Antonio Freeman (9 games)
11, Corey Harris (4 games)
9, Del Rodgers (2 games)
9, Desmond Howard (3 games)

Most Kickoff Returns (game)
7, Del Rodgers, at Dallas, Jan. 16, 1983
7, Antonio Freeman, at Dallas, Jan. 14, 1996
6, Antonio Freeman, vs. Denver, Jan. 25, 1998
5, Corey Harris, at Dallas, Jan. 8, 1995

Most Yards Gained on Kickoff Returns (career)
413, Antonio Freeman (9 games)
277, Desmond Howard (3 games)
253, Corey Harris (4 games)

Most Yards Gained on Kickoff Returns (game)
154, Desmond Howard, vs. New England, Jan. 26, 1997
148, Antonio Freeman, at Dallas, Jan. 14, 1996
132, Corey Harris, at Dallas, Jan. 8, 1995

Highest Kickoff Return Average (career - 10 returns)
23.0, Corey Harris (11-253) (4 games)
20.7, Antonio Freeman (20-413) (9 games)

Highest Kickoff Return Average (game - 3 returns)
38.5, Desmond Howard, vs. New England, Jan. 26, 1997 (4-154)
29.7, Corey Harris, at Detroit, Jan. 8, 1994 (3-89)
26.4, Corey Harris, at Dallas, Jan. 8, 1995 (5-132)

Longest Kickoff Returns
*#99, Desmond Howard, vs. New England, Jan. 26, 1997 (touchdown)
51, Corey Harris, at Dallas, Jan. 8, 1995
49, Desmond Howard, vs. Carolina, Jan. 12, 1997

PUNTING

Most Punts (game)
8, Donny Anderson, at Dallas, Dec. 31, 1967
8, Ron Widby, at Washington, Dec. 24, 1972
7, Craig Hentrich, vs. New England, Jan. 26, 1997
6, Max McGee, at New York Giants, Dec. 30, 1962
6, Donny Anderson, vs. Oakland, Jan. 14, 1968
6, Craig Hentrich, vs. San Francisco, Jan. 4, 1997

Best Punting Average (game - 4 punts)
45.2 yards, Max McGee, at Philadelphia, Dec. 26, 1960
44.0 yards, Craig Hentrich, at Dallas, Jan. 8, 1995
43.2 yards, Craig Hentrich, vs. San Francisco, Jan. 4, 1997

Longest Punts
64 yards, Boyd Dowler, vs. New York Giants, Dec. 31, 1961
63 yards, Craig Hentrich, vs. San Francisco, Jan. 4, 1997
62 yards, Craig Hentrich, at Dallas, Jan. 8, 1995

PUNT RETURNS

Most Punt Returns (career)
19, Willie Wood (10 games) (##6 in 2 Super Bowls)
14, Robert Brooks (10 games)
10, Antonio Freeman (9 games)
9, Desmond Howard (3 games) (##6 in 1 Super Bowl)

Most Punt Returns (game)
##6, Desmond Howard, vs. New England, Jan. 26, 1997
5, Willie Wood, vs. Oakland, Jan. 14, 1968
4, Irv Comp, at New York Giants, Dec. 17, 1944
4, Willie Wood, vs. Dallas, Dec. 31, 1961
4, Antonio Freeman, at Dallas, Jan. 14, 1996

Most Yards Gained on Punt Returns (career)
214, Robert Brooks (10 games)
210, Desmond Howard (3 games)
143, Antonio Freeman (9 games)

Most Yards Gained on Punt Returns (game)
117, Desmond Howard, vs. San Francisco, Jan. 4, 1997
#90, Desmond Howard, vs. New England, Jan. 26, 1997
72, Antonio Freeman, vs. Atlanta, Dec. 31, 1995

Highest Punt Return Average (career - 9 returns)
23.3, Desmond Howard (9-210) (3 games) (#38.5 in 1 Super Bowl)
*15.3, Robert Brooks (14-214) (10 games)
14.3, Antonio Freeman (10-143) (9 games)

Highest Punt Return Average (game - 3 returns)
24.0, Antonio Freeman, vs. Atlanta, Dec. 31, 1995 (3-72)
15.7, Robert Brooks, vs. Tampa Bay, Jan. 4, 1998 (3-47)
15.0, Desmond Howard, vs. New England, Jan. 26, 1997 (6-90)

Longest Punt Returns
76 yards, Antonio Freeman, vs. Atlanta, Dec. 31, 1995 (touchdown)
71 yards, Desmond Howard, vs. San Francisco, Jan. 4, 1997 (touchdown)
46 yards, Desmond Howard, vs. San Francisco, Jan. 4, 1997

Most Sacks (career - since 1982)
8, Reggie White (13 games)
4, Sean Jones (8 games)
4, Keith McKenzie (6 games)
3, Tony Bennett (2 games)
3, Bryce Paup (4 games)
3, LeRoy Butler (13 games)

Most Sacks (game - since 1982)
#3, Reggie White, vs. New England, Jan. 26, 1997
2, Reggie White, at Detroit, Jan. 8, 1994
2, Bryce Paup, vs. Detroit, Dec. 31, 1994
2, Sean Jones, vs. Atlanta, Dec. 31, 1995
2, Keith McKenzie, at San Francisco, Jan. 11, 1998

Blocked Kicks
1, Bernardo Harris, at Dallas, Jan. 14, 1996 (punt)
1, Bob Kuberski, vs. Tampa Bay, Jan. 4, 1998 (field goal)

Service By Player (games played)
13, LeRoy Butler (1993-97)
13, Mark Chmura (1993-97)
13, Doug Evans (1993-97)
13, Brett Favre (1993-97)
13, Mike Prior (1993-97)
13, Reggie White (1993-97)

13, Frank Winters (1993-97)
11, Ray Nitschke (1960-62, 1965-67, 1972)
11, Earl Dotson (1993, 1995-97)
11, Craig Hentrich (1994-97)
11, Dorsey Levens (1994-97)
11, Terry Mickens (1994-97)

* NFL Record
** Shares NFL Record
 # Super Bowl Record
Shares Super Bowl Record

PACKERS NO. 1 IN POSTSEASON

On the heels of five straight playoff appearances for the first time in team history and a second consecutive Super Bowl appearance, the Packers continue to own the best winning percentage in postseason play in National Football League history. They have won 22 of 31 playoff games since their first-ever postseason contest – the 1936 NFL championship (a 21-6 victory over the Boston Redskins) – for an overall winning percentage of .710. NFC foes Dallas (.627), San Francisco (.622) and Washington (.600) follow at a distance. The all-time standings:

POSTSEASON GAME COMPOSITE STANDINGS

	W	L	Pct.	Pts.	Opp.
Green Bay Packers	22	9	.710	745	528
Dallas Cowboys	32	19	.627	1,254	932
San Francisco 49ers	23	14	.622	936	712
Washington Redskins*	21	14	.600	738	625
Oakland Raiders**	21	15	.583	855	659
Pittsburgh Steelers	21	15	.583	801	707
Denver Broncos	13	11	.542	518	604
Miami Dolphins	17	15	.531	700	650
Buffalo Bills	14	13	.519	648	612
Carolina Panthers	1	1	.500	39	47
Chicago Bears	14	14	.500	579	552
Indianapolis Colts***	10	10	.500	360	389
Jacksonville Jaguars	2	2	.500	83	116
New York Jets	5	6	.455	216	200
Philadelphia Eagles	9	11	.450	359	369
Detroit Lions	7	9	.438	352	377
New England Patriots****	7	9	.438	300	332
Seattle Seahawks	3	4	.429	128	139
New York Giants	14	19	.424	551	616
Kansas City Chiefs*****	8	11	.421	301	384
Cincinnati Bengals	5	7	.417	246	257
Minnesota Vikings	14	20	.412	613	746
Tennessee Oilers+	9	13	.409	371	533
St. Louis Rams++	13	20	.394	501	697
San Diego Chargers+++	7	11	.389	332	428
Cleveland Browns++++	11	19	.367	596	692
Tampa Bay Buccaneers	2	4	.333	68	125
Atlanta Falcons	2	5	.286	139	181
Arizona Cardinals+++++	1	4	.200	81	134
Baltimore Ravens	0	0	.000	0	0
New Orleans Saints	0	4	.000	56	123

* One game played when franchise was in Boston (lost 21-6).
** 12 games played when franchise was in Los Angeles (won 6, lost 6, 268 points scored, 224 points allowed).
*** 15 games played when franchise was in Baltimore (won 5, lost 7, 264 points scored, 262 points allowed).
**** Two games played when franchise was in Boston (won 26-8, lost 51-10).
***** One game played when franchise was in Dallas Texans (won 20-17).
+ 22 games played when franchise was in Houston (won 9, lost 13, 371 points scored, 533 points allowed).
++ One game played when franchise was in Cleveland (won 15-14), 32 games played when franchise was in Los Angeles (won 12, lost 20, 486 points scored, 683 points allowed).
+++ One game played when franchise was in Los Angeles (lost 24-16).
++++ Franchise in suspension until 1999 season.
+++++ Two games played when franchise was in Chicago (won 28-21, lost 7-0), three games played when franchise was in St. Louis (lost 30-14, lost 35-23, lost 41-16).

TEAM PLAYOFF RECORDS

YARDS GAINED

Most Net Yards Gained
479, vs. Carolina, Jan. 12, 1997
466, at Dallas, Jan. 16, 1983
401, at Philadelphia, Dec. 26, 1960

Fewest Net Yards Gained
195, vs. Dallas, Dec. 31, 1967
210, vs. San Francisco, Jan. 4, 1997
211, at Washington, Dec. 24, 1972

FIRST DOWNS

Most First Downs
23, vs. Baltimore, Dec. 26, 1965
23, vs. Atlanta, Dec. 31, 1995
22, at Philadelphia, Dec. 26, 1960
22, vs. St. Louis, Jan. 8, 1983
22, vs. Carolina, Jan. 12, 1997

Fewest First Downs
7, vs. Boston Redskins at New York, Dec. 13, 1936
10, vs. New York Giants, Dec. 10, 1939
10, at Washington, Dec. 24, 1972
11, at New York Giants, Dec. 17, 1944

RUSHING

Most Yards Gained Rushing
223, at Philadelphia, Dec. 26, 1960
204, vs. Cleveland, Jan. 2, 1966
201, vs. Carolina, Jan. 12, 1997

Fewest Yards Gained Rushing
31, at Dallas, Jan. 16, 1994
33, at Chicago Bears, Dec. 14, 1941
48, at Dallas, Jan. 14, 1996

Most Rushing Attempts
51, vs. New York Giants, Dec. 10, 1939
48, at New York Giants, Dec. 17, 1944
47, vs. Cleveland, Jan. 2, 1966

Fewest Rushing Attempts
12, at Dallas, Jan. 14, 1996
13, at Dallas, Jan. 16, 1994
17, at Dallas, Jan. 16, 1983

FORWARD PASSING

Most Passes Attempted
46, at Dallas, Jan. 8, 1995
45, at Dallas, Jan. 16, 1994
42, vs. Denver, Jan. 25, 1998

Fewest Passes Attempted
10, vs. New York Giants, Dec. 10, 1939
11, at New York Giants, Dec. 17, 1944
15, vs. San Francisco, Jan. 4, 1997

Most Passes Completed
28, at Dallas, Jan. 16, 1994
25, vs. Denver, Jan. 25, 1998
24, vs. Atlanta, Dec. 31, 1995

Fewest Passes Completed
3, at New York Giants, Dec. 17, 1944
7, vs. New York Giants, Dec. 10, 1939
8, at New York Giants, Dec. 11, 1938

Most Net Yards Passing
327, at Dallas, Jan. 16, 1994
308, at Dallas, Jan. 16, 1983
294, at San Francisco, Jan. 6, 1996

Fewest Net Yards Passing
71, vs. San Francisco, Jan. 4, 1997
73, at New York Giants, Dec. 17, 1944

96, vs. New York Giants, Dec. 10, 1939
96, at New York Giants, Dec. 30, 1962

Most Touchdown Passes
4, at Dallas, Jan. 1, 1967
4, vs. St. Louis, Jan. 8, 1983
3, vs. New York Giants, Dec. 31, 1961
3, at Detroit, Jan. 8, 1994
3, vs. Atlanta, Dec. 31, 1995
3, at Dallas, Jan. 14, 1996
3, vs. Denver, Jan. 25, 1998

Most Passes Had Intercepted
3, vs. New York Giants, Dec. 10, 1939
3, at New York Giants, Dec. 17, 1944
3, at Dallas, Jan. 8, 1983
2, vs. Boston Redskins at New York, Dec. 13, 1936
2, at Chicago Bears, Dec. 14, 1941
2, vs. Baltimore, Dec. 26, 1965
2, at Dallas, Jan. 16, 1994
2, at Dallas, Jan. 14, 1996
2, vs. Tampa Bay, Jan. 4, 1998

SCORING

Most Points Scored
41, vs. St. Louis, Jan. 8, 1983
37, vs. New York Giants, Dec. 31, 1961
37, vs. Atlanta, Dec. 31, 1995
35, vs. Kansas City, Jan. 15, 1967
35, vs. San Francisco, Jan. 4, 1997
35, vs. New England, Jan. 26, 1997

Fewest Points Scored
3, at Washington, Dec. 24, 1972
9, at Dallas, Jan. 8, 1995
13, at Philadelphia, Dec. 26, 1960
13, vs. Baltimore, Dec. 26, 1965 (ot)

Largest Margins of Victory
37 points, vs. New York Giants, Dec. 31, 1961 (37-0)
27 points, vs. New York Giants, Dec. 10, 1939 (27-0)
25 points, vs. Kansas City, Jan. 15, 1967 (35-10)
25 points, vs. St. Louis, Jan. 8, 1983 (41-16)

Most Touchdowns Scored
5, at Dallas, Jan. 1, 1967
5, vs. Kansas City, Jan. 15, 1967
5, vs. St. Louis, Jan. 8, 1983
5, vs. Atlanta, Dec. 31, 1995
5, vs. San Francisco, Jan. 4, 1997
4, vs. New York Giants, Dec. 31, 1961
4, vs. Los Angeles Rams, Dec. 23, 1967
4, at Detroit, Jan. 8, 1994
4, vs. New England, Jan. 26, 1997

Most Field Goals Scored
##4, vs. Oakland, Jan. 14, 1968
3, vs. New York Giants, Dec. 31, 1961
3, at New York Giants, Dec. 30, 1962
3, vs. Detroit, Dec. 31, 1994
3, vs. Carolina, Jan. 12, 1997
3, at San Francisco, Jan. 11, 1998

Most (One-Point) Points After Touchdown
5, vs. Kansas City, Jan. 15, 1967
5, vs. St. Louis, Jan. 8, 1983
5, vs. San Francisco, Jan. 4, 1997
4, vs. New York Giants, Dec. 31, 1961
4, at Dallas, Jan. 1, 1967
4, vs. Los Angeles Rams, Dec. 23, 1967
4, at Detroit, Jan. 8, 1994
4, vs. Atlanta, Dec. 31, 1995

Most Safeties

PUNTING

Most Punts
10, at New York Giants, Dec. 17, 1944
8, vs. Boston Redskins at New York, Dec. 13, 1936
8, vs. Dallas, Dec. 31, 1967
8, at Washington, Dec. 24, 1972

Fewest Punts
1, vs. St. Louis, Jan. 8, 1983
2, vs. Carolina, Jan. 12, 1997
3, vs. Cleveland, Jan. 2, 1966
3, at Dallas, Jan. 16, 1994
3, at Dallas, Jan. 14, 1996

Highest Average (4 punts)
45.20 yards, at Philadelphia, Dec. 26, 1960
44.00 yards, at Dallas, Jan. 8, 1995
43.25 yards, vs. Kansas City, Jan. 15, 1967

PUNT RETURNS

Most Punt Returns
*8, at New York Giants, Dec. 17, 1944
6, vs. Baltimore, Dec. 26, 1965
##6, vs. New England, Jan. 26, 1997
5, vs. Boston Redskins at New York, Dec. 13, 1936
5, at Chicago Bears, Dec. 14, 1941
5, at Philadelphia, Dec. 26, 1960
5, vs. Dallas, Dec. 31, 1967

Most Yards, Punt Returns
117, vs. San Francisco, Jan. 4, 1997 (3 returns)
98, at New York Giants, Dec. 17, 1944 (8 returns)
#90, vs. New England, Jan. 26, 1997 (6 returns)

KICKOFF RETURNS

Most Kickoff Returns
7, at Dallas, Jan. 16, 1983
7, at Dallas, Jan. 14, 1996
6, at Dallas, Jan. 1, 1967
6, at Dallas, Jan. 16, 1994
6, at Dallas, Jan. 8, 1995
6, vs. Denver, Jan. 25, 1998

Most Yards, Kickoff Returns
154, vs. New England, Jan. 26, 1997 (4 returns)
148, at Dallas, Jan. 16, 1983 (7 returns)
148, at Dallas, Jan. 14, 1996 (7 returns)
144, at Dallas, Jan. 8, 1995 (6 returns)

PENALTIES

Most Penalties
11, at Dallas, Jan. 14, 1996
9, at San Francisco, Jan. 11, 1998
9, vs. Denver, Jan. 25, 1998
8, at Dallas, Jan. 8, 1995

DEFENSIVE RECORDS

TOTAL YARDS GAINED

Fewest Net Yards Allowed
116, vs. Boston Redskins at New York, Dec. 13, 1936
130, vs. New York Giants, Dec. 31, 1961
161, vs. Cleveland, Jan. 2, 1966

Most Net Yards Allowed
453, vs. St. Louis, Jan. 8, 1983
450, at Dallas, Jan. 8, 1995
419, at Dallas, Jan. 14, 1996

FIRST DOWNS

Fewest First Downs Allowed
*6, vs. New York Giants, Dec. 31, 1961

8, vs. Boston Redskins at New York, Dec. 13, 1936
8, vs. Cleveland, Jan. 2, 1966
9, vs. New York Giants, Dec. 10, 1939
9, vs. Baltimore, Dec. 26, 1965
9, vs. Detroit, Dec. 31, 1994

Most First Downs Allowed
28, vs. St. Louis, Jan. 8, 1983
27, at Dallas, Jan. 8, 1995
27, at Dallas, Jan. 14, 1996
26, at San Francisco, Jan. 6, 1996

RUSHING

Fewest Yards Allowed Rushing
*-4, vs. Detroit, Dec. 31, 1994
21, vs. Atlanta, Dec. 31, 1995
31, vs. New York Giants, Dec. 31, 1961

Most Yards Allowed Rushing
277, at Chicago Bears, Dec. 14, 1941
187, at Dallas, Jan. 1, 1967
179, vs. Denver, Jan. 25, 1998

FORWARD PASSING

Fewest Opponent Passes Attempted
12, at Chicago Bears, Dec. 14, 1941
12, vs. Baltimore, Dec. 26, 1965
14, at Washington, Dec. 24, 1972
15, at New York Giants, Dec. 11, 1938

Most Opponent Passes Attempted
65, at San Francisco, Jan. 6, 1996
54, vs. Atlanta, Dec. 31, 1995
51, vs. St. Louis, Jan. 8, 1983

Fewest Opponent Passes Completed
5, at Chicago Bears, Dec. 14, 1941
5, vs. Baltimore, Dec. 26, 1965
7, vs. Boston Redskins at New York, Dec. 13, 1936
7, at Washington, Dec. 24, 1972
8, at New York Giants, Dec. 11, 1938
8, at New York Giants, Dec. 17, 1944
8, vs. Cleveland, Jan. 2, 1966

Most Opponent Passes Completed
32, vs. St. Louis, Jan. 8, 1983
32, at San Francisco, Jan. 6, 1996
30, vs. Atlanta, Dec. 31, 1995
28, at Dallas, Jan. 16, 1994

Fewest Opponent Net Yards Passing
32, vs. Baltimore, Dec, 26, 1965
48, at Chicago Bears, Dec. 14, 1941
91, vs. Boston Redskins at New York, Dec. 13, 1936

Most Opponent Net Yards Passing
347, vs. St. Louis, Jan. 8, 1983
339, vs. Atlanta, Dec. 31, 1995
330, at Dallas, Jan. 8, 1995

Most Opponent Touchdown Passes
3, at Dallas, Jan. 16, 1994
2, at New York Giants, Dec. 11, 1938
2, vs. Oakland, Jan. 14, 1968
2, vs. St. Louis, Jan. 8, 1983
2, at Dallas, Jan. 8, 1995
2, vs. Atlanta, Dec. 31, 1995
2, at Dallas, Jan. 14, 1996
2, vs. New England, Jan. 26, 1997

Most Opponent Passes Intercepted
6, vs. New York Giants, Dec. 10, 1939
4, at New York Giants, Dec. 17, 1944
4, vs. New York Giants, Dec. 31, 1961

4, vs. New England, Jan. 26, 1997
vs. San Francisco, Jan. 4, 1997

SCORING

ost Opponent Points Scored
, at Dallas, Jan. 14, 1996
, at Dallas, Jan. 16, 1983
, at Dallas, Jan. 8, 1995

west Opponent Points Scored
vs. New York Giants, Dec. 10, 1939
vs. New York Giants, Dec. 31, 1961
vs. Boston Redskins at New York, Dec. 13, 1936
at New York Giants, Dec. 17, 1944
at New York Giants, Dec. 30, 1962
vs. Los Angeles Rams, Dec. 23, 1967
vs, Tampa Bay, Jan. 4, 1998

pponent Largest Margins of Victory
, at Dallas, Jan. 8, 1995 (35-9)
, at Chicago Bears, Dec. 14, 1941 (33-14)
, at Washington, Dec. 24, 1972 (16-3)

ost Opponent Touchdowns Scored
at Dallas, Jan. 8, 1995
at Dallas, Jan. 14, 1996
at Chicago Bears, Dec. 14, 1941
at Dallas, Jan. 16, 1983
vs. Denver, Jan. 25, 1998
at New York Giants, Dec. 11, 1938
at Dallas, Jan. 1, 1967
at Detroit, Jan. 8, 1994
at Dallas, Jan. 16, 1994
vs. New England, Jan. 26, 1997

ost Opponent Field Goals Scored
at Washington, Dec. 24, 1972
at Dallas, Jan. 16, 1983
six times

ost Opponent (One-Point) Points After Touchdown
at Dallas, Jan. 8, 1995
at Dallas, Jan. 14, 1996
at Dallas, Jan. 16, 1983
vs. Denver, Jan. 25, 1998
at Chicago Bears, Dec. 14, 1941
at Dallas, Jan. 1, 1967
at Detroit, Jan. 8, 1994
at Dallas, Jan. 16, 1994
vs. New England, Jan. 26, 1997

ost Safeties
vs. Detroit, Dec. 31, 1994

PUNTING

ost Opponent Punts
0, vs. Boston Redskins at New York, Dec. 13, 1936
0, at New York Giants, Dec. 17, 1944
at New York Giants, Dec. 11, 1938
vs. Baltimore, Dec. 26, 1965
vs. Dallas, Dec. 31, 1967
vs. Detroit, Dec. 31, 1994
vs. New England, Jan. 26, 1997
at New York Giants, Dec. 30, 1962
vs. Kansas City, Jan. 15, 1967

ewest Opponent Punts
*0, vs. St. Louis, Jan. 8, 1983
at Detroit, Jan. 8, 1994
at Dallas, Jan. 16, 1994
at New York Giants, Dec. 11, 1938
vs. Cleveland, Jan. 2, 1966
at Dallas, Jan. 1, 1967
at Dallas, Jan. 16, 1983
at Dallas, Jan. 8, 1995

4, vs. Tampa Bay, Jan. 4, 1998
4, vs. Denver, Jan. 25, 1998

Opponent Highest Average (4 punts)
46.60 yards, vs. Cleveland, Jan. 2, 1966
46.50 yards, at Washington, Dec. 24, 1972

PUNT RETURNS

Most Opponent Punt Returns
5, vs. Baltimore, Dec. 26, 1965
4, vs. Boston Redskins at New York, Dec. 13, 1936
4, vs. New England, Jan. 26, 1997

Most Yards, Opponent Punt Returns
87, at Chicago Bears, Dec. 14, 1941 (3 returns)
43, vs. Boston Redskins at New York, Dec. 13, 1936
(4 returns)
32, at New York Giants, Dec. 17, 1944 (3 returns)

KICKOFF RETURNS

Most Opponent Kickoff Returns
7, vs. Oakland, Jan. 14, 1968
7, vs. St. Louis, Jan. 8, 1983
7, vs. Carolina, Jan. 12, 1997
6, vs. New York Giants, Dec. 31, 1961
6, at Dallas, Jan. 1, 1967
6, vs. Kansas City, Jan. 15, 1967
6, vs. Atlanta, Dec. 31, 1995
6, vs. New England, Jan. 26, 1997

Most Yards, Opponent Kickoff Returns
186, vs. Detroit, Dec. 31, 1994 (5 returns)
178, vs. St. Louis, Jan. 8, 1983 (7 returns)
173, at Dallas, Jan. 16, 1983 (5 returns)

PENALTIES

Most Penalties
12, at Chicago Bears, Dec. 14, 1941
11, at New York Giants, Dec. 17, 1944
8, at San Francisco, Jan. 6, 1996

Fewest Penalties
**0, at Philadelphia, Dec. 26, 1960
2, at New York Giants, Dec. 11, 1938
2, vs. New England, Jan. 26, 1997
3, vs. Boston Redskins at New York, Dec. 13, 1936
3, vs. Baltimore, Dec. 26, 1965
3, vs. Cleveland, Jan. 2, 1966
3, vs. Los Angeles Rams, Dec. 23, 1967
3, vs. Tampa Bay, Jan. 4, 1998

* *NFL Record*
** *Shares NFL Record*
# *Super Bowl Record*
Shares Super Bowl Record

PACKERS' PRO HALL OF FAMERS

The Green Bay Packers boast 19 individuals who spent the majority of their careers with the club in the Pro Football Hall of Fame in Canton, Ohio. The Packers' total is second only to that of the Chicago Bears, who have 25. The New York Giants, with 15, are third, while the Pittsburgh Steelers and Washington Redskins share fourth place with 14 apiece.

In addition, five other players who played briefly for Green Bay — defensive end Len Ford, linebacker Ted Hendricks, guard/coach Walt Kiesling, kicker Jan Stenerud and safety Emlen Tunnell — have their busts displayed in the Hall of Fame.

Biographies of the Packers' 19 primary HOF players follow:

1963 — Earl L. (Curly) Lambeau, Founder, player, coach, vice president (1919-49). Founded Packers in 1919 and served as team's only coach through 1949 season. Also played halfback from '19 through '29, a period during which he pioneered forward pass in professional football. Led Packers to six world championships and is one of only five coaches to record more than 200 coaching victories in the NFL (others are Don Shula, George Halas, Tom Landry and Chuck Noll). Had coaching record of 212-106-21 (.656) with Packers. Also coached Chicago Cardinals (1950-51) and Washington Redskins (1952-53). Born April 9, 1898, in Green Bay. Died June 1, 1965, at age of 67.

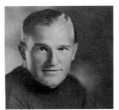

1963 — Robert (Cal) Hubbard, T (1929-33, 1935). Also played for New York Giants, Pittsburgh Pirates. A legendary athlete, he was one of pro football's first genuine giants — a massive 6-ft. 5-inch, 250-pounder who was a devastating blocker on offense and relentless pursuer on defense as a premier, two-way performer. Was an All-Pro choice in each of first three years (1931, '32, '33) such selections were made. Selected to NFL's All-50 Year Team in 1970 and to All-Time Two-Way Team in 1994. Played college football at Centenary, Geneva. Born October 31, 1900, in Keytesville, Mo. Died Oct. 17, 1977, at age of 76.

1963 — Don Hutson, E/DB (1935-45). Made third-most touchdown receptions (99) in pro football history, an all-time NFL record until broken by Steve Largent and subsequently surpassed by Jerry Rice. Credited with inventing pass patterns, he led league in receiving 8 years and in scoring 5 seasons, both also lifetime marks. Also played defensive back and placekicked. Named to NFL's All-50 Year Team in 1970, later was selected to league's 75th Anniversary and All-Time Two-Way teams in 1994. Led NFL in receiving yards in 7 seasons, an all-time record. Also holds league record for most points scored in one quarter (29). Played collegiately at Alabama. Named to four Pro Bowls. Born Jan. 31, 1913, in Pine Bluff, Ark. Died June 26, 1997, at age of 84.

1963 — Johnny (Blood) McNally, HB (1929-33, 1935-36). Also played for Milwaukee Badgers, Duluth Eskimos, Pottsville Maroons, Pittsburgh Pirates. An elusive runner and gifted pass receiver, he played major role in Packers' drive to first three championships in 1929, '30 and '31. Also helped Packers win a fourth world title in '36. Going into 1998 season, still held 19th place in Packer lifetime scoring six decades after departing Green Bay scene, with 230 points. Collegiate star at St. John's (Minn). Born Nov. 27, 1903, in New Richmond, Wis. Died Nov. 28, 1985, at age of 82.

1964 — Clarke Hinkle, FB (1932-41). A four-time All-Pro selection (1936, '37, '38, '41). One of the most versatile players in NFL annals, he was tough, bruising runner, fine blocker, good receiver and excellent placekicker as well as shrewd, hard-hitting linebacker. Fourth-ranking rusher in Packers' history with 3,860 yards in 1,171 carries. Was selected to NFL's All-Time Two-Way Team in 1994. Played college football at Bucknell. Named to three Pro Bowls. Born Apr. 10, 1909, in Toronto, Ohio. Died Nov. 9, 1988, at age of 79.

1964 — Mike Michalske, G (1929-35, 1937). Also played for New York Yankees (1927-28) before joining Packers. Rated one of game's greatest guards during pro football's "two-way" era. Two-time All-Pro selection (1931 and 1935). A true 60-minute player, he was known as "Iron Mike" because of his great stamina and durability. Best asset was exceptional quickness, which made him equally effective on both offense and defense. Played college football at Penn State. Born April 24, 1903, in Cleveland. Died Oct. 26, 1983, at age of 80.

1966 — Arnie Herber, QB (1930-40). Also played for New York Giants (1944-45). Pro football's first great long passer. Won three National Football League passing titles and was All-Pro selection in 1932. Teamed with Don Hutson to form NFL's first feared passing combination in mid-'30s. Ranks fifth in Packer annals with 64 career touchdown passes over his 11 seasons. Tough, durable athlete and accomplished punter as well as great passer. A Green Bay native, he played college football at Regis (Denver). Born April 2, 1910, in Green Bay. Died Oct. 14, 1969, at age of 59.

1971 — Vince Lombardi, Coach and General Manager (1959-67). General Manager only in 1968. Also assistant coach for New York Giants (1954-58) and head coach of Washington Redskins (1969). Directed Packers to five NFL championships in seven years (1961-62 and 1965-66-67), a feat without precedent or parallel in pro football history. His 1966 and 1967 teams also made history by winning first two Super Bowls. Packers won nine of 10 playoff games under his leadership and overall compiled a 98-30-4 record, a glittering .758 winning percentage, as he never had a losing season. Lombardi, a guard, played his college football at Fordham, where he was one of the legendary "Seven Blocks of Granite." Born June 11, 1913, in Brooklyn, N.Y. Died Sept. 3, 1970, at age of 57.

1974 — Tony Canadeo, HB (1941-44, 1946-52). Became only the third 1,000-yard rusher in pro football history when he gained 1,052 yards in 1949. Still ranks as No. 3 ground gainer in Packers' annals with 4,197 yards in 1,025 attempts, a 4.1 average. A durable, all-purpose halfback, he was an accomplished blocker, capable passer and good receiver in addition to being a highly effective kick returner. Also played defensive back during early years of his career. Played college football at Gonzaga, where he acquired nickname of "Grey Ghost." Born May 5, 1919, in Chicago.

1976 — Jim Taylor, FB (1958-66). Also played for New Orleans Saints (1967). Rushed for over 1,000 yards five straight seasons (1960-64). Heading into '98 campaign, still is NFL's 15th ranking career rusher with 8,597 yards over his 10 seasons. Also owns league's ninth highest lifetime total of rushing touchdowns — 83. Is Packers' all-time leading ground gainer with 8,207 yards to his credit during his nine seasons in Green Bay. Had 26 career 100-yard rushing games. Played his college football at LSU. Named to five Pro Bowls. Born Sept. 20, 1935, in Baton Rouge, La.

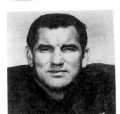

1977 — Forrest Gregg, T (1956, 1958-70). Also played with Dallas Cowboys (1971). Drafted No. 2 in 1956. Was named All-Pro eight times (including All-Pro at both Guard and Tackle in 1965) and nine times to the Pro Bowl. Called by Lombardi the "finest player I've ever coached." Voted to NFL's 75th Anniversary Team in 1994. Holds the Packer record for durability with 187 consecutive games played. Head Coach of the Green Bay Packers 1984-87. Also served as head coach of Cleveland Browns (1975-77) and Cincinnati Bengals (1980-83). Played college football at SMU. Born Oct. 18, 1933, in Birthright, Texas.

1977 — Bart Starr, QB (1956-71). Drafted in 17th round in 1956. Became the winningest quarterback in football, directing the Packers to 6 Western Division Titles, 5 World Titles, 2 Super Bowl victories, and was named MVP in Super Bowls I and II. Led the League in passing in 1962, 1964 and 1966, and was named to the Pro Bowl four times. In 1972 he coached Packers' quarterbacks. Head Coach of the Green Bay Packers 1975-83. He played college football at Alabama. Born Jan. 9, 1934, in Montgomery, Ala.

1978 — Ray Nitschke, MLB (1958-72). Drafted in third round in 1958 after playing fullback at Illinois. Most Valuable Player in 1962 NFL Title game vs. N.Y. Giants. Named to the NFL's All-50 Year and 75th Anniversary teams. All-Pro in 1964, 1965 and 1966; Pro Bowl 1964. Had 25 career interceptions. Born Dec. 29, 1936, in Elmwood Park, Ill. Died March 8, 1998, at age of 61.

1980 — Herb Adderley, CB (1961-69). Also played for Dallas Cowboys (1970-72). Packers' No. 1 draft choice (Michigan State) in 1961. Five-time All Pro at cornerback. Played in five Pro Bowls, four of first six Super Bowls (two with Green Bay, two with Dallas). Had 48 career intercepts (39 with Packers), ran 7 back for TDs (second-highest total in NFL history). Born June 8, 1939, in Philadelphia.

1981 — Willie Davis, DE (1960-69). Also played for Cleveland (1958-59). A 17th round draft choice, he came to Packers from Browns in 1960 trade. Became one of premier pass rushers in pro football history, winning All-Pro honors five times and selection to Pro Bowl five times. Holds all-time Packers record for career fumble recoveries (21) and is tied for second-longest consecutive game streak (162) in Green Bay annals. Helped Packers win five NFL titles during 1960s. Played college football at Grambling. Elected to Packers' Board of Directors in 1994. Born July 24, 1934, in Lisbon, La.

PACKERS' PRO HALL OF FAMERS

1981 — Jim Ringo, C (1953-63). Also played for Philadelphia (1964-67). Seventh round draft choice out of Syracuse in 1953. Went on to win All-Pro honors eight times, seven as a Packer, and played in 10 Pro Bowls, seven as a Packer. Highly durable performer, once held NFL record for most consecutive games played (183). Helped Packers win back-to-back NFL titles in 1961-62. Traded to Philadelphia in 1964. Born Nov. 21, 1931, in Orange, N.J.

1986 — Paul Hornung, HB (1957-62, 1964-66). One of the most versatile players in pro football history, he won NFL scoring title three consecutive years (1959-60-61), setting all-time league record of 176 points in 1960. Also shares league single-game playoff scoring record, 19 points. All-Pro selection two times and named to Pro Bowl twice. Averaged 4.2 yards per rush, caught 130 passes and kicked 66 field goals during nine-year career. Third ranking scorer in Packers' history with 760 points. Bonus choice (first player selected overall) in 1957 NFL draft. Played college football at Notre Dame, winning Heisman Trophy in 1956. Born Dec. 23, 1935, in Louisville, Ky.

1989 — Willie Wood, FS (1960-71). Wrote several NFL teams asking for a tryout coming out of USC in 1960 before Packers signed him as free agent. Went on to become recognized as a premier free safety, winning all-NFL honors six straight years beginning in 1963. A Pro Bowl selection eight times, he also played in six NFL championship games, helping Packers win five titles. Starting free safety for Green Bay in Super Bowls I and II, broke open a close contest in third quarter of SBI, intercepting a Len Dawson pass and returning 50 yards to the K.C. 5, triggering a 35-10 Packer victory. Had 48 career interceptions, returned for 699 yards. Won NFL title in 1962 with nine thefts and also captured a league punt return crown in 1961 with a 16.1 average. One of only six free agents to make Hall of Fame. Born Dec. 23, 1936, in Washington, D.C.

1995 — Henry Jordan, DT (1959-69). Also played for Cleveland (1957-58). Originally a fifth round draft choice of Browns, came to Green Bay in 1959 trade. Named All-Pro five straight seasons (1960-64), he also was selected to play in the Pro Bowl four times. One of team's more colorful personalities, missed only two games in his first 12 seasons. Played in seven NFL title games (including 1957 with Cleveland), plus first two Super Bowls. Had 3½ sacks in 1967 Western Conference Championship win over Rams. Played college football at Virginia. Born Jan. 26, 1935, in Emporia, Va. Died Feb. 21, 1977, at age of 42.

Other players in Hall of Fame who played for Green Bay

**Len Ford
1976**

**Ted Hendricks
1990**

**Walt Kiesling
1966**

**Jan Stenerud
1991**

**Emlen Tunnell
1967**

INDUCTED FALL, 1970
Bernard "Boob" Darling, C, 1927-31
Curly Lambeau, B-Coach, 1919-49
Lavvie Dilweg, E, 1927-34
Verne Lewellen, B, 1924-32
Jug Earp, C, 1922-32
Johnny "Blood" McNally, B, 1929-33, 1935-36
Cal Hubbard, T, 1929-33, 1935
Mike Michalske, G, 1929-35, 1937

INDUCTED JANUARY, 1972
Hank Bruder, G, 1931-39
Don Hutson, E-DB, 1935-45
Milt Gantenbein, E, 1931-40
Cecil Isbell, B, 1938-42
Chas. "Buckets" Goldenberg, G-B, 1933-45
Joe Laws, B, 1934-45
Arnie Herber, B, 1930-40
Russ Letlow, G, 1936-42, 1946
Clarke Hinkle, B, 1932-41
George Svendsen, C-LB, 1935-37, 1940-41

INDUCTED JANUARY, 1973
Charley Brock, C-LB, 1939-47
Bob Monnett, B, 1933-38
Tony Canadeo, B, 1941-44, 1946-52
Buford "Baby" Ray, T, 1938-48
Larry Craig, B-E, 1939-49
Andy Uram, HB, 1938-43
Bob Forte, B, 1946-53
Dick Wildung, T, 1946-51, 1953
Ted Fritsch, B, 1942-50
H.L."Whitey" Woodin, G, 1922-31

INDUCTED JANUARY, 1974
Al Carmichael, RB, 1953-58
Dave Hanner, DT, 1952-64
Fred Cone, FB-K, 1951-57
Billy Howton, E, 1952-58
Bobby Dillon, DB, 1952-59
John Martinkovic, E, 1951-56
Howie Ferguson, FB, 1953-58
Jim Ringo, C, 1953-63
Bill Forester, LB, 1953-63
Tobin Rote, QB, 1950-56

INDUCTED JANUARY, 1975
Don Chandler, K, 1965-67
Ron Kramer, TE, 1957, 1959-64
Willie Davis, DE, 1960-69
Vince Lombardi, Coach-GM, 1959-68
Paul Hornung, HB-K, 1957-62, 1964-66
Max McGee, E, 1954, 1957-67
Henry Jordan, DT, 1959-69
Jim Taylor, FB, 1958-66
Jerry Kramer, G, 1958-68
Fred "Fuzzy" Thurston, G, 1959-67

INDUCTED JANUARY, 1976
Joseph "Red" Dunn, B, 1927-31
Bob Skoronski, T, 1956, 1959-68
Hank Gremminger, DB, 1956-65
Jesse Whittenton, DB, 1958-64
Gary Knafelc, E, 1954-62
Carl "Bud" Jorgensen, Trainer, 1924-70

INDUCTED JANUARY, 1977
Howard "Cub" Buck, T, 1921-25
Bart Starr, QB, 1956-71
Forrest Gregg, T, 1956, 1958-70
A.B. Turnbull, Pres., 1923-27
Charlie Mathys, B, 1922-26
Willie Wood, S, 1960-71

INDUCTED FEBRUARY, 1978
Boyd Dowler, WR, 1959-69
Paul "Tiny" Engebretsen, G, 1934-41
Lon Evans, G, 1933-37
Ray Nitschke, LB, 1958-72
George Calhoun, Pub. Dir., 1919-46

INDUCTED FEBRUARY, 1979
Nate Barragar, C, 1931-32, 1934-35
Carroll Dale, E, 1965-72
Elijah Pitts, RB, 1961-69, 1971
Pete Tinsley, G-LB, 1938-39, 1941-45
Dominic Olejniczak, Pres., 1958-82

1980
(No inductions)

INDUCTED FEBRUARY, 1981
Herb Adderley, DB, 1961-69
Ken Bowman, C, 1964-73
Chester "Swede" Johnston, 1931, 1934-38
Lee H. Joannes, Pres., 1930-47

INDUCTED FEBRUARY, 1982
Lou Brock, 1940-45
Gale Gillingham, G, 1966-74, 1976
Dave Robinson, LB, 1963-72
Jack Vainisi, Scout, 1950-60

INDUCTED FEBRUARY, 1983
Donny Anderson, RB, 1966-71
Fred Carr, LB, 1968-77
Carl Mulleneaux, E, 1938-41, 1945-46
Contributor, Fred Leicht

INDUCTED FEBRUARY, 1984
John Brockington, RB, 1971-77
Dan Currie, LB, 1958-64
Ed Jankowski, B, 1937-41
Contributor, F.N. Trowbridge, Sr.

INDUCTED FEBRUARY, 1985
Phil Bengtson, Coach-GM, 1959-70
Bob Jeter, DB, 1963-70

Earl "Bud" Svendsen, C-LB, 1937, 1939

INDUCTED FEBRUARY, 1986
Lee Roy Caffey, LB, 1964-69
Irv Comp, B, 1943-49
Contributor, Wilner Burke, 1938-81

INDUCTED MARCH, 1987
Chester Marcol, K, 1972-80
Deral Teteak, LB-G, 1952-56
Contributor, Dr. E.S. Brusky, 1962-90

INDUCTED FEBRUARY, 1988
Lionel Aldridge, DE, 1963-71
Bob Mann, E, 1950-54
Contributor, Jerry Atkinson

INDUCTED FEBRUARY, 1989
Zeke Bratkowski, QB, 1963-68, 1971
Ron Kostelnik, DT, 1961-68

1990
(No inductions)

INDUCTED FEBRUARY, 1991
Harry Jacunski, E, 1939-44
Jan Stenerud, K, 1980-83
Contributor, Gerald L. Clifford

INDUCTED FEBRUARY, 1992
Lynn Dickey, QB, 1976-77, 1979-85
Larry McCarren, C, 1973-84
Contributor, Al Schneider

INDUCTED MARCH, 1993
Willie Buchanon, CB, 1972-78
Johnnie Gray, S, 1975-83
Contributor, Art Daley

INDUCTED MARCH, 1994
Paul Coffman, TE, 1978-85
Gerry Ellis, FB, 1980-86
Contributor, Dr. W. Webber Kelly

INDUCTED MARCH, 1995
HOF Founder, William Brault

INDUCTED MARCH, 1996
John Anderson, LB, 1978-89
Contributor, Lee Remmel

INDUCTED MARCH, 1997
John "Red" Cochran, Coach-Scout, 1959-66, 1971-present
Ezra Johnson, DE, 1977-87
Travis Williams, RB-KR, 1967-70

INDUCTED MARCH, 1998
Ken Ellis, CB, 1970-75
Mark Murphy, S, 1980-85, 1987-91
Hon. Robert J. Parins, Pres., 1982-89

46 / 1957

N HUTSON	End	...DON HUTSON
BERT "CAL" HUBBARD	Tackle	...ROBERT "CAL" HUBBARD
KE MICHALSKE	Guard	...MIKE MICHALSKE
ARLEY BROCK	Center	...CHARLEY BROCK
ARLES "BUCKETS" GOLDENBERG	Guard	...CHARLES "BUCKETS" GOLDENBERG
WARD "CUB" BUCK	Tackle	...HOWARD "CUB" BUCK
VERN "LAVVIE" DILWEG	End	...LaVERN "LAVVIE" DILWEG
NIE HERBER	Quarterback	...ARNIE HERBER
HNNY (BLOOD) McNALLY	Halfback	...JOHNNY (BLOOD) McNALLY
RNE LEWELLEN	Halfback	...TONY CANADEO
ARKE HINKLE	Fullback	...CLARKE HINKLE

1969 (50th Anniversary All-Time Packer Team)

OFFENSE

N HUTSON	End
YD DOWLER	End
BERT "CAL" HUBBARD	Tackle
ED "FUZZY" THURSTON	Guard
M RINGO	Center
RRY KRAMER	Guard
RREST GREGG	Tackle
RT STARR	Quarterback
UL HORNUNG	Running Back
ARKE HINKLE	Running Back
M TAYLOR	Running Back

DEFENSE

LARRY CRAIG	End
LaVERN "LAVVIE" DILWEG	End
WILLIE DAVIS	End
ROBERT "CAL" HUBBARD	Tackle
HENRY JORDAN	Tackle
DAVE HANNER	Tackle
RAY NITSCHKE	Linebacker
DAVE ROBINSON	Linebacker
BILL FORESTER	Linebacker
HERB ADDERLEY	Defensive Back
JESSE WHITTENTON	Defensive Back
BOBBY DILLON	Defensive Back
WILLIE WOOD	Defensive Back

1976
(Iron Man and Modern Era All-Time Packer Teams)

IRON MAN ERA TEAM

DON HUTSON	End
MILT GANTENBEIN	End
ROBERT "CAL" HUBBARD	Tackle
MIKE MICHALSKE	Guard
CHARLEY BROCK	Center
CHARLES "BUCKETS" GOLDENBERG	Guard
BUFORD "BABY" RAY	Tackle
LARRY CRAIG	Blocking Back
JOHNNY (BLOOD) McNALLY	Halfback
TONY CANADEO	Halfback
CLARKE HINKLE	Fullback

MODERN ERA TEAM

OFFENSE

YD DOWLER	Wide Receiver
B SKORONSKI	Tackle
ED "FUZZY" THURSTON	Guard
M RINGO	Center
RRY KRAMER	Guard
RREST GREGG	Tackle
N KRAMER	Tight End
AX McGEE	Wide Receiver
RT STARR	Quarterback
UL HORNUNG	Running Back
M TAYLOR	Running Back

DEFENSE

WILLIE DAVIS	End
HENRY JORDAN	Tackle
DAVE HANNER	Tackle
LIONEL ALDRIDGE	End
DAVE ROBINSON	Left Linebacker
RAY NITSCHKE	Middle Linebacker
FRED CARR	Right Linebacker
HERB ADDERLEY	Left Cornerback
BOB JETER	Right Cornerback
WILLIE WOOD	Safety
BOBBY DILLON	Safety

ecialists: Punter-DICK DESCHAINE, Placekicker-DON CHANDLER

(Iron Man and Modern Era Teams chosen by vote of fans from 29 states in 1976 Packers game program poll)

ALL-PRO SELECTIONS

ALL-LEAGUE SELECTIONS

1931 — E Lavvie Dilweg; T Cal Hubbard; G Mike Michalske; HB Johnny (Blood) McNally

1932 — C Nate Barragar; HB Arnie Herber; T Cal Hubbard

1933 — T Cal Hubbard

1936 — G Lon Evans; FB Clarke Hinkle; E Don Hutson;
T Ernie Smith

1937 — G Lon Evans; FB Clarke Hinkle

1938 — FB Clarke Hinkle; E Don Hutson; G Russ Letlow

1939 — E Don Hutson

1940 — E Don Hutson

1941 — FB Clarke Hinkle; E Don Hutson; HB Cecil Isbell

1942 — E Don Hutson; HB Cecil Isbell

(*Official selection discontinued in 1943)

PRESS ASSOCIATION ALL-PRO SELECTIONS

1943 — FB Tony Canadeo (AP, INS); E Don Hutson (AP, UP, INS)

1944 — E Don Hutson (AP, UP, INS)

1945 — C Charley Brock (AP, UP, INS); FB Ted Fritsch (UP); E Don Hutson (AP, UP)

1946 — FB Ted Fritsch (AP, UP, INS)

1947 — FB Tony Canadeo (UP); E Larry Craig (UP)

1950 — HB Billy Grimes (INS); C Clayton Tonnemaker (INS)

1954 — HB Bobby Dillon (AP); LB Roger Zatkoff (UP)

1956 — S Bobby Dillon (UP); E Billy Howton (AP, UP)

1957 — HB Bobby Dillon (AP); E Billy Howton (AP, UP); C Jim Ringo (AP)

1958 — HB Bobby Dillon (AP, UP); C Jim Ringo (AP)

1959 — C Jim Ringo (AP, UPI)

1960 — LB Bill Forester (AP, UPI); T Forrest Gregg (AP); HB Paul Hornung (AP, UPI); T Henry Jordan (AP, UPI); G Jerry Kramer (AP); C Jim Ringo (AP, UPI)

1961 — LB Dan Currie (AP, UPI); LB Bill Forester (AP, UPI); T Forrest Gregg (UPI); HB Paul Hornung (AP, UPI); T Henry Jordan (AP, NEA, UPI); C Jim Ringo (AP, NEA, UPI); FB Jim Taylor (NEA); G Fuzzy Thurston (AP, NEA, UPI); HB Jesse Whittenton (AP, NEA, UPI)

1962 — HB Herb Adderley (AP, UPI); LB Dan Currie (AP, NEA, UPI): E Willie Davis (AP); LB Bill Forester (AP, NEA, UPI); T Forrest Gregg (AP, NEA, UPI); T Henry Jordan (AP); G Jerry Kramer (AP, NEA, UPI); E Ron Kramer (AP); C Jim Ringo (AP, NEA, UPI); FB Jim Taylor (AP, NEA, UPI); G Fuzzy Thurston (UPI)

1963 — HB Herb Adderley (AP); LB Bill Forester (UPI); T Forrest Gregg (AP, NEA, UPI); T Henry Jordan (AP, NEA, UPI); G Jerry Kramer (AP, NEA, UPI); C Jim Ringo (AP, NEA, UPI); HB Willie Wood (NEA)

1964 — E Willie Davis (AP, NEA, UPI); T Forrest Gregg (AP, NEA, UPI); T Henry Jordan (AP, UPI); LB Ray Nitschke (AP, NEA, UPI); HB Willie Wood (AP, NEA, UPI)

1965 — HB Herb Adderley (AP, NEA, UPI); E Willie Davis (AP, NEA, UPI); G/T Forrest Gregg (AP, UPI); LB Ray Nitschke (UPI); HB Willie Wood (AP, NEA, UPI)

1966 — HB Herb Adderley (AP, NEA, UPI); LB Lee Roy Caffey (AP, UPI); E Willie Davis (AP, NEA, UPI); T Forrest Gregg (AP, NEA, UPI); G Jerry Kramer (AP, UPI); LB Ray Nitschke (AP, NEA, UPI); QB Bart Starr (AP, NEA, UPI); HB Willie Wood (AP, NEA, UPI)

1967 — E Willie Davis (AP, NEA, UPI); T Forrest Gregg (AP, UPI); DB Bob Jeter (AP, NEA, UPI); G Jerry Kramer (AP, UPI); LB Dave Robinson (AP, NEA, UPI); HB Willie Wood (AP, UPI)

1968 — LB Dave Robinson (UPI); HB Willie Wood (UPI)

1969 — HB Herb Adderley (AP); G Gale Gillingham (NEA); LB Dave Robinson (AP, NEA, UPI)

1970 — G Gale Gillingham (AP, NEA, UPI)

1971 — RB John Brockington (AP, NEA, UPI); G Gale Gillingham (AP, NEA, UPI)

1972 — RB John Brockington (UPI All-NFC); DB Ken Ellis (AP All-Pro, UPI All-NFC); K Chester Marcol (AP All-Pro, UPI All-NFC, PFWA All-Pro, NEA All-Pro)

1973 — RB John Brockington (AP All-Pro, NEA All-Pro, UPI All-NFC); DB Ken Ellis (AP All-Pro, UPI All-NFC)

1974 — DB Ken Ellis (UPI All-NFC); G Gale Gillingham (AP All-Pro, NEA All-Pro, UPI All-NFC, Sporting News All-NFC); LB Ted Hendricks (AP All-Pro, NEA All-Pro, UPI All-NFC, PFWA All-Pro, Pro Football Weekly All-NFC, Sporting News All-NFC); K Chester Marcol (AP All-Pro, NEA All-Pro, UPI All-NFC, PFWA All-Pro, Pro Football Weekly All-NFC, Sporting News All-NFC)

1975 — LB Fred Carr (Sporting News All-NFC)

1978 — DB Willie Buchanon (AP All-Pro, PFWA All-Pro)

1980 — WR James Lofton (NEA All-Pro, PFWA All-Pro, UPI All-NFC, Pro Football Weekly All-NFC)

1981 — WR James Lofton (AP All-Pro, NEA All-Pro, PFWA All-Pro, Pro Football Weekly All-NFC, Sporting News All-NFC)

ALL-PRO SELECTIONS

1982 — LB Mike Douglass (Pro Football Weekly All-NFC); WR James Lofton (College & Pro Football Newsweekly All-Pro)

1983 — WR James Lofton (PFWA All-Pro)

1984 — WR James Lofton (NEA All-Pro)

1985 — WR James Lofton (NEA All-Pro)

1988 — LB Tim Harris (NEA All-Pro, Sports Illustrated All-Pro)

1989 — LB Tim Harris (AP All-Pro, NEA All-Pro, UPI All-NFC, PFWA All-Pro, Sports Illustrated All-NFL, College & Pro Football Newsweekly All-Pro, Football Digest All-NFL, Pro Football Weekly All-NFL, Sporting News All-NFL); G Rich Moran (NEA All-Pro); WR Sterling Sharpe (AP All-Pro, UPI All-NFC, PFWA All-Pro, Pro Football Weekly All-NFC, Sporting News All-NFC)

1990 — C James Campen (USA Today All-Pro); WR Sterling Sharpe (UPI All-NFC)

1992 — S Chuck Cecil (College & Pro Football Newsweekly All-Pro); TE Jackie Harris (NEA All-Pro); WR Sterling Sharpe (AP All-Pro, NEA All-Pro, UPI All-NFC, Pro Football Weekly/PFWA All-NFL, College & Pro Football Newsweekly All-Pro, Football Digest All-Pro, Sporting News All-Pro)

1993 — S LeRoy Butler (AP All-Pro, UPI All-NFC, Pro Football Weekly/PFWA All-Pro, Sports Illustrated All-Pro, Sporting News All-Pro, Football Digest All-Pro, Football News All-NFC); K Chris Jacke (AP All-Pro, College & Pro Football Newsweekly All-Pro); WR Sterling Sharpe (AP All-Pro, UPI All-NFC, Pro Football Weekly/PFWA All-Pro, Sports Illustrated All-Pro, Sporting News All-Pro, College & Pro Football Newsweekly All-Pro, Football Digest All-Pro, Football News All-NFC); DE Reggie White (UPI All-NFC, Sporting News All-Pro, College & Pro Football Newsweekly All-Pro, Football Digest All-Pro, Football News All-NFC)

1994 — LB Bryce Paup (UPI All-NFC, USA Today All-Pro, Football News All-NFC); DE Reggie White (UPI All-NFC, Sports Illustrated All-Pro, Football News All-NFC)

1995 — WR Robert Brooks (USA Today All-Pro); TE Mark Chmura (College & Pro Football Newsweekly All-Pro, Football Digest All-Pro, Football News All-NFC); QB Brett Favre (AP All-Pro, UPI All-NFC, Pro Football Weekly/PFWA All-Pro, Sports Illustrated All-Pro, Sporting News All-Pro, USA Today All-Pro, College & Pro Football Newsweekly All-Pro, Football Digest All-Pro, Football News All-NFC); DE Reggie White (AP All-Pro, UPI All-NFC, Pro Football Weekly/PFWA All-Pro, Sports Illustrated All-Pro, Sporting News All-Pro, USA Today All-Pro, College & Pro Football Newsweekly All-Pro, Football Digest All-Pro, Football News All-NFC)

1996 — S LeRoy Butler (AP All-Pro, UPI All-NFC, Pro Football Weekly/PFWA All-Pro, Sports Illustrated All-Pro, Sporting News All-Pro, USA Today All-Pro, Football Digest All-Pro, Football News All-NFC); QB Brett Favre (AP All-Pro, UPI All-NFC, Pro Football Weekly/PFWA All-Pro, Sports Illustrated All-Pro, Sporting News All-Pro, USA Today All-Pro, College & Pro Football Newsweekly All-Pro, Football Digest All-Pro, Football News All-NFC); PR Desmond Howard (UPI All-NFC, Pro Football Weekly/PFWA All-Pro, Sporting News All-Pro, USA Today All-Pro, College & Pro Football Newsweekly All-Pro, Football Digest All-Pro, Football News All-NFC); S Eugene Robinson (Sports Illustrated All-Pro); DE Reggie White (UPI All-NFC, College & Pro Football Newsweekly All-Pro, Football News All-NFC)

1997 — S LeRoy Butler (AP All-Pro, Pro Football Weekly All-Pro, Sports Illustrated All-Pro, Sporting News All-Pro, USA Today All-Pro, College & Pro Football Newsweekly All-Pro, Football News All-NFC); CB Doug Evans (Football Digest All-Pro); QB Brett Favre (AP All-Pro, Pro Football Weekly All-Pro, Sports Illustrated All-Pro, Sporting News All-Pro, USA Today All-Pro, College & Pro Football Newsweekly All-Pro, Football Digest All-Pro, Football News All-NFC); P Craig Hentrich (College & Pro Football Newsweekly All-Pro); ST Travis Jervey (Pro Football Weekly All-Pro); RB Dorsey Levens (Football News All-NFC); DE Reggie White (Football News All-NFC); LB Brian Williams (USA Today All-Pro)

PACKERS ON NFL ALL-TIME TEAMS

All-50 Year Team
(selected in 1970)

Cal Hubbard	Tackle
Don Hutson	End
Jerry Kramer	Guard
Ray Nitschke	Linebacker

Two-Way Team
(selected in 1994)

Clarke Hinkle	Back
Cal Hubbard	Tackle
Don Hutson	End

75th Anniversary Team
(selected in 1994)

Forrest Gregg	Tackle
Ted Hendricks	Linebacker
Don Hutson	Wide Receiver
Ray Nitschke	Linebacker
Jan Stenerud	Kicker
Reggie White	Defensive End

Most Valuable Player / Player of the Year
1941   Don Hutson, E (NFL)
1942   Don Hutson, E (NFL)
1961   Paul Hornung, HB (AP, UPI, TSN, MC)
1962   Jim Taylor, FB (AP, NEA)
1966   Bart Starr, QB (AP, UPI, TSN, NEA)
1995   Brett Favre, QB (AP, TSN, FW, MC)
1996   Brett Favre, QB (AP, TSN, FW, MC)
1997   Brett Favre, QB (AP)

Offensive MVP / Player of the Year
1995   Brett Favre, QB (AP, PW, UPI-NFC)
1996   Brett Favre, QB (UPI-NFC)

Defensive MVP / Player of the Year
1989   Tim Harris, LB (NEA)
1995   Reggie White, DE (UPI-NFC)

Super Bowl MVP
I   Bart Starr, QB
II   Bart Starr, QB
XXXI   Desmond Howard, KR

Pro Bowl MVP
1982   John Jefferson (tie)

Rookie of the Year
1959   Boyd Dowler, E (UPI)

NFC Rookie of the Year
1971   John Brockington, RB (UPI, TSN, NEA)
1972   Chester Marcol, K (UPI, TSN)
1972   Willie Buchanon, CB (NEA)

Offensive Rookie of the Year
1971   John Brockington, RB (AP)

Defensive Rookie of the Year
1972   Willie Buchanon, CB (AP)
1984   Tom Flynn, S (PW)

Coach of the Year
1959   Vince Lombardi (AP, UPI)
1961   Vince Lombardi (TSN)
1989   Lindy Infante (AP, TSN)

NFC Coach of the Year
1972   Dan Devine (UPI, FW)
1989   Lindy Infante (UPI, FW)

NFL-Official NFL award (Joe F. Carr Trophy); AP-Associated Press; UPI-United Press International; TSN-The Sporting News; FW-Pro Football Writers of America; PW-Pro Football Weekly; NEA-Newspaper Enterprise Association; MC-Maxwell Club of Philadelphia (Bert Bell Trophy)

PRO BOWL SELECTIONS

1938 — FB Clarke Hinkle, QB Cecil Isbell, G Russ Letlow

1939 — B Frank Balazs, C Charley Brock, QB Hank Bruder, FB Larry Buhler, QB/E Larry Craig, G Paul Engebretsen, E Milt Gantenbein, G Charles Goldenberg, C Tom Greenfield, QB Arnie Herber, FB Clarke Hinkle, E Don Hutson, QB Cecil Isbell, E Harry Jacunski, HB Ed Jankowski, T Paul Kell, HB Jim Lawrence, HB Joe Laws, T Bill Lee, G Russ Letlow, E Allen Moore, E Carl Mulleneaux, T Baby Ray, T Charles Schultz, T Ernie Smith, C Earl Svendsen, G Pete Tinsley, HB Andy Uram, QB Dick Weisgerber, G Gust Zarnas

1940 — C Charley Brock, FB Clarke Hinkle, E Don Hutson, E Carl Mulleneaux

1941 — QB/E Larry Craig, E Don Hutson, QB Cecil Isbell

1942 — C Charley Brock, QB/E Larry Craig, E Don Hutson*, QB Cecil Isbell*

1950 — HB Billy Grimes, C Ed Neal

1951 — HB Billy Grimes, T Dick Wildung

1952 — E Billy Howton, G Deral Teteak, E Abner Wimberly

1953 — DT Dave Hanner, E John Martinkovic, LB Clayton Tonnemaker

1954 — DT Dave Hanner, E John Martinkovic, LB Roger Zatkoff

1955 — DB Bobby Dillon, FB Howie Ferguson, E Billy Howton, E John Martinkovic, LB Roger Zatkoff

1956 — DB Bobby Dillon, E Billy Howton, QB Tobin Rote, LB Roger Zatkoff

1957 — DB Bobby Dillon, E Billy Howton, C Jim Ringo

1958 — DB Bobby Dillon, C Jim Ringo

1959 — LB Bill Forester, T Forrest Gregg, RB Paul Hornung, C Jim Ringo, S Emlen Tunnell

1960 — LB Dan Currie, LB Bill Forester, T Forrest Gregg, RB Paul Hornung, DT Henry Jordan, C Jim Ringo, QB Bart Starr, FB Jim Taylor

1961 — LB Bill Forester, T Forrest Gregg, DT Henry Jordan, E Max McGee, C Jim Ringo, QB Bart Starr, FB Jim Taylor, DB Jesse Whittenton

1962 — LB Bill Forester, T Forrest Gregg, G Jerry Kramer, TE Ron Kramer, RB Tom Moore, C Jim Ringo, QB Bart Starr, FB Jim Taylor*, S Willie Wood

1963 — CB Herb Adderley, DE Willie Davis, T Forrest Gregg, DT Henry Jordan, G Jerry Kramer, C Jim Ringo, FB Jim Taylor, DB Jesse Whittenton

1964 — CB Herb Adderley, DE Willie Davis, T Forrest Gregg, LB Ray Nitschke, FB Jim Taylor, S Willie Wood

1965 — CB Herb Adderley, LB Lee Roy Caffey, DE Willie Davis, WR Boyd Dowler, S Willie Wood

1966 — CB Herb Adderley, DE Willie Davis, T Forrest Gregg, DT Henry Jordan, LB Dave Robinson, T Bob Skoronski, QB Bart Starr, S Willie Wood

1967 — CB Herb Adderley, K Don Chandler, DE Willie Davis, WR Boyd Dowler, T Forrest Gregg, DB Bob Jeter, G Jerry Kramer, LB Dave Robinson, S Willie Wood

1968 — RB Donny Anderson, WR Carroll Dale, T Forrest Gregg, S Willie Wood

1969 — WR Carroll Dale, G Gale Gillingham, DB Bob Jeter, LB Dave Robinson, S Willie Wood

1970 — LB Fred Carr, WR Carroll Dale, G Gale Gillingham, S Willie Wood

1971 — RB John Brockington, G Gale Gillingham

1972 — RB John Brockington, DT Bob Brown, LB Fred Carr, K Chester Marcol

1973 — RB John Brockington, CB Willie Buchanon*, LB Jim Carter, CB Ken Ellis, G Gale Gillingham*

1974 — CB Willie Buchanon, CB Ken Ellis, G Gale Gillingham, LB Ted Hendricks, K Chester Marcol

1975 — LB Fred Carr, KR Steve Odom

1978 — CB Willie Buchanon, DE Ezra Johnson, WR James Lofton, RB Terdell Middleton

1980 — WR James Lofton

1981 — WR James Lofton

1982 — TE Paul Coffman, WR John Jefferson, WR James Lofton, C Larry McCarren

1983 — TE Paul Coffman, WR James Lofton, C Larry McCarren

1984 — TE Paul Coffman, WR James Lofton

1985 — WR James Lofton

1989 — RB Brent Fullwood, LB Tim Harris, QB Don Majkowski*, WR Sterling Sharpe

1990 — WR Sterling Sharpe

1992 — S Chuck Cecil, QB Brett Favre, WR Sterling Sharpe

1993 — S LeRoy Butler, QB Brett Favre, WR Sterling Sharpe*, DE Reggie White

1994 — LB Bryce Paup, WR Sterling Sharpe*, DE Reggie White*

1995 — TE Mark Chmura, QB Brett Favre, DE Reggie White

1996 — S LeRoy Butler, QB Brett Favre, TE Keith Jackson, DE Reggie White, C Frank Winters

1997 — S LeRoy Butler, TE Mark Chmura, QB Brett Favre*, ST Travis Jervey, RB Dorsey Levens, DE Reggie White*

*selected, but did not play

note: Game not held following 1943-49 seasons

Team	W	L	T	Pct.	PF	PA		W	L	Pct.	PF	PA
				— REGULAR SEASON —						— POSTSEASON —		
Arizona*	39	21	4	.641	1,078	823		1	0	1.000	41	16
Atlanta	10	9	0	.526	439	352		1	0	1.000	37	20
Baltimore	0	0	0	.000	0	0		0	0	.000	0	0
Buffalo	2	5	0	.286	127	179		0	0	.000	0	0
Carolina	1	0	0	1.000	31	10		1	0	1.000	30	13
Chicago	67	81	6	.455	2,392	2,609		0	1	.000	14	33
Cincinnati	4	4	0	.500	138	172		0	0	.000	0	0
Cleveland**	8	6	0	.571	313	285		1	0	1.000	23	12
Dallas	9	9	0	.500	380	377		2	4	.333	134	181
Denver	3	4	1	.438	165	141		0	1	.000	24	31
Detroit***	69	59	7	.537	2,696	2,437		2	0	1.000	44	36
Indianapolis****	18	19	1	.487	804	837		1	0	1.000	13	10
Jacksonville	1	0	0	1.000	24	14		0	0	.000	0	0
Kansas City	1	5	1	.214	85	121		1	0	1.000	35	10
Miami	1	8	0	.111	131	224		0	0	.000	0	0
Minnesota	36	36	1	.500	1,451	1,300		0	0	.000	0	0
New England	3	3	0	.500	160	103		1	0	1.000	35	21
New Orleans	13	4	0	.765	459	334		0	0	.000	0	0
N.Y. Giants	22	20	2	.523	704	752		4	1	.800	111	37
N.Y. Jets	2	5	0	.286	97	130		0	0	.000	0	0
Oakland+	2	5	0	.286	95	130		1	0	1.000	33	14
Philadelphia	20	9	0	.690	610	433		0	1	.000	13	17
Pittsburgh	18	11	0	.621	689	489		0	0	.000	0	0
St. Louis++	39	43	2	.476	1,858	1,967		1	0	1.000	28	7
San Diego	5	1	0	.833	170	80		0	0	.000	0	0
San Francisco	22	25	1	.469	922	1,000		3	0	1.000	85	41
Seattle	4	3	0	.571	188	156		0	0	.000	0	0
Tampa Bay	24	13	1	.645	741	546		1	0	1.000	21	7
Tennessee+++	3	3	0	.500	96	131		0	0	.000	0	0
Washington++++	13	12	1	.519	459	434		1	1	.500	24	22

* Franchise location known as Phoenix prior to 1994, located in St. Louis prior to 1988, and located in Chicago prior to 1960
** Franchise in suspension until 1999 season
*** Franchise located in Portsmouth, Ohio, prior to 1934 and known as Spartans
**** Franchise located in Baltimore prior to 1984
\+ Franchise located in Los Angeles from 1982-94
\+\+ Franchise located in Los Angeles prior to 1995 and located in Cleveland prior to 1946
\+\+\+ Franchise located in Houston prior to 1997
\+\+\+\+ Franchise located in Boston prior to 1937 and known as Braves prior to 1933

NOTE: Results of combined teams are not recognized by NFL in series records

PACKERS VS. DEFUNCT TEAMS
(1921-52)

*Baltimore Colts	0-1-0		Kansas City Blues	2-0-0
Boston Yanks	3-0-0		Louisville Colonels	1-0-0
Brooklyn Dodgers/Tigers	10-0-0		Milwaukee Badgers	9-0-1
Card-Pitt	2-0-0		Minneapolis Marines/Redjackets	8-0-0
Cincinnati Reds	1-0-0		New York Bulldogs/Yanks	2-3-0
Cleveland Bulldogs	1-0-0		New York Yankees	1-0-1
Cleveland Indians	1-0-0		Phil-Pitt Steagles	1-0-0
Columbus Panhandles	2-0-0		Pottsville Maroons	1-2-0
Dallas Texans	5-0-0		Providence Steam Roller	4-0-1
Dayton Triangles	2-0-0		Racine Legion/Tornadoes	4-3-1
Detroit Panthers	2-0-0		Rochester Jeffersons	1-0-0
Duluth Kelleys/Eskimos	3-1-1		Rock Island Independents	1-3-1
Evansville Crimson Giants	1-0-0		St. Louis All-Stars	1-0-1
Frankford Yellowjackets	5-4-1		St. Louis Gunners	1-0-0
Hammond Pros	3-0-0		Staten Island Stapletons	4-0-0

Franchise folded after '50 season, replaced in '53 by current team which moved to Indianapolis in 1984

ARIZONA*

1921 — Tie, 3-3 (C)
1922 — Cardinals, 16-3 (C)
1924 — Cardinals, 3-0 (C)
1925 — Cardinals, 9-6 (C)
1926 — Cardinals, 13-7 (GB)
         Packers, 3-0 (C)
1927 — Packers, 13-0 (GB)
         Tie, 6-6 (C)
1928 — Packers, 20-0 (GB)
1929 — Packers, 9-2 (GB)
         Packers, 7-6 (C)
         Packers, 12-0 (C)
1930 — Packers, 14-0 (GB)
         Cardinals, 13-6 (C)
1931 — Packers, 26-7 (GB)
         Cardinals, 21-13 (C)
1932 — Packers, 15-7 (GB)
         Packers, 19-9 (C)
1933 — Packers, 14-6 (C)
1934 — Packers, 15-0 (GB)
         Cardinals, 9-0 (Milw)
         Cardinals, 6-0 (C)
1935 — Cardinals, 7-6 (GB)
         Cardinals, 3-0 (Milw)
         Cardinals, 9-7 (C)
1936 — Packers, 10-7 (GB)
         Packers, 24-0 (Milw)
         Tie, 0-0 (C)
1937 — Cardinals, 14-7 (GB)
         Packers, 34-13 (Milw)
1938 — Packers, 28-7 (Milw)
         Packers, 24-22 (Buffalo)
1939 — Packers, 14-10 (GB)
         Packers, 27-20 (Milw)
1940 — Packers, 31-6 (Milw)
         Packers, 28-7 (C)
1941 — Packers, 14-13 (Milw)
         Packers, 17-9 (GB)
1942 — Packers, 17-13 (C)
         Packers, 55-24 (GB)
1943 — Packers, 28-7 (C)
         Packers, 35-14 (Milw)
1945 — Packers, 33-14 (GB)
1946 — Packers, 19-7 (C)
         Cardinals, 24-6 (GB)
1947 — Cardinals, 14-10 (GB)
         Cardinals, 21-20 (C)
1948 — Cardinals, 17-7 (Milw)
         Cardinals, 42-7 (C)
1949 — Cardinals, 39-17 (Milw)
         Cardinals, 41-21 (C)
1955 — Packers, 31-14 (GB)
1956 — Packers, 24-21 (C)
1962 — Packers, 17-0 (Milw)
1963 — Packers, 30-7 (StL)
1967 — Packers, 31-23 (StL)
1969 — Packers, 45-28 (GB)
1971 — Tie, 16-16 (StL)
1973 — Packers, 25-21 (GB)
1976 — Cardinals, 29-0 (StL)
1982 — **Packers, 41-16 (GB)
1984 — Packers, 24-23 (GB)
1985 — Cardinals, 43-28 (StL)
1988 — Packers, 26-17 (P)
1990 — Packers, 24-21 (P)

*Franchise location known as Phoenix prior to 1994, located in St. Louis prior to 1988, and located in Chicago prior to 1960
**NFC First-Round Playoff

ATLANTA

1966 — Packers, 56-3 (Milw)
1967 — Packers, 23-0 (Milw)
1968 — Packers, 38-7 (A)
1969 — Packers, 28-10 (GB)
1970 — Packers, 27-24 (GB)
1971 — Falcons, 28-21 (A)
1972 — Falcons, 10-9 (Milw)
1974 — Falcons, 10-3 (A)
1975 — Packers, 22-13 (GB)
1976 — Packers, 24-20 (A)
1979 — Falcons, 25-7 (A)
1981 — Falcons, 31-17 (GB)
1982 — Packers, 38-7 (A)
1983 — Falcons, 47-41 (A) OT
1988 — Falcons, 20-0 (A)
1989 — Packers, 23-21 (Milw)
1991 — Falcons, 35-31 (A)
1992 — Falcons, 24-10 (A)
1994 — Packers, 21-17 (Milw)
1995 — *Packers, 37-20 (GB)
*NFC Wild Card Playoff

BALTIMORE

BUFFALO

1974 — Bills, 27-7 (GB)
1979 — Bills, 19-12 (B)
1982 — Packers, 33-21 (Milw)
1988 — Bills, 28-0 (B)
1991 — Bills, 34-24 (Milw)
1994 — Bills, 29-20 (B)
1997 — Packers, 31-21 (GB)

CAROLINA

1996 — *Packers, 30-13 (GB)
1997 — Packers, 31-10 (C)
*NFC Championship

CHICAGO

1921 — *Staleys, 20-0 (C)
1923 — Bears, 3-0 (GB)
1924 — Bears, 3-0 (C)
1925 — Packers, 14-10 (GB)
         Bears, 21-0 (C)
1926 — Tie, 6-6 (GB)
         Bears, 19-13 (C)
         Tie, 3-3 (C)
1927 — Bears, 7-6 (GB)
         Bears, 14-6 (C)
1928 — Tie, 12-12 (GB)
         Packers, 16-6 (C)
         Packers, 6-0 (C)
1929 — Packers, 23-0 (GB)
         Packers, 14-0 (C)
         Packers, 25-0 (C)
1930 — Packers, 7-0 (GB)
         Packers, 13-12 (C)
         Bears, 21-0 (C)
1931 — Packers, 7-0 (GB)
         Packers, 6-2 (C)
         Bears, 7-6 (C)
1932 — Tie, 0-0 (GB)
         Packers, 2-0 (C)
         Bears, 9-0 (C)
1933 — Bears, 14-7 (GB)
         Bears, 10-7 (C)
         Bears, 7-6 (C)
1934 — Bears, 24-10 (GB)
         Bears, 27-14 (C)
1935 — Packers, 7-0 (GB)
         Packers, 17-14 (C)

1936 — Bears, 30-3 (GB)
         Packers, 21-10 (C)
1937 — Bears, 14-2 (GB)
         Packers, 24-14 (C)
1938 — Bears, 2-0 (GB)
         Packers, 24-17 (C)
1939 — Packers, 21-16 (GB)
         Bears, 30-27 (C)
1940 — Bears, 41-10 (GB)
         Bears, 14-7 (C)
1941 — Bears, 25-17 (GB)
         Packers, 16-14 (C)
         **Bears, 33-14 (C)
1942 — Bears, 44-28 (GB)
         Bears, 38-7 (C)
1943 — Tie, 21-21 (GB)
         Bears, 21-7 (C)
1944 — Packers, 42-28 (GB)
         Bears, 21-0 (C)
1945 — Packers, 31-21 (GB)
         Bears, 28-24 (C)
1946 — Bears, 30-7 (GB)
         Bears, 10-7 (C)
1947 — Packers, 29-20 (GB)
         Bears, 20-17 (C)
1948 — Bears, 45-7 (GB)
         Bears, 7-6 (C)
1949 — Bears, 17-0 (GB)
         Bears, 24-3 (C)
1950 — Packers, 31-21 (GB)
         Bears, 28-14 (C)
1951 — Bears, 31-20 (GB)
         Bears, 24-13 (C)
1952 — Bears, 24-14 (GB)
         Packers, 41-28 (C)
1953 — Bears, 17-13 (GB)
         Tie, 21-21 (C)
1954 — Bears, 10-3 (GB)
         Bears, 28-23 (C)
1955 — Packers, 24-3 (GB)
         Bears, 52-31 (C)
1956 — Bears, 37-21 (GB)
         Bears, 38-14 (C)
1957 — Packers, 21-17 (GB)
         Bears, 21-14 (C)
1958 — Bears, 34-20 (GB)
         Bears, 24-10 (C)
1959 — Packers, 9-6 (GB)
         Bears, 28-17 (C)
1960 — Bears, 17-14 (GB)
         Packers, 41-13 (C)
1961 — Packers, 24-0 (GB)
         Packers, 31-28 (C)
1962 — Packers, 49-0 (GB)
         Packers, 38-7 (C)
1963 — Bears, 10-3 (GB)
         Bears, 26-7 (C)
1964 — Packers, 23-12 (GB)
         Packers, 17-3 (C)
1965 — Packers, 23-14 (GB)
         Bears, 31-10 (C)
1966 — Packers, 17-0 (C)
         Packers, 13-6 (GB)
1967 — Packers, 13-10 (GB)
         Packers, 17-13 (C)
1968 — Bears, 13-10 (GB)
         Packers, 28-27 (C)
1969 — Packers, 17-0 (GB)
         Packers, 21-3 (C)
1970 — Packers, 20-19 (GB)
         Bears, 35-17 (C)
1971 — Packers, 17-14 (C)

CHICAGO (continued)
Packers, 31-10 (GB)
1972 — Packers, 20-17 (GB)
Packers, 23-17 (C)
1973 — Bears, 31-17 (GB)
Packers, 21-0 (C)
1974 — Bears, 10-9 (C)
Packers, 20-3 (Milw)
1975 — Bears, 27-14 (C)
Packers, 28-7 (GB)
1976 — Bears, 24-13 (C)
Bears, 16-10 (GB)
1977 — Bears, 26-0 (GB)
Bears, 21-10 (C)
1978 — Packers, 24-14 (GB)
Bears, 14-0 (C)
1979 — Bears, 6-3 (C)
Bears, 15-14 (GB)
1980 — Packers, 12-6 (GB) OT
Bears, 61-7 (C)
1981 — Packers, 16-9 (C)
Packers, 21-17 (GB)
1983 — Packers, 31-28 (GB)
Bears, 23-21 (C)
1984 — Bears, 9-7 (GB)
Packers, 20-14 (C)
1985 — Bears, 23-7 (C)
Bears, 16-10 (GB)
1986 — Bears, 25-12 (GB)
Bears, 12-10 (C)
1987 — Bears, 26-24 (GB)
Bears, 23-10 (C)
1988 — Bears, 24-6 (GB)
Bears, 16-0 (C)
1989 — Packers, 14-13 (GB)
Packers, 40-28 (C)
1990 — Bears, 31-13 (GB)
Bears, 27-13 (C)
1991 — Bears, 10-0 (C)
Bears, 27-13 (C)
1992 — Bears, 30-10 (GB)
Packers, 17-3 (C)
1993 — Packers, 17-3 (GB)
Bears, 30-17 (C)
1994 — Packers, 33-6 (C)
Packers, 40-3 (GB)
1995 — Packers, 27-24 (C)
Packers, 35-28 (GB)
1996 — Packers, 37-6 (C)
Packers, 28-17 (GB)
1997 — Packers, 38-24 (GB)
Packers, 24-23 (C)
*Bears known as Staleys prior to 1922
**Western Division Playoff

CINCINNATI
1971 — Packers, 20-17 (GB)
1976 — Bengals, 28-7 (C)
1977 — Bengals, 17-7 (Milw)
1980 — Packers, 14-9 (GB)
1983 — Bengals, 34-14 (C)
1986 — Bengals, 34-28 (Milw)
1992 — Packers, 24-23 (GB)
1995 — Packers, 24-10 (GB)

CLEVELAND*
1953 — Browns, 27-0 (GB)
1955 — Browns, 41-10 (C)
1956 — Browns, 24-7 (Milw)
1961 — Packers, 49-17 (C)
1964 — Packers, 28-21 (Milw)
1965 — **Packers, 23-12 (GB)
1966 — Packers, 21-20 (C)

1967 — Packers, 55-7 (Milw)
1969 — Browns, 20-7 (C)
1972 — Packers, 26-10 (C)
1980 — Browns, 26-21 (C)
1983 — Packers, 35-21 (Milw)
1986 — Packers, 17-14 (C)
1992 — Browns, 17-6 (C)
1995 — Packers, 31-20 (C)
*Franchise in suspension until 1999 season
**NFL Championship

DALLAS
1960 — Packers, 41-7 (GB)
1964 — Packers, 45-21 (D)
1965 — Packers, 13-3 (Milw)
1966 — *Packers, 34-27 (D)
1967 — *Packers, 21-17 (GB)
1968 — Packers, 28-17 (D)
1970 — Cowboys, 16-3 (D)
1972 — Packers, 16-13 (Milw)
1975 — Packers, 19-17 (D)
1978 — Cowboys, 42-14 (Milw)
1980 — Cowboys, 28-7 (Milw)
1982 — **Cowboys, 37-26 (D)
1984 — Cowboys, 20-6 (D)
1989 — Packers, 31-13 (GB)
Packers, 20-10 (D)
1991 — Cowboys, 20-17 (Milw)
1993 — Cowboys, 36-14 (D)
**Cowboys, 27-17 (D)
1994 — Cowboys, 42-31 (D)
**Cowboys, 35-9 (D)
1995 — Cowboys, 34-24 (D)
+Cowboys, 38-27 (D)
1996 — Cowboys, 21-6 (D)
1997 — Packers, 45-17 (GB)
*NFL Championship
**NFC Divisional Playoff
+NFC Championship

DENVER
1971 — Packers, 34-13 (Milw)
1975 — Broncos, 23-13 (D)
1978 — Broncos, 16-3 (D)
1984 — Broncos, 17-14 (D)
1987 — Tie, 17-17 (Milw) OT
1990 — Broncos, 22-13 (D)
1993 — Packers, 30-27 (GB)
1996 — Packers, 41-6 (GB)
1997 — *Broncos, 31-24 (San Diego)
*Super Bowl XXXII

DETROIT*
1930 — Packers, 47-13 (GB)
Tie, 6-6 (P)
1932 — Packers, 15-10 (GB)
Spartans, 19-0 (P)
1933 — Packers, 17-0 (GB)
Spartans, 7-0 (P)
1934 — Lions, 3-0 (GB)
Packers, 3-0 (D)
1935 — Packers, 13-9 (Milw)
Packers, 31-7 (GB)
Lions, 20-10 (D)
1936 — Packers, 20-18 (GB)
Packers, 26-17 (D)
1937 — Packers, 26-6 (GB)
Packers, 14-13 (D)
1938 — Lions, 17-7 (GB)
Packers, 28-7 (D)
1939 — Packers, 26-7 (GB)
Packers, 12-7 (D)

1940 — Lions, 23-14 (GB)
Packers, 50-7 (D)
1941 — Packers, 23-0 (GB)
Packers, 24-7 (D)
1942 — Packers, 38-7 (Milw)
Packers, 28-7 (D)
1943 — Packers, 35-14 (GB)
Packers, 27-6 (D)
1944 — Packers, 27-6 (Milw)
Packers, 14-0 (D)
1945 — Packers, 57-21 (Milw)
Lions, 14-3 (D)
1946 — Packers, 10-7 (Milw)
Packers, 9-0 (D)
1947 — Packers, 34-17 (GB)
Packers, 35-14 (D)
1948 — Packers, 33-21 (GB)
Lions, 24-20 (D)
1949 — Packers, 16-14 (Milw)
Lions, 21-7 (D)
1950 — Lions, 45-7 (GB)
Lions, 24-21 (D)
1951 — Lions, 24-17 (GB)
Lions, 52-35 (D)
1952 — Lions, 52-17 (GB)
Lions, 48-24 (D)
1953 — Lions, 14-7 (GB)
Lions, 34-15 (D)
1954 — Lions, 21-17 (GB)
Lions, 28-24 (D)
1955 — Packers, 20-17 (GB)
Lions, 24-10 (D)
1956 — Lions, 20-16 (GB)
Packers, 24-20 (D)
1957 — Lions, 24-14 (GB)
Lions, 18-6 (D)
1958 — Tie, 13-13 (GB)
Lions, 24-14 (D)
1959 — Packers, 28-10 (GB)
Packers, 24-17 (D)
1960 — Packers, 28-9 (GB)
Lions, 23-10 (D)
1961 — Lions, 17-13 (Milw)
Packers, 17-9 (D)
1962 — Packers, 9-7 (GB)
Lions, 26-14 (D)
1963 — Packers, 31-10 (Milw)
Tie, 13-13 (D)
1964 — Packers, 14-10 (D)
Packers, 30-7 (GB)
1965 — Packers, 31-21 (D)
Lions, 12-7 (GB)
1966 — Packers, 23-14 (GB)
Packers, 31-7 (D)
1967 — Tie, 17-17 (GB)
Packers, 27-17 (D)
1968 — Lions, 23-17 (GB)
Tie, 14-14 (D)
1969 — Packers, 28-17 (D)
Lions, 16-10 (GB)
1970 — Lions, 40-0 (D)
Lions, 20-0 (D)
1971 — Lions, 31-28 (D)
Tie, 14-14 (Milw)
1972 — Packers, 24-23 (D)
Packers, 33-7 (GB)
1973 — Tie, 13-13 (GB)
Lions, 34-0 (D)
1974 — Packers, 21-19 (Milw)
Lions, 19-17 (D)
1975 — Lions, 30-16 (Milw)
Lions, 13-10 (D)
1976 — Packers, 24-14 (GB)

DETROIT (continued)
　　　Lions, 27-6 (D)
1977 — Lions, 10-6 (D)
　　　Packers, 10-9 (GB)
1978 — Packers, 13-7 (D)
　　　Packers, 35-14 (Milw)
1979 — Packers, 24-16 (Milw)
　　　Packers, 18-13 (D)
1980 — Lions, 29-7 (Milw)
　　　Lions, 24-3 (D)
1981 — Lions, 31-27 (D)
　　　Packers, 31-17 (GB)
1982 — Lions, 30-10 (GB)
　　　Lions, 27-24 (D)
1983 — Lions, 38-14 (D)
　　　Lions, 23-20 (Milw) OT
1984 — Packers, 41-9 (GB)
　　　Lions, 31-28 (D)
1985 — Packers, 43-10 (GB)
　　　Packers, 26-23 (D)
1986 — Lions, 21-14 (GB)
　　　Packers, 44-40 (D)
1987 — Lions, 19-16 (GB) OT
　　　Packers, 34-33 (D)
1988 — Lions, 19-9 (Milw)
　　　Lions, 30-14 (D)
1989 — Packers, 23-20 (Milw) OT
　　　Lions, 31-22 (D)
1990 — Packers, 24-21 (D)
　　　Lions, 24-17 (GB)
1991 — Lions, 23-14 (D)
　　　Lions, 21-17 (GB)
1992 — Packers, 27-13 (D)
　　　Packers, 38-10 (Milw)
1993 — Packers, 26-17 (Milw)
　　　Lions, 30-20 (D)
　　　**Packers, 28-24 (D)
1994 — Packers, 38-30 (Milw)
　　　Lions, 34-31 (D)
　　　**Packers, 16-12 (GB)
1995 — Packers, 30-21 (GB)
　　　Lions, 24-16 (D)
1996 — Packers, 28-18 (GB)
　　　Packers, 31-3 (D)
1997 — Lions, 26-15 (D)
　　　Packers, 20-10 (GB)
Franchise located in Portsmouth, Ohio, prior to 1934 and known as Spartans
***NFC Wild Card Playoff*

INDIANAPOLIS*
1953 — Packers, 37-14 (GB)
　　　Packers, 35-24 (B)
1954 — Packers, 7-6 (B)
　　　Packers, 24-13 (Milw)
1955 — Colts, 24-20 (Milw)
　　　Colts, 14-10 (B)
1956 — Packers, 38-33 (Milw)
　　　Colts, 28-21 (B)
1957 — Colts, 45-17 (Milw)
　　　Packers, 24-21 (B)
1958 — Colts, 24-17 (Milw)
　　　Colts, 56-0 (B)
1959 — Colts, 38-21 (B)
　　　Colts, 28-24 (Milw)
1960 — Packers, 35-21 (GB)
　　　Colts, 38-24 (B)
1961 — Packers, 45-7 (GB)
　　　Colts, 45-21 (B)
1962 — Packers, 17-6 (B)
　　　Packers, 17-13 (GB)
1963 — Packers, 31-20 (GB)

　　　Packers, 34-20 (B)
1964 — Colts, 21-20 (GB)
　　　Colts, 24-21 (B)
1965 — Packers, 20-17 (Milw)
　　　Packers, 42-27 (B)
　　　**Packers, 13-10 (GB) OT
1966 — Packers, 24-3 (Milw)
　　　Packers, 14-10 (B)
1967 — Colts, 13-10 (B)
1968 — Colts, 16-3 (GB)
1969 — Colts, 14-6 (B)
1970 — Colts, 13-10 (Milw)
1974 — Packers, 20-13 (B)
1982 — Tie, 20-20 (B) OT
1985 — Colts, 37-10 (I)
1988 — Colts, 20-13 (GB)
1991 — Packers, 14-10 (Milw)
1997 — Colts, 41-38 (I)
Franchise located in Baltimore prior to 1984
***Western Conference Championship*

JACKSONVILLE
1995 — Packers, 24-14 (J)

KANSAS CITY
1966 — *Packers, 35-10 (Los Angeles)
1973 — Tie, 10-10 (Milw)
1977 — Chiefs, 20-10 (KC)
1987 — Packers, 23-3 (KC)
1989 — Chiefs, 21-3 (GB)
1990 — Chiefs, 17-3 (GB)
1993 — Chiefs, 23-16 (KC)
1996 — Packers, 27-20 (KC)
Super Bowl I

MIAMI
1971 — Dolphins, 27-6 (Mia)
1975 — Dolphins, 31-7 (GB)
1979 — Dolphins, 27-7 (Mia)
1985 — Dolphins, 34-24 (Mia)
1988 — Dolphins, 24-17 (Mia)
1989 — Dolphins, 23-20 (Mia)
1991 — Dolphins, 16-13 (Mia)
1994 — Dolphins, 24-14 (Milw)
1997 — Packers, 23-18 (GB)

MINNESOTA
1961 — Packers, 33-7 (Minn)
　　　Packers, 28-10 (Milw)
1962 — Packers, 34-7 (GB)
　　　Packers, 48-21 (Minn)
1963 — Packers, 37-28 (Minn)
　　　Packers, 28-7 (GB)
1964 — Vikings, 24-23 (GB)
　　　Packers, 42-13 (Minn)
1965 — Packers, 38-13 (Minn)
　　　Packers, 24-19 (GB)
1966 — Vikings, 20-17 (GB)
　　　Packers, 28-16 (Minn)
1967 — Vikings, 10-7 (Milw)
　　　Packers, 30-27 (Minn)
1968 — Vikings, 26-13 (Milw)
　　　Vikings, 14-10 (Minn)
1969 — Vikings, 19-7 (Milw)
　　　Vikings, 9-7 (Milw)
1970 — Packers, 13-10 (Milw)
　　　Vikings, 10-3 (Minn)
1971 — Vikings, 24-13 (GB)
　　　Vikings, 3-0 (Minn)
1972 — Vikings, 27-13 (GB)
　　　Packers, 23-7 (Minn)

1973 — Vikings, 11-3 (Minn)
　　　Vikings, 31-7 (GB)
1974 — Vikings, 32-17 (GB)
　　　Packers, 19-7 (Minn)
1975 — Vikings, 28-17 (GB)
　　　Vikings, 24-3 (Minn)
1976 — Vikings, 17-10 (Milw)
　　　Vikings, 20-9 (Minn)
1977 — Vikings, 19-7 (Minn)
　　　Vikings, 13-6 (GB)
1978 — Vikings, 21-7 (Minn)
　　　Tie, 10-10 (GB) OT
1979 — Vikings, 27-21 (Minn) OT
　　　Packers, 19-7 (Milw)
1980 — Packers, 16-3 (GB)
　　　Packers, 25-13 (Minn)
1981 — Vikings, 30-13 (Milw)
　　　Packers, 35-23 (Minn)
1982 — Packers, 26-7 (Milw)
1983 — Vikings, 20-17 (GB) OT
　　　Packers, 29-21 (Minn)
1984 — Packers, 45-17 (Milw)
　　　Packers, 38-14 (Minn)
1985 — Packers, 20-17 (Minn)
　　　Packers, 27-17 (Minn)
1986 — Vikings, 42-7 (Minn)
　　　Vikings, 32-6 (GB)
1987 — Packers, 23-16 (Minn)
　　　Packers, 16-10 (Milw)
1988 — Packers, 34-14 (Minn)
　　　Packers, 18-6 (GB)
1989 — Vikings, 26-14 (Minn)
　　　Packers, 20-19 (Minn)
1990 — Packers, 24-10 (Milw)
　　　Vikings, 23-7 (Minn)
1991 — Vikings, 35-21 (GB)
　　　Packers, 27-7 (Minn)
1992 — Vikings, 23-20 (GB) OT
　　　Vikings, 27-7 (Minn)
1993 — Vikings, 15-13 (Minn)
　　　Vikings, 21-17 (Milw)
1994 — Packers, 16-10 (GB)
　　　Vikings, 13-10 (Minn) OT
1995 — Packers, 38-21 (GB)
　　　Vikings, 27-24 (Minn)
1996 — Vikings, 30-21 (Minn)
　　　Packers, 38-10 (GB)
1997 — Packers, 38-32 (GB)
　　　Packers, 27-11 (Minn)

NEW ENGLAND
1973 — Patriots, 33-24 (NE)
1979 — Packers, 27-14 (GB)
1985 — Patriots, 26-20 (NE)
1988 — Packers, 45-3 (Milw)
1994 — Patriots, 17-16 (NE)
1996 — *Packers, 35-21 (New Orleans)
1997 — Packers, 28-10 (NE)
Super Bowl XXXI

NEW ORLEANS
1968 — Packers, 29-7 (Milw)
1971 — Saints, 29-21 (Milw)
1972 — Packers, 30-20 (NO)
1973 — Packers, 30-10 (Milw)
1975 — Saints, 20-19 (NO)
1976 — Packers, 32-27 (Milw)
1977 — Packers, 24-20 (NO)
1978 — Packers, 28-17 (Milw)
1979 — Packers, 28-19 (Milw)
1981 — Packers, 35-7 (NO)
1984 — Packers, 23-13 (NO)

NEW ORLEANS (continued)
1985 — Packers, 38-14 (Milw)
1986 — Saints, 24-10 (NO)
1987 — Saints, 33-24 (NO)
1989 — Packers, 35-34 (GB)
1993 — Packers, 19-17 (NO)
1995 — Packers, 34-23 (NO)

N.Y. GIANTS
1928 — Giants, 6-0 (GB)
Packers, 7-0 (NY)
1929 — Packers, 20-6 (NY)
1930 — Packers, 14-7 (GB)
Giants, 13-6 (NY)
1931 — Packers, 27-7 (GB)
Packers, 14-10 (NY)
1932 — Packers, 13-0 (GB)
Giants, 6-0 (NY)
1933 — Giants, 10-7 (Milw)
Giants, 17-6 (NY)
1934 — Packers, 20-6 (Milw)
Giants, 17-3 (NY)
1935 — Packers, 16-7 (GB)
1936 — Packers, 26-14 (NY)
1937 — Giants, 10-0 (NY)
1938 — Giants, 15-3 (NY)
*Giants, 23-17 (NY)
1939 — *Packers, 27-0 (Milw)
1940 — Giants, 7-3 (NY)
1942 — Tie, 21-21 (NY)
1943 — Packers, 35-21 (NY)
1944 — Giants, 24-0 (NY)
*Packers, 14-7 (NY)
1945 — Packers, 23-14 (NY)
1947 — Tie, 24-24 (NY)
1948 — Giants, 49-3 (Milw)
1949 — Giants, 30-10 (GB)
1952 — Packers, 17-3 (NY)
1957 — Giants, 31-17 (GB)
1959 — Giants, 20-3 (NY)
1961 — Packers, 20-17 (Milw)
*Packers, 37-0 (GB)
1962 — *Packers, 16-7 (NY)
1967 — Packers, 48-21 (NY)
1969 — Packers, 20-10 (Milw)
1971 — Giants, 42-40 (GB)
1973 — Packers, 16-14 (New Haven)
1975 — Packers, 40-14 (Milw)
1980 — Giants, 27-21 (NY)
1981 — Packers, 27-14 (NY)
Packers, 26-24 (Milw)
1982 — Packers, 27-19 (NY)
1983 — Giants, 27-3 (NY)
1985 — Packers, 23-20 (GB)
1986 — Giants, 55-24 (NY)
1987 — Giants, 20-10 (NY)
1992 — Giants, 27-7 (NY)
1995 — Packers, 14-6 (GB)
*NFL Championship

N.Y. JETS
1973 — Packers, 23-7 (Milw)
1979 — Jets, 27-22 (GB)
1981 — Jets, 28-3 (NY)
1982 — Jets, 15-13 (NY)
1985 — Jets, 24-3 (Milw)
1991 — Jets, 19-16 (NY) OT
1994 — Packers, 17-10 (GB)

OAKLAND*
1967 — **Packers, 33-14 (Miami)
1972 — Raiders, 20-14 (GB)
1976 — Raiders, 18-14 (O)

1978 — Raiders, 28-3 (GB)
1984 — Raiders, 28-7 (LA)
1987 — Raiders, 20-0 (GB)
1990 — Packers, 29-16 (LA)
1993 — Packers, 28-0 (GB)
*Franchise located in Los Angeles
from 1982-94
**Super Bowl II

PHILADELPHIA
1933 — Packers 35-9 (GB)
Packers, 10-0 (P)
1934 — Packers, 19-6 (GB)
1935 — Packers, 13-6 (P)
1937 — Packers, 37-7 (Milw)
1939 — Packers, 23-16 (P)
1940 — Packers, 27-20 (GB)
1942 — Packers, 7-0 (P)
1946 — Packers, 19-7 (P)
1947 — Eagles, 28-14 (P)
1951 — Packers, 37-24 (GB)
1952 — Packers, 12-10 (Milw)
1954 — Packers, 37-14 (P)
1958 — Packers, 38-35 (GB)
1960 — *Eagles, 17-13 (P)
1962 — Packers, 49-0 (P)
1968 — Packers, 30-13 (GB)
1970 — Packers, 30-17 (Milw)
1974 — Eagles, 36-14 (P)
1976 — Packers, 28-13 (GB)
1978 — Eagles, 10-3 (P)
1979 — Eagles, 21-10 (GB)
1987 — Packers, 16-10 (GB) OT
1990 — Eagles, 31-0 (P)
1991 — Eagles, 20-3 (GB)
1992 — Packers, 27-24 (Milw)
1993 — Eagles, 20-17 (GB)
1994 — Eagles, 13-7 (P)
1996 — Packers, 39-13 (GB)
1997 — Eagles, 10-9 (P)
*NFL Championship

PITTSBURGH*
1933 — Packers, 47-0 (GB)
1935 — Packers, 27-0 (GB)
Packers, 34-14 (P)
1936 — Packers, 42-10 (Milw)
1938 — Packers, 20-0 (GB)
1940 — Packers, 24-3 (Milw)
1941 — Packers, 54-7 (P)
1942 — Packers, 24-21 (Milw)
1946 — Packers, 17-7 (GB)
1947 — Steelers, 18-17 (Milw)
1948 — Steelers, 38-7 (P)
1949 — Steelers, 30-7 (Milw)
1951 — Packers, 35-33 (Milw)
Steelers, 28-7 (P)
1953 — Steelers, 31-14 (P)
1954 — Steelers, 21-20 (GB)
1957 — Packers, 27-10 (P)
1960 — Packers, 19-13 (P)
1963 — Packers, 33-14 (Milw)
1965 — Packers, 41-9 (P)
1967 — Steelers, 24-17 (GB)
1969 — Packers, 38-34 (P)
1970 — Packers, 20-12 (P)
1975 — Steelers, 16-13 (Milw)
1980 — Steelers, 22-20 (P)
1983 — Steelers, 25-21 (GB)
1986 — Steelers, 27-3 (P)
1992 — Packers, 17-3 (GB)
1995 — Packers, 24-19 (GB)
*Steelers known as Pirates prior to
1941

ST. LOUIS*
1937 — Packers, 35-10 (C)
Packers, 35-7 (GB)
1938 — Packers, 26-17 (GB)
Packers, 28-7 (C)
1939 — Rams, 27-24 (GB)
Packers, 7-6 (C)
1940 — Packers, 31-14 (GB)
Tie, 13-13 (C)
1941 — Packers, 24-7 (Milw)
Packers, 17-14 (C)
1942 — Packers, 45-28 (GB)
Packers, 30-12 (C)
1944 — Packers, 30-21 (GB)
Packers, 42-7 (C)
1945 — Rams, 27-14 (GB)
Rams, 20-7 (C)
1946 — Rams, 21-17 (Milw)
Rams, 38-17 (LA)
1947 — Packers, 17-14 (Milw)
Packers, 30-10 (LA)
1948 — Packers, 16-0 (GB)
Rams, 24-10 (LA)
1949 — Rams, 48-7 (GB)
Rams, 35-7 (LA)
1950 — Rams, 45-14 (Milw)
Rams, 51-14 (LA)
1951 — Rams, 28-0 (Milw)
Rams, 42-14 (LA)
1952 — Rams, 30-28 (Milw)
Rams, 45-27 (LA)
1953 — Rams, 38-20 (Milw)
Rams, 33-17 (LA)
1954 — Packers, 35-17 (Milw)
Rams, 35-27 (LA)
1955 — Packers, 30-28 (Milw)
Rams, 31-17 (LA)
1956 — Packers, 42-17 (Milw)
Rams, 49-21 (LA)
1957 — Rams, 31-27 (Milw)
Rams, 42-17 (LA)
1958 — Rams, 20-7 (GB)
Rams, 34-20 (LA)
1959 — Rams, 45-6 (Milw)
Rams, 38-20 (LA)
1960 — Rams, 33-31 (Milw)
Packers, 35-21 (LA)
1961 — Packers, 35-17 (GB)
Packers, 24-17 (LA)
1962 — Packers, 41-10 (Milw)
Packers, 20-17 (LA)
1963 — Packers, 42-10 (GB)
Packers, 31-14 (LA)
1964 — Rams, 27-17 (GB)
Tie, 24-24 (LA)
1965 — Packers, 6-3 (Milw)
Rams, 21-10 (LA)
1966 — Packers, 24-13 (GB)
Packers, 27-23 (LA)
1967 — Rams, 27-24 (LA)
**Packers, 28-7 (Milw)
1968 — Rams, 16-14 (Milw)
1969 — Rams, 34-21 (LA)
1970 — Rams, 31-21 (GB)
1971 — Rams, 30-13 (LA)
1973 — Rams, 24-7 (LA)
1974 — Packers, 17-6 (Milw)
1975 — Rams, 22-5 (LA)
1977 — Rams, 24-6 (Milw)
1978 — Rams, 31-14 (LA)
1980 — Rams, 51-21 (LA)
1981 — Rams, 35-23 (LA)
1982 — Packers, 35-23 (Milw)

ST. LOUIS (continued)
1983 — Packers, 27-24 (Milw)
1984 — Packers, 31-6 (Milw)
1985 — Rams, 34-17 (LA)
1988 — Rams, 34-7 (GB)
1989 — Rams, 41-38 (LA)
1990 — Packers, 36-24 (GB)
1991 — Rams, 23-21 (LA)
1992 — Packers, 28-13 (GB)
1993 — Packers, 36-6 (Milw)
1994 — Packers, 24-17 (GB)
1995 — Rams, 17-14 (GB)
1996 — Packers, 24-9 (StL)
1997 — Packers, 17-7 (GB)
*Franchise located in Los Angeles prior to 1995 and located in Cleveland prior to 1946
**Western Conference Championship

SAN DIEGO
1970 — Packers, 22-20 (SD)
1974 — Packers, 34-0 (GB)
1978 — Packers, 24-3 (SD)
1984 — Chargers, 34-28 (GB)
1993 — Packers, 20-13 (SD)
1996 — Packers, 42-10 (GB)

SAN FRANCISCO
1950 — Packers, 25-21 (GB)
        49ers, 30-14 (SF)
1951 — 49ers, 31-19 (SF)
1952 — 49ers, 24-14 (SF)
1953 — 49ers, 37-7 (Milw)
        49ers, 48-14 (SF)
1954 — 49ers, 23-17 (Milw)
        49ers, 35-0 (SF)
1955 — Packers, 27-21 (Milw)
        Packers, 28-7 (SF)
1956 — 49ers, 17-16 (GB)
        49ers, 38-20 (SF)
1957 — 49ers, 24-14 (Milw)
        49ers, 27-20 (SF)
1958 — 49ers, 33-12 (Milw)
        49ers, 48-21 (SF)
1959 — Packers, 21-20 (GB)
        Packers, 36-14 (SF)
1960 — Packers, 41-14 (Milw)
        Packers, 13-0 (SF)
1961 — Packers, 30-10 (GB)
        49ers, 22-21 (SF)
1962 — Packers, 31-13 (Milw)
        Packers, 31-21 (SF)
1963 — Packers, 28-10 (Milw)
        Packers, 21-17 (SF)
1964 — Packers, 24-14 (Milw)
        49ers, 24-14 (SF)
1965 — Packers, 27-10 (GB)
        Tie, 24-24 (SF)
1966 — 49ers, 21-20 (SF)
        Packers, 20-7 (Milw)
1967 — Packers, 13-0 (SF)
1968 — 49ers, 27-20 (SF)
1969 — Packers, 14-7 (Milw)
1970 — 49ers, 26-10 (SF)
1972 — Packers, 34-24 (Milw)
1973 — 49ers, 20-6 (SF)
1974 — 49ers, 7-6 (SF)
1976 — 49ers, 26-14 (GB)
1977 — Packers, 16-14 (Milw)
1980 — Packers, 23-16 (Milw)
1981 — 49ers, 13-3 (Milw)
1986 — 49ers, 31-17 (Milw)
1987 — 49ers, 23-12 (GB)

1989 — Packers, 21-17 (SF)
1990 — 49ers, 24-20 (GB)
1995 — *Packers, 27-17 (SF)
1996 — Packers, 23-20 (GB) OT
        *Packers, 35-14 (GB)
1997 — **Packers, 23-10 (SF)
*NFC Divisional Playoff
**NFC Championship

SEATTLE
1976 — Packers, 27-20 (Milw)
1978 — Packers, 45-28 (Milw)
1981 — Packers, 34-24 (GB)
1984 — Seahawks, 30-24 (Milw)
1987 — Seahawks, 24-13 (S)
1990 — Seahawks, 20-14 (Milw)
1996 — Packers, 31-10 (S)

TAMPA BAY
1977 — Packers, 13-0 (TB)
1978 — Packers, 9-7 (GB)
        Packers, 17-7 (TB)
1979 — Buccaneers, 21-10 (GB)
        Buccaneers, 21-3 (TB)
1980 — Tie, 14-14 (TB) OT
        Buccaneers, 20-17 (Milw)
1981 — Buccaneers, 21-10 (GB)
        Buccaneers, 37-3 (TB)
1983 — Packers, 55-14 (GB)
        Packers, 12-9 (TB) OT
1984 — Buccaneers, 30-27 (TB) OT
        Packers, 27-14 (GB)
1985 — Packers, 21-0 (GB)
        Packers, 20-17 (TB)
1986 — Packers, 31-7 (Milw)
        Packers, 21-7 (TB)
1987 — Buccaneers, 23-17 (Milw)
1988 — Buccaneers, 13-10 (GB)
        Buccaneers, 27-24 (TB)
1989 — Buccaneers, 23-21 (GB)
        Packers, 17-16 (TB)
1990 — Buccaneers, 26-14 (TB)
        Packers, 20-10 (Milw)
1991 — Packers, 15-13 (GB)
        Packers, 27-0 (TB)
1992 — Buccaneers, 31-3 (TB)
        Packers, 19-14 (Milw)
1993 — Packers, 37-14 (TB)
        Packers, 13-10 (GB)
1994 — Packers, 30-3 (GB)
        Packers, 34-19 (TB)
1995 — Packers, 35-13 (GB)
        Buccaneers, 13-10 (TB) OT
1996 — Packers, 34-3 (TB)
        Packers, 13-7 (GB)
1997 — Packers, 21-16 (GB)
        Packers, 17-6 (TB)
        *Packers, 21-7 (GB)
*NFC Divisional Playoff

TENNESSEE*
1972 — Packers, 23-10 (H)
1977 — Oilers, 16-10 (GB)
1980 — Oilers, 22-3 (GB)
1983 — Packers, 41-38 (H) OT
1986 — Oilers, 31-3 (GB)
1992 — Packers, 16-14 (H)
*Franchise located in Houston prior to 1997

WASHINGTON*
1932 — Packers, 21-0 (B)
1933 — Tie, 7-7 (GB)
        Redskins, 20-7 (B)

1934 — Packers, 10-0 (B)
1936 — Packers, 31-2 (GB)
        Packers, 7-3 (B)
        **Packers, 21-6 (New York)
1937 — Redskins, 14-6 (W)
1939 — Packers, 24-14 (Milw)
1941 — Packers, 22-17 (W)
1943 — Redskins, 33-7 (Milw)
1946 — Packers, 20-7 (W)
1947 — Packers, 27-10 (Milw)
1948 — Redskins, 23-7 (Milw)
1949 — Redskins, 30-0 (W)
1950 — Packers, 35-21 (Milw)
1952 — Packers, 35-20 (Milw)
1958 — Redskins, 37-21 (W)
1959 — Packers, 21-0 (GB)
1968 — Packers, 27-7 (W)
1972 — Redskins, 21-16 (W)
        +Redskins, 16-3 (W)
1974 — Redskins, 17-6 (GB)
1977 — Redskins, 10-9 (W)
1979 — Redskins, 38-21 (W)
1983 — Packers, 48-47 (GB)
1986 — Redskins, 16-7 (GB)
1988 — Redskins, 20-17 (Milw)
*Franchise located in Boston prior to 1937 and known as Braves prior to 1933
**NFL Championship
+NFC Divisional Playoff

Now boasting a winning record on *Monday Night Football* for the first time in a decade-and-a-half, the Packers make the league-maximum three appearances on ABC-TV's prime-time series for the third consecutive season.

Meeting archrival Minnesota for the second straight year (and only the second time ever) on *MNF*, Green Bay waits until Week 5 of the season (Oct. 5) to hit prime time, facing the Vikings in Lambeau Field after a Metrodome duel in 1997.

A little over a month later (Nov. 9) at Three Rivers Stadium, the Packers square off with the Pittsburgh Steelers on *Monday Night Football* for the first time in the all-time series between two of the NFL's longest-standing members.

Then, escaping the cold December chill of Green Bay, the Packers venture to Tampa to face the rising Bucs. Tampa Bay, which has not played host to a Monday night game in 15 years (much less played in a Monday night game period), welcomes the Green and Gold to its new Raymond James Stadium on Dec. 7. Ironically, prior to this year (the Buccaneers travel to Detroit for a Monday night contest early in the season), the Floridians' last appearance on *Monday Night Football* came against these same Packers, a 12-9 Green Bay victory in overtime Dec. 12, 1983, at Tampa Stadium.

A part of the *Monday Night Football* television series for the sixth consecutive season after a seven-year absence, the Packers now stand 14-12-1 on the program which consistently ranks among the nation's top 10.

For the third straight year, Green Bay will have a team-record four prime-time games in all. And for a second consecutive season, the Packers will face divisional rival Detroit on ESPN, though this year's matchup will occur at the Pontiac (Mich.) Silverdome in a rare Thursday night affair, Oct. 15.

The Packers hold a 6-4 mark on the combined ESPN/TNT prime-time series, including a 4-2 record on this year's venue, ESPN.

Even 15 years later, the Packers continue to hold the distinction of being a part of the highest scoring game in Monday night history — a 48-47 track meet with the Washington Redskins on Oct. 17, 1983, in front of 55,255 spectators at Lambeau Field. Facing the then-reigning Super Bowl champions, the Packers prevailed in a contest which featured 11 touchdowns, 11 extra points and six field goals in the final tally.

Jan Stenerud's 20-yard FG with but 54 seconds remaining decided the issue, though a final, dramatic flourish was added when the 'Skins' Mark Moseley missed a 39-yard field goal try as time expired.

The 95-point production surpassed the previous Monday Night Football scoring mark by a whopping 11 points — set Dec. 20, 1982, when San Diego outscored Cincinnati 50-34. The contest also represented the highest scoring game in the Packers' history, surpassing Green Bay's 52-35 loss at Detroit in 1951.

MONDAY NIGHT FOOTBALL (14-12-1)
(All games played on ABC-TV)

Date		Result
O12, 1970	—	Packers 22, @ San Diego 20
N 9, 1970	—	Baltimore 13, Packers 10 (@ Milw.)
N 1, 1971	—	Packers 14, Detroit 14 (@ Milw.)
N22, 1971	—	@ Atlanta 28, Packers 21
O16, 1972	—	Packers 24, @ Detroit 23
S17, 1973	—	Packers 23, N.Y. Jets 7 (@ Milw.)
N26, 1973	—	@ San Francisco 20, Packers 6
O21, 1974	—	@ Chicago 10, Packers 9
S29, 1975	—	@ Denver 23, Packers 13
N21, 1977	—	@ Washington 10, Packers 9
O 1, 1979	—	@ Packers 27, New England 14
S20, 1982	—	Packers 27, @ N.Y. Giants 19
S26, 1983	—	@ N.Y. Giants 27, Packers 3
O17, 1983	—	@ Packers 48, Washington 47
D12, 1983	—	Packers 12, @ Tampa Bay 9 (ot)
O15, 1984	—	@ Denver 17, Packers 14
O21, 1985	—	@ Chicago 23, Packers 7
S22, 1986	—	Chicago 25, @ Packers 12
N 8, 1993	—	@ Kansas City 23, Packers 16
O31, 1994	—	Packers 33, @ Chicago 6
S11, 1995	—	Packers 27, @ Chicago 24
S 9, 1996	—	@ Packers 39, Philadelphia 13
O14, 1996	—	@ Packers 23, San Francisco 20 (ot)
N18, 1996	—	@ Dallas 21, Packers 6
S 1, 1997	—	@ Packers 38, Chicago 24
O27, 1997	—	Packers 28, @ New England 10
D 1, 1997	—	Packers 27, @ Minnesota 11

OTHER PRIME-TIME GAMES (6-4-0)

Date		Result
D 2, 1990	—	@ Minnesota 23, Packers 7 (ESPN)
O17, 1991	—	Chicago 10, @ Packers 0 (TNT)
D13, 1992	—	Packers 16, @ Houston 14 (ESPN)
O10, 1993	—	@ Packers 30, Denver 27 (TNT)
D12, 1993	—	Packers 20, @ San Diego 13 (ESPN)
O20, 1994	—	@ Minnesota 13, Packers 10 (ot) (TNT)
S24, 1995	—	Packers 24, @ Jacksonville 14 (TNT)
D10, 1995	—	@ Tampa Bay 13, Packers 10 (ot) (ESPN)
N24, 1996	—	Packers 24, @ St. Louis 9 (ESPN)
N 2, 1997	—	@ Packers 20, Detroit 10 (ESPN)

Non-league games are indicated by an asterisk (*). Beginning with 1921, the Packers' first season in the National Football League, non-league game results are not reflected in won-lost record, as well as in seasonal totals of points forward, points against and attendance. Overtime games are indicated by the '+' symbol. The Packers' league-high 12 NFL championship seasons are highlighted in gold.

1919 (10-1-0, .909)

Head Coach: Earl "Curly" Lambeau

			GB	Opp.	Attend.
S 14	Menominee North End A.C.	W	53	0	
S 21	Marinette Northerners	W	61	0	
S 28	New London	W	54	0	
O 5	Sheboygan Company C	W	87	0	
O 12	Racine	W	76	6	
O 19	@ Ishpeming	W	33	0	3,000
O 26	Oshkosh Professionals	W	85	0	
N 2	Milwaukee Maple Leaf A.C.	W	53	0	
N 9	Chicago Chilar A.C.	W	46	0	
N 16	@ Stambaugh Miners	W	17	0	2,500
N 23	@ Beloit Professionals	L	0	6	

Home: 8-0 **Away:** 2-1   565   12

1920 (9-1-1, .900)

Head Coach: Earl "Curly" Lambeau

			GB	Opp.	Attend.
S 26	Chicago Boosters	T	3	3	1,200
O 3	Kaukauna American Legion	W	56	0	
O 10	Stambaugh Miners	W	3	0	800
O 17	Marinette Professionals	W	25	0	
O 24	De Pere	W	62	0	3,500
O 31	Beloit Fairies	W	7	0	2,000
N 7	Milwaukee All-Stars	W	9	0	
N 14	@ Beloit Fairies	L	3	14	
N 21	Menominee Professionals	W	19	7	800
N 25	Stambaugh Miners	W	14	0	
N 28	Milwaukee Lapham A.C.	W	26	0	

Home: 9-0-1 **Away:** 0-1   227   24

1921 (3-2-1, .600)
Sixth (tie)

Head Coach: Earl "Curly" Lambeau

			GB	Opp.	Attend.
O 23	Minneapolis Marines	W	7	6	6,000
O 30	Rock Island Independents	L	3	13	6,000
N 6	Evansville Crimson Giants	W	43	6	
N 13	Hammond Pros	W	14	7	
N 20	@ Chicago Cardinals	T	3	3	2,000
N 27	@ Chicago Staleys	L	0	20	7,000
*D 4	Racine Legion (@ Milw)	T	3	3	6,200

Home: 3-1 **Away:** 0-1-1 (9,000)   70   55

1922 (4-3-3, .571)
Seventh (tie)

Head Coach: Earl "Curly" Lambeau

			GB	Opp.	Attend.
O 1	@ Rock Island Independents	L	14	19	3,500
O 8	Racine Legion	L	6	10	3,603
O 15	@ Chicago Cardinals	L	3	16	3,500
O 22	@ Milwaukee Badgers	T	0	0	6,000
O 29	Rock Island Independents	T	0	0	8,000
N 5	Columbus Panhandles	W	3	0	2,000
N 12	Minneapolis Marines	W	14	6	2,000
N 19	@ Racine Legion	T	3	3	3,000
N 26	Milwaukee Badgers	W	13	0	
*N 30	Duluth Kelleys	W	10	0	2,000
D 3	Racine Legion (@ Milw)	W	14	0	4,500

Home: 3-1-1 **Away:** 0-2-2 (16,603)   70   54
Neutral: 1-0 (4,500)

1923 (7-2-1, .778)
Third (tie)

Head Coach: Earl "Curly" Lambeau

			GB	Opp.	Attend.
S 30	Minneapolis Marines	W	12	0	3,008
O 7	St. Louis All-Stars	T	0	0	2,831
O 14	Chicago Bears	L	0	3	4,451
O 21	Milwaukee Badgers	W	12	0	5,000
O 28	Racine Legion	L	3	24	2,800
N 4	@ St. Louis All-Stars	W	3	0	750
N 11	@ Racine Legion	W	16	0	3,500
N 18	@ Milwaukee Badgers	W	10	7	5,400
N 25	Duluth Kelleys	W	10	0	
N 29	Hammond Pros	W	19	0	

Home: 4-2-1 **Away:** 3-0 (9,650)   85   34

1924 (7-4-0, .636)
Sixth

Head Coach: Earl "Curly" Lambeau

			GB	Opp.	Attend.
S 28	@ Duluth Kelleys	L	3	6	2,200
O 5	@ Chicago Cardinals	L	0	3	2,852
O 12	Kansas City Blues	W	16	0	2,800
O 19	Milwaukee Badgers	W	17	0	4,150
O 26	Minneapolis Marines	W	19	0	2,500
N 2	Racine Legion	W	6	3	4,000
N 9	Duluth Kelleys	W	13	0	2,700
N 16	@ Milwaukee Badgers	W	17	10	3,800
N 23	@ Chicago Bears	L	0	3	6,000
N 27	@ Kansas City Blues	W	17	6	1,542
N 30	@ Racine Legion	L	0	7	2,200

Home: 4-1-2 **Away:** 3-2-1 (35,300)   151   61   57,087

1925 (8-5-0, .615)
Ninth

Head Coach: Earl "Curly" Lambeau

			GB	Opp.	Attend.
S 20	Hammond Pros	W	14	0	3,000
S 27	Chicago Bears	W	14	10	5,389
O 4	@ Rock Island Independents	L	0	3	3,000
O 11	Milwaukee Badgers	W	31	0	2,300
O 18	Rock Island Independents	W	20	0	5,000
O 25	Rochester Jeffersons	W	33	13	2,700
N 1	@ Milwaukee Badgers	W	6	0	2,300
N 8	@ Chicago Cardinals	L	6	9	3,000
N 15	Dayton Triangles	W	7	0	3,000
N 22	@ Chicago Bears	L	0	21	6,898
N 26	@ Pottsville Maroons	L	0	31	3,500
N 28	@ Frankford Yellowjackets	L	7	13	10,000
D 6	@ Providence Steam Roller	W	13	10	10,000

Home: 4-1-2 **Away:** 3-2-1 (35,300)   151   61   57,087

1926 (7-3-3, .700)
Fifth

Head Coach: Earl "Curly" Lambeau

			GB	Opp.	Attend.
S 19	Detroit Panthers	W	21	0	4,500
S 26	Chicago Bears	T	6	6	7,000
O 3	Duluth Eskimos	T	0	0	2,500
O 10	Chicago Cardinals	L	7	13	5,000
O 17	Milwaukee Badgers	W	7	0	3,000
O 24	Racine Tornadoes	W	35	0	
O 31	@ Chicago Cardinals	W	3	0	2,500
N 7	@ Milwaukee Badgers	W	21	0	4,300
N 14	Louisville Colonels	W	14	0	1,300
N 21	@ Chicago Bears	L	13	19	7,500
N 25	@ Frankford Yellowjackets	L	14	20	10,000
N 28	@ Detroit Panthers	W	7	0	1,000
D 19	@ Chicago Bears	T	3	3	10,000

Home: 4-1-2 **Away:** 3-2-1 (35,300)   151   61

ALL-TIME RESULTS BY SEASON

1927 (7-2-1, .778)
Second

Head Coach: Earl "Curly" Lambeau

			GB	Opp.	Attend.
S 18	Dayton Triangles	W	14	0	3,600
S 25	Cleveland Bulldogs	W	12	7	4,500
O 2	Chicago Bears	L	6	7	5,500
O 9	Duluth Eskimos	W	20	0	4,000
O 16	Chicago Bears	W	13	0	4,500
O 23	New York Yankees	W	13	0	11,000
*O 30	@ Milwaukee Eagles	W	22	7	2,700
N 6	@ Chicago Cardinals	T	6	6	3,500
N 13	Dayton Triangles	W	6	0	2,500
N 20	@ Chicago Bears	L	6	14	6,000
N 24	@Frankford Yellowjackets	W	17	9	9,000
			113	43	54,100

Home: 6-1 (35,600) **Away:** 1-1-1 (18,500)

1928 (6-4-3, .600)
Fourth

Head Coach: Earl "Curly" Lambeau

			GB	Opp.	Attend.
S 23	Frankford Yellowjackets	L	9	19	6,500
S 30	Chicago Bears	T	12	12	8,500
O 7	New York Giants	L	0	6	7,000
O 14	Chicago Cardinals	W	20	0	4,200
O 21	@ Chicago Bears	W	16	6	15,000
O 28	Dayton Triangles	W	17	0	3,100
N 4	Pottsville Maroons	W	26	14	5,000
N 11	New York Yankees	T	0	0	5,000
N 18	@ New York Giants	W	7	0	12,000
N 25	@ Pottsville Maroons	L	0	26	1,600
N 29	@ Frankford Yellowjackets	L	0	2	8,000
D 2	@ Providence Steam Roller	T	7	7	9,000
D 9	@ Chicago Bears	W	6	0	14,000
			120	92	98,900

Home: 3-2-2 (39,300) **Away:** 3-2-1 (59,600)

1929 (12-0-1, 1.000)
First

Head Coach: Earl "Curly" Lambeau

			GB	Opp.	Attend.
S 22	Dayton Triangles	W	9	0	5,000
S 29	Chicago Bears	W	23	0	13,000
O 6	Chicago Cardinals	W	9	2	6,000
O 13	Frankford Yellowjackets	W	14	2	9,000
O 20	Minneapolis Redjackets	W	24	0	6,000
O 27	@ Chicago Cardinals	W	7	6	8,000
N 3	@ Minneapolis Redjackets	W	16	6	3,000
N 10	@ Chicago Bears	W	14	0	13,000
N 17	@ Chicago Cardinals	W	12	0	10,000
N 24	@ New York Giants	W	20	6	25,000
N 28	@ Frankford Yellowjackets	T	0	0	8,500
D 1	@ Providence Steam Roller	W	25	0	6,500
D 8	@ Chicago Bears	W	25	0	6,000
*D 15	@ Memphis Tigers	L	6	16	
			198	22	119,000

Home: 5-0 (39,000) **Away:** 7-0-1 (80,000)

1930 (10-3-1, .769)
First

Head Coach: Earl "Curly" Lambeau

			GB	Opp.	Attend.
S 21	Chicago Cardinals	W	14	0	8,000
S 28	Chicago Bears	W	7	0	10,000
O 5	New York Giants	W	14	7	11,000
O 12	Frankford Yellowjackets	W	27	12	8,000
O 19	@ Minneapolis Redjackets	W	13	0	
O 26	Minneapolis Redjackets	W	19	0	6,000
N 2	Portsmouth Spartans	W	47	13	7,500
N 9	@ Chicago Bears	W	13	12	22,000
N 16	@ Chicago Cardinals	L	6	13	12,000
N 23	@ New York Giants	L	6	13	37,000
N 27	@ Frankford Yellowjackets	W	25	7	5,000
N 30	@ Staten Island Stapletons	W	37	7	9,500
D 7	@ Chicago Bears	L	0	21	20,000
D 14	@ Portsmouth Spartans	T	6	6	4,500
			234	111	

Home: 6-0 (50,500) **Away:** 4-3-1

1931 (12-2-0, .857)
First

Head Coach: Earl "Curly" Lambeau

			GB	Opp.	Attend.
S 13	Cleveland Indians	W	26	0	5,000
S 20	Brooklyn Dodgers	W	32	6	7,000
S 27	Chicago Bears	W	7	0	13,500
O 4	New York Giants	W	27	7	14,000
O 11	Chicago Cardinals	W	26	7	8,000
O 18	Frankford Yellowjackets	W	15	7	6,000
O 25	Providence Steam Roller	W	48	20	
N 1	@ Chicago Bears	W	6	2	30,000
N 8	Staten Island Stapletons	W	26	0	7,000
N 15	@ Chicago Cardinals	L	13	21	8,000
N 22	@ New York Giants	W	14	10	35,000
N 26	@ Providence Steam Roller	W	38	7	5,000
N 29	@ Brooklyn Dodgers	W	7	0	10,000
D 6	@ Chicago Bears	L	6	7	18,000
			291	94	

Home: 8-0 **Away:** 4-2 (106,00)

1932 (10-3-1, .769)
Second

Head Coach: Earl "Curly" Lambeau

			GB	Opp.	Attend.
S 18	Chicago Cardinals	W	15	7	3,500
S 25	Chicago Bears	T	0	0	13,000
O 2	New York Giants	W	13	0	5,500
O 9	Portsmouth Spartans	W	15	10	5,500
O 16	@ Chicago Bears	W	2	0	17,500
O 23	Brooklyn Dodgers	W	13	0	5,000
O 30	Staten Island Stapletons	W	26	0	
N 6	@ Chicago Cardinals	W	19	9	8,323
N 13	@ Boston Braves	W	21	0	16,500
N 20	@ New York Giants	L	0	6	17,000
N 24	@ Brooklyn Dodgers	W	7	0	17,000
N 27	@ Staten Island Stapletons	W	21	3	3,500
D 4	@ Portsmouth Spartans	L	0	19	10,000
D 11	@ Chicago Bears	L	0	9	5,000
			152	63	

Home: 5-0-1 **Away:** 5-3 (94,823)

(1st season home games also played in Milwaukee)

1933 (5-7-1, .417)
Third, Western Division

Head Coach: Earl "Curly" Lambeau

			GB	Opp.	Attend.
S 17	Boston Redskins (GB)	T	7	7	5,000
S 24	Chicago Bears (GB)	L	7	14	12,000
O 1	New York Giants (Milw)	L	7	10	12,467
O 8	Portsmouth Spartans (GB)	W	17	0	5,200
O 15	Pittsburgh Pirates (GB)	W	47	0	4,000
O 22	@ Chicago Bears	L	7	10	19,000
O 29	Philadelphia Eagles (GB)	W	35	9	3,007
N 5	@ Chicago Cardinals	W	14	6	5,000
N 12	@ Portsmouth Spartans	L	0	7	7,500
N 19	@ Boston Redskins	L	7	20	16,399
N 26	@ New York Giants	L	6	17	17,000
*N 30	@ Staten Island Stapletons	W	21	0	3,000
D 3	@ Philadelphia Eagles	W	10	0	9,500
D 10	@ Chicago Bears	L	6	7	7,000
			170	107	123,073

Home: 3-2-1 (41,674) **Away:** 2-5 (81,399)

1934 (7-6-0, .538)
Third, Western Division

Head Coach: Earl "Curly" Lambeau	GB	Opp.	Attend.
S 16 Philadelphia Eagles (GB) ....W	19	6	5,000
S 23 Chicago Bears (GB)........................L	10	24	13,500
S 30 New York Giants (Milw)................W	20	6	11,000
O 7 Detroit Lions (GB) L	0	3	7,500
O 14 Cincinnati Reds (GB) ....W	41	0	3,000
O 21 Chicago Cardinals (GB) ....W	15	0	4,000
O 28 @ Chicago Bears............................L	14	27	11,000
N 4 @ Boston Redskins ....W	10	0	23,722
N 11 @ New York Giants L	3	17	22,000
N 18 Chicago Cardinals (Milw) L	0	9	3,000
N 25 @ Detroit Lions ....W	3	0	12,000
N 29 @ Chicago Cardinals L	0	6	1,738
D 4 @ St. Louis Gunners ....W	21	14	6,300
	156	112	123,760

Home: 4-3 (47,000) **Away:** 3-3 (76,760)

1935 (8-4-0, .667)
Second, Western Division

Head Coach: Earl "Curly" Lambeau	GB	Opp.	Attend.
S 15 Chicago Cardinals (GB) L	6	7	10,000
S 22 Chicago Bears (GB)........................W	7	0	13,600
S 29 New York Giants (GB) ....W	16	7	10,000
O 6 Pittsburgh Pirates (GB) ....W	27	0	5,000
O 13 Chicago Cardinals (Milw) L	0	3	13,000
O 20 Detroit Lions (Milw) ....W	13	9	9,500
O 27 @ Chicago Bears............................W	17	14	29,386
N 10 Detroit Lions (GB) ....W	31	7	12,000
N 17 @ Detroit Lions L	10	20	12,500
N 24 @ Pittsburgh Pirates ....W	34	14	12,902
N 28 @ Chicago Cardinals L	7	9	7,500
D 8 @ Philadelphia Eagles ....W	13	6	4,000
	181	96	139,388

Home: 5-2 (73,100) **Away:** 3-2 (66,288)

1936 (10-1-1, .909)
First, Western Division

Head Coach: Earl "Curly" Lambeau	GB	Opp.	Attend.
S 13 Chicago Cardinals (GB) ....W	10	7	8,900
S 20 Chicago Bears (GB)........................L	3	30	14,312
O 4 Chicago Cardinals (Milw) ....W	24	0	11,000
O 11 Boston Redskins (GB) ....W	31	2	6,100
O 18 Detroit Lions (GB) ....W	20	18	13,500
O 25 Pittsburgh Pirates (Milw) ....W	42	10	10,000
N 1 @ Chicago Bears............................W	21	10	31,346
N 8 @ Boston Redskins ....W	7	3	11,220
N 15 @ Brooklyn Dodgers ....W	38	7	25,325
N 22 @ New York Giants ....W	26	14	20,000
N 29 @ Detroit Lions ....W	26	17	22,000
D 6 @ Chicago Cardinals ....T	0	0	4,793
	248	118	178,496

Home: 5-1 (63,812) **Away:** 5-0-1 (114,684)

NFL Championship	GB	Opp.	Attend.
D 13 Boston Redskins (@ New York) ....W	21	6	29,545

Western Tour	GB	Opp.	Attend.
*J 1 Brooklyn Dodgers (@ Denver) ....W	21	13	6,000
*J 10 Salinas Icebergs (@ San Fran.) ....W	42	7	2,500
*J 17 @ Los Angeles Bulldogs ....W	49	0	12,000
*J 24 Chicago Bears (@ Los Angeles)........T	20	20	10,000
*J 31 Chicago Bears (@ Los Angeles) ....W	17	14	12,000

1937 (7-4-0, .636)
Second (tie), Western Division

Head Coach: Earl "Curly" Lambeau	GB	Opp.	Attend.
S 12 Chicago Cardinals (GB)....................L	7	14	10,000
S 19 Chicago Bears (GB)........................L	2	14	16,658
O 3 Detroit Lions (GB) ....W	26	6	17,553
O 10 Chicago Cardinals (Milw)...............W	34	13	16,181
O 17 @ Cleveland Rams ....W	35	10	12,100
O 24 Cleveland Rams (GB)......................W	35	7	8,600
O 31 @ Detroit Lions ....W	14	13	21,311
N 7 @ Chicago Bears............................W	24	14	44,977
N 14 Philadelphia Eagles (Milw).............W	37	7	13,340
N 21 @ New York Giants L	0	10	38,965
N 28 @ Washington Redskins L	6	14	30,000
	220	122	229,685

Home: 4-2 (82,332) **Away:** 3-2 (147,353)

1938 (8-3-0, .727)
First, Western Division

Head Coach: Earl "Curly" Lambeau	GB	Opp.	Attend.
S 11 Cleveland Rams (GB)......................W	26	17	8,247
S 18 Chicago Bears (GB)........................L	0	2	15,172
S 25 Chicago Cardinals (Milw)...............W	28	7	18,000
S 28 Chicago Cardinals (@ Buffalo)........W	24	22	10,678
O 9 Detroit Lions (GB) L	7	17	21,968
O 16 Brooklyn Dodgers (Milw)................W	35	7	11,892
O 23 Pittsburgh Pirates (GB) ....W	20	0	12,142
O 30 @ Cleveland Rams ....W	28	7	18,843
N 6 @ Chicago Bears............................W	24	17	40,208
N 13 @ Detroit Lions ....W	28	7	45,139
N 20 @ New York Giants L	3	15	48,279
	223	118	250,568

Home: 4-2 (87,421) **Away:** 3-1 (152,469)
Neutral: 1-0 (10,678)

NFL Championship	GB	Opp.	Attend.
D 11 @ New York Giants L	17	23	48,120

1939 (9-2-0, .818)
First, Western Division

Head Coach: Earl "Curly" Lambeau	GB	Opp.	Attend.
S 17 Chicago Cardinals (GB) ....W	14	10	11,792
S 24 Chicago Bears (GB)........................W	21	16	19,192
O 1 Cleveland Rams (GB) L	24	27	9,988
O 8 Chicago Cardinals (Milw)...............W	27	20	18,965
*O 15 @ St. Louis Gunners ....W	31	0	11,000
O 22 Detroit Lions (GB) ....W	26	7	22,558
O 29 Washington Redskins (Milw)...........W	24	14	24,308
N 5 @ Chicago Bears............................L	27	30	40,537
N 12 @ Philadelphia Eagles ....W	23	16	23,862
N 19 @ Brooklyn Dodgers ....W	28	0	19,843
N 26 @ Cleveland Rams ....W	7	6	30,691
D 3 @ Detroit Lions ....W	12	7	30,699
	233	153	252,435

Home: 5-1 (106,803) **Away:** 4-1 (145,632)

NFL Championship	GB	Opp.	Attend.
D 10 New York Giants (Milw)...................W	27	0	32,279

Pro Bowl	GB	Opp.	Attend.
*J 14 NFL All-Stars (@ Los Angeles) ....W	16	7	18,000

1940 (6-4-1, .600)
Second, Western Division

Head Coach: Earl "Curly" Lambeau

		GB	Opp.	Attend.
S 15	Philadelphia Eagles (GB) ....W	27	20	11,657
S 22	Chicago Bears (GB).........................L	10	41	22,557
S 29	Chicago Cardinals (Milw)...............W	31	6	20,234
O 13	Cleveland Rams (GB)......................W	31	14	16,299
O 20	Detroit Lions (GB) L	14	23	21,001
O 27	Pittsburgh Steelers (Milw)............W	24	3	13,703
N 3	@ Chicago Bears L	7	14	45,434
N 10	@ Chicago Cardinals ....W	28	7	11,364
N 17	@ New York Giants L	3	7	28,262
N 24	@ Detroit Lions ....W	50	7	26,019
D 1	@ Cleveland Rams ....T	13	13	16,249
		238	155	232,779

Home: 4-2 (105,451)   **Away:** 2-2-1 (127,328)

1941 (10-1-0, .909)
First (tie), Western Division

Head Coach: Earl "Curly" Lambeau

		GB	Opp.	Attend.
S 14	Detroit Lions (GB) ....W	23	0	16,734
S 21	Cleveland Rams (Milw) ....W	24	7	18,463
S 28	Chicago Bears (GB).........................L	17	25	24,876
O 5	Chicago Cardinals (Milw)...............W	14	13	10,000
O 12	Brooklyn Dodgers (Milw)................W	30	7	15,621
O 19	@ Cleveland Rams ....W	17	14	13,086
O 26	@ Detroit Lions ....W	24	7	30,269
N 2	@ Chicago Bears ....W	16	14	46,484
*N 9	@ Kenosha Cardinals......................W	65	2	7,200
N 16	Chicago Cardinals (GB) ....W	17	9	15,495
N 23	@ Pittsburgh Steelers ....W	54	7	15,202
N 30	@ Washington Redskins ....W	22	17	35,594
		258	120	241,824

Home: 5-1 (101,189)   **Away:** 5-0 (140,635)

Western Division Playoff

		GB	Opp.	Attend.
D 14	@ Chicago Bears.............................L	14	33	43,425

1942 (8-2-1, .800)
Second, Western Division

Head Coach: Earl "Curly" Lambeau

		GB	Opp.	Attend.
S 27	Chicago Bears (GB)..........................L	28	44	20,007
O 4	@ Chicago Cardinals ....W	17	13	24,897
O 11	Detroit Lions (Milw) ....W	38	7	19,500
O 18	Cleveland Rams (GB).......................W	45	28	12,847
O 25	@ Detroit Lions ....W	28	7	19,097
N 1	Chicago Cardinals (GB) ....W	55	24	14,782
N 8	@ Cleveland Rams ....W	30	12	16,473
N 15	@ Chicago Bears L	7	38	42,787
N 22	@ New York Giants ....T	21	21	30,246
N 29	@ Philadelphia Eagles ....W	7	0	13,700
D 6	Pittsburgh Steelers (Milw)............W	24	21	5,138
		300	215	219,474

Home: 4-1 (72,274)   **Away:** 4-1-1 (147,200)

1943 (7-2-1, .778)
Second, Western Division

Head Coach: Earl "Curly" Lambeau

		GB	Opp.	Attend.
S 26	Chicago Bears (GB)..........................T	21	21	23,675
O 3	@ Chicago Cardinals ....W	28	7	15,563
O 10	Detroit Lions (GB) ....W	35	14	21,396
O 17	Washington Redskins (Milw) L	7	33	23,058
O 24	@ Detroit Lions ....W	27	6	41,463
O 31	@ New York Giants ....W	35	21	46,208
N 7	@ Chicago Bears L	7	21	43,425
N 14	Chicago Cardinals (Milw) ....W	35	14	10,831
N 21	@ Brooklyn Dodgers ....W	31	7	18,992
*N 28	New London (Conn.) Diesels			
	(@ Bristol, Conn.) ....W	62	14	10,000
D 5	@ Phil-Pitt Steagles (@ Phil.) ....W	38	28	34,294
		264	172	278,905

Home: 2-1-1 (78,960)   **Away:** 5-1 (199,945)

1944 (8-2-0, .800)
First, Western Division

Head Coach: Earl "Curly" Lambeau

		GB	Opp.	Attend.
S 17	Brooklyn Tigers (Milw) ....W	14	7	12,994
S 24	Chicago Bears (GB) ....W	42	28	24,362
O 1	Detroit Lions (Milw).......................W	27	6	18,556
O 8	Card-Pitt (GB)................................W	34	7	16,535
*O 14	Philadelphia Eagles (@ Nashville) L	13	38	20,000
O 22	Cleveland Rams (GB).......................W	30	21	18,780
O 29	@ Detroit Lions ....W	14	0	30,844
N 5	@ Chicago Bears.............................L	0	21	45,553
N 12	@ Cleveland Rams ....W	42	7	17,166
N 19	@ New York Giants L	0	24	56,481
N 26	@ Card-Pitt (@ Chicago) ....W	35	20	7,158
		238	141	248,429

Home: 5-0 (91,227)   **Away:** 3-2 (157,202)

NFL Championship

		GB	Opp.	Attend.
D 17	@ New York Giants ....W	14	7	46,016

1945 (6-4-0, .600)
Third, Western Division

Head Coach: Earl "Curly" Lambeau

		GB	Opp.	Attend.
S 30	Chicago Bears (GB) ....W	31	21	24,525
O 7	Detroit Lions (GB) ....W	57	21	20,463
O 14	Cleveland Rams (GB) L	14	27	24,607
O 21	Boston Yanks (Milw) ....W	38	14	20,846
O 28	Chicago Cardinals (GB) ....W	33	14	19,221
N 4	@ Chicago Bears L	24	28	45,527
N 11	@ Cleveland Rams L	7	20	28,686
N 18	@ Boston Yanks ....W	28	0	31,923
N 25	@ New York Giants ....W	23	14	52,681
D 2	@ Detroit Lions L	3	14	23,468
		258	173	291,947

Home: 4-1 (109,662)   **Away:** 2-3 (182,285)

1946 (6-5-0, .545)
Third (tie), Western Division

Head Coach: Earl "Curly" Lambeau

		GB	Opp.	Attend.
S 29	Chicago Bears (GB).........................L	7	30	25,049
O 6	Los Angeles Rams (Milw) L	17	21	27,049
O 13	@ Philadelphia Eagles ....W	19	7	36,127
O 20	Pittsburgh Steelers (GB) ....W	17	7	22,588
O 27	Detroit Lions (GB)...........................W	10	7	23,564
N 3	@ Chicago Bears L	7	10	46,321
N 10	@ Chicago Cardinals ....W	19	7	30,681
N 17	@ Detroit Lions ....W	9	0	21,055
N 24	Chicago Cardinals (GB) L	6	24	16,150
D 1	@ Washington Redskins ....W	20	7	33,691
D 8	@ Los Angeles Rams L	17	38	46,838
		148	158	329,113

Home: 2-3 (114,400)   **Away:** 4-2 (214,713)

1947 (6-5-1, .545)
Third, Western Division

Head Coach: Earl "Curly" Lambeau

		GB	Opp.	Attend.
S 28	Chicago Bears (GB) ....W	29	20	25,461
O 5	Los Angeles Rams (Milw) ....W	17	14	31,613
O 12	Chicago Cardinals (GB) L	10	14	25,562
O 19	Washington Redskins (Milw) ....W	27	10	28,572
O 26	Detroit Lions (GB) ....W	34	17	25,179
N 2	Pittsburgh Steelers (Milw) L	17	18	30,073
N 9	@ Chicago Bears ....W	20	46,112	←
N 16	@ Chicago Cardinals L	20	21	40,086
N 23	@ New York Giants ....T	24	24	27,939
N 30	@ Los Angeles Rams ....W	30	10	31,040
D 7	@ Detroit Lions ....W	35	14	14,055
D 14	@ Philadelphia Eagles L	14	28	24,216
		274	210	349,908

Home: 4-2 (166,400)   **Away:** 2-3-1 (183,508)

1948 (3-9-0, .250)
Fourth, Western Division

Head Coach: Earl "Curly" Lambeau

			GB	Opp.	Attend.
S 17	@ Boston Yanks	W	31	0	15,443
S 26	Chicago Bears (GB)	L	7	45	25,546
O 3	Detroit Lions (GB)	W	33	21	24,206
O 10	Chicago Cardinals (Milw)	L	7	17	34,369
O 17	Los Angeles Rams (GB)	W	16	0	25,119
O 24	Washington Redskins (Milw)	L	7	23	13,433
O 31	@ Detroit Lions	L	20	24	16,174
N 7	@ Pittsburgh Steelers	L	7	38	26,058
N 14	@ Chicago Bears	L	6	7	48,113
N 21	New York Giants (Milw)	L	3	49	12,639
N 28	@ Los Angeles Rams	L	10	24	23,874
D 5	@ Chicago Cardinals	L	7	42	26,072
			154	290	291,046

Home: 2-4 (135,312)   **Away:** 1-5 (155,734)

1949 (2-10-0, .167)
Fifth, Western Division

Head Coach: Earl "Curly" Lambeau

			GB	Opp.	Attend.
S 25	Chicago Bears (GB)	L	0	17	25,571
O 2	Los Angeles Rams (GB)	L	7	48	24,308
O 7	@ New York Bulldogs	W	19	0	5,099
O 16	Chicago Cardinals (Milw)	L	17	39	18,464
O 23	@ Los Angeles Rams	L	7	35	37,546
O 30	Detroit Lions (Milw)	W	16	14	10,855
N 6	@ Chicago Bears	L	3	24	47,218
N 13	New York Giants (GB)	L	10	30	20,151
N 20	Pittsburgh Steelers (Milw)	L	7	30	5,483
N 27	@ Chicago Cardinals	L	21	41	16,787
D 4	@ Washington Redskins	L	0	30	23,200
D 11	@ Detroit Lions	L	7	21	12,576
			114	329	247,258

Home: 1-5 (104,832)   **Away:** 1-5 (142,426)

1950 (3-9-0, .250)
Fifth (tie), National Conference

Head Coach: Gene Ronzani

			GB	Opp.	Attend.
S 17	Detroit Lions (GB)	L	7	45	22,096
S 24	Washington Redskins (Milw)	W	35	21	14,109
O 1	Chicago Bears (GB)	W	31	21	24,893
O 8	New York Yanks (GB)	L	31	44	23,871
O 15	@ Chicago Bears	L	14	28	51,065
O 19	@ New York Yanks	L	17	35	13,661
N 5	@ Baltimore Colts	L	21	41	12,971
N 12	Los Angeles Rams (Milw)	L	14	45	20,456
N 19	@ Detroit Lions	L	21	24	17,752
N 26	San Francisco 49ers (GB)	W	25	21	13,196
D 3	@ Los Angeles Rams	L	14	51	39,323
D 10	@ San Francisco 49ers	L	14	30	20,797
			244	406	274,190

Home: 3-3 (118,621)   **Away:** 0-6 (155,569)

1951 (3-9-0, .250)
Fifth, National Conference

Head Coach: Gene Ronzani

			GB	Opp.	Attend.
S 30	Chicago Bears (GB)	L	20	31	24,666
O 7	Pittsburgh Steelers (Milw)	W	35	33	8,324
O 14	Philadelphia Eagles (GB)	L	37	24	18,489
O 21	Los Angeles Rams (Milw)	L	0	28	21,393
O 28	@ New York Yanks	W	29	27	7,351
N 4	Detroit Lions (GB)	L	17	24	18,800
N 11	@ Pittsburgh Steelers	L	7	28	20,080
N 18	@ Chicago Bears	L	13	24	36,771
N 22	@ Detroit Lions	L	35	52	32,247
D 2	New York Yanks (GB)	L	28	31	14,297
D 9	@ San Francisco 49ers	L	19	31	15,121
D 16	@ Los Angeles Rams	L	14	42	23,698
			254	375	241,237

Home: 2-4 (105,969)   **Away:** 1-5 (135,268)

1952 (6-6-0, .500)
Fourth, National Conference

Head Coach: Gene Ronzani

			GB	Opp.	Attend.
S 28	Chicago Bears (GB)	L	14	24	24,656
O 5	Washington Redskins (Milw)	W	35	20	9,657
O 12	Los Angeles Rams (Milw)	L	28	30	21,693
O 18	@ Dallas Texans	W	24	14	14,000
O 26	Detroit Lions (GB)	L	17	52	24,656
N 2	Philadelphia Eagles (Milw)	W	12	10	10,149
N 9	@ Chicago Bears	L	41	28	41,751
N 16	@ New York Giants	W	17	3	26,723
N 23	Dallas Texans (GB)	W	42	14	16,340
N 27	@ Detroit Lions	L	24	48	39,101
D 7	@ Los Angeles Rams	L	27	45	49,822
D 14	@ San Francisco 49ers	L	14	24	17,579
			295	312	296,127

Home: 3-3 (107,151)   **Away:** 3-3 (188,976)

1953 (2-9-1, .182)
Sixth, Western Conference

Head Coach: Gene Ronzani#

			GB	Opp.	Attend.
S 27	Cleveland Browns (Milw)	L	0	27	22,604
O 4	Chicago Bears (GB)	L	13	17	24,835
O 11	Los Angeles Rams (Milw)	L	20	38	23,353
O 18	Baltimore Colts (GB)	W	37	14	18,713
O 24	@ Pittsburgh Steelers	L	14	31	22,918
O 31	@ Baltimore Colts	L	35	24	33,797
N 8	@ Chicago Bears	T	21	21	39,889
N 15	Detroit Lions (GB)	L	7	14	20,834
N 22	San Francisco 49ers (Milw)	L	7	37	16,378
N 26	@ Detroit Lions	L	15	34	52,607
D 6	@ San Francisco 49ers	L	14	48	31,337
D 12	@ Los Angeles Rams	L	17	33	23,069
			200	338	330,334

Home: 1-5 (126,717)   **Away:** 1-4-1 (203,617)
Ray "Scooter" McLean and Hugh Devore served as co-head coaches for last two games of season

1954 (4-8-0, .333)
Fifth, Western Conference

Head Coach: Lisle Blackbourn

			GB	Opp.	Attend.
S 26	Pittsburgh Steelers (GB)	L	20	21	20,675
O 3	Chicago Bears (GB)	L	3	10	24,414
O 10	San Francisco 49ers (Milw)	L	17	23	15,571
O 17	Los Angeles Rams (GB)	W	35	17	17,455
O 24	@ Baltimore Colts	W	7	6	28,680
O 30	@ Philadelphia Eagles	W	37	14	25,378
N 7	@ Chicago Bears	L	23	28	47,038
N 13	Baltimore Colts (Milw)	W	24	13	19,786
N 21	Detroit Lions (GB)	L	17	21	20,767
N 25	@ Detroit Lions	L	24	28	55,532
D 5	@ San Francisco 49ers	L	0	35	32,012
D 12	@ Los Angeles Rams	L	27	35	38,839
			234	251	346,147

Home: 2-4 (118,668)   **Away:** 2-4 (227,479)

1955 (6-6-0, .500)
Third, Western Conference

Head Coach: Lisle Blackbourn

			GB	Opp.	Attend.
S 25	Detroit Lions (GB)	W	20	17	22,217
O 2	Chicago Bears (GB)	W	24	3	24,662
O 8	Baltimore Colts (Milw)	L	20	24	40,199
O 16	Los Angeles Rams (GB)	W	30	28	26,960
O 23	@ Cleveland Browns	L	10	41	51,482
O 29	@ Baltimore Colts	L	10	14	34,411
N 6	@ Chicago Bears	L	31	52	48,890
N 13	Chicago Cardinals (Milw)	W	31	14	20,104
N 20	San Francisco 49ers (Milw)	W	27	21	19,099
N 24	@ Detroit Lions	L	10	24	51,685
D 4	@ San Francisco 49ers	W	28	7	32,897
D 11	@ Los Angeles Rams	L	17	31	90,535
			258	276	463,141

Home: 5-1 (153,241)   **Away:** 1-5 (309,900)

1956 (4-8-0, .333)
Fifth (tie), Western Conference

Head Coach: Lisle Blackbourn	GB	Opp.	Attend.
S 30 Detroit Lions (GB)........................L	16	20	24,668
O 7 Chicago Bears (GB)....................L	21	37	24,668
O 14 Baltimore Colts (Milw) ....W	38	33	24,214
O 21 Los Angeles Rams (Milw) ....W	42	17	24,200
O 28 @ Baltimore Colts L	21	28	40,086
N 4 Cleveland Browns (Milw) L	7	24	28,590
N 11 @ Chicago Bears..........................L	14	38	49,172
N 18 San Francisco 49ers (GB) L	16	17	17,986
N 22 @ Detroit Lions ....W	24	20	54,087
D 2 @ Chicago Cardinals ....W	24	21	22,620
D 8 @ San Francisco 49ers L	20	38	32,433
D 16 @ Los Angeles Rams L	21	49	45,209
	264	342	387,933

Home: 2-4 (144,326)   **Away:** 2-4 (243,607)

1957 (3-9-0, .250)
Sixth, Western Conference

Head Coach: Lisle Blackbourn	GB	Opp.	Attend.
S 29 Chicago Bears (GB) ....W	21	17	32,132
O 6 Detroit Lions (GB)......................L	14	24	32,120
O 13 Baltimore Colts (Milw) L	17	45	26,322
O 20 San Francisco 49ers (Milw) L	14	24	18,919
O 27 @ Baltimore Colts ....W	24	21	48,510
N 3 New York Giants (GB) L	17	31	32,070
N 10 @ Chicago Bears..........................L	14	21	47,153
N 17 Los Angeles Rams (Milw) L	27	31	19,540
N 24 @ Pittsburgh Steelers ....W	27	10	29,701
N 28 @ Detroit Lions L	6	18	54,301
D 8 @ Los Angeles Rams L	17	42	70,572
D 15 @ San Francisco 49ers L	20	27	59,100
	218	311	470,440

Home: 1-5 (161,103)   **Away:** 2-4 (309,337)

1958 (1-10-1, .091)
Sixth, Western Conference

Head Coach: Ray "Scooter" McLean	GB	Opp.	Attend.
S 28 Chicago Bears (GB)....................L	20	34	32,150
O 5 Detroit Lions (GB)......................T	13	13	32,053
O 12 Baltimore Colts (Milw) L	17	24	24,553
O 19 @ Washington Redskins L	21	37	25,228
O 26 Philadelphia Eagles (GB) ....W	38	35	31,043
N 2 @ Baltimore Colts L	0	56	51,333
N 9 @ Chicago Bears..........................L	10	24	48,424
N 16 Los Angeles Rams (GB) L	7	20	28,051
N 23 San Francisco 49ers (Milw) L	12	33	19,786
N 27 @ Detroit Lions L	14	24	50,971
D 7 @ San Francisco 49ers L	21	48	50,793
D 14 @ Los Angeles Rams L	20	34	54,634
	193	382	449,019

Home: 1-4-1 (167,636)   **Away:** 0-6 (281,383)

1959 (7-5-0, .583)
Third (tie), Western Conference

Head Coach: Vince Lombardi	GB	Opp.	Attend.
S 27 Chicago Bears (GB) ....W	9	6	32,150
O 4 Detroit Lions (GB) ....W	28	10	32,150
O 11 San Francisco 49ers (GB) ....W	21	20	32,150
O 18 Los Angeles Rams (Milw) L	6	45	36,194
O 25 @ Baltimore Colts L	21	38	57,557
N 1 @ New York Giants L	3	20	68,837
N 8 @ Chicago Bears..........................L	17	28	46,205
N 15 Baltimore Colts (Milw) L	24	28	25,521
N 22 Washington Redskins (GB) ....W	21	0	31,853
N 26 @ Detroit Lions ....W	24	17	49,221
D 6 @ Los Angeles Rams ....W	38	20	61,044
D 13 @ San Francisco 49ers ....W	36	14	55,997
	248	246	528,879

Home: 4-2 (190,018)   **Away:** 3-3 (338,861)

1960 (8-4-0, .667)
First, Western Conference

Head Coach: Vince Lombardi	GB	Opp.	Attend.
S 25 Chicago Bears (GB)....................L	14	17	32,150
O 2 Detroit Lions (GB) ....W	28	9	32,150
O 9 Baltimore Colts (GB) ....W	35	21	32,150
O 23 San Francisco 49ers (Milw) ....W	41	14	39,914
O 30 @ Pittsburgh Steelers ....W	19	13	30,155
N 6 @ Baltimore Colts L	24	38	57,808
N 13 Dallas Cowboys (GB) ....W	41	7	32,294
N 20 Los Angeles Rams (Milw) L	31	33	35,763
N 24 @ Detroit Lions L	10	23	51,123
D 4 @ Chicago Bears ....W	41	13	46,406
D 10 @ San Francisco 49ers ....W	13	0	53,612
D 17 @ Los Angeles Rams....................W	35	21	53,445
	332	209	496,970

Home: 4-2 (204,421)   **Away:** 4-2 (292,549)

NFL Championship	GB	Opp.	Attend.
D 26 @ Philadelphia Eagles L	13	17	67,325

1961 (11-3-0, .786)
First, Western Conference

Head Coach: Vince Lombardi	GB	Opp.	Attend.
S 17 Detroit Lions (Milw) L	13	17	44,307
S 24 San Francisco 49ers (GB) ....W	30	10	38,669
O 1 Chicago Bears (GB) ....W	24	0	38,669
O 8 Baltimore Colts (GB) ....W	45	7	38,669
O 15 @ Cleveland Browns ....W	49	17	75,049
O 22 @ Minnesota Vikings ....W	33	7	42,007
O 29 Minnesota Vikings (Milw) ....W	28	10	44,116
N 5 @ Baltimore Colts ....W	21	45	57,641
N 12 @ Chicago Bears..........................W	31	28	49,711
N 19 Los Angeles Rams (GB) ....W	35	17	38,669
N 23 @ Detroit Lions ....W	17	9	55,662
D 3 New York Giants (Milw) ....W	20	17	47,012
D 10 @ San Francisco 49ers L	21	22	55,722
D 17 @ Los Angeles Rams....................W	24	17	49,169
	391	223	675,072

Home: 6-1 (290,111)   **Away:** 5-2 (384,961)

NFL Championship	GB	Opp.	Attend.
D 31 New York Giants (GB) ....W	37	0	39,029

1962 (13-1-0, .929)
First, Western Conference

Head Coach: Vince Lombardi	GB	Opp.	Attend.
S 16 Minnesota Vikings (GB) ....W	34	7	38,669
S 23 St. Louis Cardinals (Milw) ....W	17	0	44,885
S 30 Chicago Bears (GB) ....W	49	0	38,669
O 7 Detroit Lions (GB) ....W	9	7	38,669
O 14 @ Minnesota Vikings ....W	48	21	41,475
O 21 San Francisco 49ers (Milw) ....W	31	13	46,010
O 28 @ Baltimore Colts ....W	17	6	57,966
N 4 @ Chicago Bears ....W	38	7	48,753
N 11 @ Philadelphia Eagles ....W	49	0	60,671
N 18 Baltimore Colts (GB) ....W	17	13	38,669
N 22 @ Detroit Lions L	14	26	57,578
D 2 Los Angeles Rams (Milw) ....W	41	10	46,833
D 9 @ San Francisco 49ers ....W	31	21	53,769
D 16 @ Los Angeles Rams....................W	20	17	60,389
	415	148	673,005

Home: 7-0 (292,404)   **Away:** 6-1 (380,601)

NFL Championship	GB	Opp.	Attend.
D 30 @ New York Giants ....W	16	7	64,892

1963 (11-2-1, .846)
Second, Western Conference

Head Coach: Vince Lombardi

			GB	Opp.	Attend.
S 15	Chicago Bears (GB)	L	3	10	42,327
S 22	Detroit Lions (Milw)	W	31	10	45,912
S 29	Baltimore Colts (GB)	W	31	20	42,327
O 6	Los Angeles Rams (GB)	W	42	10	42,327
O 13	@ Minnesota Vikings	W	37	28	42,567
O 20	@ St. Louis Cardinals	W	30	7	32,224
O 27	@ Baltimore Colts	W	34	20	60,065
N 3	Pittsburgh Steelers (Milw)	W	33	14	46,293
N 10	Minnesota Vikings (GB)	W	28	7	42,327
N 17	@ Chicago Bears	L	7	26	49,166
N 24	San Francisco 49ers (Milw)	W	28	10	45,905
N 28	@ Detroit Lions	T	13	13	54,016
D 7	@ Los Angeles Rams	W	31	14	52,357
D 14	@ San Francisco 49ers	W	21	17	31,031
			369	206	628,844

Home: 6-1 (307,418) **Away:** 5-1-1 (321,426)

Playoff Bowl

			GB	Opp.	Attend.
*J 5	Cleveland Browns (@ Miami)	W	40	23	54,921

1964 (8-5-1, .615)
Second (tie), Western Conference

Head Coach: Vince Lombardi

			GB	Opp.	Attend.
S 13	Chicago Bears (GB)	W	23	12	42,327
S 20	Baltimore Colts (GB)	L	20	21	42,327
S 28	@ Detroit Lions	W	14	10	59,203
O 4	Minnesota Vikings (GB)	L	23	24	42,327
O 11	San Francisco 49ers (Milw)	W	24	14	47,380
O 18	@ Baltimore Colts	L	21	24	60,213
O 25	Los Angeles Rams (Milw)	W	17	27	47,617
N 1	@ Minnesota Vikings	W	42	13	44,278
N 8	Detroit Lions (GB)	W	30	7	42,327
N 15	@ San Francisco 49ers	L	14	24	38,483
N 22	Cleveland Browns (Milw)	W	28	21	48,065
N 29	@ Dallas Cowboys	W	45	21	44,975
D 5	@ Chicago Bears	W	17	3	43,636
D 13	@ Los Angeles Rams	T	24	24	40,735
			342	245	643,893

Home: 4-3 (312,370) **Away:** 4-2-1 (331,523)

Playoff Bowl

			GB	Opp.	Attend.
*J 3	St. Louis Cardinals (@ Miami)	L	17	24	56,218

1965 (10-3-1, .769)
First (tie), Western Conference

Head Coach: Vince Lombardi

			GB	Opp.	Attend.
S 19	@ Pittsburgh Steelers	W	41	9	38,383
S 26	Baltimore Colts (Milw)	W	20	17	48,130
O 3	Chicago Bears (GB)	W	23	14	50,852
O 10	San Francisco 49ers (GB)	W	27	10	50,852
O 17	@ Detroit Lions	W	31	21	56,712
O 24	Dallas Cowboys (Milw)	W	13	3	48,311
O 31	@ Chicago Bears	L	10	31	45,664
N 7	Detroit Lions (GB)	T	7	12	50,852
N 14	Los Angeles Rams (Milw)	W	6	3	48,485
N 21	@ Minnesota Vikings	W	38	13	47,426
N 28	@ Los Angeles Rams	L	10	21	39,733
D 5	Minnesota Vikings (GB)	W	24	19	50,852
D 12	@ Baltimore Colts	W	42	27	60,238
D 19	@ San Francisco 49ers	T	24	24	45,710
			316	224	682,200

Home: 6-1 (348,334) **Away:** 4-2-1 (333,866)

Western Conference Championship

			GB	Opp.	Attend.
D 26	Baltimore Colts (GB)	+W	13	10	50,484

NFL Championship

J 2	Cleveland Browns (GB)	W	23	12	50,777

1966 (12-2-0, .857)
First, Western Conference

Head Coach: Vince Lombardi

			GB	Opp.	Attend.
S 10	Baltimore Colts (Milw)	W	24	3	48,650
S 18	@ Cleveland Browns	W	21	20	83,943
S 25	Los Angeles Rams (GB)	W	24	13	50,861
O 2	Detroit Lions (GB)	W	23	14	50,861
O 9	@ San Francisco 49ers	L	20	21	39,290
O 16	@ Chicago Bears	W	17	0	48,573
O 23	Atlanta Falcons (Milw)	W	56	3	48,623
O 30	@ Detroit Lions	W	31	7	56,954
N 6	Minnesota Vikings (GB)	L	17	20	50,861
N 20	Chicago Bears (GB)	W	13	6	50,861
N 27	@ Minnesota Vikings	W	28	16	47,426
D 4	San Francisco 49ers (Milw)	W	20	7	48,725
D 10	@ Baltimore Colts	W	14	10	60,238
D 18	@ Los Angeles Rams	W	27	23	72,416
			335	163	758,282

Home: 6-1 (349,442) **Away:** 6-1 (408,840)

NFL Championship

			GB	Opp.	Attend.
J 1	@ Dallas Cowboys	W	34	27	74,152

Super Bowl I

J 15	Kansas City Chiefs (@ L.A.)	W	35	10	61,946

1967 (9-4-1, .692)
First, NFL Central

Head Coach: Vince Lombardi

			GB	Opp.	Attend.
S 17	Detroit Lions (GB)	T	17	17	50,861
S 24	Chicago Bears (GB)	W	13	10	50,861
O 1	Atlanta Falcons (Milw)	W	23	0	49,467
O 8	@ Detroit Lions	W	27	17	57,877
O 15	Minnesota Vikings (Milw)	L	7	10	49,601
O 22	@ New York Giants	W	48	21	62,585
O 30	@ St. Louis Cardinals	W	31	23	49,792
N 5	@ Baltimore Colts	L	10	13	60,238
N 12	Cleveland Browns (Milw)	W	55	7	50,074
N 19	San Francisco 49ers (GB)	W	13	0	50,861
N 26	@ Chicago Bears	W	17	13	47,513
D 3	@ Minnesota Vikings	W	30	27	47,693
D 9	@ Los Angeles Rams	L	24	27	76,637
D 17	Pittsburgh Steelers (GB)	W	17	24	50,861
			332	209	754,921

Home: 4-2-1 (352,586) **Away:** 5-2 (402,335)

Western Conference Championship

			GB	Opp.	Attend.
D 23	Los Angeles Rams (Milw)	W	28	7	49,861

NFL Championship

D 31	Dallas Cowboys (GB)	W	21	17	50,861

Super Bowl II

J 14	Oakland Raiders (@ Miami)	W	33	14	75,546

1968 (6-7-1, .462)
Third, NFL Central

Head Coach: Phil Bengtson

			GB	Opp.	Attend.
S 15	Philadelphia Eagles (GB)	W	30	13	50,861
S 22	Minnesota Vikings (Milw)	L	13	26	49,346
S 29	Detroit Lions (GB)	L	17	23	50,861
O 6	@ Atlanta Falcons	W	38	7	58,850
O 13	Los Angeles Rams (Milw)	L	14	16	49,646
O 20	@ Detroit Lions	T	14	14	57,302
O 28	@ Dallas Cowboys	W	28	17	74,604
N 3	Chicago Bears (GB)	L	10	13	50,861
N 10	@ Minnesota Vikings	L	10	14	47,644
N 17	New Orleans Saints (Milw)	W	29	7	49,644
N 24	@ Washington Redskins	W	27	7	50,621
D 1	@ San Francisco 49ers	L	20	27	47,218
D 7	Baltimore Colts (GB)	L	3	16	50,861
D 15	@ Chicago Bears	W	28	27	46,435
			281	227	734,754

Home: 2-5 (352,080) **Away:** 4-2-1 (382,674)

1969 (8-6-0, .571)
Third, NFL Central

Head Coach: Phil Bengtson

			GB	Opp.	Attend.
S 21	Chicago Bears (GB)	W	17	0	50,861
S 28	San Francisco 49ers (Milw)	W	14	7	48,184
O 5	@ Minnesota Vikings	L	7	19	60,740
O 12	@ Detroit Lions	W	28	17	58,384
O 19	@ Los Angeles Rams	L	21	34	78,947
O 26	Atlanta Falcons (GB)	W	28	10	50,861
N 2	@ Pittsburgh Steelers	W	38	34	46,403
N 9	@ Baltimore Colts	L	6	14	60,238
N 16	Minnesota Vikings (Milw)	L	7	9	48,321
N 23	Detroit Lions (GB)	L	10	16	50,861
N 30	New York Giants (Milw)	W	20	10	48,156
D 7	@ Cleveland Browns	L	7	20	82,137
D 14	@ Chicago Bears	W	21	3	45,216
D 21	St. Louis Cardinals (GB)	W	45	28	50,861
			269	221	780,170

Home: 5-2 (348,105)   **Away:** 3-4 (432,065)

1970 (6-8-0, .429)
Third (tie), NFC Central

Head Coach: Phil Bengtson

			GB	Opp.	Attend.
S 20	Detroit Lions (GB)	L	0	40	56,263
S 27	Atlanta Falcons (GB)	W	27	24	56,263
O 4	@ Minnesota Vikings	W	13	10	47,967
O 12	@ San Diego Chargers	W	22	20	53,064
O 18	Los Angeles Rams (GB)	L	21	31	56,263
O 25	Philadelphia Eagles (Milw)	W	30	17	48,022
N 1	@ San Francisco 49ers	L	10	26	59,335
N 9	Baltimore Colts (Milw)	L	10	13	48,063
N 15	Chicago Bears (GB)	W	20	19	56,263
N 22	@ Minnesota Vikings	L	3	10	47,900
N 26	@ Dallas Cowboys	L	3	16	67,182
D 6	@ Pittsburgh Steelers	W	20	12	46,418
D 13	@ Chicago Bears	L	17	35	44,957
D 20	@ Detroit Lions	L	0	20	57,387
			196	293	745,347

Home: 4-3 (369,104)   **Away:** 2-5 (376,243)

1971 (4-8-2, .333)
Fourth, NFC Central

Head Coach: Dan Devine

			GB	Opp.	Attend.
S 19	New York Giants (GB)	L	40	42	56,263
S 26	Denver Broncos (Milw)	W	34	13	47,957
O 3	Cincinnati Bengals (GB)	L	20	17	56,263
O 10	@ Detroit Lions	L	28	31	54,418
O 17	Minnesota Vikings (GB)	L	13	24	56,263
O 24	@ Los Angeles Rams	L	13	30	75,351
N 1	Detroit Lions (Milw)	T	14	14	47,961
N 7	@ Chicago Bears	L	17	14	55,049
N 14	@ Minnesota Vikings	L	0	3	49,784
N 22	@ Atlanta Falcons	L	21	28	58,850
N 28	New Orleans Saints (Milw)	L	21	29	48,035
D 5	@ St. Louis Cardinals	T	16	16	50,443
D 12	Chicago Bears (GB)	L	31	10	56,263
D 19	@ Miami Dolphins	L	6	27	76,812
			274	298	789,712

Home: 3-3-1 (369,005)   **Away:** 1-5-1 (420,707)

1972 (10-4-0, .714)
First, NFC Central

Head Coach: Dan Devine

			GB	Opp.	Attend.
S 17	@ Cleveland Browns	W	26	10	75,771
S 24	Oakland Raiders (GB)	L	14	20	56,263
O 1	Dallas Cowboys (Milw)	W	16	13	47,103
O 8	Chicago Bears (GB)	W	20	17	56,263
O 16	@ Detroit Lions	W	24	23	54,418
O 22	Atlanta Falcons (Milw)	L	9	10	47,967
O 29	Minnesota Vikings (GB)	L	13	27	56,263
N 5	San Francisco 49ers (Milw)	W	34	24	47,897
N 12	@ Chicago Bears	W	23	17	55,701
N 19	@ Houston Oilers	W	23	10	41,752
N 26	@ Washington Redskins	L	16	21	53,039
D 3	Detroit Lions (GB)	W	33	7	56,263
D 10	@ Minnesota Vikings	W	23	7	49,784
D 17	@ New Orleans Saints	W	30	20	65,881
			304	226	764,365

Home: 4-3 (368,019)   **Away:** 6-1 (396,346)

NFC Divisional Playoff

			GB	Opp.	Attend.
D 24	@ Washington Redskins	L	3	16	53,140

1973 (5-7-2, .429)
Third, NFC Central

Head Coach: Dan Devine

			GB	Opp.	Attend.
S 17	New York Jets (Milw)	W	23	7	47,124
S 23	Detroit Lions (GB)	T	13	13	55,495
S 30	@ Minnesota Vikings	L	3	11	48,176
O 7	@ New York Giants (New Haven, Conn.)	W	16	14	70,050
O 14	Kansas City Chiefs (Milw)	T	10	10	46,583
O 21	@ Los Angeles Rams	L	7	24	80,558
O 28	@ Detroit Lions	L	0	34	43,616
N 4	Chicago Bears (GB)	L	17	31	53,231
N 11	St. Louis Cardinals (GB)	W	25	21	52,922
N 18	@ New England Patriots	L	24	33	60,525
N 26	@ San Francisco 49ers	L	6	20	49,244
D 2	New Orleans Saints (Milw)	W	30	10	46,092
D 8	Minnesota Vikings (GB)	L	7	31	53,830
D 16	@ Chicago Bears	W	21	0	29,157
			202	259	736,603

Home: 3-2-2 (355,277)   **Away:** 2-5 (381,326)

1974 (6-8-0, .429)
Third, NFC Central

Head Coach: Dan Devine

			GB	Opp.	Attend.
S 15	Minnesota Vikings (GB)	L	17	32	55,131
S 22	@ Baltimore Colts	W	20	13	35,873
S 29	Detroit Lions (Milw)	W	21	19	45,970
O 6	Buffalo Bills (GB)	L	7	27	51,919
O 13	Los Angeles Rams (Milw)	W	17	6	45,938
O 21	@ Chicago Bears	L	9	10	50,623
O 27	@ Detroit Lions	L	17	19	51,775
N 3	Washington Redskins (GB)	L	6	17	55,288
N 10	Chicago Bears (Milw)	W	20	3	46,567
N 17	@ Minnesota Vikings	W	19	7	47,924
N 24	San Diego Chargers (GB)	W	34	0	50,321
D 1	@ Philadelphia Eagles	L	14	36	42,030
D 8	@ San Francisco 49ers	W	6	7	47,475
D 15	@ Atlanta Falcons	L	3	10	10,020
			210	206	636,854

Home: 4-3 (351,134)   **Away:** 2-5 (285,720)

1975 (4-10-0, .286)
Third (tie), NFC Central

Head Coach: Bart Starr

			GB	Opp.	Attend.
S 21	Detroit Lions (Milw)	L	16	30	50,781
S 29	@ Denver Broncos	L	13	23	52,491
O 5	Miami Dolphins (GB)	L	7	31	55,396
O 12	@ New Orleans Saints	L	19	20	51,371
O 19	@ Dallas Cowboys	W	19	17	64,189
O 26	Pittsburgh Steelers (Milw)	L	13	16	52,258
N 2	Minnesota Vikings (GB)	L	17	28	55,378
N 9	@ Chicago Bears	L	14	27	48,738
N 16	@ Detroit Lions	L	10	13	76,356
N 23	New York Giants (Milw)	W	40	14	50,150
N 30	Chicago Bears (GB)	W	28	7	46,821
D 7	@ Minnesota Vikings	L	3	24	46,147
D 14	@ Los Angeles Rams	L	5	22	59,312
D 21	Atlanta Falcons (GB)	W	22	13	38,565
			226	285	747,953

Home: 3-4 (349,349) **Away:** 1-6 (398,604)

1976 (5-9-0, .357)
Fourth, NFC Central

Head Coach: Bart Starr

			GB	Opp.	Attend.
S 12	San Francisco 49ers (GB)	L	14	26	54,628
S 19	@ St. Louis Cardinals	L	0	29	48,842
S 26	@ Cincinnati Bengals	L	7	28	44,103
O 3	Detroit Lions (GB)	W	24	14	54,758
O 10	Seattle Seahawks (Milw)	W	27	20	54,983
O 17	Philadelphia Eagles (GB)	W	28	13	55,115
O 24	@ Oakland Raiders	L	14	18	52,232
O 31	@ Detroit Lions	L	6	27	74,582
N 7	New Orleans Saints (Milw)	W	32	27	52,936
N 14	@ Chicago Bears	L	13	24	52,907
N 21	Minnesota Vikings (Milw)	L	10	17	53,104
N 28	Chicago Bears (GB)	L	10	16	56,267
D 5	@ Minnesota Vikings	L	9	20	43,700
D 12	@ Atlanta Falcons	W	24	20	23,116
			218	299	721,273

Home: 4-3 (381,791) **Away:** 1-6 (339,482)

1977 (4-10-0, .286)
Fourth, NFC Central

Head Coach: Bart Starr

			GB	Opp.	Attend.
S 18	@ New Orleans Saints	W	24	20	56,250
S 25	Houston Oilers (GB)	L	10	16	55,071
O 2	@ Minnesota Vikings	L	7	19	47,143
O 9	Cincinnati Bengals (Milw)	L	7	17	53,653
O 16	@ Detroit Lions	L	6	10	78,452
O 23	@ Tampa Bay Buccaneers	W	13	0	47,635
O 30	Chicago Bears (GB)	L	0	26	56,002
N 6	@ Kansas City Chiefs	L	10	20	62,687
N 13	Los Angeles Rams (Milw)	L	6	24	52,948
N 21	@ Washington Redskins	L	9	10	51,498
N 27	Minnesota Vikings (GB)	L	6	13	56,267
D 4	Detroit Lions (GB)	W	10	9	56,267
D 11	@ Chicago Bears	L	10	21	33,557
D 18	San Francisco 49ers (Milw)	W	16	14	44,902
			134	219	752,332

Home: 2-5 (375,110) **Away:** 2-5 (377,222)

1978 (8-7-1, .531)
Second, NFC Central

Head Coach: Bart Starr

			GB	Opp.	Attend.
S 3	@ Detroit Lions	W	13	7	51,187
S 10	New Orleans Saints (Milw)	W	28	17	54,336
S 17	Oakland Raiders (GB)	L	3	28	55,903
S 24	@ San Diego Chargers	W	24	3	42,755
O 1	Detroit Lions (Milw)	W	35	14	54,601
O 8	Chicago Bears (GB)	W	24	14	56,267
O 15	Seattle Seahawks (Milw)	W	45	28	52,712
O 22	@ Minnesota Vikings	L	7	21	47,411
O 29	Tampa Bay Buccaneers (GB)	W	9	7	55,108
N 5	@ Philadelphia Eagles	L	3	10	64,214
N 12	Dallas Cowboys (Milw)	L	14	42	55,256
N 19	@ Denver Broncos	L	3	16	74,965
N 26	Minnesota Vikings (GB)	+T	10	10	51,737
D 3	@ Tampa Bay Buccaneers	W	17	7	67,754
D 10	@ Chicago Bears	L	0	14	34,306
D 17	@ Los Angeles Rams	L	14	31	42,500
			249	269	861,012

Home: 5-2-1 (435,920) **Away:** 3-5 (425,092)

1979 (5-11-0, .313)
Fourth, NFC Central

Head Coach: Bart Starr

			GB	Opp.	Attend.
S 2	@ Chicago Bears	L	3	6	56,515
S 9	New Orleans Saints (Milw)	W	28	19	53,184
S 16	Tampa Bay Buccaneers (GB)	L	10	21	55,498
S 23	@ Minnesota Vikings	+L	21	27	46,524
O 1	New England Patriots (GB)	W	27	14	52,842
O 7	@ Atlanta Falcons	L	7	25	56,184
O 14	Detroit Lions (Milw)	W	24	16	53,930
O 21	@ Tampa Bay Buccaneers	L	3	21	67,186
O 28	@ Miami Dolphins	L	7	27	47,741
N 4	New York Jets (GB)	L	22	27	54,201
N 11	Minnesota Vikings (Milw)	W	19	7	52,706
N 18	@ Buffalo Bills	L	12	19	39,679
N 25	Philadelphia Eagles (GB)	L	10	21	50,023
D 2	@ Washington Redskins	L	21	38	51,682
D 9	Chicago Bears (GB)	L	14	15	54,207
D 15	@ Detroit Lions	W	18	13	57,376
			246	316	849,478

Home: 4-4 (426,591) **Away:** 1-7 (422,887)

1980 (5-10-1, .344)
Fourth (tie), NFC Central

Head Coach: Bart Starr

			GB	Opp.	Attend.
S 7	Chicago Bears (GB)	+W	12	6	54,381
S 14	Detroit Lions (Milw)	L	7	29	53,099
S 21	@ Los Angeles Rams	L	21	51	63,850
S 28	Dallas Cowboys (Milw)	L	7	28	54,776
O 5	Cincinnati Bengals (GB)	W	14	9	55,006
O 12	@ Tampa Bay Buccaneers	+T	14	14	64,854
O 19	@ Cleveland Browns	L	21	26	75,548
O 26	Minnesota Vikings (GB)	W	16	3	55,361
N 2	@ Pittsburgh Steelers	L	20	22	52,165
N 9	San Francisco 49ers (Milw)	W	23	16	54,475
N 16	@ New York Giants	L	21	27	72,368
N 23	@ Minnesota Vikings	W	25	13	47,234
N 30	Tampa Bay Buccaneers (Milw)	L	17	20	54,225
D 7	@ Chicago Bears	L	0	61	57,176
D 14	Houston Oilers (GB)	L	3	22	53,201
D 21	@ Detroit Lions	L	3	24	75,111
			231	371	942,830

Home: 4-4 (434,524) **Away:** 1-6-1 (508,306)

1981 (8-8-0, .500)
Second (tie), NFC Central

Head Coach: Bart Starr

			GB	Opp.	Attend.
S 6	@ Chicago Bears	W	16	9	62,411
S 13	Atlanta Falcons (GB)	L	17	31	55,382
S 20	@ Los Angeles Rams	L	23	35	61,286
S 27	Minnesota Vikings (Milw)	L	13	30	55,012
O 4	@ New York Giants	W	27	14	73,684
O 11	Tampa Bay Buccaneers (GB)	L	10	21	55,264
O 18	San Francisco 49ers (Milw)	L	3	13	50,171
O 25	@ Detroit Lions	L	27	31	76,063
N 1	Seattle Seahawks (GB)	W	34	24	49,467
N 8	New York Giants (Milw)	W	26	24	54,138
N 15	Chicago Bears (GB)	W	21	17	55,338
N 22	@ Tampa Bay Buccaneers	L	3	37	63,251
N 29	@ Minnesota Vikings	W	35	23	46,025
D 6	Detroit Lions (GB)	W	31	17	54,481
D 13	@ New Orleans Saints	W	35	7	45,518
D 20	@ New York Jets	L	3	28	56,340
			324	361	913,831

Home: 4-4 (429,253) **Away:** 4-4 (484,578)

1982 (5-3-1, .611)
Third, NFC

Head Coach: Bart Starr

			GB	Opp.	Attend.
S 12	Los Angeles Rams (Milw)	W	35	23	53,694
S 20	@ New York Giants	W	27	19	68,405
N 21	Minnesota Vikings (Milw)	W	26	7	44,681
N 28	@ New York Jets	L	13	15	53,872
D 5	Buffalo Bills (Milw)	W	33	21	46,655
D 12	Detroit Lions (GB)	L	10	30	51,875
D 19	@ Baltimore Colts	T	20	20	25,920
D 26	@ Atlanta Falcons	W	38	7	50,245
J 2	@ Detroit Lions	L	24	27	64,377
			226	169	459,724

Home: 3-1 (196,905) **Away:** 2-2-1 (262,819)
Games Lost to Strike: S26 Miami Dolphins (GB), 03 Philadelphia
Eagles (Milw), 010 @ Chicago Bears, 017 Tampa Bay Buccaneers
(GB), 024 @ Minnesota Vikings, 031 Chicago Bears (GB),
N7 @ Tampa Bay Buccaneers

NFC First-Round Playoff

			GB	Opp.	Attend.
J 8	St. Louis Cardinals (GB)	W	41	16	54,282

NFC Divisional Playoff

J 16	@ Dallas Cowboys	L	26	37	63,972

1983 (8-8-0, .500)
Second (tie), NFC Central

Head Coach: Bart Starr

			GB	Opp.	Attend.
S 4	@ Houston Oilers	+W	41	38	44,073
S 11	Pittsburgh Steelers (GB)	L	21	25	55,154
S 18	Los Angeles Rams (Milw)	W	27	24	54,037
S 26	@ New York Giants	L	3	27	75,308
O 2	Tampa Bay Buccaneers (GB)	W	55	14	54,272
O 9	@ Detroit Lions	L	14	38	67,738
O 17	Washington Redskins (GB)	W	48	47	55,255
O 23	Minnesota Vikings (GB)	+L	17	20	55,236
O 30	@ Cincinnati Bengals	L	14	34	53,349
N 6	Cleveland Browns (Milw)	W	35	21	54,089
N 13	@ Minnesota Vikings	W	29	21	60,113
N 20	Detroit Lions (Milw)	+L	20	23	50,050
N 27	@ Atlanta Falcons	+L	41	47	35,688
D 4	Chicago Bears (GB)	W	31	28	51,147
D 12	@ Tampa Bay Buccaneers	+W	12	9	50,763
D 18	@ Chicago Bears	L	21	23	55,807
			429	439	852,079

Home: 5-3 (429,240) **Away:** 3-5 (422,839)

1984 (8-8-0, .500)
Second, NFC Central

Head Coach: Forrest Gregg

			GB	Opp.	Attend.
S 2	St. Louis Cardinals (GB)	W	24	23	53,738
S 9	@ Los Angeles Raiders	L	7	28	46,269
S 16	Chicago Bears (GB)	L	7	9	55,942
S 23	@ Dallas Cowboys	L	6	20	64,222
S 30	@ Tampa Bay Buccaneers	+L	27	30	47,487
O 7	San Diego Chargers (GB)	L	28	34	54,045
O 15	@ Denver Broncos	L	14	17	62,546
O 21	Seattle Seahawks (Milw)	L	24	30	52,286
O 28	Detroit Lions (GB)	W	41	9	54,289
N 4	@ New Orleans Saints	W	23	13	57,426
N 11	Minnesota Vikings (Milw)	W	45	17	52,931
N 18	Los Angeles Rams (Milw)	W	31	6	52,031
N 22	@ Detroit Lions	L	28	31	63,698
D 2	Tampa Bay Buccaneers (GB)	W	27	14	46,800
D 9	@ Chicago Bears	W	20	14	59,374
D 16	@ Minnesota Vikings	W	38	14	51,197
			390	309	874,281

Home: 5-3 (422,062) **Away:** 3-5 (452,219)

1985 (8-8-0, .500)
Second, NFC Central

Head Coach: Forrest Gregg

			GB	Opp.	Attend.
S 8	@ New England Patriots	L	20	26	49,488
S 15	New York Giants (GB)	W	23	20	56,149
S 22	New York Jets (Milw)	L	3	24	53,667
S 29	@ St. Louis Cardinals	L	28	43	48,598
O 6	Detroit Lions (GB)	W	43	10	55,914
O 13	Minnesota Vikings (Milw)	W	20	17	54,674
O 21	@ Chicago Bears	L	7	23	65,095
O 27	@ Indianapolis Colts	W	10	37	59,708
N 3	Chicago Bears (GB)	L	10	16	56,895
N 10	@ Minnesota Vikings	W	27	17	59,970
N 17	New Orleans Saints (Milw)	W	38	14	52,104
N 24	@ Los Angeles Rams	L	17	34	52,710
D 1	Tampa Bay Buccaneers (GB)	W	21	0	19,856
D 8	Miami Dolphins (GB)	L	24	34	52,671
D 15	@ Detroit Lions	W	26	23	49,379
D 22	@ Tampa Bay Buccaneers	W	20	17	33,992
			337	355	820,870

Home: 5-3 (401,930) **Away:** 3-5 (418,940)

1986 (4-12-0, .250)
Fourth, NFC Central

Head Coach: Forrest Gregg

			GB	Opp.	Attend.
S 7	Houston Oilers (GB)	L	3	31	54,065
S 14	@ New Orleans Saints	L	10	24	46,383
S 22	Chicago Bears (GB)	L	12	25	55,527
S 28	@ Minnesota Vikings	L	7	42	60,478
O 5	Cincinnati Bengals (Milw)	L	28	34	51,230
O 12	Detroit Lions (GB)	L	14	21	52,290
O 19	@ Cleveland Browns	W	17	14	76,438
O 26	San Francisco 49ers (Milw)	L	17	31	50,557
N 2	@ Pittsburgh Steelers	L	3	27	52,831
N 9	Washington Redskins (GB)	L	7	16	47,728
N 16	Tampa Bay Buccaneers (Milw)	W	31	7	48,271
N 23	@ Chicago Bears	L	10	12	59,291
N 27	@ Detroit Lions	W	44	40	61,199
D 7	Minnesota Vikings (GB)	L	6	32	47,637
D 14	@ Tampa Bay Buccaneers	W	21	7	30,099
D 20	@ New York Giants	L	24	55	71,351
			254	418	865,375

Home: 1-7 (407,305) **Away:** 3-5 (458,070)

1987 (5-9-1, .367)
Third, NFC Central
Head Coach: Forrest Gregg

Date	Opponent		GB	Opp.	Attend.
S 13	Los Angeles Raiders (GB)	L	0	20	54,983
S 20	Denver Broncos (Milw)	+T	17	17	50,624
O 4	@ Minnesota Vikings	W	23	16	13,911
O 11	Detroit Lions (GB)	+L	16	19	35,779
O 18	Philadelphia Eagles (GB)	+W	16	10	35,842
O 25	@ Detroit Lions	W	34	33	27,278
N 1	Tampa Bay Buccaneers (Milw)	+	17	23	50,308
N 8	Chicago Bears (GB)	L	24	26	53,320
N 15	@ Seattle Seahawks	L	13	24	60,963
N 22	@ Kansas City Chiefs	W	23	3	34,611
N 29	@ Chicago Bears	L	10	23	61,638
D 6	San Francisco 49ers (GB)	L	12	23	51,118
D 13	Minnesota Vikings (Milw)	W	16	10	47,059
D 19	@ New York Giants	L	10	20	51,013
D 27	@ New Orleans Saints	L	24	33	68,364
			255	300	696,811

Home: 2-5-1 (379,033)   **Away:** 3-4 (317,778)
Game Lost to Strike: S27 @ Tampa Bay Buccaneers

1988 (4-12-0, .250)
Fifth, NFC Central
Head Coach: Lindy Infante

Date	Opponent		GB	Opp.	Attend.
S 4	Los Angeles Rams (GB)	L	7	34	53,769
S 11	Tampa Bay Buccaneers (GB)	L	10	13	52,584
S 18	@ Miami Dolphins	L	17	24	54,409
S 25	Chicago Bears (GB)	L	6	24	56,492
O 2	@ Tampa Bay Buccaneers	L	20	27	40,003
O 9	New England Patriots (Milw)	W	45	3	51,932
O 16	@ Minnesota Vikings	W	34	14	59,053
O 23	Washington Redskins (Milw)	L	17	20	51,767
O 30	@ Buffalo Bills	L	0	28	79,176
N 6	@ Atlanta Falcons	L	0	20	29,952
N 13	Indianapolis Colts (GB)	L	13	20	53,492
N 20	Detroit Lions (Milw)	L	9	19	44,327
N 27	@ Chicago Bears	L	0	16	62,026
D 4	@ Detroit Lions	L	14	30	28,124
D 11	Minnesota Vikings (GB)	W	18	6	48,892
D 18	@ Phoenix Cardinals	W	26	17	44,586
			240	315	810,584

Home: 2-6 (413,255)   **Away:** 2-6 (397,329)

1989 (10-6-0, .625)
Second, NFC Central
Head Coach: Lindy Infante

Date	Opponent		GB	Opp.	Attend.
S 10	Tampa Bay Buccaneers (GB)	L	21	23	55,650
S 17	New Orleans Saints (GB)	W	35	34	55,809
S 24	@ Los Angeles Rams	L	38	41	57,701
O 1	Atlanta Falcons (Milw)	W	23	21	54,647
O 8	Dallas Cowboys (GB)	W	31	13	56,656
O 15	@ Minnesota Vikings	L	14	26	62,075
O 22	@ Miami Dolphins	L	20	23	56,624
O 29	Detroit Lions (Milw)	+W	23	20	53,731
N 5	Chicago Bears (GB)	W	14	13	56,556
N 12	@ Detroit Lions	L	22	31	44,324
N 19	@ San Francisco 49ers	W	21	17	62,219
N 26	Minnesota Vikings (Milw)	W	20	19	55,592
D 3	Tampa Bay Buccaneers	W	17	16	58,110
D 10	Kansas City Chiefs (GB)	W	3	21	56,694
D 17	@ Chicago Bears	W	40	28	44,781
D 24	@ Dallas Cowboys	L	20	10	41,265
			362	356	872,444

Home: 6-2 (445,335)   **Away:** 4-4 (427,109)

1990 (6-10-0, .375)
Fourth, NFC Central
Head Coach: Lindy Infante

Date	Opponent		GB	Opp.	Attend.
S 9	Los Angeles Rams (GB)	W	36	24	57,685
S 16	Chicago Bears (GB)	L	13	31	58,938
S 23	Kansas City Chiefs (GB)	L	3	17	58,817
S 30	@ Detroit Lions	W	24	21	64,509
O 7	@ Chicago Bears	L	13	27	59,929
O 14	@ Tampa Bay Buccaneers	L	14	26	67,472
O 28	Minnesota Vikings (Milw)	W	24	10	55,125
N 4	San Francisco 49ers (GB)	L	20	24	58,835
N 11	@ Los Angeles Raiders	W	29	16	50,855
N 18	@ Phoenix Cardinals	W	24	21	46,878
N 25	Tampa Bay Buccaneers (Milw)	W	20	10	53,677
D 2	@ Minnesota Vikings	L	7	23	62,058
D 9	Seattle Seahawks (Milw)	L	14	20	52,015
D 16	@ Philadelphia Eagles	L	0	31	65,627
D 22	Detroit Lions (GB)	L	17	24	46,700
D 30	@ Denver Broncos	L	13	22	46,943
			271	347	906,063

Home: 3-5 (441,792)   **Away:** 3-5 (464,271)

1991 (4-12-0, .250)
Fourth, NFC Central
Head Coach: Lindy Infante

Date	Opponent		GB	Opp.	Attend.
S 1	Philadelphia Eagles (GB)	L	3	20	58,991
S 8	@ Detroit Lions	L	14	23	43,132
S 15	Tampa Bay Buccaneers (GB)	W	15	13	58,114
S 22	@ Miami Dolphins	L	13	16	56,583
S 29	@ Los Angeles Rams	L	21	23	54,736
O 6	Dallas Cowboys (Milw)	L	17	20	53,695
O 17	Chicago Bears (GB)	L	0	10	58,435
O 27	@ Tampa Bay Buccaneers	W	27	0	40,275
N 3	@ New York Jets	+L	16	19	67,435
N 10	Buffalo Bills (Milw)	L	24	34	52,175
N 17	Minnesota Vikings (GB)	L	21	35	57,614
N 24	Indianapolis Colts (GB)	W	14	10	42,132
D 1	@ Atlanta Falcons	L	31	35	43,270
D 8	@ Chicago Bears	L	13	27	62,353
D 15	Detroit Lions (GB)	L	17	21	43,881
D 21	@ Minnesota Vikings	W	27	7	52,860
			273	313	845,681

Home: 2-6 (425,037)   **Away:** 2-6 (420,644)

1992 (9-7-0, .563)
Second, NFC Central
Head Coach: Mike Holmgren

Date	Opponent		GB	Opp.	Attend.
S 6	Minnesota Vikings (GB)	+L	20	23	58,617
S 13	@ Tampa Bay Buccaneers	L	3	31	50,051
S 20	Cincinnati Bengals (GB)	W	24	23	57,272
S 27	Pittsburgh Steelers (GB)	W	17	3	58,724
O 4	@ Atlanta Falcons	L	10	24	63,769
O 18	@ Cleveland Browns	L	6	17	69,268
O 25	Chicago Bears (GB)	L	10	30	59,435
N 1	@ Detroit Lions	W	27	13	60,594
N 8	@ New York Giants	L	7	27	72,038
N 15	Philadelphia Eagles (Milw)	W	27	24	52,689
N 22	@ Chicago Bears	W	17	3	56,170
N 29	Tampa Bay Buccaneers (Milw)	W	19	14	52,347
D 6	Detroit Lions (Milw)	W	38	10	49,469
D 13	@ Houston Oilers	L	16	14	57,285
D 20	Los Angeles Rams (GB)	W	28	13	57,796
D 27	@ Minnesota Vikings	L	7	27	61,461
			276	296	936,985

Home: 6-2 (446,349)   **Away:** 3-5 (490,636)

1993 (9-7-0, .563)
Third, NFC Central

Head Coach: Mike Holmgren

			GB	Opp.	Attend.
S 5	Los Angeles Rams (Milw)	W	36	6	54,648
S 12	Philadelphia Eagles (GB)	L	17	20	59,061
S 26	@ Minnesota Vikings	L	13	15	61,077
O 3	@ Dallas Cowboys	L	14	36	63,568
O 10	Denver Broncos (GB)	W	30	27	58,943
O 24	@ Tampa Bay Buccaneers	W	37	14	47,354
O 31	Chicago Bears (GB)	W	17	3	58,945
N 8	@ Kansas City Chiefs	L	16	23	76,742
N 14	@ New Orleans Saints	W	19	17	69,043
N 21	Detroit Lions (Milw)	W	26	17	55,119
N 28	Tampa Bay Buccaneers (GB)	W	13	10	56,995
D 5	@ Chicago Bears	L	17	30	62,236
D 12	@ San Diego Chargers	W	20	13	57,930
D 19	Minnesota Vikings (Milw)	L	17	21	54,773
D 26	Los Angeles Raiders (GB)	W	28	0	54,482
J 2	@ Detroit Lions	L	20	30	77,510
			340	282	968,426

Home: 6-2 (452,966) **Away:** 3-5 (515,460)

NFC Wild Card Playoff			GB	Opp.	Attend.
J 8	@ Detroit Lions	W	28	24	68,479
NFC Divisional Playoff					
J 16	@ Dallas Cowboys	L	17	27	64,790

1994 (9-7-0, .563)
Second, NFC Central

Head Coach: Mike Holmgren

			GB	Opp.	Attend.
S 4	Minnesota Vikings (GB)	W	16	10	59,487
S 11	Miami Dolphins (Milw)	L	14	24	55,011
S 18	@ Philadelphia Eagles	L	7	13	63,922
S 25	Tampa Bay Buccaneers (GB)	W	30	3	58,551
O 2	@ New England Patriots	L	16	17	57,522
O 9	Los Angeles Rams (GB)	W	24	17	58,911
O 20	@ Minnesota Vikings	+L	10	13	63,041
O 31	@ Chicago Bears	W	33	6	47,381
N 6	Detroit Lions (Milw)	W	38	30	54,995
N 13	New York Jets (GB)	W	17	10	58,307
N 20	@ Buffalo Bills	L	20	29	79,029
N 24	@ Dallas Cowboys	L	31	42	64,597
D 4	@ Detroit Lions	L	31	34	76,338
D 11	Chicago Bears (GB)	W	40	3	57,927
D 18	Atlanta Falcons (Milw)	W	21	17	54,885
D 24	@ Tampa Bay Buccaneers	W	34	19	65,076
			382	287	974,980

Home: 7-1 (458,074) **Away:** 2-6 (516,906)

NFC Wild Card Playoff			GB	Opp.	Attend.
D 31	Detroit Lions (GB)	W	16	12	58,125
NFC Divisional Playoff					
J 8	@ Dallas Cowboys	L	9	35	64,745

(1st season all home games again played in Green Bay)

1995 (11-5-0, .688)
First, NFC Central

Head Coach: Mike Holmgren

			GB	Opp.	Attend.
S 3	St. Louis Rams	L	14	17	60,104
S 11	@ Chicago Bears	W	27	24	64,855
S 17	New York Giants	W	14	6	60,117
S 24	@ Jacksonville Jaguars	W	24	14	66,744
O 8	@ Dallas Cowboys	L	24	34	64,806
O 15	Detroit Lions	W	30	21	60,302
O 22	Minnesota Vikings	W	38	21	60,332
O 29	@ Detroit Lions	L	16	24	73,462
N 5	@ Minnesota Vikings	L	24	27	62,839
N 12	Chicago Bears	W	35	28	59,996
N 19	@ Cleveland Browns	W	31	20	55,388
N 26	Tampa Bay Buccaneers	W	35	13	59,218
D 3	Cincinnati Bengals	W	24	10	60,318
D 10	@ Tampa Bay Buccaneers	+L	10	13	67,557
D 16	@ New Orleans Saints	W	34	23	50,132
D 24	Pittsburgh Steelers	W	24	19	60,649
			404	314	986,819

Home: 7-1 (481,036) **Away:** 4-4 (505,783)

NFC Wild Card Playoff			GB	Opp.	Attend.
D 31	Atlanta Falcons	W	37	20	60,453
NFC Divisional Playoff					
J 6	@ San Francisco 49ers	W	27	17	69,311
NFC Championship					
J 14	@ Dallas Cowboys	L	27	38	65,135

1996 (13-3-0, .813)
First, NFC Central

Head Coach: Mike Holmgren

			GB	Opp.	Attend.
S 1	@ Tampa Bay Buccaneers	W	34	3	54,102
S 9	Philadelphia Eagles	W	39	13	60,666
S 15	San Diego Chargers	W	42	10	60,584
S 22	@ Minnesota Vikings	L	21	30	64,168
S 29	@ Seattle Seahawks	W	31	10	59,973
O 6	@ Chicago Bears	W	37	6	65,480
O 14	San Francisco 49ers	+W	23	20	60,716
O 27	Tampa Bay Buccaneers	W	13	7	60,627
N 3	Detroit Lions	W	28	18	60,695
N 10	@ Kansas City Chiefs	L	20	27	79,281
N 18	@ Dallas Cowboys	L	6	21	65,032
N 24	@ St. Louis Rams	W	24	9	61,499
D 1	Chicago Bears	W	28	17	59,682
D 8	Denver Broncos	W	41	6	60,712
D 15	@ Detroit Lions	W	31	3	73,214
D 22	Minnesota Vikings	W	38	10	59,306
			456	210	1,005,737

Home: 8-0 (482,988) **Away:** 5-3 (522,749)

NFC Divisional Playoff			GB	Opp.	Attend.
J 4	San Francisco 49ers	W	35	14	60,787
NFC Championship					
J 12	Carolina Panthers	W	30	13	60,216
Super Bowl XXXI					
J 26	New England Patriots (@ N.O.)	W	35	21	72,301

1997 (13-3-0, .813)
First, NFC Central

Head Coach: Mike Holmgren

			GB	Opp.	Attend.
S 1	Chicago Bears	W	38	24	60,766
S 7	@ Philadelphia Eagles	L	9	10	66,803
S 14	Miami Dolphins	W	23	18	60,075
S 21	Minnesota Vikings	W	38	32	60,115
S 28	@ Detroit Lions	L	15	26	78,110
O 5	Tampa Bay Buccaneers	W	21	16	60,100
O 12	@ Chicago Bears	W	24	23	62,212
O 27	@ New England Patriots	W	28	10	59,972
N 2	Detroit Lions	W	20	10	60,126
N 9	St. Louis Rams	W	17	7	60,093
N 16	@ Indianapolis Colts	L	38	41	60,928
N 23	Dallas Cowboys	W	45	17	60,111
D 1	@ Minnesota Vikings	W	27	11	64,001
D 7	@ Tampa Bay Buccaneers	W	17	6	73,523
D 14	@ Carolina Panthers	W	31	10	70,887
D 20	Buffalo Bills	W	31	21	60,108
			422	282	1,017,930

Home: 8-0 (481,494) **Away:** 5-3 (536,436)

NFC Divisional Playoff			GB	Opp.	Attend.
J 4	Tampa Bay Buccaneers	W	21	7	60,327
NFC Championship					
J 11	@ San Francisco 49ers	W	23	10	68,987
Super Bowl XXXII					
J 25	Denver Broncos (@ San Diego)	L	24	31	68,912

RESULTS BY SEASON SUMMARY

The Green Bay Packers own a 540-440-36 regular-season record in their 77 seasons of play in the National Football League (1921-97) — a .549 winning percentage.
The Packers are 210-120-13 (.631) in Green Bay and were 105-61-3 (.630) in Milwaukee for an overall home mark of 315-181-16 (.631). The Packers played league games in Milwaukee on an annual basis from 1933-94.
On the road, Green Bay stands 225-259-20 (.466), a mark which includes two neutral site contests.
The Packers played independent football during the 1919-20 seasons.

	OVERALL RECORD				— HOME — GREEN BAY			MILWAUKEE			AWAY		
Year	**W**	**L**	**T**	**Pct.**	**W**	**L**	**T**	**W**	**L**	**T**	**W**	**L**	**T**
1921	3	2	1	.600	3	1	0	-	-	-	0	1	1
1922	4	3	3	.571	3	1	1	-	-	-	*1	2	2
1923	7	2	1	.778	4	2	1	-	-	-	3	0	0
1924	7	4	0	.636	5	0	0	-	-	-	2	4	0
1925	8	5	0	.615	6	0	0	-	-	-	2	5	0
1926	7	3	3	.700	4	1	2	-	-	-	3	2	1
1927	7	2	1	.778	6	1	0	-	-	-	1	1	1
1928	6	4	3	.600	3	2	2	-	-	-	3	2	1
1929	12	0	1	1.000	5	0	0	-	-	-	7	0	1
1930	10	3	1	.769	6	0	0	-	-	-	4	3	1
1931	12	2	0	.857	8	0	0	-	-	-	4	2	0
1932	10	3	1	.769	5	0	1	-	-	-	5	3	0
1933	5	7	1	.417	3	1	1	0	1	0	2	5	0
1934	7	6	0	.538	3	2	0	1	1	0	3	3	0
1935	8	4	0	.667	4	1	0	1	1	0	3	2	0
1936	10	1	1	.909	3	1	0	2	0	0	5	0	1
1937	7	4	0	.636	2	2	0	2	0	0	3	2	0
1938	8	3	0	.727	2	2	0	2	0	0	*4	1	0
1939	9	2	0	.818	3	1	0	2	0	0	4	1	0
1940	6	4	1	.600	2	2	0	2	0	0	2	2	1
1941	10	1	0	.909	2	1	0	3	0	0	5	0	0
1942	8	2	1	.800	2	1	0	2	0	0	4	1	1
1943	7	2	1	.778	1	0	1	1	1	0	5	1	0
1944	8	2	0	.800	3	0	0	2	0	0	3	2	0
1945	6	4	0	.600	2	1	0	2	0	0	2	3	0
1946	6	5	0	.545	1	2	0	1	1	0	4	2	0
1947	6	5	1	.545	2	1	0	2	1	0	2	3	1
1948	3	9	0	.250	2	1	0	0	3	0	1	5	0
1949	2	10	0	.167	0	3	0	1	2	0	1	5	0
1950	3	9	0	.250	2	2	0	1	1	0	0	6	0
1951	3	9	0	.250	1	3	0	1	1	0	1	5	0
1952	6	6	0	.500	1	2	0	2	1	0	3	3	0
1953	2	9	1	.182	1	2	0	0	3	0	1	4	1
1954	4	8	0	.333	0	3	0	2	1	0	2	4	0
1955	6	6	0	.500	3	0	0	2	1	0	1	5	0
1956	4	8	0	.333	0	3	0	2	1	0	2	4	0
1957	3	9	0	.250	1	2	0	0	3	0	2	4	0
1958	1	10	1	.091	1	2	1	0	2	0	0	6	0
1959	7	5	0	.583	4	0	0	0	2	0	3	3	0
1960	8	4	0	.667	3	1	0	1	1	0	4	2	0
1961	11	3	0	.786	4	0	0	2	1	0	5	2	0
1962	13	1	0	.929	4	0	0	3	0	0	6	1	0
1963	11	2	1	.846	3	1	0	3	0	0	5	1	1
1964	8	5	1	.615	2	2	0	2	1	0	4	2	1
1965	10	3	1	.769	3	1	0	3	0	0	4	2	1
1966	12	2	0	.857	3	1	0	3	0	0	6	1	0
1967	9	4	1	.692	2	1	1	2	1	0	5	2	0
1968	6	7	1	.462	1	3	0	1	2	0	4	2	1
1969	8	6	0	.571	3	1	0	2	1	0	3	4	0
1970	6	8	0	.429	2	2	0	2	1	0	2	5	0
1971	4	8	2	.333	2	2	0	1	1	1	1	5	1
1972	10	4	0	.714	2	2	0	2	1	0	6	1	0
1973	5	7	2	.429	1	2	1	2	0	1	2	5	0
1974	6	8	0	.429	1	3	0	3	0	0	2	5	0
1975	4	10	0	.286	2	2	0	1	2	0	1	6	0
1976	5	9	0	.357	2	2	0	2	1	0	1	6	0
1977	4	10	0	.286	1	3	0	1	2	0	2	5	0
1978	8	7	1	.531	2	1	1	3	1	0	3	5	0
1979	5	11	0	.313	1	4	0	3	0	0	1	7	0
1980	5	10	1	.344	3	1	0	1	3	0	1	6	1
1981	8	8	0	.500	3	2	0	1	2	0	4	4	0
1982	5	3	1	.611	0	1	0	3	0	0	2	2	1
1983	8	8	0	.500	3	2	0	2	1	0	3	5	0

RESULTS BY SEASON SUMMARY

Year	OVERALL RECORD W	L	T	Pct.	— HOME — GREEN BAY W	L	T	MILWAUKEE W	L	T	AWAY W	L	T
1984	8	8	0	.500	3	2	0	2	1	0	3	5	0
1985	8	8	0	.500	3	2	0	2	1	0	3	5	0
1986	4	12	0	.250	0	5	0	1	2	0	3	5	0
1987	5	9	1	.367	1	4	0	1	1	1	3	4	0
1988	4	12	0	.250	1	4	0	1	2	0	2	6	0
1989	10	6	0	.625	3	2	0	3	0	0	4	4	0
1990	6	10	0	.375	1	4	0	2	1	0	3	5	0
1991	4	12	0	.250	1	4	0	1	2	0	2	6	0
1992	9	7	0	.563	3	2	0	3	0	0	3	5	0
1993	9	7	0	.563	4	1	0	2	1	0	3	5	0
1994	9	7	0	.563	5	0	0	2	1	0	2	6	0
1995	11	5	0	.688	7	1	0	-	-	-	4	4	0
1996	13	3	0	.813	8	0	0	-	-	-	5	3	0
1997	13	3	0	.813	8	0	0	-	-	-	5	3	0
Totals	**540**	**440**	**36**	**.549**	**210**	**120**	**13**	**105**	**61**	**3**	**#225**	**259**	**20**

* includes one neutral site victory
\# includes two neutral site victories

LARGEST MARGINS
(since 1921 — league games only)

. . .OF VICTORY

1. 53 points (56-3) Oct. 23, 1966, vs. Atlanta at Milw.
2. 49 points (49-0) Sept. 30, 1962, vs. Chicago Bears
   49 points (49-0) Nov. 11, 1962, at Philadelphia
4. 48 points (55-7) Nov. 12, 1967, vs. Cleveland at Milw.
5. 47 points (47-0) Oct. 15, 1933, vs. Pittsburgh
   47 points (54-7) Nov. 23, 1941, at Pittsburgh
7. 43 points (50-7) Nov. 24, 1940, at Detroit
8. 42 points (45-3) Oct. 9, 1988, vs. New England at Milw.
9. 41 points (41-0) Oct. 14, 1934, vs. Cincinnati
   41 points (55-14) Oct. 2, 1983, vs. Tampa Bay
11. 38 points (45-7) Oct. 8, 1961, vs. Baltimore
12. 37 points (43-6) Nov. 6, 1921, vs. Evansville
    *37 points (37-0) Dec. 31, 1961, vs. N.Y. Giants
    37 points (40-3) Dec. 11, 1994, vs. Chicago
15. 36 points (57-21) Oct. 7, 1945, vs. Detroit at Milw.
16. 35 points (35-0) Oct. 24, 1926, vs. Racine
    35 points (42-7) Nov. 12, 1944, at Cleveland
    35 points (41-6) Dec. 8, 1996, vs. Denver
19. 34 points (47-13) Nov. 2, 1930, vs. Portsmouth
    34 points (41-7) Nov. 13, 1960, vs. Dallas
    34 points (34-0) Nov. 24, 1974, vs. San Diego

. . .OF DEFEAT

1. 56 points (56-0) Nov. 2, 1958, at Baltimore
2. 54 points (61-7) Dec. 7,1980, at Chicago
3. 46 points (49-3) Nov. 21, 1948, vs. N.Y. Giants at Milw.
4. 41 points (48-7) Oct. 2, 1949, vs. L.A. Rams
5. 40 points (40-0) Sept. 20, 1970, vs. Detroit
6. 39 points (45-6) Oct. 18, 1959, vs. L.A. Rams at Milw.
7. 38 points (45-7) Sept. 26, 1948, vs. Chicago Bears
   38 points (45-7) Sept. 17, 1950, vs. Detroit
9. 37 points (51-14) Dec. 3, 1950, at L.A. Rams
10. 35 points (42-7) Dec. 5, 1948, at Chicago Cardinals
    35 points (52-17) Oct. 26, 1952, vs. Detroit
    35 points (35-0) Dec. 5, 1954, at San Francisco
    35 points (42-7) Sept. 28, 1986, at Minnesota
14. 34 points (48-14) Dec. 6, 1953, at San Francisco
    34 points (34-0) Oct. 28, 1973, at Detroit
    34 points (37-3) Nov. 22, 1981, at Tampa Bay

*playoff game

A decade-and-a-half later, Green Bay continues to own the National Football League record for most overtime games played in one season — a mark set by the club in 1983 when it was involved in five sudden death decisions, winning two while losing three. The Packers' most recent OT experience came on Oct. 14, 1996, at Lambeau Field in a Monday night game with San Francisco, one they captured in dramatic fashion when Chris Jacke drilled a 53-yard field goal just under four minutes into the extra period, ending a four-game overtime losing streak by Green Bay.

Green Bay has played in 21 total contests which have gone into overtime, standing 6-10-4 in the regular season and 1-0 in the postseason for an overall mark of 7-10-4.

The lone postseason occurrence was a historic 13-10 victory over the Baltimore Colts in a Western Conference playoff game — the first overtime game in which the Packers ever were involved — in Green Bay's Lambeau Field Dec. 26, 1965, on a 25-yard Don Chandler field goal.

In addition to regular and postseason play, the Packers have played five overtime games in preseason action. Capsules of the Packers' regular and postseason overtime games follow:

REGULAR SEASON (6-10-4)

Nov. 26, 1978-Green Bay 10, Minnesota 10, at Green Bay; Packers win toss. Both teams have possession of the ball four times.

Sept. 23, 1979-Minnesota 27, Green Bay 21, at Minnesota; Vikings win toss. Kramer throws 50-yard touchdown pass to Rashad at 3:18.

Sept. 7, 1980-Green Bay 12, Chicago 6, at Green Bay; Bears win toss. Parsons punts and Nixon returns 16 yards. Five plays later, Marcol returns own blocked field goal attempt 24 yards for touchdown at 6:00.

Oct. 12, 1980-Green Bay 14, Tampa Bay 14, at Tampa Bay; Packers win toss. Teams trade punts twice. Lee returns second Tampa Bay punt to Green Bay 42. Dickey completes three passes to Buccaneers' 18, where Birney's 36-yard field goal attempt is wide right as time expires.

Dec. 19, 1982-Baltimore 20, Green Bay 20, at Baltimore; Packers win toss. K.Anderson intercepts Dickey's first-down pass and returns to Packers' 42. Miller's 44-yard field goal attempt blocked by G.Lewis. Teams trade punts before Stenerud's 47-yard field goal attempt is wide right. Teams trade punts again before time expires in Colts' possession.

Sept. 4, 1983-Green Bay 41, Houston 38, at Houston; Packers win toss. Stenerud kicks 42-yard field goal at 5:55.

Oct. 23, 1983-Minnesota 20, Green Bay 17, at Green Bay; Packers win toss. Scribner's punt downed on Vikings' 42. Ricardo kicks 32-yard field goal eight plays later at 5:05.

Nov. 20, 1983-Detroit 23, Green Bay 20, at Milwaukee; Packers win toss. Scribner punts and Jenkins returns 14 yards to Green Bay 45. Murray's 33-yard field goal attempt is wide left at 9:32. Whitehurst's pass intercepted by Watkins and returned to Green Bay 27. Murray kicks 37-yard field goal four plays later at 8:30.

Nov. 27, 1983-Atlanta 47, Green Bay 41, at Atlanta; Packers win toss. K.Johnson returns interception 31 yards for touchdown at 2:13.

Dec. 12, 1983-Green Bay 12, Tampa Bay 9, at Tampa Bay; Packers win toss. Stenerud kicks 23-yard field goal 11 plays later at 4:07.

Sept. 30, 1984-Tampa Bay 30, Green Bay 27, at Tampa Bay; Packers win toss. Scribner punts 44 yards to Tampa Bay 2. Epps returns Garcia's punt three yards to Green Bay 27. Scribner's punt downed on Buccaneers' 33. Ariri kicks 46-yard field goal 11 plays later at 10:32.

Sept. 20, 1987-Green Bay 17, Denver 17, at Milwaukee; Packers win toss. Del Greco's 47-yard field goal attempt is short. Teams trade punts. Elway intercepted by Noble who returns 10 yards to Green Bay 34. Davis fumbles on next play and Smith recovers. Two plays later, Karlis's 40-yard field goal attempt is wide left. Time expires two plays later with Packers on own 23.

Oct. 11, 1987-Detroit 19, Green Bay 16, at Green Bay; Lions win toss. Prindle's 42-yard field goal attempt is wide left. Packers punt downed on Detroit 17. Prindle kicks 31-yard field goal 16 plays later at 12:26.

Oct. 18, 1987-Green Bay 16, Philadelphia 10, at Green Bay; Packers win toss. Hargrove scores on seven-yard run 10 plays later at 5:04.

Oct. 29, 1989-Green Bay 23, Detroit 20, at Milwaukee; Lions win toss. Sanders touchback on Jacke kickoff. On first play, Murphy intercepts Lions' Peete and returns it three yards to Lions' 26. Fullwood gains five yards on three plays to set up Jacke's 38-yard field goal at 2:14.

Nov. 3, 1991-New York Jets 19, Green Bay 16, at New York; Packers win toss. Thompson returns kickoff 30 yards to Packers' 39. Green Bay drives to New York 24 where Jacke's 42-yard field goal attempt is wide right. Jets drive to 50. Aguiar's punt is fumbled by Sikahema and recovered by New York at Packers' 23. After 2 plays, Leahy kicks 37-yard field goal at 9:40.

Sept. 6, 1992-Minnesota 23, Green Bay 20, at Green Bay; Vikings win toss. Jacke kicks off to Vikings' 23 where Allen returns 2 yards to 25. After Minnesota punt, Packers take over at Green Bay 33. On third play, Majkowski is intercepted by Glenn at Vikings' 48. On Minnesota's first play from scrimmage, Allen runs 17 yards before fumbling at Packers' 35. Teams trade punts. Packers punt a second time in overtime session with Vikings taking over at their 42. On second play, Allen runs 45 yards up middle to Packers' 11. One play later, Reveiz kicks 26-yard field goal at 10:20.

Oct. 20, 1994-Minnesota 13, Green Bay 10, at Minnesota; Vikings win toss. Ismail returns kickoff 22 yards to 2 Minnesota drives 62 yards on eight plays, Reveiz kicking a game-winning, 27-yard field goal with 4:26 elapsed.

Dec. 10, 1995-Tampa Bay 13, Green Bay 10, at Tampa Bay; Buccaneers win toss. Edmonds returns kickoff 23 yar to 24. Tampa Bay drives 48 yards in seven plays, the big play being a 23-yard completion from Dilfer to Copeland to t Packers' 37. Husted kicks 47-yard field goal 3:46 into extra period.

Oct. 14, 1996-Green Bay 23, San Francisco 20, at Green Bay; 49ers win toss. Carter returns kickoff 23 yards to 2 After San Francisco fails to pick up a first down, Packers take over at their own 44. Green Bay covers only 21 yards six plays to reach the 49ers' 35, the key play being a 13-yard completion from Favre to Beebe on third down, befo setting up for a 53-yard field goal attempt. Jacke sends his kick — the longest field goal to win an overtime game NFL history — squarely down the middle with five to 10 yards to spare at 3:41.

POSTSEASON (1-0)

Dec. 26, 1965-Green Bay 13, Baltimore 10, at Green Bay; Packers win toss. Moore returns kickoff to Packers' 2 Chandler punts and Haymond returns nine yards to Colts' 41. Gilburg punts and Wood makes fair catch at Packers' 2 Chandler punts and Haymond returns one yard to Colts' 41. Michaels misses 47-yard field goal. Packers win at 13: on 25-yard field goal by Chandler.

JUST FOR THE RECORD

Founded as a town team in 1919, a year when Woodrow Wilson was in the White House, the Green Bay Packers carry an overall winning percentage of .571 into the 1998 National Football League season, having played a total of 1,383 games. Over their 79 years of existence, the Packers have won 766 games, lost 569 and tied 48.

The 1,383-game total includes a record of 540-440-36 (.549) in regular-season play and a league-best mark of 22-9-0 (.710) in playoff action. In addition, the Packers went 19-2-1 (.886) playing independent football from 1919-20.

Green Bay stands 173-115-9 (.598) all-time in preseason games.

ALL-TIME RECORD				NFL REGULAR-SEASON RECORD				PLAYOFF RECORD			
W	L	T	Pct.	W	L	T	Pct.	W	L	T	Pct.
766	569	48	.571	540	440	36	.549	22	9	0	.710

PRESEASON RECORD				OTHER NON-LEAGUE GAMES RECORD				INDEPENDENT RECORD (1919-20)			
W	L	T	Pct.	W	L	T	Pct.	W	L	T	Pct.
173	115	9	.598	12	3	2	.765	19	2	1	.886

1921 (4-0-0)

		GB	Opp.	Attend.
S 25	Chicago Boosters	13	0	3,500
O 2	Rockford Maroons	49	0	
O 9	Chicago Cornell-Hamburgs	40	0	
O 16	Beloit Fairies	7	0	5,000

1922 (0-1-0)

S 24	@ Duluth Kelleys	2	6	

1923 (1-0-0)

S 23	Hibbing Miners	10	0	2,670

1924 (2-0-0)

S 14	Ironwood Legionaires	15	0	
S 21	Chicago Bears	5	0	4,000

1925 (1-0-0)

S 13	Iron Mountain All-Stars	48	6	4,000

1926 (1-0-0)

S 12	Iron Mountain	79	0	3,000

1927 (1-0-0)

S 11	Milwaukee Badgers	34	0

1928 (1-0-0)

S 16	Minneapolis Marines	19	0	5,000

1929 (1-0-0)

S 15	Portsmouth Spartans	14	0	5,000

1930 (1-0-0)

S 14	Oshkosh All-Stars	46	0

1932 (1-0-0)

S 11	Grand Rapids Maroons	45	0	3,000

1934 (1-0-0)

S 9	Fort Atkinson Blackhawks (GB)	28	7	4,000

1935 (4-0-0)

A 31	@ Merrill Fromm Foxes	33	0	1,500
S 2	@ Chippewa Falls Marines	22	0	6,000
S 4	@ Stevens Point	40	0	1,500
S 8	La Crosse Old Style Lagers (GB)	49	0	2,500

1936 (1-0-0)

S 5	Wisconsin Cardinals of Madison (GB)..	62	0	2,000

1937 (0-1-0)

S 1	College All-Stars (@ Chicago)	0	6	84,560

1938 (1-0-0)

S 5	Cedar Rapids (Iowa) Crush (@ Ironwood, Mich.)	75	0	5,000

1939 (2-0-1)

		GB	Opp.	Attend.
A 25	Pittsburgh Pirates (GB) (Game 1)	7	7	9,416
A 25	Pittsburgh Pirates (GB) (Game 2)	17	0	9,416
S 4	Southwest College All-Stars (@ Dallas)	31	20	

1940 (2-0-0)

A 29	College All-Stars (@ Chicago)	45	28	84,567
S 2	Washington (Milw)	28	20	14,798

1941 (1-0-1)

A 23	N.Y. Giants (GB)	17	17	10,800
S 7	Philadelphia (Milw)	28	21	10,000

1942 (2-1-0)

A 30	@ Brooklyn Dodgers	21	16	9,874
S 7	Washington (@ Baltimore)	7	28	55,000
S 13	Western Army All-Stars (Milw)	36	21	20,000

1943 (2-0-0)

S 5	Washington (@ Baltimore)	23	21	45,000
S 11	Phil-Pitt Steagles (@ Pittsburgh)	28	10	19,369

1944 (1-1-0)

S 4	Washington (@ Baltimore)	7	20	40,000
S 10	Boston Yanks (@ Buffalo)	28	0	17,372

1945 (2-2-0)

A 30	College All-Stars (@ Chicago)	19	7	92,753
S 13	@ Philadelphia	21	28	90,218
S 19	Pittsburgh (@ Hershey, Pa.)	38	12	14,521
S 23	@ Washington	7	21	27,125

1946 (0-3-0)

S 6	Philadelphia (Milw)	6	7	25,000
S 10	Washington (@ Denver)	31	35	21,000
S 20	@ N.Y. Giants	21	35	50,000

1947 (3-1-0)

A 23	N.Y. Giants (GB)	17	14	15,000
A 29	@ Pittsburgh	17	24	31,507
S 14	Boston Yanks (Milw)	14	10	17,895
S 21	Washington (@ Baltimore)	31	21	18,186

1948 (3-0-0)

A 29	N.Y. Giants (@ Minneapolis)	7	0	15,000
S 5	Pittsburgh (GB)	9	7	13,900
S 11	Washington (@ Birmingham, Ala.)	43	0	27,000

1949 (2-3-0)

A 20	Philadelphia (GB)	0	35	18,785
A 24	N.Y. Giants (@ Syracuse, N.Y.)	14	7	20,000
A 28	@ Pittsburgh	3	9	13,578
S 11	N.Y. Bulldogs (@ Rock Island, Ill.)	7	3	
S 18	Washington (Milw)	24	35	12,873

1950 (3-1-0)

A 12	Cleveland (@ Toledo, Ohio)	7	38	10,000
A 16	Chicago Cardinals (GB)	17	14	20,136
A 29	N.Y. Giants (@ Boston)	10	0	12,053
S 10	Baltimore Colts (Milw)	16	14	17,191

1951 (2-3-0)

		GB	Opp.	Attend.
A 25	Chicago Cardinals (GB)	17	14	16,168
S 9	Philadelphia (Milw)	10	14	19,282
S 12	San Francisco (@ Minneapolis)	0	20	19,021
S 16	Pittsburgh (@ Buffalo)	6	35	13,458
S 23	Washington (@ Alexandria, Va.)	14	7	6,000

1952 (2-4-0)

A 16	N.Y. Giants (Milw)	0	7	22,000
A 23	Cleveland (GB)	14	21	22,215
A 29	Pittsburgh (@ Latrobe, Pa.)	6	7	10,000
S 7	@ Chicago Cardinals	7	38	15,497
S 14	Washington (@ Kansas City)	13	7	6,500
S 17	Pittsburgh (@ Minneapolis)	23	10	21,000

1953 (1-4-0)

A 22	N.Y. Giants (@ Minneapolis)	31	7	20,560
A 29	Chicago Cardinals (@ Spokane, Wash.)	7	13	17,000
S 5	Washington (GB)	6	13	16,425
S 12	Pittsburgh (Milw)	23	26	16,859
S 19	@ Cleveland	13	21	22,336

1954 (2-4-0)

A 14	Chicago Cardinals (@ Minneapolis)	10	27	21,000
A 21	Cleveland (GB)	13	14	15,747
A 28	@ Pittsburgh	36	14	14,012
S 4	Philadelphia (@ Hershey, Pa.)	13	24	6,134
S 11	Washington (@ Raleigh, N.C.)	31	3	16,000
S 18	N.Y. Giants (Milw)	27	38	17,000

1955 (2-4-0)

A 13	N.Y. Giants (@ Spokane, Wash.)	31	24	15,000
A 20	Cleveland (@ Akron, Ohio)	7	13	22,000
A 27	Pittsburgh (GB)	14	16	16,912
S 3	Philadelphia (@ Charleston, W.V.)	10	24	12,500
S 10	Washington (@ Winston-Salem, N.C.)	31	33	13,000
S 17	Chicago Cardinals (Milw)	37	28	18,000

1956 (4-1-0)

A 18	Philadelphia (Milw)	27	6	12,138
A 25	N.Y. Giants (GB)	17	13	16,448
S 1	@ Cleveland	21	20	15,456
S 8	Washington (@ Winston-Salem, N.C.)	10	17	13,500
S 15	Chicago Cardinals (@ St. Louis)	29	21	31,454

1957 (5-0-1)

A 16	Chicago Cardinals (@ Miami)	24	16	20,820
A 24	Chicago Cardinals (@ Austin, Texas)	17	14	20,000
A 28	Philadelphia (Milw)	16	13	17,101
S 7	N.Y. Giants (@ Boston)	13	10	23,000
S 14	Washington (@ Winston-Salem, N.C.)	20	17	15,000
S 21	Pittsburgh (@ Minneapolis)	10	10	17,226

1958 (2-3-0)

A 20	Pittsburgh (Milw)	0	3	17,294
S 1	Philadelphia (GB)	20	17	17,857
S 6	N.Y. Giants (@ Boston)	41	20	27,013
S 13	Washington (@ Winston-Salem, N.C.)	14	23	12,000
S 20	Chicago Cardinals (@ Minneapolis)	24	31	18,520

1959 (4-2-0)

A 15	Chicago Bears (Milw)	16	19	28,286
A 23	@ San Francisco	24	17	18,916
A 29	Philadelphia (@ Portland, Ore.)	45	28	25,456
S 5	N.Y. Giants (@ Bangor, Maine)	0	14	20,000
S 12	Washington (@ Winston-Salem, N.C.)	20	13	15,000
S 20	Pittsburgh (@ Minneapolis)	13	10	18,081

1960 (6-0-0)

		GB	Opp.	Attend.
A 13	Pittsburgh (@ New Orleans)	20	13	17,400
A 22	N.Y. Giants (@ Jersey City, N.J.)	16	7	26,500
A 27	Chicago (Milw)	35	7	35,118
S 5	St. Louis (GB)	35	14	20,668
S 11	Dallas (@ Minneapolis)	28	23	20,151
S 17	Washington (@ Winston-Salem, N.C.)	41	7	8,000

1961 (5-0-0)

A 11	@ Dallas	30	7	30,000
A 18	@ St. Louis	31	10	31,056
A 26	Chicago (Milw)	24	14	42,560
S 4	N.Y. Giants (GB)	20	17	33,452
S 9	Washington (@ Columbus, Ga.)	31	24	18,000

1962 (6-0-0)

A 3	College All-Stars (@ Chicago)	42	20	65,000
A 10	@ Dallas	31	7	54,500
A 18	St. Louis (@ Jacksonville)	41	14	18,250
A 25	Chicago (Milw)	35	21	44,326
S 3	N.Y. Giants (GB)	20	17	38,669
S 8	Washington (@ Columbus, Ga.)	20	14	16,000

1963 (5-1-0)

A 2	College All-Stars (@ Chicago)	17	20	65,000
A 10	Pittsburgh (@ Miami)	27	7	26,500
A 17	@ Dallas	31	10	53,121
A 24	Chicago (Milw)	26	7	44,592
S 2	N.Y. Giants (GB)	24	17	42,327
S 7	Washington (@ Cedar Rapids, Iowa)	28	17	13,500

1964 (3-2-0)

A 8	St. Louis (@ New Orleans)	7	20	63,000
A 15	N.Y. Giants (GB)	34	10	42,327
A 22	Chicago (Milw)	21	7	46,920
A 29	@ Dallas	35	3	60,057
S 5	@ Cleveland	17	20	83,736

1965 (4-1-0)

A 14	N.Y. Giants (GB)	44	7	50,837
A 21	Chicago (Milw)	31	14	47,066
A 28	@ Dallas	12	21	67,954
S 4	@ Cleveland	30	14	83,118
S 11	St. Louis (GB)	31	13	50,858

1966 (3-2-0)

A 5	College All-Stars (@ Chicago)	38	0	72,000
A 12	Chicago (Milw)	10	13	47,034
A 20	@ Dallas	3	21	75,504
A 27	Pittsburgh (GB)	17	6	50,861
S 3	N.Y. Giants (Milw)	37	10	47,102

1967 (6-0-0)

A 4	College All-Stars (@ Chicago)	27	0	70,934
A 12	Pittsburgh (GB)	31	20	50,861
A 18	Chicago (Milw)	18	0	47,126
A 28	@ Dallas	20	3	78,087
S 2	@ Cleveland	30	21	84,236
S 9	N.Y. Giants (GB)	31	14	50,861

1968 (4-2-0)

A 2	College All-Stars (@ Chicago)	34	17	69,917
A 10	N.Y. Giants (GB)	14	15	50,867
A 19	Chicago (Milw)	7	10	47,127
A 24	@ Dallas	31	27	72,014
A 31	Pittsburgh (Milw)	21	17	47,268
S 7	@ Cleveland	31	9	84,917

1969 (4-2-0)

		GB	Opp.	Attend.
A 9	N.Y. Giants (GB)	22	21	50,861
A 16	Chicago (Milw)	9	19	47,014
A 23	@ Dallas	13	31	73,764
A 30	@ Cleveland	27	17	85,532
S 6	Pittsburgh (GB)	31	19	50,861
S 13	Atlanta (@ Canton, Ohio)	38	24	17,411

1970 (3-0-3)

A 8	N.Y. Giants (GB)	31	31	56,263
A 15	Chicago (Milw)	6	6	47,298
A 22	@ Dallas	35	34	72,389
A 30	@ Oakland	37	7	53,395
S 5	Cincinnati (Milw)	10	10	47,411
S 12	Buffalo (GB)	34	0	56,161

1971 (2-4-0)

A 7	Chicago (Milw)	0	2	47,248
A 14	Pittsburgh (GB)	13	16	56,263
A 21	Miami (Milw)	10	7	47,286
A 28	Oakland (GB)	13	17	56,263
S 4	@ Cincinnati	24	27	55,477
S 10	@ Buffalo	20	14	37,301

1972 (4-2-0)

A 5	Cincinnati (GB)	24	14	56,263
A 12	@ Miami	14	13	75,332
A 19	@ Houston	3	20	46,460
A 27	Chicago (Milw)	10	7	47,222
S 2	St. Louis (GB)	10	31	56,263
S 9	Kansas City (Milw)	20	0	47,281

1973 (3-2-1)

A 4	Chicago (Milw)	13	13	47,222
A 11	Buffalo (GB)	10	3	56,267
A 18	Houston (Milw)	33	14	47,302
A 26	@ Kansas City	21	16	75,231
S 1	Pittsburgh (GB)	22	30	56,267
S 8	@ Cincinnati	10	13	55,863

1974 (4-2-0)

A 2	@ Buffalo	16	13	30,119
A 10	St. Louis (Milw)	13	0	43,000
A 17	Chicago (GB)	20	10	53,106
A 24	Denver (GB)	21	31	56,267
A 30	@ Miami	10	21	54,666
S 6	Cincinnati (Milw)	26	24	46,605

1975 (2-4-0)

A 9	Buffalo (GB)	23	6	56,267
A 16	Chicago (Milw)	13	9	52,051
A 23	@ Cincinnati	10	27	49,752
A 30	New England (Milw) ....(ot)	17	20	51,769
S 6	@ Kansas City	3	31	35,543
S 13	San Francisco (GB)	3	24	56,267

1976 (2-4-0)

A 31	Cincinnati (GB)	17	23	50,245
A 7	Tampa Bay (Milw)	10	6	53,421
A 15	@ New England	16	14	28,448
A 20	@ Buffalo	0	37	33,706
A 28	N.Y. Giants (GB)	16	20	56,267
S 3	Atlanta (Milw)	7	26	54,989

1977 (2-4-0)

A 6	Cincinnati (GB)	23	20	51,178
A 13	New England (Milw)	3	38	53,244
A 20	@ Tampa Bay	7	10	49,045
A 27	Washington (Milw)	9	13	55,021
S 3	Cleveland (GB)	14	19	53,180
S 10	Philadelphia (GB)	24	16	32,217

1978 (1-3-0)

		GB	Opp.	Attend.
A 5	Kansas City (GB)	14	17	54,453
A 11	@ Washington	12	20	30,881
A 19	St. Louis (GB)	23	17	50,423
A 26	Cincinnati (Milw)	14	17	54,927

1979 (3-1-0)

A 4	Kansas City (GB)	14	10	53,994
A 11	@ Cincinnati	5	20	44,284
A 18	Buffalo (GB)	7	6	54,857
A 25	Atlanta (Milw)	45	35	55,416

1980 (0-4-1)

*A 2	San Diego (@ Canton, Ohio)	0	0	19,972
A 9	@ Dallas	14	17	54,876
A 16	Baltimore (Milw)	3	17	49,223
A 23	@ Buffalo	0	14	24,086
A 30	Denver (GB)	0	38	53,060

1981 (3-1-0)

A 8	@ Dallas	21	17	55,087
A 15	Oakland (Milw)	34	14	54,710
A 22	@ Denver	7	17	72,450
A 29	Cleveland (GB)	35	18	56,191

1982 (2-2-0)

A 14	N.Y. Jets (GB)	21	19	53,531
A 20	Cincinnati (Milw)	41	27	52,636
A 29	@ L.A. Raiders	3	24	40,906
S 4	@ New England	27	41	39,888

1983 (1-3-0)

A 6	Cleveland (GB)	20	21	39,202
A 12	@ Seattle	21	38	54,443
A 20	Philadelphia (GB)	14	27	48,867
A 27	@ St. Louis	39	27	33,041

1984 (2-2-0)

A 4	@ Dallas	17	31	43,371
A 11	Chicago (Milw)	17	10	48,253
A 18	@ L.A. Rams	24	27	41,185
A 25	Indianapolis (GB)	34	17	54,979

1985 (1-3-0)

A 10	@ Dallas	3	27	41,847
A 17	@ N.Y. Giants	2	10	35,798
A 24	Atlanta (Milw)	28	24	49,703
A 31	N.Y. Jets (GB)	20	30	56,753

1986 (1-3-0)

A 9	N.Y. Jets (@ Madison, Wis.)	38	14	73,959
A 16	N.Y. Giants (Milw)	14	22	41,774
A 23	@ Cincinnati	12	34	44,261
A 30	New England (GB)	9	16	50,642

1987 (0-4-0)

A 15	Denver (@ Phoenix)	14	20	67,500
A 22	Washington (@ Madison, Wis.)	0	33	64,768
A 29	Cincinnati (GB)	28	28	44,515
S 5	Cleveland (Milw) ....(ot)	24	30	37,707

1988 (1-2-1)

		GB	Opp.	Attend.
A 6	N.Y. Giants (GB)	3	34	41,455
A 13	@ Indianapolis	21	25	53,720
A 19	Kansas City (Milw)	21	21	32,361
A 27	N.Y. Jets (@ Madison, Wis.) ....(ot)	27	24	42,098

* Game called with 5:29 remaining due to severe thunder and lightning.

1989 (3-1-0)

		GB	Opp.	Attend.
A 12	N.Y. Jets (Milw)	28	27	22,931
A 19	Indianapolis (GB)	23	24	30,218
A 26	Buffalo (@ Madison, Wis.)	27	24	30,432
S 1	@ New England	16	0	26,549

1990 (1-3-0)

A 11	Cleveland (GB)	10	25	52,625
A 18	New Orleans (@ Madison, Wis.)	27	13	47,848
A 25	Atlanta (Milw)	14	17	51,609
A 31	@ Kansas City	14	27	42,806

1991 (2-2-0)

A 3	New England (GB)	28	7	52,852
A 10	@ New Orleans	20	31	55,730
A 17	Buffalo (@ Madison, Wis.)	35	24	51,077
A 24	Cincinnati (Milw)	(ot) 16	19	52,390

1992 (1-3-0)

A 8	Kansas City (GB)	21	13	54,322
A 16	N.Y. Jets (@ Madison, Wis.)	7	24	41,517
A 22	@ L.A. Rams	(ot) 13	16	41,252
A 29	New England (Milw)	10	24	47,152

1993 (1-4-0)

J 31	L.A. Raiders (@ Canton, Ohio)	3	19	23,863
A 7	Kansas City (Milw)	21	29	51,655
A 14	New Orleans (@ Madison, Wis.)	17	26	59,523
A 20	@ New England	17	21	24,909
A 27	Indianapolis (GB)	41	10	56,811

1994 (3-1-0)

		GB	Opp.	Attend.
A 6	L.A. Rams (@ Madison, Wis.)	14	6	52,149
A 13	Miami (Milw)	24	31	52,759
A 19	@ New Orleans	13	10	54,714
A 26	New England (GB)	24	20	57,722

1995 (3-1-0)

A 5	New Orleans (@ Madison, Wis.)	27	17	49,071
A 13	@ Pittsburgh	36	13	49,025
A 19	Indianapolis	17	20	55,624
A 25	Washington	35	23	58,824

1996 (3-1-0)

A 2	New England	24	7	57,918
A 11	Pittsburgh	24	17	59,284
A 17	@ Baltimore	17	15	62,025
A 24	@ Indianapolis	6	30	49,081

1997 (5-0-0)

J 26	Miami	20	0	59,089
J 31	New England	7	3	60,778
A 8	@ Oakland	37	24	42,956
A 16	Buffalo (@ Toronto)	35	3	53,896
A 22	N.Y. Giants (@ Madison, Wis.)	22	17	76,704

PACKERS' THANKSGIVING DAY RECORD
(10-17-2, .379)

Date	Opponent	W/L	Score	Date	Opponent	W/L	Score
11/ 25/20	Stambaugh Miners	W	14-0 (NL)	11/ 27/52	@ Detroit Lions	L	48-24
11/ 30/22	Duluth Kelleys	W	10-0 (NL)	11/ 26/53	@ Detroit Lions	L	34-15
11/ 29/23	Hammond Pros	W	19-0	11/ 25/54	@ Detroit Lions	L	28-24
11/ 27/24	@ Kansas City Blues	W	17-6	11/ 24/55	@ Detroit Lions	L	24-10
11/ 26/25	@ Pottsville Maroons	L	31-0	11/ 22/56	@ Detroit Lions	W	24-20
11/ 25/26	@ Frankford Yellowjackets	L	20-14	11/ 28/57	@ Detroit Lions	L	18-6
11/ 24/27	@ Frankford Yellowjackets	W	17-9	11/ 27/58	@ Detroit Lions	L	24-14
11/ 29/28	@ Frankford Yellowjackets	L	2-0	11/ 26/59	@ Detroit Lions	W	24-17
11/ 28/29	@ Frankford Yellowjackets	T	0-0	11/ 24/60	@ Detroit Lions	L	23-10
11/ 27/30	@ Frankford Yellowjackets	W	25-7	11/ 23/61	@ Detroit Lions	W	17-9
11/ 26/31	@ Providence Steam Roller	W	38-7	11/ 22/62	@ Detroit Lions	L	26-14
11/ 24/32	@ Brooklyn Dodgers	W	7-0	11/ 28/63	@ Detroit Lions	T	13-13
11/ 30/33	@ Staten Island Stapletons	W	21-0 (NL)	11/ 26/70	@ Dallas Cowboys	L	16-3
11/ 29/34	@ Chicago Cardinals	L	6-0	11/ 22/84	@ Detroit Lions	L	31-28
11/ 28/35	@ Chicago Cardinals	L	9-7	11/ 27/86	@ Detroit Lions	W	44-40
11/ 22/51	@ Detroit Lions	L	52-35	11/24/94	@ Dallas Cowboys	L	42-31

(NL) = non-league game which is not reflected in club's won-lost record

UPPER MIDWEST SHRINE GAMES (22-23-3)
(1950-82, 1984-94 games played at Milwaukee,
all others played at Green Bay)

Year	Result	Attendance
1950	Packers 16, Baltimore 14	17,191
1951	Philadelphia 14, Packers 10	19,282
1952	N.Y. Giants 7, Packers 0	22,000
1953	Pittsburgh 26, Packers 23	16,859
1954	N.Y. Giants 38, Packers 27	17,000
1955	Packers 37, Chicago Cardinals 28	18,000
1956	Packers 27, Philadelphia 6	12,138
1957	Packers 16, Philadelphia 13	17,101
1958	Pittsburgh 3, Packers 0	17,294
1959	Chicago Bears 19, Packers 16	28,286
1960	Packers 35, Chicago 7	35,118
1961	Packers 24, Chicago 14	42,560
1962	Packers 35, Chicago 21	44,326
1963	Packers 26, Chicago 7	44,592
1964	Packers 21, Chicago 7	46,920
1965	Packers 31, Chicago 14	47,066
1966	Chicago 13, Packers 10	47,034
1967	Packers 18, Chicago 0	47,126
1968	Chicago 10, Packers 7	47,127
1969	Chicago 19, Packers 9	47,014
1970	Packers 6, Chicago 6	47,298
1971	Chicago 2, Packers 0	47,248
1972	Packers 10, Chicago 7	47,222
1973	Packers 13, Chicago 13	47,222
1974	Packers 13, St. Louis 0	43,000
1975	Packers 13, Chicago 9	52,051
1976	Atlanta 26, Packers 7	54,989
1977	Washington 13, Packers 9	55,021
1978	Cincinnati 17, Packers 14	54,927
1979	Packers 45, Atlanta 35	55,416
1980	Baltimore 17, Packers 3	49,223
1981	Packers 34, Oakland 14	54,710
1982	Packers 41, Cincinnati 27	52,636
1983	Cleveland 21, Packers 20	39,202
1984	Packers 17, Chicago 10	48,253
1985	Packers 24, Atlanta 24	49,703
1986	N.Y. Giants 22, Packers 14	41,774
1987	Cleveland 30, Packers 24 (ot)	37,707
1988	Packers 21, Kansas City 21 (ot)	32,361
1989	Packers 28, N.Y. Jets 27	22,931
1990	Atlanta 17, Packers 14	51,609
1991	Cincinnati 19, Packers 16 (ot)	52,390
1992	New England 24, Packers 10	47,152
1993	Kansas City 29, Packers 21	51,655
1994	Miami 31, Packers 24	52,759
1995	Indianapolis 20, Packers 17	55,624
1996	Packers 24, Pittsburgh 17	59,284
1997	Packers 20, Miami 0	59,089

BISHOP'S CHARITIES GAMES (19-17-1)
(All games played at Green Bay)

Year	Result	Attendance
1961	Packers 20, N.Y. Giants 17	33,452
1962	Packers 20, N.Y. Giants 17	38,669
1963	Packers 24, N.Y. Giants 17	42,327
1964	Packers 34, N.Y. Giants 10	42,327
1965	Packers 44, N.Y. Giants 7	50,837
1966	Packers 17, Pittsburgh 6	50,861
1967	Packers 31, Pittsburgh 20	50,861
1968	N.Y. Giants 15, Packers 14	50,861
1969	Packers 22, N.Y. Giants 21	50,861
1970	Packers 31, N.Y. Giants 31	56,263
1971	Pittsburgh 16, Packers 13	56,263
1972	St. Louis 31, Packers 10	56,263
1973	Pittsburgh 30, Packers 22	56,267
1974	Denver 31, Packers 21	56,267
1975	San Francisco 24, Packers 3	56,267

Year	Result	Attendance
1976	N.Y. Giants 20, Packers 16	56,267
1977	Cleveland 19, Packers 14	53,180
1978	Kansas City 17, Packers 14	54,453
1979	Packers 14, Kansas City 10	53,994
1980	Denver 38, Packers 0	53,060
1981	Packers 35, Cleveland 18	56,191
1982	Packers 21, N.Y. Jets 19	53,531
1983	Philadelphia 27, Packers 14	48,867
1984	Packers 34, Indianapolis 17	54,979
1985	N.Y. Jets 30, Packers 20	56,753
1986	New England 16, Packers 9	50,642
1987	Cincinnati 28, Packers 20	44,515
1988	N.Y. Giants 34, Packers 3	41,455
1989	Indianapolis 24, Packers 23	30,218
1990	Cleveland 25, Packers 10	52,625
1991	Packers 28, New England 7	52,852
1992	Packers 21, Kansas City 13	54,322
1993	Packers 41, Indianapolis 10	56,811
1994	Packers 24, New England 20	57,722
1995	Packers 35, Washington 23	58,824
1996	Packers 24, New England 7	57,918
1997	Packers 7, New England 3	60,778

PACKERS vs. COLLEGE ALL-STARS (6-2)
(All games played at Chicago)

Year	Result	Attendance
1937	All-Stars 6, Packers 0	84,560
1940	Packers 45, All-Stars 28	84,567
1945	Packers 19, All-Stars 7	92,753
1962	Packers 42, All-Stars 20	65,000
1963	All-Stars 20, Packers 17	65,000
1966	Packers 38, All-Stars 0	72,000
1967	Packers 27, All-Stars 0	70,934
1968	Packers 34, All-Stars 17	69,917

PACKERS vs. NFL ALL-STARS (1-0)
(Played at Los Angeles)

Year	Result	Attendance
1939	Packers 16, All-Stars 7	18,000

BIRTH OF A TEAM AND A LEGEND

On the evening of August 11, 1919, a score or more of husky young athletes, called together by Curly Lambeau and George Calhoun, gathered in the dingy editorial room of the old *Green Bay Press-Gazette* building on Cherry Street and organized a football team. They didn't know it, but that was the beginning of the incredible saga of the Green Bay Packers.

There had been some preliminary talk and planning and that night's decision wasn't announced until two days later, but the big step had been taken. So August 11 is as good a birthday as any.

Actually the initial spark had been struck a few weeks before during a casual street corner conversation between Curly Lambeau and George Calhoun. It was apparently one of those "Why not get up a football team?" remarks, but once they got interested they wasted no time.

FIRST THEY TALKED Curly's employer at the Indian Packing Company into putting up some money for equipment.

Because the team's jerseys had been provided by the packing company, which also permitted the use of its athletic field for practice, the club was identified in its early publicity as a project of the company. With this tie-in the name "Packers" was a natural, and Packers they have been ever since, although the corporation had practically faded out of the picture before that first season was half over.

That first season the team won 10 games and lost only one against other teams from Wisconsin and Upper Michigan. Games were played in an open field with no fences or bleachers, and interested fans "passed the hat." But the team was so successful by 1921 that Lambeau was backed by two officials of the packing plant in obtaining a franchise in the new national pro football league that had been formed in 1920. Cash customers didn't quite pay the freight and at the end of the season it had to be forfeited.

THIS WAS the first in a long series of troubles that the now famous team overcame, for in 1922 Lambeau gained other backers and bought the franchise back for $250. Troubles continued during that season. One game was rained out and the insurance company wouldn't pay off because the official amount of rain was one one-hundredth of an inch short of that required in the policy.

Another storm late in the season when the Packers were scheduled to play the Duluth Kelleys, however, proved the founding of the modern community corporation. A.B. Turnbull, general manager of the *Green Bay Press-Gazette*, told the Packers to play anyway. He then went out and helped organize the businessmen of Green Bay in the support of the team, and the Green Bay Football Corporation was formed.

FROM THOSE MODEST and somewhat tenuous beginnings, the Packers have gone on to earn national stature and virtual world-wide recognition by winning more championships (12) over the intervening 70-plus years than any other team in professional football.

The fact that these achievements have come while representing a city of just around 100,000 inhabitants, in competition with the country's population giants, has endeared them to the nation's football fans, many of whom are intrigued by the David vs. Goliath concept and the Packers' unique status as a publicly-owned corporation.

INEVITABLY, PROCEDURES at Packers games have come a long way since the sandlot years of 1919-20 when the club was subsisting on the contents of George Calhoun's hat. Then there were no ushers, no cheerleaders, no band and no public address system — the latter hadn't been invented yet. There weren't even any seats at first, and it didn't cost anything to get in.

When the Packers began their existence in 1919, they played on approximately the same site as the now abandoned City (East) Stadium, but with a mighty difference. Hagemeister Park, as it was called, was just a big vacant lot with a football gridiron marked on it.

There were no gates because there wasn't any fence. Spectators just dropped off the Walnut Street streetcar and walked over to the sideline, or drove their own cars and parked about 10 yards behind the ropes stretched around the playing field.

If they felt like it they either sat in their automobiles or on top of them, but most preferred to get out and follow the play up and down the field. By moving as the play progressed, you always had a "50-yard line" location and were handy to any donnybrook that might require a little help. In fact, when things got exciting the crowd sometimes spilled right onto the field, surrounded the scrimmage in a big circle and virtually took part in every play. Teams didn't huddle in those days, or the fans would have been in that too.

When the half ended, teams grabbed blankets and adjourned to opposite end zones where they relaxed and talked over the tactics of the next half. Nothing private about those huddles. The crowd formed a ring around the players, a practice encouraged since it made a handy wind break. Fans weren't bashful about joining the discussions either, sometimes with surprising results. At least one early game was pulled out of the fire by a spectator's halftime suggestion.

In 1920 a section of stands was built — just a small bleacher with a capacity of a couple hundred — on one side of the field, and a fee charged to sit there. The next year a portable canvas fence was erected around the whole field and a regular admission charge inaugurated.

WHEN HAGEMEISTER Park was dug up in 1923 to make way for East High School, the Packers shifted to the new baseball grounds out on the end of Main Street. This was called Bellevue Park because it was just east of the old Hagemeister Brewery, which was renamed the Bellevue Products Co. during Prohibition. Things were Big Time out there, with crowds of 4,000 to 5,000 storming the fences to boo the hated Chicago Bears.

The Packers used Bellevue in 1923-24, but it was obviously inadequate and too far out, lacking about every facility needed for football. Agitation to build a new stadium somewhere near the original site culminated in the erection of old City Stadium just back of the new high school.

The new plant was barely completed in time for the 1925 opening, but was an immediate success, the Bear game that year drawing a record crowd of 5,389. It was a typical small town park of its day, with wooden fences and stands on both sides between the 30-yard lines. Seating capacity was gradually increased until it seated 15,000 by 1934, with the end zones still uncovered. With the filling in of the area around the end lines the ultimate capacity of 25,000 was reached.

AFTER WORLD WAR II, City Stadium gradually faded from its once proud position as one of the favored fields in the National Football League to an inadequate and obsolete installation. As pro crowds increased it was impossible to expand the stadium any further. With limited capacity, the Packers found it increasingly difficult to schedule top opponents at home. September 29, 1957, was a proud day for Green Bay and its Packers. A million-dollar modern stadium with a seating capacity of 32,150 was dedicated. In 1961, the stadium was expanded to 38,669, to 42,327 in 1963, to 50,852 in 1965 when the name was changed to Lambeau Field, to 56,263 in 1970, and to 56,926 following the first addition of private boxes in 1985. With the building of 36 more private boxes and 1,920 club seats in the south end zone, seating was upped to 59,543 in 1990. A subsequent, 1995 expansion of 90 private boxes in the north end zone, which also included an auxiliary press box, gave the stadium a total of 198 boxes and a new capacity of 60,790.

The Packers' colorful saga, spanning 79 years, can be divided roughly into eight chapters. They take us from the "Iron Man" period of the first decade under founder Curly Lambeau to the present day, which finds Mike Holmgren presiding as the 11th head coach in the team's history.

THE IRON MAN ERA — With good financial backing, Lambeau began to pick up college stars from all over the country, plus some unknowns who were going to turn out to be "greats." And in 1929 Green Bay won the national professional football championship. It repeated in 1930 and in 1931 with a team featuring such all-time pro greats as Red Dunn, Verne Lewellen, Cal Hubbard, Bo Molenda, Jug Earp, Mike Michalske, Johnny (Blood) McNally, Bill Kern, Arnie Herber, Clarke Hinkle, Lavvie Dilweg, Tom Nash, Milt Gantenbein and Hank Bruder. Many games 12 or 13 players would go for almost the full 60 minutes. These teams were hailed all over the country as some of the greatest ever.

THE HUTSON PERIOD — Trouble flared again soon afterward. A fan fell from the stands, sued and won a $5,000 verdict and the insurance company went out of business. The Packers went into receivership and were just about to fold when Green Bay businessmen came to the rescue again, raised $15,000 in new capital and reorganized the club. About this time a rather slight, lanky end by the name of Don Hutson came to the club. From his first game on, Hutson became the terror of the league and the secret of Green Bay's next three championships. With Herber and Cecil Isbell pitching and Hutson catching anything they threw at him despite any kind of a stop-Hutson defense, Green Bay won championships in 1936, 1939 and 1944, and all during the Hutson era the Packers always finished in the first division.

RONZANI REGIME — After Hutson's retirement, Packer fortunes again went into a decline. The disastrous pro football war brought on another financial crisis after the 1949 season. In the midst of it Lambeau resigned to take a position as head coach of the Chicago Cardinals. Then began another major reorganization and rebuilding effort with Gene Ronzani of the Bears hired as head coach. Nearly $125,000 was raised in a giant stock sale all over the state. Ronzani's teams improved each of the first three seasons until 1952. The Packers were in the thick of the title chase until the last weeks of the season. In 1953 the team played erratic ball and Ronzani resigned with two games remaining on the schedule.

BLACKBOURN TAKES OVER — The Packers

overhauled their front office and coaching staff in 1954, hiring Verne Lewellen, all-time Packers great, attorney and businessman, as general manager. Reaching into the college ranks for a head coach was the next step in the rebuilding plans and Lisle Blackbourn, coach of Marquette University, was signed to a contract. During the four-year Blackbourn regime, the Packers won 17 while losing 31.

McLEAN MOVES UP — Likable Ray "Scooter" McLean moved up from being an outstanding assistant coach to guide the destiny of the Packers for 1958. McLean resigned in December after a 1-10-1 record, the worst in Packer history in his lone season as head coach.

THE LOMBARDI ERA — In 1959, the Packers announced the signing of New York Giants assistant Vince Lombardi as head coach and general manager.

In his first season, Lombardi lifted the Packers to a 7-5 record and unanimously was voted 'Coach of the Year.' Then in 1960, the Packers captured the Western Division title and went on to win World Championships in 1961, 1962, 1965, 1966 and 1967. Never finishing lower than second since 1960, his teams became the standard of football excellence and the Packers franchise one of the most successful. Over a nine-year span as head coach, Lombardi's teams racked up 98 victories against 30 losses and 4 ties for a remarkable .758 winning percentage. Even more noteworthy, however, is the record of Lombardi coached teams in postseason play. In 10 division playoff and World Championship games, the Packers emerged victorious nine times.

BENGTSON PERIOD — Following the third consecutive title in 1967, Lombardi turned over the head coaching duties to Phil Bengtson and one year later announced that he was leaving Green Bay to coach and manage the Washington Redskins. Bengtson coached the Packers from 1968-1970, compiling a 20-21-1 record, and in December of 1970 resigned.

THE DEVINE DAYS — Dan Devine, one of the three most successful coaches in the nation's collegiate ranks, succeeded Bengtson as head coach and general manager in January of 1971. After settling for a 4-8-2 record during his first season, Devine and the Packers appeared on the road to new heights when 1972 produced a 10-4 record and the team's first Central Division title since 1967. But the Packers' Super Bowl hopes dissolved in the second half of '73 and they slipped to a 5-7-2 mark. They continued their recession in '74, emerging with a 6-8 record, and

Devine resigned.

THE STARR TREK — The most successful field general in pro football history as Green Bay's quarterback of the '60s, Bart Starr accepted the challenge to lead the Packers out of the NFL wilderness, agreeing to a three-year contract as head coach and general manager on December 24, 1974. Starr, who had led the Packers to five world championships from 1961 through 1967, asked for "the prayers and patience of Packer fans everywhere...We will earn everything else."

Although he had to settle for a 4-10 record in the baptismal season of a massive rebuilding project, Starr gave Packers fans new hope by assembling a sound organization and restoring a positive attitude, underscored by three victories in the last five games of the 1975 season. He continued the resurgent trend in 1976, leading the Packers to a 5-9 record, highlighted by a three-game, mid-season winning streak. Major and key injuries slowed the comeback in 1977 but a strong finish produced a 4-10 mark. Hopes soared in 1978 when the Packers posted their first winning slate since 1972, an 8-7-1 record, only to be temporarily dampened in '79 by a record rash of injuries which spawned a 5-11 mark. Another injury epidemic, one which saw 27 players on injured reserve during the course of the season, struck in 1980, forcing the Packers to settle for a 5-10-1 record.

Rebounding strongly in 1981, they rallied from a disappointing 2-6 start to mount one of the most dramatic comebacks in Green Bay history, closing with a 6-2 rush (an 8-8 mark) and coming within one victory of the playoffs.

The Packers continued the upsurge in 1982, when they qualified for the playoffs for the first time since 1972 by posting a 5-3-1 record during a strike-interrupted season. They then embellished that performance by routing St. Louis 41-16 in the first game of the NFL's Super Bowl Tournament before bowing to Dallas (37-26) despite a record-setting, 466-yard offensive effort. Starr was relieved of his head coaching duties on December 19, 1983, after the Packers finished the '83 season with an 8-8 record and missed the NFL playoffs on the final week of the year.

GREGG ERA — On December 24, 1984, Starr was replaced by Forrest Gregg, a former teammate and one of the premier offensive tackles in the history of the game as a player, who had maneuvered Cincinnati into Super Bowl XVI following the 1981 season. Gregg, whose Bengals' 19-6 record over the 1981-82 seasons was the best in pro football, received a five-year contract.

In taking over, he declared, "I took this job to field a winning team. That will happen."

Gregg's prediction began to bear fruit in the second half of the 1984 season when the Packers rebounded from an injury-ridden 1-7 start to win seven of their last eight games.

Because of injury and other complications, however, the 1985 season followed the '84 script, the Packers getting off to a slow 3-6 start before mounting a strong finish to again close at 8-8 by winning five of their last seven games.

Gregg, convinced the time had come to rebuild a team which had gone 8-and-8 three years in succession and was "starting to get old" at that level, made sweeping personnel changes in 1986. The young and inexperienced Packers, their task complicated by injuries to key performers, got off to an 0-6 start, then began to mature in mid-season and went on to finish with a 4-and-12 record.

Following the 1987 season, which saw the Packers finish third in the NFC Central with a 5-9-1 record, Gregg resigned (January 15, 1988) to become head coach at his alma mater, Southern Methodist University.

INFANTE SIGNS ON — Nineteen days later (February 3), Cleveland Browns offensive coordinator Lindy Infante became the 10th head coach in Packers history. Recognized throughout the NFL as a brilliant innovator, the 47-year-old University of Florida alumnus received a five-year contract.

With turnovers and kicking problems plaguing his offense, Infante's first Packers team had to settle for a 4-and-12 record, but left fans with hopes for 1989 and the future by winning the last two games to mount a strong finish.

Building upon that positive note, Infante orchestrated a dramatic upsurge in '89, escorting the Packers to a 10-6 record — their best in 17 years — and within one game of the National Football League playoffs, spicing that turnabout with a league-record four one-point victories.

In 1990, subsequent high hopes for the team's first postseason berth in a non-strike year since 1972 evaporated when the Packers — with a contending, 6-5 record after 11 games — saw a potential playoff opportunity expire in the face of a season-ending, five-game losing streak.

The Packers' field fortunes continued to decline in 1991, the record falling to 4-12, and Infante was relieved of his duties on December 22 by new Executive Vice President/General Manager Ron Wolf, who had been hired November 27 with full authority to run the organization's football operation.

THE PRESENT — Mike Holmgren, architect of one of the NFL's most potent attacks as offensive coordinator for the perennially successful, then four-time Super Bowl champion San Francisco 49ers, was named by Wolf to succeed Infante as the 11th head coach in Packers history on January 11, 1992. Holmgren, sought after by five other NFL clubs, received a five-year contract.

Getting his team on track after an 0-and-2 start, the former USC field general directed the Packers to a 9-and-7 record and within striking range of the playoffs. He thus became only the third head coach in Packers history to post a winning record in his first season, a record punctuated by a six-game winning streak, longest by a Packers team since 1965.

In 1993, his second season at the controls, Holmgren took his team to the next level — the playoffs — despite the loss of four starters to injuries and a nagging turf toe problem which hampered the Packers' principal offensive weapon, wide receiver Sterling Sharpe, over the last half of the season.

Surmounting these handicaps, the Green and Gold forged a second straight 9-and-7 record — against a considerably more demanding schedule — to qualify for postseason play for the first time since 1982, then posted a last-minute, come-from-behind victory over the Detroit Lions (28-24) in their first playoff assignment before falling to the repeating Super Bowl champion Dallas Cowboys (27-17) in their second, a divisional playoff.

In 1994, the Packers continued to experience success under Holmgren, staking a third consecutive 9-and-7 regular-season mark and making it to the playoffs for the second year in a row — registering both of these achievements for the first time since the memorable "Titletown" days of the '60s.

Riding a three-game winning streak into the postseason, they parlayed a record defensive performance and a turnover-free offensive effort into a 16-12 victory over the Detroit Lions in their initial playoff game — their first home playoff game since 1983 — holding the incomparable Barry Sanders to minus-one yard rushing in 13 attempts in the process. The Packers advanced despite playing without the services of their All-Pro wide receiver Sharpe, whose brilliant Green Bay career had been ended by a neck injury diagnosed after the team's regular-season finale. As had been the case a year earlier, their postseason came to a close at Dallas in their second game, the Cowboys prevailing in a divisional playoff, 35-9.

Closing ranks with highly productive results following the loss of Sharpe, the 1995 Packers put together one of the hallmark seasons in their history. Winning six of their last seven games, they captured their first NFC Central Division championship since 1972, then made their best postseason showing in over a quarter-century, forging all the way to the National Football Conference Championship Game for the first time since 1967.

En route, they closed out the regular season with an 11-5 record — their best since 1966, when they posted a 12-2 mark in capturing the NFL title — and followed that accomplishment by dispatching the Atlanta Falcons, 37-20, in a first-round playoff at Lambeau Field.

Building upon that triumph, the Packers mounted one of the premier performances in their postseason history, formally dethroning the defending Super Bowl champion San Francisco 49ers in their own 3Com Park, 27-17. Again, however, the Packers' dreams of a third trip to the Super Bowl subsequently foundered in Dallas, where they fell to the Cowboys, 38-27, in the NFC title game, after leading 27-24 at the end of three quarters.

Putting nearly three decades of disappointment and frustration emphatically behind them, the Packers richly rewarded their long-patient faithful in 1996 with a season for the ages. Shunting aside eight of their first nine regular-season opponents, they swept to a 13-3 record and their second consecutive NFC Central Division championship, then charged through the playoffs to capture their first Super Bowl title since 1967, dispatching the New England Patriots 35-21 in SB XXXI at the Louisiana Superdome.

Displaying impressive consistency on both sides of the football, they documented their superiority, outscoring the three opponents by a substantial margin, 100 to 48, in their postseason sweep.

Appropriately enough, the first two playoff wins were registered before their ecstatic loyalists in Lambeau Field — a 35-14 triumph over the 49ers in a divisional playoff matchup and a 30-13 victory over the upstart Carolina Panthers in the NFC title game.

In annexing a 12th NFL championship, extending their own league record, the Packers joined an elite group of teams which have won three-or-more Super Bowls — the Dallas Cowboys, San Francisco 49ers, Pittsburgh Steelers, Oakland/Los Angeles Raiders and Washington Redskins.

Thirty years earlier, Green Bay had won the first two Super Bowls following the 1966 and 1967 seasons, thus becoming the first team to "repeat."

The Packers thus entered the 1997 season with an opportunity to win back-to-back Super Bowls for a second time — and came breathtakingly close to achieving their objective.

Sweeping to a second consecutive 13-3 mark, their victory total equaling a club record, they primed for the playoffs by closing out the regular season with a five-game winning streak, their second of the campaign. Having earned home-field advantage for their initial postseason test by winning a third straight NFC Central Division title, they launched their bid in workmanlike fashion, turning back Tampa Bay in divisional playoff for the third straight time in the year, 21-7, thereby padding their all-time home-field, postseason record to 12-0 and extending the longest such winning streak in pro football history.

Faced with the need to win on the road to assure a return trip to the NFL's ultimate game, the Packers proceeded to smother the 49ers on a soggy, rain-swept afternoon in San Francisco's 3Com Park a week later, holding them without an offensive touchdown en route to a 23-10 victory in the NFC Championship Game and a berth in Super Bowl XXXII at San Diego.

The latter subsequently proved to be a see-saw affair, one which found the Green and Gold trailing Denver at halftime, 17-14. Hopes of a repeat were high, however, when quarterback Brett Favre guided them 85 yards to a third touchdown and a 24-24 tie early in the fourth quarter. But the Broncos later scored with only 1:45 remaining and a last-minute Packers drive for a deadlock fell short when a Favre pass for tight end Mark Chmura was incomplete inside the Denver 20-yard line with only 28 seconds remaining, sealing a 31-24 Denver win.

1919
• Packers founded at meeting in editorial rooms of *Green Bay Press-Gazette*, August 11.

1921
• J.E. Clair of Acme Packing Company granted National Football League franchise for Green Bay Packers, August 27.
• Packer-Bear series launched at Chicago (November 27), Packers losing 20-0 decision to Chicago Staleys, who changed name to Bears in 1922.

1922
• Packers disciplined for using college players under assumed names, Clair turns franchise back to league, January 28. E.L. "Curly" Lambeau promises to obey rules, uses $50 of own money to buy back franchise for $250.
• Bad weather, low attendance plague Packers, merchants raise $2,500, public non-profit corporation set up under direction of A.B. Turnbull to operate team with Lambeau as manager, coach.

1923
• Andrew B. Turnbull is elected first president of Green Bay Football Corporation.

1925
• Packers beat Bears for first time, 14-10, in fourth regular-season meeting.
• East (old City) Stadium built, with initial capacity of 6,000.

1927
• Packers surprise "Big Town" skeptics, shut out football Yankees, 13-0, in first New York appearance (October 23).

1929
• Packers sign back Johnny "Blood" McNally, tackle Cal Hubbard, guard Mike Michalske and win first National Football League championship, posting unbeaten 12-0-1 record.

1930
• Packers win second straight NFL title, this time with 10-3-1 record.

1931
• Packers capture third consecutive NFL championship, extending unbeaten streak to 22 games, finish 12-2-0.

1932
• Packers just miss winning fourth straight title on 10-3-1 mark, Bears winning crown with 7-1-6 record because ties not counted in standings.

1934
• Fan falls from stands at East (old City) Stadium, sues Packers and wins $5,000 verdict. Insurance company goes out of business and Packers go into receivership, about to fold, but Green Bay businessmen come to rescue, raise $15,000 in new capital and reorganize club.

1935
• Don Hutson of Alabama, to become most feared pass receiver in pro football history, signed by Packers.

1936
• Packers make Russ Letlow, University of San Francisco guard, their No. 1 choice in first NFL Draft.
• Packers win fourth NFL championship, first under playoff system. Post 11-1-1 record, defeating Boston Redskins for title in New York's Polo Grounds, 21-6 (December 13).

1938
• Packers win Western Division championship, lose to Giants in NFL title game at New York, 23-17 (December 11).

1939
• Packers repeat for Western Division title, rout Giants in title game at Milwaukee, 27-0 (December 10).

1941
• Packers tie Bears for Western Division title, fall to Bears in Chicago playoff, 33-14 (December 14).

1944
• With Ted Fritsch scoring both touchdowns, Packers beat Giants 14-7 at New York's Polo Grounds for sixth NFL title (December 17).

1945
• Don Hutson catches 4 TD passes, kicks 5 PATs in second quarter against Detroit at Milwaukee, sets all-time one-quarter scoring record of 29 points as Packers win 57-21, October 7.

1949
• Packers play intra-squad game at East (old City) Stadium on Thanksgiving Day, raise $50,000 to stay afloat financially.
• Packers, 3-9-0 in 1948, dip to all-time low under Curly Lambeau, 2-10-0.

1950
• Lambeau resigns to become vice president, head coach of Chicago Cardinals.
• Gene Ronzani, ex-Chicago Bear star, named Packer head coach, V.P.
• Stock drive nets $118,000, puts Packers on sound financial basis.
• Packers change team colors to green and gold, eliminating navy blue.

1953
• Packers play their first game in new Milwaukee County Stadium (September 27).
• Ronzani resigns with two games remaining; Hugh Devore and Ray "Scooter" McLean named co-coaches.

1954
• Lisle Blackbourn, Marquette University coach, is named as team's coach.

1957
• City Stadium (renamed Lambeau Field in 1965), completed just in time for season opener, is dedicated (September 29) with 21-17 victory over Bears.
• Packers post 3-9-0 mark following 4-8-0 in '56, Blackbourn resigns.

1958
• Assistant coach Ray "Scooter" McLean promoted to head coach.
• Dominic Olejniczak elected seventh president of Green Bay Packers, Inc., April 28.
• McLean resigns following 1-10-1 record, poorest in Packer history.

1959
• Vince Lombardi, offensive coach of N.Y. Giants, named as Packers' head coach and GM, February 4.
• Packers post 7-5-0 record, their first winning season in 12 years.

1960
• Packers win Western Division title, first since '44, but lose to Eagles in NFL title game, 17-13 (December 26).
• Paul Hornung, scores 176 points, new NFL record.

1961
• Packers rout N.Y. Giants, 37-0, for seventh NFL championship in first title game ever played in Green Bay, December 31.

1962
• Packers beat Giants in New York, 16-7, for second straight league crown (December 30).

1965
• E.L. "Curly" Lambeau, Packers' founder and first coach, dies at age 67 (June 1).
• Packers defeat Baltimore, 13-10, at Green Bay in sudden death Western Conference playoff (the first overtime game in team's history) on Don Chandler's 25-yard field goal at 13:39 of second overtime (December 26).
• Packers beat Cleveland Browns, 23-12, for ninth NFL title, January 2.

1966
• Game-ending end zone interception by Tom Brown enables Packers to down Cowboys, 34-27, in Dallas for second straight NFL title (January 1, 1967).

1967
• Packers defeat Kansas City of AFL, 35-10, at Los Angeles in first Super Bowl, January 15.
• Packers edge Cowboys, 21-17, for third consecutive NFL title on last minute, one-yard sneak by Bart Starr in 13-below zero temperature at Lambeau Field (December 31).

1968
• Packers beat Oakland, 33-14, in Super Bowl II at Miami, January 14; game has first $3 million gate in history.
• Lombardi steps down as Packers head coach, stays as general manager; Phil Bengtson named coach (February 1).

1969
• Lombardi resigns to become part-owner, executive-vice president and head coach of Washington Redskins; Bengtson named Packers' GM.

1970
• Lombardi dies at age 57, September 3.
• Bengtson resigns, December 21.

1971
• Dan Devine, University of Missouri coach, named as Packers' head coach and general manager.

1972
• Packers win first Central Division title since '67 (10-4-0), but lose to Redskins in divisional playoff at Washington, 16-3 (December 23).

1974
• Devine resigns December 16, following 5-7-2 mark in '73 and 6-8-0 in '74.
• Bart Starr, who quarterbacked Packers to five NFL titles in seven years during '60s, named head coach and general manager, December 24.

1982
• Judge Robert J. Parins elected Packers president (May 31), succeeding Dominic Olejniczak, becoming first full-time chief executive in team's history.
• Packers build 55,000-square foot indoor practice facility.
• Packers gain playoffs for first time since 1972 and defeat St. Louis in first round (41-16) before losing to Dallas (37-26).

1983
• Bart Starr released as head coach (December 19).

• Former Packers great Forrest Gregg named head coach (December 24), agreeing to five-year contract.

1985
• Packers build 72 private boxes at Lambeau Field, increasing stadium seating capacity to 56,926.

1986
• Packers report first $2 million annual profit in their history ($2,029,154).
• Green Bay Packers Foundation, a vehicle to assure continued contributions to charity, established (Dec. 30).

1987
• Fred N. Trowbridge, longtime Packer treasurer and executive committee member, dies (March 14).
• Packers report first $3 million profit in their history ($3,018,000).

1988
• Forrest Gregg resigns to become head coach at his alma mater, Southern Methodist University (January 15).
• Lindy Infante, offensive coordinator of Cleveland Browns, named as Packers' head coach, agreeing to five-year contract (February 3).
• Packers report $2,839,270 profit, then second-highest in team history.

1989
• Judge Robert J. Parins retires as President of Packer Corporation and is elected Honorary Chairman of the Board (June 5).
• Bob Harlan is elected president and chief executive officer of Packer Corporation, succeeding Judge Parins (June 5).
• Packers announce plans for construction of 1,920 club seats — a "first" for Lambeau Field — in south end zone and 36 additional private boxes at a projected cost of $8,263,000 (August 22).

1990
• Packers extend Head Coach Lindy Infante's contract two years — through the 1994 season (January 16).

1991
• Michael R. Reinfeldt, former Pro Bowl safety and Los Angeles Raiders executive, becomes Packers' Chief Financial Officer (January 7).
• The names of the Packers' players and coaches elected to the Pro Football Hall of Fame are placed in permanent display on the green walls between floors of Lambeau Field's private boxes, on both sides of the stadium, with team's championship years emblazoned above club seats in the south end zone.
• Tom Braatz, executive vice president of football operations, relieved of his duties (November 20).
• Ron Wolf, director of player personnel for New York Jets and a veteran of 29 years as a pro football scout and executive, is named executive vice president and general manager by president Bob Harlan, with full authority to run the Packers' football operation (November 27).
• Lindy Infante is relieved of his duties as head coach by executive vice president and general manager Ron Wolf (December 22).

1992
• Mike Holmgren, offensive coordinator of the San Francisco 49ers, is named by Wolf as the 11th head coach in Packers' history (January 11).
• Treasurer John R. Underwood reports Packer

Corporation profit of $2.17 million on 1991-92 operations (May 27).
- Holmgren becomes only third head coach in Packers' history to have winning record in his first season (9-7).

1993
- Packers sign Reggie White, most sought-after unrestricted free agent, as free agency comes to NFL (April 8).
- Treasurer John R. Underwood reports then-record Packer Corporation profit of $4.96 million before booking of $4.1 million for club's share of NFL's litigation settlement with players (May 26).
- New 20,500 square-foot addition to Packers' training quarters, housing a 84-by-70 foot gymnasium and new public relations and marketing offices, is completed in July.
- Packers shut out Los Angeles Raiders, 28-0, in -22 degree wind chill, gain playoffs for first time since 1982 (December 26).

1994
- Packers defeat Detroit Lions in wild-card playoff, 28-24, for first postseason victory since January, 1983 (January 8).
- Packers extend contract of Ron Wolf as executive vice president/general manager for three additional years, through 1999 (March 31).
- President Bob Harlan announces plans to construct 90 additional private boxes and an auxiliary press box in Lambeau Field's north end zone area in 1995 (April 21).
- Treasurer John R. Underwood reports Packer Corporation profit of $1.95 million on 1993-94 operations (May 25).
- The Don Hutson Center, Packers' new, $4.67-million indoor practice facility, is dedicated (July 18).
- Packers extend contract of Head Coach Mike Holmgren for three additional years, through 1999 season (August 25).
- President Bob Harlan announces that, beginning with the 1995 season, the Packers will leave Milwaukee and play their entire 10-game home schedule at Green Bay's Lambeau Field (October 12).
- Packers end 62-year Milwaukee stay on a winning note, shade Atlanta Falcons at County Stadium 21-17 (December 18).
- Mounting 28-6 halftime lead, Packers defeat Tampa Bay 34-19, qualify for NFL playoffs for second year in a row. In the process, Packers close season with a 9-7 record, thus posting third consecutive winning campaign for first time since 1965-66-67 (December 24).
- Packers defeat Detroit in wild-card playoff game, 16-12, recording 15th postseason victory in team history and maintaining club's spotless home playoff record (December 31).

1995
- Wide receiver Sterling Sharpe, Packers' career receptions leader, is released "with reluctance" (February 28).
- Treasurer John R. Underwood reports Packer Corporation profit of $2.03 million at organization's annual stockholders meeting (May 31).
- Construction of 90 additional private boxes in Lambeau Field's north end zone is completed, increasing stadium capacity to 60,790 (August).

- Packers defeat Pittsburgh Steelers, 24-19, at Lambeau Field in regular-season finale (December 24), clinch first NFC Central Division championship since 1972.
- Packers beat Atlanta Falcons, 37-20, in first-round playoff game, maintain team's perfect (9-0) home playoff record (December 31).

1996
- Packers stun defending Super Bowl champion San Francisco, 27-17, in divisional playoff contest in 49ers' 3Com Park (January 6).
- Treasurer John R. Underwood reports then-record Packer Corporation profit of $5,440,628 at organization's annual stockholders meeting (May 29).
- Packers complete $4-million Lambeau Field project in August, installing a second replay board and two new scoreboards to fully enclose the stadium.
- The design of a stamp bearing likeness of former Packers coach Vince Lombardi is unveiled in Lambeau Field (November 3).
- Packers clinch second consecutive NFC Central Division championship with 41-6 victory over Denver Broncos (December 8).

1997
- Packers vanquish San Francisco 49ers, 35-14, in divisional playoff in Lambeau Field (January 4).
- Packers beat Carolina Panthers in NFC Championship Game, 30-13, earn trip to Super Bowl for first time since 1967 (January 12).
- Packers defeat New England Patriots, 35-21, in Super Bowl XXXI at Louisiana Superdome in New Orleans (January 26), claim 12th NFL title.
- With the wind chill registering a frigid 0 to 10 degrees below zero during a three-hour parade through the city, an estimated 200,000 enthusiastic fans welcome Packers home from Super Bowl victory. Another 60,000 jam Lambeau Field for official program hailing the new World Champions (January 27).
- Packers extend contract of Ron Wolf as executive vice president/general manager for three additional years, through 2002 (April 8).
- Treasurer John R. Underwood reports, at annual stockholders meeting, then-record net income for Packer Corporation of $5,877,061 for fiscal 1996 (May 28).
- Work is completed on installation of new playing surface, including modern heating and irrigation systems, in Lambeau Field (June 15).
- Don Hutson, most feared pass receiver in pro football history, dies at age 84 (June 26)
- Packers establish own website, www.packers.com, on internet (July 23).
- Packers' two practice fields are named Clarke Hinkle Field and Ray Nitschke Field in honor of two of team's Pro Football Hall of Fame members, Executive Vice President/General Manager Ron Wolf announces (July 24).
- Quarterback Brett Favre signs a new seven-year contract, longest in Packers history, and one making him — at time of signing — highest-paid player in the history of professional football (July 25).
- Gross Avenue in neighboring Village of Ashwaubenon is renamed and dedicated as Holmgren Way in honor of Packers head coach (August 17). Street, poetically, intersects Lombardi Avenue.
- Largest crowd ever to see a Packers play a game in

Wisconsin, 76,704, turns out to watch the Packers defeat the New York Giants in a preseason finale at Camp Randall Stadium in Madison, Wis. (August 22).

- At a special meeting, Packers' stockholders approve the issuance of additional stock for the first time since 1950 (November 13), with offering of 400,000 shares at $200 per share.
- Packers' designated national clearing house receives 55,000 phone calls concerning new stock issue within 24 hours following announcement of sale (November 14).
- Packers clinch postseason berth for record fifth straight year (December 1) with 27-11 victory over Minnesota Vikings.
- Packers capture third consecutive NFC Central Division title via 17-6 victory over Buccaneers in Tampa (December 7), earn first-round bye in playoffs and right to host divisional playoff.

1998
- Gaining berth in NFC Championship for third straight year, Packers defeat Tampa Bay, 21-7, in divisional playoff (January 4).

- Packers earn second consecutive trip to the Super Bowl with 23-10 victory over 49ers at San Francisco in NFC Championship Game (January 11).
- Last-minute drive falls short of tie, Packers lose to Denver Broncos, 31-24, in Super Bowl XXXII at San Diego (January 25). Record, world-wide audience of 800 million, in 147countries, views game on television.
- More than 25,000 fans turn out in Lambeau Field to welcome Packers home from Super Bowl XXXII (January 27).
- Legendary linebacker Ray Nitschke, a member of the Pro Football Hall of Fame, dies in Florida at the age of 61 (March 8).
- Packers President Bob Harlan announces that stock sale, which ended March 16, yielded nearly 106,000 new shareholders, more than $24 million (March 17).
- With huge increase in number of "owners," Packers, make corporate history, hold annual stockholders' meeting in Lambeau Field for first time in team annals (July 8). For the third consecutive year, Treasurer John R. Underwood reports record net income for the Packer Corporation, $6,718,628 for fiscal 1997.

TEAM INTERNET SITE: PACKERS.COM

Launched in 1997, packers.com is the official internet site of the Green Bay Packers.

The site is a valuable resource for both fans and the media, containing all of the team's official press releases, the most up-to-date depth chart and player rosters, game and cumulative statistics, plus bios of all players, coaches and key front office personnel. Audio of selected press conferences also will air live on packers.com.

Breaking team news is posted on the home page of packers.com simultaneously with its release to the media. Fans also can sign up for a special email list, which will give them notice of late-breaking information as well as of other special occurences on the site.

There are many special features which are unique to packers.com, including the newest toy, Lambeau Cam, which allows one the opportunity to see inside the Packers' stadium 365 days a year, 24 hours a day. Other popular items on the site are weekly, in-season chats with Green Bay players; an 'Ask The Packers' section which allows fans to ask players and coaches questions, the best of which are answered on the site; game highlights from the Packer Radio Network; and video clips, both historical and of current games and press conferences.

A special Kids section as well as an extensive History section, which includes a data base of every player who ever played for the team, are other popular areas of the site. Fans interested in learning about the Packers' civic endeavors can tap into the Community section.

The latest and best in officially-licensed team merchandise also can be purchased from the Packer Pro Shop, on a secured basis through the site or by going directly to packerproshop.com.

Many Green Bay fans were able to successfully utilize packers.com to purchase stock in the team when shares were offered late in 1997 for the first time in 47 years.

Packers.com is produced by Digital Magic Interactive of Green Bay in conjunction with the Green Bay Packers.

Earl (Curly) Lambeau
1921-49

Gene Ronzani
1950-53

Lisle Blackbourn
1954-57

Ray (Scooter) McLean
1958

ORDER BASED ON CAREER VICTORIES

Coach	Years	Regular Season				Postseason				Career			
		Won	Lost	Tied	Pct.	Won	Lost	Tied	Pct.	Won	Lost	Tied	Pct.
Early (Curly) Lambeau*	1921-49	209	104	21	.657	3	2	0	.600	212	106	21	.656
Vince Lombardi	1959-67	89	29	4	.746	9	1	0	.900	98	30	4	.758
Mike Holmgren	1992-97	64	32	0	.667	9	4	0	.692	73	36	0	.670
Bart Starr	1975-83	52	76	3	.408	1	1	0	.500	53	77	3	.410
Dan Devine	1971-74	25	27	4	.482	0	1	0	.000	25	28	4	474
Forrest Gregg	1984-87	25	37	1	.405	0	0	0	.000	25	37	1	.405
Lindy Infante	1988-91	24	40	0	.375	0	0	0	.000	24	40	0	.375
Phil Bengtson	1968-70	20	21	1	.488	0	0	0	.000	20	21	1	.488
Lisle Blackbourn	1954-57	17	31	0	.354	0	0	0	.000	17	31	0	.354
Gene Ronzani**	1950-53	14	31	1	.315	0	0	0	.000	14	31	1	.315
Ray (Scooter) McLean***	1958	1	10	1	.125	0	0	0	.000	1	10	1	.125
TOTALS		**540**	**+440**	**36**	**.549**	**22**	**9**	**0**	**.710**	**562**	**+449**	**36**	**.554**

* Records do not reflect 1919-20 seasons when Packers played independent football and other non-NFL games

** Resigned after 10 games in 1953

*** Record does not include final two games of 1953 season, when he served as co-head coach with Hugh Devore (0-2 record)

\+ Record includes two losses in 1953 with Ray (Scooter) McLean and Hugh Devore serving as co-head coach

Vince Lombardi
1959-67

Phil Bengtson
1968-70

Dan Devine
1971-74

Bart Starr
1975-83

Forrest Gregg
1984-87

Lindy Infante
1988-91

Mike Holmgren
1992-present

ALL-TIME ASSISTANT COACHES

Name	Years
Austin, Bill	1959-64
Bengtson, Phil	1959-67
Blache, Greg	1988-93
Bratkowski, Zeke	1969-70, 1975-81
Brock, Charley	1949
Brooks, Larry	1994-98
Brunner, John	1983
Bullough, Hank	1988-91
Burns, Jerry	1966-67
Carpenter, Lew	1975-85
Champion, Jim	1980
Clark, Joe	1988-91
Cochran, John "Red"	1959-66, 1971-74
Colbert, Jim	1975
Coughlin, Tom	1986-87
Cromwell, Nolan	1992-98
Curry, Bill	1977-79
Davis, Charlie	1988-91
Devore, Hugh	1953
Doll, Don	1971-73
Dotsch, Rollie	1971-74
Drulis, Chuck	1951-53
Evans, Dick	1970
Fears, Tom	1962-65
Fichtner, Ross	1980-83
Flajole, Ken	1998
Geis, Wayne "Buddy"	1988-91
Gregg, Forrest	1969-70
Gruden, Jon	1992-94
Gustafson, Burt	1971-74, 1977
Hanner, Dave	1965-79, 1982
Haskell, Gil	1992-97
Hearden, Tom	1954-55, 1957
Hecker, Norb	1959-65
Hilton, John	1986
Holland, Johnny	1995-98
Hutson, Don	1944-48
Jauron, Dick	1986-94
Johnston, Kent	1992-98
Kettela, Pete	1981-82
Kiesling, Walt	1945-48
Kiffin, Monte	1983
Kinard, Billy	1974
Klapstein, Earl	1956
Knight, Virgil	1984-91
Kotal, Eddie	1942-43
Kuhlmann, Hank	1972-74
LeBeau, Dick	1976-79
Lewis, Sherman	1992-98
Lind, Jim	1992-98
Lindsey, Dale	1986-87
Lord, Bob	1975-78
Lovat, Tom	1980, 1992-98

Name	Years
Mariucci, Steve	1992-95
Marshall, John	1980-82
McCormick, Tom	1967-68
McLaughlin, Leon	1975-76
McLean, Ray "Scooter"	1951-57
McMillan, Ernie	1978-83
Meyer, John	1975-83
Meyers, Bill	1982-83
Modzelewski, Dick	1984-87
Molenda, Bo	1947-48
Mornhinweg, Marty	1995-96
Morton, Jack	1957-58
Moseley, Dick	1988-91
Moss, Perry	1974
Nolting, Ray	1950
Paterra, Herb	1984-85
Peete, Willie	1987-91
Plasman, Dick	1950-52
Polonchek, John	1972-74
Priefer, Chuck	1984-85
Rehbein, Dick	1979-83
Reid, Andy	1992-98
Reid, Floyd "Breezy"	1958
Reynolds, Gary	1998
Rhodes, Ray	1992-93
Richards, Ray	1958
Riederer, Russ	1991
Riley, Ken	1984-85
Roach, Paul	1975-76
Robinson, Wayne	1968-69
Roland, Johnny	1974
Rymkus, Lou	1954-57
Schnelker, Bob	1966-71, 1982-85
Sefcik, George	1984-87
Sherman, Mike	1997-98
Shurmur, Fritz	1994-98
Skorich, Nick	1958
Smith, Richard "Red"	1935-43
Snyder, Bob	1949
Starr, Bart	1972
Stidham, Tom	1949
Stuber, Abe	1956
Sydney, Harry	1994-98
Taylor, John "Tarz"	1950-52
Tippett, Howard	1988-91
Trafton, George	1944
Urich, Richard "Doc"	1981-83
Valesente, Bob	1992-98
vonAppen, Fred	1979-80
Voris, Dick	1961-62
Wampfler, Jerry	1984-87
Wietecha, Ray	1965-70

ALL-TIME ROSTER

1921-1997
(Players listed below are those who have played in at least one regular-season or playoff game with the Packers)

A

Aberson, Cliff (B), No College 1946
Abrams, Nate (E), No College 1921
Abramson, George (G/T), Minnesota 1925
Acks, Ron (LB), Illinois 1974-76
Adams, Chet (T), Ohio State 1943
Adderley, Herb (DB), Michigan State 1961-69
Adkins, Bob (B), Marshall 1940-41, 45
Affholter, Erik (WR), Southern California 1991
Afflis, Dick (G), Nevada 1951-54
Agajanian, Ben (K), New Mexico 1961
Albrecht, Art (T), Wisconsin 1942
Aldridge, Ben (B), Oklahoma A&M 1953
Aldridge, Lionel (DE), Utah State 1963-71
Allerman, Kurt (LB), Penn State 1980-81
Amsler, Marty (DE), Evansville 1970
Amundsen, Norm (G), Wisconsin 1957
Anderson, Aric (LB), Millikin 1987
Anderson, Bill (TE), Tennessee 1965-66
Anderson, Donny (RB), Texas Tech 1966-71
Anderson, John (LB), Michigan 1978-89
Anderson, Vickey Ray (FB), Oklahoma 1980
Ane, Charlie (C), Michigan State 1981
Apsit, Marger (B), Southern California 1932
Archambeau, Lester (DE), Stanford 1990-92
Ard, Billy (G/T), Wake Forest 1989-91
Ariey, Mike (T), San Diego State 1989
Arthur, Mike (C), Texas A&M 1995-96
Ashmore, Roger (T), Gonzaga 1928-29
Askson, Bert (TE), Texas Southern 1975-77
Atkins, Steve (RB), Maryland 1979-81
Auer, Todd (LB), Western Illinois 1987
Austin, Hise (DB), Prairie View A&M 1973
Avery, Steve (FB), Northern Michigan 1991
Aydelette, Buddy (G), Alabama 1980

B

Bailey, Byron (HB), Washington State 1953
Bain, Bill (T), Southern California 1975
Baker, Frank (E), Northwestern 1931
Baker, Roy (B), Southern California 1928-29
Balazs, Frank (B), Iowa 1939-41
Baldwin, Al (E), Arkansas 1950
Banet, Herb (B), Manchester 1937
Barber, Bob (DE), Grambling State 1976-79
Barnes, Emery (DE), Oregon 1956
Barnes, Gary (E), Clemson 1962
Barnett, Solon (T), Baylor 1945-46
Barragar, Nate (C), Southern California 1931-32, 34-35
Barrett, Jan (E), Fresno State 1963
Barrie, Sebastian (DE), Liberty 1992
Barry, Al (G), Southern California 1954, 57
Barry, Norm (B), Notre Dame 1921
Barton, Don (B), Texas 1953
Bartrum, Mike (TE), Marshall 1995
Barzilauskas, Carl (DT), Indiana 1978-79
Basing, Myrt (B), Lawrence 1923-27
Basinger, Mike (DE), Cal-Riverside 1974
Baxter, Lloyd (C), Southern Methodist 1948
Beach, Sanjay (WR), Colorado State 1992
Beasey, Jack (B), South Dakota 1924
Beck, Ken (DT), Texas A&M 1959-60
Becker, Wayland (E), Marquette 1936-38
Beebe, Don (WR), Chadron State 1996-97
Beekley, Bruce (LB), Oregon 1980
Bell, Albert (WR), Alabama 1988
Bell, Ed (G/T), Indiana 1947-49
Bennett, Earl (G), Hardin-Simmons 1946
Bennett, Edgar (RB), Florida State 1992-96

Bennett, Tony (LB), Mississippi 1990-93
Berezney, Paul (T), Fordham 1942-44
Berrang, Ed (E), Villanova 1952
Berry, Connie (E), North Carolina State 1940
Berry, Ed (DB), Utah State 1986
Bettencourt, Larry (C), St. Mary's (Calif.) 1933
Bettis, Tom (LB), Purdue 1955-61
Beverly, David (P), Auburn 1975-80
Bieberstein, Adolph (G), Wisconsin 1926
Bilda, Dick (B), Marquette 1944
Billups, Lewis (CB), North Alabama 1992
Biolo, John (G), Lake Forest 1939
Birney, Tom (K), Michigan State 1979-80
Blaine, Ed (G), Missouri 1962
Bland, Carl (WR), Virginia Union 1989-90
Bloodgood, Elbert (B), Nebraska 1930
Boedeker, Bill (B), Kalamazoo 1950
Boerio, Chuck (LB), Illinois 1952
Bolton, Scott (WR), Auburn 1988
Bone, Warren (DE), Texas Southern 1987
Bono, Steve (QB), UCLA 1997
Bookout, Billy (DB), Austin 1955-56
Boone, J.R. (B), Tulsa 1953
Borak, Fritz (E), Creighton 1938
Borden, Nate (DE), Indiana 1955-59
Borgognone, Dirk (K), Pacific 1995
Bowdoin, Jim (G), Alabama 1928-31
Bowman, Ken (C), Wisconsin 1964-73
Boyarsky, Jerry (NT), Pittsburgh 1986-89
Boyd, Elmo (WR), Eastern Kentucky 1978
Boyd, Greg (DE), San Diego State 1983
Bracken, Don (P), Michigan 1985-90
Brackins, Charlie (QB), Prairie View A&M 1955
Bradley, Dave (G), Penn State 1969-71
Brady, Jeff (LB), Kentucky 1992
Braggs, Byron (DE), Alabama 1981-83
Branstetter, Kent (T), Houston 1973
Bratkowski, Zeke (QB), Georgia 1963-68, 71
Bray, Ray (G), Western Michigan 1952
Breen, Gene (LB), Virginia Tech 1964
Brennan, Jack (G), Michigan 1939
Brock, Charley (C/LB), Nebraska 1939-47
Brock, Lou (B), Purdue 1940-45
Brock, Matt (DE/DT), Oregon 1989-94
Brockington, John (RB), Ohio State 1971-77
Brooks, Bucky (CB), North Carolina 1996-97
Brooks, Robert (WR), South Carolina 1992-97
Bross, Mal (B), Gonzaga 1927
Broussard, Steve (P), Southern Mississippi 1975
Brown, Aaron (DE), Minnesota 1973-74
Brown, Allen (TE), Mississippi 1966-67
Brown, Bob (DT), Arkansas AM&N 1966-73
Brown, Buddy (G), Arkansas 1953-56
Brown, Carlos (QB), Pacific 1975-76
Brown, Dave (CB), Michigan 1987-89
Brown, Gary (T), Georgia Tech 1994-96
Brown, Gilbert (DT), Kansas 1993-97
Brown, Ken (C), New Mexico 1980
Brown, Robert (LB/DE), Virginia Tech 1982-92
Brown, Tim (HB), Ball State 1959
Brown, Tom (DB), Maryland 1964-68
Browner, Ross (DE/NT), Notre Dame 1987
Bruder, Hank (B), Northwestern 1931-39
Brunell, Mark (QB), Washington 1993-94
Bucchianeri, Mike (G), Indiana 1941, 44-45
Buchanon, Willie (DB), San Diego State 1972-78
Buck, Cub (T), Wisconsin 1921-25
Buckley, Terrell (CB), Florida State 1992-94
Buhler, Larry (B), Minnesota 1939-41
Buland, Walt (T), No College 1924
Bullough, Hank (G), Michigan State 1955, 58
Bultman, Art (C), Marquette 1932-34
Burgess, Ronnie (DB), Wake Forest 1985
Burnette, Reggie (LB), Houston 1991
Burris, Paul (G), Oklahoma 1949-51
Burrow, Curtis (K), Central Arkansas 1988
Burrow, Jim (DB), Nebraska 1976

Bush, Blair (C), Washington 1989-91
Butler, Bill (B), Chattanooga 1959
Butler, Frank (C/T), Michigan State 1934-36, 38
Butler, LeRoy (CB/S), Florida State 1990-97
Butler, Mike (DE), Kansas 1977-82, 85

C

Cabral, Brian (LB), Colorado 1980
Cade, Mossy (DB), Texas 1985-86
Caffey, Lee Roy (LB), Texas A&M 1964-69
Cahoon, Ivan (T), Gonzaga 1926-29
Caldwell, David (NT), Texas Christian 1987
Campbell, Rich (QB), California 1981-84
Campen, James (C), Tulane 1989-93
Canadeo, Tony (B), Gonzaga 1941-44, 46-52
Cannava, Al (B), Boston College 1950
Cannon, Mark (C), Texas-Arlington 1984-89
Capp, Dick (TE/LB), Boston College 1967
Capuzzi, Jim (B), Cincinnati......................1955-56
Carey, Joe (G), Illinois Tech 1921
Carlson, Wes (G), St. John's 1926
Carmichael, Al (HB), Southern California 1953-58
Carpenter, Lew (B), Arkansas 1959-63
Carr, Fred (LB), Texas-El Paso 1968-77
Carreker, Alphonso (DE), Florida State 1984-88
Carroll, Leo (DE), San Diego State 1968
Carruth, Paul Ott (RB), Alabama 1986-88
Carter, Carl (CB), Texas Tech 1992
Carter, Jim (LB), Minnesota...........1970-75, 77-78
Carter, Joe (E), Southern Methodist 1942
Carter, Mike (WR), Sacramento State 1970
Casper, Charley (B), Texas Christian.............1934
Cassidy, Ron (WR), Utah State 1979-81, 83-84
Cecil, Chuck (S), Arizona 1988-92
Chandler, Don (K), Florida.......................1965-67
Cheek, Louis (T), Texas A&M 1991
Cherry, Bill (C), Middle Tenn. State 1986-87
Chesley, Francis (LB), Wyoming....................1978
Childs, Henry (TE), Kansas State 1984
Chmura, Mark (TE), Boston College 1993-97
Choate, Putt (LB), Southern Methodist 1987
Christman, Paul (QB), Missouri 1950
Cifelli, Gus (T), Notre Dame 1953
Cifers, Bob (B), Tennessee 1949
Clancy, Jack (WR), Michigan 1970
Clanton, Chuck (DB), Auburn 1985
Claridge, Dennis (QB), Nebraska 1965
Clark, Allan (RB), Northern Arizona 1982
Clark, Greg (LB), Arizona State.....................1991
Clark, Jessie (FB), Arkansas 1983-87
Clark, Vinnie (CB), Ohio State 1991-92
Clavelle, Shannon (DE), Colorado 1995-97
Clayton, Mark (WR), Louisville 1993
Clemens, Bob (FB), Georgia 1955
Clemens, Cal (B), Southern California 1936
Clemons, Ray (G), St. Mary's (Calif.) 1947
Cloud, Jack (FB), William & Mary 1950-51
Cobb, Reggie (RB), Tennessee 1994
Cody, Ed (B), Purdue 1947-48
Coffey, Junior (RB), Washington 1965
Coffman, Paul (TE), Kansas State 1978-85
Coleman, Keo (LB), Mississippi State 1993
Collier, Steve (T), Bethune-Cookman 1987
Collins, Albin (HB), Louisiana State 1951
Collins, Brett (LB), Washington 1992-93
Collins, Mark (CB), Cal State-Fullerton 1997
Collins, Patrick (RB), Oklahoma 1988
Collins, Shawn (WR), Northern Arizona 1993
Comp, Irv (B), St. Benedict 1943-49
Compton, Chuck (DB), Boise State 1987
Comstock, Rudy (G), Georgetown 1931-33
Concannon, Jack (QB), Boston College..........1974
Cone, Fred (FB/K), Clemson 1951-57
Conway, Dave (K), Texas 1971
Cook, James (G), Notre Dame 1921

Cook, Kelly (RB), Oklahoma State................1987
Cook, Ted (E/DB), Alabama 1948-50
Cooke, Bill (DE), Massachusetts 1975
Cooney, Mark (LB), Colorado 1974
Corker, John (LB), Oklahoma State 1988
Coughlin, Frank (T), Notre Dame 1921
Coutre, Larry (HB), Notre Dame 1950, 53
Cox, Ron (LB), Fresno State 1996
Craig, Larry (E/B), South Carolina 1939-49
Crawford, Keith (CB), Howard Payne 1995
Cremer, Ted (E), Auburn 1948
Crenshaw, Leon (DT), Tuskegee 1968
Crimmins, Bernie (G/B), Notre Dame 1945
Croft, Milburn (T), Ripon..........................1942-47
Cronin, Tommy (HB), Marquette....................1922
Croston, Dave (T), Iowa 1988
Crouse, Ray (RB), Nevada-Las Vegas 1984
Crowley, Jim (HB), Notre Dame 1925
Crutcher, Tommy (LB), Texas Christian 1964-67, 71-72
Cuff, Ward (B), Marquette.............................1947
Culbreath, Jim (FB), Oklahoma 1977-79
Culver, Al (T), Notre Dame 1932
Cumby, George (LB), Oklahoma 1980-85
Curcio, Mike (LB), Temple 1983
Currie, Dan (LB), Michigan State 1958-64
Curry, Bill (C), Georgia Tech 1965-66
Cvercko, Andy (G), Northwestern 1960
Cyre, Hector (T), Gonzaga 1926

D

Dahms, Tom (T), San Diego State 1955
Dale, Carroll (WR), Virginia Tech..............1965-72
Danelo, Joe (K), Washington State 1975
Daniell, Averell (T), Pittsburgh 1937
Danjean, Ernie (LB), Auburn 1957
Darkins, Chris (RB), Minnesota.....................1997
Darling, Bernard (C), Beloit 1927-31
Davenport, Bill (HB), Hardin-Simmons 1931
Davey, Don (DE/DT), Wisconsin 1991-94
Davidson, Ben (DE), Washington 1961
Davis, Dave (WR), Tennessee A&I 1971-72
Davis, Harper (B), Mississippi State 1951
Davis, Kenneth (RB), Texas Christian 1986-88
Davis, Paul (G), Marquette............................1922
Davis, Ralph (G), Wisconsin 1947-48
Davis, Rob (LS), Shippensburg 1997
Davis, Tyrone (TE), Virginia 1997
Davis, Willie (DE), Grambling State 1960-69
Dawson, Dale (K), Eastern Kentucky 1988
Dawson, Gib (HB), Texas 1953
Dean, Walter (FB), Grambling State 1991
Deeks, Don (T), Texas 1948
Dees, Bob (T), Southwest Missouri State 1952
Degrate, Tony (DE), Texas 1985
Del Gaizo, Jim (QB), Tampa 1973
Del Greco, Al (K), Auburn 1984-87
DeLisle, Jim (DT), Wisconsin 1971
Dellenbach, Jeff (C/G), Wisconsin 1996-97
DeLuca, Tony (NT), Rhode Island 1984
Dennard, Preston (WR), New Mexico 1985
Dent, Burnell (LB), Tulane 1986-92
Deschaine, Dick (P), No College 1955-57
Detmer, Ty (QB), Brigham Young 1992-95
Dickey, Lynn (QB), Kansas State 1976-77, 79-85
Didier, Clint (TE), Portland State 1988-89
Dillon, Bobby (DB), Texas 1952-59
Dilweg, Anthony (QB), Duke 1989-90
Dilweg, Lavvie (E), Marquette...................1927-34
Dimler, Rich (DT), Southern California 1980
DiPierro, Ray (G), Ohio State 1950-51
Disend, Leo (T), Albright 1940
Dittrich, John (G), Wisconsin 1959
Don Carlos, Waldo (C), Drake......................1931
D'Onofrio, Mark (LB), Penn State 1992
Donohoe, Mike (TE), San Francisco..........1973-74

Dorsett, Matthew (CB), Southern 1995
Dorsey, Dean (K), Toronto 1988
Dorsey, John (LB), Connecticut............................1984-88
Dotson, Earl (T), Texas A&I..................................1993-97
Dotson, Santana (DT), Baylor 1996-97
Douglas, George (C), Marquette 1921
Douglass, Bobby (QB), Kansas 1978
Douglass, Mike (LB), San Diego State 1978-85
Dowden, Corey (CB), Tulane......................................1996
Dowden, Steve (T), Baylor 1952
Dowler, Boyd (WR), Colorado 1959-69
Dowling, Brian (QB), Yale..1977
Drechsler, Dave (G), North Carolina 1983-84
Dreyer, Wally (B), Wisconsin.....................................1950
Drost, Jeff (DT), Iowa..1987
Drulis, Chuck (G), Temple 1950
Duckett, Forey (CB), Nevada-Reno 1994
Duford, Wilfred (B), Marquette 1924
Duhart, Paul (B), Florida..1944
Dukes, Jamie (C), Florida State 1994
DuMoe, Bill (E), No College 1921
Dunaway, Dave (WR), Duke 1968
Duncan, Ken (P), Tulsa..1971
Dunn, Red (B), Marquette 1927-31
Dunningan, Pat (E), Minnesota..................................1922

E

Earhart, Ralph (B), Texas Tech 1948-49
Earp, Jug (C), Monmouth.......................................1922-32
Eason, Roger (G), Oklahoma 1949
Ecker, Ed (T), John Carroll 1950-51
Edwards, Earl (DT), Wichita State.............................1979
Ellerson, Gary (FB), Wisconsin.............................1985-86
Elliott, Burton (B), Marquette 1921
Elliott, Carlton (E), Virginia 1951-54
Elliott, Tony (DB), Central Michigan 1987-88
Ellis, Gerry (FB), Missouri......................................1980-86
Ellis, Ken (CB), Southern......................................1970-75
Enderle, Dick (G), Minnesota 1976
Engebretsen, Paul (G), Northwestern 1934-41
Engelmann, Wuert (B), South Dakota State 1930-33
Enright, Rex (FB), Notre Dame 1926-27
Epps, Phillip (WR), Texas Christian 1982-88
Estep, Mike (G), Bowling Green 1987
Ethridge, Joe (T), Southern Methodist 1949
Evans, Dick (E), Iowa 1940, 43
Evans, Doug (CB), Louisiana Tech 1993-97
Evans, Jack (B), California 1929
Evans, Lon (G), Texas Christian 1933-37

F

Falkenstein, Tony (FB), St. Mary's (Calif.) 1943
Fanucci, Mike (DE), Arizona State............................1974
Faverty, Hal (C/LB), Wisconsin.................................1952
Favre, Brett (QB), Southern Mississippi.................1992-97
Faye, Allen (E), Marquette 1922
Feasel, Greg (T), Abilene Christian 1986
Feathers, Beattie (B), Tennessee..............................1940
Ferguson, Howie (FB), No College 1953-58
Ferragamo, Vince (QB), Nebraska 1985-86
Ferry, Lou (T), Villanova 1949
Fields, Angelo (T), Michigan State 1982
Finnin, Tom (T), Detroit 1957
Fitzgerald, Kevin (TE), Wisconsin-Eau Claire............1987
Fitzgibbons, Paul (B), Creighton 1930-32
Flaherty, Dick (E), Marquette 1926
Flanigan, Jim (LB), Pittsburgh.............................1967-70
Fleming, Marv (TE), Utah 1963-69
Flowers, Bob (C/LB), Texas Tech..........................1942-49
Floyd, Bobby Jack (FB), Texas Christian 1952
Flynn, Tom (S), Pittsburgh 1984-86
Folkins, Lee (DE), Washington 1961
Fontenot, Herman (RB), Louisiana State 1989-90
Ford, Len (DE), Michigan 1958

Forester, Bill (LB), Southern Methodist 1953-63
Forte, Aldo (G), Montana 1947
Forte, Bob (B), Arkansas 1946-53
Francis, Joe (B), Oregon State.............................1958-59
Frankowski, Ray (G), Washington..............................1945
Franta, Herb (T), St. Thomas 1930
Franz, Nolan (WR), Tulane 1986
Frase, Paul (DE), Syracuse 1997
Freeman, Antonio (WR), Virginia Tech 1995-97
Freeman, Bob (DB), Auburn 1959
Fries, Sherwood (G/LB), Colorado State 1943
Fritsch, Ted (B), Stevens Point Teachers' 1942-50
Frutig, Ed (E), Michigan 1941, 45
Fuller, Joe (CB), Northern Iowa 1991
Fullwood, Brent (RB), Auburn 1987-90
Fusina, Chuck (QB), Penn State 1986

G

Gabbard, Steve (T), Florida State 1991
Galbreath, Harry (G), Tennessee 1993-95
Gantenbein, Milt (E), Wisconsin 1931-40
Garcia, Eddie (K), Southern Methodist 1983-84
Gardella, Gus (FB), No College 1922
Gardner, Milton (G), Wisconsin............................1922-26
Garrett, Bob (QB), Stanford 1954
Garrett, Len (TE), New Mexico Highlands 1971-73
Gassert, Ron (DT), Virginia 1962
Gatewood, Lester (C), Baylor 1946-47
Gavin, Buck (B), No College 1921, 23
Gaydos, Kent (WR), Florida State 1975
Getty, Charlie (T), Penn State 1983
Gibson, Paul (WR), Texas-El Paso 1972
Gillette, Jim (B), Virginia 1947
Gillingham, Gale (G), Minnesota 1966-74, 76
Gillus, Willie (QB), Norfolk State...............................1987
Girard, Jug (B), Wisconsin.....................................1948-51
Glass, Leland (WR), Oregon 1972-73
Glick, Eddie (B), Marquette 1921-22
Gofourth, Derrel (G/C), Oklahoma State 1977-82
Goldenberg, Charles (G/B), Wisconsin 1933-45
Goodman, Les (RB), Yankton 1973-74
Goodnight, Clyde (E), Tulsa 1945-49
Gordon, Dick (WR), Michigan State 1973
Gordon, Lou (T), Illinois 1936-37
Gorgal, Ken (DB), Purdue 1956
Grabowski, Jim (RB), Illinois.................................1966-70
Grant, David (DE), West Virginia................................1993
Gray, Cecil (T), North Carolina 1992
Gray, Jack (E), No College 1923
Gray, Johnnie (S), Cal State-Fullerton 1975-83
Green, Jessie (WR), Tulsa 1976
Greene, Tiger (S), Western Carolina 1986-90
Greeney, Norm (G), Notre Dame...............................1933
Greenfield, Tom (C/LB), Arizona 1939-41
Greenwood, David (S), Wisconsin..............................1986
Gregg, Forrest (T), So. Methodist 1956, 58-70
Gremminger, Hank (DB), Baylor 1956-65
Griffen, Harold (C), Iowa 1928
Grimes, Billy (HB), Oklahoma A&M 1950-52
Grimm, Dan (G), Colorado 1963-65
Gros, Earl (FB), Louisiana State............................1962-63
Grove, Roger (B), Michigan State 1931-35
Gruber, Bob (T), Pittsburgh 1987
Gueno, Jim (LB), Tulane 1976-80

H

Hackbart, Dale (DB), Wisconsin 1960-61
Hackett, Joey (TE), Elon 1987-88
Haddix, Michael (FB), Mississippi State.................1989-90
Hadl, John (QB), Kansas 1974-75
Haley, Darryl (T), Utah 1988
Hall, Charlie (CB), Pittsburgh 1971-76
Hall, Mark (DE), Southwestern Louisiana 1989-90
Hallstrom, Ron (G), Iowa 1982-92

Hamilton, Ruffin (LB), Tulane 1994
Hampton, Dave (RB), Wyoming 1969-71
Hanner, Dave (DT), Arkansas 1952-64
Hanny, Frank (T), Indiana 1930
Hansen, Don (LB), Illinois 1976-77
Hansen, Hal (FB/E), Minnesota 1923
Harden, Derrick (WR), Eastern New Mexico 1987
Harden, Leon (S), Texas-El Paso 1970
Harding, Roger (C), California 1949
Hardy, Kevin (DT), Notre Dame 1970
Hargrove, James (RB), Wake Forest 1987
Harrell, Willard (RB), Pacific 1975-77
Harris, Bernardo (LB), North Carolina 1995-97
Harris, Corey (WR/CB/KR), Vanderbilt....................1992-94
Harris, Jack (B), Wisconsin 1925-26
Harris, Jackie (TE), Northeast Louisiana 1990-93
Harris, Leotis (G), Arkansas 1978-83
Harris, Tim (LB), Memphis State 1986-90
Harris, William (TE), Bishop 1990
Harrison, Anthony (DB), Georgia Tech 1987
Hart, Doug (DB), Texas-Arlington 1964-71
Hartnett, Perry (G), Southern Methodist 1987
Hartwig, Keith (WR), Arizona 1977
Harvey, Maurice (S), Ball State 1981-83
Hathcock, Dave (DB), Memphis State 1966
Hauck, Tim (S), Montana 1991-94
Havig, Dennis (G), Colorado 1977
Haycraft, Ken (E), Minnesota 1930
Hayden, Aaron (RB), Tennessee 1997
Hayes, Chris (S), Washington State 1996
Hayes, Dave (E), Notre Dame 1921-22
Hayes, Gary (DB), Fresno State 1984-86
Hayes, Norb (E), Marquette 1923
Hayhoe, Bill (T), Southern California 1969-73
Hays, George (DE), St. Bonaventure 1953
Hearden, Les (HB), St. Ambrose 1924
Hearden, Tom (B), Notre Dame 1927-28
Heath, Stan (QB), Nevada 1949
Hefner, Larry (LB), Clemson 1972-75
Held, Paul (QB), San Jose State 1955
Helluin, Jerry (DT), Tulane 1954-57
Henderson, William (FB), North Carolina 1995-97
Hendrian, Dutch (B), Princeton.................................1924
Hendricks, Ted (LB), Miami (Fla.) 1974
Henry, Urban (DT), Georgia Tech 1963
Hentrich, Craig (P), Notre Dame 1994-97
Herber, Arnie (B), Regis 1930-40
Hickman, Larry (FB), Baylor 1960
Highsmith, Don (RB), Michigan State 1973
Hill, Don (B), Stanford 1929
Hill, Jim (DB), Texas A&I 1972-74
Hill, Nate (DE), Auburn 1988
Hilton, John (TE), Richmond 1970
Himes, Dick (T), Ohio State 1968-77
Hinkle, Clarke (FB), Bucknell 1932-41
Hinte, Hal (E), Pittsburgh 1942
Hobbins, Jim (G), Minnesota 1987
Hoffman, Gary (T), Santa Clara 1984
Holland, Darius (DT/DE), Colorado 1995-97
Holland, Johnny (LB), Texas A&M...........................1987-93
Holler, Ed (LB), South Carolina 1963
Hollinquest, Lamont (LB), Southern California 1996-97
Holmes, Jerry (CB), West Virginia 1990-91
Hood, Estus (DB), Illinois State 1978-84
Hope, Charles (G), Central (Ohio) State 1994
Horn, Don (QB), San Diego State 1967-70
Hornung, Paul (B), Notre Dame 1957-62, 64-66
Houston, Bobby (LB), North Carolina State 1990
Howard, Desmond (WR/KR), Michigan......................1996
Howard, Lynn (B), Indiana 1921-22
Howell, John (B), Nebraska 1938
Howton, Billy (E), Rice 1952-58
Hubbard, Cal (T), Centenary, Geneva.............1929-33, 35
Huckleby, Harlan (RB), Michigan...........................1980-85
Hudson, Bob (RB), Northeastern (Okla.) State 1972
Huffman, Tim (G/T), Notre Dame 1981-85
Hull, Tom (LB), Penn State 1975

Humphrey, Donnie (DE), Auburn 1984-86
Hunt, Ervin (DB), Fresno State 1970
Hunt, Kevin (T), Doane 1972
Hunt, Mike (LB), Minnesota 1978-80
Hunter, Art (C), Notre Dame 1954
Hunter, Scott (QB), Alabama 1971-73
Hunter, Tony (RB), Minnesota 1987
Hutchins, Paul (T), Western Michigan 1993-94
Hutson, Don (E/DB), Alabama 1935-45
Hyland, Bob (C), Boston College 1967-69, 76

I

Ilkin, Tunch (T), Indiana State 1993
Iman, Ken (C), Southeast Missouri State...............1960-63
Ingalls, Bob (C/LB), Michigan 1942
Ingram, Darryl (TE), California 1992-93
Ingram, Mark (WR), Michigan State 1995
Isbell, Cecil (B), Purdue 1938-42
Ivery, Eddie Lee (RB), Georgia Tech 1979-86

J

Jacke, Chris (K), Texas-El Paso 1989-96
Jackson, Johnnie (S), Houston.................................1992
Jackson, Keith (TE), Oklahoma 1995-96
Jackson, Mel (G), Southern California 1976-80
Jacobs, Allen (HB), Utah 1965
Jacobs, Jack (B), Oklahoma 1947-49
Jacunski, Harry (E), Fordham 1939-44
Jakes, Van (CB), Kent State 1989
James, Claudis (WR), Jackson State 1967-68
Jankowski, Ed (B), Wisconsin 1937-41
Jansante, Val (E), Duquesne 1951
Jay, Craig (TE), Mount Senario 1987
Jefferson, John (WR), Arizona State 1981-84
Jefferson, Norman (DB), Louisiana State 1987-88
Jenison, Ray (T), South Dakota State 1931
Jenke, Noel (LB), Minnesota 1973-74
Jennings, Jim (E), Missouri 1955
Jensen, Greg (G), No College 1987
Jensen, Jim (RB), Iowa 1981-82
Jervey, Travis (RB), The Citadel 1995-97
Jeter, Bob (DB), Iowa 1963-70
Johnson, Bill (DE), Minnesota 1941
Johnson, Charles (DT), Maryland 1979-80, 83
Johnson, Danny (LB), Tennessee State 1978
Johnson, Ezra (DE), Morris Brown 1977-87
Johnson, Glenn (T), Arizona State 1949
Johnson, Howard (G/LB), Georgia........................1940-41
Johnson, Joe (HB), Boston College 1954-58
Johnson, Kenneth (DB), Mississippi State 1987
Johnson, KeShon (DB), Arizona 1994, 97
Johnson, LeShon (RB), Northern Illinois 1994-95
Johnson, Marvin (DB), San Jose State 1952-53
Johnson, Randy (QB), Texas A&I 1976
Johnson, Reggie (TE), Florida State 1994, 97
Johnson, Sammy (RB), North Carolina 1979
Johnson, Tom (DT), Michigan 1952
Johnston, Chester (B), Marquette 1931, 34-38
Jolly, Mike (S), Michigan............................1980, 82-83
Jones, Bob (G), Indiana 1934
Jones, Boyd (T), Texas Southern 1984
Jones, Bruce (G), Alabama 1927-28
Jones, Calvin (DB), Nebraska 1996
Jones, Daryll (DB), Georgia 1984-85
Jones, Ron (TE), Texas-El Paso 1969
Jones, Scott (T), Washington 1991
Jones, Sean (DE), Northeastern 1994-96
Jones, Terry (NT), Alabama 1978-84
Jones, Tom (G), Bucknell 1938
Jordan, Charles (WR), Long Beach City 1994-95
Jordan, Henry (DT), Virginia 1959-69
Jordan, Kenneth (LB), Tuskegee 1994
Jorgenson, Carl (T), St. Mary's (Calif.) 1934

Joyner, Seth (LB), Texas-El Paso 1997
Jurkovic, John (NT), Eastern Illinois 1991-95

K

Kahler, Bob (B), Nebraska 1942-44
Kahler, Royal (T), Nebraska 1942
Katalinas, Leo (T), Catholic Univ. 1938
Kauahi, Kani (C), Hawaii 1988
Keane, Jim (E), Iowa 1952
Keefe, Emmett (T), Notre Dame 1921
Kekeris, Jim (T), Missouri 1948
Kell, Paul (T), Notre Dame 1939-40
Kelley, Bill (E), Texas Tech 1949
Kelly, Joe (LB), Washington 1995
Kemp, Perry (WR), California (Pa.) 1988-91
Kercher, Bob (DE), Georgetown 1944
Kern, Bill (T), Pittsburgh 1929-30
Keuper, Ken (B), Georgia 1945-47
Kiel, Blair (QB), Notre Dame 1988-91
Kiesling, Walt (G), St. Thomas 1935-36
Kilbourne, Warren (T), Minnesota 1939
Kimball, Bobby (WR), Oklahoma 1979-80
Kimmel, J.D. (DT), Houston 1958
Kinard, Billy (B), Mississippi 1957-58
Kinder, Randy (CB), Notre Dame 1997
King, David (DB), Auburn 1987
King, Don (DT), Kentucky 1956
King, Don (DB), Southern Methodist 1987
Kirby, Jack (B), Southern California 1949
Kitson, Syd (G), Wake Forest 1980-81, 83-84
Klaus, Fee (C), No College 1921
Kliebhan, Adolph (B), No College 1921
Knafelc, Gary (E), Colorado 1954-62
Knapp, Lindsay (G), Notre Dame 1996
Knutson, Gene (DE), Michigan 1954, 56
Knutson, Steve (T), Southern California 1976-77
Koart, Matt (DE), Southern California 1986
Koch, Greg (T), Arkansas 1977-85
Koncar, Mark (T), Colorado 1976-77, 79-81
Konopasek, Ed (T), Ball State 1987
Koonce, George (LB), East Carolina 1992-97
Kopay, Dave (RB), Washington 1972
Kostelnik, Ron (T), Cincinnati 1961-68
Kotal, Eddie (B), Lawrence 1925-29
Kovatch, John (E), Notre Dame 1947
Kowalkowski, Bob (G), Virginia 1977
Kramer, Jerry (G), Idaho 1958-68
Kramer, Ron (TE), Michigan 1957, 59-64
Kranz, Keneth (B), Milwaukee Teachers 1949
Krause, Larry (RB), St. Norbert 1970-71, 73-74
Kroll, Bob (S), Northern Michigan 1972-73
Kuberski, Bob (DT), Navy 1995-97
Kuechenberg, Rudy (LB), Indiana 1970
Kurth, Joe (T), Notre Dame 1933-34
Kuusisto, Bill (G), Minnesota 1941-46

L

LaBounty, Matt (DE), Oregon 1995
Ladrow, Wally (HB), No College 1921
Lally, Bob (LB), Cornell 1976
Lambeau, Earl "Curly" (B), Notre Dame 1921-29
Lammons, Pete (TE), Texas 1972
Lande, Cliff (E), Carroll 1921
Landers, Walt (B), Clark 1978-79
Lane, MacArthur (RB), Utah State 1972-74
Lankas, Jim (FB), St. Mary's (Calif.) 1943
Larson, Bill (TE), Colorado State 1980
Larson, Fred (C), Notre Dame 1925
Larson, Kurt (LB), Michigan State 1991
Laslavic, Jim (LB), Penn State 1982
Lathrop, Kit (DT), Arizona State 1979-80
Lauer, Dutch (E), Detroit 1922
Lauer, Larry (C), Alabama 1956-57
Laughlin, Jim (LB), Ohio State 1983

Lawrence, Jim (B), Texas Christian 1939
Laws, Joe (B), Iowa 1934-45
Leaper, Wes (E), Wisconsin 1921, 23
Lee, Bill (T), Alabama 1937-42, 46
Lee, Mark (CB), Washington 1980-90
Leigh, Charlie (RB), No College 1974
Leiker, Tony (DE), Stanford 1987
LeJeune, Walt (G), Heidelberg 1925-26
Leopold, Bobby (LB), Notre Dame 1986
Lester, Darrell (C), Texas Christian 1937-38
Letlow, Russ (G), San Francisco 1936-42, 46
Levens, Dorsey (RB), Georgia Tech 1994-97
Lewellen, Verne (B), Nebraska 1924-32
Lewis, Cliff (LB), Southern Mississippi.................1981-84
Lewis, Gary (TE), Texas-Arlington 1981-84
Lewis, Mark (TE), Texas A&M 1985-87
Lewis, Mike (NT), Arkansas A&M 1980
Lewis, Ron (WR), Florida State 1992-94
Lewis, Tim (CB), Pittsburgh 1983-86
Lidberg, Carl (FB), Minnesota 1926, 29-30
Lipscomb, Paul (T), Tennessee 1945-49
Livingston, Dale (K), Western Michigan 1970
Lofton, James (WR), Stanford............................1978-86
Logan, David (NT), Pittsburgh 1987
Logan, Dick (G), Ohio State 1952-53
Lollar, Slick (FB), Samford 1928
Long, Bob (WR), Wichita 1964-67
Longwell, Ryan (K), California 1997
Loomis, Ace (B), La Crosse St. Teachers 1951-53
Losch, Jack (B), Miami (Fla.) 1956
Lucky, Bill (DT), Baylor 1955
Lueck, Bill (G), Arizona 1968-74
Luhn, Nolan (E), Tulsa 1945-49
Luke, Steve (DB), Ohio State 1975-80
Lusteg, Booth (K), Connecticut 1969
Lyle, Dewey (E), Minnesota 1922-23
Lyman, Del (T), UCLA.......................................1941

M

Maas, Bill (NT), Pittsburgh 1993
Mack, Red (WR), Notre Dame 1966
MacLeod, Tom (LB), Minnesota 1973
Maddox, George (T), Kansas State 1935
Majkowski, Don (QB), Virginia 1987-92
Malancon, Rydell (LB), Louisiana State 1987
Malone, Grover (B), Notre Dame 1921
Mandarich, Tony (T), Michigan State....................1989-91
Mandeville, Chris (DB), California-Davis 1987-88
Manley, Leon (G), Oklahoma 1950-51
Mann, Bob (E), Michigan...................................1950-54
Mann, Erroll (K), North Dakota 1968, 76
Mansfield, Von (DB), Wisconsin 1987
Marcol, Chester (K), Hillsdale 1972-80
Marks, Larry (B), Indiana 1928
Marshall, Rich (DT), Stephen F. Austin 1965
Martell, Herman (E), No College 1921
Martin, Charles (DE), Livingston 1984-87
Martinkovic, John (DE), Xavier 1951-56
Mason, Dave (DB), Nebraska 1974
Mason, Joel (E), Western Michigan......................1942-45
Mason, Larry (RB), Troy State 1988
Massey, Carlton (DE), Texas 1957-58
Masters, Norm (T), Michigan State 1957-64
Mataele, Stan (NT), Arizona 1987
Mathys, Charlie (B), Indiana 1922-26
Matson, Pat (G), Oregon 1975
Matthews, Al (DB), Texas A&I 1970-75
Matthews, Aubrey (WR), Delta State 1988-89
Mattos, Harry (B), St. Mary's (Calif.) 1936
Matuszak, Marv (LB), Tulsa 1958
Mayer, Frank (G), Notre Dame 1927
Mayes, Derrick (WR), Notre Dame 1996-97
McAuliffe, Jack (HB), Beloit 1926
McBride, Ron (RB), Missouri 1973
McCaffrey, Bob (C), Southern California................1975

McCarren, Larry (C), Illinois 1973-84
McCloughan, Dave (CB), Colorado 1992
McConkey, Phil (WR), Navy 1986
McCoy, Mike C. (DB), Colorado.............................1976-83
McCoy, Mike P. (DT), Notre Dame........................1970-76
McCrary, Hurdis (B), Georgia 1929-33
McDonald, Dustin (G), Indiana 1935
McDougal, Bob (B), Miami (Fla.) 1947
McDowell, John (G), St. John's (Minn.) 1964
McElmurry, Blaine (S), Montana.........................1997
McGarry, John (G), St. Joseph's (Ind.)...................1987
McGaw, Walter (G), Beloit 1926
McGeary, Clarence (DT), North Dakota State 1950
McGee, Buford (FB), Mississippi 1992
McGee, Max (E), Tulane 1954, 57-67
McGeorge, Rich (TE), Elon 1970-78
McGill, Lenny (CB), Arizona State 1994-95
McGrew, Sylvester (DE), Tulane 1987
McGruder, Michael (CB), Kent State 1989
McGuire, Gene (C), Notre Dame 1996
McHan, Lamar (QB), Arkansas 1959-60
McIlhenny, Don (HB), Southern Methodist 1957-59
McIntyre, Guy (G), Georgia 1994
McJulien, Paul (P), Jackson State 1991-92
McKay, Roy (B), Texas 1944-47
McKenzie, Keith (DE/LB), Ball State.....................1996-97
McLaughlin, Joe (LB), Massachusetts 1979
McLaughlin, Lee (G), Virginia 1941
McLean, Ray (B), No College..........................1919-21
McLeod, Mike (DB), Montana State 1984-85
McMahon, Jim (QB), Brigham Young 1995-96
McMath, Herb (DT), Morningside 1977
McMichael, Steve (DT), Texas 1994
McMillan, Ernie (T), Illinois 1975
McNabb, Dexter (FB), Florida 1992-93
McNally (Blood), Johnny (B), St. John's 1929-33, 35-36
McPherson, Forrest (T), Nebraska.......................1943-45
Meade, Mike (FB), Penn State 1982-83
Meilinger, Steve (E), Kentucky 1958, 60
Melka, James (LB), Wisconsin 1987
Mendoza, Ruben (G), Wayne State 1986
Mercein, Chuck (RB), Yale 1967-69
Mercer, Mike (K), Northern Arizona......................1968-69
Merrill, Casey (DE), California-Davis 1979-83
Merrill, Mark (LB), Minnesota..............................1982
Merriweather, Mike (LB), Pacific 1993
Mestnik, Frank (FB), Marquette 1963
Meyer, Jim (T), Illinois State 1987
Michaels, Lou (K), Kentucky 1971
Michaels, Walt (G), Washington & Lee 1951
Michalske, Mike (G), Penn State 1929-35, 37
Michels, John (T), Southern California 1996-97
Mickens, Terry (WR), Florida A&M 1994-97
Middleton, Terdell (RB), Memphis State 1977-81
Midler, Lou (DE), Minnesota..............................1941
Mihajlovich, Lou (DE), Indiana 1954
Milan, Don (QB), Cal Poly-San Luis Obispo 1975
Millard, Keith (DE), Washington State 1992
Miller, Don (B), Wisconsin 1941-42
Miller, Don (B), Southern Methodist 1954
Miller, John (T), Boston College 1960
Miller, John (LB), Mississippi State 1987
Miller, Ookie (C), Purdue 1938
Miller, Paul (B), South Dakota State 1936-38
Miller, Tom (E), Hampden-Sydney 1946
Mills, Stan (B), Penn State 1922-23
Minick, Paul (G), Iowa 1928-29
Mitchell, Charles (B), Tulsa 1946
Mitchell, Roland (CB/S), Texas Tech 1991-94
Moffitt, Mike (WR), Fresno State 1986
Moje, Dick (E), Loyola (Calif.).............................1951
Molenda, Bo (B), Michigan 1928-32
Monaco, Ron (LB), South Carolina 1987
Monnett, Bob (B), Michigan State 1933-38
Monroe, Henry (DB), Mississippi State......................1979
Moore, Allen (E), Texas A&M 1939
Moore, Blake (C/G), Wooster 1984-85

Moore, Brent (DE), Southern California 1987
Moore, Rich (DT), Villanova 1969-70
Moore, Tom (HB), Vanderbilt 1960-65
Moran, Rich (G), San Diego State 1985-93
Moresco, Tim (DB), Syracuse 1977
Morgan, Anthony (WR), Tennessee......................1993-96
Morris, Jim Bob (DB), Kansas State 1987
Morris, Larry (RB), Syracuse 1987
Morris, Lee (WR), Oklahoma 1987
Morrissey, Jim (LB), Michigan State 1993
Moselle, Dom (B), Superior State 1951-52
Mosley, Russ (B), Alabama 1945-46
Moss, Perry (QB), Illinois 1948
Mott, Joe (LB), Iowa 1993
Mott, Norm (B), Georgia 1933
Mullen, Roderick (CB/S), Grambling State..............1995-97
Mulleneaux, Carl (E), Utah State.................1938-41, 45-46
Mulleneaux, Lee (C), Northern Arizona 1938
Murphy, Mark (S), West Liberty State 1980-85, 87-91
Murray, Jab (T), Marquette 1921-24

<h2>N</h2>

Nadolney, Romanus (G), Notre Dame 1922
Nash, Tom (E), Georgia 1928-32
Neal, Ed (DT/T), Tulane 1945-51
Neal, Frankie (WR), Fort Hays State 1987
Neill, Bill (NT), Pittsburgh................................1984
Nelson, Bob (NT), Miami (Fla.) 1988-90
Neville, Tom (T/G), Fresno State 1986-88, 92
Newsome, Craig (CB), Arizona State 1995-97
Nichols, Hamilton (G), Rice 1951
Niemann, Walter (C), Michigan 1922-24
Nitschke, Ray (LB), Illinois 1958-72
Nix, Doyle (DB), Southern Methodist 1955
Nixon, Fred (WR), Oklahoma 1980-81
Noble, Brian (LB), Arizona State 1985-93
Noonan, Danny (NT), Nebraska 1992
Norgard, Al (E), Stanford 1934
Norseth, Mike (QB), Kansas 1990
Norton, Jerry (DB), Southern Methodist 1963-64
Norton, Marty (B), No College 1925
Norton, Rick (QB), Kentucky 1970
Nussbaumer, Bob (B), Michigan 1946
Nuzum, Rick (C), Kentucky 1978
Nystrom, Lee (T), Macalester 1974

<h2>O</h2>

Oakes, Bill (T), Haskell 1921
Oates, Brad (T), Brigham Young..............................1981
Oats, Carleton (DT), Florida A&M 1973
O'Boyle, Harry (B), Notre Dame 1928, 32
O'Connor, Bob (T), Stanford 1935
Odom, Steve (WR), Utah 1974-79
O'Donahue, Pat (DE), Wisconsin 1955
O'Donnell, Dick (E), No College 1924-30
Odson, Urban (T), Minnesota 1946-49
Oglesby, Alfred (NT), Houston 1992
Ohlgren, Earl (DE), Minnesota 1942
Okoniewski, Steve (DT), Montana 1974-75
Oliver, Muhammad (CB), Oregon 1993
Olsen, Ralph (E), Utah 1949
Olsonoski, Larry (G), Minnesota 1948-49
O'Malley, Tom (QB), Cincinnati 1950
O'Neil, Ed (LB), Penn State...............................1980
Orlich, Dan (E), Nevada 1949-51
Osborn, Dave (RB), North Dakota..........................1976
O'Steen, Dwayne (CB), San Jose State 1983-84
Owens, Rip (G), Lawrence 1922

<h2>P</h2>

Palumbo, Sam (LB/C), Notre Dame 1957
Pannell, Ernie (T), Texas A&M 1941-42, 45
Pape, Orrin (B), Iowa 1930

Papit, Johnny (HB), Virginia 1953
Parilli, Babe (QB), Kentucky 1952-53, 57-58
Parker, Freddie (RB), Mississippi Valley State 1987
Parlavecchio, Chet (LB), Penn State 1983
Paskett, Keith (WR), Western Kentucky 1987
Paskvan, George (B), Wisconsin 1941
Patrick, Frank (QB), Nebraska 1970-72
Patterson, Shawn (DE), Arizona State 1988-91, 93
Patton, Ricky (RB), Jackson State 1979
Paulekas, Tony (C), Washington & Jefferson 1936
Paup, Bryce (LB), Northern Iowa......................1990-94
Payne, Ken (WR), Langston 1974-77
Pearson, Lindell (HB), Oklahoma 1952
Peay, Francis (T), Missouri 1968-72
Pederson, Doug (QB), Northeast Louisiana 1996-97
Pelfrey, Ray (E), Eastern Kentucky 1951-52
Perkins, Don (FB), Platteville St. Teachers...........1943-45
Perko, Tom (LB), Pittsburgh.............................1976
Perry, Claude (T), Alabama 1927-35
Pesonen, Dick (DB), Minnesota-Duluth 1960
Peterson, Les (E), Texas............................1932, 34
Peterson, Ray (B), San Francisco 1937
Petitbon, John (DB), Notre Dame 1957
Petway, David (S), Northern Illinois 1981
Pickens, Bruce (CB), Nebraska 1993
Pisarkiewicz, Steve (QB), Missouri 1980
Pitts, Elijah (RB), Philander Smith.................1961-69, 71
Pitts, Ron (CB), UCLA 1988-90
Ploeger, Kurt (DE), Gustavus Adolphus 1986
Pointer, John (LB), Vanderbilt 1987
Pope, Bucky (WR), Catawba 1968
Powers, Sammy (G), No College 1921
Prather, Guy (LB), Grambling State 1981-85
Pregulman, Merv (G), Michigan 1946
Prescott, Harold (E), Hardin-Simmons 1946
Preston, Roell (WR/KR), Mississippi 1997
Prior, Mike (S), Illinois State 1993-97
Pritko, Steve (E), Villanova 1949-50
Prokop, Joe (P), Cal Poly-Pomona 1985
Provo, Fred (B), Washington 1948
Psaltis, Jim (DB), Southern California 1954
Purdy, Pid (B), Beloit 1926-27
Pureifory, Dave (DL), Eastern Michigan.............1972-77
Purnell, Frank (FB), Alcorn A&M........................1957

Q

Quatse, Jess (T), Pittsburgh 1933
Query, Jeff (WR), Millikin 1989-91
Quinlan, Bill (DE), Michigan State 1959-62

R

Radick, Ken (E), Marquette 1930-31
Rafferty, Vince (C), Colorado 1987
Randolph, Al (DB), Iowa 1971
Randolph, Terry (DB), American International 1977
Ranspot, Keith (E), Southern Methodist 1942
Rash, Lou (DB), Mississippi Valley State 1987
Ray, Baby (T), Vanderbilt 1938-48
Redick, Cornelius (WR), Cal State-Fullerton 1987
Regnier, Pete (B), Minnesota 1922
Reichardt, Bill (FB), Iowa 1952
Reid, Floyd (HB), Georgia 1950-56
Renner, Bill (P), Virginia Tech 1986-87
Rhodemyre, Jay (C/LB), Kentucky 1948-49, 51-52
Rice, Allen (RB), Baylor 1991
Richard, Gary (DB), Pittsburgh.........................1988
Riddick, Ray (E), Fordham 1940-42, 46
Ringo, Jim (C), Syracuse 1953-63
Risher, Alan (QB), Louisiana State 1987
Rison, Andre (WR), Michigan State 1996
Rivera, Marco (G), Penn State 1997
Roach, John (QB), Southern Methodist 1961-63
Robbins, Tootie (T), East Carolina 1992-93
Roberts, Bill (HB), Dartmouth..........................1956

Robinson, Bill (HB), Lincoln (Mo.) 1952
Robinson, Charley (G), Morgan State 1951
Robinson, Dave (LB), Penn State 1963-72
Robinson, Eugene (S), Colgate 1996-97
Robinson, Michael (CB), Hampton 1996
Robison, Tommy (G), Texas A&M 1987
Roche, Alden (DE), Southern Univ. 1971-76
Rodgers, Del (RB), Utah 1982, 84
Rohrig, Herman (B), Nebraska 1941, 46-47
Roller, Dave (DT), Kentucky 1975-78
Romine, Al (HB), Alabama 1955, 58
Rosatti, Rudy (T), Michigan 1924, 26-27
Rose, Al (E), Texas 1932-36
Rose, Bob (C), Ripon 1926
Rosenow, Gus (B), Wisconsin 1921
Roskie, Ken (B), South Carolina 1948
Ross, Dan (TE), Northeastern 1986
Rote, Tobin (QB), Rice 1950-56
Rowser, John (DB), Michigan 1967-69
Rubens, Larry (C), Montana State 1982-83
Rubley, T.J. (QB), Tulsa 1995
Rudzinski, Paul (LB), Michigan State 1978-80
Ruettgers, Ken (T), Southern California.............1985-96
Ruetz, Howard (DT), Loras 1951-53
Rule, Gordon (DB), Dartmouth 1968-69
Rush, Clive (E), Miami (Ohio) 1953
Ruzich, Steve (G), Ohio State 1952-54

S

Salem, Harvey (T), California 1992
Salsbury, Jim (G), UCLA 1957-58
Sample, Chuck (B), Toledo 1942, 45
Sampson, Howard (DB), Arkansas 1978-79
Sams, Ron (G), Pittsburgh 1983
Sandifer, Dan (DB), Louisiana State 1952-53
Sandusky, John (T), Villanova 1956
Sarafiny, Al (C), St. Edward's 1933
Satterfield, Brian (FB), North Alabama 1996
Sauer, George (B), Nebraska 1935-37
Saunders, Russ (FB), Southern California...............1931
Scales, Hurles (DB), North Texas State................1975
Schammel, Francis (G), Iowa 1937
Scherer, Bernie (E), Nebraska 1936-38
Schlinkman, Walt (FB), Texas Tech 1946-49
Schmaehl, Art (FB), No College 1921
Schmidt, George (C), Lewis 1952
Schmitt, John (C), Hofstra 1974
Schneidman, Herm (B), Iowa 1935-39
Schoemann, Roy (C), Marquette 1938
Schroeder, Bill (WR), Wisconsin-La Crosse 1994, 97
Schroll, Charles (G), Louisiana State 1951
Schuette, Carl (C/DB), Marquette 1950-51
Schuh, Jeff (LB), Minnesota 1986
Schuh, Harry (T), Memphis State 1974
Schultz, Charles (T), Minnesota 1939-41
Schwammel, Ade (T), Oregon State 1934-36, 43-44
Scott, Patrick (WR), Grambling State 1987-88
Scott, Randy (LB), Alabama 1981-86
Scribner, Bucky (P), Kansas 1983-84
Secord, Joe (C), No College 1922
Seeman, George (E), Nebraska 1940
Seibold, Champ (T), Wisconsin 1934-38, 40
Self, Clarence (B), Wisconsin 1952, 54-55
Serini, Wash (G), Kentucky 1952
Shanley, Jim (HB), Oregon 1958
Sharpe, Sterling (WR), South Carolina 1988-94
Sharper, Darren (CB/S), William & Mary 1997
Shelley, Dexter (B), Texas 1932
Shield, Joe (QB), Trinity (Conn.)......................1986
Shirey, Fred (T), Nebraska 1940
Shumate, Mark (NT), Wisconsin 1985
Sikahema, Vai (RB/KR), Brigham Young.................1991
Simmons, Davie (LB), North Carolina 1979
Simmons, John (DB), Southern Methodist 1986
Simmons, Wayne (LB), Clemson.....................1993-97

Simpkins, Ron (LB), Michigan 1988
Simpson, Nate (RB), Tennessee State 1977-79
Simpson, Travis (C), Oklahoma 1987
Sims, Joe (T/G), Nebraska 1992-95
Singletary, Reggie (T), North Carolina State 1991
Skaugstad, Daryle (NT), California 1983
Skeate, Gil (FB), Gonzaga 1927
Skibinski, Joe (G), Purdue..........................1955-56
Skinner, Gerald (T), Arkansas.....................1978
Skoglund, Bob (DE), Notre Dame 1947
Skoronski, Bob (T), Indiana...........................1956, 59-68
Sleight, Elmer (T), Purdue...........................1930-31
Smith, Barry (WR), Florida State 1973-75
Smith, Barty (RB), Richmond 1974-80
Smith, Ben (E), Alabama 1933
Smith, Blane (LB), Purdue 1977
Smith, Bruce (B), Minnesota 1945-48
Smith, Donnell (DE), Southern Univ. 1971
Smith, Earl (E), Ripon................................1922
Smith, Ed (B), New York Univ. 1937
Smith, Ed (HB), Texas Mines......................1948-49
Smith, Ernie (T), Southern California...............1935-37, 39
Smith, Jermaine (DT), Georgia 1997
Smith, Jerry (G), Wisconsin 1956
Smith, Kevin (FB), UCLA 1996
Smith, Ollie (WR), Tennessee State.............1976-77
Smith, Perry (DB), Colorado State................1973-76
Smith, Red (G), Notre Dame 1927, 29
Smith, Rex (E), Wisconsin Teachers..............1922
Smith, Warren (G), Western Michigan 1921
Smith, Wes (WR), East Texas State 1987
Snelling, Ken (B), UCLA 1945
Snider, Malcolm (T/G), Stanford 1972-74
Sorenson, Glen (G), Utah State 1943-45
Spagnola, John (TE), Yale 1989
Sparlis, Al (G), UCLA 1946
Spears, Ron (DE), San Diego State 1983
Spencer, Joe (T), Oklahoma A&M 1950-51
Spencer, Ollie (T), Kansas..........................1957-58
Spilis, John (WR), Northern Illinois................1969-71
Spinks, Jack (G), Alcorn A&M......................1955-56
Sproul, Dennis (QB), Arizona State...............1978
Stachowicz, Ray (P), Michigan State............1981-82
Staggers, Jon (WR), Missouri 1972-74
Stahlman, Dick (T), DePaul 1931-32
Stanley, Walter (WR), Mesa State 1985-88
Stansauk, Don (T), Denver 1950-51
Starch, Ken (RB), Wisconsin 1976
Staroba, Paul (WR), Michigan 1973
Starr, Bart (QB), Alabama 1956-71
Starret, Ben (B), St. Mary's (Calif.) 1942-45
Steen, Frank (E), Rice...............................1939
Steiner, Rebel (DB), Alabama 1950-51
Stenerud, Jan (K), Montana State 1980-83
Stephen, Scott (LB), Arizona State 1987-91
Stephens, John (RB), Northwestern (La.) State 1993
Stephenson, Dave (G/C), West Virginia.........1951-55
Sterling, John (RB), Central Oklahoma 1987
Stevens, Bill (QB), Texas-El Paso 1968-69
Stewart, Steve (LB), Minnesota 1979
Stills, Ken (S), Wisconsin 1985-89
Stokes, Tim (T), Oregon.............................1978-82
Stonebraker, John (E), Southern California.................1942
Strickland, Fred (LB), Purdue......................1994-95
Sturgeon, Lyle (T), North Dakota State 1937
Sullivan, Carl (DE), San Jose State 1987
Sullivan, John (DB), California 1986
Sullivan, Walter (G), Beloit 1921
Summerhays, Bob (B), Utah 1949-51
Summers, Don (TE), Boise State 1987
Sutton, Mickey (CB), Montana 1989
Svendsen, Earl (C), Minnesota 1937, 39
Svendsen, George (C/LB), Minnesota..........1935-37, 40-41
Swanke, Karl (T/C), Boston College 1980-86
Switzer, Veryl (B), Kansas State 1954-55
Sydney, Harry (FB), Kansas 1992
Symank, John (DB), Florida 1957-62

Szafaryn, Len (T), North Carolina 1950, 53-56

Tagge, Jerry (QB), Nebraska 1972-74
Tassos, Damon (G), Texas A&M 1947-49
Taugher, Claude (FB), Marquette 1922
Taylor, Aaron (G), Notre Dame 1995-97
Taylor, Cliff (RB), Memphis State 1976
Taylor, Jim (FB), Louisiana State..................1958-66
Taylor, Kitrick (WR), Washington State 1992
Taylor, Lenny (WR), Tennessee 1984
Taylor, Willie (WR), Pittsburgh.....................1978
Teague, George (S), Alabama 1993-95
Temp, Jim (DE), Wisconsin.........................1957-60
Tenner, Bob (E), Minnesota 1935
Teteak, Deral (LB/G), Wisconsin 1952-56
Thomas, Ben (DE), Auburn 1986
Thomas, Ike (DB), Bishop 1972-73
Thomas, Lavale (RB), Fresno State 1987-88
Thomason, Bobby (QB), Virginia Military 1951
Thomason, Jeff (TE), Oregon 1995-97
Thompson, Arland (G), Baylor 1981
Thompson, Aundra (WR), East Texas State............1977-81
Thompson, Clarence (B), Minnesota 1939
Thompson, Darrell (RB), Minnesota 1990-94
Thompson, John (TE), Utah State 1979-82
Thurston, Fuzzy (G), Valparaiso 1959-67
Timberlake, George (LB/G), Southern California 1955
Timmerman, Adam (G), South Dakota State 1995-97
Tinker, Gerald (WR), Kent State 1975
Tinsley, Pete (G/LB), Georgia 1938-39, 41-45
Toburen, Nelson (LB), Wichita State 1961-62
Tollefson, Chuck (G), Iowa 1944-46
Tomczak, Mike (QB), Ohio State 1991
Toner, Tom (LB), Idaho State 1973, 75-77
Tonnemaker, Clayton (LB/C), Minnesota 1950, 53-54
Torkelson, Eric (RB), Connecticut 1974-79, 81
Traylor, Keith (LB), Central Oklahoma 1993
Troup, Bill (QB), South Carolina 1980
Tuaolo, Esera (NT/DE), Oregon State..............1991-92
Tullis, Walter (WR), Delaware State 1978-79
Tunnell, Emlen (S), Iowa 1959-61
Turner, Maurice (RB), Utah State 1985
Turner, Rich (NT), Oklahoma 1981-83
Turner, Wylie (DB), Angelo State..................1979-80
Turpin, Miles (LB), California 1986
Tuttle, George (E), Minnesota 1927
Twedell, Francis (G), Minnesota 1939

Uecker, Keith (G/T), Auburn 1984-85, 87-88, 90-91
Uram, Andy (B), Minnesota 1938-43
Urban, Alex (E), South Carolina 1941, 44-45
Usher, Eddie (B), Michigan..........................1922, 24

Vairo, Dominic (E), Notre Dame 1935
Vandersea, Phil (LB/DE), Massachusetts..........1966, 68-69
Van Dyke, Bruce (G), Missouri 1974-76
Van Every, Hal (B), Minnesota.....................1940-41
Vanoy, Vernon (DT), Kansas.......................1972
Van Sickle, Clyde (C), Arkansas..................1932-33
Vant Hull, Fred (G), Minnesota 1942
Van Valkenburg, Pete (RB), Brigham Young 1974
Vataha, Randy (WR), Stanford 1977
Veingrad, Alan (T), East Texas State 1986-87, 89-90
Verba, Ross (T), Iowa................................1997
Vereen, Carl (T), Georgia Tech 1957
Vergara, George (E), Notre Dame 1925
Viaene, David (T), Minnesota-Duluth 1992
Villanucci, Vince (NT), Bowling Green 1987
Vogds, Evan (G), Wisconsin 1948-49

Voss, Lloyd (DT), Nebraska......................................1964-65
Voss, Walter (E), Detroit...1924

W

Wafer, Carl (DT), Tennessee State 1974
Wagner, Bryan (P), Cal State-Northridge...............1992-93
Wagner, Buff (B), Carroll (Wis.) 1921
Wagner, Steve (DB), Wisconsin 1976-79
Walker, Cleo (C/LB), Louisville 1970
Walker, Malcolm (C), Rice 1970
Walker, Randy (P), Northwestern (La.) State 1974
Walker, Sammy (CB), Texas Tech..............................1993
Walker, Val Joe (DB), Southern Methodist 1953-56
Wallace, Calvin (DE), West Virginia Tech 1987
Walsh, Ward (RB), Colorado 1972
Washington, Chuck (DB), Arkansas 1987
Watts, Elbert (DB), Southern California 1986
Weathers, Clarence (WR), Delaware State 1990-91
Weatherwax, Jim (DT), Cal St.-L.A. 1966-67, 69
Weaver, Gary (LB), Fresno State 1975-79
Webb, Chuck (RB), Tennessee 1991
Webber, Dutch (E), Kansas State 1928
Webster, Tim (K), Arkansas 1971
Weddington, Mike (LB), Oklahoma 1986-90
Wehba, Ray (E), Southern California 1944
Weigel, Lee (RB), Wisconsin-Eau Claire 1987
Weisgerber, Dick (B), Williamette 1938-40, 42
Weishuhn, Clayton (LB), Angelo State 1987
Wellman, Mike (C), Kansas 1979-80
Wells, Don (E), Georgia......................................1946-49
Wells, Terry (RB), Southern Mississippi. 1975
West, Ed (TE), Auburn..1984-94
West, Pat (B), Southern California 1948
Wheeler, Lyle (E), Ripon 1921-23
Whitaker, Bill (DB), Missouri 1981-82
White, Adrian (S), Florida 1992
White, Gene (DB), Georgia 1954
White, Reggie (DE), Tennessee 1993-97
Whitehurst, David (QB), Furman 1977-83
Whittenton, Jesse (DB), Texas Western 1958-64
Wicks, Bob (WR), Utah State 1974
Widby, Ron (P), Tennessee 1972-73
Widell, Doug (G), Boston College 1993
Wildung, Dick (T), Minnesota 1946-51, 53
Wilkens, Elmer (E), Indiana 1925
Wilkerson, Bruce (T), Tennessee 1996-97
Wilkins, Gabe (DE/DT), Gardner-Webb 1994-97
Willhite, Kevin (RB), Oregon 1987
Williams, A.D. (E), Pacific.......................................1959
Williams, Brian (LB), Southern California 1995-97
Williams, Clarence (DE), Prairie View A&M 1970-77
Williams, Delvin (RB), Kansas 1981
Williams, Gerald (DE), Auburn 1997
Williams, Howard (DB), Howard 1962-63
Williams, Kevin (RB), UCLA 1993
Williams, Mark (LB), Ohio State 1994

Williams, Perry (RB), Purdue 1969-73
Williams, Travis (RB/KR), Arizona State 1967-70
Williams, Tyrone (CB), Nebraska..........................1996-97
Willis, James (LB), Auburn 1993-94
Wilner, Jeff (TE), Wesleyan (Conn.) 1994-95
Wilson, Ben (FB), Southern California 1967
Wilson, Charles (WR), Memphis State 1990-91
Wilson, Faye (B), Texas A&M 1930-31
Wilson, Gene (E/DB), Southern Methodist............1947-48
Wilson, Marcus (RB), Virginia 1992-95
Wilson, Milt (G), Wisconsin Teachers........................1921
Wilson, Ray (S), New Mexico 1994
Wimberly, Abner (E), Louisiana State 1950-52
Wingle, Blake (G), UCLA...1985
Wingo, Rich (LB), Alabama 1979, 81-84
Winkler, Francis (DE), Memphis State 1968-69
Winkler, Randy (G), Tarleton State 1971
Winslow, Paul (HB), North Carolina Central 1960
Winter, Blaise (DE/NT), Syracuse 1988-90
Winters, Chet (RB), Oklahoma 1983
Winters, Frank (C/G), Western Illinois 1992-97
Winther, Wimpy (C), Mississippi 1971
Withrow, Cal (C), Kentucky 1971-73
Witte, Earl (B), Gustavus Adolphus...........................1934
Wizbicki, Alex (B), Holy Cross 1950
Wood, Bobby (T), Alabama.......................................1940
Wood, Willie (S), Southern California 1960-71
Woodin, Whitey (G), Marquette 1922-31
Woods, Jerry (S), Northern Michigan 1990
Woodside, Keith (RB), Texas A&M 1988-91
Workman, Vince (RB), Ohio State 1989-92
Wortman, Keith (G), Nebraska.............................1972-75
Wright, Randy (QB), Wisconsin............................1984-88
Wright, Steve (T), Alabama 1964-67
Wunsch, Harry (G), Notre Dame 1934

Y

Young, Billy (G), Ohio State 1929
Young, Glenn (DB), Purdue 1956
Young, Paul (C), Oklahoma 1933

Z

Zarnas, Gust (G), Ohio State 1939-40
Zatkoff, Roger (LB), Michigan 1953-56
Zeller, Joe (G), Indiana 1932
Zendejas, Max (K), Arizona 1987-88
Zeno, Lance (C), UCLA...1993
Zimmerman, Don (WR), Northeast Louisiana 1976
Zoll, Carl (G), No College....................................1921-22
Zoll, Dick (G), Indiana..1939
Zoll, Martin (G), No College 1921
Zorn, Jim (QB), Cal Poly-Pomona.............................1985
Zuidmulder, Dave (B), St. Ambrose 1929-31
Zupek, Al (E), Lawrence 1946
Zuver, Merle (C), Nebraska.....................................1930

PACKERS PRESIDENTS

Andrew B. Turnbull...1923-1927
Ray E. Evrard...1928
Dr. W.W. Kelly 1929
Lee Joannes...1930-1947
Emil R. Fischer 1948-1952
Russell W. Bogda 1953-1957
Dominic Olejniczak...April 28, 1958 to May 31, 1982
The Honorable Robert J. Parins.............................June 1, 1982 to June 5, 1989
Bob Harlan...June 5, 1989 to present

Year	Name	Pos.	School
1936	Russ Letlow	G	San Francisco
1937	Ed Jankowski	B	Wisconsin
1938	Cecil Isbell	B	Purdue
1939	Larry Buhler	B	Minnesota
1940	Hal Van Every	B	Minnesota
1941	George Paskvan	B	Wisconsin
1942	Urban Odson	T	Minnesota
1943	Dick Wildung	T	Minnesota
1944	Merv Pregulman	G	Michigan
1945	Walt Schlinkman	FB	Texas Tech
1946	John Strzykalski	B	Marquette
1947	Ernie Case	QB	UCLA
1948	Earl (Jug) Girard	B	Wisconsin
1949	Stan Heath	QB	Nevada
1950	Clayton Tonnemaker	C	Minnesota
1951	Bob Gain	T	Kentucky
1952	Babe Parilli	QB	Kentucky
1953	Al Carmichael	HB	Southern California
1954	Art Hunter	T	Notre Dame
1955	Tom Bettis	LB	Purdue
1956	Jack Losch	HB	Miami (Fla.)
1957	Paul Hornung	HB	Notre Dame
1957	Ron Kramer	E	Michigan
1958	Dan Currie	C	Michigan State
1959	Randy Duncan	QB	Iowa
1960	Tom Moore	HB	Vanderbilt
1961	Herb Adderley	DB	Michigan State
1962	Earl Gros	FB	Louisiana State
1963	Dave Robinson	DE	Penn State
1964	Lloyd Voss	T	Nebraska
1965	Donny Anderson	HB	Texas Tech
1965	Larry Elkins	WR	Baylor
1966	Jim Grabowski	FB	Illinois
1966	Gale Gillingham	T	Minnesota
1967	Bob Hyland	C/G	Boston College
1967	Don Horn	QB	San Diego State
1968	Fred Carr	LB	Texas-El Paso
1968	Bill Lueck	G	Arizona

Year	Name	Pos.	School
1969	Rich Moore	DT	Villanova
1970	Mike McCoy	DT	Notre Dame
1970	Rich McGeorge	TE	Elon
1971	John Brockington	RB	Ohio State
1972	Willie Buchanon	CB	San Diego State
1972	Jerry Tagge	QB	Nebraska
1973	Barry Smith	WR	Florida State
1974	Barty Smith	RB	Richmond
1975	None (dealt to L.A. Rams in John Hadl trade)		
1976	Mark Koncar	T	Colorado
1977	Mike Butler	DE	Kansas
1977	Ezra Johnson	DE	Morris Brown
1978	James Lofton	WR	Stanford
1978	John Anderson	LB	Michigan
1979	Eddie Lee Ivery	RB	Georgia Tech
1980	Bruce Clark	DT	Penn State
1980	George Cumby	LB	Oklahoma
1981	Rich Campbell	QB	California
1982	Ron Hallstrom	G	Iowa
1983	Tim Lewis	CB	Pittsburgh
1984	Alphonso Carreker	DE	Florida State
1985	Ken Ruettgers	T	Southern California
1986	None (dealt to San Diego in Mossy Cade trade)		
1987	Brent Fullwood	RB	Auburn
1988	Sterling Sharpe	WR	South Carolina
1989	Tony Mandarich	T	Michigan State
1990	Tony Bennett	LB	Mississippi
1990	Darrell Thompson	RB	Minnesota
1991	Vinnie Clark	CB	Ohio State
1992	Terrell Buckley	CB	Florida State
1993	Wayne Simmons	LB	Clemson
1993	George Teague	S	Alabama
1994	Aaron Taylor	G	Notre Dame
1995	Craig Newsome	CB	Arizona State
1996	John Michels	T	Southern California
1997	Ross Verba	T	Iowa
1998	Vonnie Holliday	DT	North Carolina

1936

February 8, 1936
1   RUSS LETLOW, G, San Francisco, 7
2   J.W. WHEELER, T, Oklahoma, 16
3   BERNIE SCHERER, E, Nebraska, 25
4   THERON WARD, B, Idaho, 34
5   DARRELL LESTER, C, Texas Christian, 43
6   BOB REYNOLDS, T, Stanford, 52
7   WALLY FROMHART, B, Notre Dame, 61
8   WALLY CRUICE, B, Northwestern, 70
9   J.C. WETSEL, G, Southern Methodist, 79

1937

December 12, 1936
1   ED JANKOWSKI, B, Wisconsin, 9
2   AVERELL DANIELL, T, Pittsburgh, 19
3   CHARLES (BUD) WILKINSON, T, Minnesota, 29
4   EARL SVENDSEN, C, Minnesota, 39
5   DEWITT GIBSON, T, Northwestern, 49
6   MERLE WENDT, E, Ohio State, 59
7   MARV BALDWIN, T, Texas Christian, 69
8   LES CHAPMAN, T, Tulsa, 79
9   GORDON DAHLGREN, G, Michigan State, 89
10 DAVE GAVIN, T, Holy Cross, 99

1938

December 12, 1937
1   CECIL ISBELL, B, Purdue, 7
2   MARTY SCHREYER, T, Purdue, 22
3   CHUCK SWEENEY, E, Notre Dame, 37
4   ANDY URAM, B, Minnesota, 47
5   JOHN KOVATCH, E, Northwestern, 57
6   PHIL RAGAZZO, T, Case Western Reserve, 67
7   JOHN HOWELL, B, Nebraska, 77
8   FRANK BARNHART, G, Northern Colorado, 87
9   PETE TINSLEY, G, Georgia, 97
10 TONY FALKENSTEIN, B, St. Mary's (Calif.), 107

1939

December 9, 1938
1   LARRY BUHLER, B, Minnesota, 9
2   CHARLEY BROCK, C, Nebraska, 19
3   LYNN HOVLAND, G, Wisconsin, 29
4   LARRY CRAIG, E, South Carolina, 39
5   FRANCIS TWEDELL, T, Minnesota, 49
6   PAUL KELL, T, Notre Dame, 59
7   JOHN HALL, B, Texas Christian, 69
8   VINCE GAVRE, B, Wisconsin, 79
9   CHARLEY SPRAGUE, E, Southern Methodist, 89
10 (to Brooklyn Dodgers), 99
11 DAN ELMER, C, Minnesota, 109
12 BILL BADGETT, T, Georgia, 119
13 TOM GREENFIELD, C, Arizona, 129
14 ROY BELLIN, B, Wisconsin, 139
15 JOHN YERBY, E, Oregon, 149
16 FRANK BALAZS, B, Iowa, 159
17 JACK BRENNAN, G, Michigan, 169
18 CHARLES SCHULTZ, T, Minnesota, 179
19 WILLARD HOFER, B, Notre Dame, 189
20 BILL GUNTHER, B, Santa Clara, 199

1940

December 9, 1939
1   HAL VAN EVERY, B, Minnesota, 9
2   LOU BROCK, B, Purdue, 19
3   ESCO SARKKINEN, E, Ohio State, 29
4   DICK CASSIANO, B, Pittsburgh, 39
5   MILLARD WHITE, T, Tulane, 49
6   GEORGE SEEMAN, E, Nebraska, 59
7   J.R. MANLEY, G, Northwestern, 69

8   JACK BROWN, B, Purdue, 79
9   DON GURITZ, G, Northwestern, 89
10 PHIL GASPAR, T, Southern California, 99
11 AMBROSE SCHINDLER, B, Southern
       California, 109
12 BILL KERR, E, Notre Dame, 119
13 MEL BREWER, G, Illinois, 129
14 RAY ANDRUS, B, Vanderbilt, 139
15 ARCHIE KODROS, C, Michigan, 149
16 JIM GILLETTE, B, Virginia, 159
17 AL MATUZA, C, Georgetown, 169
18 JIM REEDER, T, Illinois, 179
19 VINCE EICHLER, B, Cornell, 189
20 HENRY LUEBCKE, T, Iowa, 199

1941

December 10, 1940
1   GEORGE PASKVAN, B, Wisconsin, 7
2   (did not draft)
3   BOB PAFFRATH, B, Minnesota, 21
4   (did not draft)
5   ED FRUTIG, E, Michigan, 37
6   HERMAN ROHRIG, B, Nebraska, 46
7   BILL TELESMANIC, E, San Francisco, 57
8   BILL KUUSISTO, G, Minnesota, 66
9   TONY CANADEO, B, Gonzaga, 77
10 MIKE BYELENE, B, Purdue, 86
11 PAUL HEIMENZ, C, Northwestern, 97
12 MIKE ENICH, T, Iowa, 106
13 ED HEFFERNAN, B, Notre Dame, 117
14 DEL LYMAN, T, UCLA, 126
15 JONNY FRIEBERGER, E, Arkansas, 137
16 ERNIE PANNELL, T, Texas A&M, 146
17 BOB SAGGAU, B, Notre Dame, 157
18 HEIGE PUKEMA, B, Minnesota, 166
19 BOB HAYES, E, Toledo, 177
20 JIM STRASBAUGH, B, Ohio State, 186
21 JOE BAILEY, C, Kentucky, 194
22 BRUNO MALINOWSKI, B, Holy Cross, 200

1942

December 22, 1941
1   URBAN ODSON, T, Minnesota, 9
2   RAY FRANKOWSKI, G, Washington, 24
3   BILL GREEN, B, Iowa, 39
4   JOE KRIVONAK, G, South Carolina, 49
5   PRESTON JOHNSTON, B, Southern Methodist, 59
6   JOE ROGERS, E, Michigan, 69
7   NOAH LANGDALE, T, Alabama, 79
8   GENE FLICK, C, Minnesota, 89
9   TOM FARRIS, B, Wisconsin, 99
10 JIMMY RICHARDSON, B, Marquette, 109
11 BRUCE SMITH, B, Minnesota, 119
12 BILL APPLEGATE, G, South Carolina, 129
13 JIM TRIMBLE, T, Indiana, 139
14 TOM KINKADE, B, Ohio State, 149
15 FRED PRESTON, E, Nebraska, 159
16 BOB INGALLS, C, Michigan, 169
17 GEORGE BENSON, B, Northwestern, 179
18 HORACE (DEACON) YOUNG, B, Southern
       Methodist, 189
19 HENRY WORONICZ, E, Boston College, 194
20 WOODY ADAMS, T, Texas Christian, 199

1943

April 8, 1943
1   DICK WILDUNG, T, Minnesota, 8
2   IRV COMP, B, St. Benedict, 23
3   ROY McKAY, B, Texas, 38

ALL-TIME PACKERS DRAFTS

4   NICK SUSOEFF, E, Washington State, 48
5   KEN SNELLING, B, UCLA, 58
6   LESTER GATEWOOD, C, Baylor, 68
7   NORM VERRY, T, Southern California, 78
8   SOLON BARNETT, G, Baylor, 88
9   BOB FORTE, B, Arkansas, 98
10 VAN DAVIS, E, Georgia, 108
11 TOM BROCK, C, Notre Dame, 118
12 RALPH TATE, B, Oklahoma State, 128
13 DON CARLSON, T, Denver, 138
14 MIKE WELCH, B, Minnesota, 148
15 RON THOMAS, G, Southern California, 158
16 JIM POWERS, T, St. Mary's (Calif.), 168
17 HAROLD PRESCOTT, E, Hardin-Simmons, 178
18 EDDIE FORREST, C, Santa Clara, 188
19 LLOYD WASSERBACH, T, Wisconsin, 198
20 MARK HOSKINS, B, Wisconsin, 208
21 EARL BENNETT, G, Hardin-Simmons, 218
22 GEORGE ZELLICK, E, Oregon State, 228
23 GENE BIERHAUS, E, Minnesota, 238
24 GEORGE MAKRIS, G, Wisconsin, 258
25 PETE SUSICK, B, Washington, 258
26 BUD HASSE, E, Northwestern, 268
27 DICK THORNALLY, T, Wisconsin, 278
28 BOB RAY, B, Wisconsin, 288
29 BRUNEL CHRISTENSEN, T, California, 293
30 KEN ROSKIE, B, Southern California, 298

1944

April 19, 1944
1   MERV PREGULMAN, G, Michigan, 7
2   TOM KUZMA, B, Michigan, 22
3   BILL McPARTLAND, T, St. Mary's (Calif.), 38
4   MICKEY McCARDLE, B, Southern California, 49
5   JACK TRACY, E, Washington, 60
6   ALEX AGASE, G, Illinois, 71
7   DON WHITMORE, T, Alabama, 82
8   BOB KOCH, B, Oregon, 93
9   VIRGIL JOHNSON, E, Arkansas, 104
10 ROY GIUSTI, B, St. Mary's (Calif.), 115
11 BILL BAUGHMAN, C, Alabama, 126
12 DON GRIFFIN, B, Illinois, 137
13 BERT GISSLER, E, Nebraska, 148
14 LOU SHELTON, B, Oregon State, 159
15 CHARLEY CUSICK, G, Colgate, 170
16 HUGH COX, B, North Carolina, 181
17 KERMIT DAVIS, E, Mississippi State, 192
18 BOB JOHNSON, C, Purdue, 203
19 JIM COX, T, Stanford, 214
20 CLIFF ANDERSON, B, Minnesota, 225
21 JOHN PERRY, B, Duke, 236
22 PETE DeMARIA, G, Purdue, 247
23 LEN LISS, T, Marquette, 258
24 RAY JORDAN, B, North Carolina, 269
25 AL GRUBAUGH, T, Nebraska, 280
26 A.B. HOWARD, E, Mississippi State, 291
27 PAUL PALADINO, B, Arkansas, 302
28 BOB BUTCHOFSKY, B, Texas A&M, 313
29 RUSS DEAL, G, Indiana, 319
30 ABEL GONZALES, B, Southern Methodist, 325

1945

April 8, 1945
1   WALT SCHLINKMAN, B, Texas Tech, 11
2   CLYDE GOODNIGHT, E, Tulsa, 27
3   JOE GRAHAM, E, Florida, 43
4   DON WELLS, T, Georgia, 54
5   CASEY STEPHENSON, B, Tennessee, 65
6   TOBY COLLINS, T, Tulsa, 76

7   LAMAR DINGLER, E, Arkansas, 87
8   HAL HELSCHER, B, Louisiana State, 98
9   RALPH HAMMOND, C, Pittsburgh, 109
10 ED PODGORSKI, T, Lafayette, 120
11 BILL HACKETT, B, Ohio State, 131
12 MARV LINDSEY, B, Arkansas, 142
13 BOB McCLURE, T, Nevada, 153
14 HARRY PIEPER, C, California, 164
15 BOB KULA, B, Minnesota, 175
16 FRANK HAZARD, G, Nebraska, 186
17 ED JEFFERS, T, Oklahoma State, 197
18 BILL PRENTICE, B, Santa Clara, 208
19 WARREN FULLER, E, Fordham, 219
20 FRED NEILSEN, T, St. Mary's (Calif.), 230
21 BOB GILMORE, B, Washington, 241
22 LLOYD BAXTER, C, Southern Methodist, 252
23 NOLAN LUHN, E, Tulsa, 263
24 NESTOR BLANCO, G, Colorado Mines, 274
25 BILL CHESTNUT, B, Kansas, 285
26 JIM THOMPSON, B, Washington State, 296
27 JIM EVANS, E, Idaho, 307
28 HAMILTON NICHOLS, G, Rice, 318
29 JOHN FRIDAY, B, Ohio State, 324
30 BILLY JOE ALDRIDGE, B, Oklahoma State, 330

1946

January 14, 1946
1   JOHNNY STRZYALSKI, B, Marquette, 6
2   BOB NUSSBAUMER, B, Michigan, 16
3   ED CODY, B, Purdue, 26
4   JOHN FERRARO, T, Southern California, 36
5   ART RENNER, E, Michigan, 46
6   BERT COLE, T, Oklahoma State, 56
7   GRANT DARNELL, G, Texas A&M, 66
8   JOE McAFEE, B, Holy Cross, 76
9   STEVE CONROY, B, Holy Cross, 86
10 BILLY HILDEBRAND, E, Mississippi State, 96
11 TOM HAND, C, Iowa, 106
12 GEORGE HILLS, G, Georgia Tech, 116
13 JIM HOUGH, B, Clemson, 126
14 DEAN GAINES, T, Georgia Tech, 136
15 J.P. MILLER, G, Georgia, 146
16 BOYD MORSE, E, Arizona, 156
17 JOE BRADFORD, C, Southern California, 166
18 BILL DeROSA, B, Boston College, 176
19 RALPH GRANT, B, Bucknell, 186
20 HOWARD BROWN, G, Indiana, 196
21 ANDY KOSMAC, C, Louisiana State, 206
22 MAURICE STACY, B, Washington, 216
23 CHICK DAVIDSON, T, Cornell, 226
24 JOHN NORTON, B, Washington, 236
25 ED HOLTSINGER, B, Georgia Tech, 246
26 JOE CAMPBELL, E, Holy Cross, 256
27 FRANCIS SAUNDERS, T, Clemson, 266
28 AL SPARLIS, G, UCLA, 276
29 RALPH CLYMER, G, Purdue, 286
30 JOERVIN HENDERSON, C, Missouri, 296

1947

December 16, 1946
1   ERNIE CASE, B, UCLA, 5
2   BURR BALDWIN, E, UCLA, 19
3   PAUL (BUDDY) BURNS, Oklahoma, 30
4   GENE WILSON, E, Southern Methodist, 39
5   DICK CONNORS, B, Northwestern, 51
6   MONTE MONCRIEF, T, Texas A&M, 61
7   BOB McDOUGAL, B, Miami (Fla.), 71
8   BOB KELLY, B, Notre Dame, 80
9   TOM MOULTON, C, Oklahoma State, 91

342

10 GEORGE HILLS, G, Georgia Tech, 99
11 BOB SKOGLUND, E, Notre Dame, 80
12 JACK MITCHELL, B, Oklahoma, 121
13 DENVER CRAWFORD, T, Tennessee, 129
14 JIM CALLAHAN, E, Southern California, 140
15 TED SCALISSI, B, Ripon, 150
16 JIM GOODMAN, T, Indiana, 159
17 DICK MILLER, G, Lawrence, 171
18 BRAD ECKLUND, C, Oregon, 180
19 BOB WEST, B, Colorado, 189
20 TEX REILLY, B, Colorado, 201
21 RON SOCKOLOV, T, North Carolina, 261
22 HERB ST. JOHN, G, Georgia, 219
23 FRED REDEKER, B, Cincinnati, 231
24 HERM LUBKER, E, Colorado, 240
25 BOB PALLADINO, B, Notre Dame, 249
26 JERRELL BAXTER, T, North Carolina, 261
27 RAY SELLERS, E, Georgia, 270
28 JERRY CARLE, B, Northwestern, 279
29 BILL HOGAN, B, Kansas, 289
30 RALPH OLSEN, E, Utah, 296

1948

December 19, 1947
1   EARL (JUG) GIRARD, B, Wisconsin
2   ED SMITH, B, Texas Mines
3   WAYMAN SELLERS, E, Georgia
4   LARRY OLSONOSKI, G, Minnesota
5a DON RICHARDS, T, Arkansas
    (from Detroit Lions)
5b JAY RHODEMYRE, C, Kentucky
6   BOB CUNZ, T, Illinois
7   (to New York Giants)
8   GEORGE WALMSLEY, B, Rice
9   BOB HODGES, T, Bradley
10 BOB RENNEBOHM, E, Wisconsin
11 PERRY MOSS, B, Illinois
12 FRED PROVO, B, Texas
13 LOU AGASE, T, Illinois
14 TRAVIS RAVEN, B, Texas
15 (to Washington Redskins)
16 KEN BALGE, E, Michigan State
17 CHARLEY TATOM, T, Texas
18 FLOYD THOMAS, C, Arkansas
19 HERB ST. JOHN, G, Georgia
20 DON ANDERSON, B, Rice
21 FRED KLING, B, Missouri
22 CLYDE BIGGERS, T, Catawba
23 STAN HEATH, B, Nevada
24 AUBREY ALLEN, T, Colorado
25 STAN GORSKI, E, Northwestern
26 DON SHARP, C, Tulsa
27 JOHN PANELLI, B, Notre Dame
28 CLARENCE McGEARY, T, North Dakota State
29 MIKE MILLS, E, Brigham Young
30 RALPH EARHART, B, Texas Tech

1949

December 21, 1948
1   STAN HEATH, B, Nevada
2   DAN DWORSKY, C, Michigan
3   LOUIS FERRY, T, Villanova
4   BOB SUMMERHAYS, B, Utah
5   GLENN LEWIS, B, Texas Tech
6   JOE ETHRIDGE, T, Southern Methodist
7   (to Los Angeles Rams)
8   DAN ORLICH, E, Nevada
9   EVERETT FAUNCE, B, Minnesota
10 (to Los Angeles Rams through Detroit Lions)
11 HARRY LARCHE, T, Arkansas State

12 REBEL STEINER, E, Alabama
13 AL MASTRANGELI, C, Illinois
14 BOBBY WILLIAMS, C, Texas Tech
15 KEN COOPER, B, Vanderbilt
16 GENE REMENAR, T, West Virginia
17 PAUL DEVINE, B, Heidelberg
18 FLOYD LEWIS, G, Southern Methodist
19 BOBBY FOLSOM, E, Southern Methodist
20 LARRY COONEY, B, Penn State
21 KENNETH KRANZ, B, Milwaukee Teachers
22 JOHN KORDICK, B, Southern California
23 BILL KELLEY, E, Texas Tech
24 JIMMY FORD, B, Tulsa
25 FRANK LAMBRIGHT, G, Arkansas

1950

January 21-22, 1950
1   CLAYTON TONNEMAKER, C, Minnesota, 3
2   TOBIN ROTE, QB, Rice, 16
3   GORDY SOLTAU, E, Minnesota, 29
4   LARRY COUTRE, RB, Notre Dame, 42
5   (to Pittsburgh Steelers), 55
6   JACK CLOUD, B, William & Mary, 68
7   LEON MANLEY, T, Oklahoma, 81
8   HARRY SZULBORSKI, B, Purdue, 94
9   ROGER WILSON, E, South Carolina, 107
10 BOB MEALEY, T, Minnesota, 120
11 GENE LORENDO, E, Georgia, 133
12 ANDY PAVICH, E, Denver, 146
13 CARLTON ELLIOTT, E, Virginia, 156
14 FRED LEON, T, Nevada, 172
15 GENE HUEBNER, C, Baylor, 185
16 FRANK KUZMA, B, Minnesota, 198
17 HAL OTTERBACK, G, Wisconsin, 211
18 ARNOLD GALIFFA, QB, Army, 224
19 EARL ROWAN, T, Hardin-Simmons, 237
20 JIM HOWE, B, Kentucky, 250
21 GENE EVANS, B, Wisconsin, 263
22 CHUCK BEATTY, C, Penn State, 276
23 GEORGE MATTEY, G, Ohio State, 289
24 DON DEPLH, B, Dayton, 302
25 FRANK WATERS, B, Michigan State, 315
26 CLAUDE RADTKE, E, Lawrence, 328
27 BILL OSBOURNE, B, Nevada, 346
28 HERM HERING, B, Rutgers, 354
29 BEN ZARANKA, E, Kentucky, 367
30 RAY MALLOUF, B, Southern Methodist, 380
    (chosen off of New York Bulldogs roster)

1951

January 18-19, 1951
1   BOB GAIN, T, Kentucky, 4
2   ALBIN COLLINS, HB, Louisiana State, 15
3   FRED CONE, FB, Clemson, 26
4   (to Cleveland Browns), 40
5   WADE STINSON, HB, Kansas, 51
6   SIDMUND HOLOWENKO, T, John Carroll, 62
7   BILL SUTHERLAND, E, St. Vincent, 76
8   (to Cleveland Browns), 87
9   DICK McWILLIAMS, T, Michigan, 98
10 BOB NOPPINGER, E, Georgetown, 112
11 GEORGE ROOKS, FB, Morgan State, 123
12 CARL KREAGER, C, Michigan, 134
13 ED STEPHENS, HB, Missouri, 148
14 RAY BAUER, E, Montana, 159
15 JOE ERNST, QB, Tulane, 170
16 DICK AFFLIS, T, Nevada, 184
17 RAY PELFREY, B, Eastern Kentucky, 195
18 ED PETELA, FB, Boston College, 206
19 JIM LIBER, HB, Xavier, 220

20   DICK JOHNSON, T, Virginia, 231
21   ART EDLING, E, Minnesota, 242
22   ART FELKER, E, Marquette, 256
23   TUBBA CHAMBERLAIN, T,
        Wisconsin-Eau Claire, 267
24   DICK CHRISTIE, FB, Nebraska-Omaha, 278
25   CHARLES MONTE, HB, Hillsdale, 292
26   BILL MILLER, T, Ohio State, 303
27   BOB BOSSONS, C, Georgia Tech, 314
28   BILL AYRE, HB, Abilene Christian, 328
29   RALPH FIELER, E, Miami (Fla.), 339
30   ED WITHERS, HB, Wisconsin, 350

========= 1952 =========

January 17, 1952
1   BABE PARILLI, QB, Kentucky, 3
2   BILLY HOWTON, E, Rice, 14
3   BOBBY DILLON, DB, Texas, 27
4   (to Cleveland Browns), 38
5   DAVE HANNER, DT, Arkansas, 51
6   TOM JOHNSON, T, Michigan, 62
7   BILL REICHARDT, FB, Iowa, 75
8   MEL BECKET, C, Indiana, 86
9   DERAL TETEAK, G, Wisconsin, 99
10a BUD ROFFLER, HB, Washington State, 103
        (from Chicago Bears)
10b ART KLEINSCHMIDT, G, Tulane, 110
11   BILLY BURKHALTER, HB, Rice, 123
12   BILL WILSON, T, Texas, 134
13   BILLY HAIR, HB, Clemson, 147
14   JACK MORGAN, T, Michigan State, 158
15   BOBBY JACK FLOYD, FB, Texas Christian, 171
16   JOHNNY COATTA, QB, Wisconsin, 182
17   DON PETERSON, HB, Miami (Ohio), 219
18   HOWARD TISDALE, T, Stephen F. Austin, 206
19   JOHN PONT, HB, Miami (Ohio), 219
20   CHARLES BOERIO, C, Illinois, 230
21   HERB ZIMMERMAN, G, Texas Christian, 243
22   KARL KLUCKHORN, E, Colgate, 254
23   FRANK KAPRAL, G, Michigan State, 267
24   JOHN SCHUETZNER, E, North Carolina, 278
25   CHARLES LaPRADD, T, Florida, 291
26   CHARLES STOKES, T, Tennessee, 302
27   I.D. RUSSELL, B, Southern Methodist, 315
28   BILL BARRETT, HB, Notre Dame, 326
29   BILL STRATTON, B, Lewis, 339
30   JACK FULKERSON, T, Southern Mississippi, 350

========= 1953 =========

January 22, 1953
1   AL CARMICHAEL, HB, Southern California
2   GIL REICH, HB, Kansas
3   BILL FORESTER, DT, Southern Methodist
4   GIB DAWSON, HB, Texas
5   ROGER ZATKOFF, T, Michigan
6   BOB KENNEDY, G, Wisconsin
7   JIM RINGO, C, Syracuse
8   LAUREN HARGROVE, HB, Georgia
9   FLOYD HARRAWOOD, T, Tulsa
10 VICTOR RIMKUS, G, Holy Cross
11 JOE JOHNSON, HB, Boston College
12 DICK CURRAN, HB, Arizona State
13 BOB ORDERS, C, West Virginia
14 CHARLES WRENN, T, Texas Christian
15 GENE HELWIG, HB, Tulsa
16 JOHN HLAY, FB, Ohio State
17 BILL GEORGES, E, Texas
18 JIM PHILBEE, HB, Bradley
19 BILL LUCKY, T, Baylor

20   JOHN HARVILLE, HB, Texas Christian
21   BOB CONWAY, HB, Alabama
22   BILL TURNBEAUGH, T, Auburn
23   BILL MURRAY, E, American International
24   JIM HASLAM, T, Tennessee
25   IKE JONES, E, UCLA
26   GEORGE BOZANIC, HB, Southern California
27   JAMES McCONAUGHEY, E, Houston
28   ZACK JORDAN, HB, Colorado
29   HENRY O'BRIEN, G, Boston College
30   AL BARRY, G, Southern California

========= 1954 =========

January 28, 1954
1a   ART HUNTER, T, Notre Dame, 2
1b   VERYL SWITZER, HB, Kansas State, 3
        (from New York Giants)
2   BOB FLECK, T, Syracuse, 14
3   GEORGE TIMBERLAKE, G, Southern California, 26
4   (to Washington Redskins for Johnny Papit), 38
4   TOM ALLMAN, FB, West Virginia, 39
        (from Baltimore Colts)
5   MAX McGEE, E, Tulane, 50
6   (to Detroit Lions for Gus Cifelli), 62
7   SAM MARSHALL, T, Florida A&M, 74
8   JIMMIE WILLIAMS, T, Texas Tech, 86
9   DAVE DAVIS, E, Georgia Tech, 98
10 GENE KNUTSON, E, Michigan, 110
11 KEN HALL, E, North Texas State, 122
12 BILL OLIVER, HB, Alabama, 134
13 MIKE TAKACS, G, Ohio State, 146
14 DAVE JOHNSON, HB, Rice, 158
15 (to San Francisco 49ers for Ben Aldridge), 170
16 DESMOND KOCH, HB, Southern California, 182
17 J.D. ROBERTS, G, Oklahoma, 194
18 EMERY BARNES, E, Oregon, 206
19 KEN HALL, C, Springfield, 218
20 HERBERT LOWELL, G, Pacific, 230
21 ART LIEBSCHER, HB, Pacific, 242
22 BILL BUFORD, T, Morgan State, 254
23 CLINT SATHRUM, QB, St. Olaf, 266
24 MARVIN TENNEFOSS, E, Stanford, 278
25 JACK SMALLEY, T, Alabama, 240
26 RALPH BAIERL, T, Maryland, 302
27 HOSEA SIMS, E, Marquette, 314
28 EVAN SLONAC, FB, Michigan State, 326
29 JERRY DUFEK, T, St. Norbert, 338
30 TERRY CAMPBELL, QB, Washington State, 350

========= 1955 =========

January 27-28, 1955
1   TOM BETTIS, LB, Purdue, 4
2   JIM TEMP, DE, Wisconsin, 16
3   BUDDY LEAKE, HB, Oklahoma, 28
4   (to Cleveland Browns for Jerry Helluin), 40
5   HANK BULLOUGH, G, Michigan State, 52
6   NORM AMUNDSEN, G, Wisconsin, 64
7   BOB CLEMENS, FB, Georgia, 76
8   JOHN CROUCH, E, Texas Christian, 88
9   ED CULPEPPER, T, Alabama, 100
10 GEORGE ROGERS, T, Michigan, 136
11 RON CLARK, HB, Nebraska, 124
12 ART WALKER, T, Michigan, 136
13 ED ADAMS, FB, North Carolina, 148
14 FRED BAER, HB, Michigan, 160
15 GEORGE MACHOUKAS, C, Toledo, 172
16 CHARLIE BRACKINS, QB, Prairie View A&M, 184
17 ED BEIGHTOL, QB, Maryland, 196
18 DOYLE NIX, DB, Southern Methodist, 208

19   ROBERT CARTER, T, Grambling State, 220
20a   CARL BOLT, HB, Southern Mississippi, 232
20b   BOB ANTKOWIAK, T, Bucknell, 235
        (from New York Giants for John Bauer)
21   LAVELL ISBELL, T, Houston, 244
22   BILL BRUNNER, FB, Arkansas Tech, 256
23   ELTON SHAW, T, Louisiana State, 268
24   CHARLES BRYANT, G, Nebraska, 280
25   NATE BORDEN, E, Indiana, 292
26   JIM JENNINGS, E, Missouri, 304
27   BOB PERINGER, E, Washington State, 316
28   JACK SPEARS, T, Tennessee-Chattanooga, 328
29   SAM PINO, FB, Boston University, 340
30   BOB SALA, FB, Tulane, 352

1956

Nov. 29, 1955 (Rounds 1-3), Jan. 17, 1956 (4-30)
1   JACK LOSCH, HB, Miami (Fla.), 7
2   FORREST GREGG, T, Southern Methodist, 19
3   (to Los Angeles Rams in Tom Dahms trade), 31
4   CECIL MORRIS, G, Oklahoma, 43
5   BOB SKORONSKI, T, Indiana, 55
6   BOB BURRIS, HB, Oklahoma, 67
7   HANK GREMMINGER, E, Baylor, 79
8   RUSS DENNIS, E, Maryland, 91
9   GORDON DUVALL, FB, Southern California, 103
10   BOB LAUGHERTY, FB, Maryland, 115
11   MIKE JUDOCK, C, Miami (Fla.), 127
12   MAX BURNETT, HB, Arizona, 139
13   JAMES MENSE, C, Notre Dame, 151
14   CHARLIE THOMAS, FB, Wisconsin, 163
15   BUDDY ALLISTON, G, Mississippi, 175
16   CURTIS LYNCH, T, Alabama, 187
17   BART STARR, QB, Alabama, 199
18   STAN INTIHAR, E, Cornell, 211
19   KEN VAKEY, E, Texas Tech, 223
20   CLYDE LETBETTER, G, Baylor, 235
21   HAL O'BRIEN, FB, Southern Methodist, 247
22   JOHN POPSON, HB, Furman, 259
23   JESSE BIRCHFIELD, G, Duke, 271
24   DON WILSON, C, Rice, 283
25   FRANZ KOENEKE, E, Minnesota, 295
26   DICK GOEHE, T, Mississippi, 307
27   DICK KOLIAN, E, Wisconsin, 319
28   BOB LANCE, QB, Florida, 331
29   VESTER NEWCOMB, C, Southwest J.C., 343
30   ROD HERMES, QB, Beloit, 354

1957

Nov. 27, 1956 (Rounds 1-4), Jan. 31, 1957 (5-30)
BONUS CHOICE: PAUL HORNUNG, HB, Notre Dame
1   RON KRAMER, E, Michigan, 3
2   JOEL WELLS, HB, Clemson, 17
3   DALTON TRUAX, T, Tulane, 28
4   CARL VEREEN, T, Georgia Tech, 40
5   (to Cleveland Browns for Don King), 51
6   (to Cleveland Browns for John Sandusky), 62
6   JACK NISBY, G, Pacific, 69
        (from Chicago Cardinals for Tom Dahms)
7   FRANK GILLIAM, E, Iowa, 75
8   GEORGE BELOTTI, C, Southern California, 86
9   KEN WINEBURG, HB, Texas Christian, 99
10   GARY GUSTAFSON, G, Gustavus Adolphus, 110
11   JIM ROSEBORO, HB, Ohio State, 123
12a   ED SULLIVAN, C, Notre Dame, 134
12b   GLENN BESTOR, B, Wisconsin, 144
        (from New York Giants for Jack Spinks)
13   JIM MORSE, HB, Notre Dame, 147
14   RUDY SCHOENDORF, T, Miami (Ohio), 158

15   PAT HINTON, G, Louisiana Tech, 171
16   ED BUCKINGHAM, T, Minnesota, 182
17   DON BOUDREAUX, T, Houston, 195
18   CREDELL GRENN, HB, Washington, 206
19   ERNIE DANJEAN, G, Auburn, 219
20   PERCY OLIVER, G, Illinois, 230
21   CHARLES MEHRER, T, Missouri, 243
22   RON QUILLIAN, QB, Tulane, 254
23   JOHN SYMANK, DB, Florida, 267
24   CHARLES LEYENDECKER, T, Southern
        Methodist, 278
25   JERRY JOHNSON, T, St. Norbert, 291
26   BUDDY BASS, E, Duke, 302
27   MARTIN BOOHER, T, Wisconsin, 315
28   DAVE HERBOLD, G, Minnesota, 326
29   HOWARD DARE, RB, Maryland, 339

1958

Dec. 2, 1957 (Rounds 1-4), Jan. 28, 1958 (5-30)
1   DAN CURRIE, C, Michigan State, 2
2   JIM TAYLOR, FB, Louisiana State, 14
3a   DICK CHRISTY, HB, North Carolina State, 26
3b   RAY NITSCHKE, B, Illinois, 35
        (from New York Giants for John Martinkovic)
4   JERRY KRAMER, G, Idaho, 38
5   JOE FRANCIS, QB, Oregon State, 50
6   KEN GRAY, T, Howard Payne, 61
7   DOUG MAINSON, QB, Hillsdale, 74
8   MIKE BILL, C, Syracuse, 85
9   NORM JAROCK, HB, St. Norbert, 98
10   CARL JOHNSON, T, Illinois, 109
11   HARRY HORTON, E, Wichita, 122
12   WAYNE MILLER, E, Baylor, 133
13   GENE COOK, E, Toledo, 146
14   HARRY HAUFFE, T, South Dakota, 157
15   TOM NEWELL, HB, Drake, 170
16   ARLEY FINLEY, T, Georgia Tech, 181
17   JOE REESE, E, Arkansas Tech, 181
18   CHARLES STRID, G, Syracuse, 205
19   (to Chicago Bears for Lee Hermsen), 218
20   JOHN DUBOISE, HB, Trinity (Texas), 229
21   JERRY KERSHNER, T, Oregon, 242
22   DICK MAGGARD, HB, College of Idaho, 253
23   JACK ASHTON, G, South Carolina, 266
24   JOHN JERECK, T, Detroit, 277
25   LARRY PLENTY, HB, Boston College, 290
26   ESKER HARRIS, G, UCLA, 301
27   NEIL HABIG, C, Purdue, 314
28   DAVE CROWELL, G, Washington State, 325
29   ROBERT HAYNES, T, Sam Houston State, 338
30   JOHN PETERS, T, Houston, 349

1959

Dec. 2, 1958 (Rounds 1-4), Jan. 21, 1959 (5-30)
1   RANDY DUNCAN, QB, Iowa, 1
2   ALEX HAWKINS, HB, South Carolina, 13
3   BOYD DOWLER, E, Colorado, 25
4   (to Cleveland Browns for Len Ford), 37
5   (to Washington Redskins for J.D. Kimmel), 49
5   ANDY CVERCKO, G, Northwestern, 55
        (from Pittsburgh Steelers for Dick Christy)
6   WILLIE TAYLOR, C, Florida A&M, 61
7a   BOBBY JACKSON, HB, Alabama, 73
7b   GARY RAID, T, Williamette, 83
        (from New York Giants for Al Berry)
8a   BUDDY MAYFIELD, E, South Carolina, 85
8b   BOB LARABA, HB, Texas-El Paso, 95
        (from Cleveland Browns for Dick Deschaine)
9   GEORGE DIXON, HB, Bridgeport, 97

10 SAM TUCCIO, G/T, Southern Mississippi, 109
11 BOB WEBB, QB, St. Ambrose, 121
12 LARRY HALL, G, Missouri Valley, 133
13 JIM HURD, FB, Albion, 145
14 JIM KERR, G, Arizona State, 157
15 DICK TETEAK, G, Wisconsin, 169
16 DAN EDGINGTON, E, Florida, 181
17 TOM SECULES, HB, William & Mary, 193
18 DICK NEARENTS, T, Eastern Washington, 205
19 BILL BUTLER, HB, Chattanooga, 217
20 CHUCK SAMPLE, FB, Arkansas, 229
21 DAVE SMITH, FB, Ripon, 241
22 CHARLES ANDERSON, E, Drake, 253
23 ORVILLE LAWVER, T, Lewis and Clark, 265
24 JOE HERGERT, C, Florida, 277
25 LEROY HARDEE, HB, Florida A&M, 289
26 KEN HIGGINBOTHAM, E, Trinity (Texas), 301
27 TIM BROWN, HB, Ball State, 313
28 JERRY EPPS, G, West Texas State, 325
29 JOHN FLARA, HB, Pittsburgh, 337
30 DICK EMERICH, T, West Chester, 349

1960

date unknown
1 TOM MOORE, HB, Vanderbilt, 5
2 BOB JETER, HB, Iowa, 17
3 (to Chicago Cardinals for Lamar McHan), 29
4 (to Cleveland Browns for Henry Jordan), 41
5 DALE HACKBART, DB, Wisconsin, 51
   (from Detroit Lions for Ollie Spencer)
5 (to Cleveland Browns for Bob Freeman), 53
6 MIKE WRIGHT, T, Minnesota, 65
7 KIRK PHARES, G, South Carolina, 77
8 DON HITT, C, Oklahoma State, 89
9 FRANK BRIXIUS, T, Minnesota, 101
10 (to Chicago Cardinals for Ken Beck), 113
11 RON RAY, T, Howard Payne, 125
12 HARRY BALL, T, Boston College, 137
13 PAUL WINSLOW, HB, North Carolina Central, 149
14 JON GILLIAM, C, East Texas State, 161
15 GARNEY HENLEY, HB, Huron, 173
16 JOHN LITTLEJOHN, HB, Kansas State, 185
17 JOE GOMES, HB, South Carolina, 197
18 ROYCE WHITTINGTON, T, Southwestern
    Louisiana, 209
19 RICH BROOKS, E, Purdue, 221
20 GILMER LEWIS, T, Oklahoma, 233

1961

December 27-28, 1960
1 HERB ADDERLEY, DB, Michigan State
2 RON KOSTELNIK, T, Cincinnati
3 PHIL NUGENT, QB, Tulane
4a PAUL DUDLEY, HB, Arkansas
4b JOE LeSAGE, G, Tulane
    (from Philadelphia Eagles for Bob Freeman)
5 JACK NOVAK, G, Miami (Fla.)
6 LEE FOLKINS, DE, Washington
7 LEWIS JOHNSON, HB, Florida A&M
8 (to Cleveland Browns for Bob Jarus)
9 VESTER FLANAGAN, T, Humboldt
10a ROGER HAGBERG, FB, Minnesota
    (from Dallas Cowboys for Fred Cone)
10b BUCK McLEOD, T, Baylor
11 VAL KECKIN, QB, Southern Mississippi
12 JOHN DENVIR, T, Colorado
13 ELIJAH PITTS, HB, Philander Smith
14 NELSON TOBUREN, LB, Wichita
15 RAY LARDANI, T, Miami (Fla.)

16 CLARENCE MASON, E, Bowling Green
17 JIM BREWINGTON, T, North Carolina Central
18 ARTHUR SIMS, B, Texas A&M
19 LELAND BONDHUS, T, South Dakota State
20 RAY RATKOWSKI, HB, Notre Dame

1962

December 4, 1961
1 EARL GROS, FB, Louisiana State
2 ED BLAINE, G, Missouri
3 GARY BARNES, E, Clemson
    (from New York Giants for Joel Wells)
3 (to Cleveland Browns for John Roach)
4 RON GASSERT, DT, Virginia
5a CHUCK MORRIS, HB, Mississippi
    (from Baltimore Colts for Lamar McHan)
5b JON SCHOPF, G, Michigan
6a JOHN SUTRO, T, San Jose State
    (from Baltimore Colts for Dale Hackbart)
6b OSCAR DONAHUE, E, San Jose State
7 GARY CUTSINGER, T, Oklahoma State
8 JAMES TULIS, HB, Florida A&M
9 PETE SCHENK, DB, Washington State
10 GATE WEIDNER, QB, Colorado
11 JIM THRUSH, T, Xavier
12a JOE THORNE, HB, South Dakota State
    (from Dallas Cowboys for Steve Meilinger)
12b TOM PENNINGTON, K, Georgia
13 TOM KEPNER, T, Villanova
14 ERNEST GREEN, HB, Louisville
15 ROGER HOLDINSKY, HB, West Virginia
16 JAMES FIELD, DB, Louisiana State
17 JUNIAS BUCHANON, T, Grambling State
18 BOB JOINER, QB, Presbyterian
19 JERRY SCATTINI, DB, California
20 MIKE SNODGRASS, C, Western Michigan

1963

December 3, 1962
1 DAVE ROBINSON, DE, Penn State
2 TOM BROWN, DB, Maryland
3a DENNIS CLARIDGE, QB, Nebraska
    (from Pittsburgh Steelers for Tom Bettis)
3b TONY LISCIO, T, Tulsa
4a LIONEL ALDRIDGE, G, Utah State
    (from New York Giants for Paul Dudley)
4b CARLTON SIMONS, C, Stanford
5a JACK CVERKO, G, Northwestern
    (from Washington Redskins for Ben Davidson)
5b DAN GRIMM, T, Colorado
6a JOHN SIMMONS, E, Tulsa
    (from Dallas Cowboys)
6b JAN BARRETT, E, Fresno State
7a GARY KRONER, HB, Wisconsin
    (from Cleveland Browns for Ernie Green)
7b OLIN HILL, T, Furman
    (from Pittsburgh Steelers)
7c TODD TURNLYE, LB, Virginia
8a KEITH KINDERMAN, HB, Florida State
    (from Dallas Cowboys)
8b LOUIS RETTINO, FB, Villanova
9 BILL FREEMAN, T, Missouri Southern
10 EARL McQUISTON, G, Iowa
11 MARV FLEMING, E, Utah
12 DARYLE LAMONICA, QB, Notre Dame
13 BILL KELLUM, T, Tulane
14 ED HOLLER, LB, South Carolina
15 GENE BREEN, LB, Virginia Tech
16 COOLIDGE HUNT, FB, Texas Tech

17 THURMAN WALKER, E, Illinois
18 LOUIS HERNANDEZ, G, Texas-El Paso
19 HERMAN HAMP, Fresno State
20 BOBBY BREZINA, HB, Houston

==== 1964 ====

December 2, 1963
1   LLOYD VOSS, T, Nebraska
2   JON MORRIS, C, Holy Cross
3a ODE BURRELL, HB, Mississippi State
    (from Baltimore Colts)
3b JOE O'DONNELL, G, Michigan
    (from New York Giants in Bill Quinlan/John
    Symank trade)
3c TOMMY CRUTCHER, LB/FB, Texas Christian
4a BOB LONG, WR, Wichita
    (from Philadelphia Eagles for Ed Blaine)
4b PAUL COSTA, HB, Notre Dame
5a DUKE CARLISLE, HB, Texas
    (from Dallas Cowboys for Gary Barnes)
5b STEVE WRIGHT, T, Alabama
6   (to Dallas Cowboys for Jerry Norton)
7   DICK HERZING, T, Drake
8   KEN BOWMAN, C, Wisconsin
9   JOHN McDOWELL, T, St. John's (Minn.)
10 ALLEN JACOBS, HB, Utah
11 JACK PETERSON, T, Nebraska-Omaha
12 DWAINE BEAN, HB, North Texas State
13 JACK MAURO, T, Northern Michigan
14 TOM O'GRADY, WR, Northwestern
15 ALEX ZENKO, T, Kent State
16 ANDREW IRELAND, HB, Utah
17 LEONARD ST. JEAN, E, Northern Michigan
18 MIKE HICKS, G, Marshall
19 JOHN BAKER, E, Virginia Union
20 BILL CURRY, C, Georgia Tech

==== 1965 ====

November 28, 1964
1a DONNY ANDERSON, HB, Texas Tech
    (from Philadelphia Eagles as part of Jim
    Ringo/Earl Gros/Lee Roy Caffey trade)
1b LARRY ELKINS, WR, Baylor
2   ALPHONSE DOTSON, T, Grambling State
3   (to New York Giants)
3   ALLEN BROWN, E, Mississippi
4   WALLY MAHLE, HB, Syracuse
5a JAMES HARVEY, T, Mississippi
    (from Pittsburgh Steelers)
5b DOUG GOODWIN, FB, Maryland State
6a RICK KOEPER, T, Oregon State
    (from Pittsburgh Steelers)
6b BILL SYMONS, HB, Colorado
7a JUNIOR COFFEY, HB, Washington
7b JERRY ROBERTS, B, Baldwin-Wallace
    (from New York Giants for Turnley Todd)
7c ROGER JACOBAZZI, T, Wisconsin
    (from San Francisco 49ers)
8   MIKE SHINN, E, Kansas
9   LARRY BULAICH, HB, Texas Christian
10 RICH MARSHALL, T, Stephen F. Austin
11 JIM WEATHERWAX, T, Cal State-Los Angeles
12 GENE JETER, HB, Arkansas-Pine Bluff
13 ROY SCHMIDT, G, Long Beach State
14 JOHN PUTMAN, FB, Drake
15 CHUCK HURSTON, T, Auburn
16 PHIL VANDERSEA, FB, Massachusetts
17 STEVE CLARK, K, Oregon State
18 JEFF WHITE, E, Texas Tech

19 LEN SEARS, T, South Carolina
20 JAMES CHANDLER, HB, Benedictine

==== 1966 ====

November 27, 1965
1a JIM GRABOWSKI, FB, Illinois
    (from Detroit Lions for Ron Kramer)
1b GALE GILLINGHAM, T, Minnesota
2   TOM CICHOWSKI, T, Maryland
3a FRED HERON, T, San Jose State
3b TONY JETER, E, Nebraska
    (from Cleveland Browns)
4   JOHN RODERICK, HB, Southern Methodist
5   (to Los Angeles Rams)
6   (to Washington Redskins for Bill Anderson)
7   RAY MILLER, DE, Idaho
8   KEN McLEAN, WR, Texas A&M
9   RON RECTOR, HB, Northwestern
10 SAM MONTGOMERY, HB, Southern
11 RALPH WENEL, G, San Diego State
12 JIM MANKINS, FB, Florida State
13 ED KING, LB, Southern California
14 RON HANSON, E, North Dakota State
15 GRADY BOLTON, T, Mississippi State
16 ROBERT SCHULTZ, DE, Wisconsin-Stevens Point
17 DAVE HATHCOCK, DB, Memphis State
18 JIM JONES, DE, Nebraska-Omaha
19 DAVE NORTON, TE, Southern California
20 ED MARAS, E, South Dakota State

==== 1967 ====

March 14, 1967
1a BOB HYLAND, C/G, Boston College, 9
    (from Pittsburgh Steelers as part of Tony
    Jeter/Lloyd Voss trade)
1b DON HORN, QB, San Diego State, 25
2a DAVE DUNAWAY, WR, Duke, 41
    (from Los Angeles Rams for Tom Moore)
2b JIM FLANIGAN, LB, Pittsburgh, 51
3   JOHN ROWSER, DB, Michigan, 78
4   TRAVIS WILLIAMS, RB, Arizona State, 93
    (from Washington Redskins for Ron Rector)
4   (to St. Louis Cardinals for 3rd round pick in
    1968), 105
5a DWIGHT HOOD, DT, Baylor, 116
    (from Pittsburgh Steelers for Ron Smith)
5b DICK TATE, DB, Utah, 130
    (from Dallas Cowboys for Hank Gremminger)
5c JAY BACHMAN, C, Cincinnati, 132
6   STEW WILLIAMS, FB, Bowling Green, 158
7a BOB ZIOLKOWSKI, T, Iowa, 161
    (from New York Giants for Allen Jacobs)
7b BILL POWELL, G/LB, Missouri, 184
8   CLARENCE MILLS, DT, Trinity (Texas), 210
9   HARLAND REED, TE, Mississippi State, 236
10 BILL SHEAR, K, Cortland State, 262
11 DAVE BENNETT, QB, Springfield, 287
12 MIKE BASS, DB, Michigan, 314
13 KEITH BROWN, WR, Central Missouri, 340
14 CLAUDIS JAMES, HB, Jackson State, 366
15 JAMES SCHNEIDER, DT, Colgate, 392
16 FRED CASSIDY, HB, Miami (Fla.), 418
17 JEFF ELIAS, TE, Kansas, 444

==== 1968 ====

January 30-31, 1968
1a FRED CARR, LB, Texas-El Paso, 5
    (from New Orleans Saints for Jim Taylor)
1b BILL LUECK, G, Arizona, 26

2   (to Los Angeles Rams in Ben Wilson trade), 53
3a BILL STEVENS, QB, Texas-El Paso, 67
    (from St. Louis Cardinals for Fred Heron)
3b DICK HIMES, T, Ohio State, 81
4a BRENDAN McCARTHY, FB, Boston College, 92
    (from Pittsburgh Steelers for Dick Arndt)
4b JOHN ROBINSON, WR, Tennessee State, 108
5a STEVE DUICH, T, San Diego State, 121
    (from Pittsburgh Steelers for Kent Nix)
5b FRANCIS WINKLER, DE, Memphis State, 137
6   WALTER CHADWICK, HB, Tennessee, 164
7   ANDY BEATH, DB, Duke, 191
8   TOM OWENS, G, Missouri-Rolla, 218
9   BOB APISA, FB, Michigan State, 245
10a RICHARD CASH, T, Northeast Missouri State, 260
    (from New York Giants for Dave Hathcock)
10b RON WORTHEN, C, Arkansas State, 272
11 GORDON RULE, DB, Dartmouth, 299
12 DENNIS PORTER, DT, Northern Michigan, 325
13 FRANK GEISELMAN, WR, Rhode Island, 353
14 JOHN FARLER, WR, Colorado, 380
15 RIDLEY GIBSON, DB, Baylor, 407
16 AL GROVES, DT, St. Norbert, 434
17 KEN ROTA, HB, North Dakota State, 461

1969

January 28-29, 1969
1   RICH MOORE, DT, Villanova, 12
2   DAVE BADLEY, T, Penn State, 38
3   JOHN SPILIS, WR, Northern Illinois, 64
4   PERRY WILLIAMS, FB, Purdue, 90
5   BILL HAYHOE, T, Southern California, 116
6a RON JONES, TE, Texas-El Paso, 134
    (from Pittsburgh Steelers in Dick Capp trade)
6b KEN VINYARD, K, Texas Tech, 142
7   LARRY AGAJANIAN, DT, UCLA, 168
8   DOUG GOSNELL, DT, Utah State, 194
9   DAVE HAMPTON, RB, Wyoming, 220
10 BRUCE NELSON, T, North Dakota State, 246
11 LEON HARDEN, DB, Texas-El Paso, 272
12 TOM BUCKMAN, TE, Texas A&M, 298
13 CRAIG KOINZAN, LB, Doane, 324
14 RICH VOLTZKE, HB, Minnesota, 350
15 DAN ECKSTEIN, S, Presbyterian, 376
16 DICK HEWINS, WR, Drake, 402
17 JOHN MACK, RB, Central Missouri, 248

1970

January 27-28, 1970
1a MIKE McCOY, DT, Notre Dame, 2
    (from Chicago Bears)
1b RICH McGEORGE, TE, Elon, 16
2   AL MATTHEWS, CB, Texas A&I, 41
3   JIM CARTER, LB, Minnesota, 68
4a KEN ELLIS, WR, Southern, 93
4b SKIP BUTLER, K, Texas-Arlington, 96
    (from Baltimore Colts)
5   CECIL PRYOR, DE, Michigan, 120
6   ERVIN HUNT, DB, Fresno State, 145
7   CLEO WALKER, C, Louisville, 172
8   TIM MJOS, RB, North Dakota State, 197
9   BOB REINHARD, G, Stanford, 224
10a RUSS MELBY, DT, Weber State, 248
10b FRANK PATRICK, TE, Nebraska, 251
    (from Washington Redskins)
11 DAN HOOK, LB, Humboldt State, 276
12 FRANK FOREMAN, WR, Michigan State, 300
13 DAVE SMITH, RB, Utah, 328
14 BOB LINTS, G, Eastern Michigan, 353
15 MIKE CARTER, WR, Sacramento State, 380

16 JIM HEACOCK, S, Muskingum, 405
17 LARRY KRAUSE, RB, St. Norbert, 432

1971

January 28-29, 1971
1   JOHN BROCKINGTON, RB, Ohio State, 9
2   (to San Francisco 49ers), 37
2   VIRGIL ROBINSON, RB, Grambling State, 46
    (from Los Angeles Rams)
3   CHARLIE HALL, CB, Pittsburgh, 62
4   (to Los Angeles Rams), 90
5   (to San Diego Chargers), 115
5a DONNELL SMITH, DE, Southern, 116
    (from Washington Redskins)
5b JIM STILLWAGON, LB, Ohio State, 124
    (from Washington Redskins)
6   SCOTT HUNTER, QB, Alabama, 140
7a DAVE DAVIS, WR, Tennessee A&I, 168
7b JAMES JOHNSON, WR, Bishop, 175
    (from Oakland Raiders)
8   WIN HEADLEY, C, Wake Forest, 193
9   BARRY MAYER, RB, Minnesota, 216
10 KEVIN HUNT, T, Doane, 246
11 JOHN LANIER, RB/TE, Parsons, 271
12 GREG HENDREN, G/C, California, 296
13 JACK MARTIN, RB, Angelo State, 324
14 LeROY SPEARS, DE, Moorhead State, 348
15 LEN GARRETT, TE, New Mexico Highlands, 374
16 JACK O'DONNELL, G, Central (Okla.) State, 402
17 MONTY JOHNSON, S, Oklahoma, 427

1972

February 1-2, 1972
1a WILLIE BUCHANON, CB, San Diego State, 7
1b JERRY TAGGE, QB, Nebraska, 11
    (from San Diego Chargers)
2   CHESTER MARCOL, K, Hillsdale, 34
3   (to Minnesota Vikings), 59
4   ERIC PATTON, LB, Notre Dame, 86
5   (to New Orleans Saints), 111
6a NATE ROSS, CB, Bethune-Cookman, 138
6b DAVE PUREIFORY, LB, Eastern Michigan, 142
    (from Chicago Bears)
6c BOB HUDSON, RB, Northeastern (Okla.) St., 147
    (from Los Angeles Rams)
7   BILL BUSHONG, DT, Kentucky, 163
8   LELAND GLASS, WR, Oregon, 190
9   (to Baltimore Colts), 215
10 KEITH WORTMAN, G, Nebraska, 242
11 DAVE BAILEY, WR, Alabama, 266
12 MIKE RICH, RB, Florida, 294
13 JESSE LAKES, RB, Central Michigan, 319
14 LARRY HEFNER, LB, Clemson, 346
15 RICH THONE, WR, Arkansas Tech, 371
16 CHARLES BURRELL, DT, Arkansas AM&N, 398
17 (to San Diego Chargers), 423

1973

January 30-31, 1973
1   BARRY SMITH, WR, Florida State, 21
2   (to Dallas Cowboys in Ike Thomas/Ron Widby
    trade), 46
3   TOM MacLEOD, LB, Minnesota, 74
4   (to Los Angeles Rams in Tommy Crutcher
    trade), 99
5   (to Oakland Raiders in Carleton Oats trade), 124
6   TOM TONER, LB, Idaho State, 152
7   JOHN MULLER, G/T, Iowa, 177
8   HISE AUSTIN, DB/WR, Prairie View, 202
9   RICK BROWN, LB, South Carolina, 230

ALL-TIME PACKERS DRAFTS

10 LARRY ALLEN, S/LB, Illinois, 255
11 PHIL ENGLE, G, South Dakota State, 280
12 LARRY McCARREN, C, Illinois, 308
13 TIM ALDERSON, S, Minnesota, 333
14 JIM ANDERSON, DT, Northwestern, 358
15 REG ECHOLS, WR, UCLA, 386
16 KEITH PRETTY, TE, Western Michigan, 411
17 HAROLD SAMPSON, DT, Southern, 436

1974

January 29-30, 1974
1   BARTY SMITH, RB, Richmond, 12
2   (to Miami Dolphins in Jim Del Gaizo trade), 38
3   (to San Diego Chargers in Jim Hill trade), 54
4   (to San Francisco 49ers in Al Randolph trade), 90
5   STEVE ODOM, WR, Utah, 116
6a DON WOODS, RB, New Mexico, 134
     (from Chicago Bears)
6b KEN PAYNE, WR, Langston, 142
7   BART PURVIS, T, Maryland, 168
8a MONTE DORIS, LB, Southern California, 194
8b NED GUILLET, S, Boston College, 200
     (from New Orleans Saints)
9   HAROLD HOLTON, G, Texas-El Paso, 220
10 DOUG TROSZAK, DT, Michigan, 246
11 ERIC TORKELSON, RB, Connecticut, 272
12 RANDY WALKER, P, Northwestern (La.)
     State, 298
13 EMANUEL ARMSTRONG, LB, San Jose State, 324
14 ANDY NELOMS, DT, Kentucky State, 350
15 DAVE WANNSTEDT, T, Pittsburgh, 376
16 MARK COONEY, LB, Colorado, 402
17 RANDY WOODFIELD, WR, Portland State, 428

1975

January 28-29, 1975
1   (to Los Angeles Rams in John Hadl trade), 9
2   (from Baltimore Colts in Tom McLeod trade, later
     sent to Los Angeles Rams in John Hadl trade), 28
2   (to Miami Dolphins), 36
2   BILL BAIN, G, Southern California, 47
     (from Washington Redskins in Dave Robinson
     trade)
3   WILLARD HARRELL, RB, Pacific, 58
     (from San Diego Chargers in Bob Brown trade)
3   (to Los Angeles Rams in John Hadl trade), 61
4   STEVE LUKE, S, Ohio State, 88
5   (to Dallas Cowboys in Jack Concannon trade), 113
6   (to Los Angeles Rams in Harry Schuh trade), 140
7   TONY GIAQUINTO, WR, Central Connecticut, 165
8   (to Baltimore Colts in Ted Hendricks trade), 192
9   JAY LYNN HODGIN, RB, South Carolina, 217
10 WILLIAM COOKE, DE, Massachusetts, 244
11 BOB MARTIN, DE, Washington, 269
12 CARLOS BROWN, QB, Pacific, 296
13 BOB FUHRMAN, S, Utah State, 321
14 STAN BLACKMON, TE, North Texas State, 348
15 RANDY ALLEN, WR, Southern, 373
16 BOB McCAFFREY, C, Southern California, 400
17 TOM RAY, DB, Central Michigan, 425

1976

April 8-9, 1976
1   (to Los Angeles Rams in John Hadl trade), 8
1   MARK KONCAR, T, Colorado, 23
     (from Oakland Raiders for Ted Hendricks)
2   (to Los Angeles Rams in John Hadl trade), 39
3   (to Pittsburgh Steelers in Bruce Van Dyke
     trade), 70

3   MIKE McCOY, DB, Colorado, 72
     (from Kansas City Chiefs in MacArthur Lane
     trade)
4   TOM PERKO, LB, Pittsburgh, 101
4   (from Philadelphia Eagles, later sent to
     Houston Oilers in Lynn Dickey trade), 117
5   AUNDRA THOMPSON, RB, East Texas State, 132
6   (to Kansas City Chiefs through Houston Oilers in
     Paul Robinson trade), 166
7   (to Cincinnati Bengals in Pat Matson trade), 192
8   JIM BURROW, DB, Nebraska, 218
9   JIM GUENO, LB, Tulane, 245
10 JESSIE GREEN, WR, Tulsa, 274
11 CURTIS LEAK, WR, Johnson C. Smith, 301
12 MEL JACKSON, G, Southern California, 328
13 BRADLEY BOWMAN, DB, Southern
     Mississippi, 355
14 JOHN HENSON, RB, Cal Poly-San Luis
     Obispo, 386
15 JERRY DANDRIDGE, LB, Memphis State, 413
16 MIKE TIMMERMANS, G, Northern Iowa, 440
17 RAY HALL, TE, Cal Poly-San Luis Obispo, 467

1977

May 3-4, 1977
1a MIKE BUTLER, DE, Kansas, 9
1b EZRA JOHNSON, DE, Morris Brown, 28
     (from Oakland Raiders as compensation for Ted
     Hendricks)
2   GREG KOCH, T, Arkansas, 39
3   (to Houston Oilers), 66
3   RICK SCRIBNER, G, Idaho State, 74
     (from Denver Broncos)
4   (to Pittsburgh Steelers), 93
5   NATE SIMPSON, RB, Tennessee State, 122
6   TIM MORESCO, DB, Syracuse, 149
7a DERREL GOFOURTH, C, Oklahoma State, 172
7b RELL TIPTON, G, Baylor, 176
8   DAVID WHITEHURST, QB, Furman, 206
9   JOEL MULLINS, T, Arkansas State, 233
10 JIM CULBREATH, RB, Oklahoma, 260
11 TERRY RANDOLPH, DB, American-
     International, 290
12 (to Oakland Raiders), 317

1978

May 2-3, 1978
1a JAMES LOFTON, WR, Stanford, 6
1b JOHN ANDERSON, LB, Michigan, 26
     (from Oakland Raiders in Mike McCoy trade)
2   MIKE HUNT, LB, Minnesota, 34
3   ESTUS HOOD, DB, Illinois State, 62
4   (forfeited)
5a MIKE DOUGLASS, LB, San Diego State, 116
5b WILLIE WILDER, RB, Florida, 128
     (from Pittsburgh Steelers in Dave Pureifory
     trade)
6   LEOTIS HARRIS, G, Arkansas, 144
7   GEORGE PLASKETES, LB, Mississippi, 172
8   DENNIS SPROUL, QB, Arizona State, 172
9   KEITH MYERS, QB, Utah State, 228
10a LARRY KEY, RB, Florida State, 256
10b MARK TOTTEN, C, Florida, 259
     (from New York Giants in 1976 Joe Danelo trade)
11 TERRY JONES, DT, Alabama, 284
12 EASON RAMSON, TE, Washington State, 312

1979

May 3-4, 1979
1. EDDIE LEE IVERY, RB, Georgia Tech, 15
2. STEVE ATKINS, RB, Maryland, 44
3. CHARLES JOHNSON, DT, Maryland, 71
4. (to New York Jets in Carl Barzilauskas trade), 98
5. (to New York Jets in Carl Barzilauskas trade), 125
6. DAVIE SIMMONS, LB, North Carolina, 153
7a. HENRY MONROE, DB, Mississippi State, 180
7b. RICH WINGO, LB, Alabama, 184
   (from San Diego Chargers in Willie Buchanon trade)
8a. RON CASSIDY, WR, Utah State, 193
   (from San Francisco 49ers in Steve Knutson trade)
8b. RICK PARTRIDGE, P, Utah, 208
9. JOHN THOMPSON, TE, Utah State, 235
10. FRANK LOCKETT, WR, Nebraska, 264
11. MARK THORSON, DB, Ottawa (Kan.), 290
12. BILL MOATS, P, South Dakota, 318

1980

April 29-30, 1980
1a. BRUCE CLARK, DT, Penn State, 4
1b. GEORGE CUMBY, LB, Oklahoma, 26
   (from San Diego Chargers in 1979 Willie Buchanon trade)
2. MARK LEE, DB, Washington, 34
3. SYD KITSON, G, Wake Forest, 61
4. FRED NIXON, WR, Oklahoma, 87
5. (to Los Angeles Rams in Rick Nuzum trade), 137
6. KARL SWANKE, T/C, Boston College, 143
7. BUDDY AYDELETTE, T, Alabama, 169
8. TIM SMITH, S, Oregon State, 199
9. KELLY SAALFELD, C, Nebraska, 226
10. JAFUS WHITE, S, Texas A&I, 253
11. RICKY SKILES, LB, Louisville, 283
12. JAMES STEWART, DB, Memphis State, 310

1981

April 28-29, 1981
1. RICH CAMBELL, QB, California, 6
2. GARY LEWIS, TE, Texas-Arlington, 35
3. RAY STACHOWICZ, P, Michigan State, 62
4. RICHARD TURNER, DT, Oklahoma, 105
5. (to Los Angeles Rams in Mike Wellman trade), 132
5. BRYON BRAGGS, DT, Alabama, 117
   (from Washington Redskins)
6. (to New York Giants in Randy Dean trade), 145
7. BILL WHITAKER, DB, Missouri, 172
8. LARRY WERTS, LB, Jackson State, 200
9. TIM HUFFMAN, T, Notre Dame, 227
10. NICKIE HALL, QB, Tulane, 255
11. FORREST VALORA, LB, Oklahoma, 282
12. CLIFF LEWIS, LB, Southern Mississippi, 311

1982

April 27-28, 1982
1. RON HALLSTROM, G, Iowa, 22
2. (to San Diego Chargers in John Jefferson trade), 40
3. DEL RODGERS, RB, Utah, 71
4. ROBERT BROWN, LB, Virginia Tech, 98
5. MIKE MEADE, FB, Penn State, 126
6. CHET PARLAVECCHIO, LB, Penn State, 152
7. JOE WHITLEY, DB, Texas-El Paso, 183
8. THOMAS BOYD, LB, Alabama, 210
9. CHARLES RIGGINS, DE, Bethune-Cookman, 237

10. EDDIE GARCIA, K, Southern Methodist, 264
11. JOHN MACAULAY, C, Stanford, 294
12. PHILLIP EPPS, WR, Texas Christian, 321

1983

April 26-27, 1983
1. TIM LEWIS, CB, Pittsburgh, 11
   (from New Orleans Saints for Bruce Clark)
1. (to San Diego Chargers in John Jefferson trade), 20
2. DAVE DRECHSLER, G, North Carolina, 48
3. (to Houston Oilers in Angelo Fields trade), 58
4. MIKE MILLER, WR, Tennessee, 104
5. BRYAN THOMAS, RB, Pittsburgh, 132
6. RON SAMS, G, Pittsburgh, 160
7. JESSIE CLARK, FB, Arkansas, 188
8. CARLTON BRISCOE, DB, McNeese State, 216
9. ROBIN HAM, C, West Texas State, 243
10a. BYRON WILLIAMS, WR, Texas-Arlington, 253
   (from Houston Oilers)
10b. JIMMY THOMAS, DB, Indiana, 271
11. BUCKY SCRIBNER, P, Kansas, 299
12. JOHN HARVEY, DT, Southern California, 327

1984

May 1-2, 1984
1. ALPHONSO CARREKER, DE, Florida State, 12
2. (to New York Jets), 39
3. DONNIE HUMPHREY, DE, Auburn, 72
4. JOHN DORSEY, LB, Connecticut, 99
5. TOM FLYNN, S, Pittsburgh, 126
6. RANDY WRIGHT, QB, Wisconsin, 153
7. DARYLL JONES, DB, Georgia, 181
8. (to Denver Broncos in Greg Boyd trade), 207
9. (to Kansas City Chiefs in Charlie Getty trade), 240
10. GARY HOFFMAN, T, Santa Clara, 267
11. MARK CANNON, C, Texas-Arlington, 294
12a. LENNY TAYLOR, WR, Tennessee, 313
   (from San Diego in Derrel Gofourth trade)
12b. MARK EMANS, LB, Bowling Green, 323

1984 USFL SUPPLEMENTAL

June 5, 1984
1. BUFORD JORDAN, RB, McNeese State, 12
2. CHUCK CLANTON, DB, Auburn, 39
3. JOHN SULLIVAN, DB, California, 72

1985

April 30-May 1, 1985
1. KEN RUETTGERS, T, Southern California, 7
2. (to Buffalo Bills), 42
3. RICH MORAN, C/G, San Diego State, 71
4. WALTER STANLEY, WR, Mesa State, 98
5. BRIAN NOBLE, LB, Arizona State, 125
6. MARK LEWIS, TE, Texas A&M, 155
7a. ERIC WILSON, LB, Maryland, 171
   (from Minnesota Vikings in Jan Stenerud trade)
7b. GARY ELLERSON, RB, Wisconsin, 182
8. KEN STILLS, S, Wisconsin, 209
9. MORRIS JOHNSON, G, Alabama A&M, 239
10. RONNIE BURGESS, CB, Wake Forest, 266
11. JOE SHIELD, QB, Trinity (Conn.), 294
12. JIM MEYER, P, Arizona State, 323

1986

April 29-30, 1986
1. (to San Diego Chargers in Mossy Cade trade), 14
2. KENNETH DAVIS, RB, Texas Christian, 41
3. ROBBIE BOSCO, QB, Brigham Young, 72

4a TIM HARRIS, LB, Memphis State, 84
   (from Buffalo Bills)
4b DAN KNIGHT, T, San Diego State, 98
5 MATT KOART, DE, Southern California, 125
6 BURNELL DENT, LB, Tulane, 143
7 ED BERRY, DB, Utah State, 183
8 MICHAEL CLINE, NT, Arkansas State, 210
9 BRENT MOORE, LB, Southern California, 236
10 GARY SPANN, LB, Texas Christian, 263
11 (to Cincinnati Bengals in Mike Obravac trade), 294
12 (to Buffalo Bills in Preston Dennard trade), 331

=== 1987 ===

April 28-29, 1987
1 BRENT FULLWOOD, RB, Auburn, 4
2 JOHNNY HOLLAND, LB, Texas A&M, 41
3a DAVE CROSTON, T, Iowa, 61
3b SCOTT STEPHEN, LB, Arizona State, 69
   (from Atlanta Falcons)
3c FRANKIE NEAL, WR, Fort Hays State, 71
   (from Los Angeles Raiders in James Lofton trade)
4 LORENZO FREEMAN, DT, Pittsburgh, 89
5 (to San Diego Chargers in 1985 Mossy Cade trade), 115
6 WILLIE MARSHALL, WR, Temple, 145
7a TONY LEIKER, DT, Stanford, 172
7b BILL SMITH, P, Mississippi, 191
   (from Cleveland Browns in 1985 John Jefferson trade)
8 JEFF DROST, DT, Iowa, 198
9 GREGG HARRIS, G, Wake Forest, 228
10 DON MAJKOWSKI, QB, Virginia, 255
11 PATRICK SCOTT, WR, Grambling State, 282
12 (to Seattle Seahawks in 1986 Dan Ross trade), 312
12 NORMAN JEFFERSON, DB, Louisiana State, 335
   (from New York Giants in Phil McConkey trade)

=== 1988 ===

April 24-25, 1988
1 STERLING SHARPE, WR, South Carolina, 7
2 SHAWN PATTERSON, DE, Arizona State, 34
3 KEITH WOODSIDE, RB, Texas A&M, 61
4a ROLLIN PUTZIER, NT, Oregon, 88
   (from Los Angeles Raiders in 1987 James Lofton trade)
4b CHUCK CECIL, S, Arizona, 89
5 DARRELL REED, LB, Oklahoma, 116
6 NATE HILL, DE, Auburn, 144
7 GARY RICHARD, CB, Pittsburgh, 173
8 PATRICK COLLINS, RB, Oklahoma, 200
9 NEAL WILKINSON, TE, James Madison, 228
10 BUD KEYES, QB, Wisconsin, 256
11 (to Seattle Seahawks in 1987 Dave Brown trade), 284
12 SCOTT BOLTON, WR, Auburn, 312

=== 1989 ===

April 23-24, 1989
1 TONY MANDARICH, T, Michigan State, 2
2 (choice to Cleveland Browns in selection swap and for Herman Fontenot), 31
3a MATT BROCK, DE, Oregon, 58
3b ANTHONY DILWEG, QB, Duke, 74
   (from Cleveland Browns)
4 JEFF GRAHAM, QB, Long Beach State, 87
5 (to Cleveland Browns), 114
5a JEFF QUERY, WR, Millikin, 124

   (from Washington Redskins)
5b VINCE WORKMAN, RB, Ohio State, 127
   (from Cleveland Browns)
6 CHRIS JACKE, K, Texas-El Paso, 142
7 MARK HALL, DE, Southwestern Louisiana, 169
8a THOMAS KING, S, Southwestern Louisiana, 198
8b BRIAN SHULMAN, P, Auburn, 206
   (from Washington Redskins)
9 SCOTT KIRBY, T, Arizona State, 225
10 BEN JESSIE, CB, Southwest Texas, 254
11 CEDRIC STALLWORTH, CB, Georgia Tech, 281
12 STAN SHIVER, S, Florida State, 310

=== 1990 ===

April 22-23, 1990
1a TONY BENNETT, LB, Mississippi, 18
   (from Cleveland Browns in 1989 Draft Day trade)
1b DARRELL THOMPSON, RB, Minnesota, 19
2 LeROY BUTLER, DB, Florida State, 48
3 BOBBY HOUSTON, LB, North Carolina State, 75
4 JACKIE HARRIS, TE, Northeast Louisiana, 102
5 CHARLES WILSON, WR, Memphis State, 132
6 BRYCE PAUP, LB, Northern Iowa, 159
7 LESTER ARCHAMBEAU, DE, Stanford, 186
8 ROGER BROWN, CB, Virginia Tech, 215
9 KIRK BAUMGARTNER, QB, Wisconsin-Stevens Point, 242
10 JEROME MARTIN, S, Western Kentucky, 269
11 HARRY JACKSON, FB, St. Cloud State, 299
12 KIRK MAGGIO, P, UCLA, 325

=== 1991 ===

April 21-22, 1991
1 VINNIE CLARK, CB, Ohio State, 19
2 ESERA TUAOLO, NT, Oregon State, 35
3a DON DAVEY, DE, Wisconsin, 67
3b CHUCK WEBB, RB, Tennessee, 81
   (from San Francisco 49ers)
4 (to San Francisco 49ers), 95
5 (to San Francisco 49ers), 122
5 JEFF FITE, P, Memphis State, 135
   (from New York Jets)
6a WALTER DEAN, RB, Grambling State, 149
6b JOE GARTEN, C/G, Colorado, 164
   (from Miami Dolphins)
7a FRANK BLEVINS, LB, Oklahoma, 169
   (from Cleveland Browns for Brent Fullwood)
7b REGGIE BURNETTE, LB, Houston, 176
8 JOHNNY WALKER, WR, Texas, 203
9 DEAN WITKOWSKI, LB, North Dakota, 229
10 RAPIER PORTER, TE, Arkansas-Pine Bluff, 262
11 J.J. WIERENGA, DE, Central Michigan, 289
12 LINZY COLLINS, WR, Missouri, 316

=== 1992 ===

April 26-27, 1992
1 TERRELL BUCKLEY, CB, Florida State, 5
2 MARK D'ONOFRIO, LB, Penn State, 34
3 ROBERT BROOKS, WR, South Carolina, 62
4 EDGAR BENNETT, RB, Florida State, 103
5a DEXTER McNABB, FB, Florida, 119
5b ORLANDO McKAY, WR, Washington, 130
   (from San Francisco 49ers)
6 (to Phoenix Cardinals for Tootie Robbins), 146
6 MARK CHMURA, TE, Boston College, 157
   (from San Francisco 49ers)
7 CHRIS HOLDER, WR, Tuskegee, 190
8 (to Pittsburgh Steelers through San Francisco 49ers), 203
9a TY DETMER, QB, Brigham Young, 230

9b SHAZZON BRADLEY, NT, Tennessee, 240
    (from Los Angeles Raiders)
10 ANDREW OBERG, T, North Carolina, 257
11 GABE MOKWUAH, LB, American International, 287
12 BRETT COLLINS, LB, Washington, 314

1993

April 25-26, 1993
1a WAYNE SIMMONS, LB, Clemson, 15
1b GEORGE TEAGUE, S, Alabama, 29
    (from Dallas Cowboys)
2 (to Dallas Cowboys), 46
3 EARL DOTSON, T, Texas A&I, 81
4 (to San Diego Chargers through New England
    Patriots), 99
5a MARK BRUNELL, QB, Washington, 118
    (from Tampa Bay Buccaneers as compensation
    for Vince Workman)
5b JAMES WILLIS, LB, Auburn, 119
    (from Chicago Bears)
5 (to New York Jets), 129
6a DOUG EVANS, CB, Louisiana Tech, 141
    (from Seattle Seahawks for Dave McCloughan)
6b PAUL HUTCHINS, T, Western Michigan, 152
    (from Los Angeles Raiders)
6c TIM WATSON, S, Howard, 156
7 BOB KUBERSKI, DT, Navy, 183
8 (to Dallas Cowboys), 213

1994

April 24-25, 1994
1 AARON TAYLOR, G, Notre Dame, 16
2 (to San Francisco 49ers), 53
3 LeSHON JOHNSON, RB, Northern Illinois, 84
    (from San Francisco 49ers)
3 (to Arizona Cardinals through Miami Dolphins), 89
4 (to Los Angeles Raiders), 120
4 GABE WILKINS, DE, Gardner-Webb, 126
    (from San Francisco through Los Angeles
    Raiders)
5a TERRY MICKENS, WR, Florida A&M, 146
5b DORSEY LEVENS, RB, Georgia Tech, 149
    (from Denver Broncos through San Francisco
    49ers)
6a JAY KEARNEY, WR, West Virginia, 169
    (from Atlanta Falcons through Los Angeles
    Raiders)
6b RUFFIN HAMILTON, LB, Tulane, 175
    (from San Diego Chargers through San Francisco
    49ers)
6c BILL SCHROEDER, WR, Wisconsin-LaCrosse, 181
6d PAUL DUCKWORTH, LB, Connecticut, 190
    (from Philadelphia Eagles through San Francisco
    49ers)
7 (to Denver Broncos in 1993 Doug Widell
    trade), 212

1995

April 22-23, 1995
1 CRAIG NEWSOME, CB, Arizona State, 32
2 (to Miami Dolphins in Keith Jackson/Mark Ingram
    trades), 53
3a DARIUS HOLLAND, DT, Colorado, 65
    (from Carolina Panthers)
3b WILLIAM HENDERSON, GB, North Carolina, 66
    (from Jacksonville Jaguars in Mark Brunell trade)
3c BRIAN WILLIAMS, LB, Southern California, 73
    (from Seattle Seahawks as compensation for
    Corey Harris)

3d ANTONIO FREEMAN, WR, Virginia Tech, 90
4 JEFF MILLER, T, Mississippi, 117
5 (to Washington Redskins through Los Angeles
    Raiders), 152
5a JAY BARKER, QB, Alabama, 160
    (from Cleveland Browns)
5b TRAVIS JERVEY, RB, The Citadel, 170
    (from Jacksonville Jaguars in Mark Brunell trade)
6 CHARLIE SIMMONS, WR, Georgia Tech, 173
7 ADAM TIMMERMAN, G, South Dakota State, 230

1996

April 20-21, 1996
1 JOHN MICHELS, T, Southern California, 27
2 DERRICK MAYES, WR, Notre Dame, 56
3a MIKE FLANAGAN, C, UCLA, 90
3b TYRONE WILLIAMS, CB, Nebraska, 93
    (free agency compensatory pick)
4 CHRIS DARKINS, RB, Minnesota, 123
5 (to Arizona Cardinals through Kansas City Chiefs
    for Lindsay Knapp), 161
6 (to Philadelphia Eagles for Joe Sims), 197
6 MARCO RIVERA, G, Penn State, 208
    (free agency compensatory pick)
7a KYLE WACHHOLTZ, QB, Southern California, 240
7b KEITH McKENZIE, LB, Ball State, 252
    (free agency compensatory pick)

1997

April 19-20, 1997
1 ROSS VERBA, T, Iowa, 30
2 DARREN SHARPER, S, William & Mary, 60
3 BRETT CONWAY, K, Penn State, 90
4 JERMAINE SMITH, DT, Georgia, 126
5 ANTHONY HICKS, LB, Arkansas, 160
6 (to Oakland Raiders), 193
7a CHRIS MILLER, WR, Southern California, 213
    (from Oakland Raiders)
7b JERALD SOWELL, FB, Tulane, 231
7c RONNIE McADA, QB, Army, 240
    (free agency compensatory pick)

1998

April 18-19, 1998
1 VONNIE HOLLIDAY, DT, North Carolina, 19
2 (to Detroit Lions through Miami Dolphins), 60
3 JONATHAN BROWN, DE, Tennessee, 90
4 ROOSEVELT BLACKMON, CB, Morris Brown, 121
5 COREY BRADFORD, WR, Jackson State, 150
    (from Kansas City Chiefs for Wayne Simmons)
5 (to Oakland Raiders), 152
6a SCOTT McGARRAHAN, FS, New Mexico, 156
    (from Oakland Raiders)
6 (to Jacksonville Jaguars for Paul Frase), 182
6b MATT HASSELBECK, QB, Boston College, 187
    (free agency compensatory pick)
7 EDWIN WATSON, FB, Purdue, 218

1998 NFL SUPPLEMENTAL

July 9, 1998
2 MIKE WAHLE, T, Navy, 2

(All times local p.m.)

SUNDAY, SEPTEMBER 6 (First Weekend)
1. Arizona at Dallas 3:05
2. Atlanta at Carolina 1:01
3. Buffalo at San Diego 1:15
4. **Detroit at Green Bay 12:01**
5. Jacksonville at Chicago 12:01
6. Miami at Indianapolis...............................3:15
7. New Orleans at St. Louis 12:01
8. New York Jets at San Francisco.................1:15
9. Pittsburgh at Baltimore 1:01
10. Seattle at Philadelphia 1:01
11. Tampa Bay at Minnesota 12:01
12. Tennessee at Cincinnati 1:01
13. Washington at New York Giants................1:01
SUNDAY NIGHT
14. Oakland at Kansas City.............................7:20
MONDAY, SEPTEMBER 7
15. New England at Denver 6:20
SUNDAY, SEPTEMBER 13 (Second Weekend)
16. Arizona at Seattle 1:15
17. Baltimore at New York Jets 1:01
18. Buffalo at Miami 1:01
19. Carolina at New Orleans 12:01
20. Chicago at Pittsburgh................................1:01
21. Cincinnati at Detroit 1:01
22. Dallas at Denver 2:15
23. Kansas City at Jacksonville 1:01
24. Minnesota at St. Louis 12:01
25. New York Giants at Oakland......................1:15
26. Philadelphia at Atlanta 1:01
27. San Diego at Tennessee.........................12:01
28. **Tampa Bay at Green Bay 12:01**
SUNDAY NIGHT
29. Indianapolis at New England 8:20
MONDAY, SEPTEMBER 14
30. San Francisco at Washington...................8:20
SUNDAY, SEPTEMBER 20 (Third Weekend)
OPEN DATES: Atlanta, Carolina, New Orleans,
San Francisco
31. Baltimore at Jacksonville 4:15
32. Chicago at Tampa Bay 4:05
33. Denver at Oakland 1:15
34. Detroit at Minnesota................................12:01
35. **Green Bay at Cincinnati 1:01**
36. Indianapolis at New York Jets 1:01
37. Pittsburgh at Miami 1:01
38. St. Louis at Buffalo....................................1:01
39. San Diego at Kansas City 12:01
40. Tennessee at New England 1:01
41. Washington at Seattle 1:05
SUNDAY NIGHT
42. Philadelphia at Arizona.............................5:20
MONDAY, SEPTEMBER 21
43. Dallas at New York Giants 8:20
SUNDAY, SEPTEMBER 27 (Fourth Weekend)
OPEN DATES: Buffalo, Miami, New England,
New York Jets
44. Arizona at St. Louis 12:01
45. Atlanta at San Francisco...........................1:15
46. Denver at Washington 1:01
47. **Green Bay at Carolina 1:01**
48. Jacksonville at Tennessee 12:01
49. Kansas City at Philadelphia 1:01
50. Minnesota at Chicago................................3:15
51. New Orleans at Indianapolis...................12:01
52. New York Giants at San Diego 1:15
53. Oakland at Dallas 12:01

54. Seattle at Pittsburgh..................................4:05
SUNDAY NIGHT
55. Cincinnati at Baltimore 8:20
MONDAY, SEPTEMBER 28
56. Tampa Bay at Detroit 8:20
SUNDAY, OCTOBER 4 (Fifth Weekend)
OPEN DATES: Baltimore, Cincinnati, Jacksonville,
Pittsburgh, St. Louis, Tennessee
57. Carolina at Atlanta 1:01
58. Dallas at Washington 1:01
59. Detroit at Chicago 12:01
60. Miami at New York Jets 1:01
61. New England at New Orleans 12:01
62. New York Giants at Tampa Bay 4:15
63. Oakland at Arizona 1:05
64. Philadelphia at Denver 2:15
65. San Diego at Indianapolis 12:01
66. San Francisco at Buffalo 1:01
SUNDAY NIGHT
67. Seattle at Kansas City...............................7:20
MONDAY, OCTOBER 5
68. **Minnesota at Green Bay 7:20**
SUNDAY, OCTOBER 11 (Sixth Weekend)
OPEN DATES: Detroit, Green Bay, Minnesota,
Tampa Bay
69. Buffalo at Indianapolis 12:01
70. Carolina at Dallas 12:01
71. Chicago at Arizona 1:05
72. Denver at Seattle 1:15
73. Kansas City at New England......................1:01
74. New York Jets at St. Louis 3:15
75. Pittsburgh at Cincinnati 1:01
76. San Diego at Oakland................................1:15
77. San Francisco at New Orleans 12:01
78. Tennessee at Baltimore 1:01
79. Washington at Philadelphia 1:01
SUNDAY NIGHT
80. Atlanta at New York Giants........................8:20
MONDAY, OCTOBER 12
81. Miami at Jacksonville................................8:20
THURSDAY, OCTOBER 15 (Seventh Weekend)
OPEN DATES: Denver, Kansas City, Oakland, Seattle
82. **Green Bay at Detroit 8:20**
SUNDAY, OCTOBER 18
83. Arizona at New York Giants 1:01
84. Baltimore at Pittsburgh 1:01
85. Carolina at Tampa Bay 1:01
86. Cincinnati at Tennessee 12:01
87. Dallas at Chicago 3:15
88. Indianapolis at San Francisco 1:05
89. Jacksonville at Buffalo 1:01
90. New Orleans at Atlanta 1:01
91. Philadelphia at San Diego 1:15
92. St. Louis at Miami 4:15
93. Washington at Minnesota 12:01
MONDAY, OCTOBER 19
94. New York Jets at New England 8:20
SUNDAY, OCTOBER 25 (Eighth Weekend)
OPEN DATES: Arizona, Dallas, Indianapolis, New
York Giants, Philadelphia, Washington
95. Atlanta at New York Jets 1:01
96. **Baltimore at Green Bay 12:01**
97. Chicago at Tennessee 3:05
98. Cincinnati at Oakland 1:15
99. Jacksonville at Denver 2:15
100. Minnesota at Detroit...................................1:01

101. New England at Miami 1:01
102. San Francisco at St. Louis 12:01
103. Seattle at San Diego 1:15
104. Tampa Bay at New Orleans 12:01
SUNDAY NIGHT
105. Buffalo at Carolina 8:20
MONDAY, OCTOBER 26
106. Pittsburgh at Kansas City 7:20
SUNDAY, NOVEMBER 1 (Ninth Weekend)
OPEN DATES: Chicago, San Diego
107. Arizona at Detroit 1:01
108. Denver at Cincinnati 1:01
109. Jacksonville at Baltimore 1:01
110. Miami at Buffalo 1:01
111. Minnesota at Tampa Bay 1:01
112. New England at Indianapolis 1:01
113. New Orleans at Carolina 1:01
114. New York Giants at Washington..........1:01
115. New York Jets at Kansas City 3:05
116. St. Louis at Atlanta...................1:01
117. San Francisco at Green Bay 3:15
118. Tennessee at Pittsburgh................1:01
SUNDAY NIGHT
119. Oakland at Seattle 5:20
MONDAY, NOVEMBER 2
120. Dallas at Philadelphia.................8:20
SUNDAY, NOVEMBER 8 (Tenth Weekend)
121. Atlanta at New England 1:01
122. Buffalo at New York Jets 4:15
123. Carolina at San Francisco 1:05
124. Cincinnati at Jacksonville 1:01
125. Detroit at Philadelphia 1:01
126. Indianapolis at Miami..................1:01
127. Kansas City at Seattle.................1:15
128. New Orleans at Minnesota 12:01
129. New York Giants at Dallas 12:01
130. Oakland at Baltimore 1:01
131. St. Louis at Chicago 12:01
132. San Diego at Denver 2:15
133. Washington at Arizona 2:05
SUNDAY NIGHT
134. Tennessee at Tampa Bay 8:20
MONDAY, NOVEMBER 9
135. Green Bay at Pittsburgh 8:20
SUNDAY, NOVEMBER 15 (Eleventh Weekend)
136. Baltimore at San Diego 1:05
137. Cincinnati at Minnesota 12:01
138. Dallas at Arizona 2:15
139. Green Bay at New York Giants 4:15
140. Miami at Carolina 1:01
141. New England at Buffalo 1:01
142. New York Jets at Indianapolis 1:01
143. Philadelphia at Washington 1:01
144. Pittsburgh at Tennessee................12:01
145. St. Louis at New Orleans 12:01
146. San Francisco at Atlanta...............1:01
147. Seattle at Oakland 1:05
148. Tampa Bay at Jacksonville 4:15
SUNDAY NIGHT
149. Chicago at Detroit 8:20
MONDAY, NOVEMBER 16
150. Denver at Kansas City 7:20
SUNDAY, NOVEMBER 22 (Twelfth Weekend)
151. Arizona at Washington 1:01
152. Baltimore at Cincinnati 4:15
153. Carolina at St. Louis 3:05
154. Chicago at Atlanta 1:01
155. Detroit at Tampa Bay 1:01

156. Green Bay at Minnesota 12:01
157. Indianapolis at Buffalo 1:01
158. Jacksonville at Pittsburgh 1:01
159. Kansas City at San Diego 1:15
160. New York Jets at Tennessee 3:15
161. Oakland at Denver 2:15
162. Philadelphia at New York Giants 1:01
163. Seattle at Dallas 12:01
SUNDAY NIGHT
164. New Orleans at San Francisco 5:20
MONDAY, NOVEMBER 23
165. Miami at New England 8:20
THURSDAY, NOVEMBER 26 (Thirteenth Weekend)
166. Minnesota at Dallas 3:05
167. Pittsburgh at Detroit..................12:35
SUNDAY, NOVEMBER 29
168. Arizona at Kansas City 12:01
169. Atlanta at St. Louis 12:01
170. Buffalo at New England 4:05
171. Carolina at New York Jets 1:01
172. Indianapolis at Baltimore 1:01
173. Jacksonville at Cincinnati 1:01
174. New Orleans at Miami 1:01
175. Philadelphia at Green Bay 3:15
176. Tampa Bay at Chicago 12:01
177. Tennessee at Seattle 1:05
178. Washington at Oakland 1:15
SUNDAY NIGHT
179. Denver at San Diego 5:20
MONDAY, NOVEMBER 30
180. New York Giants at San Francisco 5:20
THURSDAY, DECEMBER 3 (Fourteenth Weekend)
181. St. Louis at Philadelphia..............8:20
SUNDAY, DECEMBER 6
182. Baltimore at Tennessee 3:15
183. Buffalo at Cincinnati 1:01
184. Dallas at New Orleans 12:01
185. Detroit at Jacksonville 1:01
186. Indianapolis at Atlanta 1:01
187. Kansas City at Denver 2:15
188. Miami at Oakland 1:15
189. New England at Pittsburgh..............1:01
190. New York Giants at Arizona 2:05
191. San Diego at Washington................1:01
192. San Francisco at Carolina 1:01
193. Seattle at New York Jets 1:01
SUNDAY NIGHT
194. Chicago at Minnesota...................7:20
MONDAY, DECEMBER 7
195. Green Bay at Tampa Bay 8:20
SUNDAY, DECEMBER 13 (Fifteenth Weekend)
196. Arizona at Philadelphia................1:01
197. Atlanta at New Orleans 12:01
198. Chicago at Green Bay 12:01
199. Cincinnati at Indianapolis 1:01
200. Dallas at Kansas City 3:15
201. Denver at New York Giants 1:01
202. Minnesota at Baltimore 4:15
203. New England at St. Louis 12:01
204. Oakland at Buffalo 1:01
205. Pittsburgh at Tampa Bay 1:01
206. San Diego at Seattle 1:05
207. Tennessee at Jacksonville 1:01
208. Washington at Carolina 1:01
SUNDAY NIGHT
209. New York Jets at Miami 8:20
MONDAY, DECEMBER 14
210. Detroit at San Francisco 5:20

1998 NFL SCHEDULE

SATURDAY, DECEMBER 19 (Sixteenth Weekend)
211. New York Jets at Buffalo 12:35
212. Tampa Bay at Washington 4:05
SUNDAY, DECEMBER 20
213. Atlanta at Detroit 1:01
214. Baltimore at Chicago 12:01
215. Cincinnati at Pittsburgh 1:01
216. Indianapolis at Seattle 1:05
217. Kansas City at New York Giants 1:01
218. New Orleans at Arizona 2:15
219. Oakland at San Diego...............................1:05
220. Philadelphia at Dallas..............................3:15
221. St. Louis at Carolina.................................1:01
222. San Francisco at New England.................1:01
223. Tennessee at Green Bay 12:01
SUNDAY NIGHT
224. Jacksonville at Minnesota 7:20
MONDAY, DECEMBER 21
225. Denver at Miami.......................................8:20

SATURDAY, DECEMBER 26 (Seventeenth Weekend)
226. Kansas City at Oakland.............................1:05
227. Minnesota at Tennessee.................11:35 a.m.
SUNDAY, DECEMBER 27
228. Buffalo at New Orleans..........................12:01
229. Carolina at Indianapolis 1:01
230. Detroit at Baltimore 1:01
231. Green Bay at Chicago 12:01
232. Miami at Atlanta 1:01
233. New England at New York Jets 1:01
234. New York Giants at Philadelphia 4:05
235. St. Louis at San Francisco 1:05
236. San Diego at Arizona 2:15
237. Seattle at Denver 2:15
238. Tampa Bay at Cincinnati...........................1:01
SUNDAY NIGHT
239. Washington at Dallas 7:20
MONDAY, DECEMBER 28
240. Pittsburgh at Jacksonville 8:20

NATIONALLY TELEVISED GAMES

(Night, Thanksgiving and Saturday games plus playoffs carried on CBS Radio Network)

REGULAR SEASON

Sunday, Sept. 6	New York Jets at San Francisco (day, CBS)
	Oakland at Kansas City (night, ESPN)
Monday, Sept. 7	New England at Denver (night, ABC)
Sunday, Sept. 13	Dallas at Denver (day, FOX)
	Indianapolis at New England (night, ESPN)
Monday, Sept. 14	San Francisco at Washington (night, ABC)
Sunday, Sept. 20	Denver at Oakland (day, CBS)
	Philadelphia at Arizona (night, ESPN)
Monday, Sept. 21	Dallas at New York Giants (night, ABC)
Sunday, Sept. 27	Minnesota at Chicago (day, FOX)
	Cincinnati at Baltimore (night, ESPN)
Monday, Sept. 28	Tampa Bay at Detroit (night, ABC)
Sunday, Oct. 4	Philadelphia at Denver (day, FOX)
	Seattle at Kansas City (night, ESPN)
Monday, Oct. 5	**Minnesota at Green Bay (night, ABC)**
Sunday, Oct. 11	Denver at Seattle (day, CBS)
	Atlanta at New York Giants (night, ESPN)
Monday, Oct. 12	Miami at Jacksonville (night, ABC)
Thursday, Oct. 15	**Green Bay at Detroit (night, ESPN)**
Sunday, Oct. 18	Dallas at Chicago (day, FOX)
Monday, Oct. 19	New York Jets at New England (night, ABC)
Sunday, Oct. 25	Jacksonville at Denver (day, CBS)
	Buffalo at Carolina (night, ESPN)
Monday, Oct. 26	Pittsburgh at Kansas City (night, ABC)
Sunday, Nov. 1	**San Francisco at Green Bay (day, FOX)**
	Oakland at Seattle (night, ESPN)
Monday, Nov. 2	Dallas at Philadelphia (night, ABC)
Sunday, Nov. 8	San Diego at Denver (day, CBS)
	Tennessee at Tampa Bay (night, ESPN)
Monday, Nov. 9	**Green Bay at Pittsburgh (night, ABC)**
Sunday, Nov. 15	**Green Bay at New York Giants (day, FOX)**
	Chicago at Detroit (night, ESPN)
Monday, Nov. 16	Denver at Kansas City (night, ABC)
Sunday, Nov. 22	Oakland at Denver (day, CBS)
	New Orleans at San Francisco (night, ESPN)
Monday, Nov. 23	Miami at New England (night, ABC)
Thursday, Nov. 26	Pittsburgh at Detroit (day, CBS)
	Minnesota at Dallas (day, FOX)

Sunday, Nov. 29	**Philadelphia at Green Bay (day, FOX)**
	Denver at San Diego (night, ESPN)
Monday, Nov. 30	New York Giants at San Francisco (night, ABC)
Thursday, Dec. 3	St. Louis at Philadelphia (night, ESPN)
Sunday, Dec. 6	Kansas City at Denver (day, CBS)
	Chicago at Minnesota (night, ESPN)
Monday, Dec. 7	**Green Bay at Tampa Bay (night, ABC)**
Sunday, Dec. 13	Dallas at Kansas City (day, FOX)
	New York Jets at Miami (night, ESPN)
Monday, Dec. 14	Detroit at San Francisco (night, ABC)
Saturday, Dec. 19	New York Jets at Buffalo (day, CBS)
	Tampa Bay at Washington (day, FOX)
Sunday, Dec. 20	Philadelphia at Dallas (day, FOX)
	Jacksonville at Minnesota (night, ESPN)
Monday, Dec. 21	Denver at Miami (night, ABC)
Saturday, Dec. 26	Minnesota at Tennessee (day, FOX)
	Kansas City at Oakland (day, CBS)
Sunday, Dec. 27	Seattle at Denver (day, CBS)
	Washington at Dallas (night, ESPN)
Monday, Dec. 28	Pittsburgh at Jacksonville (night, ABC)

POSTSEASON

Saturday, Jan. 2	AFC and NFC Wild Card Playoffs (ABC)
Sunday, Jan. 3	AFC and NFC Wild Card Playoffs (CBS and FOX)
Saturday, Jan. 9	AFC and NFC Divisional Playoffs (CBS and FOX)
Sunday, Jan. 10	AFC and NFC Divisional Playoffs (CBS and FOX)
Sunday, Jan. 17	AFC and NFC Championship Games (CBS and FOX)
Sunday, Jan. 31	Super Bowl XXXIII at Pro Player Stadium; Miami, Florida (FOX)
Sunday, Feb. 7	AFC-NFC Pro Bowl at Aloha Stadium; Honolulu, Hawaii (ABC)

PACKERS LOST IN PAST EXPANSION DRAFTS

1960..........DE Nate Borden, B Bill Butler, HB Don McIlhenny (all to Dallas)
1961..........DT Ken Beck, DB Dick Pesonen, RB Paul Winslow (all to Minnesota)
1966..........QB Dennis Claridge, RB Junior Coffey, G Dan Grimm (all to Atlanta)
1967..........C Bill Curry, B Paul Hornung, LB/DE Phil Vandersea (all to New Orleans)
1976..........LB Ken Hutcherson (to Seattle), DB Al Matthews (to Seattle), WR Barry Smith (to Tampa Bay)
1995..........RB Reggie Cobb, LB Mark Williams, RB Marcus Wilson (all to Jacksonville)

IMPORTANT NFL DATES

1998

July 7	Claiming period of 24 hours begins in waiver system. All waiver requests are no-recall and no-withdrawal
July 8	Annual Packer Stockholders Meeting; Lambeau Field, Green Bay
Mid-July	Training camps open. Clubs not permitted to open official preseason camp earlier than July 5. Veteran players cannot be required to report earlier than 15 days prior to club's first preseason game or July 15, whichever is later. The July 15 date is not applicable to clubs playing five preseason games. Except for quarterbacks and "injured" players, veterans cannot participate in any organized football activity for 10 days prior to mandatory reporting date. Bonus exemptions for NFL Europe League players must be designated by the start of training camp
July 15	Signing period ends at 3 p.m. CDT for Unrestricted Free Agents to whom June 1 tender was made by Old Club, and for Transition Players and Franchise Players who are subject to the rules for Transition Players. After this date and through 3 p.m. CST on Nov. 10, Old Club has exclusive negotiating rights with its Unrestricted Free Agents
July 15	On or after this date, a club that extends a player contract for its Franchise Player shall not be deemed to have utilized its Franchise Player designation for the period of the extension
August 1	Hall of Fame Game; Canton, Ohio: Pittsburgh vs. Tampa Bay
August 6-10	First full Preseason weekend
August 7	Drafted Rookies who have not signed with their club by this date may not be traded to any other club in 1998
August 7	Deadline for players under contract to report in order to earn a season of free agency credit
August 8-12	Deadline for club to provide written notice to certain unsigned players and the NFLPA of its intent to place them on the Exempt List if they fail to report no later than one day prior to the club's second preseason game. Any player who fails to report prior to the deadline will be ineligible to play or receive compensation for at least three games (preseason or regular season) from the time that he reports
August 25	Roster cutdown to maximum of 60 players on Active List by 3 p.m. CDT. Exemptions granted to certain NFL Europe League players expire at this time
August 30	Roster cutdown to maximum of 53 players on Active/Inactive List by 3 p.m. CDT. Remainder of NFL Europe League exemptions expire. Clubs may dress a minimum of 42 and maximum of 45 players and a Third Quarterback for each regular-season and postseason game
August 30	Simultaneously with the cutdown to 53, clubs that have players in the categories of Active/Physically Unable to Perform or Active/Non-Football Injury or Illness must take one of the following options: place player on Reserve/Physically Unable to Perform or Reserve/Non-Football Injury or Illness, whichever is applicable; ask waivers; terminate; trade; or continue to count him on Active List
August 31	After 3 p.m. CDT, clubs may establish a Practice Squad of five players by signing free agents who do not have an accrued season of free-agency credit or who were on the Active/Inactive List for less than nine regular-season games during their only Accrued Season(s). A player cannot participate on the Practice Squad for more than two seasons
September 4	All clubs are required to identify their 49-player Active List by 6 p.m. CDT on this Friday and thereafter on each Friday before a regular-season Sunday game. No later than one hour and 30 minutes prior to kickoff, clubs must identify their 45-player Active List and Third Quarterback, if any
September 5	Team Salary includes all players receiving compensation under their 1998 contracts. Top 51 rule is no longer in effect
September 6-7	Regular Season opens
September 7-8	Beginning on these dates, vested veterans terminated from the Active List or Inactive List (and from Reserve/Injured if the player was placed on Reserve/Injured after the beginning of the regular season) are entitled to receive, after the end of the regular-season schedule, Termination Pay pursuant to the terms of the 1993 CBA
September 22	Priority on multiple waiver claims is now based on the current season's standing
October 13	Beginning the day after the conclusion of the sixth regular-season weekend and continuing through the day after the conclusion of the ninth regular-season weekend, clubs are permitted to begin practicing players on Reserve/Physically Unable to Perform and Reserve/Non-Football Injury or Illness for a period not to exceed 21 days. Players may be activated during the 21-day practice period or until 3 p.m. CDT on the day after the conclusion of the 21-day period

October 13	All trading ends at 3 p.m. CDT
October 14	Players with at least four previous pension-credited seasons are subject to the waiver system for the remainder of the regular season and postseason
November 2	Deadline for 1998 for an increase in a player's Salary to be counted as Salary for the current year. Any increase in a player's 1998 Salary negotiated after this date will be treated as a Signing Bonus
November 10	Deadline (3 p.m. CST) for clubs to sign their Franchise and Transition players. If still unsigned after this date, such players are prohibited from playing in the NFL in 1998
November 10	Deadline (3 p.m. CST) for clubs to sign their Unrestricted and Restricted Free Agents to whom June 1 tender was made. If still unsigned after this date, such players are prohibited from playing in the NFL in 1998
November 10	Deadline (3 p.m. CST) for clubs to sign Drafted players. If such players remain unsigned, they are prohibited from playing in the NFL in 1998
November 28	Deadline for reinstatement of players in Reserve List categories of Retired, Did Not Report, and Exclusive Rights, and of players who were placed on Reserve/Left Squad in a previous season
December 25	Deadline for waiver requests in 1998, except for "special waiver requests" which have a 10-day claiming period, with termination or assignment delayed until after the Super Bowl
December 29	Clubs may begin signing free agent players for the 1999 season

1999

January 2-3	AFC and NFC Wild Card Playoff Games
January 9-10	AFC and NFC Divisional Playoff Games
January 17	AFC and NFC Championship Games
*January 28	First day clubs can designate Franchise or Transition players
January 31	Super Bowl XXXIII at Pro Player Stadium; Miami, Fla.
February 7	AFC-NFC Pro Bowl at Aloha Stadium; Honolulu, Hawaii
February 8	Waiver system begins for 1999. Players with at least four previous pension-credited seasons that a club desires to terminate are not subject to the waiver system until after the trading deadline
*February 11	Deadline (3 p.m. CST) for clubs to designate Franchise and Transition Players
*February 11	Expiration date of all player contracts due to expire in 1999
*February 11	Deadline for exercising options for 1999 on all players who have option clauses in their 1998 contracts
*February 11	Deadline for submission of Qualifying Offers by clubs to their Restricted Free Agents whose contracts have expired and to whom they desire to retain a Right of First Refusal/Compensation
*February 11	Deadline for clubs to submit offer of minimum salary to retain exclusive negotiating rights to their players with fewer than three seasons of free agency credit whose contracts have expired
*February 12	Free Agency period begins
*February 12	Trading period begins for 1999 after expiration of all 1998 contracts. A claiming period of three business days is in effect for waiver requests made prior to May 1
February 18-22	NFL Combine Timing and Testing at RCA Dome; Indianapolis, Ind.
March 14-18	NFL Annual Meeting; Phoenix, Ariz.
*April 12	Deadline for signing of Offer Sheets by Restricted Free Agents
*April 16	Deadline for Old Club to exercise Right of First Refusal to Restricted Free Agents
*April 17-18	64th Annual NFL Draft; New York, N.Y.
May 1	Claiming period of 10 days begins in waiver system
June 1	Deadline for Old Club to send tender to its unsigned Restricted Free Agents or to extend Qualifying Offer, whichever is greater, in order to retain rights
June 1	Deadline for Old Club to send tender to its unsigned Unrestricted Free Agents to retain rights if player is not signed by another club by July 15
June 15	Deadline for club to withdraw Qualifying Offer to Restricted Free Agents and still retain exclusive negotiating rights by substituting tender of one-year contract at 110 percent of previous year's Paragraph 5 salary (with all other terms carried forward unchanged)
July 7	Annual Packer Stockholders Meeting; Lambeau Field, Green Bay

FUTURE SUPER BOWL DATES AND SITES

*January 30, 2000	Super Bowl XXXIV; Georgia Dome; Atlanta, Ga.
*January 28, 2001	Super Bowl XXXV; Raymond James Stadium; Tampa, Fla.

*tentative date

PACKER RADIO NETWORK

Known across the NFL as simply "Jim and Max," Jim Irwin and Max McGee pair up for their 20th and final season together on the Packer Radio Network. The duo, who this past June jointly announced their intention to retire following the 1998 season, have brought the color and excitement of Green Bay Packers football to fans throughout Wisconsin and Upper Michigan in both good times and bad for two decades.

Larry McCarren, who joined Irwin and McGee on the broadcasts in 1995, enters his fourth season as the third man in the booth. It is anticipated that he will remain as an analyst in 1999, teaming with a new play-by-play announcer.

Irwin, in his 30th year as a member of the Packers' broadcast team, has been hailed as one of the most knowledgeable and authoritative play-by-play announcers in the country. He began as a color analyst on the broadcasts in 1969, serving in that role for six seasons, before assuming the play-by-play duties in 1975. Recipient of Wisconsin 'Sportscaster of the Year' recognition an unparalleled 10 times (1975-76, 1978, 1980, 1983-86 and 1988-89), Irwin, 64, also has been inducted into the Wisconsin Broadcasters Association Hall of Fame (1994) and has been awarded the 'Red Smith Award' for his contributions to state sports (1995). A native of Linn Creek, Mo., a small town in the Lake of the Ozarks region, Irwin is a 1964 graduate of the University of Missouri. His past credits include play-by-play on radio broadcasts of the Milwaukee Bucks (1979-93) and University of Wisconsin football (1969-90) and basketball.

Also sports director at WTMJ Radio, Irwin will retire from that role as well in July of 1999.

McGee, fifth all-time among Green Bay receivers and a member of the Packer Hall of Fame, provides equal amounts of colorful tales and his own unique brand of analysis. More well known for his work in the radio booth than he ever was as a player, the 66-year-old McGee is candid, droll and irreverent, applying his comments impartially whether addressing friend or foe. A native Texan, he caught 345 passes during a 12-year playing career (1954, 1957-67) with the Packers, earning selection to the Pro Bowl in 1961, then was a highly successful restaurateur/entrepreneur after retiring from the game.

McCarren, also a Packer Hall of Fame inductee, is a favorite among television viewers in northeast Wisconsin. Sports director at WFRV-TV in Green Bay, he additionally serves as host of weekly Packers-related programming during the season. He twice has been voted Wisconsin 'Sportscaster of the Year' (1995-96) by the National Sportscasters and Sportswriters Association. An iron man at center for the Packers for 12 seasons (1973-84), McCarren played in 162 consecutive games — tied for the second-longest streak in team history — and went to the Pro Bowl in 1982 and '83.

Jim Palm, long-time stats man in the booth with Irwin and McGee, also will call it quits following this season.

WTMJ Radio, which has been broadcasting the team's games since November of 1929, continues its long-standing role as the flagship station of the Packer Radio Network. That designation is set to continue beyond the turn of the century as the two parties announced a long-term extension to their radio broadcast rights agreement early in 1995.

The Packer Radio Network is made up of 70 stations in 53 markets and seven states. A complete listing of network affiliates can be found on the ensuing page.

From left, Jim Irwin, Larry McCarren and Max McGee team up to bring the color and excitement of Green Bay Packers football to listeners along the wide-ranging Packer Radio Network. The 1998 season will be a farewell tour for Irwin and McGee as the two have announced that they will retire after this year.

WISCONSIN AND UPPER MICHIGAN STATIONS

MARKET	CALL LETTERS & FREQUENCY
Antigo	WRLO 105.3 FM
Appleton	WHBY 1150 AM
Ashland	WATW 1400 AM / WBSZ 93.3 FM
Beloit	WGEZ 1490 AM
Clintonville	WFCL 1380 AM / WJMQ 92.3 FM
Duluth (Minn.)	WDSM 710 AM
Eau Claire	WBIZ 1400 AM / WBIZ 100.7 FM
Escanaba (Mich.)	WDBC 680 AM
Fond du Lac	KFIZ 1450 AM / KFIZ 107.1 FM
Fort Atkinson	WFAW 940 AM
Green Bay	WNFL 1440 AM
Hancock (Mich.)	WZRK 93.5 FM
Hayward	WRLS 92.1 FM
Iron Mountain (Mich.)	WJNR 101.5 FM
Ironwood (Mich.)	WJMS 590 AM / WIMI 99.7 FM
Ishpeming (Mich.)	WIAN 1240 AM / WJPD 92.3 FM
Janesville	WCLO 1230 AM
La Crosse	WKTY 580 AM
Lancaster	WGLR 1280 AM
Madison	WIBA 1310 AM / WIBA 101.5 FM
Manitowoc	WOMT 1240 AM
Marinette	WMAM 570 AM / WLST 95.1 FM
Marshfield	WDLB 1450 AM

MARKET	CALL LETTERS & FREQUENCY
Medford	WKEB 99.3 FM
Menomonie	WMEQ 880 AM
Milwaukee	WTMJ 620 AM
Minocqua	WMQA 1570 AM / WMQA 95.9 FM
Monroe	WEKZ 93.7 FM
New Richmond	WIXK 1590 AM / WIXK 107.1 FM
Oshkosh	WPKR 99.5 FM
Park Falls	WCQM 98.7 FM
Portage	WPDR 1350 AM / WDDC 100.1 FM
Prairie Du Chien	WPRE 980 AM / WPRE 94.3 FM
Reedsburg	WRDB 1400 AM
Rhinelander	WOBT 1240 AM / WRHN 100.1 FM
Rice Lake	WJMC 1240 AM / WJMC 96.3 FM
Richland Center	WRCO 1450 AM / WRCO 100.9 FM
River Falls	WEVR 1550 AM / WEVR 106.3 FM
Shawano	WTCH 960 AM / WOWN 99.3 FM
Sheboygan	WWJR 106.5 FM
Sparta	WCOW 97.1 FM
Stevens Point	WSPT 1010 AM
Waupaca	WDUX 92.7 FM
Wausau	WSAU 550 AM
Whitehall	WHTL 102.3 FM
Wisconsin Rapids	WFHR 1320 AM

OTHER OUT-OF-STATE STATIONS

MARKET	CALL LETTERS & FREQUENCY
Anchorage (Alaska)	KAXX 1020 AM
Davenport (Iowa)	WOC 1420 AM
Biloxi (Miss.)	KVMI 570 AM
Richton (Miss.)	WESV 96.5 FM

MARKET	CALL LETTERS & FREQUENCY
Bismarck (N.D.)	KFYR 550 AM
Fargo (N.D.)	KVOX 1280 AM
Grand Forks (N.D.)	KNOX 1310 AM

PACKERS' STADIUMS

Green Bay:

1919-22	Hagemeister Park
1923-24	Bellevue Park
1925-56	City Stadium
1957-present	Lambeau Field (known as City Stadium until 1965)

Milwaukee:

1933	Borchert Field
1934-51	State Fair Park
1952	Marquette Stadium
1953-94	County Stadium

Venerable Lambeau Field, the longest tenured NFL stadium, now is in its fourth decade of operation. Having undergone a number of major alterations in its 41 years of existence, including numerous seating additions to reach its current capacity of 60,790, the facility has become one of the most recognized and envied venues in all of professional sports.

In recent years it also has become one of *the* toughest places to play in the National Football League. Since Mike Holmgren took over as head coach in 1992, Green Bay holds an impressive 35-4 regular-season record at Lambeau, plus a 5-0 mark in the playoffs, for an overall record of 40-4 (.909). Even more imposing is the fact that the Packers have won 37 of their last 38 games in Green Bay (including the five postseason victories).

Having gone almost three full seasons at home without a defeat — their last loss at Lambeau was to the St. Louis Rams in the 1995 season opener — the Packers enter the '98 campaign with an opportunity to make NFL history. Possessor of a 23-game home winning streak (regular-season games only) heading into this season — the second-longest in league annals — Green Bay has a chance to supplant the all-time record of 27 consecutive home victories, held by the Miami Dolphins of 1971-74.

Modern in many ways — from its 198 private boxes and 1,920 club seats to its technologically-advanced sound system to its two relatively new, end zone scoreboards, each with a Sony JumboTron color replay board — Lambeau still maintains a nostalgic and intimate feel to it with totally unobstructed sightlines. Permeated by history, tradition and mystique, the view from inside can be awe-inspiring.

Erected in 1957, the structure was dedicated as City Stadium on September 29 of that year — a day which saw Green Bay topple the hated Chicago Bears, 21-17 — during ceremonies attended by then-Vice President Richard M. Nixon and National Football League Commissioner Bert Bell. It later was renamed Lambeau Field in 1965 following the death of E.L. "Curly" Lambeau, founder and first coach of the Packers.

Originally built at a cost of $960,000, an amount shared equally by the Packer Corporation and the City of Green Bay, the facility was financed by way of a bond issue which received 2-to-1 voter approval in a municipal referendum conducted April 3, 1956.

Since that time, seating additions — all of them underwritten by the Green Bay Packers, Inc. — have increased stadium capacity from its original 32,150 to 38,669 in 1961, to 42,327 in 1963, to 50,852 in 1965 and to 56,263 in 1970. Construction of the initial 72 private boxes in 1985 swelled capacity to 56,926, and a 1990 addition of 36 boxes and the 1,920 theatre-style club seats (in the south end zone on either side of the scoreboard) moved that number to 59,543.

The seventh — and perhaps final — seating addition occurred in 1995, when a $4.7-million project put 90 more private boxes and an auxiliary press box in the previously open north end zone, first giving the stadium the feel of being a complete "bowl." Also that year, just prior to the start of the season, an ultra-modern Turbosound Flashlight Loudspeaker System was put into place at the north end of Lambeau. The new audio configuration, installed at a cost of $210,000, provides highly intelligible sound throughout the stadium while minimizing reverberation off the glass of the premium seating areas.

Installed in the spring of 1997 was a new natural grass surface with a specially-designed gravel drainage system which effectively can handle up to 15 inches of rain per hour, as well as irrigation and radiant heating systems. The new heating system, which replaced the 30-year-old heating coils installed by former Packers coach Vince Lombardi, includes over 30 miles of radiant heating pipe and is capable of maintaining a root zone temperature of over 70 degrees, thus making it possible for the natural grass to continue growing throughout the winter months.

In the next two to three years, at least two other improvement projects are planned. One is to totally update and expand the stadium concourse for safety and comfort reasons, adding concession stands and restrooms. The second project calls for the current press box to be torn down and replaced by a new ultra-modern media center, along with a stadium club. Construction plans will be developed by Ellerbe Becket Architects of Kansas City, Mo.

The stadium earlier had been upgraded in 1993 with the initial installation of a $1.7-million Sony JumboTron color replay board in the north end zone. Complemented in 1996 by a new $3.5-million scoreboard project, the two scoreboards at Lambeau now rival any in the NFL, encompassing a complete listing of game score, down and distance, ball location, time of game, yardage figures and out-of-town scores with greater visibility. The larger of the two new boards, 208-feet long and 40-feet high, extends across the north end zone, while the south end zone is home to a scoreboard measuring 164-feet long and 38-feet high. In addition to the matrix portions, each complete scoreboard includes a 20-by-26 foot replay board, the original north end zone screen having been moved to the south end zone and replaced by a similar Sony replay board.

Also prominent within the stadium are the names of the 19 Packers players and coaches who have been elected to the Pro Football Hall of Fame in Canton, Ohio, which are permanently displayed on the green walls between floors of the stadium's private boxes, on both sides of the stadium. All 12 of the team's championship years (1929-30-31, 1936, 1939, 1944, 1961-62, 1965-66-67, 1996) additionally are emblazoned above the club seats in the south end zone.

With the completion of the recent scoreboard and field projects, the Packers organization has spent nearly $50 million on improvements to the stadium, club administration building and training facilities over the past 17

ATTENDANCE RECORDS

10 LARGEST HOME CROWDS

Green Bay:
60,766	Chicago, 9/1/97
60,716	San Francisco, 10/14/96
60,712	Denver, 12/8/96
60,695	Detroit, 11/3/96
60,666	Philadelphia, 9/9/96
60,649	Pittsburgh, 12/24/95
60,627	Tampa Bay, 10/27/96
60,584	San Diego, 9/15/96
60,332	Minnesota, 10/22/95
60,318	Cincinnati, 12/3/95

Milwaukee:
56,046	Dallas, 11/12/78
56,029	Seattle, 10/15/78
55,998	Seattle, 10/10/76
55,986	L.A. Rams, 11/13/77
55,963	Minnesota, 11/21/76
55,832	New Orleans, 11/7/76
55,700	Detroit, 10/1/78
55,592	Minnesota, 11/26/89
55,125	Minnesota, 10/28/90
55,119	Detroit, 11/21/93

10 LARGEST AWAY CROWDS
90,535	L.A. Rams, 12/11/55
83,943	Cleveland, 9/18/66
82,137	Cleveland, 12/7/69
80,638	Detroit, 10/16/77
80,558	L.A. Rams, 10/21/73
79,798	Detroit, 11/16/75
79,281	Kansas City, 11/10/96
79,176	Buffalo, 10/30/88
79,029	Buffalo, 11/20/94
78,947	L.A. Rams, 10/19/69

LARGEST PLAYOFF GAME CROWDS
75,546	Oakland (@ Miami), 1/14/68 (Super Bowl II)
74,152	@ Dallas, 1/1/67 (1966 NFL Championship)
72,301	New England (@ New Orleans), 1/26/97 (Super Bowl XXXI)
69,311	@ San Francisco, 1/6/96 (1995 NFC Divisional Playoff)
68,987	@ San Francisco, 1/11/98 (1997 NFC Championship)
68,912	Denver (@ San Diego), 1/25/98 (Super Bowl XXXII)
68,479	@ Detroit, 1/8/94 (1993 NFC Wild Card Playoff)
67,325	@ Philadelphia, 12/26/60 (1960 NFL Championship)
65,135	@ Dallas, 1/14/96 (1995 NFC Championship)
64,892	@ N.Y. Giants, 12/30/62 (1962 NFL Championship)

LARGEST PRESEASON GAME CROWDS
92,753	College All-Stars (@ Chicago), 8/30/45
90,218	@ Philadelphia, 9/13/45
85,532	@ Cleveland, 8/30/69
84,918	@ Cleveland, 9/7/68
84,567	College All-Stars (@ Chicago), 8/29/40
84,560	College All-Stars (@ Chicago), 9/1/37
84,236	@ Cleveland, 9/2/67
83,736	@ Cleveland, 9/5/64
83,118	@ Cleveland, 9/4/65
78,087	@ Dallas, 8/28/67
*76,704	N.Y. Giants (@ Madison, Wis.), 8/22/97
75,504	@ Dallas, 8/20/66
75,332	@ Miami, 8/12/72
75,231	@ Kansas City, 8/26/73
73,959	N.Y. Jets (@ Madison, Wis.), 8/9/86

* All-time Packers home attendance record

OTHER PACKERS ATTENDANCE RECORDS
Single Season, Total (16 games): 1,017,930 (1997)
Single Season, Home: 482,988 (1996)
Single Season, Away: 536,436 (1997)

THE LAMBEAU FIELD STORY

years, including construction of the original indoor practice structure in 1982 and replacing it with The Don Hutson Center in 1994 at a cost of nearly $4.7 million.

Unique and uncomparable, Lambeau Field now is wholly owned by the City of Green Bay, retirement of the original $960,000 indebtedness having been celebrated at a mortgage burning ceremony in May of 1978. The Packers have a lease with the city for stadium usage through the year 2013 with a team option extending through the year 2024 under the terms of a revised agreement reached in 1995.

Sold out on a season-ticket basis since 1960, the team maintained two separate ticket packages after moving all of its games to Green Bay starting with the 1995 season. 'Gold' ticket holders (made up primarily of former Milwaukee season patrons) have a three-game package consisting of the annual Midwest Shrine preseason contest plus home games two and five of the regular season. 'Green' season customers (made up of original Green Bay ticket holders) have a seven-game package consisting of the annual Bishop's Charities preseason game in addition to the remaining six regular-season contests.

Ticket prices for the 1998 season are as follows: end zone seats (sections 0-8 and 31-38) $32; seats between the 20-yard lines (sections 15-24) $39; other sideline seats (sections 9-14 and 25-30) $36; private box tickets $44; and club seats $90.

Located on the southwest edge of Green Bay and surrounded on three sides by the village of Ashwaubenon, the stadium is available for public tours daily during the months of June through August except on Packer game days. Special groups (25 or more people) can arrange for tours between May 1 and Nov. 15. The Packer Hall of Fame (920/499-4281) can provide further information on tours.

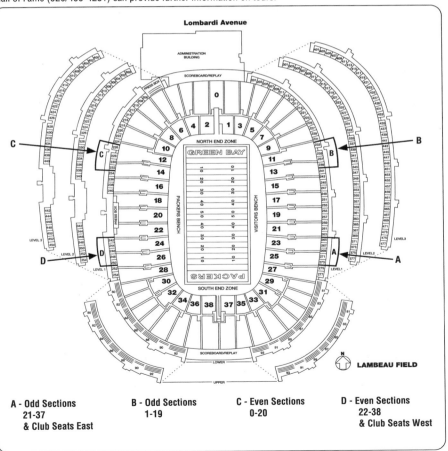

A - Odd Sections
21-37
& Club Seats East

B - Odd Sections
1-19

C - Even Sections
0-20

D - Even Sections
22-38
& Club Seats West

CREDENTIALS: All credential requests should be directed to Lee Remmel, Executive Director of Public Relations. Requests may be sent via email (martinp@packers.com), FAX (920/496-5712) or U.S. mail (P.O. Box 10628, Green Bay, WI 54307-0628). Credentials will not be mailed, unless the requesting outlet provides a Federal Express or UPS number, and should be picked up in person at the Packers' public relations office. Credentials not obtained prior to game day will be left at Press Will Call — Gate 26 (north side). The will call booth opens three hours prior to kickoff.

PHOTO CREDENTIALS will not be issued to free-lance photographers unless on a specific assignment from an accredited organization. Credentials no longer will be able to be provided to "grips" due to on-field space limitations.

MIKE HOLMGREN PRESS CONFERENCES: Head Coach Mike Holmgren regularly will hold four weekly press conferences during the regular season: Mondays and Wednesdays at 11:30 a.m. in the basement auditorium of the team's administration building, Fridays immediately following practice, as well as at the conclusion of each game. Post-game news conferences at home games will be held in the basement auditorium of the team's administration building.

During training camp, Holmgren will be available out on the practice field each day following the morning workout.

Any other requests for time with Head Coach Mike Holmgren, as well as any queries for an interview with an assistant coach, should be directed to a member of the Packers' public relations department.

PLAYER AVAILABILITY: During the regular season, the locker room is open for player interviews five days a week. On Monday, the locker room is open for 45 minutes upon completion of the players' workout. On Wednesday and Thursday, the locker room is open from 12:15-1:00 p.m. and for a half-hour following practice, beginning 10 minutes after its finish. On Friday, the locker room opens 30 minutes after the end of practice for a half-hour period. At the conclusion of all games, the locker room will be opened following the NFL's standard "cooling off" period. The locker room will be closed on the players' "off" day (generally Tuesday) and on Saturday.

The locker room is closed during training camp.

Any requests to interview players other than at the aforementioned times should be directed to a member of the Packers' public relations department.

CONFERENCE CALLS: The Packers' public relations department will arrange a conference call with the head coach and a key player of the opposing team each week during the regular season. These conference calls will be made from the media work room, located in the basement of the team's administration building, and generally will be held on Wednesday.

PRESS ROOM PHONE: The general press room phone number is 920/496-5707.

PRESS BOX PHONES: "Co-op" phones are made available to media in both press boxes at Lambeau Field. If dedicated service is desired, within the state of Wisconsin call Ameritech at 800/660-3000. Out-of-state media can order dedicated phone service by calling 800/447-7738. Please contact Don Raddatz seven to 10 days prior to the game at 920/496-7728 or by FAX at 920/739-4735 regarding any instrument needs.

GAME DAY FAX SERVICE: Telesports FAX is the Green Bay Packers' provider of FAX service for all media at home games. Service can be ordered by contacting John Dodds at 414/347-1502 (H) or 414/276-2601 (W) (mailing address: 1009 North Jackson, #608; Milwaukee, WI 53202). FAX service fees generally are the NFL's standard league-wide charge of $25.

POOL REPORTERS: As assigned by the Professional Football Writers of America (PFWA), the Green Bay pool reporter for the 1998 season is Tom Mulhern of the *Appleton Post-Crescent*.

DAVID KLINGLER — 9

Quarterback
College: Houston
NFL Exp.: 7th Season   **Packers Exp.:** 1st Season
Ht.: 6-3   **Wt.:** 215   **Born:** 2/17/69   **Acq:** FA-98

PRO: Strong-armed, highly-athletic quarterback who amassed more than 50 NCAA passing records as a collegian, he signed on with the Packers as an unrestricted free agent as the team opened training camp for the 1998 season (July 18)…A seventh-year pro, he originally was a first-round draft selection of the Cincinnati Bengals, with whom he spent his first four NFL seasons (1992-95)…Signed by Oakland as an unrestricted free agent June 8, 1996, he was with the Raiders in a backup role the past two seasons…Overall, Klingler has completed 389 of 718 passes, a 54.2 percentage, for 3,994 yards and 16 touchdowns, with 22 interceptions…Playing in 33 games over his career to date, with 24 starts, the former University of Houston field general had his best season to date in 1993 when he completed 190 of 343 passes for 1,935 yards and 6 touchdowns in 14 games, with 9 interceptions…Green Bay head coach Mike Holmgren says of him, "David, coming out of college, was the sixth player chosen in the first round of the draft, and he had had a wonderful college career in the run-and-shoot offense. He has a great arm, (but) the transition to the drop-back passing game in the NFL at times has been difficult for him. But, as far as his physical ability, he is a talented man. He gives us experience at that position – he's started 24 games in the league. And, also, there is a certain part of me that is curious to see what can happen."…**1997:** Saw action in one game for Oakland – in the fourth quarter at Carolina Nov. 2 – completing 4 of 7 passes for 27 yards, with 1 interception…**1996:** Spent majority of the 1996 season on inactive status with the Raiders as team's designated Third Quarterback…Made first appearance of the year in season finale against Seattle and finished game with 10 pass completions in 24 attempts for 87 yards…Also rushed for 36 yards on 4 carries…**1995:** Posted a 100.9 quarterback rating (33 of 47 for 395 yards, 2 TDs, 1 INT) in preseason play before suffering broken jaw in preseason contest at Detroit (Aug. 17)…Subsequently was on Bengals' inactive list for first seven regular-season games…Served as reserve quarterback in final nine league contests…Came off the bench in the fourth quarter for an injured Jeff Blake (concussion) in contest vs. Browns (Oct. 29), leading offense to a field goal and touchdown in two drives – the TD coming with only 49 seconds left to play, tying the game and forcing overtime (Blake returned in OT)…Also saw action vs. Pittsburgh (Nov. 19) and vs. Minnesota (Dec. 24)…Overall during the season, completed 7 of 15 passes for 88 yards and 1 touchdown…**1994:** Appeared in 10 league games for the Bengals, starting the first seven…Recorded career highs in completions (27) and attempts (43) in season opener vs. Cleveland (Sept. 4), throwing for 224 yards…Threw for a career-high 266 yards on 21-of-29 passing vs. New England (Sept. 18)…Suffered knee injury in rematch at Cleveland (Oct. 23)…Subsequently served as inactive Third Quarterback for the next three contests (Oct. 30 vs. Dallas, Nov. 6 at Seattle and Nov. 13 vs. Houston)…Served as the backup quarterback the next five weeks and saw action in three games – at Denver (Nov. 27), at N.Y. Giants (Dec. 11) and at Arizona (Dec. 18)…Served as inactive Third Quarterback vs. Philadelphia (Dec. 24)…Finished season having completed 131 of 231 passes for 1,327 yards and 6 touchdowns…**1993:** Started 13 league games while appearing in 14 contests overall for the Cincinnati…Posted a career-best 190 completions (on 343 pass attempts) for 1,935 yards and 6 touchdowns…Added 282 rushing yards, averaging 6.9 yards per carry…Had to leave contest vs. Cleveland (Oct. 17) after aggravating a lower back contusion he had suffered the week before at Kansas City…Served as the team's backup, but did not play, in the next two contests before coming off the bench vs. Houston (Nov. 14)…Threw a career-high 3 touchdown passes in comeback victory over Atlanta (Dec. 26)…**1992:** Started four regular-season games for Bengals as a rookie…Finished season with 47 completions in 98 passing attempts, good for 530 yards and 3 touchdowns…Fired a career-long, 83-yard pass at San Diego (Dec. 13), good for a touchdown…Drafted in the first round (the sixth pick overall) by Cincinnati in 1992.
COLLEGE: A four-time letter winner at Houston (1988-91), starting the final two years…Made wholesale

assault on NCAA passing records, setting no fewer than 51 Division I marks during a highly-productive career in the run-and-shoot offense of the Cougars, where he earned All-America honors at quarterback in both 1990 and 1991…Was a finalist for the 'Johnny Unitas Golden Arm Award,' 'Davey O'Brien Award' and *Football News* offensive 'Player of the Year' honors as a senior…Closed out college career with 9,327 yards of total offense to set Southwest Conference record, while throwing for 91 touchdowns…Passed for a career total of 9,430 yards, completing 726 of 1,262 overall attempts…Ranked second in the nation in total offense as a senior, averaging over 322 yards per game…Passed for over 400 yards in 13 of his 21 starts…Put on spectacular passing show in a 1991 contest against Louisiana Tech, throwing 6 touchdown passes in one quarter…Posted 54 touchdown passes in 1990…Redshirted in 1987…Earned B.S. degree in marketing.

PERSONAL: Given name David Ryan Klingler…Born in Lima, Ohio…Married to Katie, couple has a son, Luke (born 1/14/96)…A versatile athlete, he earned 10 varsity letters at Stratford High School in Houston, playing football (three letters) and basketball (three), in addition to running track (four)…Was an all-district choice at quarterback as both a junior and senior…Also earned all-conference honors in basketball as a guard…Hobbies include working on his ranch…Active in Christian youth work, including Fellowship of Christian Athletes, Athletes in Action and Campus for Christ…Residence: Burton, Texas.

PRO STATISTICS:

Year		G/S	Att.	Comp.	Yds.	Pct.	TD	Int.	LG	Rating
1992	Cincinnati	4/4	98	47	530	48.0	3	2	83t	66.3
1993	Cincinnati	14/13	343	190	1,935	55.4	6	9	51	66.6
1994	Cincinnati	10/7	231	131	1,327	56.7	6	9	56	65.7
1995	Cincinnati	3/0	15	7	88	46.7	1	1	33	59.9
1996	Oakland	1/0	24	10	87	41.7	0	0	20	51.9
1997	Oakland	1/0	7	4	27	57.1	0	1	8	26.2
Totals		33/24	718	389	3,994	54.2	16	22	83t	65.1

Rushing: 11 for 53 yards, 4.8 avg., LG 12 in 1992; 41 for 282 yards, 6.9 avg., LG 29 in 1993; 17 for 85 yards, 5.0 avg., LG 15 in 1994; 4 for 36 yards, 9.0 avg., LG 14 in 1996; 1 for 0 yards in 1997 for total of 74 for 456 yards, 6.2 avg., LG 29
Receptions: 1 for -6 yards in 1994

CAREER SINGLE-GAME HIGHS
Most Pass Attempts: 43, vs. Cleveland (9/4/94); **Most Pass Completions:** 27, vs. Cleveland (9/4/94); **Most Yards Passing:** 266, vs. New England (9/18/94); **Most Touchdown Passes:** 3, vs. Atlanta (12/26/93); **Most Interceptions:** 3, at Houston (9/25/94) and vs. Miami (10/2/94); **Longest Completion:** 83t, at San Diego (12/13/92)

TERRY McDANIEL — 26

Cornerback

College: Tennessee

NFL Exp.: 11th Season **Packers Exp.:** 1st Season

Ht.: 5-10 **Wt.:** 180 **Born:** 2/8/65 **Acq:** FA-98

PRO: A five-time Pro Bowl selection who signed with Green Bay on the opening day of '98 training camp practices, immediately added reliable depth and a strong leadership presence to the team's defensive backfield...Spent his first 10 NFL seasons with the Los Angeles/Oakland Raiders (1988-97)...Expected to contribute right away as the Packers' third corner in the 'nickel' package, with the capability to step in and play at a high level should either starter go down...Packers defensive coordinator Fritz Shurmur, happy to add a player of McDaniel's caliber to the squad, said, "He's a proven Pro Bowl performer and we're delighted to have him in the mix with our cover people. We look to him to be a big contributor this year. We're going to use him in our 'nickel' and 'dime' defenses, and obviously he's going to have the opportunity to compete for a cornerback position."...Begins his second decade in the NFL in 1998...Joined Packers as a free agent this past July 19...Had been waived by the Raiders on June 5...Voted to the Pro Bowl for five straight seasons from 1992-96...A veteran of 143 games with 137 starts, he has 34 career interceptions for 624 yards, including 5 touchdowns...Also has two other pro scores, both coming by way of fumble returns...**1997:** Played in 13 games overall, making 12 starts...Finished season with 50 tackles (44 solo), 1 interception and 14 passes defensed...Inactive at N.Y. Jets (Sept. 21)...Active, but did not see any playing time, vs. San Diego (Oct. 5)...Did not start, but saw action, at Seattle (Oct. 26)...Snared lone interception of the season in rematch vs. Seahawks (Dec. 14)...**1996:** Appeared in all 16 games for the eighth straight year, making 15 starts...Selected to play in his fifth consecutive Pro Bowl...Led team with 5 interceptions and 19 passes defensed...Recorded 48 tackles...Had 56-yard interception return for a touchdown vs. Minnesota (Nov. 17)...Registered a season-high 7 tackles and 1 interception among 2 passes defensed in contest at San Diego (Oct. 21)...**1995:** Started all 16 games for the fifth consecutive season and earned a fourth straight trip to the Pro Bowl...Led Raiders with 6 interceptions and 13 passes defensed as team returned to Oakland...Also posted 56 tackles...Brought back an interception 42 yards for a touchdown vs. Kansas City (Dec. 3)...Had season-high 2 interceptions among 3 passes defensed at Cincinnati (Nov. 5)...**1994:** Started all 16 games and was selected to his second straight Pro Bowl as a starter (third overall)...Led team and posted career highs in interceptions (7) and passes defensed (22)...Also led Raiders with 3 fumble recoveries...Made 61 tackles to rank seventh on the team...Returned a fumble 41 yards for a touchdown vs. Seattle (Sept. 11), accounting for the Raiders' only touchdown in a 38-9 loss...One week later at Denver (Sept. 18), returned an interception 15 yards for a touchdown, in addition to 1 forced fumble and 2 fumble recoveries...Registered 3 interceptions at New England (Oct. 9), returning one 14 yards for a score...**1993:** Appeared in his second straight Pro Bowl, making his initial start, after leading the Raiders with 5 interceptions among a team-high 14 passes defensed...Started all 16 games...Returned an interception 36 yards for a touchdown in season opener vs. Minnesota (Sept. 5)...Ranked sixth on the club with 68 tackles...Started both of Raiders' playoff games...**1992:** Led Raiders with 4 interceptions as he started all 16 games...Selected to play in his first Pro Bowl (as a reserve)...Also led club with 20 passes defensed...Finished seventh on the team with 63 tackles...Had big day in 24-0 victory over Denver (Nov. 22), making 2 interceptions among 5 passes defensed, one of which was returned to the Broncos' 1-yard line, and recovering 1 fumble...Also recorded 6 tackles in Denver contest...**1991:** Started all 16 games for the Raiders for the first time, he also started wild-card playoff contest at Kansas City (Dec. 28)...Ranked fifth on the club with 77 tackles and second with 14 passes defensed...Turned in season high with 9 tackles vs. Indianapolis (Sept. 15), adding 2 forced fumbles and 1 fumble recovery against the Colts...**1990:** Played in all 16 games, making 13 starts...Led club with 14 passes defensed and shared team honors with 3 interceptions and also 2 fumble recoveries...Also registered a career-best 2 sacks among 48 stops...Returned fumble recovery 42 yards for a touchdown vs. Denver (Sept. 9), his first pro

score...Started both of Raiders' playoff contests, including AFC Championship Game at Buffalo (Jan. 20)...**1989:** Made 15 starts while playing in all 16 games for the initial time...Finished with 68 tackles, 1 sack, 3 interceptions and 12 passes defensed...**1988:** Started first two games before suffering a broken right fibia in Week 2 at Houston (Sept. 11), ending his season...Was first Raiders rookie to start opening-day contest in the defensive backfield since Jack Tatum started at safety in 1971...Was the second of three first-round selections (ninth overall) by the then-Los Angeles Raiders in 1988.

COLLEGE: A four-time letter winner at University of Tennessee (1984-87), starting the last two-and-a-half years...Was a second-team All-America selection of *The Sporting News* and the Newspaper Enterprise Association as a senior...Also earned first-team All-Southeastern Conference recognition and academic all-conference honors his senior year, when he registered 57 tackles, 2 interceptions and 8 passes defensed...Made 68 tackles and 3 interceptions as a junior...Moved from wide receiver to cornerback prior to his sophomore season...Made 1 reception as a freshman...Redshirted in 1983...Also participated in track three years, running all sprints from the 60-meter indoors to the 400-meters...Also was a member of the SEC champion 1600-meter relay team as a freshman and junior...Earned B.A. degree in human services.

PERSONAL: Given name Terence Lee McDaniel...Nicknamed 'T-Mack'...Born in Mansfield, Ohio...Married to Janna, couple has a daughter, Shayla (born 2/6/92), and a son, Isaiah (born 3/11/96)...An all-county and all-conference selection as a running back at Saginaw (Mich.) High School...Posted 1,582 all-purpose yards as a senior...Lettered three times each in football, basketball and track...Hobbies include playing basketball...Residence: Alameda, Calif.

PRO STATISTICS:

Year		G/S	TT	Sacks	Int.	Yds.	LG	TD	FR	FF	PD
1988	L.A. Raiders	2/2	6	0	0	0	0	0	0	0	1
1989	L.A. Raiders	16/15	68	1	3	21	20	0	0	0	12
1990	L.A. Raiders	16/13	48	2	3	20	15	0	2	0	14
1991	L.A. Raiders	16/16	77	0	0	0	0	0	1	2	14
1992	L.A. Raiders	16/16	63	0	4	180	67	0	1	0	20
1993	L.A. Raiders	16/16	68	0	5	87	36	1	0	3	14
1994	L.A. Raiders	16/16	61	0	7	103	35	2	3	1	22
1995	Oakland	16/16	56	0	6	46	42	1	0	0	13
1996	Oakland	16/15	48	0	5	150	56t	1	0	0	19
1997	Oakland	13/12	50	0	1	17	17	0	0	1	14
Totals		**143/137**	**545**	**3**	**34**	**624**	**67**	**5**	**7**	**7**	**143**
Playoffs		**5/5**	**18**	**0**	**0**	**0**	**0**	**0**	**1**	**0**	**3**

Other Touchdowns: 2, 42-yard fumble return vs. Denver (9/9/90) and 41-yard fumble return vs. Seattle (9/11/94)